THE
POLITICS OF LAW
A PROGRESSIVE CRITIQUE

THE
POLITICS OF LAW
A PROGRESSIVE CRITIQUE

THIRD EDITION

EDITED BY DAVID KAIRYS

BASIC
BOOKS

A Member of The Perseus Books Group

Grateful acknowledgment is made to the following for permission to reprint previously published material: *The New Press:* Excerpts in the Introduction and chapter "Freedom of Speech" by David Kairys from *With Liberty and Justice for Some* (1993). Reprinted with the permission of The New Press. *Foundation Press:* Excerpts in the chapter "Health Law" by Rand Rosenblatt from *Law and the American Health Care System* (1997). Reprinted with the permission of The Foundation Press. *University of Chicago:* "A Black Feminist Critique of Antidiscrimination Law and Politics" by Kimberlé Crenshaw was previously published in different form as "Demarginalizing the Intersection of Race and Sex: A Black Feminist Critique of Antidiscrimination Doctrine, Feminist Theory and Antiracist Politics" in the 1989 *University of Chicago Legal Forum.* Reprinted with the permission of the University of Chicago.

Library of Congress Cataloging-in-Publication Data

Kairys, David.
    The politics of law : a progressive critique / edited by David Kairys. — 3rd ed.
    p. cm.
    Includes index.
    ISBN 0-465-05959-7
    1. Political questions and judicial power—United States. 2. Justice, Administration of—United States. 3. Law and politics. I. Title.
KF8700.P65 1998
347.73—dc21
                                97-46000
                                CIP

To W. Haywood Burns and Alan Freeman,
our co-authors, who contributed and inspired so much
and are gone too soon.

CONTENTS

ACKNOWLEDGMENTS

MANY people made important contributions to the three editions of this book. Drafts were generally circulated among the authors, and revisions benefited from input by many of them. On this edition, the editor appreciates suggestions of topics and authors from Robert Gordon, Karl Klare, Susan Silbey, Sylvia Law, and Duncan Kennedy; research assistance by Temple University law students Mark Hijar and Dwayne King; technical assistance and computer rescue by Shyam Nair, Director of Computer Services at Temple University Law School; a research grant from the Temple University Law Foundation; and editorial, production, and publicity work at Basic Books, Perseus, and HarperCollins by William Frucht, Kristen Auclair, Susan Rabiner, Susan Weinberg, and Michael Wilde. The book originated and developed with organizational bases for dialogue and support provided by the Conference on Critical Legal Studies and the National Lawyers Guild; and we continue to appreciate the contributions of the first edition editors, Philip Pochoda, Don Guttenplan, and André Schiffrin, who took a chance on an unusual book proposal.

PREFACE TO THE THIRD EDITION

THIS third edition adds fifteen new chapters, while the core of the earlier editions has been maintained, with updating and revision throughout, by substantially increasing the total number of pages. The coverage now includes a broad range of private law and public law issues, as well as all of the usual subjects taught in the first year of law school.

The new chapters cover health care, welfare, intellectual property, gay rights, affirmative action, criminal justice, environmental law, international human rights, property, civil procedure, access to courts, separation of powers, governmental takings of property, and law and literature. The book is still divided into three parts: Traditional Jurisprudence and Legal Education, Selected Issues and Fields of Law, and Progressive Approaches to the Law. The issues and fields are divided into ten broad categories: Litigation and the Legal Process, The Quality of Life, Liberty, Property, Equality, Crime and Justice, Personal Injury, Business, Labor and Social Welfare, and The Role and Structure of Government.

The new authors include professor of political science Austin Sarat, professor of English literature Julia Epstein, and law professors or practitioners Keith Aoki, Jane Baron, David Cole, Janet Halley, Charles Lawrence, Molly McUsic, Martha Minow, Joseph Singer, Gerald Torres, and Lucy Williams. The core of authors from the earlier editions include Richard Abel, Haywood Burns, Rhonda Copelon, Kimberlé Crenshaw, Elliott Currie, Jay Feinman, Alan Freeman, Peter Gabel, Robert Gordon, Morton Horwitz, Duncan Kennedy, Karl Klare, Jules Lobel, Elizabeth Mensch, Frances Olsen, Victor Rabinowitz, Rand Rosenblatt, David Rudovsky, Elizabeth Schneider, William Simon, Nadine Taub, and Cornel West.

Philadelphia
October 1997

DAVID KAIRYS

INTRODUCTION

WE Americans turn over more of our society's disputes, decisions, and concerns to courts and lawyers than does perhaps any other nation. Yet, in a society that values democracy, courts have trouble justifying their power and maintaining their legitimacy. The judiciary is a nonmajoritarian institution, whose guiding lights are usually appointed rather than elected and, even where elected, are not expected to express or implement the will of the people. Judicial legitimacy rests elsewhere: on notions of honesty and fairness and, most important, on popular perceptions of the judicial decision-making process. Judicial power of the sort we routinely accept probably requires an additional ingredient—a very American distrust of government or any form of collective action.[1]

Basic to the popular perception of the judicial process is the notion of government of law, not people.[2] Law is, in this conception, separate from—and "above"—politics, economics, culture, and the values or preferences of judges or any person. In this separation resides the law's ability to be objective, principled, and fair. Legal scholars, philosophers, and some of our best minds in a range of disciplines have long debated whether this separation accurately describes our legal system or is attainable in any system. But the ideal is problematic, even if it is, or can be, realized in practice.

The concept of government of law, not people, is so familiar, so much a part of our national identity, that its meaning can be difficult to notice, but it describes a political system that is deeply distrustful of popular government. The unstated premise is that the people cannot be fair or reasonable and should not be entrusted with decision-making power; fairness and reason must be imposed by or come from some external source—law.

Law and our particular legal system surely provide a means to articulate, organize, and record principles, rules, and prior interpretations and results. This holds the possibility of consistency, continuity, universal application, predictability, and maybe even common sense. Even if the rule of law ideal cannot be realized, rule through law, as English historian Edward P. Thompson has said, is decidedly preferable to "the exercise of unmediated force. The forms and rhetoric of law acquire a distinct identity which may, on occasion, inhibit power and afford some protection to the powerless."[3]

But government of law, not people, promises much more: to remove the human element from that enormous array of decisions and issues we turn over to judges—encompassing the common law, interpretation of statutes, and the broad reach of the federal and state constitutions—by deferring to a "higher" source, so that we may be, in this large domain, free of ourselves. If we described the higher source in terms of the creator of life or the universe, we would quickly label the thinking religious and know that it is based on faith. The power and legitimacy of this higher source rest on its claim to grounding in a sophisticated process that works by logic and reason and is separate from and independent of politics.

The separation of law from politics is supposedly accomplished and ensured by a number of perceived attributes of the legal decision-making process, including judicial subservience to the Constitution, statutes, and precedent; the quasi-scientific, objective nature of legal analysis; and the technical expertise of judges and lawyers. Together, these attributes constitute an idealized decision-making process in which (1) the law on a particular issue is preexisting, predictable, and available to anyone with reasonable legal skill; (2) the facts relevant to disposition of a case are ascertained by objective hearing and evidentiary rules that reasonably ensure that the truth will emerge; (3) the result in a particular case is determined by a rather routine application of the law to the facts; and (4) except for the occasional bad judge, any reasonably competent and fair judge will reach the "correct" decision.

Of course, there are significant segments of the bar, trends in legal scholarship, and popularly held beliefs that repudiate this idealized model. The school of jurisprudence known as Legal Realism long ago exposed its falsity. Later jurisprudential developments, such as theories resting the legitimacy of law on the existence of widely shared values, at least implicitly recognize the social and political content of law. Explicit consideration by judges of values in certain forms, such as "public policy" and "social utility," is generally acknowledged as appropriate. And it is commonly known that the particular judge assigned to a case has a significant bearing on the outcome. For many, the law's malleability is a matter of common knowledge, not a surprise or a cause for alarm.

But most of this thinking is either limited to law journals or compartmentalized, existing alongside and often presented as part of the idealized process. Despite the various scholarly trends and the open consideration of social policy and utility, legal decisions are expressed and justified in terms of the idealized process. The explicit or implicit theme of almost every judicial opinion is "the law made me do it." And this is how the courts as well as their decisions are depicted and discussed throughout society. Even the cynical views one often hears about the law, such as "the system is fixed" or "it's all politics," are usually meant to describe departures from, rather than characteristics of, the legal process.

The underlying conception envisions a legal process that, if not perverted by bias, corruption, or stupidity, will produce distinctly legal, fair rules and results untainted by politics or anyone's social values. While this perception is not monolithic or static (at various times substantial segments of society have come to question the idealized model), it has fairly consistently had more currency in the United States than in any other country.

Public debate over judicial decisions usually focuses on whether courts have deviated from the idealized decision-making process rather than on the substance of decisions or the nature and social significance of judicial power. Perceived deviations undermine the legitimacy and power of the courts, and are usually greeted with a variety of institutional and public challenges, including attacks by politicians and the press, proposals for statutory or constitutional change, and, occasionally, threats or attempts to impeach judges.

Dissatisfaction with the courts and their decisions is usually expressed in terms of this notion of deviation from the idealized model. Thus, the conservative criticism that the courts have overstepped their bounds—going beyond or outside legal reasoning and the idealized process—is now commonplace, as is the accompanying plea for judicial restraint and less intrusive government.

The authors of this book reject the idealized model and the notion that a distinctly legal mode of reasoning or analysis determines legal results. The problem is not that courts deviate from legal reasoning. There is no legal methodology or process for reaching particular, correct results. This understanding of the law has been recently most closely associated with Critical Legal Studies and many of the contributors to this book, and before that with Legal Realism.[4]

The lack of required, legally correct rules, methodologies, or results is in part a function of the limits of language and interpretation, which are subjective and value laden. More importantly, indeterminacy stems from the reality that the law usually embraces and legitimizes many or all of the conflicting values and interests involved in controversial issues and a wide and conflicting array of "logical" or "reasoned" arguments and strategies of argumentation, without providing any legally required hierarchy of values or arguments or any required method for determining which is most important in a particular context. Judges then make choices, and those choices are most fundamentally value based, or political.

For example, in the abortion controversy, the law embraces privacy, individual choice, and gender equality in sexual and reproductive matters *and* protection and preservation of life and health. One can find prior decisions of the Supreme Court placing great importance on each of these sets of values or principles. However, the law does not provide any method or process for determining neutrally or objectively which of the competing values is more important. Nor does the law provide any required method or process for determining whether or when a fetus is a life, the extent of reproductive choice, or when the courts should follow one, another, or any precedent.

Often a particular rule or result can be relatively predictable and appear to be "sensible" or "correct," but this occurs when the issue or circumstances are not controversial in a specific period or context (or when one consciously or unconsciously projects one's own values as neutral and correct). A relative societal consensus or a lack of controversy regarding particular values, issues, or results can create a false sense of determinacy. In another period or context where the same issue or circumstances are controversial, the law's indeterminacy is again readily visible. For example, the courts will now generally protect a person handing out leaflets on a street corner from interference by local officials, but before the 1930s, although the same constitutional provisions were in effect, there was no such protection (see chapter 8).

The law's variety of approaches, methods, and principles of decision making are applied selectively; every judge uses some of them some of the time and has used them all at least on occasion (and once in a while some judges originate a new one). None is required in any particular case or circumstance. The justices of the Supreme Court regularly cannot agree, for example, on the straightforward matter of how one goes about deciding an important constitutional case because there is no legally required methodology but rather many methodologies that can claim legitimacy within the legal system and from which a judge may pick and choose.

There is a distinctly legal and quite elaborate system of discourse and body of knowledge, with its own language and conventions of argumentation, logic, and even manners. In some ways these aspects of the law are so distinct and all-embracing as to amount to a separate culture. For many lawyers the courthouse, the law firm, the language, and the style become a way of life, so much so that their behavior can be difficult for nonlawyer spouses and friends to understand or accept.

But in terms of a method or process for decision making—for determining correct rules, facts, methods, or results—the law provides a wide and conflicting variety of stylized rationalizations from which courts can choose. Social and political judgments about the substance, parties, and context of a case, as well as about a range of institutional concerns, guide such choices, even when they are not the explicit or conscious basis of decision.

Adherents of the traditional view usually have no need to explain their approach. A short phrase is sufficient to gain understanding and acceptance; "the rule of law" or "government of law, not people" will easily do. But when they do try to explain, the results can be revealing. According to President Ronald Reagan's solicitor general, Charles Fried, formerly a professor at Harvard Law School and now a justice of the Supreme Judicial Court of Massachusetts, law and legal analysis bring "reason" and "neutrality" and the certainty and consistency of fair rules applied to all. But he acknowledges that law lacks an "anchor"—a set of established principles and a legal methodology that determine rules and results. "The rule of law is not quite a law of rules" and "there are no criteria about criteria" are his distracting ways of conceding that there are no legally required principles or any legal methodology that yield required results neutrally or by reason. He tries to reassure us, however, on two grounds. The "good faith" legal mind works, somewhat mysteriously but reliably, such that "you just know." Further, results do not really matter: the legal process guarantees us all freedom and liberty.[5]

Such reassurances should not be very comforting. If law is not determinate or neutral or a function of reason and logic rather than values and politics, government by law reduces to government by lawyers, and there is little justification for the broad-scale displacement of democracy. The extraordinary role of law in our society and culture is hard to justify once the idealized model is recognized as mythic.

Perhaps this is why we usually prefer to debate other issues, such as judicial restraint. The notion of judicial restraint is not merely a distraction, however. It has gained the status of a foundational principle in contemporary politics and culture and provides a window onto deeply held conceptions of law and society. The identification of judicial restraint with American freedom, democracy, and equality is among the defining political instincts of our time, despite its glaring contradictions and obvious historical inaccuracy.

Ronald Reagan solidified the popular connection of judicial restraint and conservatism with a less intrusive, more representative and democratic government. "[T]he question involved in judicial restraint," Reagan said, "is will we have a government by the people?" His attorney general, Edwin Meese III, explained that conservatives seek "to depoliticize the courts, [so they would not] usurp the authority of elected branches of our constitutional system." Fried defined the "Reagan Revolution" as assuring "less intrusive government" by two principal means, reduced taxation and judicial restraint, so courts could not replace "the self-determination of the entrepreneurs and workers who create wealth." Reagan successfully stretched these ideas to embrace the notion that conservative rules and results are not only preferable because they further values he favored, but are also legally required. To reach other, or liberal, rules or results is to deviate from the legal process and the law.[6] At the dawn of the new century and millennium, these connections are too basic and too deeply embedded in our culture and consciousness to be described merely as conventional wisdom. Yet, they are also indefensible.

Consider freedom first. If government intrusiveness is a central problem and individual freedom a central value, it is strange that the liberal courts of the 1960s have become the prime villains. Their judicial activism was largely aimed at stopping government intrusion on individuals. The liberal courts provided the individual, usually regardless of wealth or position, with wide-ranging protection from government intrusion. For example, confronted with Connecticut's ban on contraceptives, the Supreme Court of the 1960s established a new constitutional right to privacy.[7]

The liberal courts intervened to prevent other parts of the federal, state, or local governments from intruding on the people. And they did so in the absence of prior authority and often in spite of established rules and precedents to the contrary. Liberal judges were judicial activists, but their activism was used to stop government intrusion on individuals in matters of personal freedom and to promote freedom (and, usually, democracy and equality). Judicial activism is not the same as government intrusion.

The conservative justices dominating the Supreme Court since the mid-1970s have shown no reluctance to overrule precedents, to break new judicial ground, or to invalidate legislation. There was no evident hesitance, or any sign of self-reflection by staunch advocates of judicial restraint, as conservative justices invalidated legislation or governmental action that placed environmental and other restrictions on developers and businesses, limited the role of money in elections, protected free exercise of religion by nonmainstream religions, punished bias-motivated crime, placed restrictions on guns, and established affirmative action to achieve integration.[8]

Judicial activism is not consistently liberal, and judicial restraint is not consistently conservative. If one looks at the purposes and effects of particular government intrusions and places judicial activism and restraint in specific contexts, the most apparent patterns and the best generalizations are more complicated and have more to do with substantive goals than judicial means.

Conservatives tend to favor less intrusive government when it comes to regulation or interference in a free-market economy and more intrusive government when it comes to compelled conformity to religious, moral, cultural, and lifestyle norms. They champion judicial activism to prohibit government intrusion on the unrestrained operation of the market and to invalidate electoral and other reforms that tend to interfere with property rights or the advantages of wealth. Liberals tend to favor less intrusive government when it comes to individual autonomy in matters of religion, morality, culture, and lifestyle and more intrusive government when it comes to regulation of the economy and electoral and other democratic reforms. They champion judicial activism to prohibit government intrusion on personal freedom or imposition of compelled conformity. Both conservatives and liberals see themselves as protecting freedom and see each other as favoring impermissible government intrusion. Neither conservatives nor liberals seem seriously bothered by judicial interference and creativity or abandonment of established rules and precedents in furtherance of their higher goals.

These patterns are not new. Probably the most determined and successful advocates of judicial restraint in our history were liberals in the first half of the twentieth century. The conservative Supreme Court of that period invalidated economic legislation aimed at protecting working people and providing the economic safety net that we have until recently taken for granted. For example, in what is usually called the *Lockner* era, laws limiting the hours of labor were invalidated by the Supreme Court as unconstitutional infringements on the rights of employers and employees to enter into contracts. The courts were interfering with legislative intrusions into the economy. Liberals opposed this interference by advocating judicial restraint, conceived—like the conservative conception of our time—as a neutral, independent, universal, and overriding principle that transcended substantive goals or politics.[9]

Someone who favored Social Security and restriction of child labor over maximization of profits during the New Deal tended to be for judicial restraint. If one favored racial equality and justice and opposed segregation in the 1960s, one was usually for judicial activism. If one favored prohibition of abortions prior to 1973, one was for judicial restraint, but achievement of that same goal after 1973 requires a judicial activism that would not hesitate to overrule the pro-choice *Roe v. Wade* decision.

Conservatives and liberals have each tended to advocate judicial restraint when they lose control of the courts, typically justified with the lofty stated goal of stopping the courts from interfering with the will of the people. We have become accustomed to cyclic conservative and liberal swings with accompanying complaints about activism, which mainly mask the unusually broad scope of policy making by courts in our system.

The identification of conservatism and judicial restraint with democracy and equality is even stranger. There is a deep distrust of democracy in the conservative tradition and among the framers of the Constitution. The record of the Constitutional Convention reflects considerable contempt for ordinary people and popularly elected legislatures. The people are "less fit" to choose legislators than the elite of each state, defined as white men with substantial property, according to Charles Pinckney. John Dickinson saw danger in "the multitudes without property and without principle." John Jay, who with James Madison and Alexander Hamilton authored *The Federalist Papers*, thought "the people who own the country ought to govern it." In the famous *Federalist* No. 10, Madison emphasized how the constitutional scheme protected against "the mischief of factions" that stem from the "unequal distribution of property."

The Constitution reflects these views: there was direct election only of members of the House of Representatives; and state qualifications for voting, which usually required ownership of land or substantial property, were incorporated. Racial minorities, women, and even most white men could not vote. The Supreme Court early demonstrated the same approach, intervening—in an early example of conservative activism—to invalidate a state legislature's redistributive modification of property rights, and to establish, in *Marbury v. Madison* (1803), judicial review and "a government of laws, and not of men."[10]

The predominant theme of the amendments to the Constitution subsequent to the Bill of Rights has been equality and inclusion of all our people in the political process—African Americans and other minorities, women, white men irrespective of property holdings, and anyone who has reached the age of eighteen.[11] These amendments, and the array of legislation and judicial rulings that define contemporary American democracy and equality, came after the fundamental rupture of the Civil War—after the failure of the original constitutional scheme. Their adoption was not required by the Constitution or by law, nor was it inevitable. And they were consistently opposed by the conservatives of each era in which they were adopted; in many of these periods, such opposition defined conservatism.[12]

Even in the 1960s and thereafter, many or perhaps most of the significant and lasting changes were established by Congress, rather than, as conventional wisdom would have it, by the Supreme Court.[13] This is a history of progressive inclusion, equality, democracy, and protection of individual freedom, for which we can rightly be proud of our people—rather than any legacy from the founders, conservative principles or values, language in the Constitution, or legal reasoning.

The embodiment of conservative judicial dominance at the dawn of the twenty-first century is Chief Justice William Rehnquist,[14] who as a law clerk to Justice Robert Jackson in 1952 wrote a memo opposing what would become the basic American pronouncement of equality—*Brown v. Board of Education* (1954), which integrated the public schools. He wrote that the "separate but equal" principle was "right and should be reaffirmed." Another Rehnquist memo to Jackson urged approval of the all-white Democratic primary system in Texas: "It is about time the Court faced the fact that the white people of the South don't like the colored people." As a young attorney and Republican activist in Phoenix, Rehnquist actively opposed that city's public accommodations law in the early 1960s when, during a national meeting of lawyers, one of its top hotels refused to admit Jewish guests. At the helm as the Supreme Court decided in recent decades issues as vital as whether equality has gone too far was a lawyer who opposed equality at its modern beginnings and at each step along the way.[15]

Developing an approach to law, or to politics, based on a progressive understanding and tradition of freedom, democracy, and equality is a daunting task in this environment. It is complicated further by the general willingness of liberals and conservatives to let the courts have their enormous power and to accept the cyclic judicial shifts, and the accompanying condemnations of judicial activism and deviation from the idealized process, without raising any basic questions.

This arrangement has benefits. Liberals get occasional periods of judicial protection of their version of individual freedom, sometimes extending in fragments into conservative periods. Conservatives get property rights and the privileges of wealth almost always staunchly protected, and fragmentary extension of their agenda into liberal periods. Both liberals and conservatives also usually get a significant though not foolproof safeguard for the status quo and barrier to significant changes in any direction.

In recent decades, many liberals cling to the hope of rekindling the liberal judicial activism of the 1960s and to the promise of a judicial check on majoritarian excesses. However, the judicial contribution to the liberal swing in the 1960s has been exaggerated and is hard to characterize as countermajoritarian, and there is little in the way of a countermajoritarian judicial check on excesses in our historical record.[16]

There are only two periods in our entire history—from about 1937 to 1944 and from about 1961 to 1973—characterized by sustained judicial liberalism, and they correspond to periods of sustained progressive political power. This power has been based largely on popular movements, which sometimes have been able to elect liberals or progressives to high office and sometimes, but not very often, have achieved sustained success in the judicial arena. For example, there were also powerful progressive movements from 1890 to 1920, but the Supreme Court stayed staunchly conservative, unabashedly invalidating an array of liberal legislative reforms. And on the occasions crying out for a judicial check on majoritarian excess since the mid–twentieth century—the Japanese internment, the McCarthy era repression of progressives, and the criminalization of some sexual preferences come immediately to mind—the Supreme Court reacted, instead, with complicity. *Brown v. Board of Education* is surely of great importance, but it may or may not be an instance of countermajoritarian protection, and if it is thought to provide the rationale for extending and relying on judicial power, there is the difficult question of why it was not rendered long before 1954. Sustained popular pressure from progressive movements seems a necessary but not sufficient condition for sustained liberal judicial activism, and there is little historical basis for relying on the judiciary to check majoritarian excesses.

In any event, expansive judicial power is safe, familiar, and comfortable for most liberals and conservatives. But there is also afoot a deep and pervasive sense that the individual, and the American people collectively, have lost any meaningful way to affect, much less control, our own fate, and that American society and culture have lost a moral sense of direction or social purpose. Free market mania and the tendency to commodify all things human pervade our culture and our lives, yielding in the law a new and powerful discipline, law and economics, which attempts to explain and justify it all in terms of logic, reason, and "science." We seem to have adopted as our social purpose the facilitation of greed and the consolidation of wealth and resources in as few hands as possible, which we are accomplishing quite efficiently. Three decades of deregulation and tax breaks for the wealthy have yielded a near record maldistribution of wealth and resources: 10 percent of Americans own more than three-quarters of our wealth, and the real wages of working and poor people have declined or remained stagnant over several decades, including some periods characterized by rapid economic expansion.[17]

Politics has been reduced to a spectator sport—dominated by money as much as are the NFL or the NBA—in which strategy and tactics are more important than principle and the capacity to endure humiliation is more important than insight or integrity. The term for participants—*politician*—itself now connotes disgrace. Individual rights of expression no longer provide meaningful entry for people of ordinary means into a marketplace of ideas with insurmountable financial barriers to access, more akin to the stock market than the soapbox.

One result of all this is that half of the eligible voters no longer bother to vote. The media tries to bestow a mantle of legitimacy on the winners of elections no matter how ugly the contest, how minuscule the margin of victory, or how meager the turnout. In the much heralded congressional elections of 1994 that made Newt Gingrich the Speaker of the House of Representatives, the Republicans and their "Contract with America" got less than 20 percent of the eligible voters (many of whom were simply anti-Clinton), almost the same percentage went the other way, and most people stayed home. President Bill Clinton did not have much more than that 20 percent in his presidential victories, and Ronald Reagan's "landslide" victory in 1980 consisted of his getting 27 percent of the eligible voters to President Jimmy Carter's 22 percent. Our electoral system does not produce representative policies or officials or provide the winners with meaningful mandates; it yields only exaggerated legitimacy, frustrated citizens, and precarious winners.

The popular success in recent decades of conservative appeals for judicial restraint is itself reflective of the crisis of democracy. Judicial restraint will not restore democracy, nor do conservatives intend to exercise judicial restraint except selectively (when it does not interfere with their higher goals). Under cover of the judicial restraint debate, they have been moving for some time away from meaningful reform of our electoral, participatory, and democratic institutions toward enhancement of the power of the executive and judicial branches of the federal government and, more generally, toward enhancement of corporate power.[18] But the call for restraint taps into the deep public sense that democracy has broken down, and the liberal Court of the 1960s provides a good target for popular anger and frustration.

The immense power of courts and lawyers in our system is an integral part of the crisis of democracy, but not because of judicial activism or liberalism. Activism is not a deviation but part and parcel of a system of broad judicial power that impinges on democracy. The law serves, as the concept of government of law, not people, suggests, to depoliticize—removing crucial issues from the public agenda—and to cast the structure and distribution of things as they are as somehow achieved without the need for any human agency. Decisions and social structures that have been made by people—and can be unmade or remade—are depicted as neutral, objective, preordained, or even God-given, providing a false legitimacy to existing social and power relations.

The law also imposes—and removes from public scrutiny or debate—limits on the scope of democracy. For example, the economic decisions that most crucially shape our society and affect our lives—on basic social issues such as the use of our resources, investment, the environment, and the work of our people—are generally defined by the law, more so than in most every other Western democracy, as "private" and therefore not to be made democratically or by the government officials elected in the "public" sphere. This legitimizes private—mainly corporate—dominance, masks the lack of real participation or democracy, and personalizes the powerlessness it breeds.

Distrust of government in this environment should not surprise us; there isn't much to trust. Government now provides Americans at the middle and lower levels of the economic ladder little in the way of services, benefits, protection, or support in times of need. A few decades of conservatives in power has produced the kind of government and society they envisioned, perhaps best symbolized by the disparity between deteriorating, underfunded public schools (including market-driven college costs that are creating a two-tiered, class system of higher education) and a penal apparatus that is expanding without apparent limits.

The best hope and strategy is a revitalization of democracy in the broadest sense, affecting not only the electoral system but also the economy, the law, and the range of social and cultural institutions. This focus on democracy and legislatures is not based on an idealized vision of either. Legislative supremacy, for example, involves dangers and risks, and some extent and forms of judicial review further democracy. But it is hard to imagine a transition to a more humane, moral society that is not popularly driven and substantially if not primarily focused on democracy.

Such a transition would include basic reforms of the electoral system that would have widespread appeal across the political spectrum: elimination of money and all forms of bribery from elections and government; proportional representation, so that the range of people and ideas are heard and represented; and elimination of barriers to ballot access by third parties and to voting.[19] If the goal of the framers of the Constitution was, as they sometimes candidly said, to empower a national elite and to protect its reign from popular movements, they have succeeded. Their system, as it has evolved in our history and culture, spawns distrust of government and a widespread sense of futility and cynicism, which are now themselves major, maybe indispensable, ingredients for its maintenance and stability.

The role of courts, judges, and lawyers in a revitalized democracy is not easy to envision, since they currently have such enormous power, largely occupying, for example, the terrain on which basic questions of freedom, democracy, and equality are debated and resolved. Real progress on this front should be based on a contextual approach that repudiates the idealized model of judicial decision making; the very American conception of rights as absolute, individual, and without significant effects on society or others; and the cyclic, distracting debates about judicial restraint. If courts are to be restrained, the decision and the terms of restraint should not be left exclusively to courts but should be part of the process of defining and revitalizing democracy. This requires development of a realistic understanding of the range of judicial players as well as the judicial decision-making process.

Judges are the often unknowing objects, as well as among the staunchest supporters, of the myths about law and legal reasoning. While judges are usually aware of the law's gaps, conflicting mandates, and manipulability, they tend to immerse themselves in legal materials and legal reasoning, often in a state of denial about their own discretion and power to make choices.

Usually judges find confirming legal rationalizations for their choices or adopt whatever seems easiest or least controversial, which often involves ignoring or distorting contrary arguments, authorities, facts, or social realities. Some do so consciously and instrumentally, but more often their thought processes involve a less conscious or purposeful manipulation of the legal materials to provide the illusion—for themselves as well as others—that the law supports or requires what they do. In this sense, one can see them as affecting or changing the law in the course of the decision-making process, or understand the law as being or becoming what they produce or reconstitute as they weave through the legal materials and make decisions.

They sometimes feel constraints, such as an occasional moral hesitance to do what they think is expected of them, or as a fear that doing the right thing might be embarrassing to them or to the courts or other institutions. Some, particularly on appellate courts, are quite aware of and conscientiously try to resolve conflicts between their values and contrary rules or results. In such situations, however, it is still a political choice; and it is made by a person, not by "the law" and not required by legal reasoning or by the dictates or logic of any underlying social or economic system.

Decisions are predicated upon a complex mixture of social, political, institutional, experiential, and personal factors; however, they are expressed and justified, and largely perceived by judges themselves, in terms of "facts" that have been objectively determined and "law" that has been objectively and rationally "found" and "applied." Judges, like the rest of us, are immersed in the culture that pervades their daily lives and form values and prioritize conflicting considerations based on their experience, socialization, self-perceptions, hopes, and fears. The results are not, however, random; their particular backgrounds and experiences—in which law schools and the practice of law play a significant role—result in a patterning and some consistency in the ways they categorize, approach, and resolve conflicts. This is the great source of the law's power: It enforces, reflects, constitutes, and legitimizes dominant social and power relations without a need for or the appearance of control from outside and by means of social actors who largely believe in their own neutrality and the myth of nonpolitical, legally determined results.

This complex process whereby participants are encouraged to see their roles and to express themselves as neutral and objective social agents also pervades the realm of law practice. Lawyers are trained to communicate as if they have no self-interests or values and are merely promoting what the law requires, which just happens to coincide with their clients' interests. The most effective practitioners discover the art of simultaneously projecting both objectivity and principled belief in what they do, regardless of what they actually believe. The tendency or need to believe in what they do and the people and interests they represent is often overwhelming, and lawyers frequently adopt and express preposterous explanations and justifications for their clients and the positions they advocate. This is compounded by the extreme aggressiveness of the legal world. A lawyer functions in perhaps the only profession in which someone is hired and has as his or her specific responsibility to oppose and criticize everything you say or do. This all takes a heavy toll on lawyers, and burnout is common.

There is also strong pressure to take up the cause of the rich: The myth in the legal world is that, for example, finding tax breaks for people who are already sufficiently rich is somehow more interesting and personally as well as financially more rewarding than representing environmentalists, working people trying to make their workplaces safer or more fulfilling, or poor people whose legal problems bring out the lawyer's resourcefulness and ingenuity. Many lawyers devote their lives to making rich people richer even though their own values are more egalitarian and socially conscious. The reality is that the legal world provides—if one chooses it—the opportunity for quite interesting work that yields considerably more than adequate financial rewards and offers the possibility of making the world around us a somewhat better place to live.[20]

Law students, trying to understand and master legal reasoning, are commonly puzzled by the array of majority and dissenting opinions and the often pointed views of law professors regarding the cases presented to them. Differing judicial opinions each cite earlier cases and possess other apparent indicia of validity. The professor often has a theme and explanation for a string of decisions that is not found in any of the opinions. Everybody seems to have a claim to being right but the student, whose common reaction is laced with confusion, vulnerability, and insecurity. There is clear pressure to learn to "think like a lawyer," which often seems to involve abandonment of progressive values and the hope of social action (see chapter 2).

This book, in all three editions,[21] is an attempt to develop a progressive, critical analysis of current trends, decisions, and legal reasoning and of the operation and social role of the law in contemporary American society. We do not, as some progressive approaches have in the past, dismiss the law as a sham or a subterfuge; our criticism takes seriously the law's doctrines, principles, methods, and promises. Critical analysis exposes the law's proclamations of inevitability, reason, and logic as false necessity and false legitimacy, and opens up the possibility of alternatives. This provides both a deeper understanding of law and society and an essential tool for engaging in the immediate, ongoing contest over values and priorities within the law. In that contest, progressives must immerse themselves—as their opponents and the judges (and sometimes juries) they must convince do—in legal materials. Success requires effective and creative use of the rhetoric, categories, doctrines, and promises of the law and involves formulating arguments and positions in the authoritative posture every legal system adopts. The law, though indeterminate, political, and most often conservative, and though it functions to legitimate existing social and power relations, is a major terrain for political struggle that has, on occasion, yielded or encoded great gains and simply cannot be ignored by any serious progressive trend or movement.

The focus of the book is a broad range of socially important areas of law, with an emphasis on concrete, contextual analysis rather than abstract theorizing. The approach is interdisciplinary, including authors and methods based in sociology, economics, history, literature, criminology, philosophy, and political science as well as law, and draws upon the experience of law practitioners as well as teachers. We seek a theoretical and practical understanding of the law that places its institutions and individual actors in their social and historical contexts, and views the law as part of and intimately connected to society.

It is our hope that the thirty-two chapters in this third edition (fifteen of which are entirely new), while they present differing and sometimes conflicting views, will continue to provide insight, understanding, and an impetus and basis for further development to a wide variety of readers. We have attempted to minimize use of terms and references unfamiliar to non-law-trained readers, although due to space limitations it has not been possible to explain every legal term or concept used.

The book is divided into three parts. Part I is introductory, with chapters on traditional jurisprudence and legal education. Part II consists of twenty-five chapters that focus on selected issues and fields of law. These are presented in the following categories: Litigation and the Legal Process, the Quality of Life, Liberty, Property, Equality, Crime and Justice, Personal Injury, Business, Labor and Social Welfare, and the Role and Structure of Government. Part III presents five short chapters that introduce and discuss a range of progressive approaches to the law.

The reader will see reflected in this book a variety of political perspectives and methodologies, and some variance in the audiences to which the selections are addressed. While the book is intended to be more coherent as a whole than collections usually are, we have not attempted to harmonize the style or content of the contributions or to present a single, fully developed approach.

A NOTE ON THE NOTES

The bibliographic style of the notes generally follows that specified for source notes in *The Chicago Manual of Style,* published by the University of Chicago Press. However, legal citations generally follow *A Uniform System of Citations,* published by the Harvard Law Review Association, except that many words usually abbreviated have been written out to aid the non-law-trained reader. The content of the notes has generally been limited to citations to authority, and, unlike most legal writing, authorities cited with reference to a paragraph or thought, and multiple citations to a single authority, are often collected in one note.

NOTES

Portions of this introduction are drawn from my book and earlier essay on conservative decisions and approaches, *With Liberty and Justice for Some: A Critique of the Conservative Supreme Court* (New York: New Press, 1993); and *Conservative Legal Thought Revisited,* 91 Columbia Law Review 1847 (1991). I appreciate comments on an early draft from Robert Gordon and Karl Klare. The approaches and positions set out in this introduction are my own, rather than a synthesis or summary of the contributors'.

1. On a more abstract level, legitimacy also flows from the notion of popular sovereignty and a fundamental compact based on a written constitution.
2. This notion was originally expressed, of course, in terms of men. *Persons* might be a better gender-neutral substitute since *people* can sound like "the people," but I have used *people* in its popularly understood form.

3. Edward P. Thompson, *Whigs and Hunters* (New York: Pantheon, 1975), 266.

4. The development and leading tenets of Critical Legal Studies are set out in chapter 28. For a thorough bibliography, see Richard A. Bauman, *Critical Legal Studies: A Guide to the Literature* (Boulder: Westview Press/HarperCollins, 1996). On Legal Realism, see generally William Fisher, Morton Horwitz, and Thomas Reed, *American Legal Realism* (New York: Oxford University Press, 1993).

5. Charles Fried, *Order and Law, Arguing the Reagan Revolution—A Firsthand Account* (New York: Simon & Schuster, 1991), 17, 59–62, 151–54.

6. See Edwin Meese III, *With Reagan* (Washington, DC: Regnery Gateway, 1992), 318; Fried, *Order and Law,* 17, 57, 61; Robert Bork, *The Tempting of America* (New York: Free Press, 1990).

7. *Griswold v. Connecticut,* 381 U.S. 479 (1965).

8. See, for example, *Lucas v. South Carolina Coastal Council,* 505 U.S. 1003 (1992); *Dolan v. City of Tigard,* 114 S.Ct. 2309 (1994); *Nollan v. California Coastal Commission,* 483 U.S. 825 (1987); *Federal Election Commission v. National Conservative Political Action Committee,* 470 U.S. 480 (1985); *Buckley v. Valeo,* 424 U.S. 1 (1976); *First National Bank of Boston v. Bellotti,* 435 U.S. 765 (1978); *Boerne v. Flores,* 117 S.Ct. 2157 (1997); *RAV v. St. Paul,* 505 U.S. 377 (1992); *Printz v. United States,* 117 S.Ct. 2365 (1997); *City of Richmond v. Croson,* 488 U.S. 469 (1989).

9. *Lockner v. New York,* 198 U.S. 45 (1905), invalidating legislation restricting the hours of work in bakeries. See, for example, Robert L. Stern, *The Commerce Clause and the National Economy, 1933–46,* 59 Harvard Law Review 645, 659–72 (1946).

10. See Catherine Drinker Bowen, *Miracle at Philadelphia* (Boston: Little, Brown, 1966), particularly chap. 6; *The Federalist Papers* (New York: Mentor, 1961), no. 10; *Fletcher v. Peck,* 10 U.S. (6 Cranch) 87 (1810); *Marbury v. Madison,* 5 U.S. (1 Cranch) 137, 163 (1803).

11. These amendments often were not, of course, immediately or effectively implemented. The struggle over such issues does not end with an amendment, statute, or court decision, but the amendments did change the debate and provide a solid basis for setting us on a very different course.

12. See Stephen L. Schecter, "Amending the United States Constitution: A New Generation on Trial," in *Redesigning the State: The Politics of Constitutional Change,* ed. Keith G. Banting and Richard Simeon (Toronto: University of Toronto Press, 1985); Clement E. Vose, *Constitutional Change: Amendment, Politics and Supreme Court Litigation Since 1900*

(Lexington, MA: Lexington Books, 1972); Taylor Branch, *Pillar of Fire: America in the King Years, 1963–1965* (New York: Simon and Schuster, 1998) (conservative opposition to the Civil Rights Acts of 1964 and 1965). A new book that I received just as we go to press reassesses this history with a focus on issues of citizenship. See Rogers M. Smith, *Civic Ideals* (New Haven: Yale University Press, 1997).

13. See Civil Rights Acts of 1960, 1964, 1965, and 1968, 42 U.S.C. §§ 1971, 1973, 1975, 1985, 2000, 3601 (1991), covering voting, housing, employment, and public accommodations; Age Discrimination Act of 1975, 42 U.S.C. § 6101, et seq. (1991); Americans with Disabilities Act, 42 U.S.C. § 12101, et seq. (1991); 18 U.S.C. §§ 2510–21, 2701–11, 3121–27 (1991), electronic communications and surveillance provisions; Employee Polygraph Protection Act of 1988, 29 U.S.C. §§ 2001–9 (1991); Right to Financial Privacy Act of 1978, 12 U.S.C. § 3401 (1992); Freedom of Information and Privacy Acts of 1967 and 1968, 5 U.S.C. § 552 (1988).

14. See David Savage, *Turning Right: The Making of the Rehnquist Supreme Court* (New York: John Wiley & Sons, 1992), chap. 2.

15. In my view, the current conservative Court has created a dual system of equality rules that make it nearly impossible for African Americans and other minorities to make out a discrimination claim but quite easy for whites to make out a "reverse discrimination" claim. See David Kairys, *Unexplainable on Grounds Other Than Race*, 45 American University Law Review 729 (1996); *Race Trilogy*, 67 Temple Law Review 1 (1994); *With Liberty and Justice for Some*, chapter 5.

16. As used here, *countermajoritarian* does not refer simply to the usual notion that it is countermajoritarian for a court to invalidate legislation, since legislatures are majoritarian institutions. The judicial check on majoritarian excesses I address occurs when a legislature or government is acting not only through majoritarian institutions but also with majority or strong support among the people. When a majority or a very substantial portion of the people oppose a governmental action, its demise often occurs without judicial action, and a court's invalidation of it can be seen, very much like legislation, as recording or encoding a particular moment in an ongoing popular struggle. Further, when legislatures act counter to the will or inclinations of the majority of their constituents, judicial invalidation of legislation can be both majoritarian (in the sense that most people support it) and countermajoritarian (in the sense that a court is negating the action of a majoritarian institution).

17. "Economic Trends," *Business Week* (August 25, 1997): 32; Holly Sklar and Chuck Collins, "Forbes 400 World Series," *The Nation* (October 20,

1997): 6; Jane Bryant Quinn, "Your Money," *Pittsburgh Post-Gazette*, February 26, 1996.

18. See, for example, William Rehnquist, *Grand Inquests* (New York: William Morrow, 1993), 9; Fried, *Order and Law*, 67. On the rise of the executive and decline of democracy and the effects on ordinary Americans, see Donald Bartlett and James Steele, *America: What Went Wrong?* (Kansas City: Andrews & McMeel, 1992); William Greider, *Who Will Tell the People?* (New York: Simon & Schuster, 1992).

19. See David Kairys, "Why Not Democracy?" *Poverty and Race* 4 (1995): 13–18; "With Only 20 Percent of the Vote, the Republicans Have No Mandate," *Philadelphia Inquirer*, November 21, 1994; Kairys, *With Liberty and Justice for Some*, chapter 3 and conclusion. On proportional representation, see generally Douglas Amy, *Real Choices/New Voices* (New York: Columbia University Press, 1993); *Proportional Representation, The Case for a Better Election System* (Northampton, MA: Crescent Street Press, 1997), pamphlet available from the Center for Voting and Democracy, P. O. Box 60037, Washington, D.C. 20039.

20. See Gary Bellow, *Steady Work: A Practitioner's Reflections on Political Lawyering*, 31 Harvard Civil Rights–Civil Liberties Law Review 297 (1996); David Kairys, *Law and Politics*, 52 George Washington Law Review 243, 260–62 (1984).

21. The book originated in 1979 as a project of the Theoretical Studies Committee of the National Lawyers Guild and proceeded, at first informally and later formally, as a joint project with the Conference on Critical Legal Studies. The first edition was published in 1982, the second in 1990.

I

TRADITIONAL JURISPRUDENCE AND LEGAL EDUCATION

1 ELIZABETH MENSCH

THE HISTORY OF MAINSTREAM LEGAL THOUGHT

THE most corrosive message of legal history is the message of contingency.[1] Routinely, the justificatory language of law parades as the unquestionable embodiment of Reason and Universal Truth; yet even a brief romp through the history of American legal thought reveals how quickly the Obvious Logic of one period becomes superseded by the equally obvious, though contradictory, logic of subsequent orthodoxy. The account that follows is a short, and necessarily superficial, summary of the major changes that have taken place in American legal thought since the start of the nineteenth century. There will be no attempt to examine the complex causes of those changes, nor any effort to locate them in social or economic context. The goal is more limited: to describe the legal consciousness of distinct (although overlapping) periods of American legal thought. Since the effort is to reconstruct the world view of those who have been most directly concerned with making, explaining, and applying legal doctrine, many theorists who have written on the fundamental questions of jurisprudence are omitted. This is an account of conventional, and therefore often wholly unreflecting and unselfconscious, legal consciousness.[2]

PRECLASSICAL CONSCIOUSNESS (1776–1885)

During the contentious period that immediately followed the Revolution, elite American jurists devoted themselves to reestablishing legal authority. As the embodiment of reason and continuity, law seemed to offer the only source of stability in a nation where republicanism, if conceived only as local participatory democracy, would quickly dissolve into the disruptive passions of the people who had now so rashly been declared sovereign.[3] The ultimate expression of this response was the Constitution, serving simultaneously as the declared expression of popular sovereignty ("We the people . . . ") and as a distinctly *legal* text, to be interpreted authoritatively only by those learned in the profession.[4]

In a flowery vocabulary drawn from the natural-law tradition, late-eighteenth- and early-nineteenth-century legal speakers made extravagant claims about the role of law and lawyers. They described law as reflecting here on earth the universal principles of divine justice, which, in their purest form, reigned in the Celestial City. Their favorite legal quotation, for rhetorical purposes, was taken from the Anglican theologian Hooker: "Of law no less can be acknowledged, than that her seat is the bosom of God; her voice the harmony of the world."[5]

Similarly, lawyers portrayed their own professional character as the truest embodiment of republican virtue. Ideally, within each well-educated lawyer reason had subdued the unruly passions, and that triumph rendered the lawyer fit to consecrate himself to the service of law, as a "priest at the temple of justice." In this role the lawyer/priest was to act, not as an instrument of his client's unbridled will, but as a "trustee" for the interests of the whole community. As adviser and guardian, he would attempt to elicit elevated rather than base motives in his clients, guiding them to promote a social order consistent with those universal principles that were ordained by God and most clearly understood by lawyers.

This special trusteeship meant that lawyers played a vital political role in the new democracy, where principle and legal right continually faced the threat of mass assault. Leaders of the bar often described lawyers as sentinels, placed on the dangerous outposts of defense, preserving the virtue of the republic from the specifically democratic threats of irrational legislation and mob rule. Not surprisingly, many nineteenth-century jurists cited with satisfaction de Tocqueville's observation that the legal profession constituted a distinctively American aristocracy, providing order in an otherwise unstable democracy.

The universal principle that seemed to require the most zealous protection was the sanctity of private property, which was conceived as the surest foundation for both ordered political liberty and economic stability. With something approaching paranoia, American jurists explained that the redistributive passions of the majority, if ever allowed to overrun the barrier of legal principle, would sweep away the nation's whole social and economic foundation. Thus Joseph Story, upon his inauguration as professor of law at Harvard, announced that the lawyer's most "glorious and not infrequently perilous" duty was to guard the "sacred rights of property" from the "rapacity" of the majority. Only the "solitary citadel" of justice stood between property and redistribution; it was the lawyer's noble task to man that citadel, whatever the personal cost. "What sacrifice could be more pure than in such a cause? What martyrdom more worthy to be canonized in our hearts?"[6]

The ornate legal rhetoric of the period obscured a number of dilemmas deep at the core of early American legal theory. First, despite the rhetorical appeal to natural law as a source of legitimacy, American jurists lived in an intellectual context which no longer took for granted a close epistemological link between God, human reason, and the laws of nature. Most jurists readily conceded that natural law alone was too indeterminate to guide judicial decision making in specific cases; natural law provided divine sanction but yielded few concrete rules or results. Moreover, pure natural-law theory could lead in unwanted directions. The notion of natural reason upon which it rested, for example, could be translated to mean the natural reason of the sovereign people—Thomas Paine's common sense—rather than the reason of trained lawyers. That suggested precisely the unlimited popular will which most jurists feared. Furthermore, the moral content of natural-law theory often led in contradictory directions. One key example was the right to property: while an enlightenment natural-law tradition asserted the sanctity of private property, an older (and alarmingly popular) natural-law tradition located all social and economic inequality in original sin.[7]

Most early-nineteenth-century lawyers thus conceded (as had Hooker himself) that the most immediate, practical source and definition of law could be found in the consensual basis of positive law. That did not necessarily mean statutes, which were suspect given their origin in unpredictable legislative assemblies.[8] Instead, it meant the text of the Constitution, rooted in a generalized consent to authority as distributed and exercised within a federal institutional structure separate and apart from direct majoritarian rule at any given time. Positive law also meant the complex, ancient forms of the English common law, whose legitimacy derived not from universal moral principle rooted in natural reason but from the tacit consent evident from custom and long usage.[9] It was the extraordinary technicality of the common law that provided lawyers with their claim to expertise and served, by its very artificiality, to distinguish legal reasoning from the "commonsense" reason of the general populace.[10] Moreover, common-law rules, however quirky, seemed able to supply the certainty and formal predictability impossible to find in the vague morality of natural law.

The precise relation between natural-law and common-law forms was inevitably problematic. Occasionally judges announced that the common law and natural law were identical, but that claim was inherently implausible. Many technical rules of the common law were purely whimsical, rooted exclusively in the English legal tradition and often derived from the history of feudal property relations which Americans had explicitly repudiated. Some rules had already been declared wholly inapplicable to the New World, where they had been modified, in quite various ways, in each of the colonies. Even in England there had been obvious changes within the supposed changelessness of the common law. Thus, it was hard to argue that each common-law rule was an expression of immutable, universal truth.

Early leading jurists like Hamilton and Marshall recognized that one could secure emerging property rights more coherently by locating them in the positive law of the constitutional text, thereby severing them from the debatable vagaries of both the natural-law and the common-law traditions. An important example is *Fletcher v. Peck*, where in 1810 Marshall deftly blended natural law and selective analogy to common law to protect vested property rights from legislative redistribution, but relied on the contract clause of the Constitution as the ultimate basis for decision.[11]

Meanwhile, in private law, the potential conflict between natural-law conceptions and the common-law tradition, as well as between contradictory assertions within natural law, was obscured in the early nineteenth century by a surprisingly self-confident assurance that one could always reach a just conclusion by employing two techniques of legal reasoning: liberality of interpretation and implication. By the first, judges and treatise writers meant a willingness to interpret technical common-law rules—which were still unquestioningly assumed to form the bulk of the law—with a flexible, progressive American spirit and, in particular, with concern for commercial utility. Lord Mansfield in England, who had often drawn on civil law to modify rigid common-law rules in the name of commercial good sense, was often cited as an example to be followed by enlightened American decision makers.

This notion of utility became a key mediating concept in liberal interpretation. It suggested that one did not have to choose *between* a strict, rigid adherence to common-law technicalities and the less certain demands of substantive justice, nor *between* commercial utility and the moralistic claims of traditional natural law. Instead, it was common to cite utility as a justification for departing from common-law rules, often on the claim that the common law itself, properly understood by liberal judges like Mansfield, had always allowed for utilitarian change; and then further to explain that in the form of commercial "reasonableness," utility was implicit in natural reason and therefore in the whole natural-law and civil-law tradition. Thus, modern departures from common-law rules could be seen as both consistent with the long "changing change-lessness" of the common-law tradition and also as evidence of the common law's link to natural reason and universal principle.[12]

The technique of implied intent, also basic to early-nineteenth-century legal thought, performed a similar function. Often, judges appealed to the intent of the parties as a basis for decision making, which coincided with the increased use of contract imagery in judicial opinions. The emphasis on implied intent did not, however, necessarily evidence concern with the actual, subjective intent of individual parties. Instead, it represented a fusion of subjective intent with socially imposed duty. Legal thinkers confidently assumed that they could find the "law" within the obligations inherent in particular social and commercial relations, obligations which, it could be claimed, parties intended to assume when they entered the relationship.

For example, in his important treatise on contract law, Parsons devoted over 90 percent of the pages to a description of various types of parties (e.g., agents, guardians, servants) and relational contexts (e.g., marriage, bailment, service contracts, sale of goods).[13] Each category represented a social entity with its own implicit duties and reasonable expectations. A party entering into a particular relationship would be said to have intended to conform to the standards of reasonable behavior that inhered in such a relationship. Specific rules could then be defended or modified depending upon whether they promoted the principles and policies basic to that relationship (encouraged transactions in goods, promoted honorable dealing between merchants, etc.). Subjectivity and free will were thus combined with the potentially conflicting imposition of objective, judicially created obligations; and both notions were integrated into the amorphous blend of natural law, positive law, morality, and utility, which made up the justificatory language of early-nineteenth-century law.

In retrospect, that amorphous blend might be viewed as an early form of sophisticated American legal pragmatism. Nevertheless, despite the confidence with which early-nineteenth-century judges invoked liberality and implied intent, the conceptual mush they made of legal theory posed serious problems for the emerging liberal conception, in constitutional law, of a sovereignty limited by private legal rights. Public-law thinking was dominated by the Lockean model of the individual right holder confronting a potentially oppressive sovereign power. Within that world view, there ideally existed a realm of pure private autonomy, free from state intrusion. In that realm individuals owned property protected from the encroachment of others and made self-willed, freely bargained-for choices. Of course there was also a legitimate public realm, comprised of state and federal institutions entrusted with maintaining public order and serving clearly delineated public functions. Nevertheless, the public realm and the private were clearly and strictly bounded. They were conceived as wholly separate, in-or-out categories that could allow for no blurring or intermeshing. It was, in effect, the strict boundary between public and private that jurists of the early nineteenth century promised to guard with such everlasting zeal.

Yet, in order to justify protecting private rights from public power, it was necessary to conceive of the private as purely private. This demanded, in turn, a fully rationalized structure of private law, which, in theory, did no more than protect and facilitate the exercise of private will and which could also give concrete, objective content to the private rights supposedly protected by the Constitution. The loose hodgepodge of conflicting premises that made up early-nineteenth-century private law was woefully deficient for that purpose, and the great thrust of nineteenth-century legal thought was toward higher and higher levels of rationalization and generalization. Eventually, that process produced a grandly integrated conceptual scheme that seemed, for a fleeting moment in history, to bring coherence to the whole structure of American law, and to liberal political theory in general.

CLASSICAL LEGAL CONSCIOUSNESS (1885–1935)

The nineteenth century's process of legal rationalization resulted in the abstraction of law from both particularized social relations and substantive moral standards. By the "rule of law" classical jurists meant quite specifically a structure of positivised, objective, formally defined rights. They viewed the legal world not as a multitude of discrete, traditional relations but as a structure of protected spheres of rights and powers. Logically derivable boundaries defined for each individual her own sphere of pure private autonomy while simultaneously defining those spheres within which public power could be exercised freely and absolutely.

This conception of social action as the exercise of absolute rights and powers within bounded spheres extended to all possible relations. In a way inconceivable to the early nineteenth century, the relation of private parties to each other was seen as deeply analogous to the relation of private parties to states, of states to each other and to federal powers, etc. Through this process of analogic refinement run rampant, the boundary between public and private repeatedly reproduced itself. For example, quasi-contracts, which constituted the public sphere within contract law, were to be carefully distinguished from contracts based on intent; and contract law generally was to be kept wholly distinct from the more public realm of torts. Furthermore, within the private sphere, women were relegated to the utterly "private" realm of familial domesticity, leaving to men the more "public" sphere of economic activity.[14] Within this elaborate structure of spheres and analogies, the key legal question, in every instance of dispute, was whether the relevant actors had stayed within their own protected sphere of activity or had crossed over the boundary and invaded the sphere of another. To the classics, freedom *meant* the legal guarantee that rights and powers would be protected as absolute within their own sphere, but that no rightholder/powerholder would be allowed to invade the sphere of another.

Within the classical scheme, judges assumed the utterly crucial task of boundary definition. Necessarily, this task required objectivity and impartiality. Other actors were free, within their own spheres, to exercise unbridled will in pursuit of their particular (subjective) moral, political, or economic goals. In contrast, the judicial role of boundary finding required the exercise of reason—a reason now conceived, not as embodying universal moral principles and knowledge of the public good, but strictly as the application of objective methodology to the task of defining the scope of legal rights. Upon the supposed objectivity of that method hinged the liberal faith that the rule of law resolved the conflict between freedom as private, civil right and freedom as the republican ideal of public participation and civic virtue.

The supposed judicial objectivity upon which the classical structure depended was based in turn upon the intersection of constitutional language and an increasingly generalized, rationalized conception of private law. First, jurists pointed out that by enacting the Constitution, the sovereign American people had unequivocally (and wisely) adopted a government premised on private rights and strictly limited public powers. Thus, while it was certainly the exalted function of the judiciary to protect private rights from uncontrolled public passion, this function required merely the application of positive constitutional law—there was no painful choice to be made between positive law and natural rights.

Second, and of prime importance, the objective definition given to rights protected by the Constitution could be found within the common-law tradition, which had been wonderfully cleansed of both messy social particularity and natural-law morality. Classical jurists claimed that as a result of an enlightened, scientific process of rationalization, the common law could now properly be reconceived as based upon a few general and powerful—but clearly positivised—conceptual categories (like property and free contract), which had also been incorporated into the Constitution as protected rights. Christopher Columbus Langdell, the Harvard professor who established the case method in the law school classroom, taught that all of the specific rules within common-law cases (at least the "correct" rules) could be logically derived from those general categories. For example, expanding upon that model, Williston's monumental treatise on contracts assumed that from the general principle of free contract one could derive the few central doctrines around which the treatise was organized—offer and acceptance, consideration, excuse, etc.—and from the logic of those central doctrines one could derive all of the specific rules that made up the law of contracts.[15] Those rules could then be applied, rigidly and formally, to *any* particular social context; in fact, failure to do so would be evidence of judicial irrationality and/or irresponsibility. Moreover, because every rule was based upon the principle of free contract, the logical coherence of contract doctrine, correctly applied, ensured that private contracting was always an expression of pure autonomy. With no small amount of self-congratulation, classical jurists contrasted their conceptualization of private autonomy to Parson's description of contract law as something to be found *within* numberless particular social relations. In retrospect, Parsons could be viewed as naive and unscientific.

The new rationalization of common law meant that the old conflict between formal "rules" and substantive "justice" seemed resolved.

Common-law rules were no longer a quirky relic from the English feudal past. Instead, they were both an expression and a definition of rights, and of course the protection of rights constituted the highest form of justice. Furthermore, as integrated into the constitutional law structure, the rationalization of private law meant that the boundary between the realm of private autonomy and the realm of public power could be objectively determined by reference to specific common-law doctrine.

The notorious case of *Coppage v. Kansas* provides a clear example of the classical approach.[16] In that case the Kansas state legislature had passed a statute outlawing yellow-dog contracts (i.e., contracts in which workers agreed not to engage in union activities). The question was whether this was a reasonable exercise of police power (i.e., fell within the bounded sphere of public power) or whether it constituted an invasion of private contract right, a right considered implicit in the even more general category of liberty protected by the Fourteenth Amendment.

An earlier case, *Adair v. United States*, had declared that a similar federal regulation was invalid.[17] Through the Fourteenth Amendment the constitutional protection of liberty as against the federal government was made applicable to the states—evidence of the deep analogy now perceived in what were once thought to be quite different relationships. In response to the argument that *Adair* controlled, however, Kansas argued that its statute was designed specifically to outlaw contracts formed under coercion. Since workers had no realistic choice but to accept the terms obviously imposed by employers, the agreement to sign yellow-dog contracts was not an expression of freedom, and it was no violation of liberty to regulate a "choice" that was never freely made. The Court refused to accept that argument, *not* because it denied the obvious inequality between workers and employers, but because freedom of contract as a legal category had to be defined objectively, which meant according to common-law doctrine. Since the common law had excluded economic pressure from its definition of duress as a legal excuse for non-performance of contracts, then *by definition* yellow-dog contracts were not formed under duress and were therefore freely entered. It then followed logically that the statute constituted an invasion of liberty protected by the Constitution.

Cases like *Coppage* are now commonly cited as representing a judiciary determined to impose its own economic biases on the country. This both trivializes the underlying power of the classical conceptual scheme and, more significantly, trivializes the importance of the realist assault that revealed its incoherence. In fact, courts during the classical period described a police power as absolute in its sphere as were private rights in theirs, and they by no means overruled all legislation designed to regulate corporate power. Their key claim was that they could objectively "find" the boundary that separated private from public, and it was that supposed objectivity that gave the appearance of coherence and reality to the legal (and social/political) model of bounded rights and powers. That basic model, although in bankrupt form, is with us still, despite the realist challenge that demolished its premises. The message the model conveys is that actual power relations in the real world are by definition legitimate.

THE REALIST CHALLENGE (1920–1940)

The realist movement was part of the general twentieth-century revolt against formalism and conceptualism. As applied to law, that revolt was directed against the whole highly conceptualized classical legal structure, which even by the early 1920s had begun to appear barren. In part that barrenness derived from the outmoded view of "science" it represented. While Langdell's science of law was a science of clean principles deductively applied, early realists pointed out that the natural sciences had long since abandoned that approach, having adopted instead an inductive, experimental methodology that stressed empirical inquiry. Meanwhile, the social sciences in America, which had gained prominence since the Civil War with the emergence of the Progressive movement, were emphasizing social-scientific fact-gathering as the only way to understand the complex social reality of a mass industrialized and urbanized economy.[18]

More specifically and politically, realism was also a reaction against Supreme Court decisions that had invalidated progressive regulatory legislation favored even by many business leaders. Realists drew upon an early Progressive critique of property rights that had sought to blur the distinction between public and private so as to justify regulating and rendering accountable the vast accumulations of private power that had come to characterize the large-scale American economy by the close of the nineteenth century. That meant recognizing the growing importance of government—especially administrative agencies—in an advanced industrial economy. Thus the realists urged judges to eschew the rigid, abstract formalism of constitutionally protected property and contract rights in favor of increasing deference to the legislative adjustment of competing claims, enacted in the service of a larger "public interest."[19]

Meanwhile, in private law, enlightened, progressive judges should be willing to sacrifice rigid adherence to the logic of doctrine for the sake of doing a more commonsense and overtly policy-oriented "justice" within the particular context of each case.[20] In turn, that policy orientation required the collection of social and economic data, both for the sake of sensible policy decision making and also for the sake of understanding the role of legal actors within a complex social structure. The realists thus removed law from its sphere of autonomous logic, and placed it squarely within the larger political/social system.

At their most critical extreme, moreover, the realists also conducted a thoroughgoing logical assault upon conventional legal reasoning, cutting so deeply into the premises of American legal thought that subsequent legal thinkers are still struggling to rebuild a convincingly coherent structure. Chiefly, the realists undermined all faith in the objective existence of "rights" by challenging the coherence of the key legal categories that gave content to the notion of bounded public and private spheres. Traditionally, legal discourse had justified decisions by making reference to rights. An opinion, for example, would set out as a reason for finding the defendant liable that she had invaded the property rights of the plaintiff—or, similarly, would justify declaring a statute unconstitutional by saying that it violated the right of property. Yet, as the realists pointed out, such justifications are inevitably circular. There will be a right if, and *only* if, the court finds for the plaintiff or declares the statute unconstitutional. Rights are not a preexisting fact of nature, to be found somewhere "out there," but a function of legal decision making itself. What the court cites as the *reason* for the decision—the existence of a right—is, in fact, only the *result*. Rights are thus artificial, a function of social decision making, not a discernable reflection of reality itself.

Moreover, perfectly logical but contradictory arguments can always be generated about whether or not one has a particular right. As a matter of pure logic, nothing, for example, is excluded from the state's legitimate concern for the public welfare—as categories, public and private are utterly reversible. Similarly, as between two conflicting private rights, logical arguments can always be made for either side. My private right to be secure from the invasion of a nuisance, like the chemicals a neighbor sprays on her lawn, conflicts with her right to use her property freely. My right to be secure from "unfair" competition conflicts with her freedom to engage in unbridled freedom on the market. The legal system cannot simply protect rights, but must always choose between two perfectly logical but mutually exclusive rights.[21]

The realist attack upon the logic of rights theory was closely linked to an attack upon the logic of precedent. The realists pointed out that no two cases are ever exactly alike. There will always be some difference in the multitude of facts surrounding them. Thus, the "rule" of a former case can never simply be applied to a new case; rather, the judge must *choose* whether or not the ruling in the former case should be extended to include the new case. That choice is essentially a choice about the relevancy of facts, and those choices can never be logically compelled. Given shared social assumptions, some facts might seem obviously irrelevant (e.g., the color of socks worn by the offeree should not influence the enforceability of a contract), but decisions about the relevance of other distinguishing facts are more obviously value-laden and dependent on the historical context (e.g., the relative wealth of the parties).

That dilemma does not vanish when the "law" to be applied comes not from cases but from the language of statutory or constitutional provisions, or the language of a private contract. There was a time when words were thought to have a fixed, determinant content, a meaning partaking of objective Platonic forms. In the absence of a belief in Platonic intelligible essences, however, no interpretation or application of language can be logically required by the language itself. Words are created by people in history, and their definition inevitably varies with particular context and with the meaning brought to them by the judges who are asked to interpret them. That act of interpretation is, in every instance, an act of social choice.

Thus, the realists claimed that the effort of the nineteenth century to cleanse law of messy social particularity and moral choice was inevitably a failure. There was *no such thing* as an objective legal methodology behind which judges could hide in order to evade responsibility for the social consequences of legal decision making. Every decision they made was a moral and political choice.[22]

Furthermore, the realists understood, as had the classics, that the whole structure of the classical scheme depended upon the coherence of private law and the public/private distinction. Thus, the realists spent little time attacking the methodology of constitutional law and concentrated instead upon undermining the coherence of the key private-law categories that purported to define a sphere of pure autonomy. For example, in his essay "Property and Sovereignty," Morris Cohen pointed out that property is necessarily public, not private.[23] Property *means* the legally granted power to withhold from others. As such, it is created by the state and given its only content by legal decisions that limit or extend the property owner's power over others. Thus, property is really an (always conditional) delegation of sovereignty, and property law is simply a form of public law. Whereas the classics (and liberal theorists generally) had drawn a bright line separating (private) property from (public) sovereignty, Cohen collapsed the two categories.

Hale made a similar point about the supposed private right of free contract: state enforcement of a contract right represents, like property, a delegation of sovereign power.[24] Moreover, he also pointed out that coercion, including legal coercion, lies at the heart of every "freely" chosen exchange. Coercion is inherent in each party's legally protected threat to withhold what is owned; that right to withhold creates the right to force submission to one's own terms. Since ownership is a function of legal entitlement, every bargain is a function of that legal order. Thus, there is no "inner" core of free, autonomous bargaining to be protected from "outside" state action. The inner and outer dissolve into each other.

The realist critique did not, by itself, mandate any particular form of social or economic organization. At the extremes, for example, neither centralized state economic planning nor radical deconcentration of industry was logically entailed by their arguments, nor was any particular arrangement that fell between those extremes. Instead, their goal was to clear the air of beguiling but misleading conceptual categories (as termed by Felix Cohen, "transcendental nonsense") so that thought could be redirected to the two levels that required attention before sensible and responsible economic and political decisions could be made: first, to a close, contextual examination of social reality—to *facts*, rather than the nonexistent spheres of classicism; and second, to ethics, for if social decision making was inevitably moral choice, then policymakers needed some basis upon which to make their choices.[25]

Potentially, however, the realist collapse of spheres also carried with it the collapse of the whole structure of American legal thought. Realism had effectively undermined the fundamental premises of liberal legalism, particularly the crucial distinction between legislation (subjective exercise of will) and adjudication (objective exercise of reason). Inescapably, it had also suggested that the whole liberal world view of (private) rights and (public) sovereignty mediated by the rule of law was only a mirage, a pretty fantasy that masked the reality of economic and political power.

Since the realists, American jurists have dedicated themselves to the task of reconstruction; indeed, the realist message was so corrosive that many of the most influential realists evaded the full implications of their own criticism and quickly sought instead to articulate a new justification for legal reasoning's old claim to objectivity and legitimacy. That effort seemed especially crucial after the rise of fascism in Europe. If the rule of law was mere illusion, then where could one look for protection against totalitarian statism?[26] Nevertheless, the modern search for a new legitimacy, however earnest, was destined always to have a slightly defensive tone. After realism, American legal theorists had, as it were, eaten of the tree of knowledge, and there could be no return to the naive confidence of the past.

ATTEMPTS AT MODERN RECONSTRUCTION (1940–PRESENT)

During the 1940s, Laswell and McDougal at Yale followed out the implications of realism by announcing that since law students were destined to be the policymakers of the future, Yale should simply abandon the traditional law school curriculum and teach students how to make and implement policy decisions.[27] Their simultaneously antidemocratic and antilegalist message was a bit jarring; most of the major postrealist reconstructors of American legal thought have been more rhetorically restrained. Indeed, much of the reconstruction has consisted of simply conceding a number of key realist insights and then attempting to incorporate those insights into an otherwise intact doctrinal structure. What were once perceived as deep and unsettling logical flaws have been translated into the strengths of a progressive legal system. For example, the indeterminacy of rules has become the flexibility required for sensible, policy-oriented decision making; and the collapse of rights into contradiction has been recast as "competing interests," which are inevitable in a complex world and which obviously require an enlightened judicial balancing. In other words, we justify as legal sophistication what the classics would have viewed as the obvious abandonment of legality.

The most elaborate attempt to resurrect the legitimacy of the whole American lawmaking structure can be found in the extraordinarily influential Hart and Sacks legal process materials of the 1950s.[28] Those materials were premised on a vision of American society which, it seemed for a time, offered a viable alternative to the classical world view. Hart and Sacks started by explaining that the critical view of law as a "mask for force, providing a cover of legitimacy" for the exercise of political and economic power, was based on "the fallacy of the static pie." According to Hart and Sacks, the "pie" of both tangible and intangible goods was in fact ever expanding, and a primary, shared purpose of social life was to keep the pie growing.

Within the Hart and Sacks description of American society, the essentially private actors who shared the goal of expansion also shared a belief in the stability afforded by the institutional settlement (by law) of the few disputes that were likely to arise, and more specifically in the particular distribution of functions that was set out in the American Constitution. That distribution was itself designed to ensure both the maximization of valid human wants and a "fair" (although not necessarily equal) distribution of tangible and intangible goods.

The effect was to postulate not particular substantive rights but rather a shared social value in the *process* by which rights were defined—a shared value in distinct institutional competencies. That implied, in turn, a differentiation of the processes by which judges, in contrast to legislators and administrators, reached decisions. According to Hart and Sacks, judges had the competence to settle questions that lent themselves to a process of "reasoned elaboration"—that could, in other words, be settled by reference to general, articulated standards which could be applied in all like cases. That process was contrasted with the "unbuttoned discretion" enjoyed by legislators.

Similarly, in considering statutes, judges were bound to a process of "sound" and "purposive" interpretation. Sound interpretation required not foolish literalism, but feeling bound to a statute's underlying purpose and place in the American legal structure generally. A basic, perhaps quaint, assumption was that legislation is generally enacted in pursuit of rational public policy objectives, not for the sake of private interest groups or self-interested advantage.

The shift from an emphasis on substance to an emphasis on process seemed for a time to satisfy the realist critique of substantive rights. It also implicitly recognized a point that had often seemed to elude the more reductionist realists, with their modernist, fundamentalist zeal for bare facts: judging, if properly understood as a culture, exists only as a complex interrelationship between legal theory and judicial act. The vocabulary of doctrine, even if logically indeterminate, is hardly irrelevant to the process of judging. Nevertheless, the legal process materials still rested on the distinction between reasoned elaboration and discretion, which in turn rested on the availability of principled, objective, substantive categories to which judges could make reference. More generally, it also rested on the complacent, simplistic assumption that American society consisted of happy, private actors cheerfully maximizing their valid human wants while sharing their profound belief in institutional competencies. That may have reflected the mind-set of many in the 1950s, but by the end of the 1960s it seemed oddly out of touch with a pluralist reality, and with a nation bitterly divided against itself.

Another response to the collapse of clear conceptual categories has been less self-consciously articulated than Hart and Sacks's, but pervades modern case law. The prevailing pattern is to accept as inevitable and "in the nature of things" the absence of clear boundaries between categories. Instead, boundaries are portrayed as fluid, or blurred, meaning that many particular examples will occupy a mushy middle position, which includes attributes of two nonetheless distinct categories. Thus, the collapse of spheres is not total, and the goal is to deal comfortably with a world made up largely of middle positions.

This blurring of boundaries cuts across all doctrinal lines. For example, under traditional rules of jurisdiction, a state court could exercise jurisdiction only over a defendant who was within the borders of the state; the line was as clear as the state's boundary marker. That straightforward "in or out" conception has now given way to a conception that recognizes "presence" as often a middle ground, sort-of-in sort-of-out notion, to be determined by standards of "fair play and substantial justice" and by a "balance" of the interests of the relevant parties and forums.[29] Similarly, whereas classical doctrine had drawn a clear line, at the moment of formation, between contract and no contract, modern reference to reliance breaks down that clarity by recognizing a sort-of contract prior to formation, based on one party's reasonable reliance on the other's precontract negotiating promises.[30] The same notion also breaks down the once sharp contract/tort distinction (i.e., obligations agreed to by the parties as distinct from obligations imposed by law), since reliance is the basis of neither a recognized tort nor a fully contractual cause of action.

In constitutional law, the line between public and private, once the mainstay of legal coherence, can now be located only by applying a puzzling array of increasingly refined and contextual "tests." For example, in the state action cases, to determine whether an ostensibly private actor is to be charged with state accountability under the Fourteenth Amendment, we must measure the degree of "state involvement" to see if it is sufficiently "significant," a process that can be accomplished only by "weighing facts and sifting circumstances" in a particular case.[31] Thus we learn that an actor performing a "public function" remains private unless the function in question is one "traditionally" and "exclusively" a public one (ownership of town, or voting, but not education or dispute resolution, e.g.), and that activities authorized by the state are not chargeable to the public if they are not "encouraged" but merely "approved" or "acquiesced in."[32] Similarly, in the space of eight short years, the Supreme Court treated large privately owned shopping centers as, first, functionally public, then, functionally public and formally private at the same time, and, finally, formally private for all purposes.[33]

Closely paralleling the emergence of blurred boundaries has been the breakdown of the deep sense of analogy and uniformity that once characterized classical thought. Private-law categories such as property or contract were then thought to have fixed meanings that did not vary with differences in context. That uniformity was conceived to be crucial to the ideal of rationality and formal equality. Now, however, it is common to concede that rights may vary depending upon status and relationship. As Justice Robert Jackson explained in *United States v. Willow River Power Company*, simply because a particular water-flow level might constitute property as between two private parties, that did not necessarily mean that the same flow constituted property as between a private party and the federal government.[34]

Despite the breakdown of boundaries and uniform, generally applicable categories, modern American legal thought continues to be premised on the distinction between private law and public law. Private law is still assumed to be *about* private actors with private rights, making private choices, even though sophisticated judges tend quite frankly to refer to public policy when justifying private-law decision making. Similarly, the major postrealist reconstructors of private-law theory, like Edward Levi and Karl Llewellyn, acknowledged the necessary role of policy choice in legal decision making but described judicial choices as still specifically "legal" because judges worked within a long-established common law tradition, which exerted a steadying (if not precisely "logical") constraint. By training, judges acquire a "craft-consciousness," which leads them to respond to new situations through a "reworking of the heritage" rather than through unguided impulse. The result is neither unbridled choice nor inflexible formalism but "continuity with growth" and "vision with tradition."[35] The new private-law heroes were therefore not the rigorous Willistonians, who refused to acknowledge the role of social change in shaping law, but (once again) Mansfield in England, America's own preclassical nineteenth-century judges, and, in more recent times, Benjamin Cardozo.

As an example of enlightened decision making, Levi described with admiration Cardozo's opinion in *McPherson v. Buick Motors Company*.[36,37] There, Cardozo had modified the classical privity of contract rule (according to which a manufacturer's liability for personal injuries due to a defective product extended only to those with whom he had directly entered a contract) in order to hold Buick liable for a "foreseeable" injury to a party not in privity. As justification, Cardozo had specifically referred to changes in automobile retailing practices, because of which only retailers, and rarely consumers, directly contracted with manufacturers. Under the privity rule, consumers would almost always be left unprotected when defective cars caused injuries, an "anomalous" result, Cardozo said, which he did not want to reach.

Cardozo, however, did not speak to the question of policy alone. He also justified his decision by referring to the category of "abnormally dangerous" products, which had evolved as an exception to the privity rule, and to the standard of "foreseeability" upon which he claimed that exception was based. Using the notion of foreseeability, Cardozo masterfully suggested that his decision was a reasoned application of past doctrine, not simply a result-oriented exercise of judicial policy choice. Nevertheless, the skilled craft of the opinion obscured rather than solved the key realist point: for every rule there is bound to be a counterrule, *because* the choice to be made is always between the contradictory claims of freedom and security. In their extreme form here, that would mean freedom as complete absence of manufacturer liability versus consumer security as manufacturer liability for all injuries caused by use of his product. Cardozo used the tort doctrine of foreseeability to mediate those extremes, yet no jurist of his time knew better than Cardozo just how manipulable the doctrine of foreseeability could be. It was Cardozo's decision in *Palsgraf* which rendered a statistically foreseeable injury to a railroad passenger "unforeseeable" because of its odd mode of occurrence—at an utterly individualized level, there was too little closeness in the relationship between the risk undertaken (which was to the property interest of a different passenger) and the personal injury suffered by Mrs. Palsgraf.[38] At the most general, social level of statistical probability, of course, risk is always foreseeable; yet in their complete particularity individual injuries can never be "foreseen." Legal logic offers no reason for drawing the line at any single point between the general and the particular. Recasting the problem as one of a supposedly neutral public policy does not resolve the dilemma, for we have now learned that trite, conventional economic policy arguments can be made for *either* freedom or security.

As with policy, modern private-law thinking has both conceded and evaded the inevitability of value choice in legal decision making. The great postrealist treatise writers, Corbin on contracts and Prosser on torts, appeal at least as often to presumably neutral, shared standards of substantive "justice" and "reasonableness" as they do to fixed rules. But the vocabulary of modern treatises is still the vocabulary of classical doctrine—questions of justice emerge *within* discussions of offer and acceptance, the elements of a cause of action in negligence, etc. The message is that we can advance beyond the silly stage of formalism while still retaining the basic structure and premises of classical thought. Both Prosser and Corbin, however, leave unresolved the old conflict between formal rules and general standards of substantive justice; and neither explains where, within liberalism's supposed subjectivity of values, one is to find a source for objective standards of justice.

The most sophisticated version of private-law reconstruction can be found in the Sales Article of the Uniform Commercial Code—essentially Llewellyn's revamping of traditional contract law. Like Corbin and Prosser, Llewellyn relied on standard doctrine for most of his vocabulary, but he also sought to replace a formalistic application of rules with standards of good faith and reasonableness. Those standards were to be known, not through logically unassailable principles or through the abstract universals of natural law, but through a judicial understanding of actual intent and reasonable expectations within each specific fact situation and within the customs and usages of specific trades. This was Llewellyn's famous "situation-sense," perhaps best described as a form of narrative sensibility rooted in common law traditionalism. It was, Llewellyn insisted, distinctly "legal" because it drew on the common law tradition of craft, reason, and principle, and at the same time saw (universal) reason as embodied *within* the particularity of specific commercial practice.

Llewellyn's "singing reason," as he perhaps unfortunately termed it, has already raised methodological problems.[39] The facts of particular customs or situations tend to elude objective judicial determination, so that some courts have simply refused to hear all of the conflicting testimony with which they are confronted. The choice as to relevancy, of course, remains a *choice*; and even if objectively "known," the precise role of custom and usage in relation to traditional rules is still problematic. It is commonly said, for example, that custom and usage can be used to interpret contracts but not to create them, yet it is unclear why the line should be drawn at that point, or whether the distinction is even an intelligible one. Equally problematic is the precise relation between reason and custom—a problem as old as the coexistence of a natural-law and a (supposedly customary) common-law tradition.[40] Without standards of reasonableness *outside* existing practice, singing reason is simply ratification of the status quo—the "is" automatically becomes the "ought." Yet absent a fully developed natural-law theory, the source of any external normative standard remains elusive. Moreover, taking custom and usage as a source of legal standards does not really avoid the problem of self-referencing, which was inevitable in rights theory, since social practice and reasonable expectations are, like "free" bargains, in large measure a *function* of the legal order. The wholly spontaneous custom and usage is rare, if it exists at all. Thus, by reflecting "custom," the law in large measure reflects only itself, and the nagging problem of legitimacy reemerges.

The mix of policy, situation sense, and leftover classical doctrine that now makes up the body of private law provides scant basis for a rationalization of constitutional rights. The search for some coherent foundation for rights analysis, particularly for judicial review, has been the preoccupation of modern constitutional law theorists. From the legal process school, which in its various forms dominated mainstream academic thought about constitutional law at least until the 1970s, came two major responses to realism—the strategy of deference, and the strategy of craft. The deference approach focused on the relative "competence" of institutions, demanding extraordinary justification for judicial override of democratically elected legislatures. The emphasis on craft, however, sought to rescue legal reasoning from a realist assimilation into generalized "policy making" by claiming for it a unique status as "reasoned elaboration," and demanding from judicial opinions a sufficient level of intellectual rigor, fit to be called "principled" decision making. Typical of the call for deference was the influential work of Alexander Bickel; typical of the call for craft was the equally influential work of Herbert Wechsler.

During the New Deal, the Supreme Court virtually abandoned to the legislature the field of economic regulation, once subject to invalidation under the categories of property and free contract. Deference in that area, however, left unresolved the fate of other supposed constitutional rights. For some theorists, deference simply became the preferred model for all cases. Bickel created a new category, somewhere between general principle and mere expediency, which he called prudence.[41] A prudent Supreme Court would avoid judicial review by using procedural grounds (e.g., problems of ripeness or standing) to justify a refusal to reach the merits. The Court could thereby avoid both the criticism that it stood in the way of the democratic majority (the basic argument against judicial review) and the criticism that it legitimated, by finding constitutional, action that seemed to violate fundamental rights. One of Bickel's examples was the notorious *Korematsu* case, where the Supreme Court upheld the detention of all Japanese-Americans living on the West Coast in holding camps during World War II.[42] Bickel argued that the Court should have dodged the question rather than label the detention and its underlying statute constitutional. He argued that the exercise of such prudence would have gained the trust of the country and placed the Court in the position of "teacher" in the public discussion of values. Then, when a time of *real* crisis to the Constitution arose, the Court would have been in a position to act on principle, with the backing of the people.

Bickel's "passive virtues" inevitably represented something of a retreat from the juristic model of rights and sovereignty. The person in a concentration camp is presumably not comforted with the knowledge that her case has been prudently decided on procedural rather than constitutional grounds; and a Court unprepared to make hard decisions in such a case is in a weak position to then hold out legal rights as the ultimate protection against totalitarianism. Bickel maintained that the prudent Court could still act when the dictator's troops came marching down Massachusetts Avenue, but his claim rang a bit hollow.

Moreover, the Bickel approach of deference to the legislative process, while on the surface the most obvious answer to the claim that judicial review is undemocratic, evades questions about the nature of our particular form of representation. The American legislative model is not, under our federalist constitutional structure, itself a model of pure, participatory consensualism; its particular form is not more unquestionably democratic or legitimate than is judicial review. *Both* are part of a total constitutional structure, as interpreted by past legal decision making. In fact, an attack on any single part of that structure inevitably calls into question the legitimacy of the whole structure. Also, so-called free political choice, as enacted into legislation, takes place within a system of legally protected economic power, which is a function of past legal decision making and which profoundly affects outcomes in the political decision-making process. The Court, by suddenly avoiding judicial review, cannot escape responsibility for the social decisions that are made.

Alternatively, Wechsler advocated not passive retreat, but a return to crafted opinions clearly based on "general" and "neutral" substantive principles, as the only sound basis for judicial review.[43] He complained,

for example, that in the *Brown* case the Court rested its decision on sociological fact rather than on constitutional principle.[44] Yet he also
acknowledged that the only available, general principle that seemed to
cover the case was "freedom of association," which quickly confronts an
equally neutral and general but contradictory principle barring forced
association. As he conceded, at the level of pure, ahistorical generality
there was no logical resolution; yet the necessary move to greater particularity raises the dilemma of necessarily illogical choice somewhere
between abstract, transcendental generality and ad hoc, "unprincipled"
case-by-case decision making. While the Wechsler goal was lofty, representing a return to the ideal of substantive rationality, the choices judges
made seemed doomed to be always, in the end, arbitrary.

Even as the legal academics called for judicial restraint and more intel-
lectually satisfying opinions, the federal judiciary, led by the Warren
Court, was extending the scope and expanding the content of personal
liberty and equality rights as had no other Supreme Court in U.S. history.
During the Warren Court period the federal courts revolutionized criminal procedure law, created modern antidiscrimination law, recaptured the
First Amendment from the shambles of McCarthyism, and restructured
American politics through reapportionment. In response, the legal process
school directed its criticism at the Warren Court's "activism," charging
usurpation of power or, even when applauding the results, denouncing
the Court's opinions for being ad hoc or unprincipled.

In reaction to that critical tradition, however, a new generation of liberal legal scholars was emerging. Many of these scholars celebrated the
Warren Court, even believing, however naively, that determined litigators could persuade the Supreme court to deploy constitutional interpretation to usher in a new era of substantive social justice. Such an era
would see the realization of the failed promise of the New Deal—that
Americans would be entitled as of right to minimum guarantees of education, housing, health care, and welfare assistance.[45] The big challenge
for these emerging liberal constitutionalists was to square their substantive vision of social justice with their fervent belief in legalism and the
rule of law, against the shaky backdrop of the corrosive realist tradition.
Thus the *Harvard Law Review*, in a rare "editorial" in its February 1970
issue, expressed its "endorsement" of the "activism" of the Warren Court,
yet remained troubled due to a "strong preference" for "principled as
opposed to result-oriented adjudication," coupled with a "mistrust of
interest balancing" (a legacy of realism), as "unprincipled" and leaving far
too much to "the individual judge's predilections."[46]

In the 1970s, liberal legal scholars seemingly took up this call, seeking to justify, with appeals to "principle," substantive results inspired by or implicit in the most liberal of the Warren Court's activist decisions. Ironically, this enterprise was launched during the same period that the Supreme Court first became the "Burger Court," in 1969, and then, by 1972, contained four justices appointed by Richard Nixon. Yet, seemingly oblivious to the possibility that conservatives might come to dominate the federal judiciary once again, ultraliberal Judge J. Skelly Wright (of the D.C. Circuit) published in 1971 an article in the *Harvard Law Review* affirming the frank assertion of ethical values by federal judges, and in fact calling for a judicial form of existential moral choice.[47] Others sought harder to stay within the boundaries of "principled" legal decision making, vacillating between a more or less veiled reliance on natural-law theory (David Richards, Kenneth Karst, Ronald Dworkin, Lawrence Tribe), and recourse to a model, somewhat more sophisticated than Hart and Sacks's, of shared American values (Harry Wellington, Michael Perry).[48] John Ely, criticizing both approaches, has attempted to take a stand somewhere between the assertion of affirmative substantive rights and complete deference.[49] He has postulated instead a supposedly value-neutral "participation-oriented, representation-reinforcing" standard for judicial review. Drawing on Justice Harlan Fiske Stone's suggestion, Ely argues that the judiciary should actively scrutinize only that legislation (1) "which restricts those political processes which can ordinarily be expected to bring about repeal of undesirable legislation," or (2) which is based on "prejudice against discrete and insular minorities."[50] Yet this approach too rests on a conception of substantive values—the value of participation within this particular form of representative structure and the "badness" of prejudice as opposed to all those other values which the legislature would be left free to implement.[51] As in the Hart and Sacks materials, the nagging problem of asserting objective, substantive values within a system premised on a pluralistic subjectivity of values inevitably reemerges. No less than jurists of the early nineteenth century, constitutional scholars are still bedeviled by the absence of a coherent conception of natural reason upon which to base substantive decisions.[52]

After the 1980s it was difficult to identify any perspective as "mainstream" legal thought, especially in constitutional law. Some scholars were, in fact, despairingly proclaiming the "death of law."[53] Others, wistfully seeking to perpetuate the spirit of the bygone era of the Warren Court, still attempted to fashion substantive moral content from the multiplicity inherent in the subjectivity of value. As in the monumental

A Theory of Justice, where John Rawls tried to transform procedure into moral principle, many modern liberal scholars continued to pursue the alchemical goal of turning process into substance.[54] Thus, in the 1980s, there was for a time an emphasis on "dialogic" values and "hermeneutic" traditions.[55] Some have attempted to revive, in constitutional law, the classical republican ideal of civic virtue through deliberative process, and others, the world view of the Hart and Sacks legal process school.[56,57]

By the 1990s, meanwhile, the Supreme Court itself seemed by many to be characterized by a return to an almost classical conservative formalism with respect to property[58] and contract,[59] by vigorous judicial activism as against regulation or redistribution,[60] and by refusal to acknowledge historical or social reality as having any relevance to judicial decision making.[61] Nevertheless, this Supreme Court, while usually considered "conservative," does not speak with a single voice. As against Justice Scalia's insistent formalism, for example, others (in particular, O'Connor, Souter, and sometimes Kennedy) have reinserted into constitutional law a contextual, essentially common-law methodology, requiring a close reading of facts in relation to and constrained by precedent.[62] Following in the tradition of Justice Harlan, this methodology is almost Llewellynesque in its insistence on constraint through craft and narrative sensibility. An open question is whether the method of common-law judging can serve to contain the Court's sometimes apparent ideological conflicts.

Traditionally, both ideological conservatives and ideological liberals on the Supreme Court have implicitly adopted the Enlightenment's stark state/individual model of the polity, with little attention to other mediating structures within the social order—structures that range from local school boards and voluntary private organizations to state governments. Typically, by reference to the Enlightenment model, liberals have sided with the individual in areas of personal liberty and criminal rights but with the state in areas of economic rights, while the reverse has been true for the conservatives. At the level of pure logic, neither side is obviously correct, which is why choices often seem logically uncompelled and hence political.[63] Justice O'Connor, in particular, has consistently urged the Court to eschew that model by giving greater deference to authoritative mediating bodies within the polity; and during the 1996–97 term a concern with federalism issues became a dominant theme. Given the initial Madisonian rejection of pure, local participatory democracy, however, and also given the huge expansion of national economic and political power generally, the objectivity of any principle according to which the Court distributes authority as between local groups and between state and federal governments may be illusory. Without an essentialist epistemology that recognizes some matters as "by their very nature" local (as earlier courts once believed), how does one define the boundaries that mark spheres of autonomy?

Now, much legal scholarship vaguely described as "conservative" is dominated by economic analysis. Sometimes the highly influential law and economics movement is described as an outgrowth of realism, given its emphasis on factual results as described economically (actual costs) rather than on doctrinal categories. Others, however, see it as a return to classicism given its foundational model of the market as an autonomous sphere of pure freedom and voluntary choice.

Whatever the movement's relation to realism, its pivotal moment came with the publication of Coase's "Problem of Social Cost."[64] Coase brilliantly undercut the conventionally presumed naturalness and economic rationality of either preventing the external costs of economic activity by regulation, or else forcing their internalization through required compensation. Coase argued that costs are reciprocal. Protecting or compensating "victims" of factory pollution, for example, imposes a cost on factory production no less real than the damage "caused" by pollution. In other words, our commonsense notion of cause, upon which traditional liability rules were implicitly premised, is analytically irrelevant.

As a second key point, Coase also argued that a perfectly free market, with no transaction costs, is indifferent to the judicial assignment of rights: through the process of market exchange legal rights will end up belonging to those who find them most valuable. It followed that in the real world of imperfect markets and transaction costs, courts should "mimic the market" in order to achieve "efficiency;" courts should assign rights where they will be most valuable, thereby (despite an oft-ignored elision of subjective and objective valuation), preventing allocatively inefficient results that a necessarily imperfect market might be unable to remedy. Richard Posner, the most influential scholar of the law and economic movement, has argued that common-law courts have, in fact, over time, tended to mimic market exchange results, despite judicial rhetorical appeal to traditional doctrinal categories, not economics, in explaining those results; and Posner has used the mode of economic analysis in a wide array of legal issues, including sexuality and adoption, where some seem to find its application grotesque.[65]

Criticism abounds. Economic analysis is not always consistent with the libertarian strand in conservative thought; meanwhile, those on the left tend to direct their criticism toward the formalist, neoclassical foundational assumption of exchange freedom, which obscures the reality of inequality. Posner, however, does not deny that reality, insisting only that an unhampered exchange still represents an instance of freedom, a positive human good, and is, virtually by definition, value-enhancing even for the less powerful party to an exchange. Furthermore, with the recent collapse of the nonmarket economies of the Soviet bloc, the superiority of market exchange as, at the very least, a price-setting mechanism, seems undeniable.

Nevertheless, to repeat Hale's realist critique somewhat differently, a free market reaches "efficient" results only with respect to any given set of entitlements; efficiency is necessarily a function of the distribution of legally protected entitlement, and will be modified by any modification in that distribution. Given that circularity, the notion of efficiency, while analytically useful, still speaks to the underlying question of legitimacy only at the margins, so to speak, not at the core. Perhaps symptomatic of that marginality is the crabbed, instrumental reasoning the law and economics movement presupposes. Reason's primary purpose is now defined as self-interested wealth maximization in a world of subjective value, perhaps all-too stark an abandonment of the nineteenth century's wistful longing for a reason capable of discerning, at least fleetingly, the glimmering image of that law which reigns in the Celestial City.

Meanwhile, the most promising direction from left legal scholars has been to eschew the formulation of yet one more grand, integrative scheme of constitutional law jurisprudence. Instead, there is a new willingness to learn from those who have traditionally been marginalized and excluded by mainstream legal thought—especially women and persons of color. This "outsider" jurisprudence which is now emerging understands "rights" only in relation to moral practice and as situated in historical and experiential context.[66] It is the most hopeful sign of the future we now have.

NOTES

1. See especially Robert Gordon, *Historicism in Legal Scholarship*, 90 Yale Law Journal 1017 (1981), and *Comment: The Historical Contingency of the Role of History*, 90 Yale Law Journal 1057 (1981).

2. This chapter originally drew extensively upon Duncan Kennedy, "Toward an Historical Understanding of Legal Consciousness: The Case of Classical Legal Thought in America, 1850–1940," in *Research in Law and Sociology*, ed. S. Spitzer, vol. 3 (Greenwich, CT: JAI Press, 1980). Other accounts, far more thorough than this chapter, now include Neil Duxbury, *Patterns of American Jurisprudence* (Oxford, UK: Oxford University Press, 1995); Laura Kalman, *Legal Realism at Yale: 1927–1960* (Chapel Hill: University of North Carolina Press, 1986); John Henry Schlegel, *American Legal Realism and Empirical Social Science* (Chapel Hill: University of North Carolina Press, 1995); Gary Minda, *Post Modern Legal Movements: Law and Jurisprudence at Century's End* (New York: NYU Press, 1995); Anthony Chase, *Law and History: The Evolution of the American Legal System* (New York: New Press, 1997).

3. See generally Gordon Wood, *The Creation of the American Republic, 1776–1787* (Chapel Hill: University of North Carolina Press, 1969).

4. See Elizabeth Mensch and Alan Freeman, *A Republican Agenda for Hobbesian America?* 41 University of Florida Law Review 581 (1989).

5. This assertion and some of the others that follow are based upon a reading of collected but unpublished nineteenth-century addresses, speeches, and other miscellaneous examples of legal discourse. The collection is to be found, uncataloged under a single title, in the Cornell Law School Library. Hooker's quotation is still inscribed in large letters on the wall of the Harvard Law School Library.

6. Joseph Story, *Discourse upon the Inauguration of the Author as Dane Professor of Law* (Cornell Law School Collection, 1829). See also R. Kent Newmyer, "Harvard Law School, New England Legal Culture, and the Antebellum Origins of American Jurisprudence," *Journal of American History,* 74 (1987): 814.

7. For a seventeenth-century version, see Christopher Hill, "The Religion of Gerrard Winstanley," in *The Collected Essays of Christopher Hill,* vol. 2 (Amherst: University of Massachusetts Press, 1986), 185–252. See also Norman Cohn, *The Pursuit of the Millennium* (New York: Harper & Brothers, 1961).

8. See Morton Horwitz, *The Transformation of American Law, 1780–1860* (Cambridge, MA: Harvard University Press, 1977), 257.

9. For the general importance of Hooker for early American constitutional theory, see Elizabeth Mensch, "Images of Self and Images of Polity in the Aftermath of the Reformation," *Graven Images,* 3 (1996): 249–64.

10. The claim was as old as the confrontation between Sir Edward Coke and King James I, in which Coke explained that whereas others besides judges

(especially the king) had excellent natural reason, they did not have the "artificial reason" of the law, which "is an art which requires long study and experience, before that a man can attain to the cognizance of it." 12 Coke's Reports 63, 65, 77 English Reports 1342, 1343 (King's Bench, 1608).

11. 10 U.S. (6 Cranch) 87 (1810). For Marshall's debt to Hamilton, see C. Peter McGrath, *Yazoo: Law and Politics in the New Republic* (Providence, RI: Brown University Press, 1966), 70.

12. Again, nineteenth-century jurists were able to draw on a long English tradition for such notions. See Matthew Hale, "Considerations Touching the Amendment and Alteration of Law," in *A Collection of Tracts Relative to the Law of England*, ed. Francis Hargrave, vol. 1 (Dublin: W. Colles, 1787), 249.

13. Theophilus Parsons, *Law of Contracts* (Boston: Little, Brown, 1855).

14. See generally Frances Olsen, *The Family and the Market: A Study of Ideology and Legal Reform,* 96 Harvard Law Review 1497 (1983). For the rich history describing the sphere of domesticity as containment of the more radical assertion of female equality that followed the American Revolution, see Mary Beth Norton, *Liberty's Daughters: The Revolutionary Experience of American Women, 1750–1800* (Boston: Little, Brown, 1980).

15. Samuel Williston, *The Law of Contracts* (New York: Baker, Voorhis, 1920).

16. *Coppage v. Kansas,* 236 U.S. 1 (1915).

17. *Adair v. United States,* 208 U.S. 161 (1908).

18. See Duxbury, *Patterns of American Jurisprudence,* 79–97.

19. See Frank Michelman, *Possession vs. Distribution in the Constitutional Idea of Property,* 72 Iowa Law Review 1319, 1334–37 (1987). For a good judicial example, see *Pennsylvania Coal Co. v. Mahon,* 260 U.S. 393, 416–22 (1922), Brandeis dissenting.

20. As an early example of that approach, see Roscoe Pound, *Mechanical Jurisprudence,* 8 Columbia Law Review 605 (1908).

21. See generally Alan Freeman and Elizabeth Mensch, *The Public-Private Distinction in American Law and Life,* 36 Buffalo Law Review 237 (1988).

22. For one of the best single examples of the realist assault upon the objectivity of rights theory and legal analysis in general, see Felix Cohen, *Transcendental Nonsense and the Functional Approach,* 35 Columbia Law Review 809 (1935).

23. Morris Cohen, *Property and Sovereignty,* 13 Cornell Law Quarterly 8 (1927).

24. Robert Hale, *Bargaining, Duress and Economic Liberty,* 43 Columbia Law Review 603 (1943); Robert Hale, "Coercion and Distribution in a Supposedly Non-Coercive State," *Political Science Quarterly,* 38 (1923): 470. See also Elizabeth Mensch, *Freedom of Contract as Ideology,* 33 Stanford Law Review 753 (1981).

25. See, for example, F. Cohen, *The Ethical Basis of Legal Criticism,* 41 Yale Law Journal 201 (1931).

26. For a discussion of this dilemma and of American realism in general, see Edward Purcell, *The Crisis of Democratic Theory: Scientific Naturalism and the Problem of Value* (Lexington: University of Kentucky Press, 1973).

27. Howard Laswell and Myres McDougal, *Legal Education and Public Policy: Professional Training in the Public Interest,* 52 Yale Law Journal 203 (1943).

28. Henry Hart and Albert Sacks, *The Legal Process: Basic Problems in the Making and Application of Law,* tentative ed. (Cambridge: Harvard University Press, 1958).

29. *International Shoe Co. v. State of Washington,* 326 U.S. 310 (1945), the landmark modern case on personal jurisdiction.

30. *Hoffman v. Red Owl Stores, Inc.,* 26 Wis. 2d 683 (1965).

31. See *Burton v. Wilmington Parking Authority,* 365 U.S. 715 (1961).

32. See *Flagg Bros., Inc. v. Brooks,* 436 U.S. 149 (1978).

33. Compare *Amalgamated Food Employees Union v. Logan Valley Plazak,* 391 U.S. 308 (1968), with *Lloyd Corp. v. Tanner,* 407 U.S. 551 (1972), with *Hudgens v. NLRB,* 424 U.S. 507 (1976).

34. *United States v. Willow River Power Co.,* 324 U.S. 499 (1945).

35. Karl Llewellyn, *The Common Law Tradition: Deciding Appeals* (Boston: Little, Brown, 1960).

36. Edward Levi, *An Introduction to Legal Reasoning* (Chicago: University of Chicago Press, 1948).

37. *McPherson v. Buick Motors Co.,* 217 N.Y. 382 (1916).

38. *Palsgraf v. Long Island R.R.,* 248 N.Y. 339, 162 N.E. 99 (1928). See also John Noonan, Jr., *Persons and Masks of the Law* (New York: Farrar, Straus & Giroux, 1976), 111, for the contextual reality behind the case.

39. Llewellyn, *The Common Law Tradition.*

40. See, for example, Franklin Schultz, *The Firm Offer Puzzle: A Study of Business Practice in the Construction Industry,* 19 Chicago Law Review 237 (1952).

41. Alexander Bickel, *The Passive Virtues,* 75 Harvard Law Review 237 (1952).

42. *Korematsu v. United States,* 323 U.S. 214 (1944).

43. Herbert Wechsler, *Toward Neutral Principles of Constitutional Law,* 73 Harvard Law Review 1 (1959). See generally Gary Peller, *Neutral Principles in the 1950's,* 21 University of Michigan Journal of Law Reform 561 (1988).

44. *Brown v. Board of Education,* 347 U.S. 483 (1954).

45. The paradigmatic example of this effort is Frank Michelman, *On Protecting the Poor Through the Fourteenth Amendment,* 83 Harvard Law Review 7 (1969).

46. *With the Editors,* 83 Harvard Law Review vii (1970). This section is usually omitted from the bound volumes found in libraries but may be found in the individual paperbound issue as originally published.

47. See J. Skelly Wright, *Professor Bickel, The Scholarly Tradition, and the Supreme Court,* 84 Harvard Law Review 769 (1971), which is also an excellent review of Alexander Bickel's work, especially that directed critically at the Warren Court.

48. For a good overview, see Paul Brest, *The Fundamental Rights Controversy: The Essential Contradictions of Normative Constitutional Scholarship,* 90 Yale Law Journal 1063 (1981).

49. John Ely, *Democracy and Distrust: A Theory of Judicial Review* (Cambridge, MA: Harvard University Press, 1980).

50. *United States v. Carolene Products Company,* 304 U.S. 144, 152, n. 4 (1938).

51. See Paul Brest, *The Substance of Process,* 42 Ohio State Law Journal 131 (1981).

52. For an important analysis of this dilemma at a philosophical level, see Alasdair MacIntyre, *After Virtue,* 2d ed. (South Bend, IN: University of Notre Dame Press, 1984), especially chapters 1–8.

53. See Owen Fiss, *The Death of the Law?* 72 Cornell Law Review 1 (1986). For a thorough overview of the jurisprudential scene at the close of the 1980s, see Gary Minda, *The Jurisprudential Movements of the 1980's,* 50 Ohio State Law Journal 599 (1989).

54. John Rawls, *A Theory of Justice* (Cambridge, MA: Harvard University Press, 1971). For an excellent critique, see Robert Paul Wolff, *Understanding Rawls* (Princeton, NJ: Princeton University Press, 1977).

55. See Robert Cover, *The Supreme Court, 1982 Term—Foreword: Nomos and Narrative,* 97 Harvard Law Review 1 (1983); Martha Minow, *Interpreting Rights: An Essay for Robert Cover,* 96 Yale Law Journal 1860 (1987). See generally Mark Tushnet, *Anti-Formalism in Recent Constitutional Theory,* 83 Michigan Law Review 1502 (1985).

56. See *Symposium: The Republican Civic Tradition,* 97 Yale Law Journal 1493–1723 (1988). For a critical response, see Mensch and Freeman, *A Republican Agenda for Hobbesian America?*

57. See David Shapiro, *Courts, Legislatures, and Paternalism,* 74 Virginia Law Review 519 (1988). See also Steven Burton, *An Introduction to Law and Legal Reasoning* (Boston: Little, Brown, 1985).

58. See *Nollan v. California Coastal Commission,* 107 S.Ct. 3141 (1987).

59. See *Patterson v. McLean Credit Union,* 109 S.Ct. 2363 (1989).

60. Powerful examples are the Court's use of the First Amendment to insulate corporate power from public regulation (*First National Bank v. Bellotti,* 435 U.S. 765 [1978]; *Consolidated Edison Co. v. Public Service Commission,* 447 U.S. 530 [1980]) and the use of the equal protection clause to prevent a democratically elected local legislature from redistributing contract access in order to redress a long-standing condition of racial inequality (*City of Richmond v. J. A. Croson Co.,* 109 S.Ct. 706 [1989]).

61. See *Wards Cove Packing Co. v. Atonio,* 109 S.Ct. 2115 (1989).

62. For an emphasis on precedent that surprised many, see, of course, *Casey v. Planned Parenthood of Eastern Pennsylvania,* 112. S.Ct. 2791 (1992), especially part 3.

63. See generally Alan Freeman and Elizabeth Mensch, "Sandra Day O'Connor," in *The Justices of the United States Supreme Court,* ed. L. Friedman and F. Israel (Broomall, PA: Chelsea House, 1997), 1759, 1772–80, on the question of both contextual constitutional law decision making and federalism.

64. Ronald Coase, *The Problem of Social Cost,* 3 Journal of Law and Economics 1–44 (1960).

65. See Richard Posner, *Economic Analysis of Law* (Boston: Little, Brown, 1973), 18.

66. See chapter 32 by Cornel West, chapter 16 by Kimberlé Crenshaw, and chapter 14 by Charles Lawrence in this volume, and Mari Matsuda, *Public Response to Racist Speech: Considering the Victim's Story,* 87 Michigan Law Review 2320 (1989). For a recent analysis of American jurisprudence from a critical perspective, see Duncan Kennedy, *A Critique of Adjudication (fin de siècle)* (Cambridge, MA: Harvard University Press, 1997). For a serious and thorough critique of modern social theory, generally, that employs a postmodern perspective and then poses theology as the only serious alternative, see John Milbank, *Theology and Social Theory: Beyond Secular Reason* (Oxford: Blackwell, 1990).

2 DUNCAN KENNEDY

LEGAL EDUCATION AS TRAINING FOR HIERARCHY

LAW schools are intensely political places despite the fact that they seem intellectually unpretentious, barren of theoretical ambition or practical vision of what social life might be. The trade-school mentality, the endless attention to trees at the expense of forests, the alternating grimness and chumminess of focus on the limited task at hand, all these are only a part of what is going on. The other part is ideological training for willing service in the hierarchies of the corporate welfare state.

To say that law school is ideological is to say that what teachers teach along with basic skills is wrong, is nonsense about what law is and how it works; that the message about the nature of legal competence, and its distribution among students, is wrong, is nonsense; that the ideas about the possibilities of life as a lawyer that students pick up from legal education are wrong, are nonsense. But all this is nonsense with a tilt; it is biased and motivated rather than random error. What it says is that it is natural, efficient, and fair for law firms, the bar as a whole, and the society the bar services to be organized in their actual patterns of hierarchy and domination.

Because students believe what they are told, explicitly and implicitly, about the world they are entering, they behave in ways that fulfill the prophecies the system makes about them and about that world. This is the linkback that completes the system: students do more than accept the way things are, and ideology does more than damp opposition. Students act affirmatively within the channels cut for them, cutting them deeper, giving the whole a patina of consent, and weaving complicity into everyone's life story.

In this chapter, I take up in turn the initial first-year experience, the ideological content of the law school curriculum, and the noncurricular practices of law schools that train students to accept and participate in the hierarchical structure of life in the law.

THE FIRST-YEAR EXPERIENCE

A surprisingly large number of law students go to law school secretly wishing that being a lawyer could turn out to mean something more, something more socially constructive than just doing a highly respectable job. There is the fantasy of playing the role an earlier generation associated with Brandeis: the role of service through law, carried out with superb technical competence and also with a deep belief that in its essence law is a progressive force, however much it may be distorted by the actual arrangements of capitalism. For a few, there is a contrasting, more radical notion that law is a tool of established interests, that it is in essence superstructural, but that it is a tool that a coldly effective professional can sometimes turn against the dominators. Whereas in the first notion the student aspires to help the oppressed and transform society by bringing out the latent content of a valid ideal, in the second the student imagines herself as part technician, part judo expert, able to turn the tables exactly because she never lets herself be mystified by the rhetoric that is so important to other students.

Then there are the conflicting motives, which are equally real for both types. People think of law school as extremely competitive, as a place where a tough, hardworking, smart style is cultivated and rewarded. Students enter law school with a sense that they will develop that side of themselves. Even if they disapprove, on principle, of that side of themselves, they have had other experiences in which it turned out that they wanted and liked aspects of themselves that on principle they disapproved of. How is one to know that one is not "really" looking to develop oneself in this way as much as one is motivated by the vocation of social transformation?

There is also the issue of social mobility. Almost everyone whose parents were not members of the professional/technical intelligentsia seems to feel that going to law school is an advance in terms of the family history. This is true even for children of high-level business managers, so long as their parents' positions were due to hard work and struggle rather than to birth into the upper echelons. It is rare for parents to actively *disapprove* of their children going to law school, whatever their origins. So taking this particular step has a social meaning, however much the student may reject it, and that social meaning is success. The success is bittersweet if one feels one should have gotten into a better school, but both the bitter and the sweet suggest that one's motives are impure.

The initial classroom experience sustains rather than dissipates ambivalence. The teachers are overwhelmingly white, male, and deadeningly straight and middle class in manner. The classroom is hierarchical with a vengeance, the teacher receiving a degree of deference and arousing fears that remind one of high school rather than college. The sense of autonomy one has in a lecture, with the rule that you must let teacher drone on without interruption balanced by the rule that teacher can't *do* anything to you, is gone. In its place is a demand for a pseudoparticipation in which one struggles desperately, in front of a large audience, to read a mind determined to elude you. It is almost never anything as bad as *The Paper Chase* or *One-L*, but it is still humiliating to be frightened and unsure of oneself, especially when what renders one unsure is a classroom arrangement that suggests at once the patriarchal family and a Kafkalike riddle state. The law school classroom at the beginning of the first year is culturally reactionary.

But it is also engaging. You are learning a new language, and it *is* possible to learn it. Pseudoparticipation makes one intensely aware of how everyone else is doing, providing endless bases for comparison. Information is coming in on all sides, and aspects of the grown-up world that you knew were out there but didn't understand are becoming intelligible. The teacher offers subtle encouragements as well as not-so-subtle reasons for alarm. Performance is on one's mind, adrenaline flows, success has a nightly and daily meaning in terms of the material assigned. After all, this is the next segment: one is moving from the vaguely sentimental world of college, or the frustrating world of office work or housework, into something that promises a dose of "reality," even if it's cold and scary reality.

It quickly emerges that neither the students nor the faculty are as homogeneous as they at first appeared. Some teachers are more authoritarian than others; some students other than oneself reacted with horror to the infantilization of the first days or weeks. There even seems to be a connection between classroom manner and substantive views, with the "softer" teachers also seeming to be more "liberal," perhaps more sympathetic to plaintiffs in the torts course, more willing to hear what are called policy arguments, as well as less intimidating in class discussion. But there is a disturbing aspect to this process of differentiation: in most law schools, it turns out that the tougher, less policy-oriented teachers are the more popular. The softies seem to get less matter across, they let things wander, and one begins to worry that their niceness is at the expense of a metaphysical quality called rigor, thought to be essential to success on bar exams and in the adult world of practice. Ambivalence reasserts itself. As between the conservatives and the mushy centrists, enemies who scare you but subtly reassure you may seem more attractive than allies no better anchored than yourself.

There is an intellectual experience that somewhat corresponds to the emotional one: the gradual revelation that there is no purchase for committed liberal (let alone radical) thinking on any part of the smooth surface of legal education. The issue in the classroom is not left against right, but pedagogical conservatism against moderate, disintegrated liberalism. All your teachers are likely to deny or at least deemphasize the political character of the classroom and of their various subject matters, though some *are* likely to be obviously sympathetic to progressive causes, and some may even be moonlighting as left lawyers. Students are struggling for cognitive mastery and against the sneaking depression of the preprofessional. The actual intellectual content of the law seems to consist of learning rules—what they are and why they have to be the way they are—while rooting for the occasional judge who seems willing to make them marginally more humane. The basic experience is of double surrender: to a passivizing classroom experience and to a passive attitude toward the content of the legal system.

The first step toward this sense of the irrelevance of liberal or left thinking is the opposition in the first-year curriculum between the technical, boring, difficult, obscure legal case and the occasional case with outrageous facts and a piggish judicial opinion endorsing or tolerating the outrage. The first kind of case—call it a cold case—is a challenge to interest, understanding, even to wakefulness. It can be on any subject, so long as it is of no political or moral or emotional significance. Just to understand what happened and what's being said about it, you have to learn a lot of new terms, a little potted legal history, and lots of rules, none of which is carefully explained by the casebook or the teacher. It is difficult to figure out why the case is there in the first place, difficult to figure out whether you have grasped it, and difficult to anticipate what the teacher will ask and what one should respond.

The other kind of case—call it a hot case—usually involves a sympathetic plaintiff—say, an Appalachian farm family—and an unsympathetic defendant—say, a coal company. On first reading, it appears that the coal company has screwed the farm family by renting their land for strip mining, with a promise to restore it to its original condition once the coal has been extracted, and then reneging on the promise. And the case should include a judicial opinion that does something like award a meaningless couple of hundred dollars to the farm family rather than making the coal company perform the restoration work. The point of the class discussion will be that your initial reaction of outrage is naive, non-legal, irrelevant to what you're supposed to be learning, and maybe substantively wrong into the bargain. There are "good reasons" for the awful result, when you take a legal and logical "large" view, as opposed to the knee-jerk passionate view; and if you can't muster those reasons, maybe you aren't cut out to be a lawyer.

Most students can't fight this combination of a cold case and a hot case. The cold case is boring, but you have to do it if you want to become a lawyer. The hot case cries out for response, seems to say that if you can't respond you've already sold out; but the system tells you to put away childish things, and your reaction to the hot case is one of them. Without any intellectual resources, in the way of knowledge of the legal system and of the character of legal reasoning, it will appear that emoting will only isolate and incapacitate you. The choice is to develop some calluses and hit the books, or admit failure almost before you've begun.

THE IDEOLOGICAL CONTENT OF LEGAL EDUCATION

One can distinguish in a rough way between two aspects of legal education as a reproducer of hierarchy. A lot of what happens is the inculcation through a formal curriculum and the classroom experience of a set of political attitudes toward the economy and society in general, toward law, and toward the possibilities of life in the profession. These have a general ideological significance, and they have an impact on the lives even of law students who never practice law. Then there is a complicated set of institutional practices that orient students to willing participation in the specialized hierarchical roles of lawyers. Students begin to absorb the more general ideological message before they have much in the way of a conception of life after law school, so I will describe this formal aspect of the educational process before describing the ways in which the institutional practice of law schools bear on those realities.

Law students sometimes speak as though they learned *nothing* in school. In fact, they learn skills, to do a list of simple but important things. They learn to retain large numbers of rules organized into categorical systems (requisites for a contract, rules about breach, etc.). They learn "issue spotting," which means identifying the ways in which the rules are ambiguous, in conflict, or have a gap when applied to particular fact situations. They learn elementary case analysis, meaning the art of generating broad holdings for cases so they will apply beyond their intuitive scope, and narrow holdings for cases so that they won't apply where it at first seemed they would. And they learn a list of balanced, formulaic, pro/con policy arguments that lawyers use in arguing that a given rule should apply to a situation despite a gap, conflict, or ambiguity, or that a given case should be extended or narrowed. These are arguments like "the need for certainty" and "the need for flexibility," "the need to promote competition" and the "need to encourage production by letting producers keep the rewards of their labor."

One should neither exalt these skills nor denigrate them. By comparison with the first-year students' tendency to flip-flop between formalism and mere equitable intuition, they represent a real intellectual advance. Lawyers actually do use them in practice; and when properly, consciously mastered, they have "critical" bite. They are a help in thinking about politics, public policy, ethical discourse in general, because they show the indeterminacy and manipulability of ideas and institutions that are central to liberalism.

On the other hand, law schools teach these rather rudimentary, essentially instrumental skills in a way that almost completely mystifies them for almost all law students. The mystification has three parts. First, the schools teach skills through class discussions of cases in which it is asserted that law emerges from a rigorous analytical procedure called legal reasoning, which is unintelligible to the layperson but somehow both explains and validates the great majority of the rules in force in our system. At the same time, the class context and the materials present every legal issue as distinct from every other—as a tub on its own bottom, so to speak—with no hope or even any reason to hope that from law study one might derive an integrating vision of what law is, how it works, or how it might be changed (other than in any incremental, case-by-case, reformist way).

Second, the teaching of skills in the mystified context of legal reasoning about utterly unconnected legal problems means that skills are taught badly, unself-consciously, to be absorbed by osmosis as one picks up the knack of "thinking like a lawyer." Bad or only randomly good teaching generates and then accentuates real differences and imagined differences in student capabilities. But it does so in such a way that students don't know when they are learning and when they aren't, and have no way of improving or even understanding their own learning processes. They experience skills training as the gradual emergence of differences among themselves, as a process of ranking that reflects something that is just "there" inside them.

Third, the schools teach skills in isolation from actual lawyering experience. "Legal reasoning" is sharply distinguished from law practice, and one learns nothing about practice. This procedure disables students from any future role but that of apprentice in a law firm organized in the same manner as a law school, with older lawyers controlling the content and pace of depoliticized craft training in a setting of intense competition and no feedback.

THE FORMAL CURRICULUM: LEGAL RULES AND LEGAL REASONING

The intellectual core of the ideology is the distinction between law and policy. Teachers convince students that legal reasoning exists, and is different from policy analysis, by bullying them into accepting as valid in particular cases arguments about legal correctness that are circular, question-begging, incoherent, or so vague as to be meaningless. Sometimes these are just arguments from authority, with the validity of the authoritative premise put outside discussion by professorial fiat. Sometimes they are policy arguments (e.g., security of transaction, business certainty) that are treated in a particular situation as though they were rules that everyone accepts but that will be ignored in the next case when they would suggest that the decision was wrong. Sometimes they are exercises in doctrinal logic that wouldn't stand up for a minute in a discussion between equals (e.g., the small print in a form contract represents the "will of the parties").

Within a given subfield, the teacher is likely to treat cases in three different ways. There are the cases that present and justify the basic rules and basic ideas of the field. These are treated as cursory exercises in legal logic. Then there are cases that are anomalous—"outdated" or "wrongly decided" because they don't follow the supposed inner logic of the area. There won't be many of these, but they are important because their treatment persuades students that the technique of legal reasoning is at least minimally independent of the results reached by particular judges and is therefore capable of criticizing as well as legitimating. Finally, there will be an equally small number of peripheral or "cutting-edge" cases the teacher sees as raising policy issues about growth or change in the law. Whereas in discussing the first two kinds of cases the teacher behaves in an authoritarian way supposedly based on his objective knowledge of the technique of legal reasoning, here everything is different. Because we are dealing with "value judgments" that have "political" overtones, the discussion will be much more freewheeling. Rather than every student comment being right or wrong, all student comments get pluralist acceptance, and the teacher will reveal himself to be mildly liberal or conservative rather than merely a legal technician.

The curriculum as a whole has a rather similar structure. It is not really a random assortment of tubs on their own bottoms, a forest of tubs. First, there are contracts, torts, property, criminal law, and civil procedure. The rules in these courses are the ground rules of late-nineteenth-century laissez-faire capitalism. Teachers teach them as though they had an inner logic, as an exercise in legal reasoning, with policy (e.g., commercial certainty in the contracts course) playing a relatively minor role. Then there are second- and third-year courses that expound the moderate reformist program of the New Deal and the administrative structure of the modern regulatory state (with passing reference to the racial egalitarianism of the Warren Court). These courses are more policy oriented than first-year courses, and also much more ad hoc.

Liberal teachers teach students that limited interference with the market makes sense and is as authoritatively grounded in statutes as the ground rules of laissez-faire are grounded in natural law. But each problem is discrete, enormously complicated, and understood in a way that guarantees the practical impotence of the reform program. Conservative teachers teach that much of the reform program is irrational or counterproductive or both, and would have been rolled back long ago were it not for "politics." Finally, there are peripheral subjects, like legal philosophy or legal history, legal process, clinical legal education. These are presented as not truly relevant to the "hard" objective, serious, rigorous analytic core of law; they are a kind of playground or finishing school for learning the social art of self-presentation as a lawyer.

It would be an extraordinary first-year student who could, on his own, develop a theoretically critical attitude toward this system. Entering students just don't know enough to figure out where the teacher is fudging, misrepresenting, or otherwise distorting legal thinking and legal reality. To make matters worse, the most common kind of liberal thinking the student is likely to bring with her is likely to hinder rather than assist in the struggle to maintain some intellectual autonomy from the experience. Most liberal students believe that the liberal program can be reduced to guaranteeing people their rights and to bringing about the triumph of human rights over mere property rights. In this picture, the trouble with the legal system is that it fails to put the state behind the

rights of the oppressed, or that the system fails to enforce the rights formally recognized. If one thinks about law this way, one is inescapably
dependent on the very techniques of legal reasoning that are being mar-
shalled in defense of the status quo.

This wouldn't be so bad if the problem with legal education were that
the teachers *misused* rights reasoning to restrict the range of the rights of
the oppressed. But the problem is much deeper than that. Rights discourse
is internally inconsistent, vacuous, or circular. Legal thought can generate
equally plausible rights justifications for almost any result. Moreover, the
discourse of rights imposes constraints on those who use it that make it difficult for it to function effectively as a tool of radical transformation. Rights
are by their nature "formal," meaning that they secure to individuals legal
protection for as well as from arbitrariness—to speak of rights is precisely
not to speak of justice between social classes, races, or sexes. Rights discourse, moreover, presupposes or takes for granted that the world is and
should be divided between a state sector that enforces rights and a private
world of "civil society" in which individuals pursue their diverse goals. This
framework is, in itself, a part of the problem rather than of the solution. It
makes it difficult even to conceptualize radical proposals such as, for example, decentralized democratic worker control of factories.

Because it is incoherent and manipulable, traditionally individualist,
and willfully blind to the realities of *substantive* inequality, rights discourse is a trap. As long as one stays within it, one can produce good
pieces of argument about the occasional case on the periphery where
everyone recognizes value judgments have to be made. But one is without guidance in deciding what to do about fundamental questions and
fated to the gradual loss of confidence in the convincingness of what one
has to say in favor of the very results one believes in most passionately.

Left liberal rights analysis submerges the student in legal rhetoric but,
because of its inherent vacuousness, can provide no more than an emotional stance against the legal order. It fails liberal students because it
offers no base for the mastery of ambivalence. What is needed is to think
about law in a way that will allow one to enter into it, to criticize it without utterly rejecting it, and to manipulate it without self-abandonment
to *their* system of thinking and doing.

STUDENT EVALUATION

Law schools teach a small number of useful skills. But they teach them
only obliquely. It would threaten the professional ideology and the acad-

emic pretensions of teachers to make their students as good as they can be at the relatively simple tasks that they will have to perform in practice. But it would also upset the process by which a hierarchical arrangement analogous to that of law school applicants, law schools, and law firms is established within a given student body.

To teach the repetitive skills of legal analysis effectively, one would have to isolate the general procedures that make them up, and then devise large numbers of factual and doctrinal hypotheticals where students could practice those skills, knowing what they were doing and learning in every single case whether their performance was good or bad. As legal education now works, on the other hand, students do exercises designed to discover what the "correct solution" to a legal problem might be, those exercises are treated as unrelated to one another, and students receive no feedback at all except a grade on a single examination at the end of the course. Students generally experience these grades as almost totally arbitrary—unrelated to how much you worked, how much you liked the subject, how much you thought you understood going into the exam, and what you thought about the class and the teacher.

This is silly, looked at as pedagogy. But it is more than silly when looked at as ideology. The system generates a rank ordering of students based on grades, and students learn that there is little or nothing they can do to change their place in that ordering, or to change the way the school generates it. Grading as practiced teaches the inevitability and also the justice of hierarchy, a hierarchy that is at once false and unnecessary.

It is unnecessary because it is largely irrelevant to what students will do as lawyers. Most of the process of differentiating students into bad, better, and good could simply be dispensed with without the slightest detriment to the quality of legal services. It is false, first, because inasmuch as it does involve the measuring of the real and useful skills of potential lawyers, the differences between students could be "leveled up" at minimal cost, whereas the actual practice of legal education systematically accentuates differences in real capacities. If law schools invested some of the time and money they now put into Socratic classes in developing systematic skills training, and committed themselves to giving constant, detailed feedback on student progress in learning those skills, they could graduate the vast majority of all the law students in the country at the level of technical proficiency now achieved by a small minority in each institution.

Law schools convey their factual message to each student about his or her place in the ranking of students along with the implicit corollary that place is individually earned, and therefore deserved. The system tells you that you learned as much as you were capable of learning, and that if you feel incompetent or that you could have become better at what you do, it is your own fault. Opposition is sour grapes. Students internalize this message about themselves and about the world, and so prepare themselves for all the hierarchies to follow.

INCAPACITATION FOR ALTERNATIVE PRACTICE

Law schools channel their students into jobs in the hierarchy of the bar according to their own standing in the hierarchy of schools. Students confronted with the choice of what to do after they graduate experience themselves as largely helpless: they have no "real" alternative to taking a job in one of the firms that customarily hire from their school. Partly, faculties generate this sense of student helplessness by propagating myths about the character of the different kinds of practice. They extol the forms that are accessible to their students; they subtly denigrate or express envy about the jobs that will be beyond their students' reach; they dismiss as ethically and socially suspect the jobs their students won't have to take.

As for any form of work outside the established system—for example, legal services for the poor and neighborhood law practice—they convey to students that, although morally exalted, the work is hopelessly dull and unchallenging, and that the possibilities of reaching a standard of living appropriate to a lawyer are slim or nonexistent. These messages are just nonsense—the rationalizations of law teachers who long upward, fear status degradation, and above all hate the idea of risk. Legal services practice, for example, is far more intellectually stimulating and demanding, even with a high caseload, than most of what corporate lawyers do. It is also more fun.

Beyond this dimension of professional mythology, law schools act in more concrete ways to guarantee that their students will fit themselves into their appropriate niches in the existing system of practice. First, the actual content of what is taught in a given school will incapacitate students from any other form of practice than that allotted graduates of that institution. This looks superficially like a rational adaptation to the needs of the market, but it is in fact almost entirely unnecessary. Law schools teach so little, and that so incompetently, that they cannot, as now constituted, prepare students for more than one career at the bar. But the reason for this is that they embed skills training in mystificatory nonsense and devote most of their teaching time to transmitting masses of ill-digested rules. A more rational system would emphasize the way to learn law rather than rules, and skills rather than answers. Student capacities would be more equal as a result, but students would also be radically more flexible in what they could do in practice.

A second incapacitating device is the teaching of doctrine in isolation from practice skills. Students who have no practice skills tend to exaggerate how difficult it is to acquire them. There is a distinct lawyers' mystique of the irrelevance of the "theoretical" material learned in school, and of the crucial importance of abilities that cannot be known or developed until one is out in the "real world" and "in the trenches." Students have little alternative to getting training in this dimension of things after law school. It therefore seems hopelessly impractical to think about setting up your own law firm, and only a little less impractical to go to a small or political or unconventional firm rather than to one of those that offer the standard package of postgraduate education. Law schools are wholly responsible for this situation. They could quite easily revamp their curricula so that any student who wanted it would have a meaningful choice between independence and servility.

A third form of incapacitation is more subtle. Law school, as an extension of the educational system as a whole, teaches students that they are weak, lazy, incompetent, and insecure. And it also teaches them that if they are willing to accept extreme dependency and vulnerability for a probationary term, large institutions will (probably) take care of them almost no matter what. The terms of the bargain are relatively clear. The institution will set limited, defined tasks and specify minimum requirements in their performance. The student/associate has no other responsibilities than performance of those tasks. The institution takes care of all the contingencies of life, both within the law (supervision and backup from other firm members; firm resources and prestige to bail you out if you make a mistake) and in private life (firms offer money but also long-term job security and delicious benefits packages aimed to reduce risks of disaster). In exchange, you renounce any claim to control your work setting or the actual content of what you do, and agree to show the appropriate form of deference to those above and condescension to those below.

By comparison, the alternatives are risky. Law school does not train you to run a small law business, to realistically assess the outcome of a complex process involving many different actors, or to enjoy the feeling of independence and moral integrity that comes of creating your own job to serve your own goals. It tries to persuade you that you are barely competent to perform the much more limited roles it allows you, and strongly suggests that it is more prudent to kiss the lash than to strike out on your own.

THE MODELING OF HIERARCHICAL RELATIONSHIPS

Law teachers model for students how they are supposed to think, feel, and act in their future professional roles. Some of this is a matter of teaching by example, some of it a matter of more active learning from interactions that are a kind of clinical education for lawyerlike behavior. This training is a major factor in the hierarchical life of the bar. It encodes the message of the legitimacy of the whole system into the smallest details of personal style, daily routine, gesture, tone of voice, facial expression—a plethora of little p's and q's for everyone to mind. Partly, these will serve as a language—a way for the young lawyer to convey that she knows what the rules of the game are and intends to play by them. What's going on is partly a matter of ritual oaths and affirmations—by adopting the mannerisms, one pledges one's troth to inequality. And partly it is a substantive matter of value. Hierarchical behavior will come to express and realize the hierarchical selves of people who were initially only wearers of masks.

Law teachers enlist on the side of hierarchy all the vulnerabilities students feel as they begin to understand what lies ahead of them. In law school, students have to come to grips with implications of their social class and sex and race in a way that is different from (but not necessarily less important than) the experience of college. People discover that preserving their class status is extremely important to them, so important that no alternative to the best law job they can get seems possible to them. Or they discover that they want to rise, or that they are trapped by student loans in a way they hadn't anticipated. People change the way they dress and talk; they change their opinions and even their emotions. None of this is easy for anyone, but liberal students have the special set of humiliations involved in discovering the limits of their commitment and often the instability of attitudes they thought were basic to themselves.

Another kind of vulnerability has to do with one's own competence. Law school wields frightening instruments of judgment, including not only the grading system but also the more subtle systems of teacher approval in class, reputation among fellow students, and out-of-class faculty contact and respect. Liberal students sometimes begin law school with an apparently unshakable confidence in their own competence and with a related confidence in their own left analysis. But even these apparently self-assured students quickly find that adverse judgments—even judgments that are only imagined or projected onto others—count and hurt. They have to decide whether this responsiveness in themselves is something to accept, whether the judgments in question have validity and refer to things they care about, or whether they should reject them. They have to wonder whether they have embarked on a subtle course of accommodating themselves intellectually in order to be in the ball park where people win and lose teacher and peer approval. And they have, in most or at least many cases, to deal with actual failure to live up to their highest hopes of accomplishment within the conventional system of rewards.

A first lesson is that professors are intensely preoccupied with the status rankings of their schools, and show themselves willing to sacrifice to improve their status in the rankings and to prevent downward drift. They approach the appointment of colleagues in the spirit of trying to get people who are as high up as possible in a conventionally defined hierarchy of teaching applicants, and they are notoriously hostile to affirmative action in faculty hiring, even when they are quite willing to practice it for student admissions and in filling administrative posts. Assistant professors begin their careers as the little darlings of their older colleagues. They end up in tense competition for the prize of tenure, trying to accommodate themselves to standards and expectations that are, typically, too vague to master except by a commitment to please at any cost. In these respects, law schools are a good preview of what law firms will be like.

Law professors, like lawyers, have secretaries. Students deal with them off and on through law school, watch how their bosses treat them, how they treat their bosses, and how "a secretary" relates to "a professor" even when one does not work for the other. Students learn that it is acceptable, even if it's not always and everywhere the norm, for faculty to treat their secretaries petulantly, condescendingly, with a perfectionism that is a matter of the bosses' face rather than of the demands of the job itself, as though they were personal body servants, utterly impersonally, or as objects of sexual harassment. They learn that "a secretary" treats "a professor" with elaborate deference, as though her time and her dignity meant nothing and his everything, even when he is not her boss. In general, they learn that humane relations in the workplace are a matter of the superior's grace rather than of human need and social justice.

These lessons are repeated in the relationships of professors and secretaries with administrators and with maintenance and support staff. Teachers convey a sense of their own superiority and practice a social segregation sufficiently extreme so that there are no occasions on which the reality of that superiority might be tested. As a group, they accept and willingly support the division of labor that consigns everyone in the institution but them to boredom and passivity. Friendly but deferential social relations reinforce everyone's sense that all's for the best, making hierarchy seem to disappear in the midst of cordiality when in fact any serious challenge to the regime would be met with outrage and retaliation.

All of this is teaching by example. In their relations with students, and in the student culture they foster, teachers get the message across more directly and more powerfully. The teacher/student relationship is the model for relations between junior associates and senior partners, and also for the relationship between lawyers and judges. The student/student relationship is the model for relations among lawyers as peers, for the age cohort within a law firm, and for the "fraternity" of the courthouse crowd.

In the classroom and out of it, students learn a particular style of deference. They learn to suffer with positive cheerfulness interruption in mid-sentence, mockery, ad hominem assault, inconsequent asides, questions that are so vague as to be unanswerable but can somehow be answered wrong all the same, abrupt dismissal, and stinginess of praise (even if these things are not always and everywhere the norm). They learn, if they have talent, that submission is most effective flavored with a pinch of rebellion, to bridle a little before they bend. They learn to savor crumbs, while picking from the air the indications of the master's mood that can mean the difference between a good day and misery. They learn to take it all in good sort, that there is often shyness, good intentions, some real commitment to your learning something behind the authoritarian facade. So it will be with many a robed curmudgeon in years to come.

Then there is affiliation. From among many possibilities, each student gets to choose a mentor, or several, to admire and depend on, to become sort of friends with if the mentor is a liberal, to sit at the feet of if the mentor is more "traditional." You learn how he or she is different from other teachers, and to be supportive of those differences, as the mentor learns something of your particular strengths and weaknesses, both of you trying to prevent the inevitability of letters of recommendation from corrupting the whole experience. This can be fruitful and satisfying, or degrading, or both at once. So it will be a few years later with your "father in the law."

There is a third, more subtle, and less conscious message conveyed in student/teacher relations. Teachers are overwhelmingly white, male, and middle class; and most (by no means all) black and women law teachers give the impression of thorough assimilation to that style, or of insecurity and unhappiness. Students who are women or black or working class find out something important about the professional universe from the first day of class: that it is not even nominally pluralist in cultural terms. The teacher sets the tone—a white, male, middle-class tone. Students adapt. They do so partly out of fear, partly out of hope of gain, partly out of genuine admiration for their role models. But the line between adaptation to the intellectual and skills content of legal education and adaptation to the white, male, middle-class cultural style is a fine one, easily lost sight of.

While students quickly understand that there is diversity among their fellow students and that the faculty is not really homogeneous in terms of character, background, or opinions, the classroom itself becomes more rather than less uniform as legal education progresses. You'll find Fred Astaire and Howard Cosell over and over again, but never Richard Pryor or Betty Friedan. It's not that the teacher punishes you if you use slang or wear clothes or give examples or voice opinions that identify you as different, though that might happen. You are likely to be sanctioned, mildly or severely, only if you refuse to adopt the highly cognitive, dominating mode of discourse that everyone identifies as lawyerlike. Nonetheless, the indirect pressure for conformity is intense.

If you, alone in your seat, feel alienated in this atmosphere, it is unlikely that you will do anything about it in the classroom setting itself, however much you gripe about it with friends. It is more than likely that you'll find a way, in class, to respond as the teacher seems to want you to respond—to be a lot like him, as far as one could tell if one knew you only in class, even though your imitation is flawed by the need to suppress anger. And when some teacher, at least once in some class, makes a remark that seems sexist or racist, or seems unwilling to treat black or women students in quite as "challenging" a way as white students, or treats them in a more challenging way, or cuts off discussion when a woman student gets mad at a male student's joke about the tort of "offensive touching," it is unlikely that you'll do anything then either.

It is easy enough to see this situation of enforced cultural uniformity as oppressive, but somewhat more difficult to see it as training, especially if you are aware of it and hate it. But it is training nonetheless. You will pick up mannerisms, ways of speaking, gestures, that would be "neutral" if they were not emblematic of membership in the universe of the bar. You will come to expect that as a lawyer you will live in a world in which essential parts of you are not represented, or are misrepresented, and in which things you don't like will be accepted to the point that it doesn't occur to people that they are even controversial. And you will come to expect that there is nothing you can do about it. One develops ways of coping with these expectations—turning off attention or involvement when the conversation strays in certain directions, participating actively while ignoring the offensive elements of the interchange, even reinterpreting as inoffensive things that would otherwise make you boil. These are skills that incapacitate rather than empower, skills that will help you imprison yourself in practice.

Relations among students get a lot of their color from relations with the faculty. There is the sense of blood brotherhood, with or without sisters, in endless speculation about the Olympians. The speculation is colored with rage, expressed sometimes in student theatricals or the "humor" column of the school paper. ("Put Professor X's talents to the best possible use: Turn him into hamburger." Ha, ha.) There is likely to be a surface norm of noncompetitiveness and cooperation. ("Gee, I thought this would be like *The Paper Chase*, but it isn't at all.") But a basic thing to learn is the limits of that cooperativeness. Very few people can combine rivalry for grades, law review, clerkships, good summer jobs, with helping another member of their study group so effectively that he might actually pose a danger to them. You learn camaraderie and distrust at the same time. So it will be in the law-firm age cohort.

And there is more to it than that. Through the reactions of fellow students—diffuse, disembodied events that just "happen," in class or out of class—women learn how important it is not to appear to be "hysterical females," and that when your moot court partner gets a crush on you, and doesn't know it, and is married, there is a danger he will hate you when he discovers what he has been feeling. Lower-middle-class students learn not to wear an undershirt that shows, and that certain patterns and fabrics in clothes will stigmatize them no matter what their grades. Black students learn without surprise that the bar will have its own peculiar forms of racism, and that their very presence means affirmative action, unless it means "he would have made it even without affirmative action." They worry about forms of bias so diabolical even they can't see them; and wonder whether legal reasoning is intrinsically white. Meanwhile, dozens of small changes through which they become more and more like other middle- or upper-middle-class Americans engender rhetoric about how the black community is not divided along class lines. On one level, all of this is just high school replayed; on another, it's about how to make partner.

The final touch that completes the picture of law school as training for professional hierarchy is the placement process. As each firm, with the tacit or enthusiastically overt participation of the schools, puts on a conspicuous display of its relative status within the bar, the bar as a whole affirms and celebrates its hierarchical values and the rewards they bring. This process is most powerful for students who go through the elaborate procedures of firms in about the top half of the profession. These include, nowadays, first-year summer jobs, dozens of interviews, fly-outs, second-year summer jobs, more interviews, and more fly-outs.

This system allows law firms to get a *social* sense of applicants, a sense of how they will contribute to the nonlegal image of the firm and to the internal system of deference and affiliation. It allows firms to convey to students the extraordinary opulence of the life they offer, adding the allure of free travel, expense-account meals, fancy hotel suites, and parties at country clubs to the simple message of big bucks in a paycheck. And it teaches students at fancy law schools, students who have had continuous experience of academic and careerist success, that they are not as "safe" as they thought they were.

When students at Columbia or Yale paper dorm corridors with rejection letters, or award prizes for the most rejection letters and for the most unpleasant single letter, they show their sense of the meaning of the ritual. There are many ways in which the boss can persuade you to brush his teeth and comb his hair. One of them is to arrange things so that almost all students get good jobs, but most students get their good jobs through twenty interviews yielding only two offers.

By dangling the bait, making clear the rules of the game, and then subjecting almost everyone to intense anxiety about their acceptability, firms structure entry into the profession so as to maximize acceptance of hierarchy. If you feel you've succeeded, you're forever grateful, and you have a vested interest. If you feel you've failed, you blame yourself, when you aren't busy feeling envy. When you get to be the hiring partner, you'll have a visceral understanding of what's at stake, but by then it will be hard even to imagine why someone might want to change it.

Inasmuch as these hierarchies are generational, they are easier to take than those baldly reflective of race, sex, or class. You, too, will one day be a senior partner and, who knows, maybe even a judge; you will have mentees and be the object of the rage and longing of those coming up behind you. Training for subservience is training for domination as well. Nothing could be more natural and, if you've served your time, more fair than that you as a group should do as you have been done to, for better and for worse. But it doesn't have to be that way, and remember, you saw it first in law school.

I have been arguing that legal education is one of the causes of legal hierarchy. Legal education supports it by analogy, provides it a general legitimating ideology by justifying the rules that underlie it, and provides it a particular ideology by mystifying legal reasoning. Legal education structures the pool of prospective lawyers so that their hierarchical organization seems inevitable, and trains them in detail to look and think and act just like all the other lawyers in the system. Up to this point I have presented this causal analysis as though legal education were a machine feeding particular inputs into another machine. But machines have no consciousness of one another; inasmuch as they are coordinated, it is by some external intelligence. Law teachers, on the other hand, have a vivid sense of what the profession looks like and of what it expects them to do. Since actors in the two systems consciously adjust to one another and also consciously attempt to influence one another, legal education is as much a product of legal hierarchy as a cause of it. To my mind, this means that law teachers must take personal responsibility for legal hierarchy in general, including hierarchy within legal education. If it is there, it is there because they put it there and reproduce it generation after generation, just as lawyers do.

THE STUDENT RESPONSE TO HIERARCHY

Students respond in different ways to their slowly emerging consciousness of the hierarchical realities of life in the law. Looking around me, I see students who enter wholeheartedly into the system—for whom the training "takes" in a quite straightforward way. Others appear, at least, to manage something more complex. They accept the system's presentation of itself as largely neutral, as apolitical, meritocratic, instrumental, a matter of craft. And they also accept the system's promise that if they do their work, "serve their time," and "put in their hours," they are free to think and do and feel anything they want in their "private lives."

This mode of response is complex because the promise, though sincerely proffered, is only sometimes realized. People who accept the messages at face value are surprisingly often disappointed, at least to hear them tell it twenty years later. And since the law is neither apolitical nor meritocratic nor instrumental nor a matter of craft (at least not exclusively these things), and since training for hierarchy cannot be a matter merely of public as opposed to private life, it is inevitable that they do in fact give and take something different than what is suggested by the overt terms of the bargain. Sometimes people enact a kind of parody: they behave in a particularly tough, cognitive, lawyerlike mode in their professional selves, and construct a private self that seems on the surface to deliberately exaggerate opposing qualities of warmth, sensitivity, easygoingness, or cultural radicalism.

Sometimes one senses an opposite version: the person never fully enters into "legal reasoning," remaining always a slightly disoriented, not-quite-in-good-faith role player in professional life, and feels a parallel inability ever to fully "be" their private self. For example, they may talk "shop" and obsess about the day at work, while hating themselves for being unable to "relax," but then find that at work they are unable to make the tasks assigned them fully their own, and that each new task seems at first an unpleasant threat to their fragile feelings of confidence.

For committed liberal students, there is another possibility, which might be called the denunciatory mode. One can take law school work seriously as time serving and do it coldly in that spirit, hate one's fellow students for their surrenders, and focus one's hopes on "not being a lawyer" or on a fantasy of an unproblematically leftist legal job on graduation. This response is hard from the very beginning. If you reject what teachers and the student culture tell you about what the first-year curriculum means and how to enter into learning it, you are adrift as to how to go about becoming minimally competent. You have to develop a theory on your own of what is valid skills training and what is merely indoctrination, and your ambivalent desire to be successful in spite of all is likely to sabotage your independence. As graduation approaches, it becomes clearer that there are precious few unambiguously virtuous law jobs even to apply for, and your situation begins to look more like everyone else's, though perhaps more extreme. Most (by no means all) students who begin with denunciation end by settling for some version of the bargain of public against private life.

I am a good deal more confident about the patterns that I have just described than about the attitudes toward hierarchy that go along with them. My own position in the system of class, sex, and race (as an upper-middle-class white male) and my rank in the professional hierarchy (as a Harvard professor) give me an interest in the perception that hierarchy is both omnipresent and enormously important, even while I am busy condemning it. And there is a problem of imagination that goes beyond that of interest. It is hard for me to know whether I even understand the attitudes toward hierarchy of women and blacks, for example, or of children of working-class parents, or of solo practitioners eking out a living from residential real-estate closings. Members of those groups sometimes suggest that the particularity of their experience of oppression simply cannot be grasped by outsiders, but sometimes that the failure to grasp it is a personal responsibility rather than inevitable. Often it seems to me that all people have at least analogous experiences of the oppressive reality of hierarchy, even those who seem most favored by the system—that the collar feels the same when you get to the end of the rope, whether the rope is ten feet long or fifty. On the other hand, it seems clear that hierarchy creates distances that are never bridged.

It is not uncommon for a person to answer a description of the hierarchy of law firms with a flat denial that the bar is really ranked. Lawyers of lower-middle-class background tend to have far more direct political power in the state governments than "elite" lawyers, even under Republican administrations. Furthermore, every lawyer knows of instances of real friendship, seemingly outside and beyond the distinctions that are supposed to be so important, and can cite examples of lower-middle-class lawyers in upper-middle-class law firms, and vice versa. There are many lawyers who seem to defy hierarchical classification, and law firms and law schools that do likewise, so that one can argue that the hierarchy claim that everyone and everything is ranked breaks down the minute you try to give concrete examples. I have been told often enough that I *may* be right about the pervasiveness of ranking, but that the speaker has never noticed it himself, himself treats all lawyers in the same way, regardless of their class or professional standing, and has never, except in an occasional very bizarre case, found lawyers violating the egalitarian norm.

When the person making these claims is a rich corporate lawyer who was my prep school classmate, I tend to interpret them as a willful denial of the way he is treated and treats others. When the person speaking is someone I perceive as less favored by the system (say, a woman of lower-middle-class origin who went to Brooklyn Law School and now works for a small, struggling downtown law firm), it is harder to know how to react. Maybe I'm just wrong about what it's like out there. Maybe my preoccupation with the horrors of hierarchy is just a way to wring the last ironic drop of pleasure from my own hierarchical superiority. But I don't interpret it that way. The denial of hierarchy is false consciousness. The problem is not whether hierarchy is there, but how to understand it, and what its implications are for political action.

An enlarged version of this chapter entitled *Legal Education and the Reproduction of Hierarchy* is available in pamphlet form from the author.

II

SELECTED ISSUES AND FIELDS OF LAW

3 MARTHA MINOW

POLITICS AND PROCEDURE

WHEN I tell practicing lawyers that I teach Civil Procedure, I usually receive one of two reactions: either "I never understood that course" or "That's the one subject I use every day in my practice." It could be that the difference between these two answers lies in whether the interlocutor is a trial attorney; actually most attorneys do not regularly go into court or gain familiarity with the procedural rules. Yet I have even had the same person give me both reactions. Why is the course dealing with the procedural aspects of civil (noncriminal) trials both so elusive and so important? One explanation stems from strong competition among potential guiding ideals or explanations for the system of rules known as civil procedure.

Hypothesis 1: Procedure is justice, so procedural rules should not bend in the face of temporary situational concerns. This view makes procedure markedly distinct from substance and from the merits of individual cases, and therefore sets procedure apart with its own separate logic and demands; ordinary intuitions are not relevant or helpful.

Hypothesis 2: Procedure is the servant of justice, so procedural rules should not stand in the way of just results in particular circumstances. This view supports the proliferation of exceptions, waivers, ambiguities, or other interpretations of procedural rules that make the rules themselves difficult if not impossible to state, know, or use apart from claims about the merits of particular cases.

Hypothesis 3: The distinction between procedure and substance is an illusion and cannot be maintained. Procedural values can generate the same amount of compelling argument as values in other areas of law. Indeed, procedural rules influence and are influenced by substantive law even as procedural rules refer to highly valued and yet competing norms apart from the substantive norms.

Any of these theories alone would be sufficient to explain the confusion and frustration created by the field of procedure. Taken together, they assure its elusiveness, and help us understand its importance, which is best understood by focusing on a concrete example that presents both a procedure and an underlying substance that matter a great deal. I focus here on the landmark case *Walker v. Birmingham*.[1]

THE PROCEDURE AND THE SUBSTANCE

In *Walker v. Birmingham*, a majority of the United States Supreme Court enforced contempt citations against individuals who disobeyed a state court's temporary restraining order, which they believed was unconstitutional, without first filing a motion to dissolve that order. The Court stated it was simply applying a preexisting procedural rule, the collateral bar rule, which prevents individuals from raising any substantive challenge to a court order if they disobey the order prior to bringing the challenge to court. The Court explained that courts must preserve their ability to direct the methods for challenging judicial orders to ensure that individuals do not become the judges in their own cases. The strict requirement of a hearing on the substance of the issue was particularly noteworthy in this case, however, because the individuals involved included Rev. Martin Luther King, Jr., and the challenged restraining order forbade his plans for a nonviolent march to protest the racial segregation and racially motivated violence in Birmingham.[2]

By Birmingham city ordinance, drinking fountains, bathrooms, and dressing rooms had to be segregated by race.[3] Bus transportation under Supreme Court rulings had to be desegregated if public. The Birmingham government's response was to privatize the bus company and perpetuate racial segregation. Ambulances, police wagons, even elevators were segregated by race, as were theaters, ball parks, jail cells, hospitals, cemeteries, and hotels. Interracial marriage was banned. A city rule deemed it a crime for African Americans and whites to play cards, checkers, or dice together. Ordered by a federal court to provide equal recreational facilities for blacks and whites, the city closed all of its sixty-eight parks, thirty-eight playgrounds, six swimming pools, and four golf courses. Despite the Supreme Court's decision in *Brown v. Board of Education* in 1954, as of 1963 all Birmingham public schools were still racially segregated, by order of the local school board. The public library was open only to whites.

Segregation was maintained through violence. The Ku Klux Klan beat freedom riders who tried to integrate the city bus terminal, as ordered by a court. Birmingham had been nicknamed "Bombingham" because so many homes and churches of African American leaders had been bombed. Segregation was also maintained through law. Lawyers, police, sheriffs, and judges enforced the Jim Crow regime. Notable among these officials was Bull Conner, the Public Safety Commissioner who was known to send police dogs after African Americans who assembled peaceably and lawfully.

The judicial order in question in *Walker v. Birmingham* banned a peaceful protest march King had planned for that Good Friday and Easter Sunday.[4] King's group tried to obtain a permit for the march and learned in no uncertain terms that a permit would not be granted then or ever. The city filed a complaint seeking an injunction to restrain the march. It was issued at 9:00 P.M. by a state circuit court judge in a hearing held in the absence of King, his colleagues, and his lawyers. The judge was, of course, part of the government that implemented racial segregation and ducked orders opposed to it. Approximately thirty-six hours passed between the issuance of the order and the Good Friday march; no effort to challenge the order was made before the weekend.[5] King, Ralph Abernathy, and sixty others proceeded with the march as scheduled and were arrested; more were arrested two days later at the second march. On the Monday following the second march, attorneys for King and other petitioners appeared in court, seeking to dissolve the restraining order. The city moved for the protesters to show why they should not be held in contempt. The judge found them guilty of contempt and refused to consider the constitutionality of the injunction because they had disobeyed it before trying to obtain judicial relief.

The Supreme Court itself later struck down the city ordinance underlying the court's order as a patent violation of the First Amendment's guarantee of freedom of speech in a subsequent lawsuit brought by individuals who had not disobeyed the order.[6] Thus, in *Walker v. Birmingham,* the Supreme Court defended protection of a procedural rule (Do not disobey a court order without first challenging it in court) despite the apparent futility of following that rule and despite the obvious unconstitutionality of the order in question. King served his sentence for contempt in solitary confinement, and there read a statement from eight local white clergymen calling for an end to the demonstrations. King's response, "Letter from a Birmingham Jail," became a classic document in the struggle for civil rights, and indeed, in American letters.[7]

PROCEDURE IS JUSTICE, SO PROCEDURES SHOULD NOT BEND

Walker is a vivid illustration of the view that procedural rules should not bend in the face of substantive claims. By refusing to let King and the other defendants raise any substantive objections to the restraining order they had violated, the Supreme Court in *Walker* upheld a procedural requirement in the face of compelling substantive injustice. By endorsing and enforcing the collateral bar rule, the Court explicitly identified values of procedure independent of substantive justice.

In this respect, the Court echoed Western philosophic traditions and a powerful school of legal thought, both of which advance the view that justice at core is procedural. For example, philosopher Stuart Hampshire has written, "[T]he basic concept of justice, taken by itself is primarily procedural, prescribing that there just be careful and unbiased weighing of arguments on both sides."[8] Underscoring this view of justice is a particular conception of the judicial system: the adversarial system, predicated on a fair chance for competing sides to be heard by an unbiased decision maker. The rules governing such hearings and prescribing the roles for adversaries and judge thus become central to justice, and maintaining fidelity to those rules and roles matters more to the system for ensuring justice than do the results in any particular case.

Similarly, the focus on procedure as the essence of justice animates an influential school of legal theory that emerged in the United States after the end of World War II. Legal process theorists seek a morality of process, independent of results. They maintain that the common interests in a diverse democratic society are better and more successfully articulated in procedural rather than substantive terms.[9] Accordingly, the proper elements of process are framed by a comparison of the competence of legal institutions, including courts and legislatures, and the application of reason, neutral as to ends or results. Preserving procedural regularity—predictable application of regulations governing the processing of disputes—is valuable quite apart from the results in particular cases. Procedural regularity promotes the competence of the courts and their reputation for fairness.

Less abstractly, the commitment to the rules of procedure regardless of injustices produced in particular cases is routinely invoked to support rigorous application of procedural deadlines. The Federal Rules of Civil Procedure, drafted by an advisory group appointed by the Supreme Court and gaining force of law under a congressional delegation, include a rule explaining how to compute time periods, and some sixteen rules establish specific numerical time periods for filing pieces of paper or responding to pieces of paper produced in the course of litigation. Selection of the specific time periods and rules for computing them is intended to produce an orderly, predictable mechanism for pursuing cases, even if compelling arguments and issues would be foreclosed by strict application of these deadlines. (At the same time, the rules themselves afford avenues for avoiding or challenging strict application of deadlines because of substantive issues; this is an example of hypothesis 2: Procedural rules should not stand in the way of substantive justice).[10]

If the strict application of the collateral bar rule in *Walker* thus illustrates the commitment to orderly, predictable means rather than particular substantive ends, I find it unsatisfactory. The collateral bar rule as a procedural rule does not, in my view, express values important enough to trump substance. Nor would the orderly mechanisms of judicial actions be seriously jeopardized by creating exceptions to, or even by abolishing, the collateral bar rule.

The goal of procedural regularity is not undermined by allowing people who first disobey a rule then to proceed, in their defense, to challenge the rule in a hearing on a motion to hold them in contempt. Consider the common practice allowing criminal defendants to challenge the laws under which their violations are charged. Thus, a defendant charged with distributing obscene literature can challenge the obscenity statute as an unconstitutional infringement of his freedom of speech. Admittedly, criminal laws are adopted by legislatures, and in contrast, the orders protected by the collateral bar rule are judicial orders. Why, though, should this difference justify a different treatment for the offender who wishes to challenge the validity of the underlying norm?

The usual explanation points to the contrasting powers and places of the judiciary and the legislature in a system that includes both separation of powers and judicial review. Committed to dispersing power, the founders of this republic allocated different responsibilities to the judiciary, the legislature, and the executive, while also placing each branch in a position to check and monitor the others. In the federal system, one house of the legislature retains the power to approve or disapprove of the executive's nominations of judges. In turn, the judiciary interprets the laws enacted by the legislature and exercises the power to assess, ultimately, whether those laws comport with the Constitution. Hence, one could argue, the judiciary needs to protect a higher level of compliance with its enactments than does the legislature.

Another explanation would highlight the relative weakness of the judiciary, which has neither power of the budget, as does the legislature, nor power over the police, as does the executive. Accordingly, the judiciary must erect stricter requirements and show less toleration for disobedience than the other branches. Yet, the courts are not so weak as to need to erect high barriers to those who disagree with their decisions. The courts would retain the contempt sanction, including fines and jail sentences, for those who fail to offer convincing reasons for their disobedience in the face of an outstanding judicial order. California has rejected the collateral bar rule for its courts and found it possible still to conduct orderly judicial business.[11]

Having said all this, I must at the same time acknowledge the value of the attitude toward procedural rules that is manifested in *Walker v. Birmingham*. Ironically, I learned the value most emphatically in a case involving the collateral bar rule, when I helped the American Civil Liberties Union write an amicus curiae brief. Friends enticed me to participate by saying, "Here's a chance to challenge the collateral bar rule." So of course I agreed.[12]

The facts were these. *The Providence Journal* sought the Federal Bureau of Investigation (FBI) logs and memoranda summarizing the content of telephone conversations involving Raymond L. S. Patriarca, a purported leader of an organized crime syndicate. The FBI had destroyed the tape recordings themselves after discovering that they resulted from electronic surveillance conducted without a warrant and in violation of Patriarca's rights. Citing concerns about invading the personal privacy of Patriarca, the FBI declined the newspaper's request for the materials and the First Circuit agreed. After Patriarca died in 1985, the *Journal* again requested the information from the FBI, and the FBI turned it over. Then, Patriarca's son, Raymond J. Patriarca, filed suit against the FBI and the *Journal*, alleging improper release of the information and seeking an injunction to prevent publication of the materials. The district court judge issued a temporary restraining order; the newspaper's publisher decided to publish one article revealing the FBI information and another concerning the judicial action. Patriarca moved for contempt but did not pursue the motion. The district court judge appointed a federal prosecutor to pursue the matter and then found the *Journal* guilty of criminal contempt under the collateral bar rule.[13]

The Court of Appeals for the First Circuit reversed the decision, basing its action on language in *Walker* suggesting that a transparently invalid order would not be subject to the collateral bar rule. The First

Circuit judge who wrote the opinion emphasized that they had before them an injunction against publishing news—which is a prior restraint of pure speech, unlike a restraint of speech involving conduct, as in the march in *Walker*. The First Circuit later reheard the case *en banc* and modified the decision to require a publisher to make a good faith effort to seek emergency relief even when faced with what appears to be a transparently invalid prior restraint of speech, but imposed this obligation prospectively only. Thus, the *Journal* had won—until the special prosecutor pursued the case before the Supreme Court.[14]

At this juncture, I became involved, and I drafted a heartfelt defense of the exception to the collateral bar rule for transparently invalid injunctions. Finally, I thought and hoped, the Court would correct the mistake of *Walker v. Birmingham*, or at least mitigate its effects. I relished the chance to talk with Floyd Abrams, the lawyer for the *Journal* and one of the leading First Amendment lawyers in the United States. Here we were, in a big case presenting big issues before the United States Supreme Court. This, I thought, is why I wanted to be a lawyer.

One day Floyd called me and said he thought he had found a winning argument for the case. The federal statute and federal regulations governing federal courts explicitly empower the Justice Department's Solicitor General or his designee to argue suits in the Supreme Court "in which the United States is interested."[15] Surely this was such a case, and yet it was pursued in the Supreme Court by a special prosecutor, not by the Solicitor General. Indeed, the special prosecutor who had pursued the *Providence Journal* case to the Supreme Court had tried unsuccessfully to obtain authorization from the Solicitor General to file the suit in the Supreme Court. A procedural glitch!

But how technical and remote from my vision of challenging the collateral bar rule in the pursuit of substantive justice. I sputtered something to Floyd about hoping that the Court would address the big issues about the First Amendment and the collateral bar rule. Floyd reminded me that the *Journal* had won in the First Circuit, so our goal should be to keep that decision in place. He clearly had in mind his role as the *Journal*'s lawyer; I had law reform and precedent setting in mind, which is the luxury, perhaps, of law professor friends of the court who file amicus briefs.

Floyd's argument worked. The Supreme Court held that the special prosecutor lacked authority to represent the United States before the Supreme Court, and dismissed the case for want of jurisdiction.[16] The *Providence Journal* won, and a procedural requirement supplied the reason. A procedural rule that cannot bend, regardless of the merits, provides an avenue for litigants who may not be so able to win on the merits, or who would rather not take the risk of arguing the merits.

PROCEDURE AS "HANDMAIDEN": SUBSTANCE SHOULD PREVAIL

Charles Clark, a leading scholar and judge who helped to author the federal procedural rules, once described procedural rules as the "handmaiden" of justice. Judith Resnick, a contemporary procedure expert, has criticized this gendered language and more pervasive exclusion of women and subordination of women's concerns in the rules governing procedure.[17] This debate actually underscores the appeal and problems with hypothesis 2: Procedure should serve substantive justice and give way in the face of the merits of particular cases.

It is probably wise to identify elements of this view before criticizing it. First, there is an assumption: Justice is defined more by actual results—who wins, who loses—than by the design of the system overall. Second, there is a recognition of problems with the contrasting approach: Procedural rules that do not bend can be deployed merely for tactical or strategic advantages, regardless of the intention of the procedural rule. Finding tactical value in a rule because it enables particular victories regardless of the merits does little to advance the purposes of procedural regularity. Moreover, widespread strategic uses of procedural rules threaten to undermine public confidence in the legal system. How often do we hear people object to "legal loopholes" and "lawyers' technicalities" when the results of a lawsuit turn on procedure rather than substance? Finally, there is the resolution: Procedural rules can be drafted to permit adjustments in the face of substantive concerns while leaving in place a procedural system that can work with regularity.

Thus, modern rules of civil procedure include many avenues for subordinating procedural rules to substance. One example appears in Federal Rules of Civil Procedure 60(b): A court may relieve a party from a final judgment or order upon a proper showing of "mistake" or "excusable neglect," "newly discovered evidence," "fraud," or "any other reason justifying [such] relief." There could hardly be a more explicit statement that the rest of the procedural rules are intended to support a fair result; no procedural rulings are to prevent reconsidering the matter in the face of these kinds of reasons.

In a recent, remarkable decision involving public aid to students in parochial schools, the Supreme Court invoked FR 60(b) to permit relief from an injunction that had received the Court's approval twelve years previously.[18] That injunction forbade New York City from sending public school teachers into parochial schools to provide remedial education to children who were eligible for help under a federal statute. The Court rejected arguments for FR 60(b) relief premised on alleged significant changes in factual conditions. Also unavailing were claims that a change in the law occurred when five justices indicated in an opinion an interest in reconsidering the prior approval of the injunction. Nonetheless, the Court concluded that its intervening decisions had interpreted the Establishment Clause's prohibition on governmental establishment of religion in ways that undermined the assumptions at work when the Court approved the injunction. In the intervening years, changing membership on the Court expanded the number of justices willing to give religion more room and assistance in the ongoing tension between a ban on state establishment of religion and a guarantee of individual rights to the free exercise of religion. Yet rather than wait for a new case to announce the shifting trend, the Court reopened an old case. It used FR 60(b) to bypass the time limitation set by another procedural rule, governing reconsideration of an already decided case.[19]

Now, let's explore the metaphoric treatment of procedure. Locks and keys highlight the regulation of access so crucial to procedure. The metaphors "servant" and "handmaiden" do not adequately capture the refined view of procedure's role. Instead, consider this one: Procedural rules are a kind of scaffold supporting the constant effort to build and rebuild justice. Too much attention to preserving the scaffold misses the point of the enterprise, and the scaffold can and should be moved around as needed by the larger project. The scaffold should be stable enough to stand upon while remaining capable of being dismantled and reassembled as needs change.

Curiously, this conception could even be proffered to explain in substantive terms the collateral bar rule as it developed in the federal courts. The *Walker* Court relied heavily on a previous case that arose when workers disobeyed a court order against labor strikes.[20] One set of substantive concerns prevailed in that case—concerns for order and protection of employer interests rather than concerns for worker rights in the context of struggles over labor relations. Scholars have documented the direct influence of injunctions in altering the course of the labor movement in this country. This is a case of procedure used to support a particular substantive result. Forty years after the labor case enforcing the collateral bar rule, however, the Supreme Court itself rejected the collateral bar rule in one labor case; the Court explicitly found the procedural rule, enforced by a state court, should bend in the face of the federal regulation of labor relations and the shift in power relations achieved through legislative struggle.[21]

Over the objection of the dissenting justices, the majority in *Walker* decided to ignore this intervening case limiting the collateral bar rule and affirmed the contempt of court decision against King. The justices in majority apparently were influenced by their view of the substantive merits, at least according to one dissenting opinion. Justice Brennan suggested that the majority was wrongly influenced by national events occurring after the facts involved in the suit: urban riots in other cities apparently strengthened the resolve of the justices in the majority to enforce the collateral bar rule and its adherence to procedural regularity.[22] In addition, the majority justices themselves announced but neglected to apply the substantive justice exception to the collateral bar rule for judicial orders that are "transparently invalid," which I later tried to invoke in the *Providence Journal* case. It seems hard to imagine a better candidate for the exception to the rule than the situation at issue in *Walker* itself: an ex parte order banning a peaceful civil rights protest march in a city run by racist demagogues whose refusal of a parade permit was simply one of the daily acts of racial domination.

Surely, the Supreme Court justices knew that no defense of purely procedural values could prevent the watching world from reading their opinion as exonerating those who administered racial apartheid in Birmingham.

Perhaps for this reason, the procedure-minded majority emphasized the very substantive value advocated by King and the other defendants. The value of equality, treating all people alike, infuses the closing of the majority opinion:

> The rule of law that Alabama followed in this case reflects a belief that in the fair administration of justice no man can be judge in his own case, however exalted his station, however righteous his motives, and irrespective of his race, color, politics, or religion.[23]

In a demonstration that footnotes really matter, the Court then cited in footnote a judicial decision enforcing the collateral bar rule after an individual tried to organize a campaign to interfere with court-ordered desegregation of a public high school.[24] The substantive message could not be more pointed. The same equal protection clause informing the struggle against Jim Crow segregation animates the rule that requires all persons to pursue their grievances in court the same way. The same collateral bar rule applied to King would protect school desegregation orders and the promise (which seemed more likely then) of racial justice pursued through judicially mandated school reforms. Procedure, in this case, *is* substance. Equal application of the law is the ultimate goal of the defendants, too, implied the not-so-subtle Court.

Yet, whose view of justice, fairness, or correct results should prevail? This general problem is compounded by the question, When should procedure give way to permit debates over substance? Discretion would go to the judge about not only the interpretation of the merits but also the weight of procedural rules in light of the merits, if procedure is subordinate to substance. Steady preservation of procedural rules for their own sake avoids or postpones such disputes while also potentially affording litigants another combat arena, the interpretation of the procedural rules.

Yet even this cannot cover up the Court's basic conclusion. King and others had to lose their liberty despite an unjust order, an unjust local process, and an unjust state legal system. Procedural integrity required this sacrifice so the *federal* judiciary could command sufficient respect to preside over the efforts to remedy American apartheid. Was this the right calculus? Should an unjust law ever compel obedience? King's "Letter from a Birmingham Jail" addressed this directly. He argued that one could advocate breaking some laws and obeying others because of the distinction between just and unjust laws:

> An unjust law is a code that a majority inflicts on a minority that is not binding on itself. This is difference made legal. On the other hand a just law is a code that a majority compels a minority to follow that it is willing to follow itself. . . .
>
> There are some instances when a law is just on its face and unjust in its application. For instance, I was arrested Friday on a charge of parading without a permit. Now there is nothing wrong with an ordinance which requires a permit for a parade, but when the ordinance is used to preserve segregation and to deny citizens the First Amendment privilege of peaceful assembly and peaceful protest, then it becomes unjust. In no sense do I advocate evading or defying the law as the rabid segregationist would do. This would lead to anarchy. One who breaks an unjust law must do it *openly, lovingly* . . . and with a willingness to accept the penalty. I submit than an individual who breaks a law that conscience tells him is unjust,

and willingly accepts the penalty by staying in jail to arouse the conscience of the community over its injustice, is in reality expressing the highest respect for law.[25]

For good or for ill, the drafters of the Federal Rules of Civil Procedure directed that substantive concerns should come into play in both the interpretation and administration of the rules. Rule 1 provides this interpretive guide for the rest of the rules: "They shall be construed and administered to secure the just, speedy, and inexpensive determination of every action." When in doubt about the meaning of a particular rule, the doubt should be resolved in light of these substantive goals. One small problem is that the three goals point in potentially quite different directions. Speed sometimes accompanies low expense, but not always. Justice sometimes accompanies speed, but sometimes a quick decision undermines justice. And justice may be overshadowed by high expenses even as it may be thwarted by inadequate resources for witnesses, experts, and time to be heard. Efficiency sometimes is fairness and sometimes prevents it. Justice sometimes takes a million tiny moves, the involvement of many parties, and time for people and institutions to change.

PROCEDURE AND SUBSTANCE CANNOT BE SEPARATED

A third position, which may already have reared its head in the previous discussion, suggests that procedure and substance cannot be separated and that efforts to distinguish them fail. In the context of *Walker*, is the commitment to social order a substantive or procedural value? Is the strategic use of a procedural rule substantive or procedural? Is the commitment to using the same rules for everyone procedural or substantive in a society marked by racial and class divisions?

There remains considerable disagreement, even among those who think procedure and substance cannot be separated. Adherents to the legal process view would argue that procedure and substance cannot be divided, because at its heart the substance of justice is procedure; over time, substance collapses into procedure and the maintenance of a procedural system rather than the results in particular cases. Equal application of the law, in both its procedural and substantive aspects, *is* a substantive value, and perhaps the most important one.

Others will emphasize the political context, and political tilt, of adjudication, whether the crucial element determining the result of a given case is procedural or substantive. Who were the more powerful litigants?

What were the political views of the judge? How were interest group politics arrayed at the time? These issues would seem more important to some observers than efforts to sort out procedural and substantive rules and norms.

Still others will identify the ways in which technical efforts to distinguish procedure and substance fall apart. A vivid if complex example appears in a particularly technical area that exemplifies student frustrations with procedure, the area known as the *Erie* doctrine. Cases that come into federal court solely because the defendants and plaintiffs are citizens of different states have no federally forged substantive claims; therefore, the Supreme Court has ruled that the substantive norms in such cases should be state norms.[26] By definition, however, the litigants come from different states, and thus different state laws potentially could apply. No problem, ruled the Supreme Court when it explicitly addressed the issue, the state law to be used will be identified by looking to how the state in which the federal court sits would select among potentially relevant state laws if the case arose in state court.[27] That some of those very state choice-of-law rules themselves call for assessment of "better law" or characterization of the case in terms of substantive categories already blurs the line between procedure and substance.

But the real problem appears in the next question: How much of the case in federal court is to be governed by state law, whatever the particular state law chosen? The statute of limitations governing the claim? Whether the case is tried to a judge or a jury? The rules governing the lengths and typefaces used in lawyers' briefs? One justice in an influential opinion argued that the answer to such questions should lie in the distinction between procedure and substance, because "no one doubts federal power over procedure" even though the "line between procedural and substantive law is hazy."[28]

Yet another famous justice wrote, "Neither 'substance' nor 'procedure' represent the same invariants. Each implies different variables depending upon the particular problem for which it is used."[29] The effort to distinguish which parts of a case should be governed by state norms and which should be governed by federal norms itself could be viewed as both a procedural issue (selecting the rule of law) and a substantive issue (allocating power between the major levels of government). In the meantime, historians have effectively demonstrated the very real substantive effects of rulings in this technical area, influences of the power of railroads and other corporations in relation to individual workers and consumers.[30] A good reminder for any reader of procedural cases, then, is to ask about the historical context for the case and its practical effects.

Finally, some observers will emphasize that procedure and substance cannot be separated because each embrace competing purposes and values; each of these values are subject to contested interpretation in individual circumstances. No norms used in a living legal system are static; all are sufficiently general to permit multiple interpretations, and indeed the brilliance of a democratic, adversarial legal system is its capacity to transmute conflicts among people and institutions into fights among lawyers about the meanings of words. Procedural rules reflect political choices and invite contests over interpretation just as do any other kind of rule. Procedural rules, like the collateral bar rule and rules about statutes of limitations, combine the just and the arbitrary; procedural law is filled with arguments people use to express disagreements and to settle disputes. Those arguments draw upon conflicting visions of society, the meanings of justice, what can and cannot be sacrificed, and everything else people argue about. People fight as intensely about the content and application of rules about procedure as they do about the norms of property, torts, criminal law, and constitutional law.

ELUSIVE AND IMPORTANT

As a descriptive matter, each of the three hypotheses has something to offer. Procedural rules deserve respect regardless of their effect on the results in a particular case, but sometimes procedural rules should bend in light of substantive concerns. At the same time, distinctions between substance and procedure crumble even as competing procedural values vie with other kinds of purposes.

Since a lot seems to turn on each of these competing theories, and yet each has something illuminating to offer, it should be no wonder that procedure is elusive and important. Yet even taken together, the hypotheses barely scratch the surface of the complexity of American rules and practices of judicial procedure. Still, if you pay attention to fights over the relative priority of procedure and substance, you may come to appreciate the drama and stakes rather than feel exacerbated by the ambiguity and complexity of the resulting trail of rules and decisions.

Indeed, the tensions between procedure and substance reverberate throughout the American legal system, as illustrated in three more examples. The first could be called the "access to court" problem. Procedural rules are integrally related to how much a system of justice does, and should, focus upon the ending of disputes, and how much instead it should stress the declaration and enforcement of particular norms. The relative proportion of fully litigated trials, court-sponsored mediations, and out-of-court settlements reflect rules about attorneys' fees, filing dates, discovery (the investigative stages of litigation), jurisdiction, and choice of law. A comparison with the criminal justice system is apt. No one can understand the American criminal justice process by looking only at prosecutions that go to trial, given the vast majority of cases that result in plea bargains without trial.[31] A similar ratio occurs in the civil system, and reflects procedural practices and rules. A procedural system must be able to gather and process disputes in an orderly and timely fashion because justice delayed is justice denied.[32] When time and economic pressures lead parties to negotiate settlements out of court, justice of a sort can be done, especially in restoring control over the disputes to the parties. Rigorous and even costly procedural requirements can press disputants back from court into private negotiations and influence the shape of justice in the shadow of the law.

Second, procedural rules depend upon and govern the roles of legal actors who proceed with substantive arguments and decisions. As a result, no substantive argument can be made separate from procedure; each reflects the role held by the individual lawyer or judge, which itself is governed by procedural rules. For advocates in ongoing litigation, procedural rules set the guidelines for the play, or battle, under way while also affording an arena for advantage outside the merits of the contractual, tort, or other civil dispute. Procedural rules direct the day-to-day work of judges, offer constraints, and afford avenues out of constraints. Procedural rules provide policy makers, such as chief judges, court managers, and legislators, opportunities to affect the flow and resolution of cases, the accessibility of the justice system, and the experiences ordinary people have with law.

Finally, procedural rules are written, interpreted, and enforced by people who themselves have substantive interests and purposes.[33] A study of procedure affords insight into the heart of a formal legal system without the distraction of blood, money, and morals on the surface of the rules, as they are in criminal law, contract and corporate law, tort law, and family law. A formal legal system depends upon language and texts authored by people with the hope of governing actions and powers of private and public persons. Language depends upon communities of speakers and readers, yet language always admits of ambiguities, which in turn permit contests and discretionary exercises of the very people whose actions were to be constrained. The centrality of persons, politics, and contexts to law thus can be well illustrated even in the lawyers' law of procedure, and thus the human features of all of law can be laid bare. Words themselves cannot constrain power, but the aspiration to use words to do so can provide levers in struggles over power and control.

Procedural rules are often difficult to grasp and use but crucial to the practice of law. Perhaps more surprising, though, is the significance of procedure to critical understandings of the deployments and exercises of power by people performing varied roles in the justice system.

NOTES

Thanks to Christine Desan and David Kairys for helpful comments, and to Owen Fiss for my first encounter with *Walker v. Birmingham*.

1. *Walker v. Birmingham*, 388 U.S. 307 (1967).
2. King was awarded the Nobel Peace Prize for his efforts in the struggle for civil rights. He was murdered in Memphis in 1968.
3. See generally Martin Luther King, Jr., *Why We Can't Wait* (New York: Harper & Row, 1964), 39–75.
4. Bull Connor's government was to be replaced on the Monday following Easter Sunday, giving even more significance to the date of the scheduled march. See Hal Scott Shapiro, *The Collateral Bar Rule—Transparently Invalid: A Theoretical and Historical Perspective*, 24 Columbia Journal of Law and Social Problems 510, 570 (1991). See generally David Luban, *Legal Modernism* (Ann Arbor: University of Michigan Press, 1994), 209–82.
5. Indeed, the marchers made a deliberate decision not to wait for judicial consideration before marching because similar efforts to build a movement of nonviolent protest against segregation had been stalled and ultimately terminated by the tardiness of judicial review (King, *Why We Can't Wait*).
6. *Shuttlesworth v. City of Birmingham*, 394 U.S. 147 (1969).
7. See generally Luban, *Legal Modernism*.
8. Stuart Hampshire, *Innocence and Experience* (Cambridge, MA: Harvard University Press, 1989), 62.

9. Hart and Sacks, *The Legal Process,* ed. William Eskridge (Westbury, NY: Foundation Press, 1994).

10. See 28 U.S.C. §§ 2071, 2072 (Rule-making power, power to prescribe rules of procedure); FR 6(a),(d),(e); FR 12(a); FR 14(a); FR 15(a); FR 26(a); FR 27(a)(2); FR 36(a); FR 38(a); FR 56; FR 59; FR 62(a); FR 65(b); FR 68; FR 72; FR 74; FR 81(c). FR 86 also specifies the dates upon which time amendments to the rule were to become effective. For examples of rules that avoid strict application of deadlines, see FR 1, 16, 60(b).

11. *In re Berry,* 68 Cal. 2d 137, 65 Cal. Rptr., 273, 436 P.2d 273 (1968).

12. See Brief Amicus Curiae of the American Civil Liberties Union, et al., *United States v. Providence Journal Company and Charles M. Hauser,* no. 87-65. This is a friend of the court brief, submitted with party approval, to offer relevant perspectives on a matter before the court.

13. *In re Providence Journal Co.,* 820 F.2d 1342, 1344 (1st Cir. 1986). *Providence Journal Co. v. Federal Bureau of Investigation,* 602 F.2d 1010 (1st Cir. 1979), cert. denied, 444 U.S. 1071 (1980). *Patriarca v. Federal Bureau of Investigation,* 630 F.Supp. 993 (D.R.I. 1986). The court relied on FR 42(b) (*Patriarca,* 630 F.Supp., 1004). The court sentenced the executive editor to a suspended jail sentence of eighteen months and two hundred hours of community service and fined the *Journal* $100,000 (Ibid., 1345).

14. This is a hearing before all the members of that court, not simply the three members assigned to usual appellate hearings. The en banc procedure permits the court to strive for consistency and guard against the risk that results when cases turn on the luck of the draw in the assignment of three judges to a particular case. *In re Providence Journal Co.,* 820 F.2d 1354 (1st Cir. 1987).

15. See 28 U.S.C. § 518(a).

16. *United States v. Providence Journal Co. and Charles M. Hauser,* 485 U.S. 693 (1988).

17. Charles E. Clark, *The Handmaid of Justice,* 23 Washington University Law Quarterly 297 (1938), and Judith Resnick, *Housekeeping: The Nature and Allocation of Work in Federal Trial Courts,* 24 Georgia Law Review 909 (1990).

18. *Agostini v. Felton,* 1997 WL 338583 *1 (June 23, 1997), continuation of *Aguilar v. Felton,* 473 U.S. 402 (1985).

19. A dissenting opinion vigorously criticizes the majority for pressing FR 60(b) to an unprecedented and aberrational use in rehearing a twelve-year-old case. See ibid., *34, Ginsburg dissenting, joined by Stevens, Souter, and Breyer.

20. See *Walker,* 313, citing *Howat v. State of Kansas,* 258 U.S. 181 (1922).

21. See William Forbath, *Law and the Shaping of the American Labor Movement* (Cambridge, MA: Harvard University Press, 1991); see *Walker v. Birmingham,* Brennan dissenting, joined by Warren and Fortas, discussing abuses of ex parte injunctions in the context of labor relations. *In re Green,* 369 U.S. 689 (1962).

22. *Walker,* 349, Brennan dissenting, joined by Warren and Fortas: "We cannot permit fears of 'riots' and 'civil disobedience' generated by slogans like 'Black Power' to divert our attention from what is at stake here."

23. *Walker,* 320–21.

24. Ibid., 321 n. 16, discussing *Kasper v. Brittain,* 245 F.2d 92.

25. Martin Luther King "Letter from a Birmingham Jail," A. J. Muste Memorial Institute Essay Series, no. 1 (April 1973).

26. *Erie v. Tompkins,* 304 U.S. 64 (1938), overturning *Swift v. Tyson,* 41 U.S. (16 Pet.) 1 (1842).

27. *Klaxon Co. v. Stentor Electric Manufacturing Co.,* 313 U.S. 487 (1941).

28. See *Guaranty Trust Co. v. York,* 326 U.S. 99 (1945); *Ragan v. Merchant's Transfer & Warehouse Co.,* 337 U.S. 530 (1949).

29. See *Guaranty Trust Co. v. York,* 326 U.S. 99, 108 (1945) (Frankfurter delivered the opinion for the Court).

30. See Edward Purcell, *Litigation and Inequality: Federal Diversity Jurisdiction in Industrial America, 1870–1958* (New York: Oxford University Press, 1992).

31. See Robert E. Scott and William J. Stuntz, *Plea Bargaining as Contract,* 101 Yale Law Journal 1909, 1909 n. 1 (1992), citing a plea bargain rate of 86 percent for federal criminal cases in 1989 and 91 percent for state felony cases in selected jurisdictions in 1988.

32. See Marc Galanter and Mia Cahill, *"Most Cases Settle": Judicial Promotion and Regulation of Settlements,* 46 Stanford Law Review 1339, 1342 (1994), stating that 4 percent of civil cases proceeded through trial in 1994.

33. Stephen Subrin, *How Equity Conquered Common Law: The Federal Rule of Civil Procedure in Historical Perspective,* 135 University of Pennsylvania Law Review 909 (1987).

4 AUSTIN SARAT

GOING TO COURT: ACCESS, AUTONOMY, AND THE CONTRADICTIONS OF LIBERAL LEGALITY

AN independent judiciary, responsive to constitutional norms and solicitous of minority rights, stands at the symbolic center of those legal systems committed to liberal values. It is the institutional embodiment of liberal legality of the kind to which America is at least theoretically committed. Liberal legality traces its roots back to the classical liberalism of the mid–eighteenth century; it holds that law and politics are and should be separate, that legal judgments should be made impartially and should adhere to rules articulated and known in advance, that power should be exercised in accordance with the rule of law, that government should recognize and respect rights, and that freedom rather than equality should be the highest political value.[1] At the center of liberal legality is the ideal of legal autonomy, of law above and outside politics, but also of law's openness and availability to socially and politically disadvantaged groups, to those seeking redress for injuries inflicted, protection from future harm, or vindication of their membership in the community.[2] The centrality of courts in the legitimation of liberal legality depends on both their appearing to be autonomous and their accessibility. Autonomy without accessibility would produce an arid, scholastic irrelevance. Alternatively, accessibility without autonomy would collapse the distinction between law and politics on which liberalism depends. Courts that are accessible and, at the same time, can maintain the appearance of autonomy are in a critical position to vindicate liberal legality's promise of rights. They give meaning to the claim that law provides a terrain of contestation on which the powerless can hold the powerful to account by insisting that their legitimating rhetoric be turned into action.[3]

Despite a radically changed political and legal environment, the Supreme Court's decision in *Brown v. Board of Education* perhaps best exemplifies the symbolic importance of the judiciary. Even today that case stands as a beacon of hope to the poor and the disadvantaged.[4] *Brown's* significance involves more than even its remarkable willingness to say no to one of the great shames of American history. *Brown* was an occasion for the ideological rebirth of America, an occasion that tells a story of struggle and liberation and points the way for a new engagement with the problem of how men and women of different backgrounds and races might live together as equals. But *Brown* is also a story of how courts apparently can be mobilized in the service of social transformation. J. Harvie Wilkinson contends that "*Brown* may be the most important political, social, and legal event in America's twentieth-century history. Its greatness lay in the enormity of the injustice it condemned, in the entrenched sentiment it challenged, in the immensity of law it both created and overthrew."[5] It showed that courts could and would use their power to address, if not undo, injustice even if that injustice was sown deeply into the fabric of American life.

Brown marked a radical departure in the style and substance of our law. It unsettled as much as it resolved; it opened up new avenues for contestation and inspired new ideas about how Americans should think about law, rights, and the roles and responsibilities of courts in promoting social justice. In the last half-century the drama of *Brown*, of an appeal to law to make good on its promises, has been repeatedly reenacted in courtrooms across the United States. And, even today, it provides a powerful template and touchstone through which contemporary political struggles can be seen.[6]

Brown is an invitation to use the courts to carry on social struggle. Yet as attractive as that invitation has been, and continues to be, it is one contingently and variously taken up by disadvantaged persons and groups. The so called lure of litigation, while powerful, is by no means irresistible.[7] In spite of the continuing importance of *Brown* and the similarly rare though dramatic instances when the judiciary sides with the disadvantaged in their quest for social justice, disadvantaged citizens have a complicated relationship to the promise of rights and the judiciary's role in the symbolic structure of liberal legality. They live in an approach-avoidance relation to courts. They feel the symbolic pull of law even as they simultaneously see through and around its mystifications.[8] As Kristin Bumiller notes, such people are "attracted to the 'radiance of the

Law'" though they acknowledge the law's limitations and its unresponsiveness as well as its occasional irrelevance to their social situation.[9] When the courts do side with the poor, the weak, and the vulnerable, they keep alive hope that law will matter to those with few other places to turn for help.

Yet it would not be accurate to suggest that it is false consciousness that draws the disadvantaged to court. What McCann and Silverstein argue about social movement activists, namely that they view "law, litigation, and legal tactics in a skeptical, politically sophisticated manner," is generally also true of members of disadvantaged groups.[10] When they turn to the law it is because it is the best of a series of not very good alternatives. Doing so provides a resource that temporarily alters the balance of power, and, as Sally Merry notes, "with experience, the court gradually ceases to be a place for awe and fear . . . and becomes a somewhat pliant, if excruciatingly complex, institution which, with pressure and patience, can sometimes be made to yield help. It comes to seem like a flawed instrument which must be played with skill and finesse."[11]

From the point of view of liberal legality itself, litigation, especially litigation brought by disadvantaged groups seeking to vindicate their rights, is a mixed blessing. On one hand, such litigation demonstrates and reaffirms the continuing hold of rights as against more radical political action and the continuing allegiance of relatively powerless people to a social and political system that is the source of their disadvantage. On the other hand, such litigation always threatens to expose the gap between rights on the books and rights in action, and, as the current controversy surrounding the so-called litigation explosion suggests, it will be taken by some as indicative of an unhealthy breakdown of informal means of social control.

In this chapter I explore some of the contradictory qualities of citizen participation in the judicial process as well as the way citizen participation exposes some of the contradictions of liberal legality. I ask whether the contradictions that arise from such participation are in part responsible for the strength and resiliency of liberal legality.

THE MEANING OF PARTICIPATION IN THE JUDICIAL PROCESS

I use the term *participation* to refer to legal activities by which private citizens, acting individually or in organized groups, seek to influence the actions of officials charged with administering, enforcing, or interpreting the law.[12] The participatory activities I am interested in here include those through which citizens seek to enlist the courts to help remedy some individual problem or achieve some individual goal as well as those that seek to shape public policies through judicial action.

Modes of participation in the judicial process vary in terms of what political theorist Carl Cohen calls their breadth, depth, and range.[13] *Breadth* refers to the number of people who actually participate in the legal process, who bring cases to court, or alternatively to the proportion of a society's social and political problems that are litigated.[14] A fully participatory legal order would be one in which all citizens seeking to use courts had the opportunity to do so, in fact as well as in theory. It would also be one in which all citizens affected by a decision might and did participate in determining it. Of course no legal order can come close to this ideal of full participation.

The second dimension of participation is its *depth*, a measure of the participants' involvement in activities "to identify issues, formulate proposals, weigh evidence in argument on all sides, express convictions and explain their grounds and in general to foster and strengthen deliberation."[15] The deeper the participation provided, the more democratic is the process in which that participation occurs—presuming always that the opportunity for and extent of citizen participation are already fairly broad. The deep participation of a few is no substitute for the participation of the many.

The discussion of the depth of participation also raises the empirical question of exactly what constitutes participation. To file a lawsuit, for example, one does not necessarily, or even usually, have to engage in deliberation or in the process of reasoned argument. Filing may be a purely formal act, the real importance of which has little or nothing to do with adjudication or any other legal process. It may be a symbolic act, a way of letting off steam not actually meant to initiate legal proceedings. In fact, in most cases brought to courts the resultant litigation does not lead to prolonged engagement in deliberative activities; it serves instead only to facilitate processes of private bargaining in which the explicit involvement of the courts is purposely minimized.[16]

Range refers to the scope of the issues on which citizens' involvement occurs. Once it is known how many people can and do participate and how deeply they are involved with the legal system, it becomes possible to ask about the range of issues and concerns they become involved with. The greater the range of participation, the more democratic the legal order. A fully democratic legal order would, in theory, open most if not all questions to citizen input and would respond to most if not all types of problems citizens encounter and desire to bring to it.

Legal orders in general, and courts in particular, establish rules, procedures, and frameworks within which participation can occur. Variation in the strictness of such limitations reflects the tensions and contradictory impulses toward autonomy and accessibility built into liberal legal orders. These contradictions play out in different ways at different times and in different domains of legal contestation. At some times and in some domains the courts seem very accessible; at other times and in other domains they may seem quite inaccessible.

THE CONTRADICTIONS OF CITIZEN PARTICIPATION

Citizen participation, no matter how it is defined, occupies an ambiguous and contradictory position in liberal legal theory and orders. Liberalism limits popular participation by prescribing the means through which it may be exercised and proscribing its exercise in entire portions of the state apparatus. While citizens are invited to play a part in the selection of legislators and even, in some jurisdictions, of judges, they are not, with rare exceptions, expected to play a directive role in decisions about the application, enforcement, or interpretation of legal norms. The litigant comes to court seeking an authoritative declaration of rights and duties in light of applicable legal rules rather than on the basis of the relative power of the parties to the litigation. In this ideology, judicial decisions are made according to rules, discretion is to be limited, and the pressure of citizen demands is deemed to be out of place.[17] Fair procedure, the morality of the game rather than responsiveness, is the key to legal justice in the liberal state. As Nonet and Selznick argue,

> Law is elevated "above" politics; that is, the positive law is held to embody standards that public consent, authenticated by tradition or by constitutional process, has removed from political controversy. The authority to interpret this legal heritage must therefore be kept insulated from the struggle for power and uncontaminated by political influence. In interpreting and applying the law, jurists . . . have a claim to the last word because their judgments are thought to obey an external will and not their own.[18]

Liberal legality derives its claims to legitimacy in large part from this sense that law is autonomous and above the play of politics. In an autonomous legal order the business of law is supposed to be technical. At issue are questions solely about the meaning and applicability of legal rules. Decisions must be made in a disinterested and impartial manner. Citizen participation designed to influence or pressure legal officials threatens the capacity of those officials to make legally correct decisions, as well as the legitimacy of any decisions they make.

Yet liberal legality allows citizens to mobilize the law through carefully defined channels. Participation is necessary, but also carefully scrutinized. For example, rules of standing, which govern access to courts, require individuals to demonstrate that they have suffered a "real injury" before they are allowed to present their case. Thus citizen participation in the legal order is generally instrumental and defensive. The legal culture "assumes that each citizen will voluntarily and rationally pursue his own interests, with the greatest legal good of the greatest number presumptively arising from the selfish enterprises of the atomized mass."[19] When citizens litigate, they generally do so individually, and the legal system proceeds case by case. Responsibility for broad-based social decisions, in theory, is assigned to legislative bodies presumably directly responsive to popular sentiment.

Moreover, even where participation is encouraged, liberal theory stresses the limits of citizen competence. Participation is facilitated by the intervention of trained legal specialists. Lawyers speak the language of the law, and they serve clients by exercising professional judgment and responding to particular problems.[20] The lawyer mediates between the citizen and legal order, acting as gatekeeper and partisan advocate for a limited cause.

Citizen participation is not, however, completely denigrated. One need only note the importance of the jury in Anglo-American legal theory to recognize that that theory is not perfectly consistent in its attitude toward citizen participation. Indeed, rhetorically, the jury receives far more than its due as a domesticator of state power and an avenue for direct citizen involvement. While jury service is one of the most intensive and remarkable forms of citizen participation, it is clearly anomalous, the exception rather than a model from which generalizations can be drawn in understanding the role of citizens in a liberal legal order.

In general the role of citizens is never as extensive or deep as it is when they take on the mantle of jurors. In the usual pattern, participation is limited to the activities associated with the initiation of the legal process or the presentation of facts and arguments before a competent tribunal. Participation becomes litigation, complaint, and petition on one hand

and a highly ritualized form of discourse, generally carried out by paid intermediaries on the other. In this sense, citizen participation in the legal order is typically limited and indirect. Due process, not popular sovereignty, is the governing ethos.

The rules of due process themselves provide a formula for the participation of all citizens in the legal process. Although they do not allow citizens to select those who will judge them, the rules do require that individuals be heard by those who sit in judgment and be allowed to take part in a contest of reason and argument. "It confers on the affected parties a particular form of participation . . . that of presenting proofs and reasoned arguments for a decision in their favor."[21] Yet while liberal legal theory guarantees citizens a role as plaintiff, complainant, defendant, or respondent in procedures in which their lives, liberties, or property are at stake, the precise contours of such participation—what it requires and when it must be made available—are by no means fixed or clear. Expansion of the scope of due process to include more of the implementation and enforcement of the law is thus both an acknowledgment by the state of the expanded reach of its powers and an uncertain opportunity to participate in the exercise of those powers.

By treating citizen participation in the legal system as an aspect of due process, liberal theory transforms broad claims for participation into narrow arguments for access to legal justice. In the American legal tradition access to justice and due process of law are inseparable, and both are considered to be prerequisites of justice itself. The right to one's day in court, the right to be heard, and the right to take part in procedures through which one's fate is determined all provide the basic substance of due process, which is in turn at the heart of liberal legality's conceptions of fairness and justice.

Moreover, in liberal legal theory access to justice not only is essential in ensuring fairness to individuals but also is portrayed as necessary in domesticating the exercise of power. Citizen initiative, complaint, and involvement provide an opportunity to check and oppose the arbitrary use of state power. The image of a public official or agency called to account by a citizen before an independent, impartial court of law occupies a central place in liberal thought.[22] As Justice John Marshall Harlan put it,

> Perhaps no characteristic of an organized and cohesive society is more fundamental than its erection and enforcement of a system of rules defining the various rights and duties of the members enabling them to govern

their affairs and definitively settle their differences in an orderly, predictable manner. . . . It is to courts . . . that we ultimately look for the
implementation of a regularized, orderly process of dispute settlement. . . .
[Yet] without due process of law, the state's monopoly over techniques for
binding conflict resolution could hardly be said to be acceptable under
our scheme of things. Only by providing that the social enforcement
mechanism must function strictly within these bounds can we hope to
maintain an ordered society that is also just.[23]

Along with the right to vote, the right to participate in the legal
process is fundamental to liberal theory. It is both through elections and
through appeals to autonomous legal institutions, especially the courts,
that citizens can preserve all their other rights. In turn, liberal theory
contends, the general anticipation of accessible legal justice and of the
ability to participate in the legal order transforms all social relationships
and shapes the way individuals experience the meaning of citizenship.
"This anticipation matters both on account of its deterrent effects on the
behavior of those who must contemplate being voted on or sued and on
account of its effects on the potential participant's own understanding of
society and his or her place in it."[24]

Moreover, by making legal justice accessible, the legal order invites citizens to participate in rituals of affirmation.[25] By accepting the invitation
to employ legal processes, citizens in effect affirm their faith in legal
norms and their belief in the relevance of those norms to the social order.
When citizens bring their grievances to legal institutions they express a
hope that their status as rights holders will be recognized, that their
rights, once recognized, will be realized in practice, and that that realization will in fact make a difference in their lives.[26]

Access to justice and citizen participation help to legitimate the legal
order by making law appear open, available, and responsive to those with
significant grievances and needs. Of course, not all grievances and needs
are legally cognizable, but paradoxically the law, precisely by limiting
access, is able to strengthen the perceived boundary between law and politics as well as the perceived subservience of legal decision makers to the
model of rules. The legitimacy of liberal legality thus depends in important ways on maintaining a precarious balance between autonomy and
accessible justice, between justice accessible according to rules and justice
available on demand. This is a balance that, in a liberal legal order, moves
and changes over time. Law encourages demands for increased access by
recognizing new rights and yet sometimes responds to social conflict by

restricting rights. The history of citizen participation in the legal order is, as a result, a history not of even and predictable progress but instead of reform and resistance.

Access to justice and citizen participation are not, however, uniformly aids to the legitimacy of law. Indeed, they may pose threats to that legitimacy in several ways. First, to the extent that the legal order coexists with democratic or representative political institutions, citizen participation in the legal system may appear inadequate by comparison. What has been called the majoritarian dilemma in other contexts works in the legal order to push for an expanded role for citizens.[27] Restrictions on access, no matter how well justified in theory, will always appear suspicious and unjustified in the context of the majoritarian presumption. Democratic participation establishes a standard and an expectation against which the rather limited forms of participation available in the legal order may appear inadequate. This tension requires apologists for liberal legality to work hard to maintain the distinction between politics, in which participation is acknowledged to be more fully appropriate, and law, in which impartiality, neutrality, objectivity, and reason allegedly provide the essence of decision.[28] This requires a delicate ideological balancing act. Acknowledging the limits of impartiality and reason in legal decisions would legitimate and encourage demands for deeper and more extensive participation than a liberal legal order could easily accommodate. Thus, as participation demands greater citizen involvement and responsiveness on the part of legal institutions, it threatens the very legitimacy it helps to establish.

The contradictory relationship between participation and the legitimacy of liberal legality is seen in yet another way in demands that access to justice be made available more widely and more equally. Arguments about access to justice typically begin with the observation that access is unevenly and unequally distributed throughout the population.[29] The recognition of unequal access threatens legal legitimacy by pointing to gaps and inadequacies in the fulfillment of its own self-proclaimed commitment to equal justice under the law. Discovery of systematic inequality in the ability and opportunity to use legal institutions thus undermines faith in the capacity of law to treat all citizens with dignity and to serve all who merit its service.

At the same time, those arguments typically call for reforms in legal rules and practices or in the provision of legal services, which suggests that law itself can overcome this defect and that the problems of those without adequate access can be properly addressed through legal change. Demands for equalizing access to justice ultimately communicate a symbolic message . . . that formal justice can be attained within a capitalist legal system and, once attained, will produce substantive justice. They define the problem as a "gap" . . . between the promise of redistributing lawyers' services and the performance. The proximate goal of closing the gap is thereby substituted for the ultimate goal of justice. In place of questions about the capacity of legal reform to effect fundamental change in political, economic and social institutions, we are directed back to the legal system conceived as an autonomous entity, to be evaluated by the unique standards of formal justice.[30]

Critique turns into affirmation, and threats to legal legitimacy turn into support.

A third aspect of citizen participation that may challenge the legitimacy of law arises when contact with the legal system disillusions or disappoints citizens. Here there is a high price to pay for the ideological mystifications of liberal legality. Citizens promised majestic and impartial judgment encounter bureaucratic irrationality and political bias. To the extent that citizen participation in the legal system acquaints citizens with the reality of the day-to-day operation of the legal system, it may diminish respect for and belief in the idealized visions of law on which the ideology of liberal legality depends.[31] On the other hand, where citizens come to see the gap between the law's ideals and its practices, legal legitimacy may not be damaged if they revise their expectations and develop a more pragmatic approach to law, or if they blame failures on officials or incumbents while continuing to credit and endorse the legal order's aspirations.[32] In any case, citizen participation holds the potential for undermining the claims of liberal legality even as it appears to signify acceptance of them.

There is, of course, more to citizen participation than its impact on legal legitimacy. For both the legal order and the citizens who use it, participation has instrumental effects that, like those associated with legitimacy, are contradictory.

At the level of the legal order itself, access to justice and citizen participation play an important role in keeping law in touch with the social order in which it is embedded. This is not to say that litigation is the only vehicle through which legal institutions can learn about their environment. Every legal system relies upon a mix of proactive and reactive intelligence-gathering mechanisms. The balance between proactive and reactive elements found in a legal order varies over time in response to specific problems. The more reactive a legal order, the more it depends on citizens to detect the problems, articulate the disputes, or uncover the violations upon which legal policy can be based. Thus, to some extent, the limits of legal policy are effectively set by citizens. The legal system that relies on reactive methods is unable to act on matters that "citizens are unable to see, fail to notice, or choose to ignore."[33]

Such a legal order can regulate how much it learns about social problems by raising or lowering barriers to citizen participation. Citizens may want to bring matters to the attention of legal officials in order to demand redress or explanation, but they may be unable to meet the qualifications or standards the law establishes. Alternatively, their intentions may be diverted by lawyers who serve as the major channeling and linking devices for citizen participation in the legal order. Yet the greatest barriers to participation undoubtedly reside in the articulation and linkage of the prevailing legal ideology and the social relations in which potential legal problems arise.[34] In America today, despite the frequent complaints about excessive litigation, "the reluctance of citizens to mobilize the law is so widespread . . . that it may be appropriate to view legal inaction as the dominant pattern of empirical legal life."[35]

The greater the reliance on reactive methods of citizen participation, the more the legal system will reflect the biases, prejudices, and moral diversity of the society in which it is embedded. The legal order participates in a pattern of selective enforcement determined by the citizenry. "Each citizen determines for himself what within his private world is the law's business and what is not; each becomes a kind of legislator beneath the formal surface of legal life."[36] Seen in this light, the decision not to participate is in itself a form of participation, an important determinant of the reach, scope, and capacity of legal control.[37]

The refusal of citizens to bring problems to the attention of legal officials may result from the internalization of an ideology of self-blame, a predominant cultural preference for private resolution, doubts about the efficacy of legal intervention, individual cost-benefit calculations, or a crisis of legitimacy in which the appropriateness of the entire structure of legal control is questioned. In addition, citizens may avoid invoking legal processes because those processes appear relatively predictable—the "haves" come out ahead—so citizens feel they can surmise what the legal decision would be and act in accordance with that prediction. The refusal to bring problems to law, no matter what their cause, sets the effective boundaries of law, the extent to which legal institutions have the chance to respond to social problems.

When people do turn to law, when they seek to participate in the legal process, their participation extends or reinforces the reach of legal norms. Barbara Yngvesson's description of show cause or complaint hearings in the district courts of two Massachusetts communities provides a vivid demonstration of this fact. Her study focuses on "the negotiation of meaning in neighbor and family conflicts." Analyzing exchanges between complainants and the clerks who handle their complaints, Yngvesson found that "the clerk plays a dominant role by controlling the language in which issues are framed. . . . He silences some interpretations and privileges others, constructing the official definition of what constitutes order and disorder in the lives of local citizens."[38]

According to Yngvesson, "law creates the social world by 'naming' it; legal professionals are empowered by their capacity to reveal rights and define wrongs, to construct the meanings of everyday events (as just or unjust, as crime or normal trouble, as private nuisance or public grievance) and thus to shape cultural understandings of fairness, of justice, and of morality." She argues that the way law names the world and the way legal professionals construct meanings is hegemonic, but she insists that hegemony

> assumes plurality: "[I]t does not just passively exist as a form of dominance. It has continually to be renewed, recreated, defended, and modified. It is also continually resisted, limited, altered, challenged by pressures not at all its own." . . . The interpretation of key symbols . . . is contested, while the dominance of a particular structure of differences in society is left unquestioned.[39]

Plurality, resistance, and contestation suggest the fragility of the legal power, yet Yngvesson insists that they are fully compatible with a situation in which "the hearings thus become arenas where particular notions of order and rights are articulated and reinforced."[40] In this sense participation is as necessary in determining the penetration of law as it is in shaping the structure of legal intelligence. Citizen participation in the legal order involves officially recognized legal norms to regulate social behavior. It brings those norms to bear in situations in which their previous presence was insufficient to protect rights or secure redress for injury, or it uses them in preference to informal, private, customary canons of behavior.

In any society, then, the invocation of law is one measure of law's social significance and its centrality in the total system of normative ordering. This is not to say that the penetration of law and legal norms can be understood fully by measuring the level of citizen participation. Surely that is not the case. The relevance of legal norms is seen in the way those norms are incorporated into the culture and come to order social relations.[41] This incorporation, what some have called "the living law" and others "hegemony," is the true measure of the law's influence.[42,43] But that influence is unlikely to endure long without the regular mobilization and application of legal norms to particular cases that citizen participation may engender.

Here again just as citizen participation reveals contradictions in liberal legal orders, it too is rife with contradictions. Just as participation may be said to increase the range of legal intelligence and the penetration of legal norms, so too may it strain the institutional capacity of legal institutions and challenge the authority of existing legal norms. Too much participation or participation that is too intense threatens the ability of a liberal legal order to function effectively by dramatically exposing the gap between its ideology and what it can and generally does deliver. Legal institutions do not, or so the argument goes, possess the institutional resources or capacity to deal with a high volume and wide range of citizen demands. Typical is the complaint of former judge Simon Rifkind concerning the so-called litigation explosion. "The courts," Rifkind argues, "are being asked to solve problems for which they are not institutionally equipped or not as well equipped as other available institutions."[44]

Even as it informs and extends the reach of legal norms, participation constrains the ways legal institutions can act to satisfy the demands made upon them. The capacity of the legal order to function effectively depends, as Lawrence Friedman reminds us, on an imbalance between rights proclaimed and rights actually claimed.[45] Because not all citizens can or will seek to vindicate the full range of rights available to them, the legal order can be more generous in its recognition of rights. A legal order in which the full range of recognized rights is in fact realized by the entire citizenry is extremely unlikely.

From the point of view of the legitimate and instrumental needs of liberal legality, the appropriate balance of participation and nonparticipation and the appropriate intensity of participation cannot be determined empirically; nevertheless, the maintenance of such a balance is an important condition to effective legal control. Too much participation, and the institutions of law are overwhelmed; too little, and they are isolated. The precariousness of the balance between these alternatives, however, is a measure not just of the fragility of liberal legality but also of its adaptability.

Participation by poor and disadvantaged citizens in a liberal legal
order invites criticism and challenge. Citizen participation frequently
requires legal institutions to examine and revise laws and to scrutinize
the rules and procedures of other parts of the state apparatus. The universal promises and commitments of the rule of law provide a standard
against which its performance can be measured. Citizens disempowered in the political process may be able to employ legal institutions as
arenas of struggle. That participation may involve a demand that the
interests served by liberal legality live up to their legitimating ideology
and an attempt to use that ideology in political struggles against prevailing structures of power. Thus it is now widely recognized that, as
Samuel Johnson observed, law sometimes "supplies the weak with
adventitious strength."

CITIZEN PARTICIPATION AND LAW'S POWER

The hegemony of liberal legality is measured in the extent to which it
can induce its most disadvantaged citizens to fight their battles on the
terrain of liberal legality itself. Although going to court may be one way
of resisting existing structures of power, it assures those who exercise
political power that that resistance will remain inscribed within what
Michel de Certeau calls a strategic domain defined by those against
whom the resistance is directed.[46] This is as true of dramatic constitutional cases such as *Brown* as it is of the daily litigation fought out in
courts across the United States.

The contradictory yet resilient ideology of liberal legality is not simply
invented and communicated in a unidirectional process. Instead it is produced in concrete and particular social relations such as citizen participation in the judicial process. Thus Merry is correct when she suggests that
court contests provide an important site for the examination of power.
For her such an examination reveals that legal power is exercised at the
level of culture and consciousness. Courts are powerful in that they convey hegemonic ideologies. She argues that courts work

> not just by the imposition of rules and punishments but also by the capac-
> ity to construct authoritative images of social relationships and actions,
> images that are symbolically powerful. Law provides a set of categories
> and frameworks through which the world is interpreted. Legal words and
> practices are cultural constructs which carry powerful meanings not just
> to those trained in law . . . but to the ordinary person as well.[47]

The participation of poor and disadvantaged people in the judicial process reminds us that law influences how those people imagine life. The social world is understood in legal categories that in turn circumscribe its potential and define its limitations.[48] Yet litigants bring their own understandings to bear; they deploy and use liberal legality's ideology strategically to advance their interests and goals. They press their understandings in and on law and, in so doing, invite adaptation and change in the practices of judges, lawyers, and other legal officials. Thus law exists as "moving hegemony."[49] This concept, as Yngvesson explains, allows us to recognize the "coexistence of discipline and struggle, of subjection and subversion and direct attention toward a dynamic analysis of what it means to be caught up in power."[50] The exercise of power in liberal legality is always conflictual and dynamic, and courts provide one crucial arena in which that conflict and dynamism occur. That the resulting ideology of liberal legality is contradictory makes it no less powerful.

NOTES

1. For a more extended discussion of liberal legality, see Roberto Unger, *Law in Modern Society: Toward a Criticism of Social Theory* (New York: Free Press, 1976), 176–81.

2. As Roberto Unger has argued, autonomy is a quite recent legal notion that developed with the emergence of liberal culture and social institutions. Its viability is linked to the viability of that culture and those institutions. See Unger, *Law in Modern Society.*

3. E. P. Thompson, *Whigs and Hunters: The Origins of the Black Act* (New York: Pantheon, 1975).

4. For an exploration of the cultural significance of *Brown*, see Carol Greenhouse, "A Federal Life: *Brown* and the Nationalization of the Life Story," in *Race, Law, and Culture: Reflections of Brown v. Board of Education*, ed. Austin Sarat (New York: Oxford University Press, 1997).

5. J. Harvie Wilkinson, *From Brown to Bakke: The Supreme Court and School Integration: 1954–1978* (New York: Oxford University Press, 1979), 6. See *Introduction*, 93 Yale Law Journal 981 (1984).

6. Ours is a time of revision and mixed views about *Brown* and its legacy. While some commentators have noted that it has not resulted in the elim-

ination of racism in American society (see Charles Lawrence, "'One More River to Cross'—Recognizing the Real Injury in *Brown:* A Prerequisite to Shaping New Remedies," in *Shades of Brown: New Perspectives on School Desegregation,* ed. Derrick Bell [Jackson: University of Mississippi Press, 1980]), or even of segregation in public education (see Gary Orfield, *The Reconstruction of Southern Education* [New York: Wiley, 1969]), others suggest that *Brown* has been given too much credit for sparking racial progress (see Gerald Rosenberg, *The Hollow Hope: Can Courts Bring About Social Change?* [Chicago: University of Chicago Press, 1991], chapter 2). Still others see it as a continuing and powerful symbol of the quest for rights (see Lawrence Friedman, *Total Justice* [New York: Russell Sage, 1985]).

7. Michael McCann and Helena Silverstein, "Rethinking Law's Allurements: A Relational Analysis of Social Movement Lawyers in the United States," in *Cause Lawyering: Political Commitments and Professional Responsibilities,* ed. Austin Sarat and Stuart Scheingold (New York: Oxford University Press, forthcoming).

8. Austin Sarat, *"The Law Is All Over": Power, Resistance, and the Legal Consciousness of the Welfare Poor,* 2 Yale Journal of Law and the Humanities 343 (1990).

9. Kristin Bumiller, *The Civil Rights Society: The Social Construction of Victims* (Baltimore: Johns Hopkins University Press, 1988), 107.

10. McCann and Silverstein, "Rethinking Law's Allurements," 9.

11. Sally Merry, *Getting Justice and Getting Even: Legal Consciousness Among Working Class Americans* (Chicago: University of Chicago Press, 1990), 142.

12. Sidney Verba and Norman Nie, *Participation in American Politics* (New York: Harper & Row, 1975), 1.

13. Carl Cohen, *Democracy* (New York: Free Press, 1971).

14. Richard Miller and Austin Sarat, *Grievances, Claims, and Disputes: Assessing the Adversary Culture,* 15 Law & Society Review 525 (1980–81).

15. Cohen, *Democracy,* 17–18.

16. Robert Mnookin and Lewis Kornhauser, *Bargaining in the Shadow of the Law,* 88 Yale Law Journal 950 (1979).

17. Lon Fuller, *The Inner Morality of Law* (New Haven: Yale University Press, 1971), and Theodore Lowi, *The End of Liberalism,* 2d ed. (New York: Norton, 1979), chapter 11.

18. Philippe Nonet and Philip Selznick, *Law and Society in Transition: Toward Responsive Law* (New York: Harper & Row, 1978), 571.

19. Donald Black, *The Mobilization of Law,* 2 Journal of Legal Studies 138 (1973).

20. Austin Sarat and William Felstiner, *Divorce Lawyers and Their Clients: Power and Meaning in the Legal Process* (New York: Oxford University Press, 1995).

21. Lon Fuller, "The Forms and Limits of Adjudication," in *American Court Systems*, ed. Sheldon Goldman and Austin Sarat (San Francisco: W. H. Freeman, 1978), 45.

22. See Bruce Ackerman, *Reconstructing American Law* (Cambridge: Harvard University Press, 1984).

23. *Boddie v. Connecticut*, 401 U.S. 371, 374 (1971).

24. Frank Michelman, *The Supreme Court and Litigation Access Fees—II*, 1974 Duke Law Journal 527, 536 (1974).

25. See Martha Minow, *Interpreting Rights: An Essay for Robert Cover*, 96 Yale Law Journal 1860, 1877 (1987).

26. Stuart Scheingold, *The Politics of Rights* (New Haven: Yale University Press, 1974).

27. See John Hart Ely, *Democracy and Distrust* (Cambridge: Harvard University Press, 1980).

28. Owen Fiss, *Objectivity and Interpretation*, 34 Stanford Law Review 739 (1982).

29. See, for example, Jerome Carlin, Jan Howard, and Sheldon Messinger, *Civil Justice and the Poor* (New York: Russell Sage, 1967).

30. Richard Abel, *Socializing the Legal Profession*, 5 Law and Policy Quarterly 401 (1979).

31. See Merry, *Getting Justice*, chapter 7, and Sarat and Felstiner, *Divorce Lawyers and Their Clients*, chapter 4.

32. Patricia Ewick and Susan Silbey, *Conformity, Contestation, and Resistance: An Account of Legal Consciousness*, 26 New England Law Review 731 (1992).

33. Black, *The Mobilization of Law*, 130.

34. Bumiller, *The Civil Rights Society*.

35. Black, *The Mobilization of Law*, 133. See also Miller and Sarat, *Grievances, Claims, and Disputes*.

36. Black, *The Mobilization of Law*, 142.

37. Roger Cobb and Charles Elder, *Participation in American Politics* (Baltimore: Johns Hopkins University Press, 1972).

38. Barbara Yngvesson, *Making Law at the Doorway: The Clerk, the Court, and the Construction of Community in a New England Town*, 22 Law and Society Review 409, 410 (1988).

39. Barbara Yngvesson, *Inventing Law in Local Settings: Rethinking Popular Legal Culture*, 98 Yale Law Journal 1691, 1693 (1989).

40. Yngvesson, *Making Law at the Doorway,* 444.
41. Austin Sarat and Thomas R. Kearns, "Beyond the Great Divide: Forms of Legal Scholarship and Everyday Life," in Austin Sarat and Thomas R. Kearns, eds., *Law in Everyday Life* (Ann Arbor: University of Michigan Press, 1993).
42. Eugen Ehrlich, *Fundamental Principles of the Sociology of Law* (New York: Arno, 1975).
43. Antonio Gramsci, *Selections from the Prison Notebooks* (New York: International, 1971).
44. Simon Rifkind, *Are We Asking Too Much of Our Courts?* 70 Federal Rules Decisions 5 (1976).
45. Lawrence Friedman, *The Idea of Rights as a Social and Legal Concept,* 27 Journal of Social Issues 189 (1971).
46. Michel de Certeau, *The Practice of Everyday Life,* trans. Steven F. Rendall, (Berkeley: University of California Press, 1984), 36–37.
47. Merry, *Getting Justice,* 8–9.
48. Robert Gordon, *Critical Legal Histories,* 36 Stanford Law Review 57 (1984).
49. Raymond Williams, *Marxism and Literature* (New York: Oxford University Press, 1977), 114.
50. Barbara Yngvesson, *Virtuous Citizens, Disruptive Subjects: Order and Complaint in a New England Court* (New York: Routledge, 1993), 121.

5 JANET E. HALLEY

GAY RIGHTS AND IDENTITY IMITATION: ISSUES IN THE ETHICS OF REPRESENTATION

GAY and lesbian advocates often claim that gay rights are just like rights already established for racial minorities or women by the black civil rights movement and the women's movement. Particularly when they argue to judges, who are formally if not actually constrained by precedent, and even when they make more general political appeals, advocates are opportunists looking for a simile: "Your honor, this is just like a race discrimination case; this is just like a sex discrimination case."

And indeed, sexual orientation and sexual identities have formed the basis for important social movements that look like other identity-based movements. Gay men and lesbians, transgendered people, and other sexual dissidents have been able to create legal change and legal controversy on issues falling under almost every traditional rubric of law. Sexually identified progressives have legal reform aspirations and achievements affecting contract, tort, procedure, constitutional law, civil rights, family law, trusts and estates, employment law, housing law, taxation, regulation, and more.[1] They have grassroots and national organizations, including NAACP-like national legal reform offices staffed with full-time lawyers. They also have ferocious opponents convinced that, if progressives realize any of their reform aspirations, the entire national character will collapse. Sexual orientation and sexuality movements have the look and feel of identity movements of the contemporary sort.

But in important ways, they lack the substance. "Identity politics" is usually waged on assumptions that identity inheres in group members, that group membership brings with it a uniformly shared range (or even a core) of authentic experience and attitude, that the political and legal interests of the group are similarly coherent, and that group members are thus able to draw on their own experiences to discern those interests and to establish the authority they need to speak for the group. I will call these the "coherentist" assumptions about identity politics. Sexual orientation and sexuality identities do not support those assumptions very well.

Take lesbian identity for an example. One is a lesbian not because of anything in oneself but because of social interactions or the desire for social interactions: It takes two women, or at least one woman imagining another, to make a lesbian. Lesbians have a huge range of experience and attitude relating to their sexual orientation: We don't agree on issues as basic as whether being women makes lesbians really different from gay men. We are famously unable to agree with one another about what our collective political and legal interests are—for example, we don't agree about whether access to marriage should be a movement priority—and we are notoriously ready to punish any woman who purports to speak for us.

Similar things can be said about gay men; homosexuals; bisexuals (generic or male and female); transvestites; pre-op, post-op, and non-op transsexuals; transgendered people; people living with AIDS/HIV; and sexual and gender dissidents of various ever-changing descriptions. Even more complex challenges to the coherentist assumptions about identity politics emerge when attention focuses on the question of the merger, exile, coalition, and secession of these constituencies. Are gay men and lesbians—or, more properly, gay men on one hand and lesbians on the other—"homosexuals?" Are bisexuals "homosexuals" or traitors? Is there a single social movement that seeks to relieve the social suffering of women who regard femininity as an engine of repression, of transsexuals who identify as women born in men's bodies, or of people with AIDS notwithstanding differences in the ways they became infected and in their access to expensive new treatments?

Sexual orientation and sexuality movements are perhaps unique among contemporary identity movements in harboring an unforgiving, corrosive critique of identity itself, and they have launched significant activist and theoretical impulses in the direction of a "post-identity politics." The term *queer* was adopted by some movement participants in part to frustrate identity formation around dissident sexualities. And academic and street-level queer theory challenges the coherentist assumptions about identity politics. The keynote of this critique of identity is deep, strong constructivism. Starting with the finding that modern homosexual identities have emerged only in fairly recent historical times, queer theory suggests that they do not exist prior to, but are instead produced by, their politics. Noting that homosexual identity and heterosexual identity are diacritically related—that each negatively defines and makes possible the social urgency of the other—queer theory suggests that homosexual identities create a necessary condition for the oppression of homosexual people; that is, the existence of a class of heterosexuals anxious to confirm their immunity from the designation *homosexual.* Queer theory argues that identity is not the core truth and safe zone of authenticity and authority posited by our most widely shared assumptions about identity politics; instead it suggests that identity may be part of the problem.[2]

This insight poses ethical questions that are particularly pressing for advocates of identity groups. K. Anthony Appiah states the issue:

> Demanding respect for people as blacks and as gays requires that there are some scripts that go with being an African-American or having same-sex desires. There will be proper ways of being black and gay, there will be expectations to be met, demands to be made. It is at this point that someone who takes autonomy seriously will ask whether we have not replaced one kind of tyranny with another. If I had to choose between the worlds of the closet and the world of gay liberation, or between the world of *Uncle Tom's Cabin* and Black Power, I would, of course, choose in each case the latter. But I would like not to have to choose. I would like other options. . . .
>
> It is a familiar thought that the bureaucratic categories of identity must come up short before the vagaries of actual people's lives. But it is equally important to bear in mind that a politics of identity can be counted on to transform the identities on whose behalf it ostensibly labors. Between the politics of recognition and the politics of compulsion, there is no bright line.[3]

The coherentist assumptions about identity politics make Appiah's statement appear merely disloyal. Those assumptions posit that identity preexists its articulation in politics, and thus they assume away the constructive power of identity advocacy. They also assume away any difference between what Appiah, "black and gay," might opt to do or become and the script set out for him in the politics of identity. But if advocacy constructs identity, if it generates a script that identity bearers must heed, and if that script restricts group members, then identity politics compels its beneficiaries. Identity politics suddenly is no longer mere or simple resistance: It begins to look like power.

Appiah's challenge rests on the critical insight that power can be exercised not only to make people do things they would not otherwise do, but also to make them become people they would not otherwise be. One important theory of this second function of power was offered by the Marxist political theorist Louis Althusser, who posited that ideology could

> "recruit . . ." subjects amongst the individuals . . . or "transform . . ." the individuals into subjects . . . by that very precise operation which I have called *interpellation* or hailing, and which can be imagined along the lines of the most commonplace everyday police (or other) hailing: "Hey, you there!"

Althusser elaborated this notion of "interpellation" further:

> Assuming that the theoretical scene I have imagined takes place in the street, the hailed individual will turn around. By this mere one-hundred-and-eighty-degree physical conversation, he becomes a *subject*. Why? Because he has recognised that the hail was "really" addressed to him, and that "it was *really him* who was hailed" (and not someone else).[4]

Althusser's description of interpellation has often been criticized for its depiction of the subject as abject, as completely powerless to resist or reshape the hail issued by ideology. That is an important criticism, but here I want to emphasize that his description is incomplete because it assumes that the interpellative call will always come from above, from a high center of power. Dealing with the challenge of Appiah's observation, however, requires us to imagine that interpellation, with all its invisible subjections, can come from below, from within resistant social movements.

As long as law and legal institutions help to build and protect identity-generating social hierarchies, legal reformers must invoke identity. But whenever activists invoke identity in ways that transform it, they may approach and even cross the dangerous line that Appiah specifies between advocacy and coercion; they may interpellate subjects just as invidiously as Althusser's imagined cop in the street. How should a critical politics of law think about the possible coercive effects of identity-based advocacy? The features of queer legal movements that make them particularly inapt examples of the coherentist assumptions about identity politics also make them correspondingly useful for probing this long-deferred question.

SOME PRELIMINARY QUESTIONS

Departing from the coherentist assumptions about identity politics opens up some new versions of familiar problems. First, the coherentist assumptions make it important to know whether a given identity claim carries an accurate description of the identity base. But the question of accuracy is much more complex if identity claims have the power to transform the very identities they describe. Then, an identity claim's accuracy may be the product not of truth telling but of its own social constructive power. So the question of accuracy must be complemented by additional questions such as: Does a description of the movement make people see group members to be "like that," or does it make people see themselves as "like that?" Does a description of the group bring the group into existence or reposition its boundaries? To borrow a telling phrase of Ian Hacking, does a description help to "make up people?"[5]

Second and third, identity politics is frequently waged as a debate over whether a particular representational act, seen as a strategic move, is either useful or dangerous, and whether the act, seen as a self-interested or self-confirming gesture on the part of the person or subgroup making it, is ethically acceptable or unacceptable. The first question is the question of strategy; the second is the question of "speaking for others."[6] On the coherentist assumptions about identity politics, these questions are sometimes framed with great facility because everyone supposedly knows who is being benefited or harmed, and who is being spoken for by whom. But without those assumptions, the questions of strategy and of speaking for others bring with them prior questions: Useful or dangerous to whom? Ethically acceptable or unacceptable according to what normative view of identification or representation?

Fourth, the coherentist assumptions about identity politics make it possible to have an extremely rich discourse of loyalty among group members. This is a useful political tool, allowing collective action often at the expense of group member liberty. The discourse of loyalty encourages group members to believe that they can identify each other readily, to measure the degree to which group members are behaving in a way that fosters the group's interests, and to punish dissidents for disloyalty. The coherentist assumptions also make it possible to tell when one is speaking to outsiders, and thus they support strictures against airing dirty linen in public. But without stable assumptions about who belongs to the group and what their interests are, and about who can speak for the group, disloyalty loses much of its sting as an accusation and a new

normative project opens up, of intragroup and non-group-based justifications for political action.[7]

These reframed questions about identity politics are particularly pressing for advocates of identity groups. Movement advocates enact two different meanings of the term *representation*. They represent subordinated
groups both in that they function as agents sent by the group on some
mission for material change, and in that they manage the discursive rendering of the group. Keeping the second function of advocates in mind
puts critical pressure on an important new branch of writing about the
ethical obligations of lawyers representing disempowered social groups.[8]
It posits that lawyers acting for subordinated social groups have a duty to
strive for transparency in representing them. Lawyers for social groups
should take the client group as they find it in the social world, defer if at
all possible to its selection of goals, and strive to speak for it only by saying what it would say itself if it were embodied as a lawyer. They are
bound not only by the duties of loyalty normally imposed on lawyers
representing clients, but also by the thicker and more culturally nuanced
duties of loyalty imposed by coherentist identity politics—up to and possibly including a duty to withdraw from representation if the lawyer is
not a bona fide member of the identity group. But as William H. Simon
argues, lawyers' decisions to represent one client and not another and to
resolve conflicts within and between client groups will "affect the contours of organizational power" among the disempowered. Lawyers not
only have special power to affect the goals and strategies of social
groups—they can do things that alter the social definition of the group
itself. They can "make up people" in ways that weak constructivist views
of group formation ignore.[9]

To probe this form of power, we need an ethics of representation that
always keeps in focus the double meaning of representation. This ethical
inquiry should be conducted on an assumption that asking the advocates
of gay, women's, or disabled peoples' rights to give up "like race" similes
would be like asking them to write their speeches and briefs without
using the word *the*. "Like race" arguments are so intrinsically woven into
American discourses of equal justice that they can never be entirely for-
gone. Indeed, analogies are probably an inescapable mode of human
inquiry and are certainly so deeply ingrained in the logics of American
adjudication that any proposal to do without them altogether would be
boldly utopian and beyond my aim here.[10] The following pages suggest
that only some "like race" arguments are unjustifiably coercive; others,
even though inescapable, join sexual constituencies to race constituencies

in a shared exposure to danger that identity politics cannot even apprehend, that identity-based coalition politics can at least address, and that
may cause us to seek identity-indifferent norms of distributive justice for
adequate terms of analysis.

IDENTITY AS IMITATION

The imitative relationship between gay rights and sexuality movements
and the women's rights movement has been vexed in the extreme and
warrants sustained ethical and strategic attention. In this chapter, I defer
that examination for a while in order to focus on the problems raised by
"like race" arguments.

The central legal achievement of litigation waged on behalf of the
black civil rights movement was a historic succession of equal protection
holdings: State-sponsored segregation was declared a violation of the
Constitution and the Supreme Court began to test its presumption (first
announced in a case unsuccessfully challenging the Japanese American
internment) that other forms of race discrimination would also be found
unconstitutional.[11] Seeking to find room under the aegis of these key
equality precedents, gay and lesbian advocates often find themselves saying that sexual orientation is like race, or that gay men and lesbians are
like a racial group, or that anti-gay policies are like racist policies, or that
homophobia is like racism.

Thus early antidiscrimination briefs filed by the ACLU Lesbian and
Gay Rights Project sought heightened scrutiny by arguing that homosexuals are like racial minorities: They derived from the race discrimination
cases four or five "indicia of suspectness" and then argued that homosexuals as a group shared them.[12] The analogies appear in lawyers' political
rhetoric as well: During the 1993 debates over Clinton's effort to reform
military anti-gay policy, one prominent gay legal advocate called the
exclusion of homosexuals from the military "the apartheid of the closet,"
and movement activists urged Clinton to imitate President Harry
Truman's executive order banning racial discrimination in the military by
abolishing anti-gay policy with a Trumanesque stroke of the pen.[13]

To be sure, the "like race" analogy is not the handiwork of lawyers
only. At about the same time that national gay rights litigators were presenting "indicia of suspectness" similes to courts, activist and theoretical
works argued that homosexuals should understand themselves to constitute a community similar to those based on minority ethnicity. And
there are forms of imitation that seem almost unconscious, as if they

were so deeply embedded in our culture of reform activism that they are repeated unthinkingly. For example, every time gay, lesbian, bisexual, and transgendered communities stage a massive demonstration in Washington, D.C., they imitate the black civil rights movement's great 1963 march on Washington in detail, selecting the Lincoln Memorial as the event's grand proscenium and waging behind-the-scenes struggles over whether to frame the march as a bid for inclusion in America or as a more radical critique of it.[14]

These imitations of identity present problems in three ranges of potential social obligation: within sexual orientation constituencies; between sexual orientation constituencies and the first constituencies of the civil rights model, African Americans and other racial minorities; and at the intersections—to borrow a term from critical race theory— between race and sexual orientation constituencies.

PROBLEMS WITHIN SEXUAL ORIENTATION CONSTITUENCIES

To understand the internal dynamics, it is helpful to think about the position of identity-based thinking in modern pro-gay movements. Two useful distinctions are suggested by Eve Kosofsky Sedgwick and John Boswell. Sedgwick distinguishes "minoritizing" understandings of sexual orientation difference, in which homosexual and heterosexual modes of life are understood to be taxonomically and socially distinct, from "universalizing" ones, which suppose homoerotic potential to be characteristically human. The former include not only civil rights models of homosexual difference but "gay identity, 'essentialist,' [and] third-sex models"; the latter include "bisexual potential, 'social constructionist,' and 'sodomy' models" and Adrienne Rich's "lesbian continuum."[15]

Boswell offers a parallel distinction between real and nominal understandings of sexual orientation identities. As Boswell notes, "Realists consider categories to be the footprints of reality. . . . They exist because humans perceive a real order in the universe and name it. . . . On the other hand, . . . [nominalists argue] that categories are only the names (Latin: *nomina*) of things agreed upon by humans, and that the 'order' people see is their creation rather than their perception." Thus, on a nominalist view, "the category 'homosexuality' . . . does not so much describe a pattern or behavior inherent in human beings as it creates and establishes it," while realists insist that the "heterosexual/homosexual dichotomy exists in speech and thought because it exists in reality."[16]

Strikingly, minoritizing understandings tend to be realist, and universalizing ones tend to be nominalist.

These framings reflect not merely a range of descriptive options: People have self-understandings tied to minoritizing and universalizing, realist and nominalist, models of sexual orientation. This is in part why these matters have such a sharp ethical bite.

Ontologies of race are similarly understandable as either universalizing or minoritizing, realist or nominalist. When gay advocates turn to legal argumentation, particularly to claims of equal protection rights, their "like race" arguments tap into a deeply universalizing model of race, the integrationist ideal. Martin Luther King's famous invocation of race indifference in his "I Have a Dream" speech exemplifies the universalism of much civil rights–era activism. His prayer-like invocation of a future in which "my four little children will one day live in a nation where they will not be judged by the color of their skin, but by the content of their character" is shocking to leftist sensibilities now only because the political meaning of race universalism has become so much more ambiguous since 1963.[17]

Arguments that anti-gay policies are like racist policies often maintain this universalizing representation of race. Thus Ninth Circuit Judge William A. Norris, in his brave 1997 speech attacking the military "don't ask, don't tell" policy, likened it to de jure racial segregation (it was "nothing more than another variation on the theme of invidious discrimination"), likened resistance to it to the black civil rights movement (crediting "all the countless gay men and lesbians . . . who have had the fortitude to expose themselves to the forces of bigotry, just as the Little Rock Nine did forty years ago on the steps of Central High"), and predicted that society and even federal judges would soon say of it—as Arkansas Governor Michael Huckabee had recently said of racial segregation at Central High—"Today, we come to say, once and for all, that what happened here forty years ago was simply wrong. It was evil. And we renounce it."[18] This is very moving and very constructive, in part because it claimed only that the moral violation at Central High was like the moral violation of military anti-gay policy—not that blacks and gays are alike.

But often pro-gay advocates draw minoritizing models out of the legal representations of race groups, invoking a pictorial resemblance between racial minorities and gay men, lesbians, and bisexuals. I will consider the ethical implications of the bid to shift our understanding of race implied in these "like race" similes. But first it seems necessary to observe the way in which these gestures operate within and among sexual orientation constituencies. The fact that minoritizing understandings of homo-/heterosexual difference are so adaptable to the "like race" approach to advocacy means that pro-gay lawyers will be more likely to use them, and maybe also more likely to respond with indifference, obtuseness, and even hostility when universalizing models are proposed. At the same time the utility to lawyers of minoritizing models makes those models more salient, more widely diffused, and more likely to take the shape of an identity script than they would otherwise be. The questions of accuracy, strategy, speaking for others, and loyalty are all implicated in the resulting dynamics.

Consider two pictorialist "like race" arguments that have been particularly controversial: the arguments that gay men and lesbians are like racial minorities because they share an "immutable characteristic" or are a "discrete and insular minority." Immutability was one of the indicia of suspectness derived by gay rights litigators from judicial opinions treating legislation disadvantaging race groups and women as presumptively invalid—as "suspect." Some courts, in the course of justifying this aspect of equal protection doctrine, had observed that race and sex were "immutable characteristics," and pro-gay advocates argued that homosexual orientation was one too. In a related move, gay advocates looked to "the most famous footnote in constitutional law," footnote 4 of the Supreme Court's 1938 decision in *United States v. Carolene Products*. In this footnote Justice Stone laid out a new vision of the judicial role in enforcing the equal protection clause. The proposal was that courts were particularly obliged to protect minority groups that are chronically vulnerable in the political process, and a good way of limiting the resulting judicial interference with political decision making would be to accord special protection only to groups that were "discrete and insular"—paradigmatically racial, national, and religious minorities.[19] Pro-gay advocates argued that homosexuals were similarly discrete and insular and thus similarly vulnerable to exclusion and domination by legislative majorities.

Neither footnote 4 nor the many courts that observed that race and sex are immutable characteristics supplied their logic. The idea behind discreteness and insularity seems to have been that visually identifiable, socially and geographically isolated minorities were particularly susceptible to exclusion from or domination in the hurly-burly of pluralistic bargaining. The idea behind immutability must have been that racial discrimination was particularly invidious because its victims could do nothing to sidestep it: Blacks could not change the color of their skin and thus come into compliance with the majority's preference for whiteness.

Major criticisms can be launched against these theories of subordination. For example, Bruce Ackerman cogently used organization theory to argue that anonymous and diffuse groups (homosexuals being his prime example) can be just as subject to chronic exclusion from the political process as discrete and insular ones; and an unexamined and bizarre premise of the "immutable characteristic" justification for heightened judicial protection seems to be that, if blacks could change the color of their skin, white majorities would be more justified in asking them to do so and punishing them with discrimination if they did not.[20] "Like race" pictorialism is, moreover, bad coalition politics because it concedes that groups that are not "like race" have no claim to courts' equal protection solicitude; and it is bad for the development of equal protection theory, among judges and elsewhere, because it promotes the idea that the traits of subordinated groups, rather than the dynamics of subordination, are the normatively important thing to notice.[21] The coherentist assumptions about identity politics may make it hard to see that group traits— such as discreteness, insularity, a perception of immutability, and a focus on closetedness—are the effect rather than the predicate of subordinating dynamics. They certainly have worked to obscure footnote 4's primary focus on invidious majoritarian prejudice and the immutability cases' persistent primary concern with the irrelevance of the purportedly immutable trait to legitimate state concerns. The critique of coherentist identity politics and simple good equal protection doctrine merge here in a rejection of "like race" pictorialism.

It was a bold move for gay rights advocates to say that homosexuals were marked by an immutable characteristic, inasmuch as a considerable proportion of anti-gay discrimination (unlike racial discrimination) is animated by a desire to convert lesbians and gay men to heterosexuality or to prevent gay people from coming into existence in the first place. And it was part of the bold new outness of post-Stonewall gay communities in the Castro and Greenwich Village areas to claim that gay men and lesbians lived in discrete and insular enclaves (like racial and ethnic communities).

But there were some hard questions to ask about these representations. First are a series of questions that arise from the claim they make to represent homosexuals generally. Of course, the "like race" similes took the minoritizing view of homo-/heterosexual definition and tended to suppress, hide, or deny universalizing ones. This tendency reached its apogee when gay rights advocates claimed that some preliminary and equivocal scientific studies suggesting human sexual orientation might have some biological components proved decisively that homosexuality was a biological trait like race.[22] The coherentist criticism of these arguments would be that they are inaccurate. But they may have been worse than that: They may have "made up people" in the sense that they persuaded gay men and lesbians that they were "like that." I think they did. In fact, I think they created a demand for gay gene experiments, which in turn did a great deal of interpellating of their own.

Second, how should we think about the problem of speaking for others involved in the selection of minoritizing representations for legal advocacy? The questions of strategy and speaking for others are linked here. Gay advocates who used these "like race" similes often did so because they believed they might work, might secure significant legal advances for gay men and lesbians across the board and relieve widespread suffering imposed on them by state-sponsored discrimination. "It doesn't matter that the simile is a little inaccurate," they would say. "Judges fall for it, and once we secure some legal rights no one will remember the rhetoric we used to obtain them." This justification balances material benefits against "merely" symbolic harms. That framing of the "like race" debate carries with it coherentist assumptions about pro-gay identity politics, however, and avoids the critical twist on the question: Useful for whom? If the immutability argument had become the predicate for a legal victory, for instance, the resulting antidiscrimination case law could have left bisexuals out in the cold—after all, they can switch. And this was not merely a risk of future harm; it displaced bisexuals as outsiders, nonmembers of the constituency on whose behalf gay and lesbian advocates spoke. This is a particularly striking case of interpellation from below.

One way to avoid the ethical dilemmas posed here is to ask the question of loyalty. Here is a dangerous point in intragroup politics. When group members promote a duty of loyalty they implicitly ask internal dissenters to fall silent. But in this case, as in the case of double binds generally, the question of loyalty is a wash. Where pro-gay activists stake their arguments in universalizing forms, anti-gay activists can co-opt them, saying that homosexuality is a mere choice or a mere set of acts from which one can abstain. Anti-gay discrimination emerges in this formation as an effort to prevent the "spread" of homosexuality. But where pro-gay activists stake their arguments in minoritizing forms, anti-gay activists can co-opt them too, representing homosexuals as pathological deviants who should be cured, killed, aborted, or at least hidden from view. Under these circumstances, it seems clear that the strategic move is not to ensure the ascendancy of one model or the other, but to inhabit their crosscutting vulnerabilities more consciously.

So the ethical weight of advocates' minoritizing representations must be gauged. The preference of critical theory is clear: Lawyers should not impose minoritizing representations on the lively insubordination of queer politics. In stating that preference, critical theory has my deepest sympathies. But what about sincerely minoritized group members and their desires for representation? What about the fact that sometimes minoritizing representations do work in the sense that they facilitate actual legal reform? (Imagine trying to argue a lesbian coparent adoption case without making any reference to immutability.) And what about the note of communalism that sounds in so many critical appeals for universalizing, nominalizing representations? The current wild race-to-the-courthouse individualism is disturbing precisely because it lacks any mechanism for intracommunal dialogue, but if such a dialogue were possible, who would be invited to join in it and how could it be conducted without coercion? However hard these questions are, they can be stated more clearly and understood more simply if we bracket, or pretermit, "like race" similes when we deal with them.

PROBLEMS BETWEEN SEXUAL ORIENTATION AND RACIALLY IDENTIFIED CONSTITUENCIES

To be blunt, "like race" similes have caused considerable friction between gay and racial constituencies. "To equate homosexuality with race is to give a death sentence to civil rights," says Martin Luther King's niece Alveda Celeste King.[23] The African American host of a call-in radio show objects to gay rights ordinances, saying: "A lot of blacks are upset that the feminist movement pimped off the black movement. Now here comes the gay movement. Blacks resent it very much, because they do not see a parallel, nor do I."[24] Colin Powell, then Chairman of the Joint Chiefs of Staff and perhaps the most prominent African American in mainstream politics, fought vigorously to maintain the military's anti-gay practices and specifically objected to "like race" similes: "Homosexuality is not a benign . . . characteristic, such as skin color or whether you're Hispanic or Oriental. . . . It goes to one of the most fundamental aspects of human behavior."[25] These arguments go beyond criticizing particular "like race" analogies, such as the immutability argument, to claim civil rights legalism as peculiarly dedicated to racial justice and to resist quite broadly the overall effort of gay constituencies to frame their justice claims in civil rights terms. What is at stake here? How should gay-friendly analysis understand these challenges and respond to them?

These questions suggest that the question of loyalty is a dangerous device for unpacking the ethics of representation. When the question is "Loyal to whom?" the coherentist assumptions about identity politics make it easy to respond with glib composure, "To us." But those assumptions were put into question by the very issue of whether bisexuals belong to the group of homosexuals, and they are demonstrably useless in the face of black resistance to "like race" arguments.

The controversy over "like race" arguments surely turns in part on obligations that pro-gay advocates owe to people who suffer not, or not only, sexual orientation discrimination, but race discrimination. It is axiomatic that pro-gay advocates should do everything they can to pursue racial justice, so a key question emerges: How is identity imitation a way of becoming involved, indirectly but materially, in racial struggles, and how should we understand the resulting representational opportunities and normative tensions? Attached to that question is a deeper one, which I believe is an unacknowledged threat to identity politics generally: Does identity imitation provide or block access to deep, identity-indifferent questions of distributive justice?

The intermovement ethics of representation posed by "like race" claims has been articulated in several ways: first, the assumption that African American criticism of these arguments can only be homophobic, on one hand, or that it is authoritative because of the social epistemology of its speakers on the other; second, the argument that civil rights for gay men and lesbians are a natural right that cannot be trammeled by an ethics of representation; third, the argument that gay civil rights claims should be muted because the stigma attached to same-sex sexuality, indeed to sexuality, might contaminate civil rights law for other constituencies; and fourth, the argument that gay "like race" articulations threaten either to transfer civil rights resources from racial minorities to gay constituencies or to transfer civil rights meanings between the groups in ways that will put racial justice claims in jeopardy.

First, to the challenge that gay "like race" arguments "pimp off the black movement," coherentist identity politics has two immediate answers, one amenable to gay coherentists, the other amenable to black coherentists. The former decry black criticism of gay "like race" arguments as manifestations of unregenerate anti-gay sentiment, while the latter call for deference to it as an authoritative expression by those in a position to know what is and is not "like race." Neither response is any more adequate than the coherentist assumptions upon which it is founded.

Second, believers in natural or formal rights have another answer: If gay rights are required by abstract justice, there can be no intelligible ethical constraint on their assertion. That is, if rights are natural, primordial entitlements, they cannot justifiably be encumbered at all, ever. We have heard this argument in the marriage debates, when proponents of the gay marriage campaign assert that individual gay men and lesbians have a justice-based right to marry that supersedes any obligations arising from less primordial normativities, such as the feminist critique of marriage. I take some satisfaction in the fact that, having let fly this boomerang, gay marriage campaigners encounter it again when individual gay men and lesbians defend their decisions to sue to obtain marriage licenses even though their cases would likely produce bad law because of bad timing or bad venue. As this dismal series of exchanges indicates, the natural rights argument is deeply tautological: In the absence of any agreed-upon metaphysics of formal rights, it merely posits that rights are by definition entitlements that trump all other claims. It is a deeply individualist, deeply foundationalist argument, just as hostile to collective approaches to law reform as it is to any political, historical, or institutional analysis of rights discourse. Finally, no one on the left believes the natural rights argument except when he or she seeks immunity from strategic or communal criticism: Those who assert it in support of gay marriage would probably be unwilling to say that Thurgood Marshall was wrong to craft a strategic run-up to *Brown v. Board of Education* and to suppress inopportune litigation when he could; and critical race theorists who defended rights discourse against the attack mounted by critical legal studies did so not in terms of formal rights but in terms of a rhetorically alert pragmatism.

Third, an argument against "like race" assertions that may carry more water worries about contagion that homosexual stigma could bring to other areas of the law. It is, after all, entirely plausible that the stigma attached to homosexuals would facilitate legal retrogression harming racial minorities. Full-time gay rights litigators often comment on the fact that, when they say "Your Honor," they are often giving the judge his or her first opportunity to meet an openly gay person. Judicial homophobia exists, and it seriously affects the outcome of cases.[26] What if the resulting bad law is worse than anything that would have emerged in a race discrimination case, but is cited and followed in later race discrimination cases?

Case law, because of its analogical developmental style, is apt for mediating such movement-to-movement harms. Indeed, the danger seems to have materialized in *Bowers v. Hardwick* (1986), aside from *Romer v. Evans* (1996) the most important Supreme Court decision on a gay rights issue to date.[27] Michael Hardwick was engaged in fellatio with another man in the bedroom of his own home when a police officer came into the room to serve an arrest warrant on him. (There are good reasons to think that this intrusion was part of a campaign of anti-gay harassment that the Atlanta police were conducting against gay men generally and against Hardwick in particular.)[28] Prosecutors obtained a second indictment, this time on a charge of consensual sodomy.

With the help of the ACLU of Georgia, Hardwick challenged the sodomy charge, claiming that Georgia's statute violated his rights to privacy under the Constitution. The privacy theory he invoked depended on cases that women's rights lawyers had won in their decades-long effort to establish rights to reproductive autonomy, particularly contraception and abortion. When the Supreme Court rejected Hardwick's claim that constitutional privacy rights protected him from arrest for a private consensual act of same-sex sodomy, they did so in shockingly harsh and dismissive terms that involved the Court in an ugly display of homophobia. The majority opinion derided arguments upon which Hardwick had prevailed in the Court of Appeals as "facetious," and the concurring opinion of Chief Justice Burger gratuitously cited Blackstone to describe same-sex sodomy as "the infamous *crime against nature*," "an offense of 'deeper malignity' than rape, a heinous act 'the very mention of which is a disgrace to human nature.'"[29]

As disastrous as this defeat was for pro-gay legalism, it was at least as ominous for women's rights to reproductive freedom: *Hardwick* so deeply undermined the foundation of *Roe v. Wade* (1973) that abortion rights advocates seriously faced the possibility that the Supreme Court could overturn it.[30] In hindsight it seems at least possible that some justices welcomed *Hardwick* onto their docket because its association with a stigmatized group gave them a chance to slam the door on privacy doctrine and to put *Roe* in jeopardy.

If this is what happened—of course no one can say for sure whether it did—the gay rights litigation campaign set the stage for a crisis in the women's reproductive freedom campaign. But if women's rights advocates had approached Hardwick and his lawyers when they were considering whether to pursue a federal case and had argued that the stigma associated with male-male fellatio was dangerous for the continued stability of reproductive rights that were crucial to women, they would have implicitly asked him to accept that stigma as a premise for his action. It was entirely appropriate to argue that his case should not have been framed as a privacy claim because doing so misrepresented the public nature of the harm inflicted on him, to argue that he should not file a lawsuit because the law in his district was not ripe to support his claim, or even to argue that fitting his claim to the existing structure of reproductive rights distorted them, but to ask him to forgo a claim because its overlay of stigma might injure others would have been to ask him to cooperate with—indeed, by his silence to reaffirm—a profound insult to his dignity. Asking homosexuals to modify their justice claims precisely because they are exposed to acute and almost autonomic vilification is to ask them to accommodate, accept, and through the "speech act of a silence" to endorse that condition.[31] That's asking too much.

Fourth, the gravest argument against "like race" claims, and civil rights imitation generally, is that they may exhaust or divert civil rights resources—hard resources such as jobs or funds for police retraining, or soft ones such as a social and cultural appetite for antidiscrimination—away from the traditional constituencies of civil rights law to new constituencies that need it less. This is, I think, what some African American critics apprehend when they object to gay rights legislation because it would "steal away the civil rights from under our very noses," when they worry that "the civil rights bandwagon is getting so full that it's not moving anywhere."[32] It seems extremely plausible to me that gay men and lesbians—who, relative to African Americans, are whiter and far more likely to be economically just fine, thank you—don't need antidiscrimination protection as acutely as racial minorities but are more likely to get it. If antidiscrimination protection is a zero sum, moreover, we will not only get it but also take it away from people of color.

Particularly where hard resources are involved, it is alarmingly easy to see that winner-take-all civil rights contests can take shape. Affirmative action programs are rife with such contests, which pit one recognized civil rights constituency against another. For instance, in minority business enterprise programs, blacks and Latinos have had ample opportunity to observe white women speed ahead of them in contests for finite resources.[33] Increasingly we must tackle the problem as a question about whether a particular racial group with a unique history of racial disadvantage should take resources earmarked for affirmative action away from another racial group with a quite different history of racial disadvantage. For instance, magnet schools can become so attractive that their admissions policies are fraught with multiracial conflicts in which the position of Asian Americans is deeply anomalous.[34]

If we maintain coherentist assumptions about identity groups, the problems are hard enough. We have about three choices then: we could (1) engage in a crude exercise in ranking oppressions; (2) undertake a distributive justice analysis borrowed from liberal theory, imagining the contesting groups as big homogeneous individuals; or (3) (the perennial cop-out of leftist multiculturalism) object to the size of the pie and go home. But two kinds of problems can make it hard to keep neat fences around resource disputes. First, a group seeking to engage in a zero-sum contest might not already have a civil rights identity, so the question of whether it should be construed in identity terms needs to be answered. Should learning disabilities be understood to be "like race" such that allocating educational resources to learning-disabled children is done through an antidiscrimination paradigm?[35] Here distributive justice meets identity politics, and the hardest problem is dealing with their analytic incommensurability. Second, the resource at stake might not be hard, like a finite public school budget, but might involve malleable cultural tolerances. Was the "ebonics" controversy about budget allocations dedicated to bilingual education or about respect and recognition? Here distributive justice meets critical theory, and the encounter throws up another range of problems sounding in analytic incommensurability. African American objections to gay "like race" claims, understood sympathetically, involve both challenges.

The argument that homosexuality is not a status "like race" but a classification based on conduct is deeply mistaken. This is not because the converse is true; homosexuals do engage in homosexual acts. Rather, the distinctive danger attached to people currently designated homosexual arises because the relationships between sexual orientation identity and homosexual conduct are so slippery that they are always capable of becoming the vehicle for homosexual panic.[36] This does not make sexual orientation "like race," but it is a sufficient reason to invoke antidiscrimination norms to protect those harmed when vilified conduct and identity pinch. What interests me here is the second problem, the argument that gay rights claims draw resources away from racial minorities that desperately need them. While it is quite possible that they may do so, in two important settings where this criticism was raised—the conflicts over gays in the military and gay rights ordinances—the impact of gay rights claims on black civil rights is better understood not as a struggle over a concrete zero-sum resource, but as a linguistic process in which black and gay civil rights constituencies, having become signs of one another, interact to shape soft limits affecting both constituencies.

Gay advocates sought a repeal of military anti-gay regulations in expressly "like race" terms. It would be possible to see this effort as a bid for hard resources. The analysis would posit repeal as a way to increase the number of white people eligible for a limited supply of government subsidized jobs. It would anticipate that white decision makers in the military would feel more social solidarity with white gay troops than with black troops of any sexuality and would promote the former more readily than the latter. Seen in this way, lifting the ban would have transferred a public resource from racial minorities to a new group of eligible whites.

This is an easy argument to make, so it is particularly striking that virtually no one made it.[37] A different justification for military anti-gay policy—unit cohesion—won the day, and it carries a subtler racial meaning. Apparently, the integration of women into the military, combined with the energetic sexual controversy provoked by the 1993 debates over military anti-gay policy, contributed to an upsurge in the number of sexual harassment complaints. In those complaints black men have been disproportionately accused.[38] It seems at least likely that this disproportion emerges because black men are perceived by white women as sexually threatening in a way that white men are not. That is to say that disruptions in the male homosocial environment of the military has increased the level of sexual hostility there, and that sexual hostility in the United States defaults so readily to racialized tropes that black men in uniform face heightened danger.

Perhaps Colin Powell based his ferocious defense of military anti-gay policy—a defense in which unit cohesion was the centerpiece—on something like this reasoning. But note that this is not a resource allocation problem. To make it look like one, you would have to say that the good of safety in the sexual culture is a finite resource that gay advocates implicitly propose to appropriate from black men in particular. But sexual tranquillity is not a finite resource: Everyone could have it just as easily as no one. Under these circumstances it seems more direct to say that the ethics of "like race" arguments need to be worked out on a hypothesis that racial and sexual meanings are interconnected in complex discursive webs. Perhaps the best heuristic for understanding ethical challenges to "like race" arguments, then, is not the zero-sum competition between divergent coherentist identity groups but the dynamics of language.

How those dynamics might work is suggested by a second controversy in which African American critiques of gay "like race" claims were even more salient: the furor over gay rights ordinances and their attempted repeal through state constitutional amendments. The centerpiece of anti-gay resistance here was a claim that gay rights are special rights. It is conventional to read this claim to say "*not* like race." As Jane Schacter and Margaret Russell have amply documented, conservative activists running anti–gay rights campaigns amplified the voices of African American critics who said, "Gays were never declared three-fifths of human by the Constitution," "I can't go into a closet and hang up my race when it's convenient," and "We will not agree to them saying they're just like us."[39] But more covertly the anti–gay rights campaign deployed a "like race" claim that mediated race and sexual orientation as indicators of each other and created rather than competed for a zero sum of antidiscrimination commitment.

The key is the rich range of signification packed into the term *special rights*. The pro-gay ordinances that gave rise to the struggle added "sexual orientation" to a list of grounds already declared out of bounds for employers and public accommodations to consider. These grounds included race, ethnicity, and national origin—the classic civil rights grounds—as well as a hodgepodge of additional grounds that many civil rights laws now specify, from disability to marital status to veteran status and so on.

Special rights fundamentally misdescribed these reforms. Civil rights legislation bans especially bad treatment based on race, sex, and other specified grounds and provides remedies and thus deterrence designed to put victims of discrimination on a level playing field with everyone else. It is formally neutral—men can sue for sexual discrimination, whites can sue for racial discrimination. Traditional civil rights legislation is "special" only in the sense—held by almost nobody—that it invidiously removes a few arbitrarily distrusted grounds of decision from the free market.[40] But there are three versions of antidiscrimination enforcement, all of them associated historically with very specified attention to racial minorities, women, and disabled people, that are more or less accurately described as special treatment.

First, the entire "suspect classification" and "tiers of scrutiny" edifice built in Supreme Court doctrine under the equal protection clause recognizes that blacks are more likely to be hurt by race discrimination than whites, that women are more likely to be hurt by sex discrimination than men. This approach moves beyond formal equality to antisubordination and is, in one sense, special: When considering any given axis of discrimination, it gives the chronically subordinated group particularized attention.

A second deviation from formal equality appears in arguments that equality requires accommodations to the particular needs of a protected group. These arguments are historically associated with efforts to integrate women and disabled people. And they involve "special treatment": When we say that women's equality rights include the right to pregnancy leave or that a wheelchair user's equality rights include the right to a ramp, we are saying that there is something particular, distinctive, and special about their situation that requires attention. (The sophisticated justification for special rights of this kind is to point out that they are necessitated by norms that are special in themselves: workplaces that appear neutral but really assume male workers, public spaces that appear universally accessible but actually assume ambulatory users. But that justification only intensifies the specialty of this form of special rights.)

At the time of the ordinance struggles, both of these takes on antidiscrimination were controversial, but a third take—affirmative action—was the subject of a racial justice firestorm. Like antisubordination models of antidiscrimination, affirmative action notices that blacks, not whites, need special assistance in a racially stratified society, that women, not men, are likely to be bypassed when higher paying jobs are being distributed. And like "special accommodation" models of antidiscrimination, affirmative action goes beyond prohibiting discrimination to require affirmative steps to alleviate its effects. Affirmative action is "special treatment," then, in the senses that it undertakes positive steps for particular groups. Of course, by no stretch of historical accuracy is it a special right: Mainstream and constitutional law debates over affirmative action have stalled on the question of whether it is permissible, never having gotten to the question of whether it is legally mandatory. But it is a special remedy in several senses of the term.

The "special rights" campaign against gay rights ordinances was designed to ride on a strong anti–affirmative action backlash and on milder backlashes against antisubordination and special accommodation models of antidiscrimination, which were primarily about white resentment of race-based redistribution, less acutely about male resentment of sex-based redistribution, and probably only marginally about accommodations for physical and other disabilities. In that sense, "special right's" subliminal "like race" analogy harmed gay men and lesbians rather than helped them. At the same time, four elements of the "special rights" campaign hurt racial minorities and women. First, the association of homo-

sexuals with various special treatment backlashes united social conservatives with libertarian conservatives, facilitating a formidable coalition.
Second, to the extent that the three forms of "special treatment" antidiscrimination focus primarily on racial and gender justice, the latter were
under an unacknowledged subtextual attack. Third, the stigma attached
to homosexuality made for an easy identification of the queer—"differing in some odd way from what is usual or normal: strange, . . . peculiar"[41]—with the special, and muffled pro-gay activists when they tried to
defend the ordinances as normal civil rights law. Fourth, possibly most
damaging, the "special rights" accusation generated popular confusion
about the relationship between formally neutral civil rights laws and
affirmative action: If people could be convinced to vote against the former, thinking they were the same as the latter, the very idea of civil rights
legislation was undermined.

This episode amply justifies African American alarm about gay civil
rights "like race" claims. But note that the question is not whether gay
men and lesbians steal the civil rights from under African Americans'
noses but whether an unholy alliance of social and libertarian conservatives will do so. The danger arises not because blacks and gays are alike or
different, but because they can be flashed as signs of each other in a discourse that operates so smoothly it can remain virtually silent. And
antidiscrimination fatigue is not the exogenous starting point of this
operation but its product. This pattern does not support ethical constraints on gay men and lesbians deciding whether to make civil rights
claims, although it does suggest that imagining a rights-claiming project
without anticipating or resisting the racial resignifications it may produce
is to fail to imagine it well at all.

PROBLEMS AT THE INTERSECTIONS

We have become accustomed to thinking of the intersections between
sexual orientation and race as instantiated in persons—the black gay
man, the Latina lesbian—who inhabit a subordinated position in two or
more categorical systems and who are thus particularly affected by anything said about their interrelations. But if my reading of "like race"
claims in the gays-in-the-military debate and the special rights campaign
is right, the seams joining and dividing sexual orientation and race are
everywhere.

In a contribution to the intersectionality literature that expressly
addresses feminist "like race" arguments, Trina Grillo and Stephanie

Wildman discourage white women from using "like race" analogies to illuminate sexism. They note, "Analogizing sex discrimination to race discrimination makes it seem that all the women are white and all the men African-American. The experiential reality of women of color disappears."[42] Two ontological claims about racial and gender categories underlie this critique, and the ethics of intersectional representation are better understood without them. First, Grillo and Wildman posit, "To analogize gender to race, one must assume that each is a distinct category, the impact of which can be neatly separated, one from the other."[43] But the chief dangers of intersectionality arise not because the categorical systems are supposed to be independent, but because they are understood to impinge quite immediately on one another. Second, Grillo and Wildman posit that it is the reality of women of color that is obscured. Similarly, Schacter warns, "The categorical lines drawn in the discourse of equivalents around protected groups *erase or distort the identities* of people who are part of more than one group."[44] For all their critique of feminist essentialism, these and many other intersectional formulations retain a strong ontological commitment to real identities. But "like race" arguments pose hard ethical challenges at intersections, because they place the ontology of identity itself at risk in ways that are differently controversial in racial and sexual orientation discourses. To see this we need to shift from persons to discourses, from coherentist identity politics to critical theory.

If intragay identity wars can be roughly described as a tension between universalizing and minoritizing and between realist and nominalist understandings, so can disagreements about the ontology of racial differences. Minoritizing understandings emerge in ethnic solidarity, politics-of-recognition multiculturalist, and nationalist discourses of race; and universalizing understandings emerge in integrationist, hybridizing, mestiza, and strong social constructivist models. I will describe the related, less notorious tensions between realist and nominalist understandings in a moment; for now I'll simply note that they are implicated here just as they are in the framing of sexual orientation. My proposal is that gay "like race" arguments can tighten or loosen these tensions within racial discourse and that this meta-intersectionality, if you will, is possibly more political than the face-to-face, largely phenomenological intersectionalities emphasized by Grillo and Wildman and others. Moreover, the interpellative difficulties that vex intragay ethics of representation are recapitulated here across a broader range of differences.

To put it simply, a "like race" argument that A is like B also implicitly claims that B is like A. Operating meta-intersectionally, "like race" claims can create interpellative links between gay minoritizing representations and racial universalizing ones, or (almost but not quite conversely) between gay nominal representations and racial realist ones.

Consider an example of the former case. When gay rights advocates began to invoke the "immutable characteristic" simile, they were working from a set of scattered, sketchy rationales occurring at happenstance in the race and sex discrimination cases. By translating these immutable characteristic references into an indicia of suspectness checklist and implying that its items were not merely sufficient but necessary conditions for heightened judicial protection, they invited judges to harden up the law in this area. Judges did just that: Federal district courts increasingly stipulated for immutability not as a mere factor but as a prerequisite for heightened scrutiny, even as they persistently concluded that sexual orientation was not an immutable characteristic. This development has made it harder for groups distinguished by theoretically mutable characteristics—fat people, for instance—to make antidiscrimination claims ("Why don't they just lose weight?").[45] Moreover, the immutable characteristic rationale is spring-loaded to harm racial minorities: Its hidden assumption that racial discrimination would be morally acceptable if blacks could change the color of their skin leaps into prominence when employers tell black women on their payrolls that they can't wear braids, or Latino employees that they can't speak Spanish ("Why can't they just conform to white cultural norms?").[46] Gay advocates making the immutability argument, then, bear some responsibility for a legitimation of universalizing understandings of race and a delegitimation of—indeed, a constriction of the social space for—minoritizing ones.

Almost conversely, there is a subtle tension between queer nominalism and a certain tendency of critical race-representational choices to hew to realism. Racial realism is not the sole property of nationalist and other minoritizing racial understandings; it appears also in hybridizing, mestiza, and strong social constructivist versions of race universalism. To look at just one example, in the coda "On Categories" to her book *The Alchemy of Race and Rights*, Patricia Williams makes a series of nominalizing gestures: "[W]hile being black has been the most powerful *social attribution* in my life, it is only one of a number of *governing narratives* or *presiding fictions* by which I am constantly reconfiguring myself in the world." "*[T]erms* like 'black' and 'white' do not begin to capture the rich ethnic and political diversity of *my subject*." So far so nominalist. But "I prefer African-American in my own conversational usage because it effectively evokes *the specific cultural dimensions of my identity*, but in this book I use most frequently the term black in order to accentuate *the unshaded monolithism of color itself* as *a social force*."⁴⁷ Those are the last words in this important strong constructivist, racial nominalist book. I suppose we could agree that they bring in a certain realism.

Queer theory, on the other hand, is notoriously ready to abandon realism in its enraptured embrace with nominalism. The result in legal argumentation is a shift away from "like race" pictorialism and toward remedial theories that focus on the distinctive social and discursive dynamics of gay injury. My own argument that equal protection arguments should emphasize not who we are but how we are thought, Kendall Thomas's argument that sodomy laws should be understood to violate not a right to privacy but a right to be free from cruel and unusual punishment, Lisa Duggan's recommendation that "like race" arguments be replaced with "like the *relationship* between the state and religion," and Toni Massaro's argument that equal protection claims should forego "thick" social description and go "thin" all are crafted to make room for universalizing, particularly queer, understandings of sexual orientation in civil rights discourse.⁴⁸

For reasons known only to themselves, a majority of the Supreme Court in 1996 issued a gay rights decision, *Romer v. Evans*, that adopts an extreme form of nominalism. Holding Colorado's Amendment 2—which had barred the state in any of its subdivisions and agencies from entertaining *any* claim of discrimination based on homosexual status—unconstitutionally irrational, the Court persistently refused to base its decision on any social description of the group harmed by the challenged law. It describes and populates the class under consideration in a self-consciously nominal gesture: "the *named* class, a class *we shall refer to as* homosexual persons or gay men and lesbians." This is "a single *named* group" defined by "a single *trait*." "Homosexuals, by state decree, *are put* in a solitary class": The amendment "*classifies* homosexuals . . . to *make them* unequal to everyone else"; "[i]t is a *classification of persons undertaken for its own sake*" and in that sense is a "status-based enactment." "[C]lass legislation . . . [is] obnoxious."⁴⁹

It remains uncertain whether *Romer's* nominalism will appear in other equal protection decisions. But it is clear that, if it appears in the context of racial discrimination, it will be inflected by an important racial trope there with no counterpart in the constitutional discourse of sexual orientation: the maxim, drawn from Justice Harlan's dissent in *Plessy v.*

Ferguson, that "our Constitution is colorblind."[50] If understanding the distinctive dangers of race requires attention to "the unshaded mono-lithism of color itself as a social force," a queer shift toward nominalism could contribute, perhaps dangerously, to its doctrinal erasure. This is an ethical problem for gay advocates to consider, and to do so we will have to make simultaneous use of distributive and critical tools that are not now designed to work well together.

When we say that something is "like race," we imply that we know what race is like. But do we? Ever since the Supreme Court's decision in *Adarand Constructors v. Pena,* which held that race-based affirmative action could be subjected to the same degree of judicial scrutiny that courts must apply to acts of overt anti-black racism, there has been a strong strategic reason for equal protection rights claims to take a new form, "*not* like race."[51] As Stuart Minor Benjamin indicates in a fascinating article on Native Hawaiian rights claims, the considerable edifice of special programs now dedicated under federal law to federally recognized mainland Indian tribes and under Hawaiian state law to Native Hawaiian cultural preservation could be erased from the landscape if native groups were understood to be "like race."[52] This reversal in the normative content of intragroup comparisons could hardly have been anticipated twenty years ago, but it is now part of the context of any "like race" claim.

In a situation this volatile, in which so many different kinds of social harms are so finely connected, it seems important to exercise considerable caution. Working within coherentist identity constituencies is not enough; forming coalitions across them, though crucial, is also not enough. When identity can be deployed to harm its own subjects, the search for equal justice also requires that we move beyond identity politics altogether.

NOTES

1. The best survey of this broad effort for legal change is the excellent monthly newsletter *Lesbian/Gay Law Notes,* ed. Arthur S. Leonard (New York Law School, 57 Worth St., New York, NY 10013).
2. Though disparate and internally disputatious, queer theory is probably all alike in being unimaginable without Michel Foucault's *The History of*

Sexuality, vol. 1, trans. Robert Hurley (New York: Vintage, 1980 [1978]). Some key documents in the development of queer theory are: Eve Kosofsky Sedgwick, *Epistemology of the Closet* (Berkeley: University of California Press, 1990); David M. Halperin, *One Hundred Years of Homosexuality* (New York: Routledge, 1990); Henry Abelove, Michèle Aina Barale, and David M. Halperin, eds., *The Lesbian and Gay Studies Reader* (New York: Routledge, 1993); and Michael Warner, ed., *Fear of a Queer Planet: Queer Politics and Social Theory* (Minneapolis: University of Minnesota Press, 1993).

3. K. Anthony Appiah, "Identity, Authenticity, Survival: Multicultural Societies and Social Reproduction," in *Multiculturalism,* ed. Amy Gutmann (Princeton, NJ: Princeton University Press, 1994), 162–63.

4. Louis Althusser, "Ideology and Ideological State Apparatuses (Notes Towards an Investigation)," in *Lenin and Philosophy and Other Essays,* trans. Ben Brewster (New York: Monthly Review Press, 1971), 162–63 (footnote omitted).

5. Ian Hacking, "Making Up People," in *Reconstructing Individualism: Autonomy, Individuality, and the Self in Western Thought,* ed. Thomas C. Heller, Morton Sosna, and David E. Wellbery (Stanford, CA: Stanford University Press, 1986), 222–36.

6. See Gayatri Chakravorty Spivak, "Can the Subaltern Speak?" in *Marxism and the Interpretation of Culture,* ed. Cary Nelson and Lawrence Grossberg (Chicago: University of Chicago Press, 1988), 271; Linda Alcoff, *The Problem of Speaking for Others,* 20 Cultural Critique 5 (1991–92).

7. For a fascinating examination of loyalty to an identity group, see Ronald Garet, *Self-Transformability,* 655 Southern California Law Review 121 (1991). David B. Wilkins provides a rigorous examination of how a group member who affirms loyalty to the group should respond when group-based demands come into conflict with his individual ethical commitments; see *Should a Black Lawyer Represent the Ku Klux Klan?* 63 George Washington Law Review 1030 (1995).

8. See particularly Gerald P. Lopez, *Rebellious Lawyering: One Chicano's Vision of Progressive Law Practice* (Boulder, CO: Westview Press,1992); Lucie White, *Subordination, Rhetorical Survival Skills, and Sunday Shoes: Notes on the Hearing of Mrs. G.,* 38 Buffalo Law Review 1 (1990); and Anthony V. Alfieri, *Reconstructive Poverty Law Practice: Learning Lessons of Client Narratives,* 100 Yale Law Journal 2107 (1991).

9. William H. Simon, *The Dark Secret of Progressive Lawyering: A Comment on Poverty Law Scholarship in the Post-Modern, Post-Reagan Era,* 48 University of Miami Law Review 1099, 1102–3 (1994); William B.

Rubenstein, *Divided We Litigate: Addressing Disputes Among Group Members and Lawyers in Civil Rights Campaigns,* 106 Yale Law Journal 1623 (1997).

10. Sharon Rush, *Equal Protection Analogies—Identity and "Passing": Race and Sexual Orientation,* 13 Harvard Black Letter Law Journal 65 (1997); see also Cass R. Sunstein, *On Analogical Reasoning,* 106 Harvard Law Review 741 (1993).

11. *Brown v. Board of Education,* 347 U.S. 483 (1954); *Korematsu v. United States,* 324 U.S. 885 (1945).

12. Under the equal protection clause, courts recognize some classifications as "suspect" because their use in legislation or regulation always raises a judicial suspicion that invidious discrimination is at work. State action disadvantaging members of a "suspect classification" is subject to heightened judicial scrutiny. The "indicia of suspectness" were group traits that courts had often noted when holding that race groups and women were differentiated by "suspect classifications." For a gay-rights brief hypostasizing these traits, see Brief of Amici Curiae Lambda Legal Defense and Education Fund, Inc. et al., in *Watkins v. United States Army,* No. 85-4006 (9th Cir.) (Aug. 30, 1988). See chapters 15–17.

13. Gay advocates' briefs went beyond the Supreme Court's suggestion that there were "indicia of suspectness," *San Antonio Independent School Dist. v. Rodriguez,* 411 U.S. 1, 28 (1973), both by adding items like immutability and by presenting them as separate predicates rather than as factors in an inquiry into the dynamics of subordination. William N. Eskridge, Jr., *Race and Sexual Orientation in the Military: Ending the Apartheid of the Closet,* 2 Reconstruction 52 (1993); Clinton Collins, Jr., "Officers Insubordination a Greater Threat than Gays in Uniform," *Star Tribune,* February 5, 1993, 19A; Melissa Healy, "Clinton Aides Urge Quick End to Military Ban on Gays," *Los Angeles Times,* January 8, 1993, A1.

14. Steven Epstein, *Gay Politics, Ethnic Identity: The Limits of Social Constructionism,* 93–94 Socialist Review 9 (1987); Scott A. Sandage, "A Marble House Divided: The Lincoln Memorial, the Civil Rights Movement, and the Politics of Memory, 1939–1963," *Journal of American History* 80, no. 1 (June 1993): 135.

15. Sedgwick, *Epistemology of the Closet,* 89.

16. John Boswell, "Revolutions, Universals, and Sexual Categories," in *Hidden from History: Reclaiming the Gay and Lesbian Past,* ed. Martin Duberman, Martha Bauml Vicinus, and George Chauncey, Jr. (New York: Meridian, 1989), 17, 18–19.

17. Martin Luther King, Jr., "I Have a Dream," in *A Testament of Hope: The*

Essential Writings and Speeches of Martin Luther King, Jr., ed. James M. Washington (San Francisco: Harper & Row, 1986), 217, 220. On the gradual and partial displacement of the universalizing model by the minoritizing model of race in the black civil rights movement, and the attendant increase in the importance of identity politics, see Harvard Sitkoff, *The Struggle for Black Equality* (New York: Hill & Wang, 1981).

18. William A. Norris, "Acceptance Speech," delivered at the Lambda Liberty Awards Ceremony, Los Angeles, CA, October 16, 1997 (available at Stanford Law School's Robert Crown Law Library website, collecting primary documents about military anti-gay policy, http://dont.stanford.edu: 8080).

19. *United States v. Carolene Products,* 304 U.S. 144 (1938).

20. Bruce Ackerman, *Beyond Carolene Products,* 98 Harvard Law Review 713 (1985).

21. Jane S. Schacter, *The Gay Civil Rights Debate in the States: Decoding the Discourse of Equivalents,* 29 Harvard Civil Rights–Civil Liberties Law Review 283 (1994).

22. For a discussion of these arguments, see Halley, *Sexual Orientation and the Politics of Biology: A Critique of the Argument from Immutability,* 46 Stanford Law Review 503 (1994).

23. Teresa Moore, "King's Niece Slams Gay Rights: Oakland NAACP Chief Deplores Her Statement," *San Francisco Chronicle,* August 20, 1997, A17.

24. Lena Williams, "Blacks Rejecting Gay Rights as a Battle Equal to Theirs," *New York Times,* June 28, 1993, A1.

25. John Lancaser, "Why the Military Supports the Ban on Gays: Arguments Ranging from Privacy to AIDS Offered Against Clinton's Rights Pledge," *Washington Post,* January 28, 1993, A8.

26. For discussion of a case in which a judge dismissed a domestic violence complaint involving a lesbian couple with disparaging remarks about "your funny relationships," another in which, in ruling against a gay plaintiff challenging the military's anti-gay policy, the judge referred to him as a "homo," and another in which the judge sentenced the murderers of a gay man to less than a life sentence, saying he didn't "care much for 'queers,'" see David S. Buckel, "Unequal Justice for Gays in Hostile Courtrooms," *National Law Journal,* August 18, 1997, A20.

27. 478 U.S. 186 (1986); 116 S.Ct. 1620 (1996).

28. Kendall Thomas, *Beyond the Privacy Principle,* 92 Columbia Law Review 1431 (1992).

29. *Hardwick,* 478 U.S. 194, 197 (quoting 4 W. Blackstone, *Commentaries* *215).

30. 410 U.S. 113 (1973).

31. Sedgwick, *Epistemology of the Closet*, 3.

32. Alveda Celeste King, quoted in Moore, "King's Niece Slams Gay Rights"; Jim Simon, "Battle Lines Blur over Gay-Rights Bill," *Seattle Times*, February 27, 1994, A1.

33. See, for example, Steven A. Holmes, "U.S. Acts to Open Minority Program to White Bidders," *New York Times*, August 15, 1997, A1.

34. Selena Dong, *"Too Many Asians": The Challenge of Fighting Discrimination Against Asian Americans and Preserving Affirmative Action*, 47 Stanford Law Review 1027 (1995); Paul Brest and Miranda Oshige, *Affirmative Action for Whom?* 47 Stanford Law Review 855 (1995).

35. Like gay men and lesbians, people with disabilities have quite deliberately and self-consciously framed their justice claims in "like race" terms. On this "like race" analogy in the psychology of deaf identity formation, see Neil S. Glickman, "The Development of Culturally Deaf Identities," in *Culturally Affirmative Psychotherapy with Deaf Persons*, ed. Neil S. Glickman and Michael A. Harvey (Mahwah, NJ: Lawrence Erlbaum, 1996), 115, passim; in deaf grassroots activism, see Sharon N. Barnartt, "Action and Consensus Mobilization in the Deaf President Now Protest and Its Aftermath," *Research in Social Movements, Conflicts and Change* 17 (1994): 115; and in deaf antidiscrimination rights claiming, see Mary Ellen Maatman, *Listening to Deaf Culture: A Reconceptualization of Difference Analysis Under Title VII*, 13 Hofstra Labor Law Journal 269 (1996). On the way in which framing learning disabilities as an antidiscrimination identity occludes the redistributive problems, see Mark Kelman and Gilian Lester, *Jumping the Queue* (Cambridge, MA: Harvard University Press, forthcoming).

36. For my own expositions of this argument, see *Reasoning About Sodomy: Act and Identity In and After Bowers v. Hardwick*, 79 *Virginia Law Review* 1721 (1993); and "The Status/Conduct Distinction in the 1993 Revisions to Military Anti-Gay Policy: A Legal Archaeology," *GLQ: A Journal of Lesbian and Gay Studies* 3 (1996): 159.

37. The closest thing I've found is the strangely fretful prediction, that lifting the ban might increase the appeal of military service to black gay men and lesbians and to low-income white homosexuals and thus change the demographics of the armed services, of John Sibley Butler, "Homosexuals and the Military Establishment," *Society* 31, no. 1 (1993): 13.

38. Steve Komarow, "Army Forced Rape Charges, Women Say," *USA Today*, March 12, 1997, 1A (reporting NAACP's charges that, in all thirteen criminal sex harassment investigations at the Aberdeen Proving Ground, defendants were black men and accusers were white women).

39. Schacter, *The Gay Civil Rights Debate in the States*; Margaret M. Russell, *Lesbian, Gay and Bisexual Rights and the "Civil Rights Agenda,"* 1 African-American Law and Policy Report 33 (1994). Social conservatives have encouraged African Americans to regard gay civil rights claims with alarm. In his notorious "What Homosexuals Do" speech to Congress, then-Representative William Dannemeyer warned, "The road to Selma did not lead to the right to sodomy. . . . The freedom train has been highjacked" (*Congressional Record,* 135th Cong., House [June 29, 1989]: 3511, 3512). In the gays-in-the-military debate of 1993, the Reverend Lou Sheldon, head of the evangelical Christian Traditional Values Coalition, repeated the simile: "The freedom train to Selma never stopped at Sodom" (Cindy Loose, "Gay Activists Summon Their Hopes, Resolve," *Washington Post,* April 18, 1993, A1). The degree to which African American alarm was indigenous and the degree to which it was fomented by white conservatives is unclear. I suppose it was some of both.

40. For a discussion of the attenuation of this strand of libertarianism in the United States, see Kelman and Lester, *Jumping the Queue,* chapter 8, nn. 30–33.

41. "Queer," *Webster's Third New International Dictionary of the English Language, Unabridged* (Springfield, MA: Merriam-Webster, 1981).

42. Trina Grillo and Stephanie M. Wildman, "Obscuring the Importance of Race: The Implication of Making Comparisons between Racism and Sexism (or Other -Isms)," in *Critical Race Theory: The Cutting Edge,* ed. Richard Delgado (Philadelphia: Temple University Press, 1995), 568.

43. Ibid. For related arguments that are less directly focused on "like race" arguments, see Kimberlé Crenshaw, chap. 16 of this volume; Angela P. Harris, *Race and Essentialism in Feminist Legal Theory,* 42 Stanford Law Review 581 (1990).

44. Schacter, *The Gay Civil Rights Debate in the States,* 29 Harvard Civil Rights–Civil Liberties Law Review 283, 285n.13.

45. *Cassista v. Community Foods, Inc.,* 5 Cal. 4th 1050, 1065, 856 P. 2d 1143, 1153, 22 Cal. Rptr. 2d 287, 297 (1993).

46. On the relationship of cultural traits and racial group membership in antidiscrimination law, see Paulette M. Caldwell, *A Hair Piece: Perspectives on the Intersection of Race and Gender,* 1991 Duke Law Journal 365; Karl E. Klare, *Power/Dressing: Regulation of Employee Appearance,* 26 New England Law Review 1395 (1992).

47. Patricia J. Williams, *The Alchemy of Race and Rights* (Cambridge, MA: Harvard University Press, 1991), 256–57 (emphases added).

48. Halley, *Sexual Orientation and the Politics of Biology,* 568; Thomas, *Beyond*

the Privacy Principle; Lisa Duggan, "Queering the State," *Social Text* 39 (1994): 1; Toni Massaro, *Gay Rights, Thick and Thin,* 49 Stanford Law Review 45 (1996).

49. *Romer v. Evans,* at 1623 (see Janet Halley, *Romer v. Hardwick,* 68 Colorado Law Review 429, 439–40 [1997]), 1628, 1625, 1629 (quoting *The Civil Rights Cases,* 109 U.S. at 3, 24 (1883).

50. *Plessy v. Ferguson,* 165 U.S. 537 (1896) (Harlan, J., dissenting).

51. 115 S.Ct. 2097 (1995); see also *City of Richmond v. J. A. Croson Co.,* 488 U.S. 469 (1989).

52. Stuart Minor Benjamin, *Equal Protection and the Special Relationship: The Case of Native Hawaiians,* 106 Yale Law Journal 537 (1996). See also *Morton v. Mancari,* 417 U.S. 535, 553–55 (1974), distinguishing race from tribe in order to hold that affirmative action precedents do not apply to the "special relationship" between federally recognized tribes and the United States.

6

RAND E. ROSENBLATT

HEALTH LAW

HEALTH care delivery and health law are characterized by three basic tensions as we move into the twenty-first century. These tensions provide a revealing view of American society and offer an exceptional opportunity to address important questions about the nature and role of law.

First, imbalances of knowledge and power are pervasive in health care and have a deeply ambiguous significance. On one hand, we want the physician to take us under his or her parental wing, heal us, and reconnect us with the rest of humanity. On the other hand, we fear our dependence on another fallible human being.

Second, even in a society as enamored with the economic market as the United States, health care continues to be perceived as different from other commodified goods and services. If a poor person cannot afford to own a car, that is merely life in a market society, where almost all of us face some sense of limited resources. But if a poor person cannot afford to pay a doctor's fee and therefore is refused admission to a hospital and gives birth to a child in a car in the hospital parking lot, that is shocking (but before 1986, not necessarily illegal).[1] We can all imagine ourselves in that situation.

The impulse toward inclusion and solidarity is matched—in our time and place, overmatched—by the contrary impulse to exclude the poor, the immigrant, the person of color, the "other" from "our" schools, neighborhoods, suburbs, and health insurance groups so as to protect ourselves and those with whom we identify from the costs of the dispossession that our society inflicts on many of the "others."

In the 1991 and 1992 elections, large numbers of middle-income American voters were concerned about lack of health insurance due to unemployment, preexisting medical conditions, and eroding fringe benefits and favored health reform legislation that would assure access to quality care for all or most of the population. This impulse toward equality and inclusion was then systematically attacked by insurance industry advertisements and journalism, which focused on what well-off groups would lose by joining larger, less healthy, and more needy groups of people. Some analysts consider a key turning point to have been a front-page *New York Times* article in late 1993 emphasizing that suburban residents could find themselves in the same "health alliance," or insurance purchasing pool, as poor residents of New York City. Popular support for President Bill Clinton's reform plan rapidly eroded, and the chance to "join other advanced industrial democracies in guaranteeing health care insurance coverage as a signature feature of citizenship" was lost, probably for a long time.[2]

Unlike other failures to enact national health reform, this one did not result in continuation of the provider-dominated status quo. Rising health care costs, employer and government resistance to cost increases, and an aggressive pattern of commodifying and consolidating vast sectors of the economy have had a dramatic impact on health care delivery. Since the late 1980s, this immensely complex and varied set of services, products, professions, and institutions has been increasingly treated as a trillion-dollar-a-year industry to be transformed by entrepreneurial restructuring. As happened in England in the sixteenth and nineteenth centuries with respect to the market generally, the speed and extent of this revolution have in turn generated a legislative response as society tries to protect itself through law from the full logic of the market.[3] This active process of market transformation and resistance is the third reason that health law offers unusual opportunities for understanding the nature and role of law.

In the managed care era of the 1990s, the issue of dependence and vulnerability ("quality of care") and the issue of equality and solidarity ("access and financing") tend to merge. In this system, denial and rationing no longer happen only to the uninsured, racial minorities, and other outsiders (although they still happen far more often to them); now they also happen to members of the managed care system as part of the system's very design.

For example, a forty-year-old employee with a family history of heart disease is hospitalized with severe chest pains while on an overseas business trip. When he returns home, he sees his long-time family doctor, who is paid through his employer's HMO. Unknown to the employee, the HMO reduces the family doctor's income if he makes too many referrals to specialists. Thus, the family doctor convinces the employee that he does not need to see a cardiologist, even though the employee offers to pay for the referral himself. A few months later, the employee dies of heart failure.

The contrast in this case between medical coverage at home and abroad is striking: In the foreign country, the sense of solidarity is so strong that the foreign health system covers the hospital costs of the American stranger. Back home, he is treated as a stranger—as a statistical object and a source of income—by his own family doctor and thereby made vulnerable to his doctor's undisclosed self-interest, divided loyalty, and perhaps corrupted judgment. The access issue is also acute: He is prevented even from buying his way out of the system about whose nature he is not informed.

American health law is currently a major arena in which the struggle over these kinds of choices is being played out. As in the other areas of law explored in this book, legal traditions in health law contain both the potential to curb harmful power and hierarchy and the potential to reinforce and legitimate it.

THREE MODELS OF HEALTH LAW

American health law has been and is shaped by three models or perspectives. The first, which dominated judicial decisions and legislation from around 1880 until the 1960s, is that of professional authority and autonomy. The more or less self-conscious purpose of health law during this period was to guarantee the autonomy of individual physicians, particularly those engaged in the private practice of medicine. In virtually every area of law that touched on health care delivery—such as the locality rule that prevented nationally recognized medical experts from testifying against doctors charged with medical malpractice, the doctrine that neither physicians nor hospitals had a duty to render emergency care, and judicial enforcement of bylaws insulating doctors from control by hospital boards of trustees—prevailing legal principles empowered the individual doctor in private practice to do as he saw fit and insulated him from review and control by patients, hospitals, corporate employers, insurance companies, government, courts (including juries), and even other physicians.

A second perspective, which became prominent around 1960 and continues to the present, presumes and unevenly enforces a modestly egalitarian social contract. This perspective, which became influential at the same time in torts, contracts, constitutional law, administrative law, and many other fields, holds that patients and society as a whole, as well as physicians and other providers, have legitimate rights and interests.[4] In this view, the role of law is to achieve a fair resolution of those interests in the face of the highly unequal relationships that often exist between patients on one hand and doctors, hospitals, and insurance companies on the other. Because of this inequality, the law must enforce a social contract to achieve fair relationships and outcomes. Major components of the social contract have been a conception of health insurance as social insurance (explored below), federal statutes creating and financing social insurance for the elderly (Medicare) and a substantial number of the poor (Medicaid), and judicial doctrines interpreting those statutes as creating legal rights for patients and providers and thereby limiting government discretion. By the standards of the rest of the developed world, notably western Europe and Canada, the American social contract has been limited and uneven— hence the phrase *modestly egalitarian.*

The third perspective holds that however modest by international standards, the American social contract is far too regulatory and redistributive and should be replaced by legal principles appropriate to full-fledged market competition. Faith in unregulated markets had dominated legal thought in general from the late nineteenth to the mid-twentieth centuries and re-emerged with great strength in the early 1970s as the "law and economics movement." As applied to health law, its strategy has been the large reduction of regulation, redistribution, and professional power and a reconception of health insurance as a market transaction between insurers and economically rational individuals. In place of government and medical authority, the market competition model elevates contracts, drafted and enforced by employers and managed care entities, that define health benefits, physician practice patterns, quality of care standards, and patient remedies.[5]

All three perspectives are now contending actively for influence and present significantly different strategies for resolving the key issues of quality, access, and financing. However, this struggle among perspectives is not among equals, and each model has serious drawbacks. The model of professional authority permits no internal or external cost constraints . and hence is no longer supported by employer and government payers. The model of a modestly egalitarian social contract has not generated the political support needed to confront effectively the organized interests that undermine its egalitarian goals. The model of market competition is in the dominant position, but it cannot create the conditions for its own socially desirable and therefore legitimate functioning.

QUALITY OF CARE

From the perspective of the professional authority model, the power to define and enforce quality of care should be delegated to the medical profession itself and to the "independent" medical staffs of hospitals. The problem of patient vulnerability to harm is said to be solved by rigorous training, credentialing, and intraprofessional review and by an ethos that defines the doctor as primarily committed to the patient's well-being. This perspective acknowledges that medical errors of various types will occur but attempts to minimize their number and consequences by a strong conception of professionalism, including the expectation that errors will be reported to professional mentors or peers and rectified as soon and as fully as possible.[6]

There can be little doubt that professionalism of this sort is an essential component of defining and maintaining quality of care. But as necessary as it is, professional authority alone is not a sufficient method for achieving higher quality of care. First, American physicians have often achieved only local professional consensus; research has revealed remarkable geographic variations among demographically similar populations in rates of hospitalization and surgery for various conditions.[7] In other words, the profession itself often has not been able to define on a regional or national basis a standard of quality of care for various conditions. Second, common sense tells us that for peers who have no clear authority over one another, who are dependent on one another for income and reputation, and who have been socialized to project perfectionism rather than to reveal doubts and insecurities, it is extremely difficult, if not impossible, to call one another to account.

The social contract model responds to this problem by permitting the trier of fact to find the professional standard itself deficient, either in the light of a "best practice" advocated by some experts but not yet adopted by the profession or on the basis of a nonprofessional evaluation of what reasonable care requires.[8] This was the lesson of Judge Learned Hand's famous opinion in *The T. J. Hooper*: "A whole calling may have unduly lagged in the adoption of new and available devices. . . . Courts must in the end say what is required; there are precautions so imperative that even their universal disregard will not excuse their omission."[9]

Whether a judgment of this sort will actually have an impact is another question. The profession or industry has declined to adopt the precaution, most likely based on at least a rough comparison, from the industry's perspective, of the costs of taking the precaution compared with the benefits (avoided costs) of fewer harms. Will tort liability change the calculus? For example, in *Gonzales v. Nork*, a hospital failed to notice that a charming physician had persuaded thirty-eight patients, most of whom did not need surgery, to let him perform risky spinal operations that he was not qualified to do. He paralyzed many of them and then falsified his records to hide his responsibility. To the hospital's defense that it had followed industry accreditation standards in monitoring quality of care, the trial judge responded that those standards were deficient; they did not, for example, require the hospital to make a record of the doctor's demonstrated shortcomings, thereby precluding institutional awareness of ongoing problems.[10] The hospital was ordered to pay one-half of the $3.7 million in damages.

Whether such tort liability changes practices, particularly those of complex organizations such as hospitals, is probably affected by many variables, such as the visibility of the negligence, the number of people affected at one time, the size of the damages, the transaction costs of bringing multiple or class actions, the number of sellers in the market, and the degree of political mobilization and influence of the victims. We know that physicians, manufacturers, and insurers seem to think that tort liability makes a difference, because they spend large sums of money lobbying legislatures to reduce plaintiffs' rights and remedies. Indeed, as discussed below, the absence of effective tort liability for managed care health plans under the federal ERISA law is thought by many to have encouraged risky versions of market competition.

On the other hand, physician-dominated hospitals like that in the *Gonzales* case are particularly resistant to change. Even if the hospital were not covered by insurance and had to pay its share of $3.7 million, that rare payout might still be much cheaper, both in terms of money and medical staff dynamics, than careful monitoring of the quality of care delivered by dozens of independent physicians on whose patient referrals the hospital depends for its financial survival. Indeed, the prospect of tort liability under a social contract model did not seem to result in significant change in how the hospital industry functioned. In 1988, fifteen years after the *Gonzales* opinion, a *Wall Street Journal* reporter won a Pulitzer Prize for an article again revealing the inadequacies of hospital accreditation.[11]

In place of the concepts of quality offered by the professional authority and egalitarian social contract perspectives, the market competition model offers a series of radically different propositions. First, the patient is assumed to be a rational economic actor who, if using his or her own

after-tax dollars to pay for the care, would not consent to tests or procedures whose benefit was less than their cost. But in addition to the difficulty of patients or doctors determining benefit, traditional tax-subsidized
employment-based insurance (and Medicare) paying doctors on a fee-
for-service basis shielded both doctors and patients from having to consider costs. Under this system, any increment in safety or possible health
benefit for an individual patient was considered an improvement in quality of care.

The goal of the market competition model is to eliminate this distorted decision making and create the conditions in which health care
consumers will behave rationally—that is, under economic constraint.
There are many proposed strategies for trying to accomplish this, including much higher deductibles that force patients to spend their own
money, medical savings accounts that allow patients to keep what they
do not spend on health care, and reduced or eliminated tax subsidies for
health insurance. Market advocates also want to free health care consumers from the inefficiencies of the tort system, which is seen as a
wasteful lottery. In this vision, consumers should be free to waive their
tort remedies and consent to binding arbitration and even to a lowered,
or at least "HMO custom," standard of care.[12]

The central dilemma for the market approach is that when individuals
are seriously ill, their rationality is affected by their personal situation, as
indeed it should be. The seriously ill patient will try to draw on community or pooled insurance resources to the maximum extent possible,
because it is usually to his or her benefit to do so. But spending for the
last increment of marginal benefit is exactly what the market competition
model wishes to avoid. Private market-based health insurance (discussed
more fully below), particularly in its managed care form, is the mechanism by which people are said to consent to limits on their care in
advance, when they are still healthy.

Once doctors are serving a defined population for a fixed, prepaid premium, the concept of quality itself can be reconceived from a focus on
the individual patient to a focus on the insured group. Dr. David Eddy is
a major advocate of this approach:

> These two facts—the broad, population-based responsibility and the
> financial constraints—converge to define the objective of a health plan
> and the proper measure of quality. The objective is to maximize the health
> of the population it serves, subject to the limits on its resources, and the
> proper measure of quality is how well it does that.[13]

"Quality" thus means discouraging patients from using tests and procedures that do not seem to yield much benefit in terms of lives saved or other measures, such as mammograms for women under fifty or a second day in the hospital for normal vaginal deliveries, and increasing the use of tests and procedures that do yield proven benefits, such as mammograms for women over fifty or prenatal care. Eddy concedes that this definition of quality will cause some harm to subsets of people who would benefit from the disfavored services, but he argues that this is justified by maximizing the overall benefit to the insured population and by the principle of fair allocation of resources.

This approach poses a particular challenge to physicians and to the ethos of professional commitment to the well-being of individual patients. Eddy forthrightly tells his medical colleagues that

> practitioners need to develop an allegiance to the entire membership of the health plan. This will be difficult for those who see themselves as serving as their patients' advocate in a struggle with administrators and insurers. That perception is incorrect. When physicians hoard resources for their own patients, they are not taking from administrators or insurers; they are taking from other patients . . . [and] the result will . . . be . . . higher costs and lower quality.[14]

The work of Eddy and other advocates of market competition involves an eloquent and fascinating effort to articulate what might be termed market-based communitarianism. Society or a smaller group (the insured pool) demands that individuals subordinate their personal interests to the needs of the group. The proper mechanism for doing this is not the political process but private entities (health plans, insurers, and physicians themselves) operating in and through the market. Health plans can offer different coverage options at different prices; the degree to which the individual must subordinate herself to the limits of group resources depends on which subgroup she can afford to join, or which interventions she can afford to pay for out of her own unpooled resources. The final, morally critical link in the chain is that the competition must be "managed," or regulated by law, so as to be "socially desirable." In the words of market advocate Alain Enthoven, managed competition should not involve "no rules," but "new rules" that allow consumers to choose (and thereby reward) competing health plans based on their quality and efficiency rather than on slick advertising and market segmentation (enrolling only or primarily the healthy).[15]

In addition to the explicit inequalities built into this system and the tolerance of many of its advocates for leaving forty million people uninsured, its actual implementation has given rise to four large problems. First, little in current American law (unlike, say, the rules governing the British National Health Service) requires health plans to use the savings gained from limiting care to improve care for others or for the group as a whole.[16] There may well be health plans that do transfer resources in this way, but whether and to what extent they do so are largely voluntary matters influenced by institutional traditions and market conditions. On the other hand, we know that the top executives of many health plans and for-profit health services corporations, even ones serving the poor, have been paid lavish salaries and stock bonuses, yielding compensation at the top end in the hundreds of millions, while the incomes of many categories of practicing physicians are falling.[17] Vast personal wealth derived from health care underscores the need for law requiring the allocation of most saved resources to patient needs.

Second, "scientific" methods of defining and measuring the costs and benefits of health care interventions are developing, controversially and expensively. Not surprisingly, the managed care industry has implemented many rough-hewn policies, such as sharp restrictions on referrals to specialists and deep discounts from clinical laboratories, which do not cause much harm to the vast majority of healthy people but which have had significantly adverse consequences for the seriously ill.

Third, there is not yet a well-functioning market that rewards health plans for providing high-quality care. Partly this is because quality of any sort is still hard to define, measure, and communicate to prospective enrollees. In addition, many employees do not have the income or bargaining power to have any freedom of choice, and many employers offer only one health plan, if any, making it impossible for consumers to express their preferences through the market.

Fourth, the extensive media attention given to personal tragedies allegedly caused by health plan denials of care, and public reaction to these stories, suggest that most Americans expect health plans to take care of them competently if they become seriously ill. The principle that an individual's welfare must be subordinated to that of the group does not play well when referral restrictions and laboratory discounts lead to preventable deaths.

The relationship of American health law to the market competition conception of quality has been complex and evolving. On one hand, a small number of state court opinions have held that HMOs and managed care plans have a duty of care to their enrollees, although the content of that duty has only rarely been defined. On the other hand, from 1980 to 1995, the federal Employee Retirement Income Security Act (ERISA), which covers virtually all private (but not governmental) employment, was interpreted by most federal courts as protecting health benefit plans (but not their physicians) against state medical malpractice and other damage actions. Since ERISA itself does not provide for compensatory or punitive damages, the result was an immense deregulation of insurer, HMO, and managed care practices. No matter how negligent or irresponsible, an insurer or HMO could deny coverage or authorization for care, impose crushing financial incentives on physicians, or fail to investigate the credentials and malpractice experience of its doctors without fear of monetary liability other than the value of the benefits covered by the contract.[18]

Beginning in 1995, federal ERISA law began to change. The circumstances of that change support the classic critical legal studies view of judicial doctrine as a specialized branch of political discourse. Between 1980 and 1995, the Supreme Court interpreted the federal ERISA statute as preempting virtually all state law, including tort and contract actions, that "referred to" or "related to" employment-based health benefits plans. The reasoning for this position was linked to a market conception of health benefits: Congress was deemed to have intended that employers (and, for the 12 percent of unionized workers, their unions) make trade-offs between costs and benefits without interference from varying and potentially inconsistent state laws.

Suddenly, in the *Travelers* decision of 1995, without explanation or any relevant congressional action, the Supreme Court unanimously changed course, opining that Congress had not intended to preempt areas of "traditional state concern" except in limited circumstances.[19] The lower courts quickly followed this new direction and began remanding to state courts claims against HMOs based on quality as opposed to quantity of care. At the same time, while monetary recovery under ERISA is still limited to the value of contractual benefits, some federal courts have begun to interpret ERISA's due process and fiduciary requirements in a more patient-protective and egalitarian way.[20]

The only change between 1994 and 1995 was not doctrinal or legal, but rather broadly political: The Clinton and other federal health reform plans had been spectacularly defeated, and the media began intense exposure of the failings of managed care plans. The supposition is that the Supreme Court realized that its ERISA decisions had created a major regulatory vacuum that the federal government was unlikely to fill, that the relatively unregulated health care market was causing serious problems, and that therefore it was prudent to restore to the states some of their traditional power over health insurance and health care delivery. This move was made easier, of course, by the "states rights" or "devolution" approach popular in the Republican Congress, in the Clinton administration, and among the politically conservative justices.

Having apparently obtained some degree of restored regulatory authority, state governments find themselves thrust into the intense political-legal debate among the three perspectives on health law and policy. A few state intermediate courts of appeals have articulated an egalitarian social contract approach to ERISA and health plan liability, but the ultimate fate of these early doctrinal initiatives remains to be seen.[21] According to the *New York Times*, fifteen states enacted "comprehensive consumer rights laws" regarding managed care in 1997, and six others, including New York and California, had done so before 1997.[22]

Aside from considerable uncertainty about the continuing scope of ERISA preemption, the true significance of these laws lies in their frequently impenetrable details and in the balance of political forces that will surround their interpretation and implementation. For example, Texas's new managed care liability law, widely hailed as the first in the nation, while declaring that insurers and managed care entities have a duty to exercise "ordinary care when making health care treatment decisions and [are] liable for damages . . . proximately caused by . . . failure to exercise such ordinary care," defines the applicable standard as "that degree of care that a . . . managed care entity of ordinary prudence would use under the same or similar circumstances."[23] The Texas law thus straddles all three of the health law perspectives: egalitarian social contract to the extent that it creates a clearer duty to consumers, professional authority to the extent that it adopts a professional/industry standard of care, and market competition to the extent that it validates industry practices developed under conditions of market competition. Moreover, by structuring this new consumer protection as private tort lawsuits, the Texas statute is delegating to the courts the power to decide the concrete meaning of the mix of perspectives.

ACCESS AND FINANCING

The perspective of the professional authority model on access and financing is clear: Physicians should have control as to which patients to serve, and health care financing should maximize the independence and income of the medical profession.[24] To be sure, many physicians did provide charitable care, both as part of their membership on the medical staffs of charitable hospitals and because prior to the widespread growth of health insurance in the 1940s, many patients could only afford to pay reduced or "sliding scale" fees. But the amount and quality of this care was largely at the discretion of the individual physician, and the inferior standard of care at public hospitals serving the poor was well known.

Until the 1970s, American health law generally supported physician control over access and financing. With respect to access, a famous 1901 decision, *Hurley v. Eddingfield,* which has never been questioned by any other court, held that a physician had no legal duty to render even emergency care to a patient who had tendered his fee.[25] Interestingly, Dr. Eddingfield's lawyers, and the Indiana Supreme Court decision in his favor, did not refer to traditions of professional autonomy, perhaps because that also would have drawn attention to the professional ethic of serving those in need. Rather, the *Hurley* opinion equated the doctor's relations with prospective patients with the market freedom of any other seller of goods and services—without any intention, of course, of allowing the physician services market to move in the direction of salaried or prepaid care. Thus the market competition model was used to support and validate professional autonomy.

In the 1970s, American courts began to apply an egalitarian social contract approach to hospitals, requiring them to render at least "stabilizing" emergency care. In 1986, Congress created a social contract through the Emergency Medical Treatment and Active Labor Act (EMTALA), which requires all hospitals that accept Medicare funding (virtually all hospitals in the United States) to examine all patients who come to emergency rooms, not limited to those eligible for Medicare, to determine whether they have an emergency medical condition and, if they do, to provide appropriate stabilization or, in the case of childbirth, treatment. The statute authorizes the federal Department of Health and Human Services to impose civil penalties on physicians who fail to render the required services.[26]

With respect to financing, insurance contracts typically were written or interpreted in ways that required insurers to pay for virtually any service that physicians performed.[27] The enormous cost inflation that resulted from this provider-dominated financing led to attempted government regulation beginning in the 1970s, and to "private regulation" of the doctor-patient relationship by market forces beginning in the 1980s.

From the perspective of an egalitarian social contract, health insurance is seen as a way of assuring that the basic human need for health care is met with funds derived from the group or community. Once the decision is made to spread these costs as widely as possible, a government-mandated system—perhaps, but not necessarily, administered by government as well—is the most efficient solution. Compulsory universal or near-universal social insurance for health care minimizes the problem of free riders, people who try to avoid paying their share, and greatly reduces administrative costs, because there is little or no need for the marketing and underwriting (risk-selection) functions characteristic of private market-based health insurance. Other features include distribution of benefits according to health care needs rather than ability to pay (possibly qualified by cost-sharing requirements), and collective pricing, whereby everyone pays the same tax rate or premium, with lower-risk individuals effectively subsidizing higher-risk individuals.[28]

Every other industrialized nation has undertaken an approach involving some form of social insurance for health care. A limited version of it for the elderly, Medicare, was adopted in the United States in 1965 and is now subject to major reform bills in Congress that promise reduced provider payments and elimination of fee-for-service reimbursement in favor of managed care. National health insurance for the whole population has been prominently but unsuccessfully on the American political agenda at several points in our history, most recently in 1993–94.

The majority of Americans are covered by voluntary, tax-subsidized health insurance obtained through their employers or other voluntary groups such as unions and professional associations, although the number of Americans covered by private insurance has been falling since 1980.[29] From the 1940s until the mid–1960s this system functioned in many respects as voluntary, non-governmental social insurance through community rating practiced by Blue Cross and Blue Shield. Under community rating, Blue Cross set a single premium level for individuals and another for families, particularly for policies sold to groups of employees. No distinction was made between individuals or groups on the basis of their actual experience or predicted health needs. Where Blue Cross had a large share of the market, the result was similar to social insurance, because the community-rated premium assured more affordable coverage to higher-risk individuals and groups.

Not surprisingly, this voluntary system broke down. From the perspective of market competition, health insurance is not a social mechanism for paying for the health care needs of a population. Rather, insurance is seen as a transaction between two economically rational actors, an individual or group of aggregated individuals and an insurance company. What each of these actors is trying to achieve, according to this model, is maximum economic utility. The individual or group wants the lowest possible price for the desired insurance coverage. The insurance company wants the maximum profit. The logic of this perspective leads to market fragmentation, the exact opposite of social insurance's universalism. In the market, individuals want to associate themselves with the lowest possible risk group and exclude or jettison people with serious illnesses or other high-cost characteristics. Insurance companies want to segregate risk pools as much as possible so as to charge low competitive prices to healthy groups and high, actuarially appropriate premiums to people with high-cost characteristics.[30]

The dynamics predicted by the market model did in fact take place, because American law and social values allowed and indeed encouraged them to do so. In the 1940s and thereafter, commercial health insurers charged each employee group according to its actual or predicted experience. As the commercial insurers began to pick off the low-risk employee groups, Blue Cross's community rating became increasingly impractical, and Blue Cross also moved to experience rating, effectively segregating individual policyholders in a high-risk, high-cost segment of the market. This kind of market phenomenon is so familiar to Americans that to many of us it must appear to be just the way the world works and not caused by American law and values. Yet in nations with strong traditions of universal health insurance, such as Canada, Great Britain, and the Scandinavian countries, market competition of this sort is regarded as antisocial and threatening to individual security.[31]

Under experience rating, access to affordable health insurance in the United States was linked to the individual's ability to join a large group of low-risk employees. Once in such a group and "entitled" to health benefits, most people felt securely protected not only against the risk of unusually large or catastrophic costs but also against many or most of the routine costs of health care. The implicit American social contract of the 1950s and 1960s, at least for employees of large, prosperous corporations, was that if the employee was a dedicated, conscientious worker, he or she could expect in return stable long-term employment, rising wages, and secure pension and health benefits. Of course, this system did not include millions of employees of smaller companies, agricultural and domestic workers (composed predominantly of African Americans,

Mexican Americans, and other minority groups in many parts of the United States), the unemployed, and many others.

The striking development of the 1980s and 1990s has been the collapse of this implicit social contract for previously favored blue-collar and white-collar workers, and even for professional and managerial employees. The causes of this phenomenon are complex and include remarkable developments in technology and global market competition. The political, social, and legal values of individual nations also have played a major role in influencing policy and legal responses to these forces.[32]

The deep shift in American health law to a market competition approach to financing was marked by *McGann v. H & H Music Co.* (1991).[33] John McGann, an employee of H & H Music, discovered that he was afflicted with AIDS in December 1987 and soon submitted his first claims for reimbursement under H & H Music's group medical plan, which provided for lifetime medical benefits of up to $1 million to all employees. In July 1988, H & H Music informed its employees that, effective August 1, changes would be made in their medical coverage. These changes included a $5,000 lifetime cap on benefits payable for AIDS-related claims. No limitation was placed on any other catastrophic illness. H & H Music also became self-insured under the new plan, thereby insulating itself under ERISA from any state law requiring benefits or prohibiting discrimination in benefits.

McGann sued H & H Music under section 510 of ERISA, claiming that the provision limiting coverage for AIDS-related expenses was directed specifically at him in retaliation for exercising his rights under the medical plan, and for the purpose of interfering with his rights under the plan. The company conceded that the benefit reduction was prompted by the knowledge of McGann's illness and that McGann was the only beneficiary then known to have AIDS, but the district court ruled for the company on the grounds that the employer had an absolute right to alter the terms of the plan regardless of its intent in making the alterations. The Fifth Circuit affirmed, holding that while ERISA protected beneficiaries' rights under the plan, once the employer had changed the plan in a procedurally valid manner, McGann no longer had any rights to benefits other than those specified in the revised plan.

The *McGann* case generated passionate criticism. A letter to the Solicitor General, the American Association of Retired Persons, the American Hospital Association, the American Medical Association, the National Commission on AIDS, the National Governors' Association, and the United States Conference of Mayors characterized the Fifth

Circuit's decision as an "outrage" that "will add to the ranks of the unin-sured." Indeed, in the wake of the *McGann* decision, many health plans did reduce or eliminate AIDS coverage.[34]

The Fifth Circuit in *McGann* and other circuits in other cases justified their decisions on an explicitly market-based vision of ERISA. ERISA was said to stand for the proposition that benefit termination decisions are most "appropriately influenced by forces in the marketplace and, when appropriate, by federal legislation." But in what sense was the deci-sion by H & H Music to cap AIDS benefits a market decision? The bar-gaining process over benefits is almost always between insurance compa-nies or brokers and the employer. Based on the opinion's account, we do not know how much bargaining actually took place or which party took the initiative to raise what issues. Was the employer or the insurance company the first to target employees with AIDS as "the problem?" Was there an actuarial basis for this focus, as compared to other conditions or services that might contribute as much as or more to increased costs? Does it affect our sense of the adequacy of this market that employees, much less employees with AIDS, do not appear to have been represented in the bargaining? Even if we characterize AIDS caps as market decisions, do they have significant external effects that ought to be regulated, such as a shifting of costs to public programs, premature disability, and death?

From the perspective of market competition, differential treatment of persons with AIDS or HIV positive status is "fair discrimination." If health insurance is an aggregation of individual deals, with each pur-chaser seeking to pay only for his "own" and similar risks, then insurers must charge higher premiums to individuals with higher risk of illness, injury, or death. Just as it may seem reasonable to charge higher life and health insurance premiums on the basis of age, use of tobacco, and high-risk occupations, why is it not reasonable to test for HIV status and charge higher premiums or deny insurance to HIV-positive people, who have a demonstrably higher risk of illness and death than persons who are not HIV-positive?[35]

One response to this question, or at least a direction for discussion, is that as a society we do not treat all statistically discernible increased risks the same. "Even the American Academy of Actuaries (AAA) . . . [declared in] a 1986 report . . . that 'laws, regulations, and public opin-ion all constrain risk classification systems within the broad guidelines of social acceptability.'"[36] Indeed, in a shift to the egalitarian social contract model, the federal Americans With Disabilities Act of 1990 (ADA), which had not been enacted when the events in *McGann* occurred, and interpretive guidelines issued by the Equal Employment Opportunity Commission (EEOC), now require employers to justify diagnosis-specific benefit limitations with actuarial data or other bona fide business reasons.[37]

While the concept of fair discrimination may justify, at least within the market perspective, testing health insurance applicants for HIV status, it does not justify what happened to McGann. Indeed, if insurance companies may weed out high-risk individuals before they gain entrance to the standard risk pool, does not fairness require that standard-risk individuals who gain entrance to the insured pool not be weeded out after their risk has materialized? Is not the whole point of the insurance bargain that a standard-risk individual is insured if the (unlikely) risk does occur?

Underwriting and market theory, as usually presented, do not address the question of the length of time of the insurance contract, or that insurers typically reserve the right to amend the policy at any time, or that employers can terminate one contract and begin another and thereby knowingly de-select the risks that have materialized. There is at least some middle ground between "lifetime vesting" of benefits once illness has been diagnosed and plenary discretion to cut off or limit benefits to any category of insured at any time. For example, Congressman William Hughes's proposed Group Health Plan Nondiscrimination Act would prohibit reduction in benefits on the basis of particular diseases or medical conditions for insured people who are undergoing treatment for such conditions and who have filed claims based on such treatment. Under this bill, differential lifetime benefits could not be based on diseases or conditions unless the plan was the product of collective bargaining or the plan could prove that such differentials were needed to enable the plan to continue.[38]

Statutes such as EMTALA, the ADA, and the proposed Group Health Plan Nondiscrimination Act, while providing some limited access and financing to some of the population, remain squarely within the "modestly egalitarian" mode and do not purport to secure universal entitlement to health care. The failure to enact any federal health reform plan in 1994, the current political preoccupation with balancing the federal budget, the achievement of at least temporary health care cost containment through market-based managed care, the erosion of traditional public and charitable hospitals, and the erosion of Medicaid, together with the strong political tide against equality and redistribution, all suggest that tens of millions of Americans will remain without health insurance and adequate access to care, and that the market competition model of health law and policy will remain the dominant though not the only perspective.

PROSPECTS FOR THE FUTURE

American health care delivery has undergone unprecedented change in the past ten years. The medical profession, which consolidated its power over licensing, medical education, hospitals, and health care financing almost a century ago, and long-established, influential hospitals have been swept up in an entrepreneurial convulsion. The nature of the doctor-patient relationship and concepts of quality of care built up over decades, if not longer, are being profoundly challenged. The American system of social insurance and redistribution, always weaker than that of other industrialized nations, is being reduced and even dismantled.

Not surprisingly, the perspectives that gave at least some coherence to health law and policy are in disarray. The model of professional authority was undermined by its own greed and irresponsibility; employers, government, and citizens will no longer pay for sharply increasing costs and ineffective quality assurance. The model of modest egalitarianism could not mobilize the citizenry to overcome entrenched interests or impose on those interests the discipline needed to control costs and achieve quality. The model of market competition has indeed been able to discipline physicians and hospitals (to what ends?) but not its own entrepreneurs; the vision of socially desirable competition managed by law has not come about, in part because the existing market and its law have generated powerful and wealthy entities who are strong enough to resist socially desirable regulation.

Consider the story about the employee returning from abroad at the beginning of this chapter, which is drawn from an actual case, *Shea v. Esensten* (1997).[39] From the perspective of professional authority, the HMO's corruption of the physician's judgment with financial incentives to deny care is outrageous and illegitimate, albeit a pact that the doctor "agreed to" (but how voluntarily?). But the professional model also holds that the doctor has no duty to tell the patient anything except as required by professional custom, which requires little if any disclosure.[40]

If this case were being tried under state tort law, a court might adopt the egalitarian social contract perspective, go beyond "industry custom" (which, because financial incentive systems are regarded as proprietary information, probably could not even be ascertained), and hold the

HMO liable for "medically inappropriate decisions [that] result from defects in the design or implementation of cost containment mechanisms."[41] The patient would still have to convince the trier of fact that the HMO's financial incentives were defective, which raises all the problems of defining a standard of care. Nevertheless, it seems likely that a system that foreseeably leads physicians to take serious risks with their patients' lives by denying referrals to specialists would be considered defective. Whether liability based on this standard would lead to changes in the industry raises all the questions discussed above in connection with *The T. J. Hooper* and *Gonzales.*

However, the Eighth Circuit ruled in *Shea* that ERISA preempted state law claims regarding HMO financial incentives, because such incentives are part of plan administration as opposed to the practice of medicine. The issue of whether, and under what circumstances, financial incentives and other internal HMO arrangements are part of an ERISA plan is a cutting-edge issue in health law, and the ultimate resolution could be different than the one reached in *Shea.*[42] Be that as it may, the court could have interpreted ERISA's "fiduciary duty" along the lines of the social contract "defective" standard set out above, but it did not.

Instead, it adopted a position much closer to the market competition perspective: The HMO had a duty to disclose to the patient the existence and nature of the financial incentives. To be sure, such disclosure may be helpful in particular cases, including this one, where the patient apparently had the funds, knowledge, and inclination to seek out a specialist. But in the great majority of cases, disclosure might be worse than useless. If the disclosure was simply a hard-to-understand paragraph buried in a packet of brochures and forms, it would function, as do the cigarette warning labels, as the basis for an argument that the patient had consented to this type of care. Finally, even if an HMO were found liable under some interpretation of fiduciary duty, ERISA still does not provide compensatory or punitive damages. Congress clearly could amend ERISA to establish both a standard of care and damages, but the market has already generated powerful interests that will resolutely oppose any such development.

As an intellectual matter, the way forward is clear: The three perspectives need to be integrated constructively. Managed competition seems to be an important tool for realizing quality, accountability to consumers, and careful trade-offs in the face of limited resources. At the same time, egalitarianism and socially desirable market competition are desperately interdependent; only an educated citizenry with adequate purchasing power (created in part by subsidies generated by a progressive tax system), coupled with a government strongly committed to the general welfare, can make this kind of competition work. In turn, professional autonomy is needed to help maintain the human and individualized dimensions of health care delivery and to serve as a check on entrepreneurial and bureaucratic tendencies. Articulating such integration is perhaps a useful first step. Beyond that, creating the social and political conditions in which this type of synthesis could emerge is the current challenge and opportunity.

NOTES

I wish to thank Ann E. Freedman for very helpful comments. Portions of this chapter are drawn from Rand E. Rosenblatt, Sylvia A. Law, and Sara Rosenbaum, *Law and the American Health Care System* (New York: Foundation Press, 1997).

1. See *Campbell v. Mincey,* 413 F.Supp. 16 (N.D. Miss. 1975); *Burditt v. United States Dept. of Health and Human Services,* 934 F.2d 1362 (5th Cir. 1991), enforcing the Emergency Medical Treatment and Active Labor Act of 1986 (EMTALA), 42 U.S.C. § 1395dd.

2. See Tom Redburn, "Conflict Is Seen Between Regions in Health Care," *New York Times,* November 5, 1993, A1; see also Rachel Kreier, "State Boundaries on Health Opposed," *New York Times,* March 20, 1994, section 13LI, 1; Mark A. Peterson, *Health Care into the Next Century,* 22 Journal of Health Politics, Policy, and Law 291 (1997).

3. See R. H. Tawney, *Religion and the Rise of Capitalism* (Pelican, 1938 [1926]), 36–39 passim; Karl Polanyi, *The Great Transformation* (Beacon, 1957 [1944]).

4. See Gary T. Schwartz, *The Beginning and the Possible End of the Rise of Modern American Tort Law,* 26 Georgia Law Review 601 (1992); Rand E. Rosenblatt, "Social Duties and the Problem of Rights in the American Welfare State," in *The Politics of Law: A Progressive Critique,* ed. David Kairys (New York: Pantheon, 1990), 94–96, 104–10.

5. See Alain C. Enthoven, *Health Plan* (Reading, MA: Addison-Wesley, 1980); Mark A. Hall and Gerard F. Anderson, *Health Insurers' Assessment of Medical Necessity,* 140 University of Pennsylvania Law Review 1637

(1992); Clark C. Havighurst, *Altering the Applicable Standard of Care,* 49 Law and Contemporary Problems 265 (Spring 1986); *Corcoran v. United Healthcare, Inc.,* 965 F.2d 1321 (5th Cir. 1992), cert. denied, 506 U.S. 1033 (1992); *Visconti v. U.S. Healthcare,* 857 F.Supp. 1097 (E.D. Pa. 1994), rev'd on other grounds sub nom. *Dukes v. U.S. Healthcare, Inc.,* 57 F.3d 350 (3d Cir. 1995). For critical discussion of this model, see Rand E. Rosenblatt, *Health Care, Markets, and Democratic Values,* 34 Vanderbilt Law Review 1067 (1981); David M. Frankford, *Privatizing Health Care: Economic Magic to Cure Legal Medicine,* 66 Southern California Law Review 1 (1992).

6. On physician response to medical error, see Charles Bosk, *Forgive and Remember: Managing Medical Failure* (Chicago: University of Chicago Press, 1979). On physician commitment to patient well-being and the tensions with respect to that goal, see Rand E. Rosenblatt, *Medicaid Primary Care Case Management, the Doctor-Patient Relationship, and the Politics of Privatization,* 36 Case Western Reserve Law Review 915, 923–930 (1985–86).

7. See John Wennberg, "Dealing with Medical Practice Variations: A Proposal for Action," *Health Affairs* 3 (Summer 1984): 6.

8. See *United Blood Services v. Quintana,* 827 P.2d 509 (Colo. 1992).

9. *The T. J. Hooper,* 60 F.2d 737, 740 (2d Cir. 1932), ruling that industry custom or lack thereof cannot justify a tugboat's failure to use radio weather reports to avoid a dangerous storm. See also *United Blood Services v. Quintana,* 827 P.2d 509 (Colo. 1992).

10. *Gonzales v. Nork* (Cal. Sup. Ct., Sacramento Cty., no. 228566, November 19, 1973; hereafter cited as *Gonzales*). The remarkable 130-page trial court opinion by Judge B. Abbott Goldberg was not published in the judicial reporters. Excerpts are printed as an appendix in Sylvia Law and Steve Polan, *Pain and Profit: The Politics of Malpractice* (New York: Harper & Row, 1978), 215–45. Appellate opinions can be found at 573 P.2d 458 (Cal. 1978) and 131 Cal. Rptr. 717 (Cal. App. 1976). The trial court's ruling on the deficiency of the industry standards is in Law and Polan, *Pain and Profit,* 243, 244.

11. See Walt Bogdanich, "Prized by Hospitals, Accreditation Hides Perils Patients Face," *Wall Street Journal,* October 12, 1988, 6; Walt Bogdanich, *The Great White Lie: How America's Hospitals Betray Our Trust and Endanger Our Lives* (New York: Simon & Schuster, 1991) 215–17, passim.

12. See Clark C. Havighurst, *Altering the Applicable Standard of Care,* 49 Law and Contemporary Problems 265 (Spring 1986); Richard Epstein,

Medical Malpractice: The Case for Contract, 1976 American Bar Foundation Research Journal 87; Randall Bovbjerg, *The Medical Malpractice Standard of Care: HMOs and Customary Practice,* 1975 Duke Law Journal 1375.

13. David M. Eddy, "Rationing Resources While Improving Quality: How to Get More for Less," 272 *JAMA* 817, 820 (1994).

14. Ibid., 823.

15. On socially desirable competition, see Alain C. Enthoven, *Health Plan* (Reading, MA: Addison-Wesley, 1980), 126; Alain C. Enthoven, "The History and Principles of Managed Competition," *Health Affairs* 12 (supplement, 1993): 24, 29, describing the "rules of competition."

16. Federal and state HMO legislation does require HMOs to offer variously defined benefits, but these are usually stated so generally as not to constrain HMOs' allocation of resources to profits or services. Some state regulations and government and private payers require HMOs to have certain staffing levels and facilities, and this operates as a modest constraint on profits. Until very recently, medical malpractice law has not served as much of a deterrent, because of the general reasons discussed above and ERISA preemption discussed below.

17. See George Anders, *Health Against Wealth* (Boston: Houghton Mifflin, 1996) 55–73, detailing HMO CEO annual compensation of $5 million to $20 million; Jeanne Kassler, M.D., *Bitter Medicine: Greed and Chaos in American Health Care* (New York: Birch Lane Press, 1994), xi–xii, 63–92, which tells how the chairman of the Hospital Corporation of America received income and stock options worth $127 million in 1992.

18. See *Kuhl v. Lincoln National Health Plan,* 999 F.2d 298 (8th Cir. 1993), cert. denied, 114 S.Ct. 694 (1994); *Shea v. Esensten,* 107 F.3d 625 (8th Cir. 1997); *Visconti v. U.S. Healthcare,* 857 F. Supp. 1097 (E.D. Pa. 1994), rev'd on other grounds sub nom.; *Dukes v. U.S. Healthcare, Inc.,* 57 F.3d 350 (3d Cir. 1995); *Kearney v. U.S. Healthcare, Inc.,* 859 F.Supp. 182 (E.D. Pa. 1994). ERISA does provide for injunctive relief and attorney's fees.

19. *New York State Conference of Blue Cross and Blue Shield Plans v. Travelers Ins. Co.,* 514 U.S. 645 (1995).

20. On the quality-quantity distinction, see *Dukes v. U.S. Healthcare, Inc.,* 57 F.3d 350 (3d Cir. 1995), and other cases discussed in Rosenblatt, Law, and Rosenbaum, *Law and the American Health Care System,* 1019–34. On trends in duties under ERISA, see *Shea v. Esensten,* 107 F.3d 625 (8th Cir. 1997), holding that the HMO has a fiduciary duty under ERISA to disclose its financial incentives to providers, but not ruling and remanding

on important remedies issues; *Crocco v. Xerox Corp.*, 956 F.Supp. 129 (D. Conn. 1997), holding that where a plan's contract with a utilization review company specifies that the contractor's coverage decisions are advisory only, the plan administrator owes fiduciary duty to the enrollee to make an independent judgment regarding coverage.

21. See *Pappas v. Asbel*, 675 A.2d 711 (Pa. Super. 1996); *Frappier v. Wishnov*, 678 So.2d 884 (Fla. App. 1996).

22. Milt Freudenheim, "Pioneering State for Managed Care Fights for Change: California Thinks Again," *New York Times*, July 14, 1997, A1, D8.

23. Senate Bill 386, amending Title 4, Texas Civil Practice and Remedies Code, by adding chapter 88, §§ 88.002(A), 88.001(10).

24. With respect to access, the American Medical Association's Principles of Medical Ethics have long asserted that "except in emergencies, [physicians shall] be free to choose whom to serve" (American Medical Association, Council on Ethical and Judicial Affairs, *Code of Medical Ethics* [1994], xiv). Prior to 1957, the AMA principles did contain ethical duties and statements in favor of charitable care, but these were not legally enforceable and were eliminated. See Rand E. Rosenblatt, *Medicaid Primary Care Case Management*, 915, 925 n.37.

25. *Hurley v. Eddingfield*, 59 N.E. 1058 (Ind. 1901). Even cases that held that hospitals had a duty to render emergency care did not extend that duty to on-call physicians. See *Thompson v. Sun City Community Hospital*, 688 P.2d 605 (Ariz. 1984).

26. See Emergency Medical Treatment and Active Labor Act, 42 U.S.C. § 1395; *Burditt v. United States Department of Health and Human Services*, 934 F.2d 1362 (5th Cir. 1991).

27. See *Van Vactor v. Blue Cross Association*, 365 N.E. 2d 638 (Ill. App. Ct. 1977).

28. See Deborah A. Stone, *The Struggle for the Soul of Health Insurance*, 18 Journal of Health Politics, Policy, and Law 287 (1993).

29. In 1994, 69.2 percent of the population (including the elderly) had private insurance, and 60.8 percent of the non-elderly population had insurance based on employment (Health Insurance Association of America, *Source Book of Health Insurance Data 1995* (1996), 17 (figure 2.1).

30. See Mark V. Pauly, "Risk Variation and Fallback Insurers in Universal Coverage Insurance Plans," *Inquiry* 29 (1992): 137, explaining and justifying this position; David M. Frankford, *Neoclassical Health Economics and the Debate over National Health Insurance: The Power of Abstraction*, 18 Legal and Social Inquiry 351, 366–81 (1993); Stone, *The Struggle for*

the Soul of Health Insurance, 292–308, explaining and criticizing this position).

31. See Maurizio Ferrera, *The Rise and Fall of Democratic Universalism: Health Care Reform in Italy, 1978–1994,* 20 Journal of Health Politics, Policy, and Law 275, 300 (1995).

32. See Lester C. Thurow, *The Future of Capitalism* (New York: W. Morrow, 1996), 1–19, 27–28, passim; Donald L. Barlett and James B. Steele, *America: What Went Wrong?* (Kansas City: Andrews & McNeel, 1992).

33. *McGann v. H & H Music Co.,* 946 F.2d 401 (5th Cir. 1991), cert. denied, 506 U.S. 981 (1992).

34. See Kathlynn L. Butler, *Comment: Securing Employee Health Benefits Through ERISA and the ADA,* 42 Emory Law Journal 1197, 1230, n.215 (1993), regarding the joint letter; Milt Freudenheim, "Patients Cite Bias in AIDS Coverage by Health Plans," *New York Times,* June 1, 1993, A1, D2.

35. Karen A. Clifford and Russel P. Iuculano, *Commentary: AIDS and Insurance: The Rationale for AIDS-related Testing,* 100 Harvard Law Review 1806, 1807, 1808, 1810, 1814–15 (1987).

36. Benjamin Schatz, *Commentary: The AIDS Insurance Crisis: Underwriting or Overreaching?* 100 Harvard Law Review 1782, 1792, 1794 (1987). See also Deborah A. Stone, *The Rhetoric of Insurance Law: The Debate over AIDS Testing,* 15 Law and Social Inquiry 385 (1990), brilliantly placing the rhetoric and assumptions of Clifford and Iuculano, and Schatz, in the wider context of the meaning of insurance.

37. Americans With Disabilities Act, 42 U.S.C. §§ 12101–213. Provisions relevant to discrimination in insurance both as a fringe benefit of employment and as a "public accommodation" include sections 12112 (defining "discrimination") and 12201 (setting forth permitted risk selection practices but prohibiting use of such practices as a "subterfuge" to evade the purposes of the act). Interpretive guidelines issued by the EEOC can be found at 1993 Daily Labor Report (BNA) 109 d22 (June 9, 1993).

38. The Hughes bill is excerpted and discussed in Butler, *Securing Employee Health Benefits Through ERISA and the ADA* 1231–35, nn.217–33. See also Alan I. Widiss and Larry Gostin, *What's Wrong with the ERISA 'Vacuum'? The Case Against Unrestricted Freedom for Employers to Terminate Employee Health Care Plans,* 41 Drake Law Review 635, 645–54 (1992), analyzing possible legislative responses to *McGann.*

39. *Shea v. Esensten,* 107 F.3d 625 (8th Cir. 1997).

40. See *Varol v. Blue Cross and Blue Shield of Michigan,* 708 F. Supp. 826 (E.D. Mich. 1989), in which psychiatrists unsuccessfully asserted that

their agreement to participate in managed mental health services plan was not knowing or voluntary. Regarding professional norms of disclosure, see *Canterbury v. Spence,* 464 F.2d 772 (D.C. Cir. 1972); Jay Katz, M.D., *The Silent World of Doctor and Patient* (New York: The Free Press, 1984), 1.

41. *Wickline v. State of California,* 239 Cal. Rptr. 810, 819 (Cal. App. 1986), petition for review dismissed, 741 P.2d 613 (Cal. 1987).

42. See *Dukes v. U.S. Healthcare, Inc.,* 57 F.3d 350, 359 (3d Cir. 1995); *Law and the American Health Care System,* 1997 Supplement, "Note: What Is a 'Plan'? Revisited"; *American Drug Stores v. Harvard Pilgrim Health Care,* 1997 Westlaw 528087 (D. Mass, August 15, 1997).

7 GERALD TORRES

ENVIRONMENTAL LAW

IT would not be an exaggeration to say that now we are all environmentalists to some degree. A poll taken in 1989 revealed a commitment of some 80 percent of the population to the proposition that the environment ought to be protected regardless of cost. But if there is such a widespread commitment to environmental values, how do we explain or understand the rise of the essentially anti-environmentalist "wise use" movement, or the judicial limitations on environmental regulations through parsimonious readings of legislative intent, or the closing of the courthouse door to public litigants?[1]

The apparently prevalent support for environmental values produces curious results when we actually get down to cases. Respect for wilderness is tempered by a broad conception of property rights; pollution control is widely supported except when it frustrates economic activity or a development scheme. One can also see such contradictions embedded in our national self-conception, which includes the myth of the rugged individual side by side with our collective pride in the monumental grandeur of our wilderness lands. Environmental law reflects these tensions, and in recent years its protective regulatory impulses have been locked in a titanic struggle with advocates of deregulation, smaller government, revitalized states rights, and the free market.

To understand fully the modern law governing environmental pollution and the regulation of the risks associated with it, or the modern law related to resource use and conservation, one first has to understand property rights and the power of the state to regulate those rights, the law regulating governmental action, and the law of torts, especially the law of nuisance. Environmental law emerged as a field in the late 1960s and early 1970s. Yet even a brief investigation reveals that the issues, analyses, and principles that continue to guide this area of the law have deep roots in our jurisprudence. Thus, anyone who has turned to this chapter to understand the politics embedded in what has come to be known as environmental law should recognize many of the themes that are raised in the chapters on property, torts, and takings and should realize that the focus cannot be limited to legal doctrine or law but must include political science, history, science, economics, and philosophy as well.[2] The development of law in this area mirrors the ideological structure that guides most of our law, and the rhetoric of environmentalism has often masked the many strategic and tactical compromises that mark the major environmental statutes and decisions.[3]

THE EVOLUTION OF MODERN ENVIRONMENTAL LAW

Most conventional accounts root modern environmentalism in the progressive conservation movement of the late nineteenth and early twentieth centuries. While sharing a common heritage, the aims of the modern environmental movement differ significantly from those of the progressive conservation movement. Where the primary policy focus of progressive conservationism was on the need to create a sphere of scientific expertise for policy making free from politics and on the need for the efficient use of natural resources, the modern environmental movement is principally concerned with defending and preserving those physical amenities, such as clean air and water, thought to be essential for a high quality of life. Despite the different orientation toward both democratic participation and regulation for the protection of environmental quality, several elements of the conservation movement were critical to the evolution of modern environmental law.

The crucial first element was the incorporation of "scientific management" criteria into the regulation of resource use. Scientific management advocates emphasized the need to develop a corps of technically trained professionals to properly manage resource use. In the adoption of these criteria, perhaps most important was the advocacy of multiple use-sustained yield principles in forestry, and multiple-purpose river development. These principles were combined with the idea that the public lands should be efficiently managed while keeping the land available for as many uses as were deemed appropriate and for ensuring the survivability of renewable public resources. The mining laws, focusing as they did on the efficient production of a nonrenewable resource, were, of course, a distinct exception to these ideas. Their evolutions through the various rights of way laws designed to facilitate mineral exploration remain impediments to current roadless forest policy. In addition to the excep-

tions of the mining law, the various reclamation acts, which were aimed
at encouraging small farming by bringing water to the arid west, failed to
fulfill their democratic functions or their development goals and stand in
direct contradiction with dominant environmentalist values. The twin
ideals of efficiency as the lodestar of policy and multiple use–multiple
users as both a scientific principle and a technique for mediating conflict
continue to be important in the construction of resource and environmental policy.[4]

Second, the division of resource responsibility and the resultant conflict between the Department of the Interior and the Department of
Agriculture over federal land policy presaged the kinds of inside-the-
government intrigues that continue to bedevil the crafting of coherent
environmental policy across a range of issues. The famous battles
between Richard Ballinger and Gifford Pinchot, pitting as they did a representative of the preservationist camp with one of the fathers of scientific management, gave lie to the idea of policy formulation removed
from politics.[5] That struggle, while historically complicated, also mirrors
the continuing contention between those two aspects of the environmental movement.

Part of what the conventional telling of the early story reveals is the
capture of the regulatory process by the powerful interests that the
process was supposed to regulate. The classic example in the environmental context is the roles of both the Forest Service and the Bureau of
Land Management in the destruction of forest and rangeland. Each
agency was supposed to manage the lands under its jurisdiction with the
goal of achieving efficient resource use consistent with preservation or
recreational values and environmental quality. Yet the resource use mandate has swamped all else and has led the agencies to view the timber and
cattle industries as their first priorities. Capture of agencies by their
"clientele" is the typical, if not completely accurate, story of the evolution
of the progressive conservation movement, and it remains one of the
principal grounds for current struggles over the environment.

Current opponents of environmental regulation frequently claim, for
example, that the Environmental Protection Agency has been taken over
by environmentalists to the detriment of sound policy development.
These divisions continue to be fought out in resource, lands, and forest
policy and in the regulation of pesticides and other "economic poisons,"
as pesticides were characterized in the early statutes. Yet one of the consequences of regulation is that it ultimately mobilizes the targets of regulation. Even if agencies are not captured by the regulated parties, virtually

every regulation precipitates a legal challenge. Given enough political clout, these interests can cause an agency to redirect its focus. In some ways, this is the danger of turning to law. It permits the temporary winners to sit back and assume victory when what is really needed is continued political action.

Yet despite the dominance of this lineage, debates over resource use and what would come to be called "environmental amenities" was not completely within the framework of scientific management. A prominent counterpoint to the idea of expertise as the sole basis for policy formulation was found in the emergence of the national parks movement and in environmental pioneers such as John Muir.[6] Their vision of nature as valuable for its own sake was at odds with dominant policy makers but continues to inform significant segments of the environmental movement today. Similarly, although much later, Aldo Leopold promoted the idea of ecological regulation with the concept of biotic communities, localized but deeply integrated natural systems. He advocated the protection of these communities based upon a land ethic, which he defined as the set of attitudes and obligations that "tend to preserve the integrity, stability, and beauty of the biotic community."[7] The notions of interconnectedness and interdependencies of natural systems inform regulatory approaches to species protection and to the current enforcement strategies in pollution prevention.

The modern law of environmental protection sprang from this conflicting beginning. Yet the environmental movement and environmental law are not just the precipitate of debates over resource use filtered through the emerging regulatory state of the New Deal. The tangled threads that came together in the 1960s reflected the earlier debates, but also reflected insights from the new science of ecology and popular concern with the effects of industrial production on the quality of human life. In many ways the wealth of post–World War II America created the circumstances that allowed the average person to be concerned with environmental amenities. Samuel Hays documents what he calls the postwar "rediscovery of the countryside."[8] According to Hays, the increased demand for environmental quality led to conflicts with urban forces that had conventionally viewed the countryside as land nobody wanted and thus suitable for the effluvia of urban life. In fact, the vast expansion of the economy after the war produced a demand for a better quality of life and led to the increased use of petrochemical-based fertilizers and pesticides. The increased use of chemicals in agriculture after World War II promised the "green revolution" and simultaneously precipitated the fear of environmental contamination that was captured in Rachel Carson's environmental classic, *Silent Spring*. This demand for a better environment, although it was not called that at the time, precipitated many of the local political struggles that came together as the environmental movement in the late 1960s and 1970s.

The welter of local disputes was driven initially not by top-down federal regulations, but by the application of local law. The law of pollution control certainly predates the New Deal debates and has its roots in early statutes such as the Rivers and Harbors Act and in common law tort doctrine, primarily but not exclusively that governing nuisance. Nuisance law is part of the law governing the relations between landowners. The common law of nuisance protects owners or occupiers of land from the intentional conduct of other landowners that is unreasonable and causes substantial harm to the use and enjoyment of real property. This rather abstract construction has been the basis for a variety of claims and has had a substantial impact on the evolution of many industries. It has been used to restrain uses of property that produce smoke, noise, odor, or vibration, or any other conduct that substantially interferes with a property owner's quiet enjoyment of the land.

The idea of quiet enjoyment is a term of art that legal writers include in the basic bundle of rights that any property owner has in equal measure with every other. This, of course, produces the contradiction that any action that stops me from doing what I want to do on my property is, in some way, an interference with *my* right of quiet enjoyment of my property. This conflict is mediated by the idea that the only uses that will be prohibited will be those that are unreasonable and which substantially interfere with the use another landowner wants to make of her property. Yet this again is merely an abstraction that has taken on concrete expression in a dizzying array of cases ranging from the regulation of odors arising from a feedlot, to run off from sewage treatment plants and sanitary landfills, to contamination from a lead smelter, and virtually everything in between. In a classic teaching case that illustrates the conflicts over remedies, the court found that an injunction to stop a smelter would not be an appropriate remedy, even though continuing to allow the activity rendered the plaintiffs' land worthless.[9] The smoke and fumes were destroying the timber on neighboring lands, a classic nuisance, but the court reasoned that to enjoin the smelter would be to drive it and all its economic activity out of the state, a position the court could avoid through the sound exercise of its discretion. Damages would be enough. Only time and changes in popular attitudes would ultimately change the calculus that courts applied.[10]

The private law doctrine of nuisance also allowed the development of public law rationales for the regulation of specific land uses in advance of an actual conflict between private landowners. As this book's discussion of takings law indicates (see chapter 27), the common law of nuisance continues to have a prominent role in legal thinking about the legitimate range of government power to control private land use decisions.[11] But in addition to providing a basis for the rational development of land use plans, nuisance law also allowed judges to fashion remedies for ameliorating specific harms short of prohibiting the offending behavior. Courts were able to do this by pointing to examples of similar private activity that does not produce the complained of harm and requiring the adoption of similar techniques. In the statutory context this approach is reflected in the requirement that industries adopt the best available pollution control technology. That statutory requirement has clear common law roots.

DEBATES INSIDE THE ENVIRONMENTAL MOVEMENT

Putting aside the critiques raised by opponents of environmentalism, there are many contending impulses in both the law and the social movement. These contradictory pressures are understandable when seen as expressions of the historic evolution of environmentalism as both a political and a legal movement.

One of the principal conflicts reflects differences in substantive preferences as between conservationists and preservationists. An example of this conflict arose over the issue of public land management. The conservationist wing of the environmental movement was deeply skeptical of the natural wildland values advanced by some. To them the priority of natural values, whether as to land or rivers, smacked of a desire to freeze the world as it is rather than to view all resources as ultimately available for use if wisely managed.

The other conspicuous conflict is that between devotees of scientific policy making and those who prefer to rely on the incremental and piecemeal evolution of policy wrought through the case-by-case ordering dictated by private litigation based upon common law rights. This is a false dichotomy, though, because the conflict is really about nothing more than where politics will intervene in the crafting of environmental policy. These conflicts might be understood within the context of a commitment to localism and within an ecological framework that posits the interconnectedness of natural systems and the corresponding connectedness of legal doctrine and regulatory systems. The popular admonition "think globally and act locally" masks conflicts between regions, media, and interests.

The Environmental Protection Agency (EPA) was created during the Nixon administration in response to vast public pressure for the federal government to take leadership in the area of environmental protection.[12] The agency was formed through the agglomeration of a variety of programs taken from other departments and placed under one administration. One of the upshots of this genesis was to leave the agency responsible to a vast number of congressional committees, each of which could exercise its oversight function on the agency. Not only did this make the agency answer to many masters, but it also made it subject to varieties of parochial legislative concerns. The concern over agency capture that has dominated much of the debate over bureaucratic governance and that animated the conventional story of progressive conservationism is best understood in the context of the EPA as capture of the congressional subcommittee to whom the EPA must answer. The agency has labored against this parochialism in an effort to construct a coherent enforcement strategy consistent with the legislative mandates under which it functions. Yet the evolution of modern federal environmental law can be understood from the perspective of this legislative structure and as a response to popular political demands for national action on the environment.

The federal structure of environmental management reflects the historic conflicts between preservationists and conservationists and attempts to mediate regional difference by yielding regulatory power to the states through a process of delegation of federal authority. The federal pollution control statutes typically create a national floor for various pollutants in various media below which states may not fall, so that states may not compete for business by putting their citizens at too great an environmental risk.[13] In the pollution and toxin control contexts, the regulatory benchmark has been the protection of human health. Yet even here there have been traditional exceptions explained by the desire to balance health benefits with economic costs. This is true even in those statutes that are apparently cost insensitive. The regulation of worker safety, if it can be understood as a subspecies of environmental protection, is one example where courts have built in cost-benefit calculations where the statute does not clearly require it. In the regulation of toxins, for example, there is a clear division between those toxins that are merely the residue of production processes and those that are produced precisely for their toxic properties. The Federal Insecticide, Fungicide, and Rodenticide Act is one prominent example of the self-conscious adoption of cost-benefit assessments as an essential part of the regulatory design precisely because the nature of the industry is to introduce toxic substances into the environment.

THE EMERGING ISSUES

Much of the current debate in environmental law centers on the extent to which risk assessment and cost-benefit analysis ought to be made fundamental elements in the design of all environmental regulation. Suffice to say that at this point environmental statutes typically have as a guiding principle, besides the goal of protection of human health, the notion that the polluter ought to pay for the cost of pollution. At least initially, that principle has animated the discussion of the propriety of routinely requiring cost-benefit assessments of regulations. One of the ways the polluter-pays principle informed the discussion of cost-benefit analysis was to ask how risks ought to be apportioned in conditions of scientific uncertainty. When dealing with substances that are potentially toxic at extremely low exposure levels, who ought to be made to bear the cost of that uncertainty? Does the polluter-pays principle carry with it a corollary of prudence? The early debate over the regulation of risk was often framed in terms of false positives and false negatives and dose response curves. Test results are ultimately only as good as our confidence in them. A false positive in a test for toxicity, for example, is a test result incorrectly indicating toxicity. Who should bear the risks of such mistakes?

The arguments ran essentially this way: The cost of reducing risk to an acceptable level, especially where both the chance of false positives and the marginal cost of providing safety were high, ought not to be placed on the producer. Barring the scenario of catastrophic event, the private law of tort should be able to compensate the damaged parties and, in any event, would provide a realistic account of the costs. The contrary position was essentially that the producer ought to account for all costs associated with the introduction of a product into the stream of commerce. The risk of a false positive is a cost that ought to be borne by the producer, especially because that cost could be recaptured through the pricing structure. Stated in polluter-pays terms, the costs associated with risk ought to be borne by the producer of the risk.

Yet the debate over the incorporation of cost-benefit calculations into every environmental regulation that is not legislatively required to be cost-insensitive is not limited to the question of toxic exposures in conditions of scientific uncertainty. Environmental regulation that does not systematically incorporate cost-benefit analyses is subject to the more general critique that the net reduction in wealth associated with regulatory costs is itself a health harm that ought to be part of the agency calculation. *Health costs* in this context typically refers to costs associated with unemployment: increases in stress, substance abuse, domestic violence, and the like. In fairness, however, it should also include losses of health insurance benefits that accompany employment. The issue of agency consideration of cost factors should be recognized largely as a matter of legislative limitations on agency discretion. The courts have been willing to require agencies to provide economic justifications for their regulations even where the statute does not explicitly require or mention cost-benefit analysis. For example, in *Industrial Union Department, AFL-CIO v. American Petroleum Institute,* a fractured Supreme Court ruled that a new worker safety standard regulating benzene exposure levels was faulty because the agency had not made a finding that the exposure risks associated with the prior standards were "significant."[14] They reached this conclusion despite the absence of statutory language requiring such a finding.

Where the agency is instructed to regulate for human health or safety regardless of the costs, the agency can hardly be faulted for carrying out its legislative mandate. Where the agency is given a wider birth in applying its legislative mandate, the courts are largely limited to assessing whether the agency has adopted a reasonable interpretation of its statutory obligations. The reasons for a particular mandate may be complex, but they are typically legislative reasons and thus are subject to the critiques raised by public choice theory (discussed below).

This was made clear in the famous case of *Chevron U.S.A. v. National Resources Defense Council,* where the EPA's "bubble" policy was challenged. The bubble policy was designed to permit the agency to consider an entire plant a "stationary pollution source" under the Clean Air Act and regulate the entire pollution discharge of the factory.[15] This regulation represented a significant change from the way stationary pollution sources had been regulated in the past. Previously, the agency had taken the position that the statute required regulation of each individual source of air pollution, rather than permitting polluters to net their emissions. The question was the validity of the enforcing agency's interpretation of their operative statute. Here the Court held that the "unambiguously expressed intention of Congress" should be given effect. However, where legislative intention is "silent or ambiguous with respect to the specific issue," the only question left for the court to decide is whether the agency's choice was a "reasonable interpretation" and thus permissible within a reading of the statutes general intent. According to the Court, if the agency was acting reasonably and the Congress had not explicitly spoken, then courts should defer to the agency judgment. Given the wide latitude a court must give to agency determinations, no court has yet held that a high dollar amount per life saved is proof of the unreasonableness of a regulation, although *Corrosion Proof Fittings v. EPA* might have come close in the context of the Toxic Substances Control Act that required the EPA to choose the least burdensome means of determining acceptable risk.[16]

No one can oppose the argument that a cost-benefit analysis ought to be required in virtually every instance of environmental regulation, because such analysis merely requires that a decision to act in a certain way not be taken if the costs of that action outweigh the benefits. What could be wrong with that? Especially if, as suggested above, the failure to incorporate cost-benefit analyses systematically may result in the net reduction in wealth production and such reduction is itself a health harm. The principal problem, of course, is the assumption that all costs and benefits can be stated in the form of some universal equivalent that permits their easy comparison. If everything can be reduced to its dollar value, the ability to choose would be made easier but not automatic. There are always extreme examples that seem to make the case for across-the-board application of cost-benefit analyses. In the *Corrosion Proof Fittings* case, for example, the court noted that the agency, although under the statutory obligation to choose the least burdensome regulation, still chose a regulation that would have cost the asbestos industry $74 million per life saved. In addition to this cost, the regulation would have saved only three lives over thirteen years, according to projections.[17]

But even such an example begs at least two other questions. First, is it possible in specific instances to craft a scale of equivalencies that would make a comparison of costs meaningful? Second, is it desirable to do so? The first problem arises, of course, because there are many unmarketed costs and benefits. In order to convert them to dollar amounts or some other market equivalent, the analyst must first generate an imaginary market. The results will only be as good as the technique. The confidence level generated by the results of the construction of an imaginary market must be high, because what it is attempting to assess is the weight people would assign to preferences that they have otherwise not revealed. It may be, in fact, that there are good reasons for the absence of market prices for commodities that are being regulated or protected. That, of course, leads to the second question. We may have decided that we don't want to value everything according to the same scale. This may be a problem for economics, but it is also a problem for politics, and the institutions of politics are the sites we have chosen to contest those decisions. The politics of regulation may produce the additional difficulty posed by "one size fits all" regulatory regimes that limit innovation and occasionally produce unintended negative consequences. The recent debate over the safety of airbags designed to save the average adult but proving fatal to children is instructive in this regard.

It may also be that through political contestation we have resolved to control some behavior or regulate some activity even though the benefits do not seem to outweigh the costs. That may in some sense be irrational, but it is not politically impermissible and can only be criticized in specific local ways, because such a determination almost always is made with resort to other values that ought to change our conception about how irrational the decision makers are being. In other words, a general critique based only on objectively quantifiable values may miss elements of the decision-making process that are critical to understanding the internal logic of the decision.

A good local example is in Austin, Texas, where the city chose to preserve Barton Springs, a spring-fed swimming pool in a downtown park, at the cost of substantial upstream regulation and despite alternative swimming pools being available. This is irrational only based on an analysis of costs that fail to consider the importance of culture and tradition to the people of Austin.

The more general critique is in some ways more compelling even if harder to document. That argument is that the general wealth effects associated with the costs of environmental regulation may produce more social harm than good. The classic examples are where the health costs associated with unemployment are not considered when the costs of environmental regulations cause the closure of a plant, or where automobile regulations result in the increased cost for cars, leading poor people to drive older, smaller, or less safe cars. In the first instance it is obviously true that the cost of regulation resulting in increased unemployment can and perhaps ought to be calculated. It is also true that the production of economic surplus fuels both the demand and capacity for the production of environmental amenities. Yet the harder inquiry the general critique usually avoids is the inquiry into the distribution of the economic harms and benefits of less regulation of demonstrably harmful activity. These questions have fueled what has come to be called the environmental justice movement.

While the environmental justice movement is thought to be a new civil-rights, urban twist on environmental policy, most of the pollution control statutes were designed to minimize the environment insults that urban residents would be required to endure. What is new about the environmental justice movement is its conscious insertion of a racial dimension to the assessment of the fairness of one policy or enforcement choice over another. The movement dates back to two signal events. First was the historic 1979 Urban Environment Conference held in Detroit under the aegis of both the Sierra Club and the Urban League. The conference focused on the relationship between civil rights groups and environmental groups and on the need for the latter to expand their mandate to include the improvement of quality of urban life. The notion driving the civil rights groups was that environmentalists had defined environmental issues largely to the exclusion of central city residents. In addition, there were those unionists and environmentalists who were pressing the more mainstream environmentalists to take account of the impact of environmental regulation on jobs. Because the meeting was in Detroit, this claim focused on the impact of the Clean Air Act on auto industry jobs. The conference brought together elements of both movements and sought to craft an environmental agenda that took account of traditional civil rights concerns.

Second was the protest by rural black residents in North Carolina against the placement of a polychlorinated biphenyl landfill in their community. That protest led to the request by Congressman Walter Fauntroy that the Government Accounting Office investigate the socioeconomic and racial composition of the communities surrounding hazardous waste landfills in the South. The study found that three of the four major hazardous landfill sites located in the South were in poor black communities. The confluence of race and poverty seemed more than mere coincidence. This intuition was support by a later study conducted in 1987 by the United Church of Christ Commission on Racial Justice, which came to the same conclusion as the GAO study and further found that race was the most significant variable associated with the location of commercial waste facilities.

The initial Church of Christ study and others done by people such as sociologist Robert Bullard have been subjected to withering critique as well as less politically committed studies. Yet the basic perception that racial and ethnic minorities and the poor carry a disproportionate share of the environmental burdens of our industrial society has largely been substantiated. The reasons given for the observed inequality range from accusations of garden-variety racism to more complicated and sophisticated analyses of the interplay of race and poverty. One major result of the focus on race, poverty, and environmental policy has been the issuance of an executive order requiring all federal agencies to consider the environmental impact of their activities on minority and poor communities.[18] In addition to this planning mandate, the executive order required agencies to give the public a meaningful chance to participate in agency decision making that affects the human environment.

There are critics of such efforts to democratize the creation of environmental policy. Some are ideological opponents, others are the direct descendants of the proponents of the scientific policy-making wing of the progressive conservation movement, and still others are advocates of what has come to be know as public choice theory.[19] Public choice theory is the application of free-market economic theory to politics. It emphasizes the pathologies and limitations of collective action and provides the theoretical framework for delegitimizing both regulation and attempts to make politics more democratic. According to this theory, regulation merely provides the opportunity for private persons to capture unearned gains by using the power of the state and empowers politicians to extract economic surplus for their own advantage. Both eventualities operate as a drag on the economy and produce more harm than good.

Public choice theory rests on three major premises. First, political action does not necessarily produce or even reflect the will of the people because of the problem of what has come to be called "preference cycling." This essentially means that people cannot get what they want out of politics because group choice outcomes are logically indeterminate and largely the result of who controls the agenda. This premise maintains that the way choices are structured often determines which choices are made.

Second, the theory maintains that the individual cost of political participation outweighs any particular benefit, and thus there is a disincentive to participation in civic life. This being so, electoral politics will result in a state dominated by special interests that will make policy at the expense of the public good. This claim, of course, has run into what has come to be called the "paradox of voting." While turnout for elections in the United States is typically lamentably low, people do vote despite the irrationality of doing so that the theory posits. Since the second premise ought to yield the prediction that people will not vote because the costs outweigh the benefits, it has to explain why people bother to go to the polls. Similarly, people who value their time most, according to this theory, ought to be the ones who participate least, but in fact such is not the case.

Third, building on the first two premises (although the literature that forms the classics in this field actually marks a different chronological order), the theory holds that the narrowly organized interests extract unearned benefits at the expense of the disorganized electorate. This is called "rent seeking." Public officials are merely the state actors for narrow private interests. Thus, to prevent the appropriation of unearned profit and because there are deep pathologies in all forms of collective action, the most prudent course is to limit government and the power that it can wield.

I have differentiated the descendants of the scientific policy-making wing of the progressive conservation movement from public choice theorists. The distinctions between these groups arise in the specific context of the environmental justice movement largely in respect to their attitudes toward democratic politics. According to the proponents of scientific policy making, lay groups should be excluded from agency decision making because of their lack of technical expertise and the need to depoliticize public policy. Public choice theorists would exclude them to prevent policy corruption by special-interest rent-seeking behavior.

Advocates of public choice theory thus would limit regulation because it is, by hypothesis, hopelessly corrupted by the pathologies of politics. In fact, rather than democratize policy making, as suggested by the partisans of the environmental justice movement, the role of government in the regulation of the environment ought to be more rigidly circumscribed. The claims that are made for democratization are translated by public choice theorists into the merest fig leaf for special interests. Rather than giving those interests greater sway, they should be analyzed in terms of rent-seeking behavior, and that behavior should be limited rather than rewarded. Public choice theory fits hand in glove with free-market critics of environmental policy making. Yet, as critics of public choice theory point out, the brute application of economic models to political activity systematically understates the value associated with participation in decision making, especially where it directly relates to the quality of life for local residents. Participation of the local community is critical for the

legitimacy of the choices made when the community will bear the consequences of those decisions.

Much of the current skirmishing in environmental law is taking place
within the context of the fight over property rights, the appropriate role
of government, especially governmental interference with the workings
of the market, and the importance of risk assessment in the fashioning of
both pollution control and pollution avoidance strategies. But there is
another side of the environmental movement that continues to have a
powerful influence on the debate: environmental ethics, perhaps first
captured in the work of John Muir and Aldo Leopold and later developed in a more systematic way in the work of Mark Sagoff and Paul
Taylor.[20]

The respect for nature at the core of environmental ethics begins
with a belief that the human species is merely one among many that
depend on the earth and each other for survival. This attitude of interdependency rests upon a conviction that the human species is not
inherently superior to others but, because of its capacity for rational
reflection, may owe a greater degree of care for the earth and its inhabitants. The earth may be in our custody, but it is not in our control.
This position regards the passion for efficiency that drives the economic critique of environmental regulation as essentially wrongheaded,
not because we shouldn't care about costs, but because an obsessive
focus on costs leads us to value the wrong things. Moreover, so this
position maintains, to the extent that environmental policy is concerned about justice it is only by beginning with a respect for nature
and other living things in a way that does not always give a trump to
immediate human concerns that questions of justice may be framed
adequately. Distributive, restitutive, and generational claims of justice
rely in some important ways on attitudes that take nature (recognizing
our place in it) as an end in itself.

These views have influenced law largely in the development of policies
relating to species and habitat protection. The Supreme Court of
Minnesota has said:

> Over ten years ago this court cited conservationist Aldo Leopold for his
> espousal of a "land ethic" which envisions a community of interdepen-
> dent parts. . . . We reaffirm our statement that the state's environmental
> legislation had given this land ethic the force of law, and imposed on the
> courts a duty to support the legislative goal of protecting our state's envi-
> ronmental resources.[21]

Similarly, at the federal level, the Endangered Species Act counsels an attitude of prudence that is fully consistent with many of the tenets of environmental ethics, as are the statutes creating and protecting wilderness.[22] Many of the environmental groups thought to be "radical" are basically motivated by popular versions of environmental ethics. This part of the environmental movement has also seen particular expression in the realm of international environmental policy, where the conflict between rich and poor nations or between the developed world and the developing world over resource use are most intense.

Many conflicting currents, both contemporary and historical, are captured in the field of environmental law. But, like much else these days, environmental law is now part of the debate over federalism and the proper scope of national state power as well as a familiar target for those who want to challenge the power of the government to regulate private economic prerogatives. Yet despite the attacks, whether from the states rights advocates or from the advocates of laissez-faire economics, a popular national commitment to core environmental values remains relatively clear: pollution control to protect public health, regulation for a safe workplace, and preservation of wilderness and species habitat.

NOTES

1. See "Concern for Environment," *New York Times,* July 2, 1989, 18; Robert Percival, Alan Miller, Christopher Schroeder, and James Leape, *Environmental Regulation: Law Science and Policy* (Boston: Little, Brown, 1996), 113; *Lujan v. Defenders of Wildlife,* 504 U.S. 555 (1992); *Bennett v. Spear,* 117 S.Ct. 1154 (1997).

2. See Daniel A. Farber, *Eco-Pragmatism* (Chicago: University of Chicago Press, 1997); William H. Rodgers, Jr., *Environmental Law* (St. Paul, Minn.: West, 1994), 39–46.

3. There are hundreds of statutes that could legitimately be called environmental statutes, but most commentators typically focus on the National Environmental Policy Act, 42 U.S.C. §§ 4321–70d (1969); the Clean Air Act, 42 U.S.C. §§ 7401–671q; the Clean Water Act, 33 U.S.C. §§ 1251–387; the Federal Insecticide, Fungicide, and Rotenticide Act, 7 U.S.C. §§ 136–136y; the Toxic Substances Control Act, 15 U.S.C. §§

2601–92; the Solid Waste Disposal Act (as amended by the Resource Conservation and Recovery Act), 42 U.S.C. §§ 6901–92k; and the Comprehensive Environmental, Response, Compensation, and Liability Act, 42 U.S.C. §§ 9601–75.

4. See the Federal Land Policy Management Act, PL 94–579, 90 Stat. 2744; Forest and Rangeland Renewable Resources Planning Act of 1974, PL 93–378, 88 Stat. 476; 16 U.S.C. § 1600 et seq.; the Multiple-Use Sustained Yield Act of 1960, 16 U.S.C. §§ 528–31 (1960); the Mining Act of 1872, 30 U.S.C. § 22 (1872); the Right-of-Way Act, 32 Stat. 43 (1882); the Reclamation Act of 1902, 32 Stat. 388 (1902). The reclamation acts tried to tie receipt of "federal water" to small land holding in order to make productive land available to the average person who was willing to work hard and to prevent the subsidization of land speculators.

5. Gifford Pinchot was a leader of the scientific conservation movement and head of the Division of Forestry (now the Forest Service) under presidents McKinley, Roosevelt, and Taft. His nemesis was Richard Ballinger, secretary of the interior under Taft. A struggle arose between Ballinger and Pinchot because Pinchot believed Ballinger to be abandoning the principles of conservation outlined in the Roosevelt administration. Ballinger ultimately prevailed when Taft fired Pinchot.

6. See Joseph Sax, *Mountains Without Handrails* (Ann Arbor: University of Michigan Press, 1980).

7. Aldo Leopold, *A Sand County Almanac and Sketches Here and There* (Oxford: Oxford University Press, 1968), 224–25. See also *Application of Christensen*, 417 N.W. 2d 607, 615 (Minn. 1988).

8. Samuel P. Hays, *Beauty, Health, and Permanence: Environmental Politics in the United States, 1955–1985* (Cambridge, UK: Cambridge University Press, 1987), 138–39.

9. *Madison v. Ducktown Sulphur, Copper & Iron Co.*, 113 Tenn. 331, 83 S.W. 658 (Tenn. 1904).

10. There is substantial debate in the historical literature over just how willing American courts were to balance the value of the polluting behavior against the environmental damage. See Lawrence M. Friedman, *A History of American Law* (New York: Simon & Schuster, 1973); Morton Horwitz, *The Transformation of American Law, 1780–1860* (Cambridge, MA: Harvard University Press, 1977).

11. See Richard Epstein, *Takings: Private Property and the Power of Eminent Domain* (Cambridge, MA: Harvard University Press, 1985); *Lucas v. South Carolina Coastal Council*, 505 U.S. 1003 (1992).

12. For an excellent discussion of the founding of the EPA and the problems attendant to its peculiar genesis, see Richard Lazarus, *The Tragedy of Distrust in the Implementation of Federal Environmental Law*, 54 Law and Contemporary Problems 311 (1991).

13. See Kirsten H. Engle, *State Environmental Standard-Setting: Is There a "Race" and Is It "To the Bottom"?* 48 Hastings Law Journal 271 (1997).

14. *Industrial Union Department, AFL-CIO v. American Petroleum Institute*, 448 U.S. 607 (1980).

15. *Chevron U.S.A. v. NRDC*, 467 U.S. 837 (1984).

16. *Corrosion Proof Fittings v. EPA*, 947 F.2d 1201 (5th Cir. 1991).

17. Ibid., 1222.

18. Executive Order 12898, "Federal Actions to Address Environmental Justice in Minority and Low Income Populations," 59 Fed. Reg. 7629 (1994). Three basic types of agencies affect the distribution of environmental burdens. First are those agencies that implement and administer environmental laws. Second are those that control or conduct activities directly affecting the environment. Third are those that affect the environment through the management (including permitting) or funding of other activities.

19. The critiques of these theories largely rest on the failure of the proponents of the theories to validate them empirically. See Donald P. Green and Ian Shapiro, *Pathologies of Rational Choice Theory* (New Haven: Yale University Press, 1994); see also Philip P. Frickey and Daniel A. Farber, *Law and Public Choice: A Critical Introduction* (Chicago: University of Chicago Press, 1991).

20. Mark Sagoff, *The Economy of the Earth: Philosophy, Law, and the Environment* (Cambridge, UK: Cambridge University Press, 1988); Paul W. Taylor, *Respect for Nature: A Theory of Environmental Ethics* (Princeton, NJ: Princeton University Press, 1986).

21. *Application of Christensen*, 417 N.W. 2d 607, 615 (Minn. 1988).

22. Endangered Species Act, 16 U.S.C. §§ 1531–34 (1973).

8 DAVID KAIRYS

FREEDOM OF SPEECH

THE basic principle that individuals and groups are free to express different and unpopular views without prior restraint or punishment has gained a unique acceptance in the United States, for which we are rightly proud. It is a necessary element of any free and democratic society, indispensable to both the individual and society generally. Without freedom of expression, the individual is not truly free and cannot be an active participant or maintain self-respect and dignity while functioning with others as part of society. Expression is not just something people do; it is, in the deepest sense, an integral part of what people are. Society cannot effectively resolve conflict or competing demands and interests, generate new ideas, function democratically, or maintain stability unless individuals are free to express themselves. The downside of free speech is that on occasion people are exposed to ideas that they find stupid, upsetting, or offensive, but this is a minimal price—and sometimes those very same ideas later gain widespread acceptance.

While the principle is sound, free speech means much more than this in American politics and culture. Free speech is often discussed as if it defined a political or economic system rather than a series of rules prohibiting governmental limits on individual expression. It is what makes us good, and better than other countries and people. Freedom of speech is at the core of our national identity.

Yet the American celebration of free speech is unsettling, contradictory, and quite complex. The invocation of free speech gains wide acceptance when formulated generally and abstracted from current controversies or when aimed at repressive practices in other countries. But specific applications in the United States are regularly greeted with contempt, evident in the recurring controversies over flag burning, demonstrations by neo-Nazis, and, most recently, "indecency" on the Internet. There is considerably less than a consensus about or a widespread understanding of the basic aspects of American speech law that truly distinguish it from more restrictive laws and practices prevalent almost everywhere else in the world. The rejection of limits on unfettered dissent and criticism, expression in a variety of places and a variety of ways, the presumption of the primacy of expression over competing concerns, the presumption against restriction of speech based on its content (the "content barrier")—all are controversial on the home field of free speech and may no longer command support from a majority of the population.

And despite all the rhetoric about free speech and our democratic political process, a very large proportion of us—perhaps most—feel silenced and disenfranchised. There is a widespread recognition across the political spectrum that the American people lack the effective means to be heard or to translate their wishes into reality through the political process. There is, and has been for some time, a crisis of democracy and freedom that has been ignored by public officials and the media.

In contemporary politics, law, and culture, free speech and First Amendment–based free speech rights are idealized, their scope and degree of acceptance are exaggerated, and their shortcomings are hidden and ignored. The myths run deep, sustained and based to a significant extent on mythic stories and analyses of the origin and history of free speech in the United States. Despite persistent but nonspecific references to "our traditions" in legal and popular literature, no right of free speech as we know it existed, either in law or practice, until a basic transformation of the law governing speech during the period from about 1919 to 1940. Before the transformation, one spoke publicly only at the discretion of local, and sometimes federal, authorities, who often prohibited what they or influential segments of the community did not want to hear. Until very recently, it was commonly assumed in the courts and law reviews that there were no significant court decisions on freedom of speech before World War I and that shortly thereafter speech was legally protected by the Supreme Court and has remained so ever since. Popular literature regularly extends these misconceptions to embrace the idea that freedom of speech is a cornerstone of the Constitution and the basis of our country.

A candid look at that history provides a concrete and even inspiring example of popularly instigated and achieved social and cultural change and helps us understand the current state of American free speech and democracy.

A BRIEF HISTORY OF FREE SPEECH IN THE UNITED STATES, 1791–1940

For all that has been written about freedom of speech, there is little that acknowledges the pre–World War I history or recognizes the profound change in the law in the twentieth century, and even less that attempts to analyze that change. A particular aspect of speech—speaking, gathering, and distributing literature in public places—has been emphasized here because it is the subject of the Supreme Court cases that best illustrate the transformation in the law and because this aspect played a major role in the events leading to the transformation.[1]

THE TRANSFORMATION OF FREE SPEECH LAW

In 1894, the Reverend William F. Davis, an evangelist and longtime active opponent of slavery and racism, attempted to preach the Gospel on Boston Common, an open, public park. For his first attempt, Davis was incarcerated for a few weeks in the Charles Street Jail; the second time, he was fined and appealed the sentence. Davis believed that there was a "constitutional right of citizens to the use of public grounds and places without let or hindrance by the City authorities."[2]

The Supreme Court of Massachusetts disagreed. In an opinion by Oliver Wendell Holmes—perhaps most famous as a justice of the Supreme Court of the United States for his later decisions protecting freedom of speech—the court upheld Davis's conviction based on a city ordinance that prohibited "any public address" on public grounds without a permit from the mayor. Holmes, like almost all state and lower federal court judges, viewed such an ordinance as simply a city regulation of the use of its park, which was within the city's rights as owner of the property. Davis had no basis, in the Constitution or elsewhere, to claim any limits on this property right:

> That such an ordinance is constitutional . . . does not appear to us open to doubt. . . . For the Legislature absolutely or conditionally to forbid public speaking in a highway or public park is no more an infringement of the rights of a member of the public than for the owner of a private house to forbid it in his house.[3]

The Supreme Court of the United States unanimously affirmed in *Davis v. Massachusetts* (1897), quoting Holmes's analogy to a private house. In the only reference to the Constitution, the Court said that it "does not have the effect of creating a particular and personal right in the citizen to use public property in defiance of the Constitution and laws of the State." Nor did the Court find any constitutional or other limit on the mayor's authority to deny permission selectively or for any reason: "The right to absolutely exclude all right to use, necessarily includes the authority to determine under what circumstances such use may be availed of, as the greater power contains the lesser."[4]

From the adoption of the First Amendment (1791) to the beginning of the basic legal transformation (1919), a variety of social and religious activists demanded recognition of freedom of speech. The most significant of these—the abolitionists, the anarchists, the Industrial Workers of the World, the Socialist party, and the early labor and women's movements—were sometimes successful in speaking, gathering, and distributing literature publicly. Federal and state courts, however, repeatedly refused to protect any form of speech. The change came in the 1930s (after a series of dissenting opinions starting in 1919), exemplified by a decision arising from the labor movement's attempt to organize workers in Jersey City, New Jersey.

Labor organizers had regularly been denied freedom of speech, which they generally saw as inseparable from the right to organize unions, except in cities with progressive or socialist mayors. After Congress passed the National Labor Relations Act (NLRA) in 1935, the Congress of Industrial Organizations (CIO) sought to explain its provisions and the benefits of unions and collective bargaining to working people throughout the country. Nowhere was their reception more hostile than on the Jersey City turf of political boss and mayor Frank Hague.

The CIO planned to distribute literature on the streets and to host outdoor meetings, but permits for these activities were denied by Hague, who made it clear that labor organizers were not welcome in Jersey City. Many organizers were cast out of town, usually by being put on a ferry to New York. Hague promised local businesses that they would have no labor troubles while he was mayor; his response to the CIO was: "I am the law."[5]

In *Hague v. CIO* (1939), the Court said:

> Wherever the title of streets and parks may rest, they have immemorially been held in trust for the use of the public and, time out of mind, have been used for purposes of assembly, communicating thoughts between citizens, and discussing public questions. Such use of the streets and public places has, from ancient times, been a part of the privileges, immunities, rights, and liberties of citizens.[6]

This was a direct repudiation of both the doctrinal basis and the result in *Davis,* and it first established the basic concept of free speech now taken for granted.[7] However, the *Hague* Court did not explicitly overrule *Davis,* discuss the lack of free speech prior to its decision, or even acknowledge that it had made a fundamental change in legal doctrine.

Rather, the opinion was an inspiring exposition of a right to freedom of speech based on natural law and long-standing principle. Like all such conceptions, it is essentially timeless and without a social context. In the quoted passage, the streets and parks have "immemorially" been held for the people and used for speech "time out of mind," and the right of free speech stems "from ancient times." But there is no indication as to what time or place the Court was referring; it certainly had never been so in the United States—or anywhere else—before this very case, as the Court had itself ruled in *Davis.* Judges often depict even such basic changes as part of a seamless continuum.

Davis is the only Supreme Court decision addressing these basic free speech issues before the transformation began, but state and lower federal court decisions, as well as the practice throughout the country, confirm that there was no tradition of or legally protected right to free speech as we know it prior to the transformation. The supposed existence of such a tradition and such rights is a long-standing myth.

THE CONSTITUTION AND THE EARLY POPULAR UNDERSTANDING

The Constitution, as ratified in 1787, did not mention freedom of speech, although historians and legal scholars generally agree that the Bill of Rights, in the form of amendments adopted four years later, was promised and necessary to secure ratification. There is considerable controversy, however, about how the framers of the Constitution and the population generally viewed freedom of speech before and during the constitutional drafting and ratification process. The traditional view that freedom of speech was widely supported—which has been translated into the current popular notion that free speech was the founding principle of our country—is usually documented, if at all, by eloquent but largely rhetorical writings in this century by Harvard law professor Zechariah Chafee, Jr. This view has been challenged based on convincing historical research, principally by historian Leonard Levy.[8]

The controversy has suffered from a lack of concreteness: freedom of speech as we know it consists of several specific concepts and rules guaranteeing most basically the ability, without restraint, punishment, or content-based limitation, to criticize government and public officials and private institutions and individuals; to express one's views in public places; and to associate with others for political purposes. Although the Constitution and the First Amendment were popularly understood to embody basic notions of political freedom, including at least a repudiation of judicial or other actions that prohibit in advance publication by the press (called prior restraints), the other aspects of free speech as we know it developed throughout our two-hundred-year history.

For example, English and American law at the time of the Constitution's framing essentially rendered criticism of the government or its officials a criminal act. This offense, called seditious libel, was based on the conception of a monarch and government as divine and above reproach. The truth of a criticism was considered a basis for aggravation rather than mitigation of the crime because a correct criticism was more likely to create discord and contempt for the government. Although seditious libel is completely incompatible with our current conception of free speech, it was a crime in every state at the time the Constitution was adopted. Furthermore, Levy's review of the writings and speeches of the framers of the Constitution and the leaders of the Revolution shows that none of them—including even Thomas Jefferson and Thomas Paine—opposed criminalization of seditious libel. Some of the framers advocated reforms of the law of seditious libel, including adoption of truth as a defense and the determination of libel by the jury. But they still favored the criminalization of criticism of the government and its officials, which in some form was—and still is—the law in almost every other country, including the Western democracies.

Levy suggests that the First Amendment, explicitly directed at and limiting only Congress, was not viewed by its framers as changing existing law and merely constituted a reservation to the states of the power to regulate speech, press, and religion. The seeds of popular belief in free speech as we know it came later, perhaps in response to the Sedition Act of 1798.

The Federalists, our first political party, undaunted by the First Amendment to their Constitution, became dissatisfied with the ineffectiveness of common law seditious libel prosecutions aimed at silencing their political opponents. In 1798, they pushed through Congress by a narrow margin the Sedition Act, which made it a crime to "write, print, utter or publish . . . any false, scandalous and malicious writings against the government of the United States, or either House of Congress . . . or the President with the intent to defame . . . or to bring them into contempt or disrepute."

Although the act also contained two protective devices—truth was made a defense, and the jury was to decide whether the words were seditious—Federalist judges quickly negated their effect. They refused to distinguish between statements of fact and opinion, and they ruled that the defendant must prove the truth of every minute detail to establish the truth defense. Overall, they treated the First Amendment as if it only codified preexisting law and prohibited only prior censorship, which had been prohibited in England since 1695 and in the colonies since 1725.

The most prominent person prosecuted under the Sedition Act was Matthew Lyon, a member of Congress critical of the Federalists. Lyon was imprisoned and his house sold to pay his fine (nevertheless he was reelected in the next election). The longest prison term, two years, was served by a laborer for erecting a sign on a post that read, in part, "no stamp act, no sedition . . . downfall to the tyrants of America, peace and retirement to the president." The act was "never invoked against alien enemies, or possible traitors, but solely against editors and public men whom the Federalists under President Adams desired to silence or deport in order to suppress political opposition."[9]

The act and consequent prosecutions were extremely unpopular, and convictions were difficult to obtain without manipulation of the composition of juries (which, as a result, were comprised almost entirely of Federalists) and active bias by Federalist judges. "Popular indignation at the Act and the prosecutions wrecked the Federalist Party."[10] Jefferson pardoned all those convicted (although the Republicans also used the act to prosecute their opponents), and the government repaid their fines.

The Supreme Court never reviewed any of the common law or statutory sedition cases, but several legal doctrines that restricted expression were adopted by the lower courts and would be repeatedly resurrected later. The two foremost were the "bad tendency" doctrine, which allowed prosecution for words that could, in however remote or indirect a fashion, contribute to disorder or unlawful conduct sometime in the future; and the "constructive intent" doctrine, which ascribed to the speaker or writer the intent to cause such remote and indirect consequences. These doctrines were used, for example, to justify prosecutions of abolitionists for merely advocating an end to slavery, because their words might be heeded and contribute to a slave revolt. In addition, the public streets, sidewalks, and parks were controlled for purposes of expression by local authorities, as the Court later reaffirmed in *Davis*.

These were the rules governing speech until the transformation, which resulted from popular demands and political movements by people at all levels of society, led most prominently by the labor movement of the 1930s, and from social and cultural changes, rather than from any language in the Constitution, legacy from the framers, or legal reasoning.[11]

THE LIBERAL PARADIGM

The expansion of speech rights, after a regression in the 1950s, resumed in the 1960s and early 1970s, when the civil rights and antiwar movements demanded and received heightened enforcement and a substantial enlargement of speech rights.[12] The result was a set of rules that are best described as the liberal paradigm. The freedom of speech that is a favorite of American political rhetoric has been a mainstay of liberal and progressive thought. Some conservatives have also favored it, but it has always been controversial, and the main opposition has come from conservatives, starting with the Federalists and continuing to today.

The liberal paradigm can be capsulized with a few basic rules. Speech is first categorized as either protected or unprotected based on its subject matter. Protected speech cannot be infringed or burdened unless the government is furthering a compelling interest that cannot be furthered by means less restrictive of speech—called in constitutional law the "strict scrutiny" standard. The worst violations are prohibitions of speech (prior restraints) and restrictions on the content of speech (piercing the "content barrier"), which together are what we call and condemn as censorship.

The categories of unprotected speech usually referred to are obscenity, child pornography, defamation, fraud, incitement to imminent lawless action ("clear and present danger"), and "fighting words." All other speech is protected, although there is a hierarchy among the various protected categories. Political speech is the most protected because it has the highest social value, furthering society's interest in free and open debate as well as the individual's interest in expression. Commercial speech, speech by corporations or individuals in pursuit of their business interests, is less protected.

The way in which protected speech is communicated—the mode of speech—is subject to the strict scrutiny standard and also to reasonable regulation of the time, place, and manner. It can be direct or symbolic and verbal, written, or graphic (and technological advances may well add more to the list)—including a book or leaflet, a speech, a demonstration, picketing, door-to-door canvassing, burning a flag—as long as it does not conflict with a compelling government interest. But it is always subject to reasonable regulation of the time, place, and manner, which includes commonsense limits, so that a loud assembly at night in a residential neighborhood is more subject to limitation or prohibition than the same assembly in a downtown area during working hours.

The most important free-speech right for people of ordinary means has been the right to assemble, express themselves, and distribute literature in public places—the right denied Reverend Davis but vindicated in *Hague*. The property-based reasoning of *Davis* was firmly and repeatedly overruled in the fifty years following the transformation: Government property or facilities open to the general public and not restricted to some particular, incompatible use were presumptively available for peaceable assembly, expression, and distribution of literature. The centrality of this right is recognized every time we conclude that societies in which the government suppresses such activities are authoritarian or totalitarian—their people are not free.

In the post-transformation period, particularly in the 1930s and the 1960s, the Court protected and extended speech rights against a wide range of proposed justifications for limiting them. The hostile reactions of passersby, or even a majority of the community, who disagree with expressed views was found insufficient to limit speech, because the basic idea is to allow and protect expression of a wide range of ideas and perspectives. If speech rights were limited on this ground, expression would be subject to the approval of the views expressed by the potential audience, the government, or popular sentiment—amounting to what has generally been called a "listener's veto." If listeners have a veto—whether they are in the audience or in the legislatures—there cannot be free speech.

The Court rejected the listener's veto and found matters such as littering associated with speech or demonstrations and the need for crowd control insufficient to limit speech. In addition, certain ancillary rights were recognized as necessary to exercise speech rights effectively, such as the right to distribute literature and to solicit funds or sell literature or goods in support of the views expressed. In a 1943 case, the Court noted that "the pamphlets of Thomas Paine were not free of charge." Speech rights were also extended to cover new and unforeseen public places as lifestyles and the places people frequent changed: In 1946 speech rights were applied to "company towns" and in 1968 to privately owned shopping centers.[13]

The Court recognized and overcame the theoretical and practical impediments to free speech and enabled—for the first time in the history of the world—people of ordinary means and status to enter the social discourse and speak their minds freely and publicly. These rules and the resulting openness and freedom of our public places are the essence of American free speech.

THE REALITY OF FREE SPEECH

As important as the development of the liberal paradigm was, the ideal of free speech is often assumed to be or confused with the reality. The short-comings of even the most protective version of American speech law have been generally ignored, even by some of its most ardent advocates in liberal circles.

Free speech rules are not as clear as they seem and in fact embody basic contradictions. Almost all human activity involves some form of expression, so the real list of unprotected categories is much larger than acknowledged. All government activity and all the fields of law, from antitrust and regulation of the stock market to torts, contracts, and employment law, in some basic sense involve regulation of expression without application of the strict rules that we associate with free speech. It would be easier to list the small number of protected categories than the very large number of unprotected ones.

Further, no principle or standards distinguish the unprotected from the protected categories, and they are both under- and overinclusive. The unprotected categories represent expression that can be described as of minimal social value, but so can a lot of other speech that has escaped that status, such as racist speech. And the protected categories include much that is of little or no social value. The very judgment of social value or the lack thereof—the project of distinguishing protected from unprotected speech—cannot be accomplished neutrally or objectively and collides with the core concept of free speech. We do not have free speech or open debate if anyone—whether they claim membership in a legislature or the Supreme Court—is allowed to decide what ideas have value or deserve protection.

The most protected category, political speech, is difficult to define and seems to depend on the whimsy of what is currently (or has been) controversial. For example, an electric utility's promotional advertising was viewed as commercial rather than political speech because it "related solely to the economic interests of the speaker and audience," which is a fair characterization of much electoral speech routinely considered political.[14] Further, new ideas are often expressed and advocated for the purpose of persuading us that something perceived as ordinary or proper should be considered controversial and political. For example, the women's movement of the 1960s advanced the idea that much of the relationship between men and women traditionally considered personal requires social intervention to provide protection and equality for women. It is circular and, again, contrary to the basic notion of free speech to require that such ideas be demonstrably political or controversial in advance of their advocacy in order for their advocacy to be fully protected.

This doctrinal puzzle is further complicated because the protected-unprotected distinction does not seem to matter when it collides with some of the other rules, such as the content barrier and the aversion to prior restraints. In those situations, even unprotected speech is often accorded strict protection, depriving the term *unprotected* of meaning or significance.

The content barrier is itself another long-standing myth. The unprotected categories are content based; they are defined by the disfavored content of the ideas expressed. Some content distinctions are allowed whereas others are not, and there is no principle or set of standards defining the distinctions.

The result of this doctrinal tangle is extensive discretion for the judges and justices administering speech rules, not the absolute free speech rights we celebrate each Fourth of July. The speaker, demonstrator, and writer are not as free as we so easily proclaim but must cope with a variety of unclear, indeterminate principles and rules, and with outcomes that depend ultimately on very political judgment calls.

The effectiveness and usefulness of our speech rights are also diminished by the reality that effective communication in modern society is expensive. People of ordinary means must rely on the Constitution for a means of communication and organization. People with power and money do not need to picket, demonstrate, or distribute leaflets on the street. The mass media continuously express their perspectives, both explicitly and implicitly, by "more respectable"—and more effective—means.

Most basically, freedom of speech has been exclusively defined by the historically and culturally specific set of speech rights developed in the transformation period, mainly the 1930s, and the scope and importance of these rights in contemporary society are regularly exaggerated. Freedom of speech as we know it simply does not provide people of ordinary means entree to society's dialogue on the issues of the day. Rather, beyond a variety of person-to-person speech activities, we are free to demonstrate, picket, hand out literature, gather in the streets, sing, chant, and sometimes yell and scream. These activities, which most people find difficult to participate in, effectively amount to *displays of displeasure or discontent*, without the means to explain why we are displeased much less actually to participate in any social dialogue. These displays of displeasure often will not even gain a spot on the local news unless some violation of the law, injury, destruction of property, or stunt accompanies them. If they do appear, they will usually be unexplained, without description of their context, and frequently misrepresented.

Our ability to communicate is haphazard, burdensome, lacking an effective means to explain or persuade; and our messages are filtered, edited, and censored by media organizations mostly interested in pleasing the public and making profits rather than in communication, education, or social dialogue. It should not be surprising that so many Americans across the political spectrum perceive themselves and their views as excluded from public discourse.

Essentially, the law and society have frozen the scope and nature of our speech rights at levels appropriate to the 1930s, when specific audiences were geographically centered, and speaking, gathering, and distributing literature in public places were primary means of communication. The speech rights conceived in that period do not provide access to our current means of communication. Technological, social, and cultural changes have rendered the fruits of the free speech struggle and the transformation of speech law somewhat obsolete. Television, radio, newspapers, and direct mail now constitute the battleground and the marketplace of ideas.

The Internet is widely touted as a great democratizing innovation—as television once was—but its potential and the directions in which it is developed will be determined, in the current environment, by commercial rather than social or technological possibilities and concerns. The Internet is already suffering the fate of every other media form that demonstrates the potential to draw large audiences—consolidation and commercial control.

In the absence of mass-based demands, we have allowed no meaningful inroads into the mass media for people or groups without substantial money or power. The ordinary person or group of ordinary persons has no means, based in the Constitution or elsewhere, to engage meaningfully in that dialogue on the issues of the day that the First Amendment is so often heralded as promoting and guaranteeing.

Recent changes in the ownership, control, and output of the mass media lend even more significance to the absence of the voices of the mass and great variety of Americans. The information and ideas available in our homes, newsstands, movie theaters, and book and video stores are increasingly controlled by a small number of multinational corporations that have no tradition, understanding, or interest in journalism or social dialogue. After World War II, 80 percent of the newspapers were independently owned. In the mid-1980s, forty-six corporations controlled most of the newspapers, magazines, television and radio stations, books, and movies in the United States. In the early 1990s, that number was reduced to twenty-three; and in the early twenty-first century, about "a half-dozen large corporations will own all the most powerful media outlets."[15] There are more varied forms of media and, with innovations such as cable and satellite television, more choices in some segments, but the range of media is increasingly owned and controlled by a very small number of people.

This level of centralization and monopolization of the media is a phenomenon usually associated with totalitarian or authoritarian countries, except that it is privately rather than governmentally controlled. That may seem preferable in a society that values private ownership, but it amounts to extremely centralized control over the information and ideas available to the public without the responsibility, accountability, or popular-selection process associated with government officials. Elected officials surely do not always live up to our expectations, but their mandate is to serve the public interest, they are not immune from replacement and public pressure, and they are selected by a democratic process. We never got to vote for or against Rupert Murdoch, S. I. Newhouse, or Robert Maxwell, nor was there any public debate or choice when General Electric bought RCA and NBC.

Yet a handful of such people and corporations control the information and ideas available to us, and they all have pretty much the same social and political outlook. They are economic conservatives whose philosophy emphasizes free markets (while they typically have close alliances and relationships with big government). They are sometimes liberal on issues of personal freedom and, at least after they got into the media business, always liberal on free press issues. They entered the media business because it provided a better opportunity for profits than other businesses or investments. Their overriding concern is profits, not ideas. Some provide the managers of their media outlets more leeway than others, but those managers also hardly reflect the diversity of views or the range of people in the United States. Like all successful businesspeople, they do not antagonize their major customers (large advertisers), the sources of their raw materials (often government), or the regular consumers of their product—the people who watch, listen, and read, an increasingly captive audience because there is no real competition.

This consolidation has fundamentally changed the media. We should not be surprised that in an earlier era, when tobacco ads were a major source of media revenue, the media helped the tobacco industry cover up the dangers of smoking (or that the now-diversified tobacco companies still influence content).[16] The corporate standard-bearers of free speech acknowledge and sometimes glorify their avoidance of ideas or controversy. Local television news and increasingly national news and overall television programming have become a domain of fear, viciousness, snooping, and trivia.[17]

THE CONSERVATIVE RETRENCHMENT

In recent decades, free-speech law has shifted drastically further from its transformation-period emphasis on enhancing the ability of ordinary people to express themselves meaningfully. Although some previous rulings and principles protecting speech have been reaffirmed, the media and public officials have been inexplicably silent as the conservative-dominated Supreme Court has experimented with what already looks like a dismantling of the basic system of free speech.[18]

The conservative speech retrenchment has three major elements: The Court has narrowed and restricted the free-speech rights available to people of ordinary means, enlarged the free-speech rights available to wealthy people and corporations, and erected a free-speech barrier to public access to the media and to important electoral, economic, and social reforms.[19] While all this has occurred, the media and government officials have drawn the public's attention almost exclusively to other free speech issues—such as flag burning—shifting what should be a debate about the retrenchment of vital speech rights to an often inflammatory discourse on whether we have allowed free speech to go too far.

Speech in Public Places

The Court has recently limited the range and scope of speech activities in public places that provided people of ordinary means the ability to reach a substantial number of other people. The key decisions removed the protection of speech activities in transit terminals and privately owned shopping malls, the two places in which large numbers of people still congregate; upheld a blanket prohibition of posting signs on any city-owned buildings, poles, or other property; approved new limits on expression at state fairgrounds, residential neighborhoods, open portions of military facilities maintained like civilian communities, and areas near foreign embassies; limited access for competing viewpoints to a government-sponsored fundraising drive and an administrative communications network; and approved of censorship of a high-school newspaper in which articles on divorce and teenage pregnancy had been removed by administrators.[20]

The analytical vehicle for most of these decisions has been the "public forum" doctrine, an elaborate, often complicated set of speech-limiting rules made up by conservative justices over the last few decades. Chief Justice Rehnquist's majority opinion in the leading transit terminal case, which dealt with a ban of leafleting and related speech activities in the New York City area airports, defines a public forum as government property that has either (1) "traditionally been available for public expression" and has "as a principal purpose . . . free exchange of ideas" or (2) been specifically designated by the government as a public forum.

The airport terminals did not qualify as traditional forums for two reasons. First, there has not been a tradition of exercise of free speech at airport terminals because "it is only in recent years [that] it has become a common practice." Of course, there were no airport terminals when the First Amendment was drafted. Rehnquist means that only very long traditions count, and therefore the list of public forums is basically closed and fixed, not open to new developments or changing circumstances. Second, exercise of free speech is not "a principal purpose" of airport terminals. True enough, but neither is it a principal purpose of public streets, sidewalks, and parks. The sidewalks in small or large urban areas are meant to be used for walking from place to place, shopping, and gathering—like open airport terminal passageways. With very few exceptions, governments do not construct or maintain public streets, sidewalks, or parks for the purpose of providing a forum for speech, nor do people use such facilities generally for the purpose of hearing speakers. Freedom of speech on public streets, sidewalks, and parks is not a matter of physical characteristics, natural functions, or original purposes but a social decision, in our case made and enforced by courts.

Nor had the government designated these terminals as public forums; they were designated for any and all lawful public access and activity except exercise of speech rights. The air passengers, shoppers, and passersby at airport terminals are subjected to considerable noise, crowds, and activities that communicate a broad range of verbal, written, and symbolic messages whose contents include cultural, intellectual, commercial, religious, sexual, and political matters (the New York airports had large stores, including Bloomingdales, in two of them). These are not monasteries or facilities where the additional messages at issue might startle or contrast with the regular activity. Only the messages of people who wish to distribute leaflets and solicit funds in support of their causes are excluded. The public forum doctrine subordinates this reality to governmental whim: It lets the government agency challenged for infringing on speech decide for itself whether it is required to allow speech at all, amounting to what might be called a government veto.

Rehnquist did not focus on—or even consider—the vital social and constitutional concerns at stake, or even the physical or functional similarities or differences, in terms of the underlying notion of free speech, between this government property and public places where speech has been protected. The analysis is, typically these days, technical, mechanical, and unpredictable in its doctrinal twists and turns; but there is a passage that is startling to anyone familiar with the history of free speech. Rehnquist offered the following explanation (or underlying principle) of the public forum doctrine: "Where the government is acting as a *proprietor*, managing its internal operations, rather than acting as lawmaker with the power to regulate or license, its actions will not be subjected to the heightened review" (emphasis added). This is a return to the reasoning of the *Davis* case.

The portion of the ban that prohibited solicitation was upheld because passengers "may have to alter their path," "traffic is impeded," and there are "risks of duress." Leafleting (on which Rehnquist's view gained four votes, only one short of a majority) can cause "congestion," and "those who accept material may often simply drop it on the floor . . . creating an eyesore, a safety hazard, and additional cleanup work." In the liberal paradigm, blocking a walkway, impeding traffic, duress, and littering could be prohibited, but leafleting and solicitation of funds in furtherance of protected speech could not be banned unless they conflict with some government interest of considerably more importance.

The scope and import of this new doctrine were perhaps best revealed in a 1990 case concerning political speech on a public sidewalk leading to and from the entrance of a post office. A sidewalk is the most traditional public forum, but that did not matter. Justice O'Connor, a relative moderate on this Court who has written many of the public forum opinions, declared that "the mere physical characteristics of the property cannot dictate forum analysis." The Bush administration used the public forum doctrine as a basis for arguing that exercise of basic free speech rights can be prohibited on the public sidewalk on Constitution Avenue near the Vietnam Veterans' Memorial.[21] The public forum doctrine limits speech to the mainstream media and isolates the mass of people from other messages.

THE CONTENT BARRIER

Another new doctrine was announced by Justice Rehnquist in a 1986 case involving zoning of adult movie theaters, and it has since been applied by conservative justices to political and all other speech. Because obscenity is a long-established unprotected category of speech, there has been little controversy about zoning schemes that limit the locations of adult bookstores and movie theaters. However, in *Renton v. Playtime Theatres* (1986) the Court faced zoning regulations that effectively banned such theaters entirely.[22] The city of Renton, Washington, prohibited location of adult movie theaters within one thousand feet of any residence, church, or park and within one mile of any school. This would restrict only a small portion of a large or medium-sized city; but in Renton these restrictions covered 94 percent of the city, and the remaining 6 percent was already in use, unusable, or unsuited for a theater. The zoning regulation effectively constituted a total or near-total ban.

Nevertheless, Rehnquist, for the majority, treated it as a time, place, and manner regulation (the formulation of which might be: no time, no place, and no manner) and concluded that it was reasonable by analyzing its terms in the abstract rather than in the context of this particular small town. Such analysis was extraordinary enough, but he also had to deal with the content basis of the regulation, because even a time, place, and manner regulation is not supposed to be content based. The result was a new conception of the content barrier and content neutrality.

Renton's regulation set up special restrictive zoning rules explicitly made applicable only to theaters that show "adult motion pictures." All other movie theaters could locate more or less anywhere, but theaters that showed movies with that particular content were greatly restricted or banned. Nevertheless, Rehnquist concluded that the regulation was content neutral. This feat was accomplished with the "secondary effects" doctrine: content neutrality is satisfied as long as the "predominant" purpose of the measure was directed at "secondary effects" rather than content. Rehnquist found this measure content neutral because, even though it explicitly singled out a particular content of speech, the city was predominantly concerned with preventing crime, maintaining property values, and preserving the "quality of urban life," which, the city simply asserted (no proof was offered) and he simply accepted, were undercut and threatened by adult movie theaters.

This doctrine introduces a purpose element to First Amendment law similar to the more widely known role of intent in discrimination cases. In the liberal paradigm, a government action that infringed on or burdened protected speech triggered strict scrutiny and constituted a violation of the First Amendment unless the government demonstrated a compelling interest. The secondary effects doctrine means that there is no violation unless it is also proved that the government's *purpose* was to infringe on or burden speech. If the government had some other purpose—directing its action at secondary effects rather than at speech—there is no First Amendment violation even though protected speech has in fact been infringed or burdened. Because the Court also accepts very generally stated alternative purposes and does not scrutinize the good faith or basis of an asserted alternative purpose, it is easy for governments to get away with all manner of free speech violations. If the doctrine develops as it has in establishment and exercise of religion and equal-protection cases, the Court will not even require that the alternative purpose be the government's actual purpose; generally stated possible alternative purposes, thought up by lawyers or justices after the fact, will be sufficient to justify a denial of free speech. Malicious purposes can seldom be proved, of course; benign motives are available to explain malignant acts, and the Court does not even require an explanation if malice cannot be proved or a benign purpose can be imagined.

This new doctrine fundamentally undercuts the whole notion of free speech, because speech can be denied based on its content as long as there is some generally stated alternative purpose. Further, what Rehnquist calls secondary effects were the believed, anticipated, or feared effects that led to, or formed the purpose or motivation for, the content-based regulation. Stated another way, the city enacted a regulation to avoid the effects of the content that the regulation was explicitly aimed at. There is nothing really secondary about this at all, and there are no multiple concerns or intentions among which one can be predominate. What Rehnquist calls a "predominate concern . . . with the secondary effects" is simply the purpose and intended results of the regulation and has nothing to do with its content neutrality or lack of content neutrality. This "purpose doctrine," which excuses what would otherwise be constitutional violations unless there is proof of a malicious purpose, is being applied by the conservative Court majority to the range of civil rights and civil liberties.[23]

ACCESS TO THE MASS MEDIA

The Court unanimously invalidated a Florida statute, responding to widespread claims of electoral corruption stemming in part from false charges made on the eve of elections, that created a "right of reply" requiring any newspaper that "assails" the character or record of an electoral candidate to publish the candidate's reply.[24] This has been a rather standard requirement for broadcast media, until recently subject to the broader access rules of the "fairness doctrine" (which is not limited to candidates), and is often required of newspapers and broadcast media in western Europe, where reply rights are favored and defamation suits are usually disfavored. A distinction has been drawn between prohibiting expression of any viewpoint by the media—censorship—and requiring the media to include, in addition to its own views, the views of others. Chief Justice Burger's opinion found no meaningful difference between censorship and compelled access and seems to foreclose any government attempt to provide popular access at least to the print media, particularly since electoral candidates present the strongest claim.

There does not appear to be a principled or sensible reason for allowing required access in the broadcast media and absolutely forbidding it in the print media. Newspapers traditionally have been more serious and intellectual and less focused on entertainment, but they are doing their best these days to dispel that distinction (which is far too subjective in any event). The decision upholding the fairness doctrine was largely based on the "scarcity" of available outlets, but the number of broadcast outlets has increased whereas the number of print outlets has diminished (to one in most markets) so that the print medium is now at least as monopolistic as the broadcast medium. Although newspapers have history on their side, there is no meaningful social or constitutional difference.

In the transformation era, the Court vindicated the interests of individuals and society in free speech and open discourse that theretofore had been subject to government control and censorship. The practices of governments that closed channels of communication or selectively excluded people or messages from the marketplace of ideas were forbidden. This struggle is not over, as the principles and results of the new conservative Court make all too clear. But those newspapers earlier denied access to the marketplace of ideas, together with their successors in the modern press and mass media, have *become* the marketplace of ideas. Absolute freedom of the press now conflicts with meaningful freedom of speech, and we should seek some accommodation that preserves the best of both traditions. If we continue to define and treat the mass media as if they were just another leafleteer on a street corner who not only must be protected from government censorship but also must be shielded from all claims to access by others, we are once again excluding the mass of people from the social dialogue and the marketplace of ideas. A much broader range of people and ideas must gain access to our media or free speech will have lost its meaning.

MONEY AND SPEECH

Following the Watergate scandal, which led to the resignation of President Richard Nixon, there was strong public sentiment for reform of the electoral system to reduce corruption and the effects of money—particularly large amounts of money—on elections. Congress enacted electoral reform measures that placed a variety of monetary limits on campaign contributions and expenditures. In *Buckley v. Valeo* (1976) a majority struck down many of those limits as violations of the free speech rights of rich people.[25] That case and succeeding decisions have essentially made it constitutionally impermissible for Congress or any state legislature effectively to reduce the role of money in elections.

There is certainly an important connection between money and speech to the extent that campaign funds are used for speech (rather than for polls, consultants, rents, and so on) because the expenditure of money is necessary for the most effective forms of protected speech. But writing a check is not speaking. In the liberal paradigm, such activities so connected or intertwined with speech enjoyed protection, but not to the same extent as "pure speech," the spoken and written word.

Because the purpose of Congress was to improve the electoral system, stop corruption, and thereby further democracy by reducing the role of money in elections, the effect on speech would seem incidental or secondary.[26] But the Court did not see it that way. Concluding that money *is* speech, the Court applied strict scrutiny and invalidated various limits on expenditures by campaigns and individuals (while upholding the limits on contributions). For example, the limits that the act set on campaign expenditures for presidential elections ($10 million prior to nomination and $20 million in the general election, which hardly require bare-bones campaigns) and by candidates on their own behalf ($25,000, which would make it difficult for a rich candidate to buy an election) were invalidated.

The Court found these limits—and the goal of reducing the effects of money in elections—unacceptable because they "restrict the voices of people and interest groups that have money to spend." Campaigns draw funds, and should be able to spend them, in amounts that "normally vary with the size and intensity of the candidate's support." This is the language of the marketplace, not of ideas but of campaign funds. According to the Court, campaigns draw funds in proportion to their support, and if this means the ones that draw the most funds will most often win, that's just the operation of a free market. The problem with this conception is that elections are a type of market phenomenon in which every person, not every dollar, is supposed to have equal weight. And campaigns draw funds mostly in proportion to their attractiveness to rich people.

In succeeding cases, the conservatives struck down other electoral reform measures, including one that limited the power of political action committees (PACs). Congress limited the amount of money a PAC could independently spend ($1,000) in support of a presidential candidate who has opted to receive public financing. This created a trade-off: If the candidate took public campaign financing, then a PAC's support of him or her was limited, but there was no limit if the candidate opted not to receive public funds. The reform was challenged by the National Conservative Political Action Committee, which wished to exceed the limit in support of President Ronald Reagan's reelection although he was receiving public campaign financing. Justice Rehnquist's majority opinion in *Federal Election Commission v. National Conservative Political Action Committee* (1985) stressed the rights of contributors to band together and spend what they wish (and have). In *First National Bank of Boston v. Bellotti* (1978) the Court also recognized, for the first time, free speech rights of corporations, which have been used to invalidate local legislation aimed at reducing the influence of corporations on the outcomes of public referendums.[27]

Note the different role and significance given to money in this line of cases and the cases dealing with people of ordinary means trying to raise money as they hand out leaflets: Contributions by rich people are constitutionally protected; contributions by ordinary people solicited in public places are an inconvenience to others that justifies limiting speech rights. The conservatives have created different speech rules for the haves and the have-nots.

The Court forbade Congress and local legislatures to interfere with the political privileges of wealth and established what amounts to a First Amendment right to buy elections and referenda. Not surprisingly, money has increasingly dominated elections and politics. The First Amendment as interpreted by today's conservatives constitutes a constitutional barrier to political reform much like the constitutional barrier to economic reform erected by conservative justices in the *Lockner* era of the early 1900s.

VOTING AND REPRESENTATIONAL RIGHTS

In the 1960s, the Court recognized a fundamental right to vote and to ballot access based in the First and Fourteenth Amendments and enforced with the "strict scrutiny" standard. However, even then, the right was sometimes subordinated to maintenance of the two-party system. In the 1990s, as public opinion was increasingly dissatisfied with the two parties and the political process, the conservative Court rejected strict scrutiny and moved toward constitutional enshrinement of the two-party system and away from the tradition of inclusion of all our people in the political process.

In two leading cases, the Court upheld state laws prohibiting write-in voting and third-party nomination of a candidate nominated by one of the major parties (called "fusion").[28] The Court said, "No right is more precious in a free country" than the right to vote, but the states must maintain "the integrity of the democratic system," emphasizing the states' strong interest in avoiding "unrestrained factionalism" and approving of state rules that "favor" the two major parties.

While write-in voting and fusion are not the most important aspects of participation in the political process, there is something much deeper at stake. The conservative Court is restricting voting and electoral activity to the two-party system. Stated another way, the avoidance of "unrestrained factionalism" is the avoidance of real political choices that has characterized our political process and fomented so much popular discontent. The two parties, vying for a narrow band of moderates that increasingly decide elections, muddle their messages and principles and turn off most of the eligible voters. While meaningful reform lies in the direction of removing money and all forms of bribery from elections, proportional representation systems now adopted in all but a handful of democratic countries, and removal of barriers to ballot access and voting, the Court has been erecting constitutional barriers to change that encrust the current system. Unrestrained factionalism is not something to be avoided by a systemic muzzling and muddling of political discourse and voter choice. We need more, not fewer, factions—more parties and more democracy—and the ability to make meaningful political choices.[29]

As we stray in this period of conservative dominance further from the ideal of free speech we celebrate, it becomes easier to see the ideological aspects of free speech in the United States. The struggle for free speech up to the transformation, waged largely by progressives and finally realized by the labor, civil rights, and other progressive movements, has been falsely redefined as a set of preexisting natural rights whose essence and history are legal rather than political. A false pride in the legal system has displaced a source for genuine pride in the people.

This recast version of freedom of speech serves in our society to validate and legitimize existing social and power relations and to mask the lack of real participation and democracy. After two hundred years, American democracy must mean more than voting in elections devoid of content or context and the right to picket when you're really upset. Our celebration of free speech should be tempered by the realization that its continued vitality even here is not at all assured, and should be channeled into efforts to protect transformation-era speech rights and to expand public access to the media and participation and democracy regarding the decisions that affect our lives.

NOTES

I appreciate comments on early drafts of the original version of this chapter that appeared in the first edition from Thomas Emerson, Marge Frantz, David Montgomery, Victor Rabinowitz, David Rudovsky, and James Weinstein. Portions of this chapter were drawn from my chapters on expression and participation in the political process in David Kairys, *With Liberty and Justice for Some: A Critique of the Conservative Supreme Court* (New York: New Press, 1993).

1. The history summarized here is available with more detail and documentation in the earlier editions of this book: 1st ed. (New York: Pantheon), chapter 7; rev. ed. (New York: Pantheon), chapter 11. The most helpful secondary sources on the incidents, cases, and trends that comprise the pretransformation history are Leon Whipple, *The Story of Civil Liberty in the United States* (Westport, CT: Greenwood Press, 1927); Leon Whipple, *Our Ancient Liberties* (New York: Da Capo Press, 1927); Zechariah Chafee, Jr., *Free Speech in the United States* (Cambridge, MA: Harvard University Press, 1941); Norman Dorsen, Paul Bender, and Burt

Neuborne, *Emerson, Haber, and Dorsen's Political and Civil Rights in the United States*, vol. 1 (Boston: Little, Brown, 1976), 20–51; Thomas Emerson, *The System of Freedom of Expression* (New York: Random House, 1970); John Roche, *The Quest for the Dream* (New York: Macmillan, 1963); Jerold Auerbach, *Labor and Liberty* (New York: Bobbs-Merrill, 1966); Jerold Auerbach, "The Depression Decade," in *The Pulse of Freedom*, ed. Alan Reitman (New York: W. W. Norton, 1975); Paul Murphy, *World War I and the Origin of Civil Liberties in the United States* (New York: W. W. Norton, 1979); David Rabban, *The First Amendment in Its Forgotten Years*, 90 Yale Law Journal 514 (1981).

2. *Boston Globe*, May 11, 1987.

3. *Commonwealth v. Davis*, 162 Mass. 510, 511 (1895).

4. *Davis v. Massachusetts*, 167 U.S. 43 (1897).

5. See Dayton McKean, *The Boss* (Boston: Houghton Mifflin, 1940); Irving Bernstein, *The Turbulent Years* (Boston: Houghton Mifflin, 1970); Richard Connors, *A Cycle of Power* (Metuchen, NJ: Scarecrow Press, 1971).

6. *Hague v. CIO*, 307 U.S. 496 (1939).

7. That concept was best articulated in the famous opinions of Justices Holmes and Brandeis starting in 1919. See, for example, Brandeis's concurring opinion in *Whitney v. California*, 274 U.S. 357, 375–76 (1927).

8. See Zechariah Chafee, Jr., *How Human Rights Got into the Constitution* (Boston: Boston University Press, 1952); Leonard Levy, *Emergence of a Free Press* (New York: Oxford University Press, 1985); David M. Rabban, *The Ahistorical Historian: Leonard Levy on Freedom of Expression in Early American History*, 37 Stanford Law Review 795 (1985).

9. Whipple, *The Story of Civil Liberty*, 21, 25–27. On the history of the Alien and Sedition Acts (Act of June 25, 1798, 1 Stat. 570; Act of July 14, 1798, 1 Stat. 596), see Whipple, *The Story of Civil Liberty*, 21–27; James Stephens, *Digest of the Criminal Law* (New York: Macmillan, 1904), 96–99; Frank Anderson, "The Enforcement of the Alien and Sedition Laws," in *Annual Report of the American Historical Association* (1912), 113–26; Chafee, *Free Speech*, 18, 27.

10. Whipple, *The Story of Civil Liberty*, 27.

11. Free speech in the 1950s is discussed in detail in the earlier editions. See David Kairys, "Freedom of Speech," in *The Politics of Law: A Progressive Critique*, rev. ed., ed. David Kairys (New York: Pantheon, 1990), 250–59.

12. See *Barenblatt v. United States*, 360 U.S. 109 (1959); *Dennis v. United States*, 341 U.S. 494 (1951); *Lawson v. United States* and *Trumbo v. United States*, 176 F.2d 49 (D.C. Cir. 1949), cert. denied, 339 U.S. 934 (1950), the "Hollywood 10" case. The ACLU also succumbed, including its

expulsion of well-known labor activist Elizabeth Gurley Flynn from its board, but rescinded and repudiated its actions in 1976.

13. *Murdock v. Pennsylvania,* 319 U.S. 105, 111 (1943); *Marsh v. Alabama,* 326 U.S. 501 (1946); *Amalgamated Food Employees Union Local 590 v. Logan Valley Plaza,* 391 U.S. 308 (1968).

14. *Central Hudson Gas v. Public Services Commission,* 447 U.S. 557, 561 (1980).

15. Ben H. Bagdikian, *The Media Monopoly,* 3d ed. (Boston: Beacon Press, 1990), 3–4. See also Don Hazen and Julie Winokur, *We the Media: A Citizen's Guide to Fighting for Media Democracy* (New York: New Press, 1997); Eric Barnouw et al., *Conglomerates and the Media* (New York: New Press, 1997).

16. Bagdikian, *Media Monopoly,* chapter 9; Kenneth E. Warner, "Cigarette Advertising and Magazine Coverage of the Hazards of Smoking," *New England Journal of Medicine* 326 (1992): 307–8; "Cigarette Maker Cuts Off Agency That Made Smoking-Ban TV Ads," *New York Times,* April 6, 1988, A1.

17. See David Kairys, *Foreword to Noble Lies and the First Amendment: A Symposium on the Death of Discourse,* 64 University of Cincinnati Law Review 1195 (1996).

18. For cases reaffirming some protective aspects of speech law, see *Texas v. Johnson,* 491 U.S. 397 (1989), invalidating a conviction for flag burning; *Reno v. ACLU,* 117 S.Ct. 2329 (1997), invalidating a ban of "indecency" on the Internet. Some of the retrenchment decisions came as early as the mid-1970s, before conservatives fully dominated the Court, requiring and sometimes getting the votes of liberals or moderates on the Court.

19. See generally Kairys, *With Liberty and Justice for Some.*

20. *International Society for Krishna Consciousness v. Lee,* 505 U.S. 672, 830 (1992); *Hudgens v. NLRB,* 424 U.S. 507 (1976), overruling *Amalgamated Food Employees Union v. Logan Valley Plaza,* 391 U.S. 308 (1968); *Members of the City Council v. Taxpayers for Vincent,* 466 U.S. 789 (1984); *Heffron v. International Society for Krishna Consciousness,* 452 U.S. 640 (1981); *Frisby v. Schultz,* 487 U.S. 474 (1988); *Greer v. Spock,* 424 U.S. 828 (1976); *Boos v. Barry,* 485 U.S. 312 (1988); *Cornelius v. NAACP Legal Defense and Education Fund,* 473 U.S. 788 (1985); *Perry Educational Association v. Perry Local Educational Association,* 460 U.S. 37 (1983); *Hazelwood School District v. Kuhlmeier,* 484 U.S. 260 (1988).

21. *United States v. Kokinda,* 497 U.S. 720 (1990) (O'Connor's opinion was for a plurality of four); *Henderson v. Lujan,* 964 F.2d 1179 (D.C. Cir. 1992), rejecting the administration's claim but suggesting that similar sidewalks near important attractions may be restricted.

22. *Renton v. Playtime Theatres,* 475 U.S. 41 (1986).

23. See Kairys, *With Liberty and Justice for Some,* 183–86; see also *Rust v. Sullivan,* 500 U.S. 173 (1991), approving a regulation that forbade doctors in federally funded medical facilities to discuss abortion or to refer a patient to another facility that provided or discussed abortion services.

24. *Miami Herald Publishing Company v. Tornillo,* 418 U.S. 241 (1974).

25. *Buckley v. Valeo,* 424 U.S. 1 (1976).

26. See *United States v. O'Brien,* 391 U.S. 367 (1968), where a liberal majority initiated the "incidental effects" doctrine.

27. *Federal Election Commission v. National Conservative Political Action Committee,* 470 U.S. 480 (1985); *First National Bank of Boston v. Bellotti,* 435 U.S. 765 (1978).

28. *Burdick v. Takushi,* 504 U.S. 428 (1992); *Timmons v. Twin Cities Area New Party,* 117 S.Ct. 1364 (1997). The Court has also gutted the Voting Rights Act; see *Shaw v. Reno,* 509 U.S. 630 (1993); *Miller v. Johnson,* 115 S.Ct. 2475 (1995).

29. On these reforms, see my Introduction, n. 17.

9 RHONDA COPELON

THE INDIVISIBLE FRAMEWORK OF INTERNATIONAL HUMAN RIGHTS: BRINGING IT HOME

THE year 1998 marks the 50th anniversary of the Universal Declaration of Human Rights (UDHR), drafted when the capitalist world was constrained by the Soviet Union, and when want and war and the industrialized hatred of the Nazi Holocaust were recent memories.[1] The UDHR was designed to elaborate the commitment, inaugurated in the UN Charter, to promote human rights as indispensable to international as well as domestic peace and security. As a "common standard of achievement for all peoples and nations," the UDHR prohibits all forms of discrimination and is the foundation of an indivisible concept of rights. In contrast to the negative approach of the U.S. Bill of Rights, it recognizes as inseparable and interdependent—indivisible—political and civil rights and social, economic, and cultural rights.

In other words, the promise of the UDHR cannot be met by simply protecting liberty or simply providing food. These are inseparable and interdependent in that the opportunity to exercise liberty will influence the production and distribution of food, at the same time as hunger is antithetical to the enjoyment of liberty and full participation in society. Threatening to resign over U.S. opposition to the economic and social rights aspect of indivisibility, Eleanor Roosevelt, who chaired the Human Rights Commission from 1946 to 1952 and was instrumental in negotiating the UDHR, put it succinctly: "You can't talk civil rights to people who are hungry."[2]

Notwithstanding Eleanor Roosevelt's contribution and the broad acceptance of the UDHR among nations today, its indivisible platform has been consistently undercut rather than embraced by the United States in both foreign and domestic policy. As the cold war deepened, advocating for implementation of human rights in the United States was suspect as "communist." In the United Nations, the plan to embody the UDHR in one treaty was abandoned in favor of two treaties approved in 1966: the International Covenant on Civil and Political Rights (ICCPR), dubbed first-generation rights, and the International Covenant on Economic, Social, and Cultural Rights (ICESCR), dubbed second-generation rights. The hostility of U.S. policy makers to economic and social rights as true rights continues to this day.[3]

Although the UDHR has been the cornerstone of human rights movements in many parts of the world, it is virtually unknown in the United States to social justice activists and attorneys as well as to the legal establishment and the general public. The same is true of the six major widely ratified human rights treaties, including the two 1966 covenants, which establish interpretative and monitoring committees; it is also true of numerous UN declarations, resolutions, and conference agreements that have elaborated the UDHR's broad human rights program.[4] Even the U.S. ratification of three of these treaties, which came in 1992 with many limitations, received minimal attention.

The need to overcome this ignorance in the United States is particularly compelling today. The commitment to civil rights, including the legitimacy of affirmative action, is under siege. Balancing the budget and devolution of power to the states, or the "race to the bottom," is undoing already inadequate public commitments to social welfare and a safety net for the poor. Women, particularly women of color, bear disproportionately the brunt of poverty and privatization. Fundamentalist movements continue their attack on reproductive and sexual rights while gender violence and discrimination against women and sexual minorities continue largely unabated. And, except for the highly skilled, the labor force outside the home is being devalued, downsized, and demoralized.

Conditions endured by poor and working people, women, and minority peoples in South American and African countries are distinct but inseparable from conditions in the United States as well as from the influence of U.S. policy. Controlled by the highly industrialized donor nations, the international financial institutions along with multinational corporations are transforming mixed economies into ruthless market economies. By conditioning debt relief and the promise of new loans on a country's acceptance of structural adjustment policies, they strip away or privatize essential public services. Pressure to relinquish trade barriers without effective countervailing protection subjects impoverished workers to unmitigated exploitation. A resurgence of the arms race among both Northern Hemisphere manufacturers and Southern Hemisphere buyers diverts resources from social needs and retools the repressive, violent capacity of states. Fundamentalist movements, which thrive in desperate times, are also being stoked by tacit and active support from Northern governments, particularly when they promise openness to the global market.[5]

It may seem ironic or naive even to suggest that something so fragile or abstract as international human rights could be a counterweight to these local and global trends. Human rights "law" bears little resemblance to the formalities that we associate with law. The International Court of Justice entertains only the cases brought by states, which only occasionally involve human rights, and has no mandatory enforcement capacity. The proposed permanent International Criminal Court now under negotiation may be similarly limited and will deal only with gross violence or persecution, not with everyday human rights violations. Human rights "enforcement" is dispersed among political commissions, treaty committees, and special rapporteurs or working groups who investigate violations. For the most part, enforcement depends on states' voluntary responses to public scrutiny and shaming. Indeed, the insight that law is inseparable from politics is nowhere more fitting than in the sphere of human rights. Nor does the universality of human rights make them less indeterminate or susceptible to manipulation than domestic rights. The substance and potential of international human rights depends ultimately on the courage, persistence, and vision of human rights movements.

A sense of both individual and collective entitlement—embodying a vision of a better society and world—is thus a cornerstone of popular resistance and the source of human rights norms and accountability. Representing norms and claims of universal and fundamental dimension, international human rights acquire impact through popular organizing and demand. Building a human rights movement and culture in the United States, within the law and the society generally, offers not only an alternative vision of social organization and justice on our soil; it could also affect the manner in which the United States exercises its power in the international arena.

To do this, we must confront the myth that the U.S. Constitution is the best in the world. Domestically, the myth obscures the fact that the Constitution was drawn to protect the interests of white, male, propertied men and that the legitimation of slavery was at its heart and remains today its unredressed legacy. Internationally, the United States perpetuated this myth as an instrument of the cold war, at the same time as it worked to narrow, distort, and obfuscate the indivisible international framework of human rights. The myth is under challenge today as many countries have adhered, at least formally, to the international framework. The new South African constitution, for example, entrenches the indivisibility principle and puts ours to shame.

While the media stokes notions of superiority here by giving increasing attention to human rights violations abroad, the systemic failure to apply the human rights lens at home continues. Recently, I mentioned to a high school teacher that my work involves international women's human rights. Immediately, she said, "Oh yes, all my kids are really upset about female genital mutilation." "What about wife battering or health care here?" I asked.

THE BASIC ELEMENTS OF THE HUMAN RIGHTS FRAMEWORK

Negative is a word that aptly describes the U.S. framework of civil rights and civil liberties in a number of ways: Rights are limited to constraints on government; they do not reach private conduct, they do not include the most basic social and economic needs, and since about 1980, even the most limited conception of state responsibility has been essentially dismantled. For example, the current Supreme Court emphasizes that the liberty protected by the Fourteenth Amendment does not require government to take even minimal measures to protect that liberty from private violations, to enable its exercise, or even to insulate it from purposeful state suppression and discrimination. As Chief Justice Rehnquist pronounced in the infamous *DeShaney* decision, which stripped abused children of any claim to state or constitutional protection: "[Nothing] in the language of the Due Process Clause itself requires the State to protect life, liberty and property of its citizens against invasion by private actors. The Clause is phrased as a limitation on the State's power to act, not as a guarantee of minimal levels of safety and security."[6]

The international human rights system contains both negative and positive rights and imposes upon states both negative and positive obligations. The provision of basic needs—rather than, as here, accompanied by accusations of individual moral fault or the practical deficiencies of the poor—is recognized internationally as a human right and a sovereign responsibility. The International Covenant on Economic, Social, and Cultural Rights (ICESCR), so widely ratified as to be binding customary international law, protects the "right of everyone to the enjoyment of the highest attainable standard of physical and mental health." This involves the provision of not only preventative and curative health care but also the protection of healthful environmental, social, and occupational conditions. The ICESCR also recognizes "the right of everyone to an adequate standard of living . . . , including adequate food, clothing and housing, and to the continuous improvement of living conditions." Work for all—including participation in trade unions, fair terms, equality, safety, and leisure—is a human right. Social security, insurance, and assistance for families are human rights. Education is a human right, including free compulsory primary education as well as access to affordable higher education. Participation in cultural life and enjoyment of the benefits of scientific progress are human rights.[7]

Some aspects of these rights, such as primary education, are immediate obligations, and some, such as equitable distribution of sufficient food, require international cooperation. In general, the state's obligation is to "take steps, individually and through international assistance and cooperation, . . . to the maximum of its available resources, with a view to achieving progressively the full realization of the[se] rights by all appropriate means."[8] The UN Committee on Economic, Social, and Cultural Rights, along with international jurists, have identified the concept of a "minimum core" that must be guaranteed to all. While the extent of progressive implementation depends on resources, there is no excuse in a highly industrialized country such as the United States not to approach maximal realization. At the least, retrogression is forbidden. Cutbacks on social welfare programs and privatization of basic services are presumptively a violation of these human rights whether they be demanded by the international monetary institutions of Southern Hemisphere countries through structural adjustment policies (SAPs) or imposed domestically through devolution to the states, slashing of welfare programs, or privatization of public sector services. Privatization of public service institutions, whether of health care or water, is a violation unless the state retains control so as to fulfill its obligation to ensure both minimal and progressive access to needed services on a nondiscriminatory basis. Furthermore, the ICESCR permits only developing countries to limit the equal enjoyment of these rights to non-nationals.[9]

Moreover, international political and civil rights—the closest parallel to the negative rights approach of the U.S. Constitution—transcend our own. In terms of the scope of substantive rights, the right to life contained in the ICCPR clearly envisages progressive abolition of the death penalty as a goal and explicitly forbids execution of juveniles, a prohibition nonetheless approved by the U.S. Supreme Court. The right to be free from torture is explicit; and the protection extended to cruel, inhuman, and degrading "*treatment* or punishment" is not simply a post-conviction remedy, as is the Eighth Amendment. Freedom of speech is protected, but "propaganda for war . . . [and] advocacy of national, racial or religious hatred that constitutes incitement to discrimination, hostility or violence shall be prohibited." Linguistic minorities cannot be denied "the right, in community with the other members of their group, . . . to use their own language." Non-refoulement—sending immigrants back to danger—is prohibited.[10]

The ICCPR binds states not only to "respect" but also to "ensure" the enjoyment of these rights. It specifically requires that they "adopt such legislative or other measures as may be necessary to give effect to the rights recognized in the present Covenant" and to "ensure . . . an effective remedy for violations." This is an important springboard for the obligation to take positive steps to implement social and economic rights in order to protect political and civil rights.[11]

There are a number of dimensions to this positive obligation. The right to be free from torture, for example, requires that states institute systemic preventive measures against official misconduct—training, monitoring, and sanctions, for example. The positive obligation also requires states to protect human rights against private deprivation. Life, liberty, and security of person, for example, must be protected against privately inflicted harm through investigation, punishment, and preventive measures. Thus, the right to life entails an obligation to prevent and punish political assassination and kidnapping by paramilitary operations, as well as murder, gender violence, and child abuse by private individuals.[12]

Moreover, the positive obligations transcend the use of criminal penalties or judicial remedies. The UN Human Rights Committee has recognized the need for affirmative health and social welfare initiatives to avert infant malnutrition and epidemics and abortion-related mortality. In the European human rights system, the right to privacy and family life has been interpreted to require provision of legal counsel necessary to its protection.[13] The same principle should require Medicaid funding of abortion for poor women given that abortion is legal or recognized as protected.

In sum, in the international system, even political and civil rights involve state responsibility to ensure them positively. This is in sharp contrast to the U.S. approach, which views positive measures as an optional matter for legislation. Indeed, it is striking that in the United States we rarely speak of state responsibility in regard to rights. By contrast, in the international system the concept of state responsibility is fundamental, and in every human rights treaty the scope of state responsibility is articulated explicitly. State responsibility—whether it be to respect, ensure, protect, or fulfill the human right at issue—is one of the cornerstones of the human rights frameworks. How to implement and measure these responsibilities is increasingly a focus of human rights bodies and jurists.[14]

International antidiscrimination principles also depart significantly from the U.S. model. The scope of protected classes is much broader, including "discrimination of any kind, such as race, colour, sex, language, religion, political or other opinion, national or social origin, property, birth *or other status*." While discrimination on the basis of sexual orientation has not yet been squarely recognized as an "other status," the Human Rights Committee has recently recognized sexual orientation discrimination as sex discrimination and, in its comments on the U.S. report under the ICCPR, criticized the U.S. Supreme Court's decision in *Bowers v. Hardwick* as inconsistent with the Covenant.[15]

Moreover, state responsibility under international law to eliminate discrimination explicitly extends to the private sphere and covers disproportionate impact as well as intentional discrimination. In slightly different language, the Race and Women's conventions define discrimination as including distinctions that impair or nullify the equal enjoyment of rights "in the political, economic, social, cultural, civil or any other field." Both conventions also emphasize the need to address the cultural foundations of racial and gender hierarchy, stereotypes, and discrimination. Given the particular significance of private sphere discrimination to the status of women, the Women's Convention contains specific articles requiring that states foster equality in the private sphere affecting work, family relations, and access to goods and services.[16]

Both Conventions also call for temporary affirmative action measures where needed to secure the "full and equal enjoyment and exercise of human rights and fundamental freedoms" and accelerate de facto equality. In the Women's Convention, positive measures to provide assistance and prevent discrimination based on pregnancy are accepted explicitly.[17]

Finally, the Supreme Court's proliferation of barriers to the justiciability of rights claims is also out of line with international standards. Most of the international instruments emphasize the right to an accessible and effective judicial remedy for violations. And, like many national systems, their complaint procedures do not condition the ability to challenge violations on narrow concepts of injury or standing; rather, the risk of injury or the impact of disadvantage, such as stigma, are recognized forms of injury.[18]

The U.S. Bill of Rights and the current interpretation of it by the Supreme Court—far from the beacon imagined and proclaimed in the United States—amount to a mere shadow of the universal version.

THE POLITICAL CONSTRUCTION OF IGNORANCE

The apparent acceptance by the United States government of the broad, indivisible concept of human rights contained in the UDHR was hard won and short lived. As the U.S. representative to the UN Human Rights Commission during the Truman administration, Eleanor Roosevelt—deeply affected by the Great Depression and World War II and convinced that economic and social rights were essential to lasting security and peace in the world—pressed the United States into accepting the UDHR. Ultimately, however, the U.S. vote to approve the UDHR had more to do with the desire to show up the Soviet Union, which was among the abstainers, than with a commitment to the declaration's principles.[19] The prospect of international scrutiny of U.S. domestic policy would not be part of the bargain, nor would the international framework be recognized as a touchstone for domestic policy.

From the outset, however, the civil rights movement understood the potential of the human rights system to encourage domestic change. In 1947 and 1951, petitions were filed with the United Nations documenting and challenging de jure racial segregation, racial violence, and the status of African Americans in the Unites States. While these initiatives contributed to the formal repudiation of school segregation by the Eisenhower administration and the Supreme Court, the cold war and Southern opposition to racial equality produced a rightwing backlash against international accountability that continues to the present.[20]

The Bricker Amendment to the UDHR sought to preclude ratification of human rights treaties. Although never formally approved by Congress, its substance was adopted as policy by the Eisenhower administration.[21] The State Department openly used human rights as a selective tool of foreign policy—selective in the sense of focusing on violations of political and civil rights abroad committed by the Soviet Union and its allies. Advocates of international accountability of the United States were branded as disloyal.[22] This selectivity played a significant role in shaping opinion in the United States.

Attention to egregious human rights violations occurring abroad but not at home generates a convenient and false sense of security and superiority in the United States. Torture and inhuman treatment, for example, among the most frequently condemned international obligations, appear as a characteristic of the jails of dictators not democracies. Even those in the United States who suffer inhuman treatment—in the form of police brutality or physical and psychological debilitation in custody, including rape and sexual harassment—rarely name it as such. The Constitution does not explicitly protect against torture or inhuman treatment. Despite recent ratification of the UN Convention Against Torture (CAT), Congress restricted its scope and excluded U.S. officials from the purview of the civil damage remedy enacted to implement it. Thus, torture and inhuman treatment in the United States—whether committed by state officials or as a result of state tolerance of private abuse such as marital rape or other forms of severe domestic violence—have been obscured.[23]

Inattention to the international framework of human rights as a measure of domestic policy is also bolstered by the myth that the U.S. Constitution, particularly the Bill of Rights, is the best and most effective guarantor of human rights in the world. This bias is further ensured by the lack of human rights education as part of educational curricula at all levels. Neither international law nor human rights are required courses in most law schools, let alone in other contexts. Accordingly, today there is little popular sense of entitlement to the full range of human rights or knowledge of the principle of governmental responsibility. The United States has also used the myth of constitutional superiority to hold itself above international scrutiny and continues to do so today in its refusal to ratify the ICESCR and the Women's and Child Rights Conventions and in the limits it imposes when it does ratify human rights treaties.

In the international arena, the United States has consistently deprecated social and economic rights—the second-generation rights—as simply aspirations: They are not real rights to which States could be held accountable, and they involve too much intrusion into domestic policy. While the issues of definition and standard setting are indeed challenging, this deference to sovereignty or self-determination in regard to economic and social rights ironically evaporates when U.S. foreign aid or the assistance of the World Bank or International Monetary Fund are at issue. There, for example, extensive economic restructuring is demanded in return for debt relief and continuing international assistance.[24]

U.S. hostility to social and economic rights as mandated entitlements together with the myth of constitutional superiority has hindered popular knowledge as well as advocacy in the United States of the UDHR's indivisible framework. On the domestic level, neither the welfare rights movement of the 1960s nor its legal advocates made the UDHR or the ICESCR a theme or used them as a normative frame of reference. Major U.S.-based international human rights groups traditionally have excluded economic and social rights from their purview, although this is under review today. And significantly, grass roots movements have begun explicitly campaigning for human rights, including economic rights.[25]

Until recently, it may have seemed that the New Deal social welfare programs of the 1930s and the civil rights legislation of the mid-1960s were a permanent part of the legal landscape, albeit not by constitutional compulsion. Thus, just over a decade ago, a leading U.S. human rights scholar argued that the United States had become a welfare state and that "[t]he welfare system and other rights granted by legislation (for example, laws against racial discrimination) are so deeply imbedded as to have near constitutional sturdiness."[26] Given the recent stripping away of social welfare entitlements, the need for attention to the international framework as a normative basis for social and economic rights in the Constitution is pressing.

The indivisible human rights framework survived the cold war despite U.S. machinations to truncate it in the international arena. The framework is there to shatter the myth of the superiority of the U.S. version of rights, to rebuild popular expectations, and to help develop a culture and jurisprudence of indivisible human rights. Indeed, in the face of systemic inequality and crushing poverty, violence by official and private actors, globalization of the market economy, and military and environmental depredation, the human rights framework is gaining new force and new dimensions. It is being broadened today by the movements of people in different parts of the world, particularly in the Southern Hemisphere and significantly of women, who understand the protection of human rights as a matter of individual and collective human survival and betterment. Also emerging is a notion of third-generation rights, encompassing collective rights that cannot be solved on a state-by-state basis and that call for new mechanisms of accountability, particularly affecting Northern countries. The emerging rights include human-centered sustainable development, environmental protection, peace, and security.[27] Given the poverty and inequality in the United States as well as our role in the world, it is imperative that we bring the human rights framework to bear on both domestic and foreign policy.

TOWARD AN INDIVISIBLE HUMAN RIGHTS STRATEGY: ADVANCES AND CHALLENGES IN WOMEN'S HUMAN RIGHTS ADVOCACY

Recent advances by women's human rights movements should provide inspiration, strategic insight, and some hope for U.S. domestic activists. Although the UDHR prohibited sex discrimination, and the covenants reiterated and expanded this prohibition, and despite the Women's Convention, which became effective in 1981, violence and discrimination against women were largely invisible in the human rights arena until 1993.[28] Subsequent to the 1985 World Conference on Women in Nairobi, women, particularly in the Southern Hemisphere, began to organize using human rights as a framework and vision. The initial focus was on violence against women because of the near universality of its occurrence, the gravity of its effects, and its centrality to the classic human rights paradigm.

There were significant obstacles. International non-governmental organizations (NGOs) contended that women's claims would dilute existing human rights; that gender violence was merely a common crime; and that the state-centered human rights framework could not reach gender violence. At base, the view that violence and other violations of women's human rights are not important or are adequately encompassed by "neutral" rules was and remains a great obstacle to effective protection.

However, a global campaign for human rights and the 1993 World Conference on Human Rights in Vienna broke the gender sound barrier. The recognition of violence against women as a human rights violation and of the responsibility of governments to integrate gender into all human rights and related programs were the major innovations of the Vienna Conference. The following year, the General Assembly approved the Declaration on the Elimination of Violence Against Women, which for the first time recognized gender violence as a human rights violation and delineated state responsibility to prevent, punish, and eliminate official, community, and intimate violence. While in 1992 most in the human rights field questioned whether rape was a war crime, today the International Criminal Tribunal for the former Yugoslavia has charged rape as torture and enslavement, and the International Criminal Court negotiations have accepted sexual violence as among the gravest war crimes. As a result of domestic pressure, increased occasions for international review, and an increasing political recognition of the costs of gender violence, nations are beginning to pass laws against domestic violence.[29]

These advances are the product of continuing mobilization, but rhetoric does not transform into action by magic. While feminist scholars provided a theoretical basis for challenging the exclusion of women and asserting state responsibility for systemic private conduct, the most important factor was that women, organized with a sense of entitlement and a powerful vision, were a force that could not be stopped.[30] Ironically, these historical advances occurred less because of the salience of the issue of women's rights to the delegates than because of its seeming insignificance in a conference that nearly did not take place because of the intensity of the international tension over universality and sovereignty issues.

At the same time, the campaign to have gender violence recognized as a vehicle for bringing women into the human rights arena confronts the distinction between first- and second-generation rights. It has been difficult to focus attention and resources on the economic and social underpinnings of gender violence. Thus, when the Inter-American Convention on the Prevention, Punishment, and Elimination of Violence Against Women was being negotiated, the positive obligations to take social and economic measures to eliminate violence were watered down and excluded from the petition procedure before the Inter-American Commission on Human Rights.[31] The danger of this development is not unfamiliar to U.S. activists. As implementation of the norm against gender violence draws more and more activists to violence-specific remedies—prosecution, heightened penalties, incarceration, protective orders, and training of police and judicial personnel, for example—the economic, social, political, and cultural underpinnings of violence are pushed to the margins of human rights concerns.

At the 1994 International Conference on Population and Development (ICPD), women took the next step despite tremendous opposition to the human rights perspective. There a convergence of women's movements concerned with women's health and human rights accomplished another amazing, albeit partial, paradigm shift. The ICPD Programme of Action articulated the foundation for transforming targeted fertility reduction programs into a concrete and a more indivisible women-centered human rights program. It recognized sexual and reproductive health and reproductive rights as human rights, emphasizing decision making free of violence, coercion, and discrimination, as well as the responsibility of states to ensure broad health care services, education, gender equality, and empowerment and participation by women's NGOs in policy making and implementation. While religious fundamentalists led by the Vatican were able to limit women's autonomy rights by excluding sexual rights and eliminating the call to consider the decriminalization of abortion, these defects were partially remedied at the Fourth World Conference on Women.[32]

It is significant that the ICPD Program framed its detailed positive program for health, education, and women's empowerment as human rights. The force of the women's lobby and its explicit reliance on human rights principles in Cairo in 1994, together with the acknowledged inutility of the population control approach and cost of women's subordination, laid the foundation for this success. The U.S. delegation strongly supported the recognition of reproductive decision-making rights and the need for progress on the abortion issue against a fundamentalist coalition led by the Vatican. It also ultimately supported the indivisible framework in Cairo. Otherwise, it would have been isolated among countries and appeared inconsistent with the Clinton administration's domestic focus, at the time, to improve health care coverage. Women were also able to qualify the potential privatization of reproductive health care by a recognition that states are ultimately responsible for the quality and accessibility of the necessary care.[33] However, the strength of the indivisible framework in the ICPD Programme is in part connected to the fact that reproductive health care serves not only women but also those whose object is fertility control.

Nevertheless, the ICPD Program revealed another layer of resistance to implementing the full indivisible framework. Some called it "What happened to the 'D' in ICPD?" There was a concerted women's lobby on the development issues, which challenged the problem of unsustainable development, overproduction, and overconsumption in the Northern Hemisphere and among Southern Hemisphere elites and called for an end to SAPs and for increased dedication of both international or foreign aid and domestic resources to social welfare funding. These issues are merely mentioned but not developed in the Cairo Program.[34]

Worldwide development issues—specifically poverty, enabling economic environments, and social integration—were the focus of the World Summit on Social Development, which preceded the Beijing Women's Conference in 1995. There a caucus of women's human rights NGOs participated alongside a broad range of women's economic and social policy NGOs. The historic tension between social and economic *goals* and social and economic *rights* was reflected in a reluctance of the summit to incorporate the human rights framework consistently. Nevertheless, as a result primarily of the work of the women's human rights NGOs, the summit plan does begin with a commitment to the realization of the full range of human rights, including economic, social, and cultural rights and the right to development.[35]

The Beijing Platform for Action (1995), whose subject is the lives and needs of women, was the product of an extraordinary synergy between women delegates and a broad, seasoned NGO lobby. The human rights perspective is pervasive. Most of the chapters—for example, armed conflict, power and decision making, health, education, children, the economy—incorporate an explicit human rights perspective. The Beijing Platform also took a step toward greater concreteness with regard to mitigating (but not undoing) macroeconomic policies and their effect on women's poverty. It also directed the restructuring, but not the stripping away, of safety nets and supportive programs addressed to poor women. These were to be strengthened as basic entitlements.[36]

In the aftermath of these conferences, women are faced with ignorance of or resistance to the new women-centered indivisible rights frameworks as well as the draining away of resources necessary to implement the core economic and social programs. Recognizing the gap between rhetoric and accomplishment, the Vienna and ICPD Programs, the Summit Report, and the Beijing Platform are nevertheless being used by women in many parts of the world to define and legitimate their demands for both human rights and social change.[37] In the United States, the Clinton administration established an Inter-Agency Council on Women to pursue the implementation of the Beijing Platform. While this gives women a limited route to influence government policy, particularly in the State Department, the potential of the Beijing Platform is not felt because many U.S. women are unaware of its provisions, and many who are aware do not use it as a platform for action or an instrument of accountability.

BRINGING THE INTERNATIONAL FRAMEWORK HOME

The uses of international legal norms and commitments in shaping domestic policy, vision, and jurisprudence are many. Human rights implementation in the international arena relies primarily on publicity and shaming rather than on mandatory enforcement mechanisms. The same could be true domestically. Moreover, the ability to use domestic courts, legislatures, and other institutions to enforce and entrench human rights is essential to giving them force. This requires integration of the international frameworks and agreements into popular education and social justice advocacy to build a culture that accepts and demands human rights as the basis of a decent social order.

Under the Constitution, treaties are part of the law of the land. Unless inconsistent with a later federal statute or the Constitution, domestic law should be construed to facilitate the implementation of treaty obligations.[38] Thus, the recent U.S. ratification in 1992 of three treaties—the Political and Civil Covenant, the Race Convention, and the Torture Convention—provides a concrete legal foundation for domestic human rights advocacy. These ratifications, however, are subject to a plethora of reservations, declarations, and understandings—too numerous to discuss here but designed, like the Bricker Amendment, to negate most of the aspects of international human rights that are more protective than constitutional standards.[39]

But these limitations are also subject to challenge and circumvention; they are not written in stone. For example, the United States has declared that all these treaties are "non-self-executing," meaning that Congress must provide implementing legislation before they can be the basis of a legal claim. While the validity of this limitation will be adjudicated by the federal courts, U.S. officials concede that the norms guaranteed still must be observed by all state and federal officials, including judges.[40] It is also notable that the United States neglected to limit the positive obligation in the ICCPR to "ensure" the enjoyment of rights.

Once ratified, treaties provide periodic formal opportunities for domestic educational work and shaming at the international level. NGOs can participate in developing and disseminating critiques of the compliance reports that the United States is required to provide quadrennially to the responsible treaty committee. The critiques of the Human Rights Committee on U.S. compliance with the ICCPR should be widely used. While the United States has refused to accept the individual complaints procedures established by the treaties and administered by these committees, it is, by virtue of its approval of the OAS Charter and the American Declaration on the Rights and Duties of Man [sic], subject to the petition procedure of the Inter-American Commission on Human Rights (IACHR), which can consider the same range of issues.[41]

Treaties are not the only source of legal obligation. Customary international norms that reflect the consensus of nations are, on the same basis as treaties, binding on all officials. Because of the U.S. focus on political and civil rights and its disproportionate influence in the human rights system, many treaty norms—for example, torture and inhuman treatment, prolonged arbitrary detention, racial discrimination, and aspects of gender discrimination—are considered customary by U.S.

authorities today. The near-universal ratification of the ICESCR also renders it an expression of customary norms. The list of customary norms is also expanding to encompass weapons of mass destruction of human life and dangers to the environment. Customary norms are both self-executing and justiciable as laws of the United States and therefore provide a basis for individual legal claims, interpretation of domestic law, and the development and implementation of new legislation.[42]

Other agreements, such as UN General Assembly resolutions and the consensus programs and platforms of thematic international conferences, could be integrated into policy-oriented advocacy at all levels and in all branches of government. Though often described as non-binding commitments, they contain declarations and commitments that, because of their consensus nature, build customary norms and identify priorities for concrete implementation by governments and intergovernmental organizations. Their potential as a tool in domestic advocacy in the United States is as yet unrealized.

Ultimately, the most significant source of evolving human rights norms and implementation are the human rights movements themselves. If law can ever be said to be autonomous—a questionable proposition at best—it is least so in the field of human rights, which explicitly depends on political will rather than force. The evolution and efficacy of human rights law is inseparable from the processes by which individuals, activists, and NGOs begin to conceptualize, as human rights concerns, the abuses they suffer, the unmet needs they have, and the better societies they envision.[43]

NOTES

1. Universal Declaration of Human Rights, approved December 10, 1948, GA Res. 217A, UN Doc. A/810 at 56 (1948).
2. Blanche Wiesen Cook, "Eleanor Roosevelt and Human Rights: The Battle for Peace and Planetary Decency," in *Women and Foreign Policy,* ed. Ed Crapol (Westport, CT: Greenwood Press, 1987), 113.
3. See, e.g., Irving Kristol, "Human Rights: The Hidden Agenda," in Walter Laqueur and Barry Rubin, *The Human Rights Reader* (New York: Meridian, 1990), 393–94. Paradoxically, although civil rights groups were

often branded as "communist" in the 1950s, the Eisenhower administration supported the desegregation cases in the Supreme Court, culminating in *Brown v. Board of Education*, 347 U.S. 483 (1954), on foreign policy grounds, to deflect the Soviet Union's and international critiques of U.S. democracy. See, e.g., Gerald Horne, *Black and Red: W. E. B. DuBois and the Afro-American Response to the Cold War, 1944–1963*; Mary L. Dudiziak, *Desegregation as a Cold War Imperative*, 41 Stanford Law Review 1 (1988). International Covenant on Economic, Social and Cultural Rights (ICESCR), January 3, 1976, U.N.G.A. Res. 2200A, 21 UN GAOR Supp. (No. 16) at 49, UN Doc. A/6313 (1966); International Covenant on Civil and Political Rights (ICCPR), March 23, 1976, G.A. Res. 2200A, 21 UN GAOR, Supp. No. 16 at 52, UN Doc. A/6316 (1966). Notably, the naming of the generations occurred in reverse order to the chronology of their approval by the UN. See Philip Alston, *U.S. Ratification of the Covenant on Economic, Social, and Cultural Rights: The Need for an Entirely New Strategy*, 84 American Journal International Law 365 (1990); Dorothy Q. Thomas, *Advancing Rights Protection in the United States: An Internationalized Advocacy Strategy*, 9 Harvard Human Rights Journal 15 (1996).

4. Six human rights treaties establish treaty committees to provide ongoing monitoring of state adherence through state reporting and in some cases through individual petition procedures. These include the ICESCR and ICCPR, supra n. 3; Convention Against Torture (CAT), June 26, 1987, G.A. res. 39/46, annex, 39 UN GAOR Supp. (No. 51) at 197, UN Doc. A/39/51 (1984); International Convention on the Elimination of All Forms of Racial Discrimination, January 4, 1969, 660 U.N.T.S. 195 (1969); Convention on the Elimination of All Forms of Discrimination Against Women, September 3, 1979, U.N.G.A. Res. 34/180, 34 UN GAOR, Supp. (No. 46) 194, UN Doc. A/34/830 (1979); Convention on the Rights of the Child, November 20, 1989, U.N.G.A. Res. 25, 44 UN GAOR, Supp. (No. 99), UN Doc. A/RES/44/25 (1989). There are also many other norm-setting multilateral human rights treaties including genocide, slavery-like practices, and labor standards. See Henry J. Steiner and Philip Alston, *International Human Rights in Context: Law, Politics, and Morals* (Oxford, UK: Clarendon Press, 1996).

5. For discussion of the impact of global economic policies, see, e.g., Fourth World Conference on Women, Platform for Action and Beijing Declaration and Platform for Action, Report on the Fourth World Conference on Women, UN Doc. A/CONF.177/20 (17 October 1995), DPI/1766/Wom–95–39642 (New York: United Nations, February 1996),

ch. 2, 4(A) (hereinafter "Beijing Platform for Action"). Regarding Northern support for extremist religious movements, see Graham E. Fuller, *Algeria: The Next Fundamentalist State* (Santa Monica, CA: Rand [Arroyo Center/U.S. Army], 1996).

6. *DeShaney v. Winnebago County Department of Social Services,* 489 U.S. 189 (1989). See also *Harris v. McRae,* 448 U.S. 297 (1980).

7. ICESCR, articles 6–15.

8. Ibid., articles 14, 11(2), and 2.

9. See General Comments adopted by the UN Committee on Economic, Social, and Cultural Rights, in Compilation of General Comments and General Recommendations Adopted by Human Rights Treaty Bodies, HRI/Gen/1/Rev. 2 (March 29, 1996), 49–87 (hereinafter Compilation); see also Asbjorn Eide, *Realization of Social and Economic Rights and the Minimum Threshold Approach,* 10 Human Rights Law Journal 35 (1989); ICESCR, article 2(3).

10. CPR, articles 6, 7, 20, 27; CAT, article 3; *Sanford v. Kentucky,* 492 U.S. 361 (1989); *Estelle v. Gamble,* 429 U.S. 97 (1976).

11. Convention Against Torture (hereafter CAT), article 2; see Craig Scott, *The Interdependence and Permeability of Human Rights Norms: Towards a Partial Fusion of the International Covenants on Human Rights,* 27 Osgoode Hall Law Journal 769 (1989).

12. CAT, supra n. 4, article 3; *Velasquez Rodriquez* case, 28 I.L.M. 294 (1989); See Brief Amicus Curiae by International Women's Human Rights Law Clinic (IWHR) and Center for Constitutional Rights (CCR) in *Doe v. Doe,* Docket No. 96–6224 (2d Cir. appeal withdrawn), arguing that treaty and customary international law regarding gender violence justify congressional enactment of positive measures in the Violence Against Women Act), specifically, the federal cause of action to redress gender-based violence (on file with author); Human Rights Committee, comment on article 6.

13. Human Rights Committee, Comment 6 (5) on article 6 in Compilation, supra n. 9, at 7; see also Comment 2 on article 2, id. at 4; Comment 20 (8–11) on article 7 (torture and ill-treatment), id. at 31–32; *Concluding Observations of the Human Rights Committee: Peru,* 4 International Human Rights Reporter 481 para. 15 (1997); *Airey* case, 2 European Court of Human Rights (series A) 305 (1979); contrast *Lassiter v. Department of Social Services,* 452 U.S. 18 (1981).

14. See Compilation, supra n. 9 at 49–87; Asbjorn Eide, supra n. 9 at 35.

15. UDHR, supra n. 1, article 2; ICCPR, supra n. 3, articles 2(1), 26; ICE-SCR, supra n. 3, article 2(2); emphasis added. The covenants also separately

state the obligation of states to ensure the equality of men and women in respect to the covenants' rights. ICCPR, supra n. 3, article 3; ICESCR, supra n. 3, article 3; *Toonen v. Tasmania,* reprinted in UN GAOR, Hum. Rts. Comm., 15th Sess., Case No. 448/1992 (1994). Compare *Baehr v. Lewin,* 52 P.2d 44 (Haw. 1993), and *Baehr v. Miike,* 910 P.2d 112 (Haw. 1996); Concluding Observations of the Human Rights Committee: U.S.A., 53rd Sess., 1413th mtg., UN Doc. CCRP/C/79/Add.50 (1995), para. 28 (hereinafter Concluding Observations: U.S.A.); *Bowers v. Hardwick,* 478 U.S. 186 (1986). See also Beijing Platform for Action, para. 96, infra n. 32; Alice Miller and Larry Helfer, *Sexual Orientation and Human Rights: Toward a United States and Transnational Jurisprudence,* 9 Harvard Human Rights Journal 611 (1996).

16. Race Convention, articles 1, 4, 7, 11, 16; Women's Convention, articles 1–5; contrast the Supreme Court's decisions discussed in detail in chapters 12–16.

17. Race Convention, supra n. 4, articles 1(4), 2(2); Women's Convention, article 4. Both conventions provide that affirmative action is not to be considered discrimination so long as it does not maintain unequal or separate standards or outlast the point when "the objectives of equality of opportunity and treatment have been achieved." Ibid.; see also Race Convention, articles 1(4), 2(2).

18. Compare *Toonen v. Tasmania,* CCPR/C/46/D/488/1992, supra n. 15, stigma resulting from criminalization of same-sex sodomy is part of injury, with *Allen v. Wright,* 468 U.S. 737 (1984), stigma resulting from government's tax exemption to racially discriminatory private schools is not a cognizable injury. See also Nadine Strossen, *Recent U.S. and International Judicial Protection of Individual Rights: A Comparative Legal Process Analysis and Proposed Synthesis,* 41 Hastings Law Journal 805 (1990).

19. Cook, supra n. 2.

20. See Civil Rights Congress, *We Charge Genocide: The Historic Petition to the United Nations for Relief from a Crime of the United States Government Against the Negro People,* 2d. ed. (New York: International, 1970), 3; Horne, Dudziak and Thomas, supra n. 3; Brief for the United States as Amicus Curiae at 6, *Brown v. Board of Education,* 347 U.S. 483 (1954).

21. See Louis Henkin, *U.S. Ratification of Human Rights Conventions: The Ghost of Senator Bricker,* 89 American Journal of International Law 341 (1995); Hearings on S.J. Res. 1 and S.J. Res. 43 Before a Subcomm. of the Senate Comm. on the Judiciary, 83d Cong., 1st Sess. 825 (1953), Statement of Secretary of State John Foster Dulles.

22. See Dorothy Q. Thomas, supra n. 3 at 26 quoting State Department circular No. 175 stating: "Treaties should be designed to promote United States interests by securing action by foreign governments in a way deemed advantageous to the United States. Treaties are not to be used as a device for the purpose of effecting internal social change, or to try to circumvent the constitutional procedures established in relation to what are essentially matters of domestic concern" citing *U.S. Ratification of the International Covenants on Human Rights* 13, Hurst Hannum and Dana D. Fischer, eds. (1993); Kristol, supra n. 3 at 396.

23. Human Rights Watch/Women's Rights Project, *Sexual Abuse of Women in U.S. State Prisons* (New York: Human Rights Watch, 1996); Torture Victims Protection Act, 28 U.S.C. § 1350n., provides a civil damage action implementing the UN Convention Against Torture and excluding U.S. officials from its scope. Concluding Observations: U.S.A., supra n. 15 at paras. 279, 281–282, 285–286. See Rhonda Copelon, *Recognizing the Egregious in the Everyday: Domestic Violence as Torture*, 25 Columbia Human Rights Law Review 291 (1994). Report of the Special Rapporteur on Violence Against Women, Its Causes and Consequences (Coomaraswamy) (hereinafter, Special Rapporteur: Domestic Violence), Economic and Social Council, UN Doc. E/CN.4/1996/53 (5 February 1996), paras. 42–50 at pp. 12–13.

24. See "Comment on Objections to Economic and Social Rights" in Steiner and Alston, *International Human Rights in Context,* 267–68; Philip Alston, *U.S. Ratification of the Covenant on Economic, Social and Cultural Rights: The Need for an Entirely New Strategy,* 84 American Journal of International Law 365 (1990); Roberta Clark and Joan French, "Issues in the Enforceability of Human Rights: A Caribbean Perspective," in *From Basic Needs to Basic Rights,* ed. Margaret A. Schuler (New York: Institute for Women, Law, and Development, 1995), 103.

25. See Aryeh Neier, "Human Rights," in *The Oxford Companion to Politics of the World,* ed. J. Krieger (1993), 403, cited in Steiner and Alston, *International Human Rights in Context.* Human Rights Watch, for example, has begun to examine social and economic rights where linked with violations of civil and political rights. Conversation with Alison Collins, October 6, 1997. See n. 43 for grass roots initiatives.

26. Louis Henkin, "International Human Rights and Rights in the United States," cited in Steiner and Alston, *International Human Rights in Context,* 272.

27. Stephen Marks, *Emerging Human Rights: A New Generation for the 1980s?,* 33 Rutgers Law Review 435 (1981). See, e.g., UN Declaration on the

Right to Development, GA Res. 41/128, annex, 41 UN GAOR Supp. (No. 53) at 186, UN Doc. A/41/53 (1986); Beijing Platform for Action, supra n. 5.

28. UDHR, supra n. 1, articles 2, 26; ICCPR, supra n. 3, articles 2(1), 3, 4(1), 26; ICESCR, supra n. 3, articles 2(2), 3. Article 3 of both Covenants added a discrete provision that all the rights therein be ensured equally to women and men. See Johannes Morsink, *Women's Rights in the Universal Declaration*, 13 Human Rights Quarterly 299 (1991).

29. For a history of the global human rights campaign and UN negotiations through the 1995 Beijing Conference, see Felice Gaer, *Never the Twain Shall Meet?* in *American Bar Association, Instruments of Change* (forthcoming, 1998) (on file with author); Charlotte Bunch and Niamh Rielly, *Demanding Accountability: The Global Campaign and Vienna Tribunal for Women's Human Rights* (New Jersey: Center for Women's Global Leadership, 1994); Niamh Rielly, *Without Reservation: The Beijing Tribunal on Accountability for Women's Human Rights* (New Jersey: Center for Women's Global Leadership, 1996). UN World Conference on Human Rights, Vienna Declaration and Programme of Action, adopted June 25, 1993, reprinted in 32 International Legal Materials 1661 (1993), 14 Human Rights Law Journal 325 (1993). UN Declaration on the Elimination of Violence Against Women, UN Doc. A/48/104 (23 February 1994); see *Prosecutor v. Gagovic et al.* (FOCA) IT–96–23; Special Rapporteur: Domestic Violence, supra n. 23, annex.

30. See, e.g., Alda Facio, *El Sexismo en el Derecho de los Derechos Humanos* (manuscript on file with author, 1988), in *La Mujer Ausente* (Santiago, Chile: ISIS International, 1991); Charlotte Bunch, *Women's Rights as Human Rights: Towards a Re-Vision of Human Rights,* 12 Human Rights Quarterly 486 (1990); Hilary Charlesworth, Christine Chinkin, and Shelly Wright, *Feminist Approaches to International Law,* 85 American Journal of International Law 613 (1991); Rebecca J. Cook, *Women's International Human Rights Law: The Way Forward,* 15 Human Rights Quarterly 230 (1993); Berta Esperanza Hernandez-Truyol, *Concluding Remarks Making Women Visible: Setting an Agenda for the Twenty-First Century,* 69 St. John's Law Review 231 (1994); Celina Romany, *Women as Aliens: A Feminist Critique of the Public/Private Distinction in International Human Rights Law,* 6 Harvard Human Rights Journal 87 (1993); Copelon, *Domestic Violence as Torture*, supra n. 23.

31. Inter-American Convention on the Prevention, Punishment, and Elimination of Violence Against Women, 3 International Human Rights

Reporter 232 (1994); Berta Esperanza Hernandez-Truyol, *Women's Rights as Human Rights—Rules, Realities, and the Role of Culture,* 21 Brooklyn Journal of International Law 605 (1996).

32. See ICPD Program of Action, Report of the International Conference on Population and Development, A/CONF.171/13 (October 18, 1994) (hereafter ICPD POA). See Adrienne Germain and Rachel Kyte, *The Cairo Consensus* (New York: International Women's Health Coalition, 1995). For an excellent statement of a truly indivisible program developed by the women's NGOs, see *Reproductive Health and Justice: International Women's Health Conference for Cairo '94, January 24–28, 1994, Rio de Janiero* (New York: International Women's Health Coalition, 1994) (hereinafter Rio Statement). In the Beijing Platform for Action, women's sexual rights—"to have control and make decisions over . . . their sexuality"—as well as the obligation of states to consider the decriminalization of abortion were written into UN consensus documents for the first time, at paragraphs 96 and 106k, respectively; see Beijing Platform for Action, supra n. 5. For a fuller discussion of the background, political tensions, and decisions of the ICPD along with its implications for human rights, see Rhonda Copelon and Rosalind Petchesky, "Toward an Interdependent Approach to Reproductive and Sexual Rights as Human Rights: Reflections on the ICPD and Beyond," in *From Basic Needs to Basic Rights,* 343–68, supra n. 24.

33. ICPD POA, supra n. 32, para. 15.13.

34. See Rio Statement, supra n. 32; Copelon and Petchesky, supra n. 32.

35. Report of the World Summit for Social Development, A/CONF.166/9 (19 April 1995); see Gaer, supra n. 29.

36. Beijing PFA, supra n. 32, paras. 58–60.

37. See, e.g., Women's Environment and Development Organization, *Promise Kept, Promise Broken? A Survey of Governments on National Action Plans to Implement the Beijing Platform* (New York: WEDO, 1997); South African Ministry for Welfare and Population Development, *A Green Paper for Public Discussion: Population Policy for South Africa?* (Pretoria, 1995).

38. See *Murray v. Schooner Charming Betsy,* 6 U.S. (2 Cranch) 64, 118 (1804).

39. Having signed the Economic and Social Covenant and the Women's and Child Conventions, the United States is also bound to take no action inconsistent with the rights they protect; see Henkin, "International Human Rights and Rights in the United States." For reservations, declarations, and understandings regarding the ICCPR, see U.S. Senate Committee on Foreign Relations Report on the International Covenant

on Civil and Political Rights, 31 I.L.M. 645 (1992). These involve notably the death penalty, the definition and applicability of torture, and the standard of discrimination. Regarding ratification of the Race Convention, the "Helms Proviso" intends to nullify the obligation to conform U.S. law to the Convention. 140 Congressional Record S7634 (daily ed. June 24, 1994) (Statement of Sen. Pell). But see Concluding Observations: U.S.A. supra n. 15, at para. 295, calling upon U.S. to address prejudice against minority groups and women, including "where appropriate, the adoption of affirmative action" and also to conform its laws to the ICCPR. See also para. 303.

40. UN Human Rights Committee Press Releases Concerning the Review of the First Report of the United States under the ICCPR, Human Rights Committee 1401st meeting, 33, UN Doc.HR/CT.400 (March 29–30, 1995); Concluding Observations: U.S.A., supra n. 15 at para. 276.

41. See ibid., for comment of the Human Rights Committee to the U.S. report under the ICCPR. Ann Fagan Ginger, *The Energizing Effect of Enforcing a Human Rights Treaty in Symposium: The Ratification of the International Covenant on Civil and Political Rights,* 42 DePaul Law Review 1341 (1993). The U.S. reports to the Committee Against Torture and the Committee to End Racial Discrimination are overdue. The IACHR hears complaints of violations of the American Declaration as well as complaints arising under other treaties or instruments to which the United States is bound. See "Other Treaties" Subject to the Consultative Jurisdiction of the Court (Art. 64 of the American Convention on Human Rights), Advisory Opinion OC–1/82 of September 24, 1982, Inter-Am.Ct.H.R. Ser. A, No. 1 (1982).

42. Statute of the International Court of Justice, article 38(1); see *The Paquete Habana,* 175 U.S. 677 (1900); *Filartiga v. Pena,* 630 F. 2d 876 (2d Cir. 1980); International Court of Justice, Advisory Opinion on the Legality of the Threat and Use of Nuclear Weapons Under International Law, Gen Assembly Doc. A/51/218, paras. 73, 30 (July 19, 1996).

43. For U.S. based organizations that are integrating international human rights into domestic program, see Thomas, supra n. 22 at nn. 40–48. Additional initiatives include Human Rights, USA, a community organizing project in four cities (Atlanta, Minneapolis, San Antonio, and St. Louis) and national resource center jointly sponsored by the Center for Human Rights Education in Atlanta; University of Minnesota Human Rights Center; Street Law, Incorporated (Georgetown Law School); Human Rights Educators Network of Amnesty International; Kensington

Welfare Rights Union (Philadelphia); Workers Center for Human Rights, Oxford, Miss.; and Ella Baker Center for Human Rights, Oakland (police brutality). Groups who have sought to implement international human rights in domestic courts in the United States include Center for Constitutional Rights, International Human Rights Law Group, ACLU Southern California, and the International Women's Human Rights Law Clinic (CUNY Law School).

10 JOSEPH WILLIAM SINGER

PROPERTY

PROPERTY RIGHTS SERVE HUMAN VALUES. THEY ARE RECOGNIZED TO
THAT END, AND ARE LIMITED BY IT.

Chief Justice Joseph Weintraub
Supreme Court of New Jersey
State v. Shack (1971)

THE institution of private property is alive and well. The nations of eastern Europe and the former Soviet Union have been converting to market economies, a transformation that has been nothing short of a revolution. And the push to privatize government institutions by transferring them to private owners seems to have caught on around the world. Evidence of this change can be seen in Latin America, Africa, Asia and, closer to home, in Canada and Mexico. Private property appears to be sweeping the world.

The United States has witnessed a burgeoning "property rights" movement, accompanied by the end to the federal entitlement to welfare and a renewed commitment to end the era of "big government" by reducing regulation. Both businesses and owners of land are increasingly angry about environmental regulations and local zoning laws that limit their ability to develop their land. Laws have been passed in a number of states granting remedies to land owners whose property is significantly harmed by government regulations. Several bills have been introduced in Congress to prevent implementation of regulations that "take" more than some specified percentage of the property's fair market value unless the owner is compensated for the loss. Other proposed bills require agencies to undertake complicated cost-benefit analyses of new regulations, ostensibly to prevent passage of regulations that overburden property owners and businesses. The Supreme Court has been increasingly receptive to these arguments, sending signals to lower courts and to legislatures to better protect property rights.

The movement to deregulate and respect private property is based on a particular conception of the meaning of private property. Ultimately, this conception of property as ownership rests on the assumption that every property interest has an identifiable owner and that the owner has absolute or almost absolute rights to use his or her property as he or she sees fit. This is the classical conception of property. Property is conventionally understood as comprising a bundle of rights, including the right to use the property, the right to exclude nonowners, the power to transfer it, and absolute, or almost absolute, control over the thing that is owned. The problem is that these conventional understandings contradict one another. It is not possible for property rights to be absolute and also to comprise this complete bundle. Some rights in the bundle conflict with other rights in the bundle; the property rights of one person impinge on, and interfere with, both the property and personal rights of others. Absolute property rights are self-defeating.

This chapter will explain and criticize the classical conception of property by focusing on (1) the sources of property rights, (2) the problem of competing property rights, (3) the historical origins of property law, and (4) the distribution of property.

FORMAL AND INFORMAL SOURCES OF PROPERTY RIGHTS

The classical view suggests that property rights have their origin in labor and possession. Rights theorists such as John Locke explained that individuals work the land and gather crops and therefore deserve property rights. Utilitarian philosophers such as Jeremy Bentham suggested that property rights promote investment by granting secured expectations. Individual labor and first possession appear to create legitimate interests that others should respect. The case of *Pierson v. Post* is often used to make this point.[1] The case concerns a hunt for a wild fox and the question is whether ownership is established by active pursuit, physical capture, or mortal wounding. All parties agree that possession or labor, in some form, establishes ownership rights.

This classical view is suspect. Historically, it is not true that property rights in the United States are generally based on first possession. In fact, virtually all the land in the United States was originally owned by American Indian nations, and under both colonial and U.S. law, title was transferred from the tribes to the United States government before individual titles could vest. Thus, all titles to land in the United States have their source in a government grant or sale rather than in individual settlement. It is true that public law gave title to settlers in some cases, but settlement was not enough; title vested in private owners only if federal law provided as much. In many cases, title was not given to first settlers but to those who were given formal title by the government *before* settlement, either on the basis of a sale of the land by the government to the highest bidder or on a first come, first served basis.

Nor has labor been a consistent source of property rights. The labor of slaves was expropriated for more than a hundred years. No compensation for this stolen labor was ever given by the United States in the form of reparations. When the Civil War ended, many called for "forty acres and a mule"—that is, for the state to grant property rights to the freedmen. Yet this never occurred; instead, ownership of the plantations was vested in the former slave owners who had rebelled against the United States, rather than being granted to the slaves who had worked the land.

Although women continue to perform most of the labor in the household, they do this for free, or, more accurately, without any direct compensation from the labor market. Men as a group are heavily dependent on this uncompensated labor, as is the economy in general. In contrast, most of the work traditionally performed by men is monetarily compensated by means of an employment contract, by sale, or by investment. This social division of uncompensated versus compensated labor has a lot to do with the fact that women as a class are poorer than men, as well as the fact that the poverty rate for children is almost twice the poverty rate for adults. In 1991, 21.8 percent of all children were living in poverty, as opposed to 11.4 percent of adults aged 18–64 and 12.4 percent of adults over 65.[2]

The labor and first possession theses therefore mask tensions in property law between alternative sources of property rights. Sometimes, property law allocates rights to those who have been denominated owners by formal documents of title, such as government patents (grants of ownership), deeds, leases, wills, contracts, or trusts. At other times, property law grants rights on the basis of informal arrangements such as actual possession or labor.

Consider the law of adverse possession. Many owners have placed the fences or hedges around their property in positions that do not correspond precisely to the physical boundaries described in the deed they were given when they purchased the land. Adverse possession laws state that if an owner visibly occupies land for a long enough period of time, that person becomes the owner, taking title away from the "true owner." Adverse possession law demonstrates a *tension* between formal title and informal possession as sources of property rights. This tension pervades the law of property, as well as the law of contract. Sometimes the law allocates property rights on the basis of formal title and sometimes it allocates property rights on the basis of informal social arrangements. These informal arrangements include behavior that creates expectations the law will respect. Adverse possession is a major example of actual possession prevailing over formal title in allocating property rights. It also allows the possession by a current owner to dispossess a prior owner, contrary to the theory that first possession establishes the source of rights.

Family relationships are another major example in which actual behavior and social arrangements may constitute a source of property rights that prevails over formal title. Upon divorce, most states will divide the property acquired during the marriage between husband and wife based on a variety of factors, regardless of who holds title to the property. In practice, this rule historically has had the effect of transferring substantial property from a husband to a wife when the man worked outside the home and the woman worked in the home for no salary. Oral promises constitute another example of informal arrangements superseding formal ones; the statute of frauds requires an agreement in writing to transfer interests in land, but a variety of doctrines relax this requirement. Even in the absence of a promise, courts sometimes assign property rights on the basis of actual arrangements or informal understandings even when they contradict formal arrangements.

In *Rase v. Castle Mountain Ranch*, an owner of a large ranch in Montana gave friends, neighbors, and employees permission to build summer cabins around a lake located on his land.[3] In reliance on that permission, they expended substantial amounts of money to build houses; yet the owner of the land gave them no formal property rights, such as a lease or an easement (a permanent, irrevocable right to do something on land owned by another person). The cabin owners occupied their homes for fifty years. Then the original owner died, and his brother took over the property and sold it to an out-of-state developer, who promptly notified the cabin owners that they had thirty days to leave the land. The court ruled that the cabin owners had the right to retain control of their cabins for a limited period of time (thirteen years) but that the new owner could take control of the cabins if the cabin owners were interested in selling the cabins immediately to him. As a formal matter, the cabin owners only had naked permission to occupy the land; property law terms this right a "license," which is ordinarily revocable at will by the grantor. Despite this, the court created a "constructive trust" to convert the revocable license into a more permanent easement—a right of way over another's land that cannot be revoked by the owner of the land. Another doctrine, easement by estoppel, would achieve the same result.

These doctrines demonstrate that the source of property rights is sometimes formal title and sometimes informal social relationships or customs or understandings. They also demonstrate that, although owners are generally immune from losing their ownership rights without their consent, a variety of property rules give nonowners the power to take away an owner's rights by entering into particular kinds of relationships with the owner.

CONFLICTS OF PROPERTY RIGHTS

All property rights are limited by the rights of others, and most issues involving property law can be reconceptualized as conflicts *among* property rights. The rights that go along with full ownership are most basically the right to exclude, the privilege to use one's property, immunity from loss without one's consent, and the power to transfer during one's life or at death. Each of these rights has significant limits that demonstrate tensions within the concept of property itself and within the rules governing the ownership and use of property.

The Supreme Court has said that the "power to exclude has traditionally been considered one of the most treasured strands in an owner's bundle of property rights."[4] Yet public accommodations laws and fair housing laws substantially limit the owner's right to exclude nonowners on the ground of race, sex, religion, or other protected categories. In fact, these laws grant members of the public the right to enter restaurants and stores and to rent or buy homes over the objections of the owners of those properties. They do so to ensure that each person has the right to acquire property. The right to buy or use property open to use by others conflicts with the right to exclude and to determine when to sell. In order to establish a market that treats each person as an equal individual, capable of contracting and using property without exclusion, owners' powers to determine when and to whom to open their property must be limited.

Public accommodation statutes cannot be legitimately understood as minor or exceptional limits to the right to exclude. It was not until 1964 (almost 100 years after the Civil War ended) that federal law clearly limited the rights of property owners to exclude on the basis of race. Racial discrimination in housing remains a problem today. Hardly a year goes by when one of my students does not tell me that a landlord refused to rent when he saw the student, giving an excuse such as a policy against renting to students. Federal law has prohibited discrimination in housing against families with children since 1988, but such discrimination is rampant in practice. Many landlords refuse to rent to unmarried couples or gay or lesbian tenants. The laws that require access to public accommodations or housing constitute important, invasive, and significant limits on the right to exclude.

Public accommodation and fair housing laws demonstrate a fundamental tension in property law between norms of exclusion and norms of access. Private homeowners have a legal right to choose their dinner guests on any basis, including a racially discriminatory one, while public accommodations have a duty to serve the public without unjust discrimination. This tension creates choices for judges and legislatures. Should a shopping mall be able to exclude teenagers from hanging around after school? Should it have the right to exclude homeless people? Should a private eating club have the right to exclude women when most of the male partners at major law firms in the city belong to the club and transact business discussions there?

These conflicts are not properly conceptualized only as tensions between property and equality. They are tensions within the concept of property itself. The right to exclude is well understood; the right of access is often ignored. The Civil Rights Act of 1866 states that every person shall have the same right to contract and to purchase property "as is enjoyed by white citizens."[5] This statute has been interpreted to prevent individuals from refusing to enter contracts because of the purchaser's race. The right to contract to purchase property means the right to force the seller to sell if the only reason for the refusal to sell is the race of the buyer. If this right were not recognized, then the ability to purchase property would differ depending on the race of the buyer. Thus, the right to buy property (without regard to one's race) conflicts with the owner's right to determine when to sell. Property entails a tension or contradiction between the norm of access and the norm of exclusion, the right to buy versus the right to choose when to sell.

Similar conflicts arise when we move from the right to exclude to the privilege to use property. In a 1978 case the Exxon Corporation asked the Supreme Court of Texas to reaffirm earlier decisions holding that a property owner could drill to withdraw water without regard to the effects on others. The earlier cases involved owners who drilled wells on their land that effectively withdrew water from underneath neighboring land, drying up their neighbors' wells. But Exxon's withdrawal of water threatened to sink all the homes in the county, thereby destroying everyone else's property rights. The Texas Supreme Court found that Exxon's rights had reached their limit.[6] The security of everyone's property depended on each owner having due regard for a proper balance between one's own interests and those of one's neighbors. The free use of Exxon's property had to be limited to prevent Exxon from causing substantial harm to the neighbors' land.

Nuisance law, which prevents an owner from certain uses of his or her own property, is premised on the conflict between the owner's right to use the property as he or she sees fit and the right of others not to have their property harmed by actions on or off their land. Just as property law must draw a line between the right to exclude and the right of access, it must draw a line between the privilege to use property and the right to be secure from harm to one's property interests by neighboring conduct. In recent years, this doctrine has been used by neighbors to stop polluters on neighboring land and to recover damages for the contamination of property caused by toxic waste deposited by another owner.

The law of servitudes and future interests can also be understood through the tensions that characterize its rules. Servitudes involve land use restrictions imposed on future owners of particular parcels of property for the benefit of other owners in the neighborhood. For example, a real estate developer may include in the deed of sale a clause stating that the buyer agrees to use the property only for residential purposes. A buyer who opens a law office in her home violates this restriction. These restrictions are intended to benefit the owners of the neighboring property (the parcels whose owners have the right to enforce the restriction) while curtailing the free use rights of the owners of the restricted parcels. If the free use of one's property were the dominant ideal and goal, then servitudes should not be imposed on future owners who did not voluntarily agree to those restrictions created by past owners of the land. If, on the other hand, the right to control neighboring land use for one's benefit is the primary goal, then servitudes represent an ingenious device to create a new kind of property right.

For example, a residential neighborhood devoted to senior citizens can be created through the use of servitudes (as long as one complies with fair housing laws that prohibit discrimination against children except in certain narrowly defined senior citizen housing complexes). This provides an elderly purchaser the security of knowing that children would not move in next door, but it is exclusionary and significantly infringes on the free use rights of owners in the neighborhood. The servitude against the residence of children in the neighborhood could prevent an elderly couple from taking in their grandchildren in an unanticipated crisis.

Future interests pose similar dilemmas. A grandfather leaves property to his granddaughter in his will and further provides that she will lose the income from the trust if she gets married. The granddaughter gets married. Is the restraint on marriage enforceable? The case poses a conflict between the donor's power to control the behavior of the future owner of the property and the freedom of the granddaughter to use the property as she sees fit without meddlesome interference in her private life from her ancestor.

In all these cases, it is unhelpful to address a question about property law by saying, "I am in favor of deregulation; the government should stop telling people what to do and just enforce people's property rights." This tells us nothing since most situations involve conflicts among property rights or conflicts between property rights and other rights. An attachment to the ideal of property cannot tell us what to do in these situations. One must make value judgments about the appropriate contours of social relationships to define the content of property law.

HISTORICAL ORIGINS OF PROPERTY RIGHTS

Throughout the nineteenth century, the common law of property in the United States revolved around the *estates system*, a complicated regulatory framework designed to limit and systematize property rights into established channels. This system originated in the rules that mediated the relations between lords and tenants and between the generations in the feudal era. Feudal property law created a vast social hierarchy with a few lords owning most of the land and then parceling it out to vassals who would provide them services. In turn, those vassals would "subinfeudate" the land, giving possession of it to subvassals who would provide specified services for them. At the bottom of the feudal ladder were the peasants who worked the land and who had very few rights; they were subject to the jurisdiction, and the whim, of the feudal lords above them.

As the feudal system developed, the lords tried to evade certain "incidents" of ownership that were similar to taxes; they did so by the process of subinfeudation. To restore royal revenues, a variety of laws were issued that had the effect, over time, of pushing property rights downward from the lords to the peasants who worked the land. The primary principle was the prohibition of subinfeudation; instead of lords creating new lord-tenant relationships beneath them in a big hierarchical chain, the new rules encouraged transfer of title from the lord/owner to a new owner. This principle eventually became known as the principle of promoting the "alienability" of property. It has enormous impact under current law. It both pushes owners in the direction of consolidating ownership rights in a single owner and, in many cases, limits the power of prior owners to control the behavior of future owners.

The underlying premise of the estates system, as it exists today, is that strict regulation of property rights is necessary both to prevent the reemergence of feudalism and to ensure that current generations are not unduly controlled by their great-grandparents. The goal is to move power downwards from the feudal lord to the actual possessor of the land and from donors (prior generations) to current owners to ensure that power over property is decentralized and widely dispersed. The system did this by the rules governing future interests and property transfers, which restrict the ability of owners of property to limit the future uses and ownership. The intent is to disperse ownership by preventing concentration of power in a few landed families.[7]

In the United States, it is crucial to remember that property rights have their origin in American Indian nations. The United States took the land from them and gave it to white settlers. Although the United States often provided compensation for the lands it took, it did not always do so; nor were the amounts of compensation equal to fair market value, the amount the government would have paid to U.S. citizens if it had taken the land from them.

From the beginning, English colonists justified these seizures and the conquest and displacement of American Indians by arguing that the native nations had more property than they needed, were misusing it by not developing it properly, and had a moral obligation to share it with the Europeans who needed access to it.[8] Locke attempted to characterize America as a vast unclaimed territory free for settlement by industrious Europeans. His theory, in conjunction with the colonial justifications for conquest, rationalized a massive redistribution of property from American Indian nations to the colonial powers, then to the United States and its white citizens. Both the conquest of Indian nations and the homestead laws defy the typical characterization of nineteenth-century American law as opposed to redistribution of property.

DISTRIBUTION OF PROPERTY: "EVERYONE SHOULD HAVE SOME"

John Kenneth Galbraith reports that Professor Robert Montgomery, an economist at the University of Texas, was unpopular with the Texas legislature because of his liberal views. When asked whether he favored private property, he replied, "I do—so strongly that I want everyone in Texas to have some."[9] His answer contains a brilliant insight into the nature of property. Property law and property rights have an inescapable distributive component. As Jeremy Waldron explains, "[P]eople need private property for the development and exercise of their liberty; that is why it is wrong to take all of a person's private property away from him, and that is why it is wrong that some individuals should have had no private property at all."[10]

Other analysts suggest that property rights can be legitimately limited by other ideals, such as equality and liberty, or that common law understandings of property can be legitimately regulated by administrative and legislative action. Their perspectives, while useful, obfuscate a basic fact: Both property theory and our historical practice of property law contain principles that promote the norms of decentralization and distributive justice *within the concept and institution of property itself.* Once we recognize this, it makes no sense to argue that property rights must always be limited to achieve distributive justice. Private property systems always contain within them a partial component of distributive justice, and the prevailing norms of private property, as they have operated in the United States, have always contained a tension between the norm of protecting the rights of "title holders" (however defined) and the norm of shaping property rules to ensure widespread access to the system by which such titles are acquired.

The classical view of property concentrates on protecting those who *have* property. It addresses the conditions under which people *get* property but does not include the premise that such conditions must be structured so that everyone has the *right to get* property. The classical view focuses on individual owners and the actions they have to take to acquire property rights that will then be defended by the state. It assumes that the distribution of property is a consequence of the voluntary actions of individuals rather than a decision by the state. Property law does nothing more than protect property rights acquired by individual action. Distributional questions, in this conception, are foreign to property as a system. If the community is unhappy with the distribution of property that emerges from individual actions, it is free to redistribute property through, for example, the tax system. Such a tax would be seen as an intervention because the legal system would be determining the distribution of property, which was and should be privately determined by individuals acting in their own interest. The property acquiring process is seen as free from governmental compulsion. No public policy decisions need to be made for such a system to work.

This view, though widely held, is fundamentally mistaken if we look at both property theory and the historical practice of property law in the United States.

DISTRIBUTIVE NORMS IN POLITICAL THEORIES JUSTIFYING PROPERTY

John Locke's theory of private property is the source of the classical conception of property. It has been monumentally influential in the history of the United States as a justificatory scheme. Locke justified property by arguing that individuals who took actions to mix their labor with natural resources thereby became entitled to be protected in controlling the fruits of their labor. This entitlement was based both on the moral claim of rights and on the utilitarian ground that legal protection for property justly produced or possessed through labor promoted useful work and increased social welfare. However, Locke qualified this theory by a significant proviso: Labor creates property rights *"at least where there is enough and as good left in common for others."*[11]

Lockean property rights are premised on individual actions; no general right to own property emerges from this kind of theory. One has a right to own property only if one undertakes the actions needed to generate a legitimate claim. Jeremy Waldron has characterized Locke's argument as a "special rights" theory, which is subject to two crucial criticisms.[12] First, it is not at all clear why an individual acting alone can impose any legitimate obligations on others who have agreed neither to that individual's course of action nor to the rules of the game that define what actions create enforceable property rights. Second, there is no reason to believe that individual actions should have a binding moral effect on others if those actions inhibit or prevent others from exercising similar actions.

The Lockean proviso looms large. The very legitimacy of a property system depends on conferring property rights on individuals and allowing those individuals to assert those rights against others. As Frank Michelman has explained,

In a capitalist order, one person's proprietary value (or power) is obviously relative to other people's. A constitutional system of proprietary liberty is, therefore, incomplete without attending to the configurations of the values of various people's proprietary liberties. The question of distribution is endemic in the very idea of a constitutional scheme of proprietary liberty.[13]

A system of private property not only protects the rights of those who have acquired resources but also ensures the conditions that enable individuals to acquire those resources.[14]

DISTRIBUTIVE NORMS IN HISTORICAL PRACTICE IN THE UNITED STATES

This ineluctable distributive component of private property also has pervaded both historical practice and the social understanding of property in the United States. To put the argument in its simplest form, consider that a private property system requires more than one owner. This is not a *logical* requirement. After all, the state of New Jersey, where I grew up, was originally owned by two men, Sir George Carteret and John Lord Berkeley, while the Commonwealth of Pennsylvania was originally owned by William Penn, and several other colonies were similarly "proprietary." Nonetheless, under modern understandings of what it means to create a private property system, it is not an exaggeration to say that the requirement of multiple owners is close to a *definitional* component of a private property system. In the modern view, a private property system—in order to *count* as a private property system—requires some dispersal of property ownership. If an eastern European country moved from communism to a market system by distributing all the land in the country to ten families, it would be hard to conclude that the rulers of the country understood the normative premises underlying the private property systems of western Europe and the United States.

This conception not only is suggested by the political theory justifying private property but is embedded in U.S. history. In the nineteenth century, the United States adopted a practice of transferring public lands to many of its citizens through homestead laws that sometimes attempted to give priority to actual settlers.[15] These policies were premised on the idea that property was not a special right but a general right; everyone had the right to own some. Current theorists who focus on individual labor and possession as the origins of property forget the historical practice of government land distribution to settlers. They also forget that this land was taken from American Indian nations—based on the redistributive theory that they had more than they needed, that they were not using the land efficiently, and that the citizens of the United States needed it more and would use it in a more socially efficacious manner.

DISTRIBUTIVE NORMS IN CURRENT PROPERTY LAW AT THE MACRO LEVEL

Substantial regulation of property transfers is required to ensure that sellers of land do not load it down with restrictions on use and ownership that will be enforceable far into the future. In other words, a system premised on absolute ownership rights must restrict freedom of contract (the power to transfer) to ensure that, most of the time, sellers transfer to buyers most of the interests associated with property ownership. The rules operate partially to decentralize control over property by bundling certain rights together and ensuring control in the actual possessors (buyers) of the land. By creating the "fee simple" form of property ownership (the closest thing we have to absolute ownership), power is vested in current possessors of land rather than absentee lords. The rules of the estates system, such as the rule against perpetuities, are intended to shape overall social relations to ensure a certain amount and quality of dispersal of power over land.

Another example of rules of property law that operate systemically to shape social relationships is the antidiscrimination laws discussed above, which prohibit racial discrimination in housing markets (both sale and rental) and in public accommodations (businesses serving the public). These rules regulate property use and transfer by limiting the rights of public accommodations to exclude customers on such grounds as race and by limiting the rights of housing sellers and employers to refuse to contract on invidious grounds. This complex of rules is intended to combat and prevent the establishment of a racial caste system supported by law. It is analogous at a deep level to the property rules embodied in the estates system that created the idea of absolute ownership. Both sets of rules are intended to combat pernicious forms of social hierarchy and to establish protected legal rights to participate on equal terms in the public sphere of the marketplace.

Public accommodation laws can therefore be understood as *systemic* requirements of a property system committed to abolishing apartheid. Rather than limitations of property rights, they are positive requirements of property systems that eschew legally enforceable connections between race and property ownership. In other words, they not only constitute a fundamental distributive commitment but also institute the basic values of private property systems. It is true that those values instantiate conflicts between private rights to control one's own property and rights to access the property market. At the same time, the fundamental commitment to racial equality suggests that it is appropriate to understand such laws not as limits on property rights needed to achieve equality but as requirements of property systems committed to promoting access to property rights regardless of race.

DISTRIBUTIVE JUSTICE OF PROPERTY RELATIONS AT THE MICRO LEVEL

The distributive function of property law is evident not only on the level of overall social relations but also in the context of specific ongoing relationships. One major function of nuisance doctrine is to ensure that property use, as well as ownership, does not result in an unfair distribution of burdens associated with the development of land. Land uses that are perfectly legitimate in an isolated district become illegal if located in a built-up community. Each owner is entitled to *some* benefit from his or her land, and nuisance law ensures that the benefits and burdens of conflicting property uses are not distributed unfairly. Water law has a similar structure. Owners are generally entitled to withdraw water from beneath their land and even to sell it on the market. However, when they withdraw so much water that they undermine the subjacent support for neighboring land and begin to sink the surface of land in the surrounding area, the legal system may step in to limit their activities. Use of one's property cannot unreasonably interfere with the enjoyment of neighboring land.

The nuisance idea is based on the notion that the use of property rights cannot unfairly deprive others of the ability to use their own property. It has always suggested a limitation on property rights that cannot be fully comprehended by efficiency analysis. Certain types of property use will be prohibited because they interfere too much with the property rights of others, even if the social value of the conduct seems clearly to outweigh the social value of the other's property harmed by that conduct. Nuisance is therefore based on the notion that each owner should receive some benefit from the use of his or her land, and the benefits and burdens of land ownership should not be unfairly distributed between the parties. While a developer of a subdivision with a hundred houses may be required to pay for a drainage system on neighboring land to ensure that two or three neighboring houses are not flooded, it is not clear that the owner of a single family home at the top of a hill should be required to pay for a drainage system for the hundred houses located further down the hill. Nuisance law allows contextual consideration of the appropriate distribution of benefits and burdens of land ownership and use among neighbors.

Other rules exhibit distributive concerns at the micro level. Reliance interests are protected for parties who have been granted access to the owner's property or have a long-term relationship with the owner that justifies forced sharing of property rights when the relationship ends. Such reliance interests distribute the benefits and burdens of social life by defining property rights to effectuate an appropriate balance between the interests of formal title holders and those with whom the title holder forms a relationship of mutual dependence.

The concept of entitlement may express, better than does the concept of ownership or title, the ability of property rights to be secure in certain ways and defeasible in others. Entitlement suggests a right that is not absolute and connotes the right to get a minimum—a raising up to a basic level—rather than the right to all there is. We presume only one person has title to a piece of property, while several people may have entitlements of various kinds in that property. The entitlement idea suggests a bundle of rights less capacious than fee simple absolute ownership and thus better captures the contextual definition and balancing of competing claims that characterize property rights.

PROPERTY AND SOCIAL RELATIONS

The classical ownership conception of property assumes that the institution of private property entails a commitment to a general policy of laissez-faire—abolishing or severely limiting "government regulation" of "private property." This conception of the relation between property rights and government power is the classical model of property. Under this model, private property is opposed to collective or governmental ownership. Privatization transfers power from government bureaucrats to free citizens, reducing regulation and establishing liberty—the liberty of individuals to control what they own. If property means ownership free from governmental regulation, then any regulations imposed on owners are limits on private property rights. As such, they are presumptively pernicious and bear a heavy burden of justification.

The classical model of property is dangerous because it is wrong, both as a description of the ways in which private property systems actually operate and as a prescription for fairness and efficiency. The values that undergird the classical model are legitimate; the goals of increasing individual liberty, security, and well-being are justified and admirable. But the classical model is a flawed way to obtain these goals. Although the ownership concept has virtues, it is misleading as a description of the property rights we recognize and the rules of property law that define and regulate those rights. This descriptive inaccuracy is bad enough; far worse are the moral distortions created by the ownership model. Viewing all property as about the allocation of ownership suggests that everything has an owner who has presumptive total control over it. This normative paradigm hides from our consciousness the reality that almost all property is controlled by multiple owners and that property law is less about identifying who the owner is than about adjusting relationships among multiple owners and conflicting rights holders. The concept of ownership fails us just at the moment when a conceptual vocabulary for discussing property law is most needed.

The concept of ownership and the assumption of deregulation associated with it are not adequate means to achieve any of the legitimate goals we might seek to further by adopting a private property regime. Whether one conceives of the goal as promoting liberty, protecting security and reasonable expectations, rewarding hard work, establishing justice, or promoting social welfare, the classical ownership model fails as an adequate way to think about the meaning of private property.

The failure is twofold. First, property as ownership does not adequately express or implement the values we seek to foster by granting powers to owners. Its major problem is its failure to recognize that property rights have costs; the exercise of a property right by one person affects others. To structure property rights in a just and wise manner requires us to consider those effects. To do so, we must situate property in the context of social relationships.

The second problem with the ownership conception is that it fails to recognize conflicts among property rights. When two property rights conflict, it is not possible to address the conflict by asserting that one is in favor of limiting government regulation of property; such a formula is incoherent. The ownership conception of property fails to recognize that most of the conflicts that arise over the use or control of property can be best understood as conflicts *among property owners*, not conflicts between property owners and nonowners. The ownership conception misrepresents such situations and prevents us from adequately analyzing the conflicting values and interests presented by such problems.

The danger of the ownership conception is not only theoretical. Many policy makers and members of the general public in fact think about property through the simplistic lens of the ownership model. The model is simplistic because it presumes that it is easy to determine who the owner is and that, with minor exceptions, the owner wins any dispute regarding the property. Reality is far more complicated than this. Achieving the goals and protecting the principles underlying a just property regime requires a different understanding of property.

Because the ownership model of property is flawed, a variety of historical debates that continue to flourish have been wrongly formulated. Those debates include the proper extent of government regulation of private property, the legitimacy of redistribution of property, the correct balance between efficiency and rights in formulating legal rules, the legitimacy of "paternalistic" regulation, the commodification of all valuable interests, and the relation between legislative and judicial power to formulate law. All these traditional debates about property have been wrongly formulated because they all presume a simplistic model of property. The ownership conception of property prevents us from adequately analyzing public policy issues about organization of economic life. It also fails us when it comes to making moral judgments about public policy and law both by oversimplifying legal issues and by improperly allocating burdens of proof.

For example, most people assume that zoning or environmental laws take property rights by restricting the owner's right to use the property as he or she sees fit and that they therefore bear a heavy burden of justification. But when we realize that these laws are often intended to protect the property rights of others, it becomes far less easy to conclude that regulatory laws interfere with property rights rather than *protect* property rights. Zoning law, for example, protects the property rights of homeowners by preventing neighbors from building factories in the middle of residential neighborhoods. Although the zoning law limits the rights of the owner who wishes to build the factory, it does so to protect the property rights of the homeowners.

Another conception of property is available to us. Property rights concern relationships among people regarding control of valued resources. Rather than viewing property as equivalent to ownership, we can view it as defining a setting for human life. Property institutions create multiple settings to situate human relationships. Rather than identifying an owner and presuming that owner controls a particular resource for all purposes, we can understand property as rules that structure the contours of human relationships by adjusting the relations among multiple "owners."

If we focus on the tensions that exist within the concept of property itself, and the conflicts among competing property rights holders, we see how it is possible to adopt different rules while adhering to the goal of protecting property rights. Understanding the tensions within property law also gives a basis for arguing that both the concept of property and property law as it has been implemented in practice include principles that require sharing of property and access to property by nonowners in situations in which considerations of justice or morality might counsel limitations on individualistic, selfish property claims.

NOTES

1. *Pierson v. Post,* 3 Caines' Reports 175, 2 Am. Dec. 264 (N.Y. 1805).
2. Cheryl Russell and Margaret Ambry, *The Official Guide to American Incomes* (New York: New Strategist, 1993), 278.
3. *Rase v. Castle Mountain Ranch,* 631 P.2d 680 (Mont. 1981).
4. *Loretto v. Teleprompter Manhattan CATV Corporation,* 458 U.S. 419, 435 (1982).
5. Civil Rights Act, 42 U.S.C. §§ 1981, 1982 (1866).
6. *Friendswood Development Co. v. Smith-Southwest Industries, Inc.,* 576 S.W.2d 21 (Tex. 1981).
7. This does not mean the rules operate this way completely. In fact, the consolidation of ownership rights in a single owner may give that owner power over nonowners in a way that may tend to establish the further concentration of ownership.
8. Robert A. Williams, Jr., *The American Indian in Western Legal Thought: The Discourses of Conquest* (Oxford, UK: Oxford University Press, 1990).
9. *The Little, Brown Book of Anecdotes,* ed. Clifton Fadiman (Boston: Little, Brown, 1985), 395.
10. Jeremy Waldron, *The Right to Private Property* (Oxford, UK: Clarendon Press, 1988), 329.
11. John Locke, *The Second Treatise of Government* (Indianapolis: Bobbs-Merrill, 1962 [1690]), 17.
12. Waldron, *The Right to Private Property,* 109–15, 127.

13. Frank Michelman, *Liberties, Fair Values, and Constitutional Method,* 59 University of Chicago Law Review 91, 99 (1992).

14. John A. Powell, *New Property Disaggregated: A Model to Address Employment Discrimination,* 24 University of San Francisco Law Review 363, 374 78 (1990).

15. Lawrence Friedman, *A History of American Law,* 2d ed. (New York: Simon & Schuster, 1985), 230–34, 414–19.

11 KEITH AOKI

THE STAKES OF INTELLECTUAL PROPERTY LAW

THE second largest export of the United States is not comprised of iron, wood, or plastic. It doesn't grow from the ground, and it's not assembled in factories. This increasingly vital component of the U.S. gross national product and the object of increasingly fractious international controversy is ownership and control over a broad range of intellectual properties: Mickey Mouse, McDonald's, Madonna, numinous digital bytes, and unique DNA sequences. Nor are the consequences only financial or limited to ownership and control. For example, Monsanto, a multinational agrochemical corporation based in the United States, recently genetically engineered and patented soybean and cotton seeds amenable to direct applications of another patented Monsanto product, the broad-spectrum herbicide Roundup™. These seeds are called Roundup Ready™, and they have a unique characteristic: crops will die if they are sprayed with broad-spectrum herbicides made by other companies.[1]

Not long ago, intellectual property was a somewhat eccentric and arcane area far from the center stage of American law and best left to technical experts. However, in the past few decades, intellectual property law and policy have moved to the front of the legal agenda in controversies both within and between nations. Recent domestic developments include patents in living organisms, proposals to prohibit temporary copies of computer documents in computer random access memory, and unprecedented protection of dilution of a trademark's distinct meaning. Internationally, trends such as the concentration of media protection under the umbrella of a decreasing number of transnational corporations, the uncontrolled and perhaps uncontrollable spread of digital communications networks, and the prevalence of uncompensated bioprospecting by multinational agropharmaceutical firms render national regimes of intellectual property protection problematic at the very least.[2] Arguments over what directions intellectual property law will proceed are in many ways arguments over the pace, scope, and distributive effects of globalization.[3]

The scope of national and international intellectual property protection has dramatically expanded in recent decades. At first glance this may seem beneficial to the United States and to economic development internationally. However, the expansion of protection is controversial for three reasons. First, overprotection tends to undervalue a robust public domain of ideas and materials (sources) for future creators and audiences. Second, because the basic structure for intellectual property doctrine is a "private property" model, intellectual property rights are seen as predominantly private, which allows censorship and suppresses free speech (private parties don't engage in censorship, only governmental or public bodies do). Third, ownership and assertion of increasingly strong intellectual property rights, held by fewer and fewer global firms, both negatively impacts our capacity for democracy within the United States and raises troubling international human rights and distributive issues.

U.S. COPYRIGHT, PATENT, AND TRADEMARK LAW: A PRIMER

There are three federal bodies of U.S. intellectual property laws: copyrights, patents, and trademarks. Although they are sometimes confused with one another (all three areas do overlap at their margins), each applies to different subject matter.

Copyright law protects original works such as books, music, sculpture, movies, and aspects of computer programs that are embodied or fixed in a tangible medium. Copyright protection (unlike patent) generally has not been conditioned on the particular work's novelty or nonobviousness relative to prior knowledge. However, copyright protection extends only to a work's original aspects (copyright is not available for the building blocks of ideas such as the alphabet or Arabic numerals); protects only a particular *expression* of ideas, not the underlying ideas; and usually does not confer rights over independently created or similar works.[4]

Copyright vests automatically when an author creates an original work in a fixed, tangible medium, and protection lasts for the author's life plus fifty years. Authors have the exclusive right to do or to authorize the reproduction, distribution, adaptation, public performance, and public display of their works.

Unauthorized copying even a substantial amount of copyrighted expression, however, may be excused under the fair use doctrine. The Copyright Act provides an incomplete list of factors used to determine whether a putatively infringing use is a fair use, as well as a contradictory and nonexhaustive list of examples. For example, 2 Live Crew's parody of Roy Orbison's "Oh, Pretty Woman" was found to be a fair use in a case that undermined the earlier presumption that any and all "commercial uses" of copyrighted material are "presumptively unfair."[5]

A landmark 1991 case created confusion by withdrawing copyright protection (to an unclear degree) from compilations, which had previously been protected by copyright under a kind of Lockean "sweat of the brow" labor theory.[6] The court resisted attempts by many to characterize the objects of copyright protections as fungible and commensurable bytes of information, but recently there has been strong legislative lobbying by the value-added database industries for stronger and broader legal protections for databases.

Patent law, stemming from the same constitutional clause as copyright law and granting property rights to creators for the same reasons, has developed differently. Whereas copyright law addresses original expressions of authors, patent law addresses new and useful inventions, manufactures, compositions of matter, and processes reduced to practice by inventors, as well as designs, new breeds of plants, and genetically engineered strains of plants.[7] An inventor must apply for a patent and must satisfy rigorous requirements of subject matter, novelty, utility, and nonobviousness.

A patent confers the exclusive right to make, use, or sell the invention in the United States for twenty years from the date of filing. This right includes prohibiting innocent infringers, who may have independently developed the same invention, from making, using, or selling the invention for the patent term. Also, upon issue of a patent, sufficient information must be disclosed to enable "others skilled in the art" to create the invention. This information is then published at the time of the patent grant by the Patent and Trademark Office (PTO), allowing others to manufacture the disclosed invention after patent expiration. While exclusive, patent protection is nonetheless temporally finite. This limited protection theoretically makes possible eventual recombinations of elements of existing inventions into new ones, thereby ultimately adding to the common pool of ideas and inventions that are in the public domain.

Two types of subject matter generally have been considered unpatentable: mathematical formulae and natural laws and products of nature. For fairly obvious reasons, we don't give intellectual property rights in such fundamental ideas as $E = mc^2$, the Pythagorean Theorem, the law of electromagnetism, or rain. As with the idea-expression distinction in copyright law, this dichotomy of unpatentable-patentable subject matter is subject to exceptions at the margins and has proven particularly difficult to apply in the realm of inventions incorporating elements of computer software code or genetic engineering. For example, systems using mathematical formulae may be patentable as processes, even though a component step of such a process consists of using a digital computer program. Naturally occurring products cannot be patented; however, the discoverer of such a product may be able to claim a patent in an isolated, purified, or altered form of such a natural product. After the historic and troubling *Diamond v. Chakrabarty* case, which held that genetically altered living organisms are patentable, an increasing number of patents have been granted in living organisms, including mammals and recombinant human DNA sequences.[8]

In contrast to copyright and patent law, which developed partly to protect authors and inventors from marketplace pirates, nineteenth-century common law trademark developed from attempts to protect the *public* from mistake, confusion, and deception about the source and quality of products. For much of the nineteenth century, a seller's mark was legally protected because it represented consumer goodwill toward the producer of the marked goods. It thus assured the buyer that goods were of a consistent quality if bought from the same source.

However, trademark law has tended to be sensitive to public domain concerns, granting little or no protection for "merely descriptive" or "generic" marks and names unless a trademark owner could show that the public associated the particular mark with the owner's product in a commercial setting. For "arbitrary" and "fanciful" trademarks, stronger protections were available, presumably because competitors would not need to use a descriptive mark also to label and identify their products accurately. Cheerios™ or Exxon are protected, whereas *oat cereal* or *petroleum products* are not. Trademarks also served to lower the so-called search costs to consumers, providing a compact and easily identifiable way for consumers to tell similar products apart. The trademark became an informational proxy.

Legal protection of a trademark's signaling function has been expanded to include situations in which an existing mark's (or a very close analog's) use as a signal by someone else producing dissimilar goods or services in a different market creates a likelihood of consumer confusion, as disappointed consumers transfer their dissatisfaction with the other product to the products of the original owner of the registered mark.[9] Thus, the owner of McDonald's can prevent a bagel company from calling its product "McBagel" or even a mattress manufacturer from selling a "McSleep" mattress. And infringement by a passed-off inferior good was thought of as a tort-like injury to the proprietor's consumer goodwill. Trademark law also provided an incentive to the producer to maintain such goodwill through product consistency.

Thus conceived, traditional trademark law protected both buyers and sellers and promoted efficiency in marketplace transactions. For example, I can't sell McDonald's Big Macs™, unless they really are from McDonald's. However, traditionally (at least within the United States), I could say "McDonald's Big Macs are high in cholesterol and are not healthy for you," in part because I am using the trademark in an unconfusing, critical, and arguably noncommercial context.[10]

There have been two predominant theories or models of intellectual property: The first conceives a utilitarian bargain between an author or inventor and society in which the former is granted a limited term of exclusive use in return for disclosure and circulation; the second is based on a Lockean justification for property rights going to a deserving creator. Under these traditional models, society gives the author/inventor temporally limited private property rights (literally a monopoly) in a creative work or invention in exchange for the public being able to access and use or experience the invention or creative work. An author or inventor gets a state-created right to prevent others from copying or using a creative work or invention without the author/inventor's permission. Individual creativity and innovation are thus simultaneously rewarded and encouraged. Society flourishes because the net amount of available creative works and inventions increases. This model worked relatively well for eighteenth- and nineteenth-century publishing and insured recoupment of nineteenth-century research and development costs.

However, both the utilitarian and the Lockean justifications for granting copyrights and patents rest on a contingent and not altogether unattractive vision of individual human agency, a vision of an individual transformative creator producing original works of the imagination. There are two more shadowy norms justifying protecting intellectual creations, both of which have remained relatively undeveloped in U.S. law:

justifications arising from the need to protect the customs of a community, derived from the Scottish Enlightenment philosopher David Hume, and justifications arising from the need to protect an individual's intellectual creations because they embody that individual's personhood and personality, derived from Hegelian thought.[11] All four of these theoretical strands—utilitarian, Lockean, customary, and personhood—are present in the recent tendency to maximize intellectual property protection in the United States.

FROM AUTHOR TO CONTENT PROVIDER, FROM EXPRESSION TO INFORMATION

In recent decades, legal visions of authors, originality, invention, and ownership have intersected in the areas of copyright, patent, and trademark law, resulting in the removal of increasing amounts of material from the public domain. Many of these public domain materials formerly were thought of as unowned, unownable, or commonly owned. These include DNA codes; simple words, phrases, or logos; information in databases; basic ideas; and the designs of useful articles. U.S. intellectual property laws are being reconceived, often at the behest of copyright and patent-based industries, such as media, software, or biotechnology, to recast these items in ways that remove them from the intellectual common and transmute them into private intellectual property through the intervention of creative human agency, whether through a copyright holder's authorship, a patent holder's inventorship, or a trademark owner's investment of time, money, and labor to give a trademark value.[12]

The vision of originality plays itself out in U.S. intellectual property law in two ways.[13] First, when legal recognition of authorship is added into the mix via property rights, intellectual property laws convey special rights to *creators*. The economic nature of a U.S. copyright or patent means that such rights are alienable. Is it surprising, therefore, that in our mass communications environment, control of valuable copyrighted and patented products tends to concentrate in the hands of vast corporate entities rather than in the hands of individual authors or inventors, the persons such laws were initially supposed to encourage and reward? Second, given the fungibility of U.S. intellectual property rights, a copyright, patent, or trademark owner can also prohibit anyone else from copying and selling his or her work, creating a monopoly. Thus, a regime that has in the past served to increase the amounts and types of available creative and useful intellectual productions, when pushed to a maximalist extreme, actually squelches the circulation and use of these intangible yet commodifiable items.

Works that are susceptible to being copyrighted, patented, or trademarked are easily duplicated—that is, what makes them valuable is not their specific corporeal embodiment. Whether a book, a widget, or a label on a box of cornflakes, the property that is protected is intangible. Their value derives from the exclusivity of use. You may buy the book, the widget, or the box of cornflakes and do with them what you will—except make copies. Why? In brief, because intellectual properties are similar to what economists call a "public good."

A public good has two key attributes: jointness of supply and impossibility of exclusion. A paradigmatic public good is the light supplied by a lighthouse. The light is jointly supplied to all—one more ship using the beacon doesn't diminish the beam's value to other ships—and it is difficult if not impossible to offer the beacon only to those who will pay and exclude freeloaders from the beam's navigational benefits. A lighthouse is considered a public goods problem, because no private market actor will build and run lighthouses. If there is no way to recoup expenses, a public body (funded by taxes, part of which are paid by freeloading boat owners) steps in to provide the service. With similar utilitarian roots, U.S. intellectual property laws are supposed to assist authors, inventors, and others who invest in producing intellectual works in stopping others from taking advantage of the jointness of supply and impossibility of exclusion that arises from such works. Traditionally, intellectual property rights inhered in the expressions of authors, novel and nonobvious inventions, and consumer understandings about the source of marketplace goods. Problems arise when we extend such protections to underlying ideas and information itself.[14]

The maximalist intellectual property agenda has been aided by a largely surreptitious blurring and collapse of the usual categorizing of intellectual property law. Reading almost any contemporary discussion of intellectual property policy, one is struck by the ubiquity of the use of the word *information.* The move to assume commensurability between widely divergent categories of intellectual productions by characterizing them as information has been driven in part by rapid advances in computer networking technology—copyright in particular has always had an uneasy relationship with technological change. This tendency to talk about things using their lowest common digital denominator disregards context.

It is one thing to give authors (or publishers) the right to prevent

unauthorized *copies* of a book in order to encourage investment in expensive printing presses and distribution arrangements, but it is quite
another to cede the power to prevent readers of the book from discussing
or writing about the *ideas* contained in the book. Until recently, Anglo-
American copyright law has managed to draw a strong, if at times confusing, distinction between ideas and expressions. Expressions of authors
could be copyrighted; their ideas could not be. Similarly, an inventor
could prohibit others from making or using his or her patented invention, but not the underlying laws of nature exploited by the invention. In
trademark law, preventing marketplace pirates from misrepresenting the
source of goods is different from prohibiting political groups from using
a trademarked logo to criticize corporate conduct or prohibiting other
noncommercial use.[15]

In the United States, while notions of tangible property underwent
significant relativization and disaggregation during the twentieth century, legal protection and characterization of intellectual property rights
have gone in precisely the opposite direction. This hardening of intellectual property rights is partly due to the deeply embedded image of original authorship. Intellectual property laws initially mandated legal regulation of the copying of literary works. This vision of authorship emerged
in order to encourage the production and circulation of the ideas contained in such works. However, how are we to administer rules and
incentives designed to operate in a paper-publishing world when it
becomes feasible to publish one's works to the world on a $20-per-
month home page on the Internet? The tendency to conflate all sorts of
information production and circulation confuses the important distinction between providing incentives for the creation of many different *types*
of works and providing incentives for the production of many *copies* of
works. Rewarding and encouraging authors to produce many types of
creative works now has come to justify ever-increasing property rights in
information itself, a result directly contrary to understandings of early
English and American copyright law.

In contrast to their original purpose, current U.S. intellectual property
laws increasingly assign to certain parties the exclusive rights to control
information as opposed to "creative expressions of authors" or "inventions reduced to practice."[16] Due in part to the largely unquestioned and
ubiquitous importation of "author reasoning" into intellectual property
law and policy, courts and legislatures have erred consistently on the side
of overprotecting intellectual properties. Their reasoning is inappropri-
ately linear: If a certain level of intellectual property rights encourages the

circulation and creation of intellectual works, then stronger and broader intellectual property protections will produce more circulation and creation. But there is a point where overprotection of intellectual property is as harmful to production and circulation as no protection at all. Instead of setting a balance between the rights of users and creators, the maximalist intellectual property agenda has been embarrassingly lopsided toward protecting owners, ignoring the fact that all intellectual property owners are also users.

The same thinking is replicated in arguments that call for internationalized versions of U.S. intellectual property law on a global scale, but with paradoxical effects. To the extent that intellectual property regimes provide rights in information, they undermine traditional, territorial, and political notions of sovereignty. As information reconceived as intellectual property becomes less embedded in such physical objects as books, and as author-based legal regimes begin expanding the scope of property rights in information, many decision makers begin opting for supranational intellectual property protection norms and frameworks. Such frameworks contribute to the erosion of national and territorial sovereignty, particularly because entities holding increasingly large blocks of intellectual property rights are not nations but private multinational corporations. The irony is that such entities must then return to assertions of the sovereignty of domestic intellectual property laws to underwrite their ownership claims. This pattern of thinking has produced concomitant and (at least until recently) relatively unnoticed underprotection and underappreciation of the social, cultural, economic, and political importance of a robust informational public domain that students, teachers, scientists, authors, artists, inventors, business people—indeed, all of us—may draw upon to create new works of all sorts.

THE STAKES OF INTELLECTUAL PROPERTY LAW

The expansion of the scope, justification, and vision of intellectual property protections has generated intense controversy because of its economic, technological, social, and cultural impact. Here, briefly, are some of the leading current controversies.

COMPUTERS AND THE INTERNET

The Commerce Department sought four significant changes to U.S. copyright law in its influential 1995 white paper.[17] First, the paper proposed outlawing transitory and temporary copies made in a computer's random access memory as infringements of a copyright; second, imposing a strict liability scheme of contributory infringement on Internet service providers, making them liable for copyright infringement occurring on their electronic bulletin boards and other services they provide, such as e-mail (thus creating a duty to monitor content, which in turn implicates both privacy concerns and chilling effects on speech); third, imposing criminal sanctions for tampering with copy-protected digital texts, so that even if the information contained within a digital text was not copyrightable, decompiling or reverse-engineering that information's container would be illegal; and fourth, restricting fair use by a statutory commercial-noncommercial use distinction.

Consider what this would mean when, for example, you used a computer to access the Internet. Every time you viewed and read a website on the screen of your computer monitor, you would be infringing a copyright and would be liable to the owner. This is because in order to display a screen, your computer must load a copy into its random access memory: Viewing would thus equal instant infringement. This was the scenario imagined by the drafters of the white paper, who were strongly protective of the interests of content providers. Partly due to a broad coalition of teachers, students, librarians, university administrators, and information activists concerned about the radical expansion of both copyright protection and infringement liability, the Commerce Department's white paper stalled in Congress in 1996.[18]

While direct attempts by the copyright industries to lobby Congress and supranational bodies such as the United Nations agency the World Intellectual Property Organization (WIPO) for maximal protections have met with mixed success, another strategy has been to go forward into the past by resurrecting a nineteenth-century vision of formalist contract law. Originally placed under the transparent plastic wrap of software packaging, shrink-wrap licenses have inspired digital "click-wrap" licenses—textual windows of contract terms that prompt a user to "click" assent before allowing installation of a program or access to a website. This formalist vision may be seen in the proposed changes to the Uniform Commercial Code contained in the as-yet unadopted section 2B, which would cover shrink-wrap and click-wrap licenses in the software area. These proposals represent a born-again formalist approach to contract in two ways. First, shrink-wrap and click-wrap licenses bear more than a passing resemblance to adhesion contracts and suffer from the same lack of actual agreement as well as inequalities of bargaining power. Second, these agreements make an end run around the Copyright

Act's "first sale" doctrine. The first sale doctrine allows buyers of books and other copyrighted materials to re-sell, loan, give away, or modify the book they purchased—a purchaser is only prohibited from making unauthorized copies. Furthermore, by turning putative purchasers of software into mere licensees, the approach gives software companies significantly more control than the Copyright Act allows, feeding into the unequal bargaining power problem as well as suffering from serious federal preemption questions.[19]

TRADEMARKS, COPYRIGHTS, AND FREE SPEECH

I recently received a postcard from a friend. On the front was a portrait of the slain Nigerian Nobel laureate and human rights activist, Ken Saro-Wiwa, who was executed by the Nigerian government for protesting Nigeria's violent dispossession of Ogoni farmers to allow Shell Oil to drill in the Niger delta. At the top of the postcard was a legend: "Remember Ken Saro-Wiwa." At the bottom was the familiar bright yellow Shell Oil logo, dripping with blood, accompanied by a phrase: "Boycott Shell Oil." Under the new federal antidilution statute, which protects "famous marks" such as Shell's from tarnishment, this postcard would probably constitute actionable trademark infringement.

Expansive legislative grants and broad judicial construction of such intellectual property rights have an extremely disturbing impact on free speech. In effect, the private property interest of the copyright owner trumps the public interest in free expression. Under traditional notions of intellectual property law, a balance was struck between protecting expressive works of authors, enabling public disclosure of one's invention as the sine qua non of patent protection, and requiring both actual use of a mark in commerce and the unlikeliness of consumer confusion. However, with the elision of categorical differences between intellectual works into ownable, commensurable information, something important is lost or obscured.

Taken together, intellectual property laws contemplate a large area where common phrases, words, ideas, and other information remain unowned. This intellectual commons must exist for both the public state and the private market to function. Without access to such useful, unowned, or commonly owned works and ideas, the electorate would be unable to make sound electoral choices and private market actors would be unable to make efficient market decisions. In the public sphere, a vision of a rich realm of political debate and intellectual exchange drives the First Amendment. In classic economic theory, perfect information in private markets produces efficient allocation of goods. When private market actors are able to censor the creation and circulation of works via assertion of copyrights or trademark laws, the abundantly available information envisioned by the First Amendment is no longer a reality. This squelching of expression is occurring in the private sphere, accomplished by persons or entities enforcing private property rights.

In recent decades the free speech rights of corporations and wealthy people have been enhanced in the face of serious criticisms that protecting campaign contributions and corporate speech consistently favors wealthy private interests and seriously undermines the democratic process. Increasing levels of First Amendment protection for advertising and other types of commercial speech also valorize and insulate the speech and communications of powerful private parties at the expense of less powerful or organized public interests and constituencies.[20]

Nor have we paid adequate attention to the problem of concentration in the media and the communications industry.[21] Mergers between Capital Cities–ABC and Disney, NBC and General Electric, and CBS and Westinghouse have captured U.S. headlines, as have discussions of possible mergers of other media giants. The channels of communications maintained by these media behemoths are filled with material supplied by content providers—movies, television shows, music, and so on. Corporate ownership of increasing numbers of intellectual properties underwrites these new empires. Because such ownership exists in the private sphere, the importance of the free exchange of ideas and information is troublingly obscured.

EXPORTING AMERICAN INTELLECTUAL PROPERTY LAW

At a December 1996 WIPO meeting in Geneva, copyright, media, and information industry representatives behind the Commerce Department's white paper sought to globally implement the same four problematic protections advocated in the failed white paper. The proposed Database Protection Treaty was flatly rejected, and the white paper proposals were taken under consideration for further discussion. When the copyright and information industries could not get what they wanted on the domestic level, they sought to make a supranational end run, a tactic that had some prior success with the Trade Related Aspects of Intellectual Property (TRIP) component of the General Agreement on Tariffs and Trade (GATT).[22]

Two major changes in U.S. intellectual property laws were enacted under the banner of GATT compliance after failing to gain domestic enactment on their own merits. The first was a federal antidilution component, section 43(c) of the Lanham Act. The second was the shift in the patent statute from a first-to-invent regime (meaning the first to actually reduce an invention to practice) to a first-to-file regime (which tends to favor large corporate research and development departments with staffs of patent lawyers working on time-consuming and complex patent applications). The pattern that has emerged is to whipsaw domestic and international protections against each other. The U.S. will first sign on to a multilateral treaty such as GATT, which provides for minimum standards of intellectual property protection. Next, there are moves to ratchet up domestic levels of protections, which in turn exert pressure on other treaty nations to increase protections likewise. The end result is that minimum standards of protection become driven by a maximalist agenda.

Treaties such as the TRIP component of GATT use the more neutral sounding phrase "removal of barriers to trade" when dealing with intellectual property protection. But GATT in effect says to the countries of the developing world: In exchange for reducing or eliminating tariffs on goods such as cotton so you can export them, you must agree to protect the intellectual properties of the developed world. Thus, the cotton that goes into a Mickey Mouse T-shirt will pass out of Malaysia at say, $1 a pound, returning as a T-shirt emblazoned with a trademarked image and selling for $25.

These are strange times. Transnational corporate entities whose fortunes are built on protecting their intellectual properties turn to impoverished nation-states to ensure protection for their private rights. The TRIP accord explicitly states that "intellectual property rights are private rights." The United States threatens China with severe sanctions for its laxness in policing intellectual property rights, but stops short of sanctioning human rights abuses such as prison labor (labor which may produce the Mickey Mouse T-shirts) or selling nuclear weapons components to Pakistan. The ideology of the private economic sphere has become so dominant that it tops the U.S. international agenda.

CULTURAL AND OTHER (MIS)APPROPRIATIONS

For more than two centuries, the idea that a patent would be granted for a life form seemed ridiculous. Justice William O. Douglas wrote in a 1948 case:

> [P]atents cannot issue for the discovery of the phenomena of nature. . . .
> The qualities of these bacteria, like the sun, electricity, or the qualities of
> metals, are part of the storehouse of knowledge of all men. They are man-
> ifestations of laws of nature, free to all men and reserved exclusively to
> none. . . . [The bacteria at issue] serve the ends nature originally provided
> and act quite independently of any effort of the patentee.[23]

The legal conception of unpatentable products of nature has changed.
The landmark 1980 case *Diamond v. Chakrabarty* held that genetically
altered living organisms were patentable as "manufactures" or "compositions of matter," because human agency (via newly developed genetic
engineering techniques) had effectively removed such organisms from
the category of items occurring in nature.[24] To a majority of the Supreme
Court, the scientist's discovery was "not nature's handiwork, but his own;
accordingly it is patentable subject matter." By focusing on human intervention as a crucial factor in determining patentability, the court opened
the door to patents in life forms. In later cases the PTO decided that
plant tissues and seeds were patentable and upheld a patent in the
Harvard Oncomouse (a mouse bred for easy susceptibility to cancer) on
the ground that "multicellular living organisms, including animals" are
patentable.[25]

In 1993, U.S. Commerce Secretary Ron Brown (on behalf of the
Commerce Department), listing two American men as "inventors," filed
a patent application on the cell line of a twenty-six-year-old Guaymi
woman from Panama. The "inventors" had taken some blood cells from
the woman when she was in a Panama hospital and grew them in a laboratory culture media. The Guaymi woman's cells were thought to possess a special antiviral leukemia-resistant quality. When activists began
calling attention to the Commerce Department's problematic genetic
property grab by protesting the patent claim at venues such as the
annual WIPO meeting, a meeting of members of the Biodiversity
Convention, and GATT talks, the U.S. withdrew its patent application.
Subsequently, the Commerce Department filed two more patent applications based on human cell lines taken from indigenous peoples in the
Solomon Islands and Papua, New Guinea. In reply to protests from the
ambassador of the Solomon Islands, the Commerce Department stated
its position: "Under our laws, as well as those of many countries, subject
matter relating to human cells is patentable and there is no provision for
considerations relating to the source of cells that may be the subject of a
patent application."[26]

While patenting a cell line from an indigenous person may be a particularly egregious form of biocolonialism, it may be entirely consistent with Western practices rooted in the not too distant past. For example, a high percentage of the genetic resources that the United States uses in its own agricultural production originated from uncompensated sources in the Third World. No compensation was paid for these resources because such genetic resources were seen as products of nature. At virtually the same moment it became technologically possible to alter these "products"genetically, the Supreme Court held them to be patentable. Minor bioengineered variations in a species could conceivably give rise to patent property over an entire species genome and byproducts.

With the rise of the biotechnology industry in the United States has come, with little public knowledge or debate, monopoly property rights over the genetic resources of wild animal species and crop plants (perhaps the result of centuries of cultivation) and over an individual human's genome. The modern-day gold rush called bioprospecting is underwritten by the U.S. patent system, which holds out the jackpot of monopoly to the ethnobotanist who strikes genetic gold while panning through the world's rain forests and jungles for potentially useful species of plants, insects, and animals. The indigenous knowledge and practices that first produced or singled out these resources is not considered intellectual property because it is not considered novel or original in a patent or copyright sense.

Our intellectual property laws allow authors, inventors, and trademark owners to scoop up these "raw materials" and process them, "creating" intellectual properties—songs, movies, CDs, new drugs and therapies, bioengineered seeds—to sell them back (at a premium) to the people and groups from whom the "raw materials" originated, among others. The politics of this genetic grab by the pharmaceutical, agricultural, and biotech corporations of the Northern Hemisphere are beginning to become explicit. Indigenous knowledge, cultures, dances, artifacts, and agricultural and physical resources flow out of the developing world, either for free or discounted as raw material. Processed and transformed by Western authors, inventors, and corporations into intellectual properties, they are then sent out globally, premium-priced, with their value secured by international treaty, violation of which is considered to be creating barriers to free trade. Opposition to the global politics of intellectual property is emerging by fits and starts. In 1995, the European Parliament voted to ban the patenting of life forms. In October 1993, on Gandhi's birthday, half a million Indian farmers staged a mass protest at the Indian offices of Cargill Seeds Private Ltd., a subsidiary of the largest privately held corporation in the United States. The farmers objected to the patenting of seed that had been used in their farming communities for centuries—as well as the agricultural and intellectual property provisions of the then-imminent GATT.[27]

Overall, U.S. intellectual property rights cover too much and are still expanding, generating an intellectual property smog. Between the Northern and Southern Hemispheres, the problem may be too *few* property rights of the type that would give recognition, monetary and otherwise, to the siphoned resources of the developing world.

NOTES

1. Mark Arax, "No Way Around Roundup: Monsanto's Bioengineered Seeds Are Designed to Require More of the Company's Herbicide," *Mother Jones* (January/February 1997); Robert Steyer, "Monsanto Gets Green Light on Altered Soybeans," *St. Louis Post-Dispatch*, May 26, 1995, 13D; Karen Lehman and Al Krebs, "Control of the World's Food Supply," in *The Case Against the Global Economy and for a Turn Towards the Local*, ed. Jerry Mander and Edward Goldsmith (San Francisco: Sierra Club Books, 1996), 108.

2. Federal Trademark Dilution Act of 1995, § 3, Pub. L. No. 104–374, codified at 15 U.S.C. § 1125(c)(Section 43 (c)) enacted December 1995 as part of GATT Compliance Treaty, see Uruguay Round Agreements Act, Pub. L. No. 103–465 (H.R. 5110) (December 8, 1994).

3. See generally Keith Aoki, *(Intellectual) Property and Sovereignty: Notes Towards a Geography of Authorship*, 48 Stanford Law Review 1293 (1996); Rosemary J. Coombe, *Objects of Property and Subjects of Politics: Intellectual Property Laws and Democratic Dialogue*, 69 Texas Law Review 1853 (1991); Niva Elkin-Koren, *Cyberlaw and Social Change: A Democratic Approach to Copyright Law in Cyberspace*, 14 Cardozo Arts & Entertainment Law Journal 215 (1996); Neil Weinstock Netanel, *Copyright and a Democratic Civil Society*, 106 Yale Law Journal 283 (1996).

4. See 17 U.S.C. §§ 101 et seq.; 17 U.S.C. § 102(a).

5. Fisher, *Reconstructing the Fair Use Doctrine*, infra n. 11; see also *Campbell v. Acuff-Rose Music, Inc.*, 510 U.S. 569 (1994); 17 U.S.C. § 107.

6. *Feist Publications, Inc. v. Rural Telephone Service Co.*, 499 U.S. 340 (1991); *International News Service v. Associated Press*, 248 U.S. 215 (1918); see also *National Basketball Ass'n . v. Motorola, Inc.*, 105 F.3d 841 (2d Cir. 1996).

7. 35 U.S.C. §§ 101 et seq.; see also 35 U.S.C §§ 161–64 (Plant Patent Act of 1930); 7 U.S.C. §§ 2321–582 (Plant Variety Protection Act); *Asgrow Seed v. Winterboer*, 513 U.S. 179 (1995).

8. See *Reilly v. Morse*, 56 U.S.C. (15 How.) 62 (1853) denying Samuel Morse's patent claim over the use of "electromagnetism, however deployed for making or printing intelligible characters, signs, or letters at any distance"; *Diamond v. Diehr*, 450 U.S. 175 (1981); see also *In re Alappat*, 33 F.3d 1526 (Fed. Cir. 1994); *Diamond v. Chakrabarty*, 447 U.S. 303 (1980).

9. Lanham Act, 15 U.S.C. §§ 1051 et seq. See also 15 U.S.C. § 1125(a); *Two Pesos, Inc. v. Taco Cabana, Inc.*, 505 U.S. 763 (1992).

10. Fred Barbash, "'Big Mac' v. Small Fries: Award Lean for McDonald's in Giant-Size Trial," *Washington Post*, June 20, 1997, A1 (describing the end of the longest trial in England's legal history wherein McDonald's was awarded "$98,000 in libel damages from two environmental activists who accused the fast-food giant of charges ranging from aiding the destruction of rain forests to serving unhealthful food and mistreating its workers").

11. See Wendy Gordon, *An Inquiry into the Merits of Copyright: The Challenges of Consistency, Consent and Encouragement Theory*, 41 Stanford Law Review 1343 (1989); James Boyle, *Shamans, Spleens and Software: Law and the Construction of the Information Society* (Cambridge, MA: Harvard University Press, 1996); William W. Fisher III, *Reconstructing the Fair Use Doctrine*, 101 Harvard Law Review 1659 (1987).

12. David Lange, *Recognizing the Public Domain*, 1981 Law and Contemporary Problems 147 (1981); Jessica Litman, *The Public Domain*, 39 Emory Law Journal 965 (1990); Keith Aoki, *Authors, Inventors and Trademark Owners: Private Intellectual Property and the Public Domain, Parts I and II*, 18 Columbia Journal of Law and Arts 1–73; 191–267 (1993–1994).

13. See Michel Foucault, "What Is an Author?" in *The Foucault Reader* ed. Paul Rabinow, trans. Josue V. Harari (New York: Pantheon, 1984), 101; Boyle, *Shamans, Software and Spleens*, supra n. 11; Peter Jaszi, *Towards a Theory of Copyright: The Metamorphoses of 'Authorship,'* 1991 Duke Law Journal 455 (1991); Martha Woodmansee, *The Author, Art and the Market: Re-Reading the History of Aesthetics* (New York: Columbia University Press, 1994); Mark Rose, *Authors and Owners: The Invention of Copyright* (Cambridge, MA: Harvard University Press, 1996).

14. See Paul A. Samuelson, "The Pure Theory of Public Expenditure," 36 Review of Economics and Statistics 387 (1954); Robert Cooter and Thomas Ulen, *Law and Economics* (Glenview, IL: Scott Foresman, 1988), 135; Rosemary J. Coombe, *Challenging Paternities: Histories of Copyright*, 6 Yale Journal of Law and Humanities 397 (1994).

15. *Baker v. Selden*, 101 U.S. 99 (1879); *Lotus Dev. Corp. v. Borland Int'l, Inc.*, 49 F.3d 807 (1st Cir. 1995), aff'd 4–4, 116 S. Ct. 1062 (1996); see also 17 U.S.C § 102(b); *Funk Brothers Seed v. Kalo Inoculant Co.*, 333 U.S. 127 (1948); Coombe, supra n. 3.

16. See generally Pam Samuelson, *Information as Property: Do Ruckelshaus and Carpenter Signal a Changing Direction in Intellectual Property Law?*, 38 Catholic University Law Review 365 (1989); James Boyle, *A Theory of Law and Information: Copyright, Spleens, Blackmail and Insider Trading*, 80 California Law Review 1415 (1992); see also *United States v. O'Hagan*, 1997 WL 345229 (U.S.) (Decided June 25, 1997), adopting misappropriation theory to find liability for insider trading violation of securities law.

17. National Information Infrastructure Task Force, *Intellectual Property and the National Information Infrastructure: The Report of the Working Group on Intellectual Property Rights* (Washington, DC: U.S. Government Printing Office, 1995) [hereinafter White Paper]; see also the NII Copyright Protection Act of 1995, introduced as S. 1284 and H.R. 2441, 104th Cong., 2d Sess, § 106 (1995); on RAM copies as infringement, see *MAI Systems Corp. v. Peak Computer, Inc.*, 991 F.2d 1510 (9th Cir. 1993); on Internet Service Provider vicarious liability for infringement, see *Religious Technology Center v. Netcom On-Line Communications Services, Inc.*, 907 F.Supp. 1361 (N.D.Cal. 1995).

18. Pam Samuelson, *Copyright in the Twenty-First Century: Will the Copyright Office Be Obsolete in the Twenty-First Century?*, 13 Cardozo Arts & Entertainment Law Journal 55 (1994); Julie E. Cohen, *Reverse Engineering and the Rise of Electronic Vigilantism: Intellectual Property Implications of "Lock Out" Programs*, 68 Southern California Law Review 1091 (1995); Pam Samuelson, "The Copyright Grab," *WIRED* (January 1996): 134; James Boyle, *Intellectual Property On-Line: A Young Person's Guide*, 10 Harvard Journal of Law and Technology 47 (1996).

19. See Mark Lemley, *Intellectual Property and Shrinkwrap Licenses*, 68 Southern California Law Review 1239 (1995); *ProCD, Inc. v. Zeidenberg*, 86 F.3d 1447 (7th Cir. 1996); 17 U.S.C. § 109(a); cf. the Record Rental Amendment of 1984, Pub. L. No. 98–450, codified at 17 U.S.C. § 109(b); the Computer Software Rental Amendments of 1990, Pub. L. No. 101–650, Title VII, 104 Stat. 5089 (1990); 17 U.S.C. § 301; but cf. *ProCD, Inc. v. Zeidenberg*, 86 F.3d 1447 (7th Cir. 1996).

20. See, for example, *Buckley v. Valeo*, 424 U.S. 1 (1976); *First National Bank of Boston v. Bellotti*, 435 U.S. 765 (1978); *City of Cincinnati v. Discovery Network, Inc.*, 507 U.S. 410 (1993); David Skover and Ronald Collins, *The Death of Discourse* (Boulder, CO: Westview Press, 1996); David Kairys, *With Liberty and Justice for Some* (New York: The New Press, 1993).

21. Herbert Schiller, *Information Inequality* (Florence, KY: Routledge, 1996); Ben H. Bagdikian, *The Media Monopoly*, 3d ed. (Boston: Beacon Press, 1990); Stanley A. Deetz, *Democracy in an Age of Corporate Colonization* (Albany: State University of New York Press, 1992); Kairys, supra n. 20.

22. Peter H. Lewis, "World Panel Meets to Revise Copyright Laws," *New York Times*, December 2, 1996, A1; see also archive of WIPO Database Protection materials assembled by James Love of Taxpayer Assets Project and Consumer Project on Technology available at URL: http://www.essential.org/listproc/info-policy-notes/; Pam Samuelson, "Big Media Beaten Back," *WIRED* (March 1997): 81; J. H. Reichman and Pam Samuelson, *Intellectual Property Rights in Data*, 50 Vanderbilt Law Review 51 (1997).

23. *Funk Bros. Seed Co. v. Kalo Inoculant Co.*, 333 U.S. 127, 130–31 (1980) (Douglas, J.).

24. *Diamond v. Chakrabarty*, 447 U.S. 303 (1980) (Burger, J.).

25. *Ex parte Hibberd*, 2 U.S.P.Q. 2D (BNA) 1425 (PTO Bd. Pat. App. and Int'f. 1985); *Ex parte Allen*, 2 U.S.P.Q. 2D (BNA) 1425 (PTO Bd. Pat. App. and Int'f. 1987), aff'd 846 F.2d 77 (Fed. Cir. 1988) upholding a patent in a genetically altered oyster; see Patent No. 4,736,866 (issued for a genetically altered mouse with enhanced susceptibility to cancer on April 12, 1988, to Harvard University as the assignee of "inventors" Philip Leder and Timothy Stewart); Edmund L. Andrews, "U.S. Resumes Granting Patents on Genetically Altered Animals," *New York Times*, February 3, 1993, A1.

26. Philip Bereano, "Body and Soul: The Price of Biotech," *Seattle Times*, August 20, 1995, B5; Philip L. Bereano, "The Race to Own DNA: Guaymi Tribe Was Surprised They Were Invented, Part II," *Seattle Times*, August 27, 1995, B5; see the Rural Advancement Foundation International (RAFI) Resources on the Privatization of Human Genetic Material, the Human Genome Diversity Project, and the U.S. Government's Role in Patenting Human Cell Lines' home page at URL: http://www.charm.net/~rafi/pp.html; see also Boyle, *Shamans, Spleens and Software*, supra n. 11 at 97–107; Andrew Kimbrell, "Biocolonization: The Patenting of Life and the Global Market in Body Parts," in *The Case Against the Global Economy*, supra n. 1 at 131.

27. Sandy Tolan, "Against the Grain: Multinational Corporations Peddling Patented Seeds and Chemical Pesticides Are Poised to Revolutionize India's Ancient Agricultural System," *Los Angeles Times*, July 10, 1994, Magazine section, 18; Vandanna Shiva and Radha Holla-Bhar, "Piracy by Patent: The Case of the Neem Tree," in *The Case Against the Global Economy*, supra n. 1 at 146; Bereano, supra n. 26.

12 W. HAYWOOD BURNS

LAW AND RACE IN EARLY AMERICA

Haywood Burns, to whom this volume is dedicated, died in a car accident in South Africa in 1996. This is a slightly edited version of his essay in the second edition.—Ed.

IN early 1855 white men sitting in the Kansas legislature, duly elected by other white men, passed a law that sentenced white men convicted of rape of a white woman to up to five years in prison, while the penalty for a black man convicted of the same offense was castration, the costs of the procedure to be rendered by the desexed.

The penalty of sexual mutilation appears at many points in the annals of American jurisprudence, Kansas in 1855 being but one of the more recent examples. What is special about the sentence of castration is that where it was in force, it was almost universally reserved for African Americans (and, in some cases, Indians).

Apart from what this example reveals about the sexual psychopathology of white racism in American history, it graphically demonstrates the working of law in a racist society. The nexus between law and racism cannot be much more direct than this. Indeed, the histories of the African, Asian, Latin, and Native American people in the United States are replete with examples of the law and the legal process as the means by which the generalized racism in the society was made particular and converted into standards and policies of social control. A systematic analysis of racism and law provides keen insight into the operations of both.[1]

In early-seventeenth-century colonial America, blacks and whites often existed and toiled side by side in various degrees of bondage. Though there were gradations of unfreedom, there was, at first, no clearly defined status of "slave." As the century drew to a close, however, the social reality and objective conditions changed sufficiently for the members of the colonial legislatures to recognize officially that the situations of the black person in bondage and the white person in bondage were diverging, with that of the black person becoming more debased. "Free choice" was hardly an issue for either whites or blacks who came in bondage to the New World. Still, there was a considerable difference in being, for example, an Irish indentured servant and a kidnapped African arriving in chains after the unspeakable horrors of the Middle Passage. There are vast differences between a societally enforced discrimination and an entire legal order founded explicitly on racism—a world of difference between "Irish need not apply," as reprehensible as that was, and statutory denial of legal personality, of humanity.

Black people were severed from much of their culture, language, kindred, religion, and all communication with the Old World of their fathers and mothers, from which they had been torn. The ugly sentiments of white racial superiority were beginning to sprout and rear their heads above the native soil. These facts, coupled with a growing understanding of the tremendous economic advantage to be gained from the long-term exploitation of black labor, brought about a social consensus (among whites) that sought to permanently relegate black people to the lowest stratum in a vertical relationship of white over black. This consensus found expression and implementation in the form of laws passed in colonial legislatures that made slavery for black people both a lifetime condition and a hereditary condition. Thus, through the operation of law, in this case legislated societal racism, the institution of American chattel slavery was created and perpetuated.

With the advent of the detailed and oppressive colonial slave codes of the early eighteenth century, law played a consistent role throughout the period, up to and including the American Revolution. The Revolution, of course, produced a golden opportunity to do business other than as usual. It was, after all, a revolution fought in the name of liberty and egalitarian principles. It was an opportunity that was nonetheless missed or, perhaps better said, rejected. The revolution of Jefferson, Washington, and Madison was never intended to embrace the ebony throngs of captured and enslaved people in their white midsts. It was too much for the eighteenth-century white American mind to view these captured and enslaved people fully as people. It was too much for the Founding Fathers and the economic interests they represented to tamper with that amount of property—even for those who on moral, philosophical, or religious grounds opposed slavery.

Thus, the birth of the new order in the establishment of the Republic brought with it no new day for the African on American soil. In erecting the new state, black people were still consigned to be the hewers of wood, the drawers of water. For there enshrined in the fundamental law of the land, the new Constitution itself, was the guaranteed continuation of the slave trade, the guaranteed return of fugitive slaves, and the counting of black persons as three-fifths human beings for purposes of taxation and political representation.

The pre-Revolutionary slave codes were more than ample models for the post-Revolutionary slave codes, which continued their detailed, oppressive harshness into the nineteenth century and into the new and expanding nation. The nineteenth-century slave codes provide an excellent example of law and state operating to impose a given social order. The slave codes legislated and regulated in minute detail every aspect of the life of a slave and of black/white interaction; assured white-over-black dominance; and made black people into virtual nonpersons, refusing to recognize any right of family, free movement, choice, and legal capacity to bring a suit or to testify where the interest of a white person was involved. This legal structure defining a black person's place in society was reinforced by statutes requiring cruel and brutal sanctions for any black man or woman who forgot his or her place and stepped, or even tried to step, out of it.

Even in the so-called Free States there was ample borrowing from the statutory schemes of the slavocracy to enforce a societal (white) view of the black person's rightful station in life. Thus, northern states systematically resorted to legislative devices to impose their collective view on the lives of "free" blacks, restricting them in employment, education, the franchise, legal personality, and public accommodation.

The legal issue of the status of black people in pre–Civil War America came to a head in 1857 in the case of *Dred Scott v. Sanford*, which proved to be one of the most important judicial decisions in the history of the black experience with the law.[2] Dred Scott, a slave who had been taken to a free territory by his master, attempted to sue for his freedom based upon the theory that residence in a free state had made him free.

As Chief Justice Taney put it, "The question is simply this: Can a negro, whose ancestors were imported into this country, and sold as slaves, become a member of the political community formed and brought into existence by the Constitution of the United States, and as such become entitled to all the rights, and privileges, and immunities, guaranteed by that instrument to the citizen . . . ?"[3]

The Court's answer was, simply, "No." In ruling that Dred Scott, and by extension, any other black person, could not be a citizen under the Constitution, Taney went back to the founding of the Republic, examining what he declared was the public view of the black race at that point and tracing its history through time: "[T]he public history of every European nation displays it in a manner too plain to be mistaken. [T]hey (the black race) had for more than a century before been regarded as beings of an inferior order, and altogether unfit to associate with the white race, either in social or political relations; and so far inferior, that they had no rights which the white man was bound to respect . . . ."[4] This ringing Taney dictum dashed the hopes of black people and abolitionists who had looked to the courts to resolve one of the most troubling questions of racial justice of the day. The majority's decision and its view of black people as inferior brought down a rain of criticism on the Court from the North and caused cries of joy to rise from below the Mason-Dixon line. It also set the stage for the oncoming War Between the States.

Logically, the Civil War should have made a decided difference in this racial legal dynamic. It did not, for though slavery itself was destroyed by the cataclysmic confrontation, the racism and economic exploitation undergirding slavery remained very much intact. Thus, even after the Emancipation Proclamation, after the war and the Thirteenth Amendment, the South set out to win the peace, despite having lost the war. The states of the South, where well over 90 percent of the nation's black people then lived, countered the emancipation by putting in place a series of laws known as the Black Codes, designed to approximate as closely as possible, in view of the legal abolition of slavery, a white-over-black, master/servant society. This legal order governed movement, marriage, work relations, and most major aspects of the freedperson's life.

In fact, there are many ways in which the Black Codes very much resembled the pre–Civil War slave codes. Laws were instituted against vagabonds to curtail black men from moving away from the land. Sharecropping and the convict-lease laws were designed to keep the former slaves on the land. Unlike other statutes, the vagabond- and convict-leasing statutes were not racial in their terms; however, their purpose and effect were entirely clear. The Southern economy was predicated upon a large, exploited black labor force; and except for the brief and bright interregnum of Reconstruction, the law and the state throughout the last years of the nineteenth century and the early years of the twentieth operated to preserve the old order and to wring maximum advantage from white hegemony over an oppressed and economically ravaged black populace.

It was the law as well that played a crucial role in "the strange career of Jim Crow." In an uneven and nonsystematic way, culture and mores had provided for a separation of the races in many aspects of American life. For most of the nation's history, that was not even much of an issue because the presence of slavery took care of any need for social definition. However, during the late 1800s, states began to systematically codify separation of the races, *requiring* segregation literally from the hospital where one was born to the cemetery where one was laid to rest. Segregation no longer was open to local option, custom, and usage but was the state's legal order of the day. These developments occurred at the same point in time that an increasingly conservative Supreme Court was narrowing its interpretation of the Thirteenth, Fourteenth, and Fifteenth Amendments—the Civil War amendments. These trends culminated in the *Plessy v. Ferguson* decision of the Supreme Court in 1896, in which "separate but equal" was approved as the law of the land, and the seal of approval of the nation's highest court was placed upon our own American brand of apartheid.[5]

The use of the legal system to create and protect a racially segregated society was coincident with government's manipulation of the law to disenfranchise black citizens. Beginning with the Mississippi constitutional convention of 1890, revising the state's constitution through a series of legal stratagems and artifices—and greatly aided by the extralegal depredations of lynch law—black people were stripped of the ballot and any real semblance of black political power. The poll tax, the literacy test, and the Grandfather Clause were legal devices employed in the service of this racist cause to desired effect.

As a result of state uses of the law in this fashion, black Americans entered the twentieth century segregated, sundered from full and free participation in American life, and politically powerless to do much about it. This situation largely obtained through the century, with minor indications of change and advancement from time to time but with no real major breakthrough in the wall of apartheid and powerlessness until the movements of the twentieth century and the Supreme Court decision in *Brown v. Board of Education*.[6]

Brown and the struggle that followed in its wake—much of which involved use of the law to support and effect positive social change—obviously represent a highly significant advance in black Americans' quest for liberation. It would be an analytical mistake of considerable proportion, however, to view *Brown* as the end of explicitly racist legislation and court decisions, and the advent of civil rights laws as indicative of the end of the relationship among racism and the law and the state. For all our gains, America remains a country deeply infected by racism.

NOTES

1. For good general treatment and historical overview, see Derrick Bell, Jr., *Race, Racism, and American Law* (Boston: Little, Brown, 1980); Derrick Bell, Jr., *And We Are Not Saved* (New York: Basic Books, 1987); Albert P. Blaustein and Robert I. Zangrando, eds., *Civil Rights and the American Negro* (New York: Trident Press, 1968); John Hope Franklin and Alfred A. Moss, Jr., *From Freedom to Slavery* (New York: Knopf, 1988); Paul Finkelman, *Slavery in the Courtroom* (Washington, DC: Library of Congress, 1985); Thomas F. Race Gossett, *The History of an Idea in America* (Dallas: Southern Methodist University Press, 1963); Oscar Handlin, *Race and Nationality in American Life* (Boston: Little, Brown, 1957); A. L. Higginbotham, *In the Matter of Color*, vol. 1 (New York: Oxford University Press, 1980); Winthrop Jordan, *White Over Black* (Chapel Hill: University of North Carolina Press, 1968). Although this chapter focuses mainly on the history of black people and American law, a similar analysis would apply to the historical experiences of other persons of color in the United States.
2. 19 How. (60 U.S.) 393 (1857).
3. Ibid., 403.
4. Ibid., 407.
5. 163 U.S. 537 (1896).
6. 347 U.S. 483 (1954).

13 ALAN FREEMAN

ANTIDISCRIMINATION LAW FROM 1954 TO 1989: UNCERTAINTY, CONTRADICTION, RATIONALIZATION, DENIAL

Alan Freeman, to whom this volume is dedicated, died after a long illness in 1995. This is a shortened version of his essay in the second edition.—Ed.

IT took thirty-three years to go from the promise of the Emancipation Proclamation in 1863 to the bleak reality of "separate but equal" endorsed by *Plessy v. Ferguson* in 1896. In the second half of the twentieth century, it took about the same time, thirty-five years, to go from the glowing promise of *Brown v. Board of Education* in 1954 to the "Civil Rights Cases" of 1989 that enshrined the principle of "unequal but irrelevant."[1]

This development is not the product of recent historical whimsy, but is rather firmly rooted in the contradictory character of antidiscrimination law, the agenda of which was constrained from the outset by abstract principles of formal equality that would surely reassert themselves in time. It is sadly ironic that law, which offered for a time a promise of liberation from America's historic reality of caste-based oppression, and did secure some rights of equality, has also served to legitimize the persistence of rampant, racially identifiable inequality. To understand how that happened, one must look to opinions of the U.S. Supreme Court, a principal source for discovering the meaning of "civil rights."

That Court looms large in our culture. We look to its pronouncements not just for the answers to particular questions of law, but for moral guidance on our most troubling social and political issues. The Court is basically a storytelling institution. Its cases serve as instructive moral parables, presented to most people as stark, melodramatic media distillations. The Court's stories must engage dialectically with other dominant political institutions, with preexisting cultural assumption, and other sources of cultural authority (e.g., movies). In the long run, the Court offers a vision of America that normalizes the existing patterns of inequality and hierarchy.

VICTIM AND PERPETRATOR

Consider the following, all based on actual cases, as stories about the significance of race in American life:[2]

> A multiple-choice test purporting to measure "verbal ability" is used to screen applicants for the D.C. police department. Black applicants fail the test four times more frequently than whites; failure precludes admission to the training academy although the test is not predictive of successful performance on the job.

> At the behest of an *all-white* residential neighborhood in Memphis, Tennessee, bordered on the north by a black neighborhood, city officials close the white neighborhood's only thru north-south street, erecting a barrier at the northern border.

> Mobile, Alabama, with a black population of 30 percent, refuses to abandon the practice of selecting its three city commissioners on an at-large basis; no black has ever been elected to even one of the positions.

> Richmond, Virginia, onetime capital of the Confederacy, mandates that 30 percent of its construction contracts go to minority contractors, a decision based on the observation that despite its 50 percent black population, less than 1 percent of such contracts had gone to minority contractors in recent years. Aggrieved whites claim the new rule discriminates against them on account of their race.

From the perspective of one who is acquainted with American history and social reality, or one who is familiar with the experiential reality of racism, these are all easy cases: Given the ugly history of standardized testing in the United States, and the reality that such tests do not even predict job performance, how can it be fair to choose potential police officers with a device that measures little else than their racial and class background? The reality of the street closing is as stark as the whiteness of the neighborhood engineering it, whose success amply confirms the power of whites to use local government to hassle blacks. To say that the Mobile scheme is unassailable is to say that race plays little or no role in voting there, that it is mere coincidence that no black has ever been elected; in other words, to uphold the Mobile procedure requires no less than a denial of reality. As for Richmond, one can only applaud its willingness to compensate for a long and ugly past by redistributing contract access to those who have been denied it for so long.

From the perspective of what has become the dominant voice in antidiscrimination law as articulated by the Supreme Court, the cases are also easy ones. If the test claims to measure verbal ability, then it probably does and that's a good thing; the mere fact of racially disproportionate failure rate means nothing without evidence that someone employs it *purposely* to exclude blacks. The street closing is just a neutral traffic control decision, unless you can prove that the white people did it to keep *black people* out, instead of just doing it to keep *people* out, most of whom *happen to be black*. As for Mobile, it does not matter whether blacks are elected or not, since no race is entitled to representation based on its population percentage; what matters is *why* they chose the at-large system. In this case, since Mobile adopted the system in 1911, the motive could not have been exclusion of blacks from office, since then they did not let blacks vote at all. As for Richmond, its municipal officials must realize that when the Constitution says no to racial discrimination, it does so in color-blind terms, and discrimination against whites is just as illegitimate as the more traditional discrimination against blacks. You can't ask whites as a class to bear responsibility for statistical disparities, unless you can *prove* the whites were purposely excluding black from contracts. Absent that evidence, it might be that blacks just didn't want the business, which is their own fault.

The first view, the one rooted in social reality, may be characterized as the "victim" perspective. Central to the victim perspective is an insistence on concrete historical experience rather than timeless abstract norm. For black Americans, that experience has been one of harsh oppression, exclusion, compulsory reduced status, and of being perceived not as a person but as a derogatory cultural stereotype. Years of oppression have left their mark in the form of identifiable consequences of racism: residential segregation, inadequate education, overrepresentation in lowest-status jobs, disproportionately low political power, and a disproportionate share of the least and worst of everything valued most in our materialistic society. From the victim perspective, when antidiscrimination law announces that racial discrimination has become illegal, that law's promise will be tested by the only relevant measure of success—*results*.

The victim perspective focuses on the persistence of conditions traditionally associated with racist practice. The four examples are once again illustrative: racism as traditionally practiced led to discriminatory exclusion from employment, from "white" neighborhoods, from politics, and from government contracts. If those same conditions exist in virtually identical form after antidiscrimination laws have prohibited racial discrimination, the law has not yet done its job. Those conditions are presumptive violations.

The other view, which is the dominant one in American legal culture, may be termed the "perpetrator" perspective. Its concern is with rooting out the behaviors of individual bad actors who have engaged in "prejudicial" discriminatory practices. From the perpetrator perspective, the goal of antidiscrimination law is to apply timeless and abstract norms, unsullied by history or social reality. Its job is to isolate and punish racial discrimination viewed as an instance of individual badness in an otherwise nondiscriminatory social realm. Thus, we cannot find violations of antidiscrimination law in objective social conditions, but only in the actions of identifiable perpetrators who have *purposely* and *intentionally caused* harm to *identifiable victims* who will be offered a *compensatory remedy*.

Central to the perpetrator perspective is the principle of individual (or sometimes institutional) *fault*. All we need do is identify and catch the villains; having done so, we can, with confidence, place responsibility where it belongs. A corollary of this fault principle is that those who, under applicable legal doctrines, are not labeled perpetrators have every reason to believe in their own innocence and noninvolvement in the problem. One who is not a perpetrator can say "It's not my fault; I'm just an innocent societal bystander." Why should the mere bystander be called to account or implicated at all in the business of eradicating the past? This emphasis on fault provides the psychic structure of the "reverse discrimination" issue.

The perpetrator perspective also denies historical reality—in particular, the fact that we would never have fashioned antidiscrimination law had it not been for the specific historical oppression of particular races. Denial leads all too quickly to the startling claim of "ethnic fungibility"—the notion that each of us bears an "ethnicity" with an equivalent legal significance, and with identical claim to protection against "discrimination," despite the grossly disproportionate experience that generated the legal intervention in the first place. Thus, discrimination on the basis of "whiteness" gains the same disreputable status as discrimination against blacks, and efforts to improve conditions for historic victims of discrimination are struck down on grounds of "principle." The key principle is that of "color blindness," which would be the appropriate rule in a future society that had totally eliminated racial discrimination, or, more likely, had never had such a problem at all.

Looking at the four examples from the perpetrator perspective, one sees simply neutral facts. If no bad actors can be identified, then normal principles of individual responsibility apply. Those who are complaining are themselves responsible for their performance on the tests, for their inability to move to other neighborhoods or have a voice in local government, for their political ineffectiveness or failure to obtain contracts: The familiar syndrome is "blaming the victim."[3]

The victim/perpetrator dichotomy may be recast starkly as the difference between equality of results and equality of opportunity, between *de facto* and *de jure* segregation, between substantive and formal equality. Given those choices, American antidiscrimination law has remained firmly within the perpetrator mode, outlawing "intentional" discrimination, guaranteeing equality "before the law," and offering no more than equal opportunity to compete in the game of life. Yet the doctrinal history of antidiscrimination law reveals that the perpetrator form was, for a time, contradicted by results more consistent with the victim perspective. The Supreme Court produced such results not by denying any of the basic tenets of the perpetrator perspective, but by taking advantage of the plasticity of legal characterization. Among the most manipulative legal categories are remedy, causation, and intent. Manipulating all three, the Court for a time seriously toyed with the victim perspective, but never deviated from the perpetrator form. The story begins with the celebrated *Brown* case in 1954.

THE DOCTRINAL SEQUENCE

To understand the puzzling and contradictory character of antidiscrimination law, one may usefully divide the period from 1954 to 1989 into four "eras" of Supreme Court decision making. The successive eras are neither neat, nor rigid, nor the product of inexorable logic. Yet for each it is possible to describe a particular instance of legal intervention (case or statute) so at odds with received wisdom as to mark a moment of discontinuity. Moreover, within each period, typical decisions serve to characterize the style or cultural assumptions of the era. The four successive eras represent how dominant cultural forces in post–World War II America responded to the pervasive legacy of racism that had revealed itself so starkly to any observer at the beginning of the 1950s. They add up to a story of promise, intervention, retreat, and surrender. Yet the fact of that intervention, despite its contradictory rhetoric, makes it possible to look back and celebrate our success, while ignoring the objective reality of poverty and inequality that remains the pervasive legacy of racism.

THE ERA OF UNCERTAINTY (1954–1965)

Brown v. Board of Education clearly marked a break with the past. It made the qualitative leap from merely "equalizing" to declaring that "separate but equal" is "inherently unequal," heralding a period of great promise for improvement in status for black Americans. Nevertheless, despite the hoopla surrounding this most celebrated of all American Supreme Court decisions, the case served as well to usher in a period of great uncertainty. Contributing to such uncertainty were: the elusive rationale of the Court's *Brown* opinion; the Court's all-too-quick refusal to mandate remedies for the violations announced in *Brown*, instead relegating those issues to lower courts; and the consciousness of white liberals, at once utopian and myopic, who saw only the stark "southern" version of America's racial reality.

For the Court, the "question presented" by *Brown* was:

> Does segregation of children in public schools solely on the basis of race, even though the physical facilities and other "tangible" factors may be equal, deprive the children of the minority group of equal educational opportunities?

Its response was affirmative yet enigmatic:

> To separate them from others of similar age and qualifications solely because of their race generates a feeling of inferiority as to their status in the community that may affect their hearts and minds in a way unlikely ever to be undone. . . . "Segregation of white and colored children in public schools has a detrimental effect upon the colored children. The impact is greater when it has the sanction of the law; for the policy of sep-

arating the races is usually interpreted as denoting the inferiority of the Negro group. A sense of inferiority affects the motivation of a child to learn. Segregation with the sanction of law, therefore, has a tendency to [retard] the educational and mental development of Negro children and to deprive them of some of the benefits they would receive in a racial[ly] integrated school system." . . . We conclude that in the field of public education the doctrine of "separate but equal" has no place. Separate educational facilities are inherently unequal.[4]

The quoted passage raises more questions than it answers. Are segregated schools inherently unequal because they make black children feel "inferior" or because kids who are made to feel inferior do not enjoy the benefits of public education? Must schools be integrated in fact to ensure that the black children will no longer feel inferior, and therefore fulfill educational potential? Even if segregation with the "sanction of law" has a "greater" impact on the minority children, does it not have a similar impact when conditions are still segregated despite the removal of such laws?

Unfortunately, these questions are not just rhetorical. They underscore the ultimate and still unresolved uncertainty unleashed by *Brown*. From the standpoint of those who successfully litigated the *Brown* cases, the goal was a pragmatic one—to obtain the best quality education for the nation's previously segregated black children in the least amount of time. In that context, a declaration of per se illegality for segregation seemed much more efficient than case-by-case resource equalization. To integrate previously white schools did not necessarily mean integration for its own sake, but might be understood as just the quickest means of upgrading educational equality. Thus one can regard the *Brown* case as a victory for substantive educational equal opportunity—the idea that all American children should have a chance for educational success, unimpeded by artificial barriers such as racial exclusion. That view of *Brown* finds great support in the opinion itself, with its heavy rhetorical emphasis on the importance of public education, yet within twenty years of *Brown* it was clear that the case did not guarantee equal educational opportunity.

What *Brown* did do, despite its own preoccupation with education, was to outlaw all forms of state-mandated segregation, as the Court made clear in a series of decisions unexplained except by reference to *Brown*.[5] Earnest legal scholars have sought ever since to find the "principle" governing the decisions in *Brown* and its progeny. Among those offered have been "freedom of association," "color blindness," "the antidiscrimination principle," the "group-disadvantaging principle," and the like.[6] These principles, rooted in analytic notions of morality, are offered by their authors as universals against which one can test the particularity of social practices, like "racism." A properly general principle must have a scope of coverage beyond the immediate case that generates its announcement.

An antidote to the endless quest for principle is a close and direct look at social reality. Even the Supreme Court, in a 1967 case dealing with a ban on interracial marriage, conceded that such laws were attempts to institutionalize white supremacy.[7] Thus regarded, segregation, not unlike its counterpart, apartheid, was part of a historically specific and pervasive system of caste-based oppression, serving to subordinate and oppress black Americans.[8] From that perspective, it is fundamentally misguided to keep on asking what principle was implicitly announced by the *Brown* case: what the Court did was to open a window that compelled white Americans to confront at last a particular and revolting social reality.

The Court promoted uncertainty not only with its ambiguous opinion in *Brown*, but also with its nondecision a year later in *Brown II*,[9] when it declined to order remedies for the violations in the five *Brown* cases. Instead, it relegated the remedy issue to the lower courts, who were to proceed "with all deliberate speed." *Brown II* served to usher in the period of "massive resistance" in the South, and postponed the need to confront directly the implicit perpetrator/victim contradiction. On remand, one of the lower courts noted in an all-too-prescient quip that the Constitution "does not require integration. It merely forbids discrimination."[10] The statement is of course an accurate nutshell version of the perpetrator perspective.

The dominant culture of civil rights consciousness, by which I mean that of the northern white liberals whose support for the enterprise was so crucial, further served to inform the period of uncertainty. That culture was, as I have suggested, simultaneously myopic and utopian. The myopic side was the perception of America's "race problem" as constituted by the southern paradigm—state-mandated segregation reinforced by a brutal regime of enforcement, and backed by a white culture infected by "prejudice." While similar instances of prejudice existed elsewhere in the land and might be labeled "racism," the underlying premise was that racist attitudes were an aberration in American life. Typical was Gunnar Myrdal's influential account, which saw a wide gap between American racist behaviors (bad) and the American Creed (good).[11]

The utopian side was a complement to the myopic one—a belief that the race problem would go away if the overt bad behaviors were stopped.

The arduous struggles of the black civil rights movement in the South in the 1950s and 1960s, depicted on the nightly news, offered an ongoing morality play to support this consciousness. Bull Connor and Sheriff Clark, with their dogs and fire hoses and cattle prods, were pitted against decent and peaceful Americans merely seeking recognition of their constitutional rights. Ironically, these scenes made the issue of race seem easier than it would appear later on. Then northern liberals could complacently fail to notice the racism that pervaded their own lives and characterized their neighborhoods, their growing suburbs, their schools, their jobs.

Thus the era of uncertainty saw growing national acknowledgment of the egregious sort of racism that fit safely within the perpetrator model, and a gradual increase in the coverage of civil rights law, culminating in the historic enactment of the Civil Rights Act of 1964. Yet all too little attention was paid to either the other-than-southern reality of racism, or the long-delayed question of remedy.

THE ERA OF CONTRADICTION (1965–1974)

During the second era the Court could no longer avoid the perpetrator/victim issue. The perpetrator perspective is indifferent to results: yet, after years of painful struggle, including assassinations and terrorist bombings, it was surely time to deliver on the unfulfilled promise of the 1950s (e.g., *Brown*). The federal government of 1965 formed, however briefly, a unique coalition of commitment to do something about racism. No Chief Executive has ever insisted on substantive racial progress as much as Lyndon Johnson did; the Congress of 1964 and 1965 matched its Reconstruction Era counterpart in the production of civil rights statutes; and even the Supreme Court in 1965 began to wake from its post-*Brown* slumber of remedial avoidance.

In those circumstances, it is hard to imagine that the Supreme Court could have struck down discrimination in voting while leaving black voters as politically powerless as before, "desegregated" schools while leaving them substantially segregated in fact, or invalidated employment discrimination while leaving its victims in the same status as before. Yet the logic of the perpetrator perspective is consistent with "no results" in all three instances: there is no *right* to proportional political representation, there is no *right* to an integrated education, there is no *right* to a job. How could the Court adhere to the perpetrator form while nevertheless ensuring some results? Three legal concepts became crucial: remedy, causation, and intent. The perpetrator perspective insists on a neat correspondence between violation and remedy, proof of objective causation of injury by the perpetrator, and proof of "intent," that is, purposeful discrimination. Yet those three concepts are among the most manipulable in our legal culture. Examples from voting, education, and employment will illustrate how the subtle deployment of those concepts can produce the seemingly contradictory coexistence of perpetrator and victim perspective.

Federal intervention to protect voting rights took a gigantic leap forward with the Voting Rights Act of 1965. That statute was enacted in response to a record of frustration. Blacks were systematically deprived of the right to vote on the basis of race, and courts were unable to change that reality by merely outlawing specific illegal practices. The statute made its operative provisions depend on voter participation statistics and other nonreviewable administrative findings. While these findings did not constitute evidence of behaviors in themselves violations of any specific civil rights law, they were enough to trigger the act's awesome remedial machinery. The net effect of the act was to create an affirmative right to vote, instead of just a negative right to be free of discrimination in voting.

The value of the right to vote, however, given the reality of racial voting patterns, will depend on whether it translates into political power and influence for the previously disenfranchised minority. That question leads to a remedial focus on "dilution" of minority voting rights, which, in turn, illustrates how the identification of a perpetrator perspective violation can lead to a victim perspective remedy. Suppose, for example, that a municipality has gerrymandered its districts so that the entire black population is in one district while every other district is white, and there is evidence of purposeful discrimination. Suppose further that the court issues an order to the municipality that says "stop doing that," and the response is a redistricting that simply shifts a handful of people but leaves most of the black population in the original district.

If there is no specific evidence of purposeful discrimination this time, how can we decide if the new scheme has "remedied" the violation? A very slight change would seem inadequate, if it left the black community far below its representative potential. But how much is enough? The paradox is that remedy has no coherence in this context unless some notion of racial proportionality is incorporated. Moreover, instead of litigating repetitively to approach the limit of racial proportionality, why not impose such a remedy at the outset? To do so, however, is to incorporate the victim perspective.

A second typical case illustrates how the manipulation of causation to ensure remedial results serves to create victim perspective expectations. The *Brown* case announced the unconstitutionality of legally mandated school segregation; however, by relegating the remedial issues to the lower courts, the Supreme Court did nothing about the actual problem of segregation. While the Court waited, the world changed. Changing neighborhood patterns meant more and more residential segregation. By the time the Court returned to the remedy issue, in 1971 in *Swann v. Charlotte-Mecklenburg Board of Education*, to outlaw segregation but do nothing to ensure integration would be embarrassing, and undermining to the Court's credibility. Even Justice Felix Frankfurter had worried publicly during the oral argument in *Brown* that "nothing would be worse" than for the Court "to make an abstract declaration that segregation is bad and then have it evaded by tricks."[12]

But the Court could not go back in time. Thus, it had to order school districts to produce the result—racial balance—that would have followed from immediate and massive enforcement in 1955. By waiting fifteen years, however, the Court knew and simultaneously denied that changes in residential patterns would frustrate all possibility of successful integration through neighborhood school assignment. By insisting on busing to achieve meaningful racial balance, the Court created an expectation that segregation in fact was the evil to be remedied, however tenuous its relation to the historic segregation by law. From the victim perspective, the expectation became an entitlement to integrated schools. The Court rationalized its position by showing, through the use of self-contradictory presumptions, as in *Swann*, how the current conditions were "caused" by the original violation. The Court used similar presumptions in its first northern school desegregation case to extend the remedial obligation from one neighborhood to an entire city: Denver.[13]

The net effect was the creation of a nationwide perception, consistent with the victim perspective, that the problem was not just the practice of legally mandated segregation but the current pattern of racially concentrated schools. That perception gave rise to a right to attend schools in fact integrated, at least for some period of time sufficient to make credible, to black people, the claim that segregation had been outlawed.

The elusive and manipulable notion of intent is best illustrated by the third typical case, *Griggs v. Duke Power Co.*,[14] which is the centerpiece of the Era of Contradiction. *Griggs* was the only Supreme Court case that almost incorporated the victim perspective; not surprisingly, it became one of the most repudiated of cases, at least substantially overruled in 1989.

Griggs, decided under Title VII of the Civil Rights Act of 1964 rather than the Constitution, involved an ostensibly neutral practice—testing—that was probably being employed for the purpose of racial discrimination. (The employer had explicitly confined black workers to its lowest-status labor department until the effective date of Title VII in July 1965, and immediately thereafter imposed a pair of aptitude test requirements for placement in any department except labor). Yet there was no provable causal link between the racially exclusionary impact of the tests and the employer's blatantly discriminatory prior practice. The Court focused on the test itself as a practice that fell with disproportionate severity on blacks.

Title VII, according to the Court, requires the "removal of artificial, arbitrary, and unnecessary barriers to employment," and proscribes "not only overt discrimination but also practices that are fair in form, but discriminatory in operation." Speaking directly to the question of intent, the Court made it clear that "good intent" or the "absence of discriminatory intent" "does not redeem employment procedures . . . that operate as built-in headwinds for minority groups and are unrelated to measuring job capability." While not going so far as to make such practices automatic violations of the act, Chief Justice Burger's opinion placed the burden of their justification squarely on the employers, and a strict burden it was, requiring proof of *business necessity*: the practice must not only be "related to job performance," but have a "manifest relationship to the employment in question."

Thus *Griggs* set loose some new ideas. Unlike the perpetrator perspective, which inferred nothing from the mere fact of a racially disproportionate result, *Griggs* demanded the justification of ostensibly neutral practices producing such results. The shift from an emphasis on "motivation" to one on "consequences" marks a transformation of the notion of intent in antidiscrimination law. Henceforth, the intentional continuation of a course of conduct producing racially disproportionate results would be actionable, regardless of why the actor chose to continue. To so transform "intent" is to incorporate the victim perspective.

Three aspects of *Griggs* illustrate its implicit potential. With respect to its own factual context, testing, *Griggs* demanded what many knew would be an impossible standard of justification, since written tests are part of a closed world where all they correlate with is each other. Given the centrality of standardized testing in legitimating hierarchy in America, meritocracy itself might come under siege. Furthermore, since *Griggs* was about the very meaning of discrimination, there was no reason to suppose that its doctrine would be cabined. Rather, one expected its application to other employment practices, especially seniority, and to other statutory and constitutional violations, in areas such as school desegregation, voting, housing, land-use regulation, and provision of governmental services. Finally, to the extent *Griggs* presumptively invalidated selection practices with racially exclusionary results, the case subtly coerced the development of explicitly racial affirmative action programs. Employers or schools wanting to retain their "neutral" practices could use affirmative action to compensate for the exclusionary deficiencies of standard selection criteria.

Apart from *Griggs*, the Supreme Court never deviated from the rhetorical form of the perpetrator perspective, even while straining its logic with manipulation of remedy, intent, and causation doctrine. Lower courts, however, went further than the Supreme Court in explicitly extending *Griggs* to other areas. Thus the victim perspective, for a time, crept into federal law.

THE ERA OF RATIONALIZATION (1974–1984)

Without explicitly overruling any of the earlier cases, the Court in the period of rationalization employed a method of containment to defeat any deviant victim perspective expectations. Once again there was an insistence on proof of both intent and causation, coupled with an emphasis on the rhetoric rather than the results of earlier cases. To deal with the subversive *Griggs* decision the Court arbitrarily declined to extend its logic to other areas, and reduced the defensive burden of proof for employers subject to its rule. Yet it stopped short of overruling the case, leaving it applicable to cases of employment discrimination involving ostensibly neutral hiring and selection criteria.

Thus, with respect to the definition of violation under applicable antidiscrimination law, the perpetrator perspective once again became the norm, subject only to the *Griggs* exception. Simultaneously, however, the Court tolerated and even seemed to encourage vigorous remedial efforts that were in fact at odds with the perpetrator world view.

The 1974 decision in *Milliken v. Bradley*,[15] the Detroit school desegregation case, marks the moment of discontinuity that ushered in the era of rationalization. The case involved the conclusion to be drawn from two rather stark premises: first that the city of Detroit had for years quite purposely segregated its public school students by race; second, that by the 1990s there would no longer be any white students in the Detroit system. To "desegregate" the Detroit schools, then, would mean no integration at all unless the suburban (and white) school districts in the metropolitan area were made part of the solution. So concluded the district judge; yet the Supreme Court soundly defeated the result-centered expectations created by its own decisions in the Charlotte-Mecklenburg and Denver cases. Taking an atomistic view of state-created jurisdictional units as just so many actors within the perpetrator worldview, Chief Justice Burger absolved the suburban districts of responsibility, since they had not been shown to have intentionally caused the segregation in Detroit.

The notion of intent is as elusive as the variety of its forms. From the specific design to harm (associated with criminal law) one can move to "subjective" foreseeability ("intentional" torts) to "objective" foreseeability (e.g., negligence in tort) to accountability for the consequences of one's behavior (e.g., "strict" products liability). To insist on the most narrow and purposeful version in antidiscrimination law is to ensure minimalist accountability.

Such was the insistence of the Court in the era of rationalization, when it repeatedly refused to allow an inference of "intentional" discrimination despite dramatic evidence of racially disproportionate consequences. The result was a substantial contraction of the sphere of antidiscrimination law. Three of the "stories" cited in my introduction were cases decided during this period. In *Washington v. Davis*, the 1976 D.C. police case, the justices refused to extend the *Griggs* approach to cases based on constitutional antidiscrimination principles rather than statutory ones. Why? Because "[w]e have never held that the constitutional standard . . . is identical . . . and we decline to do so today."[16]

In addition, in *Davis* the Court summarily overruled all of the lower federal courts that had extended the *Griggs* rule to areas such as housing, zoning, or municipal services. Finally, *Davis* relaxed the *Griggs*-imposed burden of justification, making it easier for employers to validate their otherwise suspect employment practices. A similar insistence on the narrowest definition of intent led to defeat for the black voters subject to Mobile's at large system, in 1980; and to defeat for the black residents of Memphis burdened by the street closed at their border with the white neighborhood, in 1981.[17]

Despite these defeats, the same Court, during the same period, continued to offer some remedial promise. In 1978, 1979, and 1980, the Court decided its first three affirmative action cases.[18] In each case, affirmative action was challenged by opponents as unlawful "reverse discrimination," and in each case the Court upheld the challenged program. The most publicized of these cases was *Bakke*, involving a university admissions program specifically employing race as a criterion of admission. The Court divided into two warring camps of four justices each, one adamantly opposed, the other as adamantly in favor. Justice Powell, with his oddly pragmatic conservatism, broke the deadlock in a self-contradictory opinion that sought to have it both ways on the perpetrator/victim split.

From the perpetrator view, Powell invoked the most rigid rhetoric of color blindness, with its premise of ethnic fungibility, and rejected the notion that race could be employed in the admissions process for reasons having anything to do with securing racial justice or remedying past discrimination (absent proof of a "violation"). Nevertheless, he decided that an academic concern for the "diversity" of student populations was so compelling as a competing constitutional value, rooted in First Amendment academic freedom, as to trump the equal protection challenge of those charging reverse discrimination. Thus, in the name of a diversity that equates race with being a "farm boy from Idaho," admissions programs could continue to admit largely on the basis of race. Powell's facile assumption of equivalence becomes questionable, however, when one recognizes that the very reason for focusing on race as a relevant characteristic is our specific historical record of discrimination. To allow the admission of students because they are black is to adopt at least in part the victim perspective.

If *Washington v. Davis* marks the low point of the rationalization period, its high point was surely the 1979 decision in *United Steelworkers v. Weber*, another widely publicized "reverse discrimination" controversy. The case evolved a collective bargaining agreement providing for affirmative action efforts to eliminate conspicuous racial imbalances at Kaiser Aluminum plants. The specific controversy arose at a plant in Louisiana where, although the local work force was 39 percent black, only 1.83 percent of skilled workers were black. The plan at issue provided for training of production workers to become skilled craftworkers, with 50 percent of the trainees to be black, regardless of seniority, until the percentage of black craftworkers matched that in the local population. Weber, a white production worker with more seniority than some of the black trainees, charged the union and company with unlawful racial discrimination under Title VII of the 1964 Civil Rights Act.

In a 5 to 2 decision, the Court upheld the plan as a laudable effort to break down old patterns of segregation and hierarchy by creating job openings for blacks in areas of traditional exclusion. Implicit in this decision were two key assumptions consistent with the victim rather than the perpetrator perspective, both of which were ignored in Justice Brennan's plurality opinion. The first assumption was that statistical disparity (the 1.83 percent compared with the 39 percent) was itself enough to make out a *prima facie* case of violation under *Griggs*, which remained applicable to hiring and promotion practices. The second was that a court finding such a violation (assuming the employer could not defend the disparity) would order an affirmative action remedy not unlike the one negotiated by union and management in *Weber*. To treat the statistical disparity as a presumptive violation is to say that, given our history and social reality, conditions that *look* like those traditionally associated with racist practice are to be regarded as such. This approach relieves aggrieved members of the victim group (blacks, in this case) from the impossible perpetrator perspective burden of bringing forth specific individuals who can show they would have been trained as skilled craftworkers *but for* specific selection practices purposely utilized by the employer. By so defining the violation, its remedy follows: the employer must take affirmative steps to change the racial balance of its craftworker work force. There is no pretense of satisfying the perpetrator perspective demand that specific and identifiable victims be compensated; the remedy is a group remedy designed to confer on black workers a fair share of jobs. *Weber* thus illustrates how the *Griggs* rule and its remedial implication kept the victim perspective alive, albeit contained, at the close of the era of rationalization.

THE ERA OF DENIAL (1984–1989)

To complete the dismantling process that had begun in the period of rationalization, the Court needed to reconsider, and reject, the implicit assumptions of *Weber*. Once statistical disparities cease to be presumptive violations, and remedies mandating numerical results are no longer required (or even permitted), the reality of inequality experienced by black Americans becomes just another neutral feature of our socioeconomic landscape.

The remedial question arose first in *Firefighters v. Stotts*[19] in 1984, where the Court, speaking through John F. Kennedy appointee Byron "Whizzer" White, rejected the application of an affirmative action hiring plan (mandated by a consent decree) to a layoff situation. The district court had decided that a budget-induced layoff plan should be applied so as to preserve the percentage gains made by the affirmative action hiring required by the consent decree. Thus, according to the Supreme Court:

> The issue at the heart of this case is whether the District Court exceeded its powers in entering an injunction requiring white employees to be laid off, when the otherwise applicable seniority system would have called for the layoff of black employees with less seniority.

Just as the Court had refused in 1977 to extend the logic of the *Griggs* rule to seniority cases, the Court in *Stotts* concluded that despite the affirmative action consent decree, it was "inappropriate to deny an innocent employee the benefits of his seniority in order to provide a remedy . . . in a suit such as this."

This conclusion followed from a cold, clinical, perpetrator perspective analysis of the situation. Even though the black workers had been hired pursuant to an affirmative action plan adopted as part of a consent decree in a lawsuit charging racial discrimination in hiring, "there was no finding that any of the blacks protected from layoff had been a victim of discrimination. . . . " If they were not "victims," why had their hiring been mandated by the affirmative action plan?

The doctrine of *Stotts* was simply inconsistent with numerically grounded race-conscious affirmative action as upheld in *Weber*. Nevertheless, in the years following *Stotts*, the Court entered into a period of incoherent doctrinal instability, deciding five more affirmative action cases in 1986 and 1987. In four of them, involving hiring and promotion, the Court upheld the plans,[20] often citing *Weber* with approval, yet without any consistent majority voice. In one, the 1986 *Wygant*[21] decision, the justices followed *Stotts* in another layoff situation, largely because Justice Powell, placing pragmatism ahead of coherence, chose to insist on the perpetrator perspective only in seniority cases, while Justice O'Connor, who had joined the Court in 1984, moved only slowly and haltingly toward opposition to affirmative action.

Yet during this period of instability a new and strident voice had joined the Court. Justice Scalia, appointed in 1986 when Rehnquist was elevated to Chief Justice, was unambiguously rooted in the perpetrator perspective. In 1979 he had written:

> There [are] many white ethnic groups that came to this country in great numbers relatively late in its history—Italians, Jews, Irish, Poles—who not only took no part in, and derived no profit from, the major historic suppression of the currently acknowledged minority groups, but were, in fact, themselves the object of discrimination by the dominant Anglo-Saxon majority. [To] be sure, in relatively recent years some or all of these

groups have been the beneficiaries of discrimination against blacks, or have themselves practiced discrimination. But to compare their racial debt—I must use this term since the concept of "restorative justice" implies it; there is no creditor without a debtor—with that of those who plied the slave trade, and who maintained a formal caste system for many years thereafter, is to confuse a mountain with a molehill.[22]

Dissenting in one of the 1987 affirmative action cases, Scalia made it clear that his programmatic agenda is nothing less than the full restoration of the perpetrator perspective as the only approach to antidiscrimination law.

With a predatory flair for sniffing out the vulnerable points in prior opinions, Scalia's stinging dissent in *Johnson v. Transportation Agency* demands that *Weber* be overruled. For him, the affirmative action plan upheld in that case was nothing less than "intentional discrimination on the basis of race." According to Scalia, racially disproportionate statistical disparities are at most evidence of "societal discrimination." Societal discrimination is not only irremediable under antidiscrimination law, which requires identifiable perpetrators and victims, but is also irremediable through voluntary affirmative action plans. The latter amount to no more than insistence on racial proportionality—an unconstitutional goal. Scalia also denounced *Griggs* for coercing employers fearful of lawsuits directed at their numerical disproportion into adopting affirmative action programs that are themselves illegal "reverse discrimination," and he denounced *Bakke* for its pretense that race is just one of many "diversities."

However harsh the sound of that dissent, its voice had been present all along, though occasionally and inconsistently muted. In 1989, that voice acquired the votes needed for implementation of its remaining agenda.

Of the six major civil rights defeats issued by the Supreme Court in 1989, three are directed to the lingering victim perspective assumptions that perpetuated the viability of at least some affirmative action programs. The three, *Wards Cove Packing Co. v. Atonio*, *Martin v. Wilks*, and *City of Richmond v. J. A. Croson Co.*,[23] amount collectively to a repudiation of the implicit principles, if not the actual results, of both *Griggs* and *Weber*. These decisions compel us to deny that starkly racial differences in status have anything to do with "discrimination"; to believe that affirmative action programs amount to "reverse discrimination" against white people and as such are just as pernicious as the historical and persistent discrimination that generated civil rights law in the first place; and to deny that results matter as a measure of whether antidiscrimination law has been successful.

As described earlier, a key feature of the era of rationalization was the surgical containment of *Griggs* through the Court's renewed insistence on proof of (purposeful) intent. The decision in *Wards Cove*, the Alaska cannery case, was in one sense just a logical extension of those three cases, with the scalpel applied not just to contain but to remove *Griggs* from the body of our civil rights jurisprudence. So described, the decision surely deserves to be called a major civil rights setback: yet, it is even more dismal than that. There is a Dickensian quality to the opinion, with its excessive solicitude for employer-defendants, and its preoccupation with legal technicality (intent, causation, burden of proof) which serves to distance the victims from their own case. Its tone of reassurance—the law is still there for plaintiffs with the well-pled case—is in context about as reassuring as a promise from Uriah Heep. Justice White may have authored the opinion, but its outlook is that of Justice Scalia.

The case involved the seasonal operation of a cannery in Alaska. Even the majority conceded the existence of a two-tiered hierarchical workforce, with jobs categorized as "cannery" (unskilled and low-status) or "noncannery" (mostly skilled and higher-status). The district court found "significant disparities between the at-issue jobs (i.e., noncannery jobs) and the total workforce at the canneries." These disparities were explained specifically by the fact that "nearly all employed in the 'cannery worker' department are nonwhite." The nonwhites whose lawsuit had begun fifteen years earlier included persons of Samoan, Chinese, Filipino, Japanese, and Alaska Native descent, all but one of whom were American citizens. The racial disproportion was underscored by the fact that the employer used separate hiring channels to fill the two categories, and segregated the workers by category in housing and eating facilities.

Despite overwhelming evidence of a tradition of racial separation, which Justice Stevens characterized as bearing "an unsettling resemblance to aspects of a plantation economy," Justice White concluded that the plaintiffs had not proved even enough to require an explanation from the employer. In so doing, he deployed virtually every ideological component of the perpetrator perspective. He rebuked Justices Stevens and Blackmun for their "hyperbole," since no one had ever shown that the employer practiced "intentional" discrimination. As to the readily observable *Griggs*-type consequences, White announced that the plaintiffs could not rely on aggregates, but had to show instead how any particular hiring practice specifically *caused* discriminatory results, being sure to show how many "qualified" nonwhites were available for the jobs at issue (as opposed to requiring the employer to justify its practices as ones that selected those who are "qualified").

He reminded us that we do not wish to hold employers accountable for racially disparate situations that are not their "fault"; that if we compelled them to defend racial imbalance in lawsuits, they might take affirmative steps to create racial balance, which would of course be illegal and discriminatory; and that we would not want employers to be "potentially liable for 'the myriad of innocent causes that may lead to statistical imbalances in the composition of their work forces.'" He later characterized these undesirable and untoward consequences as a "host of evils" to be avoided. Accordingly, he substantially reduced the burden of explanation on employers once a successful case has been made out (if it ever can be under the new standards), and, in a stunning coup de grace, he reversed the *Griggs* rule that placed the burden of proof on such employers.

Wards Cove thus obliterates the implicit assumption in *Weber* that serious statistical disparities are presumptive violations of Title VII. In fact, there is very little left of the *Griggs* notion that discriminatory results should compel persuasive justification. Instead, except to the extent that *Griggs* still applies (which may be no further than North Carolina employers who adopted test and diploma requirements in 1965), the notion of "violation" has been placed firmly within the perpetrator perspective. Instead of confronting social and historical reality, antidiscrimination law has been reduced to the status of just another intentional tort, albeit one with unusually strict intent and causation requirements.

The other two 1989 cases dealt with "reverse discrimination" challenges to affirmative action programs. One case focused on procedure, the other on substance. Their combined effect is the elevation of reverse discrimination claims to a status identical to claims on behalf of discrimination's historic and traditional victims; in short, the law has been turned on its head.

In the procedural case, *Martin v. Wilks*, the Court allowed a group of white fire fighters claiming reverse discrimination to challenge a consent decree that had been entered into by the city of Birmingham, Alabama, in 1981, settling litigation begun in 1974 and providing for affirmative action hiring and promotion for black fire fighters. Seven of the nine federal appeals courts ruling on that issue had precluded such attacks as "impermissible collateral attack." The Supreme Court, by a vote of 5–4, took the opposite view. This "procedural" decision serves to invite legal attack by aggrieved whites on long-standing affirmative action programs originating in litigation, conferring on the whites a continuing right to complain about reverse discrimination in court. Its substantive implication is that this is so serious a social problem that we must offer those aggrieved a chance to vindicate their "rights."

That last observation surely gains credence from the Court's substantive decision in *City of Richmond v. J. A. Croson Co.*, involving the 30 percent set-aside for minority contractors in Richmond, Virginia, and described in my introduction. The Court struck down the program as illegal reverse discrimination under the equal protection clause of the Constitution, reasoning that the mere fact that less than 1 percent of contracts had gone to minority contractors in a city with a 50 percent black population was insufficient evidence of racial discrimination to serve as justification for the program. The opinion has a "good cop/bad cop" quality, with Justices O'Connor, White, and Rehnquist playing the former role, and, not surprisingly, Justice Scalia the latter, and with Justice Kennedy somewhere in between.

These internal differences may well be more rhetorical than real. The key point is that remedial racial classifications are henceforth to be treated as "suspect," and subjected to the same "strict scrutiny" applied in racial discrimination cases. They must justify themselves, if at all, by demonstrating the existence of a "compelling" governmental interest, which was found lacking in Richmond. Scalia would go even further and apply a per se rule of invalidity to affirmative action programs, allowing only the compensation of specific victims who have proved discrimination against themselves.

Richmond thus institutionalizes the world view of "ethnic fungibility" so central to the perpetrator outlook. Only in the messy particularity of historical and current social reality can one rediscover what it means and has meant to be black in America. Yet there is a feature of the *Richmond* opinion that is even worse than its resort to abstract, timeless, and ahistorical principle. In a singular instance of callous racial insensitivity, Justice O'Connor deviates from "principle" and becomes willing to infer discrimination from structure. She reminds us that blacks comprise 50 percent of the population of Richmond, and hold five of nine seats on the city council, leading to a "concern that a political majority will more easily act to the disadvantage of a minority." With a white majority in similar circumstances (e.g., *Mobile*), we are not even permitted to infer a racial problem. While one could dismiss O'Connor's point as facile legal argument, it may well be a warning to urban blacks who are gaining

political power that if they try to serve their own constituencies by remedying historic inequalities largely perpetrated by white political majorities serving their constituencies, they will be hauled into court as racists.

THE POLITICS OF RACE AND RIGHTS

To label Supreme Court decisions as instances of denial is to imply the
existence of a reality to which the Court is seeking to cut off our access
through its rhetorical ploys. Those realities are two: substantive inequality and the intractable persistence of racism.

These twin realities amount to a grim reversal of the utopian expectation predicted by Gunnar Myrdal, whose massive study, *An American
Dilemma*, both captured and informed the white liberal consciousness
whose support was so crucial for any racial progress. Central to Myrdal's
conception of America's "race problem" was the "principle of cumula-
tion," or the "vicious circle," which implied that the persistence of racial
stereotypes in the minds of whites served to perpetuate the poverty and
powerlessness of blacks, while the actuality of poverty and powerlessness
served to reinforce the stereotypes. Myrdal predicted that the "vicious circle" could be turned on its head and redirected toward racial progress: If
whites would allow their own better natures to operate, they would cease
to perceive blacks through a stereotypical lens, which would, in turn,
open up new political and economic possibilities for blacks, which
would, in turn, expose the falsity of the racial stereotypes, etc.

This reformist and turnabout version of the vicious circle proved
flawed in two basic ways. The view that changes in white consciousness
would follow from changes in black status depends upon a model of
white racism as a consciously held "mistaken" view, one that is educationally correctable, and at odds with one's better self: in short, racism is
a personal moral dilemma in the white mind. Recent experience suggests
that racism persists at a level much deeper than the superficial one
depicted by Myrdal's model—that it is an unconscious, culturally transmitted, and seemingly intractable feature of American life.[24]

The flip side of Myrdal's expectation is equally flawed. That changes in
consciousness (as, e.g., civil rights laws) will lead to significant changes in
status depends upon a tenuous proposition—the availability of equality
of opportunity. As suggested earlier, the important white advocates of
what has been termed "liberal interracialism" were at once myopic and
utopian. In a sense, they hoped to get results "for free." Their modest,
reformist goal was that the socioeconomic stratification of black

Americans would come to resemble that of whites. Once the obstacle of irrational racial "prejudice" was removed, blacks would advance through the rational, impersonal workings of meritocracy, facilitated by a system of public education that gave everyone an equal start. This was a vision that denied, and suppressed, the possibility that there was, in America, a *class* structure, with cultural as well as economic dimension. That structure significantly reduced upward mobility, and served to perpetuate the dominant position of those already controlling wealth and power.

Central to liberal attitude and hope, then, was what may be the single most important myth that rationalizes American social, cultural, and economic reality—formal individualistic "equality of opportunity." It was the abiding faith of folks as disparate as John Locke, Abraham Lincoln, Hubert Humphrey, and Richard Nixon. It serves not only to rationalize but to celebrate inequality, while compelling those who fail to "make it" to internalize a despairing lack of self-worth. It facilitates our callous indifference to the reality of adult inequality by loading the burden of advancement onto our children, mediated by a system of education that systematically denies the extent to which the odds of success are overwhelmingly stacked against those who start at the bottom—white or black.

No practice symbolizes the seemingly objective and neutral character of meritocracy so much as the standardized test. In this context one might better understand the Supreme Court's decision in Griggs not as necessarily insisting on equality of results, but as demanding a more credible system of equality of opportunity. Notably, Chief Justice Burger expressed a deep skepticism about mechanistic credentialism ("History is filled with examples of men and women who rendered highly effective performance without the conventional badges of accomplishment in terms of certificates, diplomas, or degrees"). No doubt he was influenced by his own background in having attended, unlike most of his judicial colleagues, a "night" law school (William Mitchell College of Law in St. Paul, Minnesota). The Court may have been rejecting mechanistic credentialism, but hoping for methods of testing that would really correlate with occupational performance.

Whatever optimism may have been the basis for *Griggs*, however, was quickly doused by the reality of post-*Griggs* litigation involving tests. In case after case, the tests demonstrably failed to satisfy the job-relatedness standard. Litigation revealed that the only thing such tests measure is job test-taking ability, so that one test will often correlate well with another test, yet fail in any statistical way to predict actual job performance.

Moreover, the tests used for tracking in public schools, or for college and university admissions, like the SAT, correlate best with one's socioeconomic background, thereby disproportionately excluding blacks and other minorities, and rewarding those who already own the predominant share of the nation's "cultural capital."[25] Thus the educational system, claiming to offer equality of opportunity, with its objective and neutral criteria of evaluation, serves instead to provide the ruling class with a "theodicy of its own privilege."[26] In that context, it is hardly surprising that the Court in *Washington v. Davis* acted quickly (within five years) to confine *Griggs* to Title VII cases—lest it be applied, as it surely would have, to SATs, and even bar exams—and, simultaneously, to make clear that the job-relatedness standard might be satisfied even if one test did no more than correlate, even weakly, with just another test. Any other result would have been seriously destabilizing to the whole structure of American meritocracy.

Unlike the utopian liberals described earlier, most pragmatic capitalists know that equality of opportunity is largely a sham, a grandiose rhetoric that rationalizes their own hierarchical advantage. Therefore, they recognize that to produce substantive results—i.e., visible jobs for blacks—without dismantling class-based obstacles for the lower class generally requires a conscious, race-based redistribution of opportunity. The paradigm of such was the affirmative action plan in *Weber*, adopted by the employer (along with the union) and upheld by the Court. It makes perfect sense, if *Weber is* viewed this way, that Justice Potter Stewart, who regularly voted to support, with some pragmatic care, the interests of capitalists, gave the majority its fifth vote. Under *Weber*, an employer may specifically correct a racial imbalance in its skilled work force, using moderate but not excessive means, without otherwise subjecting its selection criteria to scrutiny or challenge.

But such redistributive schemes are ultimately destabilizing. The race-conscious effort to increase the presence of blacks is also a concession that equality of opportunity does not work on its own. Moreover, to offer to blacks opportunities that would have otherwise gone to whites is to take away what individuals experience as vested rights or expectations even if they are more accurately regarded as unfair advantages in their social and historical context. The closer such programs come to redistribution of vested rights the more threatening they become to a mainstay of American hierarchy.

The political genius of Reagan was to rally the American people around their most cherished illusions, including the illusion of equal opportunity. He convincingly portrayed affirmative action as out of line with traditional American notions of fair play and protection of rights. Reagan's victory meant short-term gain for capitalists liberated from regulation. Nevertheless, on some issues, including affirmative action, it may have split the ruling class. With a striking purity of spirit, the Reagan team found Supreme Court justices who would take American mythology seriously, and would not bend the rules to accommodate even the pragmatic interests of sophisticated corporate executives and politicians who understood the long-term advantages of racial diversity.

The clearest example is Scalia, who infuses his opposition to affirmative action, rooted in the perpetrator world view, with a populist appeal to lower-class white "victims." For him the pragmatic capitalists are no better than the liberals:

> Yet [it] is precisely *these* groups [white ethnics not part of the "dominant Anglo-Saxon majority"] that do most of the restoring. It is they who, to a disproportionate degree, are the competitors with the urban blacks and Hispanics for jobs, housing, education—all those things that enable one to scramble to the top of the social heap where one can speak eloquently (and quite safely) of restorative justice.

I have sought in this essay to offer the corrosive clarity of realism. The goal of that effort is not, however, to promote despair, but to advocate an energetic redirection of activity. If the federal courts are to become, as they were in the past, little more than reactionary apologists for the existing order, we should treat them with the contempt they deserve. One can only hope that other political institutions will be reinvigorated.

NOTES

1. *Plessy v. Ferguson*, 163 U.S. 537 (1896); *Brown v. Topeka Board of Education*, 347 U.S. 483 (1954). I will use black-white as the model of race in America with some frequency, because I find it impossible to think about the topic without drawing heavily from the black experience, although, of course, Native Americans, Hispanics, Asian Americans and other "non-whites" also have suffered severe racial discrimination.

2. The four cases are: *Washington v. Davis*, 426 U.S. 229 (1976); *Memphis v. Greene*, 451 U.S. 100 (1981); *City of Mobile v. Golden*, 446 U.S. 55 (1980); *City of Richmond v. J. A. Croson Co.*, 488 U.S. 469 (1989).

3. See generally William Ryan, *Blaming the Victim* (New York: Pantheon, 1972).

4. *Brown v. Topeka Board of Educatiom*, 347 U.S. at 494, 495.

5. See, for example, *Gayle v. Browder*, 352 U.S. 903, aff'g per curiam 142 F.Supp. 707 (M.D. Ala. 1956) (buses); *Holmes v. City of Atlanta*, 350 U.S. 879, vacating per curiam 223 F.2d 93 (5th Cir. 1955) (municipal golf courses); *Mayor of Baltimore v. Dawson*, 350 U.S. 877, aff'g per curiam 220 F.2d 386 (4th Cir. 1955) (public beaches and bathhouses).

6. See Herbert Wechsler, *Toward Neutral Principles of Constitutional Law*, 73 Harvard Law Review 1 (1959); Richard Posner, *The DeFunis Case and the Constitutionality of Preferential Treatment of Racial Minorities*, 1974 Supreme Court Review 1, 21–26; Paul Brest, *In Defense of the Antidiscrimination Principle*, 90 Harvard Law Review 1 (1976); Owen Fiss, "Groups and the Equal Protection Clause," Philosophy and Public Affairs 5 (1976): 107.

7. *Loving v. Virginia*, 388 U.S. 1, 11 (1967).

8. See, for example, Charles Black, *The Lawfulness of the Segregation Decisions*, 69 Yale Law Journal 421 (1960). For a comparative history of racism in the United States and South Africa, see George Fredrickson, *White Supremacy: A Study in American and South African History* (New York: Oxford University Press, 1981). See also Cornel West, "Marxist Theory and the Specificity of Afro-American Oppression," in *Marxism and the Interpretation of Culture*, ed. C. Nelson and L. Grossberg (Urbana: University of Illinois Press, 1988).

9. *Brown v. Board of Education*, 349 U.S. 294 (1955).

10. *Briggs v. Elliott*, 132 F.Supp. 776, 777 (E.D.S.C. 1955).

11. Gunnar Myrdal, *An American Dilemma* (New York: Harper and Row, 1944). For a thorough, comprehensive, and sophisticated study of Myrdal's work that reveals its origins, context, production, ideology, reception, and impact, see generally D. Southern, *Gunnar Myrdal and Black-White Relations: The Use and Abuse of An American Dilemma, 1944–1969* (Baton Rouge: Louisiana State University Press, 1987). Chapter 6, for example, traces its importance for civil rights litigation, culminating with its citation in *Brown v. Board of Education*'s famous footnote 11.

12. *Swann v. Charlotte-Mecklenburg Board of Education*, 402 U.S. 1 (1971); Richard Kluger, *Simple Justice* (New York: Knopf, 1976), 572.

13. See *Keyes v. School District No. 1*, 413 U.S. 189 (1973).

14. 401 U.S. 424, 431, 432 (1971).

15. 418 U.S. 717 (1974).

16. 426 U.S. 229, 239 (1976).

17. *City of Mobile v. Golden*, 446 U.S. 55 (1980); *Memphis v. Greene*, 451 U.S. 100 (1981).

18. *Regents of the University of California v. Bakke*, 438 U.S. 265 (1978); *Weber v. Kaiser Aluminum and Chemical Corp.*, 433 U.S. 193 (1979); *Fullilove v. Klutznick*, 448 U.S. 448 (1980), federal law mandating 10 percent setaside for minority-owned business enterprises.

19. 467 U.S. 561, 572, 573 (1984).

20. *Sheet Metal Workers v. EEOC*, 478 U.S. 421 (1986); *Firefighters v. Cleveland*, 478 U.S. 501 (1986); *United States v. Paradise*, 480 U.S. 149 (1987); *Johnson v. Transportation Agency*, 480 U.S. 616 (1987).

21. *Wygant v. Jackson Board of Education*, 476 U.S. 267 (1986).

22. Antonin Scalia, *The Disease as Cure*, 1979 Washington University Law Quarterly 147, 152.

23. *Wards Cove Packing Co. v. Antonio*, 490 U.S. 642 (1989); *Martin v. Wilks*, 490 U.S. 755 (1989); *City of Richmond v. J. A. Croson Co.*, 488 U.S. 469 (1989).

24. See, for example, Charles Lawrence, *The Id, the Ego, and Equal Protection: Reckoning with Unconscious Racism,* 39 Stanford Law Review 317 (1987); Richard Delgado, *Words That Wound: A Tort Action for Racial Insults, Epithets, and Name-Calling,* 17 Harvard Civil Rights–Civil Liberties Law Review 133 (1982). For a powerful experiential account, see "Anthony Walton, Willie Horton, and Me," *New York Times Magazine* (August 20, 1989): 52. See also Mari Matsuda, *Public Response to Racist Speech: Considering the Victim's Story,* 87 Michigan Law Review 2320 (1989).

25. See, for example, McGeorge Bundy, "The Issue Before the Court: Who Gets Ahead in America?" *Atlantic Monthly* (November 1977): 48; James Fallows, "The Tests and the 'Brightest': How Fair Are the College Boards?" *Atlantic* 245 (1980): 37. On the reality of equality of opportunity, see Richard DeLone, *Small Futures* (New York: Harcourt Brace Jovanovich, 1979).

26. See Pierre Bourdieu, *Outline of a Theory of Practice* (Cambridge, UK: Cambridge University Press, 1977), 188.

14 CHARLES R. LAWRENCE III

RACE AND AFFIRMATIVE ACTION: A CRITICAL RACE PERSPECTIVE

IN 1995 Cheryl Hopwood and three other rejected White applicants sued the University of Texas Law School, claiming that the school's affirmative action admissions program violated their constitutional right to equal protection of the laws. They argued that the program amounted to reverse discrimination because their college grades and their scores on the law school admissions test were higher than those of many Black and Mexican American applicants who had been admitted.

A federal district court held that the law school admissions program was constitutional because it was necessary to remedy the continuing effects of a history of official discrimination in primary, secondary, and higher education in Texas.[1] This discrimination was "well documented in history books, case law, and [in] the record of the trial," the court said, and was "not a relic of the past." In 1994, desegregation lawsuits were pending against more than forty different Texas school districts and, although the public school population in Texas was approximately half White and half minority, the vast majority of both White and minority students attended schools that were segregated in fact if not by law. The high school graduation rate for Whites was 81.5 percent compared to 66.1 percent for Blacks and 44.6 percent for Hispanics.

At the university level, an investigation conducted by the U.S. Department of Education's Office of Civil Rights between 1978 and 1980 found that Texas had "failed to eliminate vestiges of its former de jure racially dual system . . . which segregated blacks and Whites" and that there were strong indications of discrimination against Mexican Americans. In 1994 the Office of Civil Rights found that Texas still had not eliminated its segregated system of public higher education.

Cheryl Hopwood and her co-plaintiffs appealed the district court's ruling to the Fifth Circuit Court of Appeals, where a panel of three conservative judges reversed the district court and held that the law school's affirmative action program was unconstitutional. The opening sentences of the Fifth Circuit opinion were typical of the upside-down rhetoric of what opponents of affirmative action have called reverse discrimination.

> [I]n order to increase the enrollment of certain favored classes of minority students, the University of Texas School of Law discriminates in favor of those applicants by giving substantial racial preferences in its admissions program. The beneficiaries of this system are blacks and Mexican Americans, to the detriment of whites and non-preferred minorities.[2]

According to the circuit court judges, Black and Mexican American beneficiaries of affirmative action were a "favored class" given "preference in its admissions program . . . to the detriment of whites." In fact the University of Texas had instituted affirmative action precisely because these minority groups were disfavored by traditional university admissions practices and by historical and contemporary racial discrimination in the Texas educational system.

Texas had admitted Blacks to its law school only when it was forced to do so by the Supreme Court in 1950.[3] As recently as 1960 the University of Texas segregated Mexican American students in campus housing and assigned them to a dormitory know as the Barracks, and, until the mid-1960s, a Texas Board of Regents policy prohibited Blacks from living in or visiting White dorms.[4]

But over a period of many years, affirmative action to achieve integration was working. The University of Texas Law School produced more than 650 African American and 1,300 Mexican American lawyers, including Secretary of Energy Frederico Peña and Dallas Mayor Ron Kirk, both of whom had successful careers in law practice. The entering class of fall 1997 had about one-eighth the number of African Americans (four) and almost 40 percent fewer Mexican Americans (twenty-six) as recent pre-*Hopwood* entering classes. Similar changes in admissions policies at the University of California Law School based on an anti–affirmative action referendum resulted in only one African American student entering in fall 1997, compared to twenty the year before.[5]

The Fifth Circuit simply disregarded the district court's detailed findings of fact and cavalierly denied the reality of racism in Texas. The law school admissions program was unconstitutional, said the circuit court, because it was not "colorblind." If there was past discrimination against Blacks and Mexican Americans by the state's public education system, it was a "vague and amorphous injury," and could not justify discriminating against White applicants because of their race.[6]

The Fifth Circuit's decision adopts what Alan Freeman has called the "perpetrator perspective."[7] By acting as if there has been no racism in the past, or as if past racism is in no way connected to current White privilege, the law defines racism out of existence. Slavery, segregation, genocide of native populations, and wartime incarceration of Japanese American citizens are all distant memories, unfortunate blemishes on an otherwise glorious history. If there was a time when some significant number of us were bigots, the argument goes, that time is long past, and none of us is responsible for crimes committed before we were born. Certainly, a small number of practicing racists remain, but they are social outlaws in a society committed to racial equality, outlaws subject to strong antidiscrimination laws as well as social sanction.

The Fifth Circuit court relied on a series of Supreme Court decisions of the past several years that have employed this reasoning to strike down legislation designed to remedy past and continuing discrimination against non-Whites in employment and in the area of voting rights.[8] *City of Richmond v. Croson* (1989), the first of the Supreme Court's frontal attacks on affirmative action, is a prime example of how the Court has employed historical amnesia to create a colorblind fantasy world. The Court held that the rights of White contractors had been violated when the city of Richmond, Virginia, sought to help minority contractors break into what had been virtually an all-White business. Private contractors receiving city-funded contracts were required to give 30 percent of their subcontracts to minority-owned businesses. The Court said that race could be taken into account only when an affirmative action plan was a remedy for specific past discrimination engaged in or promoted by the city. According to the Court's majority, Richmond failed to prove that minority subcontractors had been discriminated against in the past, despite the fact that less than 1 percent of city contracting dollars had been awarded to minority contractors or subcontractors in a city with a 50 percent African American population. There was "no direct evidence of race discrimination [against minority contractors] on the part of the city . . . or any evidence that the city's prime contractors had discriminated against minority owned [sub]contractors," argued the majority opinion, which went on to suggest that the huge racial disparity in contracts and jobs might have been caused by other nondiscriminatory factors such as a preference by African Americans for jobs in lower-paying industries.

Had the Court considered the historical record, it would have found abundant and uncontroverted evidence that the dearth of minorities was a direct consequence of long-standing discrimination against African American contractors in Richmond. Historian Charles Hoffer summarizes that historical record as follows:

> [N]on-minority contractors had for a century prevented African-American craftsmen from becoming businessmen, refusing them loans and finding other ways to keep them out of the larger marketplace (servicing the African-American market was permitted), while using their labor. The alliance that was to dominate city government and the awarding of city contracts was that between an old Virginia elite and a lily-white city council. While some of this elite circle believed that African-Americans ought to be allowed equality in farming and trade pursuits (so long as they were willing to accept Jim Crow laws), there was no place for African-American businessmen outside of the African-American community. That attitude persisted through the end of a white dominated City Council in 1978 and continues among the white minority of the Council and its supporters in the corporate business community.[9]

But the Court's majority blinded itself to Richmond's history of slavery and segregation, refusing to see the city's still segregated neighborhoods and schools. The justices had to deny their own life experiences in clubs, communities, and law firms that once excluded Blacks and where even today Blacks are rarely seen.

This limited vision of racism, which prohibits explicit racial exclusion but leaves intact almost all of the social practices and institutional structures of White domination, is sometimes called formal equality. It is a vision shared by most liberal and conservative judges and constitutional theorists. Because formal equality substitutes a false account for the truth of American racism, it would be more accurate, albeit less polite, to call it the big lie.

To call this vision of racial equality the big lie is not to suggest that every judge or legal theorist who believes it is an intentional liar. The big lie is seductive primarily because most Americans want to believe it is true. We want to believe we are not racists. A racist is an evil person, and most of us know that we are not cruel-hearted bigots. Moreover, if we can believe there is no racism or that there is very little, those Americans who benefit from White privilege can continue to reap its benefits while extinguishing any moral responsibility for the continued suffering of others. Thus advocates of formal equality are often deluding themselves as much as others.

The big lie begins with a rhetorical ruse that elides ideal and reality. The constitutional ideal of equality is invoked as if equality has been achieved so that now our only concern is to guard against some new inequality, such as discrimination against White males. The Constitution is colorblind, we are told.

Today's argument for colorblindness has its origin in the famous dissenting opinion of Justice Harlan in the 1896 case of *Plessy v. Ferguson*.[10] "Our constitution is color-blind, and neither knows or tolerates classes among citizens," Harlan wrote, noting his disagreement with his fellow justices on the Supreme Court. The Court's majority had held that Louisiana's law segregating passengers on public transportation did not violate the Constitution because separate accommodations for Blacks and Whites did not constitute unequal accommodations. The majority maintained that the segregation law in no way demeaned Blacks or signaled a belief in their inferiority. In an argument often echoed in today's affirmative action debate, the Court's opinion accused Blacks of mass paranoia. If the enforced separation of the two races stamped one race with a badge of inferiority, "it is not by reason of anything found in the act, but solely because the colored race chooses to put that construction upon it," said the Court.

Harlan countered that the majority was willfully blinding itself to what everybody knew: that the segregation of the races was a declaration of White supremacy. The "real meaning" of segregation, he said, is "that colored citizens are so far inferior and degraded that they cannot be allowed to sit in public coaches occupied by White citizens."

Harlan invoked the metaphor of colorblindness for a very different purpose than that of today's opponents of affirmative action, who quote his words out of context. His words declared an ideal, a mandate, and a standard, against which the Constitution should judge the state of affairs in a racist world. He was calling his colleagues' attention to the White supremacist meaning of segregation, which they sought to overlook. If slavery and segregation had legally institutionalized a racial caste system, then the equal protection clause of the Fourteenth Amendment required the disestablishment of that caste system. In other words, he was forcing his colleagues to see the racism in the purportedly neutral practice of segregation. His position was to acknowledge racial reality, not to deny it, in order to meet the constitutional ideal of equality.

This element of Harlan's dissent became the central lesson of *Brown v. Board of Education*, the 1954 landmark case that declared segregation was inherently unequal and overruled the "separate but equal" doctrine of *Plessy*.[11] Separate could not be equal, the court argued, because the purpose and effect of racial segregation was to maintain the caste system of which Justice Harlan had written. This caste system was composed of beliefs, practices, and institutions that functioned to deny Blacks full membership in the community of citizens. The equal protection clause of the Constitution required the dismantling of those racist meanings, practices, and institutions, and such dismantling could not occur without attention to the reality of racism.

We cannot desegregate a segregated institution without giving attention to race. When federal courts implemented plans to desegregate schools after the *Brown* decision, they were forced to acknowledge the race of the students they were assigning to each school. It also became clear that they could not dismantle segregation simply by taking the laws that mandated segregation off the books. Systems of White privilege in place for hundreds of years in White universities, fire departments, businesses, and labor unions would not simply dematerialize of their own inertia. Absent affirmative attention to the race of those individuals who were being included and excluded, and absent affirmative action to change the business-as-usual policies and practices, these institutions would remain all White. The dismantling of institutionalized privilege requires affirmative action.

Of course, when it became apparent that equal opportunity could not be achieved without some redistribution of opportunity, the redistribution was resisted. There was mob violence in Little Rock, Selma, and Boston, and White flight from cities when school desegregation threatened the status quo. Ultimately, the resistance to redistribution of opportunity found voice in today's politics of anti–affirmative action. These politics argue quite forthrightly that opportunity should not be "equalized" or redistributed on the basis of race. In the words of Supreme Court Justice Scalia, "In my view, government can never have a 'compelling interest' in discriminating on the basis of race in order to make up for past racial discrimination in the opposite direction. . . . [U]nder our Constitution there can be no such thing as either a debtor or creditor race."[12]

But antiredistribution and maintenance of White privilege cannot be reconciled with the *Brown* mandate unless we assume that the playing fields are already level. Unfortunately, this assumption has held sway over the years, slowing progress toward full racial justice, even as the United States appears to adhere aggressively to the principle of racial equality. Just as his colleagues in *Plessy* turned the mandate of equal protection into the lie of separate but equal, Justice Harlan's invocation of the abstract ideal of colorblindness has been transformed from a constitutional mandate for a just society into a catch phrase for the denial of racism. Today his inspirational words "our Constitution is color-blind" are quoted time and again to imply that the task of eradicating White supremacy has been completed, leaving only the bogeyman of non-White supremacy.

Just as the opponents of affirmative action use the constitutional ideal of colorblindness to argue that we have already achieved the colorblind society, they rely upon the constitutional ideal of individual rights to deny our society's continued subordination of persons based on their membership in certain racial groups. Opponents of affirmative action often argue that the equal protection clause protects individuals and not groups. Because the Constitution protects individual rights and not group rights, they argue, there can be no group injuries against a race. If there is no group injury, then there is no need for a group remedy such as affirmative action. It is a classic catch-22.

But racism is an injury to a group. White supremacy defines Blacks and other non-White races as inferior as a group. Individual Blacks are discriminated against because of their membership in the group and the entire group is injured by the system of beliefs and practices that defines and treats them as inferior. By limiting constitutional rights to individuals, the Supreme Court simply acts as if there is no such thing as a group injury and denies the only kind of remedy that responds to the way in which racism operates. No group injury means no group remedy.

Of course the Court is not wrong when it says that the purpose of the equal protection clause is to protect each and every individual without regard to his or her race. The ideology of formal equality is attractive and powerful because it starts out with a good idea, the idea of liberal individualism. Racial classifications are presumed invidious and looked upon with suspicion because when we judge a person based on her race, we disregard her unique human individuality and thereby deprive her of the dignity and freedom of self-definition and self-actualization. Race is irrelevant to our humanness and therefore to our status as citizens. This is the meaning of Justice Harlan's admonition and of Martin Luther King's challenge to us to judge one another by the content of our character rather than by the color of our skin.

The Supreme Court relies upon the strong American tradition of liberal individualism when it tells us that we can ensure human dignity and equality by promising each person fair governmental process. Using this line of reasoning, it follows that considering race in school admissions and employment decisions is suspect because it introduces a factor into the decision-making process that has nothing to do with who we are as individuals. Racial classification is wrong because by distributing benefits based on an individual's membership in a racial group we are likely to make erroneous assumptions about the attributes of that individual. It matters not whether the purpose of the policy is the perpetuation of racial subordination or its demise. The classification injures each person whose individuality it ignores.

In an ideal world, where each individual is born into a community that respects and values each individual equally, fair individual process is all that is needed. In such a world race consciousness and group-based decisions are necessarily in tension with equality and human dignity. But we do not live in such a world, and a legal theory that acts as if we do only helps to perpetuate the big lie. When an individual's rights are denied because his or her group is subjugated, only remedies creating equality for the group can offer true equality for the individual.

There is another way to think about promoting equality and human dignity that does not ignore our country's racism, sometimes called substantive equality. Consider the constitutional command of equal protection as one requiring the elimination of society's racism rather than mandating equal protection as an individual right. Such a substantive approach assumes that ridding society of racial subordination is indispensable and a prerequisite to individual dignity and equality. It understands that White supremacy hurts us all.

The recent transformations in South Africa are an inspiring example of this substantive approach to equality. There, the memory of legal apartheid is vivid, its wounds too fresh, and its ravages too enormous for the big lie to prevail. When the White supremacist government was unseated in 1994 and its laws removed from the books, it was impossible for anyone to look at White wealth and Black poverty and claim such a disparity had nothing to do with racism. To suggest, for instance, that there were no Blacks in the construction industry because they had chosen to pursue work as houseboys and maids, or that the dearth of Blacks in the universities and professional schools was unrelated to the savage inequalities of the apartheid school system, would be absurd. No one would dare tell the Black people crowded into Soweto slums that they must remain there while White people inhabit in the plush suburbs of Johannesburg because that is the natural state of things, because Blacks are genetically inferior, because the welfare system has made them dependent, because Black culture is a culture of poverty, because somehow in a free-market merit-based competitive system they have fallen to the bottom.

In South Africa, everyone, Black and White, knows that White privilege is an inheritance from a regime of White supremacy and that equality requires the redistribution of that inheritance. Justice Albie Sachs, one of President Mandela's appointees to South Africa's new Constitutional Court, takes a very different view from that of our own Supreme Court:

> From a human rights point of view, the starting point of constitutional affirmation in a post-apartheid democratic South Africa is that the country belongs to all who live in it, and not just to a small racial minority. If the development of human rights is criterion, there must be a constitutional requirement that the land be redistributed in a fair and just way, and not a requirement that says there can be no redistribution . . .
>
> Affirmative action by its nature involves the distribution of inherited rights. It is distributory rather than conservative in character.[13]

Here in the United States, we too have had to confront the reality of our racism. When Governor George Wallace stood in the doorway of the University of Alabama saying he would never submit to desegregation, when federal troops were required to escort Black children through mobs of angry Whites in Little Rock, Arkansas, when televisions broadcast scenes of Black children being attacked by police dogs and fire hoses, federal judges could not pretend that we were a colorblind society. They issued orders requiring desegregation of all-White schools, police departments, and businesses. They understood that none of this could be accomplished without attention to race.

Those first days are less than a generation ago, and we have barely begun to dismantle the legacy of American apartheid. Justice Sachs is right: Affirmative action must be redistributive. It is resistance to that redistribution that makes so many want to believe the big lie.

But:

> I am not guilty of anything. My ancestors never owned any slaves. I should not be made to pay the price of their transgressions. Their guilt does not pass on to me. I did not create *Plessy.* I regret that Reconstruction

ended in 1877. I was not even born until 1970. Racism is not my problem because I did not create it. To be sure, I do not like that the system is the way it is. If I could be all-powerful, the system would be even-Steven. It is not a creation of my intent. So I am not guilty. When you point the finger and look for someone to blame, someone who must give up something in the name of equality, don't look at me because it is not my fault.

A student in a class that I taught with Professor Mari Matsuda wrote this in response to a class discussion of affirmative action. In the same reflection piece, he also wrote:

> Funny. Last week my basement flooded. So I got out the wet-dry vacuum that my landlord provides for just this situation and started to clean it up. The ironic thing is that I did not create the flood. I did not start the rain. It was not me who improperly sealed the wall. Yet, it would be folly for me to just sit there and say, "It's not my fault. I am not guilty of creating this flood. Therefore, I will not clean it up."
>
> I view racism as my problem that I share with the rest of the country. . . . Guilt or no guilt, it is something that I must deal with whether I desire to or not. But to say that I am responsible for only that damage that I caused gets us nowhere. Indeed, the moment I fail to take responsibility for the damage caused beyond my own actions is the moment that I do become guilty. It is a lesson I learned a long time ago in elementary school. It is the sins of omission that are far worse than the sins of commission.[14]

The double-voicedness of these statements was so striking, we spoke with the student to make sure we understood his intent: "Who is speaking in the opening of your paper?"

He smiled. "It's me, it's both me," he responded.

Our young student, who doesn't want to shoulder the blame for the failure of Reconstruction, who mops up the flood in his budget-priced basement apartment, is not unlike many of the students over the years who have asked hard questions about affirmative action. Mari Matsuda and I have used a role-playing exercise in our classes to help students identify what is really at stake in the affirmative action debate. We divided the class into four groups, and assigned each a role. Group 1 was the critical race theorist/feminist activist. Picture someone like Professor Matsuda, we told the class, or Patricia Williams, whose book we had just read.[15] Group 2 was the law school dean who, while not a radical, was prepared to defend her school's affirmative action program to alumni and students. Group 3 was the student who says, "I see good arguments on both sides, but in the end I come out against affirmative action." Perhaps this person is reluctant to take a public position but will share serious misgivings about affirmative action in private conversations. From past experience, we know this describes many law students. Group 4 was the conservative activist who is an aggressive opponent of affirmative action and proud of it, perhaps someone from the Federalist Society, a conservative law student group.

We asked the students to talk about what these characters might say about affirmative action and what background beliefs they might hold. We asked that they try to use empathic skills in taking on the assigned role. Rather than caricature, we sought a real sense of how each person sees the world.

They had no problem imagining the rhetoric on all sides, and they listed several arguments in four columns on the chalkboard. In looking at what the students had written, we pointed out that the deepest ideological conflict is between two arguments at the ends of spectrum. We circled them: "redistribution" on the left, and "bell curve" on the right. Both of these start from a unified factual premise: Present distributions of wealth, power, education, and material benefits are uneven, with certain groups—women and people of color—less represented at the top. Two alternative explanations exist for this: nature and subordination. If nature is the cause and certain classes of the human species are less intelligent, aggressive, and able, the wisdom of nature—both the nature of Darwin and that of Adam Smith—is best left alone. If subordination is the cause, then antisubordination practices, including redistribution, are fair.

This, we suggested in class that day, is the reason the arguments in the middle of the board seem to go nowhere. Both the reluctant supporters ("diversity") and the reluctant opponents ("not at my expense") of affirmative action prefer to limit the terms of the debate in order to avoid talking about natural inferiority or redistribution.

In saying that people who presently have preferred tickets of admission to the marketplace have a right to keep their seats, the liberal opponents of affirmative action use a language of individualism and merit. While it was easy to see why a seat in the "Whites only" section was an unfair advantage, it is less easy to see why the recipient of a job or admission to a prestigious university has an unfair advantage once the Jim Crow signs have been taken down. If all are given an equal opportunity to compete, let the best person win. The logical extension of this argument is that those who cannot compete under existing measures are undeserving. If those who lose out in fair competition are disproportionately women and members of minority groups, that is something beyond the scope of antidiscrimination law. It belongs outside of law altogether, in the realm of what we call natural or private.

Calling exclusion natural is what theories of racial or gender inferiority do explicitly. Most people living in a century marked by unspeakable horrors done in the name of natural inferiority reject such theories completely both as a matter of fact and as a matter of ethics. No human being is naturally inferior to another, none is inevitably limited in potential at birth by virtue of race or gender.

Herein lies the rhetorical "do not enter" sign for opponents of affirmative action. Those who don't want to cross over into arguing that present distributions are fair—because of natural inferiority or natural choice ("women are risk averse and therefore take less lucrative jobs")—are left saying, "Yes, existing distributions are not always fair, but it is also unfair to penalize someone who didn't cause those distributions as the cost of achieving equality in fact. In the end, I just can't support affirmative action."

Similarly, the liberal supporter of affirmative action who prefers to emphasize the value of diversity sidesteps the question of redistribution. Arguments that we all benefit when new people and new ideas are welcomed to the workplace offer little solace to the individual who feels that his or her job was given to someone else in interest of this vague thing called diversity. The sincere institutional supporter of affirmative action who focuses on the life of the institution over the rights claims of individuals never addresses the key claim of reluctant opponents: It just isn't fair.

Without talking about structural inequality, unconscious racism, institutionalized patriarchy, and antisubordination theory, it is impossible to defend affirmative action. Redistribution is the scary word everyone wants to avoid on this side of the debate. Corporate boosters and law school deans who support affirmative action must cabin their rhetoric in the realm of maximizing institutional goals: profit making in one case, the enrichment that follows diversity in the other. Radical supporters of affirmative action are the only ones, then, who will take on the redistribution question.

My sister Paula, an Episcopal priest, tells a joke about a group of monks who taught that Christ appears in the form of the least advantaged. They always offered food and shelter to the needy who came to their door. One night as they sat down to dinner, they saw yet another hungry-looking stranger approaching the monastery. One of them looked up and said wearily, "Jesus Christ, is it you again?"

The idea that we should take in every stranger must be a joke, right? Of all the arguments we hear in support of affirmative action, there is only one, in the end, that counters the claim that it just isn't fair. It is the one no politician, no law school dean, no corporate CEO, no editor of a major daily newspaper will make. It is the argument closeted in mainstream defenses of affirmative action, and this is it: Yes, you should open your door to strangers because they are you, they are your God if you have one, they are your soul.

It is important to remember that affirmative action on behalf of racial minorities is not the first or the only step toward equality that has involved redistribution. Every gain by a previously excluded group has meant a "loss," in the most narrow self-interested sense, for the previously privileged. When women got the vote, men had less political power, but that was not a reason to deny women the vote. School integration, and even the universal right to go to school, meant that the group that previously had superior or exclusive rights to schooling had to compete for jobs with others who had been denied equal opportunity but now could get training and credentials. To define equality as encompassing only what has no effect on the previously privileged is to negate any real equality.[16]

The Constitution forbids redistribution in several specific clauses, including the contracts clause and the Fifth Amendment. Our founding document reflects the fears elites expressed at the time: those without property—the debtors and the wage laborers—might, in this new experiment called democracy, rise up and take from those who have. Thus the founders commanded that the government could neither erase debts nor take private property without just compensation. Even as they created an unprecedented system of government by the people and outlawed nobility, they conceded to the pressure to maintain slavery and to protect existing accumulations of wealth.

There is another kind of property the framers may well have protected if they had possessed the conceptual tools to do it. They feared the rising up of have-nots, the anger at privilege, the same questioning of entitlement to economic and political power that this book represents. They didn't write into the Constitution an anti–affirmative action clause, but they might have if they had thought about it.

In spite of this history it is possible to defend radical redistribution as a constitutionalist who believes that the founding document is good for the long haul. The Fourteenth Amendment, added to the Constitution after Abraham Lincoln's "Great Civil War," added a new dream to the great American experiment. It mandated equality, making ours the first nation in human history to make equality the law.

Like Frederick Douglass, we can choose to participate in the ongoing process of constitutional interpretation that makes democracy a living thing. Douglass knew the Constitution was born in slavery, with slavery written right into its text in the three-fifths clause. Nonetheless, he chose to embrace the Constitution and claim that the promise of liberty, including the aspirational language of the Preamble, included the enslaved. The long abolitionist struggle, culminating in the Reconstruction amendments, wrote slavery out of the Constitution. Out of the most bloody war of our history we were given the gift of a new Constitution, one that embraced equality.

After that great war, the substantive meaning of equality was clear. We could not pass from a nation of slavery to a nation of universally free and equal citizens without Reconstruction. Newly freed slaves needed affirmative efforts to enforce their rights and to give them the means to exercise liberty: The Freedman's Bureau's forty acres, a mule, and the vote were promises never realized, however; Reconstruction was ended by political expediency, night riders, and Jim Crow signs.

The affirmative action debate today is, as our student recognized, the legacy of 1877 and the failure of Reconstruction. Our nation was not able to make equality the law of the land, even on paper, until the Civil Rights acts passed in what some call the Second Reconstruction of the 1960s. We learned that the Civil Rights acts were not enough to erase a four-hundred-year history of racism and patriarchy. The reasons are many: antidiscrimination law is notoriously difficult to enforce, and race and gender subordination are deeply embedded in places the law is slow to reach—in psyches, cultural practices, and unconscious exclusion. Thoughtful observers, such as Justice Blackmun in the famous *Bakke* case, acknowledge that "there is no other way" than affirmative action.[17] We cannot end racism without taking account of race.

Affirmative action represents this historical knowledge. There is only one way to make equality real: to attack and dismantle inequality. Affirmative action in education and hiring alone, however, is not enough to bring about the Last Reconstruction. To make every citizen part of the polity—valued, voting, informed, active, and participating—will require a substantive theory of equality. Affirmative action is just one part of a larger claim to substantive equality.

NOTES

Much of this chapter is drawn from Charles Lawrence and Mari Matsuda, *We Won't Go Back: Making the Case for Affirmative Action* (Boston: Houghton Mifflin, 1997). The leading early writings on critical race theory are available in a collection, Kimberlé Crenshaw, Neil Gotanda, Gary Peller, Kendall Thomas, eds., *Critical Race Theory: The Key Writings That Formed the Movement* (New York: New Press, 1995).

1. *Hopwood v. State of Texas,* 861 F.Supp. 551, 554–56 (W.D. Tex. 1994).
2. *Hopwood v. State of Texas,* 78 F.3rd 932, 934 (1997).
3. *Sweat v. Painter,* 339 U.S. 629 (1950) (under the pre-*Brown* "separate but equal" rule).
4. 861 F.Supp at 555.
5. These figures were obtained from the associate dean of the University of Texas Law School. See also "Texas Students, Faculty Protest Racial Remarks," *Washington Post,* September 17, 1997, A3; "Educators Concerned About Affirmative Action," *Washington Post,* September 10, 1997, B3 (University of California figures).
6. 78 F.3rd at 949.
7. See Alan David Freeman, *Legitimizing Racial Discrimination Through Antidiscrimination Law: A Critical Review of Supreme Court Doctrine,* 62 Minnesota Law Review 1049 (1978); chapter 13 of this volume.
8. See *City of Richmond v. J. A. Croson,* 488 U.S. 469 (1989); *Adarand Constructors, Inc. v. Pena,* 515 U.S. 200 (1995); *Shaw v. Reno,* 509 U.S. 630 (1993).
9. Peter Charles Hoffer, *Blind to History: The Use of History in Affirmative Action Suits, Another Look at City of Richmond v. J. A. Croson Co.,* 23 Rutgers Law Journal 270, 289–90 (1992).
10. *Plessy v. Ferguson,* 163 U.S. 537, 559, 551, 560 (1896), Harlan dissenting.
11. *Brown v. Board of Education,* 347 U.S. 483 (1954).
12. 515 U.S. at 239, Scalia concurring.
13. Albie Sachs, *Towards a Bill of Rights in a Democratic South Africa,* 6 South African Journal on Human Rights 1, 8 (1990).

14. David Florenzo, reflection piece written for "Subordination, Traditions of Thought, and Experience," Georgetown Law Center, 1996. Our thanks to Mr. Florenzo for allowing us to reprint his work.

15. Patricia Williams, *The Rooster's Egg: On the Persistence of Prejudice* (Cambridge, MA: Harvard University Press, 1995).

16. See David Kairys, *With Liberty and Justice for Some* (New York: New Press, 1993), 140–41.

17. *Regents of the University of California v. Bakke,* 438 U.S. 265, 407 (1978).

15 NADINE TAUB AND ELIZABETH M. SCHNEIDER

WOMEN'S SUBORDINATION AND THE ROLE OF LAW

THE Anglo-American legal tradition purports to value equality, by which it means, at a minimum, equal application of the law to all persons. Nevertheless, throughout this country's history, women have been denied the most basic rights of citizenship, allowed only limited participation in the market place, and otherwise denied access to power, dignity, and respect. Women have instead been largely occupied with providing the personal and household services necessary to sustain family life.

The work women perform in the domestic sphere is barely acknowledged, let alone valued. Institutional arrangements that preclude women's economic and sexual autonomy ensure that this work will be done primarily by women. Often, though not always, these institutions are expressed in legal form.

This chapter explores two aspects of the law's role in maintaining women in an inferior status. It first considers the way the law has furthered male dominance by explicitly excluding women from the public sphere and by refusing to regulate the domestic sphere to which they are thus confined. It then examines the way the law has legitimized sex discrimination through the articulation of an ideology that justifies differential treatment on the basis of perceived differences between men and women.

THE LEGAL ORDER AND THE PUBLIC/PRIVATE SPLIT

Excluded in the past from the public sphere of marketplace and government, women have been consigned to a private realm to carry on their primary responsibilities, i.e., bearing and rearing children, and providing men with a refuge from the pressures of the capitalist world. This separation of society into the male public sphere and the female private sphere was most pronounced during the nineteenth century, when production moved out of the home.[1] But even today, women's opportunities in the public sphere are limited by their obligations in the private domestic sphere.

Men dominate both the public sphere and the private sphere. Male control in the public sphere has often been consolidated explicitly by legal means. The law, however, is in large part absent from the private sphere, and that absence, itself has contributed to male dominance and female subservience.[2] In discussing the role of law in relation to this public/private split, this section first reviews the legal means by which women have been excluded from the public sphere, and then considers the law's absence from the private sphere and how that absence furthers male dominance.[3]

LEGAL EXCLUSION FROM THE PUBLIC SPHERE

The most obvious exclusion of women from public life was the denial of the franchise. Although in colonial times unmarried, propertied women were technically entitled to vote on local issues, all state constitutions that were adopted after the War of Independence, with the temporary exception of New Jersey's, barred women from voting. This initial exclusion gained even greater significance in the 1820s and 1830s, when the franchise was extended to virtually every white male regardless of property holdings. Even after the Civil War, when black men gained the right to vote, women of all races continued to be denied the ballot. The Nineteenth Amendment, giving women the vote, finally became law in 1920 after what has been described as "a century of struggle."[4]

The amendment's passage, however, did not mean that women were automatically accorded the rights and duties that generally accompanied elector status. For example, the exclusion of women from jury duty was upheld as late as 1961, when the Supreme Court explicitly rejected the equal-protection claim of a woman accused of murdering her husband. The Court found Florida's exclusion of women who did not voluntarily register for jury service "reasonable," since:

> Despite the enlightened emancipation of women from the restrictions and protections of bygone years, and their entry into many parts of community life formerly considered to be reserved to men, woman is still regarded as the center of home and family life.[5]

Even today, women are excluded from what is viewed as a crucial test of citizenship—armed combat duty.[6] As a result, women who wish to participate on an equal basis in the military cannot do so. Moreover, because combat exclusion has been used to justify an all-male draft registration system, women have been exempted from the fundamental responsibility of deciding whether to join or resist their country's military efforts.

Women have likewise been excluded from full participation in the economy. Under English common law, not only were they barred from certain professions (such as law), but, once married, they were reduced to legal nonentities unable to sell, sue, or contract without the approval of their husbands or other male relatives.[7] Although these disabilities were initially rigidified by codification of laws, which began in the 1820s, they were gradually lifted in the middle and latter part of the nineteenth century. Starting in the 1840s, various states passed laws that gave women the right to hold certain property in their own name. Subsequent legislation, enacted over the following half-century, afforded them the right to conduct business and retain their own earnings. The enactments were, however, repeatedly subjected to restrictive judicial interpretations that continued to confirm male dominance in business matters.

Even as women moved into the paid labor force, they were limited in their work opportunities and earning power by the ideological glorification of their domestic role reflected in the law.[8] Women have been consistently excluded from certain occupational choices and denied equal earning power by statute and other governmental action. Such explicit exclusions persist today despite the promise of equal treatment contained in the Fourteenth Amendment and affirmative antidiscrimination legislation enacted in the 1960s and 1970s.[9] For example, in 1977 the Supreme Court found it legal to deny women jobs as guards in maximum-security prisons on the ground that the very presence of women would prompt sexual assaults.[10] In so holding, the Court simply ignored the fact that all guards are subject to assault by virtue of being guards and that a prison relies on the threat of future sanctions to maintain order. Women have also been and continue to be excluded from educational opportunities requisite to participation on an equal basis with men in the economy. As late as 1977, the Supreme Court upheld without opinion an appellate court decision finding that Philadelphia's two sex-segregated elite high schools were separate but essentially equal and that Philadelphia did not deny females equal protection by maintaining the dual schools.[11] Post–New Deal social-welfare legislation has likewise imposed barriers to women's participation in the public sphere.

Reflecting and reinforcing the assumption that men are breadwinners and women are homemakers, Social Security legislation has denied female workers fringe benefits available to male workers.[12] Based on the same assumption, welfare and job programs have given men priorities in job placement and job training, with the result that women seeking work have been forced to stand by and watch the most desirable positions go to men.[13]

Legislation denying women the right to determine whether and when they will bear children has also served to exclude women from the public sphere. Beginning in the 1870s, legislative restrictions began to reinforce and supplement existing religious and cultural constraints on birth control. The Comstock Law forbidding obscene material (expressly including contraceptive devices) in the United States mail was invalidated in 1938, while the Supreme Court did not invalidate state restrictions on the marital use of contraceptives until 1965 and their distribution to single persons until 1972.[14,15,16] Similarly, in the middle and late nineteenth century, most states enacted criminal statutes against abortion, although the procedure, at least in the pre-"quickening" stage, had not been a crime at the common law.[17] While a number of these statutes were liberalized in the 1960s, criminal sanctions remained in force until they were invalidated by the 1973 Supreme Court decisions.[18] Since then, provisions have been upheld that exclude abortion from Medicaid coverage and require the parents of many minors to be notified.[19] And in 1989, the Supreme Court once again signaled to the states that they would uphold restrictions on abortion.[20]

Many nongovernmental practices also help to exclude women from the public sphere. Commercial concerns have refused women credit and work; trade unions and professional associations have excluded women from skilled employment; public accommodations and business clubs have denied women entrance. Only very recently and very incompletely have governments acted to remedy this discrimination. As the introduction to this book points out, in distinguishing only between governmental and nongovernmental agencies, and ignoring distinctions based on power, the law has tolerated and tacitly approved discriminatory conduct by a variety of powerful institutions.

THE ABSENCE OF LAW IN THE PRIVATE SPHERE

While sex-based exclusionary laws have joined with other institutional and ideological constraints to directly limit women's participation in the public sphere, the legal order has operated more subtly in relation to the private sphere to which women have been relegated. On the one hand, the legal constraints against women retaining their earnings and conveying property—whose remnants endured well into the twentieth century—meant that married women could have legal relations with the outside world only through their husbands. In this sense, the law may be viewed as directing male domination in the private sphere. On the other hand, the law has been conspicuously absent from the private sphere itself. Despite the fundamental similarity of conflicts in the private sphere to legally cognizable disputes in the public sphere, the law generally refuses to interfere in ongoing family relationships. For example, the essence of the marital relation as a legal matter is the exchange of the man's obligation to support the women for her household and sexual services. Yet contract law, which purports to enforce promissory obligations between individuals, is not available during the marriage to enforce either the underlying support obligation or other agreements by the parties to a marriage to matters not involving property. A woman whose husband squanders or gives away assets during the marriage cannot even get an accounting. And while premarital property agreements will be enforced on divorce, courts' enormous discretion in awarding support and distributing property makes it highly unlikely that these decisions will reflect the parties' conduct during the marriage in regard to either the underlying support obligation or other agreements. It is as if in regulating the beginning and the end of a business partnership the law disregarded the events that transpired during the partnership and refused to enforce any agreements between the partners as to how they would behave.[21]

Similarly, tort law, which is generally concerned with injuries inflicted on individuals, has traditionally been held inapplicable to injuries inflicted by one family member on another. Under the doctrines of interspousal and parent-child immunity, courts have consistently denied recoveries for injuries that would be compensable but for the fact that they occurred in the private realm.[22] In the same way, criminal law declined to punish intentional injuries to family members. Common law and statutory definitions of rape in many states continue to carve out a special exception for a husband's forced intercourse with his wife. Wife beating was initially omitted from the definition of criminal assault on the ground that a husband had the right to chastise his wife. Even today, after courts have explicitly rejected the definitional exception and its rationale, judges, prosecutors, and police officers decline to enforce assault laws in the family context.[23]

While in recent years, there has been some modification of these doctrines, the idea that law is inappropriate in the private sphere persists. A modern example of this phenomenon is the idea that family disputes are best suited for mediation rather than more formal legal proceedings.[24]

The state's failure to regulate the domestic sphere is now often justified on the ground that the law should not interfere with emotional relationships involved in the family realm because it is too heavy-handed. Indeed, the recognition of a familial privacy right in the early twentieth century has given this rationale a constitutional dimension. The importance of this concern, however, is undercut by the fact that the same result was previously justified by legal fictions, such as the woman's civil death on marriage. More importantly, the argument misconstrues the point at which the law is invoked. Legal relief is sought when family harmony has already been disrupted. Family members, like business associates, can be expected to forgo legal claims until they are convinced that harmonious relations are no longer possible. Equally important, the argument reflects and reinforces powerful myths about the nature of family relations. It is not true that women perform personal and household services purely for love. The family is the locus of fundamental economic exchanges, as well as important emotional ties.

Isolating women in a sphere divorced from the legal order contributes directly to their inferior status by denying them the legal relief that they seek to improve their situations and by sanctioning conduct of the men who control their lives. For example, when the police do not respond to a battered woman's call for assistance or when a civil court refuses to evict her husband the woman is relegated to self-help, while the man who beats her receives the law's tacit encouragement. When the law does not allow for wage attachments or other standard collection devices to be used to enforce orders for child support, it leaves women in desperate financial straits.

But beyond its direct, instrumental impact, the insulation of women's world from the legal order also conveys an important ideological message to the rest of society. Although this need not be the case in all societies, in our society the law's absence devalues women and their functions: women simply are not sufficiently important to merit legal regulation. This message is clearly communicated when particular relief is withheld. By declining to punish a man for inflicting injuries on his wife, for example, the law implies she is his property and he is free to control her as he sees fit. Women's work is discredited when the law refuses to enforce the man's obligation to support his wife, since it implies she makes no contribution worthy of support. Similarly, when courts decline to enforce contracts that seek to limit or specify the extent of the wife's services, the law implies that household work is not real work in the way that the type of work subject to contract in the public sphere is real work. These are important messages, for denying woman's humanity and the value of her traditional work are key ideological components in maintaining woman's subordinate status. The message of women's inferiority is compounded by the totality of the law's absence from the private realm. In our society, law is for business and other important things. The fact that the law in general has so little bearing on women's day-to-day concerns reflects and underscores their insignificance. Thus, the legal order's overall contribution to the devaluation of women is greater than the sum of the negative messages conveyed by individual legal doctrines.

Finally, isolating women in a world where the law refuses to intrude further obscures the discrepancy between women's actual situation and our nominal commitment to equality. Like other collective ideals, the equality norm is expressed predominantly in legal form. Because the law as a whole is removed from women's world, the equality norm is perceived as having very limited application to women. In this way, people are encouraged to favor equality in the public sphere of government and business (e.g., "equal pay for equal work") while denigrating the need for any real change in social roles ("I'm not a woman's libber"). The law can thus purport to guarantee equality while simultaneously denying it.

In short, the law plays a powerful role, though certainly not an exclusive role, in shaping and maintaining women's subordination. The law has operated directly and explicitly to prevent women from attaining self-support and influence in the public sphere, thereby reinforcing their dependence on men. At the same time, its continued absence from the private sphere which women are relegated not only leaves individual women without formal remedies but also devalues and discredits them as a group.

Acknowledging that the public/private split currently promotes male dominance is very different from suggesting that no division between the public and private is ever acceptable. While the concern that a rigid system of legal rights and wrongs will stifle feelings is a real one, a key aspect of women's present subordinate status is the failure to recognize work now performed in the domestic sphere as a real economic contribution rather than a spontaneous and gratuitous product of emotion. Our limited understanding of patriarchal relations makes it difficult to foresee the precise institutional arrangements, and thus the legal formulations, that will mark the end of male dominance; but it is apparent that the value of "women's work" will have to be acknowledged in a fundamental sense. Much of this work will most likely move out of the home. Consequently, a large portion of the activity that now takes place in the private sphere should come to be governed by law to the same extent as activities already located in the public sphere.

Delineating the extent of human relationships and activities that should ultimately escape collective judgments and prescribing the degree to which the "personal" and the "human" should be reserved to a special private realm is even more difficult. In other areas of the law, it has been argued that there is a continued role for organized institutional political power in the quest for human freedom and that law may enhance, rather than stifle, self-realization.[25] The recognition that immunizing the family realm has thus far reinforced women's identity as man's property and obscured her subordination should spur our efforts to explore this possibility.

LEGAL CONTROLS ON REPRODUCTION AND THE PUBLIC/PRIVATE SPLIT

The relationship between legal controls on reproduction and the public/private split is not a simple one. Until 1965, a number of laws dating from the latter part of the nineteenth century that restricted access, use, and even information about contraception and abortion remained in place at both the state and federal level. In that year, a fragmented Supreme Court struck down as violative of the Constitution Connecticut's ban on use of birth control in the case of *Griswold v. Connecticut.*[26] Though no one rationale emerged clearly from the multiple opinions in *Griswold*, subsequent decisions made plain that restrictions on the procreative choice, like other family decisions, ran afoul of a constitutional right of privacy. Important among these was the 1973 *Roe v. Wade* decision, which invalidated a Texas criminal abortion law and spelled out relatively stringent standards for other abortion laws.[27] Over the next decade and a half, with the crucial exception of prohibitions on Medicaid funding, the Court struck down a variety of restrictions on abortion.

In terms of the public/private split, this process of invalidation is complex. On the one hand, the Court responded to the women's movement and other political pressures to allow women to exercise greater autonomy. On the other hand, in so doing it ignored other legal grounds for the decision, which had been offered by women's groups, in favor of a rationale that reaffirmed the public/private split.

In the decades since *Roe v. Wade*, antiabortion forces mobilized and exerted enormous pressure on the Court to overrule it. The impact of these efforts is seen in the 1977 and 1980 decisions upholding restrictions on Medicaid funding for abortions and in two major cases retrenching abortion rights.[28]

In *Webster v. Reproductive Services* (1989), the Court, stopping short of reversing *Roe v. Wade* outright, upheld Missouri provisions prohibiting the use of public employees, facilities, and public funds to perform or assist any abortion not necessary to save the woman's life and requiring physicians to perform specified tests to determine fetal viability at twenty or more weeks.[29] Two other provisions—the preamble to the law, dating the beginning of human life from the moment of conception, and a prohibition on the use of public funds, facilities, and employees for encouraging or counseling abortion—were left standing as a majority agreed they were not properly before the Court. *Planned Parenthood v. Casey* (1992) again avoided overturning *Roe v. Wade*, but Justice O'Connor's opinion replaced *Roe's* trimester approach with a standard which rests on whether state regulations of abortion impose an "undue burden" on the exercise of the right to decide whether to terminate a pregnancy.[30] In practice, *Casey* represents the Court's contradictory sensitivity to the issue of "burden." The Court upheld Pennsylvania's informed consent and mandatory twenty-four-hour waiting period requirements, but struck down a husband notification provision, showing considerable sensitivity to the problem of coercion in intimate relationships. In any event, some governmental interference with women's ability to decide whether and when they will bear children is permissible.

The effect of *Casey* and *Webster* on the public/private split is also complex. The law plays an important role in maintaining the public/private split when it denies women reproductive autonomy. As a practical matter, the inability to determine whether or when they will have children combined with the sex-based assignment of childrearing responsibilities has prevented women from participating fully in the public sphere. Women's ability to engage in political life has been constrained, and their work and educational opportunities have been limited.

Moreover, the legal rationale that has been relied on for cutting back on the constitutional protection afforded procreative choice itself reflects the notion that women do not belong in the legally protected public sphere. The cutback turns on the argument that only those rights specifically mentioned in the Constitution, the Bill of Rights, and subsequent amendments should be recognized and enforced by the judiciary. In this view, recognition of the abortion right in *Roe v. Wade* was an improper, judge-made departure from the Constitution. A particularly extreme version of this argument, the argument from original intent, gained currency during the Reagan period. Under this approach, constitutional protection should be given only those rights of importance to the decision makers at the time the Constitution was drafted or amended. Concerns of importance to those historically excluded from the decision-making process, such as reproductive autonomy, would continue to be denied protection. State and federal officials who have used this argument to defend restrictions on abortion look to the historical record and insist that neither the Founding Fathers nor the framers of the Fourteenth Amendment regarded the right to abortion as fundamental. In so doing, of course, they have ignored the inevitable consequence of their approach: to permit those already in the public sphere to limit the ability of others to join them.

Reproductive laws have functioned to maintain the public/private split in the past as well. As 281 historians told the Supreme Court considering *Webster*, abortion was particularly prevalent and visible in the nineteenth century and was not illegal for much of this nation's history.[31] From 1820 to 1860, abortion regulation in the states rejected broader English restrictions and sought to protect women from particularly dangerous forms of abortion. The nineteenth-century movement to regulate abortions, which culminated in the enforcement of restrictive legislation of the 1860s and 1870s, was one chapter in a campaign by "regulars"— the men who ultimately became practitioners and proponents of scientific medicine and who formed the American Medical Association (AMA)—to drive out the frequently female "irregulars."

One important reason the AMA succeeded in its antiabortion efforts was its ability to persuade male political leaders that "abortion constituted a threat to social order and to male authority."[32] The AMA played upon popular fears generated by the nineteenth-century movement for women's suffrage and equality that women were departing from their purely maternal role.

As described by the AMA's Committee on Criminal Abortion in 1871

> [the woman who seeks abortion] becomes unmindful of the course marked out for her by Providence, she overlooks the duties imposed on her by the marriage contract. She yields to the pleasure—but shrinks from

the pains and responsibilities of maternity; and, destitute of all delicacy and refinements, resigns herself, body and soul, into the hands of unscrupulous and wicked men. Let not the husband of such a wife flatter himself that he possesses her affection. Nor can she in turn ever merit even the respect of a virtuous husband. She sinks into old age like a withered tree, stripped of its foliage; with the stain of blood upon her soul, she dies without the hand of affection to smooth her pillow.[33]

Denying abortion was thus a way of keeping women in their place.

How, then, do legal controls on reproduction square with the general notion that the absence of law from the private sphere has furthered women's subordination? Developments in the law governing reproduction must obviously be viewed two ways. There is no question that *Casey* and *Webster* authorize legal intrusions into the private sphere and that such intrusions undercut the claim that the private sphere has been characterized by an absence of law. But at the same time, such intrusions must be understood as both a cause and effect of the public/private split. Thus in the reproductive area, unlike other areas, an absence of any state regulation seems to enhance the autonomy of many women. However, because one needs access to resources to realize this autonomy, collective support will ultimately be necessary to ensure that all women can effectuate their reproductive choices and particpate fully in all aspects of life. Those resources may not be forthcoming when reproductive choice is seen solely as a private, individual matter.

THE LEGAL IDEOLOGY OF SEXUAL INEQUALITY

As we have seen, the law has enforced male dominance through its direct impact on the lives of individual women and men, and its symbolic devaluation of women and their functions. The law has also perpetuated inequality through the articulation of an ideology that camouflages the fundamental injustice of existing sexual relations. Because the law purports to be the embodiment of justice, morality, and fairness, it is particularly effective in performing this ideological function.

Historically, women's subservient status has been associated with a view of differences between the sexes and differential legal treatment. A succession of Supreme Court decisions has legitimized that subservient status by upholding laws which, on their face, mandate that the sexes be treated differently. This section examines the principal doctrinal bases used by the Court by focusing on four illustrative Supreme Court decisions.[34] In an 1873 decision, differences between men and women were expressed in terms of gross overgeneralizations reflecting moral or religious views of women's nature and proper role. The ideology masked women's inferior treatment by glorifying women's separate role. In 1908, the differences focused to a much greater extent on the "facts" of women's physical limitations necessitated by their reproductive functions and their consequent dependence on men. These deficiencies called for special treatment for women to be on an equal footing with men. Present day ideology is even more subtle. The Supreme Court espouses a concern for sexual equality and purports to reject stereotypical overgeneralizations about the sexes; yet it refuses to recognize classifications based on reproductive capacity as sex-based, and it regards legal and social disabilities that have been imposed on women as realistic differences sufficient to justify differential treatment. By continuing to make differential treatment appear fair, the current Court provides a rationale for present inequalities.

WOMEN'S "SEPARATE SPHERE": *BRADWELL V. ILLINOIS*

In *Bradwell v. Illinois*, the Supreme Court upheld the Illinois Supreme Court's decision to refuse Myra Bradwell admission to the Illinois bar because she was a woman.[35,36] She studied law under her husband's tutelage, raised four children; ran a private school; was involved in civic work; and founded a weekly newspaper, the *Chicago Legal News*, which became an important legal publication. A feminist active in women's suffrage organizations, Myra Bradwell played an important role in obtaining Illinois legislation that removed women's legal disabilities. She took her case to the Supreme Court, arguing that admission to practice law was guaranteed by the privileges and immunities clause of the recently adopted Fourteenth Amendment.

The *Bradwell* litigation took place within the context of a particular conception of sex roles. Although women were in no way the equals of men during the colonial and Revolutionary periods, the nature of their subordination, particularly in the middle classes, changed dramatically between the end of the eighteenth century and the middle of the nineteenth century.[37] The early stages of industrial capitalism involved increasing specialization and the movement of production out of the home, which resulted in heightened sex segregation. Men went out of the house to work; and women's work, influence, and consciousness remained focused at home. Although women continued to be dependent on and subservient to men, women were no longer placed at the bottom of a hierarchy dominated by men. Rather, they came to occupy women's "separate sphere," a qualitatively different world centered on home and family. Women's role was by definition incompatible with full participation in society.

"Separate-sphere" ideology clearly delineated the activities open to women. Women's role within the home was glorified, and women's limited participation in paid labor outside the home was most often in work that could be considered an extension of their work within the home.[38] For example, native-born mill girls in the 1820s and 1830s, and immigrant women in the 1840s and 1850s, worked in largely sex-segregated factories manufacturing textiles, clothing, and shoes. Likewise, after a period of time, teaching became a woman's occupation. Unpaid charitable and welfare activities, however, were encouraged as consistent with women's domestic responsibilities.

Although ultimately quite constraining, the development of women's separate sphere had some important benefits. While the emphasis on women's moral purity and the cult of domesticity tended to mask women's inferior position, it also allowed women a certain degree of autonomy. It gave them the opportunity to organize extensively into religious and secular welfare associations, afforded access to education, and provided them with a basis for uniting with other women. Evaluations of the cult of domesticity and women's separate sphere by feminist historians have consequently ranged from the view that women were victims of this ideology to the recognition that women found a source of strength and identity in their separate world.[39]

The development of separate-sphere ideology appears in large measure to have been a consequence of changes in the conditions of production. Behavior was then further channeled by a vast cultural transformation promoted through books and magazines. The law does not seem to have played an overt role in the initial articulation of the separate-sphere ideology; but to the extent that the ideological transformation that occurred in the early part of the nineteenth century was a reaction to a strict hierarchy imposed by the previous legal order, the legal system may well have played an important part at the outset.

In any event, the law appears to have contributed significantly to the perpetuation of this ideology. Immediately following the Civil War, feminists attempted to have women expressly included in the protections of the Fourteenth and Fifteenth amendments. The failure of the Fourteenth and Fifteenth amendments to address the needs of women, and indeed for the first time to write the word "men" into the Constitution, resulted in a long-lasting division in the women's movement, which reflected differences regarding both ends and means, and which lasted at least until the 1890s. Feminists aligned with the Republican party stressed black suffrage and saw women suffrage as coming through a constitutional amendment at some future time. The more militant and effective National Woman Suffrage Association favored legal and political efforts to obtain a judicial or congressional declaration that the Wartime Amendments also secured rights for women.[40] Although Myra Bradwell's legal challenge was not known to be part of an organized strategy, her attempt to use the Fourteenth Amendment to challenge state prohibitions on occupational choices legally reflected this tack. By invoking the cult of domesticity as a legal rationale for rejecting this demand, the courts enshrined and reinforced separate-sphere ideology while deferring women's rights.

In rejecting Myra Bradwell's challenge to Illinois' prohibition on occupational choice, the Supreme Court had two options: to construe the new constitutional guarantees narrowly so as to defeat all comers, or to find special reasons for treating women differently. The majority adopted the first approach. It held that the decision was controlled by the Court's decision (the day before) in the *Slaughter-House Cases*, which held that, even after the adoption of the Fourteenth Amendment, states retained the unmediated right to regulate occupations.[41]

However, Justice Joseph Bradley, who dissented in *Slaughter-House*, opted for the second approach. His concurring opinion is the embodiment of the separate-sphere ideology.

[T]he civil law as well as nature itself, has always recognized a wide difference in the respective spheres and destinies of man and woman. Man is, or should be woman's protector and defender. The natural and proper timidity and delicacy which belongs to the female sex evidently unfits it for many of the occupations of civil life. . . . The constitution of the family organization, which is founded in the divine ordinance, as in the nature of things, indicates the domestic sphere as that which properly belongs to the domain and functions of womanhood. The harmony, not to say identity, of interests and views which belong, or should belong, to the family institution is repugnant to the idea of a woman adopting a distinct and independent career from that of her husband. . . .

It is true that many women are unmarried and not affected by any of the duties, complications, and incapacities arising out of the married state, but these are exceptions to the general rule. The paramount destiny and mission of woman are to fulfill the noble and benign offices of wife and mother. This is the law of the Creator. And the rules of civil society must be adapted to the general constitution of things, and cannot be based upon exceptional cases.

Glorification of women's destiny serves to soften any sense of unfairness in excluding women from the legal profession. Since this "paramount destiny and mission" of women is mandated by "nature," "divine ordinance," and "the law of the Creator," the civil law need not recognize the claims of women who deviate from their proper role. By conceiving of the law as the means of enforcing reality as it "is or should be," Bradley can concede that some women do live apart from men—or even that some women who live with men are capable of functioning in the public domain—without exposing the law as unreasonable.

WOMEN'S PHYSICAL DIFFERENCES: *MULLER V. OREGON*

In the nineteenth century, the persisting separate-sphere ideology legitimized and reinforced women's marginal and secondary status in the work force. Working women were suspicious, inferior, and immoral. Those women who joined the work force were predominantly single or widowed, and confined to "women's jobs," serving as a reserve supply of cheap labor. The primary identification of women with the home also provided an ideological basis for keeping women out of unions.

With industrialization and urbanization in the late nineteenth century came deplorable work conditions for all workers, which prompted unions and social reformers to press for legislation regulating conditions of work hours, and wages. By the turn of the century, both sex-neutral and sex-based protective laws had been passed and sustained against legal challenge. Women-only protective laws were enacted with the express support of such reform groups as the National Women's Trade Union League, the General Federation of Women's Clubs, and the National Consumers' League, which merged the energies of wealthy and working women. Although sex-based legislation might have conflicted with suffragists' initial argument that women were entitled to the role because they were fundamentally equal to men, it was entirely consistent with the more expedient position they had adopted in the 1890s, to the effect that women should be given the vote because their special perspective would benefit society.

Protective-labor legislation was countered legally by conservatives who, led by the American Bar Association, revived the natural-law notion of freedom of contract and located it in the due process clause of the Fourteenth Amendment. The effort culminated in *Lochner v. New York*, a decision that, in striking down maximum-hour legislation for bakers by relying on the "common understanding" that baking and most other occupations did not endanger health, cast doubt on the validity of all protective legislation.[42]

Advocates of state "protective" legislation for women could take two routes, after *Lochner*: one, to displace the "common understanding" in *Lochner* with scientific evidence that all industrial jobs, when performed more than ten hours a day, were dangerous to a worker's health; or two, by arguing that women's need for special protection justified an exception to *Lochner*.[43] In *Muller v. Oregon*, the Supreme Court was faced with a challenge to an Oregon statute that prohibited women from working more than ten hours a day in a laundry.[44] The National Consumers' League, which played the major role in the middle- and upper-class reform movement, filed an *amicus* brief, written by Louis Brandeis, Josephine Goldmark, and Florence Kelly, which attempted to combine both approaches.[45] The brief portrayed as common knowledge pseudoscientific data regarding physical differences between men and women, emphasizing the "bad effects" of long hours on women workers' health, "female functions," childbearing capacity, and job safety, and on the health and welfare of future generations. Adopting the view urged by the *amici*, the Court upheld the challenged legislation:

> that woman's physical structure and the performance of maternal functions place her at a disadvantage in the struggle for subsistence is obvious. This is especially true when the burdens of motherhood are upon her. Even when they are not, by abundant testimony of the medical fraternity continuance for a long time on her feet at work, repeating this from day to day, tends to injurious effects upon the body, and as healthy mothers are essential to vigorous offspring, the physical well-being of woman becomes an object of public interest and care in order to preserve the strength and vigor of the race. . . .
>
> Still again history discloses the fact that woman has always been dependent upon man. . . . As minors, though not to the same extent, she has been looked upon in the courts as needing special care that her rights may be preserved. . . . Though limitations upon personal and contractual rights may be removed by legislation, there is that in her disposition and habits of life which will generate against a full assertion of these rights. She will still be where some legislation to protect her seems necessary to

secure a real equality of right. . . . Differentiated by these matters from the other sex, she is properly placed in a class by herself, and legislation designed for her protection may be sustained, even when the legislation is not necessary for men and could not be sustained.[46]

Muller expresses a view of women as different from and more limited than men because of their "physical structure" and "natural functions." Although this view of women is every bit as fixed as that expressed in *Bradwell*, it purports to be grounded in physical fact. Legal reforms, such as the removal of "limitations upon personal and contractual rights," would be ineffective in changing women's rights because of women's "disposition and habits of life." These differences in physical structure and childbearing capacity are thus sufficient for women to be "properly placed in a class by themselves." Women's primary function as mother is now seen as physically incompatible with the demands of equal participation in the work force. Special work conditions for women are therefore justified.

Both social reformers and legal realists regarded the statute's survival and the Supreme Court's recognition of economic and social facts as important victories. However, as organized labor lost interest in protective legislation for men, the primary legal legacy of *Muller* was a view of women that justified excluding women from job opportunities and earning levels available to men.[47] The Court's focus on the apparently immutable facts of women's physique obscured the exploitation of workers generally and the social discrimination that assigned full-time responsibility for the household to women. As an ideological matter, the notion that women's different physiology requires special protection continues to legitimize a division of labor in which men are primary wage earners entitled to draw on the personal services of their wives, and women remain marginal workers available to replace more expensive male workers.[48]

UNEQUAL EQUAL PROTECTION: *MICHAEL M. V. SONOMA COUNTY*

Although Supreme Court opinions of the 1960s began to acknowledge some changes in woman's position, it took the rebirth of an active women's movement in the 1960s and the development of a legal arm to obtain a definitive legal determination that sex-based discrimination violated the equal-protection clause of the Fourteenth Amendment.[49] In 1971, the Supreme Court, in *Reed v. Reed*, for the first time invalidated a statute on the ground that it denied women equal protection.[50] The Court unanimously struck down an Idaho statute preferring males to females in the performance of estate administration, refusing to find generalizations about women's business experience adequate to sustain the preference. Although the actual dispute involved a relatively trivial duty, a statute that already had been repealed, and facts that presented no major threat to the established social order, the opinion appeared to voice a view of women that seemed radically different from previous judicial expressions.

Equal protection rests on the legal principle that people who are similarly situated in fact must be similarly treated by the law.[51] In *Reed*, the Court for the first time held that women and men are similarly situated. The Court recognized the social reality, through "judicial notice," that "in this country presumably due to the greater longevity of women, a large proportion of estates . . . are administered by women."[52] By recognizing a departure from traditional social roles as so obvious as to be able to rely on judicial notice, the Court appeared to presage the erosion of the "differences" ideology.

Over the next ten years, in upholding equal-protection challenges to sex-based legislation, the Supreme Court has repeatedly rejected overgeneralizations based on sex.[53] For example, in *Frontiero v. Richardson*, the Court upheld an equal-protection challenge to the military's policy of denying dependency benefits to male dependents of female servicewomen.[54] The plurality opinion criticized *Bradwell* as reflective of an attitude of "romantic paternalism" that "in practical effect, put women not on a pedestal but in a cage."[55] Similarly, in *Stanton v. Stanton*, the Court upheld an equal-protection challenge to a state statute specifying a greater age of majority for males than females with respect to parental obligation for support.[56] In so doing, the Court appeared to understand the effect of stereotypes in perpetuating discrimination and the detrimental impact that differential treatment has on women's situation.[57]

However, the Supreme Court's developing application of equal protection has not lived up to its initial promise. The Court has adopted a lower standard of review for sex-based classifications than for race-based classifications, reflecting its view that race discrimination is a more serious social problem than sex discrimination.[58] The Court has rejected only those stereotypes that it perceives as grossly inaccurate. Indeed, the Court has developed a new and more subtle view of "realistically based differences," which encompasses underlying physical distinctions between the sexes, distinctions created by law, and socially imposed differences in situation, and frequently confuses the three. In these cases, the Court simply reasons that equal protection is not violated because men and women are not "similarly situated."

The paradigmatic physical distinction between the sexes, women's reproductive capacity, has been consistently viewed by courts as a proper basis for differential treatment. The present Court does so by refusing to recognize that classifications based on pregnancy involve sex discrimination and by ignoring the similarities between pregnancy and other temporary disabilities. In *Geduldig v. Aiello*, the Supreme Court rejected an equal-protection challenge to California's disability insurance system, which paid benefits to persons in private employment who were unable to work but excluded from coverage disabilities resulting from pregnancy.[59] The Court noted that

> [w]hile it is true that only women become pregnant, it does not follow that every legislative classification concerning pregnancy is a sex-based classification like those considered in *Reed*, supra and *Frontiero*, supra. Normal pregnancy is an objectively identifiable physical condition with unique characteristics. Absent a showing that distinctions involving pregnancy are mere pretexts designed to effect an invidious discrimination against the members of one sex or the other, lawmakers are constitutionally free to include or exclude pregnancy from the coverage of legislation such as this on any reasonable basis just as with respect to any other physical condition.[60]

This position was effectively reaffirmed in *General Electric v. Gilbert*, in which the exclusion of pregnancy from General Electric's disability program was upheld in the face of a challenge under Title VII of the Civil Rights Act.[61]

Similarly, the present Court finds differential treatment justified by women's special circumstances, even when those circumstances reflect legislatively or socially imposed burdens.[62] In *Parham v. Hughes*, a plurality of the Court upheld a Georgia statute that allowed an unwed mother to sue for the wrongful death of her child, but disallowed such suits by an unwed father unless he had procured a court order legitimating the child.[63] The Court found that treating men and women differently in this fashion did not constitute impermissible sex discrimination because the two sets of parents were not similarly situated in two respects. First, under Georgia law, unwed fathers, but not unwed mothers, could legitimate their children by a unilateral act. This difference is, of course, imposed by law, not by biological necessity. Second, the Court pointed to the difficulty in ascertaining the father's identity. Here the difference in situation results primarily from socially imposed differences in child-rearing patterns, since, as a physiological matter, unless the woman is observed giving birth, there is little reason to put more faith in a woman's claim to be a particular child's parent than in a man's claim to be that child's parent. The Court's reliance on these societally imposed differences reflects its present willingness to uphold distinctions that are generally accurate though unfair to individuals and likely to perpetuate existing sex roles.

The most recent expression of the Court's current ideology of equality is a 1981 Supreme Court case, *Michael M. v. Sonoma County*, upholding California's statutory rape law, challenged by a seventeen-year-old male, which punished males having sex with a female under eighteen.[64] The thrust of his attack on the statute was that it denied him equal protection since he, not his partner, was criminally liable.

Statutory rape laws have rested historically on the legal fiction that young women are incapable of consent. They exalt female chastity and reflect and reinforce archaic assumptions about the male initiative in sexual relations and the weakness and naivete of young women.[65] Nevertheless, the Court, in *Michael M.*, found no violation of equal-protection guarantees and upheld the differential treatment as reasonably related to the goal of eliminating teenage pregnancy.

Although the Court in *Michael M.* cited its prior decisions rejecting sex-based classifications without proof of a "substantial relationship" to "important governmental objectives," it did not, in fact, apply them. No legislative history was produced in California or elsewhere to show that the purpose of the sex-based classification was to eliminate teenage pregnancy. Moreover, the experience of other jurisdictions showed that the criminalization of male, but not female, conduct bore little relation to the goal of eliminating teenage pregnancy. Instead, the Court simply stated that because females become pregnant and because they bear the consequences of pregnancy, "equalization" via differential punishment is reasonable.

> We need not be medical doctors to discern that young men and young women are not similarly situated with respect to the problems and risks of sexual intercourse. Only women may become pregnant and they suffer disproportionately the profound physical, emotional and psychological consequences of sexual activity.[66]

Thus, the Court asserts, the sex-based classification, which "serves roughly to 'equalize' the deterrents on the sexes," realistically reflects the fact that the sexes are not similarly situated.[67]

Justice Potter Stewart's concurring opinion in *Michael M.* develops the crux of this new ideology of realistically based classifications:

> The Constitution is violated when government, state or federal, invidiously classifies similarly situated people on the basis of the immutable characteristic with which they were born. . . . [W]hile detrimental gender classifications by government often violate the Constitution, they do not always do so, for the reason that there are differences between males and females that the Constitution necessarily recognizes. In this case we deal with the most basic of these differences: females can become pregnant as the result of sexual intercourse; males cannot. . . .
>
> "[A] State is not free to make overbroad generalizations based on sex which are entirely unrelated to any differences between men and women or which demean the ability or social status of the protected class." Gender-based classifications may not be based upon administrative convenience; or upon archaic assumptions about the proper role of the sexes. . . . But we have recognized that in certain narrow circumstances men and women are not similarly situated and in these circumstances a gender classification based on clear differences between the sexes is not invidious, and a legislative classification realistically based upon these differences is not unconstitutional. . . .
>
> Applying these principles to the classification enacted by the California legislature, it is readily apparent that [the statute] does not violate the Equal Protection Clause. Young women and men are not similarly situated with respect to the problems and risks associated with intercourse and pregnancy, and the statute is realistically related to the legitimate state purpose of reducing those problems and risks.[68]

Yet, the classification at issue in *Michael M.* had very little to do with biological differences between the sexes. As is seen from the total absence of supportive legislative history, the statute was not designed to address the problem of teenage pregnancy. Moreover, as Justice John Paul Stevens points out, if criminal sanctions are believed to deter the conduct leading to pregnancy, a young woman's greater risk of harm from pregnancy is, if anything, a reason to subject her to sanctions. The statute instead embodies and reinforces the assumption that men are always responsible for initiating sexual intercourse and females must always be protected against their aggression. Nevertheless, the Court's focus on the physical fact of reproductive capacity serves to obscure the social bases of its decision. Indeed, it is striking that the Court entirely fails to treat pregnancy as sex discrimination when discrimination really is in issue, while using it as a rationale in order to justify differential treatment when it is not in issue.

Like *Bradwell* and *Muller, Michael M.* affirms that there are differences between the sexes, both the physical difference of childbearing capacity and women's social role, which should result in differential legal treatment. However, because this affirmation comes at the same time as the Court claims to reject "overbroad generalizations unrelated to differences between men and women or which demean [women's] ability or social status," the Court's approval of differential treatment is especially pernicious. The fact of and harms caused by teenage pregnancy are used by the Court to avoid close analysis of the stereotypes involved and careful scrutiny of the pregnancy rationale. The role that the challenged statute plays in reinforcing those harms is never examined. The Court accepts as immutable fact that men and women are not similarly situated, particularly when pregnancy is involved. The Court then appears to favor equal rights for women, but for one small problem—pregnancy.

As an ideological matter, the separation of pregnancy and childbearing capacity, social discrimination, and even legally imposed discrimination from "invidious" discrimination, in which differential treatment is unrelated to "real" differences between men and women, perform an important function of legitimizing discrimination through the language of equality.[69] Although its doctrinal veneer is different, the Court's approach in *Michael M.* has the same effect as *Bradwell* and *Muller.* If both pregnancy and socially imposed differences in role always keep men and women from being similarly situated—thereby excluding sex-based differences from the purview of equal protection—then the real substance of sex discrimination can still be ignored. Childbearing capacity is the single greatest basis of differential treatment for women—it is a major source of discrimination in both work and family life, and the critical distinction on which the ideology of both separate spheres and physical differences rests. Yet, by appearing to reject gross generalizations about proper roles of the sexes exemplified by both *Bradwell* and *Muller,* current ideology attempts to maintain credibility by "holding out the promise of liberation."[70] By emphasizing its reliance on a reality that appears more closely tied to physical differences and the hard facts of social disadvantage, e.g., the consequences of teenage pregnancy for young girls, the Court appears sensible and compromising. Indeed, the message of the Court's approach is merely to reject "ultra feminist" androgyny while favoring equality generally. However, by excluding the core of sex discrimination, the Court is effectively removing women entirely from the reach of equal protection.

VMI: THE CONTINUING CONTRADICTIONS OF "DIFFERENCE"

In 1996, the Supreme Court ruled in *United States v. Virginia* that the Virginia Military Institute had to open its doors to women and that Virginia could not maintain sex-segregated educational institutions with different programs, resources, and alumni networks.[71] After several months of uncertainty, VMI decided to comply by admitting women and holding them to the same standards as men, including shaved heads and gauntlet running through a "rat-line" of shouting upperclassmen.[72]

In so doing, the Court faced an argument long rejected in the racial context—whether "separate but equal" facilities met a state's obligation under the equal protection clause. Virginia defended VMI's practice of excluding women in large measure by pointing to the Virginia Women's Institute for Leadership program offered to women at Mary Baldwin College. The state argued that when it comes to women and men, "separate but equal"— invalidated as to race starting with the 1954 *Brown v. Board of Education* decision—is all that is required.[73] Rather than directly considering this argument, the Court, using a technique that preceded *Brown*, focused on the many ways that the Mary Baldwin program was inferior.

The majority opinion, written by Justice Ruth Bader Ginsburg, who earlier in her career was a leading advocate for women's rights, uses language that could be interpreted to heighten the standard of judicial review in gender discrimination cases. The highest level of review, called "strict scrutiny," has been applied to race and ethnic discrimination, but sex discrimination has received "intermediate scrutiny." Intermediate scrutiny requires the government to show its action is justified by an "important" (rather than a "compelling") governmental interest and the means selected is "substantially related" (not the only means necessary) to that end. Ginsburg's opinion incorporates terms associated with strict scrutiny into new phrases—particularly "skeptical scrutiny" and "exceedingly persuasive justification"—suggesting that the Court is moving toward heightened scrutiny in sex discrimination cases. This may reflect an attempt by Ginsburg to incrementally move the Court.

In any event, the Court reaffirmed that "inherent differences" between women and men may still be a basis for constitutionally distinguishing between the sexes (although it is invalid as between races or ethnicities), as long as such differences are not used "for the denigration of either sex or for artificial constraints on an individual's opportunity." This is helpful in that the Court was explicit about the invalidity of limiting women who wish military training on the ground that most women do not want it and may not be qualified for it. However, the line between permissible and impermissible sex classifications is not clear, particularly since the Court said that gender differences "remain a cause for celebration." Will the celebration extend to allowing or glorifying different social roles? The *VMI* opinion does not offer much concrete guidance.

The legal ideology of equality shows progress from *Bradwell* to *Michael M.* to *VMI*—but less than we might expect. The Court's view of the sexes, and of women in particular, has moved from an overt, rigid conception of women's separate roles to a more subtle notion of limited differences. This more subtle notion could, of course, be put to different uses, particularly since it has now been articulated by Justice Ginsburg.

Yet, given the particular facts before it, the *VMI* Court did not consider the problem of the degree to which the assessment of qualifications is influenced by gender. Instead, the Court simply underscored that when women seek to be like men, they must be given the opportunity to do so. The Court did not reach broader questions concerning the meaning of sexual equality: Can women choose to be like women and still be equal? Should activities unique to women, such as giving birth, be specially recognized and benefited? Are there special qualities that only women, or women to a greater extent than men, possess? What are the implications of these differences of gender equality?

The *VMI* case is certainly a step forward from earlier decisions, particularly in light of the negative views of women in the military. But we have yet to see how big the step was.

NOTES

The authors gratefully acknowledge the assistance of Ann Freedman and David Kairys in the development of this chapter.

1. As David Kairys explains in the Introduction to this book, American legal doctrine distinguishes sharply between the public and the private sectors. Focusing on the question of governmental versus private control, the distinction plays an important role in disguising the limited nature of the rights afforded people in general. A distinction between public and private spheres also characterizes the law relating to women, but in this context *public* has a much broader and *private* a much narrower meaning. *Public* refers to governmental and market matters, whereas *private* refers to the domestic or family realm.

2. There is some evidence that during colonial times, when the household was the unit of production, the law intervened more directly in the home. Thus, it may be more appropriate to speak of the law's withdrawal rather than its absence from the domestic sphere.

3. This section draws heavily on Kathryn Powers's article, *Sex Segregation and the Ambivalent Directions of Sex Discrimination Law,* 1979 Wisconsin Law Review 55 (1979).

4. Eleanor Flexner, *A Century of Struggle*, rev. ed. (Cambridge, MA: Harvard University Press, 1975).

5. *Hoyt v. Florida*, 368 U.S. 57, 61 (1961). In *Taylor v. Louisiana*, 419 U.S. 522 (1975), a case involving a male rape defendant, the Supreme Court tacitly overruled *Hoyt*.

6. 10 U.S.C. § 6015; 10 U.S.C. § 8549 (Navy and Air Force). The Army and Marine Corps preclude the role of women in combat as a matter of established policy; *Rostker v. Goldberg*, 453 U.S. 57, 76 (1981), upholding the all-male draft registration scheme.

7. There is a dispute as to whether women's actual status during the colonial period corresponded to the position accorded them by law. Compare Mary Ryan, *Womanhood in America*, 2d ed. (New York: New Viewpoints, 1979), and Albie Sachs and Joan Hoff Wilson, *Sexism and the Law* (New York: Free Press, 1978), with Mary Beth Norton, *Liberty's Daughters: The Revolutionary Experience of American Women* (Boston: Little, Brown, 1980).

8. By 1978, 56 percent of all women over sixteen worked at least part of the year; in 1950 the figure was below 30 percent. Excluding farm workers, before 1900 less than 20 percent of all women were in the paid labor force. Alice Kessler-Harris, *Women Have Always Worked: A Historical Overview* (Old Westbury, NY: Feminist Press, 1981), 70, 147.

9. The Equal Pay Act of 1963 and Title VII of the Civil Rights Act of 1964 provided civil remedies for employment discrimination; private discrimination in the housing and credit markets was prohibited in 1974.

10. See *Dothard v. Rawlinson*, 433 U.S. 321, 336 (1977). See also *Phillips v. Martin Marietta Corp.*, 400 U.S. 542 (1971), suggesting that a company could legally deny jobs to women with preschool children if it could show that such children interfered more with female workers as a group than with male workers as a group.

11. See *Vorchheimer v. School District of Philadelphia*, 430 U.S. 703 (1977), affirmed by an equally divided court. Separate but equal was rejected in the racial context in 1954 (*Brown v. Board of Education*, 347 U.S. 483 [1954]).

12. See, for example, *Weinberger v. Wiesenfeld*, 420 U.S. 636 (1975); *Califano v. Goldfarb*, 430 U.S. 199 (1977); *Califano v. Westcott*, 443 U.S. 76 (1979).

13. See Barbara A. Babcock et al., *Sex Discrimination and the Law: Causes and Remedies* (Boston: Little, Brown, 1975), 782–800.

14. *United States v. Nicholas*, 97 F.2d 510 (2d Cir. 1938); see generally, Linda Gordon, *Woman's Body, Woman's Right* (New York: Penguin, 1977).

15. *Griswold v. Connecticut*, 381 U.S. 479 (1965).

16. *Eisenstadt v. Baird*, 405 U.S. 438 (1972).

17. *Roe v. Wade*, 410 U.S. 113 (1973).

18. Ibid.; *Doe v. Bolton*, 410 U.S. 179 (1973).

19. *Maher v. Roe*, 432 U.S. 464 (1977); *H. L. v. Matheson*, 450 U.S. 398 (1981).

20. *Webster v. Reproductive Services*, 109 S.Ct. 3040 (1989).

21. For a similar analogy, see Powers, *Sex Segregation*, 76.

22. Recent limitations on interspousal immunity may be due in part to the recognition of the role played by insurance, a factor that removes the situation from the private sphere and places it in the public realm.

23. The law's absence from the realm of personal relationships is even more conspicuous when the relationships lack official sanction. Lesbians, for example, are not barred from relief by intrafamily immunity doctrines only because the law does not allow them to solemnize or otherwise gain public recognition of their relationship.

24. Lisa Lerman, *Mediation of Wife-Abuse Cases: The Adverse Impact of Mediation on Women*, 7 Harvard Women's Law Journal 57, 58 (1984), citing Frank Sander.

25. See especially chapter 24 of this volume.

26. 381 U.S. 479 (1965).

27. 410 U.S. 113 (1973).

28. *Maher v. Roe*, 432 U.S. 464 (1977); *Harris v. McCrae*, 448 U.S. 297 (1980).

29. 492 U.S. 490 (1989).

30. 505 U.S. 833 (1992).

31. Brief of 281 American Historians as Amici Curiae Supporting Appellees in *Webster v. Reproductive Services*.

32. Carol Smith-Rosenberg, *Disorderly Conduct* (New York: Knopf, 1985), 235.

33. Brief of 281 Historians.

34. Much of the material regarding the first two cases has been drawn from Babcock et al., *Sex Discrimination and the Law*.

35. *Bradwell v. Illinois*, 83 U.S. (16 Wall.) 130 (1873).

36. Arabella Mansfield of Iowa had become the first woman regularly admitted to practice law in the United States in 1869.

37. See Ryan, *Womanhood in America;* Nancy F. Cott, *The Bonds of Womanhood* (New Haven, CT: Yale University Press, 1977); Kessler-Harris, *Women Have Always Worked*.

38. Only about 10 percent of all women worked in the paid labor force in the mid-1840s. The percentage did not rise above 20 percent before 1900. Kessler-Harris, *Women Have Always Worked*, 61, 70.

39. See Cott, *The Bonds of Womanhood*, 197–99.

40. See generally Ellen C. DuBois, *Elizabeth Cady Stanton and Susan B. Anthony: Correspondence, Writings, and Speeches* (New York: Schocken, 1981).

41. 83 U.S. (16 Wall.) 130, 141–42 (1873).

42. 198 U.S. 45 (1905).

43. Babcock et al., *Sex Discrimination and the Law*, 28.

44. 208 U.S. 412 (1908).

45. This brief has come to be known mistakenly as the first Brandeis brief, since Louis Brandeis actually filed it, although Josephine Goldmark, Florence Kelly, and other volunteers assembled the data. Babcock et al., *Sex Discrimination and the Law*, 29.

46. *Muller v. Oregon*, 208 U.S. at 421–22.

47. Sex-based protective legislation was considered valid until a series of court decisions between 1968 and 1973 invalidated such statutes. A few statutes, however, remain on the books today.

48. See Heidi Hartmann, "Capitalism, Patriarchy, and Job Segregation by Sex," *Signs*, 1 (1976): 137.

49. See, for example, *Hoyt v. Florida*, 368 U.S. 57 (1961).

50. 404 U.S. 71 (1971).

51. See generally Joseph Tussman and Jacobus TenBroek, *The Equal Protection of the Laws*, 37 California Law Review 341 (1949).

52. *Reed v. Reed,* 404 U.S. at 75.

53. Most of these cases have involved assumptions built into government benefit statutes that the male was the breadwinner and the female the dependent at home. See *Frontiero v. Richardson,* 411 U.S. 677 (1973); *Weinberger v. Wiesenfeld,* 420 U.S. 636 (1975); *Califano v. Goldfarb,* 430 U.S. 199 (1977); *Califano v. Westcott,* 443 U.S. 76 (1979).

54. 411 U.S. 677 (1973).

55. Ibid., 684.

56. 421 U.S. 7 (1975).

57. Ibid., 14–15.

58. In *Craig v. Boren,* 429 U.S. 190, 197 (1976), the Court articulated the standard that "to withstand constitutional challenge, classifications by gender must serve important governmental objectives and must be substantially related to achievement of those objectives."

59. 417 U.S. 484 (1974).

60. Ibid., 496, n. 20.

61. 429 U.S. 125 (1976). The Supreme Court's view of pregnancy expressed in *Gilbert* was promptly rejected by Congress. Pregnancy Discrimination Act, 26 U.S.C. § 3304(a)(12) (1976).

62. See *Schlesinger v. Ballard,* 419 U.S. 498 (1975); *Rostker v. Goldberg,* 453 U.S. 57 (1981). But see *Caban v. Mohammed,* 441 U.S. 380, 398 (1979), Stewart dissenting.

63. 441 U.S. 347 (1979).

64. 450 U.S. 464 (1981).

65. See *The Constitutionality of Statutory Rape Laws,* 27 UCLA Law Review 757, 761 (1980); *Michael M. v. Sonoma County,* 159 Cal. 3d 340, 601 P.2d 572 (1979), Mosk dissenting. Leigh Bienen, *Rape III: National Developments in Rape Reform Legislation,* 6 Women's Rights Law Reporter 170, 189 (1981).

66. 450 U.S. at 471.

67. Ibid., 473.

68. Ibid., 477–79.

69. See especially chapter 13 of this volume; Alan Freeman, *Legitimizing Racial Discrimination Through Antidiscrimination Law: A Critical Review of Supreme Court Doctrine,* 62 Minnesota Law Review 1050 (1978).

70. Ibid., 1052.

71. 116 S.Ct. 2264 (1996).

72. Mike Allen, "Defiant VMI to Admit Women, but Will Not Ease Rules for Them," *New York Times,* September 22, 1996, 1.

73. 347 U.S. 483 (1954).

16 KIMBERLÉ CRENSHAW

A BLACK FEMINIST CRITIQUE OF ANTIDISCRIMINATION LAW AND POLITICS

THE title of one of the very few Black women's studies books, *All the Women Are White, All the Blacks Are Men, But Some of Us Are Brave*, sets forth a problematic consequence of the tendency to treat race and gender as mutually exclusive categories of experience and analysis.[1] This tendency is perpetuated by a single-axis framework dominant in antidiscrimination law and reflected in feminist theory and antiracist politics that distorts the multidimensionality of Black women's experiences and undermines efforts to broaden feminist and antiracist analyses.

THE ANTIDISCRIMINATION FRAMEWORK

One way to approach the problem at the intersection of race and sex is to examine how courts frame and interpret the stories of Black women plaintiffs. Indeed, the way courts interpret claims made by Black women is itself part of Black women's experience; consequently, a cursory review of cases involving black female plaintiffs is quite revealing. To illustrate the difficulties inherent in judicial treatment of intersectionality, I will consider three employment discrimination cases: *DeGraffenreid v. General Motors, Moore v. Hughes Helicopter,* and *Payne v. Travenol.*[2]

In *DeGraffenreid*, five Black women brought suit against General Motors, alleging that the employer's seniority system perpetuated the effects of past discrimination against Black women. Although General Motors did not hire Black women prior to 1964, the court noted that "General Motors has hired . . . female employees for a number of years prior to the enactment of the Civil Rights Act of 1964." Because General

Motors did hire women—albeit *white women*—during the period that no Black women were hired, there was, in the court's view, no sex discrimination that the seniority system could conceivably have perpetuated. Moreover, reasoning that Black women could choose to bring either a sex or a race discrimination claim, but not both, the court stated:

> The legislative history surrounding Title VII does not indicate that the goal of the statute was to create a new classification of "black women" who would have greater standing than, for example, a black male. The prospect of the creation of new classes of protected minorities, governed only by the mathematical principles of permutation and combination, clearly raises the prospect of opening the hackneyed Pandora's box.

The court's conclusion that Congress did not intend to allow Black women to make a compound claim arises from its inability to imagine that discrimination against Black women can exist independently from the experiences of white women or of Black men. Because the court was blind to this possibility, it did not question whether Congress could have meant to leave this form of discrimination unredressed. Assuming therefore that there was no distinct discrimination suffered by Black women, the court concluded that to allow plaintiffs to make a compound claim would unduly advantage Black women over Black men or white women.

This negative conclusion regarding Black women's ability to bring compound claims has not been replicated in another kind of compound discrimination case—"reverse discrimination" claims brought by white males. Interestingly, no case has been discovered in which a court denied a white male's reverse discrimination claims on similar grounds—that is, that sex and race claims cannot be combined because Congress did not intend to protect compound classes. Yet, white males challenging affirmative action programs that benefit minorities and women are actually in no better position to make a race and gender claim than the Black women in *DeGraffenreid*: If white men are required to make their claims separately, they cannot prove race discrimination because white women are not discriminated against, and they cannot prove sex discrimination because Black males are not discriminated against. One would think, therefore, that the logic of *DeGraffenreid* would complicate reverse discrimination cases. That Black women's claims raise the question of compound discrimination while white males' reverse discrimination claims do not suggests that the notion of "compound class" is somehow relative or contingent on some presumed norm rather than definitive and absolute. If that norm is understood to be white male, one can understand how Black women, being "two steps removed" from being white men, are deemed to be a compound class while white men are not. Indeed, if assumptions about objectivity of law are replaced with the subjective perspective of white males, one can understand better not only why Black women are viewed as compound classes and white men are not, but also why the boundaries of sex and race discrimination doctrine are defined respectively by the experiences of white women and Black men. Consider first that when a white male imagines being a female, he probably imagines being a white female. Similarly, a white male who must project himself as Black will no doubt imagine himself to be a Black male, thereby holding constant all other characteristics except race.

Antidiscrimination law is similarly constructed from the perspective of white males. Gender discrimination, imagined from the perspective of white men, is what happens to white women; race discrimination is what happens to Black men. The dominance of the single-axis framework, most starkly represented by *DeGraffenreid*, not only marginalizes Black women but simultaneously privileges the subjectivity of white men. Under this view, Black women are protected only to the extent that their experiences coincide with those of either of the two groups. Where their experiences are distinct, Black women will encounter difficulty articulating their claims as long as approaches prevail which completely obscure problems of intersectionality.[3]

Moore v. Hughes Helicopters, Inc. presents a different way in which courts fail to understand or recognize Black women's claims. *Moore* is typical of cases in which courts refused to certify Black females as class representatives in race *and* sex discrimination actions.[4] In *Moore*, the plaintiff alleged that the employer, Hughes Helicopter, practiced race and sex discrimination in promotions to upper-level craft positions and to supervisory jobs. Moore introduced statistical evidence establishing a significant disparity between men and women, and somewhat less of a disparity between Black and white men in supervisory jobs.

Affirming the district court's refusal to certify Moore as the class representative in the sex discrimination complaint on behalf of all women at Hughes, the Ninth Circuit noted approvingly:

> Moore had never claimed before the EEOC that she was discriminated against as a female, but only as a Black female. . . . [T]his raised serious doubts as to Moore's ability to adequately represent white female employees.

The curious logic in *Moore* reveals not only the narrow scope of antidiscrimination doctrine and its failure to embrace intersectionality, but also the centrality of white female experiences in the conceptualization of gender discrimination. The court rejected Moore's bid to represent all females apparently because her attempt to specify her race was seen as being at odds with the standard allegation that the employer simply discriminated "against females." However, the court failed to see that the absence of a racial referent does not necessarily mean that the claim being made is a more inclusive one. A white woman claiming discrimination against females may be in no better position to represent all women than a Black woman who claims discrimination as a Black female and wants to represent all females. The court's preferred articulation of "against females" is not necessarily more inclusive—it just appears to be so because the racial contours of the claim are not specified.

The court's preference for "against females" rather than "against Black females" reveals the implicit grounding of white female experiences in the doctrinal conceptualization of sex discrimination. For white women, claiming sex discrimination is simply a statement that but for gender, they would not have been disadvantaged. For them there is no need to specify discrimination as *white* females because their race does not contribute to the disadvantage for which they seek redress. The view of discrimination that is derived from this grounding takes race privilege as a given.

Discrimination against a white female is thus the standard sex discrimination claim; claims that diverge from this standard appear to present some sort of hybrid claim. More significantly, because Black females' claims are seen as hybrid, they sometimes cannot represent those who may have "pure" claims of sex discrimination. The effect of this approach is that even though a challenged policy or practice may clearly discriminate against all females, the fact that it has particularly harsh consequences for Black females places Black plaintiffs at odds with white females.

The *Moore* court also denied the plaintiffs' bid to represent Black males, leaving Moore with the task of supporting her race and sex discrimination claims with statistical evidence of discrimination against Black females alone. Because she was unable to represent white women or Black men, she could not use overall statistics on sex disparity at Hughes, nor could she use statistics on race. Proving her claim using statistics on Black women alone was no small task, due to the fact that she was bringing the suit under a disparate impact theory of discrimination.

The court's rulings on Moore's sex and race claim left her with such a small statistical sample that even if she had proved that there were qualified Black women, she could not have shown discrimination under a disparate impact theory. *Moore* illustrates yet another way that antidiscrimination doctrine essentially erases Black women's distinct experiences and, as a result, deems their discrimination complaints groundless.

Finally, Black female plaintiffs have sometimes encountered difficulty in their efforts to win certification as class representatives in some race discrimination actions. This problem typically arises in cases where statistics suggest significant disparities between Black and white workers and further disparities between Black men and Black women. Courts in some cases have denied certification based on logic that mirrors the rationale in *Moore*: The sex disparities between Black men and Black women created such conflicting interests that Black women could not possibly represent Black men adequately.[5] In one such case, *Payne v. Travenol*, two Black female plaintiffs alleging race discrimination brought a class action suit on behalf of all Black employees at a pharmaceutical plant. The court refused, however, to allow the plaintiffs to represent Black males and granted the defendant's request to narrow the class to Black women only. Ultimately, the district court found that there had been extensive racial discrimination at the plant and awarded back pay and constructive seniority to the class of Black female employees. But, despite its finding of general race discrimination, the court refused to extend the remedy to Black men for fear that their conflicting interests would not be adequately addressed; the Fifth Circuit affirmed.

Even though *Travenol* was a partial victory for Black women, the case specifically illustrates how antidiscrimination doctrine generally creates a dilemma for Black women. It forces them to choose between specifically articulating the intersectional aspects of their subordination, thereby risking their ability to represent Black men, or ignoring intersectionality in order to state a claim that would not lead to the exclusion of Black men. When one considers the political consequences of this dilemma, there is little wonder that many people within the Black community view the specific articulation of Black women's interests as dangerously divisive.

In sum, several courts have proved unable to deal with intersectionality, although for contrasting reasons. In *DeGraffenreid*, the court refused to recognize the possibility of compound discrimination against Black women and analyzed their claim using the employment of white women as the historical base. As a consequence, the employment experiences of white women obscured the distinct discrimination that Black women experienced.[6]

Conversely, in *Moore*, the court held that a Black woman could not use statistics reflecting the overall sex disparity in supervisory and upper-level labor jobs because she had not claimed discrimination as a woman, but "only" as a Black woman. The court would not entertain the notion that discrimination experienced by Black women is indeed sex discrimination—provable through disparate impact statistics on women.[7]

Finally, courts such as the one in *Travenol* have held that Black women cannot represent an entire class of Blacks due to presumed class conflicts in cases where sex additionally disadvantaged Black women. As a result, in the few cases where Black women are allowed to use overall statistics indicating racially disparate treatment, Black men may not be able to share in the remedy.[8]

Perhaps it appears to some that I have offered inconsistent criticisms of how Black women are treated in antidiscrimination law: I seem to be saying that in one case, Black women's claims were rejected and their experiences obscured because the court refused to acknowledge that the employment experience of Black women can be distinct from that of white women, while in other cases, the interests of Black women were harmed because Black women's claims were viewed as so distinct from the claims of either white women or Black men that the court denied to Black females representation of the larger class. It seems that I have to say that Black women are the same and harmed by being treated differently, or that they are different and harmed by being treated the same. But I cannot say both.

This apparent contradiction is but another manifestation of the conceptual limitations of the single-issue analyses that intersectionality challenges. The point is that Black women can experience discrimination in any number of ways and that the contradiction arises from our assumptions that their claims of exclusion must be unidirectional. Consider an analogy to traffic in an intersection, coming and going in all four directions. Discrimination, like traffic through an intersection, may flow in one direction, and it may flow in another. If an accident happens in an intersection, it can be caused by cars traveling from any number of directions and, sometimes, from all of them. Similarly, if a Black woman is harmed because she is in the intersection, her injury could result from sex discrimination or race discrimination or both.

Providing legal relief only when Black women prove that their claims are based on race or on sex is analogous to calling an ambulance for the victim only after the driver responsible for the injuries is identified. But it is not always easy to identify the driver: sometimes the skid marks and the injuries simply indicate that they occurred simultaneously, frustrating efforts to determine which driver caused the harm. In these cases the tendency seems to be that no driver is held responsible, no treatment is administered, and the involved parties simply get back in their cars and zoom away.

I am suggesting that Black women can experience discrimination in ways that are both similar to and different from those experienced by white women and Black men. Black women sometimes experience discrimination in ways similar to white women's experiences; sometimes they share very similar experiences with Black men. Yet often they experience double discrimination—the combined effects of practices which discriminate on the basis of race, and on the basis of sex. And sometimes, they experience discrimination as Black women—not the sum of race and sex discrimination, but as Black women.

DeGraffenreid, Moore, and *Travenol* are doctrinal manifestations of a common political and theoretical approach to discrimination which operates to marginalize Black women. Unable to grasp the importance of Black women's intersectional experiences, not only courts, but feminist and civil rights thinkers as well have treated Black women in ways that deny both the unique compoundedness of their situation and the centrality of their experiences to the larger classes of women and Blacks. Consequently, their needs and perspectives have been relegated to the margin of the feminist and Black liberationist agendas. While it could be argued that this marginalization represents an absence of political will to include Black women, I believe that it reflects an uncritical and disturbing acceptance of dominant ways of thinking about discrimination.

Underlying dominant conceptions of discrimination, which have been challenged by a developing approach called critical race theory, is a view that the wrong which antidiscrimination law addresses is the use of race or gender factors to interfere with decisions that would otherwise be fair or neutral.[9] This process-based definition is not grounded in a bottom-up commitment to improve the substantive conditions for those who are victimized by the interplay of numerous factors. Instead, the dominant message of antidiscrimination law is that it will regulate only the limited extent to which race or sex interferes with the process of determining outcomes. This narrow objective is facilitated by the top-down strategy of using a singular "but for" analysis to ascertain the effects of race or sex. Because the scope of antidiscrimination law is so limited, sex and race discrimination have come to be defined in terms of the experiences of those who are privileged *but for* their racial or sexual characteristics. Put differently, the paradigm of sex discrimination tends to be based on the experiences of white women; the model of race discrimination tends to be based on the experiences of the most privileged Blacks. Notions of what constitutes race and sex discrimination are, as a result, narrowly tailored to embrace only a small set of circumstances which do not explicitly include the experiences of Black women.

To the extent that this general description is accurate, the following analogy can be useful in describing how Black women are marginalized in the interface between antidiscrimination law and race and gender hierarchies: imagine a basement which contains all people who are disadvantaged on the basis of race, sex, class, sexual preference, age and/or physical ability. These people are stacked—feet standing on shoulders—with those on the bottom being disadvantaged by the full array of factors, up to the very top, where the heads of all those disadvantaged by a singular factor brush up against the ceiling. Their ceiling is actually the floor above which only those who are not disadvantaged in any way reside. In efforts to correct some aspects of domination, those above the ceiling admit from the basement only those who can say that "but for" the ceiling, they too would be in the upper room. A hatch is developed through which those placed immediately below can crawl. Yet this hatch is generally available only to those who—due to the singularity of their burden and their otherwise privileged position relative to those below—are in the position to crawl through. Those who are multiply burdened are generally left below unless they can somehow pull themselves into the groups that are permitted to squeeze through the hatch.

As this analogy translates for Black women, the problem is that they can receive protection only to the extent that their experiences are recognizably similar to those whose experiences tend to be reflected in antidiscrimination doctrine. If Black women cannot conclusively say that "but for" their race or "but for" their gender they would be treated differently, they are not invited to climb through the hatch but told to wait in the unprotected margin until they can be absorbed into the broader, protected categories of race and sex.

Despite the narrow scope of this dominant conception of discrimination and its tendency to marginalize those whose experiences cannot be described within its tightly drawn parameters, this approach has been regarded as the appropriate framework for addressing a range of problems. In much of feminist theory and, to some extent in antiracist politics, this framework is reflected in the belief that sexism or racism can be meaningfully discussed without paying attention to the lives of those other than the race-, gender-, or class-privileged. As a result, both feminist theory and antiracist politics have been organized, in part, around the equation of sexism with what happens to white women and the equation of racism with what happens to the Black middle class or to Black men.

Looking at historical and contemporary issues in both the feminist and the civil rights communities, one can find ample evidence of how both communities' acceptance of the dominant framework of discrimination has hindered the development of an adequate theory and praxis to address problems of intersectionality. Not only does this adoption of a single-issue framework for discrimination marginalize Black women within the very movements that claim them as part of their constituency but it also makes the illusive goal of ending racism and patriarchy even more difficult to attain.

FEMINISM AND BLACK WOMEN: "AIN'T WE WOMEN?"

Oddly, despite the relative inability of feminist politics and theory to address Black women substantively, feminist critics and scholars borrow considerably from Black women's history. For example, "Ain't I a Woman" has come to represent a standard refrain in feminist discourse.[10] Yet the lesson of this powerful oratory is not fully appreciated because the context of the delivery is seldom examined.

In 1851, Sojourner Truth declared "Ain't I a Woman?" and challenged the sexist imagery used by male critics to justify the disenfranchisement of women.[11] The scene was a Women's Rights Conference in Akron, Ohio; white male hecklers, invoking stereotypical images of "womanhood," argued that women were too frail and delicate to take on the responsibilities of political activity. When Sojourner Truth rose to speak, many white women urged that she be silenced, fearing that she would divert attention from women's suffrage to emancipation. Truth, once permitted to speak, recounted the horrors of slavery, and its particular impact on Black women:

> Look at my arm! I have ploughed and planted and gathered into barns, and no man could head me—and ain't I a woman? I could work as much and eat as much as a man—when I could get it—and bear the lash as well! And ain't I a woman? I have born thirteen children, and seen most of 'em

sold into slavery, and when I cried out with my mother's grief, none but Jesus heard me—and ain't I a woman?[12]

By using her own life to reveal the contradiction between the ideological myths of womanhood and the reality of Black women's experience, Truth's oratory provided a powerful rebuttal to the claim that women were categorically weaker than men. Yet Truth's personal challenge to the coherence of the cult of true womanhood was useful only to the extent that white women were willing to reject the most racist attempts to rationalize the contradiction; such rationalizations were premised on the belief that because Black women were something less than real women, their experiences had no bearing on true womanhood. Thus, this nineteenth-century Black feminist not only challenged patriarchy, but she also challenged white feminists wishing to embrace Black women's history to relinquish their vested interest in whiteness.

To inherit the legacy of Truth's challenge to patriarchy, contemporary white feminists must also accept Truth's challenge to their forebears. Even today, white women's difficulty in sacrificing racial privilege renders them susceptible to Truth's critical question. When feminist theory and politics that claim to reflect *women's* experience and *women's* aspirations do not include or speak to Black women, Black women must ask: "Ain't *We* Women?" If this is so, how can the claims that "women are," "women believe," and "women need" be made when such claims are inapplicable or unresponsive to the needs, interests, and experiences of Black women?

The value of feminist theory to Black women is diminished because it evolves from a white racial context that is seldom acknowledged. Not only are women of color in fact overlooked, but their exclusion is reinforced when *white* women speak for and as *women*. The authoritative universal voice—usually white male subjectivity masquerading as nonracial, nongendered objectivity—is merely transferred to those who, but for gender, share many of the same cultural, economic, and social characteristics.[13] When feminist theory attempts to describe women's experiences through analyzing patriarchy, sexuality, or separate-spheres ideology, it often overlooks the role of race. White feminists thus ignore how their own race functions to mitigate some aspects of sexism and, moreover, how it often privileges them over and contributes to the domination of other women.[14] Consequently, feminist theory remains *white*, and its potential to broaden and deepen its analysis by addressing nonprivileged women remains unrealized.

An example of how some feminist theories are narrowly constructed around white women's experiences is found in the separate spheres literature. The critique of how separate spheres ideology shapes and limits women's roles in the home and in public life is a central theme in feminist legal thought.[15] Feminists have attempted to expose and dismantle separate spheres ideology by identifying and criticizing the stereotypes that traditionally have justified the disparate societal roles assigned to men and women. Yet this attempt to debunk ideological justifications for *women's* subordination offers little insight into the domination of Black women. Because the experiential base upon which many feminist insights are grounded is white, theoretical statements drawn from them are overgeneralized at best, and often wrong.[16] Statements such as "men and women are taught to see men as independent, capable, powerful; men and women are taught to see women as dependent, limited in abilities, and passive," are common in this literature. But this "observation" overlooks the anomalies created by crosscurrents of racism and sexism. Black men and women live in a society that creates sex-based norms and expectations which racism operates simultaneously to deny; Black men are not viewed as powerful, nor are Black women seen as passive. An effort to develop an ideological explanation of gender domination in the Black community should proceed from an understanding of how crosscutting forces establish gender norms and how the conditions of Black subordination wholly frustrate access to these norms. Given this understanding, perhaps we can begin to see why Black women have been dogged by the stereotype of the pathological matriarch or why there have been those in the Black liberation movement who aspire to create institutions and to build traditions that embrace and celebrate patriarchy.[17] For example, Black families have sometimes been cast as pathological largely because of Black women's divergence from the white middle-class female norm. The most infamous rendition of this view is found in the Moynihan report (discussed further), which blamed many of the Black community's ills on a supposed pathological family structure.

Because ideological and descriptive definitions of patriarchy are usually premised upon white female experiences, feminists and others informed by feminist literature may make the mistake of assuming that since the role of Black women in the family and in other Black institutions does not always resemble the familiar manifestations of patriarchy in the white community, Black women are somehow exempt from patriarchal norms. For example, Black women have traditionally worked outside the home in numbers far exceeding the labor participation rate of white women.[18] An analysis of patriarchy that highlights the history of white women's exclusion from the workplace might permit the inference that Black women have not been burdened by this particular gender-based discrimination. Yet the very fact that Black women must work outside the home has conflicted with normative expectations that women remain in the home, often creating emotional strife within their personal lives. Thus, Black women are burdened not only because they often have to take on responsibilities that are not traditionally feminine but, moreover, because their assumption of these roles has sometimes been interpreted within the Black community as either Black women's failure to live up to patriarchal norms or as another manifestation of racism's scourge upon the Black community.[19] This is one of the many aspects of intersectionality that cannot be understood through an analysis of patriarchy rooted in white experience.

Another example of how theory emanating from a white context obscures the multidimensionality of Black women's lives is found in feminist discourse on rape. A central political issue on the feminist agenda has been the pervasive problem of rape. Part of the intellectual and political effort to mobilize around this issue has involved the development of a historical critique of the role that law has played in establishing the bounds of normative sexuality and in regulating female sexual behavior.[20] Early carnal-knowledge statutes and rape laws are understood within this discourse to illustrate that the objective of such statutes traditionally has not been to protect women from coercive intimacy but to protect and maintain a propertylike interest in female chastity. Although feminists quite rightly criticize these objectives, to characterize rape law as reflecting male control over female sexuality is for Black women an oversimplified and ultimately inadequate account.

Rape statutes generally do not reflect *male* control over *female* sexuality, but *white* male regulation of *white* female sexuality. Historically, there has been absolutely no institutional effort to "protect" Black female chastity.[21] Courts in some states had gone so far as to instruct juries that unlike white women, Black women were not presumed to be chaste. For example: "What has been said by some of our courts about an unchaste female being a comparatively rare exception is no doubt true where the population is composed largely of the Caucasian race, but we would blind ourselves to actual conditions if we adopted this rule where another race that is largely immoral constitutes an appreciable part of the population."[22] Also, while it was true that the attempt to regulate the sexuality of white women placed unchaste women outside the law's protection, racism restored a fallen white woman's chastity where the alleged assailant was a Black man.[23] No such restoration was available to Black women.

The singular focus on rape as a manifestation of male power over female sexuality tends to eclipse the use of rape as a weapon of racial terror.[24] When Black women were raped by white males, they were being raped as Black women specifically: their femaleness made them sexually vulnerable to racist domination, while their blackness effectively denied them any protection.[25] This white male power was reinforced by a judicial system in which the successful conviction of a white man for raping a Black woman was virtually unthinkable.

In sum, both the failure of feminism to address the interplay of race and gender in constructing Black and white female sexuality and the failure to appreciate fully the close connection between historical constructions of white female sexuality and racial terrorism contribute to feminism's inability to politicize sexual violence in ways that speak to and include Black women. Sexist expectations of chastity and racist assumptions of sexual promiscuity thus combined to create a distinct set of issues confronting Black women.[26] These issues have seldom been explored in feminist literature; nor have they been prominent in antiracist politics. The lynching of Black men, the institutional practice legitimized by the oppositional representations of Black male and white female sexuality, has historically occupied the Black agenda on sexuality and violence. Consequently, those who attempt to address sexual violence against Black women are caught between members of the Black community who, perhaps understandably, view with apprehension attempts to litigate questions of sexual violence and a feminist community that reinforces this suspicion by focusing on white female sexuality. Black concerns on this issue are premised on the historical fact that the protection of white female sexuality was often the pretext for terrorizing the Black community.[27] The difficulty is further compounded by the failure of some white feminists to acknowledge adequately the relationship between the constructed images of white female sexuality and racial terrorism.

Susan Brownmiller's discussion of the Emmett Till case illustrates the problem created by a solipsistic approach to rape that places white women's sexuality at the center of the analysis.[28] Despite Brownmiller's quite laudable efforts to discuss elsewhere the rape of Black women and the racism involved in much of the hysteria over the Black male threat, her analysis of the Till case places the sexuality of white women, rather than racial terrorism, at center stage. Brownmiller states: "Rarely has one single case exposed so clearly as Till's the underlying group-male antagonisms over access to women, for what began in Bryant's store should not be misconstrued as an innocent flirtation. . . . In concrete terms, the accessibility of all white women was on review." Later, Brownmiller argues:

> And what of the wolf whistle, Till's "gesture of adolescent bravado"? We are rightly aghast that a whistle could be cause for murder but we must also accept that Emmett Till and J. W. Millam shared something in common. They both understood that the whistle was no small tweet of hubba-hubba or melodious approval for a well-turned ankle. Given the deteriorated situation . . . it was a deliberate insult just short of physical assault, a last reminder to Carolyn Bryant that this black boy, Till, had a mind to possess her.

While Brownmiller seems to categorize the case as one that evidences a conflict over possession, it is regarded in African American history as a tragic dramatization of the South's pathological hatred and fear of African Americans. Till's body, mutilated beyond recognition, was viewed by thousands so that, in the words of Till's mother, "the world could see what they did to my boy." The Till tragedy is also regarded as one of the historical events that bore directly on the emergence of the civil rights movement. Juan Williams characterized its effect well: "[W]ithout question it moved black America in a way the Supreme Court ruling on school desegregation could not match. . . . [T]he murder of Emmett Till had a powerful impact on a generation of blacks. It was this generation, those who were adolescents when Till was killed, that would soon demand justice and freedom in a way unknown in America before."[29] Brownmiller's remarkable insensitivity to the horror of the Till case illustrates how centering the perspective of white women in feminist discourse can operate to minimize racial oppression and to alienate Black women.

This contributes to the fear among some Black women that antirape agendas may undermine antiracist objectives. The politicization of rape in both feminist and antiracist discourse also illustrates how Black women are caught between ideological and political currents that coalesce and often collide in the intersection of race and gender. The multidimensional experiences and interests created by these cross currents are marginalized within feminist and antiracist politics framed around unidimensional analyses.

INTEGRATING AN ANALYSIS OF SEXISM INTO BLACK LIBERATION POLITICS

Anna Julia Cooper, a nineteenth-century Black feminist, coined a phrase that has been useful in evaluating the need to incorporate an explicit analysis of patriarchy in any effort to address racial domination. Cooper often criticized Black leaders and spokespersons for claiming to speak for the race, but failing to speak for Black women. Referring to one of Martin Delaney's public claims that where he was allowed to enter, the race entered with him, Cooper countered: "Only the Black Woman can say, when and where I enter . . . then and there the whole Negro race enters with me."[30]

Cooper's words bring to mind a personal experience involving two Black men with whom I had formed a study group during our first year of law school. One of our group members, a graduate from Harvard College, often told us stories about a prestigious and exclusive men's club that boasted memberships of several past United States presidents and other influential white males. He was one of its very few Black members. To celebrate completing our first-year exams, our friend invited us to join him at the club for drinks. Anxious to see this fabled place, we approached the large door and grasped the brass door ring to announce our arrival. But our grand entrance was cut short when our friend sheepishly slipped from behind the door and whispered that he had forgotten a very important detail. My companion and I bristled, our training as Black people having taught us to expect yet another barrier to our inclusion; even an informal one-Black-person quota at the establishment was not unimaginable. The tension broke, however, when we learned that *we* would not be excluded because of our race, but that *I* would have to go around to the back door because I was a female. I entertained the idea of making a scene to dramatize the fact that my humiliation as a female was no less painful and my exclusion no more excusable than had we all been sent to the back door because we were Black. But, sensing no general assent to this proposition, and also being of the mind that due to our race a scene would in some way jeopardize all of us, I failed to stand my ground. After all, the club was about to entertain its first Black guests— even though one would have to enter through the back door.

Perhaps this story is not the best example of the Black community's failure to address problems related to Black women's intersectionality seriously. It would be more apt if Black women, and only Black women, had to go around to the back door of the club and if the restriction came from within and not from outside the Black community. Still, this story does reflect a decreased political and emotional vigilance toward barriers to Black women's enjoyment of privileges that have been won on the basis of race but continue to be denied on the basis of sex.[31]

The story also illustrates the ambivalence among Black women about the degree of political and social capital that should be expended toward challenging gender barriers, particularly when the challenges might conflict with the antiracism agenda. While there are a number of reasons—including antifeminist ones—why gender has not figured directly in analyses of the subordination of Black Americans, a central reason is that race is still seen by many as the primary oppositional force in Black lives.[32] If one accepts that the social experience of race creates both a primary group identity as well as a shared sense of being collectively assaulted, some of the reasons that Black feminist theory and politics have not figured prominently in the Black political agenda may be better understood.[33]

The experience of racial otherness that Black women share with Black men prevents Black feminist consciousness from patterning the development of white feminism. For white women, the creation of a consciousness that was distinct from and in opposition to that of white men figured prominently in the development of white feminist politics. Yet Black women, like Black men, live in a community that has been defined and subordinated by color.[34] Even though patriarchy clearly operates within the Black community, these shared experiences of white domination render the creation of a political consciousness that is oppositional to Black men untenable.

Yet while it is true that the distinct experience of racial otherness militates against the development of an oppositional feminist consciousness, the assertion of racial community sometimes supports defensive priorities that marginalize efforts to address and dismantle patriarchy within the Black community. This marginalization is apparent where artistic portrayals of sexism within the Black community meet with stiff resistance, or where discussions about economic and family policy uncritically embrace patriarchal values that compromise the interests of Black women. Examples of both of these tendencies can been seen in recent debates over dominant images of the Black family. *The Color Purple* controversy centered on allegations that Black men were categorically denigrated in Alice Walker's novel chronicling a Black woman's struggle against domestic abuse.[35] While it is clear that Black women are not immune from domestic violence, many critics viewed the story as dan-

gerous to the interests of the Black community because it gave credence
to violent stereotypes of Black males.[36] In short, the story of a Black
woman's quest to overcome physical and emotional abuse was viewed by
many as oppositional to the larger interest in combating racism. Such
issues—to the extent that they were valid concerns—should remain private, critics claimed.

The tendency to hold patriarchal values constant in the defense of
Black interests is also illustrated in the ongoing debate over the alleged
pathology of the Black family. This can be seen in the reaction to sociological and political characterizations of the Black family as the source of
many of the Black community's social ills.

Daniel Moynihan's 1965 diagnosis of the ills of Black America
depicted a deteriorating Black family, foretold the destruction of the
Black male householder, and lamented the creation of the Black matri-
archy.[37] His conclusions prompted a massive critique from liberal sociologists and from civil rights leaders.[38] Surprisingly, while many critics characterized the report as racist for its blind use of *white* cultural norms as
the standard for evaluating *Black* families, relatively few responses argued
that the report was sexist for its endorsement of a *patriarchal* vision of the
family in which men hold traditional dominant roles.[39]

This relative insensitivity to questions of patriarchy can be seen in the
more recent controversy over the televised special *The Vanishing Black
Family*.[40] In this Bill Moyers special, the Moynihan image of the dysfunctional Black family was rehearsed along with familiar images of promiscuous, independent women and sexually irresponsible, immature Black
men.[41] One apparent theme of the special was that welfare was in part
responsible for the "vanishing" Black family because the government,
through monthly payments, replaced the role of the male in the family.
This has permitted Black men to father children carelessly and has simultaneously allowed Black women to choose state dependency over the
more appropriate choice of settling with a husband.

Like the criticism lodged against the Moynihan report decades earlier,
critics attacked the racist packaging of the program. Yet few challenged
the patriarchal assumptions upon which the conclusions of pathology
were based, such as the a priori association of female-headed families
with dysfunctionality and the implicit assumption that the answer to
welfare dependence is to reinstitute the male as the family head. White
feminists were equally culpable. There was little, if any, published
response to the Moyers report from white feminist critics. Perhaps they
were under the mistaken assumption that since the report focused on the

Black community, the problems highlighted were racial, not gender-based. Whatever the reason, the result was that the ensuing debates over the future direction of welfare and family policy proceeded without significant feminist input. The absence of a strong feminist critique of the Moynihan/Moyers model not only impeded the interests of Black women but also compromised the interests of growing numbers of white women heads of household who find it difficult to make ends meet.

William Julius Wilson's *The Truly Disadvantaged* modified much of the moralistic tone of this debate by reframing the issue in terms of a lack of marriageable Black men.[42] According to Wilson, the decline in Black marriages is not attributable to poor motivation, bad work habits, or irresponsibility, but instead is caused by structural economics which have forced Black unskilled labor out of the work force. Wilson's approach represents a significant move away from that of Moynihan/Moyers in that he rejects their attempt to center the analysis on the morals of the Black community. Yet he too considers the proliferation of female-headed households as dysfunctional per se and fails to explain fully why such households are so much in peril. Because he incorporates no analysis of the way the structure of the economy and the work force subordinates the interests of women, especially child-bearing Black women, Wilson's suggested reform begins with finding ways to put Black men back in the family. In Wilson's view, we must change the economic structure with an eye toward providing more jobs for Black men.

My criticism is not that providing Black men with jobs is undesirable; indeed, this is necessary not only for Black men themselves but for an entire community that is depressed and subject to a host of sociological and economic ills that accompany massive rates of unemployment. But as long as we assume that the massive social reorganization Wilson calls for is possible, why not think about it in ways that maximize the choices of Black women? For instance, Wilson only mentions in passing the need for day care and job training for single mothers. No mention at all is made of other practices and policies that are racist and sexist, and that contribute to the poor conditions under which nearly half of all Black women must live.[43] A more complete theoretical and political agenda for the Black underclass must take into account the specific and particular concerns of Black women; their families occupy the bottom rung of the economic ladder, and it is only through placing them at the center of the analysis that their needs and the needs of their families will be directly addressed.

EMBRACING THE INTERSECTION

If any real efforts are to be made to free Black people of the constraints and conditions that characterize racial subordination, then theories and strategies purporting to reflect the Black community's needs must include an analysis of sexism and patriarchy. Similarly, feminism must include an analysis of race if it hopes to express the aspirations of non-white women. Neither Black liberationist politics nor feminist theory can ignore the intersectional experiences of those whom the movements claim as their respective constituents. In order to include Black women, both movements must distance themselves from earlier approaches in which experiences are relevant only when they are related to certain clearly identifiable causes (for example, the oppression of Blacks is significant when based on race, of women when based on gender). The praxis of both should be centered on the life chances and life situations of people who should be cared about without regard to the source of their difficulties.

I have stated earlier that the failure to embrace the complexities of compoundedness is not simply a matter of political will, but is also due to the influence of a way of thinking about discrimination which structures politics so that struggles are categorized as singular issues. Moreover, this structure imports a descriptive and normative view of society that reinforces the status quo.

It is somewhat ironic that those concerned with alleviating the ills of racism and sexism should adopt such a top-down approach to discrimination. If their efforts instead began with addressing the needs and problems of those who are most disadvantaged and with restructuring and remaking the world where necessary, then others who are singularly disadvantaged would also benefit. In addition, it seems that placing those who currently are marginalized in the center is the most effective way to resist efforts to compartmentalize experiences and undermine potential collective action.

It is not necessary to believe that a political consensus to focus on the lives of the most disadvantaged will happen tomorrow in order to recenter discrimination discourse at the intersection. It is enough, for now, that such an effort would encourage us to look beneath the prevailing conceptions of discrimination and to challenge the complacency that accompanies belief in the effectiveness of this framework. By so doing, we may develop language which is critical of the dominant view and which provides some basis for unifying activity. The goal of this activity should be to facilitate the inclusion of marginalized groups for whom it can be said: "When they enter, we all enter."

NOTES

This chapter originated as an address given at the Conference on New Developments in Feminist Legal Theory, sponsored by the Chicago Legal Forum in October 1988. An earlier version that is more heavily footnoted appears in *Chicago Legal Forum* 139 (1989). I would like to thank Neil Gotanda, Kendall Thomas, Stephanie Phillips, Darcy Calkins, and the West Coast Fem Crits for their comments and support. I am especially indebted to David Kairys and Richard Yarborough, whose invaluable assistance made this contribution possible.

1. Gloria T. Hull et al., eds., *All the Women Are White, All the Blacks Are Men, But Some of Us Are Brave* (Old Westbury, NY: Feminist Press, 1982). For other works setting forth a feminist analysis of law from a nonwhite perspective, see Judy Scales-Trent, *Black Women and the Constitution: Finding Our Place, Asserting Our Rights (Voices of Experience: New Responses to Gender Discourse)*, 24 Harvard Civil Rights–Civil Liberties Law Review 9 (1989); Regina Austin, Sapphire-Bound, 1989 Wisconsin Law Review 539 (1989); Angela Harris, *Race and Essentialism in Feminist Legal Theory*, 42 Stanford Law Review 581 (1990); Paulette Caldwell, *A Hair Piece: Perspectives on the Intersection of Race and Gender*, 1991 Duke Law Journal 365; Taunya Banks, *Two Life Stories: Reflections of One Black Woman Law Professor*, 6 Berkeley Women's Law Journal 46 (1990–91).
2. 413 F.Supp. 142 (E.D. Mo. E.D. 1976), aff'd, 558 F.2d 480 (8th Cir. 1977), affirming the district court's decision without addressing the substance of the lower court's ruling; the court of appeals found that DeGraffenreid could not bring a gender discrimination claim due to the expiration of Title VII's statute of limitations; 708 F.2d 475 (9th Cir. 1983); 416 F.Supp. 248 (N.D. Miss. 1976), aff'd, 673 F.2d 798 (5th Cir. 1982). These are all statutory cases pursuant to Title VII of the Civil Rights Act of 1964, 42 U.S.C. § 2000e, et seq. as amended (1982).
3. Not all courts that have grappled with this problem have adopted the *DeGraffenreid* approach. Indeed, other courts have concluded that Black women are protected by Title VII. See, for example, *Hicks v. Gates Rubber*

Co., 833 F.2d 1406 (10th Cir. 1987); *Graham v. Bendix Corp.*, 585 F.Supp
1036 (N.D.Ind. 1984); *Jeffries v. Harris Community Action Association*,
615 F.2d 1025 (5th Cir., 1980). However, the very fact that the Black
women's claims are seen as aberrant suggests that sex discrimination doctrine is centered in the experience of white women. Even those courts that
have held that Black women are protected seem to accept that Black
women's claims raise issues that the "standard" sex discrimination claims
do not. See Elaine W. Shoben, *Compound Discrimination: The Interaction
of Race and Sex in Employment Discrimination*, 55 NYU Law Review 793,
803–4 (1980), criticizing the *Jeffries* Court's use of a sex-plus analysis to
create a subclass of Black women.

4. See also *Moore v. National Association of Securities Dealers*, 27 EPD (CCH)
532.238 (D.D.C. 1981); but see *Edmondson v. Simon*, 86 FRD 375
(N.D. Ill. 1980), where the court was unwilling to hold as a matter of law
that no Black female could represent without conflict the interests of both
Blacks and females.

5. See *Strong v. Arkansas Blue Cross and Blue Shield, Inc.*, 87 FRD 496 (E.
D.Ark. 1980); *Hammons v. Folger Coffee Co.*, 87 FRD 600 (W.D. Mo.
1980); *Edmondson v. Simon*, 86 FRD 375 (N.D. Ill. 1980); *Vuyanich v.
Republic National Bank of Dallas*, 82 FRD 420 (N.D. Tex. 1979); *Colston
v. Maryland Cup Corp.*, 26 Fed. Rules Serv. 940 (D. Md. 1978).

6. This reasoning of the Court in *DeGraffenreid* has been followed in subsequent decisions in the Eighth Circuit; see *Briggs v. Anderson*, 796 F.2d
1009 (8th Cir. 1986).

7. See also *Williams v. Mead Coated Board, Inc.*, 836 F.Supp. 1552 (M.D.
Ala. 1993).

8. See, for example, *Bernard v. Gulf Oil Corp.*, 890 F.2d 735 (5th Cir. 1989).

9. This interpretation of antidiscrimination law is part of a larger critique
called critical race theory. See generally Kimberlé Crenshaw, Neil
Gotanda, Gary Peller, Kendall Thomas, eds., *Critical Race Theory: The Key
Writings That Formed the Movement* (New York: New Press, 1995);
Richard Delgado, ed., *Critical Race Theory* (Philadelphia: Temple
University Press, 1995); Charles Lawrence, chapter 14 of this volume.

10. See Phyliss Palmer, "The Racial Feminization of Poverty: Women of Color
as Portents of the Future for All Women," *Women's Studies Quarterly*, 11
(Fall 1983): 3–4, posing the question why "white women in the women's
movement had not created more effective and continuous alliances with
Black women when simultaneously . . . black women have become hero-
ines for the women's movement, a position symbolized by the consistent
use of Sojourner Truth and her famous words, 'Ain't I a woman?'"

11. See Paula Giddings, *When and Where I Enter: The Impact of Black Women on Race and Sex in America* (New York: Morrow, 1984), 54.

12. Eleanor Flexner, *Century of Struggle: The Women's Rights Movement in the United States* (Cambridge, MA: Belknap Press, Harvard University Press, 1975), 91. See also Bell Hooks, *Ain't I a Woman?* (Boston: South End Press, 1981).

13. "'Objectivity' is itself an example of the reification of white male thought." Hull et al., eds., *All the Women Are White,* xxv.

14. For example, many white females were able to gain entry into previously all-white male enclaves, not through bringing about a fundamental reordering of male versus female work, but in large part by shifting their "female" responsibilities to poor and minority women.

15. Feminists often discuss how gender-based stereotypes and norms reinforce the subordination of women by justifying their exclusion from public life and glorifying their roles within the private sphere. Law has historically played a role in maintaining this subordination by enforcing the exclusion of women from public life and by limiting its reach into the private sphere. See, for example, Deborah L. Rhode, *Association and Assimilation,* 81 Northwestern University Law Review 106 (1986); Frances Olsen, *From False Paternalism to False Equality: Judicial Assaults on Feminist Community, Illinois 1869–95,* 84 Michigan Law Review 1518 (1986); Martha Minow, *Foreword: Justice Engendered,* 101 Harvard Law Review 10 (1987); Nadine Taub and Elizabeth Schneider, chapter 15 of this volume.

16. This criticism is a discrete illustration of a more general claim that feminism has been premised on white middle-class women's experience. For example, early feminist texts such as Betty Friedan's *The Feminine Mystique* (New York: Norton, 1963) placed white middle-class problems at the center of feminism and thus contributed to its rejection within the Black community. See Hooks, *Ain't I a Woman?,* 185–96.

17. See Hooks, *Ain't I a Woman?,* 94–99, discussing the elevation of sexist imagery in the Black liberation movement during the 1960s.

18. See generally Jacqueline Jones, *Labor of Love, Labor of Sorrow: Black Women, Work, and the Family from Slavery to the Present* (New York: Basic Books, 1985); Angela Davis, *Women, Race, and Class* (New York: Random House, 1981).

19. As Elizabeth Higginbotham noted, "women, who often fail to conform to 'appropriate' sex roles, have been pictured as, and made to feel, inadequate—even though as women they possess traits recognized as positive when held by men in the wider society. Such women are stigmatized

because their lack of adherence to expected gender roles is seen as a threat to the value system." Elizabeth Higginbotham, "Two Representative Issues in Contemporary Sociological Work on Black Women," in Hull et al., eds., *All the Women Are White*, 95.

20. See generally Susan Brownmiller, *Against Our Will* (New York: Simon & Schuster, 1975); Susan Estrich, *Real Rape* (Cambridge, MA: Harvard University Press, 1987).

21. See *Note: Rape, Racism, and the Law*, 6 Harvard Women's Law Journal 103, 117–223 (1983), discussing the historical and contemporary evidence suggesting that Black women are generally not thought to be chaste. See also Hooks, *Ain't I a Woman?*, 54, stating that stereotypical images of Black womanhood during slavery were based on the myth that "all black women were immoral and sexually loose"; Beverly Smith, "Black Women's Health: Notes for a Course," in Hull et al., eds., *All the Women Are White*, 110, noting that "white men for centuries have justified their sexual abuse of Black women by claiming that we are licentious, always 'ready' for any sexual encounter."

22. *Dallas v. State*, 76 Fla. 358, 79 So. 690 (1918), quoted in *Note: Rape, Racism, and the Law*, 121. Espousing precisely this view, one commentator stated in 1902: "I sometimes hear of a virtuous Negro woman but the idea is so absolutely inconceivable to me . . . I cannot imagine such a creature as a virtuous Negro woman" (ibid., 82). Such images persist in popular culture.

23. Because of the way the legal system viewed chastity, Black women could not be victims of forcible rape. One commentator has noted, "According to governing stereotypes, chastity could not be possessed by Black women. Thus, Black women's rape charges were automatically discounted, and the issue of chastity was contested only in cases where the rape complainant was a white woman." *Note: Rape, Racism, and the Law*, 126.

24. See "The Rape of Black Women as a Weapon of Terror," in Gerda Lerner, *Black Women in White America* (New York: Pantheon, 1972), 172–93. See also Brownmiller, *Against Our Will*. Even where Brownmiller acknowledges the use of rape as racial terrorism, she resists making a "special case" for Black women by offering evidence that white women were raped by the Klan as well.

25. Lemer, *Black Women in White America* (New York: Random House, 1992), 173.

26. Paula Giddings notes the combined effect of sexual and racial stereotypes: "Black women were seen as having all of the inferior qualities of white women without any of their virtues" (Giddings, *When and Where I Enter*, 82).

27. A cogent and insightful analysis of Black women's ambivalence with respect to the antirape movement, drawing on contemporary incidents such as the Charles Stuart hoax in Boston and the Central Park jogger case, is offered by Valerie Smith, "Split Affinities: The Case of Interracial Rape," in *Conflicts in Feminism*, ed. Maryanne Hirsch and Evelyn Fox Keller (New York: Routledge, Chapman, and Hall, 1990).

28. Brownmiller, *Against Our Will*, 272.

29. See Juan Williams, "Standing for Justice," in *Eyes on the Prize* (New York: Viking, 1987).

30. See Anna Julia Cooper, *A Voice from the South* (Westport, CT: Negro Universities Press, 1969 [1892]), 31.

31. To this one easily could add class.

32. An anecdote illustrates this point. A group of female law professors gathered to discuss "Isms in the Classroom." One exercise led by Pat Cain involved each participant listing the three primary factors that described herself. Almost without exception, white women in the room listed their gender either primarily or secondarily; none listed their race. All of the women of color listed their race first, then their gender. This would suggest that identity descriptions seem to begin with the primary source of opposition with whatever the dominant norm is. See Pat Cain, *Feminist Jurisprudence: Grounding the Theories*, 4 Berkeley Women's Law Journal 191 (1989–90).

33. For a comparative discussion of Third World feminism paralleling this observation, see Kumari Jayawardena, *Feminism and Nationalism in the Third World* (London: Zed Press, 1986).

34. For a discussion of how racial ideology creates a polarizing dynamic that subordinates Blacks and privileges whites, see Kimberlé Crenshaw, *Race, Reform, and Retrenchment: Transformation and Legitimation in Antidiscrimination*, 101 Harvard Law Review 1331, 1371–76 (1988).

35. Jack Matthews, "Three 'Color Purple' Actresses Talk About Its Impact," *Los Angeles Times*, January 31, 1986; Jack Matthews, "Some Blacks Critical of Spielberg's 'Purple,'" *Los Angeles Times*, December 20, 1985. But see Gene Siskel, "Does 'Purple' Hate Men?" *Chicago Tribune*, January 5, 1986; Clarence Page, "Toward a New Black Cinema," *Chicago Tribune*, January 12, 1986.

36. A consistent problem with any negative portrayal of African Americans is that they are seldom balanced by positive images. On the other hand, most critics overlooked the positive transformation of the primary male character in *The Color Purple*.

37. Daniel P. Moynihan, *The Negro Family: The Case for National Action*

(Office of Policy Planning and Research, United States Department of Labor, 1965).

38. See Lee Rainwater and William L. Yancey, *The Moynihan Report and the Politics of Controversy* (Cambridge, MA: MIT Press, 1967), 427–29, 395–97.

39. See Jacquelyne Johnson Jackson, "Black Women in a Racist Society," in *Racism and Mental Health* (Pittsburgh: University of Pittsburgh Press, 1973), 185–86.

40. *The Vanishing Black Family*, PBS Television broadcast, January 1986.

41. Columnist Mary McGrory, applauding the show, reported that Moyers found sex was as common in the Black ghetto as a cup of coffee; McGrory, "Moynihan Was Right 21 Years Ago," *Washington Post*, January 26, 1968. George Will argued that oversexed Black men were more of a menace than Bull Connor, the Birmingham police chief who in 1968 achieved international notoriety by turning firehoses on protesting schoolchildren; Will, "Voting Rights Won't Fix It," *Washington Post*, January 23, 1986.

42. William Julius Wilson, *The Truly Disadvantaged: The Inner City, the Underclass, and Public Policy* (Chicago: University of Chicago Press, 1987).

43. Wilson also does not include an analysis of the impact of gender on changes in family patterns. Consequently, little attention is paid to the conflict that may result when gender-based expectations are frustrated by economic and demographic factors. This focus on demographic and structural explanations represents an effort to regain the high ground from the Moyers-Moynihan approach, which is more psychosocial. Perhaps because psychosocial explanations have come dangerously close to blaming victims, their prevalence is thought to threaten efforts to win policy directives that might effectively address deteriorating conditions within the working-class and poor Black communities. See Kimberlé Crenshaw, "A Comment on Gender, Difference, and Victim Ideology in the Study of the Black Family" (manuscript on file with author, 1990).

17 ELLIOTT CURRIE

CRIME AND PUNISHMENT IN THE UNITED STATES: MYTHS, REALITIES, AND POSSIBILITIES

THE United States imprisons its population at a rate from five to fifteen times that of other advanced industrial societies, yet we continue to suffer the worst levels of serious violent crime in the developed world. In California, under the state's Draconian "three strikes and you're out" law, a shoplifter with two prior convictions for burglary can be sentenced to life in prison. Yet more people are murdered in the city of Los Angeles, with 3.5 million people, than in all of England and Wales, with 50 million.[1]

The stark combination of stunningly high rates of violence with equally stunning efforts at repressive control is a compelling signal that something is deeply wrong in our society, and a powerful indictment of our criminal justice policies. In a more reasonable world, this might lead us to rethink our approach to crime, and to search for more effective ways to prevent it, both inside and outside of the criminal justice system. But, with some exceptions, that isn't what has happened. Instead, we have mainly opted to continue the failed policies of the past twenty-five years. For a generation, the public discussion of crime in America has been dominated by an ideology that serves to obscure the social and political implications of our high levels of violence and incarceration, and to justify the continued expansion of a penal system that dwarfs anything in the rest of the industrial world, or in our own history.

Some version of that ideology can be encountered almost daily in editorial columns, legislative chambers, and campaign speeches. The story most Americans are likely to hear about crime and punishment goes something like this: *The reason America is plagued with violence is that we are "soft" on crime; our justice system is lenient with people who break the law, and if we want less crime we will have to get "tougher." Contrary to the claims of do-gooders and bleeding hearts, prison "works": locking up more people, for longer terms, can cut crime drastically, and indeed the reason crime has fallen somewhat in the past few years is that we have finally begun to put more criminals behind bars. But we haven't gone nearly far enough: a weak criminal justice system still lets most criminals—even chronic violent offenders—off with a slap on the wrist. And though putting more criminals behind bars is expensive, it actually saves money in the long run by reducing crime. In any case, we have no credible alternatives, other than more imprisonment, if we want to reduce crime. Some people believe that we should invest more in programs to prevent crime and to rehabilitate offenders: but we tried that in the sixties, and it didn't work. Likewise, another cherished liberal belief—that we can fight crime by attacking poverty and discrimination—has also been discredited: There is no evidence that crime is caused by poverty, inequality, or discrimination, and the misguided attempts to address those problems through government programs have, if anything, made crime worse, not better. To the extent that crime can be said to have causes at all, other than the antisocial decisions of individuals, they are moral and cultural, not social and economic: and government is powerless to do much about them, other than to increase the likelihood of punishment.*

Every one of these assertions is wrong—or, at best, extremely misleading. Yet they dominate the public discussion of crime and punishment in the United States, and they serve as the intellectual underpinning for anticrime policies that have come close to bankrupting some states while failing egregiously to protect us from the violence that continues to haunt our collective experience. They also supply the intellectual ammunition for a host of punitive measures designed to symbolize our resolve to get tough on criminals: the return of chain gangs and menial, backbreaking labor in the prisons; the rise of "three strikes and you're out" laws; the growing trend toward trying children in adult courts; proposals to return to the stocks and other brutal techniques of publicly "shaming" people who break the law. To an extraordinary degree, they have captured both political parties and much of the media.

The curious paradox is that this view has come to dominate the debate just as a very different—and far more hopeful—picture is increasingly emerging from a growing body of serious research. More and more, we are learning that the criminal justice system's ability to control crime through ever-harsher sentencing is inherently limited. At the same time, we are learning that the prospects for crime prevention and for the reintegration of offenders are much brighter than we once believed. But with scattered exceptions, we are not putting what we know into practice. Instead, we are placing most of our bets on policies that we are quite sure cannot work well. It's difficult to think of another area of social policy—with the possible exception of welfare—where the gap between knowledge and action, understanding and social policy, is so wide.

How has this happened? Why is there such a huge gap between what criminologists know and what policymakers do? There are many reasons, including a failure of nerve among too many political leaders, who have gone along with the increasingly punitive drift of public policy for fear of being typed as soft on crime. But another reason is that the realities of crime and punishment in the United States have been obscured by a set of powerful and widespread myths—often backed by forbiddingly esoteric research—that have been assiduously promoted by conservative politicians, academics, and think tanks, and uncritically repeated by a generally credulous press. The myths are, as we shall see, far off the mark; sometimes wildly so. But they have shown a remarkable staying power in the face of overwhelming evidence against them.

The focus here is on four of those myths, all of them essential pieces of the conservative ideology about crime and punishment. I call them the myth of leniency, the myth of efficacy, the myth of costlessness, and the myth of no alternatives. Put differently, the myths are that we are soft on crime; that prison "works"; that prison "pays"; and that there is little else we can do to reduce crime other than punishing offenders.

THE MYTH OF LENIENCY

In his 1996 campaign for the presidency, Senator Bob Dole described the American criminal justice system as a "liberal-leaning laboratory of leniency." And most Americans, according to opinion polls, agree—at least on the surface—that we are generally "soft" on crime. "Soft sentencing," as Senator Phil Gramm put it in a *New York Times* editorial, has led to a "plague" of violence in our cities.[2] A permissive attitude toward criminals, in this view, is only one part of a larger moral crisis in America: an overemphasis on individual rights and an excessive tolerance of misbehavior have crippled the justice system and brought the country perilously close to moral collapse. The conservative pundits William Bennett, John DiIulio, and James Walters, in the most prominent right-wing tract on crime in the 1990s, argue that the justice system has become "emasculated" by a discredited ethic of rehabilitation, and even warn of an impending violent backlash against civil liberties if we continue to allow "revolving-door justice" to flood the streets with predators. "The American public," they write, "will not accept widespread lawlessness indefinitely."

Our free democratic institutions cannot withstand much more crime without a terrible counterreaction. If violent crime continues to rise; if out-of-wedlock births continue to increase; if more children are thrown into moral poverty; if the human carnage continues to mount; then the public will demand restored order at any cost—including a more-rapid-than-you think rollback of civil liberties.[3]

The idea that our justice system is shockingly lenient with offenders, in short, is now deeply embedded in our national political culture. But how well does it stand up to reality?

Not well. By international standards, the United States has always been a relatively punitive country, and has become much more so in recent years.

Consider first how we stack up relative to other industrial countries in our use of imprisonment. The simplest measure of this is what criminologists call the "incarceration rate"—the proportion of a country's population confined in jails and prisons. In 1995, the overall incarceration rate in the United States was 600 per 100,000 (this figure does *not* include youth confined in juvenile institutions). The only country in the world with a higher rate was Russia, at 690 per 100,000 in 1995—and in some ways the comparison is misleading, because a substantial number of prisoners in Russia are behind bars for political offenses, not for street crimes. Some other countries of the former Soviet bloc also had very high rates—Romania's, for example, was 200 per 100,000, Estonia's 270—as do a few others, notably Singapore (229) and South Africa (368). But no other country in the advanced industrial world comes even close to matching the U.S. rate of imprisonment. Our closest "competitor" in Northern Europe, England, imprisoned its population at roughly 100 per 100,000, and most other Western European countries are lower. The 1995 incarceration rate in Germany and France was about 85 per 100,000, and about 65 in Sweden and Holland. Japan comes in at the bottom, with an incarceration rate of just 36 per 100,000.[4]

That we imprison our citizens at a rate from six to more than fifteen times that of other industrial democracies is, unsurprisingly, usually seen as an indication that we are an extremely punitive nation. In response, conservatives sometimes argue that a simple comparison of incarceration rates is a meaningless way to judge whether one country is more punitive than another. What really matters, in this view, is not the rate of imprisonment in proportion to a country's population, but the rate per *offense*: that is, the proportion of people incarcerated relative to the country's crime rate. If a country has a much higher level of serious crime, in short, it is likely to have a higher rate of incarceration, other things equal, and that doesn't necessarily imply that it's more punitive. The real issue, to put it another way, is what happens to offenders who've been caught and convicted of crime.

But even by this standard, the United States stands out as quite punitive in comparison with other industrial democracies, especially when it comes to less serious offenses—notably property crimes and drug crimes. Every country is likely to sentence the worst violent criminals fairly severely, and so we wouldn't expect great differences in, say, sentences for murder between countries. The disparities are most likely to appear for crimes like burglary or drug dealing. And though comparing sentencing practices across different countries is inherently tricky, the most careful studies suggest that the United States tends to treat crimes like these more harshly than do other industrial nations. Even in the 1980s, a convicted burglar was almost twice as likely to go to jail or prison in the United States as in England, and stayed behind bars, on average, more than twice as long. Even for robbery, a serious violent offense, the United States stands out: a convicted robber in the United States in the mid 1980s had a roughly similar chance as his English counterpart of going behind bars, but would serve nearly twice as long once there. We are also far more likely to put drug offenders behind bars—in 1990, English drug offenders were only half as likely to go to jail or prison as Americans—and for extremely long sentences. Nor is this disparity simply because our criminals are tougher than those in other countries: we are considerably *more* likely than the British, for example, to put first-time offenders behind bars.[5] And because American sentences have risen, often sharply, since the 1980s, these comparisons understate the relative harshness of American practice.

When we compare our penal practices with those of comparable nations, then, the argument that we have worse crime in the United States because we are unusually lenient with offenders collapses. And the myth of leniency is also countered by the growth of punishment within the United States itself. What is most extraordinary about the American experience is how stubbornly our high rates of violent crime have resisted utterly unprecedented increases in incarceration. Since the 1970s, indeed, the United States has been engaged in a profound experiment in social engineering—though it is rarely described in those terms: an experiment that has no counterpart in our history or that of any other country.

Consider the incarceration rate again. From the end of World War II through the early 1970s, the U.S. *prison* incarceration rate (that is, excluding local jails) fluctuated within a very narrow band—from a low of 92 per 100,000 (in 1972) to a high of 119 per 100,000 (in 1962). By 1995 it had reached 419. And the quadrupling of the nation's overall imprisonment rate masks even more rapid increases in some states—and for some kinds of people. The *increase* in the number of inmates in Texas prisons from 1990–1995 alone (an astonishing 67,000) is roughly equal to the entire prison population of Germany—a nation of 80 million people. Since the early 1970s, there has been a thirteenfold increase in the number of *women* in state and federal prisons. Though women are everywhere a relatively small proportion of prison populations, such is the magnitude of this increase that American women in some states are more likely to be incarcerated than the *men* in some other industrial countries. At this writing, the state of Oklahoma imprisons its female population at a rate greater than that for both sexes in every Western European country.[6]

As of 1995, fully 29 percent of black men in the United States could expect to spend some time in a state or federal prison.[7] In California, four times as many black men are "enrolled" in state prisons as are enrolled in state colleges and universities.[8] For blacks, as for women, the extraordinary increases in incarceration have been driven most powerfully by the war on drugs: between 1985 and 1995, the number of black prison inmates sentenced for drug offenses increased by more than *700 percent.* Less often discussed, but even more dramatic, is the situation of Latinos in the justice system: the number of Hispanics in America's prisons has quintupled since 1980 alone.[9]

Given the extraordinary growth of imprisonment, how is it possible to maintain that we are a "lenient" country? One way is to insist that, despite the increases in imprisonment, most offenders still get off lightly—that, as John J. DiIulio puts it, "hard time for hardened criminals is rare." That unlikely argument is sometimes backed by highly creative statistics, which are as misleading as they are startling. In the 1990s it became common to read, for example, that the "average cost" of a rape was sixty days in prison; for a robbery, just twenty-three days. Those figures found their way into mass magazines and, among others, the op-ed page of the *New York Times*.[10] They are routinely offered as evidence that "soft sentencing" has caused an explosion in crime. They are also, of course, altogether incredible—as anyone who has ever followed a serious criminal trial is well aware.

What's going on here? Where do these numbers come from? The figures do contain an element of reality; but the trick is that they are only partly about sentencing. The figures are derived from a study by a Texas economist who divided the *total number of crimes committed* by the average sentence offenders received—if they were caught and convicted. But most offenses do not result in an arrest to begin with. So what the "twenty-three days" figure for robbery really reflects is the slim chance that anyone will be arrested for the crime in the first place. Fewer than one in twelve robberies results in an arrest, and many of the arrests aren't sufficiently solid to result in a conviction. But once arrested and convicted, nine out of ten robbers are sentenced to prison or to a local jail. Once there, they will serve an average of more than four years behind bars. A convicted rapist will serve not sixty days, but more than seven years.[11]

Another widely publicized statistic, also offered as a demonstration of our weakness with people who break the law, is that "only one in 100 violent crimes results in a prison sentence."[12] Again, the figure is technically correct. But the implications drawn from it are wildly misleading. The basic problem is similar to the "sixty days for rape" canard: what the figure measures is not the courts' lenient treatment of offenders, but the fact that most violent crimes do not enter the courts at all. Over half of the more than 10 million violent crimes that appeared in the Justice Department's annual victim survey in 1994 were what the Bureau of Justice Statistics calls "simple assaults without injury"—at worst, schoolyard fights or even threats. No reasonable society would impose a prison sentence on someone for these offenses, even if they were reported to police—which most are not—and even if the perpetrators were caught, which most are not. Only about half of the *serious* assaults in the survey are reported to the police, and of those the majority never result in an arrest.[13] All told, only one in six violent crimes enters the justice system at all, and many of those are quite minor. Narrowing the statement to include only those sentenced to *prison*, moreover, cleverly obscures the fact that many violent offenders who are not sentenced to prison do go to local jails. The result, again, is that the vast majority of offenders convicted of serious crimes of violence now spend time behind bars; about nine out of ten for robbery and rape, and even higher for murder and non-negligent manslaughter. The proportions are also higher for more serious offenses *within* these categories, and higher for offenders with a prior record. And the proportions are increasing. Between 1975 and 1986, for example, the amount of prison time served per violent crime committed roughly tripled in the United States, largely because of the increased likelihood that offenders would go behind bars at all.[14] From 1990 to 1994 alone, the expected time to be served by someone convicted of murder rose by two years.[15]

DOES PRISON "WORK?"

No amount of statistical manipulation, then, can hide the stark reality: we are already quite "tough" on most serious criminals (and some who are not so serious)—more so than otherwise comparable countries, and *far* more so than in the recent past. Yet we also maintain the worst levels of violence in the developed world. That would, on the surface, appear to be a strong case that our "tough" approach to crime has been a failure. That inference has been challenged, however, from several angles.

One is to downplay the seriousness of America's crime problem in comparison with other countries. It is sometimes argued that the advanced industrial societies are more alike than different in this respect—that high crime rates, in fact, are an inevitable "cost" of growing prosperity and freedom.[16] But this argument can only be made by lumping together the most serious crimes with ones that are far less troubling—and even then, the argument is less than compelling.

International surveys of crime victimization have claimed to find rates of property crimes, and less serious forms of assault, that are as high or higher in countries like Canada, Australia, and even the Netherlands, as in the United States.[17] At best, these surveys must be taken with great caution; among other things, they are "household" surveys that are known to exclude many of the kinds of people who are most likely to be victims of crime—including the homeless, people confined in prisons or other institutions, and people who do not have telephones or who are unwilling to talk with interviewers about their experience with crime. The result is that such surveys seriously undersample the poor, the urban young, offenders, and others whose chances of victimization are greatest. And since poverty and homelessness (as well as incarceration) are far more extensive in the United States than in other industrial nations, the surveys almost certainly understate the relative amount of crime—even of less serious varieties—in the United States.

More importantly, no one seriously questions the grisly prominence of the United States when it comes to the most serious violent crimes. In the United States homicide is the third leading cause of death for black men of all ages, and the leading cause for those aged 15 to 35; it is the fifth leading cause of death among Hispanic men, seventh for Asian men, and, startlingly, even ranks among the top ten causes of death for both black and Asian *women*.[18] The United States, moreover, also exhibits a peculiarly wide gap between the risks of violent death for younger people and those for everyone else. What Americans often do not recognize is that in most industrial societies, for a young person to be murdered remains an extremely rare event. Three-quarters of all homicide deaths among children under age 14 in the entire industrial world take place in the United States. The homicide death rate among men aged 15 to 24 in 1994 in England and Wales was 1.0 per 100,000. In France it was 1.3, in Japan 0.6, and in Austria 0.4. In the United States, it was 36.8. The only countries around the world that matched or exceeded the U.S. rate of youth homicide—or, indeed, even came close—were in the Third World or the former Soviet bloc; 38 per 100,000 in Mexico, for example, 40 in Russia, and 25 in Latvia. And though the worst risks of homicide in America are among minority youth, it is important to keep in mind that the homicide death rate of *white, non-Hispanic* American youth—at about 8 per 100,000—vastly outstrips that of young people in general in most other advanced countries, in some cases by more than ten to one. Nor are the disparities confined to youth. As with incarceration rates, for example, America's exceptionalism in rates of violence often transcends the effects of gender, which is usually one of the most powerful influences on the chances of being a victim of a violent crime—or of committing one. Homicide death rates for women in the United States are higher than those for *men* in all but two of the countries of Western Europe, Finland, and Italy. The American effect also transcends age, which is also a powerful influence on the risks of being the victim of violence. The lowest risks of homicide, for example, are found among older women. But an American woman *in her sixties* is more likely to die of homicide than a young French *man* in his teens to early twenties.[19]

In the face of these extraordinary—and persistent—rates of violence, how is it possible to argue that our experiment in mass incarceration as a strategy of crime control has been a great success?

One way is to insist that crime *would* have been much worse had it not been for the enormous investment in prison. Making this argument often involves statistical analysis of great complexity, because it involves holding constant a variety of other factors—say, the poverty rate or the proportion of youth in the population—beyond our penal policies that might have influenced the crime rate, in order to isolate the effect of rapidly growing prison populations. A number of those studies have been conducted in recent years; some are routinely cited by conservatives as offering proof that the investment in prisons, despite all appearances, has indeed "worked." On closer inspection, they show something quite different.

One frequently cited study, for example, by Thomas B. Marvell and Carlisle E. Moody of the College of William and Mary, concluded that the great increases in state prison populations during the 1980s probably did reduce the overall crime rate somewhat—but mainly for property crimes, not the most troubling crimes of violence. The doubling of the prison population, they write, had "little or no impact on murder, rape, or assault." It did, apparently, reduce rates of larceny and burglary, as well as one violent crime, robbery. But even for robbery the reductions were modest. Marvell and Moody calculated that the addition of an average of 40,000 new inmates each year during the 1980s probably reduced the robbery rate by about 1.8 percent a year below what it would otherwise have been.[20] Other recent studies come to similar conclusions, as, for that matter, has most of the research on this issue since the 1970s. The findings are consistent: massive increases in imprisonment apparently have a significant, if modest, impact on some so-called high-rate crimes, especially property offenses, but a stunningly weak impact on the most serious crimes of violence.

Moreover—very importantly—these studies also tell us that the impact of *future* increases in imprisonment on violent crime is likely to be even less than in the past. Since we already incarcerate the most serious offenders we catch and convict, and for increasingly lengthy terms, boosting prison populations much higher would necessarily mean sweeping a pool of offenders into prison who are less serious, on average, than the ones already there. The "payoff" in crime reduction, accordingly, from any given increase in incarceration will correspondingly shrink.[21]

But there is an even more important problem with the assertion that prison "works." Even if we grant that extreme increases in incarceration may reduce some kinds of crime—albeit far less effectively that proponents of more prison-building have argued—no one has yet managed to show that prison "works" better than something *else* we might do with the equivalent resources. In order to make intelligent decisions about our priorities in fighting crime, in other words, it isn't enough to ask whether putting a great many people in prison reduces crime as opposed to doing *nothing* whatever—for doing nothing has never been anyone's policy agenda. The real question is whether prison "works" compared with other options. And none of these studies has shown that to be true, or, for that matter, even tried.

DOES PRISON "PAY?"

The same problem undercuts another often-heard argument in support of our current policies: that prison "pays." "All of the estimates of the cost of the prison population," argues James Q. Wilson, "suggest that the benefits in terms of crimes avoided exceed the cost by a factor of at least two to one."[22] This is a relatively new argument, which has appeared in response to growing evidence that our heedless investment in incarceration may hurt the rest of the national economy. By the 1980s, as the economic as well as social costs of massive diversion of resources into the prisons became increasingly apparent, a new set of constituencies began to weigh in against indiscriminate incarceration and in favor of developing alternatives. Gradually, local and state officials, as well as some far-sighted businesspeople, began concluding that prison might not be such a bargain after all. State officials began to realize that beyond a certain point building more prisons meant they couldn't build colleges; corporate executives began to wonder where they would find a competent work force if we continued to starve public schools in order to build prisons. Enter the "prison pays" argument, designed to prove that prison is really an economic "bargain" after all.

As with the "prison works" argument, this one is often based on statistical studies of great complexity, making it difficult for most people to evaluate it one way or another. The research involves assigning estimated costs to various kinds of crimes, a tricky business made more so because researchers also include so-called intangible costs of crime, like the pain and suffering of victims, into their calculations.[23] But also like the "prison works" argument, even those studies most often cited in support of the view that prison pays actually suggest that things are much more complicated.

The political scientist John DiIulio, for example, has been one of the most vocal proponents of the view that prisons are "a bargain, by any measure." Yet oddly, his own research shows something quite different. With a colleague, Ann M. Piehl, DiIulio attempted to calculate the costs and benefits of incarcerating the inmates of a New Jersey prison. They found that prison did indeed "pay" *for more serious offenders*: That is, after calculating what the most serious felons "cost" society when they were free, DiIulio and Piehl concluded that the total was considerably greater than what it cost to keep them behind bars. But the calculation worked in the *opposite* direction for less serious offenders. Even excluding inmates sentenced for drug offenses, DiIulio and Piehl calculated that for about a quarter of the prison population, it cost society more to imprison them than to let them remain on the streets. And when drug offenders were included, the proportion of "cost-ineffective" inmates rose sharply; for more than half the population of this prison, it cost more to incarcerate them than to allow them to roam free.[24]

What this research tells us, in short, is that critics of *indiscriminate* incarceration have been right all along. Few doubt that prison "pays"— economically and otherwise—for murderers or repeat rapists. But that isn't what the current debate over penal policy is about. The debate is over what should be done with less dangerous offenders, particularly those who have committed minor drug or property crimes. The war on drugs in particular has dramatically shifted the composition of the prison population: the proportion of state and federal inmates who have been sentenced for violent offenses fell from 57 percent in 1980 to just 44 percent in 1995, while the proportion of drug offenders tripled, from 8 to 26 percent of the inmate population.[25] And the thrust of much recent "tough" sentencing policy—like California's "three strikes" law, passed in 1994—is precisely to mandate extraordinarily lengthy sentences for relatively less serious crimes (as of the end of 1995, more California offenders had been sentenced under the three strikes law for marijuana possession than for murder, rape, and kidnapping combined).[26]

Conservative critics have tried to deny that there are significant numbers of less dangerous offenders behind bars. Another much-quoted statistic is that "93 percent of prison inmates are either violent or repeat offenders."[27] Again, the figure is technically correct, but it glosses over just what, exactly, the repeat offenders were repeating. About one in five inmates of federal prisons has been sentenced for a crime that is both minor and nonviolent—mainly low-level drug offenses—and a roughly similar proportion of state prison inmates have neither a current nor a prior sentence for a violent crime. In California, imprisoning people convicted of simple drug possession and what is familiarly called "petty with a prior"—petty theft with a previous conviction for some form of theft— costs the state roughly $400 million a year—money that consequently cannot be used for, say, drug treatment or literacy programs in the prisons.[28] Even with the most elaborate statistical manipulations, no one has managed to show that it is cost-effective to keep all of these offenders behind bars.

NO ALTERNATIVES?

Like the "prison works" argument, too, the "prison pays" argument ultimately founders on the question, Compared to what? The issue for intelligent social policy is not whether it is more cost-effective to lock up serious offenders than to do nothing, but rather, what is the most effective way to use our public resources if we want to control the kinds of crime that cause the most damage to individuals and communities? If we can get more "payoff," even in sheer economic terms, from other approaches to crime prevention, then the "prison pays" argument collapses.

Here, however, we come up against the fourth of the myths that have kept us mired in an ineffective and costly response to crime: The myth that we do not know how to do anything *else* to reduce crime other than increase the risks of punishment. "It is very hard for a free society," James Q. Wilson contends, "to figure out how effectively to deal with crime rates other than by imprisonment."[29] On its face, that assertion seems improbable, since other "free societies" have manifestly dealt with crime rates far more effectively than we have, without resorting to anything approaching our investment in imprisonment. And we now have considerable evidence from a growing body of research and experience to support a far more optimistic view of what might be possible. There are many things we could do, other than building more prisons, to reduce the crime rate in the United States. Doing them would not only make us a safer and less fearful country, but would mesh with our strongest social values in a way that simply warehousing an ever-larger proportion of our population clearly does not. Most of them, for that matter, would cost considerably less than the strategy we are now pursuing. Some of them involve changing our priorities within the criminal justice system itself; some involve supporting and expanding proven programs for vulnerable children, youth, and families; and some involve broader social action to attack the deeper roots of violence in American society. Here let me offer a thumbnail sketch of a few of each.

THE JUSTICE SYSTEM

I've argued that part of the reason for our failure to control violent crime is that we have relied too much on the criminal justice system to do the job alone. But the problem is not just that we've asked the justice system to do too much, but that we have asked it to do the wrong things. Traditionally, we have used the justice system in an almost purely reactive way. We have used most of our resources to punish offenders after the fact, little to prevent crime from occurring in the first place. Most of the people we punish are then released, at some point, with little or no effort made to prepare them for a better chance of success on the outside. And they are typically released into impoverished and often devastated communities with few social supports and minimal opportunities for legitimate success. That is clearly a prescription for futility, and it is widely understood by both scholars and practitioners that this situation needs to change. Two changes are especially crucial: making the reintegration of offenders a central priority, and shifting criminal justice resources toward the prevention of harm in the community.

Reinvesting in rehabilitation. It's often said that we tried rehabilitation in the idealistic sixties, but it failed. Both parts of the statement are wrong. Support for the idea of rehabilitation was always more rhetorical than real, even at the height of the Great Society era. In 1967, the President's Commission on Law Enforcement and the Administration of Justice lamented that "although the rehabilitation of criminals is presumably its major purpose, the custody of criminals is actually its main task."[30] And matters have mostly gone downhill since. In the 1970s, it began to be argued that "nothing works" to rehabilitate criminals. By the 1990s, even the most basic services in prisons and juvenile institutions were being cut back, often on the ground that they coddled offenders. Half of the states' juvenile facilities, for example, do not meet federal or state requirements mandating at least minimal schooling for youths behind bars. In 1994, federal funding for postsecondary education programs in prison was slashed, and the number of inmates enrolled in college-level programs accordingly fell by nearly half.[31]

The paradox is that the decimation of even the meager efforts that now exist comes just when we have more and more evidence that rehabilitation can indeed "work" for many of the people we put behind bars. Today, indeed, the issue for most criminologists is no longer *whether* rehabilitation works, but what *kind* of interventions work best, and for whom. The kernel of truth in the right's critique is that much of what now passes for rehabilitation *is* ineffective, too often both poorly conceived and poorly implemented. But programs that are carefully designed, that are designed to address the underlying problems that got offenders into trouble in the first place, and that are reasonably intensive and adequately funded, have made a difference—sometimes a striking one.[32] Two of the most encouraging examples are intensive work with serious juvenile offenders and drug treatment for prisoners.

Our current approach to youths in trouble, in most jurisdictions, represents a peculiar blend of harshness and neglect. Youths who break the law may get little attention whatsoever until they have committed several offenses, at which point the system comes down hard on them, often committing them to poorly staffed, occasionally brutal facilities where little is done to address the problems that got them into repeated trouble to begin with. The obvious alternative is to intervene earlier, and more supportively, in order to deflect the predictable trajectory into chronic lawbreaking and repeated institutionalization. Across the country, several promising programs have been developed to do just that. One approach, launched in several states, goes under the rather cumbersome name of Multisystemic Therapy (MST). MST is distinctive in two ways: it explicitly tackles youths' problems in whatever institution (or "system") they occur—the family, the school, the larger community—and it works intensively with young offenders and their families until the underlying issues are resolved, a process that may involve several contacts a week between the offender and a caseworker. An MST program for serious young offenders in South Carolina, for example, many of them violent and/or repeat offenders who would have been on their way to a youth prison in the absence of the program, cut rearrests in half among its clients, as compared to a control group of similar offenders who were given conventional juvenile-justice treatment. The program, moreover, apparently worked equally well for youths of all races, both sexes, and with widely different prior records. A similar program in Missouri slashed the number of violent offenses to less than a third that of a control group, who were offered more conventional individual counseling.[33]

A second promising strategy is drug treatment. It is estimated that as many as 60 to 70 percent of state prison inmates have a drug problem severe enough to benefit from treatment. And there is considerable recent evidence that effective treatment can strongly reduce rates of recidivism. Delaware's Key program, for example, which provided at least a year of intensive residential treatment in prison and followed it with several months of aftercare in the community, cut arrests of released inmates by more than half.[34] Drug treatment is not a panacea, and—as with other reintegrative programs—it is crucial to separate wheat from chaff. Much of what passes for drug treatment, whether in the justice system or outside it, is too spotty or too brief to have much impact. But treatment programs that enroll offenders for at least a year of intensive help, that provide comprehensive aftercare services to aid the transition into community life, and that directly confront underlying problems such as joblessness and homelessness, have produced strong results. Yet, despite the evidence of success, good treatment remains a rarity in most prison systems; until 1996, when a new 1,200-bed facility was opened, California had a total of only 400 treatment beds for an inmate population of over 140,000, more than half of whom were believed to have a substantial problem with illegal drugs.

The treatment-oriented drug court programs now blossoming in many cities are, at their best, a promising example of what can be done when the goal of reintegration is taken seriously. Though the specifics vary from place to place, the principle is to provide drug offenders with treatment as an alternative to incarceration; if they follow the program's guidelines and stay clean for a specified period of time, their charges are dropped.[35] The drug court is still a relatively new idea, and few of them now have enough of the kinds of resources—including access to effective treatment facilities or job training—that could ensure the long-term success of their clients. But the best of them are moving in that direction, and the overall premise makes eminent sense. It counters the twin problems of overincarceration and neglect that now ensure that too many minor offenders are cycled over and over again through an already over-burdened justice system.

Strategies like these are sometimes scorned as "soft on crime" by conservative critics. But the reality is that serious rehabilitation programs make demands on offenders that simply warehousing them behind bars does not. It is often said, with considerable self-righteousness, that people who "do the crime" should "do the time," preferably without supportive programs or "frills." But by itself, doing the time asks nothing of the offender. Serious reintegrative programs, on the other hand, establish a sort of social contract that makes substantial demands on both parties. Offenders agree to learn to read, learn a skill, get clean, and stay sober; society agrees to provide some of the tools to make those changes realistically possible. The principles are clear; criminal behavior will have consequences, but the consequences will be designed, as much as possible, with the aim of restoring the offender as a contributing member of the community. There is nothing revolutionary about this principle; it is how we deal with most people, most of the time, outside the justice system. Applying the principle consistently throughout the criminal justice system, however, would be a revolutionary step indeed.

Preventing community violence. A second priority is to support policing strategies that can, at least in the short run, reduce the crippling and frequently self-perpetuating level of violence in disadvantaged communities. It is crucial to be clear about what this does and does not mean. It doesn't mean throwing money at police departments, or tolerating aggressive and discriminatory police practices under the guise of fighting serious crime.

Much has been made of the supposed success of so-called zero-tolerance or quality-of-life policing—"rousting" teenagers, harrassing the homeless, targeting "squeegee men"—in the unusually sharp declines in serious crime in New York City and some other cities since the early 1990s. But little hard evidence has been offered to show that it is these strategies in particular—or any policing strategies—that have contributed to the declines. No one has yet completely disentangled all of the reasons, but serious crimes of violence have fallen much faster than less serious ones. It is difficult to understand why cracking down on "quality of life" offenses could have a *larger* impact on serious violence than on the lesser offenses it directly targets, particularly since serious crime also fell in the same period in cities like Los Angeles that did not share the New York approach to policing.

Moreover, much of the decline in cities such as New York followed extraordinary *rises* that began in the mid 1980s and brought many cities their worst-ever levels of violence. Most of the country, in short, suffered an epidemic of violence that peaked in the early 1990s, leaving us with endemic levels of violent crime that still far surpass those in any comparable developed nation. In most cities, the epidemic of violence was closely related to the epidemic of crack cocaine, which hit New York harder and earlier than most other cities. Crack settled in to become a routine, tragic, but no longer epidemic part of urban life, and a sharply improving economy in some cities has helped as well, drawing many vulnerable people into productive work and away from such high-risk settings as bars and street corners. There is also some evidence of "attrition" of the at-risk population through violence, accidents, HIV infection, or other preventable illnesses, and, on the positive side, of a cultural shift among inner-city youth sparked by the extent and impact of the tragedy on urban communities and families.[36]

The evidence for the effectiveness of more carefully targeted police strategies, however, is much stronger. This is especially true of strategies to get illegal guns off the street and to disrupt open-air drug markets, which are an enormous source of neighborhood violence and demoral-

ization.[37] Going after guns can have a special impact on the youth violence that skyrocketed in American cities after the mid 1980s; as guns
flooded inner-city communities, youths began carrying them in self-
defense, creating an upward spiral of firearms, fear, and violence (in a
1996 poll, 40 percent of inner-city eighth, tenth, and twelfth graders
reported that they carried a weapon for protection).[38] Assertive efforts by
police to crack down on guns can help to promote a kind of local disarmament, winding the spiral in the other direction and potentially bringing a dramatic improvement in the quality of community life. It is
important to be clear that supporting these efforts isn't the same as giving
police free rein to run roughshod over the rights of poor people.
Aggressive "quality of life" policing in particular is sometimes justified on
the ground that there is a necessary tradeoff between crime control and
civil liberties. But that tradeoff is mythical. There is no evidence whatever that launching a carefully targeted effort to keep illegal guns off the
streets requires violating fundamental human rights.

CHILDREN AND FAMILIES

Beyond the justice system, a serious strategy to reduce crime means making a much greater investment in programs that work with vulnerable
families and children in order to prevent violence before it happens.
Prevention programs have been the target of great scorn by conservatives
in recent years: "When someone dials 911," Newt Gingrich announced
in 1995, "they want a policeman. They don't want a social worker."[39]
Congressman Gingrich, of course, entirely missed the point of crime prevention—which is to avoid having to dial 911 in the first place. But the
comment reflected the widespread view that most of the programs touted
as "crime prevention" were nothing more than political "pork." As is
often the case, there is an element of truth in that exaggeration. At the
other end of the political spectrum, liberals have sometimes been unduly
uncritical of crime prevention programs, overselling fashionable panaceas
with little evidence of effectiveness and making extravagant claims for
programs that were minimally funded and spottily implemented. But
here, too, as with reforms within the justice system, there is compelling
evidence that the best-conceived and most seriously implemented prevention efforts have sometimes been astonishingly successful. Two examples are especially significant:

Preventing child abuse and neglect. We often talk about violent criminals as if they simply fell from the sky, or landed from Mars. But the reality is that the "thugs" we fear the most come disproportionately from

abusive families. The evidence that severe abuse or neglect is closely associated with violence—especially the kinds of brutal violent crime that
trouble us the most—has steadily accumulated in recent years; so, fortunately, has the evidence that such maltreatment is preventable.[40] Some of
the most encouraging findings come from studies of "home visiting" programs for vulnerable families. The most impressive example is Hawaii's
statewide Healthy Start program, which links high-risk families with
paraprofessional caseworkers who help parents cope with child-rearing
issues, as well as a wide range of problems—from housing crises to
unemployment—that can lead to abuse and neglect. The program,
according to careful evaluations, cut incidents of abuse and neglect by
more than half among its target families.[41]

Building the capabilities of "at-risk" youth. Although there is an obvious
case for the importance of prevention strategies that begin in early childhood, the potential of prevention doesn't end there. It is still sometimes
argued that once children are past the age of three or so, their behavioral
patterns are set in stone, for better or worse. Yet it is increasingly clear
that this view is overly pessimistic. We know how to build the capacities
of vulnerable adolescents in ways that will, among other things, keep
them out of serious crime. One of the strongest examples is the
Quantum Opportunity Program, designed in the 1980s to help
teenagers from welfare families in school and on track toward college or
advanced job training. Quantum enrolled poor teens in a comprehensive
package of activities that lasted throughout their high school years.
Students spent extra time outside regular classes learning special skills,
often high-tech skills; they were taken out of their neighborhoods to
explore job sites and to museums and the theater; and they were given a
modest stipend that was matched dollar for dollar by the program, which
created a fund that could be used for college or specialized job training.
Two years after they left the program, Quantum participants had only
half the arrests of a control group of youths from similar backgrounds.[42]

When we look at what it is about these programs that "works," some
general principles emerge, and they turn out to be very similar to those
that underlie successful rehabilitation programs in the justice system
itself. The most effective prevention programs, for example, build on the
strengths of their participants, rather than simply punishing them or
attempting to treat their presumed deficiencies. They situate their clients'
troubles in the context of the larger institutions that surround them—
including the family, schools, job and housing markets, and the wider
community—rather than trying to deal with their problems in isolation.

They provide tangible services and incentives, rather than simply offering counseling or individual "treatment." And they are sufficiently well-funded and capably staffed to be able to deliver in practice on what they promise in theory.

SOCIAL ACTION

Yet it is as much a mistake to promise too much from these prevention programs as to expect too little. The evidence is clear that even within the American context of mass poverty, economic insecurity, and community disintegration, there is much that can be done to increase the chances that children will grow up compassionate rather than predatory, that youths in trouble will be helped to achieve a productive life. But the social environment in which too many American children grow up can undercut even the best-conceived efforts to help those at risk. This does not mean we should skimp on such efforts; it means that they need to be linked with a broader attack on the social and economic forces that place so many children and their parents at risk in the first place.

This is not a new idea. Indeed, until the late 1960s it was a central part of the dominant consensus about crime and its control in the United States. The President's Crime Commission expressed that consensus concisely in 1967: "Crime flourishes," they wrote, "where the conditions of life are the worst."[43] Given such a diagnosis, the remedy was clear: "The foundation of a national strategy against crime must be an unremitting national effort for social justice." But the consensus began to unravel in the 1970s, as conservative critics began to argue that the link between crime and social disadvantage was a figment of the liberal imagination. At the extreme, it was sometimes argued that there were no "root causes" of crime at all. And by the 1980s, these views—once confined to the fringes of academic discussion—had become staples of the public debate about crime.

The kernel of truth in these arguments is that the connections between social exclusion and crime are complex, and sometimes indirect. But they are nevertheless real, and we will neither understand American violence nor confront it in enduring ways without addressing them. For what the accumulating evidence increasingly shows is that the United States has paid a high price in endemic violence as a result of its extreme adherence to the principles of the "market" in ordering its social and economic life. By comparison with most of the rest of the advanced industrial world, we have traditionally tolerated much greater extremes of economic inequality and poverty and have invested far less in the public

provision of the services—health care, family supports, income benefits—that in other nations help to include all citizens into a common
social life.

Data from the Luxemburg Income Study (LIS), an international study
of patterns of income, poverty, and social spending, illustrate these disparities. As of the early 1990s, for example, about 22 percent of U.S.
children were poor; our closest "competitors" in the developed world,
Australia and Canada, had child poverty rates of roughly 14 percent.
Most other industrial democracies were far lower—France and Germany
at about 6 percent, and Sweden, Norway, and Denmark, among others,
below 4 percent. Moreover, poor children in the United States are *poorer*,
in absolute terms, than their counterparts in other industrial nations.
Affluent children in the United States are even better off than their counterparts in Europe, but Swedish or Swiss children on the bottom rungs of
their countries' income ladder, for example, have 72 percent more real
income than the poorest American children. The combination of
absolute deprivation and harsh income inequality that afflicts American
children is compounded by a distinctively weak commitment to the provision of basic social services. The LIS also shows that the United States
devotes a much smaller portion of its national income to such measures
as public assistance, unemployment compensation, family allowances,
and disability benefits than most other industrial societies. We spend less
than 4 percent of gross domestic product on these "social protection"
measures: at the other extreme, the Scandinavian countries and the
Netherlands spend from 12 to 14 percent.[44]

The figures are cold and abstract, but they point to social policies with
enormous human consequences. American families are forced, far more
than families in other countries, to make do in a volatile market economy with little support from their government. They are much more
likely to experience a degree of social exclusion that is no longer tolerated
in most other industrial countries—even some that are considerably less
affluent than the United States overall. And this is more than just a matter of material conditions. It also represents a profound difference in values—a difference of culture. Among the industrial democracies today,
the United States stands out as a uniquely Darwinian, "sink or swim"
society, a prime example of what some critics call a "winner–loser"
culture.

And these differences *matter* in understanding our level of violent
crime. For the evidence is by now overwhelming that serious violent
crime is closely associated with extremes of economic deprivation,

inequality, and social exclusion. Crossnational studies show, for example, that countries with a wider spread of income inequality are likely to suffer higher rates of homicide (and child abuse).[45] It is not accidental that the only countries with levels of homicide that compare with ours are in Latin America and other parts of the developing world, where extremes of inequality are even sharper than ours—or in parts of the former Soviet bloc, where both income inequality and absolute poverty have increased sharply under the impact of "market oriented" reforms. Studies *within* the United States and other individual countries show the same pattern; American rates of homicide and assault, for example, rose hand-in-hand with the increasing inequality of wages among American workers from the 1970s onward.[46]

Recent research also confirms that the connection between social exclusion and violence is strongest for the poorest of the poor. The highest rates of urban violence in the United States are found in neighborhoods that are not only poor but desperately impoverished.[47] What the Crime Commission wrote thirty years ago turns out to be true: crime does indeed flourish "where the conditions of life are the worst." Again, that relationship is intensified by the meagerness of the social safety net in the United States. Crossnational research also shows, for example, that youth violence tends to be much lower in countries with a more collectivist approach to the provision of public services.[48]

As long as these enormous disparities exist, they will continue to undermine even our best efforts at prevention and rehabilitation. This does not mean, however, that such efforts are useless; on the contrary, we've seen that much can be achieved even within the American context of mass social exclusion and deprivation. But we are swimming upstream against a powerful current. By the same token, there is a positive and even hopeful message beneath these grim statistics. For what they tell us is that violence on the American scale is not inevitable. If we brought our homicide rate down even to the levels of that in Germany or France, we would save up to 15,000 American lives every year. It is not a matter of fate or even of inevitable economic or technological shifts that we suffer the level of violent crime that we do; it is in good part a reflection of structural social forces over which we have some control. The persistence of extremes of poverty and inequality and the lack of appropriate public services are things we can *do* something about, if we choose to. This is not the place to outline a blueprint for action against these social ills, but let me point to some key things it should include.

Reforming work. It is clear that an enduring response to violent crime will require a concerted attack on the extreme poverty that distinguishes us from the rest of the industrial world. But to the extent that the United States now has anything approaching an antipoverty policy, it is centered on "reforming" welfare—which means, for the most part, forcing poor women into the labor market. But what needs reforming most is the labor market itself, and especially the spread of low-wage, unstable work. The low wages at the bottom of the American pay scale distinguish us sharply from most other advanced societies, and help to explain our much higher rates of "working" poverty. Workers in the lowest tenth of the pay range in the United States, for example, earn just 38 percent of the median wage for all workers, versus 61 percent in Germany and 68 percent in Japan.[49]

It should be obvious that we won't cut the links between poverty and violence by increasing the number of poorly paid, stressful jobs and forcing poor parents to take them; if anything, the research tells us that the resulting stresses are likely to make the crime problem worse. Instead, we need to make good on the social contract that having a job should imply: that people who work should be able to earn enough to provide a decent living—and also have sufficient time away from the workplace to allow a balanced and fulfilling family life. We have made some small steps in this direction in recent years, including an expansion of the Earned Income Tax Credit (which provides modest tax breaks for working people) and, after many years of stagnation, a modest increase in the federal minimum wage. But full-time work at the current minimum wage still pays several thousand dollars less than the poverty level for a family of four. The "living wage" campaigns recently launched in several cities, demanding that employers receiving any kind of subsidy or contract from the city pay their workers at a rate much higher than the minimum and provide full benefits—are a stronger alternative. But the principle that Americans who work should earn enough to enjoy basic economic security and a stable family life should be pressed on a much broader front—including strong support for the efforts of the labor movement to organize in low-wage sectors of the economy.

Spreading work. We will also need to reverse the growing tendency for the labor force to be divided into those who work too little and those who must work too much. Both problems aggravate the family stresses and community disintegration that breed violent crime, and both result from our predilection to organize work according to what the market will bear, rather than what will best foster the healthy development of individuals, families, and communities. Mandating living wages would take us a big step in this direction, by reducing the need to take on too many hours or an extra job to pay the bills. But so would more direct measures to create more generous leaves and more flexible working arrangements. The Family and Medical Leave Act of 1993, which mandated a twelve-week unpaid leave for working parents to spend time with a baby or a sick child, was a first move in this direction—but obviously a small one. Here again, the United States is distinctive among industrial nations in the absence of provision for paid leaves—and even lags behind many countries of the developing world. Sweden, which provides a full year's leave at 90 percent of regular pay for either parent and the option of a six-hour working day until the child is eight years old, has gone the farthest; but the average among European countries is at least three months of leave with pay at or near a worker's usual salary.[50] In this country, paid leaves have been effectively resisted on the ground that they represent an unwarranted interference with the right of employers to set the terms of employment. But the result is that society as a whole is forced to pick up the pieces—to pay the taxes that support the child protective and mental health agencies, special schooling, and—not least—prisons that we deploy after the fact to deal with the effects of our national failure to ensure nurturing environments for small children.

Enhancing social services. But attacking the social exclusion that so predictably breeds violent crime will also require a commitment to more generous and universal services. The most crucial example is child care. Accessible, reliable child care can provide nurturance and supervision for many children who will not otherwise get them, especially if their parents must work too long in the low-wage labor market. By relieving the stress of combining work and child rearing, it can also reduce the risks of child abuse and neglect. And providing affordable child care could also alleviate one of the key expenses that too often keep low-income families mired in poverty. Yet here, too, the United States lags far behind many other countries. In most of Western Europe, child care for children aged three to five is virtually universal—sometimes offered in freestanding child care centers, more often in heavily subsidized preschool programs.[51] Exactly how we provide the care is much less important than that we do so one way or another.

Proposals such as these obviously go against the thrust of our present national commitment to reduce the size of the public sector and to enforce a flexible labor force. But that commitment is itself part of the problem, not part of the solution. To the extent that we allow crucial public services, from health care to income support, to wither in the name of austerity and directionless economic growth, and demand that individuals and families become ever more flexible and mobile in order to meet the presumed demands of an ever-harsher global economy, we will surely worsen the poverty, social isolation, and community disintegration that predictably breed violent crime. On this score, indeed, our current social policies reflect an extraordinary state of collective denial. We agree, across the political spectrum, that the condition of families has an enormous influence on whether children grow up compassionate or predatory. But when it comes to our commitment to the well-being of families in the real world, we want to have things both ways. We want competent, caring families that can raise children effectively, but we refuse to provide the social supports that would make this possible. We force parents to choose between draining overwork in the low-wage economy and demoralizing poverty outside it. We want parents to be self-sufficient, but we will not provide the child care that would allow them to earn a decent living without jeopardizing their children's well-being. We want parents to spend "quality" time with their children, but we reject the paid leaves or shorter hours that would allow it. We acknowledge the strong link between child abuse and violent crime, but we starve our child protective services. We say we want people to work in the legitimate labor market, but we deliberately maintain high levels of joblessness in order to soothe the stock and bond markets. Ultimately, we cannot have it both ways. In the future, we will need to choose between perpetuating the kinds of stresses and deprivations that we know breed violence, or finally bringing our social policies in line with those of the rest of the world's industrial democracies—which, not coincidentally, suffer far less violent crime.

NOTES

1. Marc Mauer, *Americans Behind Bars: U.S. and International Rates of Incarceration* (Washington, DC: Sentencing Project, 1997), 4–5; FBI, *Crime in the United States, 1995* (Washington, DC: Government Printing Office, 1996), 112, Los Angeles–England comparison; Home Office, *Notifiable Offenses, England and Wales, 1995* (London: Government Statistical Service, 1996), 6. In 1995, there were 726 homicides in England and Wales and 849 in Los Angeles.

2. Phil Gramm, "Don't Let Judges Set Crooks Free," *New York Times*, July 7, 1993.

3. William Bennet, John J. DiIulio, and James P. Walters, *Body Count* (New York: Simon & Schuster, 1996), 16.

4. Mauer, *Americans Behind Bars*, 4.

5. David Farrington and Patrick A. Langan, "Changes in Crime and Punishment in England and America in the 1980s," *Justice Quarterly*, 9, no. 1 (March 1992): 5–18; James P. Lynch, "A Cross-national Comparison of the Length of Custodial Sentences for Serious Crimes," *Justice Quarterly*, 10, no. 4 (December 1993): 653–58.

6. U.S. Bureau of Justice Statistics, *Prisoners in 1996* (Washington, DC: U.S. Department of Justice, 1997), 1–5.

7. Thomas P. Bonczar and Allen J. Beck, *Lifetime Likelihood of Going to State or Federal Prison* (Washington, DC: U.S. Bureau of Justice Statistics, 1997), 1.

8. Kathleen Connolly, Lea McDermid, Vincent Schiraldi, and Dan Macallair, *From Classrooms to Cellblocks* (San Francisco: Center on Juvenile and Criminal Justice, 1996), 1.

9. U.S. Bureau of Justice Statistics, *Prisoners in 1996*.

10. John J. DiIulio, "Crime in America: It's Going to Get Worse," *Reader's Digest* (August 1995): 57; Gramm, "Don't Let Judges Set Crooks Free."

11. Patrick A. Langan and Jodi M. Brown, *Felony Sentences in State Courts, 1994* (Washington, DC: U.S. Bureau of Justice Statistics, 1997), 5.

12. DiIulio, "Crime in America," 57.

13. U.S. Bureau of Justice Statistics, *Criminal Victimization in the United States, 1994* (Washington, DC: U.S. Department of Justice, 1996), 1–4.

14. Albert J. Reiss and Jeffrey Roth, *Understanding and Preventing Violence* (Washington, DC: National Research Council, 1993), 276.

15. Langan and Brown, *Felony Sentences in State Courts, 1994*; Patrick A. Langan, Craig Perkins, and Jan M. Chaiken, *Felony Sentences in the United States, 1990* (Washington, DC: U.S. Bureau of Justice Statistics, 1995), 8.

16. See James Q. Wilson, "The Contradictions of an Advanced Capitalist State," *Forbes* (September 14, 1992): 111–16.

17. For a discusion of some of these survey findings, see Pat Mayhew, *Findings from the International Crime Survey* (London: Home Office Research and Planning Unit, 1994).

18. U.S. Department of Health and Human Services, *Health: United States, 1995* (Washington, DC: Government Printing Office, 1996), 114–15.

19. Homicide death rate figures calculated from ibid. and World Health Organization, *World Health Statistics, 1994* (Geneva: World Health Organization, 1997).

20. Thomas B. Marvell and Carlisle E. Moody, "Prison Population Growth and Crime Reduction," *Journal of Quantitative Criminology*, 10, no. 2 (1994): 109–37.

21. On this issue, see Jorge Canela-Cacho, Jacqueline Cohen, and Alfred Blumstein, "Relationship Between the Offending Frequency of Imprisoned and Free Offenders," *Criminology*, 35, no. 1 (1997): 133–71.

22. James Q. Wilson, "Crimes and Misdemeanours," *Criminal Justice Matters* (Institute for Study and Treatment of Delinquency, London), no. 25 (Autumn 1996): 4.

23. For a recent example of this research, see Ted R. Miller, Mark A. Cohen, and Brian Wiersema, *Victim Costs and Consequences: A New Look* (Washington, DC: National Institute of Justice, 1996).

24. Anne M. Piehl and John J. DiIulio, "Does Prison Pay? Revisited," *Brookings Review* (Winter 1995): 21–25.

25. U.S. Bureau of Justice Statistics, *Prisoners in 1996,* 6.

26. Vincent Schiraldi, *Three Strikes in California: The New Apartheid?* (San Francisco: Center on Juvenile and Criminal Justice, 1996), 1.

27. See DiIulio, "Crime in America," 58.

28. Author's calculations from California Department of Corrections data. At the end of 1995, there were more than six thousand prisoners sentenced for petty theft with a prior, and more than twelve thousand for simple drug possession. The estimated cost of imprisonment per year, per offender, was $21,000, not including the costs of prison construction and financing.

29. Wilson, "Crimes and Misdemeanours."

30. President's Commission on Law Enforcement and the Administration of Justice, *The Challenge of Crime in a Free Society* (Washington, DC: Government Printing Office, 1967), 12.

31. Jessica Portner, "Jailed Youths Shortchanged on Education," *Education Week*, 16, no. 5 (October 2, 1996); Richard Tewksbury and Jon Marc Taylor, "The Consequences of Eliminating Pell Grant Funding for Students in Post-secondary Correctional Education Programs," *Federal Probation*, 60, no. 3 (September 1996): 60–63.

32. For an excellent recent review of research on programs for offenders, see Alan T. Harland, ed., *Choosing Correctional Options That Work* (Thousand Oaks, CA: Sage, 1996).

33. Scott W. Henggeler et al., "Multisystemic Therapy: An Effective Violence Prevention Approach for Serious Juvenile Offenders," *Journal of Adolescence*, 19, no. 1 (1996): 47–61.

34. James A. Inciardi, *A Corrections-based Continuum of Effective Drug Abuse Treatment* (Washington, DC: National Institute of Justice, 1996).

35. Drug Court Clearinghouse and Technical Assistance Project, *Juvenile Drug Courts: Preliminary Report* (Washington, DC: American University, 1997).

36. For a more extensive discussion, see Elliot Currie, *Crime and Punishment in America* (New York: Metropolitan Books, 1998), chapters 1 and 6.

37. Lawrence W. Sherman and Dennis P. Rogan, "Effects of Gun Seizure on Gun Violence: Hot Spots Patrol in Kansas City," *Justice Quarterly*, 12, no. 4 (December 1995): 673–93; David A. Weisburd and Lorraine Green, "Policing Drug Hot Spots: The Jersey City Drug Market Analysis Experiment," *Justice Quarterly*, 12, no. 4 (December 1995).

38. Peter Applebome, "Crime Fear Is Seen Forcing Changes in Youth Behavior," *New York Times*, January 12, 1996.

39. Cited in Gwen Ifill, "Spending in Crime Bill: Prevention or Just Pork?" *New York Times*, August 16, 1994.

40. See Cathy Spatz Widom, *The Cycle of Violence Revisited* (Washington, DC: National Institute of Justice, 1996); Carolyn Smith and Terence Thornberry, "The Relationship Between Childhood Maltreatment and Adolescent Involvement in Delinquency," *Criminology*, 33, no. 4 (1995): 451–77.

41. Center on Child Abuse Prevention Research, *Intensive Home Visitation: A Randomized Trial, Follow-up, and Risk Assessment Study of Hawaii's Healthy Start Program* (Chicago: National Committee to Prevent Child Abuse, 1996).

42. Opportunities Industrialization Centers, *Quantum Opportunity Program* (Philadelphia: OIC, 1995).

43. President's Commission, *The Challenge of Crime*, 26.

44. Lee Rainwater and Timothy M. Smeeding, *Doing Poorly: The Real Income of American Children In a Comparative Perspective* (Syracuse University, Maxwell School of Citizenship, 1995), 2–22.

45. Rosemary Gartner, "The Victims of Homicide: A Temporal and Cross-national Comparison," *American Sociological Review*, 55, no. 1 (February 1990): 92–106.

46. Richard Fowles and Mary Merva, "Wage Inequality and Criminal Activity," *Criminology*, 34, no. 2 (1996): 163–82.

47. Lauren J. Krivo and Ruth D. Peterson, "Extremely Disadvantaged Neighborhoods and Urban Crime," *Social Forces*, 75, no. 2 (December 1996): 619–50.

48. Fred C. Pampel and Rosemary Gartner, "Age Structure, Sociopolitical Institutions, and National Homicide Rates," *European Sociological Review*, 11, no. 3 (December 1995): 243–60.

49. Richard B. Freeman, "How Labor Fares in the Advanced Industrial Economies," in *Working Under Different Rules,* ed. Richard B. Freeman (New York: Russell Sage Foundation, 1994), 14.

50. Francoise Core and Vassiliki Koutsogeorgeopolou, "Parental Leave: What and Where," *OECD Observer,* no. 195 (August/September 1995): 15–20.

51. Sheila Kamerman and Alfred Kahn, *Starting Right* (New York: Oxford University Press, 1995), chapter 6.

18 DAVID COLE

TWO SYSTEMS OF CRIMINAL JUSTICE

FEW principles are more fundamental to our conception of American criminal justice than the guarantee that everyone, no matter how poor, has a right to a lawyer when facing serious criminal charges. The case establishing that principle, *Gideon v. Wainwright*, is probably the most celebrated criminal justice decision the Supreme Court has ever issued.[1] Millions have read the story in Anthony Lewis's best-selling book, *Gideon's Trumpet*, and millions more have seen the movie, starring Henry Fonda as Clarence Earl Gideon. It's a classic American story: A penniless drifter, tried without a lawyer and convicted of stealing money from a pool hall vending machine, sends a handwritten letter from prison asking for help from the Supreme Court. The Court takes his case, appoints Abe Fortas, one of the best lawyers in the country, to represent him, and then rules that all indigent defendants facing serious criminal charges have a right to a lawyer paid for by the state. On retrial, with a local trial lawyer, Gideon is acquitted. Hollywood couldn't have written it better. It is a great story, and part of what makes it great is its message: Where criminal penalties are at stake, everyone should stand on equal footing in a court of law. As the Supreme Court stated in another case that was decided about the same time as *Gideon*, "there can be no justice where the kind of trial a man gets depends on the amount of money he has."[2]

But of course everyone is not equal before the law. While the legitimacy of our criminal justice system is explicitly premised on the ideal of that equality, it is a myth. At every stage of the criminal justice system, from encounters with police officers on the beat to the appointment of lawyers for the poor to selecting jurors and enacting criminal laws, members of minority groups and the poor receive harsher treatment than white people of means.

The disparities are alarming. The vast majority of those behind bars are poor, 40 percent of state prisoners cannot read, and 67 percent of prison inmates did not have full-time employment when they were arrested. The per-capita incarceration rate among blacks is seven times that among whites. African Americans make up about 12 percent of the general population but close to half of the prison population. They serve longer sentences, have higher arrest and conviction rates, face higher bail amounts, and are more often the victims of police use of deadly force than white citizens. In 1995, one in three black men between the ages of twenty and twenty-nine was imprisoned or on parole or probation. If incarceration rates remain steady, one in four black males born today will serve time in prison during his lifetime. Nationally, for every one black man who graduates from college, one hundred are arrested.[3]

Most criminal justice scholars agree that some but not all of the disparities in incarceration are attributable to higher rates of offending by minorities and the poor.[4] But even if it were the disparity's sole cause, the previous figures raise serious questions, which I will suggest in the last section of this chapter. And differential offending rates are by no means the whole story. Consider, for example, the figures on drug use and convictions. In 1992–93, blacks made up 12 percent of the general population, and 13 percent of monthly drug users by self-reporting. But over the same period, blacks made up 35 percent of all drug arrests, 55 percent of drug convictions, and 74 percent of prison sentences for drug convictions.[5]

Minorities and the poor are also disproportionately victimized by crime. African Americans are the victims of robbery at a rate 150 percent higher than whites; they are the victims of rape, aggravated assault, and armed robbery 25 percent more often than whites. Homicide is the leading cause of death among young black men.[6] And because most crime is intraracial and intraclass, the more law enforcement resources that are directed toward protecting minority and poor communities from crime, the more often minority and poor citizens, especially those living in the inner city, will find their friends, relatives, and neighbors behind bars.

Perfect equality, of course, is by definition an ideal unrealizable in practice. But the disparities noted above do not reflect a mere failure to live up to our aspirations. They reflect a system that affirmatively depends upon the exploitation of inequality. The criminal justice system is fraught with difficult choices between safety on one hand and constitutional rights and freedoms on the other. While some constitutional rights such as the right to confront one's accusers are designed to increase the reliability of guilt determinations, many such as the rule barring use of unlawfully seized evidence affirmatively impede accurate assessments of guilt. Moreover, even rights designed to safeguard reliability exact a cost by making criminals harder to convict. The due process requirement that criminal convictions be proved beyond a reasonable doubt, for example, allows many factually guilty people to go free in order to make it more likely that innocent people are not erroneously convicted. In the end, virtually every decision to protect the rights of the criminally accused hampers law enforcement and makes us more vulnerable to crime. Obviously, crime would be much less of a problem if we were willing to live in a police state, but we would all have less privacy, less freedom, and less dignity, and fear of crime would simply be replaced by fear of official repression. Thus the administration of criminal justice in a democratic society that respects individual rights necessitates a balance of competing values.

Inequality eases the difficult task of balancing these values. The Supreme Court has repeatedly struck a "balance" not by picking one point on the continuum and defending it, but in effect by picking two points—one for the more privileged and educated, the other for the poor and less educated. For example, the Court has ruled that the Fourth Amendment bars police from searching luggage, purses, and wallets without a warrant based on probable cause to believe evidence of crime will be found. At the same time, the Court permits police officers to approach any citizen—without any legitimate basis for suspicion—and request consent to search. Furthermore, the officer need not inform the suspect that he has a right to refuse. Not surprisingly, this tactic is popular among the police and is disproportionately targeted at young black men. Thus, the privacy of the privileged is guaranteed, but the police still get their evidence through the "consent" of the underprivileged. In this way, society does not have to pay the cost in increased crime of extending to all the right of privacy enjoyed by the privileged.

Analogous double standards are evident in the legal doctrines and practices governing representation, jury selection, and criminal punishment. Each of these areas is central to the criminal justice process. Attorneys are a defendant's voice and the means by which all rights are asserted. The jury makes the most important bottom-line decision in a criminal case by determining guilt or innocence. And the sentence reflects the system's ultimate sanction for offending behavior. In each of these critical areas, double standards exist along race and class lines.

Poor defendants are assigned attorneys at state expense, as *Gideon* required, but the Court has declined to guarantee that the lawyer be competent, and indigent clients pay for their appointed lawyers' mistakes with their liberty. Throughout most of the country, criminal juries historically have been and remain disproportionately white, and despite impressive proclamations, the Supreme Court has done all too little to countermand that fact. And we are only able to maintain our ranking as first in per-capita incarceration among developed countries because the incarcerated are themselves disproportionately members of minority groups and poor. If the white per-capita incarceration rate were seven times the black rate, we would not so easily accept a "lock 'em up and throw away the key" approach to criminal justice. We are able to tolerate that policy only because the majority does not have to pay its price.

RIGHT TO COUNSEL

More than three decades after the Supreme Court decided Clarence Gideon's case, many indigent defendants are no better off than Gideon was in his original trial. There are three principal reasons for this state of affairs. First, while the Court requires appointment of counsel, it does not require that the lawyer appointed be competent. Second, the right to any legal assistance halts after trial and the first level of appeal, leaving indigent defendants without any right to legal representation for the many stages of appeal that might follow. Third, neither the states nor the federal government have allocated adequate funds to represent the poor competently.

In theory, the Supreme Court has ruled, the Sixth Amendment guarantees "effective assistance of counsel." But the Court has set the standard of effectiveness so low that virtually anyone who has made it through law school will be deemed effective. In order to establish that he or she was provided with ineffective assistance of counsel, a defendant must first overcome a "strong presumption" that the attorney was effective, by proving that the attorney's performance was "outside the range of professionally competent assistance." As one court has described this standard, "Even if many reasonable lawyers would not have done as defense counsel did at trial, no relief can be granted on ineffectiveness grounds unless it is shown that *no* reasonable lawyer, in the circumstances, would do so."[7]

Even if the defendant can overcome the strong presumption that his lawyer was effective, he must also show prejudice, which the Supreme Court has defined as "a reasonable probability that the result would have been different." Ordinarily, courts separate the question of constitutional

error from the question of the error's effect on outcome: Where a defendant shows that a constitutional violation occurred, the burden shifts to
the government to prove that the error was "harmless beyond a reasonable doubt." But for ineffectiveness claims, the Court requires the defendant to show both that his attorney performed defectively and that the
deficiency probably affected the outcome.[8] This is not merely a technical
matter, because on the necessarily hypothetical question of whether an
error (usually a failure to do something or a failure to do something competently) affected the result of a trial, where the burden lies will often
determine the outcome.

This legal standard has tangible effects, as Gregory Wilson, currently
on death row in Kentucky, has learned. Kentucky pays a maximum of
$2,500 to lawyers handling capital punishment cases for indigent clients.
Since such cases often take five hundred to a thousand hours of work, the
lawyer will earn between two and five dollars per hour. Needless to say,
lawyers don't jump at the opportunity. The judge responsible for
appointing a lawyer for Wilson hung a notice on the courthouse door
that read, in capital letters, "PLEASE HELP—DESPERATE."

William Hagedorn responded. Wilson would have been better off
without him. Hagedorn had never tried a death penalty case before, had
no office, and had only a few out-of-date law books. He worked out of a
room in his house that prominently featured a lighted Budweiser sign. A
prosecution witness described Hagedorn as "a well-known drunk."
Hagedorn filed only one pretrial motion, made no closing argument,
interviewed none of the other side's witnesses, and hired no experts to
assist him. During the most crucial testimony in the case—that of the
pathologist—Hagedorn was not present in the courtroom. Yet on March
5, 1997, the Kenton Circuit Court held that Hagedorn's representation
satisfied the constitutional standard for effective counsel.

One attorney coined the Supreme Court's ineffectiveness test the
"mirror test": "You put a mirror under the court-appointed lawyer's nose,
and if the mirror clouds up, that's adequate counsel."[9] Courts applying
the Supreme Court's standard have declined to find ineffective assistance
where defense counsel slept during portions of the trial, where counsel
used heroin and cocaine throughout the trial, where counsel allowed his
client to wear the same sweatshirt and shoes in court that the perpetrator
was alleged to have worn on the day of the crime, where counsel stated
prior to trial that he was not prepared on the law or facts of the case, and
where counsel appointed in a capital case could not name a single
Supreme Court decision on the death penalty. In one case, a capital mur-

der defendant's attorney was found effective even though he "consumed large amounts of alcohol each day of the trial . . . drank in the morning, during court recess, and throughout the evening . . . [and] was arrested [during jury selection] for driving to the courthouse with a .27 blood-alcohol content."[10] No one paying for legal representation would accept such conduct, yet the courts have ruled time and time again that such "assistance" is good enough for poor people.

The Supreme Court has exacerbated the discriminatory effects of this standard by further ruling that when an attorney mistakenly fails to make an argument on behalf of his client at the right time, the defendant is forever barred from presenting that argument to a court, even if it is meritorious. Under the "procedural default" doctrine, the Court makes defendants pay for their attorneys' mistakes, even where those mistakes are a foreseeable result of a system that tolerates the appointment of incompetent lawyers for indigent defendants. While some public defender offices provide excellent representation and some highly qualified and committed attorneys have chosen to dedicate their careers to representing the indigent, these are exceptions proving the rule that you get what you pay for. Underfunded and overworked lawyers for the poor are more likely to make mistakes than high-priced white-collar defense attorneys, thus the procedural default rule has its harshest effect on those least able to do anything about it.

A second limitation on the right to counsel for the indigent is that it extends only to trial and an initial appeal. That leaves defendants on their own for many pretrial stages of a case and for all appeals beyond the first stage. Consider, for example, the predicament of Exzavious Gibson, sentenced to death in Georgia, who filed a state habeas corpus petition in Georgia. Gibson, who has an IQ below 80 and could not afford a lawyer, had to proceed on his own in a hearing concerning the effectiveness of his prior appointed counsel. When Butts County Superior Court Judge J. Carlisle Overstreet began the hearing, he asked Gibson if he was ready to proceed:

COURT: Okay, Mr. Gibson, do you want to proceed?
GIBSON: I don't have an attorney.
COURT: I understand that.
GIBSON: I am not waiving any rights.
COURT: I understand that. Do you have any evidence you want to put on?
GIBSON: I don't know what to plead.

COURT: Huh?

GIBSON: I don't know what to plead.

COURT: I am not asking you to plead to anything, I am just asking you if
    you have anything you want to put up, anything you want to intro-
    duce to this Court.

GIBSON: But, I don't have an attorney.

The state's attorney then pointed out to the judge that Gibson was not
entitled to any assistance of counsel, and the judge directed the state to
proceed. When an observer objected that Gibson did not have anything
to write with, he was given a legal pad and a pen. The state's attorney put
on her witness, Dennis Mullis, who had been Gibson's appointed attorney at trial and on his first appeal and whose effectiveness Gibson sought
to challenge. As she conducted direct examination of Mullis, she sought
to introduce various documents. At each point, the judge asked Gibson
if he objected, but Gibson could only reply that he didn't know what to
say without an attorney. At the close of the direct testimony, the judge
asked Gibson if he wanted to cross-examine the witness:

COURT: Mr. Gibson, would you like to ask Mr. Mullis any questions?

GIBSON: I don't have any counsel.

COURT: I understand that, but I am just asking, can you tell me yes or no
    whether you want to ask him any questions or not?

GIBSON: I'm not my own counsel. . . .

COURT: I understand that, but do you want, do you, yourself, individu-
    ally, want to ask him anything?

GIBSON: I don't know.

COURT: Okay, sir. Okay, thank you, Mr. Mullis, you can go down.[11]

This hearing took place in 1996, more than thirty years after the
Supreme Court recognized what it called the "obvious truth" that
Clarence Earl Gideon could not get a fair hearing without a lawyer.
Exzavious Gibson faced a much more severe sanction—the death
penalty—and had an IQ close to retarded. Yet because he was in a post-
conviction hearing, not a trial or direct appeal, he was not entitled to any
legal assistance at all.

In cases involving long sentences there will often be as many as ten
further stages of judicial review after the trial and first appeal. A defendant with means will hire counsel to represent him or her through all
stages. Yet the Supreme Court has ruled that indigent defendants are

entitled to no legal assistance at any of those subsequent stages, leaving people such as Exzavious Gibson to fend for themselves. The Court has reasoned that once an indigent defendant has had representation at trial and a first appeal, he or she no longer needs the assistance of counsel. But such reasoning blinks at the reality presented by a virtually retarded man facing the death penalty and attempting to pursue legal claims that have never before been addressed and could not possibly have been raised at trial or in the initial appeal.

In the absence of a constitutional requirement, only a handful of states guarantee indigent prisoners legal assistance for postconviction proceedings. Most states allow judges to appoint counsel at the state's expense but leave that decision to the judge's discretion. Compensation for such services varies widely. And some states provide no right to assistance at all. In federal habeas corpus proceedings—the first and usually only time that a prisoner's federal constitutional claims are heard by a federal court—Congress provides appointed counsel only for those indigent defendants facing the death penalty.[12]

Because the Supreme Court has failed to require states to provide any counsel for so many stages of the criminal process and to demand that counsel be competent, states have little or no incentive to allocate sufficient funds for indigent defense services. Nationwide, indigent defense receives only 2 percent of our annual criminal justice expenditures, while the police and the prosecution get more than 50 percent. The national average per-capita spending on state and local indigent defense in 1990, the latest year for which figures are available, was $5.37; Arkansas spent 88 cents per capita on indigent defense that year, and Louisiana spent only 11 cents. In 1990, Kentucky spent an average of $162 on each indigent criminal case, for a total of $11.4 million, approximately one-one-thousandth of the entire state budget and four million dollars less than the University of Kentucky's athletic budget.[13]

States achieve such low defense expenditures by imposing wholly unrealistic limits on payment for indigent defense attorneys. In Alabama, for example, the statutory maximum is $1,000 for all felonies and $2,000 for capital cases. South Carolina's statutory maximum is $750. In Virginia, the maximum fee for most felonies is $350. A study prepared for the Virginia General Assembly and State Bar concluded that after taking into account overhead costs, the effective rate for appointed defense attorneys in capital cases in that state was $13 an hour.[14]

States save three times by keeping the resources for indigent defense so low. First, they save money on the defense services themselves. Second, they save money on prosecution and court costs; good defense attorneys would make the legal contest less lopsided and would require states to allocate more resources to prosecuting crime. Third, they save on the more difficult to assess but no less significant costs of constitutional rights and liberties themselves. The vindication of a criminal defendant's rights often frustrates prosecution of crime. An adjudicated violation of the Fourth or Fifth Amendment, for example, leads to exclusion of the evidence from the government's case, even where the evidence accurately proves a defendant's guilt. By assigning incompetent and underfunded lawyers to represent indigent criminal defendants, the states ensure that many defendants' rights will not be asserted effectively.

By systematically underfunding indigent criminal defense, we proclaim that we protect constitutional rights and at the same time avoid the cost that full recognition of those constitutional rights would entail. Those who can afford competent counsel will have their rights fully vindicated, but those who must rely on state-funded legal assistance will enjoy substantially less protection. Notwithstanding *Gideon,* the kind of trial a person gets depends precisely on how much money he or she has.

JURY DISCRIMINATION

The jury, according to the Supreme Court, is the "criminal defendant's fundamental 'protection of life and liberty against race or color prejudice.'"[15] The first government action that the Supreme Court ever invalidated as race discrimination was a jury selection law excluding blacks.[16] And the Court has decided more jury discrimination cases than any other type of race discrimination claim. Yet for most of our history, the all-white jury has been a staple of the American criminal justice system. Today it remains an all-too-common feature of criminal justice. The blame can be laid squarely at the Supreme Court's door. While it has made broad proclamations about extirpating racial discrimination from jury selection, the Court has tolerated a system in which jurors are to this day often selected on the basis of race.

No black person even sat on a jury in the United States until 1860.[17] Under Reconstruction, blacks began to serve on juries in the South for the first time. This development was short-lived, however, as Democratic conservatives soon regained power in the South, Klan violence intimidated Republicans and blacks alike, and the all-white jury returned.[18] In 1875, Congress made it a federal crime to exclude a juror on the basis of race, but violations of the law have rarely been prosecuted.[19] In 1880, the

Supreme Court declared unconstitutional a West Virginia law restricting jury service to white males, reasoning that it denied equal protection of the law to a black man convicted of murder by an all-white jury.[20] But in the wake of that decision, the Court permitted all-white juries to remain a pervasive feature of life in the South for at least fifty more years.[21] The Court had condemned laws explicitly excluding blacks from juries, but in response states simply avoided such obvious means of discrimination and achieved the same result through unwritten racially discriminatory jury selection practices. They repeatedly upheld convictions by all-white juries where blacks had been excluded from the jury rolls by such practices.

In 1935, the Court shifted course, invalidating a conviction in the infamous "Scottsboro Boys" case, finding that the state systematically had excluded black citizens from jury service, even though there was no law expressly disqualifying black jurors.[22] The underlying case charged nine young black men, aged thirteen to twenty, with raping two young white women on a train from Chattanooga to Memphis. The women's testimony was weak at best; one recanted her testimony altogether, and the other's testimony was starkly contrary to the physical evidence. Yet the nine men were convicted and sentenced to death in less than a week. The Communist Party then took on the defendants' cause, and the case became an international cause célèbre and an embarrassment to Alabama and the United States. The Supreme Court reversed the initial convictions on right to counsel grounds. On retrial the defendants were represented by Samuel Leibowitz, an experienced New York trial attorney. Leibowitz challenged the racial composition of the jury. He put on numerous witnesses who testified that they could not remember a black person ever serving on any jury in the county. And he showed that the jury rolls included no black citizens, with the exception of six names seemingly added during the course of the appeal in an attempt to improve the state's evidence. The state courts nonetheless rejected the jury discrimination claims and upheld another round of death sentences, but again the Supreme Court agreed to hear the case.

At oral argument in the Supreme Court, Leibowitz took the unusual step of showing the jury rolls to the justices as he made his argument. Each justice in turn examined the books with a magnifying glass as Leibowitz explained how the black names had been added during the appeal. When Justice Willis Van Devanter, sitting next to Chief Justice Charles Evans Hughes, saw the books, he whispered to Hughes, in a voice that could be heard by spectators, "Why it's plain as punch!"[23] The

Court unanimously invalidated the convictions and from that point forward paid closer attention to the discriminatory composition of jury rolls.

From 1935 to 1975, the Court reviewed an average of one jury discrimination case a year and more often than not reversed the convictions on race discrimination grounds. But all-white juries continued to remain a common feature of American criminal justice. This was so for at least two reasons. First, the Supreme Court's resources are limited, and while it was able to review about one case a year, it declined to review many more cases that raised serious questions of jury discrimination.

Second, and more important, while the Court prohibited the use of race to exclude jurors from jury rolls, until 1986 it explicitly condoned the use of race to exclude blacks from the petit juries that sit in judgment in individual cases. To this day, the so-called peremptory challenge effectively permits prosecutors to strike black jurors from the jury venire (the small pool of jurors from which a jury is chosen for a particular case), thus achieving all-white juries even where jury rolls include blacks.

The peremptory challenge allows each side to strike jurors without stating a reason. Such strikes are based on limited knowledge; often the lawyer knows little about a prospective juror other than the person's age, race, gender, and perhaps employment. As a result, peremptory strikes are by necessity driven by stereotypes. As one scholar has put it, the peremptory challenge "allows the covert expression of what we dare not say but know is true more often than not."[24] For more than a century after the Supreme Court had ruled that it was unconstitutional to exclude jurors from jury rolls because of their race, it permitted parties to use peremptory challenges to exclude jurors from petit juries on the basis of race. For more than a century, in other words, the Court condoned hypocrisy: Express race-based exclusions from the jury rolls were forbidden, but unstated race-based peremptory challenges were authorized.

The Supreme Court did not even address the validity of the long-standing practice of race-based peremptory challenges until 1965, at the height of the civil rights movement. Then it expressly upheld their validity. Robert Swain, a young black man convicted in Talladega County, Alabama, by an all-white jury of raping a young white woman, showed that no black had ever served on a petit jury in the county, even though blacks were 25 percent of the county's population. While there were a few black jurors on the jury rolls, they had been eliminated by peremptory challenges in every case, including Swain's.

The Supreme Court held that these facts did not raise even an inference of discrimination. The Court reasoned that the "essential nature of the peremptory challenge is that it is one exercised without a reason stated, without inquiry, and without being subject to the court's control," and therefore "would no longer be peremptory" if it had to be explained.[25] The Court admitted that peremptory challenges are often based on "'sudden impressions and unaccountable prejudices,'" and on "grounds normally thought irrelevant to legal proceedings or official action, namely . . . race, religion, nationality, occupation or affiliations."[26] But in reasoning that echoed the justification of segregation in *Plessy v. Ferguson*, which found no discrimination because whites were barred from riding trains with blacks just as blacks were barred from riding with whites, the Court in *Swain* explained that "[i]n the quest for an impartial and qualified jury, Negro and white, Protestant and Catholic, are alike subject to being challenged without cause."[27] Thus, at the height of the civil rights movement, in a case involving the most racially charged of crimes, in a county where peremptory challenges against blacks had been used so successfully that no one could remember a black person ever sitting on a petit jury, the Court expressly approved the practice of race-based exclusion of black jurors.

In 1986, the Supreme Court reversed *Swain* and held for the first time that race-based peremptory challenges were unconstitutional. In *Batson v. Kentucky*, the Court set forth a test that required a defendant to show only that he or she was a member of a cognizable racial group and that the prosecutor had exercised peremptory challenges to remove jurors of the same race in his or her case.[28] If the evidence raised an inference of discrimination, the burden would shift to the prosecution to advance a race-neutral explanation for its strikes.[29] The trial court would then have to determine whether the prosecutor's stated neutral reasons were genuine or pretextual.

Yet *Batson* has by most accounts done relatively little in practice to eliminate the use of race-based peremptory strikes.[30] This is not to say that it has had no effect at all. Most significantly, it repudiated *Swain*, which had explicitly countenanced race-based strikes. Now, at least, race-based strikes are not officially authorized. However, the *Batson* decision has not solved the problem.

First, the Court's test makes it extremely easy for attorneys to continue to engage in race-based peremptory challenges. The Court in *Batson* sought merely to excise those peremptories that are predicated on race itself, leaving the rest of the peremptory challenge untouched. But under that approach, courts should accept any explanation that is not race-based, no matter how ridiculous, as long as they find the prosecutor credible. Since peremptories need not even be rational, the most irrational reason, if sincerely offered and race-neutral, should suffice to defeat a *Batson* challenge.

In fact, courts have accepted virtually any race-neutral reason for a peremptory strike. Michael Raphael and Edward Ungvarsky reviewed all published decisions involving *Batson* challenges from 1986 to January 1992 and concluded that "in almost any situation a prosecutor can readily craft an acceptable neutral explanation to justify striking black jurors because of their race."[31] Courts have accepted explanations that the juror was too old, was too young, was employed as a teacher, was unemployed, or practiced a certain religion. Courts have accepted unverifiable explanations based on demeanor, such as that the juror did not make eye contact or made too much eye contact, appeared inattentive or headstrong, nervous or casual, or grimaced or smiled. Courts have accepted explanations that might in many circumstances be correlated to race, such as the fact that the juror lacked education, was single or poor, lived or worked in the same neighborhood as the defendant or a witness, or previously had been involved with the criminal justice system.[32]

A Georgia court accepted a prosecutor's explanation that he struck a black potential juror because she worked in a video store and therefore would not be "good with people." An Alabama judge accepted as race-neutral the prosecutor's explanation that he struck several black jurors because they were affiliated with Alabama State University, a predominantly black college. In *Jefferson v. State*, the prosecution used twenty-four strikes to eliminate every black person from three different juries in a single death penalty case (separate juries were chosen for a competency hearing, for the guilt/innocence phase, and for the penalty phase). In making its choices, the prosecution divided the potential jurors into four categories—"strong," "medium," "weak," and "black." The trial court found that the prosecution had race-neutral reasons for its strikes and rejected Jefferson's *Batson* challenge.[33] As one scholar has summed it up, "If prosecutors exist who . . . cannot create a 'racially neutral' reason for discriminating on the basis of race, bar exams are too easy."[34]

As a result of *Batson*'s underenforcement, prosecutors are not shy about continuing to use peremptory strikes against black jurors. A 1987 videotape of a Philadelphia district attorney training session, conducted *after* the *Batson* decision was issued, expressly advocates that prosecutors strike black jurors because of their race. The tape advises:

[Y]oung black women are very bad. There's an antagonism. I guess maybe they're downtrodden in two respects. They are women and they're black. . . . So they somehow want to take it out on somebody, and you don't want it to be you.

Let's face it, the blacks from the low-income areas are less likely to convict. I understand it. There's a resentment for law enforcement. There's a resentment for authority. And as a result, you don't want those people on your jury.

It may appear as if you're being racist, but you're just being realistic. You're just trying to win the case.[35]

When the contents of the tape were leaked to the press in 1997, the attorney who conducted the session, then running for district attorney himself, defended his instructions as perfectly appropriate.

The second flaw in *Batson* is that the test is nearly always reduced to an issue of credibility to be resolved by the trial judge. Since it is not difficult to come up with a race-neutral reason for a race-based strike, the central issue will generally be whether the prosecutor's after-the-fact justification is believable. It is very difficult for a reviewing court to second-guess a trial court's determination on such a question, since the trial court has the benefit of firsthand observation of the prosecutor's demeanor. Reviewing courts therefore defer to the trial court's finding regarding the prosecutor's motive under the deferential "clearly erroneous" standard.[36] Since most criminal cases are tried in state courts, this means that winning a *Batson* challenge generally will require convincing a state trial judge to find that the state prosecutor lied to the judge about not acting for racially motivated reasons.

While state courts today may not be as reluctant to find discrimination as they were in the post-Reconstruction, pre–New Deal period, they are still likely to be hesitant. It is no minor matter to find that an officer of the court has both lied and acted for racist reasons. In many localities, the prosecutor will have appeared regularly before the same judge, will travel in the same social circles, may well have contributed to the judge's election campaign, and may be the judge's personal friend. In any event, the vast majority of state trial courts find prosecutors' neutral explanations acceptable, and it is rare that such findings are overturned on appeal.[37]

The jury discrimination cases mark the Supreme Court's most extended effort to address the problem of race discrimination in any official setting. Justice Anthony Kennedy has proudly characterized the

Court's effort as "over a century of jurisprudence dedicated to the elimination of race prejudice within the jury selection process," and Justice Lewis Powell has generously described the Court's efforts in this area as "unceasing."[38] Yet race-based exclusion of black jurors, pronounced a violation of black criminal defendants' equal protection rights in 1880, has remained a prominent feature of our criminal justice system at least as much because of as in spite of the Supreme Court. While the Court has issued ringing pronouncements about the invidious nature of jury discrimination, its legal doctrine has permitted the discrimination to continue as long as it remains under wraps. The Court's strategy on jury discrimination might best be characterized as one of plausible deniability. Explicit race discrimination is rejected, but unstated discrimination is tolerated. As a result, the institution that decides on guilt or innocence in our criminal justice system has been and continues to be disproportionately composed of white citizens.

SENTENCING

The sentence is the criminal justice system's bottom line, and that bottom line is by no means racially neutral. Virtually every study of race and the death penalty, for example, has concluded that, all other things being equal, defendants who kill white victims are much more likely to receive the death penalty than defendants who kill black victims. From 1976 to 1995, only four white men were executed for killing black victims, while eighty black men were executed for killing white victims. More broadly, as noted at the opening of this chapter, blacks make up 12 percent of the population, but fill half the nation's jail and prison cells.[39] The per capita incarceration rate among blacks is seven times that among whites. And the problem is getting worse. In 1990, one in four young black men were under correctional supervision; now the figure is one in three.[40]

These general disparities are also reflected with respect to particular offenses. Consider federal treatment of cocaine possession and distribution. Crack cocaine is made from powder cocaine by a simple process of cooking it with baking soda. Wholesalers deal in powder; retailers deal in crack. End-users use both. Yet under the federal sentencing guidelines, a small-time crack retailer caught selling 5 grams of crack receives the same sentence as a large-scale powder cocaine dealer convicted of distributing 500 grams of powder cocaine. A suspect convicted of possessing 70 grams of powder cocaine with intent to sell it will receive a prison sentence of about two years. The same amount of crack brings 10 to 12 years. Not coincidentally, in 1992, 92.6 percent of those convicted for crimes involving crack cocaine were black, while only 4.7 percent were white; at the same time, 45.2 percent of defendants convicted for powder cocaine crimes were white, and only 20.7 percent were black.[41]

The Supreme Court has turned a blind eye to such disparities. In 1987, the Court dismissed Warren McCleskey's challenge to racial disparities in the implementation of the death penalty. A black man sentenced to death in Georgia for killing a white police officer, McCleskey argued that Georgia's death penalty was administered in a racially discriminatory way. To support his claim, he submitted the most sophisticated study ever done of racial disparity in criminal sentencing. The study, conducted by professors David Baldus, George Woodworth, and Charles Pulaski, analyzed more than two thousand murder cases in Georgia in the 1970s. Baldus and his colleagues found that defendants charged with killing white victims received the death penalty eleven times more often than defendants charged with killing black victims. Black defendants charged with killing white victims received a death sentence 22 percent of the time, while white defendants charged with killing black victims received the death penalty in 3 percent of the cases. Much of the disparity seemed attributable to Georgia prosecutors, who sought the death penalty in 70 percent of cases involving black defendants and white victims, but only 19 percent of cases involving white defendants and black victims.[42]

Raw numbers, however, can be misleading. If certain features, such as multiple murders, long criminal records, or strong eyewitness testimony, happen to be correlated with race, what appears to be a racial disparity may have a race-neutral explanation. Baldus and his colleagues therefore subjected the raw data to sophisticated statistical analysis to see if nonracial factors might explain the differences. Even after they accounted for thirty-nine nonracial variables, however, they found that defendants charged with killing white victims were 4.3 times more likely to receive a death sentence than defendants charged with killing blacks.

By a one-vote margin, the Supreme Court rejected McCleskey's challenge. It did not question the validity of the statistics but found that they did not amount to an equal protection violation. The fact that other juries imposed the death penalty more often on blacks who killed whites did not shed light on whether McCleskey's jury had been motivated by race. McCleskey could prevail only if he could prove that in his case the prosecutor had sought the death penalty, or the jury had imposed it, because of race.

But it is nearly impossible to make the showing that the *McCleskey* Court required. Long-standing rules generally bar criminal defendants from obtaining discovery from the prosecution or the jury, so defendants are precluded from discovering evidence of intent from the two actors whose discriminatory intent the Court requires them to establish.

Other challenges to sentencing disparities have failed for similar reasons. Every black defendant who has challenged the discriminatory effects of the crack-powder cocaine disparity in the federal sentencing guidelines has been rebuffed by a citation to *McCleskey* and the statement that mere disparities in result are insufficient to establish a constitutional claim. No federal court has dismissed a criminal case for racially motivated selective prosecution since 1886.

For a short-lived moment in 1995, the Georgia Supreme Court seemed to take a different approach. Georgia has a "two strikes and you're out" sentencing scheme that imposes life imprisonment for a second drug offense. Georgia's district attorneys sought this penalty against only 1 percent of eligible white defendants, but against more than 16 percent of eligible black defendants. The result: 98.4 percent of those serving life sentences under this provision were black. On March 17, 1995, the Georgia Supreme Court ruled four to three that these figures raised a prima facie case of discrimination and required prosecutors to explain the disparity.[43]

Instead of offering an explanation, however, Georgia Attorney General Michael Bowers took the unusual step of filing a petition for rehearing personally signed by every one of the state's forty-six district attorneys, all of them white. The petition argued that the Court's analysis was a "substantial step toward invalidating" the death penalty, and would "paralyze the criminal justice system," presumably because racial disparities in other areas also might have to be explained. Thirteen days later, the Georgia Supreme Court took the highly unusual step of reversing itself and held that the figures established no discrimination and required no justification. The court's new decision relied almost exclusively on the Supreme Court's decision in *McCleskey*.[44]

The mere existence of a racial disparity, of course, does not mean that intentional race discrimination has occurred. As noted above, most criminologists agree that blacks are incarcerated in greater numbers in part because they commit crime in greater proportion than do whites. But even if the disparities are not attributable to intentional discrimination as the Supreme Court defines it, they nonetheless raise serious questions about the fairness of our criminal justice policy. To see that this is so, one need only imagine the public response if the figures were reversed.

Imagine the public reaction, for example, if one in three young white men were in prison or on probation or parole. It would not be "lock 'em up and throw away the key." Or imagine how different the politics of the death penalty would be if defendants who killed black victims were 4.3 times more likely to receive the death penalty than defendants who killed white victims, and if prosecutors sought the death penalty 70 percent of the time when whites killed blacks, but only 19 percent of the time when blacks killed whites.

Indeed, turning the tables on some of these statistics is almost beyond comprehension. If the per-capita incarceration rate of the white and black communities were interchanged, more than 3.5 million white people would be incarcerated today, instead of 570,000, and we would need more than three times the prison capacity (and prosecution and court capacity) that we currently have.[45] And since white people make up about 80 percent of the national population, it would be impossible for whites to be overrepresented in prison populations to the same extent as black people are—four times their representation in the national population.

The history of marijuana laws illustrates what happens when the criminal law begins to affect large numbers of white middle- and upper-class people. The country's first marijuana users were largely minorities, mostly Mexicans.[46] By 1937, every state had criminalized marijuana. In the 1950s, federal penalties for the sale of marijuana ranged from two to five years imprisonment, a second offense brought a sentence of five to ten years, and a third brought ten to twenty years. State penalties followed suit. In 1956, Congress imposed mandatory minimum sentences for marijuana possession and sale.

In the 1960s, however, marijuana use spread to the white middle and upper classes. By 1970, some college campuses reported that at least 70 percent of the student population had tried marijuana. And as one author wrote in 1970, "the new users are the sons and daughters of the middle class, not the ethnic minorities and ghetto residents formerly associated with marijuana."[47]

As marijuana use spread to the white majority, enforcement radically decreased. Police and prosecutors began to leave users alone and instead targeted dealers and sellers. The courts also limited enforcement, invalidating convictions for procedural constitutional violations and for insufficient evidence. The legislatures amended the laws, sharply reducing penalties for possession. As one commentator described the development,

In response to the extraordinary explosion in marijuana consumption and the penetration of its use into the mainstream of American life, every state amended its penalties in some fashion between 1969 and 1972, the overall result being a massive downward shift in penalties for consumption-related offenses. Simple possession of less than one ounce was classified as a misdemeanor in all but eight states by the end of 1972.[48]

In 1973, Oregon went further and actually decriminalized possession of small amounts of marijuana, and by 1981 ten other states had followed suit.[49]

The marijuana example shows that when the effects of a criminal law are not limited to minorities and the poor, but reach the sons and daughters of the white majority, our response is not to get tough but to get lenient. This suggests that a principal reason Americans have been able to sustain an unremittingly harsh "tough on crime" attitude is precisely that the burden of punishment falls disproportionately on minority populations. The white majority could not possibly maintain its current attitude toward crime and punishment were the burden of punishment felt by the same white majority that prescribes it. Because of the stark racial divide in criminal justice, the white majority is able to gain the "benefits" of increased incarceration without paying the costs of incarcerating its own friends and family members.

CONCLUSION

On its surface, the American criminal justice system is predicated on equality. The legitimacy of punishment requires that individuals be judged by their acts, not by their status. Yet at the same time, the American system of criminal justice is predicated on race and class inequality. The privileged among us enjoy the constitutional rights we do only because we have a system that effectively denies those rights to those less privileged. Incompetent and overworked lawyers for the poor ensure that the poor's rights often will go unasserted. We have formally insisted since 1880 that race-based jury discrimination violates the Constitution, but to this day the courts continue to tolerate it as long as it remains unspoken. We have the highest per-capita incarceration rate in the developed world, but only because the burdens are disproportionately borne by the underprivileged. Some of the double standards are class-based, some are race-based, and others have both features. What all the double standards share, though, is that they exploit inequality in order to reduce the costs associated with the full enforcement of constitutional rights.

In short, we have two systems of criminal justice, and our criminal law and policy rely on maintaining these dual systems on different tracks. Our overt emphasis on the need for equality before the law demonstrates that were we to acknowledge the double standards, we would be required to reject them as a moral and ethical matter. But there is also a pragmatic case for rejecting them; as cost-saving measures, they may be self-defeating. A policy of criminal justice based on exploiting inequality will inevitably lose its legitimacy among those who get the short end of the stick. And as everyone who has ever exercised power—whether as a judge, a police officer, a president, or a parent—knows, legitimacy is critical to the enforcement of any regime of rules. By tolerating and exploiting inequality at the very core of our criminal justice system, we have surrendered that legitimacy among those sectors of our community already most vulnerable to crime.

NOTES

Portions of this chapter are drawn from David Cole, *The Uses of Inequality: Race and Class in American Criminal Justice* (New York: New Press, forthcoming).

1. *Gideon v. Wainwright*, 372 U.S. 335 (1963).
2. *Griffin v. Illinois*, 351 U.S. 12, 19 (1956).
3. David C. Lewen, *America's Addiction to Prisons*, 20 Fordham Urban Law Journal 641, 646 (1993). Michael Tonry, *Malign Neglect: Race, Crime, and Punishment in America* (New York: Oxford University Press, 1995), 4. The average sentence imposed on black offenders sentenced to incarceration in U.S. district courts in 1992 was 84.1 months, while the average sentence for white offenders was 56.8 months. Although they are only 12 percent of the population, blacks make up 31.3 percent of those arrested. Among convicted offenders, 80 percent of black defendants and 75 percent of whites are sentenced to incarceration. Bureau of Justice Statistics, *Sourcebook of Criminal Justice Statistics: 1995*, 474 (table 5.25), 408 (table 4.10), 471 (table 5.22). See also Ian Ayres and Joel Waldfogel, *A Market Test for Race Discrimination in Bail Setting*, 46 Stanford Law Review 987 (1994), finding that judges impose higher bail amounts on black defen-

dants; Marc Mauer and Tracy Huling, *Young Black Americans and the Criminal Justice System: Five Years Later* (The Sentencing Project, October 1995), 1. Henry Louis Gates, Jr., "The Charmer," *New Yorker* (April 29–May 6, 1996): 116.

4. Michael Tonry, *Malign Neglect,* 49; Alfred Blumstein, *Racial Disproportionality of U.S. Prison Populations Revisited,* 64 University of Colorado Law Review 743 (1993).

5. Mauer and Huling, supra n. 3.

6. John Hagan and Ruth Peterson, *Crime and Inequality* (Stanford: Stanford University Press, 1995), 16, 25.

7. *Rogers v. Zant,* 13 F.3d 384, 386 (11th Cir. 1994).

8. *Strickland v. Washington,* 466 U.S. 668 (1984).

9. Hal Strauss, "Indigent Legal Defense Called Terrible," *Atlanta Journal-Constitution,* July 7, 1985, 12A, quoting the vice president of the Georgia Trial Lawyer's Association.

10. *People v. Tippins,* 173 A.D.2d 512, (N.Y. App. 1991), 570 N.Y.S.2d 581 (1991); *People v. Badia,* 159 A.D.2d 577 (N.Y. App. 1990), 552 N.Y.S.2d 439 (1990); *People v. Murphy,* 96 A.D.2d 625 (N.Y.App. 1983), 464 N.Y.S.2d 882 (1983); *People v. Dalton,* 140 A.D.2d 419 (N.Y. App. 1988), 529 N.Y.S.2d 927 (1988); Stephen B. Bright, *Counsel for the Poor: The Death Sentence Not for the Worst Crime but for the Worst Lawyer,* 103 Yale Law Journal 1835, 1839 (1994), describing *Birt v. Montgomery,* 725 F.2d 587, 601 (11th Cir. 1984), cert. denied, 469 U.S. 874 (1984); *People v. Garrison,* 765 P.2d 419 (Cal. 1989), 47 Cal.3d 746 (1989).

11. Trial of Habeas Corpus Hearing in *Exzavious Gibson v. Turpin,* Civil Action No. 95-V–648 (Sup. Ct. Butts County, GA, September 12, 1996) at 2–3, 38, 51, 64, 67.

12. Randall T. Shepard, "Capital Litigation from State Court Perspective, or Rushing to Judgment in Fifteen Years," presented to a workshop for the Judges of the Seventh Circuit, Kohler, WI, May 2, 1996, 5; The Spangenberg Group, *A Study of Representation in Capital Cases in Texas* (March 1993), 129–31; The Spangenberg Group, *Right to Counsel in State Post-Conviction Death Penalty Proceedings* (April 1988); Pub. L. No. 100–690, 102 Stat. 4181 (1988), codified at 21 U.S.C. § 848q(4)(B).

13. Bureau of Justice Statistics, *Sourcebook of Criminal Justice Statistics—1993,* 2 (table 1.2), 5 (table 1.5), reporting on figures from fiscal year 1990; Edward C. Monahan, *Who Is Trying to Kill the Sixth Amendment?* Criminal Justice 24, 27 (Summer 1991).

14. Ala. Code § 15-12-21(d) (1975 & Supp. 1992). Although the statute limits reimbursement for capital cases to $1,000, the Alabama Attorney

General has interpreted it to apply separately to the guilt and sentencing phases of a capital trial, so that the effective limit is now $2,000. Op. Ala.A.G. No. 91-00206 (Mar. 21, 1991); S.C. Code Ann. § 17-3-50 (Law. Co-op. 1990); Richard Klein and Robert Spangenberg, *The Indigent Defense Crisis,* prepared for ABA Section on Criminal Justice Ad Hoc Committee on the Indigent Defense Crisis (August 1993), 6, 7; The Spangenberg Group, *A Study of Representation in Capital Cases in Virginia* (1993).

15. *McCleskey v. Kemp,* 481 U.S. 279, 310 (1987), quoting *Strauder v. West Virginia,* 100 U.S. 303, 309 (1880).

16. *Strauder v. West Virginia,* 100 U.S. 303 (1880).

17. Leon F. Litwack, *North of Slavery: The Negro in the Free States 1790–1860* (Chicago: University of Chicago Press, 1961), 102.

18. Douglas L. Colbert, *Challenging the Challenge: Thirteenth Amendment as a Prohibition Against the Racial Use of Peremptory Challenges,* 76 Cornell Law Review 1, 49–50, 62 (1990).

19. Act of March 1, 1875, ch. 114, § 4, 18 Stat. 335. See *Cassell v. Texas,* 339 U.S. 282, 303 (1950), Jackson dissenting, characterizing *ex parte Virginia* as "solitary and neglected authority" for criminal prosecutions based on racially motivated jury exclusion.

20. *Strauder v. West Virginia,* 100 U.S. 303 (1880). The same day that the Court decided *Strauder,* it also upheld a conviction of a state judge for violating the 1875 jury selection statute. *Ex parte Virginia,* 100 U.S. 339 (1880).

21. See Benno C. Schmidt, Jr., *Juries, Jurisdiction, and Race Discrimination: The Lost Promise of Strauder v. West Virginia,* 61 Texas Law Review 1401 (1983).

22. *Powell v. Alabama,* 287 U.S. 45 (1932).

23. Schmidt, *Juries, Jurisdiction, and Race Discrimination,* 1478–79, reporting the observation of Professor Herbert Wechsler, who attended the argument.

24. Barbara Allan Babcock, *Voir Dire: Preserving "Its Wonderful Power,"* 27 Stanford Law Review 545, 554 (1975).

25. *Swain v. Alabama,* 380 U.S. 220, 222 (1965).

26. Ibid., 220.

27. *Plessy v. Ferguson,* 163 U.S. 537 (1896); *Swain,* 380 U.S. at 221. Justice Rehnquist expressed the same view twenty years later, in dissenting from the Court's ruling in *Batson v. Kentucky,* 476 U.S. 79, 137–38 (1986), Rehnquist dissenting: "In my view, there is simply nothing 'unequal' about the State's using its peremptory challenges to strike blacks from the

jury in cases involving black defendants, so long as such challenges are also used to exclude whites in cases involving white defendants, Hispanics in cases involving Hispanic defendants, Asians in cases involving Asian defendants, and so on."

28. 476 U.S. 79 (1986).

29. Ibid., 96–98.

30. Kenneth J. Melilli, *Batson in Practice: What We Have Learned About Batson and Peremptory Challenges,* 71 Notre Dame Law Review 447, 503 (1996); Jere W. Morehead, *When a Peremptory Challenge Is No Longer Peremptory: Batson's Unfortunate Failure to Eradicate Invidious Discrimination from Jury Selection,* 43 DePaul Law Review 625 (1994); Jeffrey S. Brand, *The Supreme Court, Equal Protection, and Jury Selection: Denying That Race Still Matters,* 1994 Wisconsin Law Review 511, 596–613 (1994).

31. Michael J. Raphael and Edward J. Ungvarsky, *Excuses, Excuses: Neutral Explanations Under Batson v. Kentucky,* 27 University of Michigan Journal of Legal Reform 229, 236 (1993).

32. Ibid., 236–67; see also Brian J. Serr and Mark Maney, *Racism, Peremptory Challenges, and the Democratic Jury: The Jurisprudence of a Delicate Balance,* 79 Journal of Criminal Law and Criminology 1, 44–47 (1988).

33. Bryan A. Stevenson and Ruth E. Friedman, *Deliberate Indifference: Judicial Tolerance of Racial Bias in Criminal Justice,* 51 Washington and Lee Law Review 509, 521–23 (1994).

34. Sheri Lynn Johnson, *The Language and Culture (Not to Say Race) of Peremptory Challenges,* 35 William and Mary Law Review 21, 59 (1993).

35. Barry Siegel, "Storm Still Lingers Over Defense Attorney's Training Video," *Los Angeles Times,* April 29, 1997, A5 quoting from a Philadelphia district attorney training videotape.

36. *Batson,* 476 U.S. at 98 n. 21; *Hernandez,* 500 U.S. at 364.

37. Raphael and Ungvarsky, *Excuses, Excuses,* 234–35.

38. *Edmonson v. Leesville Concrete Co., Inc.,* 500 U.S. 614 (1991); *Batson v. Kentucky,* 476 U.S. 79, 85 (1986).

39. Darrell K. Gilliard and Allen J. Beck, *Prisoners in 1993* (U.S. Department of Justice, 1994), 9.

40. Michael Tonry, *Malign Neglect,* 4; Mauer and Huling, *Young Black Americans,* 1; Marc Mauer, *Young Black Men and the Criminal Justice System: A Growing National Problem* (The Sentencing Project, February 1990), 3.

41. *United States v. Clary,* 846 F.Supp. 768, 787 (E.D. Mo. 1994); see also *United States v. Walls,* 841 F.Supp. 24, 28 (D.D.C. 1994).

42. *McCleskey v. Kemp,* 481 U.S. 279, 287 (1987).

43. *Stephens v. State*, 1995 WL 116292 (Ga.S.Ct., March 17, 1995).

44. *Stephens v. State*, 1995 WL 237375 (Ga.S.Ct., March 30, 1995).

45. Calculated from 1990 figures.

46. Unless otherwise indicated, the information in the next two paragraphs is drawn from Bonnie Whitebread, *Marijuana Prohibition*, 56 University of Virgina Law Review 983 (1970).

47. Ibid., 1096.

48. Richard J. Bonnie, "The Meaning of 'Decriminalization': A Review of the Law," *Contemporary Drug Problems* (Fall 1981): 277, 278.

49. Ibid., 279; see also Bureau of Justice Statistics, U.S. Department of Justice, *Drugs, Crime, and the Justice System* (1992), 84–85, reporting that when large numbers of white middle-class youths were arrested for marijuana possession in the late 1960s and early 1970s, public complaints led Congress and eleven states to decriminalize or reduce substantially the penalties for that crime.

19 DAVID RUDOVSKY

POLICE PRACTICES

IN the 1960–61 term of the United States Supreme Court, the justices issued two landmark opinions that signaled a significant change in direction on remedies for police misconduct and on search and seizure practices. *Monroe v. Pape* presented quintessential allegations of police abuse: several heavily armed police officers broke into a home without a judicial warrant, ransacked the house and terrorized the occupants, making racial and other derogatory slurs. No contraband was found and no arrests were made. The Supreme Court ruled that these allegations stated a federal cause of action for the violation of Fourth Amendment rights under the post–Civil War Ku Klux Klan Act of 1871. In *Mapp v. Ohio*, the Court ruled that violations of the Fourth Amendment by state or local police require the exclusion of evidence improperly seized from criminal trials.[1]

While *Monroe* opened the federal courthouse doors to claims of police abuse and *Mapp* placed an important sanction on illegal search and seizures, after almost four decades and much constitutional litigation, the abuses continue, in many ways unabated. In the past five years, there have been extreme examples of abuse—the beating of Rodney King, the murder of a civilian complainant in New Orleans, the admissions of Detective Fuhrman of framing African Americans, and most recently, the stationhouse torture in New York City of a Haitian immigrant, Abner Louima. During that same period, official governmental studies and investigations of several major police departments have disclosed patterns of misconduct and corruption—including systematic use of excessive force, theft, and persistent perjury in criminal proceedings.

Establishing and enforcing proper restraints on police power is a difficult problem in any society. In the United States there is both a widespread fear of governmental abuse and a widespread tolerance of repressive measures, the latter reflecting a belief that police excesses are necessary to combat crime. As Elliott Currie shows in this volume (chapter 17), our high levels of crime and violence have social and cultural roots and have not been diminished by twenty-five years of massive imprisonment. But frustration with disorder and crime has led to a public acceptance of extraconstitutional police practices. And because police abuse is most often directed against those without political power or social status, their complaints are often dismissed or ignored.

Acceptance of a certain level of police abuse is a predictable majoritarian response to crime or to threats to the status quo. The true test of our society's commitment to constitutional constraints is how government and the courts respond to these systemic deviations from constitutional norms. Too often, the response has been indifference to even well-documented abuses and a fostering of official violence through social, political, and legal structures that reinforce patterns of unlawfulness. We know much about principles of accountability and organizational control, yet repeatedly fail to apply these basic precepts to law enforcement officials.

CIVIL REMEDIES FOR POLICE MISCONDUCT

Judicial and political efforts to remedy police abuses have produced some positive results. First, the courts have developed a set of constitutional and procedural standards that permit an abused citizen to claim damages for many forms of police misconduct. As a result, citizens and lawyers are much more willing to engage in litigation. While the impact of these lawsuits on police practices is difficult to measure, there is no question that police departments take litigation into account and, from a strictly monetary or risk management point of view, attempt to avoid some practices that will result in litigation.

Second, as a result of the widely publicized incidents of abuse and the reports of commissions established to investigate police departments, there is a broader understanding among officials, the courts and the public of the scope and causes of the problem. The Rodney King incident was a watershed in this regard, and the indictments of police in New York, New Orleans, Philadelphia and Chicago in just the past few years for remarkably similar patterns of criminal abuses of civilians have served to challenge the conventional view of police as rarely deviating from their role as protectors of the public.

Third, there has been a significant professionalization of police departments. In most law enforcement agencies, police leadership is outspokenly opposed to corruption and abuse. Police officials openly acknowledge the kinds and causes of abuses that their counterparts adamantly denied just 20 years ago. They understand how lack of training, supervision and discipline will lead to abuses, and they recognize how detrimental such practices as the "code of silence" can be to proper administration. Training and official policies are more sensitive to the rights of the community and, largely as a result of the recommendations of leading investigating commissions—most prominently, the Christopher Commission in Los Angeles and the Mollen Commission in New York City—serious changes in the supervision and evaluation of police officers and practices are now in place in some departments.

Finally, citizen's groups, particularly in minority and poor communities, have demanded accountability for police misconduct and have achieved some success in imposing greater civilian control and oversight of police departments.

There are, however, significant countervailing trends. The most prominent and troubling is the pervasive impact of the ideology of the war on crime: the police have assimilated the overriding message that as long as their actions are taken in the name of the war on crime, constitutional rights can be liberally disregarded. Doctrines and rulings that promote fairness and equality in the criminal justice system are blamed for aggravating crime and violence and many people believe that adherence to constitutional principles is incompatible with effective law enforcement. Regressive and harshly punitive legislation is passed in the name of crime control, the courts are attacked for being too soft, and the police are encouraged to use extra-legal methods to control crime and criminals.

Further, since officers learn that neither their own departments nor the courts will inquire into the legitimacy or constitutionality of their conduct as long as evidence of crime is produced, they develop a sense of impunity with regard to illegal conduct. A culture of abuse easily develops where the department, prosecutors and the courts fail to insist on adherence to constitutional norms or police accountability for misconduct.

A recent police scandal in Philadelphia illustrates this phenomenon. For several years a special narcotics squad operating in a largely black and Hispanic neighborhood systematically falsified search warrants, planted drugs on suspects, stole money and drugs, assaulted and otherwise terrorized suspects and civilians, presented perjured court testimony, and framed innocent defendants. Over 1,200 criminal cases were tainted by their misconduct, yet these officers had good reason to believe that they could act with complete impunity. Scores of civilian complaints detailing their misconduct were regularly rejected by the Police Department's Internal Affairs Division. Other officers with very good reason to know of the misconduct failed to report it, evincing the persistence of the code of silence. Prosecutors were alerted to the false testimony but refused to investigate. And judges, in case after case, "found" the often incredible testimony to be truthful.

The Rodney King and Abner Louima incidents also demonstrate the serious consequences of the failure to impose accountability. Both beatings were brutal and protracted. The officers had to be fully confident of their colleagues' silence and of their department's dismissal of any complaints made by witnesses. So sure were the officers in the King beating of their immunity from punishment, they bragged about their abuses on the police computer system and to medical personnel who treated King at the hospital. Mr. Louima was tortured in a stationhouse full of police officers. Only officers assured by prior experience and knowledge of departmental attitudes that the department would not investigate or punish this type of abuse (regardless of the credibility of the witnesses or of their own incriminating statements) could have rationally undertaken this brazen and vicious behavior.

Examples from adjudicated cases and from independent investigations provide hard documentation of the systemic flaws in the complaint processes in many police departments. It is not uncommon to find that officers who have been the subject of numerous citizen complaints of brutality are rarely disciplined and continue to serve on the force. In Los Angeles, for example, the Christopher Commission determined that several officers who have been found responsible for the illegal use of force on civilians had at the same time received performance reviews that made no mention of these findings and praised the officers' attitude toward civilians. The consequences of the department's failure to monitor and discipline these officers run far wider than the encouragement it might give them to continue to abuse civilians. The message that violence and abusive conduct will be ignored is also sent to every other officer on the force.

For its part, the Supreme Court either does not grasp the institutional causes of abuse or, as a matter of ideology, invokes the doctrines of federalism and judicial restraint to allow these conditions to persist. There is a striking disjunction between the widely recognized causes of abuse and the Court's response. The Supreme Court's rulings reflect a belief that abuse occurs in isolated instances and is caused by an occasional aberrant officer. Faced with records that reflect institutional causes, the Court recoils at the argument that the Constitution requires intervention on that level.

In several key cases the Court has refused to craft an approach that would take into account systemic patterns of abuse. In *Rizzo v. Goode,* a federal district court ruled that there was a pattern of police abuse in Philadelphia and ordered implementation of an internal police department mechanism for the review and adjudication of civilian complaints against officers.[2] The district court made the fairly obvious and well-supported finding that the failure of the police department to investigate these complaints and to discipline officers led to the high level of abuse.

The Supreme Court reversed, stating that the injunction was an impermissible intervention in the affairs of local government. As a matter of local governmental policy and police administration, the fact that the nation's fourth largest city (one with a well-earned reputation for police abuse) did not have a functioning internal review system is a cause for serious concern. The refusal of the Supreme Court to permit such a remedy demonstrates a studied ignorance of the political and social realities of police misconduct. The Court abdicated any judicial responsibility for the proven structural causes of misconduct.

The Court followed a similar doctrinal approach in *City of Los Angeles v. Lyons,* where it refused to enjoin the Los Angeles Police Department's use of the "chokehold," a practice that had resulted in 16 deaths over a period of a few years.[3] The Court ruled that *Lyons* had no standing to challenge this practice since he would not likely be subjected to it again.

The formalism of *Lyons* is disturbing both as a matter of constitutional adjudication and as a matter of social policy. *Lyons* sent a chilling message to the Los Angeles Police Department: as long as abuses like the chokehold do not become a demonstrable city "policy," the Court would not interfere. There is a direct line from *Lyons* to Rodney King; the Supreme Court bears some responsibility for the pattern of brutality in the Los Angeles Police Department that claimed King as one of its victims.

The Court did show some understanding of the link between internal police policies and abuse in *City of Canton v. Harris,* ruling that in some circumstances the failure of a police department to properly train or discipline its officers may give rise to municipal liability.[4] The causal connection between training and discipline and the incidence of abuse are well established, but the Court limited its decision to cases of "deliberate indifference" of city officials, a level of culpability approaching intentionality, and thus posing significant problems of proof. In 1997, the Court made it even more difficult to prove municipal liability.[5]

The Court has also placed substantial barriers to suits seeking damages against individual officers and officials.

The plaintiff must not only prove a constitutional violation, but to recover must defeat the defense of qualified immunity, which protects officers from damages liability unless their misconduct "violated clearly established . . . constitutional rights of which a reasonable [officer] would have known." Under this doctrine, police are not accountable for unlawful arrests, searches and seizures, excessive use of force, and other types of misconduct unless the conduct at issue had been previously proscribed. Thus, even where an officer is found to have acted unreasonably or excessively, he will not be held liable if a "reasonable" officer *could* have believed the conduct to be permissible. This dilutes the controlling constitutional standard and disallows damages except for the most egregious violations.

It is the politics of the Court, and not immutable legal doctrine, that forecloses appreciable change in the Court's approach to police misconduct. The Court regularly emphasizes the "realities" and dangers of policing without giving any serious attention or weight to the realities and dangers of abuse. This focus only on the governmental side has generated substantial deference to law enforcement officials and an array of procedural obstacles to the vindication of personal rights. Ultimately, the most important factor in the control and reduction of abuse is organizational accountability. All other remedies will fail if not accompanied by a system of training, supervision and discipline that is structured to ensure that departmental policies relative to use of force and other restrictions on the arbitrary use of power are implemented and enforced. The numerous commissions and studies which have examined the problems of police abuse are unanimous in their recommendations: only a dramatic change in the enforcement of new norms of behavior by the police will dislodge the deeply entrenched culture that currently prevails.

POLICE POWERS OF SEARCH AND SEIZURE

In the decade following the *Mapp* decision, the Court established several significant Fourth Amendment principles. First, the Court ruled that all searches conducted without a warrant are per se unreasonable, subject to only a few "jealously and carefully drawn exceptions." Government officials had to demonstrate a compelling need for an exception to the search warrant requirement.

Second, the Court required that searches, arrests, and seizures be undertaken only where probable cause existed to believe that criminal activity was afoot, and defined probable cause in a manner that required the police to have an articulable and reliable basis for their actions.

Third, in a watershed opinion, *Katz v. United States*, the Court broadened the scope of the Fourth Amendment by ruling that electronic surveillance constituted a search even where no physical trespass had occurred.[6] Placing an electronic amplifier on a telephone booth "violated the privacy upon which [the user of the booth] . . . justifiably relied." Personal privacy, not narrow property notions, was now the touchstone of the Fourth Amendment.

In developing these basic principles, the Warren Court was not insensitive to law enforcement interests. Thus, for example, the Court recognized the police power to "stop and frisk" individuals on only reasonable suspicion, it gave substantial protection to police informants (even at the risk of perjured warrants), and it allowed the seizure of blood, hair, and other personal items that are self-incriminatory.

The privacy principles were soon undermined by a differently constituted Court. One of the most remarkable developments has been the transformation of *Katz*, which broadened and deepened our notions of privacy, into a series of manipulated rules that reduce Fourth Amendment protections.

The Court's understanding of the "reasonable expectation of privacy" principle announced in *Katz* has become exceedingly narrow. The Court does not look to privacy expectations of real people or the public generally, but to its own narrow vision. We are told by the Court that we have no legitimate expectation of privacy in personal bank accounts, that we should not be surprised if the telephone company makes our records available to the government, that as passengers in cars or guests in homes we may not have a sufficient interest to object to unlawful police intrusions, and that a fenced-in backyard is not protected against aerial searches.[7] Further, the Court has ruled that society is not prepared to recognize the right of a prisoner to even limited privacy with respect to items kept in his cell—a Bible, photos of his family, personal letters, or books.

The Court's opinion in *Oliver v. United States* demonstrates just how far the Court has departed from the privacy-enhancing principles of *Katz*.[8] Oliver owned a 2,000 acre farm. The police, acting on an anonymous tip that Oliver was cultivating marijuana in his fields, entered his fenced-in property without a warrant. They ignored a "No Trespassing" sign and proceeded down a private road on the property where they eventually found a field of marijuana. The Court ruled that "open fields do not provide the setting for those intimate activities that the [Fourth] Amendment is intended to shelter from government interference or surveillance." This means that no one—whether or not they grow marijuana—has basic privacy protections in their fenced-in, posted farms.

The Court's rationalizations in such cases are often silly. The Court said that the area could be viewed from an airplane, without any reason to believe that the marijuana in the field in question could actually have been seen from the air. And if exposure to a determined snooper is sufficient to defeat a privacy interest, then *Katz* was wrongly decided, because a lipreader could determine what he was saying.

The Court has avoided such questionable distinctions in the area of agents and informers by simply declining to establish any restraints despite the serious impact on interpersonal relationships and political associations. Professor Anthony G. Amsterdam has commented: "I can conceive of no rational system of concerns and values that restrict the government's power to rifle my drawers or tap my telephone but not its power to infiltrate my home or my life with a legion of spies."[9] The Court has justified this hands-off approach by saying that you "assume the risk" that the people you deal with may be agents of the police. But is that the kind of society we want to build? Is there not a crucial difference, grounded in notions of liberty, between the normal risk we all take that a friend today may be a turncoat tomorrow, and the risk of faithlessness that is incurred when the police bribe, threaten, or otherwise convince our associates to become informers and enter our lives and premises as police agents?

Equally disturbing is the Court's approach to law enforcement techniques in the "War on Drugs." Drug courier profile stops and pretextual stops of cars result in the detention and search of tens of thousands of innocent persons every year. Yet the large percentage of these stops are predicated on nothing more than an officer's hunch and, in many cases, the decision as who to stop is informed more by the race and class of the person than any other characteristic.

Scholars and judges, while differing as to the overall intent of the Framers in drafting the Fourth Amendment, are unanimous in the conclusion that the Fourth Amendment was adopted at least in part in reaction to the abuses of the English enforcement measures in the colonies, including the notorious Writs of Assistance. The Writs of Assistance permitted British soldiers to enter colonial residences to search for violations of the customs and duties provisions. They were issued by agents of the

Crown without a showing of cause; no judicial authorization was required to search a colonial residence.

The Writs of Assistance were neither irrational nor used solely to harass the colonists. In fact, there were widespread violations of the customs laws, and the colonists were engaged in a large-scale conspiracy to thwart the collection of duties. It was predictable, therefore, that mass searches would turn up evidence in some number of cases.

Stop and search tactics in the War on Drugs are based on the same underlying assumptions: widespread searches conducted without individualized suspicion will produce evidence of criminal conduct. In both situations, it is law enforcement by serendipity; without cause that any particular individual is involved in the drug trade, police use group "profiles" or other broad-based criteria—the antithesis of individualized cause—to effect stops and searches. The drug-profile model is conceptually quite different from the model of individualized suspicion; it relies on factors that are not criminal in nature and that are often characteristic of the activities of the law-abiding persons.

Judge George C. Pratt of the United States Court of Appeals for the Second Circuit has compared the use of drug courier profiles to Alice-in-Wonderland logic.[10] Reviewing court decisions, he found that it was apparently significant if the suspect: arrived late at night or early in the morning; was one of the first to deplane or one of the last to deplane; used a one-way ticket or a round-trip ticket; carried brand-new luggage or a small gym bag, traveled alone or with a companion, acted nervously; wore expensive clothing and gold jewelry, or dressed in black corduroys, a white pullover shirt, and loafers without socks, or in dark slacks, a work shirt, and a hat, or in a brown leather aviator jacket, gold chain, with hair down to the shoulders, or in a loose-fitting sweatshirt and denim jacket; and walked rapidly through the airport, or walked aimlessly through the airport. In the operations at the Buffalo airport discussed by Judge Pratt, the police were "correct" in their stops in fewer than 2 percent of their profile encounters: of the 600 people stopped, only ten were carrying drugs. There results are typical of profile investigations. Yet the courts continue to credit these stops, rarely even considering the empirical evidence to the contrary.

Pretextual stops of automobiles are also common: police who do not otherwise have cause or suspicion that a driver is carrying drugs or weapons use an alleged traffic violation as a basis for the stop of the car to investigate possession of contraband. The Supreme Court has upheld pretextual stops as "objectively reasonable" under the Fourth

Amendment. According to the Court, as long as there was "cause" for the police action (the traffic violation), it does not matter that the police were using this reason as a pretext.

Police officials uniformly deny that race has anything to do with profiles or automobile stops, but it is apparent that race is very much a factor. For example, in a class action in federal court in Maryland involving stops on I-95, a study showed that 93 percent of all motorists violated traffic laws, and that of this group 17.5 percent were African-American and 75 percent were white. Yet, police records showed that of over 800 persons stopped on a section of I-95, 72 percent were black, 8 percent other racial minorities and only 20 percent white, almost an exact inverse from what would be expected.

Similarly, in Volusia County, Florida, videotapes and other documents relating to stops on I-95 by the Sheriff's drug squad disclosed that these stops were based in large measure on the race of the driver. Seventy percent of the motorists stopped were black or Hispanic; 80 percent of the cars that were searched were driven by blacks or Hispanics; only 1 percent of those stopped received a traffic citation; and over 500 motorists were subjected to searches and frisks without any cause or suspicion. By comparison, only 5 percent of the drivers on this stretch of I-95 were black or Hispanic, and only 15 percent of all persons convicted in Florida for traffic violations during this period were minorities.

Even where a court determines that the police have violated the Fourth Amendment, the exclusionary rule mandated by *Mapp* is often avoided. The Supreme Court has permitted the use of evidence seized in violation of the Fourth Amendment in grand jury proceedings, refused to apply the Fourth Amendment in almost all federal habeas corpus matters, and allowed the use of evidence seized under an invalid search warrant if seized in "good faith." On a percentage basis, very few criminal cases (and especially serious matters) are affected by the exclusionary rule, yet critics of the rule advocate even more limitations or total repeal. Given the lack of alternative civil or administrative remedies, such an approach will truly turn the Fourth Amendment into a voluntary honor code for the police.

Finally, we should not be sanguine about the number of cases in which courts actually suppress evidence for Fourth Amendment violations. The very low numbers may have more to do with police perjury in suppression hearings than they do with actual police practices on the streets. In a comprehensive study of police corruption and misconduct in New York City, the Mollen Commission determined that there was substantial perjury in search and seizure matters, stating that "several officers told us that the practice of police falsification in connection with such arrests is so common in certain precincts that it has spawned its own word: 'testilying.'" Thus, as in many other areas of the law, even where legal doctrine requires certain practices or procedures, the judicial process itself may stand as a barrier to the full vindication of rights.

We have witnessed tragic consequences of our failure as a society to respond to the systemic and institutional aspects of police abuse. Official misconduct endures in large part because we respond to its many manifestations in an episodic manner. As long as the courts and government treat police abuse as a series of isolated incidents, or as a regrettable by-product of the war on crime, we will continue to pay an unconscionable price for misguided policies. Police violence will be contained only if we challenge fundamental aspects of police culture and hold the police politically and legally accountable. Structural problems require structural remedies. We ignore that lesson at the peril of individual victims of abuse, the core values and institutions of constitutional government, and the very integrity of our society.

NOTES

1. *Monroe v. Pape*, 365 U.S. 167 (1961); 42 U.S.C. 1983 (1988); *Mapp v. Ohio*, 367 U.S. 643 (1961).
2. 423 U.S. 362 (1976).
3. 461 U.S. 95 (1983).
4. 489 U.S. 378 (1989).
5. *Commissioners of Bryan County v. Brown*, 117 S.Ct. (1997).
6. 389 U.S. 347 (1967).
7. See, for example, *Smith v. Maryland*, 442 U.S. 735 (1979); *California v. Ciraolo*, 476 U.S. 207 (1986).
8. 488 U.S. 445 (1989).
9. Anthony G. Amsterdam, *Perspectives on the Fourth Amendment*, 58 Minnesota Law Review 349, 365 (1974).
10. *United States v. Hooper*, 935 F.2d 484, 499 (2nd Cir. 1991), dissenting opinion.

20 RICHARD L. ABEL

TORTS

TORTS are injuries for which the law awards money damages. Some events may be both crimes and torts—O. J. Simpson was prosecuted for the murders of Nicole Brown and Ronald Goldman and held civilly liable to their families. But some torts are not crimes because the actor lacked the wrongful state of mind—a car driver who negligently injures a pedestrian. And some crimes are not torts because no one was injured— speeding on an empty highway. Compensability may turn on property rights—whether land entitles owners to freedom from the noise of an adjacent airport. Most tort claims arise without any prior agreement between the parties, as in car accidents. But some are preceded by a con- tract—the sale of a defective product or an insurer's refusal to pay an insured. And agreements may limit tort remedies—as when a parking lot disclaims liability. Contract also may define liability after the fact—most tort claims are settled rather than tried. Statutes (e.g., federal tobacco labeling requirements) and constitutional rights (e.g., equal protection and due process) may also affect tort liability.

In recent decades, a well-funded campaign by manufacturers, insurers, doctors, and other frequent tort defendants has sought, with consider- able success, to convince the public that Americans are excessively liti- gious, file frivolous claims, and persuade irresponsible juries to award excessive damages, burdening the judicial system and hurting the econ- omy. Senator Mitch McConnell, a leading proponent of "tort reform," says, "everyone is suing everyone, and most are getting big money." The Insurance Information Institute deplores that our judicial system "has been handicapped by unnecessary lawsuits, . . . exorbitant awards, and unpredictable results. . . . [T]he number of personal injury, product lia- bility, or property damage suits . . . has created a crisis." The influential columnist Jack Anderson has been even more hyperbolic: "people are suing one another with abandon; courts are clogged with litigation;

lawyers are burdening the populace with legal bills. . . . This massive, mushrooming litigation has caused horrendous ruptures and dislocations at a flabbergasting cost to the nation."[1]

The relative lack of political advocacy on behalf of tort victims has left this debate one-sided, and most Americans accept the tort defendants' position. A Harris poll found that over two-thirds of Americans believe it is too easy "for people to sue for damages when they think they have been injured or some wrong has been done to them," and almost the same proportion feels awards are "excessive."[2] However, these are false charges based on misrepresentations (addressed below): distorted anecdotes that have become urban myths and misleading or misinterpreted statistics.[3]

A VERY BRIEF HISTORY

Before the modern era, tort law was preoccupied with intentional wrongs (and still is in regions relatively unaffected by industrialization, urbanization, capitalism, and the state). Because people did not control large amounts of energy, accidents rarely caused serious injury. In societies where the means and relations of production did not generate great differences in wealth, relative status was mainly a matter of reputation. Intentional wrongs and their remedies significantly shaped reputation. Even misfortunes we see as chance, such as disease, often were attributed to a human agent (through beliefs in witchcraft and sorcery) or the wrath of ancestors or gods. In the absence of a state, redress often depended on the victim's capacity to mobilize supporters, who were more likely to be outraged by intentional wrongs.

The last few centuries have transformed tort law. Technological development made it possible for inadvertence to inflict previously unimaginable misery. Individuals can do so by driving cars or starting fires, private and public collectivities through momentary events (the Exxon oil spill and Bhopal disaster, or plane crashes) or ongoing activities (manufacturing asbestos, thalidomide, cigarettes, and IUDs, or dumping nuclear waste). The concentration of both private capital and political power, together with autocratic structures of control, have greatly augmented the potential effects of carelessness.

Mass migration and urbanization have produced a nation of strangers. They cannot enhance their standing by inflicting or revenging intentional injuries; indeed, they stand to lose status (except within deviant subcultures). Most anonymous wrongs are motivated by material gain.

Its victims, similarly, are more interested in compensation than personal revenge; but tort actions offer little redress because few criminals can pay damages. Concern about status relationships is concentrated within the family, which is increasingly nuclear. Violence and emotional abuse are endemic within that domain, but the state is reluctant to intervene for fear of underrmining intimacy, in the absence of consensus about normative standards, and because those wielding power within the family (men and parents) strongly resist interference. Aggressive competition obviously is endemic to politics and the market, but in both it is mandated, not penalized.

The same changes that reduce the salience of intentional torts increase that of negligent injuries. Strangers have less incentive to exercise care toward each other and greater difficulty in resolving conflict when injury occurs. Both features are aggravated by the deepening divides of class and race. Capitalism, technology and the division of labor increase the social distance between those who make what Calabresi calls the "decision for accidents" and their potential victims: workers and consumers of goods, services, and environmental amenities (such as air and water). Tortious behavior has come to resemble modern warfare in this respect.

As the focus of tort law has shifted from intentional wrongs among intimates to unintentional injuries among strangers, the moral tone also has changed. Although scholars disagree about the standard of care demanded by preindustrial tort law, few would deny that nineteenth-century judges adopted a highly moralistic rhetoric, allowing recovery only if defendants were morally culpable and victims wholly innocent. In the last hundred years these moral judgments have been subordinated to an equally explicit concern with compensation. Damages have been awarded to victims who previously would have been barred from recovery: charitable patients, social guests or trespassers on the land of another, gratuitous car passengers, and those whose fault contributed to the accident or who assumed the risk. Similarly, those who caused injuries have been held liable without fault merely because they were employers, manufacturers, or engaged in abnormally dangerous activities.

Changes in the experience of injury have profoundly shaped tort damages (lost earnings, medical expenses, property loss, and intangibles). Capitalism has created a proletariat that must sell its labor to live. Capitalists, by contrast, must minimize labor costs by discarding workers whose productivity is impaired. Because unemployment is tantamount to destitution, tort victims must replace lost earnings (past and future). Because capitalism erodes the obligation of mutual support outside the nuclear family and increasingly compels both spouses to work, the disabled must purchase care from strangers. Increases in the technical competence of medical professionals have been accompanied by deskilling of the laity. At the same time, medical costs have been inflated by the monopoly the state confers on professionals (as well as scientific advance). Capitalism and mass production widely disseminate consumer goods. Not only is there more to be destroyed, but most goods also are fungible (indistinguishable from others of the same kind): they are bought rather than made and readily replaced—indeed, the newer the better. Finally, the commodity form has been extended from goods, labor, and care to all forms of human experience—everything can (and increasingly must) be bought. Consequently, tort damages are granted for physical pain, disfigurement or loss of bodily function, fear, and damage to emotional relationships. The growing importance of damages for intangible injury reflects the fact that postindustrial society promises everyone a perfect life and elevates leisure and consumption over work and production.

Social fragmentation has made it very difficult for victims to mobilize collective support for their claims, increasing their dependence on both the state and the commodified assistance they must buy from lawyers. Both eagerly accept the responsibility. The state seeks a central role in enforcing norms and resolving conflict, progressively enlarging its monopoly of force. The vociferous campaign for "law and order" waged by politicians and the media justifies the continuing expansion of state coercion. Powerful bureaucracies—courts, prosecutors, police, and prison officials—develop vested interests in processing crime. The victim becomes an embarrassing anachronism—necessary to start the process but an inconvenience thereafter. Criminal prosecutions virtually supplant civil actions for intentional torts. In recent decades, the state has extended its writ to the workplace, environment, and market. Private practitioners specialize in representing tort victims in return for a contingent fee of 25 to 50 percent of the victim's recovery. Their professional associations (which recently replaced "trial lawyers" with the euphemism "consumer lawyers") stridently support fault-based private law remedies.

The Marxist critique of capitalism's exploitation and alienation of workers offers suggestive analogies with contemporary tort law. In precapitalist society injury (like work) produces "use value" unmediated by the market. Reciprocity obligates intimates to care for victims; social groups diminished by the injury support the victim's demand for redress. The capitalist legal system constructs the market for injuries as well as for labor, capital, land, and commodities. Just as capitalism denies workers control over the means of production, so legal professionalism denies tort victims control over the means of redress and medical professionalism denies victims and intimates control over the means of care. In each instance, a fraction of the dominant class mobilizes state power to protect its property—capital or professional credentials. Just as entrepreneurs combine capital with workers' labor to produce commodities with exchange value in the market, so lawyers combine their human capital (inflated by the state-created professional monopoly) with victims' injuries to produce commodities—torts—with exchange value in both the court and the market it creates (negotiated settlements). (Physicians also combine their socially constructed and state-protected expertise with victims' injuries for sale to third-party payers; both professions exploit the labor of nonprofessional employees.) Just as the capitalist insists on "managerial prerogatives" in the workplace, so the private practitioner and prosecutor demand total control over legal production. Like the worker, the victim has little say over how injuries are made into torts and crimes and is paid the bare minimum needed for survival.

CRITIQUE

There is broad agreement that the purposes of tort law are to pass moral judgment on the wrong committed, respond to the victim's needs, and encourage safety. It does all three badly.

MORAL JUDGMENT

Well into the twentieth century tort law's only goal was moral judgment: condemnation of acts endangering or injuring others and public recognition of the victim's suffering. Those held liable clearly experience tort damages as punishment. Yet tort liability is incoherent as a moral system.

Because damages are a function of the harm caused, they consistently violate the basic principle of proportionality between conduct and penalty. Punishment is too harsh when momentary inadvertence results in catastrophic injury—drivers who take their eyes off the road to tune the radio, inflicting a lifetime of agony on accident victims. It is too lenient when egregiously unsafe conduct causes little or no injury—by chance or through the intervention of others. Courts deal with these inequities haphazardly: juries stretch causation to extend liability, judges invoke proximate cause and duty to curtail it. But many injustices remain uncorrected, and all the attempts lack a principled basis. Similar problems plague defenses based on victim misconduct; again courts make ad hoc accommodations, adjusting the standard of care to victim capacity (measured by age and physical or mental disability), making crude comparisons between the parties' fault, or acknowledging environmental constraints on volition (such as employer domination of employees, or the limited choices of poor people).

Notions of fault constructed when individuals were the significant actors and technology was simple are inadequate to assign responsibility today. Many torts, especially the most serious, are caused by corporate entities, both public and private. The doctrine of respondeat superior (holding employers strictly liable for negligent employees) ensures victim compensation by obviating the need to determine which employee was responsible. Liability insurance pays most damages, but it also insulates the wrongdoer from moral judgment. Many injuries are caused by the independent acts of several unrelated defendants, among whom there is no principled basis for apportioning responsibility. Indeed, the very notion of individual responsibility is inconsistent with probabilistic theories of causation. Consequently, it seems unfair to impose liability for birth defects caused by the drug DES on all its manufacturers, because they *might* have injured the victim, when only one of them *actually* did so.

Tort theory and practice violate the moral intuitions of laypeople. Survey research reveals that both victims and the public believe that compensation ought to be divorced from fault. On one hand, those injured deserve and need compensation regardless of their own behavior. On the other, compensation should be paid by those who can most easily afford it (because they are wealthy or can spread the burden) or benefit from the activity (such as employers, manufacturers, or sellers). The attribution of fault becomes a mere rationalization for this more compelling ethical goal. Tortfeasors deeply resent moral stigmatization. Most cases are settled rather than adjudicated, and those settlements often explicitly deny any admission of fault. This contrasts sharply with many nonwestern societies, in which the response to injury focuses on the causal actor's acceptance of guilt, apology, and plea for forgiveness.

The ethical incoherence of torts is accentuated by the proliferation of different standards of care for particular situations unjustified by any principle. In preindustrial societies, liability sometimes was predicated on fault and sometimes imposed without fault, while in other instances fault went unpunished. Although nineteenth-century judges invoked fault to narrow liability, even they did not embrace fault unconditionally, as shown by the persistence of strict liability for ultrahazardous activities. The tension between fault and nonfault principles remains unresolved today. Nonfault recovery has expanded through workers' compensation, products liability, ultrahazardous activity, and no-fault automobile insurance. Some defenses have been restricted (such as assumption of risk or agreements not to sue) and others modified (comparative fault largely displaced contributory negligence). And a few jurisdictions have created comprehensive compensation programs. Yet fault principles have reappeared within every nonfault scheme: employee intoxication and employer breach of safety regulations in workers' compensation; notions of the appropriateness of ultrahazardous activities; the concept of a defect and comparative fault in products liability; criminal activity in comprehensive compensation programs. And existing fault principles have strengthened: several liability instead of joint, victim fault diminishing the liability of a reckless tortfeasor or that of a product manufacturer.

The inconsistencies just enumerated reflect difficulties in the dominant ethical framework of utilitarianism (measuring acts by their consequences). When tort law reflects nonconsequentialist ethics the results are even less satisfactory. Our inability to define the duty to help another in danger highlights the basic contradiction between egoism and altruism: we can neither embrace one extreme nor find a principled compromise. We have equal difficulty combining utilitarian and nonutilitarian ethics. We require informed consent before medical procedures out of respect for the patient's autonomy (a nonutilitarian value); but we impose liability only when the information withheld would have persuaded a reasonable person (not this patient) to reject the procedure; and the quantum of damages is the physical injury caused by the procedure rather than the violation of autonomy. We impose a general duty of reasonable care, but we also respect religious scruples against medical treatment (even when these conflict with the duty to mitigate damages) and parental rights to raise children according to personal beliefs (which may endanger the child).

Partly in response to these difficulties, and also because liberalism is uncomfortable with moral arguments that express patent and seemingly irreconcilable value dissensus, tort law has turned to the language of economics, replacing moral fault with the efficient allocation of resources, a concept that appears scientific and apolitical. I discuss below the empirical obstacles to a cost-benefit analysis of risk. But I also find it ethically unacceptable to make safety a commodity, which potential victims consume according to idiosyncratic preferences. Such "choices" inevitably reflect the enormous differences in both individual wealth and socialization.

In fact, tort law rejects many of the pivotal recommendations of economic analysis. It penalizes victims who choose too little safety (by reducing or denying recovery) but fails to punish those who waste resources by choosing too much. Economics might argue for symmetrical treatment of plaintiffs and defendants, but tort law is much more solicitous of victims. Economics might be indifferent to context, but tort law is contextually specific, distinguishing between a consumer's "choice" of an unsafe product and a worker's "choice" of an unsafe job. Indeed, the Coase theorem—a foundation of law and economics—sees tort liability as superfluous whenever plaintiff and defendant could have negotiated safety at work or in the market (the purchase of products and services such as air travel, pharmaceuticals, home appliances, and medical care). Although economics might disregard party characteristics, tort law imposes different obligations on corporate entities and individuals, entrepreneurs and consumers. Although economics would aggregate all the "costs of accidents" in calculating desired levels of safety, tort law distinguishes personal injury from property damage and lost profits. Although economics views all choices as equally "free," tort law recognizes resource constraints in the purchase of "essential" goods and services. In sum, economics offers neither an accurate description of existing tort law nor a morally superior alternative.

COMPENSATION

If moral judgment explains the origin of tort law, compensation is the contemporary preoccupation. Victims need money—often desperately— to replace lost earnings and pay medical expenses. Jurors (and many judges) are equally preoccupied with helping needy victims. Yet tort law is an unsatisfactory compensation device, both in its material consequences and as ideology.

Tort law cannot compensate consistently because liability reflects fault rather than need. Those injured by non-negligent defendants remain uncompensated. A victim at fault rarely receives full compensation. Even when the victim is found to be innocent and the defendant at fault, the consequences of liability depend on the parties' circumstances. If the defendant lacks resources and insurance, a tort judgment is an empty remedy. If defendant is no wealthier than the plaintiff, there is no social gain in shifting the financial burden from one to the other. Indeed, the goal is not to compensate the victim but to spread the financial burden as widely as possible. But tort liability does so only when the victim is an uninsured individual and the tortfeasor is either insured or a collectivity whose damages will be shared by many customers, shareholders, employees, or taxpayers.

Given the legal and financial obstacles to recovery, it is not surprising that relatively few victims succeed. Only 10 percent of American accident victims even initiate a legal claim. Only 12 percent of English accident victims disabled for at least two weeks recover *any* tort damages.[4] Lawyers are essential to successful claims but prohibited from approaching accident victims. Because the vast majority of claims are settled out of court, even the small fraction of victims who seek compensation recover only part of their damages. Economic incentives encourage tortfeasors to overcompensate small claims (because of their nuisance value) and undercompensate large ones (because victims need immediate payment and the legal system allows defendants to delay for years). Since other sources of compensation also are inadequate (loss insurance, sick pay, welfare, disability benefits, and pensions), many victims and their families are severely impoverished.

Tort damages compensate not only inadequately but also unequally, thereby symbolizing, reproducing, and intensifying existing differences. Because liberalism rejects status inequalities, tort law gradually has eliminated de jure distinctions between patients injured in charitable and profit-making hospitals, fee-paying passengers and gratuitous guests injured in automobile accidents, and business and social guests injured by landowner negligence. Yet the legal proclamation of formal equality obscures the persistence of real inequality. This has many sources.

First, some people are more likely than others to be victimized by tortfeasors who cannot or will not pay compensation. Crime victims, for instance, are disproportionately poor, racial minorities, women, and adolescent or elderly. Sovereign immunity often protects government from tortious liability; its victims are likely to be charitable patients, criminal accused, prison inmates, welfare recipients, and veterans.

Second, the process of claiming is institutionalized to varying degrees in different settings. Automobile accidents are governed by reasonably clear behavioral rules (traffic laws); because they occur in public witnesses usually are available; they create physical evidence (skid marks and dents); the police often make written reports; and at least one party is likely to be insured. Compensation almost always is available for work accidents; fellow workers encourage victims to claim and also act as witnesses; trade unions provide assistance and legal representation; and class antagonisms create a sense of entitlement. Claiming is much less well institutionalized for accidents in the home or during leisure activities: there may be no witnesses; victims tend to blame themselves; and there often is no obvious defendant. In England, damages were recovered by 29 percent of road accident victims and 19 percent of work accident victims but only 2 percent of other victims (who represented 86 percent of all victims). In the United States, claims were made in 44, 7, and 3 percent of these categories, respectively. Women, the young and old, and the unemployed are more likely to fall in the last category.

Third, the measure of damages is unequal. Tort damages are far more generous than workers' compensation payments, crime victim compensation schemes, or veterans' benefits. Victims in the last three categories are more likely to be manual workers, poor, or racial minorities. Tort damages have been arbitrarily capped in medical malpractice. Damages deliberately reproduce the existing distribution of wealth and income. The cost of preserving privilege is borne by everyone buying liability insurance, purchasing products and services, and paying taxes. Thus, all insured car owners pay the cost of compensating the privileged few who drive Rolls Royces or earn a million dollars a year. They also pay for the superior medical care consumed by victims from higher socioeconomic strata. Because nonpecuniary damages often are calculated as a multiple of pecuniary damages, the privileged also recover more for their pain and suffering. Finally, it seems likely that jurors are more solicitous of those who have lost privilege than those who never enjoyed it.

Because these biases cumulate, tort law intensifies social inequality. In England, male accident victims recovered tort damages almost twice as often as female, those 25–54 years old three times as often as the younger or older, the employed more often than the unemployed, and housewives less than a third as often as their proportion of the injured population. The mean sick pay award to women was less than half that of men.

The decision to compensate is inescapably political and unprincipled. Three illustrations must suffice. First, when adjacent landowners seek to put their property to inconsistent uses—a cattle feed lot and a residential development, for instance—one must give way, but no legal principle can choose between them. Second, because the consequences of tortious behavior ramify indefinitely in time and space and across social relations, the decision to terminate liability is hopelessly arbitrary: Spouses can recover loss of consortium but children, parents, and siblings cannot. One who witnesses the injury of an intimate can recover for emotional distress but not one who arrives on the scene minutes later or is a friend rather than a relative. A homeowner whose house is burned by a fire next door can recover but not the neighbor one house further away. Third, courts have been unable to explain when lost profits will be compensated.

Even if all these problems could be overcome (and they cannot), tort liability would be an extraordinarily inefficient mechanism for compensating victims. A very large proportion of the money paid by defendants—approximately half—is consumed by private loss and liability insurers, courts, and of course lawyers.[5]

As compensation, tort damages are no more satisfactory ideologically. Their fundamental justification is thoroughly inadequate: money cannot restore victims to the status quo ante. Damages paid years later are not the same as the wages lost or property destroyed (even if prejudgment interest is added). Many goods are not fungible. Reimbursement for medical expenses is hardly identical with never having undergone treatment. The most telling objection, however, is that money cannot be equated with nonpecuniary loss. We can better appreciate the historical contingency and cultural specificity of contemporary American tort damages by contrasting them with other responses: African customary law, for instance, which "compensated" death with livestock proportioned to the bridewealth necessary to affiliate a child to "replace" the deceased; or a workers' compensation scheme in which a lost toe is worth sixteen weeks' wages.

What cultural messages do American tort damages express? First, they affirm the existing distribution of resources. By compensating property loss, tort damages declare that a victim's worth is proportional to the value of property owned. By preserving the income streams of those who suffer physical injury, tort damages endorse the legitimacy of income differentials and the intergenerational reproduction of inequality (when children claim for the wrongful death of a parent). By excluding some victims and injuries and discouraging others from claiming, the law suggests that they are less highly valued. By relegating injured employees to workers' compensation, the law treats them like pure labor value, implicitly denying that they suffer the pain for which we compensate tort victims or enjoy the pleasures whose loss often is a significant element of tort damages (e.g., smell, taste, sexual function). Tort law proclaims the class structure of capitalist society: you are what you own, earn, and do.

Second, by monetizing intangible injuries tort law extends a fundamental concept of capitalism—the commodity form—from the sphere of production (work) to that of reproduction (producing workers).

Damages for pain and suffering extrapolate Bentham's hedonic calculus to its logically absurd conclusion, insisting that every pain suffered can be offset by an equivalent pleasure, which can be bought. Jurors must simulate a market in sadomasochism by asking what they would charge to undergo the victim's misfortune. Tort law thus extracts an involuntary present sacrifice (injury) in exchange for future gain (damages), reflecting bourgeois notions of delayed gratification and an instrumental view of the self—the very characteristics Weber stressed in identifying capitalism with the Protestant ethic.

Damages commodify unique experience by substituting the universal equivalent, money—as when a plaintiff's attorney asks the jury to assign a monetary value to each second of the victim's pain and then aggregate it over a lifetime. This dehumanization is particularly striking in two diametrically opposed situations. When injuries shorten a victim's life expectancy, damages are rationalized as enhancing present pleasure in lieu of years foregone—a secular version of the Faustian compact. A child born illegitimate or seriously disabled, who sues for wrongful life, is claiming damages for the net detriment of painful experience over the alternative of nothingness. Large awards for severe pain and suffering have several additional consequences: they salve the guilt of the unimpaired at having been spared such torment (the survivor syndrome) and rationalize their selfish desire to avoid and ignore the disabled (our new "invisible man"). Rather than evoking compassion for victims, large awards awaken envy for what is seen as a windfall and convey the erroneous impression (deliberately fostered by the insurance industry) that the tort system is working well—if anything, too well.

If damages for pain and suffering commodify experience, their recent extension to impaired relationships commodifies love. Damages are now paid for loss of the society and companionship of a parent in wrongful death actions; loss of the consortium of an injured spouse, lover, parent, or child; the experience of witnessing or learning about an injury to a loved one; mistreatment of the corpse of a loved one; misinformation about the death of a loved one; misinformation causing the breakup of a marriage; even the sorrow following damage to loved objects.

Such payments proclaim several messages. All relationships have a monetary equivalent and hence can be bought and sold. Their value depends on the extent to which the "other" resembles societal ideals of physical beauty, mental acuity, athletic ability, and emotional normality. Tort damages assume, and construct, a single scale along which everyone can be ranked—extrapolating adolescent obsession with popularity, universalizing 1950s rating-dating. They implicitly assume that an impaired partner will be discarded, like any other consumer product in our disposable society, and a replacement purchased with the damages received—tort as involuntary no-fault divorce. All relationships become a form of prostitution—the semblance of love exchanged for money—a generalization of feminist critiques of marriage. Just as society awards pain and suffering damages so the injured victim can purchase companionship that will no longer be extended out of love, so it gives damages to those who loved the victim, returning their lost "investment" so they can reinvest in unimpaired "human capital."

SAFETY

If moral judgment was the original justification for tort and compensation is its contemporary preoccupation, safety actually should be our greatest concern. Many folk sayings capture this: safety first; better safe than sorry; an ounce of prevention is worth a pound of cure. Calabresi forcefully argued this 20 years ago, convincing most scholars that reducing the cost of injuries must take priority.[6] Were we not concerned to foster safety, private law remedies would be hard to justify: criminal law expresses moral judgment more forcefully, and no-fault schemes compensate victims more efficiently.

Although tort law is not the only means of fostering safety, every alternative contains serious problems. The ideal mechanism would be self-interest: victims controlling the risks to which they are exposed. But the extreme division of labor associated with technological development, mass production of consumer goods, and the separation of workers from ownership and control of the means of production under capitalism make this impossible. Nor can we rely on altruism to inspire concern for safety in those with the power to inflict harm. Social distance, cultural difference, and class divisions undermine solicitude for others. And the market compels enterpreneurs to cut corners on safety.

Recognizing these limitations, we have created an elaborate regulatory apparatus to protect safety at work, in consumer goods and services, transportation, the environment, and recreational activities. Yet regulatory failure is manifold and notorious.[7] Regulators are swayed by political pressure, bureaucratic convenience, good relations with the regulated, and of course outright corruption. Regulation is slow and legalistic. Regulators generally have less information and expertise than the regulated and lack sufficient resources to inspect, investigate, and prosecute. Both regulators and courts are reluctant to impose severe penalties.

Legal theorists representing very different political persuasions have responded to this predicament by arguing that tort liability should be the central mechanism for promoting safety. Although they disagree whether liability ought to be strict or fault-based, they concur that the most efficient way to achieve an optimum level of safety is to internalize accident costs by making tortfeasors liable for their consequences. At least since Learned Hand offered his famous formula more than forty years ago, judges, lawyers, and legal scholars have argued that fear of liability will compel potential tortfeasors to engage in a cost-benefit analysis, taking just those safety precautions that cost less than the accidents they prevent.[8] Yet the scientific facade of this economic formulation conceals a number of fundamental theoretical flaws and empirical problems.

First, although it is possible (if often difficult) to determine the costs of safety, it is impossible to calculate the benefits of accident avoidance. Economists cannot tell us the value of bodily integrity or emotional well-being because there is no market for them. The costs of accidents can only be determined collectively—after the fact by judge or jury, before it by legislature or agency. All of these are political decisions, not the findings of positive economics. Even those elements of damage that have market values—lost earnings and medical expenses—are extremely difficult to predict far ahead. Actuarial methods can tell us only how a large population will behave, not the outcome of an individual case. Thus a central element in the cost-benefit analysis is hopelessly indeterminate.

Second, tort liability necessarily translates unequal recoveries (discussed above) into unequal risk. An entrepreneur in a competitive market *must* spend less to protect those who are less likely to claim or whose damages will be lower, i.e. the poor, unemployed, racial minorities, noncitizens, inadequately educated, young and old, and women. Thus, cheap consumer products and services are not only less effective and attractive but also more dangerous; low-paid workers suffer more frequent and more serious injuries and illnesses at work; and the underprivileged are exposed to greater environmental pollution. Whether or not the Bhopal disaster was an "accident," it was no accident that its victims were among the poorest in the third world. Nor is it chance that toxic waste dumps are overconcentrated in black ghettoes in the United States or that Taiwan is shipping radioactive waste to North Korea.[9]

Third, tort liability can produce the optimum level of safety only if the potential tortfeasor knows that the trier of fact (judge or jury) will perform the cost-benefit analysis correctly. But that calculation is theoretically impossible. The trier of fact typically asks whether the defendant failed to take specified safety precautions that would cost-effectively have avoided the injury that occurred. Yet cost-benefit analysis requires potential tortfeasors engaged in ongoing activities to evaluate *the contribution of all* possible safety precautions to reducing the costs of the entire population of accidents that *may* occur. Only a legal regime of true strict liability would place the decisional burden where it properly belongs—on the potential tortfeasor to evaluate the safety of an activity in advance rather than on the trier of fact to assign responsibility for an injury after the fact.

Fourth, every tort system, whether based on fault or strict liability, must determine if the defendant caused the plaintiff's injury. But both the natural and the social sciences describe causation in terms of probabilities. Therefore, we can talk meaningfully only about the connection between populations of causes and effects. By singling out just some of the causal agents, tort judgments inevitably hold them liable for injuries for which they were only partly responsible and fail to impose liability on others who share that responsibility. How, for example, should a court decide which injuries were caused by exposure to asbestos or tobacco?

Fifth, safety sometimes must defer to the other two goals—moral judgment and compensation. Courts often invoke the highly malleable concepts of duty and proximate cause to curtail liability because damages seem disproportionate to the defendant's moral culpability. Less often they liberally construe negligence and causation to impose liability because they find the defendant's behavior particularly reprehensible. Courts often look for the "deep pocket" defendant (large public or private entities or those likely to be insured) and then manipulate negligence and causation to rationalize the imposition of liability. Sometimes, by contrast, they refuse to find negligence or causation because the defendant seems less capable of bearing the burden than the plaintiff. Recent modifications of both the collateral source rule and joint and several liability reflect the tensions between moral judgment, compensation, and deterrence.

This focus on compensation distorts the promotion of safety in another way. When a large public or private entity is held liable (partly because it is a "deep pocket"), its organizational structure profoundly shapes how the liability message is communicated to those who actually caused the injury. Only the willfully naive could maintain that the result will be "optimum safety"—or even that this concept has any meaning. And in the vast majority of cases where insurance pays the bill, there are many reasons why liability is *not* accurately reflected in premium levels.

Indeed, if insurance perfectly transmitted liability costs to insureds much of its raison d'être would vanish.

Sixth, the efficacy of tort liability in encouraging safety rests on many dubious assumptions. Some actors are not maximizers in any simplistic sense. Charitable and governmental entities do not seek profits; indeed, an adverse judgment may augment a governmental budget and actually increase bureaucratic power. Most individuals cause accidents so rarely they have little incentive to seek information about their frequency and severity or how to avoid them. Liability is no threat to the judgment proof. Even profit-seeking enterprises may be able to shift liability costs to consumers rather than enhance safety if demand is relatively inelastic (the good or service is a necessity), the market is sufficiently concentrated to permit collusion, or accident costs are an insignificant proportion of price. Reliance on economic incentives creates another dilemma: damages may be denied or reduced to motivate careless victims to be safer; but this necessarily undermines the safety incentives of tortfeasors. Furthermore, such reasoning makes the counterintuitive assumption that victims and tortfeasors are similarly motivated.

Seventh, and perhaps most important, tort liability produces optimum safety only if *all* victims recover *all* their damages from those who negligently caused their injuries. Yet we saw above that a small fraction of victims recover anything—about one in ten in England and the United States. Caps on medical malpractice damages (and those proposed in products liability) institutionalize such inefficiency. A rational entrepreneur *must* discount safety expenditures by the likelihood of being forced to pay damages. If the market is perfectly competitive (as deterrence theory presupposes), it will drive out of business anyone who indulges in more. Most entrepreneurs are never even sued: half of all products liability litigation between 1973 and 1986 was directed at just eighty companies, and only 9 percent of manufacturers were sued in that last year.

Furthermore, the threat of damages encourages entrepreneurs to minimize *liability*, not accident costs. It creates perverse incentives: to conceal information about danger, take actions that maximize success in litigation (practicing defensive medicine by ordering unnecessary, costly, and perhaps even harmful tests), resist legitimate claims (especially those that may establish unfavorable precedents), use economic power to wage a war of attrition against claimants, and negotiate settlements that limit publicity. How else can we explain why Ford produced a Pinto with a gasoline tank it knew was explosive, Johns-Manville subjected workers to asbestos for decades after it knew they were suffering lung damage and cancer, and McDonnell-Douglas made and American Airlines flew a DC–10 they knew contained a faulty pylon and other design defects. Studies of the deterrent effect of criminal sanctions repeatedly demonstrate that certainty is more important than severity. Because full damages are rarely collected, tort liability encourages suboptimal safety.

Tort law fails as deterrence even when evaluated by its own criteria. Economic theory argues that governmental regulation ought to be unnecessary: contract can allocate risk more efficiently when the cost of transactions between the parties is low; and the threat of tort liability should achieve optimum safety in the remaining cases. Yet even the most ardent advocate of laissez-faire economics would hesitate to eliminate all speed limits, end medical malpractice liability, and abolish the Food and Drug Administration and the Federal Aviation Administration. Furthermore, if deterrent theory worked perfectly there would be *no* tort litigation: fear of liability would ensure optimum safety, and meritless lawsuits would not be brought. Yet conservatives loudly proclaim and denounce what they insist is a tort litigation explosion.

Reliance on a private law mechanism like tort to promote safety has other unfortunate consequences. The focus on liability to the particular victim subverts a collective response by all those endangered. Damages are paid only to individuals; group reparations and class actions rarely are available to those injured by the same polluter, manufacturer, common carrier, or employer. Because liability arises only when an injury has occurred tort law fails to address the underlying problem of risk. Under capitalism, private law, like private medicine, is obsessed with individual cure at the expense of collective prevention because capitalism creates a market for the former while opposing state involvement in the latter. Money damages undermine the collective interest in safety both by perpetuating the lie that they restore the victim to the status quo ante (so that greater safety is unnecessary) and by arousing jealousy of the newly wealthy victim, thereby diluting the sympathy and solidarity of potential victims.

Just as law individualizes victims (present and future), so it collectivizes tortfeasors—through the corporate form, the doctrine of respondeat superior, expansive interpretations of proximate cause (that seek a "deep pocket"), and the spread of liability insurance. This aggregation reflects the fact that tort damages have grown too large to be paid by individual defendants. The legal system further accentuates the power imbalance between individual victims and collective tortfeasors. Although the collective liability insurer can aggressively badger the individual victim for a release, the plaintiff's lawyer cannot approach victims to offer representation. Group legal service plans established in the 1930s to represent automobile accident victims were outlawed for decades. Corporations often refuse to bargain collectively with unions over safety practices on the ground that these are "management prerogatives." Thus, the individual victim (consumer, worker, traveller, breather of air and drinker of water) confronts a collective tortfeasor (enterprise, insurer, government) in the struggle over risk, whether the conflict occurs in the legislature, regulatory agency, or court, or at the negotiating table.

PROPOSALS

Criticism can lead in two directions: concrete limited reforms, feasible within the existing political framework, and more adequate solutions requiring fundamental social change. I will offer both responses, organized like the critique (even though some issues overlap and all must reconcile tensions between the goals).

Moral Judgment

Because the creation of risk is a public as well as a private wrong, endangering many besides the chance victim, it merits the official disapproval that only the state can express. Prosecutors and administrative agencies must pursue risk creators more vigorously. Since all officials respond to political pressure, actual and potential victims must organize to demand effective enforcement. Trade unions and consumer and environmental groups already do this; given the substantial free rider problem (others enjoy the benefits of such activity without contributing), they deserve state financing and legislative support.

Victims require a different response. First, we must recognize their injury and sense of grievance; damages not only fail to do this but also insinuate that the victim has enjoyed a windfall. Second, tortfeasors must acknowledge wrongdoing and apologize. In complex organizations it will be necessary to trace responsibility from the employee who physically caused the injury up through the chain of command. Settlements resolve the vast majority of claims but accept culpability instead of denying it. Third, moral judgment must occur *every* time someone is injured or endangered; even if general deterrence changed tortfeasor behavior (a doubtful proposition) it would not respond to the needs of victims. This means that all victims must be strongly encouraged to claim—by lawyers, the legal system, cultural norms, and support groups.

Finally, we must stop blaming victims. We do so now through legal doctrines like contributory negligence, comparative fault, assumption of risk, dangerous jobs, and agreements not to sue, as well as through economic arguments that workers receive a "risk premium" or consumers "choose" to purchase dangerous products and services or residents to live in unhealthy environments. Liberalism fosters these misconceptions by locating all constraint within the state, while portraying "private" behavior as free. But victims "choose" risk and injury within a structure of limited and grossly unequal economic resources; they are influenced by divergent cultural norms about their entitlement to safety; and many suffer an acute sense of political powerlessness. The concept of choice could become morally compelling only if we equalized individual circumstances—a profound challenge to those who take liberalism seriously. Furthermore, even if equal individuals should be free to choose risk, they do not forfeit our sympathy when they are injured. Suffering seems more than adequate punishment for carelessness (if any is deserved). And it still would be morally appropriate to criticize tortfeasors and require an apology.

COMPENSATION

Accidents will happen even in utopia. The popular preoccupation with compensation accurately reflects the severe personal and social dislocations they can cause. But taking compensation seriously will require new legal mechanisms. Only governmental programs can meet the criteria advanced below.

First, compensation should respond to *what* happened rather than *how* it happened, to need rather than cause or fault. It should be universally available: to those suffering congenital disability and illness as well as injury, whether or not they can identify a culpable agent, and even if they are to blame. That, after all, is how we respond to the misfortunes of those we love. We must view compensation as a social good, to be encouraged if not required, because, like education or preventive medicine, it benefits others by helping victims resume productive activities and social relationships (it has what economists call positive externalities). Victims should not have to overcome delay and cost to extract compensation from a reluctant bureaucracy or adversary. Lawyers, support groups, and government should reach out to those in need in order to overcome the differences in culture and civic competence that deter some from claiming.

Second, compensation should affirm the equal humanity of victims, both materially and symbolically. Comprehensive medical care (broadly defined to include physical and pyschological therapy) should be freely available. The state should restore all victims to the same level of income and property—whatever minimum society feels it can afford. Enlightened self-interest should make that fairly generous, since accidents happen to everyone. Those who enjoy the privileges of greater wealth and income should bear the cost of protecting them through loss insurance; potential tortfeasors would not have to carry liability insurance for this excess.[10]

Third, there should be *no* compensation for intangible harm. Despite campaigns by trial lawyers seeking to convince the public that pain and suffering damages are the inalienable entitlement of every freedom-loving American, virtually a constitutional right, surveys repeatedly demonstrate that most victims simply want defendants to acknowledge the wrong inflicted. Just as the present system of compensating pecuniary loss treats equals unequally (all people are created equal), so compensation for intangibles treats unequals equally (each human experience is unique).

The three reforms just proposed not only are mutually compatible but also reinforce each other. The trade-off between the quantum of damages awarded each victim and the number of victims benefitted is not only logical but also documented by historical experience. Workers' compensation, automobile no-fault insurance, the Swedish no-fault medical malpractice scheme and New Zealand's comprehensive compensation program all offer reduced benefits but serve everyone. Eliminating the adjudication of causation and fault and the calculation of past and future income and property loss, medical expenses, and intangible damages will enormously reduce transaction costs. It will obviate the need for lawyers (an original goal of workers' compensation). And it will drastically reduce delay, which presently inflicts great hardship on victims, forcing them to accept inadequate settlements.

I do not want to minimize the difficulty of implementing these reforms or exaggerate what they will achieve. They will elicit vigorous opposition from both the plaintiffs' bar and liability insurers (traditional adversaries who might forge an unholy alliance). But though both are adept at manipulating symbols and wield formidable material resources, hypocritical posturing has seriously eroded their public credibility. Plaintiffs' personal injury representation accounts for only six percent of lawyer effort.[11] Insurers who lose liability business probably can make more money writing loss insurance for those wishing to protect their high income streams and substantial property holdings. Besides, reformers may be able to enlist the support of capital, which would gladly give the state the burden of health and liability insurance, workers' compensation and sick pay.

Even these reforms represent only a social democratic solution to the problem of risk—ameliorating rather than eliminating the rigors of capitalism. They would reallocate the *cost* of accidents but not the accidents themselves. True, the legal system no longer would encourage tortfeasors to inflict greater risk on underprivileged victims whose liability costs are lower (because they recover fewer or smaller awards). But those with greater material, social, or educational resources still would be able to translate their privileges into lower risk when choosing consumer goods and services, a workplace, and environmental amenities, just as they would be able to buy better medical care and insure their superior wealth and income against accidental loss.

SAFETY

Without denigrating the reforms proposed above, I strongly believe that safety must be our first priority. We want to prevent accidents, not respond to them with moral condemnation and social support; the more we prevent the less important those responses become. I offer two mutually inconsistent proposals: one could be pursued incrementally within the existing social framework, while the other would require a radical transformation.

The first takes seriously the role of tort liability in deterring unsafe behavior. Many of the deficiencies criticized above can be ameliorated or eliminated. First, liability should be strict rather than fault-based. A strict liability regime encourages the tortfeasor to reduce the cost of *accidents* rather than liability. It entrusts the cost-benefit calculation to the entrepreneur (who is familiar with the risks and safety precautions) rather than the jurors (who are chosen for their ignorance of these matters). It encourages research on safety. It internalizes the cost of *all* accidents (not just those caused by the defendant's fault) in the price of the good or service, allowing the market mechanism of consumer choice to push the quantity of accidents toward the optimum level. And it lowers transaction costs by eliminating the hotly contested issue of fault (although it intensifies disputes about cause and increases claims).

Second, victim behavior should not bar or diminish recovery. Self-interest (the axiomatic foundation of economics) sufficiently discourages potential victims from exposing themselves to risk; there is no evidence that the denial of compensation makes them safer.

Third, damages should reflect *all* accident costs, however these ramify through natural fortuity, emotional bonds, or economic interdependence. For this purpose we need a comprehensive conception of the experiential consequences of injury (pain and suffering). Duty and proximate cause should not terminate liability; indeed, I would eliminate these doctrines altogether.

Fourth, claims should be actively encouraged—certainly by bar associations, possibly by individual lawyers.[12] As claimants pursue their selfish interests they simultaneously perform a public service. Furthermore, claiming is learned behavior, which should be reinforced. And encouragement will have the greatest effect on those who have been least likely to claim, helping to equalize claims rates.[13]

Many objections will be raised to this proposal. Some will maintain we cannot afford it: courts will be overburdened, prices inflated, and companies driven out of business. But these are captious criticisms. Courts exist to hear valid claims—we do not close schools because there are too many students, libraries because there are too many readers, or roads because there are too many drivers. When police, prosecutors, and prisons are overextended by rising crime rates we increase their budgets; we should be equally solicitous to private individuals who mobilize the law. If consumers purchase fewer goods or services whose prices reflect their accident costs, we have simply moved closer to the efficient allocation of resources. If we want to subsidize goods or services, there are fairer, more effective ways to do so than by leaving the random victim uncompensated. In any case, liability costs are an insignificant fraction of the cost of most goods and services. Others will decry anything that fuels American "litigiousness" and increases social conflict. But Americans actually exhibit relatively low and fairly constant rates of civil litigation, including torts.[14] And social conflict could be reduced much more effectively if tortfeasors stopped causing so many injuries and promptly acceded to claims when they were made. We do not reduce the crime rate by telling victims to stop complaining so much; why should we respond to the tort rate that way?

Perhaps the most telling objection to this proposal is its inconsistency with my earlier endorsement of no-fault compensation. But politics is not logic, and I see no practical obstacles to pursuing both reforms simultaneously: encouraging a 100 percent claims rate under a strict liability regime with an expansive concept of damages while gradually mobilizing support for universal public medical care and income maintenance. Indeed, movement toward strict liability (which merely corrects market imperfections) may create enthusiasm for no-fault compensation. If forced to choose, I would sacrifice the former to achieve the latter: the unquestionable good of universal compensation outweighs the uncertain deterrent of tort liability, especially given its very high administrative costs.

But even a strict liability regime with a 100 percent claims rate would have fatal flaws. It would continue to reproduce inequality, since tortfeasors would still find it cheaper to endanger the poor. It would violate autonomy, since the state would still set the cost of accidents and tortfeasors decide whether to inflict them. And it would undermine community, since victims would still claim as individuals. Taking seriously these three ideals in the confrontation with risk would require a commitment to democratic socialism, extending democracy from the polity to all social life.[15]

Human autonomy is the foundation of Kantian ethics. Contemporary tort law reflects this inspiration in its insistence that those exposed to danger ought to be as autonomous as possible in the confrontation with risk. Patients must give informed consent to medical procedures. Potential negligence victims must have knowledge and volition in order to "assume" a risk; the difficulty of realizing these conditions in the workplace persuaded legislatures to abrogate the doctrine. "Agreements" not to sue are unenforceable when the good or service is a necessity. Warnings put consumers on notice of risk only when they effectively communicate the danger.

The goal of autonomy in the encounter with workplace risk can be realized only through worker ownership and control of the means of production. Only in producer cooperatives will those exposed to risk also profit from that exposure and have the power to perform the cost-benefit analysis advocated by law and economics.

Rawlsian theories of justice call for equality of benefits and burdens— risk among them. This principle also is reflected in daily life. Many countries, including our own, require universal military service (at least for young men during wartime) in the belief that the threat of death or disability should be borne by all (however imperfectly that ideal is realized). None explicitly allows the wealthy to buy an exemption or substitute, as occurred during the nineteenth century; and many Americans remain deeply ashamed that the privileged were able to evade service during the Vietnam War. State guarantees of a minimal level of medical care express a rudimentary notion of equal entitlement to physical well-being. Americans are properly horrified that third-world countries tolerate markets in bodily organs and a physician proposed to create one here.

Workplace risk can be equalized only by substantially reducing the division of labor by rotating tasks—headwork and handwork, safe and dangerous. At the very least, everyone should regularly perform the most dangerous jobs—only that will awaken self-interest in reducing risk and foster empathetic understanding of the dangers that fellow workers encounter daily.

Liberalism conceptualizes the encounter with risk as a matter of individual choice: where to work and live, how to travel, what to consume, how to spend one's leisure. But individuals choose within a framework constructed by others. The most important decisions about risk—environmental pollution, the organization of work, the range of consumer goods and services—are made by collectivities (capital and state). Consequently, those exposed to risk also must respond collectively. Together they can mobilize far more information than any individual could master; collective decisionmaking also will compel individuals to reexamine their idiosyncratic risk preferences and aversions; and it will encourage individuals to take control of their lives rather than depending on others for their safety.

The organizational form best suited to promote autonomy, equality, and community in the encounter with workplace risk is the producer cooperative, whose members share ownership and management, rotate tasks, and decide collectively. Consumer cooperatives might perform a similar role; but they will encounter greater difficulty in exciting and sustaining member involvement because consumer interests are diffused across a multitude of goods and services, while those of producers are highly focused. It is so hard to organize those exposed to environmental risk that only state regulation can respond adequately. In each domain, equalizing risk requires a high degree of social, political, economic, and cultural equality.

CONCLUSION

Contemporary tort law, not surprisingly, reflects the dominant traits of late twentieth-century America: capitalist relations of production, individualism, extreme division of labor, and commodification. The unfortunate consequences for the incidence and distribution of risk and injury could be ameliorated within the existing social framework. Conservative rhetoric about law and order justifies harsher, more certain punishment for those who endanger or injure others. Numerous countries have shown that social democratic programs of health care and income main-

tenance are fully compatible with advanced capitalism and political liberalism. Laissez-faire ideology justifies strict liability as essential to efficient
resource allocation. But if we take seriously the values of autonomy,
equality, and community in the encounter with risk we must give equally
serious consideration to democratic socialism: worker ownership and
management, consumer cooperatives, equalization of benefits (resources)
and burdens (risk), and a state sufficiently powerful to regulate environmental pollution.

NOTES

I am grateful for the comments of Emily Abel, Jay Feinman, Sandra Segal Ikata, David
Kairys, Mark Delman, William Simon, and Mark Tushnet. All still would disagree with some
of what I have written and some with all of it. Adequate documentation of my arguments
would more than double the length of this chapter; a fully documented version is "A Critique
of Torts," 37 UCLA Law Review 785 (1990). Interested readers will find much of the evidence cited in my earlier articles: "A Critique of American Tort Law," 8 British Journal of
Law and Society 199 (1981); "A Socialist Approach to Risk," 41 Maryland Law Review 695
(1982); "Risk as an Arena of Struggle," 83 Michigan Law Review 772 (1985); "Blaming
Victims," 401 American Bar Foundation Research Journal (1985); "£'s of Cure, Ounces of
Prevention," 73 California Law Review 1003 (1985); "Should Tort Law Protect Property
Against Accidental Loss?" 23 San Diego Law Review 79 (1986); "The Real Tort Crisis—Too
Few Claims," 48 Ohio State Law Journal 443 (1987).

1. See Michael J. Saks, *Do We Really Know Anything About the Behavior of the
   Tort Litigation System—and Why Not?* 140 University of Pennsylvania Law
   Review 1147, 1156–63 (1992), source for the citations that follow; 132
   Congressional Record § 948–49 (daily ed., February 4, 1986); Insurance
   Information Institute, *The Lawsuit Crisis* (1986), 1–2; "U.S. Has Become
   a Nation of Lawsuits," *Washington Post,* January 25, 1985, B8.
2. Louis Harris, "Excessive Cash Settlements and Lawyers Faulted for Rise in
   Liability Suits," *Harris Survey* (Orlando, FL: Tribune Media Services, June
   9, 1986), 1.
3. See generally Saks, *Do We Really Know Anything;* Marc Galanter, *The Day
   After the Litigation Explosion,* 46 Maryland Law Review 3 (1986); Stephen
   Daniels and Joanne Martin, *Jury Verdicts and the "Crisis" in Civil Justice,* 11
   Justice System Journal 321 (1986). For example, more than half of a sample
   of South Carolina doctors overestimated median tort awards by a factor of

five or more; more than a third of the state's lawyers overestimated those awards by a factor of three or more. Donald R. Songer, *Tort Reform in South Carolina: The Effect of Empirical Research on Elite Perceptions Concerning Jury Verdicts,* 39 South Carolina Law Review 585 (1988).

4. Deborah R. Hensler et al., *Compensation for Accidental Injuries in the United States* (Santa Monica, CA: RAND, 1991); Donald Harris et al., *Compensation and Support for Illness and Injury* (Oxford: Clarendon Press, 1984); Richard L. Abel, *£'s of Cure, Ounces of Prevention,* 73 California Law Review 1003 (1985).

5. See, for example, J. Kakalik and N. Pace, *Costs and Compensation Paid in Tort Litigation* (Santa Monica, CA: RAND, 1986).

6. Guido Calabresi, *The Costs of Accidents* (New Haven, CT: Yale University Press, 1970); see Richard Posner, *Economic Analysis of Law,* 3d ed. (Boston: Little, Brown, 1986).

7. Richard L. Abel, *Risk as an Arena of Struggle,* 83 Michigan Law Review 772 (1985); *Blaming Victims,* 1985 American Bar Foundation Research Journal 401.

8. *United States v. Carroll Towing Co.,* 159 F.2d 169 (2d Cir. 1947).

9. United Church of Christ Commission on Racial Justice, *Toxic Wastes and Race in the United States: A National Report on the Racial and Socio-Economic Characteristics of Communities with Hazardous Waste Sites* (1987).

10. Richard L. Abel, *Should Tort Law Protect Property Against Accidental Loss?* 23 San Diego Law Review 79 (1986).

11. John P. Heinz and Edward O. Laumann, *Chicago Lawyers: The Social Structure of the Bar,* rev. ed. (Evanston, IL: Northwestern University Press, 1994), table 2.1.

12. Richard L. Abel, *The Real Tort Crisis—Too Few Claims,* 48 Ohio State Law Journal 443 (1987).

13. Hazel Genn, *Meeting Legal Needs? An Evaluation of a Scheme for Personal Injury Victims* (Oxford: Centre for Socio-Legal Studies; Manchester: Greater Manchester Legal Services Committee, 1982).

14. Saks, *Do We Really Know Anything;* Marc Galanter, *The Life and Times of the Big Six; or, The Federal Courts Since the Good Old Days,* 1988 Wisconsin Law Review 921; Deborah Hensler et al., *Trends in Tort Litigation: The Story Behind the Statistics* (Santa Monica, CA: RAND, 1987).

15. Richard L. Abel, *A Socialist Approach to Risk,* 41 Maryland Law Review 695 (1982).

21 MORTON J. HORWITZ

THE RISE AND EARLY PROGRESSIVE CRITIQUE OF OBJECTIVE CAUSATION

WHEN the first-year law student is taught to distinguish sharply between "actual" or "but for" causation and "proximate" or "legal" cause, the student is learning a system that did not crystallize until the 1920s. Before the successful attack of Legal Realism on the objectivity of causation, judges and lawyers thought in terms only of "actual" causes, of "chains of causation," which could be "broken" by "intervening" or "supervening" events. This historical essay is about how this paradigm of objective causation, and the related conceptualization of the "objective" will of the parties in contract law, came into being and was challenged during the late nineteenth century. It starts with freedom of contract and the rise of laissez-faire economics.

FREEDOM OF CONTRACT

The decision of the United States Supreme Court in *Lochner v. New York* (1905),[1] which struck down a maximum hours law for bakers as an unconstitutional interference with freedom of contract, expressed above all the post–Civil War triumph of laissez-faire principles in political economy and of the view that "that government is best which governs least." Closely connected to the laissez-faire position was a view of the market as a self-executing system that justly distributed rewards through voluntary agreement among individuals. The institution of contract thus represented the legal expression of free market principles, and every interference with the contract system—such as regulation of the terms and conditions of a labor contract—was treated as an attack on the very idea of the market as a natural and neutral institution for distributing rewards.[2]

Ironically, the constitutionalization of freedom of contract in *Lochner* came after two decades of astonishing change in the structure of the American economy that had resulted in the creation of giant corporations capable of exercising enormously disproportionate market power. Monopolization of the economy now would provide a catalyst for Progressive critiques of the traditional assumption of relatively equal bargaining power that had formed the foundation of legitimacy for the freedom of contract doctrine within Classical Legal Thought. The Progressive attack on freedom of contract gradually developed not only into a critique of the voluntariness of the existing system of contract but, more basically, into a challenge to the fairness and justice of the entire structure of market relations.

Roscoe Pound's powerful article on "Liberty of Contract" (1909), represented the most important early reaction of legal Progressivism to the *Lochner* decision and its progeny.[3] The freedom of contract doctrine, Pound argued, was of recent growth in the courts and represented a conception of "equal rights" between employers and employees that could only be called a "fallacy to everyone acquainted at first hand with actual industrial conditions." Pound asked, "Why then do courts persist in the fallacy? Why do so many of them force upon legislation an academic theory of equality in the face of practical conditions of inequality?"

The explanation was not that "individual judges project their personal, social and economic views into the law" or that the politics of judges had dictated these decisions. Since it had become so deeply embedded in the law, "[s]urely the sources of such a doctrine must lie deeper" in a more pervasive system of legal consciousness. Pound then proceeded to offer a series of explanations of why so great a chasm existed between "academic theory" and "practical conditions"—between what he would soon call "the law in the books" and "the law in action"—that would amount to the critical explanatory framework of Progressivism. There was "an individualist conception of justice, which exaggerates the importance of property and of contract [and] exaggerates private right at the expense of public right." While these views had come to dominate not only law, but also economics and politics, they were out of touch with "the social conception of the present." These ideas had been perpetuated by the training of judges and lawyers in an eighteenth-century natural law philosophy at the same time as they had "pretended contempt" for all forms of legal philosophy. "As a result . . . we exaggerate the importance of property and of contract . . . [and] exaggerate private right at the expense of public interest."

It is important to realize precisely how the assault on freedom of contract emerged. For every one sweeping article like Pound's great piece on "Liberty of Contract," there were twenty others which offered a more technical challenge to one or another specific aspect of contract doctrine. It was this internal critique of late-nineteenth-century contract doctrine that initially undermined the foundations of Classical Legal Thought.

The Progressive critique of freedom of contract as a constitutional doctrine began with an elaborate assault on the intellectual premises of the private law of contract. After the *Lochner* decision, most technical internal disputes within the law of contract were often displaced struggles over whether contract law could be justly characterized as a neutral and voluntary system in which the judge simply carried out the will of the contracting parties. It was this "will theory" that Progressive legal thinkers began to criticize immediately after *Lochner*.

The most striking feature of the attack on the will theory of contract is that it developed directly out of objectivism, which had arisen in the second half of the nineteenth century for the purpose of strengthening and consolidating the will theory. This shift from a subjective to an objective theory after the Civil War was part of a broader tendency to create formal and general theories that would provide uniformity, certainty, and predictability of legal arrangements.[4] Since subjective theories necessarily gave juries extensive powers to determine the actual will of the parties, the shift to an objective theory was part of a self-conscious effort of judges and jurists to establish uniformity by subordinating the fluctuating decisions of juries to judicially created formal rules.

In the process of formalizing and generalizing the system of contract law, the legal rules came to bear a more and more tenuous relationship to the actual intent of the parties. What once could be defended and justified as simply a more efficacious way of carrying out the parties' intentions came eventually to be perceived as a system that subordinated and overruled the parties' will.

An objective theory of a contract was not even the best practical approximation of the actual will of the parties, it was argued, for the law often does not even "create that relation which the parties would have intended had they foreseen." "The fact is," wrote Arthur L. Corbin, ". . . that the decision will depend upon the notions of the court as to policy, welfare, justice, right and wrong, such notions often being inarticulate and subconscious."[5] When the attack on the premises of freedom of contract began in earnest early in the twentieth century, it became immediately clear that an objective theory of contract had already sown the seeds of its own destruction. The established principles of contract, the critics maintained, could no longer be defended as simple reflections of the will of the parties or of a "meeting of minds." Objectivism could not be reconciled with individual autonomy or voluntary agreement. In fact, it demonstrated that the existing law of contract had regularly subordinated individual freedom to collective determinations based on policy or justice.

As in many other areas of the law, late-nineteenth-century contract jurisprudence had actually shifted away from post-Revolutionary natural rights theories. Its increasingly utilitarian efforts to use law to promote economic growth often sacrificed an individualized sense of justice. The claims of individualism and localism were thus frequently subordinated to the perceived need for standardization in national markets and a national economy. Subjectivism was also associated with utopian natural rights philosophy which was widely regarded as subversive of "the search for order" in a society experiencing ever increasing levels of social and economic conflict.[6]

Objectivism, in short, had prepared the way for those who wished to argue that the goals of intervention and regulation were already deeply embedded in the existing law and that the individualistic world of autonomous wills had long since passed from the scene.

The attack on objectivism in contract law was well advanced before it was extended to tort. Though there were many prior anticipations, the challenge basically crystallized as a series of reactions to the constitutionalization of freedom of contract in *Lochner*. From that time on, Progressive legal thinkers gradually elaborated the argument that since the institution of contract did not actually express the wills of private individuals, when the state either enforced or refused to enforce agreements it was only because of considerations of public policy.

An attack on the will theory of contract had been building for some time even prior to 1905. It focused first on the doctrine of "implied contracts." When courts implied a contract or a term in a contract, the critics asked, were they enforcing or overruling the parties' intentions? In his first article, written in 1870, Oliver Wendell Holmes, Jr., identified the category of implied contract as including "both contracts which are truly express, and cases which are not contracts at all."[7] But it was still too early for him to conclude anything other than that a "legal fiction" had clouded thought on the subject. Yet, recognition of both express and implied contracts had seemed to suggest that there were many contracts that could be enforced regardless of whether there was any meeting of minds or convergence of the parties' wills. Following Holmes's lead, Professor William Keener of the Harvard Law School published his treatise on *Quasi-Contract* in 1893.[8]

For the purpose of clarifying this dilemma, Keener took the willed contract as the paradigm for the "true" or "pure" contract. Among implied contracts, he distinguished between those that were "implied in fact," which were also "true" contracts because actual intention could be proven on evidence of the parties' behavior, and "implied in law" or quasi-contracts, which had nothing to do with the actual will or intention of the parties. The effect of Keener's classification was to insulate the "pure" contract from the accusation that it was simply an obligation imposed by the state. By candidly identifying quasi-contract with noncontractual principles, Keener believed he had preserved the realm of contract as the expression of individual autonomy.[9]

But the identification of a separate realm of quasi-contract did not always help to sustain the general idea that contract, correctly understood, did in fact express the parties' wills. Many legal writers after Keener actually pointed to quasi-contract as proof that the general category of contract concededly contained nonvolitional doctrines. Though this was apparently far from Keener's intention, it did nevertheless underline a deeper truth.

The publication of *Quasi-Contract* can be understood as representing the beginning of the gradual disintegration of the imperial ideal of contract as it had unfolded from early in the nineteenth century. Until the publication of Keener's treatise, the dominant impulse was toward ever increasing levels of generality and inclusiveness of contract doctrine. *Quasi-Contract* moves in the opposite direction—toward a disaggregation of concepts. The abstract ideas of the will of the parties and the meeting of minds can no longer hope to explain a series of doctrines in which courts clearly imposed their own ideas of justice on the contracting parties. Earlier in the century, legal writers had actually sought to root out all nonvoluntaristic elements in contract law. But they failed, and courts had never completely abandoned intervention in pursuit of uniformity or of justice. So that by the time Keener wrote, he was presented with a clear choice between conceding the existence of nonvoluntaristic doctrines in contract law or else excluding these elements from the definition of contract itself. In taking the latter course, he was forced both to cast doubt upon the generalizing tendencies of contract doctrine as well as to underline the frequency of nonconsensual obligation in the law.

The next step in the challenge was undertaken by those who argued that volition was often ignored even in supposedly pure contracts. It was Holmes's objective theory of contract put forth in *The Common Law* that ultimately provided the foundation for this move.[10] As we have seen, from the middle of the nineteenth century, judges and jurists had begun to retreat from the subjective theory on the ground that it undermined certainty and predictability as well as uniformity and consistency of legal results. In an increasingly national corporate economy, the goal of standardization of commercial transactions began to overwhelm the desire to conceive of contract law as expressing the subjective desires of individuals.

For a long while, however, objectivism was still primarily regarded not as in conflict with a will theory of contract but as necessarily supplementing it. For example, the function of judicial "interpretation and construction" of contracts, Holmes originally wrote, "is to work out, from what is expressly said and done, what would have been said with regard to events not definitely before the minds of the parties, if those events had been considered." In this view, while the role of judicial interference and discretion was greatly expanded compared with a model of complete deduction from the parties' intentions, the principal source of guidance remained the actual intention of the parties.

This has led Mark DeWolfe Howe to ask whether Holmes did not actually follow the orthodox view and "allow subjectivism, in the end, to control his theory of contract?" "I take it that he did not," Howe concluded, and I agree.[11] And he proceeds to argue that Holmes "was urging a revolutionary change in legal thought." "[T]he last of the contract lectures made it quite clear that Holmes saw the objective standard as no less controlling in the law of contract than it was in the law of torts and of crime," Howe declared. His goal was an increased "concentration of analytic attention upon the formal and objective aspects of obligation and a reduced concern for the subjectivities of assent."

Yet it is true that objectivism in contract law could be ambiguously understood as not necessarily in conflict with a theory based on a meeting of minds of the parties. And that is why for a long time after Holmes wrote *The Common Law*, objectivism was not understood as a frontal assault upon the will theory itself.

It was Holmes who took the argument one step further. In three sentences in "The Path of the Law" (1897), which were as influential as any he wrote, he simply assumed that the very process of implying a contract or a term in a contract was an act of judicial legislation for reasons of policy. "You always can imply a condition in a contract," he wrote. "But why do you imply it?"

It is because of some belief as to the practice of the community or of a class, or because of some opinion as to policy, or in short, because of some attitude of yours upon a matter not capable of exact quantitative measurement, and therefore not capable of founding exact logical conclusions.[12]

Here, for the first time, Holmes could not be understood ultimately to base contractual liability on the intention of the parties. It is the revolutionary moment at which objectivism is finally recognized to be incompatible with a will theory of contracts. In terms of the much-discussed question of how a "paradigm shift" occurs, it is striking that Holmes did not even try to refute the dominant paradigm from an internal perspective but instead simply asserted that it was untrue. It was still possible, after all, to account for the process by which courts imply a contractual condition in terms of the more orthodox theory of contract interpretation he used in *The Common Law.*

Now, however, Holmes simply declares that when courts interpret or construe a contract, they impose some policy on the parties regardless of any supposed intention. The bright-line distinction between contract and quasi-contract that Keener had formulated just four years earlier is denied. There is no distinction between the interpretation of real contracts and those implied in law.

The influence of Holmes' assertion was simply overwhelming and became a standard point of departure in the unfolding attack on freedom of contract. In two articles in 1903 and 1904, Clarence Ashley directly challenged the "fetish of this favorite theory of mutual assent."[13] Where courts imply conditions in a contract, they "vigorously disclaim any idea of changing the contract of the parties and argue that by interpretation they find the intent of the parties," Ashley wrote, "but this is simply a convenient fiction, and the fact remains, that absence of intent is the basis on which these rules of court rest." "As a matter of fact . . . in all these cases the courts have in reality made a new contract for the parties." What objectivism actually means is that "there does not seem to be any difference . . . between the obligation of Tort and Contract."

In 1907 George Costigan carried the implications of objectivism one step further. Teachers of contract law, he wrote, "are . . . obliged to tell our students that the 'meeting of minds' talked of in the contract cases is often a misnomer."[14] Objectivism in contract law means that "a meeting of the expressions of the parties . . . is enough to make a mutual assent contract despite the fact that in an accurate sense of the words the minds of the parties never meet at one and the same moment of time."

In many articles attacking freedom of contract such as Ashley's, Keener's distinction between contract and quasi-contract seems to have been ignored for polemical purposes. Thus, Ashley continued to write as if conditions implied in law were indistinguishable from real contracts. Since in those cases courts could easily be shown to have "in reality made a new contract for the parties," he simply asserted that this was true for contracts in general. But perhaps Holmes took advantage of precisely the same ambiguity in his famous passage in "The Path of the Law."

The first practical area of the law to bear the brunt of the attack on the will theory of contract was the law of agency, which had only recently grown in legal significance as the corporate form of business became dominant. The effort of late-nineteenth-century legal thinkers to unify most areas of agency law around will and meeting of minds had never completely succeeded, due perhaps to resistance of the judges to extending the will theory to the corporation. The law of agency thus became one of the major battlegrounds in the campaign to challenge the individualistic framework on which the constitutionalization of freedom of contract had been erected. In order to see this, we need first to see the relationship between agency law and the growth of large organizations.

The conflict between subjective and objective standards in contract met its first practical test in situations involving the law of agency. The law of agency focuses on the question of whether the principal is liable for the contracts of the agent. Since organizations conduct all of their business through agents, the rise of the corporation brought to center stage the question of the scope of authority of corporate employees. The early appearance of an objective standard in agency law suggests that the rise of the organization strongly contributed to the triumph of objective standards in contract law.

THE DOCTRINE OF OBJECTIVE CAUSATION

At the conceptual center of all late-nineteenth-century efforts to construct a system of private law free from the dangers of redistribution was the idea of objective causation. In tort law especially, where the dangers of social engineering had long been feared, the idea of objective causation played a central role in preventing the infusion of politics into law.

If tort law was to be private law, legal thinkers reasoned, its central legitimating function had to be corrective justice, the restoration of the status quo that existed before any infringement of a person's right. The plaintiff in a tort action should recover only because of an unlawful interference with his or her right, not because of any more general public goals of the state.

The idea of vindication of individual rights was intimately connected with the notion of objective causation. Only if it was possible to say objectively that A caused B's injury would courts be able to take money from A and give damages to B without being charged with redistribution. Without objective causation, a court might be free to choose among a variety of possible defendants in order to vindicate the plaintiff's claim. If the question of which of several acts caused the plaintiff's injury was open to judicial discretion, how could private law stay clear of the dangers of the political uses of law for purposes of redistribution?

There were two basic metaphors used by legal thinkers to express the idea of objective causation. The first was the notion of a distinction between "proximate" cause and "remote" cause. The idea had worked its way into the common law from Lord Bacon's *Maxims of the Law*, the first of which was: *In jure non remota causa, sed proxima spectatur* ("In law, look to proximate, not remote, causes").[15] The second, related notion, taken over from the natural sciences, was that there were objective "chains of causation" from which judges could determine scientifically which acts in a complicated series of events really caused the plaintiff's injury. A number of related legal doctrines also sought to classify situations in which separate acts constituted "intervening" or "supervening" causes sufficient to break the "chain" and hold another defendant liable. But, above all, it was necessary to find a single scientific cause and thus a single responsible defendant, for any acknowledgment of multiple causation would open the floodgates of judicial discretion.

The earliest attacks on this system of causation can be traced back to the 1870s and to efforts of young American philosophers to counter a growing movement in America toward philosophical idealism.

Along with his fellow members of the informal Metaphysical Club, Oliver Wendell Holmes, Jr., "had come very early to share their deep distrust and antagonism to the *a priori* categories of Kant and the conceptual dialectic of Hegel. A philosophy of law, an analysis of legal history, which was built on Kantian or Hegelian foundations must be repudiated and cast aside."[16] Together with future Harvard philosophers William James, Charles Peirce, and Chauncey Wright, Holmes shared membership in the Metaphysical Club with a young instructor at Harvard Law School named Nicholas St. John Green.

In the midst of his Metaphysical Club speculations in 1870, Green published an article in the recently established *American Law Review* on "Proximate and Remote Cause," which, so far as I know, was by far the earliest direct challenge to orthodox legal notions of objective causation and was not to be repeated for another fifty years. Green disputed the fundamental Baconian maxim that the law could objectively distinguish between proximate and remote causes in order to assign legal liability in a nondiscretionary manner. "The phrase 'chain of causation,' . . . embodies a dangerous metaphor," wrote Green.

> It raises in the mind an idea of one determinate cause, followed by another determinate cause, created by the first, and that followed by a third, created by the second, and so on, one succeeding another till the effect is reached. The causes are pictured as following one upon the other in time, as the links of a chain follow one upon the other in space. There is nothing in nature which corresponds to this. Such an idea is a pure fabrication of the mind.[17]

There is no single objective, proximate cause, Green argued. "To every event there are certain antecedents. . . . It is not any one of this set of antecedents taken by itself which is the cause. No one by itself would produce the effect. The true cause is the whole set of antecedents taken together."

In a passage typical of those that have led historians to see the roots of pragmatism and skepticism in these early speculations of the Metaphysical Club,[18] Green declared: "When the law has to do with abstract theological belief, it will be time to speculate as to what abstract mystery there may be in causation; but as long as its concern is confined to practical matters it is useless to inquire for mysteries which exist in no other sense than the sense in which every thing is a mystery."[19] "When [courts say that] this damage is remote, it does not flow naturally, it is not proximate," he wrote four years later, "all they mean, and all they can mean, is, that under all the circumstances they think the plaintiff should not recover. They did not arrive at that conclusion themselves by reasoning with those phrases, and by making use of them in their decision they do not render that decision clearer to others."[20]

It is important to note nevertheless that Green did not dispute the possibilities of objective causation in the physical sciences, where "there is a search for what may with some propriety, perhaps, be called the proximate cause." In the sciences, he conceded, it was possible to use causation as "not an absolute but a relative term," signifying "the nearest known cause considered in relation to the effect, and in contrast to some more distant cause."[21]

Green surveyed the uses of causation in various fields of law to demonstrate how courts manipulated the terms "proximate" and "remote" to accomplish other purposes. In contract cases, courts employed these terms to determine what damages might "reasonably be supposed to have been contemplated by the parties." In negligence cases, "misconduct is called the proximate cause of those results which a prudent foresight might have avoided." But above all, there is "no settled rule" in tort because the determination of causation "often var[ies] in proportion to the misconduct, recklessness, or wantonness of the defendant."[22] In law, moral conceptions constantly intruded upon scientific ones.

Green thus not only anticipated Holmes's famous "prediction theory" of law.[23] He also previewed what a half-century later would be the most powerful argument of the Legal Realists against the continued insistence of legal orthodoxy upon the objective character of causation in law: that because judges and jurists inevitably imported moral ideas into their determinations of legal causation, they were making discretionary policy determinations under the guise of doing science.

There are many reasons why the later Legal Realists' critique of causation doctrine largely succeeded while Green's challenge seems to have been ignored. In the realm of ideas, however, one important difference between the two periods stands out. While Green was prepared to concede that the notion of objective causation "may with some propriety" be used in the physical sciences, his Legal Realist successors were to witness an internal challenge to causation in the natural sciences themselves. Without pretensions to scientific foundations, legal conceptions of objective causation became increasingly vulnerable.

Though we may pay tribute to Green's prescience and originality, his direct influence on legal doctrine seems to have been nonexistent. If we are to find Green's influence, we must trace it through a more indirect process by which a number of his perceptions were taken up by others and gradually accumulated into a critical whole. Prescient and original as Green was, if he is to be allowed any measure of immortality, it must be either specifically through his effect on Holmes or, more generally, because of his contributions to the development of pragmatism.

CAUSATION AND IDEOLOGY

The underlying ideological issues in the controversy over legal causation were directly confronted in 1874, four years after Green wrote, by the orthodox treatise writer Francis Wharton. The recent appearance of John Stuart Mill's *Autobiography*, Wharton wrote, had "revived" the controversy on Causation originally stirred up by the publication of Mill's *System of Logic* (1843).[24] "The doctrine advocated by . . . Mill, that the cause of an event is the sum of all its antecedents," Wharton argued, was "irreconcilable with the principles of Roman and of Anglo-American law." Besides, he maintained, the inevitable result of a doctrine of multiple causation was "communism."

Wharton's major argument was that the theory of causation was different in law than it was in the natural sciences. "[P]hysicists who treat all antecedents as causes, and who can only judge of material forces, can afford no aid to jurisprudence when it undertakes to distinguish those conditions which are material, and therefore merely consecutive, from those which are moral and causal." Given the fact that the scientific definition of causation "has not, with rare exceptions, been considered, by Anglo-American courts, to call even for discussion, this shows that so far as concerns practical life, the materialistic view of causation has no ground on which to stand."

Thus far, it should be noticed, Wharton's main strategy was simply to dissociate legal causation from scientific causation. There was not yet an attempt to argue that the claims of legal science can or should be grounded on those of the natural sciences. For Wharton, the distinctively legal emphasis on moral causation was connected with the search for a free agency among the multiple antecedent causes. By the "leveling of all antecedents to the same parity," by not only failing to "distinguish between physical and moral forces" but also neglecting to "requir[e] that physical forces be directed in conformity with moral law," Mill was "denying man's moral primacy over and responsibility for nature."

The result was "the practical communism which this theory of the causal character of all antecedents promotes."

> Here is a capitalist among these antecedents; he shall be forced to pay. The capitalist, therefore, becomes liable for all disasters of which he is in any sense the condition, and the fact that he thus is held liable, multiplies these disasters. Men become prudent and diligent by the consciousness that they will be made to suffer if they are not prudent and diligent. If

they know that they will not be made to suffer for their neglects; if they know that though the true cause of a disaster, they will be passed over in order to reach the capitalist who is a remoter condition, then they will cease to be prudent. . . . No factory would be built. . . . Making the capitalist liable for everything, therefore, would end in making the capitalist, as well as the non-capitalist, liable for nothing; for there would be soon no capitalist to be found to be sued.

This seemingly sudden leap that Wharton makes from the technical question of legal causation to his warnings of destruction of capitalism is startling only if one fails to understand the systemic character of legal thought in the late nineteenth century.

Mill himself had attacked the existing doctrine of objective causation because it was associated with German idealist metaphysics, which he later noted was

in these times, the great intellectual support for false doctrines and bad institutions. . . . There never was such an instrument devised for consecrating all deep-seated prejudices. It is the main doctrinal pillar of all the areas which impede human improvement. And the chief strength of this false philosophy in the departments of morals and religion lies in the appeal which it is accustomed to make to the evidence of mathematics and of the cognate branches of physical science.[25]

Wharton's defense of objective causation and his insistence on a single responsible legal cause were repeated by all late-nineteenth-century treatise writers. For Wharton's generation the ideas of moral causation and of free agency were still regarded as intelligible and objective a priori categories. That Nicholas St. John Green alone could argue that the confusion of scientific and moral notions was precisely what made legal doctrines about causation unintelligible is evidence of his premature skepticism. In the 1870s few were yet prepared to agree that the infusion of moralism into law made it political. Indeed, it was the amoral that Wharton identified with communism. By the end of the nineteenth century, however, orthodox legal thinkers would begin to downplay the moral element in causation while emphasizing the scientific basis of objective causation in law. As they thereby implicitly conceded their own growing skepticism about the objectivity of moral categories, they also laid themselves open for the final assault on causation by the Legal Realist heirs of Nicholas Green, who could now show not only the illicit moralism of legal causation but the collapse of causation in the natural sciences as well.

There were few occasions before the twentieth century when the ideological problems underlying the question of objective causation burst forth with the clarity of a Green or a Wharton. By and large, orthodox judges and jurists continued to invoke the metaphors of "chains of causation" and "natural and probable consequences" as if these were concepts capable of objective determination.

But the skepticism of Green found another channel: the prediction theory of law articulated by Oliver Wendell Holmes, Jr. There are two separate elements in Holmes's theory. The first, expressed by his famous aphorism from "The Path of the Law" (1897), is that "[t]he prophecies of what the courts will do in fact, and nothing more pretentious, are what I mean by the law."[26] Indeed, as early as in his Harvard University lectures of 1871–1872, Holmes first expressed a similar idea virtually contemporaneously with Green's, which does suggest a reciprocal influence between Green and Holmes. Above all, Holmes's emphasis on the probabilistic nature of prediction was an effort to deny the claims of the legal system to logical or "mathematical" certainty.[27]

But there was another similar but far more practically significant shift to a prediction theory in Holmes's thought: his emphasis on foresight in the law of torts. Not only is Green's influence quite clear here but, as we shall see, the function of foresight in both Green and Holmes was to avoid the problems inherent in any claims to objectivity in legal cause.

A shift to foresight as a substitute for natural sequence had begun to appear in the case law of the 1860s. By the early 1870s, there were already "two views," Wharton noted, concerning liability for negligence:

> The first view is that a person is liable for all the consequences which flow in ordinary natural sequences from his negligence; the second, that he is liable for all the consequences that could be foreseen as likely to occur.[28]

Wharton opposed the foreseeability view and insisted on "ordinary natural sequence" as the basis for determining causation and hence liability. "If the consequence flows from any particular negligence according to ordinary natural sequence, without the intervention of any independent human agency, then such consequence, whether foreseen as probable or unforeseen, is imputable to the negligence."

More than any other writer, Wharton was responsible for clearly formulating the orthodox view of objective causation that would continue to dominate late-nineteenth-century legal thought. Only a half-century later would legal critics derisively refer to this formula as "negligence in the air."[29]

By that time, the idea of negligence as a "relational" concept had completely triumphed, and the notion of objective causation had begun to disintegrate. While he himself was something of a transitional figure with respect to the moralistic foundations of negligence, Wharton basically continued to draw on the earlier notion that it was simply just to hold an immoral actor liable for the proximate consequences of his act.

For the late nineteenth century, one judicial decision stood out as a radical rejection of the idea of objective causation; and every treatise writer, including Wharton, was forced to take a stand on its merits. In *Ryan v. New York Central Railroad* (1866), the New York Court of Appeals had held that a railroad that negligently caused a fire was liable only to the owner of an adjacent house and not to more distant owners whose houses were destroyed by the spreading fire.[30]

The court had employed traditional language in rejecting the claim of the second-house owner. Only the destruction of the first house was the proximate result of the railroad's negligence; all of the remaining injuries were remote, the court declared. Yet, even the use of traditional language offered little comfort to believers in the nondiscretionary and self-executing character of the orthodox categories. The result, limiting liability to the first house, seemed contrary to any commonsense understanding of the difference between proximate and remote consequences. And even more importantly, the court spent far more time explaining why any other result "would . . . create a liability which would be the destruction of all civilized society."

The New York court, Judge Thomas Cooley contemptuously noted, was "apparently . . . more influenced in their decision by the fact that the opposite doctrine 'would subject to a liability against which no prudence could guard, and to meet which no private fortune would be adequate,' than by a strict regard to the logic of cause and effect."[31]

The decision in *Ryan* is one of many in the period after 1840 limiting the liability of the agents of economic growth, especially the railroad. Yet, the typical judicial strategies for extending entrepreneurial immunity had rarely dealt so cynically with the idea of causation. Even though virtually all judges and jurists of the nineteenth century had also promoted doctrines limiting entrepreneurial liability, the *Ryan* decision remained an outcast through the entire period, rejected in England and most American states.

The explanation gives us some insight into the relative autonomy of legal ideas. The conception of objective causation was too central to the legitimation of the entire system of private law for it to be abandoned even in the interest of erecting another barrier to entrepreneurial liability. Many judges, to be sure, manipulated the proximate-remote distinction in other cases to limit entrepreneurial liability, but few did so as brazenly as in *Ryan*, threatening to bring the entire intellectual system into disrepute.

Wharton seems to have come closer than any treatise writer to defending the *Ryan* decision. While never explicitly endorsing it, he did cite it as illustrative of the slightly different orthodox principle that the intervention of an "independent responsible human agency" relieves a negligent defendant from liability.[32] "If a house is properly built, if it is properly watched, if a proper fire apparatus is in operation, it can be prevented, when a fire approaches from a neighboring detached house, from catching the fire." From this Wharton seems to have concluded that the owner of the second house was, in effect, contributorily negligent and thus produced a break in the chain of causation. But unlike the court in *Ryan*, even Wharton recognized a Michigan court's assertion that without an intervening cause, "the principle of justice, or sound logic . . . is very obscure, which can exempt the party through whose negligence the first building was burned from equal liability for the burning of the second."

Wharton thus sought to absorb the *Ryan* case into his own orthodox paradigm of objective causation. Indeed, he devoted considerable energy to demonstrating the terrible consequences of failing to relieve entrepreneurs of liability when an intervening cause broke the negligent chain of causation.

"Whether a railroad company is to be liable for all fires of which its locomotives are the occasion," he wrote, "is a question . . . important to the industrial interests of the land." Unless abutting landowners are "held to be personally responsible for the consequences of placing combustible materials by the side of a railroad," the "noncapitalists" will be "skipped over" and "the rich corporation" will be "attacked."

> Capital, by this process is either destroyed, or is compelled to shrink from entering into those large operations by which the trade of a nation is built up. We are accustomed to look with apathy at the ruin of great corporations, and to say, "well enough, they have no souls, they can bear it without pain, for they have nothing in them by which pain can be felt." But

no corporation can be ruined without bringing ruin to some of the noblest and most meritorious classes of the land. Those who first give the start to such corporations are men of bold and enterprising qualities, kindled, no doubt, in part by self- interest, but in part also by the delight which men of such type feel in generous schemes for the development of public resources, and the extension to new fields of the wealth and industry of the community. Those who come in, in the second place, to lend their means to such enterprises after these enterprises appear to be reliable objects of investment, are the "bloated bond-holders," consisting of professional men of small incomes, and widows and orphans whose support is dependent on the income they draw from the modest means left to them by their friends. Nor is it these alone who are impoverished by the destruction of the corporations of which I here speak. The corporation may itself be soulless, and those investing in it may deserve little sympathy, but those whom it employs are the bone and sinew of the land. There is no railroad, no manufacturing company that does not spend three-fourths of its income in the employment of labor. When the corporation's income ceases, then the laborer is dismissed. We hear sometimes of the cruelty of the eviction of laborers from their cottages at a landlord's caprice. But there are no evictions which approach in vastness and bitterness to those which are caused by the stoppage of railway improvements or of manufacturing corporations; in few cases is there such misery to the laboring classes worked, as when one of these great institutions is closed. I think I may, therefore, safely say that the question before us relates eminently to the industrial interests.[33]

It was the doctrine of independent, intervening causes on which Wharton staked his entire hopes for limiting entrepreneurial liability within the orthodox paradigm of objective causation. And it was here that the emerging doctrine of foreseeability seemed to him to pose the greatest danger. "The consequence" of any foreseeability test, Wharton wrote, "would be that the capitalist would be obliged to bear the burden, not merely of his own want of caution, but of the want of caution of all who should be concerned in whatever he should produce." If courts could argue that even intervening causes of an injury were foreseeable, the result "would be traced back until a capitalist is reached. . . . If this law be good, no man of means could safely build a steam engine, or even a house."[34]

But whether or not the choice between "natural sequence" and "foreseeability" tests had, in fact, any real effect on aggregate levels of liability, it is clear that any formulation of causation in terms of foresight presented major dangers.

We have already seen that Wharton regarded the "natural sequence" idea as a major intellectual barrier against multiple causation, which he identified as leading to "communism." But Wharton also saw an entirely different threat emanating from any reliance on a foreseeability test: the potential of redistribution through a theory of strict liability. There existed

> certain necessary though dangerous trades, of which we can say statistically that in them will be sacrificed prematurely the lives not merely of those who voluntarily engage in them, but of third persons not so assenting. Yet in such cases (e.g., gas factories and railroads), we do not hold that liability for such injuries attaches to those who start the enterprise foreseeing these consequences.[35]

In a statistical world, Wharton saw, any foreseeability test would lead to the conclusion that all risks were predictable in the aggregate. Indeed, though he was not alarmed at the prospect, Green saw similar results from a shift to a prediction theory and noted that "[w]ith events of this kind, underwriters deal."[36]

In a world of randomness, where there is no necessary connection between particular causes and effects, all we can hope to do is statistically to correlate acts and consequences in the aggregate. Wharton's individualistic notions of "moral causation" and "free agency" had begun to yield to a world of probabilities and statistical correlations.[37]

When, in 1897, Holmes declared that in law "the man of the future is the man of statistics and the master of economics,"[38] he already clearly understood the implication that flowed from the radical change in the conception of responsibility that a prediction theory entailed. Earlier, in *The Common Law* (1881), Holmes had opposed turning the state into "a mutual insurance company against accidents" that would "distribute the burden of its citizens' mishaps among all its members." Not only was "state interference . . . an evil, where it cannot be shown to be a good"; more importantly, "the undertaking to redistribute losses simply on the ground that they resulted from the defendant's act" would "offend the sense of justice," since it was based on "the coarse and impolitic principle that a man acts always at his peril."[39]

Now, however, he recognized both the pressure of organized labor for worker's compensation laws and "the inclination of a very large part of the community . . . to make certain classes of persons insure the safety of those with whom they deal." Most injuries

> with which our courts are kept busy today are mainly incidents of certain well-known businesses. They are injuries to person or property by railroads, factories, and the like. The liability for them is estimated, and sooner or later goes into the price paid by the public. The public really pays the damages, and the question of liability, if pressed far enough, is really the question how far it is desirable that the public should insure the safety of those whose work it uses.[40]

Without objective causation, the problem of assigning liability had become simply a question of the fairness of the distribution of risks, "a concealed half conscious battle on the question of legislative policy." Liability for injury had become just another cost of doing business, which could be estimated, insured against, and ultimately included in "the price paid by the public." The individualistic world of Wharton's moral causation and free agency had begun to be transformed into a world of liability insurance in which the legislative question of who should pay would ultimately undermine the self-contained, individualistic categories of private law.

With the movement for Workers Compensation after 1910, the shift to a statistical or actuarial conception of risk came to be allied with a new vision of causation as probabilistic.[41] Beginning in the 1920s, Legal Realists began the final assault on the citadel of objective causation.

The lightning rod for criticism of the old order in this area, as in many others, was Harvard Law School Professor Joseph Beale, who in 1920 offered a formalistic defense of orthodox doctrine.[42] "The rules . . . formulated by Beale," Hart and Honoré have written, "were presented in a terminology of mechanical 'forces.'" "[I]t is impossible not to sympathize with the wish to cut loose from the tradition which gave such rules birth." The "appearance of defining proximate cause in factual, policy-neutral terms was little more than a sham."[43]

In the midst of widespread attacks on courts in worker injury cases, Progressives not only sought to take these cases out of the judicial system entirely; they also wished to undermine and subvert legal doctrines that enabled judges confidently to withdraw cases from juries. Just as an entire literature developed attacking the defenses of contributory negligence and assumption of risk[44]—two other major doctrines that permitted judges to rule in favor of defendants as "a matter of law"—so too did causation become a target of those who wished to deprive the judge of any naive confidence that causation could be invoked on a neutral, objective, or scientific basis. The result was that by the time the Realist revolution had run its course, causal doctrines were substantially deprived of their power to prevent cases from being submitted to ordinarily pro-plaintiff juries.[45]

The challenge to the objectivity of causation by the Legal Realists highlighted several important themes. The notion that there were objective chains of causation with intervening and supervening causes— Beale's "mechanistic" theory—usually had operated within the legal system to favor corporate defendants over plaintiffs. Like many other questions involving jury control, traditional causation doctrine gave judges a scientific and objective basis for refusing to submit a case to a normally pro-plaintiff jury. "Courts know very well that juries are inclined to be sympathetic to plaintiffs and less so to defendants. . . . When . . . it submits the case to the jury, [the court knows] full well that its verdict may be impelled . . . by entirely extra-legal and prejudicial items."[46] To the extent that a court was able to refuse to submit a case to the jury on the grounds that there was no causation, therefore, it could deprive the plaintiff of a victory. By contrast, "if the court has decided to submit a case to the jury, it has already decided in the plaintiff's favor the only real issue of proximate cause."

The article that launched the Legal Realist attack on the orthodox theory of causation was written by Henry Edgerton, Professor of Law at George Washington University and soon to become a major New Deal figure on the United States Court of Appeals for the District of Columbia.[47] He was followed by Leon Green who, starting with his *Rationale of Proximate Cause* (1927), soon came to dominate the Legal Realist approach to the issue.[48] Green combined persistent attacks on the "legal theology" of objective causation with an insistence that the question of proximate cause needed to be determined not by judges but by juries.

The Legal Realist challenge to orthodox conceptions of causation came to a head in one of the most famous cases ever decided, *Palsgraf v. Long Island R.R.* (1928).[49] In an opinion by Judge Benjamin N. Cardozo, the New York Court of Appeals reversed a lower court judgment in favor of a plaintiff who had been injured after a bizarre series of events. The question was whether the plaintiff could recover after an explosion at one end of a Long Island Railroad station overturned a scale that fell on the plaintiff, who was standing at the other end of the platform. The explosion occurred when a railroad guard pushed a passenger into a crowded train and accidentally knocked a package of fireworks he was carrying onto the tracks.

Judge William S. Andrews's dissenting opinion, in favor of the plaintiff, was as clear a statement of the Legal Realist position on causation as any ever uttered by a judge. The explosion was clearly the actual or "but for" cause of the injury, Andrews explained. "A boy throws a stone into a pond. The ripples spread. The water level rises. The history of that pond is altered to all eternity." The real issue, however, is how to limit responsibility for these infinite consequences through some idea of proximate cause.

> What we . . . mean by the word "proximate" is, that because of convenience, of public policy, of a rough sense of justice, the law arbitrarily declines to trace a series of events beyond a certain point. This is not logic. It is practical politics. . . . It is all a question of expediency. There are no fixed rules to govern our judgment. . . . There is in truth little to guide us other than common sense.

How did Judge Cardozo's majority opinion stand in relation to this emerging Realist challenge to causation? Suprisingly, he insisted that the case was not one about causation at all. "The law of causation, remote or proximate, is . . . foreign to the case before us," he declared. Rather, the question was really about the "anterior" issue of whether the defendant owed any duty at all to the plaintiff. "The conduct of the [railroad] guard, if a wrong in its relation to the holder of the package, was not a wrong in its relation to the plaintiff, standing far away. Relative to her it was not negligence at all . . . 'Proof of negligence in the air, so to speak, will not do.'"

Cardozo's effort to shift the issue from the question of causation to one of duty was closely related to many complex issues in the history of tort theory. It seems to indicate that Cardozo had acccepted the Legal Realist critique of the objectivity of causation, and thus instead sought to find a solution in the area of duty. Did framing the analysis in terms of duty really make any difference?

From our post-Realist perspective it might be thought that the same policy considerations that would enter into determinations of proximate causation would also determine the question of duty. Yet, it appears that Cardozo, a transitional figure with respect to Realism, still thought of the duty question as capable of mediating between a purely political conception of causation and a strictly formalist conception of legal obligation.

Duty was also the central issue in Cardozo's even more famous earlier opinion in *MacPherson v. Buick* (1916).[50] In that case, the question was whether, in the absence of privity between an automobile manufacturer and a consumer (who *was* in privity with the intermediate dealer who sold him the car), the manufacturer owed any duty to the consumer not to be negligent. Cautiously embracing one of the most radical and controversial opinions of a late-nineteenth-century English judge, who suggested that everybody owed duties to the entire world not to be negligent, Cardozo directly attacked the citadel of privity.[51] The dramatic point of *MacPherson*, then, was to overthrow the traditional private law conception of duty in which one generally owed an obligation only to someone who was not a stranger. Before *MacPherson*, unless there was a legal interaction between the defendant and the plaintiff, there would be no duty.

In sharp contrast to the generalized "duties owed to the world" approach of *MacPherson* is the disaggregated and particularized private law conception of duty in Cardozo's *Palsgraff* opinion. In *Palsgraff*, we have seen, Cardozo distinguished between the duty that the railroad owed to the passenger and the duty owed to Mrs. Palsgraff. The negligence of the railroad guard "was not a wrong in its relation to the plaintiff, standing far away," Cardozo concluded. This would be the equivalent of saying in *MacPherson* that the negligence of the automobile manufacturer was a wrong in its relation to the intermediate dealer, but not in relation to the consumer with whom there was no contractual relationship. As we have seen, that is precisely the traditional view that *MacPherson* had overthrown.

It appears, therefore, that between the time of *MacPherson* and *Palsgraff*, Cardozo had begun to have second thoughts about the potentiality for unlimited liability that his view of duty in *MacPherson* seemed to entail. He thus retreated to a more individualized private-law conception of duty to restore traditional limitations on the scope of liability. Indeed, it was only after the scope of duty expanded around the turn of the century that causation prominently emerged as a separate limiting device. Before that time, limitations on the scope of duty served the same liability-limiting function that causation came to perform. So why did Cardozo not also turn to causation to limit the reach of duty?

By the time *Palsgraff* was decided, objective causation had begun to be discredited in most fields, especially in the natural sciences. The collapse of causation in the natural sciences was actually occurring at virtually the same time as *Palsgraff* was decided. When the Viennese philosopher

Friedrich Waissman lectured at Oxford University on the subject "The Decline and Fall of Causality," he pinpointed 1927, the year that Heisenberg enunciated the "uncertainty principle," as the year that "saw the obsequies" of causality in contemporary science.[52]

Moving beyond the natural sciences, Thomas Haskell points to a general decline of causal analysis in American social thought beginning around the turn of the century.[53] The attack on formalism, Haskell argues, was at bottom an attack on causation by a new generation of thinkers who "from their concrete social experience in an urbanizing, industrializing society" understood the world as radically more interdependent. "Where all is *inter*dependent," Haskell writes, "there can be no '*in*dependent variables.' . . . To insist on the interconnectedness of social phenomena in time and in social space is to insist on the improbability of autonomous action."

Haskell continues:

> Things near at hand that had once seemed autonomous and therefore suitable for causal attribution were now seen as reflexes of more remote causes. Those factors in one's immediate environment that had always been regarded as self-acting, spontaneous entities—causes: things in which explanations can be rooted—now began to be seen as merely the final links in long chains of causation that stretched off into a murky distance. One's familiar milieu and its institutions were drained of causal potency and made to appear merely secondary and proximate in their influence on one's life.

During the 1920s and 1930s, Legal Realists created the distinction between actual or "but for" causation on one hand and legal or proximate causation on the other in recognition of the collapse of objective causation. Thereafter, the question of proximate cause would be addressed, as Judge Andrews had argued, as an issue of "convenience [and] public policy."

NOTES

The portion of this chapter on objective causation first appeared in the first and second editions of this book. An enlarged version that includes freedom of contract, and from which portions of this chapter are drawn, appears in Morton Horwitz, *The Transformation of American Law, 1870–1960* (New York: Oxford University Press, 1992), chap. 2.

1. 198 U.S. 45 (1905).
2. See L. Friedman, *Contract Law in America* (Madison: University of Wisconsin Press, 1965), 184–94.
3. R. Pound, *Liberty of Contract*, 18 Yale Law Journal 454 (1909). Actually, Pound begins with a statement by Justice Harlan in *Adair v. United States*, 208 U.S. 161, 174–75 (1908).
4. See M. Horwitz, *The Transformation of American Law, 1780–1860* (Cambridge, MA: Harvard University Press, 1977), 197–201.
5. A. L. Corbin, *Offer and Acceptance, and Some of the Resulting Legal Relations*, 26 Yale Law Journal 169, 206 (1917).
6. See R. Wiebe, *The Search for Order* (New York: Hill & Wang, 1967).
7. O. W. Holmes, *Codes, and the Arrangement of the Law*, 5 American Law Review 1, 11 (1870).
8. W. Keener, *A Treatise on the Law of Quasi-Contract* (New York: Baker, Voorhis, 1893).
9. Ibid., 3–25.
10. O. W. Holmes, *The Common Law* (Boston: Little, Brown, 1881).
11. M. Howe, *Justice Oliver Wendell Holmes: The Proving Years, 1870–1882* (Cambridge, MA: Harvard University Press, 1963), 241.
12. O. W. Holmes, "The Path of the Law," in *Collected Legal Papers* (New York: Harcourt, Brace & Howe, 1920), 181.
13. Ashley, *Mutual Assent in Contract*, 3 Columbia Law Review 71 (1903); Ashley, *Should There Be Freedom of Contract*, 4 Columbia Law Review 423, 427 (1904).
14. G. Costigan, *Constructive Contracts*, 19 Green Bag 512, 513 (1907).
15. F. Bacon, "Maxims of the Law," in *Works*, vol. 7, ed. J. Spedding, R. Ellis, and D. Heath (London: Longman, 1879), 327.
16. See supra n. 11, at 151.
17. Green, *Proximate and Remote Cause*, 4 American Law Review 201, 211 (1870); reprinted in N. Green, *Essays and Notes on the Law of Tort and Crimes*, ed. J. Frank (Menasha, WI: Banta, 1933).
18. See P. Wiener, *Evolution and the Founders of Pragmatism* (Cambridge, MA: Harvard University Press, 1949), 152–71.
19. Green, *Proximate and Remote Cause*, 213.
20. Green, *Torts Under the French Law* [book review], 8 American Law Review 508, 519 (1874); reprinted in Green, *Essays and Notes*.
21. Green, *Essays and Notes*, 213.

22. Ibid., 215.

23. Howe, *Justice Oliver Wendell Holmes*, 74–76; Fisch, *Justice Holmes, the Prediction Theory of Law and Pragmatism*, 39 Journal of Philosophy 85 (1942).

24. F. Wharton, *A Suggestion as to Causation* (Cambridge: Riverside Press, 1874), 3–11. Mill's ideas on causation came to Wharton's attention through R. Hazard, *Two Letters on Causation and Freedom in Willing* (London: Longman, 1869), which contests Mill's ideas. See F. Wharton, *A Treatise on the Law of Negligence*, 2d ed. (Philadelphia: Key, 1878), § 155, at 137 n. 1.

25. J. S. Mill, "Autobiography," in *Collected Works of John Stuart Mill*, vol. 1, ed. J. Robson and J. Stillinger (Toronto: University of Toronto Press, 1981), 232.

26. Holmes, "The Path of the Law," 173.

27. See Howe, *Justice Oliver Wendell Holmes*, 74–76; Fisch, *Justice Holmes*, 24.

28. Wharton, *Negligence*, § 138, at 112.

29. *Palsgraf v. Long Island R. R. Co.*, 248 N.Y. 339, 341, 162 N.E. 99, 99 (1928), "Proof of negligence in the air, so to speak, will not do"; quoting F. Pollock, *The Law of Torts*, 11th ed. (London: Stevens, 1920), 455.

30. 35 N.Y. 210 (1866).

31. T. Cooley, *A Treatise on the Law of Torts* (Chicago: Callaghan, 1879), 76, quoting *Ryan v. New York Central R. R.*, 35 N.Y. at 216.

32. Wharton, *Negligence*, 110.

33. F. Wharton, *Liability of Railroad Companies for Remote Fires*, 1 Southern Law Review (n.s.) 729 (1876).

34. Wharton, *Negligence*, § 139 at 114–15.

35. Ibid., § 75 at 63.

36. Green, *Proximate and Remote Cause*, 215.

37. See L. Krüger, ed., *The Probabilistic Revolution*, 2 vols. (Boston: MIT Press, 1987).

38. Holmes, "The Path of the Law," 187.

39. Holmes, *The Common Law*, 96, 163.

40. Holmes, "The Path of the Law," 182–83.

41. See Friedman and Ladinsky, *Social Change and the Law of Industrial Accidents*, 67 Columbia Law Review 50 (1967); J. Weinstein, *The Corporate Ideal in the Liberal State, 1900–1918* (Boston: Beacon Press, 1968), 40–61.

42. Beale, *The Proximate Consequences of an Act*, 33 Harvard Law Review 633 (1920).

43. H. Hart and A. Honoré, *Causation in the Law* (Oxford: Clarendon Press, 1959), 91–92.

44. See Malone, *The Formative Era of Contributory Negligence,* 41 Illinois Law Review 151 (1946); Green, *Illinois Negligence Law,* 39 Illinois Law Review 36, 116, 197 (1944); Kales, *The Fellow Servant Doctrine in the United States Supreme Court,* 2 Michigan Law Review 79 (1903); James, *Assumption of Risk,* 61 Yale Law Journal 141 (1952).

45. W. Prosser and W. Keeton, *Prosser and Keeton on the Law of Torts,* 5th ed. (St. Paul, MN: West, 1984), 319.

46. Gregory, *Proximate Course in Negligence: A Retreat from "Rationalization,"* 6 University of Chicago Law Review 36, 41, 58–59 (1938).

47. Edgerton, *Legal Cause (pts. 1 & 2),* 72 University of Pennsylvania Law Review 211, 343 (1924).

48. L. Green, *Rationale of Proximate Cause* (Kansas City, MO: Vernon, 1927).

49. 248 N.Y. 339, 162 N.E. 99 (1928).

50. 217 N.Y. 382, 111 N.E. 1050 (1916).

51. M. R. Brett, afterwards Lord Esher, in *Heaven v. Pender,* L.R. 11 Q.B.D. 503 (1883). See Holmes, *A Theory of Torts,* 7 American Law Review 652 (1873).

52. See W. Wallace, *Causality and Scientific Explanation* (Ann Arbor: University of Michigan Press, 1974), 163.

53. See T. Haskell, *The Emergence of Professional Social Science* (Urbana: University of Illinois Press, 1977), 13–15, 40.

22 PETER GABEL AND JAY FEINMAN

CONTRACT LAW AS IDEOLOGY

IN 1915 the United States Supreme Court struck down a Kansas statute that prevented employers from requiring their employees to quit or refrain from joining unions because the statute interfered with the "freedom of contract" protected by the Fourteenth Amendment to the Constitution. In *Coppage v. Kansas* the Court said:

> The principle is fundamental and vital. Included in the right of personal liberty and the right of private property—partaking of the nature of each—is the right to make contracts . . . The right is as essential to the laborer as to the capitalist, to the poor as to the rich . . . [1]

The right of freedom of contract expressed in this opinion conveys a sense of personal autonomy, projecting a free market in which laborer and capitalist, rich and poor can freely transact to get what they want, unfettered by the needs of others or the dictates of government. At the same time, the image also conveys a sense of social solidarity, suggesting that the market is an arena of mutual respect in which people can hammer out their collective destiny through firm handshakes enforceable in a court of law.

The view of contract in *Coppage v. Kansas* is now generally regarded as out of date. Under modern contract law, "society may restrict the individual's freedom to contract. . . . At the very least, the state may strive to ensure that [people making contracts] do in fact bargain in acceptable ways and are not so powerful as to substitute coercion for bargain."[2] The principle of personal autonomy underlying freedom of contract has been supplemented by modern principles of cooperation and fairness to ameliorate the harshest aspects of market exchanges. The modern image of contract conveys a new sense of autonomy and solidarity, in which people are both free to act and protected from the most harmful consequences of their actions and the actions of others.

Social images like these are not restricted to contract law. The conservative movement that has transformed American politics over the last twenty years has presented a utopian image much like the traditional image of freedom of contract. For example, Ronald Reagan promised to "lift government off of the backs of the people," suggesting that it had only been "government" that had been preventing us from realizing our personal desires, and that now we could once again stand as free and equal individuals, ready to take whatever action serves our respective self-interests. Like the modern image of contract, this vision presents a way of achieving both autonomy and community.

Traditional freedom of contract and modern contract law, like the political imagery of conservative politics, express elements of people's authentic yearning for personal autonomy and social solidarity. However, the images also mask the extent to which the social order makes it difficult to achieve true autonomy and solidarity. We live within social and economic hierarchies that often leave us feeling powerless, alienated from one another, and locked into the routines of everyday activities so that it is difficult to achieve increased personal power and freedom and genuine social connection and equality. This impoverishment of our human possibilities can be overcome not by the implementation of an abstract legal principle or a political slogan but only by our own sustained efforts to transform these hierarchies, to take control over the whole of our lives, and to shape them toward the satisfaction of our real human needs. This sort of concrete, practical movement would embody the realization of the utopian content of images like these. However, the law denies the oppressive nature of the existing hierarchies, suggests instead that inequality, powerlessness, and alienation are consequences of what people have chosen through their own actions, and therefore retards the achievement of the utopian ideals.

The law is one of many vehicles for the development and transmission of ideological imagery. In order to understand the historical and present nature of the legal system, and of contract law as a part of this system, one must grasp the relationship between the utopian images transmitted through legal ideas and the socioeconomic context with which the images have been associated. This essay provides a brief introduction to a method for understanding this ideological power of law by tracing the history of contract law over the last two hundred years.

CONTRACT LAW IN THE EIGHTEENTH CENTURY

Eighteenth-century contract law would be barely recognizable to the modern lawyer. The core of eighteenth-century contract law was not the enforcement of private agreements but the implementation of customary practices and traditional norms. Indeed, in his *Commentaries on the Law of England,* written in the 1760s, Sir William Blackstone did not consider contracts to be a separate body of law at all.

In part, contracts was that portion of the law of property concerning the transfer of title to specific things from one person to another—the process by which "my horse" became "your horse." Because of this present-oriented title theory, legal enforcement of an executory agreement (an agreement under which the parties promised to render their performances at some time in the future) was not generally available. Contract law also concerned customary obligations between people related to status, occupation, or social responsibilities. For example, a patient was "contractually" obligated by custom to pay for a physician's services whether or not he actually had promised to pay prior to the rendering of the services. In all types of contracts cases, the substantive fairness of the agreement or relation was subject to scrutiny by a lay jury applying community standards of justice. If a physician sued for his fee or a seller of goods for her price, the jury could decide that even an amount agreed to by the parties was excessive and inequitable, and so award a smaller sum instead.[3]

Thus, eighteenth-century contract law did not encourage commercial exchange. The traditional image of the world presented by contract law regarded the enforcement of market transactions as often illegitimate, so a seller could never be guaranteed the price he or she had bargained for, and liability might be imposed in the absence of agreement when required by popular notions of fairness. Such a system could exist because the development of a system of production founded upon universal competition in national and world markets had not yet fully emerged, and the political worldview that justified the relatively static property relations of traditional, precapitalist society had not yet been entirely overturned.

Between the latter part of the eighteenth century and the middle of the nineteenth century, the economic and political relations that had been associated with eighteenth-century contract law were burst asunder. In this period the system of economic and social relations known as free-market capitalism achieved a full development begun several centuries earlier, and the political climate was explosively transformed in the service of those social and economic developments with the aid of violent revolutions in America and Western Europe. These changes dramatically transformed the life nations of people in Western society and brought about an equally dramatic transformation in contract law.

CONTRACT LAW IN THE NINETEENTH CENTURY

In the nineteenth century, the key changes in society were its split into capital-owning and nonowning classes, and the dissolution of traditional patterns of social relations. As to the first, the social and economic positions of those who owned capital in the form of land, money, and machinery, and those who, having been thrown off the land or out of their traditional crafts, owned only their minds and bodies, increasingly diverged. Business owners were driven irrespective of their personal will or greed to compete with one another for markets for their products and to extract, with the assistance of a developing mechanical technology, the greatest possible production from their workers at the lowest possible cost. Workers were forced to sell their labor power to owners for a wage in order to survive and thereby to subject much of their daily lives to the owners' control; at the same time, competition among them often drove wages down to bare survival levels.

The second great change in society was the dissolution of many of the traditional bonds among people that had characterized the social relations of earlier periods. The social meaning of work, property, and community were increasingly fragmented as socioeconomic processes that were characterized by competition and individual self-interest reorganized the social universe. Traditional social environments had hardly been idyllic and certainly embodied forms of alienation and class domination that ought not to be idealized. But the rise of capitalism—with its universal market in which people and things were everywhere made subject to the exigencies of money exchange—and the transformation of traditional society—a profound disruption of people's everyday experience in their homes, work, and social life—generated a dramatic and dislocating social upheaval. Within a short stretch of historical time, people experienced and were forced to adapt to the appearance of the factory, the rise of the industrial city, and a violent rupture of group life and feeling that crushed traditional forms of moral and community identity. While part of this transformation was an attempt to overturn the repressive aspects of a traditional, hierarchical society, it also created that blend of aggression, paranoia, and profound emotional isolation and anguish that is known romantically as the rugged individual.

How could people have been persuaded or forced to accept such massive disruptions in their lives? One vehicle of persuasion was the law of contracts, which generated a new ideological imagery that sought to give legitimacy to the new order. Contract law was one of many such forms of imagery in law, politics, religion, and other representations of social experience that concealed and denied the oppressive and alienating aspects of the new social and economic relations. Contract law denied the nature of the system by creating an imagery that made the oppression and alienation appear to be the consequences of what the people themselves desired.

Denial and legitimation were accomplished by representing reality in ideal terms, as if things were the way they were because the people wished them to be so.[4] This representation was not the product of conspiratorial manipulation by power-mad lawyers and judges. Instead, the legal elites tended to identify with the structure of the social and economic order because of what they perceived to be their safe (or what others might call privileged) position within it, and they expressed the legitimacy of that structure when arguing and deciding cases in their professional roles. During this period important members of the bench and bar associated themselves emotionally and intellectually with the new socioeconomic order and expressed in their professional activities the individualistic nature of the new system of human relationships. In arguing and deciding cases, they sought to fit the situation presented by each case within this individual framework as the taken-for-granted legitimate way of resolving the conflict through collective reflection. This process of reflection and decision tended, therefore, to legitimate the new competitive socioeconomic environment no matter how unjust, alienating, and oppressive it actually was. In the process of resolving a great many such cases, legal concepts were built up that embodied the new social relations. The result was a system of contract law that appeared to shape economic affairs according to universally valid, idealistic values but was in fact only an idealized expression of the new individualistic world order that also helped to constitute that order.

"Freedom of contract," later expressed in *Coppage v. Kansas,* was the legitimating image of classical contract law in the nineteenth century. It projected an ideal of free competition as the consequence of wholly voluntary interactions among many private persons, all of whom were in their nature free and equal to one another. From one point of view this was simple truth, for the practical meaning of the market system was that people conceived of as interchangeable productive units ("equality") had unfettered mobility ("freedom") in the market. From an ideological point of view, this ideal expressed the sense of personal freedom involved in the destruction of the traditional social order with its status relations and hierarchies, but it also represented a denial of psychological and economic suffering and a justification of injustice.[5] It did not take account of the practical limitations on market freedom and equality arising from class position or unequal distribution of wealth. It also ignored other meanings of freedom and equality having to do with the realization of human spirit and potential through meaningful work and mutually affirming community. The legitimation of the free market was achieved by seizing upon a narrow market-based notion of freedom and equality, and fusing it in the public mind with the genuine meaning.

The legal consequences of this process of legitimation were the separation of contract law from the law of property, the representation of all social relations as deriving from the free and voluntary association of individuals without coercion by the state, and the allocation of responsibility for the coercion worked by operation of the market to personal merit or luck. In an economy founded upon the accumulation of capital through exchange transactions occurring in a competitive market, the proper role of the state was conceived to be that of the relatively passive enforcer of the "free will" of the parties themselves, of their "freedom of contract." As a result, the nineteenth-century law of contracts consisted primarily of a series of highly formal rules ostensibly designed to realize the will of free and equal parties, as that will was objectively manifested in agreements.[6]

Some leading contracts cases taught to first-year law students illustrate the power and effects of the new framework. The rules for contract formation and performance were extensions of the principle of objectively manifested free will. A son and his wife worked for his father on the father's farm for some twenty-five years without pay, in the expectation that the father would will the farm to him on his death. When the father died without a will, the farm was divided among all his heirs. Could the son, like the eighteenth-century physician, recover in contract, if not for the farm, at least for the value of his services? No, because there was no clear expression of an agreement between father and son, without which the court would be invading the freedom of the parties if it imposed liability.[7] On the other hand, where the parties had made a definite agreement, it bound them absolutely. Thus, a builder contracted to build a schoolhouse; the partly finished building was blown down by a windstorm; and after being rebuilt, it collapsed again due to soil conditions that could not be remedied. Was the builder liable for failure to build a third time? Indeed he was, for "where a party, by his own contract, creates a duty or charge upon himself, he is bound to make it good if he may, notwithstanding any accident by inevitable necessity."[8]

The most important and in some ways the most peculiar rules of classical contract law concerned the doctrine of "consideration," which grew out of the principles of freedom and equality. Since the market was the measure of all things, only those promises were enforceable that represented market transactions—those for which the person making the promise received something, a "consideration," in return. Thus, a promise to make a gift was not enforceable because the person maing the promise did not get anything for it.[9] Further, if a person offered to sell his house to another and agreed to give the other person until Friday to decide whether to buy or not, he could change his mind and revoke the promise because it was, like a gift, a gratuity.[10] Conversely, when a bargain had been struck, it was firm, and the courts would not inquire into the "adequacy of consideration,"—that is, the fairness of the transaction. If a person promised to pay a large sum of money in return for a worthless piece of paper, the nineteenth-century court, unlike the eighteenth-century jury, would "protect" the exercise of free will between supposedly equal parties and bind him without weighing the substantive fairness of the exchange.[11]

The results in these cases may seem unfair or irrational today, but to the judges of the time they were neither. The courts could not easily have intervened to protect a party or to remedy unfairness without violating the ideological image that the source of social obligation rests only upon the bargain that the parties themselves have evinced, not upon the community's version of justice. This imagery, drawn as it was from the experience of competitive exchange and the privatization of the social order, served to deny the oppressive character of the market and the lack of real personal liberty experienced by people in their personal and work lives. Most important, it served to deny that there was a system at all that was coercively shaping and constricting the social world, because the imagery made it appear that this world was simply the perpetual realization of an infinite number of free choices made by an infinite number of voluntary actors.

CONTRACT LAW IN THE TWENTIETH CENTURY

Twentieth-century judges applying contemporary contract law would probably reach different results in these cases. The son might receive a recovery for value of the services conferred on the father. Liberalized doctrines of excuse for nonperformance might relieve the builder. In many circumstances, a "firm offer," such as the offer to sell the house upon acceptance before Friday, is binding without consideration; in other cases, a court might refuse to enforce the offer but would at least compensate the buyer for expenses incurred in reliance on the offer. And, purportedly, courts today will in extreme cases correct any gross unfairness in a bargain by applying the relatively recent doctrine of unconscionability.

Contemporary contract law views these cases differently not because twentieth-century judges are wiser or smarter than their nineteenth-century counterparts, or because a new and more equitable style of legal reasoning has somehow sprung into being through a progressive maturation of the judicial mind. The old rules disintegrated for the same reason they were conceived: there has been a transformation of social and economic life that stimulated a parallel transformation in the ideological imagery required to explain it.

The transformation from the nineteenth-century to the twentieth-century forms of American capitalism was the consequence of a variety of factors that can only be summarized here: competition among businesses produced ever larger concentrations of capital within fewer and fewer companies; workers organized in response to their collective dependence on these emerging monopolies and challenged in a revolutionary way the mythical aspects of market-based freedom and equality; exploitation of the Third World, advancing technology, and efficient organization of production facilitated the partial assimilation of the American labor movement, allowing for the payment of higher wages while deflecting more radical labor demands; this increase in the level of wages, the use of part of the economic surplus for unemployment insurance, Social Security, and other types of welfare benefits, and the greater psychological control of consumer purchases through the mass media helped to alleviate the system's persistent tendency toward underconsumption. The basic requirement for understanding contemporary contract law is to look at the socioeconomic system thus produced and to observe its transposition, through the medium of law, into an imaginary construct that accommodates the progressive elements of the attack on classical law while ultimately securing the system's appearance of legitimacy.

The essential characteristic of contemporary capitalism is a shift toward greater integration and coordination in the economy and away from the unbridled competition of the free market. Coordination is accomplished first by very large corporations that are vertically and horizontally integrated (meaning there are relatively few "horizontal" corporations at the top of the major industries that own the capital that controls "vertically" production and distribution in each industry); and second, by a massive involvement of the state in regulating and stabilizing the system. In place of the unrestricted mobility of productive units that characterized the operation of the market in the nineteenth century, we now have integration, coordination, and cooperation to maintain systemic stability through more pervasive and efficient administration.

The rise of the coordinated economy has created a major problem for the law—how to transform the ideology of "freedom and equality" and its adjunct, "freedom of contract," into a new image that might retain the legitimating power of the older images while modifying them to conform more closely to the actual organization of daily life in the modern era. The method of addressing this problem has been to transform contract law into a relatively uniform code for business transactions that is predominantly defined not by the individualist principle of unregulated free competition but by the more collective principle of competition regulated by trade custom.[12] Since most "trades" (whatever nostalgia for a bygone era that term may evoke) are actually integrated production networks subject to supervision by dominant firms, the modern law of contracts is able to retain the legitimating features of private agreement while effectuating the regulatory and stabilizing component that is a central principle of the contemporary economy.

The principle of regulated competition leads to different results in the kinds of cases mentioned earlier. The twentieth-century counterpart to the case of the son who could not recover from his father's estate because of the absence of an express promise is the 1965 Wisconsin case of *Hoffman v. Red Owl Stores*.[13] The Hoffmans were small-town bakers who were induced to sell their bakery and move to a new town in reliance on the promises of an agent of the Red Owl supermarket chain that they would be granted a franchise, which never came. Under classical contract law, the Hoffmans would be without a remedy because the formal franchise contract had never been executed; in the twentieth century, however, the Wisconsin court discarded that restricted notion of agreement and held that they could recover because their reliance on the agent's representation had been commercially reasonable. The strict nineteenth-century requirement of bargain was rejected in favor of a broader standard of social obligation more expressive of the realities of the twentieth-century capitalist economy.

Hoffman v. Red Owl is a leading case for the principle that atomistic, concrete agreement is no longer the sole principle of contract law; people's tendency to act in reliance on less formal representations must be protected as well. It also illustrates the doctrine that private economic actors have a duty to act in "good faith." Both principles embody the ethic of cooperation and coordination reflective of the modern economy.

These principles apply, in other cases also. The promise to keep open until Friday an offer to sell a house would now frequently be enforced because that is recognized as an appropriate and necessary way to do business today.[14] In rare cases, courts can even be moved to inquire into the fairness of a bargain—into the adequacy of consideration—under the recently developed doctrine of unconscionability. While this doctrine has more theoretical significance than practical effect, sometimes consumers and other parties with little economic power can be protected from the more outrageous excesses of economic predators.[15] In sum, people are conceived to be partners in a moral community where equity and the balancing of interests according to standards of fair dealing have supplanted the primitive era, when every moral tie was dissolved in "the icy waters of egotistical calculation."[16] And the state as passive enforcer of private transactions has become the state as active enforcer of the newly conceived notion of the general welfare.

LAW AND IDEOLOGY

This chapter presents a very different explanation of the role of contract law from liberal or leftist instrumental analyses, which suggest that particular rules of law or particular results "helped" capitalists by providing a framework for legal enforcement of market activity. Instrumental analyses of contract law confuse the role of direct force with the role of law in the development of sociohistorical processes. Social processes like "free-market capitalism" do not get "enforced" by "laws." Rather, these processes are accepted through social conditioning, through the collective internalization of practical norms that have their foundation in concrete socioeconomic reality. Since these norms are in part alienating and oppressive, the process of collective conditioning requires the constant threat of force and the occasional use of it. For example, if you fail to perform your part of a bargain, it may be the case that a sheriff with a gun will attach your bank account to pay the aggrieved party his or her damages. The occasional deployment of direct force serves to maintain the status quo as well as to get people to accept its legitimacy.

"The law" does not enforce anything, however, because the law is nothing but ideas and the images they signify. The law justifies the practical norms and thus contributes to the collective conditioning process. In addition, the law contributes to constituting and reconstituting the norms and the social reality that they represent, as occurred with the transformations across the historical epochs discussed above.

One important way that this justification process takes place is through judicial opinions. Judicial opinions "work" as ideology by a rhetorical process in which oppressive practical norms are encoded as "general rules" with ideological content; these "rules" then serve as the basis for a logic ("legal reasoning") that supposedly determines the outcome of the lawsuit. A key social function of the opinion, however, is not to be found in the outcome and the use of state power which may follow from it, but in the rhetorical structure of the opinion itself, in the legitimation and reconstitution of the practical norm that occurs through the application of it in the form of a "legal rule." That enforcement of bargains was much more likely to occur under nineteenth-century contract law than under eighteenth-century law is, of course, true; but this does not mean that the function of nineteenth-century contract law was to "enforce bargains." The reverse expresses the truth more accurately—that the enforcement of bargains functioned to permit the elaboration of contract law as legitimating ideology, as a kind of idealized narrative version of painful market-driven relationships.

The central point to understand from this is that contract law today constitutes in large part an elaborate attempt to conceal what is going on in the world. Contemporary capitalism bears no more relation to the imagery of contemporary contract law than did nineteenth-century capitalism to the imagery of classical contract law. Contemporary capitalism is a coercive system of relationships that more or less corresponds to the brief description given here. The proof of this statement inheres in the situations we all face in our daily lives in the functional roles to which we are consigned: lawyer, secretary, student, tenant, welfare recipient, consumer of the products and services of Exxon, Citibank, and Microsoft. Despite the doctrines of reliance and good faith, large business corporations do not generally make decisions based on their concern for others or for the natural world. Despite the doctrine of unconscionability, unfairness is rampant in the marketplace. In this reality our narrow market-based roles foster isolation, passivity, unconnectedness, and a generalized feeling of impotence. Contract law, like the other images within capitalist culture, is in significant part a denial of these painful feelings and an apology for the system that produces them.

Most of the time the socioeconomic system operates without any need for law as such because people at every level have been imbued with its inevitability and necessity. When the system breaks down and conflicts arise, a legal case comes into being. This is the "moment" of legal ideology, the moment at which lawyers and judges in *their* narrow roles seek to justify the normal functioning of the system by resolving the conflict through an idealized way of thinking about it.

But this also can be the moment for struggle against the narrow limits imposed in law on genuine values such as freedom, equality, moral community, and good faith.

We can see glimpses of that sort of struggle in the transformation from classical to modern contract law. Classical legal thought represented the world in its image of freedom of contract. Because of subsequent socioeconomic changes and because of their own perception of the falseness and injustice of that image, lawyers developed the modern image of contract, which includes more elements of interdependence, trust, and cooperation than did classical law. However, instead of holding out these ideals as a goal, in its legitimating aspect contract law presents them as already having been achieved.

The critical approach to law exposes the limits imposed on law by the ideological nature of the existing legal culture and asks whether the legal system helps or hinders the actual realization of authentic values in a meaningful sense in everyday life. For example, consider the doctrine of reliance as the basis of enforcement of a promise exemplified in *Hoffman v. Red Owl.* The current doctrine is artificially constrained by focusing on a discrete promise and a discrete act of reliance, as when the Hoffmans sold their bakery specifically because they had been promised a Red Owl franchise. We might instead recognize that people rely in intangible ways on more diffuse promises and representations; indeed, some of the most important ways people rely on each other is expressed in the continuity of behavior within institutions that are important to their lives. Workers, even unionized workers, have little choice but to rely on their employers and to consider their needs and interests when making decisions of major importance. Accordingly, contract law might prohibit an employer from firing a worker without good cause even in the absence of a specific contractual provision requiring the employer to do so,[17] and it might even prohibit a company from closing a plant in one area without taking adequate account of the importance of its continued operations to the workers and to the local community.[18]

Recently courts and legislatures have begun to recognize the power of these arguments, but in each of these instances, the power of legal ideology has constrained the recognition. In the plant closing situation, for example, workers at a U.S. Steel plant in Youngstown, Ohio, and their lawyers buttressed their political action and community organizing with legal claims that U.S. Steel was prohibited by contract and property law from simply closing the plants that were the lifeblood of the community. Although the federal trial and appeals courts recognized the enormity of the situation and the power of the workers' arguments, they failed to provide a remedy because "the mechanism [to do so] . . . is not now in existence in the code of laws of our nation."[19]

In fact, it was not the law that restrained the judges, but their own beliefs in the ideology of law. By recognizing the possibilities for social responsibility and solidarity that are immanent in the doctrine of reliance, they could have both provided the workers a remedy and helped to move contract law in a direction that would better align the legal ideals of freedom, equality, and community with the realization of these ideals in everyday life.

New developments in contract law such as these would have positive direct practical effects. But consistent with this essay's emphasis on the ideological role of contract law, their greater importance would be in revealing the legitimating aspect of traditional doctrines and providing a reflective public forum for people to press in a meaningful way for freedom, social solidarity, and authentic recognition as whole human beings. The law's treatment of a worker's rights in his or her job is intimately connected with the economic and social power structures that define what it means to be a worker and an employer. Critically rethinking contract law permits us to expose the limits of things as they are and to explore the possibility of a fundamentally different order of things.

NOTES

1. *Coppage v. Kansas*, 236 U.S. 1, 14 (1915).
2. E. Allan Farnsworth, *Contracts* (Boston: Little, Brown, 1982), 23.

3. Morton Horwitz, *The Transformation of American Law* (Cambridge, MA: Harvard University Press, 1977), chapter 6.

4. See Peter Gabel, *Reification in Legal Reasoning,* 3 Research in Law and Sociology 25 (1980).

5. See Duncan Kennedy, *The Structure of Blackstone's Commentaries,* 28 Buffalo Law Review 205 (1979).

6. See Friedrich Kessler and Grant Gilmore, *Contracts: Cases and Materials,* 2d ed. (Boston: Little, Brown, 1970), pp. 2–6.

7. *Hertzog v. Hertzog,* 29 Pa.Rep. 465 (1857).

8. *School Trustees of Trenton v. Bennett,* 27 New Jersey Law Reports 513 (1859).

9. *Kirksey v. Kirksey,* 8 Alabama Reports 131 (1845).

10. *Dickinson v. Dodds,* 2 English Law Reports, Chancery Division (Court of Appeal 1876). For the way in which American contract theorists manipulated other English precedents to support their ideas, see Grant Gilmore, *The Death of Contract* (Columbus: Ohio State University Press, 1974).

11. *Haigh v. Brooks,* 11 3 English Reports 119 (Queen's Bench 1839, Exchequer 1840).

12. See Eugene Mooney, *Old Kontract Principles and Karl's New Kode: An Essay on the Jurisprudence of Our New Commercial Law,* 11 Villanova Law Review 213 (1966).

13. 26 Wisc. 2d 683, 133 N.W.2d 267 (1965).

14. New York General Obligations Law, § 5–1109 (McKinney 1978); Uniform Commercial Code, § 2–205; Restatement (Second) of Contracts, § 87(2) (1981).

15. See Arthur Leff, *Unconscionability and the Code: The Emperor's New Clause,* 115 University of Pennsylvania Law Review 485 (1967).

16. Karl Marx and Friedrich Engels, *The Communist Manifesto* (New York: Washington Square Press, 1964), 62.

17. In the last few years courts have granted some employees limited rights against unjust termination, but they have done so without questioning the basic structure of employment. See Kenneth Casebeer, *Teaching an Old Dog New Tricks:* Coppage v. Kansas *and At-Will Employment Revisited,* 6 Cardozo Law Review 765 (1985).

18. For a discussion and critical analysis of the law on plant closings, see Joseph William Singer, *The Reliance Interest in Property,* 40 Stanford Law Review 611 (1988).

19. *Local 1330, United Steel Workers v. United States Steel Corp.,* 631 F.2d 1264, 1266 (6th Cir. 1980). For an account of the workers' struggle, see Staughton Lynd, *The Fight Against Shutdowns: Youngstown's Steel Mill Closings* (San Pedro, CA: Single Jack Books, 1982).

23 WILLIAM H. SIMON

CONTRACT VERSUS POLITICS IN CORPORATION DOCTRINE

THE traditional corporation law doctrine expounded in the law schools and the law reviews tends to disappoint both those looking for vocationally relevant technical instruction and those looking for theoretical insight into the vital business institutions of capitalism. The type of deconstructive or "trashing" analysis associated with Critical Legal Studies that finds tension and contradiction underlying a veneer of doctrinal coherence and confidence seems to have been preempted here. Mainstream lawyers have dismissed the field in terms as radical as those of the most implacable trasher. "We have nothing left," wrote Bayless Manning, "but our great empty corporation statutes—towering skyscrapers of rusted girders, internally welded together and containing nothing but wind."[1]

While the widely held belief that corporation doctrine needs overhauling is surely correct, traditional doctrine does have more significant content than Manning's remark implies. Perhaps the most important content is an implicit map of the universe of business law that situates disparate rules in a way that influences the way people learn and manipulate them. A striking feature of this map is its tendency to relegate considerations of power and public value to the periphery. The explicit content of the corporations course seems resolutely apolitical, but the implicit map expresses a vision that seems an unmistakably conservative one.

Most of the recent efforts inspired by economics to revise business doctrine have not challenged its basic premises or its political vision. They have, however, made these premises more explicit and given them more theoretical substance. This is a real achievement, but an ambitious reform effort ought to consider, not only fleshing out the conventional subject matter, but also redefining it to include a broader range of political perspectives.

In this essay I try to identify the central themes of corporation doctrine. I then try to bring to the surface some tacit political commitments of this doctrine by describing another set of concerns, once considered central to the study of business organization in America, that contemporary corporation doctrine excludes. Finally, I speculate that recent developments in business practice and economic theory might be conducive to the revival of the older, explicitly political tradition of discourse about the corporation.

WHAT CORPORATION DOCTRINE IS ABOUT— PRIVATE ORDERING

The introductory law school business course is typically called Corporations, and even when it has a broader title, such as Business Associations, it is focused largely on corporation law. Moreover, within this field, it is principally concerned with a special kind of corporation— the large publicly held enterprise. Relatively little attention is devoted to small, closely held corporations. The premise that corporations is the core business law field and that, within the field, large, publicly held businesses are central is also reflected in the allocation of scholarly effort and attention.

Throughout most of the period since World War II, corporations has been treated as, in effect, a specialized branch of contract law. This branch is concerned with the mutual adjustment or private ordering of relations among investors, lenders, and managers.

Among corporation lawyers, contract rhetoric is favored by people who tend to support judicial and legislative deference to ostensibly voluntary business arrangements, and it is sometimes resisted by those who tend to support state intervention to protect investors. But the positions of both groups can be readily embraced within contemporary mainstream contract doctrine, with its principles of fraud, duress, and unconscionability and its associated panoply of implied-in-law, nonwaivable rights and duties.[2] Both the interventionists and the noninterventionists are contractual in the sense used here. They are both primarily focused on investors, lenders, and managers, and they both treat informed bargaining among these parties as the ideal way to define relations among them (however much they differ about the extent to which practical obstacles to such bargaining warrant regulation).

From the contract perspective, the distinctive feature of corporate organization is that it involves large numbers of people engaged in a relatively long-term collaboration. Since basic contract rhetoric tends to presuppose small numbers of individuals, arm's length bargaining, and short-term relations, adjustments seem needed in the corporate field. Corporation doctrine is focused primarily on two sorts of adjustments. One has to do with the extent to which the corporation should be personified, that is, the extent to which various actors associated with the corporation should be treated as a unity. The other has to do with constraining the ability of corporate actors to abuse their discretion to take advantage of each other.

PERSONIFICATION

A problem of formality arises from the difficulty of adapting the basically individualistic rhetoric of American private law to deal with large-scale collective activity. A highly influential though largely mistaken response to this problem might be called the naive view of corporate formality. The naive view suggests that once a business fulfills certain prescribed procedural steps it should be treated as a legal "person" indistinguishable from a natural individual. Moreover, the naive view holds that the decision to treat a business as a corporate person in this manner resolves a host of specific legal issues.

Much of the modern history of corporation law has been preoccupied with a war against the naive view.[3] The war has nearly been won, but fighting continues on a few fronts, and some portion of the law school corporation course is devoted to reenacting prior victories.

From the late nineteenth century through the Depression, the debate over corporate formality was intensely politically charged. The naive view was associated with a conservative politics hostile to business regulation. Conservatives relied on the naive view of corporate personality in support of arguments that incorporated businesses should have the same rights of privacy as natural individuals, despite the relatively impersonal, materialistic nature of the businesses, and that they should have the same rights of property as natural individuals, despite the relatively greater power businesses achieved through centralized control of the property of large numbers of people.

Many who fought the naive view believed that its defeat would necessarily entail the adoption of a view of business organization more favorable to regulation. But others cautioned that rejecting the naive view did not preclude you from arguing against regulation. It just forced you to come up with a substantive reason against regulation. Moreover, the rhetorical sleight of hand involved in the naive view could be used to support regulation, and rejecting the naive view opened up as many misleading arguments against regulation as it closed. You could concede the portrayal of the corporation as a person and portray it as a rapacious, irresponsible one in need of punishment or discipline; you could deny that the corporation was a person and argue that it was just a collection of individuals, some of them widows and orphans, trying to achieve some financial security.

The critics prevailed over the naive view, but only incompletely. The battle against the naive view still has to be fought. Consider, for example, the Supreme Court's 1978 decision in *First National Bank of Boston v. Bellotti,* which struck down a state statute prohibiting corporations in certain lines of business from making political expenditures in connection with referenda on tax issues. Justice Powell's opinion for the majority seems to flirt with the naive view when it relies on earlier decisions upholding First Amendment claims by natural individuals without considering the differences between individuals and corporations that might be relevant to the First Amendment.[4] On the other hand, Justice Rehnquist's dissent, which vigorously rejects the naive view and insists on viewing the corporation as an "artificial being," seems to make the related mistake of attributing substantive significance to the *refusal* to characterize the corporation as a person.[5] In arguing for the statute as an exercise of the state's distinctively broad regulatory powers over corporations, he slights the question of whether the statute might infringe the free speech and associational rights of the shareholders.

Bellotti is something of an anachronism because it deals with an explicitly political issue, and the case is rarely found in courses or treatises on corporation law. The critique of the naive view usually occurs in connection with issues concerning the internal relations of participants in corporate activities. Consider, for example, the following:

- Is a contract purportedly negotiated on behalf of a corporation by one of its organizers prior to the completion of the incorporation process binding on the subsequently incorporated business? An answer inspired by the naive view is the contract is not binding since, if the corporation did not exist at the time it was made, it could not bind itself or authorize anyone else to do so for it.
- Can creditors of a corporation reach assets formally held by separate corporations when the corporations are affiliated by ownership,

management, and operations in what appears to be functionally a single business? The naive view suggests that they cannot be reached since the assets belong to someone other than the debtor.

- Is a contract purportedly made on behalf of a corporation binding when it would involve the corporation in an area of activity outside those specified in the statement of purposes in its charter? A naïf would be content to answer no on the ground that the corporation lacked the capacity to enter such a contract.

- May a corporate officer buy stock on the basis of undisclosed inside information? Under the naive view, one can say yes, because the officer's corporate duties are to the corporation, not to the stockholders.

- May a corporation sue an officer under antifraud provisions of the federal securities statutes for failure to disclose material facts in a transaction in which the officer sold something to the corporation? Under the naive view, one might say it cannot sue because, since the officer was an agent of the corporation, his knowledge is imputed to the corporation, and the corporation thus could not have been deceived.

In such cases, the answer associated with the naive view is wrong, at least insofar as it is offered as a substantive argument, rather than a summary of an independently grounded conclusion. Courses in corporate doctrine use such issues to teach that, while it is often convenient to treat the corporation as a unitary entity, or fictional person, one must resist the temptation to read substantive significance into this practice.

Thurman Arnold, a famous critic of the naive view, argued that the destruction of that view should lead to an understanding of the corporation as a political entity, "an integral part of our government," as he put it.[6] Arnold was not making the mistake here of attributing substantive significance to a formal matter. He simply assumed that once people stopped conflating corporations with natural individuals it would be apparent to them that the distinctively interesting issues about corporations had to do with the social effects of concentrated economic power.

But he was wrong. The naive view has been replaced by a view of the corporation, not as an aggregation of power or a center of governance, but as a "nexus of contracts." What is pernicious about the naive view to contemporary corporations scholars is not its tendency to obscure economic power, but its tendency to obscure conflicts of interest among shareholders, managers, and creditors. Contemporary doctrine would address these conflicts in contract terms. And this turns out to mean that one looks for convergent expectations of the parties, or when none are found, to solutions that promote efficiency.

DISCRETION

Although the corporate form is available to businesses of nearly every functional description, contemporary corporation doctrine focuses on large corporations with hierarchically organized management and a large number of dispersed investors who are not active in corporate affairs. Since shares in these corporations are regularly traded in public capital markets, the shareholders are a constantly changing class.

If the paradigm contract is a bargained for specification of the parties' rights and duties, then the relations of participants in large corporations seem deviant in two respects. First, the great mass of shareholders have no practical opportunities to bargain directly with each other or with the officers of the corporation. Second, it is not feasible to specify the duties of corporate officers; they need discretion to respond to myriad and largely unforeseeable contingencies. There are similar, though perhaps less intense, concerns about the relation of creditors with officers and managers and about the relation of shareholders among themselves. Contemporary corporation doctrine takes as its central problem the task of constraining the abuse of the discretion that results when direct bargaining and contractual specification are not feasible. Abuse here means the failure to maximize the value of the firm to managers, shareholders, and creditors or the expropriation by some of these participants of returns due to others.

The main focus of doctrine is on the problem of preventing officer exploitation of shareholders. The doctrine takes two general perspectives: one focuses on internal institutional mechanisms of officer accountability; the other focuses on the constraints and opportunities that result from the fact that the large corporation's shares are traded in organized national markets.

The two principal internal devices to protect shareholders from managerial discretion are fiduciary duties and voting rights. The basic idea of fiduciary duties is that officers owe unspecified, open-ended obligations to maximize the value of corporate ownership and to distribute this value in proportion to the size of share holdings. Such duties are enforceable by shareholders through derivative suits in which a single shareholder can challenge a breach on behalf of the "corporation," that is, the body of shareholders. Voting rights enable the shareholders to elect and remove the board of directors, which in theory has general managerial power over the corporation and appoints its senior officers.

But these devices have problems. While fiduciary duties by their nature do not have to be specified in advance, effective compliance and enforcement requires some degree of consensus about the conduct they prohibit, and outside the more blatant forms of officer self-dealing, this has proved difficult to achieve. Moreover, because officers of large corporations control large amounts of wealth, most of it belonging to other people, the potential loss from bad decisions is enormous relative to the returns officers expect from their own salaries and share holdings when things go well. It is thus difficult to prescribe liability for breach of duty that is sufficiently severe to deter improper conduct while preserving incentives for taking on the job. (This is particularly true of the job of the "independent" directors—part-time outsider as opposed to the inside director who is also a manager—but it is also a problem with inside directors.)

Voting rights suffer from basic recurrent dilemmas of collective action among self-interested individuals. To make effective use of voting rights the shareholder needs to invest in research about the corporation and in communication and coordination efforts with other shareholders. However, the gains from voting that effectively polices managerial responsibility accrue to all shareholders, and shareholders benefit from the efforts of their peers whether they contribute to them or not. Thus, shareholders tend to be "rationally apathetic." They usually do not engage in active monitoring either because the returns to the holdings of any one shareholder from monitoring would not warrant the costs to that shareholder (even though shareholders would benefit in the aggregate from monitoring by more than its costs) or because shareholders who would gain enough individually to justify efforts hope to "free-ride" on the efforts of their peers.

Moreover, to the extent shareholders do become active, there is a risk they will exploit other shareholders by seeking gains disproportionate to their holdings. If a majority of the shares can bind the corporation, then an individual or group that holds a majority can make decisions that disproportionately benefit themselves at the expense of the minority. (For example, they can have the corporation sell things to or buy things from other entities they own at prices favorable to the other entities.) If the rules try to constrain such exploitation by giving the minority a veto, the danger arises that the minority will threaten to block profitable moves (the loss of which would cost it less than the majority) unless they receive a disproportionate share of the gains.

In recent years, a large literature has emerged that is relatively indifferent to or dismissive of internal institutional mechanisms of accountability, and relatively sanguine about the pressures that arise from public securities markets. A shareholder can express dissatisfaction with management more easily by selling her shares than by organizing an electoral campaign. To be sure the price she receives may be discounted because of the managerial practices she disapproves of, but the fact that the securities markets continuously price the corporation's shares based in part on evaluation of managerial decisions makes the market an engine of accountability. Improper manager decisions will lower the price of shares. The fear of such a reaction will often act as a deterrent to improper decisions. If this deterrent is ineffective, the market provides a second one—the takeover. If a corporation's shares decline because of bad management, an outsider can profit by buying sufficient shares to enable her to replace existing management with a better one.

However, there are a variety of problems with this view.[7] For the market to operate as an engine of accountability, prices have to be based on rational estimates of future earnings rather than simply on fad or mob psychology, though some believe that the latter play decisive roles in price determination. Even conceding that prices are good estimates of future earnings, there are evident limitations on their ability to discipline managers. For one thing, managerial compensation in large corporations typically depends only to a small extent on stock price; thus, the incentives from price per se are weak.

The takeover threat may be more formidable, but the takeover strikes many as a crude accountability mechanism, creating as many abuses as it checks. Takeovers (including the preliminary stage of identifying targets) are slow enough and expensive enough that at best they allow managers a considerable range of ineptitude before they become a serious threat.

There is, moreover, the difficulty in designing an effective takeover process. If takeovers are made too easy, acquirers may be able to stampede target shareholders into selling at unreasonably low prices or exploit minorities once they assume control; if they are made too difficult, management will be able to immunize itself from challenge. And it may be that some takeovers themselves constitute managerial ineptitude or malfeasance by acquiring corporation executives who want to expand their empires even at the cost of corporate profitability. If they act quickly enough, they can do so without turning themselves into takeover targets.

Contemporary corporation doctrine thus consists largely of a standard repertory of institutional responses to the problem of discretion—vaguely specified contractual duties—in the relations of managers, shareholders, and creditors. There is a large range of variations and combinations of the standard responses, and no one is especially stable or commands consensus. Within the dominant perspective, debates occur between those with greater confidence in internal accountability mechanisms and those with greater confidence in capital market mechanisms, between those more concerned about managerial ineptitude and malfeasance and those more concerned about shareholder passivity and malfeasance, and between those who most fear target management self-entrenchment and those who most fear acquirer management empire building.

Critical Legal Studies critiques often suggest that mainstream doctrine tends to induce complacency about or confidence in institutions by lending a false sense of coherence and completeness to the doctrines that describe them.[8] I think this point applies less strongly to corporations than other subjects. Corporation doctrine is distinctively contentious and relatively openly chaotic. A student emerging from the corporations course would be unlikely to have a lot of confidence in the ability of any particular combination of the standard responses to deal adequately with the problem of discretion among managers, shareholders, and creditors. But such a student might well take for granted that the central problem of corporation doctrine is in fact or ought to be controlling discretion in these relationships. At least, hardly anything in the course would encourage him to think that there might be other equally important problems for corporate doctrine.

WHAT CORPORATION DOCTRINE IS NOT ABOUT—POLITICS

We can get some insight into the premises of contemporary business law doctrine by comparing the current conception of the subject matter of corporations to an earlier one. Throughout much of the nineteenth century, the subject of the nature and social function of the corporation occupied a central place in popular discourse about public affairs. It was treated as an intensely political subject. While the legal treatment of the corporation was never as openly or intensely political as the popular one, it did reflect some of the popular concerns. During this period, a large portion of the more important corporate doctrine was treated as public, often constitutional, law. As today, the subject was identified with large, managerial, controlled businesses with dispersed ownerships, but in contrast to today, the most salient issues concerned the political implications of such enterprises.[9]

One perspective that fueled much of the debate might be identified—at some risk of oversimplification—as economic republicanism. This perspective took a variety of forms and influenced positions at many points of the political spectrum. Some of its distinctive themes can be found in the polemics and programs of Jeffersonian republicanism, Jacksonian democracy, the radical republicanism of the Reconstruction Era, the Populism of the Farmer's Alliance, and the labor radicalism of the Knights of Labor.[10]

The conception of business organization in economic republicanism was political rather than contractual. First, republicanism focused on the effects of business organization on, not just investors, lenders, and managers, but on a variety of other constituencies and the larger surrounding society. Second, while bargaining among affected constituencies played a role, that role was subordinated to criteria of economic democracy. These criteria were expressed most distinctively, in inalienability rules and government support for particular kinds of enterprises.

Like socialists, the republicans focused attention on the economic basis of a democratic political order, and they saw democracy as incompatible with a drastically unequal distribution of productive resources. Like classical liberals, the republicans also emphasized the danger of a large and powerful state to democracy, and they saw an important role for private property, as a bulwark against state power. They appealed to a vision of an economy designed to encourage small-scale, internally egalitarian enterprise and to protect small capital against both the state and large capital.

Their notion of the typical economic actor was inspired by ideals of citizenship as well as of productive efficiency: a single individual or group of equals working at their own direction with their own productive resources. Widely distributed property was considered essential to secure the average citizen from subordination to an economic elite in both the public sphere and the workplace, which was itself viewed as a forum of political self-expression and solidarity.

In this vision, the state acted to support the political ideal of an independent citizenry in part through the definition of property entitlements. For example, scale could be constrained through agrarian (acreage limitations and residency requirements in public land and water grants) and antimonopoly laws. The state also established banking and credit institutions responsive to the needs of small enterprise and provided technical and marketing assistance that remedied some disadvantages of small-scale production.

Economic republicanism implied a strong preference for investment in human capital, i.e., education, as opposed to physical capital. This meant, for one thing, a system of universal public education. It also meant institutions to facilitate the sharing and development of specialized knowledge within firms and occupations. These goals were animated by the overlapping ideals of the skilled worker and the knowledgeable citizen. The skilled worker views work both as a form of self-expression and as creative participation in occupational culture. The knowledgeable citizen takes a similar view toward participation in the political processes of the community and the larger society.

The role of the market in this vision was complex. On the one hand, contractual exchange among private parties was accorded an important place. Such a process was seen as conducive to productive efficiency. Equally important, it was also seen as necessary to sufficiently decentralize the social system to ensure meaningful participation by producer-citizens in both the workplace and the community. But the market, depending on how it was defined and regulated, could also be a threat to efficiency and decentralization. For example, if contractual exchange produced far-flung, hierarchically controlled, large-scale enterprises, they undermined the goal of decentralization and threatened the autonomy of workers and local political communities. And when exchange processes left local firms and political communities defenseless against the pressures of volatile national and world markets, they further threatened autonomy.

Unrestricted exchange could also create radical uncertainty and instability incompatible with productive efficiency as well as political autonomy. In the classical tradition associated with James Harrington, nineteenth-century American economic republicans viewed investment in nonmovable or locally rooted assets as the material foundation of a prosperous, participatory polity. As with the classicists, land was the paradigmatic immovable asset, but certain kinds of education in knowledge specific to craft or occupational communities or long-term trading or collaborative relations with local partners might also qualify. Such investments gave the individual the kind of stake in the community that would motivate materially productive and political activity and the kind of independence that would protect him from subordination. (One reason why republicans considered black slavery a threat to the independence of whites was that the comparative mobility of slave as opposed to landed property discouraged slaveholders from making material or personal investments in local communities and encouraged them to oppose politically the types of public investments necessary to a vital public culture.)

Such locally rooted investments are interdependent to a greater extent than investments in readily redeployable assets. An individual would be reluctant to undertake such an investment to the extent that others seem unable or unlikely to undertake complementary investments or to the extent that others seem able and likely to withdraw their complementary investments. Unrestricted exchange threatens the solvency of the community by eroding the rootedness of investments and increasing the danger of a situation in which individuals who would want to stay if the others would stay are stampeded into withdrawing their investments because they are unable to collectively commit to stay. One reason for the hostility to speculators and intermediaries in economic republicanism is that they introduce a community-threatening liquidity to investments. (This problem is most familiar today in connection with investment in residential neighborhoods—for example, the destabilizing effects of "block-busting" real estate brokers who induce homeowners to sell quickly at low prices for fear that, if their neighbors sell before they do, prices will go still lower.)

A related concern about unrestricted exchange is that it might permit the citizen to alienate the kind of autonomy necessary to her effective functioning as a producer-citizen. This type of concern survives in contemporary prohibitions against selling one's self into slavery or slightly milder forms of subordination (e.g., debt peonage or specifically enforceable personal service obligations), but nineteenth-century republicanism had broader notions of the proper scope of inalienability. For example, the notorious "crop lien" that required the farmer to surrender the control of the growing and marketing of his crop to financial intermediaries was considered a politically objectionable infringement of autonomy.

The republican attitude toward monopoly differed from the currently dominant one in two respects. First, republicanism was suspicious of large-scale enterprise even in competitive markets where the power to restrict output and raise price above cost was small. Second, republicanism was sympathetic to certain constraints on price and wage competition that encouraged or protected small enterprise and employment relations. This sympathy was partly motivated by noneconomic concerns, but partly by notions of efficiency. Contemporary mainstream economists tend to see an exceptional role for monopoly rights, such as those conferred by patent and copyright, as an inducement to important forms of investment. The republicans had an analogous intuition, but the types of investment they focused on were different. They were especially concerned with investments in skills, in long-term cooperative business relations, and in product quality reputations. Constraints on wage and price competition were seen as an inducement to make such investments, as a way of channeling competition toward innovation in products and production (rather than toward sweating labor and shaving product quality), as well as an approach to smoothing the process of economic adjustment.

The republican ideal of economic association was most fully expressed in the late-nineteenth-century rhetoric of "cooperation." Cooperation implied a kind of flexible, solidaristic (but not radically altruistic) collaboration among equals. Cooperation could take the form of a "cooperative," a firm owned and managed by its workers, but the firm was a less important category in republican rhetoric than it is in the business rhetoric of today. In agriculture, where the cooperative ideal was most influential, cooperation was most visible in purchasing and marketing associations formed by independent owner-operator farmers. In the program of industrial cooperation of the Knights of Labor, producer cooperatives were linked to each other through unions and to their suppliers, customers, and communities through a variety of ties of varying degrees of formality.

In republican rhetoric, corporation was an antonym to cooperation. The corporation appeared as a threat to the republican program. It fostered concentration and centralization of economic power. It tended to subordinate workers to the status of wage earners and order followers. It threatened to subject local affairs to the control of managers and owners not connected to the community and to the vicissitudes of volatile, far-flung markets. And by creating highly dispersed and liquid ownership interests, it tended to preclude the republican role of ownership as a solvent of local relationships.

The concerns of republican discourse about business organization contrast strikingly with those of contemporary legal doctrine. In both visions, the corporation is central, less because of its technical legal features, than because of its connotation of large-scale, hierarchical, managerially controlled enterprise. But the issues associated with the corporation differ radically in the two visions. Political concerns are nearly invisible in contemporary corporation doctrine. So are some of the social roles that economic organization plays in the republican view, such as the reinforcement of community ties. And many of the actors who play prominent roles in the republican view—workers, suppliers, customers, local communities—have disappeared.

Now, the fact that doctrinal concerns have changed since the nineteenth century is not in itself surprising, but the extent to which the older concerns have receded in business law calls for some explanation. Although many have long regarded some features of the republican vision as anachronistic or discredited, some features, such as the emphasis on the political significance of large corporate enterprise and the concern about the possibilities of personally satisfying work in such organizations, remain prominent in the discussion of the corporation in popular discourse and in academic fields such as political science and sociology.

Nor does the fact that the concerns of the republican vision are peripheral to the preoccupations of practicing business lawyers explain their treatment in contemporary doctrine. Legal doctrine, as expounded in the law reviews and taught at the law schools, has always been somewhat aloof from practical lawyering concerns. It has rarely been reluctant to deal with matters of political or policy significance when such matters are considered important.

Moreover, the contemporary contours of corporations doctrine do not seem any more attuned to practical lawyering needs than a republican counterpart would likely be. It is widely believed that the law school corporations course is out of touch with practice. The doctrinal content of the course is really quite skimpy, and neither its curricular centrality nor the amount of time devoted to it could be justified in practical terms. And a variety of matters of fundamental practical importance—noncorporate business forms, agency, close corporations matters, nonprofit enterprise, and finance and employment matters subject to distinctive contract practices—are skimmed or ignored. In two recent books offering introductory surveys of the knowledge lawyers need for business practice, corporate doctrine gets 20 percent or less of the coverage.[11] Yet, corporate doctrine continues to receive the great majority of attention, sometimes all of it, in the great majority of introductory law school business courses.

The marginalization of partnership in contemporary doctrine is especially striking. The presumptive form of the partnership—for example, the one provided by the Uniform Partnership Act in the absence of contrary agreement—is a fairly egalitarian worker cooperative (with the qualification, also characteristic of many other types of worker cooperatives, that some workers are not owner/partners). This form corresponds substantially to the economic republican enterprise vision. However, it is also quite well established in a variety of important, quite nonutopian business contexts in contemporary America. Perhaps the most important of these is the large law firm of the sort where most graduates of elite law schools go on to practice. You would think that these students would have an intense practical interest in the dynamics of these organizations, but they have been largely invisible in the law school business curriculum.[12]

Surely part of the explanation for the definition of corporation doctrine and its central place in business law generally lies, not in practical vocational concerns, but rather in ideological ones. This doctrine and this arrangement express tacitly a vision of the social order that holds sway over legal and business elites. By taking as paradigmatic the large, hierarchically organized enterprise owned by outside investors, mainstream doctrine implies that other forms of enterprise are relatively uninteresting, marginal, or nonviable. And the relegation of political concerns and concerns for constituencies other than the three privileged ones to the periphery at worst implies that these concerns are relatively unimportant and at best suggests a limited vision of how they might be dealt with. The implication is that these outside concerns are to be dealt with either through contractual specification or through conventional forms of regulation. The republican notion that such concerns might be dealt with through the structuring of enterprises—either by general constraints on enterprise form and scale or by government support for favored structures—is implicitly denied.

The recently intensified tendency to situate corporations doctrine in the context of capital markets (and to integrate it with securities law) as opposed to situating in the context of, for example, labor markets (and integrating it with employment law) or local communities (and integrating it with local government law) encourages the marginalization of distributive issues. Some corporation scholars have generated moral interest in the various ways by which managers exploit investors, but when we consider that most of the victims of this exploitation are rich—most individually held stocks are held in the top few percentiles of the income distribution—and/or foolish—some of the risk of exploitation could be costlessly mitigated by investing through diversified funds run by professional intermediaries—it is hard to see such problems as fundamental issues of social justice. (The distributive issues with respect to investments held by intermediaries, and especially pension funds, are more interesting and important, but these are excluded from mainstream core doctrine.)

Conventionally defined doctrine seems incapacitated to confront the critical distributive issues that arise from one of the more important recent developments in connection with the large corporation—the "downsizing" of large established enterprises and the attendant loss of a broad range of previously stable and well-paying middle-class jobs, especially in middle management and manufacturing production. These developments are often entailed by the movement of capital, especially manufacturing operations, to low-wage economies abroad. The focus of corporation doctrine on investors, capital markets, and neoclassical economics makes it easy to emphasize the advantages of capital mobility. Traditional capital suppliers have benefited from many of the changes involved here. And the capital markets, with commodified products, large numbers of buyers and sellers, and widely disseminated information, lend themselves distinctively to modeling in terms of neoclassical theories that assert the efficiency of unrestrained alienation.

On the other hand, the disadvantages associated with recent mass capital movement have been visited largely on workers and local communities, who do not appear in corporation doctrine. Moreover, the limitations of neoclassical economic models that become quite apparent when the relations of corporations with workers and communities are considered are more easily ignored when these actors are banished.

Of course, legal doctrine does not entirely ignore the relations of large-scale business enterprise with workers and communities or the effects of corporate power on democratic values. There are, after all, plenty of legal rules that apply to these relations. Doctrine as expounded in the law schools and the law reviews purports to deal with these rules outside the corporation field. But in fact these rules are often peripheral and are sometimes invisible in academic doctrine.[13]

Economic concentration is the focus of antitrust law and while the quintessentially republican concerns that influenced the passage of the major statutes typically get some acknowledgment, the subject is currently dominated by an explicitly apolitical concern with consumer welfare. Concern about the influence of corporate power on the electoral and administrative processes surfaces in the law concerning campaign finance, lobbying, and official conflict of interest. Though they sometimes get attention in constitutional and administrative law, they are treated as specialized subjects.

The only major doctrinal field devoted to workers is labor law. But this field has long been preoccupied with unionized workers who have never been a majority of the work force and are now a rapidly dwindling minority. Nonunionized workers have always been nearly invisible in the law schools and the law reviews. And municipal law has remained a specialized backwater, marginalized both by the preoccupations of the general run of elite legal academics with national government and with the judiciary and by the preoccupations of several of the few practitioners of the subject with narrowly technical matters.[14]

·The core business field in which redistribution is a central focus is tax. The relegation of distributive issues to tax seems to express tacitly a preference for the tax/transfer system as a means of redistribution. (The transfer part of this mechanism, of course, gets almost no attention, but that is another story.) Republicanism traditionally opposed reliance on taxes and transfers in favor of a strategy of achieving distributive goals through the rules that determine the distribution of primary incomes, including both labor law and the rules that determine the availability of credit and assistance to small businesses. From the republican point of view, the tax/transfer approach has the dual disadvantage of increasing the dependence of ordinary citizens on the state and of leaving unconstrained the political power of the wealthy that results from their control over the investment process.

The case for broadening the perspective of corporations doctrine does not depend on belief in the superiority of the republican vision or the cooperative program. Those who have recently reconsidered elements of the program differ widely over their merits.[15] However, the preeminence of the corporate mode in contemporary doctrine does not rest on any widespread agreement about its superiority, but simply on the a priori exclusion or marginalization of alternatives and the undefended refusal to consider many of the issues that republicans considered essential to the appraisal of economic organization. Thus, the main argument for broadening the focus is to encourage greater reflectiveness about the premises of economic organization.

PROSPECTS FOR CHANGE

The American economy seems to be undergoing epochal transformation. Some aspects of this change have harmed middle- and working-class Americans and threaten to do much greater damage in the future. Other aspects seem to have at least the potential to benefit them. The future balance of harm and benefit depends on which of multiple possible trajectories of development are followed.

From the point of view of the more pessimistic scenarios—which predict the continued erosion of stable, well-paying middle- and working-class jobs, the growth of marginal and contingent employment, and the shift of production work abroad—traditional corporation law gives appropriate legal expression to the economic realities of the contemporary corporate enterprise. In this enterprise, the needs of investors and managers predominate; workers and local communities are simply suppliers of inputs who deal with the corporation through conventional contract processes.

On the other hand, an interesting feature of the more optimistic scenarios of economic development is that they would require some reformulation of traditional corporation doctrine. These scenarios suggest that the time may be auspicious for a redefinition of the field of corporate doctrine to include some of the concerns and issues emphasized in economic republicanism.

Two sets of practical developments have changed the landscape of large enterprise in ways that put increasing pressure on the boundaries of traditional corporation doctrine. One is the growth of financial intermediaries, and especially pension funds. An increasingly large portion—about half in terms of value—of ownership claims on publicly held businesses are held by banks, insurance companies, mutual funds, and pension funds. These organizations have both expertise and ability to aggregate claims that make active exercise of shareholder rights more plausible than in the case of dispersed, small-stakes shareholders. Many of these intermediaries hold their shares in trust for middle- and working-class individuals. This is notably true of pension funds whose managers hold shares to finance the current income of retirees and the retirement income of current workers. About half of private sector workers are currently covered by some pension plan, and a substantial and growing share of the nation's capital is owned by these funds.

The notion of large blocks of claims on corporate capital held by middle and working-class people, most of them employees of large corporations, has inspired the vision of a major transformation of the economy into "pension fund socialism." These suggestions are exaggerated. Without drastic changes in the rules of the game, pension funds will not claim anything approaching a majority of corporate wealth in the foreseeable future. To the extent that socialism implies that workers have control over as well as beneficial interests in capital, the current arrangements are rarely socialistic. Plans typically are not structured to permit beneficiaries to exercise shareholder rights directly. Moreover, most plans do not focus their investments in the companies in which their beneficiaries work; rather they diversify their holdings so that they do not hold more than a small fraction of the shares of any given company. (In strictly financial terms, such diversification helps beneficiaries by lowering the risk of their investments.)[16]

Nevertheless, the growth of pension capital seems to challenge the traditional boundaries of corporate doctrine. At the least it has brought to prominence a new set of shareholders—the intermediaries—whose structure and conduct have to be taken into account. Moreover, even in the conventional diversified funds, situations sometimes arise where a pension fund in which a firm's workers have substantial beneficial interests has a significant voting block on an issue, such as a takeover by an acquirer expected to initiate layoffs, in which the workers are interested. Such situations raise issues that erode the traditional distinction between shareholders and workers and the relegation of workers to separate peripheral fields.

Moreover, the growth of pension finance at least raises the possibility—and has provided a few examples—of more dramatic shifts to worker ownership. Unlike the conventional diversified fund, the employee stock ownership plan focuses its investments in the stock of the beneficiaries' employer. Such plans have been encouraged in recent years by a tax subsidy. The subsidy is structured so that employers can often capture its financial benefits without giving significant control to employees, and while a significant portion of the work force now participates in such plans, few involve serious worker control. Nevertheless, there have been some notable examples, including a few large firms, of substantial worker ownership and control, and while the tax subsidy is not conditioned on serious shifts in control, it at least legitimates them.[17]

The second set of developments that challenges traditional doctrinal contours concerns both business practice and economic theory. The developments in business practice I have in mind are often discussed in connection with the pressures of intensified foreign competition, the attenuation of demand for standardized mass-produced consumer goods, and the relative decline of the manufacturing in relation to the service sector of the economy.[18] These trends have increased the premium on the ability to make rapid adjustments to volatile market signals and to diversify products. The prototypical large enterprise throughout the period in which corporate doctrine took its modern form was a manufacturing business engaged in very long runs of standardized goods with machinery dedicated to specific operations operated by narrowly skilled workers. But this pattern seems to be changing.

At the enterprise level, managers are insisting that increased product market competition and volatility precludes them from guaranteeing wage and benefit levels of the order to which the more successful unionized manufacturing workers were once accustomed. They also claim that traditional job classifications and work rules designed to protect workers from abusive managerial discretion prevent the kind of prompt, flexible adjustment to market signals that the new environment demands. And at the same time, some of these managers are seeking better trained and motivated workers with more general skills and the capacity for judgment and discretion. For their part, workers are pressing demands for kinds of security that impinge on managers' traditional discretion over levels of employment, investment, redeployment of capital, and subcontracting.

One set of responses to these tensions involves the extension to workers of some of the traditional incidents of ownership. These include both financial incidents, such as profit sharing, bonuses, and other forms of contingent compensation. They also include various opportunities for participation in decision making either at the shop-floor level in forms such as quality-of-work life programs, or at the senior governance level, in forms such as representation on the board of directors. In addition, contractual provisions over matters such as subcontracting and plant closing now occasionally restrict discretion over matters previously considered the prerogatives of managers and owners. These developments make it increasingly difficult to separate owner/creditor/manager relations from employee relations. They also make it harder to understand employee relations in terms of contractual specification.[19]

These developments have involved analogous changes with other constituencies such as suppliers, customers, and governments. Firms are developing increasingly complex and flexible relations with suppliers involving joint investments and complex, flexible coordination (and firms are decentralizing internally by giving autonomy to divisions in ways that sometimes erode the distinction between division and supplier or customer). Governments, especially at the state and local level, have experimented with sponsoring industrial districts or regional economic networks in ways that make them active participants in the enterprises involved.[20]

At the same time economic doctrines that have begun to filter into the law schools have taken a parallel direction, in part, of course, in response to the developments in practice. In 1970, Albert Hirschman succeeded in making intelligible to neoclassical economists the centuries-old republican commonplace that encumbrances on mobility and alienation (barriers to "exit" in his jargon) can promote productive activity by increasing the relative incentives for internal participatory efforts ("voice") to improve the organization or community.[21]

Since then other economists have taken account of the role that long-term relations cemented by relatively immobile investments play in resolving important practical problems ignored in neoclassical economics. Such problems include the viability of executory bargains in a world where litigation is costly and uncertain, and the ability of people with differing levels of knowledge and information to bargain with each other.[22] The solutions to such problems often lie in mutual investments that make the parties dependent on and vulnerable to each other.

Consider, for example, the question of training workers in skills that are specific to the operations of an employer. If the employer finances the training, it risks losing its benefits because the worker may leave. If the worker finances the training, she risks losing its benefits because the employer may discharge her. Moreover, the most effective trainers may be experienced employees, and they may be unwilling to cooperate because they fear that newly trained workers will compete against and replace them. A fully specified long-term employment contract would be unenforceable against the worker and might excessively constrain the employer's ability to change or reduce employment levels in accordance with economic conditions. One response to this situation is a semiformal bargain that includes compensation arrangements that reward seniority, giving the employee an incentive to remain after the training period, and a seniority rule for layoffs, giving workers some protection against discharge before they reach the point of relatively generous compensation and neutralizing the threat of competition from junior workers.

In these circumstances, the firm has made an illiquid investment in the worker by training her; the worker has made an illiquid investment in the firm by giving up other learning and job opportunities and by accepting deferred compensation. The new institutional economists see such semiformal arrangements of mutual interdependence as material bases for the kind of flexible cooperation that obviates full contractional specification and reliance on official enforcement procedures. Once workers are seen in this manner as investors in the firm, their exclusion from the central focus of business organization seems arbitrary.

To the extent these developments in theory and practice continue, they will challenge the boundaries that have defined corporations doctrine. While they push toward a different definition of the core concerns of the doctrine, this need not necessarily be a republican one. Indeed the best-known model of an economy built partly on flexible long-term relations—Japan—seems decidedly unrepublican in its acceptance of hierarchy and paternalism.

Nevertheless, the developments in both theory and practice have an affinity for republicanism in at least some respects. First, the business reform ideal of the broadly skilled worker with discretion in the workplace is shared by economic republicanism, which associates it both with economic productivity and effective citizenship.

Second, the contemporary economists' concern with grounding long-term productive cooperative relationships in interdependent investments and their related idea of long-term employment as an investment that may require the kind of security conventionally associated with capital investments somewhat overlap the republican ideal of securing independent membership in a political community through property rights.

Third, both innovative business practice and republicanism tend to subvert the priority given in both legal doctrine and neoclassical economics to the firm as a focus of analysis by shifting attention to relations involving actors such as suppliers, customers, and local governments who are not formal members of the firm.

Fourth, both the new economic practices and republicanism challenge some conventional notions about decentralization in analogous ways. The conventional notions tend to portray decentralization in terms either of the restriction of government regulation and the enhancement of the autonomy of property generally or in terms of the devolution of government power to state and local government. They tend to take for granted that business organizations be internally centralized, and they tend to be relatively indifferent to the kind of economic centralization that arises when private enterprises grow to large size. By contrast, the newer developments occasionally have involved, in a way compatible with republicanism, efforts at internal decentralization of enterprises and experiments with the use of state power to encourage the decentralization of private market structures, for example, through the kind of credit support and technical assistance to small enterprise that was a central part of some nineteenth-century republican programs.

Of course, the developments that recall the republican program represent only one tendency in the economy. Other tendencies pose less challenge to traditional corporation doctrine and offer less promise to workers. Instead of seeking to make the production process more innovative and dynamic, managers can respond to competitive pressures by trying to lower the costs of standardized production of conventional process. This strategy dictates sweating, rather than investing in, workers, and short-term squeezing of local communities rather than cultivating dense, long-term relations.

EXPANDED FIDUCIARY DUTIES

The most prominent effort of recent years to incorporate the interests of workers, local communities, and other corporate constituencies into corporation doctrine has taken the form of proposals to reinvigorate and extend the doctrine of managerial fiduciary duties to include such constituencies.

Such proposals have surfaced most often in connection with takeover contests. Managers frequently tried to justify defensive measures by arguing that the proposed control change would injure workers or other non-shareholder constituencies. Acquirers typically responded that managers were bound to pursue only shareholder welfare in responding to a takeover bid. The managers were seconded by a group of liberal academics who have produced a remarkable historical and theoretical literature in defense of the idea of expansive duties to nonshareholder constituencies. Some of the academics carried the point considerably farther than the managers, arguing for mandatory rather than discretionary responsibilities. While the managers had argued that the courts should *permit* them to consider nonshareholder interests, these commentators thought the courts should *require* them to consider such interests, sometimes by giving the nonshareholder constituencies rights of action in court.[23]

Judicial doctrine on the extent of fiduciary duties to nonshareholder constituencies has long been vague, and the takeover cases did not add significant clarification. Proponents took heart from a dictum of the Delaware court in the *Time-Warner* takeover cases that the preservation of a distinctive "corporate culture" might be a worker or public interest warranting management efforts to defeat a control change.[24] The strongest endorsement of expanded duties in the takeover context came from the state legislatures. About two-thirds of the states amended their corporation statutes to permit managers to consider the interests of non-shareholder constituencies in responding to takeover bids. Liberal theorists seek to build on these developments to encourage a more expansive and specific set of duties to such constituencies.

In my view the potential of such developments is quite limited. Contrary to the impression given in some recent fiduciary scholarship, corporate law has never strongly constrained the ability of managers to take account of nonshareholder interests. There is not a single reported case in which a court has invalidated a management action because it subordinated the interests of shareholders to those of the public, local communities, or workers.[25] The recent statutes and case law confirm management discretion in this area, but they don't create any judicially enforceable duties. It seems unlikely that they have had much effect beyond shoring up the ability of management to resist control changes that threaten its own position.

Aside from the conservatism of the courts, the proposal to make constituency duties mandatory and enforceable by their beneficiaries has the problem that it would require courts to make business judgments of the sort that the "business judgment" rule has traditionally forbidden. Issues about fair treatment of constituencies will often depend on speculative economic issues that will be hard to resolve judicially.

Moreover, even if courts were willing and able to take on such issues, it is questionable how far they could develop fiduciary doctrine for the benefit of nonshareholders without basic change in corporate structure. As long as risky businesses are financed with capital drawn from outside the community in which they produce, responsibilities to that community and other local constituencies will have to compromise with responsibilities to outside capital suppliers. Ambitious conceptions of economic community require a high degree of internal, local finance, with attendant risks from loss of diversification. Despite the increased risks, I think there are many economically plausible opportunities for worker or community ownership of the sort envisioned in the republican literature. But without local ownership, an ambitious conception of constituency responsibility seems unworkable; and with local ownership, it would seem trivial. Local owners would be better protected by the control rights associated with ownership.

To say that a set of doctrines is grounded in ideology is not to say that these doctrines are not worth learning, even to people who find the ideology unattractive. If the doctrines are employed by the dominant actors in important institutions, then anyone who aspires to be a competent practitioner in those institutions needs to master them. At the least, however, aspirants should try to avoid confusing the power that doctrine derives from its congruence to historical and political contingency with its plausibility as a portrayal of a desirable social order. Moreover, both doctrinal and political structures are susceptible to revision and sometimes to far-reaching reconstruction. The recovery of the republican tradition, the revival of institutional economics, and the wave of innovations in business practice suggest that this may be an auspicious time for such a reconstruction of business law doctrine.

NOTES

1. Bayless Manning, *The Shareholder's Appraisal Remedy—An Essay for Frank Coker,* 72 Yale Law Journal 223, 245, n. 37 (1962); see also Bernard Black, *Is Corporate Law Trivial?* 84 Northwestern Law Review 542 (1990) (answering "yes").
2. A good discussion of the capacity of contract rhetoric to absorb the full range of mainstream opinions on corporate issues is John C. Coffee, Jr., *No Exit? Opting Out, The Contractual Theory of the Corporation, and the Special Case of Remedies,* 53 Brooklyn Law Review 919, 931–53 (1988).
3. The classic critiques are John Dewey, *The Historical Background of Corporate Legal Personality,* 35 Yale Law Journal 655 (1926), and Thurman Arnold, *The Folklore of Capitalism* (New Haven, CT: Yale University Press, 1937), 185–262. See also Morton J. Horwitz, *Santa Clara Revisited: The Development of Corporate Theory,* 88 West Virginia Law Review 173 (1985).
4. *First National Bank of Boston v. Bellotti,* 435 U.S. 765, 778–83 (1978). At one point, Justice Powell suggested that he might consider disproportionate power of corporations in the electoral process relevant to the First Amendment issue but declined to consider the matter because he found no evidence of record that there was such disproportionate power. Ibid., 789. To the extent that Powell here escapes the conceptual naïveté discussed in the text, he seems guilty of empirical naïveté.
5. Ibid., 822–25.
6. Cited in Arnold, *The Folklore of Capitalism,* 246.
7. The takeover literature is enormous. For an enthusiastic view of the takeover as an accountability mechanism, see Frank Easterbrook and Daniel Fischel, *The Proper Role of a Target's Management in Responding to a Tender Offer,* 94 Harvard Law Review 1161 (1981). For reservations, see John C. Coffee, Jr., *Regulating the Market for Corporate Control: A Critical Assessment of the Tender Offer's Role in Corporate Governance,* 84 Colorado Law Review 1145 (1984); Andrei Schleifer and Laurence Summers,

"Breach of Trust in Hostile Takeovers," in *Corporate Takeovers: Causes and Consequences*, ed. A. Auerbach (Chicago: University of Chicago Press, 1988); Reinier Kraakman, *Taking Discounts Seriously: The Implications of Discounted Share Prices as an Acquisition Motive*, 88 Colorado Law Review 891 (1988).

8. For an impressive critique of corporation doctrine from this perspective, see Gerald Frug, *The Ideology of Bureaucracy in American Law*, 97 Harvard Law Review 1276 (1984).

9. See J. Willard Hurst, *The Legitimacy of the Business Corporation in the Law of the United States* (Charlottesville: University of Virginia Press, 1970), 13–57; Lawrence Friedman, *A History of American Law* (New York: Simon & Schuster, 1973), 166–78, 446–59. Hurst's discussion reflects a tendency to associate the republican critique of the corporation with the early-nineteenth-century practice of "special" incorporation in which corporate status was typically legislatively bestowed as a special privilege that carried explicit monopoly or quasi-governmental powers and responsibilities. From this perspective, the persistence of hostility to the corporation after the advent of "general" incorporation processes that made a streamlined package of corporate attributes routinely available seems obtuse or anachronistic. The remarks in the text are intended to rebut this impression by suggesting that the republicans had a plausible critique of general incorporation.

10. See Drew McCoy, *The Elusive Republic: Political Economy in Jeffersonian America* (Chapel Hill: University of North Carolina Press, 1980); Sean Wilentz, *Chants Democratic: New York City and the Rise of the American Working Class 1788–1850* (New York: Oxford University Press, 1984); Eric Foner, *Reconstruction: America's Unfinished Revolution 1863–1866* (New York: Harper and Row, 1988); Lawrence Goodwyn, *Democratic Promise: The Populist Moment in America* (New York: Oxford University Press, 1978); George S. Kealey and Brian D. Palmer, *Dreaming of What Might Be: The Knights of Labor in Ontario 1880–1900* (Cambridge, UK: Cambridge University Press, 1982).

11. William Klein, *Business Organization and Finance* (Mineola, NY: Foundation Press, 1980); Robert Hamilton, *Fundamentals of Modern Business* (Boston: Little, Brown, 1988).

12. But see the recent efforts of Ronald Gilson and Robert Mnookin, *Sharing Among the Human Capitalists: An Economic Inquiry into the Corporate Law Firm and How Partners Split Profits*, 37 Stanford Law Review 313 (1985); see also William H. Simon, *Babbitt v. Brandeis: The Decline of the Professional Vision*, 37 Stanford Law Review 565 (1985).

13. For some pioneering efforts to broaden the focus of corporate doctrine to acknowledge conventionally excluded constituencies, see John Coffee, *Unstable Coalitions: Corporate Governance as a Multiplayer Game,* 78 Georgetown Law Journal 1495 (1990); Henry Hansmann, *When Does Worker Ownership Work?* 99 Yale Law Journal 1749 (1990). And for an interesting effort to integrate corporate materials into a treatment of labor and employment law, see Robert Rabin, Eileen Silverstein, and George Schatzki, *Labor and Employment Law* (St. Paul, MN: West, 1988).

14. But see the recent effort at invigoration by Gerald Frug, *Local Government Law,* 2d ed. (St. Paul, MN: West, 1992).

15. For example, contrast Oliver Williamson, *The Economic Institutions of Capitalism* (New York: Free Press, 1985), with Louis Putterman, "On Some Recent Explanations of Why Capital Hires Labor," *Economic Inquiry* 22 (1984): 171.

    Contemporary republicans must deal with the fact that in the one area in which republicanism has remained influential in this century—agriculture—its rhetoric has been used to rationalize policies that seem to pervert its political goals. Whether this fact suggests defects in the republican programs or simply a failure to implement them faithfully is a matter of controversy. See Grant McConnell, *The Decline of Agrarian Democracy* (Cambridge, MA: Harvard University Press, 1953).

16. See generally William H. Simon, *The Prospects of Pension Fund Socialism,* 14 Berkeley Journal of Employment and Labor Law 251 (1993).

17. See Joseph Blasi, *Employee Ownership—Revolution or Ripoff?* (Cambridge, MA: Ballinger, 1988).

18. In this and the following few paragraphs, I draw on the large recent literature on industrial structure and policy, especially on Michael Piore and Charles Sabel, *The Second Industrial Divide: Possibilities for Prosperity* (New York: Free Press, 1984), which links industrial policy issues to republican political ideals. See also Michael Best, *The New Competition: Institutions of Industrial Restructuring* (Cambridge, MA: Harvard University Press, 1990). Roberto Mangabeira Unger's *False Necessity* (Cambridge, UK: Cambridge University Press, 1988) situates the industrial policy issues in the context of a broad theory of radical democracy. A discussion of such ideas as they appear in legal doctrine appears in William H. Simon, *Social-Republican Property,* UCLA Law Review 1335 (1991).

19. See Katherine Stone, *Labor and the Corporate Structure: Changing Conceptions and Emerging Possibilities,* 55 University of Chicago Law Review 73 (1988).

20. See David Osborne, *Laboratories of Democracy* (Cambridge, MA: Harvard Businss School Press, 1988).

21. Albert Hirschman, *Exit, Voice and Loyalty* (Cambridge, MA: Harvard University Press, 1970).

22. See Williamson, *The Economic Institutions of Capitalism.*

23. Lawrence E. Mitchell, *A Theoretical and Practical Framework for Enforcing Corporate Constituency Statutes,* 70 Texas Law Review 579 (1992). See generally Lawrence E. Mitchell, ed., *Progressive Corporate Law* (Boulder, CO: Westview Press, 1995).

24. *Paramount Communications v. Time, Inc.*, 571 A.2d 1140, 1143 n. 4 (Del. 1990).

25. *Dodge v. Ford Motor Co.*, 170 N.W. 668 (Mich. 1919), which is often cited for the shareholder-agent view, did not enjoin the expansion that Henry Ford had rationalized with public interest rhetoric. It merely ordered the payout of retained earnings that exceeded the amount the court thought necessary for expansion. The case is one of the few in which a court has suggested that fiduciary duties are owed exclusively to shareholders, but it illustrates that such a principle need not constrain strongly even when it is accepted. Most corporate actions that justify nonshareholder constituencies can readily be justified in terms of shareholder interests, for example, as promoting good public relations or cementing advantageous long-term dealings. In the *Dodge* case, even though Ford had explained the decision in public interest terms, the court upheld it because there were *potential* shareholder-interest explanations for it. See generally William H. Simon, *What Difference Does It Make Whether Corporate Managers Have Public Responsibilities?* 50 Washington and Lee Law Review 1697 (1993).

24 KARL E. KLARE

CRITICAL THEORY AND LABOR RELATIONS LAW

COLLECTIVE bargaining in the United States attained its maximum extent and social impact in the decade after World War II. The unionized percentage of paid (nonagricultural) workers ("union density") peaked over 35 percent in 1945 and never fell below 30 percent until 1962. The fortunes of labor law, the part of the law of employment dealing with unions, collective bargaining, and labor-management relations, are closely linked to the prosperity of the union movement itself. So labor law, both as a practice specialty and as an academic discipline, experienced a kind of golden age in the postwar years, which lasted through the Warren Court period. This article discusses the rich body of labor law that emerged in that golden age.

The doctrines and cases examined here still form the core of labor law today and, for the most part, continue to govern the employment relationship in the collective bargaining sector. They are of vital significance to the daily lives of millions of American workers and their families. But the worlds of politics and of work have changed dramatically since labor law's formative era, and collective bargaining has much less weight as a force in American life than a generation ago. Union density began a precipitous decline in the late 1950s that continued unabated for over three decades. Private sector union density is now barely above 10 percent, no more and perhaps even less than the unionization rate before the Great Depression.[1] Unions have been largely on the political and economic defensive in recent decades.

Not surprisingly, labor law entered a sustained crisis some years ago. Employer illegality has skyrocketed, and available legal remedies seem feeble. The U.S. Supreme Court shows little of its earlier interest in or appreciation of labor law, and many of the the union and worker victories of the Warren Court era have gradually eroded. Academic fashions are attuned to these developments, and the new emphasis is on the law of individual employee rights or "employment law." (Employment law commentators and scholars frequently overlook that much cutting-edge litigation and law reform in this field is sponsored and financed by unions on behalf of employees they represent.)

The whys and hows of the decline of U.S. collective bargaining are much debated. Scholars, lawyers, and activists have canvassed a range of causal factors—increased wage competition in world trade, deregulation, changes in the nature of the contemporary employment relationship such as the replacement of career with contingent employment, developing trends in the occupational and social composition of the paid workforce, political and strategic failings of the labor movement itself, technological change, and so on. In particular, intense controversy surrounds the questions: What role, if any, has labor law played in the decline of American collective bargaining? And, what role, if any, could labor law reform play in revitalizing the union movement? Most observers sympathetic to workers and collective bargaining agree that the legal environment has been a significant, if by no means the only or even necessarily most important, factor in the decline.

This chapter does not attempt to recount these debates or to assess the current situation and prospects of labor and employment law. I do discuss one particularly ironic piece of the puzzle, the way that the union movement's postwar legal successes contributed to its present decline and crisis. But the chapter has a broader goal, to sketch new ways of understanding law and legal processes and, in particular, to develop a more critical and transformative conception of labor law and the practices of labor lawyers. For this purpose, it is worthwhile to cast light on the past and to attempt to rethink the consolidation of collective bargaining law during its liberal phase. For this purpose, I begin with a story about grocery clerks who made labor law history nearly thirty years ago.

THE *BOYS MARKETS* CASE

On February 18, 1969, unionized clerks at the Boys Markets supermarket in Cudahy, California, observed a supervisor and other nonunionized workers rearranging merchandise in the frozen-food cases. The employees complained that their collective bargaining contract assigned such work to employees within the bargaining unit and demanded that the counters be stripped of all merchandise and restocked by unionized personnel. The business-dominated media often cite work-preservation demands like this in portraying the labor movement as narrow-mindedly self-interested and as standing in the way of the consumer, progress, and the public interest. The reality for working people is ignored: public policy takes job scarcity for granted and makes no genuine commitment to full employment. Because labor has little input into national economic policy, unions seek to protect jobs on an ad hoc basis through work-preservation rules, lobbying for favorable tariff and regulatory treatment, and, particularly in recent years, through concessions ("givebacks") in collective bargaining.

The Boys Markets management declined the union's demand that the shelves be restocked. The union was therefore entitled to file a written grievance to press its interpretation of the contract. The grievance would initiate a prescribed dispute resolution process culminating either in a settlement or, if necessary, a ruling by a neutral, called an "arbitrator," on whether management had violated the contract by misassigning the frozen-food work. A settled and firm rule of law provides, however, that while a grievance is pending, the employees must return to work. No matter how patently in violation of contract, management's decisions and commands (e.g., regarding who will perform the work) must be obeyed while the grievance is being processed. For reasons that are obscure, these supermarket clerks departed from the usual process and went on strike. Likely none was aware that the incident would result in one of the most important Supreme Court labor law decisions of the postwar period.[2]

The clerks' grievance strike violated the no-strike clause contained in their collective bargaining contract, indeed, in most contracts. A no-strike clause is a union's promise that no work stoppage ("wildcat strike") will occur during the term of the contract. Ordinarily, employees are not legally protected when they strike in breach of a no-strike clause; they can be disciplined or fired. If a union authorizes or provokes a wildcat strike, it is subject to liability for monetary damages. But the delay and costs involved in either replacing employees or suing the union often make these remedies unattractive to employers. What management really wants is to get the employees back on the job. This requires an injunction, a court order compelling the employees to return to work. Failure to obey such an order would be punishable as contempt of court with fines or even prison. In this case, Boys Markets went to court seeking an injunction against the clerks' strike. The legal question that eventually reached the Supreme Court was whether courts may issue orders enjoining, and thereby breaking, grievance strikes.

The labor injunction casts a long shadow over American labor history. From the late nineteenth century through the 1930s, employers, assisted by the courts, used the injunction in thousands of cases to combat union organization and strikes. Spontaneity, courage, solidarity, and the acuteness of the sense of grievance are all critical to union success in labor disputes. Since these feelings ebb and flow, timing is obviously a crucial factor. The injunction became a favorite legal weapon of employers because it provided a mechanism for instantaneous legal intervention that could postpone strikes, often indefinitely. Moreover, the preliminary phases of injunction proceedings could traditionally occur *ex parte* (with only one party—the employer—appearing before the judge) or upon affidavits (without witnesses being subject to cross-examination). There is no right to a jury in injunction hearings. The truth had a way of getting lost in these shabby proceedings. The union's theoretical right to a subsequent review with full procedural guarantees often was meaningless once an initial, "temporary" injunction broke a strike. Hostile courts granted employers very broad labor injunctions, as in a famous case involving Eugene V. Debs in which the court order essentially prohibited any person from engaging in any conduct in furtherance of the strike.

The labor injunction became a much-despised symbol of a largely pro-employer judiciary. Generations of antiinjunction agitation finally culminated in the Norris-La Guardia Act of 1932. Section 4(a) of that law expressly prohibits the federal courts from issuing injunctions against peaceful strikes. Many states subsequently passed "little Norris-La Guardia acts" similarly curtailing state court injunctions in labor cases.

But, if the Norris-La Guardia Act and like state laws forbid injunctions against peaceful strikes, on what possible basis could the Boys Markets company ask for an injunction in the frozen-food-counter case? The company argued that the Norris-La Guardia Act must be read in light of and accommodated to another, subsequent law, section 301(a) of the Taft-Hartley Act of 1947. On its face, section 301(a) deals only with technical jurisdictional issues. It does not say anything about labor injunctions, and its explicit terms certainly do not suggest a repeal of the Norris-La Guardia Act. However, by 1970, section 301(a) had been interpreted as expressing a national labor policy of promoting industrial peace by enforcing contractual no-strike clauses and by strengthening grievance arbitration procedures.

The company therefore argued, and the Supreme Court eventually agreed, that the implicit policy of industrial peace embodied in section 301(a) trumps the explicit antiinjunction provisions of Norris-La

Guardia. Despite an act of Congress and generations of popular struggle against the hated labor injunction, the Court held, and the law remains, that employees can be enjoined from utilizing collective action to press their contract grievances, no matter how deeply or wrongly they have been injured by management. The *Boys Markets* doctrine has been extended to permit courts to enjoin even strikes protesting potentially life-threatening safety hazards.

LABOR LAW THEORY: TRADITIONAL AND CRITICAL

A case like *Boys Markets* poses difficulties for all varieties of legal theory. For conventional theory, the task is to find some neutral basis to justify this controversial exercise of activist judicial power. The embarrassment is that this is a classical instance in which the legislative history and relevant precedents are so ambiguous and conflicting that a respectable formal argument can easily be constructed for either side of the case (indeed, for several conceivable outcomes). Therefore, any claim that the Court's ruling is *legally required* is a good deal less than convincing. Indeed, eight years earlier the Supreme Court had faced the identical question and adopted precisely the opposite approach to the one ultimately taken in *Boys Markets*.[3] Had the legal situation changed since 1962? As Justice Black acidly commented in his *Boys Markets* dissent: "Nothing at all has changed . . . except the membership of the Court and the personal views of one Justice."[4]

The repertoire of lawyers' formal arguments simply cannot determinately resolve a legal problem of this kind. Judgment is required—judgment not only about the meaning and intent of words, but also about unions and industrial conflict, about where collective bargaining came from and about where it should be going. These are inescapably political judgments. One could acknowledge the ambiguity of the legal materials and still argue, in the current argot, that the *Boys Markets* result "fits" best with the "overall structure" of national labor policy, and that in this sense we can meaningfully say that the result was legally required. But "fit" and "structure" are not exactly terms of determinative precision. They are terms of judgment, redolent with political meaning. One cannot neatly separate "is" and "ought," or "being" and "becoming," in identifying the latent structure of legal doctrine. In this case, the question of "fit" comes down to the relative significance one assigns the competing antiinjunction and proarbitration principles. A judge according great weight to Norris-La Guardia tenets could easily make the case that the 1962 antiinjunction result achieved a better fit with the fundamental commitments of our labor law than the 1970 proinjunction decision in *Boys Markets*.

Radical critics have not had an easy time explaining legal phenomena like *Boys Markets* either. It is difficult to argue, in the mode of some critics, that the *capitalist system requires* that grievance strikes be enjoinable, since the law was otherwise from the 1930s until 1970. Indeed, labor law systems in the capitalist world exhibit extraordinarily diverse features even as to the most basic aspects of workplace regulation. Nor was there any discernible change between 1962 and 1970 in the level or character of class conflict that might explain the Court's shift. With hindsight we can now identify some disquieting industrial relations trends that began brewing in that period, such as increasing efforts by employers to avoid collective bargaining. But it is hard to imagine that the Court responded to or even registered these then obscure developments.

Moreover, there is a particular irony about *Boys Markets*. While it seems clearly to a reflect a repressive, antilabor spirit, unions won numerous, momentous Supreme Court victories in that period. *Boys Markets* itself was the enthusiastic product of one of the most liberal members of the postwar Court, the late Justice William J. Brennan. Many of the theoretical underpinnings upon which Brennan built were developed in a set of Warren era cases brought to and won in the Supreme Court by unions, not employers. Those precedents were intended to and did significantly enhance workers' power. The challenge is to develop a theoretical vantage enabling us to appreciate a harmful decision like *Boys Markets* as consistent with a legal framework and judicial mentality heavily infused with liberal values and genuine concern for workers' interests. Neither a more refined doctrinal exegesis, nor a radical interest/functional analysis, nor an analysis pegged to some metric of class conflict, suffices for this purpose.

The difficulty of explaining the *Boys Markets* case with available theoretical tools illustrates a broader point about efforts to construct critical perspectives on law. Critical approaches have always been caught in a tension between the critique of formalism and an aspiration to provide systemic analyses. An instinctive starting point of critical legal theory, particularly when written by lawyers, is the attack on formalism. Antiformalist critique aims to show that the prevailing rules are not preordained by the nature of things, nor are particular case results required by legal logic. To the contrary, the critics argue that legal rules and decisions are contingent and conventional—they are products of human choice. There is always room for discretion, some times more, sometimes less, in applying the rules to cases. Following the lead of the Legal Realists, contemporary critics argue that the accepted repertoire of justificatory arguments ("legal reasoning") is sufficiently ambiguous, porous, and contradictory so that particular outcomes cannot be understood as required by legal logic alone. Every instance of rule formulation and rule application involves some component, often subtle and obscure, of moral and political choice and, therefore, of decision-maker responsibility.

This is not to say that radical critics believe (as they frequently are misunderstood or misrepresented as believing) that legal reasoning is indistinguishable from general political argument or that decisional outcomes are crude derivatives of prevailing political interests. Rather, the claim is that legal reasoning is not and cannot be made nearly so autonomous from political and ethical argument as is customarily believed, even by sophisticated thinkers. Critical theory seeks to establish that, consciously or not, legal actors routinely make and express moral and political choices in the course of their work, and that therefore they play a responsible role in constructing the institutional substrata of social and political life. As it happens, this proves remarkably easy to show.

Nor do the critics believe (as they frequently are misunderstood or misrepresented as believing) that either rule-content or decisional outcomes are random and unpatterned. Quite the contrary, critical legal theory has traditionally aspired to show how legal orders systematically reflect, generate, and/or reinforce poverty, class inequality, and patriarchal, homophobic, and racial domination. Regrettably, it is also depressingly easy to show that class, gender, race, and sex-preference hierarchies and discrimination are pervasive in the legal cultures of the advanced democracies, although explaining precisely why and how law reflects and reinforces invidious domination sometimes proves a more formidable task. But whatever the difficulties, most radical legal theorists adhere to the goal of developing systemic perspectives that situate legal rules and practices within broader, structural accounts of social order and hierarchy. There is an instinctive sense that the systemic approach is what sets radical theory apart from incremental reformism and supplies it with its political bite.

The dilemma, of course, is that the antiformalism collides with and erodes systemic explanation. To attribute observed regularities in legal results to systemic principles or functions, one needs an account of the constraints on routine legal decision making that generate these patterns. That is, systemic theories, whether apologetic or critical, seem to require some version of formalism, some claim or assumption that legal orders have a built-in, determinative structure that steers routine decision making. In mainstream theory, the steering mechanism is the legal culture's overarching philosophical principles as interpreted and applied with the professionally accepted techniques of legal reasoning. The claim is that properly trained and acculturated legal craftspersons can derive appropriate answers to routine problems by applying a catalogued repertoire of argumentative techniques in order to translate communal norms into legal results. In critical theories, the role of steering mechanism typically is played either by the basic functional attributes or requirements of the social system, or by "class interest" or some similar form of elite identification. But the radicals' recurring antiformalism aims precisely to demonstrate the pervasiveness of choice, contingency, and personal agency in legal processes. Usually sooner rather than later, the critics' powerful antiformalist arsenal renders all available theories of structural constraint problematic.

Labor law theory illustrates the tension between antiformalism and systemic orientations particularly well. Labor law is often regarded as unusually accessible to radical analysis and criticism. Labor cases like *Boys Markets* frequently evidence quite transparent struggles over power in the workplace. Working people have indelibly imprinted the law of labor relations with their aspirations, values, and struggles, both in victory and anguishing defeat. Accordingly, labor law appears to lend itself naturally to discussion in terms of whether this doctrine or that case expands or diminishes worker power.

But the fact that political issues are so close to the surface in labor law can also be a liability for critical legal theory. The relative ease with which we seem to identify employees' short run, intrasystemic interests in particular legal conflicts may inhibit us from attacking a broader and deeper range of questions: Why did the doctrines and institutions of collective bargaining law develop as they have? What are the historical meanings and social functions of that distinctive institutional and intellectual practice we call labor law? How might we explain labor law's inner tensions and future prospects, particularly in this current period of crisis and transformation in American collective bargaining? How should we evaluate the postwar collective bargaining and labor law systems in terms of their own premises and in light of alternative, expanded conceptions of workplace democracy? What role, if any, can litigation and/or statutory reform play in the ongoing project of advancing workplace democracy? Can we envision radical, postliberal models that will deepen opportunities for self-determination in work while preserving the democratic prescripts already impressed upon the law by working peoples' activism? Is there any distinctive role for labor lawyers in conceiving and realizing these new models?

Until recently, those critics who have attempted systemic perspectives usually simply inserted interest analysis into a preformed theoretical structure. The social system, generally designated "capitalism" or "monopoly capitalism," is treated as a historical subject, existing prior to law. It is said to have a "deep" or "intrinsic" structure (e.g., "the relations of production"), and legal results are assumed to derive from this prelegal structure. Some leeway generally is allowed for the impact of social conflict and activism (although the contours of social struggle itself are usually thought to be determined by the conflicts ("contradictions") of the intrinsic structure). The typical discussion shows, first, that a given set of outcomes was not legally preordained; and then, if employers have won, this is said to reflect the "needs of capital," but if employees were successful, that represents a "heightened level of worker struggle."

Legal theory in this vein is comforting to received wisdom, but not very illuminating. For one thing, by taking for granted that legal phenomena reflect the vagaries of class conflict within an overall structure of system-functional imperatives, the approach avoids all the hard issues and assumes what needs to be proved. The precise questions at stake are whether legal outcomes reflect systemic constraint and social struggle, and if so, why and how this occurs. A methodology premised upon systemic determination of legal interests and outcomes is incapable of even asking these questions. In any event, what the parties' long-run interests are rarely is so transparent and one-dimensional as the model supposes.

Moreover, the approach is fundamentally circular. There is no way to describe social structures—deep, intrinsic, or otherwise—without discussing law or lawlike phenomena. There simply is no "prelegal" realm of social life to which legal outcomes can be referred, at least not in the modern age. A particularly embarrassing case of circularity is the ease with which we are told that legal outcomes and processes derive from the underlying relations of production or property ownership, as though production relations or property could meaningfully be defined without reference to legal rules. Finally, the functionalist dimensions of the approach rest on the assumption—shared, ironically, by most mainstream theories—that routine legal practices and results are powerfully determined by constraints on decision makers built into legal orders at some paramount level. But this assumption cannot survive the antiformalist critique.

New approaches are needed to break this theoretical impasse. We surely need to transcend the partial and constricted definitions of employee interests and workplace democracy available within the going system, yet we also need to get beyond prepackaged "class analysis" and unconvincing functionalist or system-logic explanations of the relationships between legal and social orders.

Conventional legal theory and the older critical approaches share a common difficulty. Both fail to appreciate the pervasiveness of human agency in the construction of legal orders; at the same time, neither adequately explains how human action in legal contexts is socially structured. Mainstream legal theory hardly makes the effort to appreciate the embeddedness of law in social context. Sophisticated postrealists recognize, of course, that law combines reason and fiat. Yet in the conventional image, discoverable logics of social order and of legal justification exist outside of history. The older critical approaches have neither a theory of human agency, nor a convincing account of social determination of legal processes. These approaches explain legal events by reference to some transhistorical logic or metastructure of history, but have great difficulty explaining where the structures come from or how they frame legal processes.

A point of departure toward resolving these difficulties may be found in the most important idea in modern social thought: the concept of the "social construction of reality." A critical approach would aim to understand law as situated in social context. This means an attempt to understand law as a "practice" or form of expression, as a contingent product of human action. Legal processes are meaning-creating activities, in the course of which people try to understand and interpret their experience and to draw connections between their images of how the world works and how people ought to act. Legal actors create symbols, relationships, and institutions. They also create, elaborate, entrench, contest, and resist *understandings*—assumptions, beliefs, and values about human character and capacity, and about social organization and justice.

Social orders are comprised of practices, and thus, legal practices partially constitute social life. But human action is *situated,* it can only occur in context and through the medium of culturally available forms, symbols, and understandings. Therefore these collectively created structures of recognition, meaning, belief, and relationship pattern and constrain human action and choice, including legal practices. The meaning structures in and through which we have experience orient our perceptions, thoughts, and feelings. They shape imagination and belief about human capacity and fulfillment. Because of this, although the structures and relationships of social life are all contingent products of human action, they often tend to appear as natural and unchangeable.

Given this understanding of legal processes as a form of practice, as situated human action, critical legal theory can deploy the tools utilized in the interpretive disciplines—social history, anthropology, literary criticism, and so on. Interpretive techniques can be used to seek clues regarding the structures of meaning, belief, and power embedded in legal discourse and institutions. All discourses are force fields of power relations. Discourse, including legal discourse, involves peculiar, hierarchical patterns of privileging, silencing, and denial which need to be unearthed and examined. But critical legal theory aspires to go beyond strictly interpretive methods. It seeks to understand why given legal practices arise in and are sustained by particular social and historical conditions; to understand how various legal practices reinforce prevailing power relations; and to develop theories of transformative practice, of emancipation from historically unnecessary restraints upon human freedom and self-realization.

The effort, then, is to go beyond the law's understanding of itself, and also beyond its immediate, instrumental consequences, to an understanding of the particular vision or visions of the world animating and expressed in a given set of legal practices and institutions, to uncover the assumptions and commitments about politics and social life legal practices embody. The goal is to appreciate how legal discourse and events inform and shape experience and belief, how they sustain and legitimate institutions and power relations. Insofar as legal institutions reinforce hierarchy and inequality in social and political life, and insofar as legal discourse endorses the dominant power arrangements or induces belief in their inevitability, legal culture can be understood as a form of legitimating ideology. While law can be a repository of emancipatory values and aspirations and of questions sharply or subtly critical of the status quo, more typically legal discourse operates to deny us access to our transformative capacities, our power to alter and abolish existing patterns of domination. By exploring, mapping, and criticizing the prevailing forms of legal consciousness, we may hope to release our political imagination and gain access to transformative possibilities immanent in our situation.

BOYS MARKETS AND THE LIBERAL PARADIGM

Ordinarily, legal culture is created and sustained by and in turn largely
has effect on people who are regularly engaged in the legal arena, e.g.,
lawyers, judges, politicians, institutional litigants, and, occasionally, academics. That is, legal culture for the most part denotes elite culture. For
this reason, the approach illustrated here has thus far proved most useful
in understanding the coherence and developmental path of legal doctrine
itself. But there are important exceptions, historical settings in which
other groups in society have influenced the development of legal culture,
and cases in which legal ideas and processes have deeply influenced popular culture. Unquestionably, American workers have left their imprint
on our law of labor relations. Somewhat more controversially, ideas and
values about industrial order emanating from the legal arena have sometimes spread beyond professional circles and influenced other participants in our highly legalized industrial relations process.

    This is particularly true with respect to the postwar, golden age of
American collective bargaining law, roughly 1945–1975. In this period,
labor law was deeply influenced by a particularly innovative and nuanced
set of ideas about the world of work. I will call this the "liberal conception" or "paradigm" of labor law, although this shorthand probably
attributes greater clarity and coherence to the ideas than warranted.
While major themes of the liberal approach were developed outside the
legal arena, lawyers, judges, and legal academics did play a significant role
in elaborating and advancing the paradigm. The liberal worldview never
held unchallenged sway; it was attacked from the conservative side
throughout the period. Nonetheless, liberal, not conservative, ideas provided the dominant grounding for the postwar development of labor law.
To a considerable extent that influence continues, although many basic
assumptions of the liberal model have eroded during and since the
Reagan years.

    Liberal labor law thinking surely contributed to and exemplified lead-
ing political ideas of the postwar period. Moreover, the liberal paradigm
permeated broader, nonelite circles. To a significant, although perhaps
unmeasurable extent, values and beliefs associated with this way of thinking about industrial organization were internalized by labor leaders and
activists, influencing their perspectives and actions. Many labor leaders
accepted assumptions about what is possible and desirable in the workplace that derive from or share themes with the postwar liberal paradigm.
This value system therefore forms an important component of the collec-

tive unconscious of the American labor movement. To the extent this is so, the latent value system of American collective bargaining law has been a legitimating ideology that has reinforced the dominant institutions for the better part of a generation. "Totalistic" or "reconstructive" criticism of labor law is therefore an indispensable task for those who wish to conceive and work toward alternative forms of workplace democracy. *Boys Markets* and related cases illustrate three major themes of the liberal paradigm.

CONFINING CONCERTED ACTIVITY

The first is a grudging attitude toward employee participation in workplace governance, and specifically hostility toward the use of employee self-help in dispute resolution. Had the Boys Markets clerks filed a grievance and left their protest at that, the law might well have provided them a remedy. But even liberal judges have limited patience with the use of strike action to vindicate employee rights.

To be sure, strikes and other forms of job action played an enormously significant part in bringing the modern labor law framework into being, and the NLRA resoundingly guarantees employees the right to strike and to engage in other forms of concerted activity. Within the liberal mindset, it is essential to validate the strike as a fundamental, if residual, right of workers. Justice Brennan often eloquently acknowledged the importance of the reserve right to strike, notably in the case of private sector, primary economic strikes (strikes against one's own employer in connection with contract negotiations).

In light of these conflicting pressures, labor law gradually evolved a conception of legitimate collective action that simultaneously *encourages* and *confines* worker self-expression through concerted activity and industrial conflict. Labor law invites and authorizes workers to articulate and advance their interests through self-organization, yet carefully regulates and blunts workers' collective action. The law impedes solidarity and mutual aid and channels collective action into narrow, institutionalized forms. These stylized frameworks of legitimate economic conflict provide rallying points for mobilizing employee energy and commitment, but, particularly as they become bureaucratized and overloaded, they can also exercise a dissipating effect on collective action.

Accepting conflict as a fact of industrial life, postwar liberalism sought to institutionalize and confine it. To meet that goal, labor law theory and doctrine had to (1) fashion a "nonideological" explanation of the causes and purposes of industrial conflict; (2) establish boundaries for the permissible use of economic weapons; and (3) develop alternative dispute-resolution mechanisms that could plausibly claim to be neutral as between capital and labor.

Liberal industrial relations and social theory strip industrial conflict of any class-based or political character and treat it as a by-product of a transnational and transhistorical logic of modernization. Industrial conflict is seen as aimed to advance intrasystemic group or sectoral interests. The precise structure of economic distribution is open to periodic renegotiation, and groups may use self-help weapons in the process. But the fundamental organization of social life is not deemed at stake in or open to revision through industrial conflict. Moreover, all groups are said to share a common interest in maximizing output (so that the pie from which each gets its slice is as large as possible). Therefore, a basic liberal ground rule is that the strike weapon should not be used to protest mid-contract grievances, much less should it be used as a mode of political expression.[5]

Accordingly, the legitimate use of economic force is largely restricted to the periodic ritual of contract negotiation in the private sector, or, in rare cases, to protesting when an employer flagrantly abuses the basic rules of the game. A great deal of labor law doctrine concerns the suppression or weakening of other forms of concerted activity considered to be unacceptably disruptive: worker protests invoking class solidarity, such as secondary boycotts; concerted activity through which employees attempt to reorganize the labor process; worker action of a "political" nature transcending the concerns of employees as employees; minority-group dissenting protests; "recognitional" picketing or strikes, designed to cut through the time-consuming legal procedures by which unions obtain representational rights; sit-ins and other trespassory strikes; certain strikes occurring in vital industries; and public employee strikes. Additionally, a central development in modern labor law is the harsh treatment accorded to the midcontract strike, as illustrated by the *Boys Markets* case. The liberal vision of collective bargaining treats the wildcat strike as a form of social deviancy, a fundamental industrial crime.

Of course, the liberal model could not simply proscribe wildcat strikes without offering some other means for employees to air their grievances and have them resolved. Just as liberal collective bargaining law prejudices collective employee action, it favors "peaceful" resolution of industrial disputes through formalized, bureaucratic channels, notably grievance arbitration. As Justice Brennan frankly stated in *Boys Markets*:

As labor organizations grew in strength and developed toward maturity, congressional emphasis shifted from protection of the nascent labor movement to the encouragement of collective bargaining and to *administrative techniques* for the peaceful resolution of industrial disputes.[6]

The most important "administrative" alternative to concerted activity is grievance arbitration. Enforced adherence to no-strike and grievance arbitration agreements became, in Justice Brennan's words, a "dominant motif," indeed, a "kingpin of federal labor policy."[7] *Boys Markets* brought this logic of liberal labor jurisprudence full circle.

Grievance arbitration represents a genuine and in some respects highly effective extension of due process into workplace life. Since employees cannot strike over every grievance, an alternative dispute resolution system often represents a good trade-off. The problem is not with arbitration in the abstract but rather with specific features of contemporary doctrine and arbitral processes. For example, the Court has invoked arbitration to divest employees of statutory rights they have *not* waived. There are problems of severe overload and breakdown in our grievance systems. Arbitral due process has significant substantive limitations because the content of arbitral law derives from the contract, that is, from the parties' relative bargaining power, not from open-ended considerations of justice. Above all, there is the tendency of liberal theory to *equate* arbitration with industrial democracy. Without doubting the contribution of a system of informal adjudication and rights enforcement, an empowered vision of workplace democracy also requires other institutional forms of a more continuous and participatory nature.

MINIMALIST FREE CONTRACT

The second, somewhat more complicated, theme exemplified by *Boys Markets* is the way contemporary labor law mobilizes the rhetoric of freedom of contract and the institution of the labor agreement to reinforce employer power. When it comes to setting wage rates and working conditions, the law most definitely does not favor administrative or regulatory techniques. There are exceptions, of course, such as minimum wage laws and occupational safety and health requirements, and this list is growing. But insofar as legal policy is concerned, most aspects of wages and working conditions are to be established through freedom of contract, i.e., bargaining processes reflecting the so-called free play of market forces.

Mainstream labor law theory endorses statutory reform to permit employees to pool their bargaining power in labor markets. As the Court stated in sustaining the NLRA: "union was essential to give laborers opportunity to deal on an equality with their employer."[8] But liberal theory has always been committed to the view that, once labor markets are collectivized, contract bargaining, not statute, should be the primary source of law and rights in the workplace. Freedom of contract is seen as a basic institutional platform of autonomy and participation in workplace governance.

This position has considerable merit, which is why American workers have fought so determinedly over the years to achieve unionization. When working well, collective contracting offers employees significant and relatively accessible opportunities to participate in determining the content of workplace rules and standards. Collective bargaining offers the advantage of flexible adaptability to local conditions and problems. Centralized administrative bodies can be captured by forces insensitive or hostile to workers' interests. In principle, collective bargaining represents a decentralized, activist alternative to clumsy or antagonistic bureaucratic power.

As will be noted later, the free contract model also has several serious drawbacks, even when working in optimal fashion. But, taking the ideal on its own terms for the moment, it is important to observe that free contract is a very general rubric, consistent with a wide array of actual and conceivable legal regimes. Freedom of contract is simply not a self-defining concept. The lived meaning of a contractual regime can only be determined in social and historical context, and by reference to its specific doctrinal and institutional embodiments. Because of its generality ("indeterminacy"), freedom of contract provided a broad framework during the postwar years within which workers' rights could be advanced on some fronts while they were curtailed and interdicted on others. From a critical point of view, free contract came to represent an institutional system that buttresses managerial power. The liberty-enhancing potential of free contract for workers was often blocked or dissipated, and authoritarian outcomes were fostered instead. To make matters worse, the alluring rhetoric of free contract made it appear as though this control and domination of employees occurred by their own consent.

By way of illustration, one source of indeterminacy within the ideal of free contract is that it simultaneously prizes and protects two conflicting moral values.[9] The first is liberty or freedom of choice, particularly freedom of action in markets. This aspect underlies the attraction of collective bargaining as a framework of employee activism and participation in workplace governance. The second value is security of expectations, the notion that we ought to be able to rely upon others to fulfill their obligations freely undertaken ("a deal is a deal"). Workers, of course, have a great interest in the security of their wages, working conditions, and continued employment that contract, in principle, provides.

The problem is that contract disputes almost invariably put these two values in conflict. Protecting plaintiffs' expectations through enhanced contract enforcement typically detracts from defendants' freedom of choice. Sometimes the predictable plaintiff and defendant groups are more or less the same sorts of people, so that the legal tension evens out in the long run; but often they are not. Resolving contract disputes therefore frequently requires the exercise of judgment about which value— security of expectations or freedom of action—to favor in particular contexts, with distinct consequences for different groups in society. This creates room for considerable political play within contract regimes. In the postwar labor context, the courts consistently exploited this political leeway within contract to favor managerial power and to defeat employees' egalitarian and participatory aspirations.

Boys Markets exemplifies these points. The case involved several relevant contractual promises. The union claimed that management had promised to assign frozen-food work to union personnel, and that the employer had also agreed to arbitrate disputes as to the meaning of the contract. The union promised not to strike during the contract term. The employees were obviously concerned for the job security provided by contractual work assignment rules, but also had an interest in freedom to act in the event they perceived their rights to be violated. The employer relied on the expectation that work would not be interrupted by strikes, but also had an interest in managerial freedom of action in administering the contract and in determining how and by whom work will be carried out. On the surface, one might say that the promises and interests were neatly balanced, and that the free contract ideal necessarily implies that, so long as the employer was willing to arbitrate the grievance, the employees could be required not to strike.

But there are at least two "gaps" or points of indeterminacy in the free contract ideal at work here. A first ambiguity involves whose interpretation of the contract should govern pending the arbitrator's definitive ruling. Labor law assumes that management's interpretation prevails, and employees must obey unless and until they win their case (which may be months or even years later, depending upon how backlogged the grievance process is). Nothing in the ideal of free contract or the notion that "a deal is a deal" requires this rule, which profoundly favors managerial freedom to manage at the expense of employee security. Free contract is perfectly consistent with the opposite premise, adopted in some legal regimes, namely that the employer must restore the status quo and abide by the union's interpretation of the contract, unless and until the arbitrator rules that it is free to do otherwise. That American law consistently takes the former approach reflects a choice in favor of managerial domination.

Second, let us assume that by striking over the frozen-food dispute the employees broke an obligation they had freely entered. It does not follow that the strike was *enjoinable* and the clerks could be compelled to work. The general notion that we are bound to observe our contractual obligations is quite indeterminate on the point of particular *remedies* for breach. As it happens, the normal remedy for breach of contract is a suit for money damages, not an injunction. The historic position of Anglo-American law, quite apart from Norris-La Guardia strictures, has been to refuse injunctions compelling people to perform service contracts, because compulsion to work intrudes too severely on employees' freedom of action, and ordinarily a suit for damages is thought adequately to protect the employer. By granting the additional and unusual remedy of an injunction, *Boys Markets* favored the employer's security of expectations regarding continuity of work operations over the employees' freedom to take action to protect their working conditions. The decision therefore reflects a distinctly political judgment in favor of workplace hierarchy and against concerted activity.

The "deal is a deal" principle has been conveniently overlooked when strict enforcement of contract terms would limit employer freedom of action. An example is the notorious *Milwaukee Spring* case, which allows employers effectively to walk away from their bargain with a union by transferring the work to a nonunion location.[10] But typically, contract enforcement has been highlighted, at the expense of employee freedom of action, due to a perception that vigorous contract enforcement can be useful to management, which, in the words of a famous 1947 Senate Report, "can reasonably expect from a collective labor agreement . . . assurance of uninterrupted operation during the term of the agreement."[11]

The collective bargaining contract is also helpful to management in other ways. Contracts foster long-range economic planning. Contractual grievance procedures provide a device by which higher-level management can monitor and control its own front-line supervisors to ensure compliance with company policy. The arbitral process provides an institutionalized mechanism for generating operating rules for the enterprise and for obtaining a modicum of employee consent and reconciliation to the hierarchical structure of workplace organization. Management can use the threat of damage actions to enlist union offficials in efforts to halt wildcat strikes. Thus, the law of the collective contract effectively co-opts unions into the uncomfortable position of performing certain managerial and disciplinary functions. Over the years, the prospect of these and similar advantages to management was deftly invoked by liberal labor theorists to encourage at least a partial employer truce with collective bargaining. *Boys Markets* culminated a long effort to conform the law to liberal claims that collective bargaining is functional for management.

There is another sense in which the free contract ideal was given a rights-narrowing content in the postwar period. Collective bargaining agreements often waive employees' statutory rights. Indeed, the collective agreement is a legal device by which employees surrender certain basic democratic rights for a price. Two centerpieces of mature collective bargaining are the union's contractual waiver of the employees' statutory right to strike and the "management's rights" clause, under which the contract carves out a sheltered area of employer prerogative exempted from employee input, protest, and even arbitral review. In effect, employees waive during the term of the contract their statutory right to coparticipation in establishing working conditions and rules. These and other waiver rules make the collective bargaining agreement an institutional form by which organized employees consent to their own domination in the workplace.

This is not to suggest that employees should never trade statutory entitlements. Although some workplace rights should be inalienable, surely in other cases employees might be well served by trading statutory entitlements (even the right to engage in certain kinds of concerted activity for limited periods of time) in return for collectively bargained benefits. But, mainstream theory to the contrary notwithstanding, the mere fact that a waiver is voluntarily bargained does not mean that the resulting arrangement is substantively just or that enforcing the bargain respects or enhances employee autonomy and self-determination. Just because the benefits were preferred to the entitlement under the circumstances does not mean that putting employees to the choice was fair to begin with. There are many circumstances in which preventing certain bargains (child labor, to use an obvious example) might enhance rather than detract from human autonomy. The moral and political significance of contract enforcement cannot be determined a priori, without reference to the social context.

The substantive justice of a bargaining regime and the degree to which it actually respects human autonomy and enhances liberty and self-determination turn on the background distribution of economic and social power and on how the particular rules and institutions constituting the market structure affect the parties' powers, endowments, and vulnerabilities. For example, if the background to bargaining is one of enormous and pervasive inequality (as is typical in the workplace), a legal regime that makes rights under employee protective statutes freely waivable effectively permits employers to deploy their economic power so as to dilute or undermine whatever victories employees have won in the legislature, with the consequence that self-determination is decreased rather than enhanced by free contract. On the other hand, if the legal regime makes it difficult or impossible to waive basic rights (and all free contract regimes restrict or prohibit at least some trade-offs), this may enhance employee power and self-determination in the workplace.[12]

Postwar labor law has been exceedingly hospitable to waivers. The dozens of waiver decisions over the years have gradually eroded the statutory rights employees won, at great sacrifice, during and since the New Deal. Cases like *Boys Markets,* vigorously enforcing the waiver of employees' fundamental right to strike, illustrate the process. The waiver rules were promulgated in the name of employee liberty and under the general banner of freedom of contract. But their cumulative effect is to give free contract a specific legal and institutional embodiment that ratifies and reinforces managerial power.

These considerations lead us to some basic deficiencies of contracting processes from the workplace democracy standpoint. Like administrative processes, collective bargaining can become overly bureaucratic and insensitive to employee need. Moreover, there is a virtue in the public focus and debate that is encouraged when workplace rights issues are brought explicitly into the political arena. But the chief disadvantage of contracting systems is that the quality of working life and the remuneration of labor are ultimately determined by the broad patterns of distribution of economic power. Although through activism and solidarity employees can influence the bargain in meaningful ways, the overall shape of the bargain is predominantly cast by the background economic context, which in our society is generally one of profound employer/employee inequality and massive corporate power, even throughout most of the dwindling unionized sector. Given this setting, any contract system will inevitably be hostage to the legally grounded structure of class domination and can never produce a fully adequate or just set of wages and working conditions.

For this reason, workplace reformers have long advocated legislative determination of at least some workplace rights, such as minimum wages, maximum hours, safety protections, and prohibition of race and gender discrimination. In Western Europe, labor and social democratic parties have sponsored much more elaborate programs of noncontract determination of workplace standards. This has led some to assume that progress toward equity in work can *only* be accomplished by a process of gradual statutory encirclement of the field now governed by contract.

This view contains more than one kernel of truth. It properly treats employment relationships as encompassing governance systems and structures of bureaucratic power, as well as bargained arrangements. And it rightly posits that transforming work in an enduringly democratic and egalitarian direction will require major changes at the social and political levels. Nonetheless, the left's traditional call for an eclipse of contract is in certain respects seriously misleading. It overlooks the decentralized and participatory virtues of adversary bargaining. It implicitly invokes a fanciful and ultimately undesirable image of an employment system with limited or no scope for individual choices about entry and exit. And hostility to contract, as such, involves the formalist error of treating contract and market too abstractly. Even within a general capitalist framework, market structures and institutions vary widely, and each particular form of market structure or contract regime has distinct, potentially significant consequences for the distribution of power. To use our example once more, whether grievance strikes may or may not be enjoined in a given legal regime might make a real difference in the quality of working life, even though enjoinability and nonenjoinability are both but variants of a market/contract system. Critical approaches to legal theory must be sensitive to the distributive consequences of market-structuring rules. The plasticity and variation of such rules can be a source of significant law reform opportunities for workplace democracy advocates.

The notion that markets are structured by legal rules that have significant distributive consequences was a fundamental insight of Legal Realism. Indirectly it influenced the theory of the National Labor Relations Act. A core notion behind the act was to redistribute power in favor of employees by "reconstructing" the background legal regime of labor markets, principally by moving from a system of individual to one of collective bargaining. As I have argued elsewhere, this change was filled with radical potential, even though the framework of labor relations was still conceived predominantly in contractual terms.[13]

The NLRA and related statutes are formulated in quite general terms. Their legal meaning is filled out by thousands upon thousands of interpretive decisions which crucially determine the institutional structure within which labor bargaining takes place. At least in theory, the labor law decisional process could have aimed systematically to reconstruct market ground rules so as to enlarge workers' power and participation opportunities. Such redistributive market reconstruction could have been designed to accord with the principles of contractual autonomy and economic efficiency, and much could have been accomplished consistent with the broad frame of congressional intent. While this was a theoretical possibility, such systematically redistributive market reconstruction was clearly not on the postwar political agenda. The operative spectrum of debate ran between the liberals, who advocated partial market reconstruction, and conservatives, who sought, if not a complete rollback to pre-NLRA days, at least NLRA interpretations involving as little departure as possible from the earlier regime of "unregulated" labor bargaining (that is, labor bargaining regulated by the heavily proemployer common law).

The liberal approach unquestionably advocated reconstruction of labor markets to the extent of fostering collective bargaining and requiring employers to treat with unions. But the prevailing view was that once law set up a collective bargaining process, it should largely recede into the background and refrain from any further attempts to redistribute power or to steer the substantive content of employment contracts. Thus, the liberal approach was a significant but inherently limited attempt to reconstruct labor markets, a position I call "minimalist" or "self-limiting market reconstruction." This diffident and restricted postwar application of the market reconstruction concept is not, as is often believed, a logical corollary of the ideal of autonomous free collective bargaining. It seems more a reflection of the political context and the decline of social unionism during the cold war.

Under this gloss on free contract, liberal collective bargaining law tolerates massive inequality in labor markets, so that the options available to employees, while not negligible, are a shadow of what they could and should be. This has always been a disquieting fact for liberal labor law theory, and postwar architects have gone to some lengths to deny it. The most common form of denial is the flat assertion that collective bargaining in and of itself rectifies bargaining imbalance and places labor and management on a level playing field. The point of this totally unconvincing though oft-repeated *ipse dixit* is to place an imprimatur of legitimacy on the outcomes of collective bargaining, no matter how parsimonious or inequitable they may be. In this sense, too, the implicit philosophy of collective bargaining law has legitimated and thereby reinforced socially unnecessary hierarchy in the workplace.

BOUNDING EMPLOYEE PARTICIPATION

A third theme of postwar labor law (not developed in *Boys Markets* itself), is that the liberal model of industrial democracy simultaneously *invites* and *limits* employee participation in workplace governance. That there will be employee participation is taken as a given in postwar politics, but the substantive focus of participation is carefully circumscribed. It is deflected away from such concerns as long-range planning for the enterprise, production methods, and the organization of the work process. The "legitimate" involvement of employees tends to be confined to the terms of sale of labor power.

A key legal formulation of these points is the distinction between "mandatory" and "permissive" subjects of collective bargaining. This doctrine determines the circumstances under which an employer is barred from making unilateral decisions and can be compelled to notify the union of proposed changes and bargain with it about them. The permissive subject rule effectively immunizes employers from collective bargaining duties concerning managerial decisions that are, in the Supreme Court's words, "fundamental to the basic direction of a corporate enterprise" or those "which lie at the core of entrepreneurial control."[14] The entrepreneurial core, of course, includes most strategic decisions, particularly decisions about capital investment in or disinvestment from the enterprise. As a general rule, the more important a management decision is, the less likely that unions can compel employers to bargain about it.[15]

The consequences of deflecting employee participation away from strategic issues have been particularly tragic in recent years with respect to the question of plant closing and relocation. In an incalculably destructive 1981 decision, the Supreme Court applied the Reaganomic "cost-benefit" obsession to scope-of-bargaining doctrine. Justice Harry A. Blackmun first provided a remarkably candid description of what he calls the "neutral purposes" of the NLRA including "defusing and channeling conflict between labor and management"—and then ruled that an employer's decision to close part of its business is outside the mandatory scope of employee participation:

> [I]n establishing what issues must be submitted to the process of bargaining, Congress had no expectation that the elected union representative would become an equal partner in the running of the business enterprise in which the union's members are employed. . . . [I]n view of an employer's need for unencumbered decisionmaking, bargaining over management decisions that have a substantial impact on the continued availability of employment should be required only if the benefit, for labor-management relations and the collective-bargaining process, outweighs the burden placed on the conduct of the business.[16]

The Court assumes employees have neither the motivation, intelligence, nor ability to participate in or contribute to strategic decision making. Likewise, in legal contemplation, employees make no investment and therefore acquire neither a stake in the direction of their company, nor any legal interest in the fruits of their labor. Nor can the surrounding community, even one dominated by and dependent upon a major enterprise, claim a legal interest to participate in or be protected from crucial capital investment decisions the company makes affecting that community.[17]

Employee participation is also constricted by the basic assumption that enterprises must be organized and directed hierarchically. Employees are bound to obey the employer's commands and operational decisions; this is deemed a natural and eternal feature of the employment relationship. Employees are thought to owe a strong "duty of loyalty" to the employer, although the employer owes no correlative duty to its employees. For example, in many instances employers are privileged in pursuit of their own goals to inflict devastating job-loss upon employees, even sometimes without a business justification, and even sometimes with a motive to retaliate for the exercise of the statutory right to unionize.

Although it is acknowledged to be uniquely suited for communication and social intercourse among employees, the workplace is not treated by law as a place for employees to congregate, express themselves, grow as individuals and collectively, or to experience their creative potential and capacity for self-governance. The legal conception of work is productivist: the workplace is a place for employees to carry out production tasks and objectives under employer command. Though employees may spend the bulk of their waking lives in the plant or office, they acquire no entitlement to regard the workplace is in any sense their own. This is explained by the largely circular argument that the workplace—both the physical premises and the existential space—belongs to the employer.

The mindset reflected in these rules and in the grudging approach of American labor law toward employee participation contrasts sharply with the prevailing attitude in Western Europe, where most of the major industrial nations have accorded employee representatives much wider consultative and participatory rights.

THE LIBERAL IMAGINATION AND POSTWAR COLLECTIVE BARGAINING LAW: DEFENSIVE DEMOCRACY

Postwar labor law is a complex weave of rights-expanding and rights-restricting doctrines and institutions. It reflects the achievements of popular struggle; in this respect, there are few comparable examples in law. Yet the struggle to humanize and democratize work is quite incomplete, not only because there were many defeats and compromises along the way, but also because changing times, needs, and possibilities constantly alter the potential meanings of workplace democracy. Thus, postwar labor law both provides the foundation for a genuine, although partial and incomplete system of industrial democracy and also grounds an institutional and ideological system that legitimates managerial power and reinforces employer control in work.

Labor law's detailed doctrine has developed in light of this tension between its democratizing and hierarchy-reinforcing aspects. Accommodation of these discordant emphases within a going system required an imaginative effort of applied political theory, one that acknowledged yet co-opted and institutionalized the emancipatory aspirations of collective bargaining, yet also staved off the more repressive approaches constantly urged by conservative and business interests. Liberal postwar labor jurisprudence elaborated a historically and culturally distinct conception of industrial democracy, which I call *defensive democracy*. Particularly when one recalls the reactionary cold war climate, the absence of a worker party or other social-democratic political presence, and the decline of CIO-style social unionism, the entrenchment of the liberal collective bargaining paradigm in the 1950s and 1960s was a remarkably successful political initiative.

Defensive workplace democracy has substantial built-in ideological and institutional limitations. While employees are guaranteed a voice in establishing working conditions and rules, their power turns largely on their market strength. Because the approach taken toward market reconstruction has been minimalist, employees are permanently subordinated to management in market clout. There are exceptions, of course, cases approaching bilateral monopoly in competition-insulated industries, and cases of strong unions facing weak, fragmented employer groups. But particularly with deregulation and the intensification of world trade competition in recent years, defensive workplace democracy is ordinarily hostage to employers' vastly superior economic resources, a precarious island of due process surrounded by a constantly threatening sea of class power, to extend Kathy Stone's apt metaphor.[18]

A second, important effect of minimalist market reconstruction has been to promote labor market segmentation—that is, to drive a wedge between the organized and unorganized sectors of the workforce—and to foster the privatization in collective bargaining of welfare functions (e.g., delivering health care) performed by the state elsewhere in the industrial world. By tying welfare to jobs rather than membership in the community, the very success of the postwar labor-management compromise had the unintended effect of decoupling the concerns of poor people and low-wage workers from the labor movement's political agenda, to the ultimate detriment of both groups. This has had profoundly damaging consequences for the interests of unrepresented, contingent, and unpaid workers, with disproportionate adverse effect on women workers and workers of color. U.S. social welfare minimalism damages the economy as a whole by encouraging firms to indulge low-wage strategies and, therefore, to waste and injure human capital and to defer the search for "high road," productivity-enhancing strategies as emphasized by our trade rivals abroad.

Even within its besieged and precarious zone, the liberal model of workplace democracy has built-in limitations. Strategic decision making in the enterprise is reserved for management. The liberal model tolerates and even encourages hierarchic and authoritarian organization of work operations. Defensive workplace democracy does not invite employees to participate directly and continuously in firm decision making and governance, nor does it routinely entitle employees to the kind of business plans and data that would inform and facilitate direct and continuous participation in decision making. In contemplation of law the day-to-day employee role is simply that of command follower. True enough, if management violates the contract, employees have a remedy through the grievance process (but not job action). But in the first instance, and throughout the period pending arbitral decision, management manages and employees obey. And because business (as opposed to labor relations) decisions are not ordinarily subject to arbitral review, employees can at most have only an indirect impact on such decisions. Thus, in daily routine, the liberal vision of industrial democracy is a defensive or reactive process of rights-enforcement within a restricted field, not a continuous, prospective, and participatory process. This is surely better than unconstrained managerial power, but it is a pale shadow of what workplace democracy can and should be.

CONCLUSION: LABOR LAW CRITIQUE, TRANSFORMATIVE LEGAL PRACTICES, AND EMPOWERED DEMOCRACY

Liberals found in collective bargaining law a superb terrain to develop approaches to general problems of cold war political theory (e.g., the strategy of institutionalizing conflict, the theory of a common interest in uninterrupted production, technological-determinist explanations of modernization). A generation later, radical activists and critical theorists can ground new approaches to workplace democracy and progressive legal practice, in part, in a rethinking of the experience of collective bargaining.

The richly textured doctrine of labor law that pervades and envelops the daily lives of all union officials and activists induces us to think about workplace problems in ways that inhibit the effort to create industrial freedom. Labor activists need to forge an entirely new vision of workplace democracy. We must go beyond the liberal legalist conception of industrial justice, in which entitlements ultimately turn on bargaining power rather than human need; in which the prerogatives of capital trump the democratic concerns of employees; and in which employee participation is deflected from the all-important decisions regarding the allocation of society's resources. An empowered conception of workplace democracy must encompass new notions of the meaning of work. It must center on the idea that work should *have* meaning, that it should be a mode of self-expression and development, that its content and purposes *matter*; on new conceptions of how to reconcile production processes with the needs and rhythms of personal life and of our physical environment; on a new set of values about the uses and allocation of social resources; and on cultural pluralism and an end to racism, sexism, homophobia, and all forms of illegitimate hierarchy in the workplace and in the labor movement.

Moreover, the problem of democratic governance in the workplace is in some respects paradigmatic of the problems of politics and law generally. The effort to conceptualize work as an experience of free, creative, and developmental expression, and the workplace as a locus of democratic self-governance, may suggest general terms in which to conceive transformative legal practices and institution-building as arenas of human self-development and self-realization. For these reasons, the enterprise of critical labor law is inspired by the hope that reflection upon resistance and transformation at the intersection of the workplace and the legal process will contribute to a broader project of articulating and contesting for a postliberal, empowered conception of democracy in politics and social life.

NOTES

Earlier versions of this chapter appeared in previous editions of this book. In the interest of conserving space for this enlarged edition, most endnote references have been deleted. Readers wishing fuller documentation will find complete case citations and other references in the 1990 revised edition.

1. Overall union density, including both public and private sectors, totals 14.5 percent, outpacing the private sector figure of 10.2 percent (11 Labor Relations Week 89 [1997]). Union density is much higher in public sector employment, where it continues to grow, although the public sector comprises a much smaller percentage of overall employment.
2. *Boys Markets, Inc. v. Retail Clerks Union, Local 770*, 398 U.S. 235 (1970).
3. See *Sinclair Refining Co. v. Atkinson*, 370 U.S. 195 (1962).
4. 398 U.S. at 256.
5. This summary of the dominant postwar industrial relations theory is drawn from Walter Korpi, "Industrial Relations and Industrial Conflict: The Case of Sweden," in *Labor Relations in Advanced Industrial Societies: Issues and Problems*, ed. Benjamin Martin and Everett M. Kassalow (Washington, DC: Carnegie Endowment for International Peace, 1980), 90–93.
6. 398 U.S. at 251 (emphasis added).
7. *Sinclair Refining Co. v. Atkinson*, 370 U.S. 195, 225, 226 (1962) (Brennan dissenting).

8. *NLRB v. Jones & Laughlin Steel Corp.*, 301 U.S. 1, 33 (1937), quoting, with a slight modification, *American Steel Foundries v. Tri-City Central Trades Council*, 257 U.S. 184, 209 (1921).

9. This argument is developed in Betty Mensch, *Freedom of Contract as Ideology*, 33 Stanford Law Review 753 (1981).

10. Milwaukee Spring Div. of Illinois Coil Spring Co., 265 N.L.R.B. 206 (1982), revised, 268 N.L.R.B 601 (1984), enforced sub nom., *United Automobile Workers v. NLRB*, 765 F.2d 175 (D.C. Cir. 1985).

11. Senate Report No. 105, 80th Cong., 1st Sess., at 16 (1947).

12. Law professors commonly object that, a priori, rules prohibiting waivers impair efficiency. Except in trivial cases, this argument is mistaken. In the presence of transaction costs and other forms of market failure, no legal regime will generate a perfectly efficient outcome, nor is it possible to determine the efficiency consequences of legal rules a priori. Whether a particular rule, including a substantive restriction on freedom of contract, will lead to relatively more or less efficient outcomes cannot be determined without detailed, contextualized analysis. That is, the claim that substantive restrictions on freedom of contract are a priori inefficient is false. See generally Duncan Kennedy and Frank Michelman, *Are Property and Contract Efficient?* 8 Hofstra Law Review 711 (1980); Karl Klare, *Workplace Democracy and Market Reconstruction: An Agenda for Legal Reform*, 38 Catholic University Law Review 1 (1988). It is also a common objection that nondisclaimable terms and prohibitions on waivers must have the consequence of decreasing the welfare of the group intended to be benefited. This argument, too, is mistaken. See Duncan Kennedy, *Distributive and Paternalist Motives in Contract and Tort Law, with Special Reference to Compulsory Terms and Unequal Bargaining Power*, 41 Maryland Law Review 563, 604–14 (1982).

13. See Karl Klare, *Judicial Deradicalization of the Wagner Act and the Origins of Modern Legal Consciousness, 1937–1941*, 62 Minnesota Law Review 265 (1978); Karl Klare, *Traditional Labor Law Scholarship and the Crisis of Collective Bargaining Law: A Reply to Professor Finkin*, 44 Maryland Law Review 731 (1985).

14. *Fibreboard Paper Products Corp. v. NLRB*, 379 U.S. 203, 223 (1964), Stewart concurring.

15. See Staughton Lynd, *Investment Decisions and the Quid Pro Quo Myth*, 29 Case Western Reserve Law Review 396, 398–403 (1979).

16. *First National Maintenance Corp. v. NLRB*, 452 U.S. 666, 676–79 (1981).

17. For an argument that the law actually does protect, or at any rate should protect, employee and community interests in continuity of investment,

see Joseph William Singer, *The Reliance Interest in Property,* 40 Stanford Law Review 611 (1988).

18. See Katherine Stone, *The Structure of Post-War Labor Relations,* 11 New York University Review of Law and Social Change 125, 131 (1982–1983).

25 LUCY A. WILLIAMS

WELFARE AND LEGAL ENTITLEMENTS: THE SOCIAL ROOTS OF POVERTY

PUBLIC policy and political rhetoric in the United States always have been ambivalent about assisting the poor, unsure about whether the poor are good people facing difficult times or bad people who refuse to fit into society. Public welfare programs in the United States originated as discretionary programs for the "worthy" poor. Local asylums or poorhouses, with wide variation and broad local administrative discretion, separated the "deserving" poor, such as the blind, deaf, insane, and eventually the orphaned, from the "undeserving"—all other paupers, including children in families.

The dominant political discourse in the United States, reinforced by our legal culture, teaches that poverty arises naturally. Either it is a twist of fate, such as victimization by a flood, drought, or other act of God (this is the case of the deserving poor, such as the blind and deaf, who deserve some sympathy because of their misfortune) or it results from an individual's willful refusal to conform to minimal social norms and obligations (the undeserving poor). In either case, the basic message is that neither the political system nor the legal system bears any responsibility for causing poverty, nor can public policy do much about poverty except to alleviate the suffering of the most abject among the deserving.

This tenet—that poverty is a natural result of cruel fate or individual failing—is deeply entrenched and broadly diffused in our politics and culture, and it is also false. To be sure, biological accident and antisocial behavior play some part. However, the persistence of poverty on a massive scale in an extremely wealthy and technologically advanced country such as the United States is largely a product of political decisions and institutions that generate and sustain a sharply unequal distribution of wealth and resources. Legal rules, norms, and practices play a central part in maintaining and legitimating poverty in the United States—although their role is predominantly invisible—by according privilege to certain interests, values, and concerns over others.

Congress enacted the Social Security Act in 1935, establishing several well-known programs, such as Social Security, Unemployment Insurance, and Aid to Dependent Children. Thirty years later, the last program (renamed Aid to Families with Dependent Children, or AFDC) was judicially interpreted to create a federal statutory entitlement to the receipt of cash assistance for certain eligible families, primarily single mothers and their children. To put it another way, the Supreme Court held that, as long as the federal statute was in place, families who met certain federal eligibility criteria had a legal right to cash assistance.

In 1996 the Republican-controlled Congress passed and Democratic President Bill Clinton signed the Personal Responsibility and Work Opportunity Reconciliation Act of 1996 (PRWORA)—"welfare reform"—which abolished the AFDC program.[1] States now receive Temporary Assistance for Needy Families block grants with fixed funding and few federal individual eligibility requirements. The new scheme eliminated the federal statutory legal right or entitlement to cash assistance for poor single-parent families.

While much of the rhetoric supporting block grants relied on the need for state discretion in framing welfare programs, the PRWORA is not about enhancing states' abilities to be "laboratories of experimentation." For more than ten years, beginning in the Reagan administration, the states had been given increased flexibility through the greatly expanded use (or misuse) of federal waivers.[2] Instead, the importance of the PRWORA is its repudiation of the concept of entitlement in welfare jurisprudence.

In the debate about ending the AFDC entitlement, the term *entitlement* was associated only with the legal right of poor people to receive governmental benefits, as distinct from the thousands of other entitlements guaranteed by our legal system. Anti-welfare politicians and commentators made it appear that, as a legal form, the term *entitlement* was an aberration or anomaly in United States legal culture.

But most legal rights and obligations can be and are routinely cast as entitlements, and they have essentially the same characteristics as welfare entitlements. Entitlements are contingent—they do not arise naturally, but are crafted by people and develop socially and historically—and have distributive consequences. The term *anti-entitlement* is not a coherent concept as a matter of legal analysis or basic jurisprudence. These politicians were not against entitlements per se but against entitlements to welfare.

Welfare entitlements were distributive—or redistributive—in a particular way: The emergence of rudimentary legal rules transferring wealth to the poor revealed that poverty was not natural. By implication, poverty could be ended by deploying more vigorous welfare entitlements or other redistributive measures, and our distribution of wealth and power would be proven to be socially constructed. If the full implications of this paradigm were to emerge, there would be no reason for a thorough redistribution of wealth not to be discussed and evaluated.

But by using this rhetorical strategy of separating welfare entitlement from all other legal entitlements, politicians were able to make *entitlement* a dirty word, to make *anti-entitlement* a seemingly coherent concept in the political arena, and to depict entitled welfare recipients as socially deviant. Welfare recipients were portrayed as responsible for many, if not most, societal problems, including crime, family degeneration, unemployment in wage work, and illegitimacy. This stereotype was bolstered by reiterating the long-standing conception of dependency as a debilitating condition that afflicts only poor people who receive help from the government. Other forms of dependency, which are central to all social relationships, were seen to cause no ill effects and to be irrelevant. These ideas framed and continue to frame the welfare policy agenda.

THE DEVELOPMENT OF AN ENTITLEMENT TO WELFARE

The complex story of how U.S. public policy treats poor people, particularly single mothers and their children, reflects the political culture's ambivalence about the causes of poverty. Claims about individual human failure and a deficit of traditional family values have always been part of the discourse. Political leaders in the early twentieth century often claimed that providing "outdoor relief" (assistance outside the context of a poorhouse or workhouse) would undermine poor people's initiative and dignity. Some elements of the reformists' movements tried to control the behavior of—or "Americanize"—poor immigrant mothers who were felt to have inadequate moral values.[3] Public provision for poor women and children has always reflected a tension between the conflicting imperatives of family care and wage work.

Welfare recipients and the development of welfare programs have always been deeply connected to low-wage labor markets. For example, the predecessors to AFDC were the "Mother's Pensions" or "Widow's Pensions" acts created in numerous states in the early twentieth century. One goal of these programs was to provide cash assistance to enable single mothers to fulfill the "woman's role" of homemaker rather than placing their children in institutions. To avoid the stigma of immorality attached to unmarried mothers or deserted wives, the proponents of these programs highlighted an image of the worthy white widow. Early programs were highly discretionary, allowing localities to exclude "immoral" women and women of color.[4]

But even for a "deserving" woman eligible for such benefits, the amount was so low that she (and often her children) had to do paid labor, such as doing laundry, sewing, or taking in boarders, or attach themselves to a male breadwinner. However, if the recipient did do wage work, she was considered a bad mother. Thus, poor women were faced with irreconcilable pressures: They were expected not to earn yet were expected to earn; they were expected to be chaste yet needed to find a man; they were expected to care for their children yet were forced to leave their children to perform paid labor.

The Social Security Act of 1935 emerged from the Great Depression, when the massive unemployment of previously employed white male voters made it politically impossible to dismiss the poor as random victims of bad luck or as antisocial people responsible for their own situation. Three main programs were enacted: a retirement income supplement or pension for the elderly, commonly known as Social Security; a program for time-limited, partial wage-replacement when income was interrupted due to unemployment, commonly known as Unemployment Compensation or Unemployment Insurance (UI); and AFDC, a much smaller program of cash assistance for children living with their mothers, commonly known as welfare.[5]

Social Security and UI were based on a different structural scheme from AFDC. Social Security and UI are social insurance programs, meaning that the benefits are funded through employer or employer-employee taxes. Eligibility for these programs is conditioned on a designated length of employment in wage work, and benefit levels are tied to the individual's work and earning history. Partly because these programs meshed well with the political culture's emphasis on individual effort and (labor) market exchange, Social Security and, to a somewhat lesser extent, UI eventually became less controversial entitlements in our culture than the welfare entitlement.

In contrast, AFDC was structured as a needs-based, transfer payment program. Eligibility for benefits was not based on earning history or tied to prior employer-employee contributions. Rather, eligibility was based on the financial need of the members of the covered group, and benefits were funded through general tax revenues.

As interpreted administratively, the Social Security Act allowed the states great discretion to condition eligibility or deny benefits based on implicit racial or perceived moral grounds. For example, Georgia closed AFDC cases in certain counties with seasonal employment whenever the county board designated the period as one of full employment, whether or not the mother was employed. The Georgia regulation also provided that earnings from full-time employment would not be supplemented by a partial AFDC grant, regardless of how low the earnings were. African American AFDC mothers were denied benefits during harvest season in rural counties, forcing them to work in the fields for substandard wages.[6]

Benefits in a number of states were conditioned upon the sexual morality of AFDC mothers through "suitable home" or "man in the house" rules: Welfare case workers conducted "midnight raids," and if they found a man in the house in the middle of the night, the mother and children were dropped from the welfare rolls on the presumption that a man with whom an AFDC recipient had a sexual relationship was willing and able to support her children.[7] These sexual behavior rules, like the Georgia work rules, were often manipulated to exclude those seen as undeserving from the rolls, frequently African Americans and children of unwed mothers.[8] In testimony in a case challenging the "suitable home" provision, one state official stated that the regulation applied if the parties had sex once every six months, another testified that it applied only if the parties had sex at least once every three months, and another said that the parties had to have had sex at least once a week.[9] Thus, even after the enactment of the Social Security Act, much of the history of care for poor single mothers and children adhered to the latent cultural principle of giving only to those who were deserving as defined through value-laden lenses.

AFDC experienced a major expansion of its scope in the 1960s in the context of heightened civil rights mobilization and the emergence of political movements and advocacy groups for the poor. Building on the conception of welfare entitlement developed by social workers in the 1930s and 1940s and the more recent legal scholarship of Charles Reich and others equating welfare benefits with private law property rights, aggressive lawyering on behalf of poor people in the 1960s and 1970s removed many of the pervasive administrative barriers and subterfuges used to keep African American women off the welfare rolls.[10]

U.S. law has never adopted a constitutional right of the needy to social support. Even in the context of the social insurance scheme of the Social Security program, benefits have been interpreted judicially to be statutory entitlements, not accrued property rights.[11] In other words, Congress can grant or eliminate eligibility for social programs by altering or removing the enabling statutory language. In addition, the Supreme Court has rejected arguments that, where welfare benefits are granted, they embody fundamental rights triggering the highest level of judicial review of discriminatory classifications.[12]

However, a major breakthrough occurred in a series of cases in the late 1960s and early 1970s. In *King v. Smith*, a challenge to a "suitable home" rule, and in subsequent cases, the Supreme Court interpreted the amorphous language of the Social Security Act "Aid . . . shall be furnished with reasonable promptness to all eligible individuals" as creating a *statutory categorical entitlement* to benefits. This interpretation meant that, as long as Congress did not rescind this language, the states were required to provide AFDC benefits, albeit in amounts determined by each state, to certain categories of eligible individuals. And in *Goldberg v. Kelly*, the Supreme Court ruled that an AFDC recipient was entitled to a fair hearing prior to the termination of benefits. The jurisprudential effect of *Goldberg* was to designate welfare as a right, or entitlement, triggering procedural due process, rather than a mere privilege.[13]

This reformulation did not eliminate the emphasis on personal blame in welfare law. For example, in *Wyman v. James* (1971) the Supreme Court upheld New York's regulations prescribing home-visit surveillance of AFDC recipients. The Court rebuffed the argument that the recipients' right to welfare was being unconstitutionally conditioned on degrading invasions of privacy. Justice Blackmun's majority opinion sidesteps crucial legal issues but recites irrelevant evidence designed to imply that Mrs. James was a bad mother whom the state needed to watch over.[14]

However, the civil rights and welfare rights movements effectively used the entitlement concept embraced by *King* and *Goldberg* in developing organizing strategies. For example, while the welfare entitlement concept was wending its way to the Supreme Court, the National Welfare Rights Organization began an unprecedented campaign to get recipients the special needs to which they were entitled under existing regulations. Organizers saw the potential of the right to a pretermination hearing as a vehicle to empower recipients—to make them less afraid of losing subsistence benefits in retaliation for taking collective action.[15]

Due to the confluence of a changing political climate, effective organizing, and the legal victories, the number of African Americans on the AFDC rolls increased dramatically, by approximately 15 percent from 1965 to 1971, although the vast majority of those receiving welfare continued to be white.[16] This development coincided with the evolution of an elaborate and sustained rightwing critique of welfare in the early 1960s that incorporated a distinctly radical edge.

THE CONCEPT OF ENTITLEMENT IN U.S. LAW

The concept of entitlement is neither a novelty nor an innovation of welfare jurisprudence. Entitlement, or right, is a central concept throughout U.S. jurisprudence and is the basic legal form utilized in the range of private law areas, such as contract and tort. For example, one is entitled to recover certain damages for breach of contract, one is entitled to sue for certain kinds of injury under tort law, and only people with contractual capacity are entitled to sell their labor. As a legal idea, the concept of an entitlement is utterly mundane.

But the substantive content and distributive effects of the range of legal entitlements are not matters of indifference, rather they reflect and enact distinct political values. Legal entitlements do not descend from the sky, but are created by human actors who make moral or philosophical decisions, explicitly or implicitly, about who is deserving or undeservingy of reward within a chosen economic structure. The politics of race, gender, and class are filtered through these choices.

Thus the legal entitlements that form the basis of private property allocations and contractual rights are not natural or neutral but chosen, and they play a significant role in determining the prevailing distribution of wealth and income, favoring certain interests and disfavoring others. These "background rules" of property and contract rights set out the array of mostly private law entitlements operative in a given society at a given moment. They also shape social roles by assigning power and responsibility in relationships, such as family relationships, landlord-tenant relationships, and so on, always eroding the independence of some in order to empower others. For example, those with greater property rights generally have greater bargaining power in the market; they are more capable of living without or replacing elsewhere the goods that the other participant in the bargain has to trade or offer.

Contrary to the dominant political imagery, which effaces the power of the state in structuring social life, the state has always intervened in social life through the design and enforcement of non-neutral, value-laden entitlements established by market-structuring background rules. The question is not when or whether government should step in; rather, it is whose interests and what distribution of power are protected by these entitlements.

More specifically, in nineteenth-century legal culture, the dominant framing of entitlement or right was grounded in ideals of independence and self-sufficiency. Rights created zones of autonomy, with the goal that individuals be immune from the needs of others and from reliance on the goodwill of others. Of course, altruistic or communitarian norms have always had a presence in common law, but in classical U.S. legal thought, liberty, independence, and fulfillment were predominantly identified with individual effort within a free-market system. From the doctrine of consideration to the concept of negligence and throughout the private law system, legal entitlements were designed largely to justify and reward individual effort and advantage-seeking exchange. In other words, one was entitled to own private property because the privileges of ownership supposedly rewarded individual effort and exchange. Freedom prevailed when individuals were able to make free decisions as equal participants within an unregulated market.

Central to this legal formulation is the presentation of wage work as freely chosen activity enabling the worker to be self-sufficient. We know, of course, that conceiving of wage labor as economic independence denies the intrinsic domination and dependency within employer-employee relationships. The designation of a free market in which all actors are equal is a legally formulated fiction that makes existing social and economic discrepancies seem natural.[17] The structure of labor markets tends to reinforce socially constructed class and racial hierarchies and existing patterns of gender subordination and dependency within work and family relationships.[18] In particular, the structure of low-wage labor often creates and contributes to increased dependency of poor single mothers in the workplace—for example, single mothers with few financial options to support their children tolerating degrading or unhealthy conditions.

To bolster its legitimationist goals, nineteenth-century legal discourse had to reconceive the economically dependent and subordinating relationship of wage labor as one supposedly based on free exchange for mutual benefit. As Nancy Fraser and Linda Gordon have documented, prior to the rise of industrial capitalism, dependence was defined as being subordinate to someone else or gaining one's livelihood by working for someone else.[19] Virtually everyone was considered dependent; there was no deviancy associated with the concept. Only those owning sufficient property to live without working were deemed independent.

With the rise of modern capitalism, as white male workers demanded electoral rights, the legal culture generated ideas that expanded and reinterpreted the concept of economic independence to include wage labor. Through the legal discourse of free markets and maximization of wealth through effort and exchange, economic inequality or capital-labor relationships of subordination were no longer thought to create dependency. Because the legal culture effaced the social dependency of capitalist wage labor and ignored the dependent position of women in families, many in elite culture, including legal culture, came to believe that structural bases of dependency had been eliminated in the United States. In contrast, the concept of dependency became tied to exclusion from wage work or receipt of social welfare programs. Rather than dependence being viewed as normal, it was cast as deviant, a result of individual fault.

However, the legal culture presented the property and contract rights that undergirded these concepts of independence, effort, and free market exchange not as governmentally created entitlements but as natural and eternal rules of social organization. In this formulation, the ultimate source of economic well-being and fulfillment was and should be freedom of contract unimpeded by government regulation or control, so that "just outcomes arise when people are permitted to do the best they can, given their circumstances."[20] Classical U.S. legal thought was an important part of a pervasive worldview that successfully induced people to forget that property ownership, wage labor, market structures, and all other relationships providing the context for individual contracting and competition were composed of an array of legal entitlements consciously fashioned by responsible political actors. Thus legal discourse naturalized poverty and supported the belief that welfare connotes dependence. Because welfare was relegated to the margins of cultural acceptability, it came to be understood as a privilege rather than as a right like every other legal entitlement.

THE CONCEPTUAL POWER OF AN ENTITLEMENT TO WELFARE

In distinguishing between favored social insurance (Social Security, Unemployment Insurance) and disfavored needs-based programs

(AFDC,) the New Deal reforms retained, albeit in updated form, the marginalized treatment of welfare benefits. So the reconceptualization of welfare as an entitlement in *King, Goldberg,* and their progeny, was an authentic political opening—despite the fact that, as a jurisprudential matter, there was nothing new in the entitlement concept. This should be seen as an important achievement of the popular mobilization of the period and, in part, of creative lawyering by deeply committed welfare rights advocates.

The establishment of welfare as an entitlement, a right to even a small amount of cash for designated individuals from tax revenues, introduced a radically destabilizing concept into U.S. legal discourse in two distinct but related ways. At its most basic level, creating an entitlement that re-distributed income exposed the socially created nature of all background rules of entitlement and exposed their distributive significance—that is, their role in maintaining inequality. In particular, the creation of an enti-tlement to welfare challenged and disrupted the nineteenth-century for-mulation of individual autonomy and independence as effort and ex-change by equal participants within an unregulated market.

First, the new welfare jurisprudence exposed rights as socially chosen, not naturally given. And if entitlements are constructed, they can be reconstructed. From a technical legal perspective that was hardly news, but the political and cultural significance of the insight was deeply desta-bilizing. It revealed or, more accurately, resurfaced the fact that all prop-erty entitlements and therefore the distribution of all wealth and power are the contingent product of political decisions. The current distribu-tion of wealth is not inevitable, and indigence is not natural; both are socially and legally constituted.

Second, the Court announced that a full-fledged legal entitlement, a property right, could accrue to someone even though he or she had not earned it through effort and market exchange. Of course, this was always true, as in the example of inheritance. But in a powerful way, the cultural legitimacy of U.S. law—and therefore the structure of grossly unequal distribution of wealth—had been tied to the romanticized ethic of effort and exchange. The concept of welfare entitlement threatened to erode this link and therefore to invite reconsideration of the precise structure of existing legal entitlements. In other words, connecting entitlement to (or placing a social value on) a formulation of effort and exchange outside traditional labor markets challenged the idea of a neutral and natural def-inition of effort and exchange.

Likewise, the creation of a legal welfare entitlement funded by general taxation (as opposed to social insurance programs) challenged definitions of autonomy and independence as having an intrinsic meaning grounded in individual effort (which preceded a legal recognition). Lawyers, of course, knew that the law had always denominated a few individuals for whom one was financially responsible; for example, the state established certain parental child support responsibilities. But the notion of a welfare entitlement conceptually exposed the false dichotomy between individual independence and communal action. An AFDC entitlement symbolized the restrictiveness of the traditional conception of individual freedom over the product of one's labor and gave an imprimatur not just to taxation for general communal purposes (such as highways and national defense) but also to taxation for the economic benefit of another individual. At the same time, welfare entitlement validated a communal investment in human capital as empowering individuals and bolstering individual independence, while serving a social good.

Thus the legal concept of welfare entitlement served as a symbol for the idea that development of individual autonomy can be enhanced when collective action transforms social interactions to make available a wider range of individual choice. Conversely, conceptualizing an entitlement to welfare (based on taxation) as similar to other existing background entitlements highlighted the fact that traditional concepts of property ownership affect future distribution of property—the background rules of private property themselves comprise a form of taxation for the benefit of the entitlement owners.

Exploding the traditional definition of independence, then, exposed the false dichotomy between wage work, seen as an equal relationship of independent market participants, and receipt of government benefits, seen as a relationship of inherent dependency. The concept of a welfare entitlement, although not the meager amount of actual benefits, theoretically gave some workers an alternative to wage work. By conceptually restructuring the role of market participants to enhance the worker's freedom of contract, a welfare entitlement challenged the invisibility of the dependency in wage work relationships created by the employer's superior market power.

Finally, in recognizing that all background rules of entitlement are socially chosen, have distributive consequences, and can be reformulated, and in challenging the naturalness of independence as individual effort within a free-market system, the creation of a welfare entitlement exposed the false dichotomy of welfare as state intervention in the market and private property and freedom of contract as nonintervention.

Enacting the background rules of a self-regulating market constitutes a government regulatory program. The state is always implicated in the outcomes of private interactions through the construction of the background rules.

Thus, a welfare entitlement made it possible to see that all "free-market" transfers are publicly regulated and exerted pressure on legal thought to take a position on the distributive consequences of state-imposed, socially constructed entitlements.

THE ATTACK ON AND DEFENSE OF WELFARE ENTITLEMENT

The welfare entitlement discourse of twenty-five years ago offered a chance to develop and diffuse public understanding that poverty is not an accident but a choice sustained by our legal system, a product of countless property, contract, and tort rights and entitlements that privilege wealth and reinforce inequality. Regrettably, we missed the opportunity to challenge traditional notions of effort and exchange, the illusory dichotomy between the independence of wage work and the dependency created by government largesse, and the dichotomy between a free market supposedly without government regulation and the welfare state supposedly based on governmental intrusion into people's lives. The political right was much more skillful in exploiting the rhetorical and cultural potential of the entitlement debate.

The welfare rights community did extraordinary legal work to establish the concept of a legal entitlement to welfare. On a political level, welfare advocates saw welfare entitlements as components of a postliberal model of democracy. The basic philosophical belief was and continues to be that a democratic culture should guarantee a minimum livelihood. Welfare rights advocates also were alert to the redistributive importance of a welfare entitlement. The entitlement concept was often effectively used in litigation and organizing to achieve subsistence funding critical to many poor people in the United States.

In hindsight, however, we did not fully apprehend and mobilize the destabilizing potential of the welfare entitlement concept and debate. The deep message of the welfare entitlement concept was the role of law in sustaining poverty through the political choices embodied in all legal rules. As such, radical lawyers and activists needed to frame a discourse that questioned the traditional distinction between state and market and exposed markets as structured by politically chosen legal entitlements.

Yet, despite ourselves, many welfare rights advocates subtly bought into this dichotomy, a dichotomy that welfare entitlement conceptually undermined. We generally envisioned an antipoverty strategy that deployed state intervention to redistribute income, focusing on the role of government in solving poverty through a top-down model of general taxation and transfer programs. We conceived our field as a branch of public regulatory law.

This strategic focus distracted us from engaging with the concept that all of social life, including structural inequalities, are embedded in and sustained by an array of private law entitlements that are subject to revision. We therefore did not integrally relate our public law antipoverty strategy to a reexamination and recasting of state-imposed background rules of private law. The background rules remained largely in the background of welfare rights thinking.

Because we did not look closely at market structures, our focus obscured the important connection of our perspectives to a critique of dependency in wage work. In other words, it often clouded the connection between the politics of welfare and the politics of wage work. Thus, while much important legal work was accomplished, we failed to envision an antipoverty strategy that furthered the transformation of legal and social relationships in all arenas, thus limiting our ability to exploit the destabilizing potential of the welfare entitlement concept. In particular, because we did not fully understand the conceptual force of welfare entitlement, we were slow to recognize the political power of and were not fully prepared conceptually to respond to the right's crusade to abolish a federal statutory welfare entitlement. We often treated that attack as fringe discourse that could be dismissed.

Welfare rights advocates in the academy generally shared the approach of legal activists in the field during the late 1960s and early 1970s. Beginning at the end of the 1970s, however, new questions concerning the value of formulating welfare as an entitlement emerged among progressive academics. The context was a debate about whether rights-based approaches were an adequate grounding for transformative lawyering.[21]

Some critics argued that the private law strategy of analogizing welfare benefits to traditional property concepts actually would inhibit redistributive politics by implanting nineteenth-century individualistic values onto social change efforts. The fear was that treating welfare as an entitlement would reinforce the image of rights as sanctuaries for independent individuals against the power of the state, thereby according a subtle but powerful normative priority to the private law status quo. Ultimately, the

argument went, an entitlement strategy would split the income maintenance movement by dividing the constituents of social insurance programs from welfare recipients.[22] In addition, sympathetic academics
argued about whether an emphasis on rule-based solutions would
accomplish the goal of eliminating poverty—that is, whether the substantive meaning of welfare entitlement was predominantly created
through legal regulations on the books or in the implementation process
by street-level bureaucrats.[23]

Certainly the concept of a welfare entitlement can be criticized, and
these debates pushed progressive legal thinkers to engage in important
implications of a rights-based strategy in various contexts. But many academics lost sight of the limitations of the rights critique itself. The
debates over rules versus discretion and interstitial versus transformative
change often distanced the academics from the frontline poverty advocates, who might have benefited from academics' perspectives in understanding the conceptual power of a welfare entitlement. Closer dialogue
between critical legal theorists and frontline practitioners would have
better prepared the welfare rights community to repel the right's effort to
suppress the destabilizing insights of *King* and *Goldberg* and to renatural-
ize the private law background rules.

Had all this occurred, the PRWORA still might have been signed into
law. But welfare rights academics and advocates did not jointly do the intellectual work necessary to understand fully and to translate into effective
political discourse the radical insights generated by combining the words
welfare and *entitlement*. In the welfare reform debate, we missed an opportunity to frame for the U.S. public something beyond just a humanitarian
plea on behalf of the unfortunate. Instead, we missed an opportunity to
expose poverty as a product of our legal system, a result of property and
contractual rights that privilege certain parties and make certain political
choices.

The antiwelfare rhetoric of the rightwing movements is indicative of
the counterattacks on the conceptual power of the welfare entitlement.
Even though welfare expenditures were a minuscule part of the federal
budget, the right had a large investment in maintaining the economic
stucture supported and legitimized by legal property, contract, and tort
background rules. Thus, the right emphasized and sought to reestablish
the apolitical nature of these background rules. Two of their prevalent
themes were especially effective.

First, the right isolated entitlement in the welfare context as an aberration, as government intervention that disrupted an otherwise supposedly

unregulated market. Second, the right continually framed poverty as the fault of individuals. To bolster this argument, they reinforced the historically resonating dichotomy between wage work as independence and the receipt of welfare as resulting in personal dependency.

Through both of these themes, the right played to the ongoing racism in our society. The timing of their attack on welfare coincided with the evolution of the welfare entitlement concept, which was in part responsible for finally opening the welfare rolls to African Americans and other people of color. As the right consciously focused on the "white backlash," particularly in the South, exploiting the racial tensions of the 1960s to advance their political agenda, AFDC—along with street crime, nondiscriminatory housing, deteriorating neighborhoods, declining property values, school busing, and affirmative action—became a code word for race.[24]

Highlighting the dichotomy between state welfare regulation and private effort and exchange, "Old Right" publications in the early 1960s attacked the welfare state for undermining rugged individualism and private property, supporting the growth of collectivism, fostering nonproductive activity and dependent citizens, contributing to crime (particularly associated to urban riots and the civil rights movement), and ultimately leading to communism. By teaching that "the have nots can take from the haves" through taxation, Barry Goldwater portrayed the welfare state as contributing to crimes of private property and riots.[25]

In 1977, conservative economist Walter Williams argued that an African American and Latin underclass was being created because of excess government intervention, in the form of direct income transfer programs, as well as indirect costs in racial hiring quotas and busing; unions, labor support of income-transfer programs disguising the "true effects of restrictions created by unions ... by casting a few 'crumbs' to those denied jobs in order to keep them quiet, thereby creating a permanent welfare class"; and minimum wage laws, by giving firms an incentive to only hire the most productive. Williams asserted that one of the "best strategies to raise the socioeconomic status of Negroes as a group is to promote a *freer* market." Other conservative authors during this decade emphasized the dichotomy between taxation as government intervention and natural private property.[26]

In the 1980s, a group of "New Right" and Reagan administration authors concluded that "the ideal conservative state keeps interference with our lives to a minimum because that maximizes our freedom to be whatever it is we are *intended to be*. ...[I]ndividual rights come from

God and the purpose of government is only to secure those rights."[27]

The second theme in the right's rhetoric—that poverty is caused by individual failure or lack of individual initiative—is frequently connected to race. In the 1960s, laziness and immorality were explicitly tied to an image of AFDC recipients as African American—the immoral sexual practices of a "growing horde of lazy Negroes" living off the public dole, "the unmarried Negro women who make a business of producing children . . . for the purpose of securing this easy welfare money." Goldwater stated that welfare "transforms the individual . . . into a dependent animal creature," evoking traditional European American caricatures of African Americans. The rise in the numbers receiving welfare was attributed to "illegitimate children fathered by men who wander from woman to woman, unworried about who will care for their offspring because they know that Aid to Dependent Children payments will." Poverty can be conquered by individual responsibility and thrift; the $20 billion spent each year on liquor and tobacco, not to mention gambling, presumably by poor people, could be invested in industrial development.[28]

In 1969, *The Public Interest,* a leading conservative public policy jounal, dichotomized dependency and independency along racial lines:

> Our welfare policies were ... perfectly rational—and quite efective—as measures for the temporary relief of *competent people* who were unemployed only because of the catastrophe of the Great Depression.... And small wonder that these programs did not work, that instead they aggravated the problem and increased the helplessness, the dependence, the despair of the Negro masses.[29]

Welfare entitlements, as an ersatz anomaly in legal thought, must be replaced by individual responsibility.

In the 1970s, the "New Right" carefully created and elevated the stereotype of the welfare queen, which was then skillfully used to full political advantage by Ronald Reagan, resulting in a stereotypical image of the welfare recipientas a socially deviant woman of color: unwed teen parent, non–wageworker, drug user, long-term recipient. By drawing constant connections between race and dysfunctional behavior, the right was ableto express blatantly racist concepts without shame. For example, in Charles Murray and Richard Herrnstein's 1994 *The Bell Curve,* ten years after Murray's *Losing Ground* (in which he had criticized welfare as creating antisocial economic incentives), they argued that welfare should be abolished because it encouraged "dysgenesis," the outbreeding of intelligent whites by genetically inferior African Americans, Hispanics, and poor whites.[30]

Emphasizing the dichotomy between independence based on effort and market exchange and dependence resulting from government largesse provided a mechanism for the "New Right" increasingly to divide wage workers from welfare recipients and channel wage workers' economic frustrations toward welfare recipients. In 1978, a Heritage Foundation monograph, after overstating the value of benefits by including multiple programs that only some poor people receive some of the time, concluded, "Many welfare families are better off financially, by their participation in several programs, than are the families of workers whose taxes pay for the welfare. . . . The key issue of welfare reform is the conflict between work and welfare."[31] This same marketing of the reductionist and misleading information to dichotomize wage work and welfare continued in 1995, when the libertarian Cato Institute used dissembling calaulations to conclude that welfare pays far more than a low-wage job in every state in the nation.[32]

Reiterating the connection of independence with work, *Issues '88: A Platform for America,* a "political platform for a stronger America" published jointly by the Heritage Foundation and the Free Congress Foundation, advocated mandatory full-time workfare programs (working off one's welfare grant, but not receiving any wage) for women receiving welfare and strongly supported the "right" of women to work at home on cottage industry piecework.[33] The proposal ignored the dependency inherent in at-home wage work: Women are still expected to do the at-home nonwage work, thus reinforcing preexisting social relations and gendered division of labor within the domesic unit; and cottage industry workers are dependent on those who distribute the homework and on other sites of production outside of the homeworker's control. The proposal discussed this "right" as a boon to the family and articulated the importance of "the right of employers to hire employees based at home," thereby avoiding unionization, higher wages, and investment in production sites.

The right's constant formulation of welfare receipt as dependency and wage work as independency has resonated with the U.S. public by playing to its historic ambivalence about assisting the poor and its internalized understanding that the property and contract rights that undergird concepts of independence, effort, and free-market exchange are natural, not socially chosen. The right portrays entitlement in the welfare context as a novel concept connected to the colloquial "getting something for nothing," receiving a benefit without effort and exchange. Thus the general public, not familiar with the centrality of the entitlement concept in the law, equated welfare entitlement with individual failure in a free market. By renaturalizing poverty and reinforcing dependency as receipt of welfare benefits, policy makers and the public have focused on the behavior of the poor instead of addressing the legal entitlements established and maintained by law and a myriad of political decisions and institutions.

But the passage of the PRWORA, ending the sixty-year federal statutory entitlement to AFDC, is not the end of the story. While billed as devolution, or relinquishment of federal government regulation, the enactment of this statute is ultimately state ratification of the background rules of private property and freedom of contract. In other words, we still live in a society that intrinsically establishes through government intervention the entitlements that maintain the current distribution of power and wealth. Thus, the radical nature of the concept of a welfare entitlement should not be lost on us; it forms a central lens through which to understand the contingency and distributive consequences of all underlying entitlements. Our role continues to be to expose those entitlements, to develop new entitlements that redistribute income and power, and to break down the false dichotomies between wage work and welfare. Understanding the progressive potential of this work and learning from our failures are critical to the development of the next generation of poverty activists and lawyers.

NOTES

1. Pub. L. No. 104–193, 110 Stat. 2105, 42 U.S.C. § 601, et seq. (Supp. 1997).
2. See Lucy A. Williams, *The Abuse of Section 1115 Waivers: Welfare Reform in Search of a Standard*, 12 Yale Law and Policy Review 8 (1994).
3. Linda Gordon, *Pitied, but Not Entitled* (New York: The Free Press, 1994), 28, 45–46. Even widows often were scrutinized for their housekeeping, cleanliness, and moral habits. Winifred Bell, *Aid to Dependent Children* (New York: Columbia University Press, 1965), 29.

4. Gordon, *Pitied, but Not Entitled,* 27. The National Congress of Mothers, in lobbying for mother's aid, initially framed the program as providing support for mothers of "the race." Ibid., 62–63. See also Bell, *Aid to Dependent Children,* 29–31, 34–35. Gordon notes that in 1931, only 3 percent of recipients of mother's pensions were African American (*Pitied, but Not Entitled,* 48, n. 41).

5. Mothers themselves were not covered by the program until 1950. Social Security Act Amendments of 1950, Pub. L. No. 81–734, § 323, 64 Stat. 477, 551 (codified as amended at 42 U.S.C. § 606 (1989)).

6. This practice was challenged in *Anderson v. Burson,* 300 F.Supp. 401 (N.D. Ga. 1968). See also Bell, *Aid to Dependent Children,* 63–67, noting that these provisions were utilized not only in the South but also in states such as New York and Michigan; Martha F. Davis, *Brutal Need: Lawyers and the Welfare Rights Movement, 1960–1973* (New Haven: Yale University Press, 1993), 62.

7. "Alabama denied AFDC payments to the children of any mother cohabiting in or outside her home with a single or married able-bodied man; in Louisiana, any home in which an illegitimate child was born subsequent to the receipt of public assistance was considered unsuitable, and the children in that home were denied benefits." *King v. Smith,* 392 U.S. 309, 311, 322 (1962).

8. Of the 184 cases closed due to the challenged regulation in a two-and-a-half-year period in Mrs. Smith's county, 182 involved African American families. In one month alone, all of the 600 terminated families in seven representative Alabama counties were African American. Davis, *Brutal Need,* 64, citing Martin Garbus, *Ready for the Defense* (New York: Farrar, Straus & Giroux, 1971), 159–61. See also Bell, *Aid to Dependent Children,* 29–39, 137–51.

9. *King v. Smith,* 392 U.S. 309, 314.

10. See William H. Simon, *The Invention and Reinvention of Welfare Rights,* 44 Maryland Law Review 1 (1991); Charles A. Reich, *The New Property,* 73 Yale Law Journal 733 (1964).

11. *Flemming v. Nestor,* 363 U.S. 603 (1960); see also *San Antonio Independent School District v. Rodriguez,* 411 U.S. 1 (1973). Note that there are some rare and narrow constitutional entitlements to certain aspects of social provision, such as appointed counsel and right to transcripts on appeal in criminal cases (*Gideon v. Wainwright,* 372 U.S. 335 [1963], *Griffin v. Illinois,* 351 U.S. 12 [1956]) and access to divorce proceedings (*Boddie v. Connecticut,* 401 U.S. 371 [1971]).

12. *Dandridge v. Williams,* 397 U.S. 471 (1970).

13. *King v. Smith*, 392 U.S. 309 (1968), invalidating Alabama's practice of disqualifying from AFDC any mother cohabiting with a man who was not obligated to provide support; 42 U.S.C. § 602 (a)(10); *Goldberg v. Kelly*, 397 U.S. 254 (1970).

14. *Wyman v. James*, 400 U.S. 309 (1971). See further discussion of *Wyman* in Thomas Ross, *The Rhetoric of Poverty: Their Immorality, Our Helplessness*, 79 Georgetown Law Journal 1499, 1522–25 (1991).

15. See generally Davis, *Brutal Need*.

16. Irwin Garfinkel and Sara S. McLanahan, *Single Mothers and Their Children: A New American Dilemma* (Washington: Urban Institute Press, 1986), 55–57.

17. For the classic U.S. law presentation of relationships of domination in wage work as relationships of equality, see *Coppage v. State of Kansas*, 236 U.S. 1, 17–18 (1915).

18. Diane Elson, "From Survival Strategies to Transformation Strategies: Women's Needs and Structural Adjustment," in *Unequal Burden: Economic Crises, Persistent Poverty, and Women's Work*, ed. L. Benería and S. Feldman (Boulder, CO: Westview Press, 1992), 26–48; Lourdes Benería and Martha Roldán, *The Crossroads of Class and Gender* (Chicago: University of Chicago Press, 1987), 40–74; Karen Hossfeld, "'Their Logic Against Them': Contradictions in Sex, Race, and Class in Silicon Valley," in *Women Workers and Global Restructuring*, ed. K. Ward (Ithaca, NY: Cornell University Press, 1990), 149–78; Shandra Talpade Mohanty, "Women Workers and Capitalist Scripts: Ideologies of Domination, Common Interests, and the Politics of Solidarity," in *Feminist Genealogies, Colonial Legacies, Democratic Futures*, ed. M. J. Alexander and C. T. Mohanty (New York: Routledge, 1997), 3–29.

19. Nancy Fraser and Linda Gordon, "A Genealogy of Dependency: Tracing a Keyword of the Welfare State," in *Critical Politics: From the Personal to the Global*, ed. P. Jones (Melbourne: Arena, 1994), 77–109.

20. Alan Schwartz, *Justice and the Law of Contracts: A Case for the Traditional Approach*, 9 Harvard Journal of Law and Public Policy 107, 107 (1986).

21. For a brief summary, see Karl E. Klare, *Legal Theory and Democratic Reconstruction: Reflections on 1989*, 25 University of British Columbia Law Review 69 (1991).

22. William H. Simon, *Rights and Redistribution in the Welfare System*, 38 Stanford Law Review 1431 (1986).

23. Compare Joel F. Handler, *Discretion in Social Welfare: The Uneasy Position in the Rule of Law*, 92 Yale Law Journal 1270 (1983), to William H. Simon, *Legality, Bureaucracy, and Class in the Welfare System*, 92 Yale Law Journal 1198 (1983).

24. See Jonathan Martin Kolkey, *The New Right, 1960–1968* (Washington: University Press of America, 1983), 252; Michael Lind, *Up From Conservatism: Why the Right Is Wrong for America* (New York: The Free Press, 1996), 119–37.

25. Barry Goldwater, "Wanted: A More Conservative GOP," *Human Events* (February 18, 1960): sec. 2, 2; Goldwater, *The Conscience of a Conservative* (1960) 69; see also Charles Mohr, "Goldwater Links the Welfare State to Rise in Crime," *New York Times,* September 11, 1964, A1; Kolkey, *The New Right,* 51–52, citing *Dan Smoot Report,* July 7, 1965, 183.

26. Walter E. Williams, "Government Sanctioned Restraints that Reduce Economic Opportunities for Minorities," *Policy Review,* no. 2 (1977): 10–19, 28 (emphasis added). See also Robert A. Nisbet, "The Dilemma of Conservatives in a Populist Society," *Policy Review,* no. 4 (1978): 91, 97, 138 (emphasis added).

27. Daniel Oliver in William F. Buckley, Jr., M. E. Bradford, Terry Eastland, Daniel Oliver, Joseph Sobran, Phyllis Schlafly, Paul M. Weyrich, R. Emmett Tyrrell, Jr., William J. Bennett, "Heaven on Earth," *Policy Review,* no. 41 (1987): 88, 90 (emphasis added).

28. Kolkey, *The New Right,* 54, citing Rockwell Report, February 1, 1963, 4; Marilyn R. Allen, *Kingdom Digest* (1960), as quoted in *Beacon-Light Herald* (March–April 1961): 33; Goldwater, *The Conscience of a Conservative,* 73; Jenkin Lloyd Jones, "The 'Bum' Factor in Welfare," *Human Events* (May 22, 1965): 8. See also Jenkin Lloyd Jones, "Tough for the Able, Too," *Human Events* (June 24, 1967): 11; Howard Kershner, "Thrift Helps Conquer Poverty," *Human Events* (February 13, 1965): 14.

29. Peter Drucker, "The Sickness of Government," *Public Interest,* 14 (1969): 14 (emphasis added); Ron Haskins and Representative Hank Brown, "A Billion Here, A Billion There: Social Spending Under Ronald Reagan," *Policy Review,* no. 49 (1989): 28.

30. Republican challenger Kirk Fordice defeated Democratic incumbent Ray Mabus in 1991, after Fordice "aired television attack ads with stark images of black welfare recipients" (Michael Shanahan, "Bush Rhetoric Hits Welfare," *Minneapolis Star Tribune,* April 26, 1992, 1A). Former Ku Klux Klan leader David Duke was elected to the Louisiana legislature with anti-welfare rhetoric that "recolored" social problems (Clarence Page, "This Drug Crackdown Targets Color," *Chicago Tribune,* December 31, 1989, 3). See generally Charles Murray and Richard Herrnstein, *The Bell Curve,* chapters 9, 13, 14, 15 (New York: The Free Press, 1994); Charles Murray, *Losing Ground* (New York: Basic Books, 1984).

31. Charles D. Hobbs, *The Welfare Industry* (Washington, DC: Heritage Foundation, 1978), 9, 69.

32. Michael Tanner, Stephen Moore, and David Hartman, "The Work and Welfare Trade-Off: An Analysis of the Total Level of Welfare Benefits by State," *Policy Analysis,* 240 (September 19, 1995): 3.

33. *Issues '88: A Platform for America* (Washington, DC: Heritage Foundation and Free Congress Foundation, 1988), vol. 1, 61–62, 226–27; vol. 3, 23–24.

26 JULES LOBEL

THE POLITICAL TILT OF SEPARATION OF POWERS

JAMES Madison wrote of separation of powers that "no political truth is certainly of greater intrinsic importance." Five years later he termed the doctrine "a first principle of free government," and for more than two hundred years Americans have viewed the constitutional structure of separation of powers set forth in the U.S. Constitution as one of our major contributions to constitutional development in the world.[1]

Yet constitutional discourse about separation of powers too often separates legal doctrine from the historical, social, and political conditions that cultivate and nurture the law and thereby ignores the interests constitutional arrangements serve. The constitutional allocation of power often is viewed mythically as a "political truth," a politically neutral process divorced from result, and the question legal scholars usually ask is whether the process is efficient, democratic, reasonable, or fair rather than what interests it might serve or policy results it might favor. While law review articles and casebooks focus on determining which legal theory—formalist or functionalist are the usual alternatives—best captures the essence of our government's structure, or on harmonizing conflicting Supreme Court decisions, a fuller understanding of separation of powers requires attention to the political, social, and economic influences and interests that underlie constitutional arrangements. This chapter examines the connection between constitutional process and constitutional outcomes—in other words, the political tilt of separation of powers.

THE ORIGINAL DESIGN

The framers of the Constitution had several goals in constructing the separation-of-powers scheme. First, they wanted to establish a stronger, more efficient federal government than had existed under the Articles of Confederation. To do so, the delegates to the Constitutional Convention agreed on an independent executive branch separate from the Congress and judiciary. The framers' preference for a tripartite scheme of government with divided powers reflected their negative experiences both with the Articles of Confederation, which lacked an independent executive and a strong judiciary, and with many of the post-Revolutionary state governments. Pennsylvania operated with a council of governors instead of a unitary executive. The Virginia scheme, which allowed the legislature to choose the governor and his cabinet, was more akin to a parliamentary system of government.

The main reason for adoption of separation of powers, though, was not to promote efficiency but to preclude the "excesses of democracy" that the framers viewed as arbitrary and tyrannical. When one understands the goal of preventing this type of "tyranny," one can see the role of the fundamental social and class interests of the framers. As historian Gordon Wood and others have argued persuasively, the central problem that led to the drafting of the 1787 Constitution was not the weaknesses of the Articles of Confederation but the growing concern over what was perceived to be an excess of democracy in the state governments.[2] It was the interferences with property and creditor rights arising out of the "inconveniences of democracy" that, according to Madison, "were evils . . . which had more perhaps than any thing else, produced this convention."[3]

Madison recognized that the factionalized disputes resulting from democracy were rooted in the "various and unequal distribution of property . . . form[ing] distinct interests in society." His main concern was not that a minority faction would gain dictatorial control but rather that majority factions would gain control of government and enact "unjust" legislation, such as legislation repudiating or relaxing debts seen as unfair to many or interfering with property rights.[4] The problem the framers such as Madison grappled with was how to create a government based on popular sovereignty that also curbed the potential of the majority to interfere with property or contract rights.

The Madisonian and Federalist solution to these vices of democracy lay in creating institutional arrangements designed to produce a spirit of moderation, to ensure that factions whose "distinct . . . interests" favored "schemes of oppression," such as renunciation of debts or violation of property rights, would be unable to "discover their own strength and act in unison" so as to control government.[5] Separation of powers, which made it difficult for a majority faction seeking radical change to gain control of the entire national government, was one of those mechanisms.

To further their goal of creating a stable government that would not act radically or impulsively, the framers added checks and balances to the "pure" doctrine of separation of powers. Separation of powers was understood by many Americans of the Revolutionary War period to require a strict demarcation of power into three independent branches to promote both efficient and limited government: Each branch could operate decisively in its limited sphere of power. But the excesses of democracy that so concerned the framers led them to look to the British experience of mixed government whereby each branch of government—the monarchy, the House of Lords, and the House of Commons—represented a different social class. Knowing that such an open class-based system was unacceptable, the framers instead divided each branch by function (although some of the framers, such as John Dickinson, openly wished the Senate to bear "as strong a likeness to the British House of Lords as possible").[6] They retained the "mixed government" perspective so that each branch would have the ability to interfere with and thereby check or balance the others. To division of power was added such features as judicial review, executive veto of legislative acts, senatorial ratification of treaties, and legislative approval of Cabinet officials, all of which reflected an intermixing and not a pure separation of power.

The Constitution's separation of powers and checks-and-balances arrangements brilliantly mediated the tension between popular control of government and the protection against redistribution of property from majoritarian rule. Checks and balances particularly help obstruct majoritarian radical change by ensuring that even if a radical political group gains control of one, or even both, elected branches of government, it will be difficult to implement its program because it can be checked by another branch. Only a sustained political movement could capture all three branches of government, and such a majority coalition would be difficult to maintain.

Divided and balanced government would lead to limited government and favor government inaction: In Montesquieu's words, such division of power "should naturally form a state of repose or inaction."[7] Madison's argument for checks and balances, that "ambition must be made to counteract ambition," reflected a Newtonian perspective that a proper government structure, like natural matter, consists of forces pushing in opposite directions so as to create equipoise.

The elitist nature of the checks and balances scheme adopted by the framers was controversial from the beginning. The anti-Federalists, and later the Jeffersonians, objected to the checks-and-balances aspects of the Constitution, particularly the presidential veto power over legislation and judicial review. More sympathetic to majoritarian radical change, they rejected mixed, balanced government, preferring instead to rely on the electorate as the basic check on governmental power. They favored a "pure" separation of power along the lines of constitutional structure that triumphed in France, which strictly divided power between the branches but did not contain such checks-and-balances features as judicial review.

The foreign policy separation-of-powers provisions also favored a substantive policy of inaction, although for different policy reasons. The newly independent United States was a weak military power having strong commercial interests and opportunities. At the time Washington assumed the presidency, the U.S. Army consisted of fewer than 840 men. As commander in chief, Washington was without any naval forces to command.[8] Faced with stronger European powers threatening to drag the country into warfare and a decentralized political system made up of fractious and bickering state governments, a cautious foreign policy based on respect for international norms was a necessity. Early U.S. foreign policy was therefore designed to avoid, as much as possible, political entanglements in European affairs. As Attorney General Edmund Jennings Randolph observed in 1795,

> An infant country, deep in debt; necessitated to borrow in Europe; without manufacture; without a land or naval force; without a competency of arms or ammunition; with a commerce, closely connected beyond the Atlantic with a certainty of enhancing the price of foreign productions, and diminishing that of our own; with a constitution more than four years old; in a state of probation, and not exempt from foes[—]such a country can have no greater curse in store for her than war. That peace was our policy has been admitted by Congress, and by France herself.[9]

The constitutional arrangements arrived at in Philadelphia reflect the strategic goal of extending commerce with Europe while avoiding political entanglements and war with European powers. The foreign affairs provisions contain several important themes: maintaining a strong central government capable of conducting foreign policy and asserting U.S. sovereignty, dividing power within that central government so the president could not unilaterally involve the new republic in disastrous overseas engagements, and ensuring that U.S. foreign policy be based on law, including international law.

The framers understood the connection between constitutional procedure and substance; their procedural choices were designed to achieve certain substantive goals. To ensure that force be used only to counter serious threats to national security, Congress, not the president, was given the power to commit the United States to armed conflict. To James Madison, the executive branch was more likely to involve us in warfare because "war is, in fact, the true nurse of executive aggrandizement."[10] Thomas Jefferson desired an "effectual check to the Dog of War," James Madison noted that Congress would be "clogging rather than facilitating war," and James Wilson, a key figure at the convention, argued that the Constitution was designed not to "hurry us into war."[11] The president's power to use armed force was narrowly circumscribed to defending against an attack on U.S. armed forces or territory. Moreover, the Constitution accorded Congress the power to issue letters of marque and reprisal, which was viewed by our early leaders as the authority to authorize a broad spectrum of armed hostilities short of declared war.

The constitutional commitment to Congress of the power to declare war was not premised solely on the perceived value of democratic decision making and open debate that the legislature could provide; it also represented a substantive judgment on the part of the framers that entry into war should be difficult. That substantive judgment was conditioned on both general principle and the historical circumstances in which the leaders of the republic found themselves.

The framers were also wary of providing the executive with unilateral power over the other key area of U.S. foreign policy in the eighteenth century, the making and terminating of treaties with foreign countries. As Alexander Hamilton noted, the "history of human conduct does not make it wise to commit interests of so delicate and momentous a kind [entering into treaties] to the sole disposal . . . of a president."[12] Thus, the Constitution expressly limits the executive's role in forming a treaty by requiring the advice and consent of two-thirds of the Senate.

Significantly, Article VI of the Constitution confers on treaties the status of supreme law of the land. While primarily intended to make treaties binding on the states, the status of treaties as domestic law also suggests that they could not be repealed or violated by executive action alone. The executive's constitutional obligation to "take care that the laws be faithfully executed" suggests that he is not empowered to repeal or ignore the law. While the text of the Constitution is silent on the issue of who could abrogate a treaty, the early leaders of the republic and drafters of the Constitution believed that the president could not do so alone. As vice president, Jefferson argued: "Treaties being declared equally with the law of the United States, to be the supreme law of the land, it is understood that an act of the legislature alone can declare them infringed and rescinded."[13]

The original understanding of the governmental structure articulated in 1787 was generally followed for the first century of the republic: Checks and balances served the purpose the framers intended, and the presidency was relatively weak in both domestic and foreign policy. Checks and balances operated to restrain congressional and state efforts to restrict property rights, and when fifty years after *Marbury v. Madison* the Supreme Court next exercised its power of judicial review over congressional legislation in the infamous *Dred Scott v. Sanford* case, it struck down an act of Congress that the Court held interfered with slaveowners' property interests in their slaves.[14] It was therefore no accident that the leading Southern politician John C. Calhoun was a strong supporter of checks and balances, defending the president's veto power and judicial review. Had the South not seceded in 1861, one can only speculate how far the Republicans could have gone in adopting their program in the face of what would have undoubtedly been strong opposition from the Supreme Court.

The executive's domestic authority was fairly limited: for example, President Washington refused to introduce "any topic which relates to legislative matters to members of either house of Congress, lest it should be suggested that he wished to influence the question before it."[15] Although a strong president such as Andrew Jackson could use the veto power to defy Congress and make the presidency more than a mere executive office, and the Civil War gave Lincoln substantial emergency power, for the most part the executive branch was relatively weak. As late as the latter part of the nineteenth century, scholars such as the young Woodrow Wilson complained of congressional dominance.

In foreign policy also the original design worked fairly well for the first century of the nation's existence. During its first significant and prolonged military conflict, the quasi-war with France in the 1790s, the Adams administration proceeded cautiously, generally following the constitutional mandate of seeking congressional approval for U.S. military actions or terminating treaties. Thus when the United States decided to abrogate its treaties of alliance and friendship with France in the late 1790s, all agreed that annulling the treaties could not be undertaken by the executive alone.[16] The administration's supporters introduced a bill into Congress to annul the treaties, reflecting their understanding of the Constitution's distribution of power.

The judiciary also played an important role in restraining executive adventurism. In *Little v. Barreme,* a unanimous Supreme Court upheld the imposition of individual liability on a naval commander for his seizure of a merchant ship suspected of trading with the French during the quasi-war.[17] The Court imposed liability on the commander despite the fact that he had acted pursuant to a presidential order, because his acts violated a congressional statute.

Even in the early years of the republic, the Constitution's foreign policy strictures were subject to differing interpretations and were at times stretched by presidents. The Madison administration's fomenting of rebellion in Florida in the early 1800s in order to obtain the territory from Spain is but one example of executive conduct of a dubious constitutional nature. Indeed, the early leaders were cautious internationally yet dreamed of empire. Jefferson claimed, "I am persuaded no constitution was ever before so well calculated as ours for extensive empire and self-government."[18] The conflict between a desire for empire and U.S. military and political weakness relative to Europe produced executive action that often threatened or even exceeded constitutional limitations. This was particularly true with respect to weaker powers on our borders: Indian tribes, at times Spain, and later Mexico.

Yet despite these inconsistencies, the first few decades of U.S. foreign policy were characterized by joint executive-legislative participation in most foreign policy decisions and generally cautious executive use of U.S. military force. Abraham Sofaer, who exhaustively studied those early years, concludes that while presidents took the lead in foreign affairs activities and sometimes engaged in activities that "exceeded the bounds of behavior by which they publicly purported to be governed," "at no time did the executive claim 'inherent' power to initiate military actions. . . . Furthermore, no President or other official of the executive branch ever claimed that Congress lacked power to control or dictate executive conduct."[19]

EMERGENCE OF THE IMPERIAL PRESIDENT

The twentieth century produced a dramatic change in our separation-of-powers scheme, with an enormous expansion of executive power over both foreign and domestic policies. By the 1970s, the distinguished historian Arthur Schlesinger termed our modern executive "the imperial president," and the eminent conservative legal scholar Philip Kurland wrote, "The separation of powers as a doctrine restraining the exercise of power by the executive branch has all but disappeared." While conservatives still write of the "fettered presidency," the true nature of our modern chief executive is best captured by the title of a recent article on the executive, "The Most Dangerous Branch."[20]

The rise of the modern, powerful executive is inextricably linked to political, social, and economic changes undergone by the United States since the end of the nineteenth century. Those changes transformed the substantive interests that the framers sought to protect, producing pressures for government action that bent and ultimately fractured the careful separation-of-powers scheme originally contained in the Constitution.

The first and probably most powerful driving force behind the growth of executive power was the changing role of the United States in the world. In the late nineteenth and early twentieth centuries, the United States turned toward globalism and international power. With the extension of U.S. power abroad, the limitations on presidential power so carefully guarded by the early leaders of the republic began to erode. The unilateral executive use of force abroad, beyond merely protecting American citizens, and the increasing use of executive agreements to bypass the treaty procedure contributed to the evisceration of the limitations on executive power. Observers as diverse as author James Bryce, editor E. L. Bodkin, and military strategist Alfred Thafer Mahan worried that the Constitution was inconsistent with these new imperial aspirations.[21]

A critical theoretical transformation began to unfold during these early years of globalism. Inherent presidential power to meet crises was for the first time seen as emanating from within the Constitution. President Theodore Roosevelt articulated a broad theory of executive emergency power. Unlike Jefferson, Roosevelt grounded this emergency power on a notion of inherent constitutional authority, stating that the president had the "legal right to do whatever the needs of the people demand, unless the Constitution or the laws explicitly forbid him to do it."[22]

The Supreme Court provided encouragement to the theory of inherent executive constitutional power to meet exigencies. In 1890, in the course of ruling that the president had the power to provide the justices with personal bodyguards, the Court noted that the president possessed broad, implied constitutional powers beyond the execution of treaties and congressional acts.[23]

The scholarly community also recognized that the new role of the United States in the world required changes in the traditional constitutional model. For an astute academic such as Woodrow Wilson, the assertion of power abroad "challenged the balance of [constitutional] parts," projecting the president "at the front of government." According to Wilson, the traditional theory of the Constitution was premised on Newtonian science, a paradigm that viewed the universe as composed of opposite forces balancing each other to create symmetry and order.[24] The metaphor of Newtonian physics underscored a dualist conception of politics and constitutional law that imposed a strict boundary on executive power.[25] Recognizing the constitutional transformation wrought by rising U.S. power, Wilson substituted Darwinian evolution for Newtonian physics as the inspiration of U.S. constitutionalism and thus provided an intellectual framework for the practical shading of legal boundaries limiting executive power.

The expansion of executive power that started at the end of the nineteenth century culminated after World War II. The United States' new role as the world's dominant superpower fed an obsession with crisis and altered our notion of national security. Every challenge to U.S. hegemony anywhere in the world began to be perceived as a threat to national security. Those perceived threats to U.S. power generated a profound sense of crisis, leading William Fulbright and others to argue that traditional democratic separation-of-powers principles had to yield to the need for strong executive power to meet the new situation and maintain U.S. power.[26] Schlesinger analogized the U.S. perspective to the state of mind of the Roman Empire:

> There was no corner of the known world where some interest was not alleged to be in danger or under actual attack. If the interests were not Roman, they were those of Rome's allies; and if Rome had no allies, then allies would be invented. . . . Rome was always being attacked by evil-minded neighbors, always fighting for a breathing space.[27]

National Security Council (NSC) Paper 68, issued in April 1950 as "the first comprehensive statement of a national strategy after World War II," foresaw "an indefinite period of tension and danger." In response, the NSC called for a massive military buildup and, as President Truman later wrote, "a great change in our normal peacetime way of doing things."[28]

Modern presidents have relied on three key constitutional sources to justify their expansion of executive power: the executive power clause, the commander in chief clause, and the executive's implied power over foreign affairs.

Presidents such as Theodore Roosevelt, Harry Truman, and Richard Nixon asserted that because Article I limits congressional power to those powers "herein granted," while Article II's grant of "executive power" has no such limitation, the president has inherent power to do either anything necessary to preserve the United States or, even more broadly, anything not explicitly forbidden by the Constitution. Even though this executive power clause argument has been condemned by commentators and some courts, the executive has continued to rely on it to assert broad power over the conduct of U.S. foreign policy. The ill-defined breadth of these presidential arguments was accurately foreseen by Daniel Webster in his 1835 address to the Senate: "Executive power is not a thing so well known, and so accurately defined, as that the written constitution of a limited government can be supposed to have conferred it in the lump. What is executive power? What are its boundaries?"[29]

Second, the executive has justified broad emergency power through resort to the commander in chief clause of Article II. The traditional limit of the commander in chief's power to that necessary to repel sudden attack or resist invasion until Congress has declared war was abandoned after the Cold War. The Justice Department argued that the president had the unilateral power to send troops to Vietnam because the interdependence of the twentieth-century world meant that all warfare anywhere in the world might "impinge directly upon the nation's security."[30] Therefore, modern presidents have articulated a constitutional power to send forces into combat whenever they detect threats to national security. Under this model, the commander in chief's powers, in Dean Rusk's approving words, "are as large as the situation requires."[31] If any threat to U.S. security around the world activates the executive's war powers, then the distinction between the executive emergency power to repel an attack and congressional power to authorize the introduction of U.S. forces into hostilities loses significance.

Finally, the executive branch often relied on the president's generic and ill-defined power as "the sole organ of foreign affairs," articulated by dicta in *United States v. Curtiss-Wright Export Corp.* in 1936, to justify broad assertion of power over foreign policy.[32] Recent administrations have asserted forcefully that the Constitution limits congressional authority to restrain the exercise of the president's power as the "sole organ" of foreign affairs power.[33]

In most cases Congress and the judiciary have assented to these assertions of executive power. Congress has delegated broad power to the president to authorize activities such as covert actions or embargoes of trade with foreign countries and has refused to enforce statutes such as the War Powers Resolution that provide limits on executive action. The judiciary often has refused to intervene in cases challenging U.S. foreign policy, as was the case during the Vietnam War. Instead, judges have sought refuge in a judicially created avenue that allows them to avoid review, called the political question doctrine.[34]

The result of executive assertiveness, congressional compliance, and judicial abstention has been a reworking of the original constitutional understandings. Post–World War II executives have repeatedly used U.S. forces without congressional authorization, allegedly for defensive purposes pursuant to their commander-in-chief power. Moreover, the 1950s witnessed the rise of covert operations involving the use of paramilitary troops to overthrow or support foreign governments as an important instrument of U.S. foreign policy. Between 1953 and 1973 the CIA used paramilitary troops in at least eight major efforts against foreign governments.[35] Because of the post-Vietnam political and legal objections to using U.S. troops to achieve foreign policy goals, the Reagan administration increasingly turned to local paramilitary operations to execute foreign policy. These covert operations are not initiated pursuant to congressional authorization, thus they violate the constitutional mandate that all U.S. uses of force be authorized by Congress.[36]

Similarly, separation of powers in the making and breaking of treaties has been undermined. There has been a spectacular rise in the number of executive agreements with other nations, which do not require ratification by two-thirds of the Senate. While the first 150 years of our nation's history produced a rough equivalence between the number of executive agreements and official treaties entered into by our government, since 1939 close to 95 percent of all international agreements entered into by the United States have been executive agreements, not treaties.[37] Moreover, twentieth-century presidents have asserted the power to terminate treaties unilaterally, a practice the Supreme Court refused to review in a case involving President Carter's termination of our treaty with Taiwan.[38]

The executive's domestic power also expanded dramatically, fueled by the changing capitalist economy in the latter part of the nineteenth century. The rise of large monopolistic or oligarchic corporations in the late nineteenth and early twentieth centuries required more government regulation. While it is certainly true, as some commentators suggest,[39] that the greater democratic legitimacy of the president provided by national elections and mass-media focus has contributed to the rise of presidential power, and that new technology has led to greater executive power, or as one scholar deterministically argued "the higher the state of technological development, the greater the concentration of political power,"[40] the critical factor behind the rise of executive power domestically was the regulatory needs of twentieth-century capitalism.

Increased national regulation required a strong central government, one that operated not primarily through division of power and the tension of checks and balance, but through harmony and cooperation between the branches, with a strong executive at its apex.[41] A broad coalition of interests, including farmers, workers, and big business, formed to support such increased government regulation.[42] As early as 1904, the *Wall Street Journal* editorialized that "[i]n the end it is probable that the corporations will find that a reasonable system of federal regulation is to their interest."[43] Gabriel Kolko argues in his study of the Progressive Era: "Progressivism was not the triumph of small business over the trusts as has often been suggested, but the victory of big business in achieving the rationalization of the economy that only the federal government could provide."[44]

Starting with the Progressive Era at the turn of the century, and dramatically escalating during the New Deal, reformers sought to transform the separation-of-powers structure of government to deal with the social and economic issues that stemmed from modern industrial capitalism. The New Deal reformers understood that the original constitutional structure protected the existing distribution of wealth and prevented the federal government from taking action necessary to stabilize the economy and protect the poor from the fluctuations of the market.[45] While the framers defined liberty negatively and structured the Constitution to check potential government action interfering with society, the New Deal viewed liberty as requiring positive federal action regulating the free market. Franklin Roosevelt and his New Dealers dramatically increased the power of the presidency and expanded the power of administrative agencies to regulate the economy. The resulting rise of the administrative state, controlled by virtually unchecked executives who were viewed as nonpartisan technicians combining executive, legislative, and judicial functions, eroded traditional separation-of-powers restraints.

The rise of the modern presidency wielding enormous power domestically and internationally has changed the original separation-of-powers scheme. The president now exercises substantial lawmaking power and in fact has been termed our chief lawmaker. Unlike the practice during the early years of the republic, the president now proposes a budget to Congress and initiates a great deal of proposed legislation. While the framers anticipated that the executive veto power would be used primarily to check the legislature's passage of unconstitutional bills, modern presidencies utilize the veto power to effectuate legislative policy, and the recent grant of presidential line-item veto power only increases executive authority. Congress's willingness to delegate expansive authority to the executive to administrate the law with only little guidance or standards, combined with the demise of the nondelegation doctrine that required clear standards from Congress, has led to the executive exercising tremendous policy-making discretion in areas as diverse as regulation of the environment, occupational safety and health, energy, and communications.[46]

Finally, the rise of so-called independent agencies—sometimes termed the "headless fourth branch of government"—also has strengthened the president, because the president usually has the power to appoint agency directors and provides supervision of agency rule making. The presidency as an institution has grown Hydra-like: As late as Herbert Hoover's day the White House staff numbered only three secretaries, a military and naval aide, and forty clerks, while today the White House staff numbers about a thousand.

REFORMIST EFFORTS AND SUBSTANTIVE POLICIES

The twin disasters of Vietnam and Watergate created pressure to restore limitations on executive powers. Even strong supporters of the growth of executive power during the 1940s and 1950s, such as Arthur Schlesinger and William J. Fulbright, began to question whether the pendulum had swung too far.[47] Congress sought to reassert its power in a series of post-Vietnam statutes, such as the War Powers Resolution of 1973, which provided automatic withdrawal of U.S. forces after sixty days absent explicit congressional approval; the Hughes-Ryan Amendment, asserting oversight over covert action; and the International Economic Emergencies Powers Act (IEEPA).[48]

Two decades later these statutes lie in shambles, wrecked by presidential defiance, congressional acquiescence, and judicial undermining. Virtually all observers recognize the War Powers Resolution to be a failure. No president ever has filed a report to start the sixty-day clock running, despite executive introduction of armed forces into hostile situations in Indochina, Iran, Lebanon, Central America, Grenada, Libya, the

Persian Gulf, Kuwait, Somalia, Bosnia, and Haiti. Congress has challenged this noncompliance only once, without a decisive result.[49] The judiciary has refused to adjudicate claims challenging executive action as a violation of the resolution, most recently holding that a challenge by a serviceman to President Bush's deployment of U.S. forces in the Persian Gulf was unjustifiable.[50] Various efforts have been made to amend the resolution by repealing its most important operative measures, including the sixty-day clock.

The reason for the failure of the post-Vietnam reforms lies in the very forces and substantive policies that underlie the transformation of our original constitutional understandings in the late nineteenth century. The reformist failure not only is a legal and institutional failure, but is primarily caused by an aggressive U.S. assertion of power in the international arena. To restore republican thought in the area of foreign affairs requires not merely procedural change but substantive reevaluation.

Old lessons have to be relearned constantly. The debate over the Iran-Contra scandal narrowly focused on such issues as what the president knew, whether the law had been violated, and whether new legislation was needed. Commentators generally ignored the causal connection between the persistent failure of the executive to heed constitutional or legal limitations in its efforts to overthrow the Nicaraguan government and an aggressive view of U.S. power in the world. Yet two decades before, the Vietnam War vividly brought this lesson into focus.

As the war in Vietnam dragged on, thoughtful commentators began to question whether our constitutional assumptions could withstand the quest for empire. The doubts that had earlier appeared in the 1890s as to whether the Constitution could function "for a conquering nation" reappeared forcefully in the 1960s. Henry Steele Commager wrote that the "abuse of power by Presidents is a reflection, and perhaps a consequence, of abuse of power by the American . . . nation." In the long run, "abuse of executive power cannot be separated from abuse of national power. If we subvert world order and destroy world peace, we must inevitably subvert and destroy our own political institutions first." The answer to abuse of executive power was, and still is, neither the removal of evil people nor the reform of insufficient laws, but rather the dissipation of the "forces, motives and fears which underlie the exercise and the rationale of excessive presidential power. "[51]

The Vietnam War also led William Fulbright to reevaluate dramatically his earlier views on empowering the presidency. The failure in Vietnam provided an occasion to rethink the messianic anticommunism that drove the United States to intervene unilaterally anywhere in the world in the name of national security. For Fulbright the conflict was clear. If "America is to become an empire, there is very little chance that it can avoid becoming a virtual dictatorship as well."[52]

While better presidents, advisers, and laws are both necessary and significant in curbing executive power, the failure of legal reforms reflects the nation's failure to alter dramatically its substantive worldview. The procedural constraints the Constitution places on executive action reflect a substantive vision of America's place and role in the world that does not comport with its new role as the dominant world power.

In domestic policy, there also has been increasing dissatisfaction with the uncontrolled power wielded by administrative agencies and the executive branch. Congress enacted the Administrative Procedures Act in 1966 to subject administrative decisions to some judicial control, and efforts have been made to bring the agencies under stricter executive control. But as in foreign policy, the power of the executive branch continues to increase, and despite reformists efforts Martin Flaherty probably is right that, as we enter the twenty-first century, "never has the executive branch been more powerful, nor more dominant over its two counterparts, than since the New Deal."[53]

THE FUTURE OF SEPARATION OF POWERS

Controversy over the Constitution's allocation of power continues unabated with the basic tensions between efficiency and checks on power, interbranch cooperation and conflict, and strong executive power and balanced government still present.

Powerful adherents from both major parties share the view that conflict and confrontation between the president and Congress must be reduced and that the constitutional separation of powers must be weakened further. Lloyd Cutler, President Carter's White House Counsel; Douglass Dillon, a distinguished public servant in the Eisenhower and Kennedy administrations; and Senator Nancy Kassebaum joined other luminaries in establishing the Committee on the Constitutional System in 1982. The frustrations Cutler and others felt during the Carter administration inspired their renewed interest in a more parliamentary system of government as a means of restoring executive authority to lead the country and act decisively. The committee's *Basic Policy Statement* asserted, "The checks and balances inspired by the experience of the Eighteenth Century have led repeatedly, in the Twentieth Century, to governmental stalemate and deadlock, to indecision and inaction in the face of urgent problems."[54] Echoing Senator Fulbright's sentiments during the early 1960s, Dillon asked whether the modern United States could "continue to afford the luxury of the separation of power."[55]

The Reagan and Bush administrations and such allies as Supreme Court Justice Antonin Scalia and legal scholars associated with the Federalist Society also favored strengthening the executive. But instead of a parliamentary system these conservatives support a "pure," formalistic separation-of-powers doctrine with a removal of many of the checks-and-balances restraints on executive power. While Cutler, Dillon, and their reformist movement sought to augment government efficiency and action through interbranch cooperation, Scalia and the Federalist theorists appear less concerned with efficiency values than with political accountability. According to prominent Federalist theorist Steven Calabresi, members of Congress represent special local interests transformed by the dramatic expansion of federal spending into "constituent service agents whose raison d'être is to recover for their constituencies as much federal largesse as possible," which "ultimately intensifies the growth in the size of the federal pie."[56] The result, according to Calabresi, "is an unmitigated redistributive disaster." "The only practicable way out of this situation is to strengthen presidential power and *unitariness*." Unitariness to Calabresi and Scalia means that all power they denote as executive should be lodged with the president, and legislation such as the Special Prosecutor Act that gives law-enforcing power—a quintessential executive power, according to Scalia—to an entity independent of presidential control is unconstitutional. The underlying policy reason for favoring formalist separation of power that removes the checks on executive power is that "the President is unique in our constitutional system as being the only official who is accountable to a national voting electorate and no one else." Thus, according to Calabresi and like-minded legal scholars, enhanced executive power favors decision making based on national and not local or special interests.

Other proponents of increased executive power favor the substantive goal of maintaining an assertive foreign policy. According to this outlook, the magnitude of the threat facing the country requires a strong president and a cooperative Congress supportive of executive initiatives. For these "interventionists," the lesson of the Vietnam War and the Iran-Contra affair is not that more congressional checks on executive power are needed but rather that such checks should be removed. The escalation of the Iran-Contra affair, for example, is ascribed to Congress's attempts to interfere with executive conduct of foreign policy.[57] Prominent interventionists comment that the constraints imposed by Congress "have undermined rather than enhanced deterrence" and "fueled potentially catastrophic constitutional confrontations with the Presidency;"[58] Vietnam and Iran-Contra require reform to "restore the Presidency to the position it held just a few administrations ago."[59] Judge Abraham Sofaer, who was legal advisor to the State Department in the Reagan administration, expressed the connection between constitutional process and the substance of national security decision making when he stated that "the President is not so powerless, nor the nation so helpless" as to accept reformist proposals that would strengthen the War Powers Resolution.[60]

While the "presidentialists" seek to expand executive power, the "balancers" hope to restore the original checks-and-balances scheme. The process-oriented balancers all seek to restrain executive power by reinvigorating congressional and judicial oversight. As Peter Shane argues in rejecting the formalist "unitary" executive position, "The Constitution's contribution to accountability depends primarily upon its structure of checks and balances. Keeping agencies attentive to multiple voices is likely to maximize the dialogue, openness and responsiveness that define accountability in its most important sense."[61] In foreign affairs, reformers such as Harold Koh advocate a new national security "charter" that would "seek to alter recurrent patterns of executive behavior by restructuring the *institutional* attributes" that contribute to executive excesses.[62] Koh's design would encourage Congress and the judiciary to become involved in foreign policy issues. Other, more specific process-oriented reforms would provide for judicial review of executive use of force pursuant to the War Powers Resolution or the Constitution.[63]

Progressives have remained on the sidelines in the modern separation-of-powers debate. Perhaps this silence stems from the predilection of most progressive activists and scholars to focus on rights, or because separation-of-powers issues tend to be abstract. A progressive critique of separation of powers requires connecting substantive policy with structural process and emphasizing the social forces underlying such structures in any historical era.

Indeed the left generally did connect policy and process during the first 150 years of our nation's history and for that reason generally rejected the main checks-and-balances features of the Constitution, particularly judicial review. As the prominent labor lawyer and socialist Louis Boudin noted in his 1932 book entitled *Government by Judiciary*,

"For a century and a quarter—ever since the decision of *Marbury v. Madison*—the Judicial Power has been the storm centre of American politics. Every popular, democratic or progressive movement since that famous adjudication . . . has had an anti-judicial point."[64] In an influential critique the Progressive Era historian Charles Beard excoriated separation of powers as a device designed by the framers "to check certain kinds of positive action that might be advocated to the detriment of established and acquired rights."[65] The left's attacks on separation of powers ranged from progressive politicians merely seeking to reform and democratize the structure of government to communist theorists such as Lenin rejecting the entire notion of separation of powers in favor of unitary government.

A progressive view of separation of powers must recognize the tensions and ambiguity contained in our constitutional structure. That structure, designed to forestall radical change in property relations, also sought to limit executive adventurism abroad, making imperial foreign policy more difficult. While favoring certain status quo substantive goals, separation of powers provides both democratic stability and a space for progressive movements to develop and grow. Our Constitution's separation of powers contains a conservative bias toward preserving existing social relations yet also provides a forum of struggle that is flexible enough to be used by popular movements to advance their aspirations.

For example, while it is correct that judicial review has played a pernicious role in the broad sweep of U.S. history, in various historical periods such as the 1950s and 1960s the judiciary has read the aspirations of oppressed groups into the text of our fundamental law. Separation of powers impedes radical changes, yet the division of government into three separate branches expands the points of access to government, increasing the potential that popular movements can influence one branch to promote social reform.[66] What is required is an understanding of the contradictory nature of the Constitution and the complex interrelationship between the Constitution as a conservative document and as a historically contested forum of struggle. That analysis must eschew an abstract, global reading of separation of powers as inherently progressive or reactionary and instead investigate the role it plays in a particular historical context.

The dominant feature of the post–New Deal separation-of-powers landscape is the rise of a powerful executive branch. In this historical era the main danger to popular movements both abroad and at home comes from an overreaching and imperial presidency. While there is no persuasive evidence that any of the three branches is more progressive or conservative than any other, there is strong evidence that the accumulation of power in one person's hands poses grave dangers. Former President Nixon's remark in a television interview with David Frost that "when the President does it, that means that it is not illegal" may be an extreme view, but it is not much different than the position the executive branch took during the Iran-Contra scandal.[67]

The Progressive and New Deal critique that separation of powers was both antidemocratic and stifling of government action eventually focused on the latter problem. The New Deal's antidote to the status quo bias of the Constitution—strengthening the executive to foster strong, effective action in both domestic and foreign crises—turned out to be even more antidemocratic than the original separation-of-powers scheme: While the president's mandate stems from a national election, that election and the subsequent administration that results from it are removed from popular control over the mechanisms of government. The vast administrative state has placed government even further from people's input. Presidential elections illustrate Madison's famous argument in *Federalist* no. 10 that a large election district encompassing a large number of interests is likely to produce a moderate representative. Moreover, the elected president is far removed from the population that elected him or her and illustrates framer Benjamin Rush's view of democracy, that although "all power is derived from the people, they possess it only on the days of their elections. After this it is the property of their rulers."[68]

The structure of the U.S. economy and foreign policy as presently constituted favors a strong executive, and only a restructuring of the polity and economy to be less hegemonic abroad and more democratic at home will reduce executive power and revitalize separation of powers. That would take a transformation equivalent to the New Deal coalition, but this time instead of creating a New Deal–style "broker state" that only represents "a concert of organized interests," the government must be opened up to participation by people now excluded.[69]

A long-term transformative vision must insist on two very different but complementary changes from our present situation. The first would be the further development of the international system of governance that would subject all states, including the United States, to the rulings and orders of international bodies such as an international court or legislature. The second change would involve reviving communalist politics in which the citizenry, often acting through local communities, plays a more active role both in determining our relations with peoples of other nations and in our national system of governance. Both changes would supplement and ultimately transform traditional separation-of-powers restraints: one by internationalizing government, the other by localizing it and making the citizenry active participants in the decision-making process. The constitutional restraints on the executive are the product of a fear of unilateral decision making by any one person. In an effective multinational system, unilateral U.S. executive power would be restrained by international, political, and legal processes. Moreover, active citizen and local participation in foreign policy making would reduce the power of the centralized government, rendering unrestrained executive adventurism abroad and administrative bureaucratic government at home less likely. The legal restraints currently provided horizontally within the national government by separation of powers would be supplemented by vertical restraints imposed by international society and popular community pressures.

The resulting normative vision probably would rely more on community interaction and less on fixed rules to govern our lives. Eschewing a reliance on fixed rules requires decision making that focuses on the particular consequences of the concrete alternative possibilities in discrete situations.[70] Frank Michelman argues that much of our constitutional dialogue occurs outside the formal channels of electoral and legislative politics; for example, in town meetings, voluntary organizations, and local government agencies. "Those are all arenas of potentially transformative dialogue."[71] To citizen activists of the last few decades, law is not merely the positivistic command of the sovereign but a product of the community's experiences and the values that it articulates.[72] This vision of law as deriving from community interaction is more multidimensional and particularized than the traditional model of liberal constitutional thought.

The possibility of these transformations lies within the shadows of the present.[73] While the bright hopes of a world government that accompanied the establishment of the United Nations have faded, the end of the Cold War, the increasing interdependence of the world's economies, and the awareness of the vulnerability of the global environment have renewed interest in multilateral institutions and cooperative approaches. In addition, the revival of scholarly interest in citizen participation in government has proceeded apace with renewed efforts at citizen participation in governmental affairs.[74] Localities have begun passing resolutions on foreign policy issues, adopting sister cities in other parts of the world and actively refusing to cooperate with federal emergency plans.[75]

Citizens across the country have engaged in acts of civil disobedience to display their disapproval of nuclear weapons, U.S. policies in Central America, and the policy of interdicting Haitian refugees. While these efforts are on the margin of current mainstream thought on foreign affairs and domestic policy, it is possible that the current citizens movement will move from the margin to the center in the twenty-first century.

NOTES

1. [James Madison], "Federalist no. 47," in The Federalist Papers, ed. J. Cooke (Middletown, CT: Wesleyan University Press, 1961), 324; James Madison, *Philadelphia National Gazette,* February 6, 1792.
2. Gordon Wood, "Democracy and the Constitution," in *How Democratic is the Constitution?* ed. R. Goldwin and W. Schambra (Washington: American Enterprise Institute, 1980), 12–13. See also Gordon Wood, *The Creation of the American Republic* (Chapel Hill: University of North Carolina Press, 1969), 166–67; *Myers v. United States,* 272 U.S. 52, 293 (1926) (Brandeis dissenting).
3. *The Records of the Federal Convention of 1787,* vol. 1, ed. M. Farrand (New Haven, CT: Yale University Press, 1966), 134–35 [hereinafter *Records*] (statements of James Madison).
4. [Madison], "Federalist no. 10," 59, 60–61.
5. Ibid., 63, 61, 64.
6. Wood, *The Creation of the American Republic,* 554.
7. Charles-Louis Montesquieu, *The Spirit of the Laws,* ed. P. Carrithers (1977), 211, cited in Cass Sunstein, *Constitutionalism After the New Deal,* 101 Harvard Law Review 421, 434 (1987).
8. Abraham Sofaer, *War, Foreign Affairs, and Constitutional Power* (Cambridge, UK: Ballinger, 1976), 116.
9. Letter from Edmund Jennings Randolph to James Monroe (June 1, 1795), cited in Jules Lobel, *The Rise and Decline of the Neutrality Act: Sovereignty and Congressional War Powers in United States Foreign Policy,* 24 Harvard International Law Journal 1, 21 (1983); see also F. Wharton, *A Digest of International Law of the United States,* 2d ed., vol. 3 (Washington, DC: Government Printing Office, 1887), 514.

10. Helvidius no. 4, in *The Writings of James Madison,* vol. 6, ed. G. Hunt (New York: C. P. Putnam's Sons, 1906), 174.

11. *The Papers of Thomas Jefferson,* vol. 15, ed. J. Boyd (Princeton, NJ: Princeton University Press, 1951), 397; *Records of the Federal Convention of 1787,* 319, 528.

12. [Alexander Hamilton], "Federalist no. 75," 505–6. See also J. Story, *Commentaries on the Constitution of the United States,* 5th ed., vol. 2 (Boston: Little, Brown, 1905), 1512.

13. *Jefferson's Manual of Senate Procedure,* reprinted in *Senate Manual,* S. Doc., 94th Cong., 1st Sess. 668 (1975); *Ware v. Hylton,* 3 U.S. (3 Dall.) 199, 261 (1796), opinion of Iredell, circuit justice; rev'd on other grounds, ibid., 285.

14. *Marbury v. Madison,* 5 U.S. (1 Cranch 137) (1803); *Dred Scott v. Sanford,* 60 U.S. (19 How.) 393 (1857).

15. Quoted in Cass Sunstein, *An Eighteenth Century Presidency in a Twenty-First Century World,* 48 Arkansas Law Review 1, 9 (1995).

16. Letter from Jefferson to James Madison, May 31, 1798, *Writings of Thomas Jefferson,* vol. 10, ed. A. Lupscomb (Washington, DC: Thomas Jefferson Memorial Association, 1903).

17. 6 U.S. (2 Cranch) 170 (1804).

18. Cited in W. Lafeber, "The Constitution and U.S. Foreign Policy: An Interpretation," in *A Less Than Perfect Union: Alternative Perspectives on the U.S. Constitution,* ed. Jules Lobel (New York: Monthly Review Press, 1988), 226.

19. Sofaer, *War, Foreign Affairs, and Constitutional Power,* 378–79.

20. Arthur Schlesinger, *The Imperial President* (Boston: Houghton Mifflin, 1973); Philip Kurland, *Watergate and the Constitution* (Chicago: University of Chicago Press, 1978), 176; Martin Flaherty, *The Most Dangerous Branch,* 105 Yale Law Journal 1725 (1996).

21. See generally Lafeber, "The Constitution and U.S. Foreign Policy," 229–34; Schlesinger, *The Imperial President,* 85–91.

22. Theodore Roosevelt, *Theodore Roosevelt: An Autobiography* (New York: Scribner, 1913), 464.

23. *In re Neagle,* 135 U.S. 64 (1890).

24. Woodrow Wilson, *Constitutional Government in the United States* (New York: Columbia University Press, 1908), 55, 59; Lafeber, "The Constitution and U.S. Foreign Policy," 231–34.

25. P. Goldstene, *The Collapse of Liberal Empire: Science and Revolution in the Twentieth Century* (New Haven, CT: Yale University Press, 1977), 11–12.

26. William J. Fulbright, *American Foreign Policy in the 20th Century Under*

an *18th-Century Constitution,* 47 Cornell Law Quarterly 1, 7 (1961); see S. Hoffman, *Gulliver's Troubles? or The Setting of American Foreign Policy* (New York: McGraw-Hill, 1968). Walter Lippmann, *The Public Philosophy* (Boston: Little, Brown, 1955), 23–24, 29, 48; see also T. Bailey, *The Man in the Street* (Gloucester, MA: P. Smith, 1964), 13; see generally *Senate Reporter* no. 797, 90th Cong., 1st Sess. 6 (1967), perception of crisis is most important cause of executive assertion of virtually unlimited war power and congressional acquiescence.

27. Schlesinger, *The Imperial President,* 184, quoting J. A. Schumpter, *Imperialism and Social Classes* (New York: A. M. Kelly, 1951) 51.

28. Stephen Ambrose, *Rise to Globalism* (Baltimore: Penguin, 1971), 189–91; see also Lafeber, "The Constitution and U.S. Foreign Policy," 222. NSC-68 became the blueprint of U.S. policy after 1950.

29. *Myers v. United States,* 272 U.S. 52, 229–30 (1926), Reynolds dissenting (emphasis in original), quoting from Daniel Webster, *The Works of Daniel Webster,* vol. 4 (Boston: Little, Brown, 1851), 186.

30. Office of the Legal Adviser, Department of State, *The Legality of United States Participation in the Defense of Viet Nam,* 75 Yale Law Journal 1085 (1965).

31. Schlesinger, *The Imperial President,* 169.

32. 299 U.S. 304, 320 (1936).

33. See, for example, *U.S. Intelligence Agencies and Activities: Risks and Control of Foreign Intelligence: Hearings Before the House Select Committee on Intelligence,* 94th Cong., 1st Sess. 1729–34 (1975), statement of Mitchell Rogovin, special counsel to director of CIA under President Ford; *Hearings Before the Senate Select Committee on Intelligence,* 96th Cong. 2d Sess. 15–19 (1980), statement of Stansfield Turner, director of the CIA under President Carter, that requirement of prior notification of all covert actions would amount to excessive intrusion into executive's constitutional powers; T. Fain et al., eds., The Intelligence Community (New York: R. R. Bowker, 1977), 714; *Intelligence Oversight Act of 1988 Hearings Before the House Committee on Foreign Affairs,* 100th Cong., 2d Sess. 114–15 (1988), testimony of Mary Lawton, counsel for intelligence policy, Justice Department.

34. See, for example, *Atlee v. Laird,* 347 F.Supp. 689 (E.D. Pa. 1972), affirmed sub nom. *Atlee v. Richardson,* 411 U.S. 911 (1973). A more recent case brought by owners of a Norwegian vessel seeking damages for the destruction of their ship by mines placed in Nicaraguan harbors by the CIA is instructive. As in *Little v. Barreme,* executive officials had acted in disregard of congressional legislation and caused damage to a commer-

cial vessel. While the Supreme Court in 1804 held the captain liable for damages, the Second Circuit Court of Appeals affirmed a decision that the Nicaraguan case presented a political question that courts should not decide. *Chaser Shipping Corp. v. United States*, 649 F.Supp. 736 (S.D.N.Y. 1986), aff'd mem., 819 F.2d 1129 (2d Cir. 1987), cert. denied, 108 S. Ct. 695 (1988).

35. Church Committee Report, *Senate Reporter* no. 75, 94th Cong., 2d Sess. 145 (1977).

36. See Jules Lobel, *Covert War and Congressional Authority: Hidden War and Forgotten Power*, 134 University of Pennsylvania Law Review 1035 (1986).

37. Senate Foreign Relations Committee, *Treaties and Other International Agreements: The Role of the U.S. Senate*, 37–40, S. Prt. 98–205, 98th Cong. 2d Sess. (Washington, DC: Government Printing Office, 1984).

38. *Goldwater v. Carter*, 444 U.S. 996 (1979).

39. See Sunstein, *An Eighteenth Century Presidency*, 3; Archibald Cox, *Watergate and the Constitution of the United States*, quoted in Kurland, *Watergate and the Constitution*, 183.

40. Franz Neumann, *The Democratic and the Authoritarian State*, quoted in Arthur S. Miller, *Social Change and Fundamental Law: America's Evolving Constitution* (Westport, CT: Greenwood Press, 1979), 247.

41. See M. J. C. Vile, *Constitutionalism and the Separation of Powers* (Oxford, UK: Clarendon, 1967), 263–93, describing the Progressive era's call for harmony and cooperation between the branches.

42. See Gabriel Kolko, *The Triumph of Conservatism: A Reinterpretation of American History, 1900–1916* (New York: Free Press of Glencoe, 1963); Gabriel Kolko, *Railroads and Regulation 1877–1916* (Westport, CT: Greenwood Press, 1965).

43. Cited in Kolko, *Railroads and Regulation*, 78.

44. Kolko, *The Triumph of Conservativism*, 284.

45. Cass Sunstein, *Constitutionalism After the New Deal*, 101 Harvard Law Review 421 (1987).

46. Sunstein, *An Eighteenth Century Presidency*, 9–10.

47. Schlesinger, *The Imperial President*.

48. Pub. L. No. 93–148, 87 Stat. 555 (1973), codified at 50 U.S.C. §§ 1541–1548 (1982). Pub. L. No. 95–223, 91 Stat. 1625 (1977), codified at 50 U.S.C. Supp. V. §§ 1701 et seq. (1982).

49. John H. Ely, *Suppose Congress Wanted a War Powers Resolution That Worked*, 88 Columbia Law Review 1379, 1381, and n. 8 (1988). The one occasion was the Lebanon crisis, when Congress negotiated a compromise

with the Reagan administration permitting troops to remain in Lebanon for eighteen months.

50. *Ange v. Bush,* 752 F.Supp. 509 (D.D.C. 1990); see also *Lowry v. Reagan,* 676 F.Supp. 333 (D.D.C. 1987); *Crockett v. Reagan,* 720 F.2d 1355 (D.C. Cir. 1983); *Sanchez-Espinoza v. Reagan,* 568 F.Supp. 596 (D.D.C. 1983), aff'd, 770 F.2d 202 (D.C. Cir. 1985).

51. H. Commager, *The Defeat of America* (New York: Simon & Schuster, 1968) 57. Presidential adviser and well-known historian Arthur Schlesinger arrived at a similar conclusion in *The Imperial President,* writing that the imperial "vision of the American role in the world unbalanced and overwhelmed the Constitution" (Schlesinger, *The Imperial President,* 168–69).

52. 115 *Congressional Record* 16618 (June 19, 1969).

53. Flaherty, *The Most Dangerous Branch,* 1727.

54. Arthur Schlesinger, *The Cycles of American History* (Boston: Houghton Mifflin, 1986), 302–3, quoting Committee on the Constitutional System, Basic Policy Statement, *After Two Centuries: Our Eighteenth Century Constitution in Today's Complex World* (1983), 3.

55. Dillon, "The Challenge of Modern Governance," in *Reforming American Government: The Bicentennial Papers on the Committee on the Constitutional System,* ed. D. Robinson (Boulder, CO: Westview Press, 1985), 28–29; David Kairys, *With Liberty and Justice for Some* (New York: New Press, 1993). See also J. William Fulbright, *The Price of Empire* (New York: Pantheon Books, 1989), 60–75, supporting a move toward a more parliamentary system.

56. Steven G. Calabresi, *Some Normative Arguments for the Unitary Executive,* 48 Arkansas Law Review 23, 34, 36, 59 (1995).

57. J. Moore, *Government Under Law and Covert Operations* (1980), reprinted in "Iran-Contra Report," *Senate Reporter* no. 216, *House Reporter* no. 433, 100th Cong., 1st Sess. at pp. 614, 617 (minority report). The minority report stated that a number of the mistakes of the Iran-Contra Affair resulted directly from the "political guerilla warfare between the legislative and executive branches" (ibid., 437, 439).

58. Ibid.

59. "Iran-Contra Report," 449, 585 (minority report).

60. Abraham Sofaer, *The Power Over War,* 50 University of Miami Law Review 33, 34 (1995).

61. Peter Shane, *Political Accountability in a System of Checks and Balances: The Case of Presidential Review of Rulemaking,* 48 Arkansas Law Review 101, 213–14 (1995).

62. Harold Koh, *Why the President (Almost) Always Wins in Foreign Affairs: Lessons of the Iran-Contra Affair*, 97 Yale Law Journal 1255, 1323 (1988).

63. John H. Ely, *War and Responsibility: Constitutional Lessons of Vietnam and Its Aftermath* (Princeton, NJ: Princeton University Press, 1993).

64. Louis Boudin, *Government by Judiciary* (New York: W. Godwin, 1932), 1.

65. Charles A. Beard, *An Economic Interpretation of the Constitution of the United States* (New York: Macmillan, 1935).

66. See Sunstein, *An Eighteenth Century Presidency*, 490.

67. Excerpts from interview with Nixon about domestic effects of Indochina war, *New York Times*, May 20, 1977, A16.

68. Quoted in W. Carpenter, *The Development of American Political Thought* (Princeton, NJ: Princeton University Press, 1930) 103.

69. For the view that the New Deal represented a "broker state," see Barton Bernstein, "The New Deal: The Conservative Achievements of Liberal Reform," in *Twentieth Century America: Recent Interpretations,* ed. Barton Bernstein and Allen J. Materson, 2d ed. (San Francisco: Harcourt Brace Jovanovich, 1972), 242, 251.

70. L. Mazor, *The Crisis of Liberal Legalism*, 81 Yale Law Journal 1032, 1052–53 (1972).

71. Frank Michelman, *Law's Republic*, 97 Yale Law Journal 1493, 1531 (1988).

72. See R. Cover, *The Supreme Court, 1982 Term—Foreword: Nomos and Narrative*, 97 Harvard Law Review 1 (1983), that law stems from community.

73. R. Falk, "The Grotian Quest," in *International Law, A Contemporary Perspective,* ed. R. Falk, F. Kratochwil, and S. Mendlovitz (Boulder, CO: Westview Press, 1985), 36.

74. B. Barber, *Strong Democracy: Participatory Democracy for a New Age* (Berkeley: University of California Press, 1984); see, for example, Michelman, *Law's Republic;* P. Brest, *Constitutional Citizenship*, 34 Cleveland State Law Review 175 (1986); P. Brest, *Further Beyond the Republican Revival: Toward Radical Republicanism*, 97 Yale Law Journal 1623 (1988).

75. M. Shuman, "Dateline Main Street: Local Foreign Policies," *Foreign Policy*, 65 (Winter 1987): 154. See R. Falk, "Introduction," in F. Boyle, *Defending Civil Resistance Under International Law* (Dobbs Ferry, NY: Transnational, 1987).

27 MOLLY S. McUSIC

REDISTRIBUTION AND THE TAKINGS CLAUSE

TO the extent that the general public gives any thought to the takings clause of the Fifth Amendment, it likely understands from its language ("nor shall private property be taken for public use, without just compensation") that the clause exists to prevent the government from taking people's property without paying a fair price and as such serves as a check on government license and a defense of personal liberty. Most historians agree that the writers and ratifiers of the Bill of Rights had that goal in mind in response to fresh memories of British soldiers confiscating horses, carriages, and other personal property from colonists without consequence (except, of course, for their ultimate expulsion).

Most legal scholars, while proposing far more complex and expansive theories and applications, generally agree that the clause is written and applied to preclude the government from singling out an individual to pay some special burden. Various scholars, for example, see the clause as a check on government caprice or unfairness. Others understand the clause as a barrier against the exploitation of weaker groups or individuals. Most everyone shares the view that the takings clause is about liberty, individual autonomy, and freedom from government overreaching.[1]

Such a takings clause seems like a good idea. Few in our society would feel well served by a government that issued laws and executive orders such as: "Bob's family shall be thrown into the street and his house converted into military barracks." But focusing narrowly on Bob's situation obscures the clause's more pervasive impact. Whatever effect takings jurisprudence may have had on enhancing liberty, its more telling impact has been on the distribution of wealth. In an important sense, the takings clause has been more about money than about liberty, more about halting redistributive measures than preserving personal freedom. Specifically, during the two historical periods in which takings analysis has played a prominent part in the Court's docket—the *Lochner* era, from roughly 1905 to 1937, and the present—the clause has been deployed chiefly to invalidate aspects of a legislative and regulatory agenda that seeks greater economic equality.

In both historical periods, prominent conservative scholars have locked on to the notion that if property were defined to include the status quo distribution of any valuable interest, then virtually any progressive legislation or regulation would take property. If property consists of the legal rights to possess, use, and dispose of any economic interest, then regulations as disparate as building codes, price controls, minimum wages, and restrictions on selling rotten meat take property, as all limit an owner's ability to use and dispose of his property as he wishes. And if every such taking violated the Constitution, then virtually any economic legislation or regulation would be prohibited and the Constitution could be used to protect wealth from populist redistributive efforts. The law either would fall outside the government's power absolutely or would require compensation. As few governments have the resources to compensate widespread regulatory schemes and such compensation would defeat any distributional purpose, the law would be precluded in either case.

These conservative scholars—well-known examples include John Lewis in the *Lochner* era and Richard Epstein in our own—have embraced this broad definition of constitutional property and the consequent view that the takings clause embodies a general antiredistributive principle that precludes far more than taking land for a post office or horses for a war. Epstein, for example, is convinced that the takings clause should prevent all public transfer and welfare programs, the minimum wage, the National Labor Relations Act, price controls on oil and gas, rent control, eviction limitations, environmental restrictions, health and safety laws, and much of the rest of twentieth-century legislation.[2]

Although neither the *Lochner* Court nor the modern Court have gone as far as these scholars hoped, both Courts expanded the prohibition on takings from isolated instances of seizing or destroying land or personal property without compensation to prohibiting generalized regulatory regimes intended to ameliorate the harsh effects of laissez-faire economic policies in a crowded, industrialized economy. In the *Lochner* era, the progressive income tax, the minimum wage, regulation of railroad rates, and restrictions on anti-union activity were all found unconstitutional.

In the present era, environmental regulations protecting coastlines and wetlands, fees and burdens on development in booming areas, and certain tenant protections have been found unconstitutional. In both periods, takings analysis has played an important role in preventing legislative and administrative measures that redistribute wealth.

This chapter begins with an account of takings analysis during the *Lochner* era, when the Court initially honed its use of the takings clause as an antiredistributive tool targeted at the major progressive programs of its day; then describes the Court's posture in the liberal period from the 1930s to the 1970s, when it stepped back from the business of invalidating economic programs and used the takings clause only sporadically to protect individuals against specific government actions; and concludes with the takings jurisprudence of the current Court. The current Court's differences with the *Lochner* Court are many, but it has used the clause similarly to invalidate liberal programs. Its relative inactivity in this area has less to do with its philosophical differences with the *Lochner* Court and more to do with the political differences between that era and this one: Given the country's conservative climate, the current Court simply has fewer opportunities to review the constitutionality of newly passed liberal economic programs.

TAKINGS JURISPRUDENCE DURING THE *LOCHNER* ERA

The *Lochner* era owes its name to a 1905 case in which the Court found a New York statute limiting the maximum hours bakers could work to sixty per week or ten per day an unconstitutional interference with liberty of contract and private property.[3] Between the Civil War and World War II, the industrialization of the United States led to a host of new social ills, including the greatest income and wealth inequality in American history. Populist legislatures responded by protecting labor unions; establishing minimum wage, maximum hour, and workplace safety laws; abolishing child labor; and regulating railroads, utilities, insurance companies, and the sale of perishable foods such as meat and dairy products. The response of the federal courts is well known: The Supreme Court alone invalidated approximately two hundred of those economic regulations.

Prior to the expanded takings analysis of the *Lochner* era, state and federal constitutional law was understood to protect economic interests only against certain narrowly defined forms of government interference: Constitutional law protected the title and possession of property, but not its use and value. In other words, an owner was protected by the Constitution if the government seized his or her land, but not if it took some action that would limit the land's use or diminish its value. There was little application of the federal (or the equivalent state) due process clause, and the takings clause simply did not apply to regulation of property.

With the onset of the *Lochner* era, the degree of property protected from legislative redistribution expanded under both the due process and the takings clauses until the two lines of analysis converged. Eventually, a majority of the Court adopted the view that the deprivation of property without due process was the equivalent of, if not in fact, a taking. Under this analysis, the Constitution began to constrain statutes and regulations that reduced and redistributed economic value.

As the *Lochner* Court began relying on the Fourteenth Amendment's prohibition on "depriv[ation] . . . of . . . liberty, or, property, without due process of law" to protect wealth and income from certain regulations, it did so by adopting a system of classifications made up of highly abstract principles and categories, which it applied to particular statutes. As the Court saw it, the due process clause protected liberty and property, and what belonged to the category of liberty and property rights was derived from the fundamental nature of those concepts. Any infringement of those rights was unconstitutional unless it fell within the police power of the government. The police power as seen by the *Lochner* Court permitted the government to regulate property, without regard to the owner's gain or loss, if the regulation advanced the public interest. If the law did not advance the public interest, then it was beyond the police power of the government and, accordingly, violated the constitutional rights of the owner. The Court's role was to patrol this boundary, separating the laws into their respective categories. The early cases were aimed primarily at regulations that affected contractual relationships such as the case of *Lochner* itself.

The Court's sympathy for due process–based objections to regulatory actions coincided with growing sympathy for takings claims where non-regulatory government action affected property use. In a series of cases, the Court began to extend its understanding of property and what constituted a taking. The Court concluded that it was insufficient merely to protect from physical seizure or title acquisition while not protecting property from government action that could render it unusable. The Court took a significant step in this direction, for example, when it held in 1871 that legislatively authorized permanent floodings were takings that required compensation.[4]

Gradually the Court began to accept the view that property encompassed every valuable economic interest and that to deprive an owner of any of those interests was to take his or her property. The most significant cases in the Court's path to this jurisprudence were the rate regulation cases, in which businesses (primarily railroads) complained that various state acts limiting rates violated the Fourteenth Amendment's due process clause. The states, through rate regulation, forced owners to run their businesses with less financial return than they could receive without the regulation. This, plaintiffs argued, amounted to a forced dedication of their businesses to the public. In these cases, the Court began regularly to hold that property was essentially taken if its market value was significantly reduced as a result of government action.

The Court also completed the logical connection between measures that interfered with contract (and had been protected by the due process clause) and those that interfered with property (and were protected by the takings clause). As the Court made clear in the "yellow dog" contract cases of 1908 and 1915 (dealing with agreements, as a condition of employment, that an employee not join a labor union), if constitutionally protected property rights included any economically valuable interest, then freedom of contract was a species of property right. A limitation on freedom of contract was an invasion of the right of property as well.[5]

By the 1920s takings analysis and due process analysis had fused in the Court's jurisprudence: The question of whether due process–protected property rights had been deprived was coterminous with the question of whether property had been taken. A regulation could take property by limiting its use or value, and such a taking would contravene the due process clause of the Fourteenth Amendment.

With the merger of takings and due process analyses, the Court determined whether regulations either were within the legislature's police power or were takings. As noted earlier, a valid exercise of the police power required that the law advance a public purpose, and this Court counted as a valid public purpose only laws that, in its view, furthered health, safety, and general welfare. Clearly excluded from this definition was "class" legislation designed to redistribute between groups or to reduce "inequalities of fortune." The police power was broad, but it clearly did not permit the state to "declar[e] in effect that the public good requires the removal of those inequalities."[6] Those laws fell on the takings side of the line.

Proving a valid nonredistributive public purpose was not a perfunctory task. The state had to show a "real or substantial" relation to the goals of health, safety, or welfare. Moreover, if the unregulated actions of the property owner were not of themselves endangering the public health, safety, or general welfare, then regulating the use of his or her property could not further the advancement of those ideals. Thus, for example, the minimum wage was unconstitutional because the Court held that the employer had neither caused nor contributed to the poverty of his employee that the law sought to alleviate.

If the Court had followed this analysis rigorously, it would have found all economic legislation unconstitutional. After all, any change in the existing rules affects economic value at least initially with some redistributive impact, and legislation of the era was intended to help reduce the inequalities of economic power and wealth in the newly industrialized United States. The Court did disallow a great mass of legislation, but the doctrinal tools for distinguishing unconstitutional class legislation from constitutional public interest legislation were flexible, and legislation that did in fact favor one class at the expense of another survived.

The Court derived its understanding of what constituted appropriate public interest legislation from state common law categories. Through analogy to common law nuisance, the Court upheld some regulations with little scrutiny because the legislature had found particular business practices harmful. Just as property rights did not include the right to commit a common law nuisance, neither did they include the right to commit a legislatively determined harm. Zoning and other land use regulations, for example, were upheld as furthering the public welfare by analogy to nuisance, although the laws did redistribute property between groups. The Court also upheld various paternalistic interventions with redistributive impact—maximum-hour legislation for women and mine workers, for example—because protecting the health and safety of those in particular need was consistent with settled usages. Regulations were approved for industries that were "affected with a public interest"—another category from common law. The Court agreed that railroads, milk producers, fire insurance, and real estate rentals were affected with the public interest, and thus some regulations of those industries were appropriate. But the Court disapproved regulations of other industries it found not affected with the public interest—gasoline, theater ticket brokers, employment agencies, and ice companies, for example.

The result of the *Lochner*-era jurisprudence was that virtually all economic measures were subject to judicial supervision, for the Court to
approve or disapprove as it saw fit, and this Court's disapproval focused
on the primary progressive legislation of its day—graduated taxes,
labor legislation, the regulation of prices, and restrictions on entry into
business.

AFTER *LOCHNER:* A DORMANT TAKINGS
JURISPRUDENCE

Politically, the *Lochner* era was overrun by the New Deal. By 1937, with
Franklin Roosevelt's appointment of Hugo Black, the Court reflected the
political preferences of the president and for the next forty years curbed
the use of the takings clause or any constitutional measure that might
limit redistributive legislation.

As a matter of jurisprudence, the change in results was accompanied
by a change in legal style. The *Lochner* Court's search for the fundamental nature of constitutionally protected property and its deliberations
about whether a law was a taking or advanced the public interest was
replaced with a balancing test. This shift in the style of legal reasoning
had begun with Justice Holmes's famous opinion in *Pennsylvania Coal v.
Mahon,* in which the Court held that a Pennsylvania statute forbidding
all coal mining that would cause the town atop the mines to cave in was
unconstitutional.[7] Rejecting the *Lochner*-era approach, Justice Holmes
asserted that the constitutional question was not one of finding the
appropriate category but of explicit balancing: All regulations take some
economic value and all regulations further some interest of the public.
There is no bright-line distinction between constitutional and unconstitutional regulations. Instead, according to Justice Holmes, regulations of
the use of property shade into confiscation by degrees, requiring compensation only when they go "too far." Whether or not a regulation was a
taking would have to "depen[d] upon the particular facts."

Adopting Justice Holmes's analysis, the post-*Lochner* Court began
deciding takings claims by weighing a variety of factors to determine if
the regulation went too far or "unfairly singled out" a property owner. By
the late 1970s the Court concluded that its takings jurisprudence since
the 1930s had involved "essentially ad hoc factual inquiries" that could
be described as a balancing of various interests of the property owner and
the public: the economic impact of the regulation on the property owner,
the extent the regulation interfered with distinct investment-backed

expectations, and the character of the governmental action.

This balancing test of the takings clause favored deference to the economic decisions of the legislature. Explicit balancing of the people's various interests is obviously subjective. But subjectively choosing between permissible and impermissible economic legislation invites the embarrassing question of what authority permits the Court to prefer its own balance over the balance struck by democratically elected officials. Thus, the balancing test's appearance of subjectivity limited the Court's own efforts to review and invalidate legislation by seemingly depriving the justices of any judicially principled avenue for overturning economic enactments.

Nor is it likely this deference to legislative redistributive efforts troubled most members of the Court. By 1937 Franklin Roosevelt had appointed a liberal majority to the Court; by the presidential election of 1952, all nine justices had been appointed by presidents Roosevelt or Truman. President Eisenhower's appointments were, from today's perspective, all liberals, and the Kennedy and Johnson appointments maintained liberal control of the Court. These justices probably had little desire to overturn the enactments of liberal legislative majorities.

During this period, the Court occasionally did find a compensable taking from various nonregulatory government actions. It found, for example, two takings in agreements made with Indian tribes whereby the tribes lost all rights to the land, and it found a taking in the government takeover of a coal mine and the destruction of a construction lien. But the Court never decided a regulatory takings claim in favor of the property owner.

This meant that the political process rather than the courts provided the primary limitations on government regulation. The political process favored regulation, and the period saw an explosion. Franklin Roosevelt's New Deal and Lyndon Johnson's Great Society both provided periods of greatly increased regulation of the economy by legislation and administrative rules designed for downward distribution of income.

By Richard Nixon's election, liberals had dominated the Court for a thirty-year stretch and had approved and upheld the New Deal and Great Society's massive regulation of economic life. By the early 1980s, however, the string of appointments by the more conservative presidents who followed Lyndon Johnson had reached a majority, and this new majority began to revive takings analysis as an instrument to protect certain property from legislative and administrative redistribution.

MODERN TAKINGS JURISPRUDENCE

Although the modern Court, in reviving the takings clause, has not formally abandoned the ad hoc balancing test of its predecessor, in most cases it has replaced it with a new doctrinal test far less sympathetic to government regulation. Rather than balancing an array of interests, the Court now focuses on whether the regulation infringes on "essential" or "fundamental" property rights and whether the regulation "substantially advances" the government's interest.

This legal style has at least three prominent parallels with *Lochner*-era jurisprudence. This Court embraces the *Lochner*-era credo that property has an essence or core meaning that can be applied in concrete cases; it requires stricter scrutiny between the means and ends of the regulation; and it insists that at least in some instances the government establish cause and effect, namely that the regulated party contributes to the harm addressed by the regulation.

This change in legal style aids the Court in increasing the level of property protection by providing a seemingly more principled basis for rejecting the value choices of the legislature. Had this Court retained the balancing test of earlier Courts but simply redrawn the line signaling how far was too far, it would have invited the charge that balancing differently is simply politics masquerading as principles. The Court's return to a modified *Lochner*-era style of legal reasoning provides a method for finding unconstitutionality in a less obviously political manner. If a legal right is deemed the essence or core of property, it follows from the language of the takings clause that eliminating that right is taking property. Applying the plain language of the clause appears less legislative (or judicially activist) than examining a number of factors to see whether a regulation has gone too far.

Defining Protected Property

The essence or core of property for this Court has been the so-called dominion interests in land—interests premised on the right to control real property. Specifically, the current Court has begun to consider the claims to possession, use, and disposition of land as essential elements of ownership protected from government regulation.

The Court took an important early step in *Loretta v. Teleprompter Manhattan CATV Corp.* (1982) when it invalidated a New York statute requiring landlords to allow cable TV installation on their property.[8] In order to facilitate cable access, the state of New York had passed a law providing that landlords could not interfere with the installation of cable television facilities upon their property and could not demand payment for such installation from any tenant or any company in excess of the amount the state commission deemed reasonable. The statute stipulated that the cable company or the tenant was responsible for the cost of installation and for indemnifying the landlord for any damage caused by the installation. In deciding that the statute did constitute a taking of the landlord's property, the Court undertook no analysis of the various interests at stake—the economic impact on the owner or the owner's expectations or the character and importance of the government's actions. Instead, the Court held that if a law destroyed the whole bundle of dominion interests by preventing an owner from possessing, using, or disposing of a portion of his her property (as a cable installation on the roof apparently did), it was a per se taking. In other words, there is no public purpose the government could demonstrate that would release it from paying compensation to all landlords.

The first specific dominion interest to be granted nearly full protection from regulatory redistribution was possession, namely the right to exclude. The Court had concluded in a 1979 case that the right to exclude "falls within this category of interests that the Government cannot take without compensation."[9] In two recent cases, *Nollan v. California Coastal Commission* (1987) and *Dolan v. City of Tigard* (1994), in which the government offered a development permit for an expanded building on the condition that the property owners grant a public easement, the Court stated that the loss of the right to exclude, inherent in the government's public easement requirement, made that requirement unconstitutional.[10]

The Court has since ventured beyond the right to exclude in enumerating its fundamental property rights and now considers various uses of land also fundamental. In *Lucas v. South Carolina Coastal Council*, the Court considered the constitutionality of a South Carolina law that prevented Mr. Lucas from building single-family houses on his beachfront property.[11] In response to a congressional mandate that states significantly reduce threats to life and property by eliminating development and redevelopment in high-hazard coastal areas, South Carolina enacted a law prohibiting the construction of any habitable structure in a designated "critical area" along its coastline, as determined by annual erosion rates. The law stipulated that no new houses could be built and no older houses rebuilt in a critical area. Lucas's entire two lots were in a critical area, having been under water or flooded twice daily by the tide over roughly half of the previous forty years. At the time the law was enacted, however, the land was high and dry, and Lucas wished to build luxury homes comparable to those of his neighbors, who had completed construction before the law was passed and now were limited only in rebuilding. The Court found a taking, again without regard to other factors, holding that the government cannot prevent all economically valuable use of property except in rare circumstances, and remanded to the South Carolina court to see if this situation fell in the category of a rare circumstance. It did not.[12]

In other cases, the Court has repeatedly said that the takings clause protects the right to undertake at least some uses of land, suggesting that regulations preventing an owner from leaving the rental business, for example, as well as those abrogating "essential uses" such as the right to build on land, are unconstitutional.

The Court also has classified a right to disposition of land as an essential attribute of property. In 1987 and again in 1997, the Court held that a statute seeking to solve the problem of fractured ownership of Indian land by prohibiting the disposition of very small land interests through a will, while permitting full use and right to dispose during the owner's lifetime, was a taking because the right to pass property is an essential property right.[13]

At the same time the Court has held that regulations of these "fundamental" property interests are per se or nearly per se takings, it has found other economic interests commonly considered property to be entitled to little protection. For example, the Court has found that economic interests such as Social Security payments, liquor licenses, and employment are not property for takings purposes. In addition, economic interests such as personal property, trade secrets, copyright, and money are all recognized by the Court as property under the takings clause but receive little protection against government regulation. In analyzing regulations affecting these interests, the Court reverts to the three-factor balancing test of the liberal era—the diminution in value, the effect on reasonable investment-backed expectations, and the character of the government action—but still seldom finds them weighing in the owner's favor.[14] For example, although taxes clearly take property and redistribute it, they appear never to be a taking.

The Court also gives relatively little protection for losses of economic value and profit even when they are connected to land use. In a long series of cases, the Court has held that regulations causing even a substantial reduction in the value of land are not a taking. This is also true for regulations directly intending to limit profits from land, such as rate regulation. The Constitution prevents only rate setting that is "confiscatory," a standard that is not necessarily met even when the rates are so low that the enterprise loses money.

The result of the Court's search for core or essential attributes of property is that it finds per se or nearly per se takings where there is an interference with the right to exclude, to control real property disposition, to leave the rental business, or to develop land, but not where regulation merely limits prices or profits or decreases market value.

JUDICIAL SCRUTINY OF PROPERTY REGULATION

In addition to singling out certain legal rights for greater constitutional protection, current Court doctrine also subjects the connection between the owner, the regulation, and the public goal to rigorous scrutiny through the "substantially advance test" when the regulation affects one of the Court's selected fundamental property interests.

Requiring a careful scrutiny between the regulation, the government's goals, and the owner's actions was a feature of *Lochner*-era jurisprudence abandoned by the liberal courts that followed. Instead, the post-*Lochner* Courts developed different levels of means-end analysis according to the nature of the rights allegedly infringed. Property or economic rights, since the late 1930s, had been subject only to "rational basis" scrutiny— a scrutiny the law would survive if any rational being could be made to see a connection between the government's desired end and the employed means. Rarely does a challenged law fail to pass rational scrutiny. Laws that involve either a "suspect classification" (claims that the law discriminates against African Americans, for example) or a restriction of a "fundamental interest" (rights such as speech and privacy) are tested by "strict" or "heightened" scrutiny, which involves more rigorous judicial demands for "important" or "compelling" governmental objectives and for "substantial" or "narrowly tailored" instrumental relationships to such objectives. A law almost never survives the kind of strict scrutiny applied to suspect classifications and fundamental rights, although, in the interregnum of takings analysis between *Lochner* and the present era, such strict scrutiny had never been required of economic regulations.

Tightening the rational relation test for takings cases began with *Nollan* in 1987. The Court invalidated a requirement for a building permit by invoking the standard that a law "substantially advance a legitimate state interest." The California Coastal Commission required the

Nollans (as it had every beachfront builder) to allow an easement for access to the public beach between their beach wall and the ocean in exchange for a permit to tear down their bungalow and build a bigger house. The Court found this requirement unconstitutional because the permit requirement did not "substantially advance a legitimate state interest."

The majority articulated two requirements for how a regulation must substantially advance a legitimate state interest in takings law. The Court described the "substantially advance" test as one that examines whether the regulation actually achieves its stated purpose through the means prescribed: a means-end test. In addition, the government must prove a proportionate relationship between the amount of public harm caused by the owner and the regulatory burden imposed: a cause-and-effect test.

In *Nollan* the Court declared both requirements but defined neither. It stated that the means-end test would require a higher level of connection than merely a "rational relationship" between the regulation and the government's goal, but it did not stipulate what level. Although the dissent claimed that the government's goal was increasing overall access to the beach (a goal that would have been advanced by requiring an easement as a condition for a permit), the Court defined the government's goal as reducing obstacles to viewing the beach and held that a beach easement was wholly unrelated to reducing viewing obstacles.

Nor did the Court elucidate its cause-and-effect test. It proposed in a footnote that to substantially advance a legitimate state interest meant that the regulation at issue rectified a harm caused by the property owners' behavior. The state's demand of an easement from the Nollans failed this test because the Nollan house (a larger house blocking the ocean view from the road) did not cause the problem the easement sought to correct (access to the ocean). The Court did not decide the issue, however, because the Nollans had not raised it.

Subsequently, the Court provided some additional hints as to the content of these requirements. In 1994, the issue of the appropriate nexus was considered again in *Dolan v. City of Tigard*. Mrs. Dolan, owner of a chain of hardware stores in the Portland, Oregon, area, had sought a building permit to expand her existing hardware store in downtown Tigard. Her plans included paving and expanding a gravel parking lot and tearing down the existing structure to replace it with a building nearly twice as large. The hardware store was in the heart of the city's central business district, with one side of the parcel abutting a creek. Pursuant to Tigard's Community Development Code, the city granted the permit on the condition that Dolan dedicate easements to the city for the purpose of flood control and reduced traffic congestion. Dolan appealed these conditions through the city's administrative process and then the Oregon courts, losing at each level. In the U.S. Supreme Court, she argued that *Nollan* required greater scrutiny of land use regulations beyond the rational relationship standard applied by the Oregon court to uphold the permit conditions. The Court agreed that there needed to be an "essential nexus" between the permit condition and the goals of the regulation but readily found such a relationship between the easement and the city's goals of flood control and reduced traffic.

Although the Court in *Dolan* did not adopt any explicit form of heightened scrutiny in applying its means-end test, the Court opinion did suggest a higher level of scrutiny might be just as appropriate in takings cases as it is in cases involving speech or privacy, stating that it saw "no reason why the Takings Clause of the Fifth Amendment, as much a part of the Bill of Rights as the First Amendment or Fourth Amendment, should be relegated to the status of a poor relation in these comparable circumstances."[15] This sentence suggested to some that the Court was endorsing the notion that the same heightened standard of review would apply to regulation of property as to speech, privacy, and other fundamental rights with the same result: Virtually no regulation would pass constitutional muster.

Dolan was herself more successful with the second meaning of the substantially advance requirement, the cause-and-effect test. This test focuses on whether the burden of the regulation is properly placed on this particular owner. One year after *Nollan*, in a separate opinion in a rent control case, Justice Scalia explained that a property regulation does not substantially advance the state's interest unless the use of the property caused the problem the state was seeking to correct or the property owner reaped unique benefits from the problem. The rent control scheme was unconstitutional under Justice Scalia's analysis because landlords did not cause the housing shortage or their tenants' poverty.[16]

In *Dolan* the Court agreed with Justice Scalia that takings analysis requires at least one form of this cause-and-effect test. In applying that test to *Dolan*, the Court held that to withstand constitutional scrutiny local governments had to prove that the permit condition imposed would proportionately counteract the harm caused by the owner's project. The effect of the government's permit conditions on Dolan could not be disproportionate to the harm she would cause with her planned use. This connection was not to be met by some general statement either, but through the local government's individualized determination of the effect of the regulation on each owner's property. The Court rejected as insufficient the studies provided by Tigard that a larger retail sale facility would increase traffic by roughly 435 additional trips per day and that the bike path would offset some of the traffic demand. Without better proof, the Court held that Tigard could not require Dolan to dedicate easements in exchange for a building permit.

THE REGULATIONS AT RISK

The substantially advance test and the definition of fundamental property interests are intertwined in the Court's analysis of takings. If the regulation extinguishes one of the fundamental attributes of property—to possess (exclude), use (build or convert to a different use or use in an economically valuable manner), or dispose (devise)—it appears that no government interest, however great, can rescue it. Thus, this Court would likely find unconstitutional (without further inquiry into singling out, or expectations or government interest) regulations that require an owner to open his or her property to the public, prohibit any development on property (such as some beach and wetlands restrictions), or prohibit all changes in the use of the property (such as complete prohibitions against converting or demolishing rental apartments). If, rather than eliminating, the regulation merely encroaches on one of these fundamental attributes of property, then the Court appears likely to find a taking by applying means-end or cause-and-effect scrutiny. For example, if the state requires a property owner to grant an easement as a condition of receiving a development permit, it has not eliminated the right to exclude but only required that an aspect of that right be forfeited in exchange for the benefit of a building permit. As such, the regulation is not a per se taking, but because it impinges on a core property right, the Court subjects the regulation to a heightened form of judicial scrutiny. Similarly, stringent limitations on exiting the rental business appear subject to a rigorous application of the substantially advance test. In terms of practical impact, the regulations most at risk of being invalidated under this Court's takings jurisprudence are environmental laws that prohibit development, some categories of development exactions, and capital mobility restrictions.

Laws that prohibit development are in clear constitutional danger. Current examples are the various environmental regulations—primarily wetlands and coastal restrictions—that can prohibit all development. The Court has explicitly decided in *Lucas* that a prohibition on building on beaches can be an unconstitutional taking, notwithstanding the law's widespread application or the government's interest in protecting life and property from hurricanes and saving public money that would otherwise be spent reconditioning beaches, insuring houses, and providing storm relief. Similarly, restrictions on all building in wetlands have been found unconstitutional, notwithstanding the national scope of the wetlands issue or the government's interest in preventing soil erosion, reducing flooding by absorbing and storing rainwater, and improving drinking water through filtering and biological treatment.

Other regulations endangered by this Court's takings approach are various development exaction schemes—so-called exotic exactions, which are conditions on development permits that do not specifically benefit the developer or development buyer. Local governments in thriving areas have increasingly turned to exactions to pay for the substantial service demands of growth because the more common form of payment in the past—property taxes and aid from state and federal governments—became less available after the 1970s. State and federal aid to local governments was reduced at a time of rising political resistance to taxes. Faced with stagnant or declining local revenue, no option of raising taxes, and expanding service demands, towns and cities began to turn to development exactions to help finance government services, some of which ran well beyond the needs created by the new development. Common examples are requirements that builders provide public benefits such as low-income housing, schools, day care centers, public parks, job training, or beach access or that they pay a fee for such services. It seems implausible that local governments will be able to prove that the new developments caused the need for these services or that the means are sufficiently related to the ends—both of which seem to be required by the Court in *Nollan* and *Dolan*.

A final category of regulations at risk prohibit property owners from changing the use of their land. Regulations such as eviction controls, condominium conversion restrictions, and mobile home park restrictions are all efforts to prevent owners from redirecting capital—stopping the apartment owner, for example, from converting his or her property into anything other than a rental property. Such measures are crucial to the effectiveness of housing regulations, especially rent control. Without limitations on an owner's capacity to evict the tenants and change the use of his or her property to something unregulated, the owner will be free to circumvent the tenant laws. While the Court has not yet squarely decided this issue, the justices have indicated (and lower courts have agreed) that if regulations prohibit owners from going out of a particular business and thus changing the use of their land, the regulations are unconstitutional.

REDISTRIBUTION AND THE MODERN TAKINGS CLAUSE

Obviously, a takings clause jurisprudence that targets some development exactions, landlord-tenant laws, and environmental regulations does not have the reach that it did in conjunction with the due process clause during the *Lochner* era. This Court has an active takings docket if it decides two cases in a year, and many Court terms see no takings cases. Compared to the 184 state laws alone that the Court invalidated between 1899 and 1937 under the due process analysis, this Court seems positively demure. Moreover, income generated from property can be taxed for the express purpose of redistribution without testing the teeth of this Court's takings clause; and the Court continues to uphold such measures as industrial health and safety regulations, minimum wage regulations, and restrictions on firing employees, all of which limit the conditions under which goods may be produced and exchanged—in effect limiting profits to owners for the purpose of expanding benefits to workers. And the measures the takings clause does obstruct—various federal and local land use measures—are relatively modest efforts to benefit the public at the expense of landowners. It is extremely unlikely that any plausible regulatory land use regime, even if unfettered by constitutional restraints, could be a major engine of redistribution.

But modern takings jurisprudence, like its counterpart in the first part of the century, does have a significant impact on redistributive efforts. This impact owes less to the wide judicial reach of the Court, as it did in the *Lochner* era, and more to its hostile regard for the relatively modest redistributive agenda of the day. In both time periods, it is the major new liberal economic programs that are at stake in the Court's takings jurisprudence.

The regulations at risk—some development exactions, certain landlord-tenant laws, and environmental land regulations—are highly effective forms of redistribution. The cost of these regulations is primarily borne by the original land owner, and because land cannot be moved, the landowner cannot thwart the purpose of the regulation by passing on the cost (as can often be the case with other forms of redistributive regulation). Because owners of undeveloped land subject to exactions and environmental laws as well as owners of rental property are wealthier than the average American, these laws likely redistribute in general from richer to poorer.

The last twenty years have seen a decrease or elimination of most methods of redistribution. Virtually all redistributive regulation now in effect was passed in the United States during the liberal phase of political domination, the New Deal and Great Society legislative programs that spanned roughly from the early 1930s until the early 1970s. Since the early 1970s, the political climate, particularly at the national level, turned in a conservative, antiregulatory direction. Republicans and conservative Democrats in Congress, gaining strength in the three decades since President Nixon's election, have been able to halt most new liberal economic legislation.

Repeated efforts to implement a federal health insurance scheme have failed, for example, and many other measures such as the minimum wage, the National Labor Relations Act, and workplace safety regulations have not kept pace with changes in the workplace and thus have lost much of their effect as redistributive measures. Much consumer regulation of such industries as transportation, communications, and energy has been halted and dismantled. Conservative politicians in Congress were also able to scale back, if not eliminate, many existing redistributive programs—public housing and welfare, for example—by freezing or reducing funding. Redistribution through the tax code also has been stymied as the federal income tax has become less progressive and Social Security and other regressive taxes have grown. Since the 1980s, overall taxation in the United States appears to have ceased to redistribute income progressively. This trend explains why the current Court's takings clause is an effective antiredistributive tool despite its narrow reach. Within this national conservative climate pockets of liberal political power remain. By President Nixon's second term, the United States had a federal bureaucracy with enormous legislative power and a fair degree of independence from other branches. Despite various efforts by several administrations, the lack of political accountability in many agencies allowed them at times to pursue a liberal agenda that could not have passed even a Democrat-controlled Congress.

During the 1960s and 1970s, state governments also tightened their regulatory grip. Although generalizations about state and local government politics are more difficult to make than at the federal level, after World War II state governments were controlled largely by rural voters and business interests. The Supreme Court undermined that status quo with a series of decisions culminating in its 1964 decision requiring "one man one vote."[17] This ended the regional voting that had permitted minority voting blocs from rural areas to control state houses. As urban areas, often with concentrated racial minority populations, increased their clout, state governments in some states did not follow the national conservative trend. This tendency was accelerated by other voting rights decisions invalidating state statutes that had served to disenfranchise poor people, a disproportionate number of whom were black.

More liberal state governments began their own mini federal redistributive schemes. This process was enhanced by the federal government's revenue-sharing program, started by President Nixon, which transferred federal money to the state along with responsibility for its administration. States expanded their bureaucracies to handle these programs, and many bureaucracies enjoyed the luxury of limited legislative oversight because funding came from the federal government or earmarked state dollars.

The shape and extent of any liberal programs in the states remained limited by voter resistance to higher taxes and the competition between states for economic development. Within those constraints, however, jurisdictions with liberal political majorities still pursued regulatory programs. This was even more likely to apply at the local level than the state level, as the new conservative majority did not reproduce itself in every locale. Residential segregation, by both race and class, as well as the suburbanization of the American landscape made possible enclaves where regulation might continue unhindered by the national or even state political environment. Land use regulation in particular traditionally has been the prerogative of local governments, and such regulation has expanded despite the antiregulatory political climate across the nation.

As a result of these political dynamics, in the late 1970s and early to mid-1980s, when the takings clause was being resuscitated by the Court, conservative political power had successfully halted downward redistribution through new taxes and legislation but had been less successful in controlling administrative agencies and local governments, which became the country's primary source of new redistributive laws. The laws under constitutional attack by the current Court's takings doctrine— environmental regulations, development exactions, and landlord-tenant laws—are in the primary new areas of regulatory effort initiated by these liberal enclaves. It was not until the 1970s, for example, that there was extensive redefinition of real property law—under laws such as the Clean Water Act, the Coastal Zone Management Act, and the Endangered

Species Act—in the interest of the environment. Similarly, exotic exactions were not widespread until the 1970s and 1980s when voter resistance to taxes at all levels of government put local governments in a financial squeeze. Finally, regulations such as eviction controls, condominium conversion restrictions, and mobile home restrictions are all relatively new; expanded tenant legal protections are, for the most part, phenomena of the last twenty years.

By protecting core property rights rather than economic value, the takings clause takes aim at only a small number of liberal economic programs. But the redistributive measures relatively unhindered by the takings clause are measures simply not taken by elected branches in the current political climate. The only fresh redistributive efforts of this era have emerged from regulatory agencies and local governments. The common characteristics of the regulations at constitutional risk—new administratively imposed, often local, land use limitations—are all the features of a politically feasible and economically effective redistributive regulation. Thus, while the takings clause leaves much of the wealth of Americans constitutionally unprotected from legislative redistribution, it strikes at wealth that is in fact being redistributed.

NOTES

Portions of this chapter were drawn from my articles *The Ghost of Lochner: Modern Takings Doctrine and Its Impact on Economic Legislation*, 76 Boston University Law Review 605 (1996), and *Looking Inside Out: Institutional Analysis and the Problems of Takings*, Northwestern University Law Review (forthcoming).

1. See, for example, Frank Michelman, *Property, Utility, and Fairness: Comments on the Ethical Foundation of "Just Compensation" Law,* 80 Harvard Law Review 1165 (1967); Saul Levmore, *Just Compensation and Just Politics,* 22 Connecticut Law Review 285 (1990).
2. Richard Epstein, *Takings: Private Property and the Power of Eminent Domain* (Cambridge, MA: Harvard University Press, 1985).
3. *Lochner v. New York,* 198 U.S. 45 (1905).
4. *Pumpelly v. Green Bay Co.,* 80 U.S. 166 (1871), construing the almost identically worded takings clause in the Wisconsin constitution.

5. *Coppage v. Kansas,* 236 U.S. 1, 14 (1915); *Adair v. United States,* 208 U.S. 161, 172 (1908).

6. *Coppage,* 236 U.S. at 17–18.

7. *Pennsylvania Coal v. Mahon,* 260 U.S. 393 (1922).

8. *Loretta v. Teleprompter Manhattan CATV Corp.,* 458 U.S. 419 (1982).

9. *Kaiser Aetna v. United States,* 444 U.S. 164, 179–80 (1979).

10. *Nollan v. California Coastal Commission,* 483 U.S. 825 (1987); *Dolan v. City of Tigard,* 512 U.S. 374 (1994).

11. *Lucas v. South Carolina Coastal Council,* 505 U.S. 1003 (1992).

12. The Court held in *Lucas* that the government could prevent all economically valuable uses of land if the common law would have prohibited them as nuisances anyway or the uses would pose grave threats to the lives and property of others. The South Carolina Supreme Court decided that under the law of South Carolina coastline building was not a nuisance (309 S.C. 424, 427 [1992]). The court made no reference to whether the law would pose a grave threat to life.

13. *Hodel v. Irving,* 481 U.S. 704, 715–16 (1987); *Babbitt v. Youpee,* 117 S.Ct. 727, 732 (1997).

14. A possible exception to this generalization occurred in *Ruckelshaus v. Monsanto Co.,* 467 U.S. 986 (1984), in which the Court found the loss of a trade secret to be an unconstitutional taking. The Court came to that decision based on the fact that the government had made an explicit promise, Monsanto had relied on the promise, and the government had then reneged. For this reason, the Court found that the reasonable investment-backed expectations of Monsanto had been destroyed.

15. *Dolan v. City of Tigard,* 512 U.S. 374, 385 (1994).

16. *Pennell v. San Jose,* 485 U.S. 1, 15 (1988), considering a rent control scheme that allowed reduction in the maximum available rent on the grounds of the tenant's hardship, Scalia dissenting.

17. *Reynolds v. Sims,* 377 U.S. 533 (1964).

III

PROGRESSIVE
APPROACHES
TO THE LAW

28 ROBERT W. GORDON

SOME CRITICAL THEORIES OF LAW AND THEIR CRITICS

MANY lawyers allied with progressive causes have reached such a state of stalemate or exhaustion that they may find it hard to remember that the last thirty years has been an amazingly creative period in the history of socially activist law. New social movements—civil rights, women's rights, welfare rights, children's rights, gay and lesbian rights, international human rights, immigrants' and farm workers' rights, environmentalism and community development—have demanded the invention of a whole new range of lawyering skills and strategies and styles of interaction with clients and client communities; and given rise to striking innovations in legal institutions: law-reform-oriented legal-services offices and "public interest" practices, new roles and remedies such as the public interest intervention in administrative proceedings, the public interest class action, the structural injunction, and the teaching of self-help "lay lawyering."

In the history of progressive legal theory as well, this has been an extraordinary period, probably the most creative since the Legal Realist movements of the 1920s and 1930s. The lawyers who have participated in the development of "critical" legal theories came from many different starting points—some of us law teachers with humanist intellectual concerns and left-liberal (civil rights and anti-Vietnam war) political involvements in the 1960s and 1970s; others radical activists who identified with neo-Marxist versions of socialism or feminism or both; still others primarily practitioners, some of them associated with the National Lawyers Guild, and who work in collective law practices, legal services offices, law school clinics, or a variety of other progressive jobs. Mostly white and male at the start, the company of critical legal theorists has greatly diversified over time in its racial, ethnic, and gender composition;

and has also come to exhibit a startling intellectual and ideological variety, to the point of turning its occasional conferences into Babels of conflicting and competing views. Yet for all their differences in jobs, origins, and outlooks, people engaged in critical thinking about law have tended to converge around certain common clusters of ideas.

To understand how these ideas developed, imagine someone who first started thinking seriously about law as a student in the late 1960s. At that time he or she would have been struck by the staggering contrast between the preoccupations of our teachers and casebooks and the world outside. When a law student now refers to the "real world," she usually means the world of practice; but in 1968, of course, "reality" was the swirling political chaos outside. The contrast between the schools and the streets—civil rights marches, burning cities, Vietnam protests—was surely one of the main factors that broke up the authority of the orthodox agenda of legal education, in a way from which it has never quite recovered.

What law teachers taught then is what most teach still, a mixture of doctrinal analysis and policy analysis. Doctrinal analysis was a kind of toned-down legal realism: we learned how to take apart the formal arguments for the outcome of the case and to pierce through them to find the underlying factors that would explain the case, a layer of "principles" and "purposes" behind the rules. Policy analysis was a quickie utilitarian method for use in close cases: it was supposed to enable us to argue for outcomes that would efficiently serve policies desired by "society" and somehow inhering in the legal system. The policies were derived either by appeal to an assumed general consensus of values (such as the "security of transactions," or "our federalism"), or to an assumed (and assumed to be good) trend of historical development. Sometimes there would be competing policies, representing conflicting "interests"; here the function of policy analysis was to provide an on-the-spot rapid-fire-from-the-hip "balancing" of the policies. A really "smart" lawyer who was adept at all these techniques would be able to discover—by the use of legal reasoning and legal craftsmanship alone—socially optimal solutions for virtually all legal problems. Indeed, the whole way of speaking about law that pervaded the opinions and casebooks and methods of argument was suffused with a deep complacency about the current forms of liberal-democratic capitalism: "private ordering" in markets usually led to free and fair outcomes; if not, the problems were correctable through legislatures presumed to represent the relevant interest groups and agencies presumed to possess technical expertise; the functions of law were the largely technical ones of proper interpretation and application of rules and principles.

Outside politics must have made it easier for law students of the late 1960s and early 1970s than it had been for those who had graduated just before then to see what was wrong with this vision of law as neutrally benevolent technique. The appeal to a deep social consensus was hardly a winner in a society apparently splintering further every day into divisions between blacks and whites, hawks and doves, men and women, hippies and straights, parents and children. The appeal to the underlying march of historical progress was in trouble for the same reason. The vision of law as a technocratic policy science administered by a disinterested elite was tarnished, to say the least, for anyone who watched the "best and the brightest" direct and justify the war in Vietnam. The fluent optimistic jargon of policy science that came out of such unspeakable slaughter and suffering seemed not only absurdly remote from any real experience but literally insane.

Under these conditions young lawyers became desperate for a more plausible and less compromised view of the social uses of law; and many of us found it in the emerging vocation of the liberal but antiestablishment activist reform lawyer, who would deploy the techniques of the system against the system, work for good, substantive rule change, more open and representative procedures and more responsive bureaucracies, and, in general, who would try to make effective and real the law's formal promises of equal justice.

Although the concrete achievements of lawyers who adopted this vocation were considerable, the focus here is how the experience of this work may have contributed to their intellectual development. The dominant message of orthodox legal training was then and still is today that a basically unalterable value consensus, a basically unchangeable system of economic and political realities, a basically frozen system of legal understandings and institutions, fix rigid outer boundaries to thinkable social change. But the history of the recent epoch was a revelation of how apparently permanently frozen practices and beliefs—including legal practices and beliefs—can suddenly become plastic and alterable, neither because of changes commanded from the centers of power nor vanguard conspiracies of the Leninist type but rather from thousands of local actions in churches, workplaces, fields, families, relationships, and schools, coalescing into broadly transformative sea changes. The extraordinary changes in racial relations and perceptions, in the roles and relations of men and women, and in beliefs about the appropriate relation of humans to their natural environment are only the most dramatic legacies of these movements.

But another legacy, sadly, was an education in the resilience and resistance of entrenched interests and ideas—in all the myriad ways in which the legal system was not a set of neutral techniques available to anyone who could seize control of its levers and switches but a game heavily loaded in favor of the wealthy and powerful. Procedure was so expensive and slow that one's side could be exhausted in a single engagement with an enemy who could fight dozens. One was likely to obtain the most favorable rule outcomes just where enforcement of them seemed most hopeless. And even the doctrinal victories peaked all too early: just as a promising line of rules opened up, it would be qualified before it became truly threatening. Antidiscrimination doctrine became quagmired at sanctioning intentional state action against individuals, not quite reaching systemic private action against groups; and started to backtrack the moment that gains by blacks began to seriously threaten the interests of middle-class whites. Equal protection doctrine flirted briefly with remedies for wealth inequalities, then scurried rapidly into retreat.[1]

Even the smallest victories of the reformers mobilized ferocious right-wing movements determined to roll them back. Conservatives have managed to replace liberal state and federal judges with conservatives; to defund and cripple legal services; to invalidate employment and education policies aimed at overcoming structural barriers to racial equality; to demolish welfare entitlements without putting in their place realistic means of caring for children and getting work at a living wage; to defeat universal access to medical care; and to weaken enforcement of the labor laws against employers who illegally fire union organizers. They have also tried (with somewhat less success) through crusades for "family values," to limit the growing power of women to control the terms on which they will bear children and remain in marriages and to reverse the increasing recognition of the legitimacy of gays and lesbians.

Critical legal theory was in some part an attempt by young law teachers and practitioners to weave this double experience of plasticity and resistance into a reworked understanding of a legal process whose orthodox interpreters kept insisting was not possible to change in any major way. The felt need for a theory that would help explain what was going on became acute; and the kind of theory that seemed called for was one that connected what happened in the legal system to a wider political, economic, and cultural context. Here orthodox legal thought had almost nothing to offer because even though liberal lawyers had learned from the legal realists that all law was social policy, their working methods kept technical (narrowly legal) issues at the forefront of legal analysis; the conventions of scholarship dictated that if social context were to be discussed at all, it could only be done casually and in passing. Activist lawyers in their excitement about the possibilities of using law to promote social change and disappointment with the pace and scope of change had to reach back to the sources of social and political theory, which their legal training had pushed out of focus. When they did, it was like discovering that what had happened to them was something they had known about all along but had partially repressed.

The main kinds of commonsense explanations available to them were what are sometimes called instrumental theories of the relationship between law and society.[2] In the *liberal* version, law is a response to social "demands." These demands are frequently those of specific interest groups that want some advantage from the state: law represents the compromise bargains of multiple conflicting interest groups. At other times the demands are more generally expressed as those of the functional "needs" of "the society" or "the economy"; e.g., "the market" needs stable frameworks for rational calculation, which the legal system responds to with contract enforcement, security interests, recording of land titles, etc.

Liberal instrumentalist theory, in short, says that societies get the law they want or need, or that whatever interests happen to be ascendant at a given moment want or need. More *radical* instrumentalist theories assume that societies are usually organized around durable *systems* of power relations of hierarchical domination—notably those of class, sex, and race—and that one of the primary functions of law is to maintain and reproduce those hierarchies. In the orthodox Marxist version of instrumentalism, for example, "bourgeois" law is a product not of just any group's demands but specifically those of the capitalist ruling class. In both versions, a "hard" world of economic actions (or "material base") determines what happens in the "soft" world of legal rules and processes (as part of the ideological "superstructure"). Also common to both versions is a deep logic theory of historical change. In the liberal version, this is usually: feudalism—mercantilism—industrial capitalism—organized capitalism—modern welfare capitalism; in the Marxist version, much the same with slightly different terms. Both versions assume that legal systems go through different stages that are necessary functions of the prevailing economic organization. Liberals, for example, explained nineteenth-century tort rules that put all the risks of accidents or product defects on workers and consumers either as functional to that stage of industrial development (because infant industries needed to keep their costs down) or as the result of a temporary (and soon remedied) imbalance of political power in favor of capitalists; the radicals said much more straightforwardly that capitalists simply imposed these costs on workers.

If one had to choose between these theories—both purposely depicted here in their crudest form and *not at all* meant to represent the best that either liberals or radicals have to offer—the radical version would have considerably more explanatory bite, since the liberal-pluralist notion that any interest group could capture the system and make it play the right tunes seems to contradict historical experience as well as the practical experience of the recently embittered lawyers. The liberal versions do not really explain why masses of people passively suffer atrocious treatment from the legal system, sometimes for decades, without effectively organizing to fight it, or why it seems to function so as to reinforce class, racial, and sexual inequalities: it seems to have a built-in tilt toward reproduction of existing power relations.

Nonetheless, anyone who thought about it would begin to see a great many problems with radical instrumentalist theories of law—especially in a society such as ours in which law has so visibly served as a resource for struggling underdogs and outgroups. The capitalists did not seem to win all the time through state policy and law: workers had been granted rights to organize and bargain collectively out of it, blacks had received the abolition of slavery and some affirmative government action promoting their rights, radicals had been granted some rights to teach and write, the poor had received some welfare entitlements, and so on. The laws that have helped emancipate women from the loss of all their property and civil capacity upon marriage, enlarged their rights to exit unwanted marriages, and won them the rights to vote, enter the professions, buy contraceptives, and sue for discriminatory treatment in the workplace, are difficult to explain as simply serving the interests of "patriarchy."

To some extent, such gains by underdogs and outgroups may be re-explained as ways that ruling groups accommodate to challenge so as to preserve hierarchies through more subtle forms of domination, but such explanations require considerable refinement of instrumentalist theories. Some writers spoke of the strategy of "corporate liberalism"—the ruling class promotes government social-welfare programs and regulation of business in order to prevent political (through popular risings) and economic (through chaotic competition) destabilization of the social order. Other writers, borrowing from European neo-Marxist sources, began to speak of law as a means of "legitimating" class society: in order to be bearable to those who suffer most from it, law must be perceived to be approximately just, so the ruling class cannot win all the time. Still others, extending the point, saw the "legitimacy" of capitalist society as importantly inhering in (among a number of other factors, such as a certain degree of social mobility, social security for everyone, and apparently meritocratic criteria for determining people's shares of income and wealth) the legal system's promises to protect rights of freedom and security for everyone in the society equally—promises that must sometimes be made good.[3] So, since the legal system must at least appear universal, it must operate to some extent independently (or with "relative autonomy," as the saying goes) from concrete economic interests or social classes. And this need for legitimacy is what makes it possible for other classes to use the system against itself, to try to entrap it and force it to make good on its utopian promises. Such promises may therefore become rallying points for organization, so that the state and law become not merely instruments of class domination but "arenas of class struggle."[4]

Once leftist lawyers became accustomed to thinking this way, a whole new set of problems and questions opened up. One was that given this view of the matter, hard-won struggles to achieve new legal rights for the oppressed began to look like ambiguous victories. The official legal establishment had been compelled to recognize claims on its utopian promises. But had these real gains only deepened the legitimacy of the system as a whole? The labor movement secured the vitally important legal rights to organize and strike, at the cost of fitting into a framework of legal regulation that certified the legitimacy of management's making most of the important decisions about conditions of work.[5]

In any case, once one begins to focus closely on problems such as these, one begins to pay much more attention to what instrumentalists think of as the "soft" or "superstructural" aspects of the legal system. If what is important about law is that it functions to "legitimate" the existing order, one starts to ask *how* it does that. And for the purposes of this project, one does not look only at the undeniably numerous, specific ways in which the legal system functions directly to help the powerful protect their wealth and privileges, to organize their own interests and keep their opponents disorganized and scared—though it is always important to do that too, to point it out as often and as powerfully as possible—but also at all the ways in which the system seems at first glance basically uncontroversial, neutral, acceptable. This is Antonio Gramsci's notion of "hegemony," i.e., that the most effective kind of domination takes place when both the dominant and dominated classes believe that the existing order, with perhaps some marginal changes, is satisfactory, or at least represents the most that anyone could expect, because things pretty much have to be the way they are.[6] So Gramsci says, and the "critical" American lawyers who have accepted his concept agree, that one must look closely at these belief systems, these deeply held assumptions about politics, economics, hierarchy, opportunity, individual merit, the proper role of government, the proper roles of men and women in the family, which are profoundly paralysis-inducing because they make it so hard for people (including the ruling groups themselves) even to *imagine* that life could be different and better.

The idea is not that ideology drugs the masses into thinking that their rulers and bosses are ideal, that life is fair and that everyone deserves his fate. Most ordinary people may well think that the system plays with a stacked deck and that the deal they got is a lousy one. Yet an ideology can still be "hegemonic" if its practical effect is to foreclose imagination of *alternative* orders. Workers may not much care for authoritarian rule at the workplace. Even so, they may not press for economic democracy, because they have bought the arguments that it would lower efficiency, leaving a smaller pie for everyone; or that they are not really competent to run the shop; or that it would be an alien order, some kind of "communism." Such arguments may now seem especially plausible after the collapse of the Soviet empire and the discrediting of "socialist" alternatives to capitalism. The existing order may inflict terrible wounds on health and personality and family life and self-respect, and still be tolerated as "the system we have, with all its faults."

Law, like religion and television images, is one of these clusters of belief—and it ties in with a lot of other nonlegal but similar clusters—that convince people that all the many hierarchical relations in which they live and work are natural and necessary. A small business is staffed with people who carry around in their heads mixed clusters of this kind: "I can tell these people what to do and fire them if they're not *very* polite to me and quick to do it, because (a) I own the business; (b) they have no right to anything but the minimum wage; (c) I went to college and they didn't; (d) they would not work as hard or as efficiently if I didn't keep after them; a business can't run efficiently without a strong top-down command structure; (e) if they don't like it they can leave," etc.—and the employees, though with less smugness and enthusiasm, believe it as well. Take the ownership claim: the employees are not likely to think they can challenge that because to do so would jeopardize their sense of the rights of ownership, which they themselves exercise in other aspects of life ("I own this house, so I can tell my brother-in-law to get the hell out of it"); they are locked into a belief cluster that abstracts and generalizes the ownership claim.

Now, the point of the work that some of the "critical" lawyers are doing is to try to describe—to make maps of—some of these interlocking systems of belief. Drawing here on the work of such "structuralist" writers as Lévi-Strauss and Piaget, they claim that legal ideas can be seen to be organized into structures, i.e., complex cultural codes.[7] The way human beings experience the world is by collectively building and maintaining systems of shared meanings that make it possible for us to interpret one another's words and actions and to protect freedom, goodness, and order from evil, pollution, and anarchy. "Law" is just one among many such systems of meaning that people construct in order to deal with one of the most threatening aspects of social existence: the danger posed by other people, whose cooperation is indispensable to us (we cannot even have an individual identity without them to help define it socially), but who may kill us or enslave us. It seems essential to have a system to sort out positive interactions (contracts, taxation to pay for public goods) from negative ones (crimes, torts, illegal searches or detentions, unconstitutional seizure of property). In the West, legal belief structures, together with economic and political ones, have been constructed to accomplish this sorting out. The systems, of course, have been largely built by elites who have thought they had some stake in rationalizing their dominant power positions, so at any given time they have tended to define rights in such a way as to reinforce existing hierarchies of wealth and privilege.

Even more important, such system building has the effect of making the social world as it is come to seem natural and inevitable. Though the structures are built, piece by interlocking piece, with human intentions, people come to "externalize" them, to attribute to them existence and control over and above human choice; and, moreover, to believe that these structures must be the way they are. Recall the example given earlier of the person who works in a small business for the "owner" of the business. It is true that the owner's position is backed up by the ultimate threat of force—if he does not like the way people behave on his property, he can summon armed helpers from the state to eject them—but he also has on his side the powerful ideological magic of a structure that gives him the "rights" of an "employer" and "owner," and the worker the "duties" of an "employee" and "invitee" on the "owner's property." The worker feels she cannot challenge the owner's right to eject her from his property if he does not like the way she behaves, in part because she feels helpless against the force he can invoke, but also because in part she not unreasonably accepts his claim as legitimate: she respects "individual rights of ownership" because the powers such rights confer seem necessary to her own power and freedom; limitations on an "owner's" rights would threaten her as well. But the analogy she makes is possible only because of his acquiescence in a belief structure—a particular version of liberal legalism—that abstracts relationships between real people (this woman and the man she "works for"; this woman and the brother-in-law she wants to eject from her house) into relations between entirely abstract categories of "individuals" playing the abstract social roles of "owner," "employee," etc.

This process of allowing the structures we ourselves have built to mediate relations among us so as to make us see ourselves as performing abstract roles in a play that is produced by no human agency is what is usually called (following Marx and such modern writers as Sartre and Lukács) reification.[8] It is a way people have of manufacturing necessity: they build structures, then act as if (and genuinely come to believe that) the structures they have built are determined by history, human nature, economic law.

Perhaps a promising tactic, therefore, of trying to struggle against being demobilized by our own conventional beliefs is to try to use the ordinary rational tools of intellectual inquiry to expose belief structures that claim that things as they are must necessarily be the way they are. There are many varieties of this sort of critical exercise, whose point is to unfreeze the world as it appears in legal discourse, or economic discourse, or just everyday common speech, as a "system" of more or less objectively determined social relations; and to reveal it as (we believe) it really is: a loose, fluid, contingent, various miscellany of practices that point toward many alternative ways of organizing social life.

Critical theories of law focus, naturally, mainly on legal discourse— the normal everyday ways lawmakers and administrators, judges, legal scholars, practicing lawyers, and law teachers argue and brief cases and talk about law and the role of law in regulating social life to one another and to their clients. Why is it that even people with an idealistic or reformist social agenda who come to law school, become lawyers, and are socialized into the system, come to believe that there's something natural, inevitable, and necessary about the way the legal system works, the social status quo? Among the many forces, political and economic, that reinforce the status quo there is a densely woven web of cultural assumptions wrapped around legal discourse, that say to lawyers: You cannot be a professional, you cannot be a realist, you cannot faithfully serve your clients and the premises of the legal system, and at the same time hope to contribute to any kind of progressive and transformative politics that would help to make this a more democratic and egalitarian society. The lessons lawyers learn from their practices are, in a phrase or two, lessons of *false legitimation* and *false necessity*. They learn that the way things are in society is about as good as they can be; and to the extent they aren't they can be fixed through marginal shifts in conventional arrangements—a little more or a little less regulation. Otherwise things are OK, and if they aren't, nothing can be done about it, without leading to economic inefficiency, totalitarian regulation, or just expensive futility, a lot of bother for bad results, or no results.

How does legal discourse accomplish this depressing, conservatizing effect? By selection and suppression; by concealing the actual complexities of legal doctrines and institutions and the social practices that law helps to structure; by privileging some legal principles as dominant and normal, and marginalizing others as deviant or exceptional.[9]

Look once again at the example of property rights. "Property rights," in American culture, have functioned as powerful symbols of individual freedom, the freedom to do as one wills with one's own, to behave as one feels like in one's own domain; as symbols of security, the castle moat protecting one from the incursions of others, especially from the state, whose officers cannot enter without a warrant or take without compensation; and as symbols of productive efficiency, providing the incentives to labor, invest, and create. But this dominant ideology of property, by facing frontward the aspects of property that seem to promote individual freedom, security, and efficiency, downplays or obscures property's other faces—some coercive and oppressive, others cooperative and benign. Stressing how property promotes the freedom of owners suppresses how it also enables the owner to control the lives and reduce to subjection those who need access to it. Stressing how property makes possible stable expectations by protecting them against arbitrary action, suppresses how property gives the owner an arbitrary discretion to wreak havoc over the lives of others—employees at will suddenly fired without cause, tenants suddenly evicted from rental housing, people who live around industrial plants who must watch their city die when the plant closes. Stressing how property provides a bulwark against coercive state action suppresses how the existence of property essentially depends upon coercive state power—without definition by laws, and enforcement by police, courts, and marshals, property would be meaningless and worthless. Stressing how property protects the lone individual's rights to exclude and enjoy suppresses the myriad ways in which property depends upon interaction and cooperation. Most basically, there can be no property rights unless a whole social system encourages people to collaborate to develop norms and enforce obligations to respect them: my in-your-face property right actually depends on collectively shared and enforced conventions of trust and cooperation. In any case, property rights are invariably relative, not absolute; they must accommodate when their exercise conflicts with the rights of others (as when my factory pollutes your stream); they are often shared rights to common resources (as in rights to fish or hunt or breathe air). Thus every legal system that recognizes property rights "regulates" their conflict with the rights of others: it's never an option *whether* to regulate, only *how* to regulate. Stressing property as the necessary incentive to productivity suppresses the need for resources to be widely available to others to make productive use of—as, for example, insisting on making all the fruits of creative labor into "intellectual property" disregards how making knowledge into property limits the ability of other creative people to make use of a common stock of ideas for innovations of their own (as is recognized in the organization of science on communist principles, with the fruits of discovery made available free of charge to all).[10]

Legal ideology provides false legitimation when it conceals the violent, coercive, arbitrary, and ugly faces of existing institutions. It reinforces false necessity by suppressing the alternative arrangements, the more democratic, egalitarian, cooperative, liberating alternatives, that our legal norms and practices also make available—sometimes those that have been available historically, but suppressed, and often those that are suggested in actual functioning practices in our society or others, and which have potential to be developed further. Contract law, for example, is actually saturated with progressive doctrines and policies: policies protecting weaker parties against advantage-taking and exploitation; policies promoting relations of loyalty, trust, solidarity, and cooperation and discouraging opportunism and strategic behavior; policies discouraging the commodification of valuable rights and relations that should not be turned into things that can be bought and sold for money; policies obliging parties to share gains, losses, or information, instead of grabbing everything they can for themselves. These tend to be framed as policies for exceptional or deviant cases.[11] What would happen if—gradually, selectively—more of them became the norm?

Critical legal theory helps to identify what's been privileged and what's been suppressed. It tries to reveal the backstage devices—the empirical assumptions, the contestable visions of society, the beliefs about directions of historical change—that mainstream legal discourse uses to close off the dark side of the status quo and embedded progressive alternatives to the status quo. As a constructive method, it describes how the alternative historical or currently functioning leeways and opportunities in the legal system might be strategically exploited and extended and generalized in the service of a progressive politics. One way of doing this is to do what Roberto Unger calls "deviationist doctrine"—to take arguments and practices that are familiar and respectable from one institutional context and to transfer them to another.[12] The most familiar general example is "economic democracy"—you take the norms of democracy— that the rulers are accountable to the ruled, that the governed should participate in making the rules that govern them, that every person should count for one and none for more than one—and apply them to the workplace. Much of this work is very specific. Kathy Stone and Karl Klare, for instance, have explored the possibilities within our basic structure of labor law and corporate governance for more participatory forms of workplace governance. Bill Simon has reached both into history and current practices of cooperatives—producer's cooperatives and housing cooperatives—for what he calls "social-republican property," models of association that, by limiting individual members' rights to accumulate and alienate property, promote equality and community without sacrificing efficiency. Another example would be Simon's work on the New Deal social workers—a historical model for street-level professional discretion that managed to help out poor clienteles without patronizing them and saw poor relief as a way-station toward political power.[13]

How has this been different from other progressive critiques and movements?

1. It takes the rhetoric and content of law seriously; it doesn't argue that law is just a mask for privilege and exploitation. The categories, principles, and rhetorics of law and legal argument deliver real resources to get some leverage on social change. Legal discourses don't just mask the realities of power and life, but participate in constructing those realities. Having a legal property right gives you real power; being able to work through the corporate form or partnership or union gives you real capacity for collective action.

2. Unlike most forms of Marxist thought, it doesn't treat capitalism as a totalizing system. There's no notion that one would need a cataclysmic crisis of capitalism to transcend it and bring about a totally new order.

On the contrary, it holds that the forms of liberal-democratic-capitalism that we are used to are only a few among the many ways of being liberal-democratic-capitalist in the world—very different from Swedish or Taiwanese capitalism for example!—and among the forms that might be brought into being, ours are both worse and better. Prototypes for some of these alternatives are all around us, in existing institutions and practices. The United States itself in its own history has experimented with many different forms of workplace organization, property holdings, compensation systems, models of gender relations, and family life. The rule systems we have incorporated into our belief structures are not found in nature but are historically contingent; they have not always existed in their present form. This discovery can be extraordinarily liberating, not (at least not usually) because there is anything so wonderful about the belief structures and institutional arrangements of the past, but because uncovering those structures makes us see how arbitrary our categories for dividing up experience are, how nonexhaustive of human potentiality. The resources for "revolutionary reform" are thus often to be found in our own traditions, customs, and practices.

3. The target of critical legal theory has usually been "illegitimate hierarchy"—meaning not only hierarchies of class, race or ethnicity, and gender, but hierarchies within races, classes, and sexes as well.

4. And finally, critical legal theory is not particularly oriented toward capture of central state machinery. The view of many critical theorists is that much of social life is constructed out of the smallest, most routine, most ordinary interactions of daily life in which some human beings dominate others and they acquiesce in such domination, all the while constructing the systems of belief that explain and justify what they are doing. It may be, as the social theorist Michel Foucault's work suggests, that much of the legitimating power of a legal system is built up out of such myriad tiny instances.[14] To the extent that is so, social activism may most usefully begin in the situation in which the activist may immediately find herself, in one's law school (if one is a student or teacher) or law office (if one is in practice), and living or work community; and focus on producing interstitial changes in beliefs, practices, and social practices. Clearly among the inspiring models here are those of the civil rights, women's, environmental, and gay and lesbian rights movements, in which large numbers of local actions have come gradually to be interlinked in national and international networks of affiliation, and are directed at changing ordinary citizens' attitudes and routines as well as government policies.

I do not want to give the impression that everyone drawn to critical legal theory has adopted the approaches I have just described. On the contrary, these approaches are hotly debated. Some of those who most fiercely dispute the validity of these approaches do so in part on political grounds. I will mention a few of these criticisms and briefly respond to them.

1. Probably the most common critique of critical legal theory has been of its central thesis that the law is not a fixed and determined system, but rather an unruly miscellany of various, multifaceted, contradictory practices, altering from time to time and from context to context as different facets of law are privileged or suppressed—for example, as the law of property stresses its exclusionary or its sharing doctrines; as the law of contract stresses its enforce-all-promises-come-hell-or-high-water or its protective doctrines; as the law of corporations stresses doctrines promoting management's authority and autonomy or its fiduciary duties to stakeholders and the public; or indeed as any body of applications emphasizes its strict rules or its equitable exceptions, defenses, or excuses. Critical theorists sometimes called this the thesis of the "indeterminacy" of law; and this has given rise to many critiques, many of them based on misunderstandings.

Some people supposed the thesis was that law was unpredictable; and pointed out reasonably enough that legal results are predictable most of the time, and lawyers make a living predicting them. Critical theorists agreed, but said that legal results were predictable not because those results were inexorably "required" by existing legal doctrines or principles but because lawyers and other interpreters tend to develop shared conventions about how to apply the law; and these conventions remain stable for a while, until something happens to destabilize them. But there are always, wholly or partly hidden, branching alternative tracks that the law might travel on instead; and under the right kind of pressure in the right circumstances, the law may switch tracks—as in 1954 when the Supreme Court switched from the *Plessy* v. *Ferguson* track of doctrine that state racially segregated facilities were constitutional if equal to the alternative *Brown* v. *Board of Education* track (a track patiently prepared through decades of NAACP litigation) that state-mandated segregation was inherently unequal and hence unconstitutional.

Other critics said the indeterminacy thesis was a form of "nihilism" and a threat to the "rule of law"—meaning, I would guess, that if lots of people get the idea that law is just a bunch of reified belief structures and is bristling with immanent alternatives, then the legal system will become the prey of demagogues, opportunists, and reactionaries, who are now restrained only by the belief that law is fixed and certain. The problem with that argument is that such people have never been much restrained. After the Civil War, for example, conservative courts effectively nullified civil rights legislation designed to promote the equal rights of freed slaves while allowing business lawyers to turn the Fourteenth Amendment into a device to protect their clients from regulation. In the present day, conservatives quote Martin Luther King, Jr., and great civil rights cases in support of their ideal of "color-blind equal opportunity," which they believe prohibits any state-backed action directed at pushing historically subordinated groups past barriers to their advancement. If conservatives are under no illusions that the legal system is immune from manipulation and alteration, it's hard to see what liberals and leftists have to gain by preserving such illusions!

2. A second criticism is that the view that law and the economy as we know them are structures inside people's heads is a form of "idealism"; it assumes that the world can be changed merely by *thinking* about it differently. This charge is, I think, partly valid and partly misleading. The charge is true in that the belief it criticizes is indeed that among the main constraints on making social life more bearable are these terrible, constricting limits on imagination; and that the structures limiting our potential are as obdurate as they are because they are collectively constructed and maintained—we *have* to use them to think about the world at all, because the world makes no sense apart from our systems of shared meanings. But the charge is not true if it means to imply that we believe that all constraints on human action are imaginary, alienated ideas of "false necessity." Obviously there are many constraints on human social activity—scarcities of desired things, finite resources of bodies and minds, production possibilities of existing and perhaps all future technologies, perhaps even ineradicable propensities for evil—that any society will have to face. What is false is to think that these constraints dictate that we are limited to some specific set of social arrangements that we are already familiar with, in history or in our own time; that the human race can live only within its real constraints in a few specific ways—e.g., that it *must* choose between (reified models of) "liberal capitalism" and "state socialist dictatorship."

There are of course other constraints of a different kind: entrenched power and privilege, which are not easily surrendered; customary inertia; fear even among the dispossessed that any change will leave them with less than they have; terror of the unknown. Obviously it takes more than reimagining the world to overcome these constraints: it takes the courage and cunning to organize with others and struggle against circumstances. But reimagination, getting to the point of seeing that change is possible, is a necessary first step. People don't revolt because their situation is bad; they can suffer in silence for centuries. They revolt when their situation comes to seem *unjust* and *alterable*. A tiny example from recent history: Until a few years ago, a working woman had to accept her employer's sexual advances as something she had invited by her dress and manner, or as an inevitable occupational risk, given natural male aggression. Feminists got together and reinterpreted this kind of interaction as "sexual harassment," something both culpable and avoidable; then by engaging in politics got it defined as a legal harm with a legal remedy.[15] That doesn't always help the victims much, because legal rights are hard to vindicate. But the process has switched many people's (including employers') views of the conduct from "It's only natural; men are like that; deal with it" to "He's a creep; that's unacceptable."

3. Other critics—especially those who pioneered what has become known as "critical race theory"—worry that the critique that "rights" lack any objective substance or reality, that they are merely shared practices that people adopt and then reify, may be dangerous to the interests of subordinated groups. Such groups have wrung whatever concessions they have from the dominant society by asserting that they have—that they almost physically possess—"rights" that are as real as chairs and tables, that the "rule of law, not of men" requires that their rights be recognized and protected as a kind of property. If "rights" are reanalyzed as conventional and contingent, subject to shifting political winds, won't that leave minorities completely unprotected?[16] I would respond this way: It's certainly true that the language of "rights" has been a powerful mobilizer of insurgency and resistance, has exerted a powerful appeal upon influential outsiders (as, for example, the Southern black civil rights movement appealed to Northern whites in the 1950s and 1960s), and has thus delivered powerful leverage for negotiating with people in authority. But the rhetoric of rights can be dangerously double-edged, as the black civil rights movement has also discovered. Floor entitlements can be turned into ceilings (you've got your rights, but that's all you'll get). Formal rights without practical enforceable content are easily substituted for real benefits. Anyway, the powerful can always assert counterrights (to vested property, to differential treatment according to "merit," to association with one's own kind) to the rights of the disadvantaged. "Rights" conflict—and the conflict cannot be resolved by

appeal to rights. The fact is that "rights" are just shorthand symbols for social practices that people collectively value and maintain. The right to be free of illegal searches and seizures is a bunch of rules governing police conduct, enforced by agencies outside the police bureaucracy. It should be possible to value, and fight for, the substantive practices that the rights only symbolically represent without mystifying and falsely objectifying the symbols themselves.

Critical race theorists and feminist legal theorists also argued that the strand of critical legal theory I have been describing was too exclusively directed at liberal legal discourse in general—that by dwelling on what seemed unexceptionable and taken-for-granted in the legal system it did not sufficiently and concretely focus on legal enactments of racism and patriarchy themselves as causes of illegitimate hierarchy. This critique was, I think, entirely valid; and fortunately a good deal of work is being done to fill the void.[17]

Ultimately, an intellectual stance that pretends to be the basis of a politics has to ask the question, Does it help give us reason for hope and a motive for action, or lead to paralysis and despair? Does being a critic of "false legitimation" and "false necessity" supply energy or direction for a progressive politics? The notion that there are no objective laws of social change is in one way profoundly depressing. Those who have come to believe it have had to abandon the most comforting hopes of socialism: that history was on its side, and that history could be accelerated through a scientific understanding of social laws. It no longer seems plausible to think that organization of the working class or capture of the state apparatus will magically bring about the conditions within which people could begin to realize the full potential for human flourishing. Such strategies have led to valuable if modest improvements in social life, as well as to stagnation, co-optation by the existing structures, and nightmare regimes of state terror. Of course, this does not mean that people should stop trying to organize the working class or other subordinated or marginalized groups or to influence the exercise of state power; it means only that they have to do so pragmatically and experimentally, with full knowledge that there are no deeper logics of historical necessity that can guarantee that what we do now will be justified later. Yet, if the real enemy is *us—all of us*—the structures we carry around in our heads, the limits on our imagination—where can we even begin? It ought to be of some value to demonstrate that, over and over again, the arguments for why nothing important can change are no good; and to point to alternatives embedded in historical and existing practices. Things seem to change in history when people break out of their accustomed ways of responding to domination, by acting as if the constraints on their improving their lives were not real and that they could change things; and sometimes they can, though not always in the way they had hoped or intended; but they never knew they could change them at all until they tried.

NOTES

1. See Alan D. Freeman, *Legitimizing Racial Discrimination Through Antidiscrimination Law: A Critical Review of Supreme Court Doctrine,* 62 Minnesota Law Review 1049 (1978); Derrick A. Bell, *And We Are Not Saved: The Elusive Quest for Racial Justice* (New York: Basic Books, 1989).

2. Some classic instrumentalist texts are David B. Truman, *The Governmental Process: Political Interests and Public Opinion* (New York: Knopf, 1951); Ralph Miliband, *The State in Capitalist Society* (New York: Basic Books, 1969).

3. See E. P. Thompson, "The Rule of Law," in *Whigs and Hunters* (New York: Pantheon, 1975); Douglas Hay et al., *Albion's Fatal Tree: Crime and Society in Eighteenth-Century England* (New York: Pantheon, 1975); Mark V. Tushnet, *A Marxist Analysis of American Law,* 1 Marxist Perspectives 96 (1978).

4. See Thompson, "The Rule of Law"; David M. Trubek, *Complexity and Contradiction in the Legal Order: Balbus and the Challenge of Critical Social Thought About Law,* 11 Law and Society Review 527 (1977).

5. See Karl Klare, chapter 24, supra.

6. See Antonio Gramsci, *Selections from the Prison Notebooks,* ed. trans. Quintin Hoare and Geoffrey Nowell-Smith (New York: International Publishers, 1971), 195–96, 246–47.

7. See, for example, Duncan Kennedy, *The Structure of Blackstone's Commentaries,* 28 Buffalo Law Review 205 (1979); Isaac D. Balbus, *Commodity Form and Legal Form: An Essay on the Relative Autonomy of the Law,* 11 Law and Society Review 571 (1977); Thomas C. Heller, "Is the Charitable Exemption from Property Taxes an Easy Case? General Concerns About Legal Economics and Jurisprudence," in *Essays on the Law and Economics of Local Governments,* ed. Daniel Rubinfeld

(Washington, DC: Urban Institute, 1979), 183–251; Al Katz, *Studies in Boundary Theory: Three Essays in Adjudication and Politics,* 28 Buffalo Law Review 383 (1979); Roberto Mangabeira Unger, *Knowledge and Politics* (New York: Free Press, 1975); Jack Balkin, *The Crystalline Structure of Legal Thought,* 39 Rutgers Law Review 1 (1986).

8. See Peter Gabel, "Reification in Legal Reasoning," in *Research in Law and Sociology,* vol. 3, ed. Stephen Spitzer (Greenwich, CT: JAI Press, 1980), 25–51.

9. For an account of critical legal thought stressing selection and suppression, see Mark Kelman, *A Guide to Critical Legal Studies* (Cambridge, MA: Harvard University Press, 1987).

10. See Joseph Singer, *The Reliance Interest in Property,* 40 Stanford Law Review 614 (1988); Carol Rose, *Property and Persuasion: Essays on the History, Theory, and Rhetoric of Ownership* (Boulder, CO: Westview, 1996); Duncan Kennedy and Frank I. Michelman, *Are Property and Contract Efficient?* 8 Hofstra Law Review 711 (1980); James Boyle, *Shamans, Software, and Spleens: Law and the Construction of the Information Society* (Cambridge, MA: Harvard University Press, 1996).

11. See Duncan Kennedy, *Distributive and Paternalist Motives in Contract and Tort Law, with Special Reference to Compulsory Terms and Unequal Bargaining Power,* 41 Maryland Law Review 563 (1982); Margaret Jane Radin, *Contested Commodities* (Cambridge, MA: Harvard University Press, 1996).

12. Roberto Mangabeira Unger, *The Critical Legal Studies Movement* (Cambridge, MA: Harvard University Press, 1986).

13. See Katherine V. W. Stone, *Labor and the Corporate Structure,* 55 University of Chicago Law Review 73 (1988); Karl Klare, *Workplace Democracy and Market Reconstruction: An Agenda for Legal Reform,* 38 Catholic University Law Review 1 (1988); William H. Simon, *Social-Republican Property,* 38 U.C.L.A. Law Review 1335 (1991); William H. Simon, *The Invention and Reinvention of Welfare Rights,* 44 Maryland Law Review 1 (1985).

14. See especially Michel Foucault, *Discipline and Punish: The Birth of the Prison,* trans. Alan Sheridan (New York: Pantheon, 1977).

15. The pioneering work in this field was Catharine A. MacKinnon, *Sexual Harassment of Working Women: A Case of Sex Discrimination* (New Haven, CT: Yale University Press, 1979).

16. See Kimberlé Williams Crenshaw, *Race, Reform, and Retrenchment: Transformation and Legitimation in Antidiscrimination Law,* 101 Harvard Law Review 1331 (1988), for a particularly powerful version of this critique.

17. See Gary Minda, *Postmodern Legal Movements: Law and Jurisprudence at Century's End* (New York: New York University Press, 1995), for sympathetic accounts of much of this work.

29 JANE B. BARON AND JULIA EPSTEIN

LANGUAGE AND THE LAW: LITERATURE, NARRATIVE, AND LEGAL THEORY

THE law is its own form of language, as any first-time reader of a statute or judicial opinion will attest. To begin with, law is characterized by a highly specialized vocabulary; students must be initiated into the proper use of such terms as *perpetuities, bills of attainder, promissory estoppel,* and scores of others integral to the basic law school curriculum. But legal usage transforms even the familiar vocabulary of ordinary speech. Pleadings, motions, affidavits, and court orders differ distinctly in form and intelligibility from newspaper articles, letters, or novels, even though they are often composed of nonspecialized terms.

What can be said in the language of the law? In theory, anything that can be said in ordinary language. In the past twenty years, two groups of scholars have called attention to the limits of legal language—highlighting what it omits, the ways it can be inaccessible, and how it tends covertly to privilege certain points of view. The first of these two groups focuses on law and literature, while the second focuses on law and narrative.

Both groups rely on materials (such as novels, plays, or stories) and theories (such as New Criticism, hermeneutics, or deconstruction) outside the usual realm of law. Both also seem to reach in the same general direction, toward the humanities. Thus, one would expect the paths of the two movements to connect or overlap in some way. Surprisingly, the connection is thin and weak. Both movements question the adequacy of legal language to express the experiences and aspirations of all members of the community—the powerless as well as the powerful—but the parallel ends there. From similar starting points, the movements travel in quite different directions.

This essay offers historical sketches of the Law and Literature and the Law and Narrative movements, analyzing their concerns and goals.[1] Both movements seek to use literary methodologies in the service of a political critique of the legal system and its operations. In neither case has the effort been entirely successful. Even the most sensitive literary or narrative analyses have a troubling tendency to reinforce rather than displace existing relations of power and subordination within the law.

LAW AND LITERATURE

Lawyers have long been interested in literature, but the nature of that interest has changed over time. As Robert Ferguson has demonstrated, until the Civil War the man of law in the United States (there were, of course, no women lawyers) was also a man of letters; the culture of the profession was a culture of art as well as of science.[2] The vision of professionalism as technical proficiency in the manipulation of formal legal doctrine developed later. Once it did, literature was no longer understood to be a part of law or of legal education. Instead, it was offered as a supplement or enrichment to dry law, something lawyers ought to consult for its broadening or humanizing perspective. This view survives today, supplemented by the view that interpretive theories and techniques developed in the context of literary texts are useful for interpreting legal texts.

THE THEMES OF LAW AND LITERATURE

The Law and Literature movement perhaps got its start in 1908, when John H. Wigmore published *A List of Legal Novels,* a "legal" novel being, in Wigmore's view, "simply a novel in which a lawyer, most of all, ought to be interested." The list, which has been often expanded and updated since its initial appearance, presumed that a lawyer had a "special professional duty to be familiar with those features of his profession which have been taken up into general thought and literature" and also that the lawyer, whose work requires him to "know human nature" could find in fiction "a catalogue of life's characters."[3]

The contemporary Law and Literature movement continues to examine literary texts with legal themes, such as Melville's *Billy Budd* and Kafka's *The Trial,* but no longer is that examination addressed solely to practicing lawyers. The notion is that literary texts depicting human encounters with the law raise fundamental questions about the role of law in society and the moral responsibilities of lawyers. A typical work in this genre might describe the way in which law is treated in plays such as *The Merchant of Venice* and *Measure for Measure*, arguing, for example, that Shakespeare's jurisprudence demonstrates that law "can help bring about social regeneration" rather than becoming "a tool of apology and unjustified repression."[4]

We call this strand of the Law and Literature movement the "moral uplift" project. The moral uplift view essentially holds that literature can humanize law, and that the experience of systematically reading literary texts can humanize lawyers. The study and practice of law, in this view, has become overly technical and codified and thereby disconnected from the essential character and values of the people it affects—law students, practitioners, and clients alike. Literature can serve to reconnect legal doctrine and those who deal with law to values from which they have become detached.

The moral uplift project argues also that literature provides a means of understanding human motivations and choices as well as human weaknesses and moments of courage—even when the literary work in question does not touch upon law directly. Indeed, many of the leading works of the more contemporary Law and Literature movement examine texts that are not "legal" in the sense Wigmore proposed, ranging from Homer's *Iliad* to Toni Morrison's *Beloved*.[5] Literature's abiding interest in the human condition calls attention to the fact that law is only one of many social institutions that shape human and social interactions. As Martha Nussbaum puts it:

> [L]iterary works typically invite their readers to put themselves in the place of people of many different kinds and to take on their experiences. . . . [T]hey promote identification and sympathy. . . .
>
> One may be told many things about people in one's own society and yet keep that knowledge at a distance. Literary works that promote identification and emotional reaction cut through those self-protective stratagems, requiring us to see and to respond to many things that may be difficult to confront.[6]

The lessons implicit in the moral uplift project ought to be of interest to legal professionals and lay citizens alike. In practice, it has not been clear whether anyone outside of a small segment of the legal academy has been listening. When great works of the humanities are offered as a source of general wisdom, it is easy to dismiss the study of literature as a study of appreciation, a not entirely necessary addition to the hard discipline of law. Once literary study is seen as just an add-on, and not a necessary component of good legal analysis, many lawyers—practitioners and academics alike—may be tempted simply to ignore it. Thus, the influence of the moral uplift project is difficult to ascertain.

We call the second strand of the Law and Literature movement the "hermeneutic" project. Hermeneutic legal scholars view legal writings such as statutes or judicial opinions as texts, shaped productions of language. Literary study offers the most elaborated set of critical techniques for reading texts, and, the hermeneutic project proposes, legal academics can and should borrow methodologies from literary critics.

However, literary critics often disagree about methodology. Like literary hermeneutics, legal hermeneutics has engendered heated controversies over such issues as intention, formalism, and the possibility of objective interpretation. Thus, the turn to literary criticism has involved legal theorists in debates over who or what controls the meaning of a text and how to establish a text's meaning. As two leading scholars of the hermeneutic project have written: "All of these controversies involve the key question of whether an interpreter can remain separate from an external text and ultimately submit to the reading demanded by the text. In what sense, if at all, do texts exert control over what their readers make of them?"[7] In this way, hermeneutic legal scholars have recast the debate over authority in law into a debate over interpretation in a literary as well as a legal sense.

Much of real-world legal practice involves interpretations of documents, statutes, opinions, and the like. In theory, then, the hermeneutic project should be as relevant to legal practitioners as to legal academics. In practice, however, the complexity of literary methodologies such as deconstruction, coupled with the hermeneutic project's almost obsessive fascination with constitutional law, have kept this strand of the Law and Literature movement fairly well confined to the legal academy.

THE POLITICS OF LAW AND LITERATURE

The politics of the Law and Literature movement are somewhat obscure. The moral improvement offered by literature renders readers more responsible, more empathic, more sensitive to others—or so it is argued—and surely these qualities are not irrelevant to people's behavior as political actors. Yet despite constant references to the quality of our communal life, politics seems curiously peripheral to the moral uplift side of Law and Literature. Indeed, critics of this strand of Law and Literature have frequently noted how little attention is paid to issues of inclusion in and, more important, exclusion from the communities of which Law and Literature so often speaks.[8]

In the mid-1980s, the moral uplift strand of Law and Literature approached politics indirectly, by addressing the hottest political dispute in the academy at the time, that between law and economics on one side and critical legal studies (CLS) on the other. To the Law and Literature movement, economic thinking represented a highly virulent form of utilitarian instrumentalism, the principal vice of which was that it regarded persons and institutions as means, rather than treating them as ends valuable and meaningful in themselves. Part of the uplift provided by literature was, in fact, to demonstrate the fallacies and dangers of this way of thinking. So, the argument goes, where instrumentalism deals primarily in abstractions, literature provides particulars; where instrumentalism relies on dry rationalism, literature reaches—and teaches the value of— the emotions; where instrumentalism sees individuals solely in terms of their preferences, literature sees individuals as, well, individuals, richer than any sum of their parts or aims.

Distrust and distaste for law and economics allied Law and Literature with CLS, but only to a limited degree. Proponents of Law and Literature tended to make their arguments about morality in law by offering pointed readings of carefully chosen works of literature. But CLS tended to emphasize the openness of texts, and the definitive readings put forward by the Law and Literature movement were at odds with both the indeterminacy thesis and the reigning literary methodology of the period, deconstruction. To propose a given reading as *the* correct interpretation of a literary work is the exact analogue of the legal strategy that the indeterminacy thesis was designed to expose and combat, that is, the presentation of the court's reading as the one mandated by law and the suppression of alternative possible readings of the precedent or statute at issue.

Moreover, the dichotomization of qualities such as reason-emotion, abstraction-particularity, and the like was, by CLS standards, naive. CLS found no shortage of such dichotomies in traditional legal thinking, but it did not accept them at face value. Rather, borrowing loosely from poststructuralism, it held the dichotomies up to critical scrutiny, examining how they functioned as rhetoric and as ways of organizing thought. For example, far from treating the reason-emotion dichotomy as natural and descriptive, as the Law and Literature movement did, CLS treated it as contingent, and then inquired whether it tended covertly to privilege one or another side. (It did.) Since the moral uplift strand of Law and

Literature enlisted the very dichotomies that CLS sought to critique, it is not surprising that the two movements identified only loosely with one another.

On the hermeneutic side, things were somewhat different. The central position of the U.S. Constitution in our governmental culture has made the political stakes involved in interpretative issues more obvious, and Edwin Meese's inflammatory originalist proposals made those stakes almost impossible to deny.[9] Moreover, the hermeneutic project's fundamental decision to look *outside* law for interpretive methodologies reflects a judgment, with important political implications, about the adequacy of law alone to provide answers to questions of interpretation. Those in the tradition of Langdell who understand law as a self-contained system will have no need for the less "scientific" and "objective" methodologies of the humanities.

For those engaged in the hermeneutic project, then, politics were everywhere. The debate within literary theory at the time legal academics turned to it (and, to a large extent, today) is a debate about power. The issue concerns who has authority over the meaning of a text—its author, its reader, its cultural and institutional uses, its words themselves, and so on. The answer to this question determines the important related issue of whether (and how) a reader/decision maker is constrained in his or her reading of texts. If, as some theories assert, neither authorial intent nor the text's words themselves determine the meaning of a text, then, it could be argued, the reader is free to read a text *in any way he or she wants*. The political implications of this line of reasoning in the legal context are significant. If neither the words nor the history of statutes and opinions determine meaning and judges are free to choose any outcomes they want, then it will be impossible to attain the rule-of-law objective of "government of law, not men."[10]

The hermeneutic project's interest in power paralleled that of CLS, but despite substantial overlap the trajectories of the two movements were somewhat different. The CLS indeterminacy critique was quite consistent with the strand of the hermeneutic project that argued that texts, intentions, and the like do not (completely) control meaning. And the methodology used to demonstrate legal indeterminacy evermore self-consciously borrowed and built on literary deconstruction. But the point of the indeterminacy critique, at least as some saw it, was to demonstrate that, appearances to the contrary notwithstanding, important questions of value in the law had not been concluded, and therefore it was still possible—indeed, imperative—to discuss politics and create a better world.

That is, once freed from the illusion that certain aspects of the world were fixed and immutable, we could discuss the sort of world we wanted and ultimately bring that world into being. But at least some of the interpretive theories that were thought to support the CLS indeterminacy critique denied the possibility of the sort of freedom the critics seemed to envision. For example, if, as some of these interpretive theories assert, we are "always already" imbedded in cultural structures that constrain what it is possible for us to imagine, then recognition of indeterminacy does not render us more free to decide what we want to be or what language can mean.

LAW AND NARRATIVE

Just as lawyers had taken an interest in literature for a substantial period of time before there was a Law and Literature movement, lawyers had something of a long-standing interest in narrative before the legal storytelling movement blossomed in the 1980s. Prior to that time, trial advocates wrote extensively on storytelling in litigation contexts, arguing that effective lawyering tends to require, along with strong cross-examination skills and the like, a case theory in the form of a story that is coherent and plausible to the finder of fact. One strand of the Law and Narrative movement picked up on this theme, agreeing that storytelling is a particularly strong and effective communication strategy but—unlike the trial advocates—arguing that many litigants might be unable effectively to employ it, either because they lack cultural familiarity with traditional storytelling conventions or because their experiences depart from the plot lines of accepted stories. This strand of interest in narrative within law has been supplemented by two others, one offering stories as evidence of facts and experiences left out of conventional legal accounts and the other offering stories—usually multiple accounts of a single event—as a challenge to the notion of objectivity in law.

THE THEMES OF LAW AND NARRATIVE

There are many ways to convey ideas. In trying to persuade another person, one might make a speech, formulate a mathematical proof, or compose an argument constructed in ordered, logical deductive or inductive steps. In what we call its "strategic" strand, the Law and Narrative movement proposed that a most effective method of persuasion is to tell a story. Stories, it is argued, employ particulars rather than abstractions and can appeal to the emotions as well as to the intellect. Because individuals are socialized to story forms from childhood (who does not understand "once upon a time" as a beginning, and "they all lived happily ever after" as an end?), arguments in the form of stories call on a widely available cultural competence.

The strategic strand of the legal storytelling movement proposed to use the accessibility of the story form in the service of arguments that might otherwise seem improbable or unintelligible. Points that others might not be prepared to hear—because those points may seem bizarre or incredible—might be rendered intelligible if transmitted through a story; the familiar format in effect renders the unfamiliar message easier to hear. So, for example, a white person unconvinced by an African American's statement about unconscious discrimination might understand the point differently if it were embedded in a story whose context, details, and plot could make the discrimination nearly undeniable. The strategic strand of the Law and Narrative movement thus offers storytelling as a particularly powerful communicative tool to be employed in the service of persuasion.[11]

The second strand of the legal storytelling movement focuses less on story form than on substance. The "evidentiary" strand of the Law and Narrative movement uses stories—usually stories of individuals' actual experiences—to supply information about the actual functioning of the law in real-world settings. For example, in deciding on policy respecting gays in the military, it may be useful to know the ways in which both closeted and uncloseted gays are treated while in the service. One way to obtain this information is to obtain and attend to their stories. Similarly, one way to learn whether existing civil rights laws adequately remedy racism is to attend to stories of discrimination experienced by people of color in an ostensibly colorblind world.[12] In this sense, the evidentiary vein of the legal storytelling movement aims to supply information missing from the law—information presumably relevant to the proper formulation of legal principles.

The stories offered for evidentiary purposes treat the described experiences as real; they tell of things that really occurred, things that informed law should take into account. A third strand of the Law and Narrative movement, the "multiple realities" strand, offers stories to challenge the idea of the real. Imagine a dispute concerning an event such as the interrogation of a prisoner in custody or a man and a woman engaging in sexual intercourse following a date. Imagine further that the participants in these events—the police officers and the suspect, the man and the woman—provide radically different accounts of the events in question, and that each of these accounts is an accurate and truthful statement of what its author experienced at the time. The very multiplicity of these inconsistent stories should give pause, raising questions about whether any single account can capture the truth.[13]

THE POLITICS OF LAW AND NARRATIVE

There is little doubt that the strands that together constitute the Law and Narrative movement are meant to be political.[14] Each is offered to show how the linguistic conventions of traditional legal discourse have the potential to—and do—operate to suppress the voices of the powerless: poor people, women, and persons of color. That is, each begins from the proposition that language both embodies and creates a power order; each seeks to expose the way in which language expresses power in order to change existing power relationships and structures.

The strategic strand of the Law and Narrative movement argues that there are many points that cannot be conveyed in the abstract forms of conventional legal argumentation. The story form is offered as a potentially more effective alternative, one that persuades less through logical rigor than by creating moments of recognition and empathy in the hearer. Conventional legal arguments, these strategists suggest, "appeal primarily to values that are already considered acceptable." Stories, on the other hand, "by their very nature can appeal to what is, by convention, still taboo in a culture. Because facts themselves capture and reflect values, what cannot be argued explicitly can be sneaked into a story."[15]

The strategic strand of the Law and Narrative movement also asks such politically charged questions as whether the highly stylized speech patterns that characterize traditional legal discourse, especially in formal settings, are equally available to everyone. Not surprisingly, they find that those patterns are not universally accessible:

> Familiar cultural images and long-established legal norms construct the subjectivity and speech of socially subordinated persons as inherently inferior to the speech and personhood of dominant groups. Social subordination itself can lead disfavored groups to deploy verbal strategies that mark their speech as deviant when measured against dominant stylistic norms. These conditions . . . undermine the capacity of many persons in our society to use the procedural rituals that are formally available to them.[16]

Unfortunately, the two arguments for the strategic use of storytelling do not fit well together. The very conventions that privilege the speech patterns of those in dominant positions render the arguments smuggled into stories suspect at best and unintelligible at worst because they depart so dramatically in form from what legal professionals have been trained to expect. This problem is confirmed by empirical research demonstrating that while clients and witnesses tend to present facts in story form, lawyers—and especially judges—are often incapable of processing the offered information because it is not presented in the inductive and deductive modes to which lawyers have become accustomed.[17]

The political goals of the evidentiary strand of the Law and Narrative movement are more straightforward. The premise of most evidentiary storytelling is that existing law is, in important instances, based on false or incomplete information; the function of stories is to provide additional data that will complete or correct the factual foundation on which doctrine rests. So, for example, one might tell a story of one's own experiences with childbirth or miscarriage to demonstrate the ways in which the current laws concerning reproductive rights fail to express the truths of female bodies. Similarly, one might recount stories of battered women's experiences in order to show that courts underestimate both the frequency of battering and the risks women face when they take steps to escape battering relationships.[18]

While the story format is a relatively new way of presenting evidence, the objectives of evidentiary stories are fairly mainstream: to reform law to reflect better the real-world context in which that law will be applied. On one level, there is little new in this sort of effort; if, for example, it could be shown through statistical evidence that some aspect of the existing tort liability system pervasively underestimated the risks of certain accidents, that showing would count as a reason for reforming the law to take account of the demonstrated risks. But the stories offered for evidentiary purposes are not perceived as mainstream for two related reasons. First, most of those writing these stories argue that the law tends to be least factually accurate when it comes to certain groups: women, minorities, and the poor. Implicit (and sometimes explicit) in the evidentiary stories, then, is a critique of existing law as nothing but a story, an untrue story, the effect of which is to privilege the experiences of dominant groups and ignore or suppress the experiences of the subordinated.

Second, the story format in which the critique is embedded to some degree undermines the critique's general point. If the argument is that the law *systematically* omits the experiences of certain groups, then no single story can support that argument because one person's experiences alone cannot demonstrate facts about group treatment. It is one thing to include a personal story or two in a more or less conventional law review article, that is, in an article that collects and analyzes large numbers of cases and statutes. It is another thing to embed discussions of cases and statutes inside a personal story, or to dispense with the case and statute discussions altogether. In the latter instance, the story may be seen as a wholly new form of argument and then criticized as unverifiable, atypical, and therefore irrelevant to the larger claim of group mistreatment.[19]

The political agenda of the multiple realities strand of the Law and Narrative movement is to challenge the idea of objectivity and neutrality in law. The point of recounting the same event from several different perspectives, or of showing the way in which our vision of an event changes if we see that event as beginning at an earlier point in time, is to demonstrate that there is no single story that can fully represent that event. What passes, then, for *the* facts of a case is some person's view. And because all viewing is situated in place, in time, and in culture, no view is impartial.

Whereas these observations might seem to be of merely philosophical interest, they are politically charged in the legal context because the aspirations of the rule of law ideal require courts to strive for, and to claim they have attained, a "neutral" or "objective" perspective on the facts. This "objectivity," the multiple reality storytellers argue, is false. More important, it masks or suppresses the other perspectives that might equally pertain to or bear on the events in question. These perspectives will also lack objectivity, but that does not render them less valid or relevant. Here again, multiple realities storytellers argue that the perspectives that tend to be suppressed or ignored by purportedly objective accounts are those of subordinated groups. So claims to objectivity are not just false but harmful, part of the way oppression is both institutionalized and disguised.

The politics of the multiple realities strand of the Law and Narrative movement are, like the politics of evidentiary storytelling, problematic. First, the point and premise of multiple realities storytelling is that there is no single true perspective that can legitimately claim authority. This claim is in tension with evidentiary storytelling, whereby accounts are offered as true and are meant to be given authority over the less true stories told by unreformed legal doctrine. Second, the epistemological claim that there is no unsituated access to knowledge, no impartial or objective way to determine the facts, is often misunderstood as an ontological claim that facts and reality do not exist at all. Finally, if there are only perspectives, each true for the perceiver and none entitled to authority, how, critics have asked, are we to avoid a slide into complete relativism?

LITERATURE, NARRATIVE, AND SOCIAL TRANSFORMATION

Legal scholars in the Law and Literature and Law and Narrative movements have begun to take into account the fact that law is a discursive practice—a system of ideas conveyed by and based in language—as well as a method of social organization and a means for state coercion. In such a view, not only do literary and legal texts reflect the belief systems that inhere in their historical moments, they also participate in shaping those belief systems and those historical moments. Thus, fictive and legal texts alike—poems, plays, novels; statutes, judicial opinions, contracts—provide particular sets of documents for studying both cultural ideas and social change. In this sense, the Law and Literature and Law and Narrative movements reflect the "linguistic turn" already made by historians and anthropologists.

A full linguistic turn requires an understanding of the ways in which law's discursive practices—its norms of speech, argumentation, and writing—both embody and implement power, as has been amply pointed out by CLS scholars. It especially requires understanding the inadequacies, distortions, and elitism of professional languages. These languages produce a set of images of precisely those people who are least likely to have access to expertise in deploying them, especially the poor and educationally disadvantaged. While the resulting images are meant to serve these groups' legal interests, the professional discourse may exclude and disempower persons who are represented in a language they have not been trained to use.

Legal scholars examining how lawyers represent clients have taken a step toward examining this paradox. Poverty lawyers in particular, especially clinical teachers operating from bases in academia, have begun to push harder along the boundaries of narrative scholarship by questioning not only whose stories get to be told, but also how and by whom those stories are told, how they are heard, and how they are interpreted and reconstructed by lawyers. Narrative scholars in this line have provided sensitive accounts of their own practices, demonstrating how—despite good intentions and technically good legal results—poverty lawyers can reconstruct their clients' stories in such a way that the client is silenced and disempowered. These stories are offered as the basis of an alternative practice, one in which lawyers challenge their own interpretive pre-understandings of client dependency, listen in new ways to the discontinuous and often contradictory strands of their clients' stories, and reempower their clients by seeing the relevance of their daily struggles, honoring their values and their agency in their own lives, and restoring the integrity of their stories through collaborative advocacy.[20]

These accounts focus usefully on the way in which poverty lawyers often have reinforced a sense of dependency in their clients and thereby falsified their clients' stories and belittled their integrity. But they do not always pay adequate attention to the larger context in which these stories arise: the impersonal and degrading bureaucratic practices of a welfare system that clients find routinely insensitive. Scholars writing these accounts have yet to take the next step not only to fight the poverty lawyer's classist and perhaps also racist and sexist assumptions about clients' dependency, but also to analyze the ways in which that dependency serves the state welfare apparatus, indeed may even be cultivated by it to maintain control over the potentially unruly poor. They only barely analyze how the poverty law office apparatus, meant to help the poor (as is the department of welfare), reinforces the induced powerlessness and dependency the poor have been made to feel, and how the law offices to which clients go for redress operate uncannily like the offices that have treated them unfairly in the first place. In other words, the stories of advocacy in action cogently assess what poverty lawyers initially miss or falsify in client narrative, and readmit the integrity of clients' subjective experiences. But they fail to weave into the complex and circular stories of unemployment, hunger, and deprivation the other strands of the narrative, those that emanate from a welfare system that depends for its operation on maintaining its clientele at or below the poverty level.

Similarly, neither the moral uplift nor the hermeneutic projects of the Law and Literature movement fully account for the ways in which legal language both expresses and implements power within law. The moral uplift strand has analyzed the operation of the legal system in works with legal themes such as *Billy Budd, Bleak House,* or *The Trial.* These analyses can expose the way in which the literal language of the law inadequately reflects the full range of human issues involved in the story, leading to results that are morally unacceptable or absurd. And consideration of works with nonlegal themes can, as participants in the moral uplift project have argued, heighten sensitivity to and empathy toward persons who might otherwise appear as "others"; this heightened awareness may enhance the possibility that justice will be done in a case involving such an "other."

Although it is undoubtedly useful to identify the limits of legal language or to enhance human sympathy, works in this vein do not sufficiently attend to the ways in which the law itself constructs the very values in which the moral uplift project takes interest. It is useful to question whether law adequately respects or responds to emotions as well as to reason, to passion as well as to intellect. But it may be more important to question whether these qualities are truly dichotomous, or whether the law, in its obsessive search for impartiality, has itself been the source of the view that reason must be disengaged and that intellect must be disinterested. Again, it is helpful to enhance sensitivity to those who are different. But it may be more helpful to question whether differences are the product of precisely the laws that purport to respond to them—laws shot through with distinctions based on gender, race, class, and the like.

The hermeneutic project is more sensitive to the hidden connections between language and power. Indeed, the point of emphasizing the degree to which any understanding of a legal text is interpretive is to expose the values animating or reflected in any particular interpretation. Yet understanding that a given interpretation is political—the product of ideologies and values—may not lead anywhere. If all interpretations embody power and reflect someone's point of view, then from what basis can any individual interpretation be criticized? In the absence of political consensus over which perspectives deserve to be privileged and which subordinated, an analysis devoted to exposing that a given interpretation instantiates some (contestable) views while suppressing others merely states the obvious.

Taking account of the way language generally and legal language in particular both embodies and entrenches power is complicated. It is not accomplished by simplistic, tendentious readings of literary works selected for unstated reasons. Nor is it accomplished by even sensitive narratives of the experiences of discrimination or of representing victims of discrimination, for these narratives too are inevitably partial products of prior linguistic structures and discursive practices. Legal scholars and clinical practitioners who tell the stories of "others"—women, minorities, the disenfranchised poor—risk appearing to appropriate, renarrate, and speak for their subjects/clients. This presents a nasty double bind, because the whole point of such legal analysis is to uncover and critique the ways in which the legal system silences the voices of "others." Another facet of this double bind—one not lost on critics of the legal storytelling movement—is that those stories of poor clients who find their way into law review articles end up serving another use as well, the promotion of a career in legal scholarship.

Such are the inconsistencies and double binds of the Law and

Literature and Law and Narrative movements. Legal scholars and literary critics alike must recognize our position as members of a privileged class, even if we are (also) women, racial minorities, gays or lesbians, or disabled. Our privilege within the academy and the legal profession inevitably affects our analyses of unprivileged positions that we do not inhabit. In addition, we must acknowledge the ambiguities and limitations inherent in textual studies, whether of poems, statutes, or personal anecdotes. Language is always slippery, its uses always suspect. If, as both the Law and Literature and Law and Narrative movements assert, power is complex, nuanced, and multilayered, then it cannot be represented by even the most sensitive literary analysis or the best-crafted story.

Yet despite these caveats, the work of interpreting the law using the methodologies and insights of narrative theory is important. It can illuminate gaps and inequities in our systems of judicial and state power and in our ability to understand the life experiences behind particular rulings, legislation, and constitutional mandates. Behind all abstract or dry legal discourse resides a story with a human face, and it is always worthwhile to uncover that story.

The Supreme Court recently recognized as much in *Johnny Lynn Old Chief v. United States*. The Court had to decide whether, when there is a risk of "unfair prejudice," a prosecutor must accept a defendant's stipulation or admission rather than providing specific evidence of one of the elements of the crime at issue. While the Court ruled for the defendant on the particular facts of the case, it was careful to note that its holding was exceptional:

> [M]aking a case with testimony and tangible things not only satisfies the formal definition of an offense, but tells a colorful story with descriptive richness. . . . Evidence thus has force beyond any linear scheme of reasoning, and as its pieces come together a narrative gains momentum. . . . This persuasive power of the concrete and the particular is often essential to the capacity of jurors to satisfy the obligations that the law places on them. . . .
>
> In sum, the accepted rule that the prosecution is entitled to prove its case free from any defendant's option to stipulate the evidence away rests on good sense. A syllogism is not a story, and a naked proposition in a courtroom may be no match for the robust evidence that would be used to prove it.[21]

Sometimes, that is to say, there is just no substitute for a good story.

NOTES

1. We do not address here the question of whether the diverse strands of interest in storytelling in the law are properly considered a movement. For an examination of this issue, see Jane B. Baron, *The Many Promises of Storytelling in Law,* 23 Rutgers Law Journal 79 (1991) (book review). There has been a turn to literature in medicine also, with a parallel division into Medicine and Literature and Medicine and Narrative movements. For an example of the former, see Howard Brody, *Stories of Sickness* (New Haven, CT: Yale University Press, 1988). For examples of the latter, see Julia Epstein, *Altered Conditions: Disease, Medicine, and Storytelling* (New York: Routledge, 1995); Katherine Montgomery Hunter, *Doctors' Stories: The Narrative Structure of Medical Knowledge* (Princeton, NJ: Princeton University Press, 1991).

2. Robert F. Ferguson, *Law and Letters in American Culture* (Cambridge, MA: Harvard University Press, 1984).

3. John H. Wigmore, *A List of Legal Novels,* 2 Illinois Law Review 574, 576, 579 (1908). Updates of the list include Richard H. Weisberg, *Wigmore's "Legal Novels" Revisited: New Resources for the Expansive Lawyer,* 71 Northwestern Law Review 17 (1976); David R. Papke, *Law and Literature: A Comment and Bibliography of Secondary Works,* 73 Law Library Journal 421 (1980).

4. John Denvir, *William Shakespeare and the Jurisprudence of Comedy,* 39 Stanford Law Review 825, 826 (1987).

5. The Law and Literature movement on which we focus here took off in the 1980s, following the publication of two influential books by James Boyd White: *When Words Lose Their Meaning: Constitutions and Reconstitutions of Language, Character, and Community* (Chicago: University of Chicago Press, 1984) and *Heracles' Bow: Essays on the Rhetoric and Poetics of the Law* (Madison: University of Wisconsin Press, 1985). The former examines, in addition to Homer's *Iliad,* such works as Jonathan Swift's *A Tale of a Tub* and Jane Austen's *Emma.* Morrison's novel *Beloved* is discussed in Robin West, *Communities, Texts, and Law: Reflections on the Law and Literature Movement,* 1 Yale Journal of Law and Humanities 129 (1988).

6. Martha Nussbaum, *Poetic Justice: The Literary Imagination and Public Life* (Boston: Beacon, 1995), 5–6.

7. Sanford Levinson and Steven Mailloux, eds., *Interpreting Law and Literature: A Hermeneutic Reader* (Evanston, IL: Northwestern University Press, 1988), xii.

8. See, for example, David Cole, *Against Literalism*, 40 Stanford Law Review 545 (1988) (book review); Mark V. Tushnet, *Translation as Argument*, 32 William and Mary Law Review 105 (1990) (book review).

9. Edwin Meese III, "Address Before the D.C. Chapter of the Federalist Society Lawyers Division," in *Interpreting Law and Literature*, 25.

10. Relatively few people who engaged in this debate took the extreme position that, in the absence of textual constraint, judges were not constrained at all. Possible limits on apparent interpretive freedom are suggested in Stanley Fish, *Dennis Martinez and the Uses of Theory*, 96 Yale Law Journal 1773 (1987) (interpretive constructs); Steven Winter, *The Cognitive Dimension of the* Agon *Between Legal Power and Narrative Meaning*, 87 Michigan Law Review 2225 (1989) (cognitive factors); Joseph William Singer, *The Player and the Cards*, 94 Yale Law Journal 1 (1984) (entrenched institutional practices).

11. For a particularly useful analysis of the strategic use of storytelling in advocacy, see Austin Sarat, *Narrative Strategy and Death Penalty Advocacy*, 31 Harvard Civil Rights–Civil Liberties Law Review 353 (1996).

12. See, for example, Patricia Williams, *The Alchemy of Race and Rights* (Cambridge, MA: Harvard University Press, 1991); Richard Delgado, *Storytelling for Oppositionists and Others: A Plea for Narrative*, 87 Michigan Law Review 2411 (1989); William N. Eskridge, Jr., *Gaylegal Narratives*, 46 Stanford Law Review 607 (1994). On the role of storytelling in Critical Race Theory, see generally Richard Delgado, ed., *Critical Race Theory: The Cutting Edge* (Philadelphia: Temple University Press, 1995), 37–96.

13. These examples are drawn from Kim Lane Scheppele, *Foreword: Telling Stories*, 87 Michigan Law Review 2073 (1989).

14. The points in this section are drawn from, and are explained at greater length in, Jane B. Baron, *Resistance to Stories*, 67 Southern California Law Review 255 (1994), and Jane B. Baron and Julia Epstein, *Is Law Narrative?* 45 Buffalo Law Review 141 (1997).

15. Gerald P. Lopez, *Lay Lawyering*, 32 UCLA Law Review 1, 33 (1984).

16. Lucie E. White, *Subordination, Rhetorical Survival Skills, and Sunday Shoes: Notes on the Hearing of Mrs. G*, 38 Buffalo Law Review 1, 4 (1990). For a similar conclusion, see W. Lance Bennett and Martha S. Feldman, *Reconstructing Reality in the Courtroom: Justice and Judgment in American Culture* (New Brunswick, NJ: Rutgers University Press, 1981), 171.

17. John M. Conley and William M. O'Barr, *Rules Versus Relationships: The Ethnography of Legal Discourse* (Chicago: University of Chicago Press, 1990).

18. See Marie Ashe, *Zig-Zag Stitching and the Seamless Web: Thoughts on "Reproduction" and the Law,* 13 Nova Law Review 355, 375 (1989); Martha R. Mahoney, *Legal Images of Battered Women: Redefining the Issue of Separation,* 90 Michigan Law Review 1 (1990).
19. The best-known critique along these lines is Daniel A. Farber and Suzanna Sherry, *Telling Stories out of School: An Essay on Legal Narratives,* 45 Stanford Law Review 807 (1993).
20. See, for example, Anthony V. Alfieri, *Reconstructive Poverty Law Practice: Learning Lessons of Client Narrative,* 100 Yale Law Journal 2107 (1991); Binny Miller, *Give Them Back Their Lives: Recognizing Client Narrative in Case Theory,* 93 Michigan Law Review 485 (1994).
21. *Johnny Lynn Old Chief v. United States,* 117 S.Ct. 644, 653–54 (1997).

30 VICTOR RABINOWITZ

THE RADICAL TRADITION
IN THE LAW

ON June 27, 1905, the founding convention of the Industrial Workers of the World (IWW) met in Chicago, pursuant to a call urging the creation of "one big industrial union" to be "founded on the class struggle." The Credentials Committee reported the attendance of nearly two hundred delegates—socialists, anarchists, members of industrial trade unions, and a handful of representatives from craft unions. The Committee recommended the seating of the delegates and also recommended the seating, as a fraternal delegate, of a lawyer from New York. A long and bitter debate followed. Daniel de Leon, speaking against the recommendation to seat the lawyer, said:

> . . . If you admit a lawyer because he nominally works and does not derive interest—though every dollar that goes into his pocket is tainted with the blood of workingmen in some way or other, because he lives upon interest indirectly—if you allow such a man in here, by what process of reasoning can you exclude the policeman? . . . I would say that I know of no lawyer who deserves any place in the labor movement. . . . What does the class struggle mean but that the material necessities of a man control his action? And will you deny that the material necessities of the lawyer will compel him to commit the crimes against the working class that every lawyer in the country commits today?[1]

Others made similar comments. The convention resolved not to seat the lawyer, after refusing to permit him to address the convention.

The New York lawyer was Louis B. Boudin. His exclusion by the IWW convention did not put an end to either his political or his legal career. He became a part of the leadership of the Socialist Party and, during World War I, was prominent in the left-wing of the party, which opposed U.S. participation in the war. He was the author of *The Theoretical System of Karl Marx*, a book highly regarded in Marxist circles. In the thirties he represented Communist Party leaders in AFL local unions who were struggling against a bankrupt and corrupt national leadership. After the formation of the CIO, he represented many of the new unions in their early and most militant struggles. He similarly acted for scores of radicals brought up on criminal charges or faced with deportation. He participated in the formation of the National Lawyers Guild. One could hardly argue that his contributions to the radical movement of his day were not considerable. In his time, he was one of the most active and most learned of the radicals in the country.

The debate over the role of the law (and the lawyer) in the class struggle has not abated since 1905, and the nature and significance of the legal system continue to be the subject of extensive discussion among progressives. In 1971 a collection of essays by radical lawyers in the United States, edited by Robert Lefcourt, was published under the title *Law Against the People*. Over half of the essays in the volume argued what the title of the collection implied, that the law as an institution is an instrument of the bourgeoisie designed to deceive and oppress the mass of the people, and the lawyer is necessarily a part of this machinery. Florynce Kennedy, a prominent militant lawyer, wrote, in characteristically blunt language:

> Ours is a prostitute society. The system of justice, and most especially the legal profession, is a whorehouse serving those best able to afford the luxuries of justice offered to preferred customers. The lawyer, in these terms, is analogous to a prostitute. The difference between the two is simple. The prostitute is honest—the buck is her aim. The lawyer is dishonest—he claims that justice, service to mankind, is his primary purpose.[2]

The Law, in this view, while pretending to be a benign, neutral force dispensing justice, equality and due process, actually is but a fraudulent cover-up for the force through which the State rules.

More recently, Critical Legal Studies, which has generally made a very positive progressive contribution to legal scholarship, has generated some writings that indict the law from a different perspective, for its indeterminacy and lack of coherence. These writings, criticized by the late Edward Sparer, sometimes repudiate the rule of law and lapse into nihilism and hopelessness.[3]

These approaches encourage cynicism about our legal structure and give up the battle that both the mass of people and a handful of lawyers have carried on for centuries—a battle for progressive, socially desirable laws and against retrogressive laws—by failing to distinguish between them or even to admit that such differentiation can exist.

This paper is written with a few assumptions in mind, which should be set down. No society of even moderate complexity, whether it be feudal, capitalist, or socialist, can exist without law. All systems of law are constructed to protect the state and its economic base. Conduct that seriously threatens the survival of the state or that would effectuate a basic change in its economic system is, *ipso facto*, "illegal." Those in whose interests the state exists will necessarily make laws to protect those interests and that state, and a government that will tolerate effective seditious conduct is almost beyond our imagination.

Having said this, there are several points to be made.

The law sets up standards and rules by which the state agrees to exercise its power and which, by definition, set limits on that exercise. These standards and limits are, of course, self-imposed, but in the long run every state finds it necessary to impose some restrictions upon itself because no structured society can exist for long if state power is lawless and completely arbitrary. Most states find it desirable to act by these standards. Thus, over the past two hundred years in the United States, there has grown up a body of law, some of it statutory, some common law, and some judge-made, that curbs the state's conduct. Similar development has taken place in every organized society, capitalist, socialist, or anywhere in between. The state relinquishes its power to act except in conformity with certain rules.

Whether those rules give adequate protection to the mass of the people will vary greatly in different situations, but the existence of rules provides some protection against totally arbitrary state action. To the degree that state power is exercised in an arbitrary (lawless) manner, the state itself becomes unstable and subject to the constant threat of revolutionary violence. When that happens for any length of time, one of the demands of the people is for a change in the law, which will check the authority of the state. This has been happening for centuries.

In a modern capitalist state, the law does more than establish standards by which the state promises to conduct its business. In such a state there is a working class sufficiently well educated and sufficiently articulate not only to carry on the role required of it in a capitalist society but also, in the long run, to demand certain action by the state. Capitalist law (and even precapitalist law in the English common-law tradition), under great pressure from the mass of the people has, from the earliest days, promised equality of treatment, fair play, due process and other abstract goals. In this country the law even promises freedom of speech, press, religion, and assembly, freedom from unreasonable search and seizure, and all of those other good things set forth in our Bill of Rights.

It is true that these promises are often broken, perhaps more often than not. It is also true that many of those who made the promises in the first place never intended that they should be kept. Governments seldom deliver on such promises of equality, justice, and freedom. But the promises are made; and the fact is that very large numbers of the people accept, believe in, and rely on these abstract principles. Often they demand that the promises be kept; they may even be willing to march and riot in the streets, and sit down in factories and churches to enforce the promises. Belief in and devotion to these principles are not confined to the working class; many members of the middle class, including, in our country, even some members of Congress and some judges, believe in these promises or are unwilling to repudiate them.

For example, the trade-union movement of this country in the 1930s, the civil rights movement of the 1950s and 1960s, and the antiwar movement of the 1960s and 1970s would not have been possible had we not had a deep tradition of respect for freedom of speech and assembly. It is a mistake to minimize the significance of that tradition in our history. This and related concepts are deeply embedded in the consciousness of most of the American people. Even though these traditions are frequently frustrated in practice, much progress has been made because these rights have been assumed and, often enough, asserted.

For who can deny that progress has been made? Certainly not one who has read Mayhew or Dickens or even Stephen's *History of the Criminal Law*.

A century and a half ago, poor people spent years in custody because they could not pay their debts; in England, many were transported to the other side of the world for such "offenses." Today there are no debtors' prisons in the United States or England, and transportation is no longer acceptable. Trade unions were once deemed unlawful conspiracies in the United States; in the past half-century, unions have been given recognition, approval, and some degree of encouragement by the state. The factory and housing conditions that characterized the growth of the industrial revolution in England and the United States have largely been ameliorated by the passage of housing, factory, and child-labor laws; the conditions under which men, women, and children customarily worked in Birmingham, England, and Lowell, Massachusetts, would be unlawful today in any advanced capitalist state. There are still short falls and gaps, but they are regarded as conditions to be corrected, rather than as conditions to be endured.

Censorship of written material has been relaxed; only several decades ago, Joyce's *Ulysses* could not be imported into the United States or transported through the mails. In an ever-increasing number of states and cities, laws protecting the rights of homosexuals have been enacted. And, of course, the greatest progress of all has been made with respect to the rights of minorities and women in our society.

The catalog could be extended at length. Let us take but a quick look at some of the major developments in our constitutional law in the recent past.

In *Gideon v. Wainwright*, the Supreme Court held that all persons charged with serious crimes are entitled to a lawyer and that the court must appoint one where the defendant is indigent. In *Miranda v. State of Arizona*, the Court held that persons in police custody must be advised of their constitutional rights and advised of their right to get legal counsel. *Mapp v. Ohio* excluded from criminal proceedings evidence illegally seized by the police. *Griswold v. Connecticut* held that a statute prohibiting the sale of contraceptives was unconstitutional, and in fact now the sale and use of contraceptives are both legal and commonplace.[4] And in the past forty years, scores of laws, both federal and state, have addressed themselves to the issue of the racism which so pervades our culture, and while progress has been uneven, only those who never experienced the apartheid which characterized much of this country fifty years ago will deny that the situation has changed for the better.

The legal and political battles waged over *Furman v. Georgia* and *Roe v. Wade* over the past three decades (and, no doubt, to be continued in the future) deserve special consideration.[5] In *Furman*, the Court held almost every state statute permitting capital punishment to be unconstitutional. *Roe* invalidated almost every state law prohibiting abortions. In all of these cases, the law moved in a progressive direction on vital social issues.

The law established by most of these cases has been under attack and in some cases ground has been lost. The *Furman* decision did not declare capital punishment to be illegal; it merely set new rules, mostly procedural, governing imposition of the death sentence. The effect of the decision has been largely canceled out by statutes in most states reinstituting capital punishment, and many of those statutes have passed constitutional examination by a Supreme Court much less liberal than the Court that decided *Furman*. Indeed, the number of executions in the midnineties was higher than in many pre-*Furman* years, responding to increasing right-wing pressure to solve the problem of crime by imposing more and more severe sanctions. Thousands of persons are on death row, awaiting the outcome of appeals from death sentences. *Roe* is also under attack in state legislatures and in Congress.

The history of the law governing capital punishment and abortion, set forth in the opinions of Justices Brennan and Marshall in *Furman* and Justice Blackmun in *Roe*, makes it clear that for such contentious issues there are pendulumlike swings over long periods of time. *Furman* and *Roe* may represent three steps forward, and we may be forced a step or two back. It seems most unlikely that we will ever revert to the pre-*Roe* situation, when all but one state banned abortion, however performed, unless done to save or preserve the life of the mother.

Hardly a term of the Supreme Court passes without further discussion of such issues. However, it is important to note that the battle lines have not been drawn on class lines. Important struggles are being waged but they are not primarily economic struggles; not rich against poor, nor capital against labor, nor capitalism against socialism. Rather the struggle is often on religious lines, and on differing views of ethics and morality. To the extent to which there are economic interests involved at all, these decisions cut across class lines.

The law as set down in cases like *Furman* and *Roe*, if viewed from a class perspective, was beneficial to the poor. The law as an institution is not necessarily reactionary and a defense of the capitalist status quo but, on the contrary, has in it a progressive element which often moves in the direction of a more humane and more bearable society. Our task is to support that movement. It will not be productive of success nor will it be truthful to advise the participants in this struggle that the law is a fraud and serves only the capitalist class. On the contrary, it is the low-income segments of our population who have gained the most in these battles and who will lose the most if the laws do not hold.

Progress in the assertion and development of human rights has always been slow, and we must not fall into the trap of viewing the history of humankind as if it extended over a mere span of a few decades. It is also true that now, as in Jefferson's day, eternal vigilance is the price of liberty, and many of the gains that have been made are constantly threatened and will continue to be threatened under a capitalist, socialist, or any other kind of economic system. Failure to exercise that vigilance exacts a heavy price.

Of course, these progressive changes in the law have not transformed our capitalist system; they have not abolished poverty, nor have they eliminated economic classes in our society. But the law was never intended to perform those tasks and, if our earlier assumptions are true, cannot be understood as having so promised. Such changes can be brought about only by political, perhaps even by extralegal or illegal, means.

None of this should be understood as suggesting that the law gives adequate protection to working men and women. This can never be so as long as there are inequalities in wealth and power, and such inequalities will always exist under capitalism. In many respects the law has not significantly improved much in two or three centuries. The election laws are, generally speaking, still rigged to frustrate the democratic process and are helpful principally to the wealthy; the tax laws still impose the heaviest burden on the working class; and the laws relating to real property still leave a tenant with little power. The anti-trust laws, the regulations governing banks and financial institutions and much of the criminal law are, as one would expect, laws written to protect the capitalist system. These conditions provide more battles for the progressive lawyer to fight. Unlike Alexander the Great, we still have more worlds to conquer.

It has been argued that legal reforms and the legal system itself have the effect of preserving the capitalist system and serve to postpone basic change. To some extent this is true. Certainly the unemployment insurance and Social Security laws, the extension of suffrage to blacks in the South, and even child-labor laws were required to bring the industrial revolution to fruition; and objectively they strengthen, not weaken, capitalism. Had these reforms not occurred, economic and social conditions would be much worse than they are; but who would advocate their repeal to bring a revolution closer? This argument puts progressives in the untenable position of advocating misery and assumes that misery will lead to progressive change.

Moreover, while capitalism was strengthened by many of these measures, it does not follow that the "ruling class" permitted such reforms in order to preserve the economic system. The contrary is true. The New Deal measures were adopted during the 1930s in the context of powerful working-class movements demanding substantial progressive changes. These demands and movements were fought tooth and nail by sections of the capitalist class, to whom President Franklin Roosevelt was the devil incarnate; Roosevelt reciprocated with his attacks on the "economic royalists." What was responsible for those laws is a complex question and beyond the scope of this paper, but there is no evidence that those laws were merely bones thrown by the leaders of capitalism to the working class to pacify it, or that they were the result of prescient and sagacious planning by United States Steel, General Motors, Chase National Bank et al.

Even more important, most of the recent changes discussed above have little to do with the preservation of the capitalist system or, for that matter, with the preservation of any economic system except to the extent that they meet the needs of the people and to that extent strengthen the state regardless of its economic system. They are certainly not merely devices of the ruling class intended to serve only the ruling class.

There is no discernible connection between the preservation of capitalism and the legalization of contraception, the legalization of abortion, the abolition of capital punishment, the effective abolition of censorship over "obscene" literature, the strengthening of the laws against search and seizure and the protection of the rights of people charged with crime. The *Roe v. Wade* controversy and the dispute over capital punishment have their basic roots in conflicting views as to religion, ethics, and morality. Capitalism will not be strengthened or weakened by the results of those battles.

It is noteworthy that many of these recent changes in our law are judge-made and not required by any legislative action. Some of these changes purport to be required by ambiguous language in our Constitution, requirements that were not discovered until about two hundred years after the Constitution was adopted. In fact, the judges who wrote those opinions were "interpreting" a Constitution which they perceived to be a flexible document to meet a current social need. They were moved in some cases by popular pressure and in some cases by what Chief Justice Warren called "the evolving standards of decency that mark the progress of a maturing society."[6]

In recent years, a new and important issue has arisen, not only in our country, but all over the world: respect for and protection of our global environment. The development of a body of law to protect the environment should be high on the agenda of progressive lawyers because here, if anywhere, it is clear that such laws are not for the protection of any class in society but for the protection and indeed survival of all of us. The problems which will face us in this area, are exceptionally difficult and without clear principles to guide us. Freedoms which have been regarded by most Americans as essential to a decent existence (such as driving an automobile) may have to be curtailed. A system involving some collective control over many of our activities, heretofore regarded as basic liberties, may be required if we are to survive. It is important that this system not be constructed in a manner which deprives persons of low income of the comforts of life while giving the wealthy the freedom to destroy life. We are only at the beginning of this new phase of the development of our law, but certainly there is enough to be done which is not in the service of capitalism.

I suggest that the law develops a dynamic and a life of its own which is independent of capitalism or any other system of economic relationships. It grows out of the pressure of the people for a better, more rational, and more bearable existence, and out of changes in the moral and ethical systems of a society that require changes in the law even when there is no economic reason or even popular demand therefore. Even the most conservative judges can be moved, on some occasions, by the horrors of capital punishment, by the fearful consequences of laws against abortion, and by the terrors of police abuse; even conservative state legislators suffer physical discomfort at having to breathe the air of Los Angeles and New York.

Any capitalist legal system in its entirety undoubtedly crystallizes class relations and masks injustice created by those relations. But what is the alternative? The exercise of naked, arbitrary power without even the forms of law can hardly constitute an improvement. English historian and disarmament activist Edward P. Thompson has made this point most eloquently:

> [T]he notion of the regulation and reconciliation of conflicts through the rule of law—and the elaboration of rules and procedures which, on occasion, made some approximate approach towards the ideal—seems to me a cultural achievement of universal significance. I do not lay any claim as to the abstract, extra-historical impartiality of these rules. In a context of gross class inequalities, the equity of the law must always be in some part sham. . . . I am insisting only upon the obvious point, which some modern Marxists have overlooked, that there is a difference between arbitrary power and the rule of law. We ought to expose the shams and inequities which may be concealed beneath this law. But the rule of law itself, the imposing of effective inhibitions upon power and the defense of the citi-

zen from power's all-intrusive claims, seems to me to be an unqualified human good. To deny or belittle this good is, in this dangerous century when the resources and pretentions of power continue to enlarge, a desperate error of intellectual abstraction. More than this, it is a self-fulfilling error, which encourages us to give up the struggle against bad laws and class-bound procedures, and to disarm ourselves before power. It is to throw away a whole inheritance of struggle *about* law, and within the forms of law, whose continuity can never be fractured without bringing men and women into immediate danger. . . .

. . . It is true that in history the law can be seen to mediate and to legitimize existent class relations. Its forms and procedures may crystallize those relations and mask ulterior injustice. But this mediation, though the forms of law, is something quite distinct from the exercise of unmediated force. The forms and rhetoric of law acquire a distinct identity which may, on occasion, inhibit power and afford some protection to the powerless. Only to the degree that this is seen to be so can law be of service in its other aspects, as ideology.[7]

Shall we proclaim that the law is a fraud; or should we as progressives interested in creating a better world use the law as a vehicle through which we seek to compel the state to keep the promises it makes—the promises contained in the Constitution and in the Fourth of July orations? When the law fails to keep these promises, is it not our duty to promote a confrontation between the people and the state to compel the latter to move toward the dream of a better world we share with all others?

There is certainly enough to be done. We can do our best to keep activists out of jail and on the streets. We can seek to extend to their ultimate limit the rights of free speech, due process, freedom from unreasonable searches, and similar rights, to make more possible major changes in our economic system. We can expose police abuse and protect the right of privacy, both in political and personal affairs. We can, as lawyers and legal workers, join with rank-and-file trade-union groups in the struggle for the establishment of democracy in the trade unions. We can use our talents to protect the rights of women to an abortion or the rights of gays to a job. We can use our imaginations to devise new methods to attack the environmental problems, which are worldwide in their scope. Many of us have legislative skills that can be put to good service.

And most important of all, we can join with other radical lawyers in developing a modern Marxist theory of the role of the law and the radical lawyer in our society. The office of such a theory will be to point a direction for such lawyers. It will help us to distinguish between reforms that carry the seeds of oppression and developments that truly represent an improvement in the lot of humankind. Such, we understand, are the tasks undertaken by this volume of essays.

NOTES

1. Proceedings of the First Convention of the Industrial Workers of the World, vol. 26 (New York: New York Labor News Co., 1905), 67–70.
2. R. Lefcourt, ed., *Law Against the People* (New York: Random House, 1971), 81.
3. Edward Sparer, *Fundamental Human Rights, Legal Entitlements, and the Social Struggle: A Friendly Critique of the Critical Legal Studies Movement,* 36 Stanford Law Review 508 (1984).
4. 372 U.S. 335(1963); 384 U.S. 436 (1966); 367 U.S. 643(1961); 408 U.S. 238 (1972).
5. 381 U.S. 479 (1965); 410 U.S. 113 (1973).
6. *Trop v. Dulles,* 356 U.S. 86 at 101. See also *Weems v. United States,* 217 U.S. 349.
7. Edward P. Thompson, *Whigs and Hunters* (New York: Pantheon, 1975), 265–66.

31 FRANCES OLSEN

THE SEX OF LAW

SINCE the rise of classical liberal thought, and perhaps since the time of
Plato, most of us have structured our thinking around a complex series of
dualisms, or opposing pairs: rational/irrational; active/passive;
thought/feeling; reason/emotion; culture/nature; power/sensitivity;
objective/subjective; abstract/contextualized; principled/personalized.
These dualistic pairs divide things into contrasting spheres or polar
opposites.[1]

This system of dualisms has three characteristics that are important to
this discussion. First, the dualisms are sexualized. One-half of each dualism is considered masculine, the other half feminine. Second, the terms
of the dualism are not equal, but are thought to constitute a hierarchy. In
each pair, the term identified as "masculine" is privileged as superior,
while the other is considered negative, corrupt, or inferior. And third,
law is identified with the "male" side of the dualisms.

SEXUALIZATION

The division between male and female has been crucial to this dualistic
system of thought. Men have identified themselves with one side of the
dualisms: rational, active, thought, reason, culture, power, objective,
abstract, principled. They have projected the other side upon women:
irrational, passive, feeling, emotion, nature, sensitivity, subjective, contextualized, personalized.

The sexual identification of the dualisms has both a descriptive and a
normative element. Sometimes it is said that men are rational, active, and
so forth, and other times it will be said that men should be rational,
active, and so forth. Similarly, the claim about women is sometimes considered to be descriptive; women simply are irrational, passive, and so
forth. A lot of people used to believe that this was an inevitable,
immutable fact about women—that women were unable to become

rational, active, and so forth. Another kind of claim is that women should be irrational, passive, and so forth, or at least that they should *not* become rational, active, and so forth—either because it is important that women remain different from men, or because irrational, passive, and so forth, are good traits *as applied to women.*

HIERARCHIZATION

The system of dualisms is hierarchized. The dualisms do not just divide the world between two terms; the two terms are arranged in a hierarchical order. Just as men have traditionally dominated and defined women, one side of the dualism dominates and defines the other. Irrational is considered the absence of rational; passive is the failure of active; thought is more important than feeling; reason takes precedence over emotion.

This hierarchy has been somewhat obscured by a complex and often insincere glorification of women and the feminine. However much men have oppressed and exploited women in the real world, they have also placed women on a pedestal and treasured them in a fantasy world. And just as men simultaneously exalt and degrade women, so, too, do they simultaneously exalt and degrade the concepts on the "feminine" side of the dualisms. Nature, for example, is glorified as something awesome, a worthy subject of conquest by male heroes, while it is simultaneously degraded as inert matter to be exploited and shaped to men's purposes. Irrational subjectivity and sensitivity are similarly treasured and denigrated at the same time. However much they might romanticize the womanly virtues, most people still believe that rational is better than irrational, objectivity is better than subjectivity, and being abstract and principled is better than being contextualized and personalized. It is more complicated than this, however, because no one would really want to *eliminate* irrational, passive, and so forth, from the world altogether. But men usually want to distance *themselves* from these traits; they want women to be irrational, passive, and so forth. To women, this glorification of the "feminine" side of the dualisms seems insincere.

LAW AS MALE

Law is identified with the hierarchically superior, "masculine" sides of the dualisms. "Justice" may be depicted as a woman, but, according to the dominant ideology, law is male, not female. Law is supposed to be rational, objective, abstract, and principled, as men claim they are; it is not supposed to be irrational, subjective, contextualized, or personalized, as men claim women are.

The social, political, and intellectual practices that constitute "law" were for many years carried on almost exclusively by men. Given that women were long excluded from the practice of law, it is not surprising that the traits associated with women are not greatly valued in law. Moreover in a kind of vicious cycle, law is considered rational and objective in part because it is highly valued, and it is highly valued in part because it is considered rational and objective.

The most interesting and promising challenges to this dominant system of thought are those made by feminists. Feminist critiques of law bear a close analogy to feminist critiques of male dominance in general and the several conflicting attitudes that various feminists have taken toward law can best be understood when viewed in this broader context.

FEMINIST STRATEGIES

Feminist strategies for attacking the dominant dualistic system of thought fall into three broad categories. The first category consists of strategies that oppose the sexualization of the dualisms and struggle to identify women with the favored side, with rational, active, and so forth. Strategies in the second category reject the hierarchy men have established between the two sides of the dualisms. This second category accepts the identification of women with irrational, passive, and so forth, but proclaims the value of these traits; they are as good as or better than rational, active, and so forth. The third category rejects both the sexualization and the hierarchization of the dualisms. Strategies in this third category question and disrupt the differences asserted between men and women, and they deny the hierarchy of rational, active, and so forth, over irrational, passive, and so forth. Rational and irrational, active and passive, and so forth, are not polar opposites, and they do not and cannot divide the world into contrasting spheres.

REJECT SEXUALIZATION

Strategies that reject the sexualization of the dualisms are like the dominant ideology in that they accept the hierarchy of rational over irrational, of active over passive, and so forth. They differ from the dominant ideology in that they reject the normative claim that women should be irrational, passive, and so forth, and for the most part they reject the descriptive assertion that women are irrational, passive, and so forth. They most strongly reject the idea that women cannot help but be irrational, passive, and so forth.

This strategy is illustrated by an essay written in 1851 by Harriet Taylor Mill. She disputed the assertion that women were naturally or universally inferior to men and argued that each individual should be free to develop his or her own abilities to their fullest, "to prove his or her capacities . . . by trial." According to Mills, "[t]he proper sphere for all human beings is the largest and highest which they are able to attain to."[2]

Harriet Taylor Mill rejected the sexualization of the dualisms but accepted the hierarchy. She used "rational" as an honorific and "irrational" as a term of derision, and argued that "reason and principle," not "sentimentalities," offered the strongest support for women's emancipation. She denied that women were inherently irrational, passive, and so forth, but asserted that women's education and situation in life tended to make them so. This was both "an injustice to the individual and a detriment to society." To deny women the opportunity to develop to their fullest potential is an effective way to prevent them from being rational, active, and so forth. "[T]he qualities which are not permitted to be exercised shall not exist." Harriet Taylor Mill dismissed as "nonsensical" the efforts of some feminists to challenge the hierarchy of rational over irrational, active over passive, and so forth. "What is wanted for women is equal rights, equal admission to all social privileges; not a position apart, a sort of sentimental priesthood."[3]

This attitude toward women's equality is widely held today. Many feminists and most liberals believe that sex roles should be a matter of individual choice. When individuals act rationally and reasonably, they should be treated accordingly. If women or men choose to be irrational, passive, and so forth, they cannot expect to be treated as though they were not. Moreover, if women do not want to bear and raise children, they should not have to do so; and if men want to nurture children they should be free to make that choice.

There is more to this category than simple sex blindness. One claim consistent with this attitude is that women have been trained to be irrational and passive and that this training should be reversed. Affirmative action for women, a departure from sex blindness, may be justified and supported as a method to counteract years of teaching women to be irrational, passive, and so forth. A different claim, also consistent with this attitude, is that women already are rational, active, and so forth, but are not recognized to be. Affirmative action might then be justified and supported as a technique for counteracting prejudiced, inaccurate views that women are irrational, passive, and so forth. The point of these strategies that reject sexualization is not that gender must be ignored, but that women are or should become rational, active, and so forth.[4]

Under these strategies, equal treatment for women is almost always an eventual goal. Equal treatment for women is generally considered to be the current norm, and gender-conscious policies are seen as a limited departure from this norm— an exception that may be justified in order to counteract and correct inequality. The result of these gender-conscious policies, according to their advocates, should be to secure to women the same power and prestige that men have, and to let women be, and be recognized to be, as rational, active, and so forth, as men claim to be (or, less ambitiously, as men really are).

REJECT HIERARCHIZATION

The second set of strategies rejects the hierarchy but accepts the sexualization. These strategies are like the dominant ideology in that they accept in general the proposition that men and women are different— that men are rational, active, and so forth, and women irrational, passive, and so forth. Also they tend to choose alternative adjectives that are a bit less value laden, or value laden in the opposite direction: rationalistic/spontaneous, aggressive/receptive, and so forth.

During the nineteenth and early twentieth centuries, a major focus of the women's movement was the exclusion of women from the public arena and the denial to women of equal opportunities. These concerns were addressed primarily by strategies in the first category, strategies that rejected the sexualization of the dualisms, rather than by strategies in the second category, strategies that rejected the hierarchy. The main exception to this was the movement for social purity and other moral reforms.

For the most part, moral reform movements led by feminists rejected the hierarchization of the dualisms and accepted their sexualization. The reformers argued that women were morally superior to men and thus had a special mission to improve society. Many of these reformers hoped that men would adopt more of the womanly virtues—especially sexual restraint—but they basically accepted the dualisms, accepted women's identification with irrational, passive, and so forth, and were generally resigned to men not changing much. Their chief focus was not on transforming men or abolishing the dualisms, but on forcing a reevaluation of the traits attributed to women.[5]

Charlotte Perkins Gilman, an early feminist who was strongly critical of many of the character traits actually prevalent among turn-of-the-century women, nevertheless wrote an eloquent endorsement of the devalued side of the dualisms. The novel, *Herland* describes a feminist utopia established in a geographically isolated setting after all the men have killed themselves off in war. Gilman passed quickly over the expediency of an implausible miraculous shift to asexual reproduction, in order to get to a description of how an all-female society might function. Although Gilman's women are stronger and more capable than the standard stereotype of the day would have allowed, and although there are some other androgynous overtones to the novel, the main message of the book is a disruption and partial reversal of the hierarchy of rational over irrational, active over passive, and so forth.[6]

A group of modern feminists has continued this disruption and partial reversal of hierarchy. Talk of "women's psychology," "women's imagination," and women's "common language" has become popular.[7] The distinction between the strategy of rejecting the hierarchy while accepting the sexualization of the dualisms, on one hand, and, on the other hand, the strategy I refer to as androgyny—rejecting the entire dualistic structure—has begun to break down.

To focus on women's experience and on women's culture, psychology, imagination, or language can be an effective way to recover what has been excluded or obscured by dominant culture; but it can also entail an acceptance of the sexualization of the dualisms. To reverse or invert the hierarchy between rational and irrational, active and passive, and so forth, could simply reinforce the dualisms and ultimately maintain dominant values. Alternatively, such a reversal will occasionally seem to be the most effective way to subvert the dualisms.[8] Moreover, an author may intend for her writing to serve one strategy and readers may use it to serve another. Although some authors articulate clear support for the maintenance of sex roles,[9] in other cases the disruption of the hierarchy between the terms of the dualisms may or may not be intended to disrupt the sexualization of the dualisms and the dualisms themselves. When this is the intention, I would classify the strategy in the third category—androgyny.

ANDROGYNY

It is possible to attack both the sexualization and the hierarchy at the same. time. Men are not more rational, objective, and principled than women, nor is it particularly admirable to be rational, objective, and principled, as the dominant male supremacist ideology has defined the terms. A number of feminists have tried over the years to adopt such a critical stance toward the dual claims of male dominance. A rejection of both the sexualization of the dualisms and the hierarchy established between the two sides of the dualisms is often accompanied by a rejection of the dualisms altogether and a disruption of conventional sex roles.

During the second half of the nineteenth century there was significant support for moderating sex-role expectations for men and women. William Leach, in his study of nineteenth-century feminism, asserts "[a]ll feminists believed that only strong, independent, but also tender men and women, who combined in their natures the best virtues of both sexes, could make good marital partners and parents." Only "symmetrically developed men and women" were considered "whole human beings."[10]

The rebirth of the women's movement has brought these ideas back into popular discourse. Some feminists argue that women are and must be both rational and irrational, objective and subjective, abstract and contextualized, and principled and personalized. Recently, feminists influenced by postmodernism, and especially by such movements as deconstruction, have begun to question the basic dichotomies themselves. This strategy challenges the border between the two terms in each of the dualisms, problematizes the straightforward opposition between them, and denies their separateness. It is rational to be irrational and objectivity is necessarily subjective."[11]

FEMINIST CRITIQUES OF LAW

Feminist criticisms of law fall into three broad categories, corresponding to the categories of feminist strategies for attacking male domination in general. The dominant ideology maintains that law is rational, objective, abstract, and principled and that rational is better than irrational, objective better than subjective, and so forth. The first category consists of those critiques that attack the claim that law is rational, objective, abstract, and principled, while agreeing that rational, objective, and so forth, are better than irrational, subjective, and so forth. These feminists argue that law should be rational, objective, and principled and struggle to improve the situation of women by trying to make law live up to its claims and actually be rational, objective, and principled. Criticisms in the second category accept that law is rational, objective, and principled but reject the hierarchization of the dualisms. Feminists holding this view often characterize law as male and patriarchal, and thus ideologically oppressive to women. The third category of criticisms rejects both the characterization of law as rational, objective, abstract, and principled and the hierarchization of rational over irrational, objective over subjective, and so forth. Law is not, cannot be, and should not aspire to be rational, objective, abstract, and principled. Once again, according to these feminists, rational and irrational, active and passive, and so forth, are not polar opposites, and they do not and cannot divide the world into contrasting spheres.

LEGAL REFORMIST

The first category of criticisms questions the accuracy of the assertion that law is rational, objective, and principled. It accepts the notion that law should be rational, objective, and principled, but points out the ways law fails to live up to this aspiration when it deals with women. In particular, reformist feminists condemn laws that deny women rights—or otherwise harm women—as irrational, subjective, and unprincipled. This has been the single most important feminist legal strategy and is the theoretical underpinning of the entire women's rights movement in law. It includes a broad range of arguments for reform, from a demand for sex blindness to the argument that to be "truly neutral" the law must take account of women's current subordination and devise rules carefully tailored to rectify and overcome this unfair inequality. Each of these arguments identifies a different aspect of law to condemn for failing to be rational, objective, and principled.

Denial of Formal Equality. For many years feminists have complained that law draws irrational distinctions between men and women. These critics have argued that law should instead really be rational and objective, by which they mean it should treat women the same way it treats men. This argument has often been successful, and courts have overturned laws preferring male to female executors, discharging parents' obligation to support daughters at a younger age than sons, and prescribing different legal drinking ages for males and females.[12]

Feminists have also argued successfully that laws should forbid employers, schools, and other important private actors from discriminating against women. These laws have been shaped and extended in part by feminist insistence that the law accord formal legal equality of treatment to men and women—that law really become rational, objective, and principled.

Denial of Substantive Equality. To achieve a substantive equality of outcome, it may be necessary for the law to take account of existing differences among people and consequently to deny formal legal equality. Thus, in some cases there will be a conflict between feminists seeking formal equality for women—"equal treatment"—and those seeking substantive equality, sometimes through "special treatment." This "equal treatment" versus "special treatment" debate takes place *within* this same broad category of legal criticism. Both sides agree that the law should be rational, objective, and principled; they just disagree about what particular outcome these traits require in a given case. Feminists urging "special treatment" claim to favor a truly neutral result and debunk certain instances of formal equality as "pseudoneutrality."[13]

Operating on an Assimilationist or "Male" Model. Another basis for feminist charges that law is not truly rational, objective, and principled is that equality is at present judged by comparing women to men. To state a claim, a woman usually has to show that she was treated worse than a man would have been. This means that sex discrimination law operates on an Assimilationist or male model.[14] Sex discrimination law serves only to allow those women who choose to act as men do to receive the rewards men receive—that is, it facilitates the first feminist strategy, the strategy that denies the sexualization of the dualisms. When the law chooses to support this feminist strategy instead of another one, it is not being rational and objective. Antidiscrimination law could require, for example, that jobs be structured so that workers can devote significant periods of time to child care without prejudice to their incomes or careers, or it could require comparable worth, that all jobs—and let us include care for one's own child—be rewarded in accordance with the skill and responsibility they entail.[15]

Exclusion of Law from the Domestic Sphere. Feminists point out that "law has been conspicuously absent from the [domestic] sphere"[16] and that this has contributed to women's subordination. On a practical level, it leaves wives without a remedy against domination by their husbands; and on an ideological level, it "devalues women and their functions." The important activities of our society are regulated by law; and when law maintains a hands-off posture, it implies "women simply are not sufficiently important to merit legal regulation." The insulation of the women's sphere conveys an important message: "In our society law is for business and other important things. The fact that the law in general has so little bearing on women's day-to-day concerns reflects and underscores their insignificance." Thus, once again law has failed truly to be rational, objective, abstract, and principled.

A distinction should be made between this description of part of the ideology and the more complicated picture of ideas and reality. The history of laissez-faire policies toward domestic life is considerably more complex than this description suggests. Laws have regulated family life, directly and indirectly, for centuries. Laws have also long reinforced the dichotomy between the "private" home and the "public" market, and they have done so in ways that have been peculiarly destructive to women.[17]

LAW AS PATRIARCHY

The second category of feminist criticisms of law accepts the descriptive claim that law is rational, objective, abstract, and principled but rejects the hierarchy of rational over irrational, objective over subjective, and so forth. These feminists identify law as part of the structure of male domination; they characterize rational, objective, and so forth, as patriarchal and condemn law for being therefore ideologically oppressive to women. The legal system is said to have a "pervasive maleness." "The whole structure of law—its hierarchical organization; its combative, adversarial format; and its undeviating bias in favor of rationality over all other values—defines it as a fundamentally patriarchal institution."[18]

Janet Rifkin has asserted that law is "a paradigm of maleness," and "the ultimate symbol of masculine authority in patriarchal society."[19] Some of Catharine MacKinnon's writing seems to agree that law is male. Objectivity is a male norm as well as law's image of itself. Law therefore "not only reflects a society in which men rule women; it rules in a male way."[20]

This conception of law leads to a less than sanguine view of legal reform. MacKinnon writes that "law will most reinforce existing distributions of power when it most closely adheres to its own highest ideal of fairness." Diane Polan warns that to the extent women articulate their grievances in terms of "equal rights" and "equal opportunities" and confine their struggle to litigation and lobbying they are giving tacit approval to the basic social order and "giving up the battle" for more radical challenges to society. Litigation and other forms of lawmaking can be effective, Polan argues, only when "they are undertaken in the context of broader economic, social, and cultural changes." Rifkin goes further. She argues that litigation "cannot lead to social changes, because in upholding and relying on the paradigm of law, the paradigm of patriarchy is upheld and reinforced." To eliminate patriarchy "the male power paradigm of law" must be "challenged and transformed."

CRITICAL LEGAL THEORY

The third category of feminist criticisms of law rejects the hierarchy of rational over irrational, objective over subjective, and so forth, and denies that law is or could be rational, objective, abstract, and principled. The feminists who endorse this third category, feminist critical legal theory, agree in part and disagree in part with the first two categories of criticism.

These feminists do not dispute the benefits obtained by legal reform feminism in the name of women's rights, but remain unconvinced by claims about the role of abstract legal theory in obtaining these benefits. The political organizing of the women's movement played a larger role in these reforms than legal reform feminists generally acknowledge. Legal reasoning and legal battles are not sharply distinguishable from moral and political reasoning and moral and political battles.

Similarly, critical legal theory feminists agree with the "law as patriarchy" feminists that law is often ideologically oppressive to women. They disagree, however, that law is male; law has no essence or immutable nature. Law is a form of human activity, a practice carried on by people. The people who carry on this activity are predominantly men, and many of them make claims about what they are doing that are just not true and could not be true. While it is true that law has been dominated by men, the traits associated with women have been only obscured, not eliminated. Law is not male. Law is not rational, objective, abstract, and principled. It is as irrational, subjective, concrete, and contextualized as it is rational, objective, abstract, and principled.

Law is not all one side of the dualisms. Law is not now and could not, consistent with what we believe, become principled, rational, and objective. The claim that law is principled is based on the belief that law consists of a few rules or principles and that these general rules provide a principled basis for deciding individual cases. But instead of this, law is actually made up of an agglomeration of lots of specific rules and some very general standards.

The rules are too specific, definite, and contextualized to count as principles. The existence of these rules is what gives law the degree of predictability that it has—but the rules are too detailed and each rule covers too few cases to make the law *principled.* For example, there is at present a rule that states may use gender-based statutory rape laws to try to reduce the incidence of teenage pregnancy, and there is another rule that age of majority for purposes of terminating parental support may not be gender-based. In *Michael M. v. Sonoma County*, the Supreme Court let stand a gender-based statutory rape law that the California Supreme Court said was intended to reduce the incidence of teenage pregnancy.[21] In *Stanton v. Stanton*, the Supreme Court struck down a Utah law that required a parent to support his son until age twenty-one but allowed him to stop supporting his daughter at age eighteen.[22] My point is not that these two rules conflict or that the cases cannot be reconciled with one another. Rather, each of these two rules applies in too few circumstances to provide any principled answer to the question of when states may use gender-based laws.

The standards, on the other hand, are too vague and indeterminate to decide cases. In each interesting disputed case, you can find at least two different broad, general standards that could seem to apply to the case and that would lead to different results. For example, the standard of noninterference in the family will often support one outcome, while the standard of protecting children will support the opposite outcome. Just as rules apply to too few cases, standards apply to too many. The legal system fluctuates between being based on rules and being based on standards, but its aspiration to be principled is not achieved. Law is not really any more abstract and principled than it is personalized and contextualized.

Nor is law rational. The efforts by feminists to work out a rational elaboration of equal rights of human beings in order to achieve rights for women has not worked and it will not work. The classic conflicts between equality of opportunity and equality of result, between natural rights and positive rights, and between rights-as-a-guarantee-of-security and rights-as-a-guarantee-of-freedom, render rights analysis incapable of settling any meaningful conflict.[23] More specifically, if one outcome will protect the plaintiff's right to freedom of action, the opposite outcome will often protect the defendant's right to security. If one outcome will protect a woman's right to formal equality of treatment, her right to substantive equality of result may seem to require a different outcome. This is why, for example, feminists found themselves on opposite sides of the *California Federal v. Guerra* case.[24] Some feminists argued that formal equality requires that the law treat pregnancy just like any other temporary disability, while other feminists maintained that substantive equality requires that women be able to give birth to children without losing their jobs—even if no other temporary absence from work is excused. Therefore, some feminists argued that women should insist on formal equality and reject any form of special maternity leave; while other feminists argued that working women need adequate maternity leave, even if no similar leaves of absence are given to men or other people who are not pregnant. Law does not provide a *rational* basis for choosing which right to recognize and protect in any particular case. Rights analysis cannot settle these conflicts but merely restates them in a new—at most somewhat obscured—form.

Finally, law is not objective. The idea that law is objective is refuted by the gradual recognition that *policy* issues appear everywhere. Every time a choice is made, every legal decision that is not obvious and uncontroversial, is a decision based on policy—which cannot be objective. Thus, it is simply a mistake to say that law is or could become rational, principled, and objective. Law is not all one side of the dualisms.

Sometimes dominant legal theory recognizes that law is not principled, rational, and objective. The dominant ideology does recognize the so-called female traits—indeed it celebrates them—but only on the periphery, or in their own "separate sphere." For example, family law may be subjective, contextual, and personalized, but commercial law is thought to be principled, rational, and objective. Similarly, the core doctrines of law are thought to be principled, rational, and objective, although there may be minor exceptions and subdoctrines that permit some influence of the subjective, contextual, and personalized. It is important for feminists to correct these misperceptions, to dissolve the ghettos of law, and to show that you cannot exclude the personalized, irrational, and subjective from any part of the law.

One way that dominant ideology makes law seem principled, rational, and objective is by banishing to the periphery of law those fields believed to be tainted by unruly, discretionary standards—fields such as family law, trust law, and the law of fiduciary obligation in general. The core subjects or the important fields of law are said to remain principled, rational, and objective. We can show, however, that although banished, family law, trusts, and fiduciary obligations continue to influence the rest of law—including those fields that were supposed to be the bastion of the so-called male principles of law. For example, the ideology of the marketplace depends upon the ideology of the family, and commercial law can be understood adequately only by recognizing the interrelationship between it and family law.[25]

Another technique by which the dominant ideology tries to make the law seem principled, rational, and objective is by separating each field between, on one hand, a set of basic rules, or a "male" core that is principled, rational, and objective and, on the other hand, a periphery of exceptions that can contain irrational and subjective elements. For example, contract law is frequently conceptualized as a set of rational, consistent, individualistic rules, softened by somewhat subjective, variable, "altruistic" exceptions, such as promissory estoppel. The basic core of contract law remains principled, rational, and objective. Feminists can disrupt this by showing that the conflict between the individualistic "rule" and the altruistic "exception" reappears with every doctrine. Every doctrine is a choice or compromise of sorts between the individualistic and altruistic impulses. This feminist analysis also problematizes what should be considered the rule and what the exception. It is not possible to separate any field of law into a core and a periphery and the traits associated with women cannot be excluded from law.[26]

CONCLUSION

As I have said, the feminist strategies for attacking legal theory are analogous to feminist strategies for attacking male dominance in general. The "reject sexualization" position resonates with the "legal reformist" position, the "reject hierarchization" with the "law as patriarchy" and the "androgyny" with "critical legal theory." But I do not want to claim that the relationship is anything more than this—an analogy or a resonance. The sets of categories are not identical, and no strategy from one set requires or entails any strategy from the other set.

First there is no necessary relationship between a person's attitude toward the sexualization of the dualisms in general and her attitude toward the identification of law with rational, objective, and principled. Moreover, someone could accept the hierarchization for some purposes—for example, could believe that it is better for law to be rational, objective, and principled—but still reject the hierarchization in general. Some feminists embrace androgyny, but still claim that law is patriarchal. Similarly, one can support feminist critical legal theory and still believe either that women are inherently or morally superior to men, the second feminist strategy, or that women should strive to act rational, active, and so forth, the first feminist strategy.

While it is apparent that I tend to support androgyny as a strategy to critique male dominance in general and critical legal theory to critique dominant legal theory, I do not wish to be understood as establishing my own hierarchy among theories. There is much to be learned from the first two categories of feminist critique, and there are risks and limitations in the third. Postmodernist efforts to rework or deconstruct the dualisms that underlie Western thought seem generally congenial with the goals of feminism, yet postmodernism in general and deconstruction in particular also have a conservative side. Just as socialism has seemed to be able to accommodate sexism, postmodernism may also be able to coexist with the subordination of women. Indeed, at times, postmodernism can appear to be a male-dominated effort to appropriate insights from feminism. It seems clear that any avant-garde movement must move forward continuously or it will become rigid and institutionalized in a bad way. As deconstruction has become respectable (and profitable) its radical potential may recede and the worries raised about it in progressive circles appear more justified. The same risk applies to feminism itself: It must move forward to resist being institutionalized and deradicalized.

Nothing in androgyny or critical legal theory will provide easy answers to concrete questions—such as "Would women really benefit from more state regulation of the family?" or "Could revised statutory rape laws protect young females without oppressing and demeaning them?" What I do hope is that by improving the theories upon which we operate we can understand better what is at stake in questions like these. I hope that by recognizing the impossibility of easy, logical answers we can free ourselves to think about the questions in a more constructive and imaginative manner. Law cannot be successfully separated from politics, morals, and the rest of human activities but is an integral part of the web of social life.

NOTES

1. See Helene Cixous, "Sorties," in *New French Feminisms,* ed. Elaine Marks and Isabelle de Courtivron (New York: Schocken, 1981), 90–91; Jacques Derrida, *Dissemination,* trans. Barbara Johnson (Chicago: University of Chicago Press, 1981); Carol P. Christ, *Diving Deep and Surfacing* (Boston: Beacon, 1980), 25; Jerry S. Clegg, *The Structure of Plato's Philosophy* (Lewisburg, PA: Bucknell University Press, 1977), 18, 100–101, 188–91; Frances Olsen, *The Family and the Market: A Study of Ideology and Legal Reform,* 96 Harvard Law Review 1497, 1570–76 (1983); Gerald Frug, *The City as a Legal Concept,* 93 Harvard Law Review 1057, 1057 (1980).

2. Harriet Taylor Mill, "Enfranchisement of Women," in John Stuart Mill and Harriet Taylor Mill, *Essays on Sex Equality,* ed. Alice S. Rossi (Chicago: University of Chicago Press, 1970), 89, 100–101; see also Mary

Wollstonecraft, *A Vindication of the Rights of Woman* (London: J. Johnson, 1792), 49–92.

3. Mill, "Enfranchisement of Women," 101, 120.

4. See Olsen, *The Family and the Market,* 1549–50.

5. See Barbara Easton, "Feminism and the Contemporary Family," in *A Heritage of Her Own: Toward a New Social History of Women,* ed. Nancy F. Cott and Elizabeth H. Pleck (New York: Simon & Schuster, 1979), 555, 556, 557; Nancy F. Cott and Elizabeth H. Pleck, "Introduction," in ibid., 11; Keith E. Melder, *Beginnings of Sisterhood* (New York: Schocken, 1977), 53; Judith Walkowitz, "The Politics of Prostitution," *Signs: Journal of Women in Culture and Society,* 6 (1980), reprinted in Catharine R. Stimpson and Ethel Spector Person, eds., *Women: Sex and Sexuality* (New York: Simon & Schuster, 1980), 145.

6. See Charlotte Perkins Gilman, *Herland* (New York: Pantheon, 1979).

7. See Carol Gilligan, *In a Different Voice: Psychological Theory and Women's Development* (Cambridge, MA: Harvard University Press, 1982); Patricia Spacks, *The Female Imagination* (New York: Knopf, 1975); Adrienne Rich, "Origins and History of Consciousness," in *The Dream of a Common Language: Poems, 1974–1977* (New York: Norton, 1978), 7.

8. See Drucilla Cornell and Adam Thurschwell, "Femininity, Negativity, Intersubjectivity," in Seyla Benhabib and Drucilla Cornell, *Feminism as Critique* (Minneapolis: University of Minnesota Press, 1987); Christ, *Diving Deep and Surfacing,* 26, 130.

9. See, for example, Jean Bethke Elshtain, "Against Androgyny," *Telos* 47 (1981): 5.

10. William Leach, *True Love and Perfect Union* (New York: Basic Books, 1980), 32.

11. See Olsen, *The Family and the Market,* 1577–78; Carolyn G. Heilbrun, *Toward a Recognition of Androgyny* (New York: Harper & Row, 1973); Ellen Piel Cook, *Psychological Androgyny* (New York: Pergamon, 1985); Wendy Doniger O'Flaherty, *Women, Androgynes, and Other Mythical Beasts* (Chicago: University of Chicago Press, 1980).

12. See *Reed v. Reed,* 404 U.S. 71 (1971); *Stanton v. Stanton,* 421 U.S. 7 (1975); *Craig v. Boren,* 429 U.S. 190 (1976).

13. See Frances Olsen, *From False Paternalism to False Equality: Judicial Assaults on Feminist Community, Illinois 1869–1895,* 84 Michigan Law Review 1518, 1518–20, 1541 (1986). For other useful critiques of the "equal treatment" versus "special treatment" debate, see Catherine MacKinnon, *Feminism Unmodified: Discourses on Life and Law* (Cambridge, MA: Harvard University Press, 1987), 32–45; Joan Scott,

"Deconstructing Equality Versus Difference: Or, The Uses of Poststructuralist Theory for Feminism," *Feminist Studies*, 14 (1988): 33.

14. See MacKinnon, *Sexual Harassment of Working Women*, 144–46.

15. Mary Joe Frug, *Securing Job Equality for Women: Labor Market Hostility to Working Mothers*, 59 Boston University Law Review 55 (1979).

16. See Nadine Taub 593

and Elizabeth M. Schneider, chapter 15 in this volume; Kathryn Powers, *Sex, Segregation, and the Ambivalent Directions of Sex Discrimination Law*, 1979 Wisconsin Law Review 55 (1979).

17. See Olsen, *The Family and the Market*, 1501–7; Frances Olsen, *The Myth of State Intervention in the Family*, 18 University of Michigan Journal of Law Reform 835 (1985).

18. Diane Polan, "Toward a Theory of Law and Patriarchy," in *The Politics of Law*, ed. David Kairys (New York: Pantheon, 1982), 294, 300, 302.

19. Janet Rifkin, *Toward a Theory of Law and Patriarchy*, 3 Harvard Women's Law Journal 83, 84, 87, 88, 92 (1980).

20. See Catherine MacKinnon, "Feminism, Marxism, Method, and the State: Toward Feminist Jurisprudence," *Signs: Journal of Women in Culture and Society*, 8 (1983): 635, 645.

21. 450 U.S. 464 (1981).

22. 421 U.S. 7 (1975).

23. See Frances Olsen, *Statutory Rape: A Feminist Critique of Rights Analysis*, 63 Texas Law Review 391 (1984); see also Joseph Singer, *The Legal Rights Debate in Analytical Jurisprudence from Bentham to Hohfeld*, 1982 Wisconsin Law Review 975 (1982); Kennedy, *Blackstone's Commentaries*; Oliver Wendell Holmes, Jr., *Privilege, Malice, and Intent*, 8 Harvard Law Review 1 (1894).

24. 479 U.S. 272 (1987).

25. See Olsen, *The Family and the Market*; see also Duncan Kennedy, *The Political Significance of the Structure of the Law School Curriculum*, 14 Seton Hall Law Review 1 (1983); Duncan Kennedy, "The Rise and Fall of Classical Legal Thought" (unpublished manuscript, 1975).

26. See Mary Joe Frug, *Rereading Contracts: A Feminist Analysis of a Contracts Casebook*, 34 American University Law Review 1065 (1985); Clare Dalton, *An Essay in the Deconstruction of Contract Doctrine*, 94 Yale Law Journal 997 (1985); Duncan Kennedy, *Form and Substance in Private Law Adjudication*, 89 Harvard Law Review 1685 (1976); Roberto Unger, *The Critical Legal Studies Movement*, 96 Harvard Law Review 561, 618–48 (1983).

32 CORNEL WEST

THE ROLE OF LAW IN PROGRESSIVE POLITICS

WHAT is the role and function of the law in contemporary progressive politics? Are legal institutions crucial terrain on which significant social change can take place? If so, how? In which way? What are progressive lawyers to do if they are to remain relatively true to their moral convictions and political goals?

In this chapter I shall attempt to respond to these urgent questions. This response will try to carve out a vital democratic left space between the Scylla of upbeat liberalism that harbors excessive hopes for the law and the Charybdis of downbeat leftism that promotes exorbitant doubts about the law. My argument rests upon three basic claims. First, the fundamental forms of social misery in American society can be neither adequately addressed nor substantially transformed within the context of existing legal apparatuses. Yet serious and committed work within this circumscribed context remains indispensable if progressive politics is to have any future at all. Second, this crucial work cannot but be primarily defensive unless significant extraparliamentary social motion or movements bring power and pressure to bear on the prevailing status quo. Such social motion and movements presuppose either grassroots citizen participation in credible progressive projects or rebellious acts of desperation that threaten the social order. Third, the difficult task of progressive legal practitioners is to link their defensive work within the legal system to possible social motion and movements that attempt to transform American society fundamentally.

Any argument regarding the role of law in progressive politics must begin with two sobering historical facts about the American past and present. First, American society is disproportionately shaped by the outlooks, interests, and aims of the business community—especially that of big business. The sheer power of corporate capital is extraordinary. This power makes it difficult even to imagine what a free and democratic society would look like (or how it would operate) if there were publicly accountable mechanisms that alleviated the vast disparities in resources, wealth, and income owing in part to the vast influence of big business on the U.S. government and its legal institutions. This is why those who focus on forms of social misery—such as the ill-fed, ill-clad, and ill-housed—must think in epochal, not apocalyptic, terms.

The second brute fact about the American past and present is that this society is a *chronically* racist, sexist, homophobic, and jingoistic one. The complex and tortuous quest for American identity from 1776 to our own time has produced a culture in which people define themselves physically, socially, sexually, and politically in terms of race, gender, sexual orientation, and "anti-American" activities. One unique feature of the country among other modern nations—with the embarrassing exceptions of South Africa and Hitler's Germany—is that race has served as the linchpin in regulating this national quest for identity. A detailed genealogy of American legal discourse about citizenship and rights, as initiated by the late Robert Cover of Yale, bears out this inescapable reality. The historical articulation of the experiential weight of African slavery and Jim Crowism to forms of U.S. patriarchy, homophobia, and anti-American (usually communist and socialist) repression or surveillance yields a profoundly conservative culture.

The irony of this cultural conservatism is that it tries to preserve a highly dynamic corporate-driven economy, a stable election-centered democracy, and a precious liberties-guarding rule of law. This irony constitutes the distinctive hybridity of American liberalism (in its classical and revisionist versions) and the debilitating dilemma of American radicalism (in its movements for racial, class, and sexual equality). In other words, American liberalism diffuses the claims of American radicals by pointing to long-standing democratic and libertarian practices, despite historic racist, sexist, class, and homophobic constraints. Hence, any feasible American radicalism seems to be but an extension of American liberalism. Needless to say, the sacred cow of American liberalism—namely, economic growth achieved by *corporate* priorities—is neither examined nor interrogated. And those that do are relegated to the margins of the political culture.

My first claim rests upon the assumption that the extension of American liberalism in response to movements for racial, class, and sexual equality is desirable yet insufficient. This is so because the extension of American liberalism leaves relatively untouched the fundamental reality that undergirds the forms of social misery: *the maldistribution of resources, wealth, and power in American society*. Yet the extension of American liberalism in regard to race, labor, women, gays, lesbians, and nature *appears* radical on the American ideological spectrum principally because it goes against the deeply entrenched cultural conservatism in the country. In fact, this extension—as seen for example in the 1930s and 1960s—takes place by means of insurgent social motion and movements convincing political and legal elites to enact legislation or judicial decrees over the majority of the population. In short, the very extension of American liberalism has hardly ever been popular among the masses of American people primarily owing to a pervasive cultural conservatism.

The law has played a crucial role in those periods in which liberalism has been extended precisely because of the power of judicial review and an elected body of officials responding to social movements—not because cultural conservatism has been significantly weeded out. The effects of these laws and policies over time have attenuated some of the more crude and overt expressions of cultural conservatism, yet the more subtle expressions permeate the culture. The existing legal apparatuses cannot adequately address or substantially transform the plight of the racially and sexually skewed ill-fed, ill-clad, or ill-housed not only because of the marginalizing of perspectives that highlight the need for a redistribution of resources, wealth, and power, but also because of the perception that the extension of American liberalism is the most radical option feasible within American political culture.

Is this perception true? Is it the case that all workable radical alternatives must presuppose economic growth achieved by corporate priorities? These questions are especially acute given the collapse of social Keynesianism in the mid 1970s—that "magic" Fordist formula of mass production undergirded by mass consumption alongside government provisions to those with no access to resources that sustained economic growth in the postwar period. The conservative project of supply-side economics and military Keynesianism of the 1980s yielded not simply a larger gap between the haves and have-nots but also a debt-financed public sphere and a more corporate-dominated economy—all in the name of "free enterprise."

If the extension of American liberalism is the only feasible radical option within American political culture, then the defensive role of progressive lawyers becomes even more important. Their work constitutes one of the few buffers against cultural conservatism that recasts the law more in its own racist, sexist, antilabor, and homophobic image. Furthermore, the work within the existing legal system helps keep alive a memory of the social traces left by past progressive movements of resistance, a memory requisite for future movements. This defensive work, though possibly radical in intent, is *liberal* practice in that it proceeds from within the legal system in order to preserve the effects of former victories threatened by the conservative offensive. Yet this same defensive work has tremendous radical potential, especially within the context of vital oppositional activity against the status quo. This is why the distinction between liberal and radical legal practice is not sharp and rigid; rather it is fluid and contingent due to the ever-changing larger social situation. Needless to say, the crucial role of this kind of legal practice—be it to defend the rights of activists, secure permits to march, or dramatize an injustice with a class suit—is indispensable for progressive politics. Yet in "cold" moments in American society—when cultural conservatism and big business fuse with power and potency—radical lawyers have little option other than defensive work. This work is often demoralizing, yet it serves as an important link to past victories and a basis for the next wave of radical action.

In our present period, radical legal practice takes two main forms: theoretical critiques of liberal paradigms in the academy that foster subcultures of radical students and professors or participation in radical organizations that engage in extraparliamentary social motion. It is no accident that the first form consists of a pedagogical reform movement within elite institutions of the legal academy. This critical legal studies (CLS) movement is symptomatic of a pessimism regarding feasible radical options in American political culture and a distance between radical legal critiques and radical legal action vis-à-vis the courts. This sense of political impotence and gulf between radical professors of law and radical lawyers results not because CLS consists of insular bourgeois theorists with little grasp of political reality. In fact, their understanding of this reality is often acute. Yet some of the CLS trashing of liberalism at the level of theory spills over to liberal legal practice. This spillover is myopic, for it trashes the only feasible progressive practice for radical lawyers vis-à-vis the courts. This myopia becomes downright dangerous and irresponsible when aimed at civil rights lawyers for whom the very effort to extend American liberalism may lead to injury or death in conservative America.

Is there any way out of this impasse? Can progressive legal practice be more than defensive? My second claim holds that there are but two ways out. In situations of sparse resources along with degraded self-images and depoliticized sensibilities, one avenue for poor people is existential rebellion and anarchic expression. The capacity to produce social chaos is the last resort of desperate people. It results from a tragic quest for recognition and survival. The civic terrorism that haunts our city streets and the criminality that frightens us is, in part, poor people's response to political neglect and social invisibility. Like most behavior in American society, it is directly linked to market activity—the buying and selling of commodities. In this case, the commodities tend to be drugs, alcohol, and bodies (especially women's bodies). These tragic forms of expression have yet to take on an explicitly political character, yet they may in the near future. If and when they do, the prevailing powers will be forced to make *political* responses, not simply legal ones that lead to prison overcrowding.

One major challenge for progressive politics is to find a way of channeling the talent and energy of poor people into forms of social motion that can have impact on the powers that rule. This second way out of the impasse is the creation of organized citizen participation in credible progressive projects. Yet American political culture mitigates against this. The status quo lives and thrives on the perennial radical dilemma of disbelief: It is hard for ordinary citizens to believe their actions can make a difference in a society whose resources, wealth, and power are disproportionately held by the big business community.

The best project progressive politics offered in recent decades was the courageous and exciting 1980s presidential campaigns of the charismatic spokesperson seeking acceptance and respect within the Democratic party: the prophetic witness of the Reverend Jesse Jackson. Yet his two campaigns reveal the weakness of American progressive politics: the obsession with televisual visibility alongside little grassroots organizing beyond elections and the inability to generate social motion outside electoral politics. In Jackson's case, it also discloses the refusal to promote democratic practices within one's own organization. Jackson has had a significant and, for the most part, salutary effect on American progressive politics. The major contribution of his efforts are that they were the first serious attempt since the Poor Peoples' Campaign of Martin Luther King, Jr., to constitute a multiracial coalition to raise the issue of the maldistribution of resources, wealth, and power. Yet, unlike King, Jackson's attempt to highlight this crucial issue was often downplayed or jettisoned by his quest for entry into the elite groupings of the centrist Democratic party. Social motion and movements in America tend to be neither rooted in nor sustained by campaigns for electoral office, no matter how charismatic the leader.

There can be no substantive progressive politics beyond the extension of American liberalism without social motion or movements. And despite the symbolic and cathartic electoral victories of liberal women and people of color, all remain thoroughly shackled by corporate priorities in the economy and in debt-ridden administrations. Under such conditions, the plight of the ill-fed, ill-clad, and ill-housed tends to get worse.

With the lethargic electoral system nearly exhausted of progressive potential—though never to be ignored owing to possible conservative politicians eager for more power—we must look toward civil society, especially to mass media, universities, religious and political groupings, and trade unions. Despite the decline of popular mobilization and political participation and the decrease of unionized workers and politicized citizens, there is a vital and vibrant culture industry, religious life, student activism, and labor stirrings.

In the midst of a market-driven culture of consumption—with its spectatorial passivity, evasive banality, and modes of therapeutic release—there is an increasing sense of social concern and political engagement. These inchoate progressive sentiments are in search of an effective mode of organized expression. Until we create some channels our progressive practice will remain primarily defensive.

How do we go about creating these channels of resistance and contestation to corporate power? What positive messages do we have to offer? What programs can we put forward? This brings me to the third claim regarding the role of law in progressive politics. In a society that suffers more and more from historical amnesia—principally due to the dynamic, past-effacing activities of market forces—lawyers have close contact with the concrete traces and residues of the struggles and battles of the past. This is in part what Alexis de Tocqueville had in mind when he called the legal elites America's only aristocracy. Needless to say, he understood continuity with the past in terms of social stability. I revise his formulation to connect continuity with the memory of the effects of progressive victories of the past inscribed in the law of a society whose link with the past is tenuous and whose present is saturated with flashing images, consumer and hedonistic sensibilities, and quick information (much of it disinformation dispensed by unreliable corporate cartels).

The role of progressive lawyers is not only to engage in crucial defensive practices—liberal practice vis-à-vis the courts—but also to preserve, recast, and build on the traces and residues of past conflicts coded in laws. This latter activity is guided by a deep historical sensibility that not only deconstructs the contradictory character of past and present legal decisions or demystifies the power relations operative in such decisions; it also concocts empowering and enabling narratives that cast light on how these decisions constitute the kind of society in which we live and how people resist and try to transform it. Progressive lawyers can be politically engaged narrators who tell analytically illuminating stories about how the law has impeded or impelled struggles for justice and freedom. Like rap artists of the best sort, progressive lawyers can reach out to a demoralized citizenry to energize them with insights about the historical origins and present causes of social misery in light of visions, analyses, and practices to change the world. Lawyers can perform this role more easily than others due to the prestige and authority of the law in American society. Progressive lawyers can seize this opportunity to highlight the internal contradictions and the blatant hypocrisy of much of the law in the name of the very ideals—fairness, protection, and formal equality—heralded by the legal system. This kind of progressive legal practice, narrative in character and radical in content, can give visibility and legitimacy to issues neglected by and embarrassing to conservative administrations as well as expose and educate citizens regarding the operations of economic and political powers vis-à-vis the courts. In this regard, historical consciousness and incisive narratives yield immanent critiques, disclose the moral lapses, and highlight the structural constraints of the law while empowering victims to transform society.

Without this kind of historical consciousness and analytical storytelling, it is difficult to create channels for resistance and challenge to corporate power. In addition, there must be an accent on the moral character of the leaders and followers in the past and present who cared, sacrificed, and risked for the struggle for justice and freedom. Progressive lawyers must highlight the *ethical* motivations of those who initiated and promoted the legal victories that further struggles for racial, sexual, and class equality within the limiting perimeters of American law.

The CLS movement is significant primarily because it introduced for the first time in legal discourse a profoundly historicist approach and theoretical orientation that highlights *simultaneously* the brutal realities of class exploitation, racial subordination, patriarchal domination, homophobic marginalization, and ecological abuse in the American past and present. By historicist approach, I mean a candid recognition that the law is deeply reflective of—though not thoroughly determined by—the political and ideological conflicts in American society. By theoretical orientation, I mean a serious encounter with social theories that accent the structural dynamics of the economy, state, and culture that shape and are shaped by the law.

Legal formalism, legal positivism, and even legal realism remained relatively silent about the brutal realities of the American past and present. This silence helped American liberalism remain for the most part captive to cultural conservatism. It also limited radical alternatives in legal studies to extensions of American liberalism. The grand breakthrough of CLS was to expose the intellectual blinders of American liberal legal scholarship and to link these blinders to the actual blood that has flowed owing to the realities hidden. It calls attention to the human costs paid by those who suffer owing to the institutional arrangements sanctioned by liberal law in the name of formal equality and liberty.

Yet CLS has not been and cannot be more than a progressive movement within a slice of the professional managerial strata in American society without connections to other social motions in American society. Academic leftist subcultures have a crucial role to play, yet they do not get us beyond the impasse.

It may well be that American culture does not possess the democratic and libertarian resources to bring about racial, sexual, and class equality. Its cultural conservatism and big business influences may impose insurmountable constraints for such a radical project. Lest we forget, there are roughly three reactionaries (Klansmen, John Birches, and so on) for every leftist in America. Yet it is precisely this kind of cynical—or is it realistic—outlook that often confines radicalism to extensions of American liberalism. How does one combat or cope with such an outlook?

There is no definitive answer to this question. The enabling and empowering response that avoids illusions is to sustain one's hope for social change by keeping alive the memory of past and present efforts and victories and to remain engaged in such struggles owing principally to the *moral* substance of these efforts. As Nietzsche noted (with different aims in mind), subversive memory and other-regarding morality are the principal weapons for the wretched of the earth and those who fight to enhance their plight. This memory and morality in the United States consists of recurring cycles of collective insurgency and violent repression, social upsurge, and establishmentarian containment. The American left is weak and feeble during periods of social stability owing to the powers of big business and cultural conservatism; it surfaces in the form of social movements (usually led by charismatic spokespersons) to contest this stability due to their moral message that borrows from the nation's collective self-definition (as democratic and free) and due to cleavages within big business and culturally conservative groups. The social movements do not and cannot last long; they indeed change the prevailing status quo, but rarely fundamentally rearrange the corporate priorities of American society. In this regard, American radicalism is more than an extension of American liberalism when it constitutes a serious and concrete threat to big business, usually in the call for substantial redistribution of resources, wealth, and power. Yet this threat, though significant, is short-lived owing to repression and incorporation. After such social movements, American radicalism is relegated to a defensive posture, that is, trying to preserve its victories by defending extensions of American liberalism.

If this crude historical scenario has merit, the major role of the law in progressive politics is threefold. First, past victories of social movements encoded in the law must be preserved in order to keep alive the memory of the past, struggle in the present, and hope for the future. Second, this preservation, though liberal in practice, is radical in purpose in that it yearns for new social motion and movements that can threaten the new social stability of big business and cultural conservatism long enough to enact and enforce more progressive laws before repression and incorporation set in. In this regard, radical American legal practice is a kind of Burkean project turned on its head. It fosters tradition not for social stability but to facilitate threats to the social order; it acknowledges inescapable change not to ensure organic reform but to prepare for probable setbacks and defeats of social movements. Third, the new memories and victories inscribed in new laws are kept alive by the defensive work of progressive lawyers in order to help lay the groundwork for the next upsurge of social motion and movements.

The interplay between the work of progressive lawyers and social change is crucial. In some cases, it is a matter of life or death for charismatic leaders or courageous followers. In other instances, it is a question of serving as the major buffer between the unprincipled deployment of naked state power and "principled" use of the courts against social movements. Such a buffer may prolong these movements and increase their progressive impact on society and culture. The moral character of these movements is important precisely because it may make repressive attackers less popular and will more than likely help sustain the memory of the movement more easily. One of the reasons the civil rights movement led by Martin Luther King, Jr., is remembered more than, say, other equally worthy ones such as the CIO-led unionization movement or the feminist movement is that its moral vision was central to its identity and accented by its major spokesperson. Needless to say, this vision appealed to the very ideals that define the national identity of many who opposed the movement.

How do progressive lawyers articulate ideals that may subvert and transform the prevailing practices legitimated by limited liberal versions of these ideals? Progressive legal practice must put forward interpretations of the precious ideal of democracy that call into question the unregulated and unaccountable power of big business; it also must set forth notions of the precious ideal of liberty that lay bare the authoritarian attitudes of cultural conservatism. This two-pronged ideological strategy should consist of an unrelenting defense of substantive democracy (in a decentralized, nonstatist fashion) and all-inclusive liberty (as best articulated in the Bill of Rights). This defense is utopian in that it tries to keep alive the possibility of social movements; it is realistic in that it acknowledges the necessity of liberal legal practices for radical lawyers to preserve the gains after social movements have been crushed or absorbed.

With solid yet insular academic leftist subcultures, eager yet sober black, brown, Asian, and red lefts, a battered yet determined labor movement (especially organized public-sector workers), beleaguered yet bold feminist and womanist progressives, scarred though proud gay and lesbian lefts, and the growing number of green and gray activists, united social motions and movements are in the making. What is needed is neither a vanguard party nor purist ideology, but rather a coming together to pursue the common goals of radical democratic and libertarian projects that overlap, especially locally and regionally and not simply within electoral politics. Democratic leadership of and by ordinary citizens in extraparliamentary modes must flourish. The social stability of the conservative and moderate administrations must be bombarded and shaken by democratic demands and libertarian protections. The profits and investments of big businesses should be scrutinized for public accountability and civic responsibility. The xenophobia and jingoism of cultural conservatives have to be morally rejected and judicially checked. A new world is in the making. Let us not allow the lethargy of American politics, the predominance of big business, and the pervasiveness of cultural conservatism to blunt the contributions we can make. Especially if some of us choose the law as the vocational terrain for progressive politics.

CONTRIBUTORS

Richard L. Abel is Connell Professor of Law at UCLA. He is the author of *Politics by Other Means: Law in the Struggle Against Apartheid; Lawyers: A Critical Reader; Speaking Respect, Respecting Speech; American Lawyers; The Law and Society Reader;* and former president of the Law and Society Association.

Keith Aoki is professor of law at the University of Oregon.

Jane B. Baron is professor of law at Temple University.

W. Haywood Burns, who died in 1996, was dean of the law school and professor of law at the City University of New York, and former president of the National Conference of Black Lawyers and the National Lawyers Guild.

David Cole is professor of law at Georgetown University and a volunteer staff attorney for the Center for Constitutional Rights. He is the author of *The Uses of Inequality: Race and Class in American Criminal Justice* (forthcoming).

Rhonda Copelon is professor of law and director of the International Women's Human Rights Law Clinic at the City University of New York, vice president of the Center for Constitutional Rights, and a member of the Advisory Committee of Human Rights Watch/Women's Rights Project. She is the co-author of *Sex Discrimination and the Law: History, Practice, and Theory.*

Kimberlé Crenshaw is professor of law at UCLA and Columbia University. She is the co-editor of *Critical Race Theory: The Key Writings That Formed the Movement.*

Elliott Currie is research associate at the Center for the Study of Law and Society and lecturer in Legal Studies at the University of California, Berkeley. He is the author of *Confronting Crime*; *Reckoning: Drugs, the Cities, and the American Future*; and *Crime and Punishment in America.*

Julia Epstein is professor of English and comparative literature at Haverford College. She is the author of *Altered Conditions: Disease, Medicine, and Storytelling*; and *The Iron Pen: Frances Burney and the Politics of Women's Writing*; and the co-editor of *Body Guards: The Cultural Politics of Sexual Ambiguity.*

Jay Feinman is Distinguished Professor of Law at Rutgers University, Camden. He is the author of *Economic Negligence: Liability of Professionals and Businesses to Third Parties for Economic Loss.*

Alan Freeman was, until his death in 1995, professor of law at the State University of New York, Buffalo. He co-authored *The Politics of Virtue* and *Property Law.*

Peter Gabel is president and professor of law at the New College of California and associate editor of *Tikkun* magazine.

Robert W. Gordon is professor of law and history at Yale University. He is the author of *The Legacy of Oliver Wendell Holmes.*

Janet E. Halley is professor of law and Robert E. Paradice Faculty Scholar at Stanford University, a former professor of English literature, and a cooperating attorney at the Lambda Legal Defense and Education Fund. She is the author of *Don't* (forthcoming).

Morton J. Horwitz is Charles Warren Professor of the History of American Law at Harvard University. He is the author of *Transformation of American Law, 1780–1860* (1977); and *Transformation of American Law, 1870–1960: The Crisis of Legal Orthodoxy* (1992).

David Kairys is professor of law at Temple University and is one of the nation's leading civil rights lawyers. He was a founding partner and is of counsel to Kairys, Rudovsky, Epstein, Messing & Rau in Philadelphia. He is the author of *With Liberty and Justice for Some: A Critique of the Conservative Supreme Court*.

Duncan Kennedy is Carter Professor of General Jurisprudence at Harvard University. He is the author of *Legal Education and the Reproduction of Hierarchy*, *Sexy Dressing, Etc.* and *A Critique of Adjudication [fin de siècle]*.

Karl E. Klare is George J. and Kathleen Waters Matthews Distinguished Professor of Law at Northeastern University.

Charles R. Lawrence III is professor of law at Georgetown University. He is co-author of *We Won't Go Back: Making the Case for Affirmative Action*; *Words That Wound: Critical Race Theory; Assaultive Speech and the First Amendment*; and *The Bakke Case: The Politics of Inequality*.

Jules Lobel is professor of law at the University of Pittsburgh and a cooperating attorney and board member of the Center for Constitutional Rights. He is the editor of *Less Than a Perfect Union: Alternative Perspectives on the Constitution*, and has co-edited the *Civil Rights Litigation Handbook*.

Molly S. McUsic is professor of law at the University of North Carolina.

Elizabeth Mensch is professor of law at the State University of New York, Buffalo. She is co-author of *The Politics of Virtue* and *Property Law*.

Martha Minow is professor of law at Harvard University. She is the author of *Not Only for Myself: Identity, Politics, and Law; Making All the Difference*; and the co-editor of *Law Stories*.

Frances Olsen is professor of law at UCLA and Overseas Fellow at Cambridge University. She is the co-author and editor of *Legal Concepts and Changing Human Relationships: Cases and Materials on Family Law* and *Feminist Legal Theory*.

Victor Rabinowitz is a founding partner and counsel to Rabinowitz, Boudin, Standard, Krinsky & Leiberman in New York. He is the author of *Unrepentent Leftist: A Lawyer's Memoir*, and a founder and former president of the National Lawyers Guild.

Rand E. Rosenblatt is professor of law and associate dean at Rutgers University, Camden. He is the co-author of *Law and the American Health Care System* and *American Health Law*.

David Rudovsky is a partner at Kairys, Rudovsky, Epstein, Messing & Rau in Philadelphia and a senior fellow at the University of Pennsylvania Law School. He is the co-author of *Police Misconduct: Law and Litigation* and *Pennsylvania Criminal Procedure*.

Austin Sarat is William Nelson Cromwell Professor of Jurisprudence & Political Science at Amherst College. He is the author of *Capital Punishment in Law and Culture* (forthcoming) and *Race, Law, & Culture: Reflections on Brown v. Board of Education* and co-author of *Divorce Lawyers and Their Clients: Power and Meaning in the Legal Process*; *Cause Lawyering: Political Commitments and Professional Responsibilities*; and *Law's Violence*.

Elizabeth M. Schneider is professor of law and chair of the Edward V. Sparer Public Interest Law Fellowship Program at Brooklyn Law School. She is co-author of *Battered Women and the Law: Cases and Materials* (forthcoming).

William H. Simon is Kenneth and Harle Montgomery Professor of Public Interest Law at the University of California, Berkeley. He is the author of *The Practice of Justice: A Theory of Lawyers' Ethics* and has worked in both corporate and legal aid practice.

Joseph William Singer is professor of law at Harvard University. He is the author of *Property Law: Rules, Policies, and Practices*.

Nadine Taub is professor of law and director of the Women's Rights Litigation Clinic at Rutgers University, Newark. She is the co-author of *The Law of Sex Discrimination* and *Sex Discrimination and the Law: History, Practice, and Theory* and co-editor of *Reproductive Laws for the 1990s*.

Gerald Torres is H.O. Head Centennial Professor of Real Property at the University of Texas. He is a member of the National Environmental Justice Advisory Committee of the Environmental Protection Agency and was Deputy Assistant Attorney General of the United States for Environmental and Natural Resources and Counsel to the Attorney General.

Cornel West is professor of Afro-American Studies at Harvard University. He is the author of *Race Matters*; *Keeping Faith*; *Roots of Violence*; and *Restoring Hope*.

Lucy A. Williams is professor of law at Northeastern University. She practiced poverty law with the Legal Assistance Foundation of Chicago and the Massachusetts Law Reform Institute.

INDEX AND TABLE OF CASES

Cases cited in the text appear in the index italicized and listed alphabetically by name of first party.

NEW REVISED EDITION

PHILOSOPHY
and SEX

EDITED BY

ROBERT BAKER and FREDERICK ELLISTON

Prometheus Books

700 East Amherst St. Buffalo, New York 14215

Published by
Prometheus Books
700 East Amherst Street
Buffalo, New York 14215

ISBN 0-87975-246-7
Library of Congress Catalog Card No. 84-63548

Contents

5

Preface to Second Edition

When, about a decade ago, the two of us set out to anthologize the recent work on philosophy and sex, our task was relatively easy. Although few reputable philosophy journals had cared to publish on the subject proper, several had begun to include essays on sexual issues that were relevant to questions of public policy. The consequent paucity of published material simplified our editorial tasks to a degree that we have only recently begun to appreciate. We had only to review the few articles that had managed to find their way into the published philosophical literature, peruse a variety of nonstandard sources, discover unpublished manuscripts, commission some essays to fill in the gaps, create a short bibliography—and find a publisher with the perspicacity and gumption to ignore the shibboleths of the profession and support the enterprise. Once we discovered the publisher, the rest took less than a year.

Timeliness, as it turned out, was on our side. *Philosophy and Sex* received instant acclaim as both a text and a reference book. Moreover, once philosophers knew a text was ready to hand, they created courses on the subject. The natural concatenation of teaching, reflection, research, and writing led, in turn, to a new generation of literature on the subject—a literature that cited *Philosophy and Sex* more than any other volume, but, ironically, was not reflected in the original volume. As time passed and the literature on philosophy and sex burgeoned, we became increasingly aware that timeliness is a quintessentially perishable commodity. Now, almost a decade after the publication of the first edition, we have undertaken to revise the anthology both by incorporating some of the more significant work published in the last decade and by bringing to the attention of philosophers some material that might otherwise be overlooked.

The resultant anthology retains most of the essays from the first edition in four of the first five sections: *Marriage, Contraception,*

7

Abortion, Conceptions of Sex. The present volume now leads off with a new section of previously published essays on *Love* and ends with four new sections on *Pornography and Censorship, Homosexuality, Pedophilia,* and *Case Studies.* Most of the materials in these sections have been extensively revised by their authors.

As a perusal of the table of contents will immediately reveal, one of the essays in the section on homosexuality could not have been revised by its author for inclusion in this volume. The author, Jeremy Bentham, has been dead for over a century. His essay "Pederasty," however, was first published in the *Journal of Homosexuality* in 1978. Since the essay is as relevant and insightful as anything currently being written on the subject, we decided to include it in this collection, not as a historical curiosity, but as an important contribution to the contemporary debate on the topic.

This edition also includes material that has not hitherto been included in any anthology on philosophy and sex, but is frequently found in similar books in other areas of social philosophy: case studies. The studies we have chosen are based on actual cases and were originally assembled for a course on human sexuality taught by Dr. Richard Cross of the Rutgers Medical School. Our hope is that they can be used to test and enrich intuitions about some of the more abstract theories developed elsewhere in this book, such as Ehman's analysis of pedophilia and Nagel's analysis of perversion, among others.

Every anthology is itself a case study in resource allocation. The addition of new material on homosexuality, love, pornography, and pedophilia, as well as the case studies, came in part at the expense of the sections in the first edition that dealt, somewhat more abstractly, with sexual language and sexual perversion. We keenly regret the loss of these sections and of a number of articles that we replaced with more current material. There are also many excellent articles on such topics as affirmative action, children's rights, population ethics, and sexual violence that we chose not to publish. Our primary reason for excluding these topics was the ready availability of material on these subjects in other anthologies. For example, since there is at present a relative abundance of moderately priced collections on feminist theory (which could be used in tandem with *Philosophy and Sex*), no essays on feminist theory proper have been included here—although, to be sure, we do include work that is an outgrowth of such a theory, e.g., Firestone's critique of love.

Similar sacrifices had to be made in the bibliography. Of necessity, the criteria for inclusion have become more restrictive; except for bibliographies, we now include only articles written by and for philosophers, primarily in philosophical journals.

Books such as these are, of course, the product of many helping hands. We would like to thank everyone who corresponded with us when we were preparing the bibliography: the librarians at Union College and Illinois Institute of Technology who helped us to track down obscure references, all of our colleagues who helped out with criticisms and comments (particularly Felmon Davis), our student aides (especially Rita Lindenberg and Phillip McFarland), our secretary Marianne Snowden, and each of the contributors. Special thanks must go to William Vitek, our bibliographer; Paul Kurtz, our publisher; and Steven L. Mitchell, our editor. We thank our families—Arlene, Meredith, and Nathanial among the Bakers, and David and Deborah among the Ellistons—for generously foregoing so much in order that we could commune with our word processors.

Lastly, we gratefully acknowledge those readers of the first edition who took the time and trouble to communicate with us about the book. We hope that the second edition will prove to be as useful, and as provocative, as the first.

Robert Baker
Union College

Frederick Elliston
Illinois Institute of Technology

Robert Baker
and Frederick Elliston

Introduction

In the "war" between philosophers and poets, the philosophers have all too willingly relinquished the field of sex to the poets. Their retreat is puzzling when one considers that all of us are born into this world as biological males or females, and that the attendant gender roles boy/girl, man/woman, husband/wife, father/mother, adulterer/adulteress mediate and perhaps even determine our lives. If anatomy is not all of destiny, sex and sexuality—especially in the institutionalized forms of courtship, marriage, and the family—are crucial in molding individuals and cultures. Surely then, intellectuals who are committed to living the examined life should not fail to devote a goodly part of their work to the analysis of sex, sexuality, and gender.

Why then have philosophers surrendered sex to the poets? In part, their refusal to deal with sex can be traced to the tradition of rejecting the body and all things corporeal. For example, in the dialogue in which Plato introduces the "war" between the philosophers and the poets, he has the Prophetess advise Socrates that the contemplation of pure beauty "is the life for men to live." She goes on to say that he "will esteem [this pure beauty] far beyond ... those lovely persons whom you and many others now gaze on with astonishment. ..." Love between persons is contaminated with "the intermixture of human flesh and colors, and all other idle and unreal shapes attendant upon morality"; whereas pure beauty is "simple, pure and uncontaminated."[1]

Writing in a similar vein, Epictetus argued that rationality and sexuality are incompatible, and hence that there is no room for sex in the truly philosophical life.

> Every habit is confirmed and strengthened by corresponding acts. ... So, if you lie in bed for ten days and then get up and try to take a fairly long walk, you will see how your legs lose their power. ... When you yield to carnal passion you must take account not only of this one defeat, but of the fact that you fed your incontinence and strengthened it. ...

11

Today when I saw a handsome woman I did not say "Would that she were mine!" and "Blessed is her husband!". . . Nor do I picture the next scene: the woman present and disrobing and reclining by my side. . . . And if the woman, poor thing, is willing and beckons, and sends to me, and even touches me and comes close to me, I still hold aloof and conquer; the refutation of this argument is something greater than the argument of "the Liar" or the "Resting" argument. This is a thing really to be proud of. . . .

The man who truly trains is he who disciplines himself to face such impressions. . . . Great is the struggle, divine the task; the stake is a Kingdom, freedom, peace, an unruffled spirit. . . . Can any storm be greater than that which springs from violent impressions to drive out reason?[2]

Except when planning utopias, the ancient philosophers tended to abandon sex to the poets because of the felt conflict between their commitment to reason and the inherent unreasonableness of sexual passion, because of a tendency to regard the sensual world as unworthy of philosophical contemplation, and—on a more personal level—because they tended to regard abnegation and the suppression of libido as intrinsically praiseworthy. For the most part the history of the philosophy of sex has been little more than a footnote to the ancients. Yet, a brief glance at this history is not altogether unrewarding.

In living their lives the great medieval philosophers Augustine and Aquinas followed the antisexual precedent of Plato and Epictetus. And while their writings form a somewhat different tradition, these medievals would undoubtedly have dismissed sex as quickly and disdainfully as their pagan predecessors if their inclinations had not been checked by the Biblical commandment to "increase and multiply and fill the earth."[3] This "blessing of fecundity," even more than St. Paul's grudging concession that marriage is better than hell, led them to consider, analyze, and defend the institution of monogamous marriage—thereby providing us not only with one of the very few bodies of philosophical literature dealing with sex, but also with a series of expositions and arguments that still shape contemporary views.

As is so frequently the case, the typical expression of medieval thought is found in the works of Thomas Aquinas, who developed what might be called the traditional eightfold truth on the subject: (1) seminal discharge defines the essence of sexual intercourse; (2) the only moral function of sexual intercourse is procreation (hence the emission of semen in any way that in itself prevents procreation is unnatural and immoral); (3) procreation naturally completes itself in the generation of an adult; (4) those who engage in sexual intercourse should provide whatever is necessary to rear any creature they procreate; (5) an unadulterous monogamous marriage is the best environment for rearing offspring to become adults;

(6) females are inferior to males; (7) the male acts as the female's governor in marriage;[4] (8) divorce is improper (note that the seventh proposition renders it unjust for a male to divorce a female, while the sixth proposition makes female generated divorces inappropriate).

It would be difficult to overestimate the significance of these eight theses for the subject of this book—indeed for the very nature of our society. To accept or reject any one of them, even the most innocuous, is to accept or reject a significant feature of one's culture. Consider proposition 1. If ever a proposition appeared to be a metaphysical irrelevancy, it does. Yet this seemingly superfluous bit of abstraction can—and possibly does —have the mundane and tragically real effect of ruining the sex life of half of the population.[5] If the implications of proposition 1 are somewhat subtle, those of the remaining seven are not. Between them they describe a monogamous, sexually inequitable, paternalistic patriarchy that proscribes divorce and alternative marital and sexual relationships, including recreational and nonprocreative sexual intercourse—for example, masturbation, contraception, oral intercourse, homosexual intercourse, and sodomy.

Contemporary society is not as rigidly traditional as the one described above, but it partakes of the tradition to a greater extent than might be apparent. This point can be underlined by considering what a society that rejects Thomas' eightfold truth might be like.

At the heart of the tradition lies the belief that sex is essentially procreative; a contratraditional view belies this "truth." So let us imagine a society that takes the essence of sex to be erotic fulfillment and that considers sex moral only to the extent that it is fulfilling. (We need not stop to consider whether this "fulfillment" is essentially self-centered, other-directed, or interactive, since this is a rough sketch rather than a blueprint.) Perhaps the most significant difference between the erotic and the procreative conceptions of sex is that if procreation is linked with parental responsibility it provides grounds for believing in a relatively stable relationship with a fair degree of permanence (and generates arguments for sexual exclusivity, and so forth); by contrast, erotic fulfillment has little need of permanence. Hence, in contratraditional society there would be no reason for linking parenthood (or, rather, what might be called "parenting"—that is, the activity of rearing a child) with sexual partnership. Such a society would be free to deny proposition 4 and to allow children to be parented by the state, by private charities, by individual volunteers, or by tribes of volunteers. The erotic act itself could be unburdened of the onus of possible parenthood by socially encouraged policies of sterilization, contraception, and abortion.

While the family has many functions in our society, its two primary functions are to provide for and protect an exclusive sexual relationship between a man and a woman and to provide for the parenting of children. Neither of these functions would be required of sex partners in contratraditional society. In such a society sex partners might be permanent "bachelors," impermanent trios, or tribes; "marriage" might exist in some vestigial form, but since there would be no sexual exclusivity and no sexually determined parenting, there would be no daughters, no sons, no husbands, no wives, no mothers, no fathers, no sisters, no brothers—at least not in the accepted sense. Sexual relations might occur in specially provided places in public buildings (say, in rooms located between the telephone booth and the toilet), or out in the open where everyone could enjoy them as either participant or spectator; or perhaps they might be restricted to more-ritual occasions or more-private locations. But sex-dictated residences, such as the family-oriented dwellings that have been a feature of Western culture since prehistoric times, would be superfluous. Contratraditional society might be the communalistic world of Plato's *Republic*, the libertine world of the Marquis de Sade, or the Harmonian world of Charles Fourier's passional phalansteries. But it would be a postmarital culture, a society without families; as such it would be different from any culture that has played a significant role in any civilization known to history.

Having sketched the possible outlines of postmarital society, we should like to suggest that however radical this society may appear, the contratraditional transfiguration of Western culture is possible—perhaps even probable—within the next few decades. And that change is the subject of this book. While no one essay deals with all aspects of this transfiguration, together they consider the advisability of rejecting the tradition. Yet, if a tradition is to be transformed rationally, it must first be understood.

The following is a selection of passages from Thomas in which he develops the eightfold tradition:

> Now, it is good for each person to attain his end, whereas it is bad for him to serve away from his proper end. Now, this should be considered applicable to the parts, just as it is to the whole being; for instance, each and every part of man, and every one of his acts, should attain the proper end. Now, though the male semen is superfluous in regard to the preservation of the individual, it is nevertheless necessary in regard to the propagation of the species. Other superfluous things, such as excrement, urine, sweat, and such things, are not at all necessary; hence, their emission contributes to man's good. Now, this is not what is sought in the case of semen, but, rather, to emit it for the purpose of generation, to which purpose the sexual act is directed. But

man's generative process would be frustrated unless it were followed by proper nutrition, because the offspring would not survive if proper nutrition were withheld. Therefore, the emission of semen ought to be so ordered that it will result in both the production of the proper offspring and in the upbringing of this offspring.

It is evident from this that every emission of semen, in such a way that generation cannot follow, is contrary to the good for man. And if this be done deliberately, it must be a sin. Now, I am speaking of a way from which, *in itself*, generation could not result; such would be any emission of semen apart from the natural union of male and female. For which reason, sins of this type are called *contrary to nature*. But, if by accident generation cannot result from the emission of semen, then this is not a reason for it being against nature, or a sin; as for instance, if the woman happens to be sterile.

Likewise, it must also be contrary to the good for man if the semen be emitted under conditions such that generation could result but the proper upbringing would be prevented. We should take into consideration the fact that, among some animals where the female is able to take care of the upbringing of offspring, male and female do not remain together for any time after the act of generation. This is obviously the case with dogs. But in the case of animals of which the female is not able to provide for the upbringing of offspring, the male and female do stay together after the act of generation as long as is necessary for the upbringing and instruction of the offspring. . . .

Now, it is abundantly evident that the female in the human species is not at all able to take care of the upbringing of offspring by herself, since the needs of human life demand many things which cannot be provided by one person alone. Therefore, it is appropriate to human nature that a man remain together with a woman after the generative act, and not leave her immediately to have such relations with another woman, as is the practice with fornicators. . . .

Now, we call this society *matrimony*. Therefore, matrimony is natural for man, and promiscuous performance of the sexual act, outside matrimony, is contrary to man's good. For this reason, it must be a sin.

Nor, in fact, should it be deemed a slight sin for a man to arrange for the emission of semen apart from the proper purpose of generating and bringing up children, on the argument that it is either a slight sin, or none at all, for a person to use a part of the body for a different use than that to which it is directed by nature (say, for instance, one chose to walk on his hands, or to use his feet for something usually done with the hands) because man's good is not much opposed by such inordinate use. However, the inordinate emission of semen is incompatible with the natural good; namely, the preservation of the species. Hence, after the sin of homicide whereby a human nature already in existence is destroyed, this type of sin appears to take next place, for by it the generation of human nature is precluded.

Moreover, these views which have just been given have a solid basis in divine authority. That the emission of semen under conditions in which offspring cannot follow is illicit is quite clear. There is the text of Leviticus (18:22-23): "thou shalt not lie with mankind as with womankind . . . and thou shalt not copulate with any beast." And in I Corinthians (6:10): "Nor the effeminate, nor liers with mankind . . . shall possess the Kingdom of God."

Also, that fornication and every performance of the act of reproduction with a person other than one's wife are illicit is evident. For it is said: "There shall be no whore among the daughters of Israel, nor whoremonger among the sons of Israel" (Deut[eronomy] 23:17); and in Tobias (4:13): "Take heed to keep thyself from all fornication, and beside thy wife never endure to know a crime"; and in I Corinthians (6:18): "Fly fornication."

By this conclusion we refute the error of those who say that there is no more sin in the emission of semen than in the emission of any other superfluous matter, and also of those who state that fornication is not a sin.

If one will make a proper consideration, the preceding reasoning will be seen to lead to the conclusion not only that the society of man and woman of the human species, which we call matrimony, should be long lasting, but even that it should endure throughout an entire life.

Indeed, possessions are ordered to the preservation of natural life, and since natural life, which cannot be preserved perpetually in the father, is by a sort of succession preserved in the son in its specific likeness, it is naturally fitting for the son to succeed also to the things which belong to the father. So, it is natural that the father's solicitude for his son should endure until the end of the father's life. Therefore, if even in the case of birds the solicitude of the father gives rise to the cohabitation of male and female, the natural order demands that father and mother in the human species remain together until the end of life.

It also seems to be against equity if the aforesaid society be dissolved. For the female needs the male, not merely for the sake of generation, as in the case of other animals, but also for the sake of government, since the male is both more perfect in reasoning and stronger in his powers. In fact, a woman is taken into man's society for the needs of generation; then, with the disappearance of a woman's fecundity and beauty, she is prevented from association with another man. So, if any man took a woman in the time of her youth, when beauty and fecundity were hers, and then sent her away after she had reached an advanced age, he would damage that woman contrary to natural equity.

Again, it seems obviously inappropriate for a woman to be able to put away her husband, because a wife is naturally subject to her husband as governor, and it is not within the power of a person subject to another to depart from his rule. So, it would be against the natural order if a wife were able to abandon her husband. Therefore, if a husband were permitted to abandon his wife, the society of husband and wife would not be an association of equals, but, instead, a sort of slavery on the part of the wife.

Besides, there is in men a certain natural solicitude to know their offspring. This is necessary for this reason: the child requires the father's direction for a long time. So, whenever there are obstacles to the ascertaining of offspring they are opposed to the natural instinct of the human species. But, if a husband could put away his wife, or a wife her husband, and have sexual relations with another person, certitude as to offspring would be precluded, for the wife would be united first with one man and later with another.[6]

In the seventeenth and eighteenth centuries most of the philosophers were bachelor males dedicated to the life of reason who viewed sex as an antirational distraction unworthy of serious comment. Insofar as they addressed themselves to sexual issues at all, it was only to reinforce the traditional view of marriage. In "Of Polygamy and Divorces," for example, David Hume defends the classic Western marriage ("an engagement entered into by mutual consent and has for its end the propagation of the species"), argues that polygamy and divorce are inimical to these ends, and concludes that "the exclusion of polygamy and divorce sufficiently recommend our present European practices with regard to marriage."[7]

Kant, too, concludes his brief remarks on sex and marriage by defending the tradition. In his precritical work *Observations on the Feeling of the Beautiful and the Sublime* (1763)[8] he takes the stance of an aesthete and extolls the virtues of femininity while decrying the education of women ("her philosophy is not to reason but to sense") as a perversion by which males, who are weakened by the power of women ("a single sly glance sets them more in confusion than the most difficult problem of science"), seek to alter the situation to their own advantage. Kant argues that since women are naturally irrational, while morality is essentially rational, they will avoid the wicked "not because it is unright, but because it is ugly." Reaffirming the traditional procreative view of the nature of sexual intercourse, Kant contends that whatever feelings or fascinations may appear to motivate us in sexual matters, "Nature pursues its great purpose, and all refinements that join together, though they may appear to stand as far from that as they will, are only trimmings and borrow their charm ultimately from that very source." Finally, he concludes that this great procreative purpose is best served by nonadulterous monogamous marriage, because promiscuity "degenerates into excess and dissoluteness." In matrimonial life the united pair should constitute a single moral person animated and governed by the understanding of the man and the taste of the wife.

In Kant's later (critical) work *Lectures on Ethics* the aesthete turns rationalist. Many of his earlier conclusions are retained, but the analyses that buttress them are radically different. He eschews the traditional conception of sexual intercourse as procreation marred by lust and reconceptualizes sex as mutual masturbation salvageable by human love. In a few key passages he originates the concept of a *sex object*. He argues that from the participants' point of view the purpose of coition is not procreation but orgasm, and develops the view that coition is essentially mutual masturbation—that is, that each participant uses the other as a *means* for attaining his own sexual satisfaction and hence does not treat the other as a full human being, as an *end* in himself. Since, for Kant, treating someone as a means rather than as an end is the essence of immorality, he has developed a rational proof of St. Paul's belief that coition is intrinsically evil. Like St. Paul, Kant allows one condition under which coition is morally permissible—nonadulterous monogamous marriage. For in marriage two persons become united as one in all things, and neither uses the other for his own purposes, but each gives himself over to the other. In other words, marriage transubstantiates immoral sexual intercourse into morally permissible human copulation by transforming a manipulative masturbatory relationship into one of altruistic unity.

> Human love is good-will, affection, promoting the happiness of others and finding joy in their happiness. But it is clear that, when a person loves another purely from sexual desire, none of these factors enter into the love. Far from there being any concern for the happiness of the loved one, the lover, in order to satisfy his desire and still his appetite, may even plunge the loved one into the depths of misery. Sexual love makes of the loved person an Object of appetite; as soon as that appetite has been stilled, the person is cast aside as one casts away a lemon which has been sucked dry. Sexual love can, of course, be combined with human love and so carry with it the characteristics of the latter, but taken by itself and for itself, it is nothing more than appetite. Taken by itself it is a degradation of human nature; for as soon as a person becomes an Object of appetite for another, all motives of moral relationship cease to function, because as an Object of appetite for another a person becomes a thing and can be treated and used as such by every one. This is the only case in which a human being is designed by nature as the Object of another's enjoyment. Sexual desire is at the root of it; and that is why we are ashamed of it, and why all strict moralists, and those who had pretensions to be regarded as saints, sought to suppress and extirpate it. . . .
>
> Because sexuality is not an inclination which one human being has for another as such, but is an inclination for the sex of another, it is a principle of the degradation of human nature, in that it gives rise to the preference of one sex to the other, and to the dishonoring of that sex through the satisfaction of desire. The desire which a man has for a woman is not directed towards her because she is a human being, but because she is a woman; that she is a human being is of no concern to the man; only her sex is the object of his desires. Human nature is thus subordinated. Hence it comes that all men and women do their best to make not their human nature but their sex more alluring and direct their activities and lusts entirely towards sex. Human nature is thereby sacrificed to sex. If then a man wishes to satisfy his desire, and a woman hers, they stimulate each other's desire; their inclinations meet, but their object is not human nature but sex, and each of them dishonors the human nature of the other. They make of humanity an instrument for the satisfaction of their lusts and inclinations, and dishonor it by placing it on a level with animal nature. Sexuality, therefore, exposes

mankind to the danger of equality with the beasts. But as man has this desire from nature, the question arises how far he can properly make use of it without injury to his manhood. . . .

The sole condition on which we are free to make use of our sexual desire depends upon the right to dispose over the person as a whole—over the welfare and happiness and generally over all the circumstances of that person. If I have the right over the whole person, I have also the right over the part and so I have the right to use that person's *organa sexualia* for the satisfaction of sexual desire. But how am I to obtain these rights over the whole person? Only by giving that person the same rights over the whole of myself. This happens only in marriage. Matrimony is an agreement between two persons by which they grant each other equal reciprocal rights, each of them undertaking to surrender the whole of their person to the other with a complete right of disposal over it. We can now apprehend by reason how a *commercium sexuale* is possible without degrading humanity and breaking the moral laws. Matrimony is the only condition in which use can be made of one's sexuality. If one devotes one's person to another, one devotes not only sex but the whole person; the two cannot be separated. If, then, one yields one's person, body and soul, for good and ill and in every respect, so that the other has complete rights over it, and if the other does not similarly yield himself in return and does not extend in return the same rights and privileges, the arrangement is one-sided. But if I yield myself completely to another and obtain the person of the other in return, I win myself back; I have given myself up as the property of another, but in turn I take that other as my property, and so win myself back again in winning the person whose property I have become. In this way the two persons become a unity of will. Whatever good or ill, joy or sorrow befall either of them, the other will share in it. Thus sexuality leads to a union of human beings, and in that union alone its exercise is possible.[9]

Whether Kant's conception of marriage and sexual intercourse is defensible, or indeed whether it even makes sense, is a question for Kant scholars. What interests us is Kant's reconceptualization of the nature of sexual intercourse, which alters the tradition in at least three significant ways: first, coition has become an essentially hedonic and self-interested act, rather than a procreative one; second, the sexual act is analyzed in terms of the manipulation of an object by a subject; and, third, sexual intercourse (even sexual intercourse entered into with procreative intent) is considered to be moral only if it is done as part of an altruistic union of two human beings. As will shortly become apparent, each of those three alterations had significant influence on later philosophical writings on sex.

If Thomas Aquinas and Kant are the most influential sexual philosophers, Arthur Schopenhauer is unique in being the first Western philosopher to recognize the significance of the subject as such and to contrast the loquaciousness of the poets to the silence of the philosophers.

We are accustomed to see poets principally occupied with describing the love of the sexes. . . .

. . . no one can doubt either the reality or the importance of the matter; and therefore, instead of wondering that a philosophy should also for once make its own this constant theme of all poets, one ought rather to be surprised that a thing which plays throughout so important a part in human life has hitherto practically been disregarded by philosophers altogether, and lies before us a raw material. The one who has most concerned himself with it is Plato, especially in the "Symposium" and the "Phaedrus." Yet what he says on the subject is confined to the sphere of myths, fables and jokes, and also for the most part concerns only the Greek love of youths. The little that Rousseau says upon our theme in the *Discours sur l'inégalité* is false and insufficient. Kant's explanation of the subject in the third part of the essay, *Über das Gefühl des Schönen und Erhabenen* is very superficial and without practical knowledge, therefore it is also partly incorrect. . . . On the other hand, Spinoza's definition, on account of its excessive näiveté, deserves to be quoted for the sake of amusement: *"Amor est titillatio, concomitante idea causae externae"* ["Love is joy with the accompanying idea of an external cause"]. *(Eth.* iv., prop. 44, dem.) Accordingly I have no predecessors either to make use of or to refute.[10]

Schopenhauer's scholarship is not all that one might have hoped it to be. He may be forgiven for having overlooked a page or so of Bishop Berkeley's *The Querist*; but his omission of Kant's critical reconceptualization of coition in the *Lectures on Ethics* and *The Philosophy of Law* and Johann Gottlieb Fichte's defense of the inequality of women in *The Science of Rights* (1795) is more serious. No less significant (but perhaps more understandable) was Schopenhauer's failure to mention William Godwin's call for the abolition of marriage in *Political Justice* (1793) and Mary Wollstonecraft's defense of the rights of women in *A Vindication of the Rights of Women* (1793).

Nonetheless, Schopenhauer's point was well taken: "one ought to be surprised," given the importance of sex and its attendant institutions, that it has been "disregarded by philosophers altogether." In reviewing the works of the major philosophers of the seventeenth and eighteenth centuries—Hobbes, Descartes, Spinoza, Leibniz, Malebranche, Locke, Berkeley, Rousseau, Fichte, Godwin, Hume, and Kant—one discovers that their writings on sex and its attendant institutions occupies less than twenty octavo-size pages, and almost all of that is by the last five philosophers named. A look at Lewis Selby-Bigge's classical anthology *British Moralists: Being Selections from Writers Principally of the Eighteenth Century*[11] makes clear that in their major essays on ethics the British moralists from Ralph Cudworth to Jeremy Bentham did not consider sexual intercourse, gender roles, marriage, or parental roles to be topics worthy of discussion. So while Schopenhauer was wrong to claim that he had no predecessors, he was essentially correct in holding that both modern and ancient philosophers had hitherto largely abandoned sex to the poets.

What then does Schopenhauer have to say in his "pioneering" work on the subject? First, that "all love, however ethereally it may bear itself, is rooted in the sexual impulse alone . . . "; second, that when we consider the power of love and love affairs, not only in our art and fiction but also in life, where it "constantly lays claim to half the powers and thoughts of the younger portion of mankind . . . embarrasses for a while even the greatest minds, [and] demands the sacrifice even of life and health," we are forced to conclude that what is involved in love and sex is more than a "trifle." Why is sexual love so significant? Because it is essentially procreative: it involves the will to life—not of individuals, but of generations. Love, Schopenhauer maintains, is a mechanism whereby the species manipulates the individual for its own ends and whereby individuals deceive themselves—not only as to their role as perpetuators of the species, but also in their relations with each other.

> . . . the sexual impulse, although in itself a subjective need, knows how to assume very skilfully the mask of an objective admiration, and thus to deceive our consciousness; for nature requires this stratagem to attain its ends. But yet that in every case of falling in love, however objective and sublime this admiration may appear, what alone is looked to is the production of an individual of a definite nature. [This] is primarily confirmed by the fact that the essential matter is not the reciprocation of love, but possession, i.e., the physical enjoyment. The certainty of the former can therefore by no means console us for the want of the latter; on the contrary, in such a situation many a man has shot himself. On the other hand, persons who are deeply in love, and can obtain no return of it, are contented with possession, i.e., with the physical enjoyment. This is proved by all forced marriages, and also by the frequent purchase of the favor of a woman, in spite of her dislike, by large presents or other sacrifices, nay, even by cases of rape. That this particular child shall be begotten is, although unknown to the parties concerned, the true end of the whole love story; the manner in which it is attained is a secondary consideration.[12]

In terms of the philosophical tradition, Schopenhauer is arguing Kant's point that although sexual intercourse is objectively procreative in nature, subjectively it is essentially hedonic and manipulative, and that, moreover, the objective aspect of sex ennobles and controls the subjective, giving it both its direction and its meaning.

> . . . every lover will experience a marvellous disillusion after the pleasure he has at last attained, and will wonder that what was so longingly desired accomplishes nothing more than every other sexual satisfaction; so that he

does not see himself much benefited by it. That wish was related to all other wishes as the species is related to the individual, thus as the infinite to the finite. The satisfaction, on the other hand, is really only for the benefit of the species, and thus does not come within the consciousness of the individual, who, inspired by the will of the species, here served an end with every kind of sacrifice, which was not his own end at all. Hence, then, every lover, after the ultimate consummation of the great work, finds himself cheated; for the illusion has vanished by means of which the individual was here the dupe of the species.[13]

He concludes his analysis of love by indicating its relationship to marriage.

Happy marriages are well known to be rare; just because it lies in the nature of marriage that its chief end is not the present but the coming generation. However, let me add, for the consolation of tender, loving natures, that sometimes passionate sexual love associates itself with a feeling of an entirely different origin—real friendship based upon agreement of disposition, which yet for the most part only appears when sexual love proper is extinguished in its satisfaction. This friendship will then generally spring from the fact that the supplementing and corresponding physical, moral, and intellectual qualities of the two individuals, from which sexual love arose, with reference to the child to be produced, are, with reference also to the individuals themselves, related to each other in a supplementary manner as opposite qualities of temperament and mental gifts, and thereby form the basis of a harmony of disposition.[14]

For all Schopenhauer's self-proclaimed iconoclasm, he does not really challenge any of the eight theses associated with the traditional view of sex and marriage: he agrees with all those he specifically mentions, and differs from Thomas only by emphasizing a point previously noted by Kant—the hedonic nature of sex when viewed subjectively. On this point Thomas is silent, but since he readily allows the importance of the concupiscible appetite, it seems doubtful that he would be prone to quarrel—or even to cavil. Indeed, with the exception of Plato (who argues that males and females are morally and intellectually equal and who embraces the ideal of communal marriage), all the philosophers considered thus far have been content to justify the indigenous practice current when they penned their analyses. Since Schopenhauer does much the same thing in his essay, there seems to be little call for noting disagreements. But the situation changes in the nineteenth century.

Centuries are shaggy creatures. The social and intellectual movements of one century tend to originate in the eighties or nineties of the previous one and to spill over into half the next. Thus, with a typical disdain for the aesthetics of chronology, the basic sexual issues of the nineteenth century start in the 1790s. And to further complicate matters, Hegel's writings of 1821 and Schopenhauer's essay of 1844 sit more easily with the "eighteenth-century" essays of Kant and Hume than with the "nineteenth century" works of Condorcet, Wollstonecraft, Godwin, Fichte, Mill, and Nietzsche. Why do we claim this? It seems significant that despite the existence of libertine lifestyles the philosophers of the seventeenth and eighteenth centuries did not seriously question the traditional view of sex and marriage, whereas, with the exceptions of the early Schopenhauer and of Hegel, the nineteenth-century writers either had serious reservations about the traditional conception of sex, gender roles, and marriage, or defended the tradition in the face of objections of critics. The polemical nature of these "later" works sets them apart in such a way that they form a "school" if not a "century."

Much of the polemic of the nineteenth-century writers had its roots in feminism, which surfaced as a political movement in France with the publication of *The Petition of the Women of the Third Estate to the King* (1789) and was quickly defended by Condorcet, who pointed out the absurdity of males crying out for equality, yet ignoring these same cries when they issued from the mouths of females. The first feminist manifesto, *Declaration of the Rights of Women*, published by Olympe des Gouges (Marie Gouze) in 1791, called for total equality between the genders ("Woman is born free and her rights are the same as those of men"), education for women, and the abolition of "the trade in women." Traditional marriage ("the tomb of trust and love") was to be replaced with a liberated marriage in which property was owned in common for the duration of the marriage, and in which bastards had full rights if acknowledged by either parent. (In nineteenth-century French law both legitimacy and property were entirely in the province of the male.)

By 1793 the political climate of France changed, causing, among other things, a strong political reaction against feminism. Olympe des Gouges was guillotined and the nascent feminist organizations withered. The ideals of feminism migrated across the channel, to be articulated and developed by Mary Wollstonecraft (and later disseminated by her daughter, Mary Shelley). By the mid-nineteenth century feminism returned to France to be espoused by Charles Fourier, Saint-Simon, and other socialists. It was embraced by Karl Marx and Friedrich Engels and accepted by all communist parties after the Second International.[15] The first self-conscious purely feminist political movement was organized in 1848 when 250 women met at Seneca Falls, New York, to found the American Women's Rights Movement. (Interestingly, most of the women were abolitionists —

the impetus for the meeting was the exclusion of Lucretia Mott and Elizabeth Cady Stanton from the proceedings of the 1840 World Anti-Slavery Convention, in London.)

Although feminist arguments changed somewhat in the years between Des Gouges and John Stuart Mill, the basic position remained the same—equality of gender roles through equal education; equal property rights; equal rights in marriage; and above all, absolute legal equality. Legal equality was stressed not because it was more significant but because it seemed to be the prerequisite of everything else. As Mill put this, his central point, in *On the Subjection of Women*, "the principle which regulates the existing relations between the two sexes—the legal subordination of one sex to the other—is wrong in itself, and now one of the chief hindrances to human improvement; and . . . it ought to be replaced by a principle of perfect equality, admitting to no power or privilege on the one side, nor disability on the other."[16]

Revolutions and counterrevolutions go hand in glove, and, not surprisingly, a counterrevolutionary antifeminism quickly developed. For the most part the ideology of the counterrevolution can be described as either traditional or libertine. Perhaps the most powerful antifeminist essay ever published in the traditionalist vein was penned by Johann Gottlieb Fichte as an appendix to his *The Science of Right*, under the title "Fundamental Principles of the Rights of the Family" (1795). In the "Principles" he attempts to deal with the questions posed by the various feminist manifestos of the 1770s: "Has woman the same rights in the state which man has?" Noting that the answer to this question was "never a more urgent problem than in our days," he argues that since both males and females are equally endowed with freedom and reason, the genders do indeed have equal rights. Their apparent inequality arises because it is questionable "how far the female sex *can desire* to exercise these rights."

Fichte's doubts derive from a theory of the nature of males and females that has its roots in Aristotelean biology. In the *Generation of Animals*[17] Aristotle argued that the female is a passive receptacle in procreation, while the male is the active generative principle. Fichte not only accepted this view of procreation but endowed it with a special significance, since he also held (on independent grounds) that (1) "the individual is permanent only as a tendency to form the species"[18] and that (2) an individual is essentially a rational, self-realizing, active agent.[19] If proposition 1 is true, then, Fichte thought, it is also true (1 a) that since individuals can give form to species only as a couple, complete individuals can exist only in a coupled relationship of the two sexes (for example, a married couple); and (1 b) that since the natural role of individuals (both complete and incomplete) is to form a species, the nature of each is determined by its sexual role. Since Fichte accepted the Aristotelean view that the female sexual role is essentially passive and since (by proposition 1a) in order to complete themselves females (and males) will couple (or marry), it follows (by proposition 1b) that females will be led through their coupling to an essentially passive role. But passivity is irrational and suicidal for rational agents, since (by proposition 2) rationality is essentially active. Thus, the female sexual role appears to be self-annihilating.

> The character of reason is absolute self-activity; pure passivity for the sake of passivity contradicts reason, and utterly cancels it. Hence, it is not against reason that the one sex should propose to itself the satisfaction of its sexual impulse as an end in itself, since it can be satisfied through activity; but it is absolutely against reason that the other sex should propose to itself the satisfaction of its sexual impulse as an end, because in that case it would make a pure passivity its end. Hence, the female sex is either not rational even in its tendencies, which contradicts our presupposition that all men should be rational, or this tendency can not be developed in that sex in consequence of its peculiar nature, which is a self-contradiction, since it assumes a tendency in nature which nature does not accept; or, finally, that sex can never propose to itself the satisfaction of its sexual impulse as its end. Such an end and rationality utterly cancel each other in that sex.
> Nevertheless, the sexual impulse of this female sex, as well as its manifestation and satisfaction, are part of the plan of nature. Hence it is necessary that the sexual impulse should manifest itself in woman under another form; and, in order to be conformable to reason, it must appear as an impulse to activity; and as a characteristic impulse of nature, it must appear as an activity exclusively appertaining to the female sex.[20]

How does the sexual impulse appear to women? Or, given proposition 1b, what is Fichte's view of the nature of the female gender?

> Woman can not confess to herself that she gives herself up—and since, in a rational being, everything is only in so far as it arises in consciousness— woman can not give herself up to the sexual impulse merely to satisfy her own impulse. But since she can give herself up only in obedience to an impulse, this impulse must assume in woman the character of an impulse to satisfy the man. Woman becomes, in this act, the means for the end of another, because she can not be her own end without renouncing her ultimate end—the dignity of reason! This dignity she maintains, although she becomes means, because she voluntarily makes herself means in virtue of a noble natural impulse—*love!*
> Love, therefore, is the form in which the sexual impulse appears to woman. But love is, to sacrifice one's self for the sake of another not in consequence of a reasoning, but in consequence of a feeling. Mere sexual impulse should never be called love; to do so is a vulgar abuse of language,

calculated to cause all that is noble in human nature to be forgotten. In fact, my opinion is that nothing should be called love but what we have just now described. Man *originally* does not feel love, but sexual impulse; and love in man is not an original, but a *communicated, derived* impulse, namely, an impulse developed through connection with a loving woman; and has, more-over, quite a different form in man to what it has in woman. Love, the no-blest of all natural impulses, is unborn only in woman; and only through woman does it, like many other social impulses, become the common pro-perty of mankind. The sexual impulse received this moral form of love in woman, because in its original form it would have canceled all morality in woman. Love is the closest point of union of nature and reason; it is the only link wherein nature connects with reason, and hence it is the most excellent of all that is natural. The Moral Law requires that man should forget him-self in the other; but love even sacrifices itself to the other.

Let me state it concisely: In an uncorrupted woman the sexual impulse does not manifest itself at all, but only love; and this love is the natural impulse of a woman to satisfy a man. It is certainly an impulse which ur-gently requires to be satisfied, but its being thus satisfied is not the satisfac-tion of the woman. On the contrary, it is the satisfaction of the man, and for woman it is only the satisfaction of her heart. Her only requirement is to love and to be loved. Only thus does the impulse which the woman feels to sacri-fice receive that character of freedom and activity which it must have in order to be rational. Perhaps there does not exist a man who does not feel the absurdity to turn this around and to assume in man a similar impulse to satisfy a need of woman; a need, in fact, which he can neither presuppose in woman nor consider himself as its tool without feeling himself disgraced to the innermost depths of his soul.

Hence, also, woman in the sexual union is not in every sense means for the object of the man. She is means for her own end, to satisfy her heart; and she is means for the end of the man only in so far as physical satisfaction is concerned.[21]

Although Fichte does not accept the Kantian view that sexual inter-course is mutual masturbation, his asymmetrical analysis reveals inter-course to be problematic, not only because the female is used by the male merely as a means, but also because to be so used she must reject ration-ality. On a superficial level Fichte's solution to the problem of the immoral nature of sexual intercourse is similar to Kant's: for both philosophers the moral salvation of copulation is achieved by the marital union of a dom-inant rational male and a sensitive loving female. Yet, though the rather conventional outward forms of their solutions are identical, the substance is radically different. For Kant, marital union makes moral the essentially manipulative (and hence inherently immoral) nature of intercourse be-cause the very fact of union dissolves the possibility of manipulation. One person can use another only if there is both a one and an other, a user and a used. But if a fusion of the one and the other truly exists, if there is but one entity and hence neither user nor used, then the very possibility of using an *other* as a means no longer exists. Thus Kant's resolution of the dilemma turns on the cataclysmic power of love to transform a coupling into a unity called a couple.

For Fichte. on the other hand, a marital union is very much a *duo*. As such, it does not eliminate the possibility of manipulation but rather provides the opportunity for reciprocal manipulation—a quid pro quo whereby each partner uses the other. The female accepts her status as a sex object in return for the male's acquiescence in his role as a love object. The function of union is to allow each to use the other for his or her own ends. Presumably this reciprocity will ensure the morality of the exchange. (Of course, this exchange would be just only if the role of love object was as desirable—or as undesirable—as that of sex object; the point of much feminist literature is that while it is not altogether unattractive to be a love object, the status of sex object is quite repellent.)

The modern reader might be tempted to dismiss Fichte as obscure, antiquated, and, hence, uninteresting. But however dated the form of his analysis may be, the substance is both contemporary and radical. For Fichte argues that women are intrinsically the equal of men and that the female gender role (feminity) is essentially antihuman. So far, his analysis is consistent with radical feminism. Like the radical feminist, he sees the situation as one in which a woman must sacrifice her femininity to her humanity or her humanity to her femininity. He opted for the latter alternative because he held the not uncommon view that the interests of the species override those of its members; hence given the species' compelling interest in preserving itself, procreation demands the sacrifice of women's humanity to their femininity. Interestingly, as radical feminists have been quick to point out, revolutionary biological innovations such as cloning, parthenogenesis, and artificial placentas are on the verge of rendering obsolete the species' interest in womankind's acquiescence in femininity. Moreover, the most radical feminists concur with Fichte's view that "man does not originally feel love, but only sexual impulse," agree with him in rejecting the female sexual role as antihuman, and hence view the nascent biological revolution as heralding a post-sexual or, perhaps, lesbian or homosexual society. Thus, had the biology of one hundred years ago been more advanced, Fichte might have been remembered as the (perhaps inadvertent) grandfather of radical feminism rather than as the godfather of male chauvinism.

Yet another ironic aspect of Fichte's work is that while he was the first philosopher to establish a cogent justification for exclusive monogamous marriage without parenting, the structure of his argumentation is basically the same as that used by Fourier to justify sexual communes and by Robert Rimmer and Nena and George O'Neill to justify open marriage (a "marriage" between cohabiting sexual partners who may share parenting but who deny any commitment to sexual exclusivity on the part of either partner). That is, Fichte was the first to advance the argument that the value of marriage is inherent in the relationship itself, and not merely, as the tradition held, a function of procreative responsibility.[22] For Fichte, as for Fourier, Rimmer, and Nena and George O'Neill, the value of marriage lay in the fact that only through marriage could one become a whole person, a full human being capable of both love and reason.

> Philosophers have hitherto considered it necessary to assign some end to marriage, and have specified that end variously. But marriage has no other end than itself; it is its own end. The marriage relation is the true mode of existence of grown persons of both sexes, required even by nature. In this relation all man's faculties develop; but out of it many, and among them the most remarkable faculties of man, remain uncultivated. Precisely as the whole existence of man has no relation to any sensuous end, so neither has its necessary mode, marriage.
>
> Marriage is a union between *two* persons—*one* man and *one* woman. A woman who has given herself up to one, can not give herself up to a second, for her whole dignity requires that she should belong only to this one. Again, a man who has to observe the slightest wish of one woman can not conform to the contradictory wishes of many. Polygamy presupposes that women are not rational beings like men, but merely willess and lawless means to gratify man. Such is, indeed, the doctrine of the religious legislation which tolerates polygamy. This religion has—probably without being clearly conscious of the grounds—drawn onesided conclusions from the destination of woman to remain passive.[23]

As we pointed out earlier, Fichte's writings on sexual philosophy were basically addressed to the question of the political rights of women. And here again he develops the classic male-chauvinist position.

> As a rule, woman is either a maid or married. If a maid, she is still under the care of her father, precisely as the unmarried young man. Herein both sexes are perfectly equal. Both become free by marriage, and in regard to their marriage both are equally free; ...
>
> If she is *married*, her whole dignity depends upon her being completely subjected, and seeming to be so subjected, to her husband. Let it be well observed, what my whole theory expresses, but what it is perhaps necessary to repeat once more emphatically—woman is not subjected to her husband in such a manner as to give him a *right of compulsion* over her; she is subjected through her own continuous necessary wish—a wish which is the condition of her morality—to be so subjected. She has the *power* to withdraw her freedom, if she could have the *will* to do so; but that is the very point: she can

not rationally will to be free. Her relation to her husband being publicly known, she must, moreover, will to appear to all whom she knows as utterly subjected to, and utterly lost in, the man of her choice.

Her husband is, therefore, the administrator of all her rights in consequence of her own necessary will; and she wishes those rights asserted and exercised only in so far as *he* wishes it. He is her natural representative in the state and in the whole society. This is her *public* relation to society. She can not even allow herself to think for a moment that she should exercise herself her rights in the state.

So far as her *private* and *internal* relation in the house is concerned, *the tenderness of the husband necessarily restores to her all and more than she has lost.* The husband will not relinquish her rights, because they are his own; and because, if he did so, he would dishonor himself and his wife before society. The wife has also rights in public affairs, for she is a citizen. I consider it the duty of the husband—in states which give to the citizen a vote on public matters—not to vote without having discussed the subject with his wife, and allowed her to modify his opinion through her own. His vote will then be the result of their common will. The father of a family, who represents not only his own but also the interests of his wife and children, ought indeed to have a greater influence and a more decisive vote in a commonwealth, than the citizen who represents only his own interests. The manner of arranging this is a problem for the science of politics.

Women, therefore, do really exercise the right of suffrage—not immediately, however, in their own person, because they can not wish to do so without lowering their dignity, but—through the influence which results from the nature of the marriage relation.[24]

Nineteenth-century antifeminism exhibited itself in the works of philosophical libertines as well as in the writings of traditionalists. The Magna Carta of libertinism is *Justine*, by the Marquis de Sade, a work that contains the defining theme of the libertine tradition—the view that in sexual matters the natural determines the moral, with a correlative rejection of social restraints on coition and sexuality. In the words of its greatest exponent, libertinism calls upon one to "break those bonds" of social constraint: "nature wills it; for a bridle have nothing but your inclinations, for laws your desires, for morality Nature's alone. . . ." Libertinism per se need not be antifeminist. Godwin's variety is certainly profeminist (see *Social Justice*, 1793), and even de Sade's version has notable profeminist elements, for example, the call for houses intended for women's libertinage and the advocacy of state institutions to relieve women of the labors of parenting. Nonetheless, it is reasonably clear that for de Sade nature dictates a somewhat lesser role for females than for males.

It is certain, in a state of Nature, that women are born *vulguivaguous*, that is to say, are born enjoying the advantages of other female animals and belonging, like them and without exception, to all males; such were, without any doubt, both the primary laws of Nature and the only institutions of those earliest societies into which men gathered. *Self-interest, egoism,* and *love* degraded these primitive attitudes. . . .

Never may an act of possession be exercised upon a free being; the exclusive possession of a woman is no less unjust than the possession of slaves; all men are born free, all have equal rights: never should we lose sight of those principles; according to which never may there be granted to one sex the legitimate right to lay monopolizing hands upon the other, and never may one of these sexes, or classes, arbitrarily possess the other. Similarly, a woman existing in the purity of Nature's laws cannot allege, as justification for refusing herself to someone who desires her, the love she bears another, because such a response is based upon exclusion, and no man may be excluded from the having of a woman as of the moment it is clear she definitely belongs to all men. The act of possession can only be exercised upon a chattel or an animal, never upon an individual who resembles us, and all the ties which can bind a woman to a man are quite as unjust as illusory.

If then it becomes incontestable that we have received from Nature the right indiscriminately to express our wishes to all women, it likewise becomes incontestable that we have the right to compel their submission, not exclusively, for I should then be contradicting myself, but temporarily. It cannot be denied that we have the right to decree laws that compel woman to yield to the flames of him who would have her; violence itself being one of that right's effects, we can employ it lawfully. Indeed! has Nature not proven that we have that right, by bestowing upon us the strength needed to bend women to our will? [25]

The later nineteenth-century philosophical libertines tended to accept de Sade's view that nature dictates the bending of the female to the will of the male, without conceding that justice mandated some profeminist revisions of the status quo. Perhaps the purest example of libertine antifeminism is Schopenhauer's essay *On Women*, which was written after, and in partial reaction to, the feminist aspects of the libertarian revolutionary movements of 1848. This essay differs markedly from his treatise of 1844. Whereas *The Metaphysics of Sexual Love* was a traditionalist defense of a monogamous union of a rational, dominant male with a sensitive, loving, submissive female, the later work bears all the earmarks of libertinism—the assimilation of the natural to the proper and the concomitant call for the revision of "unnatural" norms. In addition it is informed by a bitter misogyny and takes the radical libertine stance of rejecting monogamy as an unnatural perversion. For nature, he argues, has determined that the female is merely a mechanism by which *man*kind reproduces himself; since monogamy limits man's ability to reproduce himself, it must be replaced by polygamy.

It is only the man whose intellect is clouded by his sexual impulses that could give the name of *the fair sex* to that undersized, narrow-shouldered, broad-hipped, and short-legged race; for the whole beauty of the sex is bound up with this impulse. Instead of calling them beautiful, there would be more warrant for describing women as the unaesthetic sex....

And since women exist in the main solely for the propagation of the species, and are not destined for anything else, they live, as a rule, more for the species than for the individual....

They form the *sexus sequior*—the second sex, inferior in every respect to the first; their infirmities should be treated with consideration; but to show them great reverence is extremely ridiculous, and lowers us in their eyes. When Nature made two divisions of the human race, she did not draw the line exactly through the middle. These divisions are polar and opposed to each other, it is true; but the difference between them is not qualitative merely, it is also quantitative.

This is just the view which the ancients took of a woman, and the view which people in the East take now; and their judgment as to her proper position is much more correct than ours, with our old French notions of gallantry and our preposterous system of reverence—that highest product of Teutonico-Christian stupidity.

The laws of marriage prevailing in Europe consider the woman as the equivalent of the man—start, that is to say, from a wrong position. In our part of the world where monogamy is the rule, to marry means to halve one's rights and double one's duties. Now, when the laws gave woman equal rights with man, they ought also to have endowed her with a masculine intellect. But the fact is that just in proportion as the honors and privileges which the laws accord to women, exceed the amount which nature gives, is there a diminution in the number of women who really participate in these privileges; and all the remainder are deprived of their natural rights by just so much as is given to the others over and above their share. For the institution of monogamy, and the laws of marriage which it entails, bestow upon the woman an unnatural position of privilege, by considering her throughout as the full equivalent of the man, which is by no means the case; and seeing this, men who are shrewd and prudent very often scruple to make so great a sacrifice and to acquiesce in so unfair an arrangement.

Consequently, whilst among polygamous nations every woman is provided for, where monogamy prevails the number of married women is limited; and there remains over a large number of women without stay or support, who, in the upper classes, vegetate as useless old maids, and in the lower succumb to hard work for which they are not suited; or else become *filles de joie*, whose life is as destitute of joy as it is of honor. But under the circumstances they become a necessity; and their position is openly recognized as serving the special end of warding off temptation from those women favored by fate, who have found, or may hope to find, husbands. In London alone there are eighty thousand prostitutes. What are they but the women, who, under the institution of monogamy have come off worse? Theirs is a dreadful fate: they are human sacrifices offered up on the altar of monogamy. The women whose wretched position is here described are the inevitable set-off to the European lady with her arrogance and pretension. Polygamy is therefore a real benefit to the female sex if it is taken as a whole. And, from another point of view, there is no true reason why a man whose wife suffers from chronic illness, or remains barren, or has gradually become too old for him, should not take a second. The motives which induce so many people to become converts to Mormonism appear to be just those which militate against the unnatural institution of monogamy.[26]

In Schopenhauer's work there is a devolution of the status of woman from the deceived but sublime ladies of *The Metaphysics of Sexual Love* to the basically supine in *On Women,* while the evoiution of his conception of the male role is ever upward. In the works of the third libertine we shall consider, Friedrich Nietzsche, the subsidiary procreative role of women is a constant. The themes of libertinism abound in Nietzsche's works. Nature, albeit a nature much tempered by the "evolutionary laws" of the survival of the fittest, determines morality, and traditions that are unnatural must be rejected. Thus, since nature determines that woman's sole role is the propagation of the species, any other activity by females is perverse: *"When a woman has scholarly inclinations there is generally something wrong with her sexual nature; barrenness itself conduces to a certain virility of taste; man, if I may say so, is the barren animal."*[27]

If women are naturally incapable of creative intellectual endeavor, and if as essentially herd creatures they threaten to mire males in herd mentality (and hence must be subdued), they are nonetheless capable of fulfilling their procreatve function in the service of evolution.

"Much hath Zarathustra spoken also to us women, but never spake he unto us concerning woman."

And I answered her: "Concerning woman, one should only talk unto men."

"Talk also unto me of woman," said she; "I am old enough to forget it presently."

And I obliged the old woman and spake thus unto her:

Everything in woman is a riddle, and everything in woman hath one solution—it is called pregnancy.

Man is for woman a means: the purpose is always the child. But what is a woman for man?

Two different things wanteth the true man: danger and diversion. Therefore wanteth he woman, as the most dangerous plaything.

Man shall be trained for war, and woman for the recreation of the warrior; all else is folly.

Too sweet fruits—these the warrior liketh not. Therefore liketh he woman;—bitter is even the sweetest woman.

Better than man doth woman understand children, but man is more childish than woman.

In the true man there is a child hidden: it wanteth to play. Up then, ye women, and discover the child in man!

A plaything let woman be, pure and fine like the precious stone, illumined with the virtues of a world not yet come.

Let the beam of a star shine in your love! Let your hope say: "May I bear the Superman."[28] . . .

Not only onward shalt thou propagate thyself, but upward! For that purpose may the garden of marriage help thee!

A higher body shalt thou create, a first movement, a spontaneously rolling wheel—a creating one shalt thou create.

Marriage: so call I the will of the twain to create the one that is more than those who created it. The reverence for one another, as those exercising such a will, call I marriage.

Let this be the significance and the truth of thy marriage. But that which the many-too-many call marriage, those superfluous ones—ah, what shall I call it?

Ah, the poverty of soul in the twain! Ah, the faith of soul in the twain! Ah, the pitiable self-complacency in the twain!

Marriage they call it all; and they say their marriages are made in heaven.

Well, I do not like it, that heaven of the superfluous! No, I do not like them, those animals tangled in the heavenly toils!

Far from me also be the God who limpeth thither to bless what he hath not matched!

Laugh not at such marriages! What child hath not had reason to weep over its parents? . . .

"Lo! now hath the world become perfect!"—thus thinketh every woman when she obeyeth with all her love.

Obey, must the woman, and find a depth for her surface. Surface is woman's soul, a mobile, stormy film on shallow water.

"Man's soul, however, is deep, its current gusheth in subterranean caverns: woman surmiseth its force, but comprehendeth it not.—

Then answered me the old woman: "Many fine things hath Zarathustra said, especially for those who are young enough for them.

Strange! Zarathustra knoweth little about woman, and yet he is right about them! Doth this happen, because with women nothing is impossible?

And now accept a little truth by way of thanks! I am old enough for it!

Swaddle it up and hold its mouth: otherwise it will scream too loudly, the little truth."

"Give me, woman, thy little truth!" said I. And thus spake the old woman:

"Thou goest to women? Do not forget thy whip!"—

Thus spake Zarathustra.[29]

Nietzsche finished speaking in 1888 but actually died in 1900. Twentieth-century sexual philosophy opens with, and is almost immediately dominated by, Bertrand Russell—whose syncretic blend of feminism, libertinism, and traditionalism (best expounded in *Marriage and Morals*) constitutes virtually the entire philosophical literature on the subject until Jean-Paul Sartre's analysis in *Being and Nothingness* (1943; chapter three, section two). Aside from the works of Russell and Sartre, the only other major contributions were Ortega y Gasset's *On Love* (1939), Simon de Beauvoir's *The Second Sex* (1949), and the chapter on "The Body in Its Sexual Being" in Merleau-Ponty's *The Phenomenology of Perception* (1945). The views of these philosophers are too contemporary, too significant—and, above all, too interrelated with the essays we have anthologized —to receive the sort of summary historical treatment accorded to the works we have hitherto discussed. Unfortunately, to present their work in an appropriate manner would expand this introduction to such an extent that it would crowd out some of the works we would like to include. We believe that the least unsatisfactory resolution of this dilemma is to refrain from commenting on pre-1968 modern work on sexual philosophy and to refer interested readers to D. P. Verene's *Sexual Love and Western Morality*,[30] which contains a fine selection of and introduction to this literature.

Why do we speak of *pre-1968* literature? To appreciate the significance of the date it is important to take cognizance of the fact that of the major twentieth-century philosophers not previously mentioned—Austin, Carnap, Heidegger, Husserl, James, Peirce, Whitehead, and Wittgenstein —not one wrote on sexual philosophy. *The Encyclopedia of Philosophy* (published in 1967) has no entries under "adultery," "contraception," "engagement," "marriage," "femininism," "libertinism," "monogamy," "perversion," "procreation," "sex," or "women." *The Philosopher's Index* indicates that no articles were published on these topics in 1967. Yet in the very next year articles began to appear in philosophical journals— hence the significance of the date. But why did this begin to happen in 1968?

One hypothesis is that if the time lag between inspiration and publication is taken into account, the two primary causes were the newly emergent feminist movement, which dates from the foundation of NOW in 1965, and the almost simultaneous rebirth of libertinism in the countercultural revolution of the late sixties (for example, the "Hippie" movement). In this the genesis of the newly renascent literature on sexual philosophy seems to follow the precedent of its nineteenth-century forbears, although they are unlike most of their nineteenth-century predecessors in their inclination to be favorable toward the feminist movement. Also, two new factors that influence the literature are gay liberation and the ecology movement.

This new literature is not only a response to changing social conditions but to a new philosophical climate as well. By 1968 the "linguistic turn" had been executed and logical positivism had spent itself, leaving Anglo-American philosophers receptive to refocusing philosophical inquiry. By contrast, the existential-phenomenological tradition of Husserl, Heidegger, Sartre, Merleau-Ponty, Marcel, Ricoeur, and Ortega had retained its preoccupation with man's concrete existence. The translations of their works into English, which began to appear in the late fifties and early sixties, increasingly challenged the "analytic" tradition to address itself to mundane realities such as sex. This challenge was taken up explicitly by Thomas Nagel in his pioneering essay of 1969 "Sexual Perversion," and others have since joined the discussion.

In the present volume we have attempted to bring together essays that reflect the most significant aspects of the post-1968 literature. We have acted in the belief that sex, gender, and parenting are too significant to be the exclusive domain of the poets and too important to be left to the pragmatics of revolutionary politics. For the sexual revolution is in our midst, and philosophers have only belatedly begun to contemplate it.

NOTES

1. Plato, *Symposium*, trans. Percy Shelley (New York: Peter Pauper Press, 1967), pp. 64-65, Steph. 211-12.
2. Epictetus, *The Discourse and Manual*, trans. P. E. Matheson, (Oxford: Clarendon Press, 1916), Book 2, chap. 18, pp. 208-09.
3. Genesis 8:17.
4. Cf. Genesis 3:16.
5. Cf. Janice Moulton, "Sex and Reference," herein, pp. 34-44.
6. Thomas Aquinas, *On the Truth of the Catholic Faith*, Book 3: Providence, pt. 1, trans. Vernon J. Bourke (New York: Doubleday, 1956).
7. David Hume, *Essays Moral, Political and Literary*, vol. 1, ed. T. H. Green and T. H. Grose (London: Longmans, Green, 1875), pp. 231-39.
8. Immanuel Kant, *Observations on the Feeling of the Beautiful and the Sublime*, trans. John T. Goldthwait (Berkeley and Los Angeles: University of California Press, 1960). All quotes are from section three.
9. Immanuel Kant, *Lectures on Ethics*, trans. Louis Infield (London: Methuen and Co., Ltd., 1930), pp. 162-71.
10. Arthur Schopenhauer, "Metaphysics of the Love and the Sexes," in Edman, *The Philosophy of Schopenhauer* (New York: Random House, Modern Library), p. 334.
11. Oxford, 1893.
12. In Edman, *The Philosophy of Schopenhauer*, pp. 342-43.
13. Ibid., pp. 349-50.
14. Ibid., pp. 373-74.
15. For an exposition of the views of Fourier and Marx see David Palmer, "The

Consolation of the Wedded," herein, pp. 178-89.

16. John Stuart Mill, "The Subjection of Women" (1869), reprinted in *Three Essays by J. S. Mill* (London: Oxford University Press, World Classics Series, 1966), p. 427.

17. Book 1, chaps. 20-23.

18. *The Science of Rights* (Philadelphia: Lippincott, 1869), chap. 1, sec. 1.

19. This is the argument of Book 1 of *The Science of Rights* (Philadelphia: Lippincott, 1869).

20. Fichte, *The Science of Rights*, p. 394.

21. Ibid., sec. 4, pp. 398-401.

22. Cf. Thomas' propositions 3-5.

23. Fichte, *The Science of Rights*, pp. 406-07.

24. Ibid., pp. 440-42.

25. Marquis de Sade, *The Complete Justine* (New York: Grove Press, 1965), p. 318.

26. *Essays on Women* (New York: Simon & Schuster, Philosophers Library, 1928), pp. 450-55.

27. "Beyond Good and Evil," sec. 144 in *The Philosophy of Nietzsche* (New York: Random House, Modern Library, 1970), pp. 465-66.

28. "Child and Marriage," chap. 28 of "Thus Spake Zarathustra," trans. Thomas Common, in ibid., pp. 72-73.

29. "Old and Young Women," chap. 18 of "Thus Spake Zarathustra," in ibid., pp. 68-69.

30. New York: Harper & Row, 1972.

LOVE

Shulamith Firestone

Love: A Feminist Critique

A book on radical feminism that did not deal with love would be a political failure. For love, perhaps even more than childbearing, is the pivot of women's oppression today. I realize this has frightening implications: Do we want to get rid of love?

The panic felt at any threat to love is a good clue to its political significance. Another sign that love is central to any analysis of women or sex psychology is its omission from culture itself, its relegation to "personal life." (And whoever heard of logic in the bedroom?) Yes, it is portrayed in novels, even metaphysics, but in them it is described, or better, recreated, not analyzed. Love has never been *understood,* though it may have been fully *experienced,* and that experience communicated.

There is reason for this absence of analysis: *Women and Love are underpinnings. Examine them and you threaten the very structure of culture.*

The tired question "What were women doing while men created masterpieces?" deserves more than the obvious reply: Women were barred from culture, exploited in their role of mother. Or its reverse: Women had no need for paintings since they created children. Love is tied to culture in much deeper ways than that. Men were thinking, writing, and creating, because women were pouring their energy into those men; women are not creating culture because they are preoccupied with love.

That women live for love and men for work is a truism. Freud was the first to attempt to ground this dichotomy in the individual psyche: the male child, sexually rejected by the first person in his attention, his mother, "sublimates" his "libido"—his reservoir of sexual (life) energies—into long-term projects, in the hope of gaining love in a more generalized form; thus he displaces his need for love into a need for recognition. This process does not occur as much in the female: most women never stop seeking direct warmth and approval.

There is also much truth in the clichés that "behind every man there is a woman," and that "women are the power behind [read: voltage in] the throne." (Male) culture was built on the love of women, and at their expense. Women provided the substance of those male masterpieces; and for millennia they have done the work, and suffered the costs, of one-way emotional relationships the benefits of which went to men and to the work of men. So if women are a parasitical class living off, and at the margins of, the male economy, the reverse too is true: *(Male) culture was (and is) parasitical, feeding on the emotional strength of women without reciprocity.*

Moreover, we tend to forget that this culture is not universal, but rather sectarian, presenting only half the spectrum. The very structure of culture itself, as we shall see, is saturated with the sexual polarity, as well as being in every degree run by, for, and in the interests of male society. But while the male half is termed all of culture, men have not forgotten there is a female "emotional" half: They live it on the sly. As the result of their battle to reject the female in themselves (the Oedipus Complex as we have explained it) they are unable to take love seriously as a cultural matter; but they can't do without it altogether. Love is the underbelly of (male) culture just as love is the weak spot of every man, bent on proving his virility in that large male world of "travel and adventure." Women have always known how men need love, and how they deny this need. Perhaps this explains the peculiar contempt women so universally feel for men ("men are so dumb"), for they can see their men are posturing in the outside world.

I

How does this phenomenon "love" operate? Contrary to popular opinion, love is not altruistic. The initial attraction is based on curious admiration (more often today, envy and resentment) for the self-possession, the integrated unity, of the other and a wish to become part of this Self in some way (today, read: intrude or take over), to become important to that psychic balance. The self-containment of the other creates desire (read: a challenge); admiration (envy) of the other becomes a wish to incorporate (possess) its qualities. A clash of selves follows in which the individual attempts to fight off the growing hold over him of the other. Love is the final opening up to (or, surrender to the dominion of) the other. The lover demonstrates to the beloved how he himself would like to be treated. ("I tried so hard to make him fall in love with me that I fell in love with him myself.") Thus love is the height of selfishness: the self attempts to enrich itself through the absorption of another being. Love is being psychically wide-open to another. It is a situation of total emotional vulnerability. Therefore it must be not only the incorporation of the other, but an *exchange* of selves. Anything short of a mutual exchange will hurt one or the other party.

There is nothing inherently destructive about this process. A little healthy selfishness would be a refreshing change. Love between two equals would be an enrichment, each enlarging himself through the other: instead of being one, locked in the cell of himself with only his own experience and view, he could participate in the existence of another—an extra window on the world. This accounts for the bliss that successful lovers experience: Lovers are temporarily freed from the burden of isolation that every individual bears.

But bliss in love is seldom the case: For every successful contemporary love experience, for every short period of enrichment, there are ten destructive love experiences, post-love "downs" of much longer duration—often resulting in the destruction of the individual, or at least an emotional cynicism that makes it difficult or impossible ever to love again. Why should this be so, if it is not actually inherent in the love process itself?

Let's talk about love in its destructive guise—and why it gets that way, referring once more to the work of Theodore Reik. Reik's concrete observation brings him closer than many better minds to understanding the *process* of "falling in love," but he is off insofar as he confuses love as it exists in our present society with love itself. He notes that love is a reaction formation, a cycle of envy, hostility, and possessiveness: he sees that it is preceded by dissatisfaction with oneself, a yearning for something better, created by a discrepancy between the ego and the ego-ideal; that the bliss love produces is due to the resolution of this tension by the substitution, in place of one's own ego-ideal, of the other; and finally that love fades "because the other can't live up to your high ego-ideal any more than you could, and the judgment will be the harsher the higher are the claims on oneself." Thus in Reik's view love wears down just as it wound up: Dissatisfaction with oneself (whoever heard of falling in love the week one is leaving for Europe?) leads to astonishment at the other person's self-containment; to envy; to hostility; to possessive love; and back again through exactly the same process. This is the love process *today*. But why must it be this way?

Many, for example Denis de Rougemont in *Love in the Western World,* have tried to draw a distinction between romantic "falling in love" with its "false reciprocity which disguises a twin narcissism" (the Pagan Eros) and an unselfish love for the other person as that person really is (the Christian Agape). De Rougemont attributes the morbid passion of Tristan and Iseult (romantic love) to a vulgarization of specific mystical and religious currents in Western civilization.

I believe instead that *love is essentially a simple phenomenon—unless it has become complicated, corrupted, or obstructed by an unequal balance of power.* We have seen that love demands a mutual vulnerability or it turns destructive: the destructive effects of love occur only in a context of inequality. But if, as we have seen, (biological) inequality has always remained a constant, existing to varying degrees, then it is understandable that "romantic love" would develop. (It remains for us only to explain why it has steadily increased in Western countries since the medieval period, which we shall attempt to do in the following chapter.)

How does the sex class system based on the unequal power distribution of the biological family affect love between the sexes? In discussing Freudianism, we have gone into the psychic structuring of the individual within the family and how this organization of personality must be different for the male and the female because of their very different relationships to the mother. At present the insular interdependency of the mother/child relationship forces both male and female children into anxiety about losing the mother's love, on which they depend for physicial survival. When later (Erich Fromm notwithstanding) the child learns that the mother's love is conditional, to be rewarded the child in return for approved behavior (that is, behavior in line with the mother's own values and personal ego gratification—for she is free to mold the child "creatively," however she happens to define that), the child's anxiety turns into desperation. This, coinciding with the sexual rejection of the male child by the mother, causes, as we have seen, a schizophrenia in the boy between the emotional and the physical, and in the girl, the mother's rejection, occurring for different reasons, produces an insecurity about her identity in general, creating a lifelong need for approval. (Later her lover replaces her father as a grantor of the necessary surrogate identity—she sees everything through his eyes.) Here originates the hunger for love that later sends both sexes searching in one person after the other for a state of ego security. But because of the early rejection, to the degree that it occurred, the male will be terrified of committing himself, of "opening up" and then being smashed. How this affects his sexuality we have seen: To the degree that a woman is like his mother, the incest taboo operates to restrain his total sexual/ emotional commitment; for him to feel safely the kind of total response he first felt for his mother, which was rejected, he must degrade this woman so as to distinguish her from the mother. This behavior reproduced on a larger scale explains many cultural phenomena, including perhaps the ideal love-worship of chivalric times, the forerunner of modern romanticism.

Romantic idealization is partially responsible, at least on the part of men, for a peculiar characteristic of "falling" in love: the change takes place in the lover almost independently of the character of the love object. Occasionally the lover, though beside himself, sees with another rational part of his faculties that, objectively speaking, the one he loves isn't worth all this blind devotion; but he is helpless to act on this, "a slave to love." More often he fools himself entirely. But others can see what is happening ("How on earth he could love her is beyond me!"). This idealization occurs much less frequently on the part of women, as is borne out by Reik's clinical studies. A man must idealize one woman over the rest in order to justify his descent to a lower caste. Women have no such reason to idealize men—in fact, when one's life depends on one's ability to "psych" men out, such idealization may actually be dangerous—though a fear of male power in general may carry over into relationships with individual men, appearing to be the same phenomenon. But though women know to be inauthentic this male "falling in love," all women, in one way or another, require proof of it from men before they can allow themselves to love (genuinely, in their case) in return. For this idealization process acts to artificially equalize the two parties, a minimum precondition for the development of an uncorrupted love—we have seen that love requires a mutual vulnerability that is impossible to achieve in an unequal power situation. *Thus "falling in love" is no more than the process of alteration of male vision—through idealization, mystification, glorification—that renders void the woman's class inferiority.*

However, the woman knows that this idealization, which she works so hard to produce, is a lie, and that it is only a matter of time before he "sees through her." Her life is a hell, vacillating between an all-consuming need for male love and approval to raise her from her class subjection, to persistent feelings of inauthenticity when she does achieve his love. Thus her whole identity hangs in the balance of her love life. She is allowed to love herself only if a man finds her worthy of love.

But if we could eliminate the political context of love between the sexes, would we not have some degree of idealization remaining in the love process itself? I think so. For the process occurs in the same manner whoever the love choice: the lover "opens up" to the other. Because of this fusion of egos, in which each sees and cares about the other as a new self, the beauty/character of the beloved, perhaps hidden to outsiders under layers of defenses, is revealed. "I wonder what she sees in him," then, means not only, "She is a fool, blinded with romanticism," but, "Her love has lent her x-ray vision. Perhaps we are missing something." (Note that this phrase is most commonly used about women. The equivalent phrase about *men's* slavery to love is more often something like, "She has him wrapped around her finger," she has him so "snowed" that he is the last one to see through her.) Increased sensitivity to the real, if hidden, values in the other, however, is not "blindness" or "idealization" but is, in fact, deeper vision. It is only the *false* idealization we have described above that is responsible for the destruction. Thus it is not the process of love itself that is at fault, but its *political,* i.e., unequal *power* context: the who, why, when and where of it is what makes it now such a holocaust.

II

But abstractions about love are only one more symptom of its diseased state. (As one female patient of Reik so astutely put it, "Men take love either too seriously or not seriously enough.") Let's look at it more concretely, as we now experience it in its corrupted form. Once again we shall quote from the Reikian Confessional. For if Reik's work has any value it is where he might least suspect, i.e., in his trivial feminine urge to "gossip." Here he is, justifying himself (one supposes his Superego is troubling him):

> A has-been like myself must always be somewhere and working on something. Why should I not occupy myself with those small questions that are not often posed and yet perhaps can be answered? The "petites questions" have a legitimate place beside the great and fundamental problems of psychoanalysis.

> It takes moral courage to write about certain things, as for example about a game that little girls play in the intervals between classes. Is such a theme really worthy of a *serious* psychoanalyst who has passed his 77th year? (Italics mine)

And he reminds himself:

> But in psychoanalysis there are no unimportant thoughts; there are only thoughts that pretend to be unimportant in order not to be told.

Thus he rationalizes what in fact may be the only valuable contribution of his work. Here are his patients of both sexes speaking for themselves about their love lives:

WOMEN:

> Later on he called me a sweet girl. . . . I didn't answer . . . what could I say? . . . but I knew I was not a sweet girl at all and that he sees me as someone I'm not.

> No man can love a girl the way a girl loves a man.

> I can go a long time without sex, but not without love.

> It's like H_2O instead of water.

> I sometimes think that all men are sex-crazy and sex-starved. All they can think about when they are with a girl is going to bed with her.

> Have I nothing to offer this man but this body?

> I took off my dress and my bra and stretched myself out on his bed and waited. For an instant I thought of myself as an animal of sacrifice on the altar.

> I don't understand the feelings of men. My husband has me. Why does he need other women? What have they got that I haven't got?

> Believe me, if all wives whose husbands had affairs left them, we would only have divorced women in this country.

> After my husband had quite a few affairs, I flirted with the fantasy of taking a lover. Why not? What's sauce for the gander is sauce for the goose. . . . But I was stupid as a goose: I didn't have it in me to have an extramarital affair.

> I asked several people whether men also sometimes cry themselves to sleep. I don't believe it.

MEN (for further illustration, see *Screw*):

> It's not true that only the external appearance of a woman matters. The underwear is also important.

> It's not difficult to make it with a girl. What's difficult is to make an end

of it.

The girl asked me whether I cared for her mind. I was tempted to answer I cared more for her behind.

"Are you going already?" she said when she opened her eyes. It was a bedroom cliché whether I left after an hour or after two days.

Perhaps it's necessary to fool the woman and to pretend you love her. But why should I fool myself?

When she is sick, she turns me off. But when I'm sick she feels sorry for me and is more affectionate than usual.

It is not enough for my wife that I have to hear her talking all the time—blah, blah, blah. She also expects me to hear what she is saying.

Simone de Beauvoir said it: "The word love has by no means the same sense for both sexes, and this is one cause of the serious misunderstandings which divide them." Above I have illustrated some of the traditional differences between men and women in love that come up so frequently in parlor discussions of the "double standard," where it is generally agreed: That women are monogamous, better at loving, possessive, "clinging," more interested in (highly involved) "relationships" than in sex per se, and they confuse affection with sexual desire. That men are interested in nothing but a screw (Wham, bam, thank you Ma'am!), or else romanticize the woman ridiculously; that once sure of her, they become notorious philanderers, never satisfied; that they mistake sex for emotion. All this bears out what we have discussed—the difference in the psychosexual organizations of the two sexes, determined by the first relationship to the mother.

I draw three conclusions based on these differences:

1) That men can't love. (Male hormones? Women traditionally expect and accept an emotional invalidism in men that they would find intolerable in a woman.)

2) That women's "clinging" behavior is necessitated by their objective social situation.

3) That this situation has not changed significantly from what it ever was.

Men can't love. We have seen why it is that men have difficulty loving and that while men may love, they usually "fall in love"—with their own projected image. Most often they are pounding down a woman's door one day, and thoroughly disillusioned with her the next; but it is rare for women to leave men, and then it is usually for more than ample reason.

It is dangerous to feel sorry for one's oppressor—women are especially prone to this failing—but I am tempted to do it in this case. Being unable to love is hell. This is the way it proceeds: as soon as the man feels any pressure from the other partner to commit himself, he panics and may react in one of several ways:

1) He may rush out and screw ten other women to prove that the first woman has no hold over him. If she accepts this, he may continue to see her on this basis. The other women verify his (false) freedom; periodic arguments about them keep his panic at bay. But the women are a paper tiger, for nothing very deep could be happening with them anyway; he is balancing them against each other so that none of them can get much of him. Many smart women, recognizing this to be only a safety valve on their man's anxiety, give him "a long leash." For the real issue under all the fights about other women is that the man is unable to commit himself.

2) He may consistently exhibit unpredictable behavior, standing her up frequently, being indefinite about the next date, telling her that "my work comes first," or offering a variety of other excuses. That is, though he senses her anxiety, he refuses to reassure her in any way, or even to recognize her anxiety as legitimate. For he *needs* her anxiety as a steady reminder that he is still free, that the door is not entirely closed.

3) When he *is* forced into (an uneasy) commitment, he makes her pay for it: by ogling other women in her presence, by comparing her unfavorably to past girlfriends or movie stars, by snide reminders in front of his friends that she is his "ball and chain," by calling her a "nag," a "bitch," "a shrew," or by suggesting that if he were only a bachelor he would be a lot better off. His ambivalence about women's "inferiority" comes out: by being committed to one, he has somehow made the hated female identification, which he now must repeatedly deny if he is to maintain his self-respect in the (male) community. This steady derogation is not entirely put on: for in fact every other girl suddenly does look a lot better, he can't help feeling he has missed something—and, naturally, his woman is to blame. For he has never given up the search for the ideal; she has forced him to resign from it. Probably he will go to his grave feeling cheated, never realizing that there isn't much difference between one woman and the other, that it is the loving that *creates* the difference.

There are many variations of straining at the bit. Many men go from one casual thing to another, getting out every time it begins to get hot. And yet to live without love in the end proves intolerable to men just as it does to women. The question that remains for every normal male is, then, *how do I get someone to love me without her demanding an equal commitment in return?*

Women's "clinging" behavior is required by the objective social situation. The female *response* to such a situation of male hysteria at any prospect of mutual commitment was the development of subtle methods of manipulation, to force as much commitment as *could* be forced from men. Over the centuries strategies have been devised, tested, and passed on from mother to daughter in secret tête-à-têtes, passed around at "kaffee-klatsches" ("I never understand what it is women spend so much time talking about!"), or, in recent times, via the telephone. These are not trivial gossip sessions at all (as women prefer men to believe), but desperate strategies for survival. More real brilliance goes into one-hour coed telephone dialogue about men than into that same coed's four years of college study, or for that matter, than into most male political maneuvers. It is no wonder, then, that even the few women without "family obligations" always arrive exhausted at the starting line of any serious endeavor. It takes one's major energy for the best portion of one's creative years to "make a good catch," and a good part of the rest of one's life to "hold" that catch. ("To be in love can be a full-time job for a woman, like that of a profession for a man.") Women who choose to drop out of this race are choosing a life without love, something that, as we have seen, most *men* don't have the courage to do.

But unfortunately The Manhunt is characterized by an emotional urgency beyond this simple desire for return commitment. It is compounded by the very class reality that produced the male inability to love in the first place. In a male-run society that defines women as an inferior and parasitical class, a woman who does not achieve male approval in some form is doomed. To legitimate her existence, a woman must be *more* than woman, she must continually search for an out from her inferior definition;[1] and men are the only ones in a position to bestow on her this state of grace. But because the woman is rarely allowed to realize herself through activity in the larger (male) society— and when she is, she is seldom granted the recognition she deserves—it becomes easier to try for the recognition of one man than of many; and in fact this is exactly the choice most women make. Thus once more the phenomenon of love, good in itself, is corrupted by its class context: women must have love not only for healthy reasons but actually to validate their existence.

In addition, the continued *economic* dependence of women makes a situation of healthy love between equals impossible. Women today still live under a system of patronage: With few exceptions, they have the choice, not between either freedom or marriage, but between being either public or private property. Women who merge with a member of the ruling class can at least hope that some of his privilege will, so to speak, rub off. But women without men are in the same situation as orphans: they are a helpless sub-class lacking the protection of the powerful. This is the antithesis of freedom when they are still (negatively) defined by a class situation: for now they are in a situation of *magnified* vulnerability. To participate in one's subjection by choosing one's master often gives the illusion of free choice; but in reality a woman is never free to choose love without external motivations. For her at the present time, the two things, love and status, must remain inextricably intertwined.

Now assuming that a woman does not lose sight of these fundamental factors of her condition when she loves, she will never be able to love gratuitously, but only in exchange for security:

1) the emotional security which, we have seen, she is justified in demanding.

2) the emotional identity which she should be able to find through work and recognition, but which she is denied—thus forcing her to seek her definition through a man.

3) the economic class security that, in this society, is attached to her ability to "hook" a man.

Two of these three demands are invalid as conditions of "love," but are imposed on it, weighing it down.

Thus, in their precarious political situation, women can't afford the luxury of spontaneous love. It is much too dangerous. The love and approval of men is all-important. To love thoughtlessly, before one has ensured return commitment, would endanger that approval. Here is Reik:

> It finally became clear during psychoanalysis that the patient was afraid that if she should show a man she loved him, he would consider her inferior and leave her.

For once a woman plunges in emotionally, she will be helpless to play the necessary games: her love would come first, demanding expression. To pretend a coolness she does not feel, *then,* would be too painful, and further, it would be pointless: she would be cutting off her nose to spite her face, for freedom to love is what she was aiming for. But in order to guarantee such a commitment, she *must* restrain her emotions, she *must* play games. For, as we have seen, men do not commit themselves to mutual openness and vulnerability until they are forced to.

How does she then go about forcing this commitment from the male? One of her most potent weapons is sex—she can work him up to a state of physical torment with a variety of games: by denying his need, by teasing it, by giving and taking it back, by jealousy, and so forth. A woman under analysis wonders why:

> There are few women who never ask themselves on certain occasions "How hard should I make it for a man?" I think no man is troubled with questions of this kind. He perhaps asks himself only, "When will she give in?"

Men are right when they complain that women lack discrimination, that they seldom love a man for his individual traits but rather for what he has to offer (his class), that they are calculating, that they use sex to gain other ends, etc. For in fact women are in no position to love freely. If a woman is lucky enough to find "a decent guy" to love her and support her, she is doing well—and usually will be grateful enough to return his love. About the only discrimination women *are* able to exercise is the choice between the men who have chosen them, or a playing off of one male, one power, against the other. But *provoking* a man's interest, and *snaring* his commitment once he has expressed that interest, is not exactly self-determination.

Now what happens after she has finally hooked her man, after he has fallen in love with her and will do anything? She has a new set of problems. Now she can release the vise, open her net, and examine what she has caught. Usually she is disappointed. It is nothing she would have bothered with were *she* a man. It is usually way below her level. (Check this out sometime: Talk to a few of those mousy wives.) "He may be a poor thing, but at least I've got a man of my own" is usually more the way she feels. But at least now she can drop her act. For the first time it is safe to love—now she must try like hell to catch up to him emotionally, to really mean what she has pretended all along. Often she is troubled by worries that he will find her out. She feels like an impostor. She is haunted by fears that he doesn't love the "real" her—and usually she is right. ("She wanted to marry a man with whom she could be as bitchy as she really is.")

This is just about when she discovers that love and marriage mean a different thing for a male than they do for her: Though men in general believe women in general to be inferior, every man has reserved a special place in his mind for the one woman he will elevate above the rest by virtue of association with himself. Until now the woman, out in the cold, begged for his approval, dying to clamber onto this clean well-lighted place. But once there, she realizes that she was elevated above other women not in recognition of her real value, but only because she matched nicely his store-bought pedestal. Probably he doesn't even know who she is (if indeed by this time she herself knows). He has let her in not because he genuinely loved her, but only because she played so well into his preconceived fantasies. Though she knew his love to be false, since she herself engineered it, she can't help feeling contempt for him. But she is afraid, at first, to reveal her true self, for then perhaps even that false love would go. And finally she understands that for him, too, marriage had all kinds of motivations that had nothing to do with love. She was merely the one closest to his fantasy image: she has been named Most Versatile Actress for the multi-role of Alter Ego, Mother of My Children, Housekeeper, Cook, Companion, in *his* play. She has been bought to fill an empty space in his life; but her life is nothing.

So she has not saved herself from being like other women. She is lifted out of that class only because she now is an appendage of a member of the master class; and he cannot associate with her unless he raises her status. But she has not been freed, she has been promoted to "house-nigger," she has been elevated only to be used in a different way. She feels cheated. She has gotten not love and recognition, but possessorship and control. This is when she is transformed from Blushing Bride to Bitch, a change that, no matter how universal and predictable, still leaves the individual husband perplexed. ("You're not the girl I married.")

The situation of women has not changed significantly from what it ever was. For the past fifty years women have been in a double bind about love: under the guise of a "sexual revolution," presumed to have occurred ("Oh, c'mon Baby, where have you *been?* Haven't you heard of the sexual revolution?"), women have been persuaded to shed their armor. The modern woman is in horror of being thought a bitch, where her grandmother expected that to happen as the natural course of things. Men, too, in her grandmother's time, expected that any self-respecting woman would keep *them* waiting, would play all the right games without shame: a woman who did not guard her own interests in this way was not respected. It was out in the open.

But the rhetoric of the sexual revolution, if it brought no improvements for women, proved to have great value for men. By convincing women that the usual female games and demands were despicable, unfair, prudish, old-fashioned, puritanical, and self-destructive, a new reservoir of available females was created to expand the tight supply of goods available for traditional sexual exploitation, disarming women of even the little protection they had so painfully acquired. Women today dare not make the old demands for fear of having a whole new vocabulary, designed just for this purpose, hurled at them: "fucked up," "ballbreaker," "cockteaser," "a real drag," "a bad trip,"—to be a "groovy chick" is the ideal.

Even now many women know what's up and avoid the trap, preferring to be called names rather than be cheated out of the little they can hope for from men (for it is still true that even the hippest want an "old lady" who is relatively unused). But more and more women are sucked into the trap, only to find out too late, and bitterly, that the traditional female games had a point; they are shocked to catch themselves at thirty complaining in a vocabulary dangerously close to the old I've-been-used-men-are-wolves-they're-all-bastards variety. Eventually they are forced to acknowledge the old-wives' truth: a fair and generous woman is (at best) respected, but seldom loved. Here is a description, still valid today, of the "emancipated" woman—in this case a Greenwich Village artist of the thirties—from *Mosquitoes,* an early Faulkner novel:

> She had always had trouble with her men. . . . Sooner or later they always ran out on her. . . . Men she recognized as having potentialities all passed through a violent but temporary period of interest which ceased as abruptly as it began, without leaving even the lingering threads of mutually remembered incidence, like those brief thunderstorms of August that threaten and dissolve for no apparent reason without producing any rain.
>
> At times she speculated with almost masculine detachment on the reason for this. She always tried to keep their relationships on the plane which the men themselves seemed to prefer—certainly no woman would, and few women could, demand less of their men than she did. She never made arbitrary demands on their time, never caused them to wait for her nor to see her home at inconvenient hours, never made them fetch and carry for her; she fed them and flattered herself that she was a good listener. And yet—She thought of the women she knew; how all of them had at least one obviously entranced male; she thought of the women she had observed; how they seemed to acquire a man at will, and if he failed to stay acquired, how readily they replaced him.

Women of high ideals who believed emancipation possible, women who tried desperately to rid themselves of feminine "hangups," to cultivate what they believed to be the greater directness, honesty, and generosity of men, were badly fooled. They found that no one appreciated their intelligent conversation, their high aspirations, their great sacrifices to avoid developing the personalities of their mothers. For much as men were glad to enjoy their wit, their style, their sex, and their candlelight suppers, they always ended up marrying The Bitch, and then, to top it all off, came back to complain of what a horror she was. "Emancipated" women found out that the honesty, generosity, and camaraderie of men was a lie: men were all too glad to use them and then sell them out, in the name of *true* friendship. ("I respect and like you a great deal, but let's be reasonable. . . ." And then there are the men who take her out to discuss Simone de Beauvoir, leaving their wives at home with the diapers.) "Emancipated" women found out that men were far from "good guys" to be emulated; they found out that by imitating male sexual patterns (the roving eye, the search for the ideal, the emphasis on physical attraction, etc.), they were not only achieving liberation, they were falling into something much worse than what they had given up. They were *imitating*. And they had inoculated themselves with a sickness that had not even sprung from their own psyches. They found that their new "cool" was shallow and meaningless, that their emotions were drying up behind it, that they were aging and becoming decadent: they feared they were losing their ability to love. They had gained nothing by imitating men: shallowness and callowness, and they were not so good at it either, because somewhere inside it still went against the grain.

Thus women who had decided not to marry because they were wise enough to look around and see where it led found that it was marry or nothing. Men gave their commitment only for a price: share (shoulder) his life, stand on his pedestal, become his appendage, or else. Or else— be consigned forever to that limbo of "chicks" who mean nothing or at least not what mother meant. Be the "other woman" the rest of one's life, used to provoke his wife, prove his virility and/or his independence, discussed by his friends as his latest "interesting" conquest. (For even if she had given up those terms and what they stood for, no male had.) Yes, love means an entirely different thing to men than to women: it means ownership and control; it means jealousy, where he never exhibited it before—when she might have wanted him to (who cares if she is broke or raped until she officially belongs to him: then he is a raging dynamo, a veritable cyclone, because his property, his ego extension have been threatened); it means a growing lack of interest, coupled with a roving eye. Who needs it?

Sadly, women do. Here are Reik's patients once more:

She sometimes has delusions of not being persecuted by men anymore. At those times of her nonpersecution mania she is very depressed.

And:

All men are selfish, brutal and inconsiderate—and I wish I could find one.

We have seen that a woman needs love, first, for its natural enriching function, and second, for social and economic reasons which have nothing to do with love. To deny her need is to put herself in an extra-vulnerable spot socially and economically, as well as to destroy her emotional equilibrium, which, unlike most men's, is basically healthy. Are men worth that? Decidedly no. Most women feel that to do such tailspins for a man would be to add insult to injury. They go on as before, making the best of a bad situation. If it gets *too* bad, they head for a (male) shrink:

A young woman patient was once asked during a psychoanalytic consultation whether she preferred to see a man or woman psychoanalyst. Without the slightest hesitation she said, "A woman psychoanalyst because I am too eager for the approval of a man."

Note

1. Thus the peculiar situation that women never object to the insulting of women as a class, *as long as* they individually are excepted. The worst insult for a woman is that she is "just like a woman," i.e., no better; the highest compliment that she has the brains, talent, dignity, or strength of a man. In fact, like every member of an oppressed class, she herself participates in the insulting of others like herself, hoping thereby to make it obvious that *she* as an individual is above their behavior. Thus women as a class are set against each other ["Divide and Conquer"], the "other woman" believing that the wife is a "bitch" who "doesn't understand him," and the wife believing that the other woman is an "opportunist' who is "taking advantage" of him—while the culprit himself sneaks away free.

Robert C. Solomon

Love and Feminism

"Love. Being in love. Yuck!" Val poured more wine. . . . "I mean, it's one of those things they've erected, a bunch of nonsense *erected*—and that's the crucial word—into truth by a bunch of intelligent *men*—another crucial word. What the particular nonsense is, isn't particularly important. What's important is why they do it.

Marilyn French, The Women's Room

Is romantic love—the perennial obsession of the Western world—unfair to women, perhaps even a systematic form of rape? So it has been charged.

The charge itself is simple and persuasive. It begins with a fact, that some (many? most? almost all?) women are unhappy and unfulfilled; the fact suggests a hypothesis, that the cause of this unhappiness is the promise of romantic love, which will turn household chores into meaningful and significant acts of devotion, which will transform the biological pains and daily difficulties of having babies into cosmic events, which is said to last "forever" but normally lasts but a few months or years, followed by a lifetime in which to dwell on one's wasted opportunities. The hypothesis in turn implies a theory: that romantic love is neither "natural" nor "divine," as the (male) poets have always insisted, but rather a cultural invention, created by men for the subjugation of women.

It is, when spelled out, an extremely persuasive polemic, far more so than the murky and pious praise of love and lessons on our alleged "need for love" that have been the topic of so many predominantly male theoreticians and theologians from Plato and St. Paul to Rollo May. But it is a polemic with a tragic double bind, one that is also evident in *The Women's Room* and in the work of other authors from Virginia Woolf to Doris Lessing. In its simplest formulation, it is the feeling that

Adapted from *Love: Emotion, Myth & Metaphor* (Doubleday-Anchor, 1981)

love is a lie but nevertheless one cannot live without it.

A double bind is not a question of mere addiction, a romantic habit that we would like to break but cannot; it is rather an impossible confusion in which we both accept and at the same time reject an utterly absurd ideal of love. What I would like to do here is attack this ideal, and to suggest that we can continue to honor a more reasonable notion of romantic love, not in spite of or even in addition to but as a presupposition of feminism. The latter, I would argue, depends largely upon the former.

The "dump love" argument begins with the realization that romantic love, which has so often been promised to women (by men), is an illusion, a fraud, a myth. It does not, as promised, change one's life once and for all or turn the drudgery of housework into joy, much less forever. But not only that. It is the myth itself that has this as its ulterior motive; it is an illusion whose deconstruction reveals a political purpose. Love was invented by men, as an instrument of a kind of culture—which might be summarized as "capitalist"—in order to "keep women in their place," or in any case isolated and dependent on men, and if not happy then at least hopeful of love and complacent about their socially inferior but infinitely useful occupations. By preaching that love is always good and desirable, it is charged, men have convinced at least most women that love is more important than politics and power, thus limiting the competition to themselves. By teaching that love is "everything," men have convinced many women that it is also worth any sacrifice, and like generals in their luxurious tents behind the battle lines, they have succeeded in getting others to make the sacrifices without having to make them themselves. Within the realm of love itself, men have created an image of the "feminine," such that the virtues a woman finds or creates in herself for the sake of love are directly at odds with the virtues required for success in the world: soft, yielding, quiet, accepting versus hard, aggressive, outspoken and critical. A man can be sexy in pursuit of his career; a woman is sexy despite or in contrast to hers (unless, of course, sex is her career). For a woman, to be in love is to be submissive, and therefore disadvantaged and powerless within the relationship, second-class and degraded. If the lover or husband also insists on praising her effusely, worshipping the ground she walks on or putting her "on a pedestal," that is just so much worse, for he is disguising the fact that she is becoming the willing victim in her own political oppression even while being worshipped.

This is not the smirking cynicism of neo-Freudian male reductionist "love is nothing but . . ." theorists like Philip Slater who argue that "romantic love is a scarcity mechanism . . . whose only function is to transmute that which is plentiful [i.e., sex] into that which is in short supply. Although romantic love always verges on the ridiculous, Western peoples and Americans in particular have shown an impressive tendency to take it seriously."[1] The argument that is so well-presented in *The Women's Room* represents the personal outrage and bitter disappointment of a million or more women, only some of whom would identify themselves as "feminists" and few of whom would be able to articulate the precise mechanism by which they have been systematically shut out of power or what all of this has to do with love. But that means it is an argument to be taken especially seriously, for it is not just an academic theory that is at stake.

Now to begin with, there is much here that is no longer controversial, no longer deniable:

1. Much of what we believe about love is demonstrably false or hopelessly obscure, mere mythology and pious illusion—men merely masturbating with the archaic concept of *eros*.

2. Love is not "everything" nor is it "the answer"; it is not always good or desirable. Sometimes, and for some people, it is simply stupid.

3. Love provides private compensation for public impotence or anonymity. Indeed, it is the very essence of love that it allows us to play roles and feel "special" in our personal relationships even when—especially when—we feel overburdened or underappreciated in our jobs or in our social roles.

4. Love is a cultural creation, the product of a male-dominated society, and so, we may reasonably suppose, "erected by men," presumably not to their own disadvantage. Indeed, our current conception of romantic love is largely a literary creation, from Plato and the Bible, from the medieval poets to Shakespeare and the Brownings. On the other hand, romantic love is unknown and would be considered ludicrous in many societies around the world.

5. Love consists of personal roles which, more often than not, cast the women into the more submissive and subservient position. There cannot be any argument against the claim that the promise of love, at least, has long been used against women, by way of compensation for political impotence, as an excuse to keep them in the home (and away from the public positions of power) and as a ready rationalization for social inequities in everything from politics ("women are too emotional") to changing diapers ("women are naturally better at that sort of thing").

Indeed there can be no objection to the charge that the "feminine" role in love makes it difficult for a woman to be both romantically desirable and successful in the male-dominated world of money and power. So what is left of love to defend?

What does not follow is the conclusion that love itself is exploitative, a source of inequity or an obstacle to equality between the sexes. The fact that much of what we believe about love is illusion does not mean that love itself is illusion, nor does it follow from the fact that love is a cultural artifact that it is simply artificial, a "fiction" or a manipulative ploy. It does not follow from the fact that it was (probably) invented by men that love is disadvantageous to women (a man may have invented the wheel and the toothbrush too). It does not follow from the fact that romantic love is often used to reinforce submissive and subservient female roles that those roles are intrinsic to romantic love as such.

If, as the feminist argument charges, romantic love *required* in its structure a division into distinctively male and female roles, strictly corresponding to what has traditionally been called "masculinity" and "femininity," then I would agree that love and the love world constitute archaic emotional structures that we would be better off leaving behind us. But if, as I will argue, romantic roles are fundamentally sex-neutral and presuppose a significant degree of equality, then the much-abused neo-Victorian crypto-caveman scenario of macho "me-Tarzan" and passive-submissive, lovingly house-cleaning Jane is not at all a paradigm of love but at most one of its many historical curiosities—like Quasimodo and Esmerelda.

THE HISTORY OF LOVE

Looking back at the history of romantic love, it is no doubt true that it was "erected," in part by men, in order to fill a need in a certain kind of society, but this does not warrant the leap into the antagonistic and somewhat paranoid conclusion that the need could only have been the suppression of women. Indeed, if we look back to Plato, we find that at least one classical author of love introduced *eros* not as a weapon against women but rather as a relationship between males and between men and the gods; eros simply excluded women or at least dismissed the love of women as "vulgar" and "inferior." Reading Aristophanes, on the other hand, gives a very different impression: relations between men and women, even 2,500 years before birth control, were not that different from today. There were the same battles for power, the same charges and countercharges, with women getting the upper hand as often as men. [2]

If we follow the scholars and locate the origins of romantic love more properly in the chivalric spirit of twelfth-century France, however, we get a very different picture again; what we find is that romantic (or "courtly") love was indeed the invention of wandering free-agent knights and their poetic brethren the troubadours, but it was not at all an instrument of female oppression. Quite the contrary; courtly love quite literally placed women (often married, their husbands off to the Crusades) on pedestals, but thereby freed them from their strict identities in terms of their families, marriages, and household duties. We may now look at the "reduction" of women to their physical appearance and attractiveness as "dehumanizing," a denial of the *person,* but at its origins this celebration of individual attractiveness and personality was the first step in the individualization of women, the recognition that a woman was something more than a household convenience, an object for inter-family barter—a mother, mistress, and, literally, a possession.

It is often argued, nowadays, that romantic love is essentially an invention of capitalism, a creation of industrialized society. This is by any measure not true. Shakespeare described a fully developed conception of romantic love well over a century before the Industrial Revolution in England. It has been argued (by Linda Nicholson, for example) that the breakdown of feudalism and the origins of a market-based society gave rise to the breakdown as well of the old religious view of women as "creatures before God" and began our current capitalist insistence on evaluating people according to what they are "good for." But the truth seems to be rather that under feudalism women were evaluated and considered "worth something" only according to what they were "good for," and it is with the rise of a less regimented society that individual identity—as opposed to mere market value—came to mean anything at all. It is true, for example, as Shulamith Firestone argued in her *Dialectic of Sex,* that romantic love became more important with industrialization, but her Marxist urge to equate sexism with capitalism ignores the historical facts: that romantic love and our current conception of the feminine predates capitalism in any guise by several centuries, and that the parallel, in any case, is not with capitalism or industrialism but with the idea of individualism. Romantic love became possible with the severing of "natural" ties between a person and his or her family, the historical drama of a society of individuals—wandering knights and poets and abandoned wives and daughters—finding themselves for the first time required to make commitments rather than merely recognize predetermined allegiances, free to "devote" themselves to a master or mistress of their choice, and no longer locked into a rigid structure of arranged marriages and obligations. Because these "natural" ties were broken, love became not only desirable but a need.

Love is indeed a cultural invention, created by males perhaps but certainly to the advantage and also with the cooperation of women. Love is a cultural creation, but it is not, therefore, either arbitrary or easily dispensable. Romantic love is our primary mode of forming intimate relationships in a society in which we are all systematically uprooted and sent away from our families and communities. Though love is not the only way of achieving intimacy (friendship certainly deserves mention here), it is imminently successful in doing so. This is as true for men as for women. So it is not in the purpose or original design of romantic love that we are going to find the origins of its use against women.

LOVE AND POWER

A distinction of fundamental importance in recent literature about sexual identity has been marked out between *sex* (that is, male and female) and gender (that is, masculine and feminine). Sex is essentially a biological category, though what we *make* out of sexual differences is a matter of culture, no matter how they may be tied to history or biology by habit or some very suspiciously self-serving arguments. (Women are "naturally" this or that because of the mating habits of some species of fish.) Romantic love is from its very origins neutral to sex; homosexual and Lesbian love is just as much romantic love as unkinky, heterosexual love.

But what about gender roles? What would become of our romantic literature without *her* soft and dutiful gaze, waiting for *him* to return from the battle and give her a hard and possessive embrace? But who cares? In our non-warrior society, in which the day's battle is more than likely a screaming telephone battle with the local tax office, we can switch the above pronouns all that we want, delete as well the adjectives "soft" and "hard," dispense with the roles as well as the sexes. Yet it is part of the history of romantic love, and so part of the "dump love" argument as well, that masculine and feminine gender roles are, if not essential, at least central to love.

Years ago, in one of the more virulent classics of the genre, Shulamith Firestone argued in her *Dialectic of Sex* that it is precisely the "liberation of women from their biology," not now but several generations ago, that brought about the distinctively male invention of romantic love:

Romantic love developed in opposition to the liberation of women from their biology. . . . Male supremacy must shore itself up with artificial institutions or exaggerations of previous institutions. [3]

Romantic role models, she argues, the gender distinctions of "masculine" and "feminine," are developed *in place of* the no longer essential distinction between male and female. Gender depends not on nature but on culture; thus the question, for what purpose, and for whose benefit, has gender been created? The answer is not long forthcoming.

Romanticism is a cultural tool of male power to keep women from knowing their condition. It is especially needed—and therefore strongest— in Western countries with the highest rate of industrialization.[4]

Romantic love is thus to be understood in terms of *power,* and so viewed, the main difference between masculine and feminine gender roles becomes obvious. The argument, interestingly enough, is traced to Freud. Freud is usually considered the nemesis of feminism, but Firestone rightly credits him "as having grasped the crucial problem of modern life, sexuality."[5] But where Freud takes sexuality to be a psycho-biological problem, Firestone sees it as a political problem. Where Freud mysteriously talks about the powers of the libido, Firestone talks concretely about *power* itself. And where Freud talks murkily and unconvincingly about penis envy and castration fears, Firestone substitutes the tangible fact of family power relationships, the all-powerful father and the privileged sons.[6] Penis envy becomes privilege envy, and Firestone quite plausibly suggests that the young girl who is said to envy her brother's curious genitalia is more likely feeling deprived because she is not allowed to play her brother's rough-and-tumble games. With this switch on Freud, the theory can begin: romantic love is the extension of this power-game into adult life, a more subtle way of depriving women of "male" roles and at the same time flattering her as a "lady." Promise her anything, but offer her only love.

What Firestone is arguing, from Freud, is what Freud and many neo-Freudians prefer to ignore: the institutional nature of romantic love and its functional role, not only in the individual psyche and the family but in the power structure of society as a whole. According to Firestone's argument, now that female sexuality as such is of much less importance for survival, the institution of romantic love serves the function of introducing femininity as a matter of emotional significance, as a way of continuing archaic male-dominated institutions and power-structures. Femininity, in a word, is *impotency*. Masculinity is *potency*. To reinforce the roles, femininity is isolated in the home, while masculinity gathers further power in the marketplace. Women, in turn, find themselves seeking approval—the test of success in their feminine roles— entirely from men, while men gain their support and approval as well in a variety of friendships and business or professional relationships. The power relations thus become self-perpetuating.

The isolation of women and the exclusively male-dominated world of power are starting to break down extremely quickly on any reasonable historical scale, and this changes at least one of the key connections between romantic love, gender identity, and power. Much of the power that was once the exclusive domain of males had to do not only with the fact that they had power, but with their variable sources of recognition and approval as well. Men were not solely dependent on women for their sense of self-esteem as women were upon men. But now, as women aggressively find friendships and alliances for themselves—even to the extent that a current popular argument maintains that *only* women are even *capable* of friendship—and as women are beginning to find professional, political, and other sources of self-esteem, this source of power is becoming open to them as well. Thus, in this sense, it has become evident that it is not romantic love or gender roles as such that determine one major traditional source of asymmetrical female dependency, but an entirely distinct set of inequities which might be summarized as unequal access to approval and self-esteem. This isolation of women is now at an end, once and for all, I would argue. Even the reactionary countermovement, the "total woman" syndrome, has the ironic outcome of helping to bring about the public visibility of women speakers and "women's issues," thus destroying this sense of isolation. Romantic love, consequently, no longer remains a woman's sole source of self-esteem, a burden that, in any case, no single emotion could ever be expected to sustain.

ROMANTIC ROLES: BEYOND ANDROGYNY TOO.

Are romantic roles themselves oppressive? If by "romantic roles" one means gender roles— masculine and feminine—the answer is yes. For a woman, if being in love meant accepting a position of subservience and passivity, if being romantically attractive meant being quiet, unaggressive, and apparently helpless, then I doubt that I could argue in favor of romantic love at all. But the truth of the matter seems to be that these roles are not so automatically involved in male-female love as our cheaper novels and more reactionary politicians would suggest. Indeed, love tends to destroy these steroetypes rather than reinforce them, and in theory as well as in practice the concepts of femininity and masculinity ought to be rejected, not only in the public sphere, where they put the woman to a serious disadvantage, but in the personal sphere as well, where they still tend to turn even the best relationships into one-role, one-plot, television-like situation comedies, or worse.

There are at least three ways of overcoming sexual stereotypes. Two of them have become popularly known under the camp word "androgyny." The word is often confused with "bi-sexual," which is only one of its variations, but in any case, I tend to agree with Mary Daly when she writes that 'androgyny' makes me think of Farrah Fawcett and John Travolta scotch-taped together." The first form of androgyny (or "androgynism") insists that masculine and feminine characteristics exist together in everyone, and so it is unnecessary, the argument goes, for each individual to feel that he or she should develop only one set of sex-bound characteristics. In the public sphere, the argument is appealing, since what it says, in effect, is that everyone has the same potential and so should have the same opportunities. Its effect, in other words, is to deny the difference between men and women and to provide a single ideal of rights and potential for all, which leads one author, Joyce Trebilcot, to call it "monoandrogynism."[7] In the personal sphere, however, the same view leads logically to the idea of bi-sexuality; if we each have essentially the same masculine and feminine characteristics, then it would follow that we each also have the same masculine and feminine desires. This sounds like Freud's well-known bi-sexuality argument, but it isn't. For Freud, this was a sexual matter, a fact about biology; for the monoandrogynist, it is a matter of cultural potential, not biology at all. But here, too, we see a problem with this simple view; as a theory about *potentials*, it slips too easily between the idea that the various roles that we call "masculine" and "feminine" *can* be developed in everyone (whether or not they should be) and the idea that these roles are *already* lurking somewhere inside of us, waiting to be developed. But, alas, in our society, only one of the roles ever is, thus frustrating the other. The recognition of the cultural origins of these roles ought to lead us not to the view that they are "there in everybody" but to the more radical conclusion that they are unnecessary, unreal— they do not exist except in so far as we *will* them.

The second form of androgyny is more radical in just this sense; it denies the simple duality between masculinity and femininity and emphasizes the wide variety of gender roles, including any number of combinations of the two "pure" extremes. In effect, this breaks down the extremes while refocusing our attention on particular traits and roles rather than on the monolithic extremes, and opens up the possibility of a large variety of roles that are, traditionally speaking, neither masculine nor feminine. (Because of its pluralism, Trebilcot calls this "polyandrogynism.")

But this second form of androgyny or androgynism suggests a third possibility, which escapes the man-woman etymological orientation of "androgyny" by dismissing masculinity and femininity as roles, particularly where romantic love is involved. What we have been allowing without comment for too long is the idea that these two roles define, if not all, at least a large part of our romantic tradition. In fact, they had no place in Plato; there the crucial distinction was one of age and experience, the lover as teacher, the beloved as pupil. The notion of masculine-feminine may have played a significant part in courtly love, but the notions of chivalry and attractiveness were a matter of historical context, and not necessarily essential to the concept of love as such. As one looks at the structure of romantic love—apart from the grade "B" novels—divisions according to sex and gender have had a very small part to play, even where sex itself is concerned. Indeed, romantic love consists of roles, private roles that are only occasionally or coincidentally played out in public. But the point now to be made once and for all is that few of these roles have anything to do with sex or gender, and insofar as they do, it is not *because* they are male or female or masculine or feminine roles but only because they contain roles that are usually associated with sex and gender, such as domination and submissiveness, aggressiveness and passivity. But what happens in love is that these roles are continuously redefined, and whatever might be expected on the masculine-feminine model, what we actually do in love is something quite different. Indeed, this leads to the unexpected conclusion that masculinity and feminity are, in fact, *public* roles, and not private, and that love requires the overcoming of these roles rather than the realization of them. Femininity is a show, not an expression, and trying to be "feminine" in bed or in love is more like trying to be a comedian or a prima donna rather than a lover. Indeed, as soon as one begins to list the huge gamut of roles through which we are intimate with one another—not only the thousand varieties of sex that need have nothing to do with gender, but cooking, talking, walking, dancing, looking, scratching, fighting, driving cross country, feeding the squirrels, confessing, celebrating, crying, laughing, knowingly nodding to each other in a room full of people, sharing the events of the day, consoling one another in defeat, studying Spanish, staying in bed on Sunday, reading the funnies, bitching about the weather, whispering and occasionally whimpering—the emphasis that is so stressed on a single set of asymmetrical roles, "masculine and feminine," becomes more than embarrassing. Indeed, people who are too caught up in their "masculine" and "feminine" roles are inevitably, after the initial attraction, disappointing lovers. This has nothing to do with sexism, but only with boredom. How can you build your life around a one-act actor? Or perhaps, in some cases, a movie poster?

Beyond sex and gender means beyond *androgyny* too, beyond that one-dimensional set of man-woman identities that too many bad movies and sado-masochistic Freudian fantasies have set out for us. Love is a multiplex of personal roles of all kinds, which are being continuously redefined and reenacted and which need have nothing to do with sex or with those simple stereotypes of gender. In fact, to think of love in terms of masculinity and feminity is like having a conversation in which each party is allowed to say just one sentence. At most, one can expect a predictable performance, instead of the "anything goes" exhilaration of love.

LOVE AND EQUALITY

Romantic love, unlike many other emotions and other forms of love, *requires* equality. It may be, as Stendhal argued a century ago, that love creates rather than discovers equals; and it may also be that within the bounds of equality love divides into unequal roles, into domination and submission, for example, with sado-masochism as its extreme. But it is absolutely crucial to this emotion that one sees the other as an equal, which is not to deny either that it is possible for one person to love more than the other (which is not a question of the nature of love) or that there are other emotions, distinct from romantic love, that sometimes borrow its promiscuous name (adoration, feeling motherly or fatherly, fear, and simple possessiveness). Indeed, in a still class-ridden and unequal society, romantic love is our favorite if not most effective political equalizer. Cinderella moves from maid to princess not only in the eyes of her prince but in the eyes of the law, too, whether or not she lives thereby "happily ever after." King Edward VIII found it necessary to lower his social status to match that of the woman he loved, and with a perverse twist of this perception, Shulamith Firestone argues in *Dialectic of Sex* that men "fall in love (with women) to justify their descent into a lower caste." But what is *equality*, in a relationship?

"Equality" is one of those political glow-words with very little determinate content, like "liberty." One gives it a content by giving it a context, for example—equal work time, or equal say in an issue, equal responsibility for some specific activity or equal power. What counts as equality in a particular relationship may indeed be quite different from what counts as equality in another. The equality that is the precondition for love only consists in the demand that social differences do not matter, that both lovers are mutually willing to take up the various personal and private roles that make up intimacy. But as the notion of equality starts to become more "objective" and more concerned with social rather than personal status, once the private is measured by public criteria, the tacitly accepted roles within the relationship tend to be shattered. The quasi-political self-consciousness that replaces them undermines the intimacy of love. What was once a relationship now becomes a "partnership," which may well be more efficient, even a model of fairness and success in "having worked it out," but it isn't love. It is too dominated by foreign and critical observers, external measurements and publicly defined if nominally private roles. It was a problem that many of us had with women's liberation in the sixties (though that is by no means the only ideology that has that consequence; sex books and our modern therapeutic attitudes towards sex can do the same thing). The demands may all be completely reasonable. They may indeed force a relationship to conform with some more general and "objective" form of equity. But what is too often sacrificed is love, for love is not objective, not negotiable, not a "partnership." None of which is to say, let me quickly add, that love itself is inherently, "objectively" unequal, or that what inequality there may be necessarily gives the woman the disadvantage, or that our idea of "women's roles" cannot be changed, or that romantic love and feminism are incompatible. To the contrary, they even presuppose one another. But the problem that defies ideology and one-sided "consciousness raising" by its very nature is to bring these demands—if they must be demands rather than shared ideals—into the relationship itself. As a set of demands or ideals imposed from the outside, "equality" becomes antithetical to, rather than the precondition for, love.

The division between the public and the personal, and the quite different concerns for equality of the sexes in the public sphere (equal pay for equal work, equal access to jobs and careers, equal rights and responsibilities under the law) on the one hand and the sense of equality that is the precondition for intimacy on the other, have been commonly confused by both feminist theorists and anti-feminists alike. Shulamith

Firestone is just one of the many theorists who have argued that romantic love and "the relegation of love to the personal" is part and parcel of the manipulative ploy to "keep women in their place" and to rationalize, even idealize, their class inferiority. But love is by its very nature personal, and if it isolates women in romantic relationships, it isolates men in exactly the same way. That is what we mean by a "personal" relationship. The mistake is to think that the *overemphasis* on the personal, which is foisted upon women, to the exclusion of public roles and interests, is a feature of romantic love itself, and that the indefensible inequality in the public sphere necessarily has its counterpart in the personal sphere as well. But these are quite distinct, and to treat them together as a single problem may mean blurring the very different strategies that are required to encounter each of them.

A more vicious version of the same confusion has given birth to the outlandish conception of the "total woman," who is in fact a Medieval woman, more at home in Khomeini's Persia than contemporary America. The strategy of these anti-feminists is to systematically confuse questions about intimacy and personal relationships with questions about equality and public life. *Whatever* one says about the private, romantic, and family roles to which women have become accustomed (which is misleadingly described as their "natural" roles), nothing follows about the public roles or abilities or ambitions of women in society, in which sex and gender considerations simply drop out of the picture—or ought to. It is simply false, where public criteria are concerned, that "men and women are different by nature," since nature has nothing to do with most public functions (given, that is, that we no longer inherit our leaders through their birthright) and sex, in any case, is irrelevant to our roles. But in the personal sphere, questions of sex do indeed arise, but not of necessity, much less "by nature." They arise because we choose to make sex—and heterosexuality specifically—the basis of our most intimate relationships. But it is not difficult to find cultures in which sexual relationships are perfunctory, and other encounters—with friends or fellow workers or soldiers—are far more intimate and "meaningful." One need only look again at Plato to appreciate the power of love in which the difference in the sexes plays no part whatever. It is what we *make* of the sexes and sex that determines the roles in our personal relationships, and it is here that the slippery argument from the historical *public* place of women in certain kinds of roles, to an inference about what is "natural," and to a conclusion about the properly submissive and subservient place of women in love is particularly vicious. There is nothing "natural" about public roles, and there is nothing "natural" about personal roles either. Our roles in romance are in every case personally determined, if on the basis of public instruction, and the kinds of roles one chooses to play with one's lover cannot be dictated *a priori*. To say that a woman *ought* to be submissive, and also to say that she ought not, is nothing less than a kind of emotional fascism, a way of dismissing and degrading huge numbers of women who find that their personal preferences do not match up to the latest official line. "The totalitarian woman" might be a better designation for the conservative tendency to confuse questions about public equality with questions about personal roles; but the tendency to confuse the demand for social equality with an authoritarian attack on love is to be found on the other side as well. Romantic love *requires* equality, and to deny this or to enforce it from the outside is the denial of love as well.

Yet, it would be absurd to deny that one's personal self-image and one's public, social image are related and affect each other. So what does this mean about equality in love? First of all, that it is aided immensely by social-political-economic equality. Whatever truth may be in the argument that women have always wielded "the *real* power" at home, there is no question that status in public and status at home are mutually supportive. But more crucial to the argument here is the fact that equality in personal relationships is essential to seeing oneself as equal in social relationships as well, in part because we (unlike most people of the world) tend to take our personal identities as more real ("more myself") than our public identities. If love is an emotion *requiring* that we see one another as equals, it is therefore an important tool for equality in the public sphere as well.

But what does "equality" mean in relations? It does not mean "being the same." It does not exclude all sorts of asymmetrical and uneven roles and relationships, including the absolute domination of one person by the other. It does not require, as such, the equal division of housework or "bread earning" tasks, though these have become rather routine expectations (whether or not routinely fulfilled). Equality in love essentially means a mutually-agreed upon indeterminacy, more or less free from social strictures and limitations (short of violence and illegality, sometimes), a sense of reformulation in which one's self-images and personal roles and identity are up for grabs, in negotiation with one other person, in which there are no preordained roles or predestined status relationships, including, particularly, those which are traditionally labeled "masculine" and "feminine." Indeed, it is the heart of love that it involves the breakdown of these television stereotypes and an openness to change and mutual reevaluation which is available in very few of our experiences. It is not yet political equality (or "liberation") and equality in love is no guarantee that the public demand will be successful. But it is a self-effacing error, and an unrealistic demand for most women besides, that the demand for political equality *preclude* romantic love (with men). The latter is and has often been a means to the former.

LOVE AND ILLUSION

The central argument of *The Women's Room* is an anti-romantic version of an old argument in philosophy that is usually called "the argument from illusion." It is the fallacious but persuasive inference from the fact that one is sometimes fooled to the paranoid supposition that one might always be deceived. Quite a few years ago, Shulamith Firestone exploited this argument by attacking what she called "idealization": the fact that women tend to imagine their lovers with virtues they never had, and in return men mock-worship women, which Firestone says is an effective substitution for physical abuse—and the result is the same. (How this is so is never quite clear.) What is so obvious in Firestone is the double bind asymmetry itself: men idealize women and thereby exploit them, women idealize men and are therefore exploited. Idealization and the argument from illusion also enter into the work of a new spokesperson for the "dump love" movement, Jill Tweedie *(In The Name of Love)*, who argues that love is a pair of "rose colored glasses" that when removed . . . reveal "that what was taken to be precious is simply a bare dull pebble, like any other." But the most spectacular description of idealization as illusion is in *The Women's Room* itself, as Val describes with exquisite irony the bloated idealization of love, followed by its inevitable collapse:

> Okay. Love is one of those things you think is supposed to happen, is a fact of life, and if it doesn't happen to you, you feel cheated. You're walking around feeling rotten, you know, because it's never happened to you. So one day you meet this guy, right? And, ZING! He is gorgeous! It doesn't matter what he's doing. He may be making a point in a debate, he may be chopping up concrete on a city street, with his shirt off and his back tanned. It doesn't matter. Even if you've met him before and not thought much about him, at some moment you look at him and everything you've thought about him before goes straight out of your head. You never really saw him before! You realize that in a split second! You never saw how totally gorgeous he was![8]

Val, the narrator, then proceeds in almost obscene detail to describe his wonderful arms, his sensual month, his pithy intelligence, the desperation with which one wants him, and so on, for several salivating pages.

> Then one day, the unthinkable happens. You are sitting together at the breakfast table and you're a little hung over, and you look across at beloved, beautiful golden beloved, and beloved opens his lovely rosebud mouth showing his glistening white teeth, and beloved says something stupid. Your whole body stops midstream: your temperature drops. Beloved has never said anything stupid before. You turn and look at him; you're sure you misheard. You ask him to repeat. And he does . . .

Thus, the doubt begins, but that's only the start, and soon you see that he is *always* saying stupid things—and suddenly you see that he's skinny, or flabby or fat. His teeth are crooked, his toenails are dirty and he farts in bed. So on now in the other direction. The initial idealizations were all *falsehoods*. Now you see you've been had:

> And you hate yourself for having deluded yourself about him (you tell yourself it was HIM you were deluded about—not love), and you hate him for having believed your delusions, and you feel guilty and responsible and you try, slowly, to disengage. But now, just try to get rid of him! He clutches, he clings, he doesn't understand. How could you want to separate from a deity?

Love always involves idealization, and, indeed, idealization, like hallucination and flattery, can be abused to deceive either oneself or a lover. But the problem with the argument is that it flatly fails to make the distinction between innocent fantasy and celebration on the one hand and self-deception and illusion on the other. All emotions, not only love, are blind (that is, myopic) in that they see what they want to see, emphasize what they want to emphasize, celebrate what they want to celebrate. Without that element of enthusiasm, birthdays and anniversaries would be just another day, life would be grey, and even family and friends would be reduced to social security numbers and vital statistics. *All* values are idealizations in this sense; all hopes and plans are fantasies, and even daydreams are, in one sense, false. Yes, we do disappoint one another (women as well as men, though this would never be known from *The Women's Room*), but to infer from this that our fantasies are fraudulent, much less that love is itself an illusion, is a piece of painful self-deception.

THE DOUBLE BIND

> Except for her (Camille's) passion for Bernard, she is tough and fun. Don't ask what it is about Bernard that makes her so adore him. It is not Bernard, but love itself. She believes in love, goes on believing in it against all odds. Therefore, Bernard is a little bored. It is boring to be adored. At thirty-eight, she should be tough and fun, not adoring. When he leaves her, a month or two from now, she will contemplate suicide. Whereas, if she had been able to bring herself to stop believing in love, she would have been tough and fun and he would have adored her forever. Which would have bored her. She then would have had to be the one to tell him to clear out. It is a choice to give one pause.[9]

The genius of *The Women's Room*—perhaps as opposed to *The Dialectic of Sex*—is in its descriptions, presented for the most part in a flat matter-of-fact familiarity that leaves many people who reject the tone of the book incapable of saying what is wrong with it. But the first thing to see about the above illustration, and a hundred others like it, is its unwarranted one-sidedness. French tells us that the dilemma is symmetrical, that it is the same for Bernard as for Camille, but Bernard remains a mere name for us; the problem is all Camille's. It has been said that French is unsympathetic to her male characters, but this isn't true. She *has* no male characters, no men with problems and paradoxes themselves, just cardboard figures who periodically fall down on, blow away from or on occasion confess to their disappointed female lovers. But French, unlike Firestone, for example, doesn't put the blame on men. She blames love itself, and idealization is the key to love.

The Women's Room is built on a brutal dichotomy, between an overidealized and impossible form of love—expecting love to be everything: instant happiness, creativity, undying devotion, adoring and being adored "forever"—and the disillusioning facts of our lives: that love doesn't last, that love isn't everything, that one can be in love and still be unhappy, suffer from writer's block, feel insecure and inadequate. But what remains intact is the ideal itself, unattainable, a bitter disappointment and a cruel promise. What we do not get, unfortunately, is a less pregnant but still desirable promise of love that is more in tune with experience, and thus not so prone to disillusionment.

The refrain of *The Women's Room,* "but of course, she would not think of blaming love," should have been about blaming certain ideas we have about love, not love itself. The danger of confusing love with illusion is more than the personal unhappiness it causes: its cost also includes creating a serious obstacle in the public fight for women's equality. Even if one assumes that the battle for equality will entail antagonism with men on a public level, it is sheer folly, and also unnecessary, to carry that antagonism into intimate relationships which, despite certain utopian hopes and radical experiments to the contrary, may well be indispensable in our society, at least for the present and the foreseeable future. But the argument goes beyond this, too: for if, as I have argued, romantic love actually *requires* a sense of equality, then love provides, rather than works against, the ideal of feminism. Historically, romantic love (and Christian love, too) were powerful forces in breaking down the old hierarchies and roles. Today, that conception is still at work, in spite of the continuing overemphasis on sex and gender roles and despite the fact that too many feminists see love as the problem, instead of as part of the solution. Indeed, here as elsewhere in politics, projecting one's personal disappointments into the world as cynical "realism" is not the way to win adherents. Romantic love between men and women, from its very inception, has always been the primary vehicle of personal and, consequently, social equality. It has always been "feminist" in its temperament, whatever the mythologies that have sometimes been imposed on top of it. Romantic love and feminism are neither incompatible nor antagonistic; in fact, I would argue that, for the present at least, they should not try to do without one another.

NOTES

1. Philip Slater, *Pursuit of Loneliness*, p. 8.
2. In *Euripides at Bay*, for example, as well as in Aristophanes' best-known play *Lysistrada*.
3. Shulamith Firestone, *Dialectic of Sex*, p. 165.
4. Ibid., p. 166.
5. Ibid., p. 49
6. Ibid., p. 53.
7. Joyce Trebilcot, "Two Forms of Androgynism," in *Feminism and Philosophy* by Vetterling-Braggin, Elliston, and English, eds. (Littlefield Adams, 1977), pp. 70-78.
8. Marilyn French, *The Women's Room*, p. 362.
9. Ibid., pp. 210-211.

Richard Taylor

The Ethics of
Having Love Affairs

The following excerpts from Richard Taylor's book Having Love Affairs
*present the argument for the rationality and morality of extra-marital
love affairs. Part One consists of a series of analyses, arguments, and
argument fragments directed against the morality of fidelity. In Part
Two, Taylor constructs a set of rules for extra-marital love.*—Eds.

PART ONE: FIDELITY

What we call "morality" is simply blind obedience to words of command.

Havelock Ellis

. . . If love and affection are good—and they are, indeed, the ultimate
good, exceeding wealth, honor, and everything else in the joy they bring
to their possessor—then the free expression of passionate love cannot be
bad, except in its effects. And, to be sure, these effects can be so horribly
bad, so totally destructive of everything good, that it is no wonder
people still find a kind of elemental wisdom in simply restricting passionate love to the formal relationship of marriage . . . The home, it is
thought, must by all means be preserved; and having no other means of
keeping it intact, societies have resorted to rules and ceremony. Needless
to say, this does not work.

A society can, to be sure, render the legal dissolution of a marriage
impossible, as has been done in some countries; but all this has ever
achieved is the preservation of the thinnest outward appearance. A
church can, of course, with much solemnity, formalize the state of matri-

From Richard Taylor, *Having Love Affairs* (Buffalo, NY: Prometheus Books)
1982, pp. 49-50, 52-53, 58-60, 141-142, 143-146, 125, 130-132, 133, 135-139,
171-174, 178, 179-180, 181. Reprinted by permission of the publisher.

mony, even declare it incorruptible and indissoluble; but this, too, only creates the outward appearance. Marriage itself can in no way be created by any priest or servant of the state. It cannot be preserved by them nor by any other power of heaven or earth, except in appearance. Nor can it really be terminated by them; they can at best only recognize what has already ended. Marriage is entirely the work of those who enter into it. Its successes, and rewards of rejoicing, the warmth and fulfillment it gives, are theirs alone. Its failure, and the inner desolation this produces, are theirs too. The rest of the world can look on, but only they will have the blessings if they succeed, and the anguish if they do not.

Of course this implies that marriage, being the creation of two persons, can be made ethical or moral by them alone. No priest, no political functionary, no state, no church, no rules, and no laws can confer moral rightness on this relationship, nor can any of these make that relationship morally wrong. Only lovers can do these things. It is lovers who make a marriage. No priest makes it. It is lovers, or former lovers, who destroy a marriage. No court dissolves it. Really, all a church or court can do is to confer outward legality on a state of affairs that the individuals involved have already established.

This truly goes to the heart of the matter, so far as morality is concerned. For there is a popular conception to the very contrary; that is, it is widely thought, even regarded as obvious, that *only* an authorized functionary of the church or government, a clergyman or judge, can make the relationship of lovers ethical, and indeed, that marriage between lovers is the very creation of such persons or the rituals they perform. People become married, it is thought, at a stroke, by the ceremonious pronouncement of words and the signing of documents, as though there were no more to it than this. Of course that formality is required for the *legality* of a marriage relationship. This is a truism. But to suppose it to be required for the *morality* or even the existence of that relationship is a naive, even vulgar confusion of genuine morality with law. Not all that the law requires measures up to any significant moral standard, nor does everything that is forbidden by law violate morality. If it were otherwise, then the merest infractions of parking regulations, or unintentional tax delinquencies, would be violations of morality, while, on the other hand, the total and casual disregard of human suffering, which is permitted by law, would violate no moral requirement. What is required or forbidden by law is often but not always the same as what is required or forbidden by morality. To suppose that the deepest and most precious feelings of which human beings are capable—the very feelings that are the basis not only of all social life, but life itself, the feelings of love and passion between the sexes—can be significantly influenced by any outsiders at all, or that any outsider can confer either morality or immorality upon them, is to suppose what is plainly absurd. Worse than that, it is to try to chuck onto the shoulders of some functionary a responsibility that no person can possibly relinquish, namely, the responsibility of lovers to create their own marriage. They will not accomplish this through the approval of others nor the approval of their church nor even through the approval of the whole of mankind, who are forever outside that relationship and all its implications.

The purpose of what follows is to set forth, not a comprehensive ethic of marriage, but only the ethical principles and guidelines that should govern a part of that relationship, namely, that pertaining to sexual fidelity. Suddenly, with the introduction of that term, we find ourselves involved with some large misconceptions.

The first, and probably the most dangerous, of these is that the ethic unique to marriage is completely exhausted by the concept of fidelity, or in other words, that morality in marriage requires the sexual exclusivity of its partners. Other rules and guidelines, it is supposed, are of a purely practical nature, some of which are of great importance, but none of them are considered strictly moral. This mean and trivial standard gives married lovers one primary rule: Thou shalt not commit adultery. The notion is cultivated in married couples that, so long as they heed this rule, the basic requirement of morality, at least so far as marriage is concerned, has been met; if the rule is ever broken, then morality has been violated. It is thought to be that simple. Adultery is, for example, the only ground that is universally considered sufficient for divorce. And here, accordingly, we begin to see why the goodness and well-being that marriage promises are so rarely found; namely, that the ethic governing it is so grossly oversimplified.

The second misconception has to do with the concept of fidelity. Infidelity is everywhere treated as though it were simply synonymous with adultery, illustrating once more the vulgarization of the ethic which seems everywhere to accompany its ritualization. Some persons look upon the wedding band as a kind of "no trespassing" sign, and upon the marriage certificate as a type of permit or license to make love, a right which must then have been lacking until conferred by the document! Yet, as we have already noted, the real and literal meaning of fidelity is *faithfulness;* and what thinking person could imagine that there is only one way in which someone can fail to keep faith with another? Faithfulness is a state of one's heart and mind. It is not the mere outward conformity to rules. There are countless ways that it can fail which have nothing whatever to do with sexual intimacy nor, indeed, with outside persons. It can be fulfilled in various ways as well, even in spite of sexual nonexclusiveness, though this is sometimes more difficult to see.

To illustrate this, imagine a man who has long been married to one person, a man who has never lapsed from the rule of strict sexual constancy, nor has he ever appeared to, and who could never be suspected of this by anyone with the slightest knowledge of his character. This man, we shall imagine, assumes without doubt the rightness of his behavior, is scornful of anyone whose standards are less strict, would not permit a violation of this rule by anyone under his own roof, and would consider no circumstances to mitigate the breach of it. So far, so good; he is, it would seem to most persons, a faithful husband.

But now let us add to the picture that this same man, being of a passive nature and having somewhat of an aversion to sex, has never yielded to temptations for the simple reason that he has had no temptations placed before him. His intimacy with his own wife is perfunctory, infrequent, dutiful, and quite devoid of joy for himself or his spouse. They are, in fact, essentially strangers to each other's feelings. In this light, the nobility of his austere ethic begins to appear less impressive, does it not?

But we are not finished with our description. Let us add to the foregoing that these two persons appear to the world as hard workers, but are still quite poor. He works monotonously as a sales clerk in a declining drug store, we can suppose, while she adds what she can to the family's resources by putting in long hours assisting in the local public library. Appearances are misleading, however, for behind this facade of meager resources there are, unbeknown to anyone but the husband, and scrupulously kept secret from his wife, eight savings accounts, which have been built up over the years, each in his name only, and none containing less than thirty thousand dollars. At every opportunity—sometimes by shrewd dealing, often by sheer penuriousness, and always by the most dedicated selfishness—the husband squirrels away more savings, so that by this time the total, augmented by interest compounded over the years, adds up to a most impressive sum.

Has the rule of good faith been breached?

But to continue the description: We now suppose that the long suffering wife of this dreary marriage is stricken, let us say, with cancer, and undergoes a radical mastectomy as the only hope of saving her life. Whereupon whatever small affection her husband ever had for her evaporates completely. He turns sullen, distant, and only dimly aware of his wife's presence, finding all the comfort for his life in those growing and secret savings accounts. He never thinks of sexual infidelity, and congratulates himself for this, as well as for other things, such as his thrift.

Finally, let us suppose that his wife has always been a poet of considerable creative power, whose creations have never received the attention they deserve, least of all her husband's, he being only dimly aware that they even exist. Yet they are finally seen and sincerely praised by another sensitive soul having the qualities of mind necessary to appreciate them, and through his encouragement, we shall imagine, she is finally able to have a sense of meaningfulness in her life, hitherto found only meagerly in the lonely creation of poetic beauty. This same new found friend is, moreover, oblivious to the scars of her illness; he cares only for her, and, unlike her husband, his love is sincere, impulsive, passionate, imaginative, and as frequent as conditions allow.

We could expand this story, but the point of it is abundantly clear by now. It is found in answering the question: *Who has been faithless to whom?* In that answer one finds not only the essential meaning of infidelity, which is a betrayal of the promise to love, but also, by contrast, the true meaning of fidelity.

* * *

JEALOUSY

Jealousy is the most wrenching and destructive of human passions. Not only is it painful, but the pain is self-inflicted; and unlike most other emotions, no good ever comes from it, not even the release of tension or the assuaging of pride on the part of the jealous person. On the contrary, this passion is as destructive of oneself as it is of others. Other emotions, even painful ones, are usually redeemed in some way, but not jealousy. Anger, for example, though ugly, is sometimes justified, and may even produce some genuinely worthwhile result, even if it consists of no more than the salvaging of an angry person's pride. Anger is sometimes called "righteous," although jealousy can never be so described. Anxiety, although painful, is seldom self-inflicted, and sometimes has its place in warding off actual evils. Pity, though unpleasant, can sometimes be tender and even ennobling. And resentment, to take still another passion, is sometimes a goad to the correction of evils, such as injustice.

Jealousy, however, is never good for anything at all. It is a pain that is unredeemed, self-imposed, debilitating, ugly, and utterly destructive in its inward and outward effects. Rather than providing a kind of outlet for bad feelings, it has an amazing capacity for feeding on itself, festering away, nourishing depression, and defeating every good and generous impulse that could make itself felt. It does not even protect the pride of its victim, but on the contrary makes him more and more shameful both to himself and in the eyes of everyone else. To be over-powered by jealousy is the ultimate self-defeat.

*   *   *

Jealousy always has its source in something almost as ugly as itself; namely, in the attitude of possessiveness towards another person. A man is likely to look upon his wife as *his* in the sense of a personal pos-session, and with this starting point he feels quite justified in imposing rules and restrictions just as he would upon any other thing to which he claims ownership. Thus the marriage relationship, which is supposed to inspire the most exalted love and friendship, becomes instead debased, reducing a partner to a mere chattel, a *thing,* or worse than this, a thing *owned.*

There is no doubt, however, that this conception of conventional marriage is generally thought to be perfectly natural and acceptable. It is hard therefore to imagine, for example, any clergyman remonstrating with any member of his flock for having exactly this conception of conjugal love, for thinking of his wife as literally *belonging* to him. The same holds for women; that is, wives are similarly possessive of hus-bands. But strangely, the degree of possessiveness considered allowable for wives is somewhat less than for husbands. Like a man, a woman may restrict her partner's association with other persons, but his viola-tion of these restrictions is considered less serious than it would be had she been thus confined, and similarly, his outrage is deemed more to be feared than hers. Of course this is arbitrary and unfair, but nonetheless true . . . .

The question here is not, of course, how far such rights of pos-session extend between the sexes, but rather, whether any such right exists at all. It should be quite clear that it does not. No human being can be owned. Even children are not literally the property of their parents, however much some parents may wish to think otherwise. How much less so, then, is an adult an item of property. Furthermore, apart from property rights, this kind of possessiveness is inconsistent with the most basic requirement of ethics: that a person be treated, always and by everyone, as a person and not as an object. And it is likewise inconsistent with the fundamental ethical requirement of any marriage relationship, which is, very simply, that its partners love each other.

*   *   *

These last two points need to be considered separately.

A mere *object* is without mind or will, and can therefore be dealt with as we please—unless, of course, it is something owned by someone else. In this case the manner in which we treat it bears on its owner's mind and will, that is, upon the interests of another person. But considering a thing apart from its relationship to persons, it is immune to injury, and has neither rights nor interests that can be violated. A person, on the other hand, has both mind and will. He has thoughts, feelings, purposes, aspirations, and interests. This gives an individual moral significance, and it matters overwhelmingly how he is treated. Indeed, his most basic interest is in the very treatment he receives from others, for his pride, self-esteem, and everything that gives him worth depends on it.

Since, then, a person, unlike a thing, is possessed of both mind and will, the most fundamental injury to him is to treat him as though he had neither. Such treatment consists precisely in substituting your *own* mind and will for his, which is exactly what happens when anyone asserts any right of possession whatever over another person. Thus, if it is a wife's wish to do something—for instance, to paint, to write, to travel, to earn an income, to have times and places of absolute privacy, or to enjoy the company of whomever she chooses—and her husband vetoes or annuls this desire, then he quite clearly is substituting his mind and will for hers, and is treating her as though she had neither. He treats her, in short, as an object. And whatever might be said of the conventional rules of marriage and of fidelity in their narrowest sense, it is doubtful whether there can be any more degraded standard of ethics than this. To treat a person as a mere object is not just *an* abuse of that person, but *the ultimate* abuse.

Generalizing from this, it is worth noting that public moralists, most often represented by clergymen, who make it their primary business to set forth rules of morality for *others*, and even to get these rules of theirs passed into law, are not at all acting in accordance with any acceptable moral standard. They are doing the very opposite, by treating persons as though they were not persons but mere objects to be used and controlled. No civilized ethic can stand which excludes the idea of responsibility, and no responsibility can exist in anyone for those actions of his which are chosen, not by him, but by others. Through fear, law, and manipulation a moralist can sometimes achieve conformity to a rule that seems important to him, but he cannot thereby achieve anything remotely resembling morality.

With respect to the second point, namely, the requirement of love, it is quite obvious that possessive love, as it might be called, is no real expression of love at all, but its perversion. Loving an *object* is not really loving *it* at all; instead, it is an expression of self-love. A person who takes pride in his possessions, who glories in them, quite clearly does not love them for their own sake, but for his. They are just ornaments. A man's relationship to fine cars, buildings, or whatever, is exactly that of a woman's relationship to her jewelry. These are loved because they enhance their owners. It is as simple as that. Hence, for someone to love another individual possessively is precisely *not* to love that other, but only to love oneself. What must be remembered, however, is that partners of any marriage relationship are expected to love *each other*, and that *this* is the fundamental ethical requirement. There really is no other, except what is implied by this one. No one is ever asked to pledge lasting love *for himself*. This would be absurd. Accordingly, the moment that any husband or wife asserts any right of ownership over the other, at that moment the fundamental vow of marriage has been violated by withdrawing the love each swore to give, and substituting in its place a grotesque love of *oneself*. Here, it must be stressed again, is the basic infidelity or breach of faith. Sexual infidelity, as it is generally called, is at worst the expression of this more serious infidelity, namely, the corruption of love itself, and it is not always even that.

PART TWO: RULES FOR HUSBANDS, WIVES, AND LOVERS

He who lets the world, or his own part of it, choose his plan of life for him, has no need of any other faculty than the ape-like one of imitation.

—John Stuart Mill

It is one of life's paradoxes that instead of assuming ultimate responsibility for their own conduct, which no one else may usurp, many people seem to suppose that the first order of business in life is to shed it, to transfer to someone else the responsibility for their decisions and, oftentimes, their whole way of life. Thus there are people who will hardly take a step in the world without anxiously wondering how it will be viewed by others—by their church, for example, or by society as a whole, or by their neighbors. For most people, the mere admonition that an action is disapproved by the church, or frowned upon by one's community, is quite sufficient to justify the rejection of it; and in this unthinking rejection, which allows others to choose for them, they strangely suppose themselves to be following a path of morality. What they are actually doing is to remove their behavior from the realm of moral consideration altogether thus rendering themselves, in the strictest sense, irresponsible. It is astonishing the limits to which this kind of thinking has sometimes been carried. There are some who not only allow, but eagerly encourage, other people to decide for them not only their public manners and behavior, but personal matters, as well as things which are of no real significance, such as their modes of speech and dress. Here, as in everything, the question always uppermost in their minds is not how it suits *themselves,* but how it appears to *others,* to everyone *but* themselves. All of which would of course be harmless enough, but for the fact that these very people, who seem almost deliberately to have reduced their own minds and feelings to the smallest possible scope, tend to restrict the actions of others to the same narrow range. With scorns and frowns, smiles and blandishments, and sometimes by using their power to give or withhold what others need for their very survival, these people try to reduce alternative conceptions of what is allowable to conform with their own petty and unimaginative standards. Fall into step, the message seems to be, and you will fare well; or assume the responsibility for your own free choices, as nature meant you to, and you will do so at the cost of your reputation and the support of those around you. *That,* at least, is a very bad choice to put before anyone. Yet it is the constant admonition of society, this exhortation to littleness, usually in the very name of what people like to think of as "morality." It takes not only a very free spirit, but a fairly courageous one—or perhaps one who is rich enough not to care what others think—not to cave in to it.

It is in the light of all this that I am now going to propose rules or guidelines having to do with love affairs. I shall first consider three rules for people who believe their partners are so involved, and then six additional rules for those who are engaged in a love affair. The point of each proposed rule is exactly the same, namely, to reduce or eliminate the fiercely destructive power of these relationships, and to promote the love, kindness, and respect between people that is so vastly more precious than the kind of free-wheeling moralizing and condemnation that seems so appropriate to some individuals and groups.

RULES FOR THOSE WHOSE PARTNERS
ARE HAVING LOVE AFFAIRS

Rule One: Do not spy or pry.

By spying I mean any devious effort to learn whether someone is having an affair, regardless of who initiates the probe: a husband, a wife, or the partner of a marriage relationship. Its worst form is to watch, or arrange for others to watch, someone's comings and goings; but of course it also includes surreptitious looking at mail, eavesdropping, poking through waste paper, and things of this sort.

That such behavior violates the principle enunciated above is obvious, as it betrays a total lack of confidence in another person's judgment and determination of his own conduct, thus amounting to a declaration that he or she cannot be trusted. But, in addition to this, it is degrading to the spying partner. To be reduced to fishing through wastebaskets or pockets, putting one's ear to doors or telephone receivers, or, worse yet, engaging an ally to watch and report, is inherently ignominious and degrading.

But, one is tempted to reply, he or she "has a right to know." Not quite. One has perhaps a keen desire to know, but a right only to ask. Asking is, with respect to matters of this sort, the only acceptable form of inquiry. A suspected wrong on the part of one person cannot justify a clear and incontestable wrong, such as spying would be, on the part of another.

Moreover, besides being inherently disgraceful, spying is a clear breach of faith, or infidelity, in the strictest sense. It is an injury to the person spied on, of a kind that needs no more to be tolerated within marriage or a marriage relationship than within any other. To spy on a friend would be equivalent to declaring that no friendship exists at all, and a lesser standard can hardly apply within the closest and most intimate kind of friendship. Just as a person forfeits a friendship by turning from friend into spy, so too does a wife or husband, for example, forfeit a marriage in its meaningful sense.

When directed to someone who is cared about, questions concerning matters of this sort might not always yield true answers. To be sure, this is exactly the kind of information that the person asked might be most reluctant to yield. The question of the obligation to be truthful will be considered separately; here it need only be said that the desire for information does not justify the use of *any means whatever* to obtain it. Such a desire must stop short of what is base and faithless in its very nature, which means, to stop on the side of asking. Even here, asking cannot extend to quizzing and prying, to raising accusatory or prosecutorial questions, or to badgering and harassing with suspicions. Behavior of this kind has every bad quality of spying even though it is not covert. In particular, it amounts to a declaration of distrust, and an attempt to take upon oneself the role of governor and judge of another's conduct.

*   *   *

Rule Two: Do not confront or entrap.

The one who feels forsaken and deceived is sometimes tempted to walk right in on the partner, trapping her or him in circumstances with a third person where no out is available. Here the aim is not, of course, to find out what is going on, since this appears to be already known, but to humiliate in the most effective and devastating manner possible. Thus a husband or wife will return home a day earlier than announced, or turn up unexpectedly at some likely place such as a motel to which the partner has been followed. Certainly a more total victory cannot be imagined. There is nothing the "guilty" party can do when "caught" but collapse in total mortification, and to this is added the relish of a devastating humiliation delivered to the third person.

Here, one is tempted to say that sexual infidelity by itself is the ultimate faithlessness, such that no response to it can be inappropriate, and that when it occurs the relationship is already bankrupt. The one who is forsaken might as well salvage his or her remaining pride by gaining the final satisfaction that possessing clear proof of infidelity brings, thereby rubbing the mate's nose in it for the sweet and final relish.

This is beyond a doubt the fundamental and most widespread error in people's thinking on these matters; namely, that infidelity is of necessity sexual, and that an adulterous partner in marriage, for example, proves by his or her very actions that love for the other is dead and that the marriage now exists in appearance and name only. People do think this way, but it is totally the result of cultural conditioning, besides being completely false.

A Moslem man believes that if his wife is raped, by enemy soldiers for example, then she is irrevocably defiled and no longer fit to live with, so she is simply discarded. We look upon such an attitude as heartless and primitive, as one that could not exist in any intelligent and enlightened mind. But our own attitude towards sexual inconstancy is no less mindless and irrational. Like that of the Moslem man, ours is the product of nothing more than religious and cultural conditioning. Our emotional reaction to it is likely to be intense, but it is no less irrational. Like the Moslem's, it is a dreadfully destructive reaction.

Nature did not make us monogamous, nor was it ever decreed that a man's or a woman's every need could be met, finally and always, by some one person. Sometimes sexual infidelity is a mere act of playfulness, without significance, and it should be treated as such by being completely ignored. Even to wonder or inquire about it is to go too far, by giving it an importance, however small, that it simply lacks. On the other hand, sexual intimacy can involve very deep feelings, and it can assume tremendous significance in a person's life. Married people can, in fact, fall in love with outsiders. To say they should not is beside the point, for they do. Nor is this any sign of weakness or moral laxity; on the contrary, weakness is far more apt to lie on the side of those law abiding and unimaginative persons who simply never expose themselves to temptation and who take a complacent, even sometimes a disgusting pride in their strict but fundamentally timid adherence to conventional standards.

People who are strong, good, even noble, and who are utterly devoted to their own partners, nevertheless occasionally become entangled in love affairs with others. No exhortations from pulpits, no reminders of vows or promises, no inner resolutions are going to change this fact. The terse "Thou shalt not" long ago ceased to deserve any but the most simple-minded tribute. To think that even the strictest ethic of marriage can consist of this command alone is to dishonor husbands and wives by supposing that they have little capacity for feeling and thought and are unable to rise to a higher standard of conduct than to be conditioned, like apes, to a largely groundless taboo.

It is also insufficiently appreciated that while a love affair is likely to have an intense impact upon the personalities of the two people immediately involved, it is apt to be temporary in the case of people who are married, and the feelings elicited are almost never as rich and meaningful as either partner already has for the husband or wife who is there in the background. Sometimes, to be sure, a wife or husband leaves to marry someone else, but, by the very nature of things, this happens only in those cases where profound needs were unmet in the original marriage. Shortly, we shall consider this type of situation. But for now consider the case of a perfectly happy marriage wherein one or the other partner becomes entangled in a love affair. This cannot happen, you say. But it does, and fairly often. Nothing on earth is perfect.

Every man, for example, has a boundless ego, and even though he can imagine no woman more wonderful than the partner he has, he can easily imagine someone in addition to her, and often finds himself in the company of such women. Similarly, a woman may feel in every way blessed in the partner she has, but this does not mean that she will take no notice of someone who, for example, appreciates elements in her personality or talents to which her partner is somewhat insensitive. To suppose otherwise is to presume a kind of human nature that exists nowhere on earth. What, then, of a happily married wife and mother who becomes infatuated with her English professor? Or the sincerely devoted husband and father whose animal vigor seems to him suddenly and rather overwhelmingly evoked by his secretary? The mere description of such things suggests, in its banality, the proper assessment of them; namely, that love affairs arising from circumstances like these are destined to be temporary and probably brief if left to themselves. Not much can actually be made of someone's admiration of a poetic soul, or of a woman's apparent sense of collapse in the presence of sheer prowess in a man who impresses her. Very little indeed—but love affairs can be made of such things. And because the basis of these relationships is of such limited value, the affairs are likely to be of limited duration.

Putting all of this another way, we can say that a couple who have had a long and happy marriage have innumerable things holding them together, and the product of all these things is a sincere and meaningful devotion to each other. There are memories that stretch over years, many things have been undertaken together, the successes and the failures; there are likely to be children and all the memories and feelings associated with their upbringing, and so on endlessly. Such a marriage can withstand many assaults and buffetings and still remain, not wholly intact, but not really damaged either, so far as the relationship itself is concerned. If things are left to themselves, anyone having such a marriage will never abandon it in favor of a relationship that is likely to be based upon only one or two things of comparatively trivial value. The appreciation of a woman's poetic skill, her loveliness, or her felt need for more esteem than she has, may easily lead her to the singular thrill of forbidden and passionate love, but it will not by itself lead her to the destruction of a marriage that is of inestimably greater worth to her. Similarly, the lure of sex, in and of itself, will easily lead almost any man into an affair, even at considerable risk, but he will never let that destroy the good marriage he already has. Not, that is, if things are left to take their course.

And that brings us to our next rule.

Rule Three: Stay out of it.

What, then, is to be done when one is almost sure one's partner is having an affair? Nothing, really, except to try to cultivate a certain attitude of serene confidence which will serve to put things back in order more effectively than anything else. It is almost impossible not to feel jealousy and resentment, and sometimes an appalling sense of insecurity, but these should be concealed, or at least expressed to some sympathetic ear other than that of the wandering mate. Beyond that, the most effective instrument, both for the preservation of one's own self-respect and sense of balance and for putting things in their true perspective, is a sense of humor from which you are careful to exclude any bite or edge. A husband of middle age, for example, whose ego seems suddenly carried aloft by the blandishments of a young, shallow, and bosomy nurse—secretary, student, or whomever—can be fairly comical. He views everything with gravity, finds inestimable virtue and nobility where none was apparent before, is borne down by the tragic overtones of these overpowering circumstances, and solemnly plays out the comic role until, sooner or later, he sees these new things for what they are worth, which is very little—provided, however, that things are left to run their course, without wife and friends leaping into the act. A wayward wife, on the other hand, spellbound by the first man who has ever appreciated her as a person—in other words, he nourishes her vanity—is not so comical, because she is not driven by the boundless ego of most men. The watchword for her husband should be patience rather than amusement; for in her case, too, things will run their course.

Imagine, for example, a wife in love with her music teacher, her hairdresser, or whomever, a man who is in every way a lesser person than her husband. Suppose she learns, in her husband's presence, that this lover has left forever. The natural reaction of a husband to this news, so crushing to his wife, is an inward satisfaction followed by declamations to her on how worthless he was anyway and how slight is the loss. But the right response, upon which no improvement could be made, would be sympathy. This could be expressed, for example, by asking: Would you like to be alone? A response of this sort would be neither natural nor easy, which means that it would require a man of significant strength who could rise to the occasion. But it should also be noted that it is the only kind of response that is really in keeping with the lasting love he once promised her.

What most often happens, however, when a husband or a wife finds out about an affair of the other, is everything that should not happen. That is, he (or she) throws himself (herself) into the act, becoming deeply and emotionally involved in it, enlisting the support of friends, and commencing, perhaps with their help, endless remonstrations and accusations. This never has any good result, other than the temporary release of emotion, and in fact produces exactly the result that should be prevented at all cost. The partners in this love affair now feel themselves beleaguered, friendless except for each other, and thus driven to each other's arms. Foolish as this may be, it is nevertheless virtually inevitable the moment any one makes a great thing of their affair, for the needs that drew them together to begin with are now vastly increased in intensity, and the road to destruction has been made clear.

Of course there is still the real possibility that an affair can destroy a marriage relationship. Wives do leave husbands of long standing, and husbands leave wives, in favor of others who appear on the scene. Marriage relationships that have no legal protection are even more vulnerable to this threat, which can become overwhelming and can drive one to the brink of breakdown when, in addition to the threat to home and affection, there is also a threat to one's security. This is especially threatening to numerous women, who have formed an economic dependence upon their husbands. It is clearly not enough, then, to say that someone thus threatened should just disregard what is going on, as though it were of the least importance.

But here what needs to be said once more is that no good marriage relationship can be threatened by a love affair so long as others keep out of it. A bad relationship can be endangered, and many do come to exactly this end: one partner or the other yields easily to the solicitations of what certainly looks like something better. We have to add, however, that no one is obligated to maintain a bad marriage anyway, and promises spoken long ago cannot still have meaning under these circumstances.

What is a bad marriage? Simply one in which no love exists on one or both sides. Regardless of what else may be said for such a home, how good it may look to the world, that its partners present the appearance of constancy, conspicuously adhering to every conventional standard and upholding the values that are honored everywhere, however appealing they may perhaps appear in a setting which includes beautiful children, that marriage has already failed in case love is not abundant in either partner. And it is, indeed, vulnerable to destruction by the first person who shows the slightest sign of offering a love to one partner that the other has withheld.

Thus, though a wife may be ever so dutiful, faultless, and virtuous in every skill required for the making of a home, if she lacks passion, then in a very real sense she already is without a husband, or he, at least, is without a wife. Similarly, a husband who is preoccupied with himself and his work, who is oblivious to the needs of his wife and insensitive to her vanities, who takes for granted her unique talents—whether they are significant or not—and who goes about his own business more or less as though she did not exist, has already withdrawn as a husband, except in name.

Consider, for example, a husband who works late into the night and then sleeps through most of the morning, but whose wife goes to bed early and rises at dawn; they are rarely awake in bed together. If this is the general picture of their marriage, then it is really a marriage in form only, and there is not much that would be threatened if the wife happened to fall into a love affair—except, of course, her husband's ego and pride. She never promised to protect these, however.

Let us imagine a wife who is absorbed in her children and her home to such an extent that these appear spotless and beautiful to the world; she is a woman who lives her childrens' triumphs and sorrows as they grow up, glories in the praise and envy that her house evokes from others, and, in addition, pours her remaining energy into clubs, garden, church activities, and similar laudatory things. Suppose that with all this she is cold, neither imaginative nor seductive, entirely accepting of sex but very far from her husband's apparent preoccupation with it. This marriage, too, has already failed, and there is nothing but the visible shell of it left to crumble when some third person offers the basic ingredient that is missing.

What must be remembered by those persons who wish to condemn adultery is that the primary vow of marriage is to love, and that vow is not fulfilled by the kind of endless busyness exemplified in the industrious and ever generous husband or the dedicated homemaking wife. It is true that one of the partners in marriage may well be awakened to the startling realization that the other partner has been engaged in a full-fledged affair. What has to be stressed, however, is that the first infidelity may not have been committed by the one who is having an affair. The first and ultimate infidelity is to withhold the love that was promised, and which was originally represented as the reason for marriage to begin with. In such cases adultery is not infidelity, but a natural response to it.

RULES FOR LOVERS

Those who have had great love affairs are forever glad, and forever sorry, that they have ended.

La Rochefoucauld

Rule One: Fidelity

Fidelity, "extramarital fidelity" is the rule for lovers. The words "extramarital fidelity" seem at first incongruous, as though trying to combine two ideas that do not fit. Yet that is not so, for all that the expression means is that there is a faith lovers should keep with each other, and this should be obvious by now.

This kind of fidelity gives rise to additional rules, addressing the issues of truth, discretion, accommodation, trust, and constancy.

Rule Two: Be honest.

Friends and lovers have a special obligation to candor and honesty that few relationships can demand, and one that even comes close to being absolute. The reason is that they have nothing but each other. They have no home, no children, none of the other things that go into making a marriage, or even ordinary business associations, such as partnerships. They have only each other and, by common consensus, are not even supposed to have that. Here, within a love affair, there can almost never be any reason to lie except to gain an advantage over the other, and the moment that happens the possibility of genuine love has already been all but cancelled. This is not so in other human associations. In the presence of enemies, for example, one lies in self defense, and has every right and reason to do so. No one will give true answers to a bandit's questions if he can offer lies instead. Again, lawyers lie and distort to protect their clients, for that is what they are paid to do. A defending attorney who simply presented the whole, unblemished truth to a prosecutor would not be worth his fee, and could in fact be rightly thought to have betrayed his client. And even in the case of husbands and wives, as we have seen, though the presumption of truth, candor, and openness is very high, it is far from absolute. Married people have a great deal more than each other. They have a home, and very likely children, and in any case they presumably want their marriage to last.

To the extent that any of these things do not hold—if they have no children, for example—then to that extent the expectation of complete honesty is enhanced. The truth can injure sometimes, just as falsehood can, and when home and children are involved the injury can be immense.

But in the case of lovers no truth can really injure, beyond the injury to feelings. Of course the relationship itself can be destroyed, but lovers who have nothing but each other cease to have even that when serious false representations come to be considered acceptable. Here, truth can destroy nothing that lies would not destroy just as effectively. A love affair will survive a thousand unpleasant truths, but sometimes not even a single deliberate and discovered lie.

The clearest example of wrongdoing in a love affair is for one or the other partner to conceal the fact that he or she is married. A woman is unlikely to do this, for it makes little difference to the feelings of a man to discover that an intended lover is already married. It increases his sense of caution, of course, and is clearly seen as an obstacle, but a man's passions are seldom affected by such a discovery. A woman, on the other hand, is likely to lose interest, instantly and completely, in a man she learns is already married, the more so if he is happily married. And it is quite rare for a woman to have any passionate interest in a man whose wife she knows well and admires. Two men, on the other hand, can continue a close and friendly association that they have cultivated for years even though one of them is, unbeknown to the other, deeply involved with that other's wife. Indeed they can part company at the end of a pleasant day of golfing or sailing, and one of them go straightway to the arms of the other's wife. Corresponding behavior on the part of women is far less common.

There is, then, a temptation on the part of a man to conceal the fact of his marriage. He correctly perceives it as being sometimes an obstacle. In my interviews, it was in fact quite common to find women who had been lied to in just this way. I never found a man who had been thus lied to. And it is even more common for men to pretend that they expect to divorce their wives in the near or distant future—"as soon as the children are a little older," for example. Women, it seems, seldom or never say this unless it is in fact true.

The temptation to mislead someone in matters of this kind must absolutely be suppressed, for to do otherwise is sheer exploitation. A single woman—a divorcée, for example—sometimes has a keen and very understandable wish to remarry, and will go to considerable lengths to enhance that possibility. It is a sheer barbarism, violating every conception of fairness and decency, for any man to combine that wish with his own deceptions in order to gain sexual favors from her. Here his purpose would not be a love affair, but sexual indulgence for its own sake, purchased at no cost to himself and possibly at great cost to his partner.

The case is not different in kind if a man misrepresents his marriage, without actually denying the fact of it. Therefore, if a man genuinely adores his wife and takes great pride and joy in his family, he should not pretend otherwise to any partner in a love affair, and for the same reason. The difference is only a small one of degree.

Lovers have no obligation of constancy to each other, that is, of sexual exclusiveness. Having already broken the rule of monogamy, they know that they can break it again, and again. But here, too, total honesty is needed. Sometimes lovers agree to a nonexclusive relationship, in which case there is no real need to conceal other relationships. Usually, however, there is an intense desire on both sides that the affair should be an exclusive one, excepting only the wife or husband who is already there; and if this is understood, then no deviation from it should be concealed.

So it should be with respect to everything. Matters of health, wealth, comings and goings, must be entirely open. Often one is known by his partner in a love affair better than he is known by anyone else in the world. It is something about such a relationship that can be terribly frightening, but at the same time tremendously valuable. Such knowledge should therefore be clear, not something that is contaminated with all sorts of misrepresentations.

Ideally such complete knowledge should be the rule between husbands and wives, but the "should be" does not always convert to an "is." Husbands and wives are in fact sometimes deeply threatened by even the most innocuous truths, not only about each other, but sometimes about their children as well. It is unfortunate that this is so, but it is, and such personal insecurity on the part of one mate is seldom a good reason for demolishing a marriage. A truth that is innocuous to one partner can be devastating to another, and the beauty of truth, as such, can rarely match the ugliness of the devastations that are sometimes produced this way. Understandably, a husband (or a wife) can, indeed, feel degraded by the thought that there might be someone in the world to whom more honesty is owed by the other than to him (or to her). That feeling would be entirely justified if the truth were always safe, in other words, if it would not be turned around and used against the one who dared to be honest. This is how husbands and wives really should be, that is, totally and safely honest with each other. But that is not the way they typically are, and when much more is at stake than their own feelings in the matter, it is better that truth should yield than that things far more precious should be placed in jeopardy.

Lovers have nothing but each other, and while truth can injure their feelings, sometimes severely, it can seldom destroy their affection. And nothing else exists there that is threatened with destruction.

Rule Three: Do not exhibit and boast.

A love affair is an ego trip for nearly every man, often a very big one. That is rarely all it is, for if it were, his partner would quickly lose interest; but that is usually part of it, and sometimes a very large part. His temptation is therefore to make it known to the whole world, or to as much of it as he dares. To be in love is a heady thing. But for someone to be in love with you is even more inflationary to the ego. And if that other person has every practical reason not to have such feelings, if in fact the whole thing has the aspect of being something forbidden, as in the case of every love affair, then the impact on a man's ego can be intoxicating. Here, he imagines, is someone who has every incentive and many of the strongest of social pressures not to be involved with him, but who nevertheless, it seems, adores him—for no other reason, it would appear, than his own glory and greatness. That perception is essentially illusory, of course, since her affection rests far more on her needs than any qualities of greatness in him. Still, it is a pleasant, sometimes overpowering illusion, to which even men who are quite able to perceive realities in their true light easily succumb.

Rule Four: Never deliver ultimatums.

This is a rule that applies to all persons who care for each other, whether spouses, lovers, parents, whomever. Every ultimatum produces a counter-reaction and, in the area of personal relationships, they tend to destroy the relationship itself. No one can interpret an either-or option as an expression of caring. A wife who tries to modify her husband's behavior by that kind of forced choice, or a husband who thus tries to control his wife, holds a gun that can explode in the hand and never achieves the desired result except at prohibitive cost. And the same is true for lovers.

Rule Five: Do not betray.

It is rare for a really intense love affair to end happily. The emotions involved are too strong. The needs that were more or less fulfilled in the relationship are now no longer met, and the effect can be agonizing. The ending seldom comes by mutual consent; one or the other breaks things off, sometimes more or less abruptly, leaving the other lonely and depressed and, very often, sunk in anger and bitterness. For reasons that are not very clear, it seems usually to be the male partner of the affair who withdraws. Perhaps part of the reason is that in our culture men are less likely than women to form an emotional dependence on the opposite sex. If set adrift a man can turn to other things or other persons more easily than a woman. A woman is very likely to terminate an affair if she begins to suspect that she is being "used," that is, not loved for herself and the personal qualities in which she takes pride. This almost certainly happens if she discovers that her partner behaves towards, and tries to ingratiate himself with, some lesser woman in exactly the way he does with her. And again, a woman will sometimes drop an affair in great haste if she finds her security, and perhaps that of her children, imperiled. But when fears and discoveries like this do not arise to disrupt things, then a love affair runs its course, to end sooner or later, usually with less emotional damage to the male partner.

The temptation in these circumstances is for the one who feels abandoned to get even, and of course the instrument of revenge is close at hand. One needs only to betray the secret that both have held. In this we find one of the ugliest spectacles in human relationships. Two persons who, until recently, were lovers—even, as they thought, the most genuine of lovers, without ulterior motives—are suddenly converted to implacable adversaries. This also happens in divorces, but two factors usually reduce the ugliness of these cases. For one thing, there are accepted procedures for terminating a marriage, though none for terminating an affair. And for the other, the partners of a marriage usually do not possess secret knowledge of a scandalous nature that can be used against each other, though of course sometimes they do. On the other hand, lovers always do.

If a man withdraws from an affair, leaving his partner emotionally adrift, then she is likely to have letters he has written that she can mail to his wife, or perhaps his boss. A man, of course, can do the same, in case he is the one abandoned. Weapons of deadly destructiveness are always available. It is all ugly beyond description, especially when viewed in the context of the feelings that, until shortly before, had flourished.

In fact lovers, or former lovers, rarely betray each other this way, though the possibility always exists. What chiefly restrains them is simple decency, together with a perception of the damage that is going to be done to other people. If love letters are planted, for example, then the real victim of that assault is the person who discovers them, not the person who wrote them. The effect on him is severe embarrassment and resentment, but the effect on the person who finds them—his wife, for example—may be trauma. It was not she at whom the assailant was aiming. The same occurs if the sexes are reversed. On top of this is always the real danger that an established marriage, very likely a home with children, can be destroyed by such an act, and is almost certainly damaged by it. These considerations are usually sufficient to restrain any abandoned lover from acting out an impulse of vengeance.

*   *   *

Rule Six: Do not abandon.

The end of any love affair, whether gradual or abrupt, is more or less wrenching to one or both partners. It is almost certainly unrealistic to think of such a relationship ending in smiles, its partners to be friends who might henceforth enjoy each other's occasional and casual company. The very minimum expectation, however, is that they can avoid becoming enemies, though this is often not easy. Beyond that, the rule should be not to utterly abandon, whatever pressures there might be to do so. The happiness and fulfillment that were once there are gone, but the same needs persist. They cannot be fulfilled, else the affair would go on, but at least one need that both have does not have to be disregarded, and that is the need for simple friendship and respect, even if maintained at a distance.

One reason for urging this is somewhat aesthetic in character. Things that begin well, and go well, really should end well. Whatever may be the popular and vulgar condemnation and moralizing about it, a love affair is a genuinely heavenly thing to its partners, at least for awhile. No taboos can alter this fact. Something so singular and good should really be spared utter ruination by a sad or sickening ending. Even when it can no longer be possessed, the memory of it never dies, and that memory should be a sweet one. Others might understandably protest a love affair itself, but no one can reasonably object to the memory of it, and that memory may as well be one of those things that makes growing old a bit easier.

Richard Wasserstrom

Is Adultery Immoral?

Many discussions of the enforcement of morality by the law take as illustrative of the problem under consideration the regulation of various types of sexual behavior by the criminal law. It was, for example, the Wolfenden Report's recommendations concerning homosexuality and prostitution that led Lord Devlin to compose his now famous lecture "The Enforcement of Morals." And that lecture in turn provoked important philosophical responses from H. L. A. Hart, Ronald Dworkin, and others.

Much, if not all, of the recent philosophical literature on the enforcement of morals appears to take for granted the immorality of the sexual behavior in question. The focus of discussion, at least, is on whether such things as homosexuality, prostitution, and adultery ought to be made illegal even if they are immoral, and not on whether they are immoral.

I propose in this paper to consider the latter, more neglected topic, that of sexual morality, and to do so in the following fashion. I shall consider just one kind of behavior that is often taken to be a case of sexual immorality—adultery. I am interested in pursuing at least two questions. First, I want to explore the question of in what respects adulterous behavior falls within the domain of morality at all, for this surely is one of the puzzles one encounters when considering the topic of sexual morality. It is often hard to see on what grounds much of the behavior is deemed to be either moral or immoral, for example, private homosexual behavior between consenting adults. I have purposely selected adultery because it seems a more plausible candidate for moral assessment than many other kinds of sexual behavior.

The second question I want to examine is that of what is to be said about adultery if we are not especially concerned to stay within the area of its morality. I shall endeavor, in other words, to identify and to assess a number of the major arguments that might be advanced against adultery.

This article is reprinted from Richard Wasserstrom, ed., *Today's Moral Problems* (New York: Macmillan Co., 1975), with the permission of the author.

I believe that they are the chief arguments that would be given in support of the view that adultery is immoral, but I think they are worth considering even if some of them turn out to be nonmoral arguments and considerations.

A number of the issues involved seem to me to be complicated and difficult. In a number of places I have at best indicated where further philosophical exploration is required, without having successfully conducted the exploration myself. This essay may very well be more useful as an illustration of how one might begin to think about the subject of sexual morality than as an elucidation of important truths about the topic.

Before I turn to the arguments themselves, there are two preliminary points that require some clarification. Throughout the paper I shall refer to the immorality of such things as breaking a promise, deceiving someone, and so on. In a very rough way I mean by this that there is something morally wrong in doing the action in question. I mean that the action is, in a strong sense of "prima facie," prima facie wrong or unjustified. I do not mean that it may never be right or justifiable to do the action—just that the fact that it is an action of this description always counts against the rightness of the action. I leave entirely open the question of what it is that makes actions of this kind immoral in this sense of "immoral."

The second preliminary point concerns what is meant or implied by the concept of adultery. I mean by "adultery" any case of extramarital sex, and I want to explore the arguments for and against extramarital sex, undertaken in a variety of morally relevant situations. Someone might claim that the concept of adultery is conceptually connected with the concept of immorality and that to characterize behavior as adulterous is already to characterize it as immoral or unjustified in the sense described above. There may be something to this. Hence the importance of making it clear that I want to discuss extramarital sexual relations. If they are always immoral, this is something that must be shown by argument. If the concept of adultery does in some sense entail or imply immorality, I want to ask whether that connection is a rationally based one. If not all cases of extramarital sex are immoral (again, in the sense described above), then the concept of adultery should either be weakened accordingly or restricted to those classes of extramarital sex for which the predication of immorality is warranted.

One argument for the immorality of adultery might go something like this: What makes adultery immoral is that it involves the breaking of a promise, and what makes adultery seriously wrong is that it involves the breaking of an important promise. For, so the argument might continue, one of the things the two parties promise each other when they get married is that they will abstain from sexual relationships with third parties. Because of this promise both spouses quite reasonably entertain the expectation that the other will behave in conformity with it. Hence, when one of them has sexual intercourse with a third party, he or she breaks that promise about sexual relationships that was made when the marriage was entered into and defeats the reasonable expectations of exclusivity entertained by the spouse.

In many cases the immorality involved in breaching the promise relating to extramarital sex may be a good deal more serious than that involved in the breach of other promises. This is so because adherence to this promise may be of much greater importance to them than is adherence to many of the other promises given or received by them in their lifetime. The breaking of this promise may be much more hurtful and painful than is typically the case.

Why is this so? To begin with, it may have been difficult for the nonadulterous spouse to have kept the promise. Hence that spouse may feel the unfairness of having restrained himself or herself in the absence of reciprocal restraint having been exercised by the adulterous spouse. In addition, the spouse may perceive the breaking of the promise as an indication of a kind of indifference on the part of the adulterous spouse. If you really cared about me and my feelings, the spouse might say, you would not have done this to me. And third, and related to the above, the spouse may see the act of sexual intercourse with another as a sign of affection for the other person and as an additional rejection of the nonadulterous spouse as the one who is loved by the adulterous spouse. It is not just that the adulterous spouse does not take the feelings of the nonadulterous spouse sufficiently into account; the adulterous spouse also indicates through the act of adultery affection for someone other than the nonadulterous spouse. I will return to these points later. For the present it is sufficient to note that a set of arguments can be developed in support of the proposition that certain kinds of adultery are wrong just because they involve the breach of a serious promise that, among other things, leads to the intentional infliction of substantial pain on one spouse by the other.

Another argument for the immorality of adultery focuses not on the existence of a promise of sexual exclusivity but on the connection between adultery and deception. According to this argument adultery involves deception. And because deception is wrong, so is adultery.

Although it is certainly not obviously so, I shall simply assume in this essay that deception is always immoral. Thus, the crucial issue for my purposes is the asserted connection between extramarital sex and deception. Is it plausible to maintain, as this argument does, that adultery always involves deception and is, on that basis, to be condemned?

The most obvious person upon whom deceptions might be practiced is the nonparticipating spouse; and the most obvious thing about which the nonparticipating spouse can be deceived is the existence of the adulterous act. One clear case of deception is that of lying. Instead of saying that the afternoon was spent in bed with A, the adulterous spouse asserts that it was spent in the library with B or on the golf course with C.

There can also be deception even when no lies are told. Suppose, for instance, that a person has sexual intercourse with someone other than his or her spouse and just does not tell the spouse about it. Is that deception? It may not be a case of lying if, for example, he or she is never asked by the spouse about the situation. Still, we might say, it is surely deceptive because of the promises that were exchanged at marriage. As we saw earlier, these promises provide a foundation for the reasonable belief that neither spouse will engage in sexual relationships with any other person. Hence the failure to bring the fact of extramarital sex to the attention of the other spouse deceives that spouse about the present state of the marital relationship.

Adultery, in other words, can involve both active and passive deception. An adulterous spouse may just keep silent or, as is often the case, the spouse may engage in an increasingly complex way of life devoted to the concealment of the facts from the nonparticipating spouse. Lies, half-truths, clandestine meetings, and the like may become a central feature of the adulterous spouse's existence. These are things that can and do happen, and when they do they make the case against adultery an easy one. Still, neither active nor passive deception is inevitably a feature of an extramarital relationship.

It is possible, though, that a more subtle but pervasive kind of deceptiveness is a feature of adultery. It comes about because of the connection in our culture between sexual intimacy and certain feelings of love and affection. The point can be made indirectly by seeing that one way in which we can in our culture mark off our close friends from our mere acquaintances is through the kinds of intimacies that we are prepared to share with them. I may, for instance, be willing to reveal my very private thoughts and emotions to my closest friends or to my wife but to no one else. My sharing of these intimate facts about myself is, from one perspective, a way of making a gift to those who mean the most to me. Revealing these things and sharing them with those who mean the most to me is one means by which I create, maintain, and confirm those interpersonal relationships that are of most importance to me.

In our culture, it might be claimed, sexual intimacy is one of the chief currencies through which gifts of this sort are exchanged. One way to tell someone—particularly someone of the opposite sex—that you have feelings of affection and love for them is by allowing them, or sharing with them, sexual behaviors that one does not share with others. This way of measuring affection was certainly very much a part of the culture in which I matured. It worked something like this: If you were a girl, you showed how much you liked a boy by the degree of sexual intimacy you would allow. If you liked him only a little you never did more than kiss—and even the kiss was not very passionate. If you liked him a lot and if your feeling was reciprocated, necking and, possibly, petting were permissible. If the attachment was still stronger and you thought it might even become a permanent relationship, the sexual activity was correspondingly more intense and intimate, although whether it led to sexual intercourse depended on whether the parties (particularly the girl) accepted fully the prohibition on nonmarital sex. The situation for the boys was related but not exactly the same. The assumption was that males did not naturally link sex with affection in the way in which females did. However, since women did link sex with affection, males had to take that fact into account. That is to say, because a woman would permit sexual intimacies only if she had feelings of affection for the male and only if those feelings were reciprocated, the male had to have and express those feelings too, before sexual intimacies of any sort would occur.

The result was that the importance of a correlation between sexual intimacy and feelings of love and affection was taught by the culture and assimilated by those growing up in the culture. The scale of possible positive feelings toward persons of the other sex ran from casual liking, at one end, to the love that was deemed essential to, and characteristic of, marriage, at the other. The scale of possible sexual behavior ran from brief, passionless kissing or hand-holding, at one end, to sexual intercourse, at the other. And the correlation between the two scales was quite precise. As a result, any act of sexual intimacy carried substantial meaning with it, and no act of sexual intimacy was simply a pleasurable set of bodily sensations. Many such acts were, of course, more pleasurable to the participants because they were a way of saying what their feelings were. And sometimes they were less pleasurable for the same reason. The point is, however, that sexual activity was much more than mere bodily enjoyment. It was not like eating a good meal, listening to good music, lying in the sun, or getting a pleasant back rub. It was behavior that meant a great deal concerning one's feelings for persons of the opposite sex in whom one was most interested and with whom one was most involved. It was among the most authoritative ways in which one could communicate to another the nature and degree of one's affection.

If this sketch is even roughly right, then several things become somewhat clearer. To begin with, a possible rationale for many of the rules of conventional sexual morality can be developed. If, for example, sexual intercourse is associated with the kind of affection and commitment to another that is regarded as characteristic of the marriage relationship, then it is natural that sexual intercourse should be thought properly to take place between persons who are married to each other. And if it is thought that this kind of affection and commitment is only to be found within the marriage relationship, then it is not surprising that sexual intercourse should only be thought to be proper within marriage.

Related to what has just been said is the idea that sexual intercourse ought to be restricted to those who are married to each other, as a means by which to confirm the very special feelings that the spouses have for each other. Because our culture teaches that sexual intercourse means that the strongest of all feelings for each other are shared by the lovers, it is natural that persons who are married to each other should be able to say this to each other in this way. Revealing and confirming verbally that these feelings are present is one thing that helps to sustain the relationship; engaging in sexual intercourse is another.

In addition, this account would help to provide a framework within which to make sense of the notion that some sex is better than other sex. As I indicated earlier, the fact that sexual intimacy can be meaningful in the sense described tends to make it also the case that sexual intercourse can sometimes be more enjoyable than at other times. On this view, sexual intercourse will typically be more enjoyable if strong feelings of affection are present than it will be if it is merely "mechanical." This is so in part because people enjoy being loved, especially by those whom they love. Just as we like to hear words of affection, so we like to receive affectionate behavior. And the meaning enhances the independently pleasurable behavior.

More to the point, an additional rationale for the prohibition on extramarital sex can now be developed. For given this way of viewing the sexual world, extramarital sex will almost always involve deception of a deeper sort. If the adulterous spouse does not in fact have the appropriate feelings of affection for the extramarital partner, then the adulterous spouse is deceiving that person about the presence of such feelings. If, on the other hand, the adulterous spouse does have the corresponding feelings for the extramarital partner but not toward the nonparticipating spouse, the adulterous spouse is very probably deceiving the nonparticipating spouse about the presence of such feelings toward that spouse. Indeed, it might be argued, whenever there is no longer love between the two persons who are married to each other, there is deception just because being married implies both to the participants and to the world that such a bond exists. Deception is inevitable, the argument might conclude, because the feelings of affection that ought to accompany any act of sexual intercourse can only be held toward one other person at any given time in one's life. And if this is so, then the adulterous spouse always deceives either the partner in adultery or the nonparticipating spouse about the existence of such feelings. Thus extramarital sex involves deception of this sort and is for that reason immoral even if no deception vis-à-vis the occurrence of the act of adultery takes place.

What might be said in response to the foregoing arguments? The first thing that might be said is that the account of the connection between sexual intimacy and feelings of affection is inaccurate—not in the sense that no one thinks of things that way but in the sense that there is substantially more divergence of opinion than the account suggests. For example, the view I have delineated may describe reasonably accurately the concepts of the sexual world in which I grew up, but it does not capture the sexual *Weltanschauung* of today's youth at all. Thus, whether or not adultery implies deception in respect to feelings depends very much on the persons who are involved and the way they look at the "meaning" of sexual intimacy.

Second, the argument leaves unanswered the question of whether it is desirable for sexual intimacy to carry the sorts of messages described above. For those persons for whom sex does have these implications there are special feelings and sensibilities that must be taken into account. But it is another question entirely whether any valuable end—moral or otherwise—is served by investing sexual behavior with such significance. That is something that must be shown and not just assumed. It might, for instance, be the case that substantially more good than harm would come from a kind of demystification of sexual behavior—one that would encourage the enjoyment of sex more for its own sake and one that would reject the centrality both of the association of sex with love and of love with only one other person.

I regard these as two of the more difficult unresolved issues that our culture faces today in respect of thinking sensibly about the attitudes toward sex and love that we should try to develop in ourselves and in our children.

Much of the contemporary literature that advocates sexual liberation of one sort or another embraces one or the other of two different views about the relationship between sex and love. One view holds that sex should be separated from love and affection. To be sure, sex is probably better when the partners genuinely like and enjoy being with each other. But sex is basically an intensive, exciting sensuous activity that can be enjoyed in a variety of suitable settings with a variety of suitable partners. The situation in respect to sexual pleasure is no different from that of the person who knows and appreciates fine food and who can have a satisfying meal in any number of good restaurants with any number of congenial companions. One question that must be settled here is whether sex can be thus demystified; another, more important, question is whether it would be desirable to do so. What might we gain and what might we lose if we all lived in a world in which an act of sexual intercourse was no more or less significant or enjoyable than having a delicious meal in a nice setting with a good friend? The answer to this question lies beyond the scope of this essay.

The second view of the relationship between sex and love seeks to drive the wedge in a different place. On this view it is not the link between sex and love that needs to be broken, but rather the connection between love and exclusivity. For a number of the reasons already given it is desirable, so this argument goes, that sexual intimacy continue to be reserved to and shared with only those for whom one has very great affection. The mistake lies in thinking that any "normal" adult will have those feelings toward only one other adult during his or her lifetime—or even at any time in his or her life. It is the concept of adult love, not ideas about sex, that needs demystification. What are thought to be both unrealistic and unfortunate are the notions of exclusivity and possessiveness that attach to the dominant conception of love between adults in our culture and others. Parents of four, five, six, or even ten children can certainly claim, and sometimes claim correctly, that they love all of their children, that they love them all equally, and that it is simply untrue to their feelings to insist that the numbers involved diminish either the quantity or the quality of their love. If this is readily understandable in the case of parents and children, there is no necessary reason why it is an impossible or undesirable ideal in the case of adults. To be sure, there is probably a limit to the number of intimate, "primary" relationships that any person can maintain at any given time without affecting the quality of the relationship. But one adult ought surely to be able to love two, three, or even six other adults at any one time without that love being different in kind or degree from that of the traditional, monogamous, lifetime marriage. And between the individuals in these relationships, whether within a marriage or without, sexual intimacy is fitting and good.

The issues raised by a position such as the one described above are also surely worth exploring in detail and with care. Is there something to be called "sexual love" that is different from parental love or the nonsexual love of close friends? Is there something about love in general that links it naturally and appropriately with feelings of exclusivity and possession? Or is there something about sexual love, whatever that may be, that makes these feelings especially fitting? Once again, the issues are conceptual, empirical, and normative all at once: What is love? How could it be different? Would it be a good thing or a bad thing if it were different?

Suppose, though, that having delineated these problems we were now to pass them by. Suppose, moreover, that we were to be persuaded of the possibility and the desirability of weakening substantially either the links between sex and love or the links between sexual love and exclusivity. Would it not then be the case that adultery could be free from all of the morally objectionable features described thus far? To be more specific, let us imagine that a husband and wife have what is today sometimes characterized as an "open marriage." Suppose, that is, that they have agreed in advance that extramarital sex is—under certain circumstances—acceptable behavior for each to engage in. Suppose that as a result there is no impulse to deceive each other about the occurrence or nature of any such relationships and that no deception in fact occurs. Suppose, too, that there is no deception in respect to the feelings involved between the adulterous spouse and the extramarital partner. And suppose, finally, that one or the other or both of the spouses then has sexual intercourse in circumstances consistent with these understandings. Under this description, so the argument might conclude, adultery is simply not immoral. At a minimum adultery cannot very plausibly be condemned either on grounds that it involves deception or on grounds that it requires the breaking of a promise.

At least two responses are worth considering. One calls attention to the connection between marriage and adultery; the other looks to more instrumental arguments for the immorality of adultery. Both deserve further exploration.

One way to deal with the case of the "open marriage" is to question whether the two persons involved are still properly to be described as being married to each other. Part of the meaning of what it is for two persons to be married to each other, so this argument would go, is to have committed oneself to have sexual relationships only with one's spouse. Of course, it would be added, we know that that commitment is not always honored. We know that persons who are married to each other often do commit adultery. But there is a difference between being willing to make a commitment to marital fidelity, even though one may fail to honor that commitment, and not making the commitment at all. Whatever the relationship may be between the two individuals in the case just described, the absence of any commitment to sexual exclusivity requires the conclusion that their relationship is not a marital one. For a commitment to sexual exclusivity is a necessary but not a sufficient condition for the existence of a marriage.

Although there may be something to this suggestion, it is too strong as stated to be acceptable. To begin with it is doubtful that there are many, if any, *necessary* conditions for marriage; but even if there are, a commitment to sexual exclusivity is not such a condition.

To see that this is so, consider what might be taken to be some of the essential characteristics of a marriage. We might be tempted to propose that the concept of marriage requires the following: a formal ceremony of some sort in which mutual obligations are undertaken between two persons of the opposite sex; the capacity on the part of the persons involved to have sexual intercourse with each other; the willingness to have sexual intercourse only with each other; and feelings of love and affection between the two persons. The problem is that we can imagine relationships that are clearly marital and yet lack one or more of these features. For example, in our own society it is possible for two persons to be married without going through a formal ceremony, as in the common-law marriages recognized in some jurisdictions. It is also possible for two persons to get married even though one or both lacks the capacity to engage in sexual intercourse. Thus, two very elderly persons who have neither the desire nor the ability to have intercourse can nonetheless get married, as can persons whose sexual organs have been injured so that intercourse is not possible. And we certainly know of marriages in which love was not present at the time of the marriage, as, for instance, in marriages of state and marriages of convenience.

Counterexamples not satisfying the condition relating to the abstention from extramarital sex are even more easily produced. We certainly know of societies and cultures in which polygamy and polyandry are practiced, and we have no difficulty in recognizing these relationships as cases of marriages. It might be objected, though, that these are not counterexamples because they are plural marriages rather than marriages in which sex is permitted with someone other than one of the persons to whom one is married. But we also know of societies in which it is permissible for married persons to have sexual relationships with persons to whom they are not married, for example, temple prostitutes, concubines, and homosexual lovers. And even if we knew of no such societies, the conceptual claim would still, I submit, not be well taken. For suppose all of the other indicia of marriage were present: suppose the two persons were of the opposite sex; suppose they had the capacity and desire to have intercourse with each other; suppose they participated in a formal ceremony in which they understood themselves voluntarily to be entering into a relationship with each other in which substantial mutual commitments were assumed. If all these conditions were satisfied we would not be in any doubt as to whether or not the two persons were married, even though they had not taken on a commitment of sexual exclusivity and even though they had expressly agreed that extramarital sexual intercourse was a permissible behavior for each to engage in.

A commitment to sexual exclusivity is neither a necessary nor a sufficient condition for the existence of a marriage. It does, nonetheless, have this much to do with the nature of marriage—like the other indicia enumerated above, its presence tends to establish the existence of a marriage. Thus, in the absence of a formal ceremony of any sort an explicit commitment to sexual exclusivity would count in favor of regarding the two persons as married. The conceptual role of the commitment to sexual exclusivity can, perhaps, be brought out through the following example. Suppose we found a tribe that had a practice in which all the other indicia of marriage were present but in which the two parties were *prohibited* even from having sexual intercourse with each other. Moreover, suppose that sexual intercourse with others was clearly permitted. In such a case we would, I think, reject the idea that the two persons were married to each other, and we would describe their relationship in other terms, for example, as some kind of formalized, special friendship relation—a kind of heterosexual "blood-brother" bond.

Compare that case with the following one. Again suppose that the tribe had a practice in which all of the other indicia of marriage were present, but instead of a prohibition on sexual intercourse between the persons in the relationship there was no rule at all. Sexual intercourse was permissible with the person with whom one had this ceremonial relationship, but it was no more or less permissible than with a number of other persons to whom one was not so related (for instance, all consenting adults of the opposite sex). While we might be in doubt as to whether we ought to describe the persons as married to each other, we would probably conclude that they were married and that they simply were members of a tribe whose views about sex were quite different from our own.

What all of this shows is that a *prohibition* on sexual intercourse between the two persons involved in a relationship is conceptually incompatible with the claim that the two of them are married. The *permissibility* of intramarital sex is a necessary part of the idea of marriage. But no such incompatibility follows simply from the added permissibility of extramarital sex.

These arguments do not, of course, exhaust the arguments for the prohibition on extramarital sexual relations. The remaining argument that I wish to consider is—as I indicated earlier—a more instrumental one. It seeks to justify the prohibition by virtue of the role that it plays in the development and maintenance of nuclear families. The argument, or set of arguments, might, I believe, go something like this:

Consider first a far-fetched nonsexual example. Suppose a society were organized so that after some suitable age—say 18, 19, or 20—persons were forbidden to eat anything but bread and water with anyone but their spouse. Persons might still choose in such a society not to get married. Good food just might not be very important to them because they have underdeveloped taste buds. Or good food might be bad for them because there is something wrong with their digestive system. Or good food might be important to them, but they might decide that the enjoyment of good food would get in the way of the attainment of other things that were more important. But most persons would, I think, be led to favor marriage in part because they preferred a richer, more varied diet to one of bread and water. And they might remain married because the family was the only legitimate setting within which good food was obtainable. If it is important to have society organized so that persons will both get married and stay married, such an arrangement would be well suited to the preservation of the family, and the prohibitions relating to food consumption could be understood as fulfilling that function.

It is obvious that one of the more powerful human desires is the desire for sexual gratification. The desire is a natural one, like hunger and thirst, in the sense that it need not be learned in order to be present within us and operative on us. But there is in addition much that we do learn about what the act of sexual intercourse is like. Once we experience sexual intercourse ourselves—and, in particular, once we experience orgasm—we discover that it is among the most intensive, short-term pleasures of the body.

Because this is so it is easy to see how the prohibition on extramarital sex helps to hold marriage together. At least during that period of life when the enjoyment of sexual intercourse is one of the desirable bodily pleasures, persons will wish to enjoy those pleasures. If one consequence of being married is that one is prohibited from having sexual intercourse with anyone but one's spouse, then the spouses in a marriage are in a position to provide an important source of pleasure for each other that is unavailable to them elsewhere in the society.

The point emerges still more clearly if this rule of sexual morality is seen as being of a piece with the other rules of sexual morality. When this prohibition is coupled, for example, with the prohibition on nonmarital sexual intercourse, we are presented with the inducement both to get married and to stay married. For if sexual intercourse is only legitimate within marriage, then persons seeking that gratification that is a feature of sexual intercourse are furnished explicit social directions for its attainment, namely, marriage.

Nor, to continue the argument, is it necessary to focus exclusively on the bodily enjoyment that is involved. Orgasm may be a significant part of what there is to sexual intercourse, but it is not the whole of it. We need only recall the earlier discussion of the meaning that sexual intimacy has in our own culture to begin to see some of the more intricate ways in which sexual exclusivity may be connected with the establishment and maintenance of marriage as the primary heterosexual love relationship. Adultery is wrong, in other words, because a prohibition on extramarital sex is a way to help maintain the institutions of marriage and the nuclear family.

I am frankly not sure what we are to say about an argument such as the preceding one. What I am convinced of is that, like the arguments discussed earlier, this one also reveals something of the difficulty and complexity of the issues that are involved. So what I want now to do in the final portion of this essay is to try to delineate with reasonable precision several of what I take to be the fundamental, unresolved issues.

The first is whether this last argument is an argument for the *immorality* of extramarital sexual intercourse. What does seem clear is that there are differences between this argument and the ones considered earlier. The earlier arguments condemned adulterous behavior because it was behavior that involved breaking a promise, taking unfair advantage of or deceiving another. To the degree to which the prohibition on extramarital sex can be supported by arguments that invoke considerations such as these, there is little question but that violations of the prohibition are properly regarded as immoral. And such a claim could be defended on one or both of two distinct grounds. The first is that action such as promise-breaking and deception are simply wrong. The second is that adultery involving promise-breaking or deception is wrong because it involves the straightforward infliction of harm on another human being—typically the nonadulterous spouse—who has a strong claim not to have that harm so inflicted.

The argument that connects the prohibition on extramarital sex with the maintenance and preservation of the institution of marriage is an argument for the instrumental value of the prohibition. To some degree this counts, I think, against regarding all violations of the prohibition as obvious cases of immorality. This is so partly because hypothetical imperatives are less clearly within the domain of morality than are categorical ones, and even more because instrumental prohibitions are within the domain of morality only if the end that they serve or the way that they serve it is itself within the domain of morality.

What this should help us see, I think, is the fact that the argument that connects the prohibition on adultery with the preservation of marriage is at best seriously incomplete. Before we ought to be convinced by it, we ought to have reasons for believing that marriage is a morally desirable and just social institution. And such reasons are not quite as easy to find or as obvious as it may seem. For the concept of marriage is, as we have seen, both a loosely structured and a complicated one. There may be all sorts of intimate, interpersonal relationships that will resemble but not be identical with the typical marriage relationship presupposed by the traditional sexual morality. There may be a number of distinguishable sexual and loving arrangements that can all legitimately claim to be called *marriages*. The prohibitions of the traditional sexual morality may be effective ways to maintain some marriages and ineffective ways to promote and preserve others. The prohibitions of the traditional sexual morality may make good psychological sense if certain psychological theories are true, and they may be purveyors of immense psychological mischief if other psychological theories are true. The prohibitions of traditional sexual morality may seem obviously correct if sexual intimacy carries the meaning that the dominant culture has often ascribed to it, and they may seem equally bizarre if sex is viewed through the perspective of the counterculture. Irrespective of whether instrumental arguments of this sort are properly deemed moral arguments, they ought not fully convince anyone until questions such as these are answered.

MARRIAGE

John McMurtry

Monogamy: A Critique

Remove away that black'ning church
Remove away that marriage hearse
Remove away that man of blood
You'll quite remove the ancient curse.
—William Blake

I

Almost all of us have entered or will one day enter a specifically standardized form of monogamous marriage. This cultural requirement is so very
basic to our existence that we accept it for most part as a kind of intractable given—dictated by the laws of God, Nature, Government, and Good
Sense all at once. Though it is perhaps unusual for a social practice to be
so promiscuously underwritten, we generally find comfort rather than
curiosity in this fact and seldom wonder how something could be divinely
inspired, biologically determined, coerced, and reasoned out all at the
same time. We simply take for granted.

Those in society who are officially charged with the thinking function
with regard to such matters are no less responsible for this uncritical
acceptance than is the man on the street. The psychoanalyst traditionally
regards our form of marriage as a necessary restraint on the anarchic id
and no more to be queried than civilization itself. The lawyer is as undis-
posed to questioning the practice as he is to criticizing the principle of pri-

This article is reprinted from *The Monist* 56, no. 4 (1972), La Salle, Illinois, with
the permission of the author and publisher.

vate property (this is appropriate, as I shall later point out). The church-man formally perceives the relationship between man and wife to be as inviolable and insusceptible to question as the relationship between the institution he works for and the Christ. The sociologist standardly accepts the formalized bonding of heterosexual pairs as the indispensable basis of social order and perhaps a societal universal. The politician is as incapable of challenging it as he is the virtue of his own continued holding of office. And the philosopher (at least the English-speaking philosopher), as with most issues of socially controversial or sexual dimensions, ignores the question almost altogether.

Even those irreverent adulterers and unmarried couples who seem to be challenging the institution in the most basic possible way, in practice, tend merely to mimic its basic structure in unofficial form. The coverings of sanctities, taboos, and cultural habit continue to hold them with the grip of public clothes.

II

"Monogamy" means, literally, "one marriage." But it would be wrong to suppose that this phrase tells us much about our particular species of official wedlock. The greatest obstacle to the adequate understanding of our monogamy institution has been the failure to identify clearly and sys-tematically the full complex of principles it involves. There are four such principles, each carrying enormous restrictive force and together con-stituting a massive social-control mechanism that has never, so far as I know, been fully schematized. To come straight to the point, the four prin-ciples in question are as follows:

1. *The partners are required to enter a formal contractual relation:* (a) whose establishment demands a specific official participant, certain conditions of the contractors (legal age, no blood ties, and so on), and a standard set of procedures; (b) whose governing terms are uniform for all and exactly prescribed by law; and (c) whose dissolution may only be legally effected by the decision of state representatives.

The ways in which this elaborate principle of contractual requirement is importantly restrictive are obvious. One may not enter into a mar-riage union without entering into a contract presided over by a state-investured official.[1] One may not set any of the terms of the contractual relationship by which one is bound for life. And one cannot dissolve the contract without legal action and costs, court proceedings, and in many places actual legislation. (This is the one and only contract in all English-speaking law that is not dissoluble by the consent of the contracting parties.) The extent of control here—over the most intimate and putatively "loving" relationships in all social intercourse—is so great as to be difficult to catalogue without exciting in oneself a sense of disbelief.

Lest it be thought there is always the real option of entering a common-law relationship free of such encumbrances, it should be noted that: (a) these relationships themselves are subject to state regulation, though of a less imposing sort; and (much more important) (b) there are very formidable selective pressures against common-law partnerships, such as employment and job discrimination, exclusion from housing and lodging facilities, special legal disablements,[2] loss of social and moral status (consider such phrases as "living in sin" and "make her an honest woman"), family shame and embarrassment, and so on.

2. *The number of partners involved in the marriage must be two and only two* (as opposed to three, four, five, or any of the almost countless possibilities of intimate union). This second principle of our specific form of monogamy (the concept of "one marriage," it should be pointed out, is consistent with any number of participating partners) is perhaps the most important and restrictive of the four principles we are considering. Not only does it confine us to just one possibility out of an enormous range, but it confines us to that single possibility that involves the least number of people, two. It is difficult to conceive of a more thoroughgoing mechanism for limiting extended social union and intimacy. The fact that this monolithic restriction seems so "natural" to us (if it were truly "natural," of course, there would be no need for its rigorous cultural prescription by everything from severe criminal law[3] to ubiquitous housing regulations) simply indicates the extent to which its hold is implanted in our social structure. It is the institutional basis of what I will call the "binary frame of sexual consciousness," a frame through which all our heterosexual relationships are typically viewed ("two's company, three's a crowd") and in light of which all larger circles of intimacy seem almost inconceivable.[4]

3. *No person may participate in more than one marriage at a time or during a lifetime* (unless the previous marriage has been officially dissolved by, normally, one partner's death or a divorce). Violation of this principle is, of course, a criminal offense (bigamy) that is punishable by a considerable term in prison. Of various general regulations of our marriage institution, it has experienced the most significant modification, not indeed in principle, but in the extent of flexibility of its "escape hatch" of divorce. The ease with which this escape hatch is opened has increased considerably in the past few years (the grounds for divorce being more permissive than previously) and it is in this regard most of all that the principles of our marriage institution have undergone formal alteration—

that is, in plumbing rather than substance.

4. *No married person may engage in any sexual relationship with any person other than the marriage partner.* Although a consummated sexual act with another person alone constitutes an act of adultery, lesser forms of sexual and erotic relationships[5] may also constitute grounds for divorce (for example, cruelty) and are generally proscribed as well by informal social convention and taboo. In other words, the fourth and final principle of our marriage institution involves not only a prohibition of sexual intercourse per se outside one's wedlock (this term deserves pause) but a prohibition of all one's erotic relations whatever outside this bond. The penalties for violation here are as various as they are severe, ranging from permanent loss of spouse, children, chattel, and income to job dismissal and social ostracism. In this way, possibly the most compelling natural force toward expanded intimate relations with others is strictly confined within the narrowest possible circle for (barring delinquency) the whole of adult life.[6] The sheer weight and totality of this restriction is surely one of the great wonders of all historical institutional control.

III

With all established institutions, apologetics for perpetuation are never wanting. Thus it is with our form of monogamous marriage.

Perhaps the most celebrated justification over the years has proceeded from the belief in a Supreme Deity, who secretly utters sexual and other commands to privileged human representatives. Almost as well known a line of defense has issued from a similarly confident conviction that the need for some social regulation of sexuality demonstrates the need for our specific type of two-person wedlock. Although these have been important justifications in the sense of being very widely supported, they are not—having other grounds than reason—susceptible to treatment here.

If we put aside such arguments, we are left, I think, with two major claims. The first is that our form of monogamous marriage promotes a profound affection between the partners that is not only of great worth in itself but invaluable as a sanctuary from the pressures of outside society. Since, however, there are no secure grounds whatever for supposing that such "profound affection" is not at least as easily achievable by any number of *other* marriage forms (that is, forms that differ in one or more of the four principles), this justification conspicuously fails to perform the task required of it.

The second major claim for the defense is that monogamy provides a specially loving context for child-upbringing. However, here again there are no grounds at all for concluding that it does so as, or any more, effectively than other possible forms of marriage. (The only alternative type of upbringing to which it has apparently been shown to be superior is non-family institutional upbringing, which of course is not relevant to the present discussion.) Furthermore, the fact that at least half the span of a normal monogamous marriage involves no child-upbringing at all is overlooked here, as is the reinforcing fact that there is no reference to or mention of the quality of child-upbringing in any of the prescriptions connected with it.

In brief, the second major justification of our particular type of wedlock scents somewhat too strongly of red herring to pursue further.

There is, it seems, little to recommend the view that monogamy specially promotes "profound affection" between the partners or a "loving context" for child-upbringing. Such claims are simply without force. On the other hand, there are several aspects to the logic and operation of the four principles of this institution that suggest that it actually *inhibits* the achievement of these desiderata. Far from uniquely abetting the latter, it militates against them in these ways:

1. Centralized official control of marriage (which the Church gradually achieved through the mechanism of Canon Law after the fall of the Roman Empire[7] in one of the greatest seizures of social power of history) necessarily alienates the partners from full responsibility for and freedom in their relationship. "Profound closeness" between the partners—or at least an area of it—is thereby expropriated rather than promoted and "sanctuary" from the pressures of outside society prohibited rather than fostered.

2. Limitation of the marriage bond to two people necessarily restricts, in perhaps the most unilateral way possible consistent with offspring survival, the number of adult sources of affection, interest, and material support and instruction for the young. The "loving context for child-upbringing" is thereby dessicated rather than nourished, providing the structural conditions for such notorious and far-reaching problems as sibling rivalry for scarce adult attention[8] and parental oppression through exclusive monopoly of the child's means of life.[9]

3. Formal exclusion of all others from erotic contact with the marriage partner systematically promotes conjugal insecurity, jealousy, and alienation in several ways. (a) It officially underwrites a literally totalitarian expectation of sexual confinement on the part of one's husband or wife: which expectation is, *ceteris paribus*, inevitably more subject to anxiety and disappointment than one less extreme in its demand and/or

cultural-juridical backing.[10] (b) It requires so complete a sexual isolation of the marriage partners that should one violate the fidelity code the other is left alone and susceptible to a sense of fundamental deprivation and resentment. It stipulates such a strict restraint of sexual energies that there are habitual violations of the regulations, frequently if not always attended by willful deception and reciprocal suspicion about the occurrence or quality of the extramarital relationship, anxiety and fear on both sides of permanent estrangement from partner and family, and overt and covert antagonism over the prohibited act in both offender (who feels "trapped") and offended (who feels "betrayed").

The disadvantages of the four principles of monogamous marriage do not, however, end with inhibiting the very effects they are said to promote. There are further shortcomings:

1. The restriction of marriage union to two partners necessarily prevents the strengths of larger groupings. Such advantages as the following are thereby usually ruled out: (a) the security, range, and power of larger socioeconomic units; (b) the epistemological and emotional substance, variety, and scope of more pluralist interactions; (c) the possibility of extra-domestic freedom founded on more adult providers and upbringers as well as more broadly based circles of intimacy.

2. The sexual containment and isolation that the four principles together require variously stimulates such social malaises as: (a) destructive aggression (which notoriously results from sexual frustration); (b) apathy, frustration, and dependence within the marriage bond; (c) lack of spontaneity, bad faith, and distance in relationships without the marriage bond; (d) sexual fantasizing, perversion, fetishism, prostitution, and pornography in the adult population as a whole.[11]

Taking such things into consideration, it seems difficult to lend credence to the view that the four principles of our form of monogamous marriage constitute a structure beneficial either to the marriage partners themselves or to their offspring (or indeed to anyone else). One is moved to seek for some other ground of the institution, some ground that lurks beneath the reach of our conventional apprehensions.

IV

The ground of our marriage institution, the essential principle that underwrites all four restrictions, is this: *the maintenance by one man or woman of the effective right to exclude indefinitely all others from erotic access to the conjugal partner.*

The first restriction creates, elaborates on, and provides for the enforcement of this right to exclude. And the second, third, and fourth restrictions together ensure that the right to exclude is—respectively—not cooperative, not simultaneously or sequentially distributed, and not permissive of even casual exception.

In other words, the four restrictions of our form of monogamous marriage together constitute a state-regulated, indefinite, and exclusive ownership by two individuals of one another's sexual powers. Marriage is simply a form of private property.[12]

That our form of monogamous marriage is, when the confusing layers of sanctity, apologetic, and taboo are cleared away, another species of private property should not surprise us.[13] The history of the institution is so full of suggestive indicators—dowries, inheritance, property alliances, daughter sales (of which women's wedding rings are a carry-over), bride exchanges, and legitimacy and illegitimacy—that it is difficult not to see some intimate connections between marital and ownership ties. We are better able still to apprehend the ownership essence of our marriage institution, when in addition we consider: (1) that until recently almost the only way to secure official dissolution of consummated marriage was to be able to demonstrate violation of one or both partner's sexual ownership, (that is, adultery); (2) that the imperative of premarital chastity is tantamount to a demand for retrospective sexual ownership by the eventual marriage partner; (3) that successful sexual involvement with a married person is prosecutable as an expropriation of ownership—"alienation of affections"—which is restituted by cash payment; (4) that the incest taboo is an iron mechanism that protects the conjugal ownership of sexual properties, both the husband's and wife's, from the access of affectionate offspring and the offsprings' (who themselves are future marriage partners) from access of siblings and parents;[14] (5) that the language of the marriage ceremony is the language of exclusive possession ("take," "to have and to hold," "forsaking all others and keeping you only unto him/her," and so on, not to mention the proprietary locutions associated with the marital relationship ("he's mine," "she belongs to him," "keep to your own husband," "wife stealer," "possessive husband," and so on).

V

Of course, it would be remarkable if marriage in our society was not a relationship akin to private property. In our socioeconomic system we relate to virtually everything of value by individual ownership: by, that is, the effective right to exclude others from the thing concerned.[15] That we do so as well with perhaps the most highly valued thing of all—the sexual partners' sexuality—is only to be expected. Indeed, it would probably be an intolerable strain on our entire social structure if we did otherwise.

This line of thought deserves pursuit. The real secret of our form of monogamous marriage is not that it functionally provides for the needs of adults who love one another or of the children they give birth to but that it serves the maintenance of our present social system. It is an institution that is indispensable to the persistence of the capitalist order[16] in the following ways:

1. A basic principle of current social relations is that some people legally acquire the use of other people's personal powers, from which they may exclude other members of society. This system operates in the workplace (owners and hirers of all types contractually acquire for their exclusive use workers' regular labor powers) and in the family (husbands and wives contractually acquire for their exclusive use their partner's sexual properties). A conflict between the structures of these primary relations— as would obtain were there a suspension of the restrictions governing our form of monogamous marriage—might well undermine the systemic coherence of present social intercourse.

2. The fundamental relation between individuals and things that satisfy their needs is, in our present society, that each individual has or does not have the effective right to exclude other people from the thing in question.[17] A rudimentary need is that for sexual relationship(s). Therefore the object of this need must be related to the one who needs it as owned or not owned (that is, via marriage or not-marriage, or approximations thereof) if people's present relationship to what they need is to retain —again—systemic coherence.

3. A necessary condition for the continued existence of the present social formation is that its members feel a powerful motivation to gain favorable positions in it. But such social ambition is heavily dependent on the preservation of exclusive monogamy in that (a) the latter confines the discharge of primordial sexual energies to a single unalterable partner and thus typically compels those energies to seek alternative outlet, such as business or professional success[18] and (b) the exclusive marriage necessarily reduces the sexual relationships available to any one person to absolute (nonzero) minimum, a unilateral promotion of sexual shortage that in practice renders hierarchial achievement essential as an economic and "display" means for securing scarce partners.[19]

4. Because the exclusive marriage necessarily and dramatically reduces the possibilities of sexual-love relationships, it thereby promotes the existing economic system by: (a) rendering extreme economic self-interest —the motivational basis of the capitalistic process—less vulnerable to

altruistic subversion; (b) disciplining society's members into the habitual repression of natural impulse required for long-term performance of repetitive and arduous work tasks; (c) developing a complex of suppressed sexual desires to which sales techniques may be effectively applied in creating those new consumer wants that provide indispensable outlets for ever increasing capital funds.

5. The present form of marriage is of fundamental importance to (a) the continued relative powerlessness of the individual family: which, with larger numbers would constitute a correspondingly increased command of social powers; (b) the continued high demand for homes, commodities, and services: which, with the considerable economies of scale that extended unions would permit, would otherwise falter; (c) the continued strict necessity for adult males to sell their labor power and for adult women to remain at home (or vice versa): which strict necessity would diminish as the economic base of the family unit extended; (d) the continued immense pool of unsatisfied sexual desires and energies in the population at large: without which powerful interests and institutions would lose much of their conventional appeal and force;[20] (e) the continued profitable involvement of lawyers, priests, and state officials in the jurisdictions of marriage and divorce and the myriad official practices and proceedings connected thereto.[21]

VI

If our marriage institution is a linchpin of our present social structure then a breakdown in this institution would seem to indicate a breakdown in our social structure. On the face of it, the marriage institution is breaking down—enormously increased divorce rates, nonmarital sexual relationships, wife-swapping, the Playboy philosophy, and communes. Therefore one might be led by the appearance of things to anticipate a profound alteration in the social system.

But it would be a mistake to underestimate the tenacity of an established order or to overestimate the extent of change in our marriage institution. Increased divorce rates merely indicate the widening of a traditional escape hatch. Nonmarital relationships imitate and culminate in the marital mold. Wife-swapping presupposes ownership, as the phrase suggests. The Playboy philosophy is merely the view that if one has the money one has the right to be titillated—the commercial call to more fully exploit a dynamic sector of capital investment. And communes—the most hopeful phenomenon—almost nowhere offer a *praxis* challenge to private property in sexuality. It may be changing. But history, as the old man puts it, weighs like a nightmare on the brains of the living.

NOTES

1. Any person who presides over a marriage and is not authorized by law to do so is guilty of a criminal offense and is subject to several years imprisonment (for example, Canadian Criminal Code, Sec. 258.) Here and elsewhere, I draw examples from Canadian criminal law. There is no reason to suspect the Canadian code is eccentric in these instances.

2. For example, offspring are illegitimate, neither the wife nor children are legal heirs, and the husband has no right of access or custody should separation occur.

3. "Any kind of conjugal union with more than one person at the same time, whether or not it is by law recognized as a binding form of marriage—is guilty of an indictable offence and is liable to imprisonment for five years" (Canadian Criminal Code, Sec. 257, [1] [a] [ii]). Part 2 of the same section adds: "Where an accused is charged with an offence under this section, no averment or proof of the method by which the alleged relationship was entered into, agreed to or consented to is necessary in the indictment or upon the trial of the accused, nor is it necessary upon the trial to prove that the persons who are alleged to have entered into the relationship had or intended to have sexual intercourse."

4. Even the sexual revolutionary Wilhelm Reich seems constrained within the limits of this "binary frame." Thus he says: "Nobody has the right to prohibit his or her partner from entering a temporary or lasting sexual relationship with someone else. He has only the right *either to withdraw or to win the partner back*" (Wilhelm Reich, *The Sexual Revolution*, trans. T. P. Wolfe [New York: Farrar, Straus & Giroux, 1970], p. 28. Emphasis added.) The possibility of sexual partners extending their union to include the other loved party (as opposed to one partner having either to "win" against this third party or to "withdraw" altogether) does not seem even to occur to Reich.

5. I will be using "sexual" and "erotic" interchangeably throughout this paper.

6. It is worth noting here that: (*a*) man has by nature the most "open" sexual instinct—year-round operativeness and response to a wide variety of stimuli—of all the species (except perhaps the dolphin); and (*b*) it is a principle of human needs in general that maximum satisfaction involves regular variation in the form of the need-object.

7. "Roman law had no power of intervening in the formation of marriages and there was no legal form of marriage. . . . Marriage was a matter of simple private agreement and divorce was a private transaction" (Havelock Ellis, *Studies in the Psychology of Sex* [New York: Random House, 1963], vol. 2, p. 429).

8. The dramatic reduction of sibling rivalry through an increased number of adults in the house is a phenomenon that is well known in contemporary domestic communes.

9. One of the few other historical social relationships I can think of in which one person holds thoroughly exclusive monopoly over another's means of life is slavery. Thus, as with another's slave, it is a criminal offense to "receive" or "harbor" another's child without "right of possession" (Canadian Criminal Code, Sec. 250).

10. Certain cultures, for example, permit extramarital sexuality by married persons with friends, guests, or in-laws with no reported consequences of jealousy. From such evidence, one is led to speculate that the intensity and extent of jealousy at a partner's extramarital sexual involvement is in direct proportion to the

severity of the accepted cultural regulations against such involvements. In short such regulations do not prevent jealousy so much as effectively engender it.

11. It should not be forgotten that at the same time marriage excludes marital partners from sexual contact with others, it necessarily excludes those others from sexual contact with marital partners. Walls face two ways.

12. Those aspects of marriage law that seem to fall outside the pale of sexual property holding—for example, provisions for divorce if the husband fails to provide or is convicted of a felony or is an alcoholic—may themselves be seen as simply prescriptive characterizations of the sort of sexual property that the marriage partner must remain to retain satisfactory conjugal status; a kind of permanent warranty of the "good working order" of the sexual possession.

What constitutes the "good working order" of the conjugal possession is, of course, different in the case of the husband and in the case of the wife: an *asymmetry* within the marriage institution that, I gather, women's liberation movements are anxious to eradicate.

13. It is instructive to think of even the nonlegal aspects of marriage, for example, its sentiments, as essentially private-property structured. Thus the preoccupation of those experiencing conjugal sentiments with expressing how much "my very own," "my precious," the other is, with expressing, that is, how valuable and inviolable the ownership is and will remain.

14. I think the secret to the long-mysterious incest taboo may well be the fact that in all its forms it protects sexual property: not only conjugal (as indicated above) but paternal and tribal as well. This crucial line of thought, however, requires extended separate treatment.

15. Sometimes—as with political patronage, criminal possession, de facto privileges, and so forth—a *power* to exclude others exists with no corresponding "right" (just as sometimes a right to exclude exists with no corresponding power). Therefore, properly speaking, I should here use the phrase "power to exclude," which covers "effective right to exclude" as well as all nonjuridical enablements of this sort.

16. It is no doubt indispensable as well—in some form or other—to any private-property order. Probably (if we take the history of Western society as our data base) the more thoroughgoing and developed the private-property formation is, the more total the sexual ownership prescribed by the marriage institution.

17. Things in unlimited supply—like, presently, oxygen—are not of course related to people in this way.

18. This is, of course, a Freudian or quasi-Freudian claim. "Observation of daily life shows us," says Freud, "that most persons direct a very tangible part of their sexual motive powers to their professional or business activities" (Sigmund Freud, *Dictionary of Psychoanalysis*, ed. Nandor Fodor and Frank Gaynor [New York: Fawcett Publications, Premier Paperback, 1966], p. 139).

19. It might be argued that exclusive marriage also protects those physically less attractive persons who—in an "open" situation—might be unable to secure any sexual partnership at all. The force of this claim depends, I think, on improperly continuing to posit the very principle of exclusiveness that the "open" situation rules out (for example, in the latter situation, X might be less attractive to Y than Z is and yet Z not be rejected, any more than at present an intimate friend is rejected who is less talented than another intimate friend).

20. The sexual undercurrents of corporate advertisements, religious systems, racial propaganda, and so on, are too familiar to dwell on here.

21. It is also possible that exclusive marriage protects the adult-youth power structure in the manner outlined on p. 171.

David Palmer

The Consolation of the Wedded

It will be agreed that all this sanctimonious prudish world . . . that this heap of libertines and intriguers who disguise themselves behind a verbiage of fidelity, is a bigamous, trigamous and polygamous world in every degree.

Those who hasten to invalidate my thesis will surely be the most guilty in these matters, because false prudes always rise up violently against the vices from which they secretly profit.

—Charles Fourier, The New Theory of Society.

"With all established institutions," John McMurtry tells us, "apologetics for perpetuation are never wanting."[1] If that is so it is surely because the critics of those institutions are never silent. And, indeed, the criticisms directed at monogamy are many and varied. But in spite of the title of this essay, I enter the discussion as no dogmatist—neither as apologist nor as critic. I propose instead to spend these few pages in investigating some of the kinds of claims and criticisms to which the institution of marriage has been subjected in both the nineteenth and twentieth centuries. If I rise up violently against any vices, I hope that they shall be only the philosophical vices of conceptual confusion or specious argument and that these shall not be vices from which I secretly profit. First, then, what is the nature of the institution that finds such vocal critics and such a profusion of apologists?

Unfortunately, it is not clear that we can do more than list certain fairly common features of marriage. For example, there is usually a temporally extended relationship between (or among) two or more individuals; this usually involves (1) a sexual relationship; (2) the expectation of procreation; (3) certain expectations or even agreements to provide economic, physical, or psychological support for one another; and (4) a ceremonial event recognizing the creation of the marriage. However, none of these is a *necessary* condition of marriage, and if they are logically *sufficient* conditions when taken jointly, it is probably because of the inclusion of feature number 4. And, in effect, number 4 says only that *whatever* is recog-

119

nized within the social context as a marriage *is* a marriage—that is, that what is sufficient to constitute a marriage is dependent upon the social structure and institutions of the society. But of course this does not constitute a definition.

It is largely because marriage (and monogamy) is so widespread that arriving at a definition of it is so difficult. That is, the practice of marriage transcends our society and its customs, habits, legal systems, social institutions, and ways of life. Any successful attempt to define marriage would have to define it in terms of social institutions or practices that were necessarily present wherever marriage could occur; but as it turns out, there are few, if any, institutions as universal as marriage. In our society marriage may, for example, be first and foremost a legal relationship. But, unfortunately for the attempt to arrive at a definition, there is no reason to think that marriage could not exist in a prelegal society or as a religious and nonlegal relationship. Thus there seem to be no necessary conditions of marriage apart from that of involving (at least) two individuals. The concept of marriage seems to have all the marks of what philosophers call a "primitive," that is, simple or unanalyzable, concept. Hence, with respect to monogamy, we can say only that it is the practice of being married to no more than one person at a time.[2]

Given this very limited amount of essential formal structure involved in monogamous marriage, it is probably inevitable that many critiques of monogamy will turn out to be directed not at monogamy itself but at monogamy of some particular description and in some social context. Indeed, some critiques of marriage or monogamy have taken the form of an attack on one or more of the social or economic concomitants of marriage in one particular setting and thus have little to do with that relationship per se. For example, the undesirable aspects of monogamy or marriage may be a function of religious traditions that make divorce or remarriage after the death of a spouse impossible, or of a legal system of a particular state at a particular time that subordinates one spouse to another or fails to provide for a just property settlement upon termination of a marriage, or of various other social conditions and economic difficulties that are reflected in marriage and the family.

There is, of course, nothing wrong with pointing out the difficulties people face in marriage or the evils of marriage or monogamy *as a special set of customs in a particular setting*, even when those difficulties and evils are a consequence of factors quite extrinsic to marriage or monogamy per se. Yet there is always the danger that the reader, if not the author himself, may become conceptually muddled about the distinction between (1) a certain set of social practices at a certain time and place, and (2) a transplantable institution like monogamy. As a result, he will confuse a justifiable attack on the first with a justifiable attack on the second. That is to say, a monogamous relationship may be damnable either because *monogamy* is bad or because the relationship is surrounded with and contaminated by a variety of other evil and unhappy institutions and practices. Very different conclusions are warranted in one case than in the other.

Karl Marx, to whom many twentieth-century critics of marriage owe a considerable intellectual debt, was often far more careful than his followers have been to recognize this distinction between criticism of the institution of marriage and criticism of the practices and institutions that surround it. In fact, in 1842 Marx wrote approvingly of romantic love and of monogamous relationships between men and women, speaking, for example, of "the sanctification of the sex drive through *exclusiveness*, the restraint of the drive through law, the *ethical beauty* which turns nature's command into an ideal moment of spiritual union—the *spiritual essence* of marriage." [3] And in a later article he opposed the liberalization of divorce laws on the grounds of the importance to children of a family structure that could not be readily dissolved. [4]

Marx's later attacks on this exclusive relationship and the family structure were founded not on any conviction that these early views were fundamentally mistaken but rather on the discovery that love, which should be (and could be) the fundamental principle of family life, had been replaced in that role by the ownership of property. [5] Private property made a family life based on love impossible. [6] With the development of a communal economy, the division of labor, unequal division of the products of labor, and the increasing accumulation of goods, changes were brought about in the nature of the family. In fact, Marx wrestled mightily with the problem of explaining the origin of private property and the emergence of male dominance and of slavery within the family. He hoped to account for these developments in a way that did not support the capitalist economists' view that they were due to an innate desire of man to acquire goods and dominate other people. [7] That is, he hoped to show that there is nothing in the nature of the individual or of the monogamous relationship *as such* that makes monogamous marriage undesirable. He wrote, in 1846, for example, "Assume particular stages of development in production, commerce, and consumption and you will have a corresponding social constitution, a corresponding organization of the family, of order, of classes: in a word, a corresponding civil society." [8] Clearly, Marx himself, perhaps unlike his followers, placed the source of evil not in marriage or monogamy but in other social conditions and developments.

It may be that many people have been misled about the nature of

Marx's views on marriage and the family by his calls for an end to marriage and for the substitution of a new set of male-female relationships.[9] However, the suggestion that the institutions of marriage and the family should be destroyed was not based on the inherent evils of these institutions, as many later interpreters of Marx have assumed, but rather on his conviction that this would be a pragmatic means of implementing changes in yet other institutions and practices that were indeed inherently bad. But it must not be thought that the means of social reform necessarily reflect the structure of the evils of society. There may be a causal relationship between the destruction of monogamous marriage and the destruction of other institutions in the society. Yet, it does not follow from this that the evils of monogamous marriage are the cause of the evils of society.[10]

Certainly, not all critiques of monogamy have been limited to the consideration of extrinsic social and economic concomitants of marriage. A notable alternative is the sustained attack on monogamy by the early nineteenth-century French social utopian Charles Fourier. Fourier is especially interesting, not only because of his strong influence on Marx and the relative modernity of his views on society, sex, and the family, but also because his attack on monogamy is designed to show that institution—independent of other social institutions and practices—to be unsatisfactory as a model for human relationships.

Fourier held that the monogamous relationship was essentially an incomplete relationship. A complete unit of the human species in the physical or material sense consists of two individuals, two bodies—one male and one female. But man consists of more than body alone, more than material man. He also consists of soul, personality, or "passional man." And just as no male or female is materially complete alone, so no individual, and indeed no couple, is passionally complete. For, rather than two individuals, as in the case of physical man, it takes 810 individuals—810 distinct character types, in the ratio of 415 men to 395 women, to make up the complete passional man:

> ... if a thousand men were presented to form a human body, we should have to reject 999, and to the one which remained add a woman. Now if ... the integrality of the human body requires two different bodies, should we be surprised that the integrality of the soul may require two or even two thousand souls? ...
>
> When the 810 characters are brought together and fully developed, forming the complete passional man ... it will be seen that in this new order the poorest individual may develop and satisfy more of the passions of the soul than the richest potentate can do in the present day, and the greater the inequalities in fortune, intelligence, etc., the easier will association rise to a

general accord, which will be as perfect as the muscles of the body, or the various instruments of a good orchestra—the latter being an image of the human passions, which constitute an orchestra of 810 instruments.[11]

To the extent that Fourier has this metaphysical view of the nature of man, he has a basis for the claim that monogamy and the family are not the social relationships for which man is best suited—a far different kind of criticism of monogamy than we have so far seen. Fourier proposes the creation of Phalansteries—ideal communities composed of the various passional components working together in a tightly knit socialistic unit that would be so economically viable as to be able to provide all its members with a life of luxury and so emotionally harmonious as to be able to provide satisfaction for the sexual desires and emotional needs of all of its members.[12]

But even Fourier's criticism of marriage and the family is not made strictly on metaphysical grounds. If one reads on one finds that his views on marriage were influenced by sixteen other problems that beset marriage at the turn of the nineteenth century in France—all of them institutions and practices and problems not essentially connected with monogamy and many of which no longer exist.

Unfortunately, not everyone criticizing the practice of monogamy, even in this century, has been careful to determine in any clear way what is and what is not an essential part of that institution. The awkward consequence is that what is claimed to be a critique of marriage or monogamy often turns out to be a critique of factors that are essentially independent of the marriage relationship. I believe that Professor McMurtry's critique of monogamy to a large extent contains just this sort of conceptual confusion. There are, in fact, three major points that I should like to make about his critique. First, there is a consistent failure on his part to identify unambiguously the object of his attack. Is it the institution of monogamy or the social problems and practices of some particular group? Second, certain psychological criticisms he makes of monogamy, like Fourier's analysis of the passional man, presuppose, yet utterly lack, supporting empirical data. And third, his ultimate analysis of the nature of monogamous marriage—that it is essentially an ownership relation—is not only false but implausible. I shall discuss these points in order.

McMurtry talks about "our specific species of official wedlock," "our monogamy institution," "our specific form of monogamy," and "our marriage institution," all in the context of attempting to "identify clearly and systematically the full complex of principles it involves."[13] Indeed, in the very process of identifying these principles (which themselves require some critical scrutiny) he makes repeated references to local laws and attitudes making marriage, and perhaps specifically monogamy, *in those circumstances* less desirable than it might otherwise be. Such laws and attitudes include the requirement of a state-investitured official, a formal contractual agreement (about the terms of which the partners have nothing to say and the dissolution of which must be effected by a state representative), certain specific laws concerning rights of inheritance from common-law marriage, public hostility to common-law relationships, and local prejudices against sexual liaisons outside of marriage.[14]

But, as we have seen, a catalog of such ills may not be very interesting to someone concerned with the relationship apart from its local peculiarities—to someone concerned with the institution of monogamy and not with the fairness of the laws of Ontario. Needless to say, those who have defended monogamy as an institution have neither thought nor argued that the institution, no matter what its social environment and local forms, would rectify the social ills of the society or satisfy all the needs of the participants. At some times and under some conditions and for some individuals, marriage has no doubt contributed significantly to unhappiness.

But it is, after all, McMurtry's real aim to go beyond a criticism of the local conditions and the locally unique institution he has described. Indeed he seems to use this particular form of monogamy, complete with its sociogeographical and temporal context and restrictive principles, as a model on which to base his attacks on the institution as a whole. Thus, after having talked about "our marriage institutions," he suggests that *"the four principles of monogamous marriage"* (note the sudden generality) inhibit "the very effects they are said to promote."[15] Among those desirable effects are a closeness between the partners, a sanctuary from the pressures of outside society, and a loving context for child upbringing. And just how are these desired effects inhibited? Profound closeness, we are told, is "expropriated" and sanctuary from outside pressures is "prohibited" by "centralized official control of marriage."[16] But these, we respond, are certainly not problems with *monogamy*, or with a principle of "monogamous marriage." They are at most local conditions, the burden of which may be felt in marriage as elsewhere in the social structure. That is, on one hand, "centralized official control" is not necessary for marriage, but on the other hand such bureaucratic control *may* extend not only to marriage but also to one's job, residence, travel, education, and other aspects of life as well. The problem, then, is centralized official control and its effects, not marriage.

With a similar disdain for identifying clearly the object of his attack, McMurtry claims that the "number of adult sources of affection, interest, material support, and instruction for the young" is restricted by monogamy "in perhaps the most unilateral possible way consistent with offspring survival."[17] Now in the first place this is sheer hyperbole. Whether we look to the extended families of London's East End, to any number of preindustrial and tribal societies, to the Old South of Katherine Anne Porter, or to the Israeli kibbutz, there is, in general, no lack of sources of adult support for children in either the family itself or the community at large.[18] And the same is true to varying, though diminished, degrees even in a highly mobile industrial society. Furthermore, it is clear that what limits the sources of affection and support for children is not monogamy but social conditions and practices, including the type of housing, the cohesiveness of the extended family, the proximity and interest of friends and neighbors—that is, conditions that are largely extrinsic to marriage.

While listing the societal ills that are heaped at the doorstep of marriage, I might note that McMurtry also claims that there are economic disadvantages of monogamy, such as loss of "the security, range, and power of larger socioeconomic units" and loss of "the possibility of extradomestic freedom founded on more adult providers and upbringers." But here, once again, we have a criticism that presupposes a specific economic and social context for the marriage. These economic problems, if indeed they are problems at all, are not a fault especially of marriage or monogamy but a failure of the society and the individuals involved to form alliances that provide for these needs. After all, if the Israeli Kibbutz provides certain strengths that families collected into cities do not, it is not because the institution of monogamy exists in one place and not in the other. It is rather because we have failed to desire, or, perhaps, failed to combine our efforts in, cooperative ventures for the production of material needs, childcare, multifamily dwelling units, and so on—all of which are perfectly compatible with monogamous marriage.

Another class of criticisms McMurtry directs against monogamy is concerned with supposed psychological effects of the institution. We are told that monogamy "systematically promotes conjugal insecurity, jealousy, and alienation" and that it stimulates destructive aggression, apathy, frustration, dependence, lack of spontaneity, bad faith, sexual fantasizing, perversion, fetishism, prostitution, and pornography, and, presumably, that it does this to a greater extent than would other kinds of male-female relationships.[19] The obvious question here is whether and to what extent these psychological difficulties are (a) the effect of monogamy as opposed to other factors in the culture, such as the pressure to succeed in economic and social ways; (b) reducible by changes in the structure of marriage; and (c) less desirable than the psychological and social problems resulting from some other structure of male-female relationships.

So far as I am aware, McMurtry's charge amounts to little more than a bit of armchair speculation (neither more nor less supported than Fourier's analysis of passional man). McMurtry has made an empirically testable claim about the effects of marriage; it is one that most psychologists and sociologists writing on marriage do not affirm, not because they are apologists for the institution of marriage, but because they lack the requisite empirical evidence.[20] McMurtry's only indication of how he was led to these conclusions is a footnote in which we are told that cultures permitting extramarital sexuality have no reported consequences of jealousy. He is "led to speculate" that jealousy of a partner's extramarital sexual involvement is in proportion to the severity of cultural regulations against such involvements.[21] His speculations might better have led him to the conclusion that jealousy might be avoided by adherence to the principle "what's sauce for the goose is sauce for the gander." In any event, it is certain that such speculations do not begin to answer the crucial questions raised in a, b, and c, and that answers to these would be necessary before it would be reasonable to reject the institution of monogamy on grounds of the psychological harm that it does.

Finally, a third point in McMurtry's critique of monogamy is the claim that marriage is simply a form of private property in which the two partners own one another's sexual powers—marriage is ownership.[22] It would, I think, be worthwhile to briefly consider some of the similarities and differences between marriage, contracts, and ownership.

In the standard case of private property in which one owns a car, an umbrella, or a piece of land, ownership provides one with (1) the right to exclude others from access to or use of those items; (2) the right, should one so desire, to allow others access to or the use of those items; (3) the right to use those items as one sees fit, roughly to the point of not interfering with the rights of others; (4) the right to sell those items for other considerations—money, land, a car, and so on. In addition, it is also the case that (5) the items owned do not have an equal and reciprocal right to the owner. All of this, by the way, holds true in the paradigm case of ownership of human beings and their services—slavery.

By contrast, in the case of contracts one agrees to exchange services or goods with another legally recognized entity on a basis that both parties believe to be to their mutual advantage. The failure of one party to fulfill his part of his contract is in itself sufficient grounds for nonfulfillment by the other party and termination of the contract (or even restitution if that is called for). But the case is notably different if I own someone, say Jones, or his labor or services; for then there are no comparable rights or legally enforceable expectations by whatever (whomever) is owned. Now, just as the conventions of leasing and renting are different from owning, so too is contracting for a service different from owning it. *Thus it would be a gross logical error to argue that the structural similarities between these relations renders them identical.* But this is precisely what McMurtry does when he adduces the "systemic coherence" of marriage and ownership: "It would be remarkable if marriage in our society was not a relationship akin to private property. In our socioeconomic system we relate to virtually everything of value by individual ownership: that is, by the effective right to exclude others from the thing concerned."[23]

The thrust of my argument is that McMurtry has committed precisely the logical error discussed above; for marriage is yet another nonownership relation. It is not only that marriage fails to fulfill conditions of ownership but, contrary to the heart of McMurtry's analysis, marriage is not essentially "the maintenance by one man or woman of the effective right to exclude indefinitely all others from erotic access to the conjugal partner." That is, marriage in fact fails to fulfill even the *first* condition of ownership—the one that McMurtry cites as the "grounds of our marriage institution."[24]

To see that this is true we need only consider that each individual has, and after marriage retains, the sole right to enter into or refrain from sexual relations with others. It is not the right of one partner to prevent the other from engaging in sexual relationships with someone else. It is only the partner's right to ask for a termination of the marriage should this happen. Similarly, no one has the right by virtue of *marriage*, and independent of other social customs, to dispose of his partner's sexual powers as he might his private property. (One could not, for example, *sell* one's partner's sexual powers.) Thus, to attempt to assimilate marriage to ownership is surely a conceptual confusion.

If the marriage relationship is reducible to some other species of relationship at all, it is certainly more akin to what I have described as a contractual relationship than to an ownership relationship. That should not be surprising, for in this society marriage is, among other things, a kind of contract. (McMurtry himself notes that it is a unique kind of contract.[25]) I would not, however, want to suggest that marriage is essentially a contract or, indeed, that it is reducible to any other kind of relationship or institution. A contractual relationship is a legal relationship, and, while the marriage relationship may be a legal relationship in this culture, it can presumably exist in a prelegal society, or as a religious institution, or in quite different societies and under quite different social conditions. It is for this reason that I suggested earlier that the concept of marriage appears to be an irreducible one.

We can see from this investigation into some of the claims and criticisms to which the institution of monogamy has been subjected that many popular criticisms of it are in reality criticisms of social institutions, practices, and conditions with which it is in no way essentially related. Moreover, we have seen that any charges to be made on the basis of alleged psychological ills deriving from marriage require a substantial empirical basis that is not currently available. And finally, at least one interesting attempt to understand the real nature of marriage, namely, that it is "simply a form of private property," fails.

It may fairly be said that I have not provided much consolation for the wedded. But my task has merely been to show that a few of the arguments against monogamy are not as convincing as some may previously have thought. But nevertheless, while we may continue to nod assent to the assertion in *Twelfth Night* that we are "better well-hung than ill-wed," at least we no longer have any reason to deny the suggestion that we might be better off hanging together than hanging separately. And that may be some consolation.

NOTES

1. John McMurtry, "Monogamy: A Critique," herein, p. 110.

2. Monogamy contrasts with bigamy, trigamy, or any other form of polygamy. Each of these is a form of marriage in which there is marriage to more than one person at the *same time*. It is sometimes held that monogamy contrasts with digamy or deuterogamy, in which there is marriage to only one person at a time but to more than one person during a lifetime. However, in its broadest sense monogamy is compatible with digamy or deuterogamy. If we do not allow for more than one marriage during a lifetime, then we shall have to hold that we do not practice monogamy, and consequently that a critique or a defense of that institution is, from our point of view, merely academic.

3. Lloyd D. Easton and R. H. Guddat, eds., *Writings of the Young Marx on Philosophy and Society.* (Garden City, N.Y.: Doubleday, 1967), pp. 101-02. For a recent discussion of these ideas see Russell Jacoby, "The Politics of Subjectivity: Slogans of the American New Left," *New Left Review* 79 (May-June, 1973): 37-49. For an excellent discussion of the development of Marx's views on marriage and the family, including these quotations as well as central problems of the origins of male domination, I am indebted to an unpublished manuscript by Robert P. Neuman entitled "Karl Marx on Women, Marriage and the Family."

4. Easton and Guddat, *Writings*, p. 139.

5. Karl Marx, *Critique of Hegel's Philosophy of Right*, ed. J. O'Malley (Cambridge: The University Press, 1970), pp. xxxvii, 90.

6. Neuman notes that Marx was here taking up a "fundamental tenet of the 'critical utopian socialists'" and had not yet reached the point of calling for an end to private property.

7. Ibid.

8. Marx-Engels, *Werke*, 27:452. (Letter to P. V. Annenkev, Dec. 28, 1846).

9. Such as those in Marx's and Engels' *The Communist Manifesto* or *The German Ideology*.

10. Note McMurtry's talk of marriage as the "linchpin of our present social structure," p. 115. He too may be more concerned with an attack upon monogamy as a means of altering society in other ways rather than as an end in itself.

11. Charles Fourier, *Harmonian Man: Selected Writings of Charles Fourier*, ed. Mark Poster (Garden City, N.Y.: Doubleday, Anchor Books, 1971), p. 116-17.

12. But even in Fourier's case, the discovery that large communal groupings of the sort he advocates are more desirable than cities composed of families seems to be dependent upon particular economic circumstances. He says: "It is the only system adapted to the requirements of the passions; the only one by which industry can be rendered attractive . . . if economy and profits can result only from large numbers and extensive combinations, God must have based his calculation on large associations; and our political theories which would base the accord of the passions on the smallest possible union, that of a single family, are utterly absurd" (p. 124).

13. McMurtry, "Monogamy," p. 108 and elsewhere. The four principles are detailed on pp. 108-110.

14. Ibid., pp. 108-110.

15. Ibid., p. 112.

16. Ibid., p. 110.

17. Ibid., p. 111.

18. See especially Michael Young and Peter Willmett, *Family and Kinship in East London* (London: Penguin, 1960). Also, "Is the Family Universal," Melford E. Spiro, in *American Anthropologist* 56 (1954): 839-46.

19. McMurtry, "Monogamy," p. 112.

20. Even those (for example, psychologists) advocating social change, including a full range of possible marriage relationships, while claiming that conventional marriage and family life are responsible for possessiveness, jealousy, the prevailing neurotic climate, pervasive insecurity, and so on, offer no evidence. See, for example, Lawrence Casler, "Permissive Matrimony: Proposals for the Future," *The Humanist* (March/April 1974), p. 5. I am not arguing against complete freedom in these matters, but I see no reason to think changes in marriage a panacea for our emotional problems.

21. McMurtry, "Monogamy," note 10.

22. Ibid., pp. 112-113.

23. Ibid., p. 113.

24. Ibid., p. 112.

25. Ibid., p. 108.

Michael D. Bayles

Marriage, Love, and Procreation

The current era is one of that vulgar form of hedonism rejected by philosophical hedonists such as Epicurus and John Stuart Mill.[1] Apologists thinly disguise the tawdriness of a hedonism of biological pleasures by appeals to individual rights and autonomy. Far too frequently these appeals merely mask a refusal to accept responsibility. This failure to accept personal responsibility is periodically atoned for by ritualistic and ill-conceived attempts to help the poor and underprivileged people of the world.

One of the central focuses of the current vulgar hedonism has been sexual liberation. Premarital intercourse, gay liberation, no-fault divorce, open marriage (read, "open adultery"), polygamy, and orgies all have their advocates. About the only forms of sexual behavior yet to have strong advocates are pedophilia and bestiality. Any day now one may expect grade-school children to assert their right to happiness through pedophilia and animal lovers to argue that disapproval of bestiality is unfair to little lambs.

The result, especially in Western society, is an emphasis on sex that is out of all proportion to its significance for a eudaemonistic life—that is, a life worth living, including elements besides pleasure. The only ultimate test for the value of a life is whether at its end it is found to have been worth living. It is difficult to conceive of a person's thinking his life significant because it was a second-rate approximation to the sexual achievements of the notorious rabbit. However, many people seem to think such a life offers the highest ideal of a "truly human" existence, forgetting Aristotle's insight that reproduction is characteristic of all living things, not just humans.[2] Consequently, the institution of marriage has been attacked for hindering the achievement of this vulgar hedonistic ideal.

ATTACKS ON MARRIAGE

Not all attacks on the institution of marriage have been based solely on the

130

vulgar hedonistic ideal. A more broad ranging, although no more plausible, attack has recently been made by John McMurtry. His attack is directed not against marriage per se but against that form of it found in Western society—monogamy. McMurtry does not merely find that monogamous marriage hinders the achievement of the vulgar hedonistic ideal. He also claims it is at least one of the causes of the following social ills: (1) Central official control of marriage *"necessarily* alienates the partners from full responsibility for and freedom in their relationship."[3] (2) Monogamy restricts the sources of adult affection and support available to children.[4] (3) It "systematically promotes conjugal insecurity, jealousy, and alienation. . . ."[5] (4) It "prevents the strengths of larger groupings."[6] (5) It stimulates aggression, apathy, frustration, lack of spontaneity, perversion, fetishism, prostitution, and pornography.[7] (6) It serves to maintain the status quo and capitalism.[8] (7) It supports the powerlessness of the individual family by keeping it small.[9] (8) By promoting many small families it creates a high demand for homes and consumer goods and services.[10] (9) It makes it necessary for many more males to sell their labor than would be necessary if monogamy were not practiced.[11] (10) By limiting opportunities for sexual satisfaction it channels unsatisfied desire into support for various institutions and interests.[12] (11) Finally, it promotes financial profit for lawyers, priests, and so forth, in marriage and divorce proceedings.[13] Such a catalog of evils omits only a few social problems such as political corruption and environmental deterioration, although even they are hinted at in numbers 8 and 11.

Many people have hoped that the simple-mindedness that attributes all or most or even many of society's ills to a single factor would disappear. At one time private ownership of the means of production was the *bête noir* of society.[14] Recently it has been replaced in that role by unlimited population growth.[15] Both of these beasts have been slain by the St. George of reasonableness.[16] McMurtry has called forth yet another single-factor beast. There is no reason to suppose this one to be any more powerful than its predecessors.

No attempt will be made in this essay to examine in detail McMurtry's criticisms of monogamous marriage. In general they are characterized by a lack of historical and sociological perspective. It is unclear whether he is attacking the ideal of monogamous marriage as it perhaps existed a hundred years ago or as it exists today. Yet this difference is crucial. A century ago divorce was not widely recognized or accepted; today that is not true. When divorce was not recognized, concubinage and prostitution were quite prevalent, as was simply abandoning one's family.

Such practices certainly mitigated the effect of the strict social rules that McMurtry discusses. Also, he criticizes monogamy for limiting the access of children to adult affection and support, since they must rely upon their parents alone for care. But in the extended family, which existed until the urbanization of society, that limitation was considerably less common than it may be at present.

McMurtry seems to be unaware of the social realities of modern society. He emphasizes the law as it is written rather than the law in action. It is generally recognized that despite the wording of statutes, marriages can in practice now be dissolved by mutual consent.[17] Nor is adultery usually prosecuted in those states in which it is still a crime. Nor does McMurtry present any sociological evidence for the various effects that he claims monogamous marriage has. Sometimes the evidence may well be against him. For example, he claims that monogamy supports the high demand for homes. Yet, for a century in Ireland monogamy coincided with a low demand for new homes. Couples simply postponed marriage until the male inherited the home of his parents, and those who did not inherit often did not marry.[18]

Underlying McMurtry's view of monogamous marriage is the Kantian conception of the marriage contract. According to Kant, marriage "is the Union of two Persons of different sex for life-long reciprocal possession of their sexual faculties."[19] McMurtry takes the following principle to be the essential ground of monogamous marriage: "the maintenance by one man or woman of the effective right to exclude indefinitely all others from erotic access to the conjugal partner."[20] Since by "possession" Kant meant legal ownership and the consequent right to exclude others, these two views come to the same thing. They both view marriage as chiefly concerned with private ownership of the means to sexual gratification, thus combining capitalism with vulgar hedonism (although Kant was not a hedonist).

Such a view of marriage is pure nonsense. However, it has more plausibility in today's era of vulgar hedonism than it did in Kant's time. Historically, the official aims of marriage, according to the Catholic Church—which was the only church during the period of the establishment of monogamous marriage in Western society—were procreation and companionship. There was also a tendency to view it as a legitimate outlet for man's sinful nature.[21] It is this latter element that Kant and McMurtry have taken as the chief one.

In addition to the avowed purposes of marriage there were the actual social functions that it performed. The family unit was the basic social unit, not only for the education of children (that is, socialization, not formal schooling—which has only become widespread during the past century), but also for the production of necessities, including food and clothing, and for recreation. These historical functions of the extended-family unit based on monogamous marriage have been undermined by the development of industrial, urban society.[22] Consequently, the moral and legal status and functions of marriage require reexamination in the light of current social conditions.

Before undertaking such a reexamination it is necessary to distinguish between rules of marriage and attendant social rules. They are mixed together in the traditional social institution of monogamous marriage, but there is no necessity for this mix and it is probably unjustified. In particular one must distinguish between penal laws prohibiting various forms of sexual union—homosexual, premarital, adulterous—and private arranging laws granting legal recognition to the marital relationship.[23] Private arranging laws do not prescribe punishment for offenses; instead, they enable people to carry out their desires. People are not punished for improperly made marriages; instead, the marriages are invalid and unenforceable. Laws against fornication, prostitution, cohabitation, and homosexuality are almost always penal. Objections to them cannot be transferred directly to the marriage relationship. All of these penal laws could be abolished and monogamous marriage could still be retained.

It may be claimed that despite their nonpenal form, marriage laws do in fact penalize those who prefer other forms of relationship. If homosexual and polygamous relationships are not legally recognized as "marriages," then persons desiring these forms of relationship are being deprived of some degree of freedom. When considering freedom one must be clear about what one is or is not free to do. Consider, for example, the case of gambling. One must distinguish between laws that forbid gambling and the absence of laws that recognize gambling debts. The latter does not deprive people of the freedom to contract gambling debts; it simply does not allow the use of legal enforcement to collect them. Similarly, the absence of laws recognizing polygamous and homosexual marriages does not deprive people of the freedom to enter polygamous and homosexual unions. Instead, it merely fails to provide legal recourse to enforce the agreements of the parties to such unions. The absence of laws recognizing such marriages does not deprive people of a freedom they previously had, for they were never able to have such agreements legally enforced. Nor have people been deprived of a freedom they would have if there were no legal system, for in the absence of a legal system no agreements can be legally enforced. If there is a ground for complaint, then, it must be one of inequality—that one type of relationship is legally recognized but others are not. However, a charge of inequality is warranted only if there are no relevant reasonable grounds for distinguishing between relationships. To settle that issue one must be clear about the state's or society's interests in marriage.

The rest of this essay is concerned with the purposes or functions of the marriage relationship in which society has a legitimate interest. It is not possible here to set out and to justify the purposes for which governments may legislate. It is assumed that the state may act to facilitate citizens' engaging in activities that they find desirable and to protect the welfare and equality of all citizens, including future ones. Government has an especially strong responsibility for the welfare of children. Of course, these legitimate governmental or social interests and responsibilities must be balanced against other interests and values of citizens, including those of privacy and freedom from interference.

There is no attempt or intention to justify penal laws prohibiting forms of relationship other than monogamous marriage. Indeed, it is generally assumed that they ought not be prohibited and that more people will enter into them than has been the case. In such a context, monogamous marriage would become a more specialized form of relationship, entered into by a smaller proportion of the population than previously. Underlying this assumption are the general beliefs that many people are unqualified or unfit for a marital relationship and ought never to enter one and that many people marry for the wrong reasons. If true, these beliefs may explain why both marriage and divorce rates have been steadily rising in most Western countries during this century.[24]

PROMOTING INTERPERSONAL RELATIONSHIPS

Alienation from others and loss of community are perceived by many to be among the most serious ills of modern, mass society. In such a situation it seems unlikely that many would deny the need for intimate interpersonal relationships of affection. The importance of such relationships for a good or *eudaemonistic* life have been recognized by philosophers as diverse as Aristotle and G. E. Moore.[25] In considering such interpersonal relationships to be among the most valuable elements of a good life, one must distinguish between the value of a good and the strength of the desire for it. Many people have a stronger desire for life than for such interpersonal relationships, but they may still recognize such relationships as more valuable than mere life. Life itself is of little value, but it is a necessary condition for most other things of value.

Among the most valuable forms of interpersonal relationship are love, friendship, and trust. These relationships are limited with respect to the number of persons with whom one can have them. Classically, there has been a distinction between agapeic and erotic love. Agapeic love is the love of all mankind—general benevolence. The concept of erotic love is more limited. In today's world erotic love is apt to be confused with sexual desire and intercourse. But there can be and always has been sex without love and love without sex. Personal love is more restricted than either agapeic love or sexual desire. It implies a concern for another that is greater than that for most people. Hence, it cannot be had for an unlimited number of other people.[26] Similar distinctions must be drawn between friendship and acquaintance, trust of a political candidate and trust of a friend.

Such interpersonal relationships require intimacy. Intimacy involves a sharing of information about one another that is not shared with others. Moreover, it often involves seclusion from others—being in private where others cannot observe.[27] In some societies where physical privacy is not possible, psychological privacy—shutting out the awareness of the presence of others—substitutes. Consequently, these valuable interpersonal relationships require intimacy and usually physical privacy from others, and at the very least nonintrusion upon the relationship.

Moreover, these forms of interpersonal relationship require acts expressing the concern felt for the other person. In most societies acts of sexual intercourse have been such expressions of love and concern. It is not physically or psychologically necessary that sexual intercourse have this quasi-symbolic function, but it is a natural function of sexual intercourse. All that is here meant by "natural" is that in most societies sexual intercourse has this function, for which there is some psychological basis even though it is not contrary to scientific laws for it to be otherwise. Intercourse usually involves an element of giving of oneself, and one's sexual identity is frequently a central element of one's self-image. It is not, however, sexual intercourse that is intrinsically valuable but the feelings and attitudes, the underlying interpersonal relationship, that it expresses. Nonsexual acts also currently express such relationships, but sexual intercourse is still one of the most important ways of doing so. If sexual intercourse ceases to have this function in society, some other act will undoubtedly replace it in this function. Moreover, sexual intercourse will have lost much of its value.

If these interpersonal relationships of personal love and trust are of major value, it is reasonable for the state to seek to protect and foster them by according legal recognition to them in marriage. The specific forms of this recognition cannot be fully discussed. However, there is some basis for treating the partners to a marriage as one person. Historically, of course, the doctrine that the parties to a marriage are one person has supported the subjugation of women in all sorts of ways, for example, in their disability from owning property. But there is an underlying rationale for joint responsibility. Two people who, without a special reason such as taxes, keep separate accounts of income and expenditures do not have the love and trust of a couple who find such an accounting unnecessary. Moreover, in such a joint economic venture there is no point to allowing one party to sue the other. Only the advent of insurance, whereby neither spouse, but a third party, pays, makes such suits seem profitable. Another recognition of these relationships—albeit one not frequently invoked—is that one is not forced to testify against his or her spouse. More important is that neither party is encouraged to violate the trust and intimacy of the relationship, for example, by encouraging one to inform authorities about bedroom comments of his or her spouse.[28]

The character of these valuable forms of interpersonal relationship provides an argument against according marriages of definite duration legal recognition equal to that accorded those that are intentionally of indefinite duration. For it to be "intentionally of indefinite duration," neither partner may, when entering the marriage, intend it to be for a specific period of time, for example, five years, nor may the marriage contract specify such a period. The following argument is not to show that marriages for a definite duration should not be recognized, but merely to show that they should not have equal standing with those intentionally of indefinite duration. The basic reason for unequal recognition is that interpersonal relationships that are not intentionally of indefinite duration are less valuable than those that are.

Suppose one were to form a friendship with a colleague, but the two mutually agree to be friends for only three years, with an option to renew the friendship at that time. Such an agreement would indicate a misunderstanding of friendship. Such agreements make sense for what Aristotle called friendships of utility, but in the modern world these friendships are business partnerships.[29] While there is nothing wrong with business friendships, they do not have the intrinsic value of personal friendships. In becoming close personal friends with someone, one establishes a concern and trust that would be seriously weakened or destroyed by setting a time limit to the friendship. It is sometimes claimed that time limits may be set because people will only be together for a while. But one need not see a person every day or even every year to remain friends. However, extended separation usually brings about a withering away of the friendship.

Similarly, the personal relationship of love and trust in marriage is of lesser value if it is intentionally for only a definite period of time. Moreover, the entering into a relationship that is intentionally of indefinite duration and legally recognized symbolizes a strength of commitment not found in other types of relationships. While two unmarried people may claim that there is no definite limit to their mutual commitment, their commitment is always questionable. Entering into a marital relationship assures the commitment more than does a mere verbal avowal.

There are two common objections to this argument. First, it is sometimes said that there may be special reasons for making marriages of short, definite duration, for example, if one partner will only live in the area for a while. But a personal love that is not strong enough to overcome difficulties of moving to another area and possible sacrifices of employment is not as close and strong as a love that can. Many married couples make such compromises and sacrifices. Second, it is sometimes claimed that commitment is in fact stronger when not legally reinforced, when one does not need the law to support the relationship. However, this claim overlooks the fact that when a married couple's relationship rests substantially upon their legal obligations, their relationship has already begun to deteriorate. The strength of commitment is established by the willingness to enter into a legal relationship that cannot be broken simply, without any difficulties. A person who is not willing to undertake the risk of the legal involvement in divorce should he desire to terminate the relationship is probably unsure of his commitment. Moreover, the legal relationship provides security against a sudden and unexpected change in one's life—the breakup of the social aspects will take some time, giving one a chance to prepare for a new style of life. Even then the change is often very difficult.

Hence, if marriage is for the purpose of providing legal recognition of some of the most valuable interpersonal relationships, it should grant more protection and recognition to those intentionally of indefinite duration than to others. Such a conclusion does not imply that divorce should be impossible or exceedingly difficult. Friendships frequently do not last forever despite their not being intended for a limited period of time. The same may happen to a marital relationship. So while this argument supports not according legal recognition to relationships intended to be of definite duration equal to that accorded those intended to be of indefinite duration, it does not support restrictions on divorce in the latter case. Moreover, the average length of time of marriages has increased considerably since the seventeenth century. When a couple married then, one of them was likely to die within twenty years. With today's increased life expectancy, both parties may live close to fifty years after they marry.[30] Obviously, with such an increased possible length of marriage, there is a greater chance for marital breakdown and divorce. One may expect more divorces in marriages that have lasted twenty to twenty-five years simply because there are more such marriages. Nevertheless, such marriages are intentionally of indefinite duration—for life.

PROTECTING THE WELFARE OF CHILDREN

Another area of pervasive social interest that has historically centered in marriage concerns the procreation and raising of children. Society has an interest not only in the number of children born but their quality of life. This fact is in deep conflict with the current emphasis on the freedom of individuals to make reproductive decisions unfettered by social rules and restrictions. Moreover, it is an area in which social control has traditionally been weak. Child abuse is widespread, and efforts to prevent it are mediocre at best. There are few general legal qualifications or tests for becoming a parent. Yet parenthood is one of the most potentially dangerous relationships that one person can have with another. If one is a poor college teacher, then at worst a few students do not receive a bit of education they might have. But as a parent one potentially can ruin completely the lives of one's children. At the least, they may develop into psychological misfits incapable of leading responsible and rewarding lives.

Essentially, there are three areas of social interest and responsibility with respect to procreation and the raising of children. First, there is a social interest in the sheer number of children born. The current emphasis on population control makes this interest abundantly clear.[31] Second, there is a social interest in the potentialities of children. This area includes concern for genetic and congenital birth defects and abnormalities. Over 5 percent of all children born have a genetic defect. The possibility of genetic control of those who are born will soon take on major significance. Already, approximately sixty genetic diseases as well as almost all chromosomal abnormalities can be detected *in utero*, and adult carriers of about eighty genetic defects can be identified.[32] Given the possibility of genetic control, society can no longer risk having genetically disadvantaged children by leaving the decision of whether to have children to the unregulated judgment of individual couples. Some social regulations with respect to genetic screening and, perhaps, eugenic sterilization are needed. While potential parents have interests of privacy and freedom in reproductive decisions, the social interests in preventing the suffering and inequality of possibly defective children may outweigh them in certain types of cases.

Third, the care and development of those who are born is a social interest and responsibility. This interest has been recognized for some time in the form of children's homes and compulsory education. However, increasing knowledge about childhood development extends the area in which social interests and responsibility may be reasonably involved. To give an example at the most elementary level, the nutritional diet of children during their first three years is crucial for their future development. So also is their psychological support. The welfare of future generations is not a private but a social matter. It is a proper task of society, acting through its government, to ensure that the members of the next generation are not physical or psychological cripples due to the ignorance, negligence, or even indifference of parents.

Historically, society has attempted to control procreation through the institution of marriage. Society's means were primarily to stigmatize children born out of wedlock and to encourage the having of many children. It is now recognized that no useful purpose is served by stigmatizing children born out of wedlock as illegitimate. (However, some useful purpose may be served by not according children born out of wedlock all the rights of those born in wedlock, for example, inheritance without parental recognition.) The emphasis on having as many children as one can has also disappeared. It is not this historical concern with procreation that is misplaced in modern society but the forms that the concern has taken.

If society has the responsibility to protect the welfare of children, then some social regulation and control of human reproduction and development is justified. Such regulation and control need not be effected by penal laws. For example, social concern has traditionally been expressed in adoptions through regulations to ensure that those who adopt children are fit to care for them. That some regulations have been inappropriate and not reasonably related to the welfare of children is not in question. Rather, the point is that there has been regulation without penal laws, or at least without resorting primarily to penal laws. Nor can social regulation and control be solely by legislation. Legislation alone is usually ineffective; it must be supported by informal social rules and expectations.

Not only has modern biomedicine made sex possible without procreation; it has also made procreation possible without sex. The techniques of artificial insemination and fertilization, embryo transfer, ova donation, ectogenesis, and cloning now, or soon will, make it possible for people to reproduce without sexual intercourse.[33] Hence, not only may one have sex for pleasure, but one may reproduce for pleasure without sexual intercourse. Not only may people reproduce outside marriage; they are not even biologically required to have intercourse. Thus, sex and marriage may become dissociated from reproduction.

However, there are strong reasons for restricting procreation primarily to marriages of indefinite duration, which does not imply that such marriages should be restricted to procreation. Marriage has traditionally been the central social institution concerned with procreation. Consequently, if society is to exercise some control over procreation in the future, it would involve the least change in conditions to do so through marriage. Moreover, there is considerable evidence that the disruption of family life contributes to juvenile delinquency. Whether divorce or marital breakdown (with or without divorce) is a prime cause of such delinquency does not matter. The point is that the disruption of home life does seriously affect the development of children.[34] The chance of such disruption outside of a marriage that is intentionally of indefinite duration is higher than for that within. Moreover, there is some reason to believe that the presence of both mother and father is instrumental in the psychological development of children. In any case, the presence of two people rather than one provides the security that there will be someone to care for the children should one of the parents die. Generally, children are better off being with one parent than in a state orphanage, but better off still with both parents. Hence, for the welfare of children it seems best that procreation and child rearing primarily occur within the context of marriages intentionally of indefinite duration.

While society has a responsibility for the care and development of children, this general responsibility is best carried out if specific adults have obligations to care for specific children. In the past, the biological parent-child relation has reinforced the allocation of responsibility for specific children and has been a major factor in monogamy.[35] The separation of reproduction and sexual intercourse threatens disruption of this assignment. For example, if gestation occurs in an artificial womb in a laboratory, there may be no "parents," only a scientific research group. More realistically, if a woman has an embryo from ova and sperm donors transferred to her uterus, it is unclear who are the child's parents. However, if there is to be optimal care for children, specific adults must have obligations for specific children. It cannot be left to somebody in general, for then nobody in particular is likely to do it. "Let George do it" is too prevalent and careless an attitude to allow with regard to children.

McMurtry's contention that monogamy restricts the care for children is not well founded.[36] First, if there are no specific adults responsible for children, they may become "lost" in large groups and victims of the "it's not my job" syndrome. Second, monogamy per se does not cut children off from the support and care of others. One must distinguish the marital relationship from living arrangements. It is the isolated situation of the family that deprives children of such support. In many married-student housing complexes children have access to other adults. Even in general-residential neighborhoods with separate family housing units, such support is available if there is a sense of community in the neighborhood.

Given the social interests in and responsibility for the procreation and development of children, some more effective controls of parenthood appear desirable. If the primary locus of reproduction is to be within marriages of intentionally indefinite duration, then the easiest way to institute controls is to add requirements for people to enter such marriages. A few requirements such as blood tests are already generally prevalent. Alternatively, one might have a separate licensing procedure for procreation. Nonmarried couples and single people might also qualify for such licenses. Moreover, couples who want to marry but not have children would not have to meet requirements. However, the only requirements suggested below that might bar marriages are almost as important for those couples who do not have children as for those who do. If the requirements were tied to marriage they would be easier to administer. The only drawback is that unmarried people would not have to meet them. However, such requirements can and should be part of the medical practice of the "artificial" techniques of reproduction—artificial insemination and embryo transfer. And there are few if any effective methods, except generally accepted social rules, to control procreation outside of marriage.

One obvious requirement would be genetic screening. With modern medical techniques genetic problems do not imply that couples cannot become married, but they might be expected not to have children who are their genetic offspring. Artificial insemination and embryo transfer make it possible for almost everyone to have children, even though the children might not be genetically theirs. A general distinction between biological and social parenthood should be made, with legal emphasis on the latter.

More important, perhaps, is some general expectation of psychological fitness for family life and the raising of children. The difficulty with such an expectation is the absence of any clear criteria for fitness and reliable methods for determining who meets them. Perhaps, however, some formal instruction in family relations and child rearing would be appropriate. The Commission on Population Growth and the American Future has already called for an expansion of education for parenthood.[37] It is only a bit further to require some sort of minimal family education for marriage. Probably the easiest method for ensuring such education would be to make it a required subject in secondary schools. If that were done, few people would have difficulty meeting this requirement for marriage.

There should not be any financial or property qualifications for marriage.[38] Society's interest in and responsibility for the welfare of the population in general is such that governments should ensure an adequate standard of living for all persons. Were that to be done there would be no reason to impose any financial restrictions on marriage. Nonetheless, prospective parents should have more concern for their financial situation than is now frequently the case. The adequate care of children is an expensive task, financially as well as psychologically and temporally.

CONCLUSION

It may be objected that neither the argument from interpersonal relations nor that from the welfare of children specifically supports monogamous marriage. While loving relationships cannot extend to an indefinite number of people, they can extend to more than one other person. Also, a polygamous union may provide a reasonable environment for procreation. Hence, neither of the arguments supports monogamous marriage per se.

Logically, the objection is quite correct. But it is a misunderstanding of social philosophy to expect arguments showing that a certain arrangement is always best under all circumstances. The most that can be shown is that usually, or as a rule, one social arrangement is preferable to another. Practically, polygamous marriage patterns will probably never be prevalent.[39] For centuries they have been gradually disappearing throughout the world. If a disproportionate sex distribution of the population occurs in some areas or age groups (such as the elderly), then they may increase in significance. Unless that occurs, most people will probably continue to prefer marital monogamy.

More important, the burden of this paper has not been to defend the traditional ideal of marital union or even the current practice. Many of the traditional rules of marriage have been unjust, for example, the inequality between the sexes, both legally and in terms of social roles. Instead, it has been to defend social recognition of marriage of intentionally indefinite duration as a unique and socially valuable institution that society has interests in promoting and regulating. In particular, society has interests in and responsibility for promoting a certain form of valuable interpersonal relationship and protecting the welfare of children. Both of these purposes can be well served by monogamous marriage.

The image, then, is of a society with various forms of living together, but one in which marriage of intentionally indefinite duration would have a distinctive though lessened role as a special kind of socially and legally recognized relationship. There would not be laws prohibiting nonmarital forms of cohabitation. Divorce would be based on factual marital breakdown or mutual consent, with due regard for the welfare of children.

Monogamous marriage would recognize a special form of personal relationship in which reproduction and child rearing primarily occur. Given the social interest in decreasing procreation, many people might marry but not have children, and others might not marry at all. Details of the legal marital relationship have not been specified, nor could they be in this brief essay except with respect to the main social interests. Questions of inheritance, legal residence and name, social-security benefits, and so on, have not been specified. Changes in laws with respect to many of these matters can be made without affecting the arguments for the value of, social responsibility for, and interests in marriage. Above all, it is an image in which sexual intercourse plays a much smaller role in the conception of marriage and the good life in general, a society in which vulgar hedonism has at least been replaced by a broader-based *eudaemonism.*

NOTES

1. Epicurus, "Letter to Menoeceus," in *The Stoic and Epicurean Philosophers*, ed. Whitney J. Oates (New York: Modern Library, 1957), p. 31. Epicurus even wrote, "Sexual intercourse has never done a man good, and he is lucky if it has not harmed him" (Fragment 8 in *The Stoic and Epicurean Philosophers*). John Stuart Mill, *Utilitarianism*, chap. 2, especially paragraphs 1-9.

2. *De Anima* 2. 4.

3. "Monogamy: A Critique," *The Monist* 56 (1972); reprinted herein, pp. 107-118. This quote appears on page 111 of this volume (italics added). Subsequent references to McMurtry's essay are to pages in this volume.

4. Ibid., p. 111

5. Ibid.

6. Ibid.

7. Ibid., p. 112.

8. Ibid., p. 114.

9. Ibid., p. 115.

10. Ibid.

11. Ibid.

12. Ibid.

13. Ibid.

14. Karl Marx and Friedrich Engels, "Manifesto of the Communist Party," in *Basic Writings on Politics and Philosophy*, ed. Lewis S. Feuer (Garden City, N.Y.: Doubleday, Anchor Books, 1959), especially p. 24.

15. Paul R. Ehrlich, *The Population Bomb* (New York: Ballantine Books, 1968).

16. Even new Marxists perceive other sources of problems. See Milovan Djilas, *The New Class* (New York: Praeger, 1964); and, more generally, Richard T. De George, *The New Marxism* (New York: Pegasus, 1968), chap. 2. The importance of population for pollution, with which it is most frequently connected, has been contested by Barry Commoner, *The Closing Circle* (New York: Knopf, 1971), pp. 133-35. Ehrlich now clearly recognizes that various causal factors are important, al-

though he still disagrees with Commoner on the importance of population growth; see Paul R. Ehrlich et al., *Human Ecology* (San Francisco: W. H. Freeman and Company, 1973), chap. 7, esp. pp. 206, 213-15, 221.

17. Max Rheinstein, *Marriage Stability, Divorce, and the Law* (Chicago: University of Chicago Press, 1972), p. 251.

18. Edwin D. Driver, "Population Policies of State Governments in the United States: Some Preliminary Observations," *Villanova Law Review* 15 (1970): 846-47.

19. Immanuel Kant, *The Philosophy of Law*, trans. W. Hastie (Edinburgh: T. & T. Clark, 1887), p. 110.

20. McMurtry, "Monogamy," p. 112; italics in original omitted.

21. See John T. Noonan, Jr., *Contraception* (Cambridge, Mass.: Harvard University Press, 1966), pp. 312-14.

22. Keith G. McWalter, "Marriage as Contract: Towards a Functional Redefinition of the Marital Status," *Columbia Journal of Law and Social Problems* 9 (1973): 615.

23. Robert S. Summers, "The Technique Element of Law," *California Law Review* 59 (1971): 736-37, 741-45.

24. Burton M. Leiser, *Liberty, Justice and Morals* (New York: Macmillan Co., 1973), p. 126; R[oland] Pressat, *Population*, trans. Robert and Danielle Atkinson (Baltimore: Penguin Books, 1970), pp. 84, 86; U.S. Commission on Population Growth and the American Future, *Population and the American Future* (New York: Signet, New American Library, 1972), pp. 102-03.

25. Aristotle, *Nicomachean Ethics* 9. 9-12; George Edward Moore, *Principia Ethica* (Cambridge: At the University Press, 1903), pp. 188, 203-05.

26. It is thus misleading for McMurtry to write of monogamous marriage excluding "almost *countless* other possibilities of *intimate* union" with any number of persons (p. 109; my italics). On the limited nature of personal love or friendship see also Aristotle, *Nicomachean Ethics* 9. 10.

27. For a discussion of these relationships and the need for privacy, see Charles Fried, "Privacy," in *Law, Reason, and Justice*, ed. Graham Hughes (New York: New York University Press, 1969), pp. 45-69.

28. See the discussion (in another context) of such a case in Nazi Germany by H. L. A. Hart, "Positivism and the Separation of Law and Morals," *Harvard Law Review* 71 (1958): 618-20; and Lon L. Fuller, "Positivism and Fidelity to Law—A Reply to Professor Hart," *Harvard Law Review* 71 (1958): 652-55.

29. *Nicomachean Ethics* 8. 3. The vulgar hedonists treat marriage as a form of friendship for pleasure, but that is not the highest form of friendship.

30. Pressat, *Population*, p. 52.

31. For a more complete discussion see my "Limits to a Right to Procreate," in *Ethics and Population*, ed. Michael D. Bayles (Cambridge, Mass.: Schenkman Publishing Company, 1975).

32. Daniel Callahan, *The Tyranny of Survival* (New York: Macmillan Co., 1973), p. 219.

33. For a good general survey of these techniques and some suggestions for social controls, see George A. Hudock, "Gene Therapy and Genetic Engineering: Frankenstein Is Still a Myth, But It Should Be Reread Periodically," *Indiana Law Journal* 48 (1973): 533-58. Various ethical issues are discussed in Joseph Fletcher, *The Ethics of Genetic Control* (Garden City, N.Y.: Doubleday, Anchor Books, 1974).

Successful human embryo implantation and growth to term after *in vitro* fertilization has been reported in Britain (see *Time,* July 29, 1974, pp. 58-59; and *Newsweek,* July 29, 1974, p. 70).

34. President's Commission on Law Enforcement and Administration of Justice, *The Challenge of Crime in a Free Society* (New York: Avon Books, 1968), pp. 184-89.

35. Daniel Callahan, "New Beginnings in Life: A Philosopher's Response," in *The New Genetics and the Future of Man,* ed. Michael P. Hamilton (Grand Rapids, Mich.: William B. Eerdmans Publishing Company, 1972), pp. 102-03.

36. "Monogamy,' p. 111.

37. *Population and the American Future,* pp. 126-33, esp. 133.

38. For some suggested financial requirements as well as others, see Jack Parsons, *Population versus Liberty* (Buffalo, N.Y.: Prometheus Books, 1971), p. 349.

39. Even McMurtry appears to recognize this fact; see "Monogamy," p. 107.

Frederick Elliston

Gay Marriage

Over the past decade, homosexuals have both lost and gained ground in their fight for legal rights. In Boulder, Colorado; Dade County, Florida; St. Paul, Minnesota; Wichita, Kansas; and Eugene, Oregon; their legal protection against discrimination has been revoked. On the other hand, the mayor of New York City has issued a memorandum that no recipient of city funds will discriminate against an employee on the basis of sexual orientation. California successfully defeated an initiative to dismiss gay teachers. Homosexuality is becoming more acceptable in the military, and several jurisdictions and countries are taking steps to legalize consensual homosexual acts between adults in private.

In this essay, I want to examine one battle that has been fought and lost: the homosexual's right to marry. In 1971, two men petitioned the Minnesota Supreme Court to compel the state to grant them a marriage license.[1] The court denied their petition and the following year the United States Supreme Court dismissed their appeal.[2] My examination will not be a legal one tracing out the cases and precedents for their rights, but rather a moral one. Are there any sound ethical arguments for denying homosexuals the legal right to marry? I shall assess eight considerations that could be invoked to provide an ethical justification for the denial of such a legal right: 1) the historical function of marriage within our society; 2) the religious perspective on the very nature of marriage; 3) the suffering of innocent children; 4) the argument from shared values; 5) the law as promoter of values; 6) the argument from perversion implicit in most sodomy statutes; 7) the worry: What if everybody did that?; and 8) the "slippery slope" appeal—What next? I shall try to show that none of these arguments provides adequate moral grounds for outlawing homosexual marriages. I shall then offer three positive considerations in defense of legalization—appeals to freedom, love, and justice.

I

THE SEMANTIC ISSUE

Let me begin by defining a homosexual marriage. Obviously what is at issue is not the legal right of a latent homosexual to marry someone of the opposite sex. Nor is it a question of denying a practicing homosexual such a right. Though acting on such a sexual preference may constitute adultery and be grounds for divorce, it is not as such an obstacle to successful application for a marriage license. What is at stake in gay marriages is the legal right of two people of the same sex to marry one another.

For economy's sake I shall refer to the homosexual as male. But the term refers to 'homo' in the sense of *same*, as in the word "homogeneous" meaning same consistency. Thus the lesbian is a homosexual also, and the arguments to defend the right of two gay men to marry apply to two women, with slight variations.[3]

In most cases the law does not specify that the members of a marriage must be of the opposite sex. Such an assumption was, and to some extent still is, so pervasive that it was not thought necessary to build it into the law. But legal appeals of the state's refusal to grant a marriage license simply because the partners were of the same sex have failed (as documented above in footnotes one and two): heterosexuality is taken as a necessary condition of matrimony by those who enforce the law, though the law typically fails to stipulate this requirement.

One could argue that even if the state fails to stipulate this condition, its oversight is inconsequential: heterosexuality is part of the meaning of marriage in our society and monogamy is a relationship between a husband and wife, a male and female. This strategy to solve the problem by defining it out of existence is misconceived, but it does call for a careful analysis of the meaning of monogamy.

Quite literally "monogamy" means one spouse. It is a form of marriage that limits the number of participants to two. To enter into this relationship is typically to sign a legal contract.[4] No further contracts can be signed until earlier contracts have been dissolved by the state: to fail to do so is bigamy. Unlike most contracts, this one cannot be dissolved by mutual consent: though both parties may agree to a divorce, the state may in theory (though less frequently in practice) refuse to grant one, unless it is convinced that the relationship has been irreparably destroyed. The state further regulates the signing of this contract by requiring a license that is granted only if the couple satisfies several conditions—minimal age, no direct family and/or blood ties, physical and psychological health (i.e., blood tests are required, severely retarded people and those serving life sentences frequently cannot marry).

Heterosexuality is not part of the definition of monogamy. Whether or not it ought to be is better seen not as a semantic issue but as a moral one. Otherwise the problem is reduced to one of meaning, a verbal quibble that seems impossible to resolve short of linguistic fiat or an appeal to vague intuitions.[5] To keep the issue where it belongs—on the moral turf—a neutral definition of monogamy should be employed that does not beg the question of the legitimacy of homosexual marriages by loading the semantic dice at the outset. Such a minimal definition would describe monogamy as a form of marriage that limits the number of participants who may legally enter this contractual relation to two. As such, monogamy stands in contrast to other forms of marriage primarily in terms of the number of participants: polygamy allows for several husbands or wives. Should homosexuals be denied a license to enter into our form of marriage? Let me turn first to a historical justification of a negative response.

II

1. THE HISTORICAL FUNCTION OF MONOGAMY

Marriage—by which I shall henceforth mean monogamy as the form of marriage most widely practiced in our Western culture—has served a variety of functions in the past: to consolidate political power, to form international alliances, to enable men to escape the draft, to provide citizenship for bettering employment prospects, to legalize copulation, to regulate the transfer of property from one generation to another, and to legitimize offspring. The last is probably still one of the most important and prevalent functions of marriage today: it provides a secure and loving context for having and raising children.

Clearly homosexual acts are nonreproductive. No one will ever get pregnant by engaging in sex exclusively with someone of the same sex. Accordingly, one of the objections against legalizing homosexual marriages is that such an arrangement violates one of the primary functions of marriage. People marry in order to raise a family, but couples who are exclusively homosexual will never have children. Legalizing such pairings jeopardizes the traditional function of the institution of marriage. It denies the state's interest in protecting the welfare of children by according heterosexual marriages a privileged legal position.

This argument is weak for two reasons. First the principle on which it rests cuts against too many other widely and rightly accepted social practices. If we are to deny a marriage license to homosexuals on the grounds that they will never have children, then we should also deny it in the case of the professional couple who have decided to remain childless for the sake of their careers. Admittedly, they could have children but the homosexual couple never will. But it is impossible to see a significant difference if they are determined and abortion is legal.

Or consider a marriage when the husband is sterile, and the state knows it. Should the couple be denied a marriage license on the grounds that they will never fulfil the proper historical function of holy matrimony by having children? To do so would be wrong, and by analogy, I suggest, it is equally wrong for two men to be denied a marriage license for this reason and this reason alone.

Some may object that this argument by analogy collapses because it depends on the contingency of the husband's infertility and the state's knowledge of it. But consider, then, a situation where the woman is past menopause. Should the state deny a marriage license to elderly couples, say over sixty-five years of age, where it is virtually certain that the couple will remain childless? I think to do so would be wrong, and that most people would agree. Consequently, unless we are prepared to deny a marriage license to elderly and sterile couples, it is inconsistent and hence immoral to refuse the gay couple—at least on this ground alone.

Second, I think this historical argument is anachronistic. Recent contraceptive technology has provided control over fertility that makes procreation an option many can and do reject, who still choose to marry for a variety of other good reasons. The value of companionship, intimacy, social approval and support are widely recognized and marriage plays a key role in promoting and protecting these. But these are some of the same good reasons gay couples want to marry. They wish to solidify a relation with a 'significant other' whom each cares for deeply. They seek the social support that will safeguard their relationship and foster its growth. Many of the values that make marriage attractive to heterosexual, professional couples who intend to remain childless, or to elderly couples who must remain childless make it attractive to gay couples too.

In short, as a result of contraceptive technology, marriage as an institution is changing its historical function. Reasons other than having children are becoming socially more acceptable. To insist that procreation *must* be a goal of all married couples or that the institution serves only this function today is archaic and anachronistic. To allow professional and elderly couples who will not have children to marry because of other values associated with matrimony while denying gay couples this right is cruel and unfair.

A more sophisticated philosophical version of the historical argument has been put forth by the Roman Catholic Church. Based on the teachings of Saint Thomas Aquinas, the Church asserts that marriage and the family are inseparably interconnected. So I shall now turn to the arguments offered by the Church and attacked by recent critics, and extrapolate them to apply to gay marriages.

2. THE RELIGIOUS ARGUMENT

Roman Catholicism asserts that conjugal love—sex within marriage—is inseparably and necessarily tied to procreation. The argument in defense of this assertion is put forth in "Humanae Vitae"[6] and recently reaffirmed, that marriage has two inseparable functions—spiritual union and procreation of children.

This papal encyclical issued by Pope Paul in 1968 is still binding on devout and faithful Catholics. It is primarily a condemnation of contraception within marriage. Yet the arguments provided suffice to show why the Church would not sanction homosexual marriages either. Sex within marriage is acceptable and proper only insofar as each conjugal act serves two simultaneous purposes: first to unite the husband and wife in bonds of love and affection, and second to provide for the creation and transmission of new life. Insofar as the pill, I.U.D. (or Intrauterine Device), condoms, or other contraceptive devices intrude into the divinely sanctioned natural process of reproduction, they violate the second condition of moral sex, and hence are condemned as sinful by the Church. Sexual practices other than penile-vaginal intercourse—at least if they serve as a substitute rather than supplement—would also violate the natural function of sex, and would therefore be equally condemned. Clearly homosexual practices fall into this category.[7] To marry a homosexual would be to approve of sin.

Carl Cohen has offered one of the most direct and powerful attacks on this logic.[8] He contends that the inseparability premise is unsupported by rational argument and relies instead on religious fiat, that it cannot be defended by appeal to scriptures, that it contradicts the Church's own emphasis on love and its acceptance of the rhythm method, and that it betrays an unwholesome attitude toward sex as dirty and not valuable in its own right. I find his elaboration of these points convincing though I do not wish to rehearse it here. To the extent that his attack weakens the inseparability premise, it weakens Catholic opposition to homosexual marriages. The crux of the Catholic position, however, is a view of the natural function of sex as reproduction, which I shall address later.

Let me say that whatever the merits of the Catholic position, it is inconclusive as a reason for outlawing gay marriages. For why should all of society be bound by the special teachings of one religious sect? Catholics are free to refuse to marry gay couples within the Church, and it would be unjust for the law to deny them this option. By the same token it is wrong for the Roman Catholics to deny others the chance to exercise their religious freedom. If Protestants, for example, want to marry gay couples, by what right should Roman Catholics interfere? Religious opposition collapses on the secure rock of religious freedom. No sect has the moral right to use the law to impose its beliefs on others. The well-established doctrine of separation of religion and state prohibits the simplistic inference from that which is sinful to that which is illegal.

Yet, this principle of the separation of powers has recently been attacked by Lord Patrick Devlin. He contends that society has the right to use the arm of the law to enforce its public, shared morality—a set of values that has its religious base in Christianity. Before turning to Devlin, let me consider the primary value that is at issue: the welfare of children. Many people no doubt feel that legalizing gay marriages, even if it does not destroy the family as an institution, will harm its most innocent and vulnerable members—children.

3. THE WELFARE OF CHILDREN

Some people may fear that homosexual marriages could have harmful consequences, not so much for the family as an institution but for children who are its weakest and most vulnerable members. The innocent offspring of homosexuals who marry may suffer from social ridicule and confusion about their sexual identity and social roles. In order to protect the welfare of children, homosexual marriages must be illegal. Let us assess this stance by examining carefully the ways the problem of harming innocent children might arise.

First, the children could be the result of a previous marriage. So the question is: Would they be better or worse off if their mother should 'marry' another woman, or their father another man?

In part the question is an empirical one, and could be answered definitively only through a social experiment: legalize gay marriages, take a representative sample of the children of such marriages, and compare them to a control group in terms of self-esteem, personal adjustment, satisfactory social relations, career successes, delinquency or deviance, and other measures of self-worth. Ideally, the study would be longitudinal and would control for all outside factors. Less definitive data could be extrapolated through a comparison of the children of gay and straight couples. But it would then be impossible to determine how much the illegality of homosexuality and homosexual marriages affected the outcome.

Behind the question is a worry: What will happen to innocent children? One way to diminish the worry is to recognize the protective mechanisms we already have. Safeguards now exist in the form of the courts who decide, and can re-decide, custody of the children of divorced parents based on the best interests of the child. In a particular case if the court were convinced that the children would be disadvantaged by the homosexual marriage of a gay parent, the judge could reassign custody. Each case could be decided on its merits by an independent arbiter, and if homosexual marriages were harmful to children, the children could be protected.

Second, the situation could arise through the death of one spouse and the remarriage of the parent. In cases where the first parent and spouse has died, the court can effectively do little to prevent the remaining parent from taking a gay lover. The question in this situation is: Would the children be better off if the parent had the legal option to marry a gay lover? Without this option, the parent has two choices: to continue the doubly illicit affair, or to end it. In view of what many straight people will risk for sex and love, a significant number would probably choose the first option nevertheless. Then the question is: Would the children be better off if the homosexual affair is not secretive and clandestine but open, recognized, and legitimate? My own view is that the answer to this question is yes. The deception, distrust, and dishonesty that are the natural concomitants of illicit conduct, sexual or not, are disruptive in any case, and when the relationship undermined holds between a parent and child, it is inevitably damaging to the child. The statistics on delinquent children and broken homes bear ample testimony to this fact. Accordingly, the legalization of gay marriages would thus remove the social stigma mistakenly attached to innocent children and would promote the interests of the innocent.

Moreover, it is again worth noting that there is already a mechanism in place to protect the interests of children: the courts. Where children are abused, neglected, or endangered, a judge can remove them from the home and take them away from the parents. If it were true that a homosexual relationship were so harmful to the interests of the child as to endanger his/her physical or mental health, then the courts could intervene. But the contingent connection between the welfare of the child and the sexual preferences of the parent needs to be established, and to be established in each case. There is ample evidence that excessive drinking, drug abuse, and, indeed, chronic unemployment and poverty are harmful to the welfare of children, but their presence in the home does not automatically justify legal intervention by the courts to remove the children. Neither should the presence of homosexuality.

Third, the situation of children living with a gay married couple could arise through adoption. Let me first insist that this is another issue entirely. Legalizing gay marriages does not logically entail granting gay couples the right to adopt children. One can support the former and oppose the latter, yet still be consistent. Moreover, the first is exclusively a legal question and the second is more a matter of social policy. It depends partly on the practices of private adoption agencies. Secondly, the problem is miniscule: few gay couples want to adopt children to begin with, and it is difficult for many straight couples to find children to adopt. Finally, I would point out that the private adoption agency can legally form its own *ad hoc* judgment about allowing any couple to adopt children. My own view is that some gay couples would make better parents than some heterosexual couples, but I think this decision should be left to competent professionals.

Lastly, the situation of children within a homosexual marriage relationship could arise through artificial insemination by a donor, a practice that is much debated among a significant but small minority of lesbian couples. Here again I think that the legalization of gay marriages is a separate issue, that this situation rarely occurs, and that it should be decided by professionals—i.e., the doctor who would perform the operation. I think that a woman who would go to the trouble and expense of becoming pregnant in this way demonstrates sufficient dedication to parenthood that she ought to be given the freedom of choice. But even if society were to decide against her (and could somehow enforce its decision), it could still consistently support her right to marry the person of her choice.

The suffering of innocent children is a serious issue. But it is difficult to formulate a utilitarian calculus about their long-term interests. Moreover what children stand to lose is as dependent on society's attitudes as the sexual orientation of their parents.

Consider an analogy with interracial marriages. Some argued that the marriage of a white man and black woman (or vice versa) should not be permitted, because innocent children suffer. They suffer social ridicule, ostracism, reprobation, and rejection. But what was the source of their suffering? It was not interracial marriage but racism—the unfair and unwarranted discrimination against someone on the basis of their race.

Similarly, to discriminate against someone on the basis of sex, the sex of their partner, is unwarranted. In the case of both interracial and homosexual marriage, the source of the harm to children is social prejudice. These prejudices are only perpetuated by social and legal disapproval of unconventional marriages. It is indeed unfortunate if the helpless and guiltless young must bear the burden of combating bigotry among their elders. But future generations of children and adults may reap the benefits of their pain.

If one could dispense with social biases against gays, a remaining objection would be the lack of role models. How could a gay couple provide a necessary socialization into the the appropriate behavior for a boy or a girl, a man or a woman?

Single parents face the same problem of raising children of the opposite sex, and often manage to do so quite well. Moreover, we do not (any longer, at least) forbid them to divorce, or require them to remarry or to give up their children.

If, indeed, role models are desirable, a gay couple could still ensure that their children would learn them from other sources—e.g., friends, television, schools, the church, neighbors, and so forth. The actual parents are not the sole source, or always the most effective or appropriate one. It is for this reason that some children with very bad parents are able to be fine parents themselves.

Are the traditional sex roles still desirable and defensible? One could argue (with some plausibility) just the opposite—that they are oppressive to both men and women, that they restrict individual freedom, and curtail opportunities for growth and for negotiating a more flexible division of labor. It is for this reason that some feminists extol an androgenous ideal that goes beyond stereotypes.[9] They claim that our society would do better to teach children to be people first and only secondarily, if at all, to be "real men" or "true women." If traditional sex roles are sexist, then legalizing homosexual marriages may help to combat this evil.

Part of the force of this appeal to the welfare of children may turn on a latent assumption that homosexuality is a disease of sorts that may be passed on to children. To protect children from this disorder, they must be protected from homosexuals. In another essay in this volume,

Frederick Suppe examines the thesis that homosexuality is a disorder to be cured,[10] and Joseph Margolis has shown elsewhere that the psychiatric profession is itself confused on the scientific and medical status of homosexuality.[11] I shall not, therefore, pursue this line of criticism here.

But if homosexuality is not a genetically or socially transmitted disease, what is wrong with it, and what justifies society's legal condemnation of it? Lord Patrick Devlin has recently offered a provocative and much debated account of the relation of law and morality, which, if it succeeded, would justify our current practice of denying gays the right to marry. I shall now return to Devlin's appeal to social conventions.

4. THE ARGUMENT FROM SHARED MORALITY

Devlin has provided two general arguments to justify society's use of the law to enforce its moral code.[12] Though addressed more specifically to the recommendations of the Wolfenden Committee on homosexuality and prostitution, and the classic liberal principle on which it was based, his arguments can apply to society's refusal to legalize homosexual marriages.

He offers two arguments, the second of which has attracted more philosophical attention. His first is an *a posteriori* argument to establish that the law is and ought to be based on society's morals. Citing the refusal of courts to force payment of gambling debts or to accord legal status to murder contracts, he contends that the law could not function in fact if it were not based on a moral consensus. This consensus, where it exists, is not only necessary but sufficient to justify the law as it operates in our society today. His second argument, an *a priori* one, appeals more to the nature of society as a group of individuals bound together by their shared values. A threat to their common code is a threat to their existence as a society, or at least it could be. The right of society to defend itself entails the right to enforce its moral code.

This right is not an obligation, as Devlin realizes. Thus, he must confront the question: When should this right be exercized? Four elastic principles demarcate his answer. First, individual freedom of choice should be accorded maximum respect. Second, the law should be slow to act, since once a moral consensus has been enshrined in a legal statute it is difficult to change. Third, privacy should be respected. And fourth, the law should be concerned with minimal, not maximal, moral transgressions. As a test of society's ability to withstand deviant behavior, Devlin appeals to a combination of intense feelings of intolerance, indignation, and disgust. At concert pitch, they mark the breaking point of the moral code, the point at which legal intervention is warranted.

If Devlin's argument were sound and if the thought of homosexual marriages produced unanimous feelings of intolerance, indignation, and disgust in twelve randomly chosen people, then society's present stance on homosexual marriages would be warranted.[13] But, in the first place, I doubt that such emotional uniformity can be found in our pluralistic society. Though many people would not choose a homosexual marriage for themselves or their children, a few have done so and even larger numbers are prepared to accept it with equanimity. Accordingly, the emotional and moral consensus on which Devlin might defend current statutes does not exist. Some people approve of homosexual marriages and some disapprove, and this admixture of sentiment leaves the law without a social foundation.

But even if the consensus of feeling Devlin requires could be achieved, it would not provide a sound basis for either morality or the law. One could still ask: Are people misinformed about the meaning of homosexuality or the reality of homosexual lives? Are these individuals simply scapegoats for other feelings that the larger community lacks the courage to confront? Are people generally conceptually confused about pedophilia, inversion, and homosexuality, and thus led astray by the erroneous belief that gay men are child molesters or effeminate?

Finally, as H.L.A. Hart points out,[14] Devlin's argument fails to distinguish clearly between the incidental and the essential elements of a society's moral code; it provides no basis for contrasting a shift in society's moral code with its destruction. Possibly, even if people were unanimous in their emotional abhorrence of gay marriage, and were not deceived or misinformed, changing demographics would justify a changed morality. Homosexuality may have once been counterproductive, but may no longer be and people do not know it. A change in attitudes may therefore be warranted. Rather than annihilating our shared values, accepting gay marriages may improve them.

5. THE LAW AS PROMOTER OF VALUES

More recently Michael Bayles offered another version of Devlin's conservative stance. Though he is primarily intent on defending monogamy as an intentionally life-long and exclusive relation, the argument he develops could be extended to the heterosexual orientation of our marriage laws as well. He notes that the law serves two different functions: to prohibit some practices (the criminal law) and to promote others (the civil law). The practices prohibited by the criminal code are those thought to be wrong, largely (but not necessarily only) actions harmful to others, such as murder and rape. The practices promoted are socially approved, such as buying, selling, and marrying. These private-arranging laws are based on society's values—in the case of marriage, on the value of an intimate, intentionally life-long heterosexual relationship. Though Bayles believes that homosexuals ought not to be prohibited from engaging in private consenting acts, he might insist that they have no right to demand that society legalize and promote through marriage laws something of which it does not fully approve. The most a homosexual can demand is that he be left alone when his actions do not harm others. He cannot demand that society condone his relationship by institutionalizing it through law.

I believe that this argument, like Devlin's, is inconclusive because the final court of appeal is society's *actual* values, however misguided or ill-founded they may be. Any appeal to positive morality leaves open the question: Are these beliefs justified? Some apparatus is needed to sort out fact from fantasy, wisdom from folly. If the law is a promoter of values, which values or whose values does it promote? In a pluralistic society, different groups have different values and will use the law to realize them. On what basis can the law decide which of the competing sets of values to promote or protect? No appeal to existing values can answer this question.

Society's values and attitudes must be subject to rational scrutiny. Are they based on prejudice and rationalization or logic and experience? Do people just parrot what they are told or can they sincerely and consistently defend their position? Only if these values withstand a reasoned critique can they serve as a basis for the law.

Perhaps society is confused about homosexuality, biased, ignorant, or repressed, and for these reasons opposes the legalization of homosexual marriage. The mere possibility of these errors is sufficient, I think, to discredit appeals simply on the ground of popular morality.

Earlier I suggested that marriage for childless couples is a means to worthwhile ends. It can promote intimacy, trust, companionship, and love. To the extent that homosexuals seek these values, homosexual marriage is a means to legitimate ends and should be legalized.

The objection to homosexual marriage, insofar as it is warranted, must then be based on an objection to homosexuality *per se* and not just on a view of the nature and role of the law. To assess the objection, ultimately we must ask: Is homosexuality immoral? It is often claimed to be on the grounds that it is perverted or unnatural. Let us now turn to the argument from perversion.

6. HOMOSEXUALITY AND PERVERSION

Underlying the Roman Catholic position, and the visceral response of many, is the sense that homosexuality is "unnatural." The term can mean many different things: unaccepted, unacceptable, unusual, abnormal, deviant, or just repugnant. In the context of sexual behavior, the terms "unnatural" or "perverted" typically and most coherently refer to acts that are nonreproductive.

Behind the Catholic position is a mythology: God created man and woman so that the first and natural sex act was with a member of the opposite sex. This mythology is buttressed by theological arguments found in Saint Thomas Aquinas.[15] Each bodily organ has its natural function, the function it performs better than any other organ to a degree of perfection none can match. Thus, the eyes are for seeing, the ears for hearing, and genitalia for reproduction—for that is what they alone can do and what they do best.

All homosexual acts are thus unnatural: they do not serve the biological function of reproduction. Like coprophila, necrophilia, and pedophilia, they are to be condemned as a violation of God's plan. To condone homosexual marriages would be as sinful as promulgating bestiality.

One immediate difficulty with this inference from the unnatural to the immoral is overkill. It rules out all forms of fetishism, voyeurism, masturbation, and petting. But few today would indiscriminately and without qualification condemn the sex appeal of almost all Hollywood movies which to some degree are voyeuristic. Far from taking masturbation as unnatural, Masters and Johnson have taken the ability to masturbate to orgasm as the condition of mature and healthy sexuality.

More significantly for "straight couples," this logic leads to a condemnation of contraception, sex among the aged or sterile, and oral-genital sex between husband and wife. The last case is the most telling: Why should the same act suddenly become sinful when practiced by two people of the same sex? Imagine that two people love each other deeply, that they remain faithful to each other in thought and deed, that they make a commitment to succor and support each other in sickness and health and that they express their affection and special relationship by giving and receiving sexual pleasure. Such is the widely accepted, somewhat romantic view of sex and love. Imagine further that the two people find a particular form of sexual pleasure, oral-genital intercourse, the most intense and expressive, and for this reason include it in their love making. This version of the romantic view is not altogether unfamiliar or unappealing to many young, modern urbanites, and even those who find it personally unattractive or distasteful seldom find it morally repugnant. What moral difference does it add if we now inject the fact that the couple are not of the opposite sex but of the same sex? This fact alone will hardly bear the weight of our moral condemnation, especially when all the other elements of our romantic sexual mythology are present. To draw a moral distinction simply on the grounds of the gender of the participants is arbitrary and capricious.

The identification of the natural and the reproductive seems initially plausible because it captures some of our intuitions about perverted sex. Necrophilia, pedophilia, and bestiality seem wrong and are also non-procreative. But is it their sterility that accounts for their immorality? What these acts also have in common is a lack of informed, voluntary consent from all participants. The paradigm of an immoral sexual act is rape—sex with another against their will. It is this failure of *consent* rather than *conception* that makes any sexual act (perverted or not) immoral.

Beyond the question of consent, sexual acts are perhaps more a matter of aesthetics than morality, of personal preference and tastes rather than general condemnation and legal prohibition. Personal likes and dislikes, even if they have a theological basis (and perhaps especially then), are not an adequate basis for morality or law. To prove that a practice is unnatural or perverted (in the sense of being nonreproductive) is not to prove it is wrong. For example, it may be "unnatural" to use the eyes for decoration with mascara or for communication with a sly glance, but these are hardly sins, and should certainly not be illegal even if they were. An analogy with eating may reinforce this point. Lust may be likened to an appetite, which, like hunger, is strong and instinctive. The process for gratifying each has become highly ritualized and overladen with symbolic meaning. Yet it is hardly immoral to use the occasion for ingesting food as a time for entertainment or business, as an opportunity to get to know another person or exchange intimacies. To restrict eating to nutrition, its natural function, is surely ascetic, and to impose this preference on others is surely presumptuous. Outlawing all forms of the unnatural needlessly deprives life of much of its variety, excitement, and richness—indeed of much that makes us human.

7. THE UNIVERSALIZABILITY PROBLEM

Behind some opposition to homosexuality is this worry: What if everybody did that? This concern could be made into a philosophical argument along Kantian lines. For an action to be morally right, it must be based on a principle we can recommend to all people. Yet to recommend that everyone become a homosexual, or enter a homosexual marriage, is to promulgate the termination of the human race. Since this practice fails the test of universalizability, it is properly condemned as immoral.

The most apparent difficulty with this argument is that it misses the logical mark. What is disputed is not the *obligation* to be gay or to enter a gay marriage but the *right* to do so. What is at issue is the option, not the duty of everyone to marry the person of their choice regardless of gender.

There is nothing illogical about recommending that every person has such a right, the way there is something illogical about saying that everyone should lie or have the right to do so (is this recommendation itself a lie?). Moreover the fear of the consequences from according everyone this right is also groundless. The best statistical evidence from Kinsey and his researchers suggests only a minority of the population would exercise their right to enter a homosexual marriage. If one adopts a rule utilitarian perspective in which the morality of an act is determined by the social utility of adopting the practice, then homosexual marriages are warranted: in a world in which overpopulation is a serious and growing problem, this practice promises to alleviate the increasing demand on scarce resources.

8. THE SLIPPERY SLOPE

The final argument I want to consider has a logical form familiar to philosophers debating abortion, euthanasia, and other contemporary issues. The major premise is that the small and perhaps plausible step we are now proposing will soon accelerate us down the slope into a moral abyss. Thus mercy killing may seem humane, but it weakens the principle of the sanctity of human life, so that soon we will also be killing deformed babies, senile men, incapacitated women, the insane, misfits, and others deemed socially unacceptable. To avoid these atrocities we must avoid the first step.

By a similar logic one might argue that legalizing homosexual marriages will lead shortly to group marriages, polygamy, polyandry—until there is nothing left of marriage as we know it. But to destroy the institution of marriage is to undermine the family and the basis of society. To avoid such a catastrophe we must avoid the first step: we must adhere resolutely to marriage as we know it—one man and one woman in holy wedlock.

In my view, such arguments rely more on scare tactics than on clear-mindedness. They invite the reassertion of the point made earlier that prevents the slide into other forms of marriage: monogamy has not been abandoned, for the homosexual marriage at issue still involves just one spouse. Moreover, I am not convinced that the abyss is so abysmal. There may be good reasons to challenge our binary frame of reference for conceptualizing legitimate sexual behavior. The success of television shows like "Three's Company" weakens our tendency to think in two's by asserting that three is not always a crowd. Some critics like John McMurtry view the monogamous restriction to two as needless and repressive.[16] Additionally, the polygamous practices of the Mormons may provide hard data that the alternatives to monogamy are neither imprudent nor destructive. Legalizing homosexual monogamy is not necessarily a step in this direction, and even if it were it might not be so bad.

III

None of the first eight arguments in defense of current restrictive marriage laws have turned out to be sound. Of course it does not follow that none can be formulated: some may be forthcoming at a future time. In order to justify legalizing homosexual marriages, let me now offer three positive considerations.

1. MAXIMIZING FREEDOM OF CHOICE

Freedom is one of the things our society values, and rightly so. The ability to live one's life as one chooses is not only sought by most people, but used as a standard against which particular social practices and, indeed, entire societies can be judged. The law serves as both the protector and promoter of this freedom. Its failure to include homosexual marriages can be regarded as a failure to provide freedom in one of its most important areas—our intimate, personal sexual life. The fact that some cannot marry the partner of their choice marks a moral deficiency in our society.

Moral philosophers have never ceased to wax eloquent in praise of freedom—whether we refer to Kant, Hegel, Marx, Mill, or Sartre.

Indeed, John Stuart Mill, who decided the morality of an action in terms of its consequences, accords freedom almost the same value as Kant and Sartre, with their quite different deontological perspective. In his essay *On Liberty,* Mill lavishly praises the virtues of choosing a life-plan for oneself, of allowing individuals the greatest array of lifestyles until their action can be shown to violate an assignable duty to others. His principle places a moral burden on those who would oppose gay marriages to justify their infringing on each individual's freedom to choose a marriage partner as he or she will. The maximization of freedom requires the legalization of homosexual marriages.

2. THE VALUE OF LOVE

However cynical one wants to be and however extreme one's view of love, it is difficult to deny that some homosexual couples do love one another and that their lives are the better for it. They make enduring commitments in word and deed to comfort and console each other, to safeguard and secure their partner's interests, and to care for their needs. Like health and wealth, such love is a good thing, something we would choose for ourselves and those close to us.

As a ceremony, marriage serves to recognize and legitimize a relationship, and to solicit social support for what is good and valuable in it. Bayles *seems to be close* in remarking that one of the functions of the law is to promote what is of genuine value. Insofar as love is of value and homosexual relationships are loving, then homosexual marriages should be legal.

3. SEXLESS JUSTICE

According to the popular image, justice is blindfolded, indicating that certain particularities are irrelevant to considerations of fairness. The biological identity of a person is one of these facts that I consider irrelevant: whether one's partner is male or female should make no difference in the eyes of the law. The Equal Rights Amendment, which outlaws discrimination on the basis of sex, may entail the legalization of homosexual marriages. But I do not want to argue this change as a constitutional point, but as a requirement of equity or justice.

I am not sure how to refute those who believe that gender makes a moral difference. Their view strikes me as pernicious, sexist, and chauvinistic, but I concede that this response contains more rhetoric than logic. Let me therefore offer three arguments from justice.

First, the "Golden Rule" may provide some logical leverage to budge the stubborn opponent: Do unto others as you would have others do unto you! Since all of us want to be granted the right to marry the partner of our choice, the homosexual should be accorded this same right. Since we would think it wrong for anyone to try to prevent us from marrying a person of our choice, just because of their gender, we should not prevent others from doing so. This argument is not very powerful, for the staunch defender of the status quo will undoubtedly reply that the homosexual is free to marry anyone of his or her choice—anyone of the opposite sex, that is. So we are back to the question of the justification of this restriction.

Second, a Rawlsian argument might be more persuasive.[17] Imagine that you did not know whether you would be born into the world preferring partners of the same sex or the opposite sex. Imagine further that you would be condemned to frustration, embarrassment, and loneliness if you could not marry a partner with your sexual preference. Imagine finally that you are rational and concerned about your own well-being. Would you choose to have homosexual marriages legal? It seems to me that most people would and should answer yes, if this were all they knew. In short it seems to me that if we can disengage ourselves from our sexual orientation through reason or compassion, then the unfairness of discrimination against homosexuals becomes blatant. Justice as well as love and freedom require the legalization of homosexual marriages.

Third, consider an analogy with interracial marriages. To strengthen it I shall reverse the factors. Imagine a society of two races in which people could marry only individuals of the opposite race, because marriage is thought of as a way to legitimize a sexual relationship. Sex with someone of the same race is considered by that society to be unnatural and perverted, a cause for reprobation, condemnation, and expulsion. Confronted with such conjugal practices, it seems plausible for us to object that they are racist and hence unjust. Whether one is prevented from marrying someone of the opposite race (as in our society at one time) or someone of the same race (as in the hypothetical case) is immaterial. The biological contingencies of birth into a particular race ought not, if we are to be just, serve as a basis for social or legal practice. People cannot do anything about their race—it is given, perhaps a God given. To prevent someone from marrying another just because that person happens to be of the wrong race—namely the same race—strikes us quite rightly as grossly unfair. By the same logic the prohibition on same-sex marriages is just as unwarranted—not racist but "sexist" in the very broad sense of making gender differences per se into moral differences. Like race, our biological identity as male or female is something over which the average person has little control (transsexualism notwithstanding). Each of us is born into the world as a member of a particular race and endowed with a particular gender. Social policies that discriminate on the basis of gender alone fault us for something we cannot change. If ought implies can, if the focus of morality is free, voluntary actions, then sexist marriage laws are unjust.

Some might contend that the law does not discriminate on the basis of gender. After all any male can legally marry any female, more or less (i.e., with blood and age restrictions), and any female can marry any male. The law does not say that having a particular gender disqualifies you from the legal right to marry—and that is what unfair discrimination based on gender would be.

I think this position is wrong-headed, like the racist doctrine of separate but equal. If the gender or race of my partner makes any difference in the eyes of the law, then the law is sexist or racist. A racist says you cannot marry some people because of their race, and a sexist says you cannot marry some people because of their sex. Both policies are unjust: neither race nor sex should make a legal or moral difference.

The injustice would be less serious if only the right to marry were at issue. But in our society this right is tied to many other financial benefits—medical and health insurance, taxation (though now changed), and inheritance—not to mention the psychological and emotional advantages. For example, if your gay lover dies without a will, you cannot inherit half of what you have built up during your life together. If you take out a health insurance policy, you cannot receive coverage that extends to your lover. You cannot receive social security benefits or visiting rights in the intensive care ward reserved for members of the immediate family. In short, homosexual couples are denied a host of real privileges and significant advantages that accrue automatically to heterosexual pairs. This inequitable distribution based solely on the gender of the participants strikes me as a violation of the principle of justice, not a humane practice for an enlightened society. Though some could be redressed through a series of protective statutes and astute private measures, these means are cumbersome. None could compensate for the lack of social approval and psychological support that marriage provides.

IV

The Mirage of Matrimony

Let me conclude with a postscript on the desirability of holy wedlock, for it may not be as rosy as I have painted it. Some cynics might object that marriage is not all I have made it out to be. Perhaps it is only, as St. Paul suggested, a solution to fornication—at worst it is hell and at best it is a consolation. Indeed, many homosexuals might agree and choose to forego this option because they do not want to import the heterosexual problems of marriage into the gay world.

The advantages of marriage per se are difficult to disentangle from the religious mystique that enshrouds it and the social rituals that embellish it. The rigid stereotypical sex roles imposed on a husband and a wife in our culture curtail their freedom to work out their personal identities and a division of labor according to their own preferences. This restriction is a serious disadvantage, but hard to weigh against the advantages. It is difficult to sort out the value of marriage for oneself from the value of marriage per se, to separate out the contingencies that accompany marriage in a particular locale, class, or culture. Accordingly, the position I have sought to defend is that marriage may be a benefit to some and that we should not deny it to any one simply on the basis of gender. For even where it is not a benefit, people have the right to choose for themselves—even to harm themselves. Society should not use the law to prevent people from entering into a mutually agreed upon marriage, whether it be good or bad for them. All persons are entitled to the pursuit of happiness as they envisage it.

NOTES

1. *Baker vs. Nelson*, 291 Minn 310, 191 N.W. 2nd 185 Minn Sup. Ct., 1971.
2. *Baker vs. Nelson*, 41 U.S.L.W. 3167 (Us Oct. 10, 1972).
3. The variations arise because of the different roles of men and women in child bearing and child rearing. See the subsequent discussion of the family.
4. The qualification "typically" is needed to cover cases of common law marriage. There is no means whereby same-sex couples who live together can acquire the rights that opposite-sex couples acquire through the institution of common law marriage. A bill in San Francisco to grant gay couples legal rights comparable to common law marriage was recently defeated.
5. I would take the same stance against those who would argue that open marriage is a contradiction in terms because exclusivity is part of the definition of monogamy. Richard Wasserstrom suggests a strategy for opposing this semantic approach that I have not adopted in "Is Adultery Immoral?", herein, pp. 93 to 106.

6. Pope Paul VI "Humanae Vitae,"herein, pp. 167-184, and the recent Vatican Declaration on Ethics.

7. The position of the study commissioned by the Catholic Theological Society of America is far more humane and tolerant. See A. Kosnik et al., *Human Sexuality* (New York: Paulist Press, 1977) pp. 186-218.

8. See Carl Cohen, "Sex, Birth Control, and Human Life," in *Ethics* 19 (July, 1969), also reprinted in this volume pp. 185-199.

9. For a still useful selection of philosophical papers on sex roles, see *Feminism and Philosophy*, edited by Mary Vetterling Braggin, Frederick Elliston and Jane English (Totowa, NJ: Littlefield Adams, 1977).

10. See Frederick Suppe's "Curing Homosexuality," herein, pp. 391-420.

11. See Joseph Margolis, "The Question of Homosexuality" in the first edition of *Philosophy and Sex*, pp. 288-302, and his more recent "Homosexuality" in *And Justice for All*, edited by Tom Regan and Donald VanDeVeer (Totowa, NJ: Littlefield Adams, 1982), pp. 42-63.

12. See Patrick Devlin, *The Enforcement of Morals* New York: (Oxford University Press, 1965), viz ch. 1.

13. In chapter 4, dealing with marriage laws, Devlin goes further, building on the positive converse that if society generally feels a marital practice is warranted, then it should be legal.

14. See H.L.A. Hart "Immorality and Treason" in *The Listener* (July 30, 1959), pp. 162-63, and his elaboration in *Law, Liberty and Morality* (New York: Oxford University Press, 1963).

15. Thomas Aquinas, *On the Truth of the Catholic Faith* Book 3: Providence pt. 1, trans. Vernon J. Bourke (New York: Doubleday, 1956).

16. John McMurtry, "Monogamy: A Critique" in *The Monist* 56 no. 4 (1972) and pp. 107-118 of this volume.

17. John Rawls, *A Theory of Justice* (Cambridge: Harvard University Press, 1971), viz. Chapter 3.

CONTRACEPTION

Pope Paul VI

Humanae Vitae

To the venerable Patriarchs, Archbishops and other local ordinaries in peace and communion with the Apostolic See, to priests, the faithful and to all men of good will.

Venerable brothers and beloved sons:

THE TRANSMISSION OF LIFE

1. The most serious duty of transmitting human life, for which married persons are the free and responsible collaborators of God the Creator, has always been a source of great joys to them, even if sometimes accompanied by not a few difficulties and by distress.

At all times the fulfillment of this duty has posed grave problems to the conscience of married persons, but, with the recent evolution of society, changes have taken place that give rise to new questions which the Church could not ignore, having to do with a matter which so closely touches upon the life and happiness of men.

1. NEW ASPECTS OF THE PROBLEM AND COMPETENCY OF THE MAGISTERIUM

New Formulation of the Problem

2. The changes which have taken place are in fact noteworthy and of

The encyclical *Humanae Vitae* was issued July 29, 1968, at Rome. This official translation is reprinted by permission of the National Catholic News Service.

varied kinds. In the first place, there is the rapid demographic development. Fear is shown by many that world population is growing more rapidly than the available resources, with growing distress to many families and developing countries, so that the temptation for authorities to counter this danger with radical measures is great. Moreover, working and housing conditions, as well as increased exigencies both in the economic field and in that of education, often make the proper education of a large number of children difficult today. A change is also seen both in the manner of considering the person of woman and her place in society, and in the value to be attributed to conjugal love in marriage, and also in the appreciation to be made of the meaning of conjugal acts in relation to that love.

Finally and above all, man has made stupendous progress in the domination and rational organization of the forces of nature, such that he tends to extend this domination to his own total being: to the body, to psychical life, to social life and even to the laws which regulate the transmission of life.

3. This new state of things gives rise to new questions. Granted the conditions of life today, and granted the meaning which conjugal relations have with respect to the harmony between husband and wife and to their mutual fidelity, would not a revision of the ethical norms, in force up to now, seem to be advisable, especially when it is considered that they cannot be observed without sacrifices, sometimes heroic sacrifices?

And again: by extending to this field the application of the so-called "principle of totality," could it not be admitted that the intention of a less abundant but more rationalized fecundity might transform a materially sterilizing intervention into a licit and wise control of birth? Could it not be admitted, that is, that the finality of procreation pertains to the ensemble of conjugal life, rather than to its single acts? It is also asked whether, in view of the increased sense of responsibility of modern man, the moment has not come for him to entrust to his reason and his will, rather than to the biological rhythms of this organism, the task of regulating birth.

Competency of the Magisterium

4. Such questions required from the teaching authority of the Church a new and deeper reflection upon the principles of the moral teaching on marriage: a teaching founded on the natural law, illuminated and enriched by divine revelation.

No believer will wish to deny that the teaching authority of the

Church is competent to interpret even the natural moral law. It is, in fact, indisputable, as our predecessors have many times declared,[1] that Jesus Christ, when communicating to Peter and to the Apostles His divine authority and sending them to teach all nations His commandments,[2] constituted them as guardians and authentic interpreters of all the moral law, not only, that is, of the law of the Gospel, but also of the natural law, which is also an expression of the will of God, the faithful fulfillment of which is equally necessary for salvation.[3]

Conformable to this mission of hers, the Church has always provided —and even more amply in recent times—a coherent teaching concerning both the nature of marriage and the correct use of conjugal rights and the duties of husband and wife.[4]

Special Studies

5. The consciousness of that same mission induced us to confirm and enlarge the study commission which our predecessor Pope John XXIII of happy memory had instituted in March, 1963. That commission which included, besides several experts in the various pertinent disciplines, also married couples, had as its scope the gathering of opinions on the new questions regarding conjugal life, and in particular on the regulation of births, and of furnishing suitable elements of information so that the magisterium could give an adequate reply to the expectation not only of the faithful, but also of world opinion.[5]

The work of these experts, as well as the successive judgments and counsels spontaneously forwarded by or expressly requested from a good number of our brothers in the episcopate, have permitted us to measure exactly all the aspects of this complex matter. Hence with all our heart we express to each of them our lively gratitude.

Reply of the Magisterium

6. The conclusions at which the commission arrived could not, nevertheless, be considered by us as definitive, nor dispense us from a personal examination of this serious question; and this also because, within the commission itself, no full concordance of judgments concerning the moral norms to be proposed had been reached, and above all because certain criteria of solutions had emerged which departed from the moral teaching of marriage proposed with constant firmness by the teaching authority of the Church.

Therefore, having attentively sifted the documentation laid before us,

after mature reflection and assiduous prayers, we now intend, by virtue of
the mandate entrusted to us by Christ, to give our reply to these grave
questions.

II. DOCTRINAL PRINCIPLES

A Total Vision of Man

7. The problem of birth, like every other problem regarding human life, is
to be considered, beyond partial perspectives—whether of the biological or
psychological, demographic or sociological orders—in the light of an integral vision of man and of his vocation, not only his natural and earthly, but
also his supernatural and eternal vocation. And since, in the attempts to
justify artificial methods of birth control, many have appealed to the demands both of conjugal love and of "responsible parenthood," it is good to
state very precisely the true concept of these two great realities of married
life, referring principally to what was recently set forth in this regard, and
in a highly authoritative form, by the Second Vatican Council in its pastoral constitution *Gaudium et Spes.*

Conjugal Love

8. Conjugal love reveals its true nature and nobility, when it is considered
in its supreme origin, God, who is love,[6] "the Father, from whom every
family in heaven and on earth is named."[7]

Marriage is not, then, the effect of chance or the product of evolution
of unconscious natural forces; it is the wise institution of the Creator to
realize in mankind His design of love. By means of the reciprocal personal
gift of self, proper and exclusive to them, husband and wife tend towards
the communion of their beings in view of mutual personal perfection, to
collaborate with God in the generation and education of new lives.

For baptized persons, moreover, marriage invests the dignity of a sac-
ramental sign of grace, inasmuch as it represents the union of Christ and
of the Church.

Its Characteristics

9. Under this light, there clearly appear the characteristic marks and demands of conjugal love, and it is of supreme importance to have an exact
idea of these.

This love is first of all fully human, that is to say, of the senses and of the spirit at the same time. It is not, then, a simple transport of instinct and sentiment, but also, and principally, an act of the free will, intended to endure and to grow by means of the joys and sorrows of daily life, in such a way that husband and wife become only one heart and only one soul, and together attain their human perfection.

Then, this love is total, that is to say, it is a very special form of personal friendship, in which husband and wife generously share everything, without undue reservations or selfish calculations. Whoever truly loves his marriage partner loves not only for what he receives, but for the partner's self, rejoicing that he can enrich his partner with the gift of himself.

Again, this love is faithful and exclusive until death. Thus in fact, do bride and groom conceive it to be on the day when they freely and in full awareness assume the duty of the marriage bond. A fidelity, this, which can sometimes be difficult, but is always possible, always noble and meritorious, as no one can deny. The example of so many married persons down through the centuries shows, not only that fidelity is according to the nature of marriage, but also that it is a source of profound and lasting happiness and finally, this love is fecund for it is not exhausted by the communion between husband and wife, but is destined to continue, raising up new lives. "Marriage and conjugal love are by their nature ordained toward the begetting and educating of children. Children are really the supreme gift of marriage and contribute very substantially to the welfare of their parents."[8]

Responsible Parenthood

10. Hence conjugal love requires in husband and wife an awareness of their mission of "responsible parenthood," which today is rightly much insisted upon, and which also must be exactly understood. Consequently it is to be considered under different aspects which are legitimate and connected with one another.

In relation to the biological processes, responsible parenthood means the knowledge and respect of their functions; human intellect discovers in the power of giving life biological laws which are part of the human person.[9]

In relation to the tendencies of instinct or passion, responsible parenthood means that necessary dominion which reason and will must exercise over them.

In relation to physical, economic, psychological and social conditions, responsible parenthood is exercised, either by the deliberate and generous decision to raise a large family, or by the decision, made for grave motives and with due respect for the moral law, to avoid for the time being, or even for an indeterminate period, a new birth.

Responsible parenthood also and above all implies a more profound relationship to the objective moral order established by God, of which a right conscience is the faithful interpreter. The responsible exercise of parenthood implies, therefore, that husband and wife recognize fully their own duties towards God, towards themselves, towards the family and towards society, in a correct hierarchy of values.

In the task of transmitting life, therefore, they are not free to proceed completely at will, as if they could determine in a wholly autonomous way the honest path to follow; but they must conform their activity to the creative intention of God, expressed in the very nature of marriage and of its acts, and manifested by the constant teaching of the Church.[10]

Respect for the Nature and Purpose of the Marriage Act

11. These acts, by which husband and wife are united in chaste intimacy, and by means of which human life is transmitted, are, as the council recalled, "noble and worthy,"[11] and they do not cease to be lawful if, for causes independent of the will of husband and wife, they are foreseen to be infecund, since they always remain ordained towards expressing and consolidating their union. In fact, as experience bears witness, not every conjugal act is followed by a new life. God has widely disposed natural laws and rhythms of fecundity which, of themselves, cause a separation in the succession of births. Nonetheless the Church, calling men back to the observance of the norms of the natural law, as interpreted by their constant doctrine, teaches that each and every marriage act (*quilibet matrimonii usus*) must remain open to the transmission of life.[12]

Two Inseparable Aspects: Union and Procreation

12. That teaching, often set forth by the magisterium, is founded upon the inseparable connection, willed by God and unable to be broken by man on his own initiative, between the two meanings of the conjugal act: the unitive meaning and the procreative meaning. Indeed, by its intimate structure, the conjugal act, while most closely uniting husband and wife, empowers them to generate new lives, according to laws inscribed in the very being of man and of woman. By safeguarding both these essential aspects, unitive and procreative, the conjugal act preserves in its fullness the sense of true mutual love and its ordination towards man's most high calling to parenthood. We believe that the men of our day are particularly capable of seizing the deeply reasonable and human character of this fundamental principle.

Faithfulness to God's Design

13. It is in fact justly observed that a conjugal act imposed upon one's partner without regard for his or her condition and lawful desires is not a true act of love, and therefore denies an exigency of right moral order in the relationships between husband and wife. Hence, one who reflects well must also recognize that a reciprocal act of love, which jeopardizes the responsibility to transmit life which God the Creator, according to particular laws, inserted therein is in contradiction with the design constitutive of marriage, and with the will of the Author of life. To use this divine gift destroying, even if only partially, its meaning and its purpose is to contradict the nature both of man and of woman and of their most intimate relationship, and therefore, it is to contradict also the plan of God and His will. On the other hand, to make use of the gift of conjugal love while respecting the laws of the generative process means to acknowledge oneself not to be the arbiter of the sources of human life, but rather the minister of the design established by the Creator. In fact, just as man does not have unlimited dominion over his body in general, so also, with particular reason, he has no such dominion over his generative faculties as such, because of their intrinsic ordination towards raising up life, of which God is the principle. "Human life is sacred," Pope John XXIII recalled; "from its very inception it reveals the creating hand of God."[13]

Illicit Ways of Regulating Birth

14. In conformity with these landmarks in the human and Christian vision of marriage, we must once again declare that the direct interruption of the generative process already begun, and, above all, directly willed and procured abortion, even if for therapeutic reasons, are to be absolutely excluded as licit means of regulating birth.[14]

Equally to be excluded, as the teaching authority of the Church has frequently declared, is direct sterilization, whether perpetual or temporary, whether of the man or of the woman.[15] Similarly excluded is every action which, either in anticipation of the conjugal act, or in its accomplishment, or in the development of its natural consequences, proposes, whether as an end or as a means, to render procreation impossible.[16]

To justify conjugal acts made intentionally infecund, one cannot invoke as valid reasons the lesser evil, or the fact that such acts would constitute a whole together with the fecund acts already performed or to follow later, and hence would share in one and the same moral goodness. In truth, if it is sometimes licit to tolerate a lesser evil in order to avoid a greater evil or to promote a greater good[17] it is not licit, even for the gravest reasons, to do evil so that good may follow therefrom,[18] that is, to make into the object of a positive act of the will something which is intrinsically disordered, and hence unworthy of the human person, even when the intention is to safeguard or promote individual, family, or social well-being. Consequently it is an error to think that a conjugal act which is deliberately made infecund and so is intrinsically dishonest could be made honest and right by the ensemble of a fecund conjugal life.

Licitness of Therapeutic Means

15. The Church, on the contrary, does not at all consider illicit the use of those therapeutic means truly necessary to cure diseases of the organism, even if an impediment to procreation, which may be foreseen, should result therefrom, provided such impediment is not, for whatever motive, directly willed.[19]

Licitness of Recourse to Infecund Periods

16. To this teaching of the Church on conjugal morals, the objection is made today, as we observed earlier, that it is the prerogative of the human intellect to dominate the energies offered by irrational nature and to orientate them towards an end conformable to the good of man. Now, some may ask: in the present case, is it not reasonable in many circumstances to have recourse to artificial birth control if, thereby, we secure the harmony and peace of the family, and better conditions for the education of the children already born? To this question it is necessary to reply with clarity: the Church is the first to praise and recommend the intervention of intelligence in a function which so closely associates the rational creature with his Creator; but she affirms that this must be done with respect for the order established by God.

If, then, there are serious motives to space out births, which derive from the physical or psychological condition of husband and wife, or from external conditions, the Church teaches that it is then licit to take into account the natural rhythms immanent in the generative functions, for the use of marriage in the infecund periods only, and in this way to regulate birth without offending the moral principles which have been recalled earlier.[20]

The Church is consistent with herself when she considers recourse to the infecund periods to be licit, while at the same time condemning, as being always illicit, the use of means directly contrary to fecundation, even if such use is inspired by reasons which may appear honest and serious. In reality, there are essential differences between the two cases; in the former, the married couple make legitimate use of a natural disposition; in the latter, they impede the development of natural processes. It is true that, in the one and the other case, the married couple are in agreement in the positive will of avoiding children for plausible reasons, seeking the certainty that offspring will not arrive; but it is also true that only in the former case are they able to renounce the use of marriage in the fecund periods when, for just motives, procreation is not desirable, while making use of it during infecund periods to manifest their affection and to safeguard their mutual fidelity. By so doing, they give proof of a truly and integrally honest love.

Grave Consequences of Methods of Artificial Birth Control

17. Upright men can even better convince themselves of the solid grounds on which the teaching of the Church in this field is based, if they care to reflect upon the consequences of methods of artificial birth control. Let them consider, first of all, how wide and easy a road would thus be opened up towards conjugal infidelity and the general lowering of morality. Not much experience is needed in order to know human weakness, and to understand that men—especially the young, who are so vulnerable on this point—have need of encouragement to be faithful to the moral law, so that they must not be offered some easy means of eluding its observance. It is also to be feared that the man, growing used to the employment of anti-conceptive practices, may finally lose respect for the woman and, no longer caring for her physical and psychological equilibrium, may come to the point of considering her as a mere instrument of selfish enjoyment, and no longer as his respected and beloved companion.

Let it be considered also that a dangerous weapon would thus be placed in the hands of those public authorities who take no heed of moral exigencies. Who could blame a government for applying to the solution of the problems of the community those means acknowledged to be licit for married couples in the solution of a family problem? Who will stop rulers from favoring, from even imposing upon their peoples, if they were to consider it necessary, the method of contraception which they judge to be most efficacious? In such a way men, wishing to avoid individual, family, or social difficulties encountered in the observance of the divine law, would reach the point of placing at the mercy of the intervention of public authorities the most personal and most reserved sector of conjugal intimacy.

Consequently, if the mission of generating life is not to be exposed to the arbitrary will of men, one must necessarily recognize unsurmountable limits to the possibility of man's domination over his own body and its functions; limits which no man, whether a private individual or one invested with authority, may licitly surpass. And such limits cannot be determined otherwise than by the respect due to the integrity of the human organism and its functions, according to the principles recalled earlier, and also according to the correct understanding of the "principle of totality" illustrated by our predecessor Pope Pius XII. [21]

The Church Guarantor of True Human Values

18. It can be foreseen that this teaching will perhaps not be easily received by all: Too numerous are those voices—amplified by the modern means of propaganda—which are contrary to the voice of the Church. To tell the truth, the Church is not surprised to be made, like her divine founder, a "sign of contradiction," [22] yet she does not because of this cease to proclaim with humble firmness the entire moral law, both natural and evangelical. Of such laws the Church was not the author, nor consequently can she be their arbiter; she is only their depositary and their interpreter, without ever being able to declare to be licit that which is not so by reason of its intimate and unchangeable opposition to the true good of man.

In defending conjugal morals in their integral wholeness, the Church knows that she contributes towards the establishment of a truly human civilization; she engages man not to abdicate from his own responsibility in order to rely on technical means; by that very fact she defends the dignity of man and wife. Faithful to both the teaching and the example of the Saviour, she shows herself to be the sincere and disinterested friend of men, whom she wishes to help, even during their earthly sojourn, "to share as sons in the life of the living God, the Father of all men." [23]

III. PASTORAL DIRECTIVES

The Church Mater et Magistra

19. Our words would not be an adequate expression of the thought and solicitude of the Church, mother and teacher of all peoples, if, after having recalled men to the observance and respect of the divine law regarding

matrimony, we did not strengthen them in the path of honest regulation of birth, even amid the difficult conditions which today afflict families and peoples. The Church, in fact, cannot have a different conduct towards men than that of the Redeemer: She knows their weaknesses, has compassion on the crowd, receives sinners; but she cannot renounce the teaching of the law which is, in reality, that law proper to a human life restored to its original truth and conducted by the spirit of God.[24]

Possibility of Observing the Divine Law

20. The teaching of the Church on the regulation of birth, which promulgates the divine law, will easily appear to many to be difficult or even impossible of actuation. And indeed, like all great beneficent realities, it demands serious engagement and much effort, individual, family, and social effort. More than that, it would not be practicable without the help of God, who upholds and strengthens the good will of men. Yet, to anyone who reflects well, it cannot but be clear that such efforts ennoble man and are beneficial to the human community.

Mastery of Self

21. The honest practice of regulation of birth demands first of all that husband and wife acquire and possess solid convictions concerning the true values of life and of the family, and that they tend towards securing perfect self-mastery. To dominate instinct by means of one's reason and free will undoubtedly requires ascetical practices, so that the affective manifestations of conjugal life may observe the correct order, in particular with regard to the observance of periodic continence. Yet this discipline which is proper to the purity of married couples, far from harming conjugal love, rather confers on it a higher human value. It demands continual effort yet, thanks to its beneficent influence, husband and wife fully develop their personalities, being enriched with spiritual values. Such discipline bestows upon family life fruits of serenity and peace, and facilitates the solution of other problems; it favors attention for one's partner, helps both parties to drive out selfishness, the enemy of true love; and deepens their sense of responsibility. By its means, parents acquire the capacity of having a deeper and more efficacious influence in the education of their offspring; little children and youths grow up with a just appraisal of human values, and in the serene and harmonious development of their spiritual and sensitive faculties.

Creating an Atmosphere Favorable to Chastity

22. On this occasion, we wish to draw the attention of educators, and of all who perform duties of responsibility in regard to the common good of human society, to the need of creating an atmosphere favorable to education in chastity, that is, to the triumph of healthy liberty over license by means of respect for the moral order.

Everything in the modern media of social communications which leads to sense excitation and unbridled habits, as well as every form of pornography and licentious performances, must arouse the frank and unanimous reaction of all those who are solicitous for the progress of civilization and the defense of the common good of the human spirit. Vainly would one seek to justify such depravation with the pretext of artistic or scientific exigencies,[25] or to deduce an argument from the freedom allowed in this sector by the public authorities.

Appeal to Public Authorities

23. To Rulers, who are those principally responsible for the common good, and who can do so much to safeguard moral customs, we say: Do not allow the morality of your peoples to be degraded; do not permit that by legal means practices contrary to the natural and divine law be introduced into that fundamental cell, the family. Quite other is the way in which public authorities can and must contribute to the solution of the demographic problem: namely the way of a provident policy for the family, of a wise education of peoples in respect of moral law and the liberty of citizens.

We are well aware of the serious difficulties experienced by public authorities in this regard, especially in the developing countries. To their legitimate preoccupations we devoted our encyclical letter *Populorum Progressio*. But with our predecessor Pope John XXIII, we repeat: No solution to these difficulties is acceptable "which does violence to man's essential dignity" and is based only on an utterly materialistic conception of man himself and of his life. The only possible solution to this question is one which envisages the social and economic progress both of individuals and of the whole of human society, and which respects and promotes of true human values.[26] Neither can one, without grave injustice, consider divine providence to be responsible for what depends, instead, on a lack of wisdom in government, on an insufficient sense of social justice, on selfish monopolization, or again on blameworthy indolence in confronting the efforts and the sacrifices necessary to ensure the raising of living standards of a people and of all its sons.[27]

May all responsible public authorities—as some are already doing so laudably—generously revive their efforts. And may mutual aid between all the members of the great human family never cease to grow. This is an almost limitless field which thus opens up to the activity of the great international organizations.

To Men of Science

24. We wish now to express our encouragement to men of science, who "can considerably advance the welfare of marriage and the family, along with peace of conscience, if by pooling their efforts they labor to explain more thoroughly the various conditions favoring a proper regulation of births."[28] It is particularly desirable that, according to the wish already expressed by Pope Pius XII, medical science succeed in providing a sufficiently secure basis for a regulation of birth, founded on the observance of natural rhythms.[29] In this way, scientists and especially Catholic scientists will contribute to demonstrate in actual fact that, as the Church teaches, "a true contradiction cannot exist between the divine laws pertaining to the transmission of life and those pertaining to the fostering of authentic conjugal love."[30]

To Christian Husbands and Wives

25. And now our words more directly address our own children, particularly those whom God calls to serve Him in marriage. The Church, while teaching imprescriptible demands of the divine law, announces the tidings of salvation, and by means of the sacraments opens up the paths of grace, which makes man a new creature, capable of corresponding with love and true freedom to the design of his Creator and Saviour, and of finding the yoke of Christ to be sweet.[31]

Christian married couples, then, docile to her voice, must remember that their Christian vocation, which began at baptism, is further specified and reinforced by the sacrament of matrimony. By it husband and wife are strengthened and as it were consecrated for the faithful accomplishment of their proper duties, for the carrying out of their proper vocation even to perfection, and the Christian witness which is proper to them before the whole world.[32] To them the Lord entrusts the task of making visible to men the holiness and sweetness of the law which unites the mutual love of husband and wife with their co-operation with the love of God, the author of human life.

We do not at all intend to hide the sometimes serious difficulties inherent in the life of Christian married persons; for them as for everyone else, "the gate is narrow and the way is hard, that leads to life."[33] But the hope of that life must illuminate their way, as with courage they strive to live with wisdom, justice and piety in this present time,[34] knowing that the figure of this world passes away.[35]

Let married couples, then, face up to the efforts needed, supported by the faith and hope which "do not disappoint . . . because God's love has been poured into our hearts through the Holy Spirit, who has been given to us."[36] Let them implore divine assistance by persevering prayer; above all, let them draw from the source of grace and charity in the Eucharist. And if sin should still keep its hold over them, let them not be discouraged, but rather have recourse with humble perseverance to the mercy of God, which is poured forth in the sacrament of Penance. In this way they will be enabled to achieve the fullness of conjugal life described by the Apostle: "husbands, love your wives, as Christ loved the Church . . . husbands should love their wives as their own bodies. He who loves his wife loves himself. For no man ever hates his own flesh, but nourishes and cherishes it, as Christ does the Church . . . this is a great mystery, and I mean in reference to Christ and the Church. However, let each one of you love his wife as himself, and let the wife see that she respects her husband."[37]

Apostolate in Homes

26. Among the fruits which ripen forth from a generous effort of fidelity to the divine law, one of the most precious is that married couples themselves not infrequently feel the desire to communicate their experience to others. Thus there comes to be included in the vast pattern of the vocation of the laity a new and most noteworthy form of the apostolate of like to like; it is married couples themselves who become apostles and guides to other married couples. This is assuredly, among so many forms of apostolate, one of those which seem most opportune today.[38]

To Doctors and Medical Personnel

27. We hold those physicians and medical personnel in the highest esteem who, in the exercise of their profession, value above every human interest the superior demands of their Christian vocation. Let them persevere, therefore, in promoting on every occasion the discovery of solutions inspired by faith and right reason, let them strive to arouse this conviction and this respect in their associates. Let them also consider as their proper professional duty the task of acquiring all the knowledge needed in this delicate sector, so as to be able to give those married persons who consult

them wise counsel and healthy direction, such as they have a right to expect.

To Priests

28. Beloved priest sons, by vocation you are the counselors and spiritual guides of individual persons and of families. We now turn to you with confidence. Your first task—especially in the case of those who teach moral theology—is to expound the Church's teaching on marriage without ambiguity. Be the first to give, in the exercise of your ministry, the example of loyal internal and external obedience to the teaching authority of the Church. That obedience, as you know well, obliges not only because of the reasons adduced, but rather because of the light of the Holy Spirit, which is given in a particular way to the pastors of the Church in order that they may illustrate the truth.[39] You know, too, that it is of the utmost importance, for peace of consciences and for the unity of the Christian people, that in the field of morals as well as in that of dogma, all should attend to the magisterium of the Church, and all should speak the same language. Hence, with all our heart we renew to you the heartfelt plea of the great Apostle Paul: "I appeal to you, brethren, by the name of Our Lord Jesus Christ, that all of you agree and that there be no dissensions among you, but that you be united in the same mind and the same judgment."[40]

29. To diminish in no way the saving teaching of Christ constitutes an eminent form of charity for souls. But this must ever be accompanied by patience and goodness, such as the Lord himself gave example of in dealing with men. Having come not to condemn but to save,[41] he was indeed intransigent with evil, but merciful towards individuals.

In their difficulties, many married couples always find, in the words and in the heart of a priest, the echo of the voice and the love of the Redeemer.

Speak out confidently, beloved sons, with the conviction that the Spirit of God, while assisting the Magisterium in propounding doctrine, enlightens internally the hearts of the faithful, and invites them to give their assent. Teach married couples the necessary way of prayer, and prepare them to have recourse frequently and with faith to the sacraments of the Eucharist and Penance, without ever allowing themselves to be disheartened by their weakness.

To Bishops

30. Beloved and venerable brothers in the episcopate, with whom we most intimately share the solicitude of the spiritual good of the people of God,

at the conclusion of this encyclical our reverent and affectionate thoughts turn to you. To all of you we extend an urgent invitation. At the head of the priests, your collaborators, and of your faithful, work ardently and incessantly for the safeguarding and the holiness of marriage, so that it may always be lived in its entire human and Christian fullness. Consider this mission as one of your most urgent responsibilities at the present time. As you know, it implies concerted pastoral action in all the fields of human activity, economic, cultural and social; for, in fact, only a simultaneous improvement in these various sectors will make it possible to render the life of parents and of children within their families not only tolerable, but easier and more joyous, to render the living together in human society more fraternal and peaceful, in faithfulness to God's design for the world.

Final Appeal

31. Venerable brothers, most beloved sons, and all men of good will, great indeed is the work of education, of progress and of love to which we call you, upon the foundation of the Church's teaching, of which the successor of Peter is, together with his brothers in the episcopate, the depositary and interpreter. Truly a great work, as we are deeply convinced, both for the world and for the Church, since man cannot find true happiness—towards which he aspires with all his being—other than in respect of the laws written by God in his very nature, laws which he must observe with intelligence and love. Upon this work, and upon all of you, and especially upon married couples, we invoke the abundant graces of the God of holiness and mercy, and in pledge thereof we impart to you all our apostolic blessing.

Given at Rome, from St. Peter's, this 25th day of July, feast of St. James the Apostle, in the year 1968, the sixth of our pontificate.

NOTES

1. Cf. Pius IX, encyc. *Qui Pluribus*, November 9, 1846; in *PII IX P. M. Acta*, I, pp. 9-10; St. Pius X, encyc. *Singulari Quadam*, Sept. 24, 1912; in *AAS* IV (1912), p. 658; Pius XI, encyc. *Casti Connubii*, Dec. 31, 1930; in *AAS* XXI (1930), pp. 579-81; Pius XXI, allocution *Magnificate Dominum* to the episcopate of the Catholic world, Nov. 2, 1954; in *AAS* XLVI (1954), 671-72; John XXIII, encyc. *Mater et Magistra*, May 15, 1961; in *AAS* LIII (1961), p. 457.

2. Cf. Matthew 28:18-19.

3. Cf. Matthew 7:21.

4. Cf. *Catechismus Romanus Concilii Tridentini*, part 2, chap. 8, Leo XIII, encyc. *Arcanum*, Feb. 19, 1880; in *Acta Leonis XIII*, II (1881), pp. 26-29; Pius XI, encyc. *Divini Illius Magistri*, Dec. 31, 1929, in *AAS* XXII (1930), pp. 58-61; encyc.

Casti Connubii, in *AAS* XXII (1930), pp. 545-46; Pius XII, alloc. to the Italian medicobiological union of St. Luke, Nov. 12, 1944, in *Discorsi e Radiomessaggi,* 6, pp. 191-92; to the Italian Catholic union of midwives, Oct. 29, 1951, in *AAS* XLIII (1951), pp. 857-59; to the seventh Congress of the International Society of Haematology, Sept. 12, 1958, in *AAS* L (1958), pp. 734-35; John XXIII, encyc. *Mater et Magistra,* in *AAS* LIII (1961), pp. 446-47; *Codex Iuris Canonici,* Canon 1067; Can. 1968, S 1, Can. 1066 S 1-2; II Vatican Council, Pastoral Constitution, *Gaudium et Spes,* nos. 47-52.

5. Cf. Paul VI, allocution to the Sacred College, June 23, 1964, in *AAS* LVI (1964), p. 588; to the Commission for Study of Problems of Population, Family and Birth, March 27, 1965, in *AAS* LVII (1965), p. 388; to the National Congress of the Italian Society of Obstetrics and Gynecology, Oct. 29, 1966, in *AAS* LVIII (1966), p. 1168.

6. Cf. I John 4:8.

7. Cf. Ephesians 3:15.

8. Cf. Pastoral Const. *Gaudium et Spes,* no. 50.

9. Cf. St. Thomas, *Summa Theologica,* I-II, q. 94, art. 2.

10. Cf. Pastoral Const. *Gaudium et Spes,* nos. 50, 51.

11. Ibid., no. 49.

12. Cf. Pius XI, encyc. *Casti Connubii,* in *AAS* XXII (1930), p. 560; Pius XII, in *AAS* XLIII (1951), p. 843.

13. Cf. John XXIII, encyc. *Mater et Magistra,* in *AAS* LIII (1961), p. 447.

14. Cf. *Catechismus Romanus Concilii Tridentini,* part 2, chap. 8; Pius XI, encyc. *Casti Connubii,* in *AAS* XXII (1930), pp. 562-64; Pius XII, *Discorsi e Radiomessaggi,* VI (1944), pp. 191-92; *AAS* XLIII (1951), pp. 842-43; pp. 857-59; John XXIII, encyc. *Pacem in Terris,* Apr. 11, 1963, in *AAS* LV (1963), pp. 259-60; *Gaudium et Spes.* no. 51.

15. Cf. Pius XI, encyc. *Casti Connubii,* in *AAS* XXII (1930), p. 565; decree of the Holy Office, Feb. 22, 1940, in *AAS* L (1958), pp. 734-35.

16. Cf. *Catechismus Romanus Concilii Tridentini,* part 2, chap. 8; Pius XI, encyc. *Casti Connubii,* in *AAS* XXII (1930), pp. 559-61; Pius XII, *AAS* XLIII (1951), p. 843; *AAS* L (1958), pp. 734-35; John XXIII, encyc. *Mater et Magistra,* in *AAS* LIII (1961), p. 447.

17. Cf. Pius XII, alloc. to the National Congress of the Union of Catholic Jurists, Dec. 6, 1953, in *AAS* XLV (1953), 798-99.

18. Cf. Romans 3:8.

19. Cf. Pius XII, alloc. to Congress of the Italian Association of Urology, Oct. 8, 1953, in *AAS* XLV (1953), pp. 674-75; *AAS* L (1958), pp. 734-35.

20. Cf. Pius XII, *AAS* XLIII (1951), p. 846.

21. Cf. *AAS* XLV (1953), pp. 674-75; *AAS* XLVIII (1956), pp. 461-62.

22. Cf. Luke 2:34.

23. Cf. Paul VI, encyc. *Populorum Progressio,* March 26, 1967, no. 21.

24. Cf. Romans 8.

25. Cf. II Vatican Council, decree *Inter Mirifica, On the Instruments of Social Communication,* nos. 6-7.

26. Cf. encyc. *Mater et Magistra,* in *AAS* LIII (1961), p. 447.

27. Cf. encyc. *Populorum Progressio,* nos. 48-55.

28. Cf. Pastoral Const. *Gaudium et Spes,* no. 52.

29. Cf. *AAS* XLIII (1951), p. 859.
30. Cf. Pastoral Const. *Gaudium et Spes,* no. 51.
31. Cf. Matthew 11:30.
32. Cf. Pastoral Const. *Gaudium et Spes,* no. 48; II Vatican Council, Dogmatic Const. *Lumen Gentium,* no. 35.
33. Matthew 7:14; cf. Hebrews 11:12.
34. Cf. Titus 2:12.
35. Cf. I Corinthians 7:31.
36. Cf. Romans 5:5.
37. Ephesians 5:25, 28-29, 32-33.
38. Cf. Dogmatic Const. *Lumen Gentium,* nos. 35 and 41; Pastoral Const. *Gaudium et Spes,* nos. 48-49; II Vatican Council, Decree *Apostolicam Actuositatem,* no. 11.
39. Cf. Dogmatic Const. *Lumen Gentium,* no. 25.
40. Cf. I Corinthians 1:10.
41. Cf. John 3:17.

Carl Cohen

Sex, Birth Control, and Human Life

I

The 1968 encyclical letter of Pope Paul VI, *Humanae Vitae*, has caused deep dismay both within and without the Roman Catholic Church. In reaffirming categorically its absolute prohibition of all devices for birth control, the Church creates with this document a new impediment to the slowing of the rate of population growth on earth. Some underdeveloped areas of the planet, where human crowding is now extreme and the need to limit population is already desperate, are greatly influenced by the teachings of the Catholic Church. Where its prohibitions are taken seriously by poverty-stricken masses, *Humanae Vitae* will have as its direct result the discouragement of effective birth-control techniques, and therefore the creation of more new lives than can be decently fed or cared for—a greater number than would be the case if the encyclical had been more enlightened. Indirectly, its foreseeable results will be more of the suffering and misery that overpopulation necessarily imposes. It is an unhappy irony that the document whose name is "human life" will reap human death as its harvest.

My present aim is not to bemoan this encyclical further but to exhibit, through an examination of its argument, the internal weakness of the moral position it presents. The practical consequences of the conclusions of *Humanae Vitae* are simply awful; the argument it provides in defense of these conclusions is equally bad.

II

The argument begins by establishing a foundation of doctrinal principles of a very general sort regarding the nature of marriage and of con-

This article is reprinted from *Ethics* 79, no. 4 (July 1969), with the permission of the author and the University of Chicago Press.

jugal love. These principles may well be doubted by one who does not accept the teachings of the Church, but they are not at issue here. Essentially they come to this: that marriage, love, and birth must be viewed not from any narrow perspective but in the light of an integral vision of man and his vocation, both natural and supernatural. Within this vision, conjugal love is understood to flow from God Who is Love, and marriage is the deliberate institution of the Creator realizing in mankind his design of love. Through marriage husband and wife collaborate with God in the generation of new lives. In this perspective, conjugal love is understood to possess certain essential characteristics: first, that it is fully human, love of the senses and of the spirit at the same time; second, that it is an act of the free will, intended to endure and grow, and leading to greater human perfection; third, that it is total in that in it husband and wife share everything without reservation or calculation; fourth, that it is faithful and exclusive until death; and, finally, that it is fecund, destined to raise up new lives. "In the task of transmitting life, therefore," the encyclical concludes, "they [husband and wife] are not free to proceed completely at will, as if they could determine in a wholly autonomous way the honest path to follow; but they must conform their activity to the creative intention of God, expressed in the very nature of marriage and of its acts."[1]

These are the doctrinal foundations. I now propose to show that the specific conclusions of the encyclical regarding birth control are not (as they purport to be) the logical consequences of these general principles. Even if one does accept the Church's general views on marriage, he is not obliged by reason to accept its dogmas on birth control.

III

Precisely what are the conclusions at issue? Essentially, they reduce to a categorical prohibition of all control of the sex act, once begun, and all efforts or devices whose object is the blocking of conception.

> We must once again declare that the direct interruption of the generative process already begun, and above all, directly willed and procured abortion, even if for therapeutic reasons, are to be absolutely excluded as licit means of regulating birth.
>
> Equally to be excluded . . . is direct sterilization, whether perpetual or temporary, whether of the man or of the woman. Similarly excluded is every action which, whether in anticipation of the conjugal act, or in its accomplishment, or in the development of its natural consequences, proposes, whether as an end or as a means, to render procreation impossible.[2]

The encyclical does permit as licit, however, the regulation of birth through the scheduling of intercourse for infecund periods only. It is concluded that this rhythm method and sheer abstinence are the only forms of birth control that do not offend against moral principles.

IV

How does one get from the very general doctrine holding marriage to be a free, loving, and fecund relationship to the specific dogmas regarding birth control for which *Humanae Vitae* is so widely condemned? The argument requires certain additional premises; its completed form runs something like this: The love of husband and wife has many aspects, natural and supernatural, physical and spiritual. The act of sexual intercourse between them is the physical manifestation of their spiritual union. The act itself, therefore, has two meanings, *unitive* and *procreative*, both of which inhere in it. Joining in sex as lovers one of another and as the creators of new life one with another are two aspects of the same sexual act. Men have the power to *distinguish* these two aspects of sex, but no human power can rightly separate them, because *the eternal conjunction of unitive and procreative functions is willed by God.* Therefore (it is held) "each and every marriage act must remain open to the transmission of life."[3] Any single instance of sexual intercourse that does not remain open to the conception of life destroys the meaning and purpose of that intercourse, contradicts the nature of man and woman and their love, and serves, therefore, "to contradict the plan of God and His will."[4] Birth control, as it is normally practiced, the encyclical concludes, has just this consequence and must threfore be prohibited and condemned.

The crucial premise, upon which the entire argument of the encyclical depends, is the claim that sexual intercourse and procreation are *universally* and *indivisibly* conjoined. This proposition must be maintained literally and in its strongest form to support the conclusion drawn: that we must condemn "every action which, either in anticipation of the conjugal act, or in its accomplishment, or in the development of its natural consequences, proposes, whether as an end or as a means, to render procreation impossible."[5] This fundamental premise, that the unitive and procreative functions of sex are conjoined in such a way as to be totally inseparable in every case, must be gravely questioned.

About this premise—let us call it the "inseparability" premise—several things need to be said. First, it is without good foundation. Second, it is false. Third, its denial is perfectly consistent with the larger doctrines of the Catholic Church regarding marriage. Fourth, it betrays an unwholesome, essentially instrumental view of sex. Fifth, it is a premise contradicted by the Church's own view of licit birth control. Elaboration upon these claims is called for.

V

How is the inseparability premise defended in *Humanae Vitae?* Rational argument based on the merits of the case is not even attempted. Scriptural authority (even if it were persuasive) cannot be offered because it does not exist. Neither is the principle encountered in any standard version of the natural law, nor in the consciences of most honest men within or without the Catholic Church. The majority report of the Papal Commission on Birth Control could not support it. Dr. John Marshall, a member of that commission, reports that after lengthy inquiry even the four theologians of the minority group, although supporting the prohibition of birth control, acknowledged that they could not demonstrate the intrinsic evil of contraception on the basis of natural law. What then does the premise rest upon? Authority and nothing more. All that is said in its defense is that inseparability has long been part of the teaching of the Church. By accepting that teaching and repeating it, the Pope is spared the need to break from an old tradition.

Papal authority, however persuasive for some Catholics, cannot constitute proof for a moderately rational man. Too often have popes proclaimed as true and binding what has later been admitted (at a time too late to remedy the injury done) to be blatantly false. Pope Boniface VIII could influence an epoch, causing misery and promoting war, with his insistence (in *Unam Sanctam*, 1302) that "it is entirely necessary for salvation that every human creature be subject to the Roman pontiff." One of the major instruments of modern economic growth—the lending and borrowing of money with interest—was condemned by Pope Urban III (in 1185) in his ban against usury; it was, he said, self-evidently immoral. Even the notion that everyone is entitled to freedom of conscience was condemned as "a delirium" and "a pestilential error" by Pope Gregory XVI as recently as 1832.

The Church now recognizes the grave errors in many of its earlier teachings. Those mistaken doctrines did not express the will of God, all now agree, but were only the confused opinions of limited, sometimes narrow-minded men. Yet the frame of mind that leads to such wrongheadedness has not been recognized—a frame of mind in which it is presumed that the Church alone knows what God plans and knows also exactly what instruments He has decided we may use in helping Him to accomplish these plans. In elevating fallible human opinions on controversial issues to the status of divine will, this encyclical, like many before it, makes a false and deceptive appeal, seeking to shield dogma from rational criticism.

The argument of *Humanae Vitae* has precisely that character. Repeatedly Pope Paul appeals to his only available support—past teaching, the magisterium of the Church. The defense of the inseparability premise boils down to this: "It's true because we tell you it is; if you doubt us, note that we have been telling you the same thing for a very long time." Such reiteration has absolutely no probative force.

VI

The inseparability premise is false. It is hard to reach certainty in matters of this sort, of course. But granting, *arguendo*, the twofold "meaning" of sexual intercourse, its procreative and unitive functions, such evidence as experience and reflection provide would strongly suggest that in many instances it is right for these functions to be separated. Very briefly I will try to indicate the ways in which this might be shown.

1. In any utilitarian ethic the falsity of the inseparability premise could be quite convincingly established. The disutility of its consequences is so great, so sure, and so widely understood that the encyclical does not attempt—with some minor exceptions to be discussed shortly—a defense of that premise based on its consequences. Such efforts prove hopeless.

2. Perhaps utilitarian calculi will be flatly rejected by the Church, but its own larger principles cannot be disposed of so easily. On its own principles the inseparability premise is virtually impossible to defend. Recall that the entire argument arises in a context of doctrine concerning the nature of the marriage union and the character of conjugal love. Sexual intercourse in marriage, it is held, must be free and loving. But it cannot be fully so if it is flawed by the fear of a conception the couple cannot afford for reasons of economy or health. Sexual intercourse, it is held, should be total; it is love incarnate and supposes that the partners give to one another without reservations. But reservations are precisely what the inseparability premise forces upon them. They must, if it be true, either hold back in passion or have that passion marred by the awareness that total reciprocity between them risks the well-being of themselves or their family. In short, the larger aims of the Church, which include the most perfect realization of the ideals of marriage that the circumstances permit, are undermined by the conclusions of this encyclical. To oblige as alter-

natives the acceptance of the hazards of uncontrolled sexual intercourse or the avoidance of ill health and impoverishment through abstinence is to present a pair of options both foolish and cruel. Cruel because the actual consequences of forcing that choice are inhumane and can be rather accurately predicted. Foolish because that obligation runs counter to the highest ideals of the Church itself.

Whatever the origin of the institution of marriage, particular marriages are enriched and deepened when the sexual congress of the partners is free and happy, untroubled and unreserved. The passions and pleasures of sex, manifesting the intense affection of one human being for another, are blessings that ought to be supported by reason, not blemished or curtailed by the deliberate refusal to use reason. The rational control of birth requires the deliberate separation of the procreative from the unitive functions when appropriate. Because this has as consequences the encouragement of satisfying sexual intercourse, and the greater likelihood of contentment, such separation is right conduct if the strength and happiness of the marriage are ruling considerations.

3. But perhaps it will be argued that even these considerations cannot rule when the act in question is intrinsically wrong, a contravention of the will of God. The claim that God's plan is disrupted by the control of birth appears to be based on the notion (not fully explicit in the encyclical) that God intends all natural functions to be completed and that since procreation is the natural completion of sexual intercourse any act that deliberately thwarts procreation is ungodly. Final causes are divinely set; birth is the "final cause" of coition; to block the possibility of birth flowing from coition is to contravene the divine will.

The entire argument is plausible only on the assumption that God's plans and instruments are precisely known—a degree of presumption whose dangers I have remarked upon earlier. Beyond this, it is noteworthy that the principle that morality requires the absolute completion of all sexual acts is one that any rational man will find difficult to maintain, even supposing one knew what "completion" meant in every context. Such a principle would seem to commit one to the view that unless every kiss leads to intercourse God's will is frustrated, or that no attention that is sexually motivated may be given to the child since the fulfillment of that attention would lead to incest. The fact that much of our conduct in daily life is sexually toned is neither avoidable nor wrong. The greatest part of this sexual activity stops far short of consummation, but surely that is not unnatural. No sensible person denies the pervasive influence of sex or supposes that once an act takes on sexual dimensions we are obliged to pursue the relationship to full intercourse. Loving acts, including those that incorporate sexual activity, are worthy in themselves, quite apart from whether they lead to orgasm, or to new lives. There need be no misuse of natural functions or dishonesty of purpose when, deliberately and humanely, we limit the range or techniques of sex play. To insist that such play, once begun, must be pursued to its extremes would be absurd; it is no less absurd to insist that intercourse, once begun, must be pursued to its extremes and that no intelligent limits may be placed upon its techniques or consequences.

The defender of the encyclical might here rejoin that the thrust of the inseparability premise has been misconstrued in the preceding critique. It is not simply the completion of natural functions that is required (he may say) but their integrity that must be respected. It is the distortion of the act as it is being completed, the suppression of an essential aspect of its significance, that contradicts God's will.

Once again one might wonder whether the Church's view of unnatural distortion and God's view of it—if He has one—are altogether in accord and how we find that out. But putting all that aside, it would be well to see the consequences of the general application of the principle invoked here. Moving to another sphere for the sake of illustration, suppose we were to agree that artistic creation has (using terms the Church is likely to find acceptable) at least a twofold meaning. Being an application of the practical intellect, it is necessarily concerned with the quality of the art object produced. Call this its *productive* meaning. Being a satisfaction of the artist's appetite for beauty, it is necessarily concerned with the exercise of his inventive talents. Call this its spontaneous or *originative* meaning. Would we wish to say that artistic activity that is spontaneous and originative but wholly playful and exploratory, having no concern for a product (or even seeking to avoid one), is unnatural or ungodly? Consider the artist who distinguishes the exercise of his creative talents from the perfection of his created objects and pursues now one of these objectives, now the other, sometimes both conjointly. Surely his occasional separation of these functions does not convict him of dishonest or disorderly acts.

Another example, closer to that of sex, may prove more persuasive. Most men will allow that eating, in addition to its *nutritive* function, provides certain intrinsic satisfactions that we may call *gustatory*. A good meal will be rich in protein, carbohydrates, vitamins, and so on, but will also be agreeable to the palate. Eating may fulfill these functions concurrently, but is there any moral fault in eating with the intent to separate them? Sometimes, as when one is ill, we eat for the sake of nutrition, altogether without gusto. Often we eat with the deliberate intention of avoiding additional nutriment, yet relishing the taste of the dish. Many of the foods and flavors we prize are known to be without nutritive value—mushrooms, truffles, a cup of fine tea, for example—but we do not think it wrong to eat them.

In the sphere of sex the case is essentially no different. The pleasures, emotional as well as physical, derived from the satisfaction of an appetite may be separated rationally and without wrongdoing from the fulfillment of organic functions also possible through the satisfaction of that appetite. Whether it is right, or wise, to satisfy an appetite repeatedly without ever fulfilling the organic functions of such satisfaction is a question that may remain moot here. But the force of this encyclical depends upon the claim that such separation is in *every* case immoral. That claim seems plainly false.

VII

The denial of the inseparability premise is perfectly consistent with the larger doctrines of the Church regarding the purpose of marriage. The apparent stumbling block here is the notion of fecundity; every marriage, the Church holds, must be loving and total, free and faithful—and fecund. For a marriage to be fecund, however, it need not be the case that every sexual act within it be potentially so. If the married couple assumes an obligation to raise up new lives (an obligation those outside the Church may question), that obligation may be fully and honestly met without their every sexual union being open to conception. The intelligent use of birth control does not block fecundity or in any way denigrate it; indeed, the importance of fecundity is magnified by control. No honor is done to marriage by forcing fecundity upon the partners willy-nilly or depriving them of sexual satisfaction. The fecundity of human marriage is not the fecundity of animals who bear young at every season of heat because they know not what they do. When the decision to create new life is made deliberately and rationally, out of love and with a full understanding of the consequences, the act of procreation itself is enhanced. Birth is then not an accident beyond human control but the happy outcome of a free act, an act right in its purpose and good in its execution. The life brought into being, rather than being tolerated or resented as a blunder, is then wanted and loved. That is the procreative meaning of conjugal love; that, if anything, may be construed as collaboration with God. The accomplishment of these worthy goals, however, requires that fecundity *not* be tied to every passionate sexual embrace. On the doctrinal principles of the Church itself the marriage of a man and a woman—the moral union of two beings without reservations—is made potentially *more* perfect through the rational use of birth control.

VIII

Embedded in the argument of *Humanae Vitae* is a view of sex as an aspect of human life fundamentally unworthy in itself because essentially
instrumental in character. The insistence that every coition be open to
conception implicitly supposes that all sex, and every act of love sexually
toned, is at bottom a tool for the accomplishment of something else. An
uneasy distaste for fleshly things, partly disguised, is revealed in the refusal of the Church to approve of sexual intercourse for its own sake. The
intrinsic worth of sexual passion is not precisely denied, but that denial is
clearly suggested by insisting that, separated from procreation, the act is
dishonest and contravenes God's will. A more generous conception of
divine intentions might suppose sex to be a blessing that humans are peculiarly able to understand and appreciate. It might view sex as that
animal function most essentially of a loving kind and its practice (whether
fecund or not) the closest thing to the incarnation of the religious ideal of
love. Such at least is a possible view. In such a view sex might be conceived
as an element of our condition having sometimes an instrumental role,
sometimes a consummatory role, and often both. Even when not intended
to produce new life it may serve to make tangible our union with another
human creature. If it makes sense at all to infer the intentions of God, we
may reasonably suppose that so rich and delightful a dimension of human
life was designed by Him (if He is wise and loving) both as an instrument
and as a satisfaction to be enjoyed mutually, for its own and each other's
sake. To suppose narrowly that sexual intercourse must serve as an instrument in every circumstance is to demean its designer, if it has one.

That an essentially instrumental view of sex *is* implicit in the argument of *Humanae Vitae* is further evidenced by the very language it
adopts in dealing with sex; not as acts of love or of passion—which they
are and ought to be—but as the *uses* or *familiarities* of marriage are coital
acts discussed in this document. "[Q]*uilibet matrimonii usus*" must, it is
proclaimed, "remain open to the transmission of life." But sexual intercourse is not a *use* of marriage; it is one realization of it, and it may serve
as that realization whether or not it also serves, on any particular occasion,
its further instrumental function.

IX

In approving the so-called rhythm method of birth control, the Church flatly contradicts its own dogmas in this sphere and shows clearly that in its more reflective moments it too denies the "inseparable connection" of sexual intercourse and procreation. *Humanae Vitae* says straightforwardly that it is entirely proper for the married couple to "take into account the natural rhythms immanent in the generative functions, for the use of marriage in the infecund periods only, and in this way to regulate birth without offending the moral principles."[6] This form of birth regulation, the encyclical allows, remains licit *even though the married couple are engaging in sexual intercourse with the deliberate intention of avoiding the creation of new life.*

Earlier, however, the encyclical had condemned birth control in principle, that condemnation based upon the "inseparable connection, willed by God and unable to be broken by man on his own initiative," between the unitive and procreative aspects of sexual congress.[7] Can the permission of deliberate and knowing efforts to effect this very separation by the clever timing of intercourse be logically reconciled with the earlier prohibition of all such efforts? It cannot. Recognizing the difficulty, *Humanae Vitae* seeks to ward off the charge of self-contradiction, but fails.

The Pope argues that, in this matter, the Church "is coherent with herself" because there are essential differences between birth control using natural rhythms and all other common methods of achieving the same result. In fact, an examination of these claimed differences in method shows that they cannot justify the condemnation of separating unitive and procreative functions in the one case while approving it in the other.

The differences specified are only two, and neither can bear the weight the argument puts upon them. One of these amounts to nothing more than a restatement of what the rhythm method is—a system in which husband and wife are "able to renounce the use of marriage in the fecund periods when, for just motives, procreation is not desirable, while making use of it during infecund periods to manifest their affection and to safeguard their mutual fidelity. By so doing they give proof of a truly and integrally honest love."[8] Clearly it is not the manifestation of affection or the safeguarding of fidelity that differentiates the rhythm method from all others. The difference, rather, lies only in the fact that this system relies upon the timing of intercourse and no mechanical or pharmaceutical aids. But this difference has no bearing whatever upon the separability of sex and procreation. In the case of the rhythm method, as with all other methods, the fact is—and the encyclical admits—that "the married couple are concordant in the positive will of avoiding children for plausible reasons, seeking the certainty that offspring will not arrive."[9] It is precisely that will, the will to have sexual intercourse and not conceive, that had earlier been damned as a contradiction of the will of God.

The other difference specified is that upon which all the argument must rest. The claim is that with the rhythm method, the couple makes use of a "natural disposition"; with all other methods "they impede the development of natural processes."[10] The encyclical supposes, but cannot demonstrate, that only the use of timing is a "legitimate use" of nature and that drugs or diaphragms are not legitimate. In what aspect of the latter cases does the claimed illegitimacy lie? All that can be said is that in the one case instruments are not used, in the other case they are. Surely civilization, and with it the Catholic Church, has passed the point where it was considered a disruption of God's plan to accomplish worthwhile objectives with the aid of rational and humane instruments. Is it legitimate to protect health with exercise but illegitimate to do so with vaccination? Is it legitimate to fight illness with nutrition but illegitimate to do so with medicines? Surely the notion that an act is illegitimate only because instruments are used is absurd. The Church agrees unequivocally in matters of personal and public health; its hospitals are among the finest in the world. Why is the notion any less absurd in the sphere of sexual health and family well-being? No reason is or can be given.

If birth control is wrong, it is wrong not because an instrument is used but because of what is being accomplished and the intent to accomplish it. The argument of the encyclical clearly states that the (alleged) evil lies in the immoral separation of sexual love and procreation. But it is freely admitted that that separation *is* permissible to manifest affection and safeguard fidelity. If it is permissible in some cases, then it must be permissible in all cases, unless the difference between the cases distinguished bears upon the intentions with which the act is done. The differences specified do not bear upon such intentions. By simply calling the rhythm method licit and all other methods illicit, the encyclical begs the central question. Why is the one legitimate, the other not? The argument purports to exhibit a morally relevant difference, but never begins to do so.

This inconsistency is not just a minor slip; it is fatal to the entire position of *Humanae Vitae*. For that position depends utterly upon what has here been called the inseparability premise; and it is now clear that, even for the Church, where there are plausible reasons and honest love, a couple may indeed separate their desire for children from their desire for sex with each other. Both fecund and loving the marriage should be, perhaps, but even if true that principle gives no warrant for the prohibition of any humane method of birth control.

X

The leaders of the Catholic Church are far from callous men; they are fully aware of the human misery that flows from uncontrolled population growth. They understand the grave need for the global control of human numbers; hence their approval of the rhythm method. Still they argue that other forms of birth control, being intrinsically wrong, may not be practiced because it is never permissible to do what is wrong, even with a view to some larger good.

> [I]t is not licit, even for the gravest reasons, to do evil so that good may follow therefrom; that is, to make into the object of a positive act of the will something which is intrinsically disorder, and hence unworthy of the human person, even when the intention is to safeguard or promote individual, family, or social well-being. Consequently it is an error to think that a conjugal act which is deliberately made infecund and so is intrinsically dishonest could be made honest and right by the ensemble of a fecund conjugal life.[11]

This argument fails utterly; both of its premises are false. The major premise—that it is never right to do a minor evil in order that a greater good may come of it—will be denied by most reasonable men. But even granting that premise, the condemnation of birth control does not follow. In the first place, if all control of sexual intercourse with the deliberate intent of avoiding birth is dishonest and disorderly, it is so whatever the method employed to reach that end. The argument cuts as strongly against the rhythm method as against any other, since all birth control embodies the positive will to enjoy sex without procreation. More importantly, the argument depends also on the minor premise, that deliberate control of birth *is* intrinsically evil, dishonest, and disorderly. That premise *Humanae Vitae* does not and cannot establish. Even if one accepts the larger doctrinal principles of the Church regarding marriage and its essentially loving, total, faithful, and fecund character, family planning and the intelligent control of sexual intercourse to implement such planning may be approved and encouraged, not as instrumental evils but as acts wholly honest and right.

XI

Finally, *Humanae Vitae* offers, in support of its prohibition of birth control, three arguments of a totally different sort, arguments aiming not to establish the wrongness of birth control in itself but to point out the evils alleged to flow from its employment. This emphasis upon consequences rather than intrinsic quality is not characteristic of the encyclical, not in harmony with its general spirit. Moreover, the arguments appear in abbreviated form, and not the slightest effort is made to show that the consequences alleged would in fact ensue. This pragmatic interlude does not play a major role in the document. Still it is proper to give these arguments the little attention they deserve.

1. Birth-control devices, it is claimed, offer "easy means of eluding" the observance of the moral law by leading to "conjugal infidelity and the general lowering of morality."[12]

The argument is thrice bad: First, there is no evidence to show that birth control would in fact increase the frequency of marital infidelity. Indeed, it is the Church's prohibition, in combination with a couple's inability to care properly for more children, which creates frustration, forces unnatural abstinence, and may lead to extramarital intercourse. This counterclaim is, of course, equally unproved; but of the two positions it appears reasonable that the prohibition of birth control is at least as likely to encourage infidelity as its use would be.

Second, if the moral law is what the Church believes it to be, none of the consequences of the use of birth control, good or bad, are needed to enforce it or able to do so. Obedience to it as a moral law is complete only when compliance is willing and free and not forced by the sanctions of disobedience. Those who deny the existence of that law or wish to flout it can as easily deny or flout the prohibition of birth control as well.

Third, even if the consequence—sexual intercourse more widely enjoyed—were evil, and even if the general use of birth control were shown to have that consequence, it is plainly unjust to force abstinence on faithful married couples, or to compel them to rear more children than is good for them or the community, simply because the instrument that might avoid such hardship could be used improperly by others.

The argument is intolerable.

2. Birth-control devices, it is claimed, give excessive power to public authorities, placing in their hands "a dangerous weapon" that may be easily abused. "Who will stop rulers from favoring, from even imposing upon their peoples, if they were to consider it necessary, the method of contraception which they deem to be most efficacious? In such a way men . . . would reach the point of placing at the mercy of the intervention of public authorities the most personal and most reserved sector of conjugal intimacy."[13]

The scare of this argument is largely fictitious. What, precisely, is the grave danger being hinted at? Is it that governments may play a more active role in stabilizing the size of human population? Such a development would be no bad thing. Or is it that governments might force individual couples to use contraceptive devices they do not wish to use? Considering the circumstances of most sexual intercourse, that would be quite a trick, even for Big Brother. Or might it be that governments ("rulers," as the Pope perceives them) would use their power to encourage or oblige the use of contraceptives in ways contrary to the interests of citizens? There is that danger, of course, if government eludes the control of the people; but such dangers exist now, having been created by the very invention of the instruments in question. The general prohibition by the Church of all use of such instruments reduces that power not one iota. If it is the immoral use of power that we fear, it is not precepts or the banning of instruments but the strengthened control of the people over their government that is called for.

3. The final argument is the most extraordinary of all. The encyclical states: "It is also to be feared that the man, growing used to the employment of anticonceptive practices, may finally lose respect for the woman and, no longer caring for her physical and psychological equilibrium, may come to the point of considering her as a mere instrument of selfish enjoyment, and no longer as his respected and beloved companion."[14] How in the world this consequence is drawn from the use of birth control is never rationally explained, nor could it be. The imagination is staggered by the picture of continuing sexual relations harbored in the minds of the authors of this passage: the males, blinded by lust and potent as satyrs—now freed by birth control—plunge relentlessly into the females, who in spite of their frailty are reduced to instruments of carnal pleasure, to be cast aside when passion's spent. The speculation would be amusing if the circumstances were not serious. One who supposes that sex is essentially a one-sided demand placed by men on women, and that sex separated from procreation leads inevitably to the selfish use of the woman by the man, tells us far more about himself and his sexual fantasies than about birth control in the real world. The complete failure to consider the woman's desire for sex and for the pleasure of it, the implicit distorted picture of what sexual intercourse for its own sake may be, reveal enough about the authors of this document to put their competence in this entire sphere, not to speak of their authority, in gravest doubt.

It is understandable that the encyclical does not rely in any serious way upon the supposed consequences to support its conclusions. For if consequences are relevant at all, the consequences of not using birth-control devices must be weighed against the consequences of using them. And while the latter consequences are at worst controversial and at best happy, the former—the results of population growth uncontrolled or controlled only by timing or abstinence—are famine, sickness, and death for millions. Such suffering is already upon us; with the help of unenlightened dogmatism like that found in *Humanae Vitae*, far worse is in store.

The argument based on consequences the Church is obliged, for the security of its dogma on birth control, to skirt. The argument based on the intrinsic moral quality of the act itself the Church is unable, in behalf of this dogma, to defend. It is time for the dogma to be changed.

NOTES

1. Section 10. All citations in this article are from the official English-language version of the encyclical letter.
2. Section 14
3. Section 11
4. Section 13
5. Section 14
6. Section 16
7. Section 12
8. Section 16
9. Ibid.
10. Ibid.
11. Section 14
12. Section 17
13. Ibid.
14. Ibid.

ABORTION

Judith Jarvis Thomson

A Defense of Abortion

Most opposition to abortion relies on the premise that the fetus is a human being, a person, from the moment of conception.[1] The premise is argued for, but, as I think, not well. Take, for example, the most common argument. We are asked to notice that the development of a human being from conception through birth into childhood is continuous; then it is said that to draw a line, to choose a point in this development and say "before this point the thing is not a person, after this point it is a person" is to make an arbitrary choice, a choice for which in the nature of things no good reason can be given. It is concluded that the fetus is, or that we had better say it is, a person from the moment of conception. But this conclusion does not follow. Similar things might be said about the development of an acorn into an oak tree, and it does not follow that acorns are oak trees, or that we had better say they are. Arguments of this form are sometimes called "slippery-slope arguments"—the phrase is perhaps self-explanatory—and it is dismaying that opponents of abortion rely on them so heavily and uncritically.

I am inclined to agree, however, that the prospects for "drawing a line" in the development of the fetus look dim. I am inclined to think also that we shall probably have to agree that the fetus has already become a human person well before birth. Indeed, it comes as a surprise when one first learns how early in its life the fetus begins to acquire human characteristics. By the tenth week, for example, it already has a face, arms and legs, fingers and toes; it has internal organs, and brain activity is detectable.[2] On the other hand, I think that the premise is false, that the fetus is not a person from the moment of conception. A newly fertilized ovum, a newly implanted clump of cells, is no more a person than an acorn is an oak tree. But I shall not discuss any of this. For it seems to me to be of greater interest to ask what happens if, for the sake of argument, we allow the premise. How, precisely, are we supposed to get from there to the conclusion that abortion is morally impermissible? Opponents of abortion commonly spend most of their time establishing that the fetus is a person, and hardly any time explaining the step from there to the impermissibility of abortion. Perhaps they think the step too simple and obvious to require much comment. Or perhaps they are simply being economical in argument. Many of those who defend abortion rely on the premise that the fetus is not a person, but only a bit of tissue that will become a person at birth; and why pay out more arguments than you have to? Whatever the explanation, I suggest that the step they take is neither easy nor obvious, that it calls for closer examination than it is commonly given, and that when we do give it this closer examination we shall feel inclined to reject it.

I propose, then, that we grant that the fetus is a person from the moment of conception. How does the argument go from here? Something like this, I take it. Every person has a right to life. So the fetus has a right to life. No doubt the mother has a right to decide what shall happen in and to her body; everyone would grant that. But surely a person's right to life is stronger and more stringent than the mother's right to decide what happens in and to her body, and so outweighs it. So the fetus may not be killed; an abortion may not be performed.

It sounds plausible. But now let me ask you to imagine this. You wake up in the morning and find yourself back to back in bed with an unconscious famous violinist. He has been found to have a fatal kidney ailment, and the Society of Music Lovers has canvassed all the available medical records and found that you alone have the right blood type to help. They have therefore kidnapped you, and last night the violinist's circulatory system was plugged into yours so that your kidneys could be used to extract poisons from his blood as well as your own. The director of the hospital now tells you: "Look, we're sorry the Society of Music Lovers did this to you—we would never have permitted it if we had known. But still, they did it and the violinist now is plugged into you. To unplug you would be to kill him. But never mind, it's only for nine months. By then he will have recovered from his ailment and can safely be unplugged from you." Is it morally incumbent on you to accede to this situation? No doubt it would be very nice of you if you did, a great kindness. But do you *have* to accede to it? What if it were not nine months but nine years? Or longer still? What if the director of the hospital said: "Tough luck, I agree, but you've now got to stay in bed, with the violinist plugged into you, for the rest of your life. Because remember this: All persons have a right to life, and violinists are persons. Granted you have a right to decide what happens in and to your body, but a person's right to life outweighs your right to decide what happens in and to your body. So you cannot ever be unplugged from him." I imagine you would regard this as outrageous, which suggests that something really is wrong with that plausible-sounding argument that was mentioned previously.

In this case, of course, you were kidnapped; you did not volunteer for the operation that plugged the violinist into your kidneys. Can those who oppose abortion on the grounds I mentioned make an exception for a pregnancy due to rape? Certainly. They can say that persons have a right to life only if they did not come into existence because of rape; or they can say that all persons have a right to life, but that some have less of a right to life than others, in particular, that those who came into existence because of rape have less. But these statements have a rather unpleasant sound. Surely the question of whether one has a right to life at all, or how much of a right one has, should not turn on the question of whether or not one is the product of a rape. And in fact the people who oppose abortion on the ground I mentioned do not make this distinction, and hence do not make an exception in case of rape.

Nor do they make an exception for a case in which the mother has to spend the nine months of her pregnancy in bed. They would agree that that would be a great pity and hard on the mother, but would insist all the same that all persons have a right to life, and that the fetus is a person. I suspect, in fact, that they would not make an exception for a case in which, miraculously enough, the pregnancy went on for nine years, or even for the rest of the mother's life.

Some would not even make an exception for a case in which continuation of the pregnancy is likely to shorten the mother's life; they regard abortion as impermissible even to save the mother's life. Such cases are nowadays very rare, and many opponents of abortion do not accept this extreme view. All the same, it is a good place to begin: a number of points of interest come out in respect to it.

1. Let us call the view that abortion is impermissible even to save the mother's life "the extreme view." I want to suggest, first, that it does not issue from the argument I mentioned earlier without the addition of some fairly powerful premises. Suppose a woman has become pregnant, and now learns that she has a cardiac condition such that she will die if she

carries the baby to term. What may be done for her? The fetus, being a person, has a right to life; but as the mother is a person too, so has she a right to life. Presumably they have an equal right to life. How is it supposed to come out that an abortion may not be performed? If mother and child have an equal right to life, should not we perhaps flip a coin? Or should we add to the mother's right to life her right to decide what happens in and to her body, which everybody seems to be ready to grant—the sum of her rights now outweighing the fetus' right to life?

The most familiar argument here is the following. We are told that performing the abortion would be directly killing[3] the child, whereas doing nothing would not be killing the mother, but only letting her die. Moreover, in killing the child, one would be killing an innocent person, for the child has committed no crime and is not aiming at his mother's death. And then there are a variety of ways in which this argument might be continued. (1) As directly killing an innocent person is always and absolutely impermissible, an abortion may not be performed. Or, (2) as directly killing an innocent person is murder, and murder is always and absolutely impermissible, an abortion may not be performed.[4] Or, (3) as one's duty to refrain from directly killing an innocent person is more stringent than one's duty to keep a person from dying, an abortion may not be performed. Or, (4) if one's only options are directly killing an innocent person or letting a person die, one must prefer letting the person die, and thus an abortion may not be performed.[5]

Some people seem to have thought that these are not further premises that must be added if the conclusion is to be reached, but that they follow from the very fact that an innocent person has a right to life.[6] But this seems to me a mistake, and perhaps the simplest way to show this is to point out that while we must certainly grant that innocent persons have a right to life, the theses in arguments 1 through 4 are all false. Take argument 2 for example. If directly killing an innocent person is murder, and thus is impermissible, then the mother's directly killing the innocent person inside her is murder, and thus is impermissible. But it cannot seriously be thought to be murder if the mother performs an abortion on herself to save her life. It cannot seriously be said that she *must* refrain, that she *must* sit passively by and wait for her death. Let us look again at the case of you and the violinist. There you are, in bed with the violinist, and the director of the hospital says to you: "It's all most distressing, and I deeply sympathize, but you see this is putting an additional strain on your kidneys, and you'll be dead within the month. But you *have* to stay where you are all the same, because unplugging you would be directly killing an innocent violinist, and that's murder, and that's impermissible." If anything in the world is true, it is that you do not commit murder, you do not do what is impermissible, if you reach around to your back and unplug yourself from that violinist to save your life.

The main focus of attention in writings on abortion has been on what a third party may or may not do in answer to a request from a woman for an abortion. This is in a way understandable. Things being as they are, there is not much a woman can safely do to abort herself. So the question asked is, What may a third party do? And what the mother may do, if it is mentioned at all, is deduced, almost as an afterthought, from what it is concluded that a third party may do. But it seems to me that to treat the matter in this way is to refuse to grant to the mother that very status of person that is so firmly insisted on for the fetus. For we cannot simply read off what a person may do from what a third party may do. Suppose you find yourself trapped in a tiny house with a growing child—I mean a very tiny house, and a rapidly growing child; you are already up against the wall of the house and in a few minutes you'll be crushed to death. The child, on the other hand, will not be crushed to death; if nothing is done to stop him from growing he will be hurt, but in the end he will simply burst open the house and walk out a free man. Now I could well understand it if a bystander were to say: "There's nothing we can do for you. We cannot choose between your life and his, we cannot be the ones to decide who is to live, we cannot intervene." But it cannot be concluded that you too can do nothing, that you cannot attack the child to save your life. However innocent the child may be, you do not have to wait passively while it crushes you to death. Perhaps a pregnant woman is vaguely felt to have the status of a house, which we do not allow the right of self-defense. But if the woman houses the child, it should be remembered that she is a person who houses it.

I should perhaps pause to say explicitly that I am not claiming that people have a right to do anything whatever to save their lives. I think, rather, that there are drastic limits to the right of self-defense. If someone threatens you with death unless you torture someone else to death, I think you have not the right, even to save your life, to do so. But the case under consideration here is very different. In our case there are only two people involved, one whose life is threatened, and one who threatens it. Both are innocent: the one who is threatened is not threatened because of any fault; the one who threatens does not threaten because of any fault. For this reason we may feel that we bystanders cannot intervene. But the person threatened can.

In sum, a woman surely can defend her life against the threat to it posed by the unborn child, even if doing so involves its death. And this shows not merely that the theses in arguments 1 through 4 are false; it shows also that the extreme view of abortion is false, and so we need not canvass any other possible ways of arriving at it from the argument I mentioned at the outset.

2. The extreme view could of course be weakened to say that while abortion is permissible to save the mother's life, it may not be performed by a third party, but only by the mother herself. But this cannot be right either. For what we have to keep in mind is that the mother and the unborn child are not like two tenants in a small house that has, by an unfortunate mistake, been rented to both: the mother *owns* the house. The fact that she does adds to the offensiveness of deducing that the mother can do nothing from the supposition that third parties can do nothing. But it does more than this; it also casts a bright light on the supposition that third parties can do nothing. Certainly it lets us see that a third party who says "I cannot choose between you" is fooling himself if he thinks this is impartiality. If Jones has found and fastened on a certain coat that he needs to keep himself from freezing but that Smith also needs to keep from freezing, then it is not impartiality that says "I cannot choose between you" when Smith owns the coat. Women have said again and again, "This body is my body!" and they have reason to feel angry, reason to feel that it has been like shouting into the wind. Smith, after all, is hardly likely to bless us if we say to him: "Of course it's your coat; anybody would grant that it is. But no one may choose between you and Jones who is to have it."

We should really ask what it is that says "no one may choose" in the face of the fact that the body that houses the child is the mother's body. It may be simply a failure to appreciate this fact. But it may be something more interesting, namely the sense that one has a right to refuse to lay hands on people, even where it would be just and fair to do so, even where justice seems to require that somebody do so. Thus justice might call for somebody to get Smith's coat back from Jones, and yet you have a right to refuse to be the one to lay hands on Jones, a right to refuse to do physical violence to him. This, I think, must be granted. But then what should be said is not "no one may choose," but only "*I* cannot choose"—indeed not even this, but rather "*I* will not act," leaving it open that somebody else can or should, in particular that anyone in a position of authority, with the job of securing people's rights, both can and should. So this is no difficulty. I have not been arguing that any given third party must accede to the mother's request that he perform an abortion to save her life, but only that he may.

I suppose that in some views of human life the mother's body is only on loan to her, the loan not being one that gives her any prior claim to it. One who held this view might well think it impartiality to say, "I cannot choose." But I shall simply ignore this possibility. My own view is that if a human being has any just, prior claim to anything at all, he has a just, prior claim to his own body. And perhaps this need not be argued for here anyway, since, as I mentioned, the arguments against abortion we are looking at do grant that the woman has a right to decide what happens in and to her body.

But although they do grant it, I have tried to show that they do not take seriously what is done in granting it. I suggest the same thing will re-appear even more clearly when we turn away from cases in which the mother's life is at stake and attend, as I propose we now do, to the vastly more common cases in which a woman wants an abortion for some less weighty reason than preserving her own life.

3. Where the mother's life is not at stake the argument I mentioned at the outset seems to have a much stronger pull. "Everyone has a right to life, so the unborn person has a right to life." And isn't the child's right to life weightier than anything other than the mother's own right to life, which she might put forward as ground for an abortion?

This argument treats the right to life as if it were unproblematic. It is not, and this seems to me to be precisely the source of the mistake.

For we should now, at long last, ask what it comes to, to have a right to life. In some views having a right to life includes having a right to be given at least the bare minimum one needs for continued life. But suppose that what in fact *is* the bare minimum a man needs for continued life is something he has no right at all to be given? If I am sick unto death, and the only thing that will save my life is the touch of Henry Fonda's cool hand on my fevered brow, then all the same, I have no right to be given the touch of Henry Fonda's cool hand on my fevered brow. It would be fright-fully nice of him to fly in from the West Coast to provide it. It would be less nice, though no doubt well meant, if my friends flew to the West Coast and carried Henry Fonda back with them. But I have no right at all against anybody that he should do this for me. Or again, to return to the story I told earlier, the fact that for continued life the violinist needs the con-tinued use of your kidneys does not establish that he has a right to be given the continued use of your kidneys. He certainly has no right against you that *you* should give him continued use of your kidneys. For nobody has any right to use your kidneys unless you give him such a right; and nobody has the right against you that you shall give him this right. If you do allow him to go on using your kidneys, this is a kindness on your part, and not something he can claim from you as his due. Nor has he any right against anybody else that they should give him continued use of your kidneys. Certainly he had no right against the Society of Music Lovers that they should plug him into you in the first place. And if you now start to unplug yourself, having learned that you will otherwise have to spend nine years in bed with him, there is nobody in the world who must try to prevent you, in order to see to it that he is given something he has a right to be given.

Some people are rather stricter about the right to life. In their view it does not include the right to be given anything, but amounts to, and only to, the right not to be killed by anybody. But here a related difficulty arises. If everybody is to refrain from killing the violinist, then everybody must refrain from doing a great many different sorts of things. Everybody must refrain from slitting his throat, everybody must refrain from shooting him—and everybody must refrain from unplugging you from him. But does he have a right against everybody that they shall refrain from unplugging you from him? To refrain from doing this is to allow him to continue to use your kidneys. It could be argued that he has a right against us that *we* should allow him to continue to use your kidneys. That is, while he had no right against us that we should give him the use of your kidneys, it might be argued that he anyway has a right against us that we shall not now intervene and deprive him of the use of your kidneys. I shall come back to third-party interventions later. But certainly the violinist has no right against you that *you* shall allow him to continue to use your kidneys. As I said, if you do allow him to use them, it is a kindness on your part, and not something you owe him.

The difficulty I point to here is not peculiar to the right to life. It reappears in connection with all the other natural rights; and it is something that an adequate account of rights must deal with. For present purposes it is enough just to draw attention to it. But I would stress that I am not arguing that people do not have a right to life—quite the contrary, it seems to me that the primary control we must place on the acceptability of an account of rights is that it should turn out in that account to be a truth that all persons have a right to life. I am arguing only that having a right to life does not guarantee having either a right to be given the use of or a right to be allowed continued use of another person's body—even if one needs it for life itself. So the right to life will not serve the opponents of abortion in the very simple and clear way in which they seem to have thought it would.

4. There is another way to bring out the difficulty. In the most ordinary sort of case, to deprive someone of what he has a right to is to treat him unjustly. Suppose a boy and his small brother are jointly given a box of chocolates for Christmas. If the older boy takes the box and refuses to give

his brother any of the chocolates, he is unjust to him, for the brother has been given a right to half of them. But suppose that having learned that otherwise it means nine years in bed with that violinist, you unplug your-self from him. You surely are not being unjust to him, for you gave him no right to use your kidneys, and no one else can have given him any such right. But we have to notice that in unplugging yourself you are killing him; and violinists, like everybody else, have a right to life, and thus in the view we are considering, the right not to be killed. So here you do what he supposedly has a right that you shall not do, but you do not act unjustly to him in doing it.

The emendation that may be made at this point is this: the right to life consists not in the right not to be killed but rather in the right not to be killed unjustly. This runs a risk of circularity, but never mind: it would enable us to square the fact that the violinist has a right to life with the fact that you do not act unjustly toward him in unplugging yourself, thereby killing him. For if you do not kill him unjustly, you do not violate his right to life, and so it is no wonder you do him no injustice.

But if this emendation is accepted, the gap in the argument against abortion stares us plainly in the face: it is by no means enough to show that the fetus is a person, and to remind us that all persons have a right to life; we need to be shown also that killing the fetus violates its right to life, that is, that abortion is unjust killing. And is it?

I suppose we may take it as a datum that in a case of pregnancy due to rape the mother has not given the unborn person a right to the use of her body for food and shelter. Indeed, in what pregnancy could it be sup-posed that the mother has given the unborn person such a right? It is not as if there were unborn persons drifting about the world, to whom a woman who wants a child says "I invite you in."

But it might be argued that there are other ways one can have ac-quired a right to the use of another person's body than by having been in-vited to use it by that person. Suppose a woman voluntarily indulges in intercourse, knowing of the chance that it will issue in pregnancy, and then she does become pregnant. Is she not in part responsible for the pres-ence, in fact the very existence, of the unborn person inside her? No doubt she did not invite it in. But doesn't her partial responsibility for its being there itself give it a right to the use of her body?[7] If so, then her aborting it would be more like the boy's taking away the chocolates and less like your unplugging yourself from the violinist—doing so would be depriving it of what it does have a right to, and thus would be doing it an injustice.

And then, too, it might be asked whether or not she can kill it even to save her own life: If she voluntarily called it into existence, how can she now kill it, even in self-defense?

The first thing to be said about this is that it is something new. Opponents of abortion have been so concerned to make out the independence of the fetus, in order to establish that it has a right to life, just as its mother does, that they have tended to overlook the possible support they might gain from making out that the fetus is dependent on the mother, in order to establish that she has a special kind of responsibility for it, a responsibility that gives it rights against her that are not possessed by any independent person—such as an ailing violinist who is a stranger to her.

On the other hand, this argument would give the unborn person a right to its mother's body only if her pregnancy resulted from a voluntary act, undertaken in full knowledge of the chance that a pregnancy might result from it. It would leave out entirely the unborn person whose existence is due to rape. Pending the availability of some further argument, then, we would be left with the conclusion that unborn persons whose existence is due to rape have no right to the use of their mothers' bodies, and thus that aborting them is not depriving them of anything they have a right to and hence is not unjust killing.

And we should also notice that it is not at all plain that this argument really does go even as far as it purports to. For there are different kinds of cases, and the details make a difference. If the room is stuffy and I therefore open a window to air it and a burglar climbs in, it would be absurd to say, "Ah, now he can stay; she's given him a right to the use of her house—for she is partially responsible for his presence there, having voluntarily done what enabled him to get in, in full knowledge that there are such things as burglars, and that burglars burgle." It would be still more absurd to say this if I had had bars installed outside my windows precisely to prevent burglars from getting in, and a burglar got in only because of a defect in the bars. It remains equally absurd if we imagine it is not a burglar who climbs in but an innocent person who blunders or falls in. Again, suppose it were like this: people-seeds drift about in the air like pollen, and if you open your windows one may drift in and take root in your carpet or upholstery. You do not want children, so you fix up your windows with fine mesh screens, the very best you can buy. As can happen, however, and on very rare occasions does happen, one of the screens is defective; and a seed drifts in and takes root. Does the person-plant who now develops have a right to the use of your house? Surely not, despite the fact that you voluntarily opened your windows, that you knowingly kept carpets and upholstered furniture, and that you knew that screens were sometimes defective. Someone may argue that you are responsible for its rooting, that it does have a right to your house because, after all, you *could* have lived out your life with bare floors and furniture, or with sealed windows and doors. But this will not do, for by the same token anyone can avoid a pregnancy due to rape by having a hysterectomy, or by never leaving home without a (reliable!) army.

It seems to me that the argument we are looking at can establish at most that there are some cases in which the unborn person has a right to the use of its mother's body, and therefore some cases in which abortion is unjust killing. There is room for much discussion and argument as to precisely which cases, if any, are unjust. But I think we should sidestep this issue and leave it open, for the argument certainly does not establish that all abortion is unjust killing.

5. There is, however, room for yet another argument here. We all surely must grant that there may be cases in which it would be morally indecent to detach a person from your body at the cost of his life. Suppose you learn that what the violinist needs is not nine years of your life but only one hour: all you need do to save his life is to spend one hour in that bed with him. Suppose also that letting him use your kidneys for that one hour would not affect your health in the slightest. Admittedly you were kidnapped. Admittedly you did not give anyone permission to plug him into you. Nevertheless it seems to me plain you *ought* to allow him to use your kidneys for that hour—it would be indecent to refuse.

Again, suppose pregnancy lasted only an hour and constituted no threat to life or health. And suppose that a woman becomes pregnant as a result of rape. Admittedly she did not voluntarily do anything to bring about the existence of a child. Admittedly she did nothing at all that would give the unborn person a right to the use of her body. All the same it might well be said, as in the newly emended violinist story, that she *ought* to allow it to remain for that hour—that it would be indecent in her to refuse.

Now some people are inclined to use the term "right" in such a way that it follows from the fact that you ought to allow a person to use your body for the hour he needs, that he has a right to use your body for the hour he needs, even though he has not been given that right by any person or act. They may say that it follows also that if you refuse you act unjustly toward him. This use of the term is perhaps so common that it cannot be called wrong; nevertheless it seems to me to be an unfortunate loosening of what we would do better to keep a tight rein on. Suppose that the box of chocolates I mentioned earlier had not been given to both boys jointly, but was given only to the older boy. There he sits, stolidly eating his way through the box, his small brother watching enviously. Here we are likely to say: "You ought not to be so mean. You ought to give your brother some of those chocolates." My own view is that it just does not follow from the truth of this that the brother has any right to any of the chocolates. If the boy refuses to give his brother any, he is greedy, stingy, callous—but not unjust. I suppose that the people I have in mind will say it does follow that the brother has a right to some of the chocolates, and thus that the boy does act unjustly if he refuses to give his brother any. But the effect of saying this is to obscure what we should keep distinct, namely the differ-ence between the boy's refusal in this case and the boy's refusal in the earlier case, in which the box was given to both boys jointly, and in which the small brother thus had what was from any point of view clear title to half.

A further objection to so using the term "right," that from the fact that A ought to do a thing for B it follows that B has a right against A that A do it for him, is that it is going to make the question of whether or not a man has a right to a thing turn on how easy it is to provide him with it; and this seems not merely unfortunate but morally unacceptable. Take the case of Henry Fonda again. I said earlier that I had no right to the touch of his cool hand on my fevered brow, even though I needed it to save my life. I said it would be frightfully nice of him to fly in from the West Coast to pro-vide me with it, but that I had no right against him that he should do so. But suppose he isn't on the West Coast. Suppose he has only to walk across the room and place a hand briefly on my brow—and lo, my life is saved. Then surely he ought to do it; it would be indecent to refuse. Is it to be said, "Ah, well, it follows that in this case she has a right to the touch of his hand on her brow, and so it would be an injustice for him to refuse"? So that I have a right to it when it is easy for him to provide it, though no right when it is hard? It's rather a shocking idea that anyone's rights should fade away and disappear as it gets harder and harder to accord them to him.

So my own view is that even though you ought to let the violinist use your kidneys for the one hour he needs, we should not conclude that he has a right to do so; we should say that if you refuse you are, like the boy who owns all the chocolates and will give none away, self-centered and callous —indecent, in fact—but not unjust. And similarly, that even supposing a case in which a woman pregnant due to rape ought to allow the unborn person to use her body for the hour he needs, we should not conclude that he has a right to do so; we should conclude that she is self-centered, callous, indecent, but not unjust, if she refuses. The complaints are no less grave; they are just different. However, there is no need to insist on this point. If anyone does wish to deduce "he has a right" from "you ought," then all the same he must surely grant that there are cases in which it is not morally required of you that you allow that violinist to use your kidneys, and in which he does not have a right to use them, and in which you do not do him an unjustice if you refuse. And so also for mother and unborn child. Except in such cases as the unborn person has a right to demand it—and we were leaving open the possibility that there may be such cases—nobody is morally *required* to make large sacrifices, of health, of all other interests and concerns, of all other duties and commitments, for nine years, or even for nine months, in order to keep another person alive.

6. We have in fact to distinguish between two kinds of Samaritans: the Good Samaritan and what we might call the Minimally Decent Samaritan. The story of the Good Samaritan, you will remember, goes like this:

> A certain man went down from Jerusalem to Jericho, and fell among thieves, which stripped him of his raiment, and wounded him, and departed, leaving him half dead.
>
> And by chance there came down a certain priest that way; and when he saw him, he passed by on the other side.
>
> And likewise a Levite, when he was at the place, came and looked on him, and passed by the other side.
>
> But a certain Samaritan, as he journeyed, came where he was; and when he saw him he had compassion on him.
>
> And went to him, and bound up his wounds, pouring in oil and wine, and set him on his own beast, and brought him to an inn, and took care of him.
>
> And on the morrow, when he departed, he took out two pence, and gave them to the host, and said unto him, "Take care of him; and whatsoever thou spendest more, when I come again, I will repay thee." (Luke 10:30-35)

The Good Samaritan went out of his way, at some cost to himself, to help one in need of it. We are not told what the options were, that is, whether or not the priest and the Levite could have helped by doing less than the Good Samaritan did; but assuming they could have, then the fact they did nothing at all shows they were not even Minimally Decent Samaritans, not because they were not Samaritans, but because they were not even minimally decent.

These things are a matter of degree, of course, but there is a difference; it comes out perhaps most clearly in the story of Kitty Genovese, who was murdered while thirty-eight people watched or listened and did nothing at all to help her. A Good Samaritan would have rushed out to give direct assistance against the murderer. Or perhaps we had better allow that it would have been a Splendid Samaritan who did this, on the ground that it would have involved a risk of death for himself. But the thirty-eight people not only did not do this; they did not even trouble to pick up a phone to call the police. Minimally Decent Samaritanism would call for doing at least that, and their not having done so was monstrous.

After telling the story of the Good Samaritan Jesus said, "Go, and do thou likewise." Perhaps he meant that we are morally required to act as the Good Samaritan did. Perhaps he was urging people to do more than is morally required of them. At all events it seems plain that it was not morally required of any of the thirty-eight that he rush out to give direct assistance at the risk of his own life and that it is not morally required of anyone that he give long stretches of his life—nine years or nine months— to sustaining the life of a person who has no special right (we were leaving open the possibility of this) to demand it.

Indeed, with one rather striking class of exceptions, no one in any country in the world is *legally* required to do anywhere near as much as this for anyone else. The class of exceptions is obvious. My main concern here is not the state of the law in respect to abortion, but it is worth drawing attention to the fact that in no state in this country is any man compelled by law to be even a Minimally Decent Samaritan to any person; there is no law under which charges could be brought against the thirty-eight people who stood by while Kitty Genovese died. By contrast, in most states in this country women are compelled by law to be not merely Minimally Decent Samaritans, but Good Samaritans, to unborn persons inside them. This does not by itself settle anything, because it may well be argued that there should be laws in this country—as there are in many European countries—compelling at least Minimally Decent Samaritanism.[8] But it does show that there is a gross injustice in the existing state of the law. And it shows also that the groups currently working against liberalization of abortion laws, in fact working toward having it declared unconstitutonal for a state to permit abortion, had better start working for the adoption of Good Samaritan laws generally, or earn the charge that they are acting in bad faith.

I myself think that Minimally Decent Samaritan laws would be one thing, Good Samaritan laws quite another—and in fact highly improper. But we are not here concerned with the law. What we should ask is not whether anybody should be compelled by law to be a Good Samaritan but whether we must accede to a situation in which somebody is being compelled—by nature, perhaps—to be a Good Samaritan. We have, in other words, to look now at third-party interventions. I have been arguing that no person is morally required to make large sacrifices to sustain the life of another who has no right to demand them, and this even where the sacrifices do not include life itself; we are not morally required to be Good

Samaritans, or anyway, Very Good Samaritans, to one another. But what if a man cannot extricate himself from such a situation? What if he appeals to us to extricate him? It seems to me plain that there are cases in which we can, cases in which a Good Samaritan would extricate him. There you are: you were kidnapped, and nine years in bed with the violinist lie ahead of you. You have your own life to lead. You are sorry, but you simply cannot see giving up so much of your life to the sustaining of his. You cannot extricate yourself, and ask us to do so. I should have thought that—in light of his having no right to the use of your body—it was obvious that we do not have to accede to your being forced to give up so much. We can do what you ask. There is no injustice to the violinist in our doing so.

7. Following the lead of the opponents of abortion, I have throughout been speaking of the fetus merely as a person; and what I have been asking is whether or not the argument we began with, which proceeds only from the fetus' being a person, really does establish its conclusion. I have argued that it does not.

But of course there are arguments and arguments, and it may be said that I have simply fastened on the wrong one. It may be said that what is important is not merely the fact that the fetus is a person but that it is a person for whom the woman has a special kind of responsibility issuing from the fact that she is its mother. It might be argued that all my analogies are therefore irrelevant—for you do not have that special kind of responsibility for that violinist and Henry Fonda does not have that special kind of responsibility for me. And our attention might be drawn to the fact that men and women both are compelled by law to provide support for their children.

I have in effect dealt (briefly) with this argument in section 4 above; but a (still briefer) recapitulation now may be in order. Surely we do not have any such "special responsibility" for a person unless we have assumed it, explicitly or implicitly. If a set of parents do not try to prevent pregnancy, do not obtain an abortion, and then at the time of birth of the child do not put it up for adoption but rather take it home with them, then they have assumed responsibility for it, they have given it rights, and they cannot *now* withdraw support from it at the cost of its life because they now find it difficult to go on providing for it. But if they have taken all reasonable precautions against having a child, they do not simply by virtue of their biological relationship to the child who comes into existence have a special responsibility for it. They may wish to assume responsibility for it, or they may not wish to. And I am suggesting that if assuming responsibility for it would require large sacrifices, then they may refuse. A Good

Samaritan would not refuse, or, anyway, a Splendid Samaritan would not, if the sacrifices that had to be made were enormous. But then so would a Good Samaritan assume responsibility for that violinist; so would Henry Fonda, if he is a Good Samaritan, fly in from the West Coast and assume responsibility for me.

8. My argument will be found unsatisfactory on two counts by many of those who want to regard abortion as morally permissible. First, while I do argue that abortion is not impermissible, I do not argue that it is always permissible. There may well be cases in which carrying the child to term requires only Minimally Decent Samaritanism of the mother, and this is a standard we must not fall below. I am inclined to think it a merit of my account precisely that it does *not* give a general yes or a general no. It allows for and supports our sense that, for example, a sick and desperately frightened fourteen-year-old schoolgirl, pregnant due to rape, may *of course* choose abortion, and that any law that rules this out is an insane law. And it also allows for and supports our sense that in other cases resort to abortion is even positively indecent. It would be indecent in the woman to request an abortion, and indecent in a doctor to perform it, if she is in her seventh month and wants the abortion just to avoid the nuisance of postponing a trip abroad. The very fact that the arguments I have been drawing attention to treat all cases of abortion, or even all cases of abortion in which the mother's life is not at stake, as morally on a par ought to have made them suspect at the outset.

Second, while I am arguing for the permissibility of abortion in some cases, I am not arguing for the right to secure the death of the unborn child. It is easy to confuse these two things in that up to a certain point in the life of the fetus it is not able to survive outside the mother's body; hence removing it from her body guarantees its death. But they are different in important ways. I have argued that you are not morally required to spend nine months in bed, sustaining the life of the violinist; but to say this is by no means to say that if when you unplug yourself there is a miracle and he survives, you have a right to turn round and slit his throat. You may detach yourself even if this costs him his life; you have no right to be guaranteed his death by some other means if unplugging yourself does not kill him. There are some people who will feel dissatisfied by this feature of my argument. A woman may be utterly devastated by the thought of a child, a bit of herself, put up for adoption and never seen or heard of again. She may therefore want not merely that the child be detached from her but, more, that it die. Some opponents of abortion are inclined to regard this as beneath contempt, thereby showing insensitivity to what is surely a powerful source of despair. All the same, I agree that the desire for the child's death is not one that anybody may gratify, should it turn out to be possible to detach the child alive.

At this place, however, it should be remembered that we have only been pretending throughout that the fetus is a human being from the moment of conception. A very early abortion is surely not the killing of a person and so is not dealt with by anything I have said here.

NOTES

1. I am very indebted to James Thomson for discussion, criticism, and many helpful suggestions.

2. Daniel Callahan, *Abortion: Law, Choice, and Morality* (New York: Macmillan, 1970), p. 373. This book gives a fascinating survey of the available information on abortion. The Jewish tradition is surveyed in David M. Feldman, *Birth Control in Jewish Law* (New York: New York University Press, 1968), part 5; the Catholic tradition, in John T. Noonan, Jr., "An Almost Absolute Value in History," in *The Morality of Abortion*, ed. John T. Noonan, Jr. (Cambridge, Mass.: Harvard University Press, 1970).

3. The term "direct" in the arguments I refer to is a technical one. Roughly, what is meant by "direct killing" is either killing as an end in itself or killing as a means to some end, for example, the end of saving someone else's life. See note 6 for an example of its use.

4. Cf. *Encyclical Letter of Pope Pius XI on Christian Marriage*, St. Paul Editions (Boston, n.d.), p. 32: "However much we may pity the mother whose health and even life is gravely imperiled in the performance of the duty allotted to her by nature, nevertheless what could ever be a sufficient reason for excusing in any way the direct murder of the innocent? This is precisely what we are dealing with here." Noonan (*The Morality of Abortion*, p. 43) reads this as follows: "What cause can ever avail to excuse in any way the direct killing of the innocent? For it is a question of that."

5. The thesis in argument 4 is in an interesting way weaker than those in 1, 2, and 3: they rule out abortion even in cases in which both mother and child will die if the abortion is not performed. By contrast, one who held the view expressed in 4 could consistently say that one need not prefer letting two persons die to killing one.

6. Cf. the following passage from Pius XII, *Address to the Italian Catholic Society of Midwives:* "The baby in the maternal breast has the right to life immediately from God.—Hence there is no man, no human authority, no science, no medical, eugenic, social, economic or moral 'indication' which can establish or grant a valid juridical ground for a direct deliberate disposition of an innocent human life, that is a disposition which looks to its destruction either as an end or as a means to another end perhaps in itself not illicit.—The baby, still not born, is a man in the same degree and for the same reason as the mother" (quoted in Noonan, *The Morality of Abortion*, p. 45).

7. The need for a discussion of this argument was brought home to me by members of the Society for Ethical and Legal Philosophy, to whom this paper was originally presented.

8. For a discussion of the difficulties involved, and a survey of the European experience with such laws, see *The Good Samaritan and the Law*, ed. James M. Ratcliffe (New York: Peter Smith, 1966).

Alison Jaggar

Abortion and a Woman's Right To Decide

I

Philosophical discussions of abortion commonly focus on the question of how to justify abortion: In what circumstances (if any) is abortion a morally right course of action, and in what circumstances (if any) is it morally wrong?[1] Much less frequently discussed is the question concerning the responsibility for applying the results of such reflection to particular cases: given a particular pregnancy, who should decide whether or not it ought to be terminated? The first is a question in moral philosophy; the second is a question in social or political philosophy. If everyone were a totally rational and disinterested moral agent, the second question would be unimportant, for the same decision would be reached regardless of who was responsible for making it. But since the answers to the first question are notoriously diverse, the second question becomes one of great practical importance to women. It is to this second question that I will address myself. Specifically, I want to consider whether or not each woman should be legally guaranteed the sole right to decide whether or not she may have her own pregnancy terminated.

This problem is not of just narrowly feminist interest: like most feminist issues it raises more-general questions whose resolution is basic for the formulation of a comprehensive social philosophy. Among the obvious questions it raises are the extent of individual freedom in society and the obligation of the state to protect the interests of those who are unable to do so for themselves. A particularly interesting aspect of this issue is the way in which it illustrates some fundamental problems with the attempt to guarantee justice, freedom, and equality through the establishment of political rights.

In what follows I shall attempt to provide a moral justification for the

This article is reprinted from *The Philosophical Forum*, volume 5, nos. 1-2 (Fall-Winter 1973-74) with the permission of the publisher and author.

claim that each woman should have the sole legal right to decide whether or not, in her own case, an abortion should be performed. For reasons that will be given later, I shall ignore utilitarian considerations in my attempt to establish this conclusion. Instead I shall support my claim that each woman should have a legal right to abortion by appeal to an underlying moral right. The moral right to abortion for which I argue, however, is not a universal or absolute one enjoyed by all women, regardless of their social situation. Rather, it is a right whose existence depends on certain contingent features of the social situation in which women find themselves. Within our society, I shall argue, conditions are such that most women have a moral right to abortion, and, consequently, this right should be guaranteed by law. However, it is possible to describe other societies in which women do not have the sole moral right to decide on abortion, and indeed even within our own society there may be some women who do not have that right. It will be in our consideration of the reasons why the moral right to decide on abortion is only a contingent right and does not belong to all women that we shall gain fresh insight into the difficulties of attempting to formulate an ideal of the just, free, and egalitarian society in terms of legal rights.

My argument for the conclusion that each woman should legally be guaranteed the right to decide whether or not she should abort attempts to bypass a number of difficult problems that are usually thought to complicate the issue. For example, I do not appeal to the unclear and dubious "right to one's own body." I skirt the general question of population control. I make no presuppositions about the moral status of unborn human beings other than to assume they do not have a right to life so absolute that the question of abortion may never be raised; that is, I assume it to be false that there are *no* circumstances that could conceivably justify abortion, but I do not commit myself to any stand on exactly what circumstances might do so. Finally, I avoid the general question of the purposes and limits of state authority. Instead I attempt to short-circuit all these difficulties and to resolve the issue of whether each woman should have a legal right to make her own decision about abortion by appeal to two relatively uncontroversial principles. Thus, if my argument works, it should be acceptable to people of most shades of political opinion and to anyone who will admit that abortion might occasionally be justified. Before presenting my solution, however, I shall briefly survey the claims of the various candidates for the right to judge whether or not a given pregnancy should be terminated.

II

Several grounds are commonly adduced for the pregnant woman's right to decide if she should abort. They include an alleged right to privacy (the basis of the 1973 U.S. Supreme Court decision to liberalize the hitherto very restrictive abortion laws), an alleged right to her own body, and a right to determine her own future. There are also utilitarian arguments for allowing a woman to choose abortion: if a woman is reluctant to have a child, then the refusal to allow her to decide to terminate her pregnancy is said to increase the sum of unhappiness in the world, either by forcing her to seek an illegal, unsafe, and expensive abortion, or by resulting in an unwilling mother and an unwanted child. Other utilitarian arguments concern the general disutility of passing laws restricting a woman's choice when such laws are likely to be disregarded so widely that they will bring the whole legal system into disrespect.

The potential mother, however, is not the only parent with a claim to decide. The potential father also has some grounds to claim at least a share in making the decision. The father's claim rests not so much on possible property rights over the disposition of his semen (although I have heard this argument given!) as on his legal obligation to share in the economic support of the child that will result if the abortion is not performed. He might argue that he should have a choice as to whether or not he undertakes those obligations. He might also make an appeal, parallel to the mother's, to utilitarian arguments about the unwanted children of unwilling fathers.

Many people assume that the doctor or the medical personnel who are asked to perform the abortion should also have some say in deciding whether or not it should occur. In order to justify this claim, it seems necessary to assume either that abortion is a totally nonmoral question of medical technique or, alternatively, that the role of the medical staff is to act as moral rather than as medical authorities. If one rejects these assumptions, then the only other reason that I can think of for allowing the medical personnel to share in deciding whether or not a particular abortion ought to be performed is that they should not have to do something that they believe to be morally wrong.

Much stronger arguments can be brought forward in support of the state's claim to decide on cases of abortion. If the unborn is viewed as having any right to life at all, even a weak one, then it is plausible to suppose that the state has an obligation to protect that right. Additionally, if the birth of a child places a burden on the state by requiring it to provide education, health care, or economic support, then it may be reasonable to grant the state a part in making the decision about whether or not that child should be born. There is also a familiar utilitarian argument for state control of abortion, to the effect that it is for the benefit of all if the state determines the optimum population.

Since demographic decisions ultimately affect the whole world, it is even arguable that decisions about abortion ought to be made by the world community. However, although I believe that in certain circumstances this suggestion might have some merit, it is at present so wildly impractical that I shall not consider it further in this discussion. Should anyone wish to do so, it is easy to construct arguments for world-community control analogous to those that I use for the state.

Given all these conflicting claims and the variety of the grounds on which they rest, it is hard to see how to settle the question of who should decide whether or not a pregnancy should be terminated. Talk of rights is notoriously problematic, and when the alleged rights of different individuals conflict both with each other and with the state, as they do in the case of the abortion decision, the only way to resolve the conflict appears to be by appeal to utilitarian arguments. Even if the utilities and disutilities involved in a complex question such as this could be worked out, however, it is doubtful whether either side would accept them. Antiabortionists refuse to accept utilitarian arguments if they appear to threaten the alleged right to life of the unborn; correspondingly, feminists may well fear that to fall back on utilitarianism would open the way to a fresh call on women for the kind of sacrifices that they have traditionally made. Involuntary abortion and involuntary childbirth are both unacceptable to feminists, but utilitarianism cannot guarantee protection from either.

III

There are two principles that I see as the key to determining whether or not each woman has the right to decide if she should terminate her pregnancy.

The first principle is that the right to life, when it is claimed for a human being, means the right to a full human life and to whatever means are necessary to achieve this. Unfortunately I am not able to spell out precisely the necessary conditions for a full human life. This is a perennial subject of philosophical debate. To some extent, although not entirely, those conditions may be dependent on the level of development of the society in which the right to life is claimed. But certainly they go beyond the requirements for mere physiological survival to the less tangible requirements for full development as a human being, however those requirements should be construed. To be born, then, is only one of the necessary conditions for a full human life; the others presumably include nutritious food, breathable air, warm human companionship, and so on. If anyone has a right to life, she or he must be entitled to all of these.

The second principle to which I shall appeal is the principle that decisions should be made by those, and only by those, who are importantly affected by them. This principle provides the fundamental justification for democracy and is accepted by most shades of political opinion. Ideological differences arise not because of disagreement on the principle but because of disagreement on how to instantiate it.

How do these two principles apply to the issue of each woman's right to decide whether or not she should abort? The first principle suggests that if an individual or an organization does not make a genuine attempt to guarantee all of a child's needs, both before and after its birth, it cannot be viewed as the protector of that child's right to life. The protector of the child's right to life is that individual or organization that attempts to fulfill *all* the conditions necessary to the child's achieving a full human life. If an individual or organization knowingly and willfully neglects some of those necessary conditions, then there is no reason to grant it any special status as the child's protector. Hence, such an individual or organization has no special moral authority that would justify its insistence on just one of the many conditions necessary to a full human life, in circumstances where this would place the burden of fulfilling all the other conditions squarely on the shoulders of some other individual or organization. In particular, it cannot appeal to its special status as defender of the unborn's right to life in order to prohibit abortion, for it has no such special status.

The second principle entails that the decision about abortion should be made by all those whose lives are to be importantly affected by that decision. Which persons are included in that class is determined partly by certain features inherent in the situation (necessarily the lives of the woman and of the unborn are importantly affected), but it is also determined partly by the social context in which the question of abortion arises. For example, in a situation of very short food supply the whole community into which the child is to be born will be affected by the birth in a way in which it would not be affected if food were plentiful.

The two principles together entail that in our society each woman has the right to choose whether or not she should terminate her pregnancy. This conclusion follows from the application of the two principles to certain contingent features of our social organization. These features include the inadequate prenatal and postnatal health care provided by the state, the fact that the main responsibility for raising a child is laid on its biological mother, and the small proportion of the natural resources devoted to welfare.

IV

To explain this, let us look again at the main candidates for a share in making the decision about abortion. Some of those who are eligible on the basis of having their lives affected by the decision are nevertheless unable in principle to participate in making it. They include the unborn child in question and future unborn generations. The world community at large, which is eligible on the same grounds, is also excluded from a share in making the decision—this time because of practical difficulties. This leaves the potential mother, the potential father, the medical staff who are asked to perform the abortion, and the state.

It will be remembered that the father's main claim to being able to decide whether or not his unborn child should be aborted was based on the fact that his life would be affected by the birth of a child. He has a legal obligation to contribute to the child's economic support, and if he happens to be married to the mother, it is conventionally understood that he will take at least a small part in raising the child; if he lives in the same house, he can hardly avoid some contact with it. In fact, however, the father has considerable choice as to how far his life is affected by the birth of his child. He may not live in the same house, and even if he does, present conventions about parenthood indicate that he will take a much smaller part in raising the child than will the mother, perhaps almost no part at all. Again, the father's obligation to provide economic support for the child may not be legally enforced. Finally, he does not have to go through the inconveniences, and even dangers, of pregnancy and childbirth. It is true that many fathers choose voluntarily to share as much as possible in the birth and raising of their children. But the fact remains that the choice is open to the father in a way in which it is not open to the mother. Biology, law, and social conditioning work together to ensure that most women's lives are totally changed as the result of the birth of a child, while men can choose how much they wish to be involved. It is for this reason that the potential mother, rather than the potential father, should have the ultimate responsibility for deciding whether or not an abortion should be performed, although this obviously does not exclude the mother from consulting the father if she wishes. If conventions regarding the degree of parental responsibility assumed by the mother and by the father were to change, or if the law prescribing paternal child support were to be enforced more rigorously, then perhaps we might require that the father share with the mother in making the decision (he could never take over the decision completely, of course, because it is not his body that is involved). But in the present social situation the right of a woman to decide if she should abort is not limited by any right of the father.

Still less should a woman's right to decide be limited by the claims of medical personnel. Their role is to present the medical information that she requests, not to determine the moral weight to be given to that information. They are not concerned in the long-term consequences of the abortion decision except insofar as they are members of the society into which the child will be born. This is not to say that even if the medical practitioners genuinely believe that abortion is morally wrong, they should still be compelled to perform it. But neither should they be able to prevent it. In practice, if there is a difficulty in finding the medical staff prepared to perform abortions, it is an indication that medical practitioners should be drawn from a broader spectrum of the population. Specifically, they should include more women. Generally, people are not slow in recognizing their rights, and if each woman has a right to choose whether or not she should abort, then female medical staff are unlikely to have moral qualms about helping her to exercise that right.

Let us now turn to the more difficult question of the claims of the state to participate in abortion decisions. Ignoring the utilitarian argument, the claim of the state rests on two grounds: the fact that the rest of the community is affected by the birth of new members and the alleged obligation of the state to protect the rights of even its unborn citizens. If our social situation were different, either of these arguments might be strong enough to justify the state's claim. But, as things are now, neither can outweigh the right of each woman to decide.

Certainly this right is not outweighed by the effects of the birth of new members on the rest of the community. While every woman's life is enormously affected by the birth of her child, the effect of new births on the rest of our society is small. Our food supply is ample, neither overpopulation nor underpopulation is as yet a serious problem, and only a very small proportion of our resources is spent on welfare. The birth of more children still has a negligible effect on the lives of everyone except the mother. The father and the siblings may be in some degree exceptions to this, but their involvement is usually minor compared to that of the mother, who has to carry, give birth to, and raise the child. Therefore, the principle that only those who are affected importantly by a decision should share in making it indicates that, in our society, the potential mother rather than the state has the right to decide whether or not she should seek an abortion.

What about the alleged obligation of the state to protect the rights of the unborn? Feminists often try to answer this question by denying that the unborn has any rights. However, I think that this argument for state control of abortion can be answered without having to commit oneself to any stand on the difficult question of the moral status of the unborn or, indeed, to any position on the general justification of abortion. I have already argued that the rights of the unborn child cannot be separated from its rights after it is born; birth is just one necessary condition of an individual's exercising his or her right to life. But an individual's right to life is not fulfilled once she or he is born. She or he then acquires immediately a whole set of complex requirements in order to exercise her or his right to life. In our society the responsibility for fulfilling those needs falls primarily on the mother. The state does indeed provide schooling and a minimal degree of physical care for those children whose mothers are unable to support them. Such children do not usually starve or freeze to death. But, as is shown by the horrifying statistics on "battered" unwanted babies and the stunted physical and emotional development of children in state institutions, the state is far from guaranteeing the fulfillment of all their basic needs. Moreover, the offspring of a poor mother who keeps her children suffer in every way from their mother's poverty: they are malnourished, subject to disease, and perhaps aware that their very existence contributes to her poverty. For our society lays on each woman the bulk of the responsibility for protecting the right to life of her children. The state abandons most of this responsibility by refusing to guarantee for each child the necessary conditions of a full human life. Thus, since in our society the mother and not the state is the primary protector of the child's right to life, it is the pregnant woman and not the state who should decide whether or not, in her own case, abortion is justified.

So far I have ignored the utilitarian arguments surrounding the question of whether each woman has the right to decide to terminate her pregnancy. There are two reasons for this. One is that most utilitarian arguments tend to support the conclusion for which I am arguing. For example, they talk about the suffering caused by illegal abortions or about the danger of promoting a general disrespect for the law, since a law that restricts a woman's right to decide is likely to be widely disobeyed. The main utilitarian argument *against* each woman's having the legal right to decide is that it is in the general interest for the state to control population policy. At this time in history, however, state population control would be more likely to result in forced abortions than in the refusal to terminate a pregnancy; but this proposal is so offensive to the moral intuitions of most people that it would probably be seen as justified only by a dire social emergency. Hence I have ignored that argument here. The other reason why I have avoided utilitarian arguments is that, in this context, they are not usually accepted as conclusive: if they seem to be working against either side in the dispute, then that side invariably reverts to talking about human rights—the antiabortionists appealing to the rights of the unborn, the proabortionists appealing to the rights of women. For myself, I tend to believe that each woman's right to decide if she should abort could be demonstrated very well on utilitarian grounds. But, for the reasons given above, I chose other grounds to defend my claim that, in our society, no individual or group has a justified claim to restrict a woman's right to decide.

To say that each woman in our society has the moral right to decide whether or not she should terminate her pregnancy is not to say that abortion is always justified. It implies nothing about what justifies abortion. Quite possibly, in deciding whether to abort or to bear the child, a woman will make the wrong decision. But the right to decide is hers.

Her right to decide is not derived from some obscure right to her own body; nor is it part of her right to privacy. It is a contingent right rather than an absolute one, resulting from women's situation in our society. In this society each woman is primarily responsible for her own support, for the medical expenses she will incur during pregnancy and childbirth, and for providing her child with both its material and emotional needs. Because of this situation, women's lives are enormously affected by the birth of their children, whereas the community as a whole is affected only slightly. Moreover, because of this situation, each woman finds that she, rather than the state, is the primary protector of her child's right to life. Given these facts, and given the principle that those and only those who are significantly affected by a decision should share in making it, it seems plain that in this society each woman has the sole moral right to determine whether or not, in her case, abortion is justified.

V

That each woman has this moral right is the basis of my claim that our legal system should guarantee to every woman the political right to decide whether or not to terminate her pregnancy. In making this claim, however, I am aware of possible problems: What should be done about very young women? What should be done about those women who are members of minority-group cultures where it is accepted that the family as a whole takes on the responsibility for fulfilling the needs of a child? And even, what should be done about women who are so rich that once a child is born, its existence may not affect their lives in any significant way? Surely circumstances like these would make us hesitate to claim that every woman in our society has the moral right to decide whether to terminate her pregnancy?

It may well be that a few women in these and other circumstances do not have the sole moral right to decide whether or not to seek an abortion. But in our society such women are exceptional, and it is a familiar fact that the law, being general, cannot take account of the unique circumstances of every individual case. I would argue that such cases are so few that they should not be allowed to limit the general conclusion that each woman in our society should be guaranteed the legal right to decide whether or not she should have her own pregnancy terminated. Consideration of such exceptions does indicate, however, a weakness inherent in any attempt to guarantee justice in terms of legal rights. For: "Right by its very nature can consist only in the application of an equal standard; but unequal individuals (and they would not be different individuals if they were not unequal) are measurable only by an equal standard in so far as they are brought under an equal point of view, are taken from one definite side only. ... To avoid all these defects, right instead of being equal would have to be unequal."[2] And where individuals' moral rights are unequal, it is unjust that their legal rights should be the same.

The right-to-decide issue also shows why freedom and equality cannot be guaranteed simply through the establishment of political rights. As many poor women have pointed out, to grant a woman the legal right to decide whether or not she should seek an abortion does not guarantee that, in a more than trivial sense, a woman has both options open to her. If present social conditions remain unchanged, then the choice remains a merely formal rather than real choice. A real choice about abortion requires that a woman should be able to opt to have her child, as well as to abort it. This means that the full right to life of the child must be guaranteed, either by community aid to the mother who wishes to raise it herself, or by the provision of alternative arrangements that do not put the child who is not raised by its own mother at any significant disadvantage. Conversely, abortions must be made so cheap and convenient that any woman may be able to obtain one without hardship.

The latter condition is not difficult to achieve; indeed, for a number of reasons quite unconnected with women's liberation, it may well be on the way. But the former condition, while it is easy enough to state, would require social changes far-reaching enough to be accurately termed a revolution. Among other things it would require cheap or free medical care for all mothers and children, and probably, if children raised by their mothers are not to have an advantage over the others, the abandonment of the official ideology that sees the nuclear family as the ideal or normal living arrangement. In short, it would require that the community take over the responsibility for the physical and emotional welfare of all mothers and children. Therefore if a woman's right to decide whether or not she should abort is to be translated in practice into a genuine choice, uncoerced by economic stringency, it presupposes fundamental change in our most basic social institutions.

Now arises an apparent paradox. The moral right to decide for which I have been arguing is a right only for women in societies relevantly similar to this one. The existence of that right is contingent on the conditions obtaining in our society. But if these are radically altered, for example by the expenditure of a much greater proportion of our resources on welfare, then a woman's moral right to decide might be restricted. If the whole community were to assume responsibility for the welfare of mothers and children, then the application to the changed social conditions of the two principles that I used in defending the woman's right to decide would surely result in the conclusion that the community as a whole should have a share in judging whether or not a particular abortion should be performed. For the impact of new children on the whole community would be much greater, whereas the impact on the life of the mother would be considerably lessened, and might be reduced to the solely biological. Moreover, the mother's legal and conventional responsibility to protect her child's right to life would be no greater than that of any other member of the community. Of course, to say that the community as a whole should decide about abortions does not mean that the pregnant woman should not have a strong voice in making the decision: she is not just an ordinary member of the community in this matter, for it is still she who must bear and carry the child. Her wishes must therefore be accorded special weight. But she no longer would have the sole right or responsibility, depending on how one views it, for making the decision about whether or not to abort. The paradox, then, is that the attempt to guarantee the conditions in which each woman's right to decide about abortion would become a real option results in the achievement of conditions in which she no longer has that right.

The resolution of this paradox lies in the recognition that the establishment of political rights is inadequate as an ultimate social ideal. As such rights cannot guarantee justice, neither can they guarantee real freedom or equality. Unless our society is fundamentally changed, only a few women will be able to make a choice that is not determined by their economic situation. Hence, except for those fortunate few, the legal freedom to decide whether or not to abort will not result in genuine freedom of choice. And hence women's rights will not really be equal.

The abortion issue shows clearly why, in our search for justice, freedom, and equality, it may well be more fruitful to change our emphasis from the establishment of individual rights to the fulfillment of human needs. To attempt to describe an ideal society in terms of individual rights is to suggest that every society is composed of individuals whose interests inevitably conflict. This picture may be an accurate likeness of our present society, and, so long as it remains accurate, women must be granted the legal right to decide whether or not they should abort. Ultimately, however, when the community as a whole takes on the responsibility for fulfilling the needs of its members and the conflict between the interests of the individual and the interests of the rest of society is reconciled, this right will no longer be necessary. To achieve the legal right to decide about abortion is a first step on the way to women's liberation, but the last step may be the achievement of a society in which the whole notion of individual rights against the community makes no sense at all.

VI

It is sometimes objected that the foregoing argument justifies not only a woman's right to abort but also her right to kill her two-week-old baby or even her six-year-old child. The objectors assume, of course, that if this were indeed a consequence of my account, it would make my claim quite unacceptable.

My answer depends on making a distinction—not a problematic distinction between the moral status of prenatal and postnatal children, but an obvious and uncontroversial distinction between a woman's relation to her unborn child and her relation to it once it is born. She cannot sever the tie between herself and her unborn child in any way short of killing that child. She can, however, cut the connection between herself and a postnatal child without directly killing that child. Psychologically agonizing as it may be (and that empirical fact is not irrelevant to the right to abortion), one can walk away from the crying of a baby as one cannot walk away from the kicking of an unborn child. It is possible, at least in principle, to ignore the needs of a baby, whereas an unborn child will take its needs from a woman's body regardless of her willingness or her ability to give. A mother may, though at tremendous psychological cost, refuse her socially assigned responsibility for raising her child. But there is no way in which a pregnant woman can avoid the discomforts and inconveniences of her condition, nor the experience of childbirth, which not only carries an unavoidable risk to her life, but which, in our society, is sometimes very painful and often humiliating.

I have argued that the pregnant woman's right to decide on abortion results from her finding herself in a social situation that leaves her with the primary responsibility for coping with her pregnancy, the birth, and the child to be. But we must not forget, of course, that only a pregnant woman can ever be in such a situation. It is obvious that a woman's relation to her child is only partly defined by society; it is also determined by biology. It is the conjunction of the biological element with the social one that makes a woman's relation to her unborn child a unique relation of peculiar magnitude and peculiar inevitability. I have already made it clear that if the *social* aspect of the relationship were to change, then we would have to reexamine the claim that women have the sole right to decide on abortion. What I must now make explicit, in order to show that a mother's right to infanticide is not a necessary consequence of a woman's right to abortion, is that when the *biological* aspect of the relationship is changed, as it is when the child is born, then another moral reevaluation must occur, and the rights of the mother must be redefined. (So, indeed, should her responsibilities, together with the rights and responsibilities of the father and of the state, be redefined.) Consequently, it is plain that whether a woman has the right to infanticide is a question quite separate from whether she has the right to abort and must be considered on its own merits.

NOTES

1. The time to write this essay was provided by a Taft grant-in-aid of research. Some of the stimulus to do so was provided by hearing an unpublished paper, "Women's Rights, Population Control, and Marxist Ideology," read by Janet Farrell Smith at a meeting of the midwestern division of the Society for Women in Philosophy, in Chicago, February 1974.

2. Karl Marx, *Critique of the Gotha Programme,* reprinted in Karl Marx and Frederick Engels, *Selected Works of Marx and Engels* (New York: International Publishing Co., 1968), p. 324.

R. M. Hare

Abortion and the Golden Rule

If philosophers are going to apply ethical theory successfully to practical issues, they must first have a theory. This may seem obvious; but they often proceed as if it were not so. A philosopher's chief contribution to a practical issue should be to show us which are good and which are bad arguments; and to do this he has to have some way of telling one from the other. Moral philosophy therefore needs a basis in philosophical logic— the logic of the moral concepts. But we find, for example, Professor Judith Jarvis Thomson, in an article on abortion which has been justly praised for the ingenuity and liveliness of her examples, proceeding as if this were not necessary at all.[1] She simply parades the examples before us and asks what we would say about them. But how do we know whether what we feel inclined to say has any secure ground? May we not feel inclined to say it just because of the way we were brought up to think? And was this necessarily the right way? It is highly diverting to watch the encounter in the same volume between her and Mr. John Finnis, who, being a devout Roman Catholic, has intuitions which differ from hers (and mine) in the wildest fashion.[2] I just do not know how to tell whether Mr. Finnis is on safe ground when he claims that suicide is "a paradigm case of an action that is always wrong"; nor Professor Thomson when she makes the no doubt more popular claim that we have a right to decide what happens in and to our own bodies.[3] How would we choose between these potentially conflicting intuitions? Is it simply a contest in rhetoric?

In contrast, a philosopher who wishes to contribute to the solution of this and similar practical problems should be trying to develop, on the basis of a study of the moral concepts and their logical properties, a theory of moral reasoning that will determine which arguments we ought to

This article, which was the 1974 Hurst Lecture at American University, is reprinted with permission from *Philosophy & Public Affairs* 4 (Spring 1975). Copyright © 1975 R. M. Hare.

accept. Professor Thomson might be surprised to see me saying this, because she thinks that I am an emotivist,[4] in spite of the fact that I devoted two of the very first papers I ever published to a refutation of emotivism.[5] Her examples are entertaining, and help to show up our prejudices; but they will do no more than that until we have a way of telling which prejudices ought to be abandoned.

II

I shall abjure two approaches to the question of abortion which have proved quite unhelpful. The first puts the question in terms of the "rights" of the fetus or the mother; the second demands, as a necessary condition for solving the problem, an answer to the question, Is the fetus a person? The first is unhelpful at the moment, because nobody has yet proposed an even plausible account of how we might argue conclusively about rights. Rights are the stamping ground of intuitionists, and it would be difficult to find any claim confidently asserted to a right which could not be as confidently countered by a claim to another right, such that both rights cannot simultaneously be complied with. This is plainly true in the present controversy, as it is in the case of rights to property—one man has a right not to starve, another a right to hold on to the money that would buy him food. Professor Thomson evidently believes in property rights, because she curiously bases the right of a woman to decide what happens in and to her own body on her ownership of it. We might ask whether, if this is correct, the property is disposable; could it be held that by the marriage contract a wife and a husband yield up to each other some of their property rights in their own bodies? If so, might we find male chauvinists who were prepared to claim that, if the husband wants to have an heir, the wife cannot claim an absolute liberty to have an abortion? As a question of law, this could be determined by the courts and the legislature; but as a question of morals . . . ?

In the law, cash value can be given to statements about rights by translating them into statements about what it is or is not lawful to do. An analogous translation will have to be effected in morals, with "right" (adjective), "wrong," and "ought" taking the place of "lawful" and "unlawful," before the word "rights" can be a dependable prop for moral arguments. It may be that one day somebody will produce a theory of rights which links the concept firmly to those of "right," "wrong," and "ought" —concepts whose logic is even now a *little* better understood. The simplest such theory would be one which said that A has a right, in one sense of the word, to do X if and only if it is not wrong for A to do X; and that A has a right, in another sense, to do *X* if and only if it is wrong to prevent A from doing *X*; and that A has a right to do *X* in a third sense if and only if it is wrong not to assist A to do *X* (the extent of the assistance, and the persons from whom it is due, being unspecified and, on many occasions of the use of this ambiguous word "rights," unspecifiable). It is often unclear, when people claim that women have a right to do what they like with their own bodies, which of these senses is being used. (Does it, for example, mean that it is not wrong for them to terminate their own pregnancies, or that it is wrong to stop them doing this, or that it is wrong not to assist them in doing this?) For our present purposes it is best to leave these difficulties on one side and say that *if* at some future time a reliable analysis of the various senses of "rights" in terms of "wrong" or "ought" is forthcoming, then arguments about rights will be restatable in terms of what it is wrong to do, or what we ought or ought not to do. Till that happy day comes, we shall get the issues in better focus if we discuss them directly in terms of what we ought or ought not to do, or what it would be right or wrong to do, to the fetus or the mother in specified circumstances.

III

The other unhelpful approach, that of asking whether the fetus is a person, has been so universally popular that in many of the writings it is assumed that this question is the key to the whole problem. The reason for this is easy to see; if there is a well-established moral principle that the intentional killing of other innocent persons is always murder, and therefore wrong, it looks as if an easy way to determine whether it is wrong to kill fetuses is to determine whether they are persons, and thus settle once for all whether they are subsumable under the principle. But this approach has run into well-known difficulties, the basic reason for which is the following. If a normative or evaluative principle is framed in terms of a predicate which has fuzzy edges (as nearly all predicates in practice have), then we are not going to be able to use the principle to decide cases on the borderline without doing some more normation or evaluation. If we make a law forbidding the use of wheeled vehicles in the park, and somebody thinks he can go in the park on roller skates, no amount of cerebration, and no amount of inspection of roller skates, is going to settle for us the question of whether roller skates are wheeled vehicles "within the meaning of the Act" if the Act has not specified whether they are; the judge has to decide whether they are *to be* counted as such. And this is a further determination of the law.[6] The judge may have very good reasons of public interest or morals for his decision; but he cannot make it by any physical or metaphysical investigation of roller skates to see whether they are *really* wheeled vehicles. If he had not led too sheltered a life, he knew all he needed to know about roller skates before the case ever came into court.

In the same way the decision to say that the fetus becomes a person at conception, or at quickening, or at birth, or whenever takes your fancy, and that thereafter, because it is a person, destruction of it is murder, is inescapably a moral decision, for which we have to have moral reasons. It is not necessary, in order to make this point, to insist that the word "person" is a moral word; though in many contexts there is much to be said for taking this line. It is necessary only to notice that "person," even if descriptive, is not a fully determinate concept; it is loose at the edges, as the abortion controversy only too clearly shows. Therefore, if we decide that, "within the meaning of" the principle about murder, a fetus becomes a person as soon as it is conceived, we are deciding a moral question, and ought to have a moral reason for our decision. It is no use looking more closely at the fetus to satisfy ourselves that it is *really* a person (as the people do who make so much of the fact that it has arms and legs); we already have all the information that we need about the fetus. What is needed is thought about the moral question, How ought a creature, about whose properties, circumstances, and probable future we are quite adequately informed, to be treated? If, in our desire to get out of addressing ourselves to this moral question—to get it settled for us without any moral thought on our part—we go first to the physicians for information about whether the fetus is really a person, and then, when they have told us all they can, to the metaphysicians, we are only indulging in the well-known vice of philosophers (which my fellow linguistic philosophers, at any rate, ought to be on their guard against because that is the mainstay of our training)— the vice of trying to settle substantial questions by verbal maneuvers.

I am not saying that physiological research on the fetus has no bearing on moral questions about abortion. If it brought to light, for example, that fetuses really do suffer on the same scale as adults do, then that would be a good moral reason for not causing them to suffer. It will not do to show that they wriggle when pricked, for so do earthworms; and I do not think that the upholders of the rights of unborn children wish to extend these rights to earthworms. Encephalograms are better; but there are enormous theoretical and practical difficulties in the argument from encephalograms to conscious experiences. In default of these latter, which would have to be of such a sort as to distinguish fetuses radically from other creatures which the antiabortionists would not lift a finger to protect, the main weight of the antiabortionist argument is likely to rest, not on the sufferings of the fetus, but on harms done to the interests of the person into whom the fetus would normally develop. These will be the subject of most of the rest of this paper.

Approaching our moral question in the most general way, let us ask whether there is *anything* about the fetus *or* about the person it may turn into that should make us say that we ought not to kill it. If, instead of asking this question, somebody wants to go on asking, indirectly, whether the fetus is a person, and whether, *therefore*, killing it is wrong, he is at liberty to do so; but I must point out that the reasons he will have to give for saying that it is a person, and that, therefore, killing it is wrong (or that it is not a person and, therefore, killing it is not wrong) will be the very same moral reasons as I shall be giving for the answer to my more direct question. Whichever way one takes it, one cannot avoid giving a reasoned answer to this moral question; so why not take it the simplest way? To say that the fetus is (or is not) a person gives *by itself* no moral reason for or against killing it; it merely encapsulates any reasons we may have for including the fetus within a certain category of creatures that it is, or is not, wrong to kill (that is, persons or nonpersons). The word "person" is doing no work here (other than that of bemusing us).

IV

Is there then anything about the fetus which raises moral problems about the legitimacy of killing it? At this point I must declare that I have no axe to grind—I am not a fervent abortionist nor a fervent antiabortionist—I just want fervently to get to the root of the matter. It will be seen, as the argument goes on, that the first move I shall make is one which will give cheer to the antiabortionists; but, before they have had time to celebrate, it will appear that this move brings with it, inescapably, another move which should encourage the other side. We shall end up somewhere in between, but perhaps with a clearer idea of how, in principle, to set about answering questions about particular abortions.

The single, or at least the main, thing about the fetus that raises the moral question is that, if not terminated, the pregnancy is highly likely to result in the birth and growth to maturity of a person just like the rest of us. The word "person" here reenters the argument, but in a context and with a meaning that does not give rise to the old troubles; for it is clear at least that we ordinary adults are persons. If we knew beyond a peradventure that a fetus was going to miscarry anyway, then little would remain of the moral problem beyond the probably minimal sufferings caused to the mother and just possibly the fetus by terminating the pregnancy now. If, on the other hand, we knew (to use Professor Tooley's science-fiction example[7]) that an embryo kitten would, if not aborted but given a wonder drug, turn into a being with a human mind like ours, then that too would raise a moral problem. Perhaps Tooley thinks not; but we shall see. It is, to use his useful expression, the "potentiality" that the fetus has of becoming a person in the full ordinary sense that creates the problem. It is because Tooley thinks that, once the "potentiality principle" (see below) is admitted, the conservatives or extreme antiabortionists will win the case hands down, that he seeks reasons for rejecting it; but, again, we shall see.

We can explain why the potentiality of the fetus for becoming a person raises a moral problem if we appeal to a type of argument which, in one guise or another, has been the formal basis of almost all theories of moral reasoning that have contributed much that is worthwhile to our understanding of it. I am alluding to the Christian (and indeed pre-Christian) "Golden Rule," the Kantian Categorical Imperative, the ideal-observer theory, the rational-contractor theory, various kinds of utilitarianism, and my own universal prescriptivism.[8] I would claim that the last of these gives the greatest promise of putting what is common to all these theories in a perspicuous way, and so revealing their justification in logic; but it is not the purpose of this paper to give this justification. Instead, since the problem of abortion is discussed as often as not from a Christian standpoint, and since I hope thereby to find a provisional starting point for the argument on which many would agree, I shall use that form of the argument which rests on the Golden Rule that we should do to others as we wish them to do to us.[9] It is a logical extension of this form of argument to say that we should do to others what *we are glad was* done to us. Two (surely readily admissible) changes are involved here. The first is a mere difference in the two tenses which cannot be morally relevant. Instead of saying that we should do to others as we wish them (in the future) to do to us, we say that we should do to others as we wish that they had done to us (in the past). The second is a change from the hypothetical to the actual: instead of saying that we should do to others as we wish that they had done to us, we say that we should do to others as we are glad that they did do to us. I cannot see that this could make any difference to the spirit of the injunction, and logical grounds could in any case be given, based on the universal prescriptivist thesis, for extending the Golden Rule in this way.

The application of this injunction to the problem of abortion is obvious. If we are glad that nobody terminated the pregnancy that resulted in *our* birth, then we are enjoined not, *ceteris paribus*, to terminate any pregnancy which will result in the birth of a person having a life like ours. Close attention obviously needs to be paid to the "*ceteris paribus*" clause, and also to the expression "like ours." The "universalizability" of moral judgments, which is one of the logical bases of the Golden Rule, requires us to make the same moral judgment about qualitatively identical cases, and about cases which are *relevantly* similar. Since no cases in this area are going to be qualitatively *identical*, we shall have to rely on relevant similarity. Without raising a very large topic in moral philosophy, we can perhaps avoid the difficulty by pointing out that the relevant respects here are going to be those things about our life which make us glad that we were born. These can be stated in a general enough way to cover all those persons who are, or who are going to be or would be, glad that they were born. Those who are not glad they were born will still have a reason for not aborting those who would be glad; for even the former wish that, if they had been going to be glad that they were born, nobody should have aborted them. So, although I have, for the sake of simplicity, put the injunction in a way that makes it apply only to the abortion of people who will have a life just like that of the aborter, it is generalizable to cover the abortion of any fetus which will, if not aborted, turn into someone who will be glad to be alive.

I now come back to Professor Tooley's wonder kitten. He says that if it became possible by administering a wonder drug to an embryo kitten to cause it to turn into a being with a human mind like ours, we should still not feel under any obligation either to administer the drug to kittens or to refrain from aborting kittens to whom the drug had been administered by others. He uses this as an argument against the "potentiality principle," which says that if there are any properties which are possessed by adult human beings and which endow any organisms possessing them with a serious right to life, then "at least one of those properties will be such that any organism *potentially* possessing that property has a serious right to life even now, simply by virtue of that potentiality, where an organism possesses a property potentially if it will come to have that property in the normal course of its development." [10] Putting this more briefly and in terms of "wrong" instead of "rights," the potentiality principle says that if it would be wrong to kill an adult human being because he has a certain property, it is wrong to kill an organism (for example, a fetus) which will come to have that property if it develops normally.

There is one minor objection to what Tooley says which we can pass over quickly. The administration of wonder drugs is not normal development; so Tooley ought not to have used the words "in the normal course of its development"; they spoil his "kitten" example. But let us amend our summary of his principle by omitting the words "if it develops normally" and substituting "if we do not kill it." I do not think that this substitution makes Tooley's argument any weaker than it is already.

Now suppose that I discovered that I myself was the result of the administration of the wonder drug to a kitten embryo. To make this extension of the example work, we have to suppose that the drug is even more wonderful and can make kitten embryos grow into beings with human bodies as well as minds; but it is hard to see how this could make any moral difference, especially for Tooley, who rests none of his argument on bodily shape. If this happened, it would not make my reasons for being glad that I was not aborted cease to apply. I certainly prescribe that they should not have aborted an embryo kitten which the wonder drug was going to turn into *me*. And so, by the Golden Rule, I must say that I should not abort an embryo kitten to whom the wonder drug had been administered and which therefore was going to turn into a creature just like me. And, for what it is worth, this is what I would say. The fact that I confidently assert this, whereas Tooley confidently asserts the opposite— so confidently, in fact, that he thinks that this single example is enough to establish his entire case against the potentiality principle, and produces no other—just shows how inadequate intuitions are as a guide to moral conclusions. The fantastic nature of his example (like that of some of Professor Thomson's) makes it even more difficult to be certain that we are saying what we *should* say about it. Our intuitions are the result of our upbringings, and we were not brought up on cases where kittens can be turned into beings with human minds, or where people get kidnapped and have distinguished violinists with kidney failure plugged into their bloodstreams, in Professor Thomson's example.

The problem becomes more difficult if we ask whether the same argument could be used to establish that it would be wrong, if this wonder drug were invented, not to administer it to all the embryo kittens one could get hold of. I shall postpone discussion of this problem until we have discussed the similar problem of whether the potentiality principle, once established, will not force upon us an extreme conservative position not only about abortion but also about contraception, and even forbid chastity. If we allow the potentiality of procreating human beings to place upon us obligations to procreate them, shall we not have a duty to procreate all the human beings that we can, and will not even monks and nuns have to obey King Lear's injunction to "let copulation thrive"? [11] To the general problem which this raises I shall return. We shall see that it is simply the familiar problem about the right population policy, which has to be faced whatever view we take of the present question.

V

I propose to take it as established that the potentiality principle is *not* refuted by Tooley's one example, and that it therefore holds the field until somebody produces a better argument against it—which I do not expect to happen, because the potentiality principle itself can be based on the Golden Rule, as the examples already considered show, and the Golden Rule has a secure logical foundation which I have already mentioned, though I have not had room to expound it.

Why does Tooley think that, if the potentiality principle is once granted, the extreme conservative position on abortion becomes impregnable? Obviously because he has neglected to consider some other potential beings. Take, to start with, the next child that this mother will have if this pregnancy is terminated but will not have if this pregnancy is allowed to continue. Why will she not have it? For a number of alternative reasons. The most knockdown reason would be that the mother would die or be rendered sterile if this pregnancy were allowed to continue. Another would be that the parents had simply decided, perhaps for morally adequate reasons, that their family would be large enough if and when this present fetus was born. I shall be discussing later the morality of family limitation; for the moment I shall assume for the sake of argument that it is morally all right for parents to decide, after they have had, say, fifteen children, not to have any more, and to achieve this modest limitation of their family by remaining completely chaste.

In all these cases there is, in effect, a choice between having this child now and having another child later. Most people who oppose abortion make a great deal of the wrongness of stopping the birth of this child but say nothing about the morality of stopping the birth or the later child. My own intuition (on which I am by no means going to rely) is that they are wrong to make so big a distinction. The basis of the distinction is supposed to be that the fetus already exists as a single living entity all in one place, whereas the possible future child is at the moment represented only by an unfertilized ovum and a sperm which may or may not yet exist in the father's testes. But will this basis support so weighty a distinction?

First, why is it supposed to make a difference that the genetic material which causes the production of the future child and adult is in two different places? If I have a duty to open a certain door, and two keys are required to unlock it, it does not seem to me to make any difference to my duty that one key is already in the lock and the other in my trousers. This, so far, is an intuition, and I place no reliance on it; I introduce the parallel only to remove some prejudices. The real argument is this: when I am glad that I was born (the basis, it will be remembered, of the argument that the Golden Rule therefore places upon me an obligation not to stop others being born) I do not confine this gladness to gladness that they did not abort me. I am glad, also, that my parents copulated in the first place, without contraception. So from my gladness, in conjunction with the extended Golden Rule, I derive not only a duty not to abort, but also a duty not to abstain from procreation. In the choice-situation that I have imagined, in which it is either this child or the next one but not both, I cannot perform both these duties. So, in the words of a wayside pulpit reported to me by Mr. Anthony Kenny, "if you have conflicting duties, one of them isn't your duty." But which?

I do not think that any general answer can be given to this question. If the present fetus is going to be miserably handicapped if it grows into an adult, perhaps because the mother had rubella, but there is every reason to suppose that the next child will be completely normal and as happy as most people, there would be reason to abort this fetus and proceed to bring to birth the next child, in that the next child will be much gladder to be alive than will this one. The Golden Rule does not directly guide us in cases where we cannot help failing to do to *some* others what we wish were done to us, because if we did it to some, we should thereby prevent ourselves from doing it to others. But it can guide us indirectly, if further extended by a simple maneuver, to cover what I have elsewhere called "multilateral" situations. We are to do to the others affected, taken together, what we wish were done to us if we had to be all of them by turns in random order.[12] In this case, by terminating this pregnancy, I get, on this scenario, no life at all in one of my incarnations and a happy life in the other; but by not terminating it, I get a miserable life in one and no life at all in the other. So I should choose to terminate. In order to reach this conclusion it is not necessary to assume, as we did, that the present fetus will turn into a person who will be positively miserable; only that that person's expectation of happiness is so much less than the expectation of the later possible person that the other factors (to be mentioned in a moment) are outweighed.

In most cases, the probability that there will be another child to replace this one is far lower than that this fetus will turn into a living child. The latter probability is said in normal cases to be about 80 percent; the probability of the next child being born may be much lower (the parents may separate; one of them may die or become sterile; or they may just change their minds about having children). If I do not terminate in such a normal case, I get, on the same scenario, an 80 percent chance of a normal happy life in one incarnation, and no chance at all of any life in the other;

but if I do terminate, I get a much lower chance of a normal happy life in the second incarnation and no chance at all in the first. So in this case I should not terminate. By applying this kind of scenario to different cases, we get a way of dramatizing the application of the Golden Rule to them. The cases will all be different, but the relevance of the differences to the moral decision becomes clearer. It is these differences in probabilities of having a life, and of having a happy one, that justify, first of all the presumptive policy, which most people would follow, that abortions in general ought to be avoided, and secondly the exceptions to this policy that many people would now allow—though of course they will differ in their estimation of the probabilities.

I conclude, therefore, that the establishment of the potentiality principle by no means renders impregnable the extreme conservative position, as Tooley thinks it does. It merely creates a rebuttable or defeasible presumption against abortion, which is fairly easily rebutted if there are good indications. The interests of the mother may well, in many cases, provide such good indications, although, because hers is not the only interest, we have also to consider the others. Liberals can, however, get from the present form of argument all that they could reasonably demand, since in the kinds of cases in which they would approve of termination, the interests of the mother will usually be predominant enough to tip the balance between those of the others affected, including potential persons.

The effect of this argument is to bring the morality of contraception and that of abortion somewhat closer together. Important differences will remain, however. There is the fact that the fetus has a very good chance of turning into a normal adult if allowed to develop, whereas the chance that a single coitus will have that result is much lower. Further, if a general duty to produce children be recognized (as the view I have suggested requires), to kill a fetus means the nonfulfillment of this duty for a much longer period (the period from its begetting to the begetting of the next child, if any), whereas, if you do not beget a child now, you may five minutes later. Thirdly, parents become attached to the child in the womb (hence the argument, "We should all think differently if wombs were transparent"), and therefore an abortion may (whatever the compensating good) do some harm to them in addition to that (if any) done to the prospective child that is aborted; this is not so if they merely refrain from procreation. These differences are enough to account for the moral gap between contraception and abortion which will be found in the intuitions of most people; one has to be very extreme in one's views either to consider contraception as sinful as abortion or to think of abortion as *just* another alternative to contraception.

VI

We must now consider some possible objections to this view. Some of these rest on supposed conflicts with received opinion. I shall not deal at great length with these, for a number of reasons. The first is that it would be hard at the moment to point to any at all generally received opinion about abortion. But even if we could, it is a difficult question in moral philosophy, which I have discussed at length elsewhere,[13] how much attention should be paid to received opinion on moral issues. I will sum up my view, without defending it. It is that there are two levels of moral thinking. The first (level 1) consists in the application of learnt principles, which, in order to be learnt, have to be *fairly* general and simple; the second (level 2) consists in the criticism, and possibly the modification, of these general principles in the light of their effect in particular cases, actual and imagined. The purpose of this second, reflective kind of thinking is to select those general principles for use in the first kind of thinking which will lead to the nearest approximation, if generally accepted and inculcated, to the results that would be achieved if we had the time and the information and the freedom from self-deception to make possible the practice of level-2 thinking in every single case. The intuitions which many moral philosophers regard as the final court of appeal are the result of their upbringing—that is, of the fact that just these level-1 principles were accepted by those who most influenced them. In discussing abortion, we ought to be doing some level-2 thinking; it is therefore quite futile to appeal to those level-1 intuitions that we happen to have acquired. It is a question, not of what our intuitions *are*, but of what they *ought to be*—a question which can usefully be dramatized by asking, What opinions about abortion ought we to be teaching to our children?

This may help to answer two objections which often crop up. The first claims that common opinion makes a larger moral distinction between failure to procreate and killing a fetus than the present view would warrant. Sometimes this distinction is said to be founded on the more general one between omissions and acts. There are strong arguments against the moral relevance of this last distinction;[14] and if we are always careful to compare like with like in our examples, and apply the Golden Rule to them, we shall not obtain any morally relevant difference between acts and omissions, provided that we are engaged in level-2 thinking. However, it may well be that the level-1 principles, which we selected as a result of this thinking, *would* use the distinction between acts and omissions. The reason for this is that, although this distinction is philosophically very puzzling and even suspect, it is operable by the ordinary man at the commonsense level; moreover, it serves to separate from each other classes of cases which a more refined thinking would also separate, but would do so only as a result of a very protracted investigation which did not itself make use of the act-omission distinction. So the act-omission distinction serves as a useful surrogate for distinctions which really are morally relevant, although it itself is not. Thus there may be no morally relevant distinction, so far as the Golden Rule goes, between killing and failing to keep alive *in otherwise identical cases*; but if people have ingrained in them the principle that it is wrong to kill innocent adults, but not always so wrong to fail to keep them alive, they are more likely in practice to do the right thing than if their ingrained principles made no such distinction. This is because most cases of killing differ from most cases of failing to keep alive in *other* crucial ways, such that the former are very much more likely to be wrong than the latter. And in the case of abortion and failure to procreate, it is *possible* (I do not say that it is so) that the best level-1 principles for practical use would make bigger distinctions at birth and at conception than a refined level-2 thinking could possibly support. The reason is that conception and birth are dividing lines that are easily discerned by the ordinary man and that therefore a level-1 principle which uses these dividing lines in order to draw the moral line (what moral line?) *may* lead in practice to the morally best results. But if we are arguing (as we are) whether or not this is so, appeals to the intuitions of the ordinary man are entirely beside the point.

Second, we have the "thin end of the wedge" or "slippery slope" objection. If we sanction contraception, why not abortion; and if abortion, why not infanticide; and if infanticide, why not the murder of adults? As an argument against the too ready abandonment of accepted general level-1 principles this argument has some force; for, psychologically speaking, if the ordinary man or the ordinary doctor has got hold of some general principles about killing, which serve well enough in the ordinary run, and then somebody tells him that these principles ought not to be followed universally, it may well be that he will come to disregard them in cases where he ought not. The argument can be overplayed—I do not think that many doctors who have come to accept abortion are thereby made any more prone to murder their wives) but at this level the argument has *some* force, especially if, in the upbringing of the ordinary man and the ordinary doctor, enormous stress has been laid on general principles of great rigidity—such principles are naturally susceptible to thin ends of wedges. But when we are disputing at level 2 about what our level-1 principles ought to be, the argument has little force. For it may be that we could devise other, equally simple principles which would be wedge-resistant and would draw lines in different places; it may be that we *ought* to do this, if the new places were more likely, if generally recognized, to lead most often to the right results in practice. Tooley recommends such a moral line very shortly *after* birth, and his arguments have a great attraction.[15] For the present, it is enough to say that if the line proved wedge-resistant and if it separated off, in a workable manner, nearly all the cases that would be pronounced wrong by level-2 thinking from nearly all those which would be pronounced permissible, then it would be no argument against this proposal that it conflicted with people's intuitions. These intuitions, like earlier ones which made a big distinction at quickening, are the results of attempts to simplify the issues for a laudable practical purpose; they cannot without circularity be used in an appraisal of themselves. As Tooley implies, we have to find real moral reasons for distinguishing cases. If, as is sure to happen, the distinctions that result are very complicated, we have to simplify them for ordinary use as best we can, and there is no reason to assume that the simplifications which will be best are those which have been current hitherto—certainly not in a context in which circumstances have changed as radically as they have with regard to abortion.

VII

It might be objected, as we have seen, that the view I have advocated would require unlimited procreation, on the ground that not to produce any single child whom one might have produced lays one open to the charge that one is not doing to that child as one is glad has been done to oneself (namely, causing him to be born). But there are, even on the present view, reasons for limiting the population. Let us suppose that fully grown adults were producible ad lib., not by gestation in human mothers or in the wombs of cats or in test tubes, but instantaneously by waving a wand. We should still have to formulate a population policy for the world as a whole, and for particular societies and families. There would be a point at which the additional member of each of these units imposed burdens on the other members great enough in sum to outweigh the advantage gained by the additional member. In utilitarian terms, the classical or total utility principle sets a limit to population which, although higher than the average utility principle, is nevertheless a limit.[16] In terms of the Golden Rule, which is the basis of my present argument, even if the "others" to whom we are to do what we wish, or what we are glad, to have done to us are to include potential people, good done to them may be outweighed by harm done to other actual or potential people. If we had to submit to all their lives or nonlives in turn, we should have a basis for choosing a population policy which would not differ from that yielded by the classical utility principle. How restrictive this policy would be would depend on assumptions about the threshold effects of certain increases in population size and density. I think myself that even if potential people are allowed to be the objects of duties, the policy will be fairly restrictive; but this is obviously not the place to argue for this view.

One big gap in the argument of this paper is my failure to deal with the question of whether, when we are balancing the interests of the potential person into whom this fetus will turn against the interests of other people who might be born, we ought to limit the second class to other members of the same family, or include in it *any* potential person who might in some sense "replace" the first-mentioned potential person. This major question would seem to depend for its answer on a further question: To what extent will the birth or non-birth of *this* person make more or less likely the birth or non-birth of the others? This is a demographic question which at the moment baffles me; but it would obviously have to be gone into in any exhaustive account of the morality of abortion. I have, however, written (possibly too hastily) as if only other potential members of the same family need be considered. That was enough to illustrate the important principle that I was trying to explain.

VIII

Lastly, a logician might object that these potential people do not exist, and cannot be identified or individuated, and therefore cannot be the objects of duties. If I had put my own view in terms of rights or interests, the same objection could be expressed by saying that only actual people have these. Two points can be made against this objection at once. The first is a perhaps superficial one: it would be strange if there were an act whose very performance made it impossible for it to be wrong. But if the objection were correct, the act of aborting a possible person would be such an act; by preventing the existence of the object of the wrongdoing, it would remove its wrongness. This seems too easy a way of avoiding crime.

Second, there seems to be no objection in principle to condemning hypothetical acts: it would have been wrong for Nixon to stay on any longer in the presidency. And it seems a fairly safe principle that if it makes sense to make value judgments about an act that was done, it makes equal sense to make opposite judgments about the hypothetical omission to do that act. "Nixon did right to resign" makes sense; and so, therefore, does "Nixon would have done wrong not to resign." But we do commend actions which resulted in our own existence—every Sunday in thousands of churches we give thanks for our creation as well as for our preservation and all the blessings of this life; and Aristotle says that we ought to show the same gratitude to our earthly fathers as "causes of our being."[17] So it is at least meaningful to say of God or of our fathers that if they had not caused us to exist, they would not have been doing as well for us as they could. And this is all that my argument requires.

Coming now to the purely logical points, we notice that the nonactuality of the potential person (the supposed object of the duty to procreate or not abort) is a separate issue from his nonidentifiability. Unfortunately "identifiable" is an ambiguous word; in one sense I can identify the next man to occupy my carrel at the library by describing him thus, but in another sense I cannot identify him because I have no idea who he is. The person who will be born if these two people start their coitus in precisely five minutes is identified by that description; and so, therefore, is the person who would have been born if they had started it five minutes ago. Moreover (this is an additional point) if we had enough mechanical and other information, we could specify the hair color and all the other traits of that person, if we wished, with as much precision as we could the result of a lottery done on a computer whose randomizing mechanism we could minutely inspect. In this sense, therefore, the potential person is identifiable. We do not know who he will be, in the sense that we do not know what actually now existing person he will be, because he will not be identical with any actually now existing person. But it is hard to see how his inability to meet this logically unmeetable demand for identifiability with some already existing person affects the argument; he is identifiable in the sense that identifying reference can be made to him. So it cannot be nonidentifiability that is the trouble.

Is it then nonactuality? Certainly not *present* nonactuality. We can do harm to, and wrong, succeeding generations by using up all the world's resources or by releasing too much radioactive material. But suppose that this not merely made them miserable, but actually stopped them being born (for example, that the radioactive material made everybody sterile all at once). As before it seems that we can be thankful that our fathers did not do this, thereby stopping us coming into existence; why cannot we say, therefore, that if we behave as well as our fathers, we shall be doing well by our children or grandchildren, or that if we were to behave in this respect worse than our fathers, we would be doing worse by our children or grandchildren. It seems strange to say that if we behaved only a little worse, so that the next generation was half the size it would have been, we had done badly for that generation, but that if we behaved much worse, so that the succeeding generation was reduced to nil, we had not done badly for it at all.

This is obviously a very perplexing matter, and needs much more discussion. All I can hope to do here is to cast doubt on the assumption that some people accept without question, namely, that one cannot harm a person by preventing him coming into existence. True, he does not exist to be harmed; and he is not *deprived* of existence, in the sense of having it taken away from him, though he is *denied* it. But if it would have been a good for him to exist (because this made possible the goods that, once he existed, he was able to enjoy), surely it was a harm to him not to exist, and so not to be able to enjoy these goods. He did not suffer; but there were enjoyments he could have had and did not.

IX

I conclude, then, that a systematic application of the Christian Golden Rule yields the following precepts about abortion. It is prima facie and in general wrong in default of sufficient countervailing reasons. But since the wrongness of it consists, in the main, of stopping a person coming into existence and not in any wrong done to the fetus as such, such countervailing reasons are not too hard to find in many cases. And if the termination of this pregnancy facilitates or renders possible or probable the beginning of another more propitious one, it really does not take much to justify it.

I have not discussed what the law on abortion ought to be; that question would have to be the subject of another paper. I have been speaking only about the morality of terminating individual pregnancies. I will end as I began by saying that my argument has been based on a developed ethical theory, though I have not had room to expound this theory (I have done it in my books). This theory provides the logical basis of the Golden Rule. Though not *founded on* a utilitarian principle, it also provides the basis for a certain sort of utilitarianism that escapes the vices which have been decried in some other sorts.[18] But I shall not now try to defend these last assertions. If they are challenged, and if the view that I have advanced in this paper is challenged, the issue can only be fought out on the terrain of ethical theory itself. That is why it is such a pity that so many people— even philosophers—think that they can discuss abortion without making up their minds about the fundamental problems of moral philosophy.

NOTES

1. Judith Jarvis Thomson, "A Defense of Abortion," *Philosophy & Public Affairs* 1, no. 1 (Fall 1971). Reprinted in *The Rights and Wrongs of Abortion*, ed. Marshall Cohen, Thomas Nagel, and Thomas Scanlon (Princeton, N.J., 1974), hereafter cited as *RWA*; and reprinted herein, pp. 201-217.

2. John Finnis, "The Rights and Wrongs of Abortion: A Reply to Judith Thomson," *Philosophy & Public Affairs* 2, no. 2 (Winter 1973); reprinted in *RWA*.

3. Finnis, "Rights and Wrongs," p. 129; *RWA*, p. 97. Thomson, "Defense," herein, p. 310.

4. Judith Jarvis Thomson and Gerald Dworkin, *Ethics* (New York, 1968), p. 2. Cf. D. A. J. Richards, *Chicago Law Review* 41 (1973): 71, for a similar misunderstanding. I am most grateful to Professor Richards for clearing up this misunderstanding in his article "Free Speech and Obscenity Law," in *University of Pennsylvania Law Review* 123 (1974), fn. 255.

5. "Imperative Sentences," *Mind* 58 (1949), reprinted in my *Practical Inferences* (London, 1971); "Freedom of the Will," *Aristotelian Society Supp.* 25 (1951), reprinted in my *Essays on the Moral Concepts* (London, 1972).

6. Cf. Aristotle, *Nicomachean Ethics* 5, 1137b20. I owe the roller-skate example to H. L. A. Hart.

7. "Abortion and Infanticide," *Philosophy & Public Affairs* 2, no. 1 (Fall 1972): 60; *RWA*, p. 75. It will be clear what a great debt I owe to this article.

8. See my "Rules of War and Moral Reasoning," *Philosophy & Public Affairs* 1, no. 2 (Winter 1972), fn. 3; reprinted in *War and Moral Responsibility*, ed. Marshall Cohen, Thomas Nagel, and Thomas Scanlon (Princeton, N.J., 1974). See also my review of John Rawls, *A Theory of Justice*, in *Philosophical Quarterly* 23 (1973): 154 f.; and my "Ethical Theory and Utilitarianism," in *Contemporary British Philosophy*, vol. 3, ed. H. D. Lewis (London, forthcoming).

9. Matthew 7:12. There have been many misunderstandings of the Golden Rule, some of which I discuss in my "Euthanasia: A Christian View," lecture at the State University College of New York at Brockport (forthcoming).

10. Tooley, "Abortion and Infanticide," p. 55; *RWA*, pp. 70-71 (my italics).

11. Act 4, sc. 6.

12. See C. I. Lewis, *An Analysis of Knowledge and Valuation* (La Salle, Ill., 1946), p. 547; D. Haslett, *Moral Rightness* (The Hague, 1974), chap. 3. Cf. my *Freedom and Reason* (Oxford, 1963), p. 123.

13. See "The Argument from Received Opinion," in my *Essays on Philosophical Method* (London, 1971); "Principles," *Aristotelian Society* 72 (1972-73); and my "Ethical Theory and Utilitarianism."

14. Tooley, "Abortion and Infanticide," p. 59; *RWA*, p. 74. See also J. C. B. Glover's forthcoming book on the morality of killing.

15. Tooley, p. 64; *RWA*, p. 79. If the potentiality principle be granted, the number of permissible infanticides is greatly reduced, but not to nothing. See my "Survival of the Weakest," in *Documentation in Medical Ethics* 2 (1973); reprinted in *Moral Problems in Medicine*, ed. S. Gorovitz et al. (New York, forthcoming).

16. See my review of Rawls, pp. 244 f.

17. *Nicomachean Ethics* 8, 1161a17, 1163a6, 1165a23.

18. See my "Ethical Theory and Utilitarianism."

CONCEPTIONS OF SEX

Robert Baker

"Pricks" and "Chicks": A Plea for "Persons"

There is a school of philosophers who believe that one starts philosophizing not by examining whatever it is one is philosophizing about but by examining the words we use to designate the subject to be examined. I must confess my allegiance to this school. The import of my confession is that this is an essay on women's liberation.

There seems to be a curious malady that affects those philosophers who in order to analyze anything must examine the way we talk about it; they seem incapable of talking about anything without talking about their talk about it—and, once again, I must confess to being typical. Thus I shall argue, first, that the way in which we identify something reflects our conception of it; second, that the conception of women embedded in our language is male chauvinistic; third, that the conceptual revisions proposed by the feminist movement are confused; and finally, that at the root of the problem are both our conception of sex and the very structure of sexual identification.

IDENTIFICATION AND CONCEPTION

I am not going to defend the position that the terms we utilize to identify something reflect our conception of it; I shall simply explain and illustrate a simplified version of this thesis. Let us assume that any term that can be (meaningfully) substituted for x in the following statements is a term used to identify something: "Where is the x?" "Who is the x?" Some of the terms that can be substituted for x in the above expressions are metaphors; I shall refer to such metaphors as metaphorical identifications. For example, southerners frequently say such things as "Where did that girl get to?" and "Who is the new boy that Lou hired to help out at the filling station?" If the persons the terms apply to are adult Afro-Americans, then "girl" and "boy" are metaphorical identifications. The fact that the metaphorical identifications in question are standard in the language reflects the fact that certain characteristics of the objects properly classified as boys and girls (for example, immaturity, inability to take care of themselves, need for guidance) are generally held by those who use identifications to be properly attributable to Afro-Americans. One might say that the whole theory of southern white paternalism is implicit in the metaphorical identification "boy" (just as the rejection of paternalism is implicit in the standardized Afro-American forms of address, "man" and "woman," as in, for example, "Hey, man, how are you?").

Most of what I am going to say in this essay is significant only if the way we metaphorically identify something is not a superficial bit of conceptually irrelevant happenstance but rather a reflection of our conceptual structure. Thus if one is to accept my analysis he must understand the significance of metaphorical identifications. He must see that, even though the southerner who identifies adult Afro-American males as "boys" feels that this identification is "just the way people talk"; but for a group to talk that way it must think that way. In the next few paragraphs I shall adduce what I hope is a persuasive example of how, in one clear case, the change in the way we identified something reflected a change in the way we thought about it.

Until the 1960s, Afro-Americans were identified by such terms as "Negro" and "colored" (the respectable terms) and by the more disreputable "nigger," "spook," "kink," and so on. Recently there has been an unsuccessful attempt to replace the respectable identifications with such terms as "African," and "Afro-American," and a more successful attempt to replace them with "black." The most outspoken champions of this linguistic reform were those who argued that nonviolence must be abandoned for Black Power (Stokely Carmichael, H. Rap Brown), that integration must be abandoned in favor of separation (the Black Muslims: Malcolm X, Muhammad Ali), and that Afro-Americans were an internal colony in the alien world of Babylon who must arm themselves against the possibility of extermination (the Black Panthers: Eldridge Cleaver, Huey Newton). All of these movements and their partisans wished to stress that Afro-Americans were different from other Americans and could not be merged with them because the differences between the two was as great as that between black and white. Linguistically, of course, "black" and "white" are antonyms; and it is precisely this sense of oppositeness that those who see the Afro-American as alienated, separated, and noninte-gratable wish to capture with the term "black." Moreover, as any good dictionary makes clear, in some contexts "black" is synonymous with "deadly," "sinister," "wicked," "evil," and so forth. The new militants were trying to create just this picture of the black man—civil rights and Uncle Tomism are dead, the ghost of Nat Turner is to be resurrected, Freedom Now or pay the price, the ballot or the bullet, "Violence is as American as cherry pie." The new strategy was that the white man would either give the black man his due or pay the price in violence. Since conceptually a "black man" was an object to be feared ("black" can be synonymous with "deadly," and so on), while a "colored man" or a "Negro" was not, the new strategy required that the "Negro" be supplanted by the "black man." White America resisted the proposed linguistic reform quite vehemently, until hundreds of riots forced the admission that the Afro-American was indeed black.

Now to the point: I have suggested that the word "black" replaced the word "Negro" because there was a change in our conceptual structure. One is likely to reply that while all that I have said above is well and good, one had, after all, no choice about the matter. White people are identified in terms of their skin color as whites; clearly, if we are to recognize what is in reality nothing but the truth, that in this society people are conscious of skin color, to treat blacks as equals is merely to identify them by their skin color, which is black. That is, one might argue that while there was a change in words, we have no reason to think that there was a parallel conceptual change. If the term "black" has all the associations mentioned above, that is unfortunate; but in the context the use of the term "black" to identify the people formerly identified as "Negroes" is natural, inevitable, and, in and of itself, neutral; black is, after all, the skin color of the people in question. (Notice that this defense of the natural-inevitable-and-neutral conception of identification quite nicely circumvents the possible use of such seemingly innocuous terms as "Afro-American" and "African" by suggesting that in this society it is *skin color* that is the relevant variable.)

The great flaw in this analysis is that the actual skin color of virtually all of the people whom we call "black" is not black at all. The color tones range from light yellow to a deep umber that occasionally is literally black. The skin color of most Afro-Americans is best designated by the word "brown." Yet "brown" is not a term that is standard for identifying Afro-Americans. For example, if someone asked, "Who was the brown who was the architect for Washington, D.C.?" we would not know how to construe the question. We might attempt to read "brown" as a proper name ("Do you mean Arthur Brown, the designer?"). We would have no trouble understanding the sentence "Who was the black (Negro, colored guy, and so forth) who designed Washington, D.C.?" ("Oh, you mean Benjamin Banneker"). Clearly, "brown" is not a standard form of identification for Afro-Americans. I hope that it is equally clear that "black" has become the standard way of identifying Afro-Americans not because the term was natural, inevitable, and, in the context, neutral, but because of its occasional synonymy with "sinister" and because as an antonym to "white" it best fitted the conceptual needs of those who saw race relations in terms of intensifying and insurmountable antonymies. If one accepts this point, then one must admit that there is a close connection between the way in which we identify things and the way in which we conceive them —and thus it should be also clear why I wish to talk about the way in which women are identified in English.[1] (Thus, for example, one would expect Black Muslims, who continually use the term "black *man*"—as in "the black *man*'s rights"—to be more male chauvinistic than Afro-Americans who use the term "black *people*" or "black *folk*.")

WAYS OF IDENTIFYING WOMEN

It may at first seem trivial to note that women (and men) are identified sexually; but conceptually this is extremely significant. To appreciate the significance of this fact it is helpful to imagine a language in which proper names and personal pronouns do not reflect the sex of the person designated by them (as they do in our language). I have been told that in some oriental languages pronouns and proper names reflect social status rather than sex, but whether or not there actually exists such a language is irrelevant, for it is easy enough to imagine what one would be like. Let us then imagine a language where the proper names are sexually neutral (for example, "Xanthe"), so that one cannot tell from hearing a name whether the person so named is male or female, and where the personal pronouns in the language are "under" and "over." "Under" is the personal pronoun appropriate for all those who are younger than thirty, while "over" is appropriate to persons older than thirty. In such a language, instead of saying such things as "Where do you think *he* is living now?" one would say such things as "Where do you think *under* is living now?"

What would one say about a cultural community that employed such a language? Clearly, one would say that they thought that for purposes of intelligible communication it was more important to know a person's age grouping than the person's height, sex, race, hair color, or parentage. (There are many actual cultures, of course, in which people are identified by names that reflect their parentage; for example, Abu ben Adam means Abu son of Adam.) I think that one would also claim that this people would not have reflected these differences in the pronominal structure of their language if they did not believe that the differences between unders and overs was such that a statement would frequently have one meaning if it were about an under and a different meaning if it were about an over. For example, in feudal times if a serf said, "My lord said to do this," that assertion was radically different from "Freeman John said to do this," since (presumably) the former had the status of a command while the latter did not. Hence the conventions of Middle English required that one refer to people in such a way as to indicate their social status. Analogously, one would not distinguish between pronominal references according to the age differences in the persons referred to were there no shift in meaning involved.

If we apply the lesson illustrated by this imaginary language to our own, I think that it should be clear that since in our language proper nouns and pronouns reflect sex rather than age, race, parentage, social status, or religion, we believe one of the most important things one can know about a person is that person's sex. (And, indeed, this is the first thing one seeks to determine about a newborn babe—our first question is almost invariably "Is it a boy or a girl?") Moreover, we would not reflect this important difference pronominally did we not also believe that statements frequently mean one thing when applied to males and something else when applied to females. Perhaps the most striking aspect of the conceptual discrimination reflected in our language is that man is, as it were, essentially human, while woman is only accidentally so.

This charge may seem rather extreme, but consider the following synonyms (which are readily confirmed by any dictionary). "Humanity" is synonymous with "mankind" but not with "womankind." "Man" can be substituted for "humanity" or "mankind" in any sentence in which the terms "mankind" or "humanity" occur without changing the meaning of the sentence, but significantly, "woman" cannot. Thus, the following expressions are all synonymous with each other: "humanity's great achievements," "mankind's great achievements," and "man's great achievements." "Woman's great achievements" is not synonymous with any of these. To highlight the degree to which women are excluded from humanity, let me point out that it is something of a truism to say that "man is a rational animal," while "woman is a rational animal" is quite debatable. Clearly, if "man" in the first assertion embraced both men and women, the second assertion would be just as much a truism as the first.[2] Humanity, it would seem, is a male prerogative. (And hence, one of the goals of women's liberation is to alter our conceptual structure so that someday "mankind" will be regarded as an improper and vestigial ellipsis for "humankind," and "man" will have no special privileges in relation to "human being" that "woman" does not have.[3])

The major question before us is, How are women conceived of in our culture? I have been trying to answer this question by talking about how they are identified. I first considered pronominal identification; now I wish to turn to identification through other types of noun phrases. Methods of nonpronominal identification can be discovered by determining which terms can be substituted for "woman" in such sentences as "Who is that woman over there?" without changing the meaning of the sentence. Virtually no term is interchangeable with "woman" in that sentence for all speakers on all occasions. Even "lady," which most speakers would accept as synonymous with "woman" in that sentence, will not do for a speaker who applies the term "lady" only to those women who display manners, poise, and sensitivity. In most contexts, a large number of students in one or more of my classes will accept the following types of terms as more or less interchangeable with "woman." (An asterisk indicates interchanges acceptable to both males and females; a plus sign indicates terms restricted to black students only. Terms with neither an asterisk nor a plus sign are accepted by all males but are not normally used by females.)

A. NEUTRAL TERMS: *lady, *gal, *girl (especially with regard to a coworker in an office or factory), *+sister, *broad (originally in the animal category, but most people do not think of the term as now meaning pregnant cow)

B. ANIMAL: *chick, bird, fox, vixen, filly, bitch (Many do not know the literal meaning of the term. Some men and most women construe this use as pejorative; they think of "bitch" in the context of "bitchy," that is, snappy, nasty, and so forth. But a large group of men claim that it is a standard nonpejorative term of identification—which may perhaps indicate that women have come to be thought of as shrews by a large subclass of men.)

C. PLAYTHING: babe, doll, cuddly

D. GENDER (association with articles of clothing typically worn by those in the female gender role): skirt, hem

E. SEXUAL: snatch, cunt, ass, twat, piece (of ass, and so forth), lay, pussy (could be put in the animal category, but most users associated it with slang expression indicating the female pubic region), +hammer (related to anatomical analogy between a hammer and breasts). There are many other usages, for example, "bunny," "sweat hog," but these were not recognized as standard by as many as 10 percent of any given class.

The students in my classes reported that the most frequently used terms of identification are in the neutral and animal classifications (although men in their forties claim to use the gender classifications quite a bit) and that the least frequently used terms of identification are sexual. Fortunately, however, I am not interested in the frequency of usage but only in whether the use is standard enough to be recognized as an identification among some group or other. (Recall that "brown" was not a standardized term of identification and hence we could not make sense out of "Who was the brown who planned Washington, D.C.?" Similarly, one has trouble with "Who was the breasts who planned Washington, D.C.?" but not with "Who was the babe (doll, chick, skirt, and so forth) who planned Washington, D.C.?")

Except for two of the animal terms, "chick" and "broad"—but note that "broad" is probably neutral today—women do not typically identify themselves in sexual terms, in gender terms, as playthings, or as animals; *only males use nonneutral terms to identfy women.* Hence, it would seem that there is a male conception of women and a female conception. Only males identify women as "foxes," "babes," "skirts," or "cunts" (and since all the other nonneutral identifications are male, it is reasonable to assume that the identification of a woman as a "chick" is primarily a male conception that some women have adopted).

What kind of conception do men have of women? Clearly they think that women share certain properties with certain types of animals, toys, and playthings; they conceive of them in terms of the clothes associated with the female gender role; and, last (and, if my classes are any indication, least frequently), they conceive of women in terms of those parts of their anatomy associated with sexual intercourse, that is, as the identification "lay" indicates quite clearly, as sexual partners.

The first two nonneutral male classifications, animal and plaything, are prima facie denigrating (and I mean this in the literal sense of making one like a "nigger"). Consider the animal classification. All of the terms listed, with the possible exception of "bird," refer to animals that are either domesticated for servitude (to *man*) or hunted for sport. First, let us consider the term "bird." When I asked my students what sort of birds might be indicated, they suggested chick, canary (one member, in his forties, had suggested "canary" as a term of identification), chicken, pigeon, dove, parakeet, and hummingbird (one member). With the exception of the hummingbird, which like all the birds suggested is generally thought to be diminutive and pretty, all of the birds are domesticated, usually as pets (which reminds one that "my pet" is an expression of endearment). None of the birds were predators or symbols of intelligence or nobility (as are the owl, eagle, hawk, and falcon); nor did large but beautiful birds seem appropriate (for example, pheasants, peacocks, and swans). If one construes the bird terms (and for that matter, "filly") as applicable to women because they are thought of as beautiful, or at least pretty, *then there is nothing denigrating about them.* If, on the other hand, the common properties that underlie the metaphorical identification are domesticity and servitude, then they are indeed denigrating (as for myself, I think that both domesticity and prettiness underlie the identification). "Broad," of course, is, or at least was, clearly denigrating, since nothing renders more service to a farmer than does a pregnant cow, and cows are not commonly thought of as paradigms of beauty.

With one exception all of the animal terms reflect a male conception of women either as domesticated servants or as pets, or as both. Indeed, some of the terms reflect a conception of women first as pets and then as servants. Thus, when a pretty, cuddly little chick grows older, she becomes a very useful servant—the egg-laying hen.

"Vixen" and "fox," variants of the same term, are the one clear exception. None of the other animals with whom women are metaphorically identified are generally thought to be intelligent, aggressive, or independent—but the fox is. A chick is a soft, cuddly, entertaining, pretty, diminutive, domesticated, and dumb animal. A fox too is soft, cuddly, entertaining, pretty, and diminutive, but it is neither dependent nor dumb. It is aggressive, intelligent, and a minor predator—indeed, it preys on chicks—and frequently outsmarts ("outfoxes") men.

Thus the term "fox" or "vixen" is generally taken to be a compliment by both men and women, and compared to any of the animal or plaything terms it is indeed a compliment. Yet, considered in and of itself, the conception of a woman as a fox is not really complimentary at all, for the major connection between *man* and fox is that of predator and prey. The fox is an animal that men chase, and hunt, and kill for sport. If women are conceived of as foxes, then they are conceived of as prey that it is fun to hunt.

In considering plaything identifications, only one sentence is necessary. *All the plaything identifications are clearly denigrating since they assimilate women to the status of mindless or dependent objects.* "Doll" is to male paternalism what "boy" is to white paternalism.

Up to this point in our survey of male conceptions of women, every male identification, without exception, has been clearly antithetical to the conception of women as human beings (recall that "man" was synonymous with "human," while "woman" was not). Since the way we talk of things, and especially the way we identify them, is the way in which we conceive of them, any movement dedicated to breaking the bonds of female servitude must destroy these ways of identifying and hence of conceiving of women. Only when both sexes find the terms "babe," "doll," "chick," "broad," and so forth, as objectionable as "boy" and "nigger" will women come to be conceived of as independent *human beings*.

The two remaining unexamined male identifications are gender and sex. There seems to be nothing objectionable about gender identifications per se. That is, women are metaphorically identified as skirts because in this culture, skirts, like women, are peculiarly female. Indeed, if one accepts the view that the slogan "female and proud" should play the same role for the women's liberation movement that the slogan "Black is beautiful" plays for the black-liberation movement, then female clothes should be worn with the same pride as Afro clothes. (Of course, one can argue that the skirt, like the cropped-down Afro, is a sign of bondage, and hence both the item of clothing and the identification with it are to be rejected—that is, cropped-down Afros are to Uncle Tom what skirts are to Uncle Mom.)

The terms in the last category are obviously sexual, and frequently vulgar. For a variety of reasons I shall consider the import and nature of these identifications in the next section.

MEN OUGHT NOT TO THINK OF WOMEN AS SEX OBJECTS

Feminists have proposed many reforms, and most of them are clearly desirable, for example, equal opportunity for self-development, equal pay for equal work, and free day-care centers. One feminist proposal, however, is peculiarly conceptual and deeply perplexing. I call this proposal peculiarly conceptual because unlike the other reforms it is directed at getting people to think differently. The proposal is that *men should not think of women (and women should not think of themselves) as sex objects*. In the rest of this essay I shall explore this nostrum. I do so for two reasons: first, because the process of exploration should reveal the depth of the problem confronting the feminists; and second, because the feminists themselves seem to be entangled in the very concepts that obstruct their liberation.

To see why I find this proposal puzzling, one has to ask what it is to think of something as a sex object.

If a known object is an object that we know, an unidentified object is an object that we have not identified, and a desired object is an object that we desire, what then is a sex object? Clearly, a sex object is an object we have sex with. Hence, to think of a woman as a sex object is to think of her as someone to have sexual relations with, and when the feminist proposes that men refrain from thinking of women in this way, *she is proposing that men not think of women as persons with whom one has sexual relations.*

What are we to make of this proposal? Is the feminist suggesting that women should not be conceived of in this way because such a conception is "dirty"? To conceive of sex and sex organs as dirty is simply to be a prude. "Shit" is the paradigm case of a dirty word. It is a dirty word because the item it designates is taboo; it is literally unclean and untouchable (as opposed to something designated by what I call a curse word, which is not untouchable but rather something to be feared—"damn" and "hell" are curse words; "piss" is a dirty word). If one claims that "cunt" (or "fuck") is a dirty word, then one holds that what this term designates is unclean and taboo; thus one holds that the terms for sexual intercourse or sexual organs are dirty, one has accepted puritanism. If one is a puritan and a feminist, then indeed one ought to subscribe to the slogan *men should not conceive of women as sexual objects.* What is hard to understand is why anyone but a puritan (or, perhaps, a homosexual) would promulgate this slogan; yet most feminists, who are neither lesbians nor puritans, accept this slogan. Why?

A word about slogans: Philosophical slogans have been the subject of considerable analysis. They have the peculiar property (given a certain seemingly sound background story) of being obviously true, yet obviously false. "Men should not conceive of women as sex objects" is, I suggest, like a philosophical slogan in this respect. The immediate reaction of any humanistically oriented person upon first hearing the slogan is to agree with it—yet the more one probes the meaning of the slogan, the less likely one is to give one's assent. Philosophical analysts attempt to separate out the various elements involved in such slogans—to render the true-false slogan into a series of statements, some of which are true, some of which are false, and others of which are, perhaps, only probable. This is what I am trying to do with the slogan in question. I have argued so far that one of the elements that seems to be implicit in the slogan is a rejection of women as sexual partners for men and that although this position might be proper for a homosexual or puritanical movement, it seems inappropriate to feminism. I shall proceed to show that at least two other interpretations of the slogan lead to inappropriate results; but I shall argue that there are at least two respects in which the slogan is profoundly correct—even if misleadingly stated.

One plausible, but inappropriate, interpretation of "men ought not to conceive of women as sex objects" is that men ought not to conceive of women *exclusively* as sexual partners. The problem with this interpretation is that everyone can agree with it. Women are conceived of as companions, toys, servants, and even sisters, wives, and mothers—and hence not exclusively as sexual partners. Thus this slogan loses its revisionary impact, since even a male chauvinist could accept the slogan without changing his conceptual structure in any way—which is only to say that men do not usually identify or conceive of woman as sexual partners (recall that the sexual method of identification is the least frequently used).

Yet another interpretation is suggested by the term "object" in "sex object," and this interpretation too has a certain amount of plausibility. Men should not treat women as animate machines designed to masturbate men or as conquests that allow men to "score" for purposes of building their egos. Both of these variations rest on the view that to be treated as an object is to be treated as less than human (that is, to be treated as a machine or a score). Such relations between men and women are indeed immoral, and there are, no doubt, men who believe in "scoring." Unfortunately, however, this interpretation—although it would render the slogan quite apt—also fails because of its restricted scope. When feminists argue that men should not treat women as sex objects they are not *only* talking about fraternity boys and members of the Playboy Club; they are talking about all males in our society. The charge is that in our society men treat women as sex objects rather than as persons; it is this universality of scope that is lacking from the present interpretation. *Nonetheless, one of the reasons that we are prone to assent to the unrestricted charge that men treat women as sex objects is that the restricted charge is entirely correct.*

One might be tempted to argue that the charge that men treat women as sex objects is correct since such a conception underlies the most frequently used identifications, as animal and plaything; that is, these identifications indicate a sexual context in which the female is used as an object. Thus, it might be argued that the female fox is chased and slayed if she is four-legged, but chased and layed if she is two. Even if one admits the sexual context *implicit* in *some* animal and plaything identifications, one will not have the generality required; because, for the most part, the plaything and animal identifications themselves are nonsexual—most of them do not involve a sexual context. A pregnant cow, a toy doll, or a filly are hardly what one would call erotic objects. Babies do not normally excite sexual passion; and anyone whose erotic interests are directed toward chicks, canaries, parakeets, or other birds is clearly perverse. The animals and playthings to whom women are assimilated in the standard metaphorical identifications are not symbols of desire, eroticism, or passion (as, for example, a bull might be).

What is objectionable in the animal and plaything identifications is not the fact that some of these identifications reflect a sexual context but rather that—regardless of the context—these identifications reflect a conception of women as mindless servants (whether animate or inanimate is irrelevant). The point is not that men ought not to think of women in sexual terms but that they ought to think of them as human beings; and the slogan *men should not think of women as sex objects* is only appropriate when a man thinking of a woman as a sexual partner automatically conceives of her as something less than human. It is precisely this antihumanism implicit in the male concept of sex that we have as yet failed to uncover —but then, of course, we have not yet examined the language we use to identify sexual acts.

OUR CONCEPTION OF SEXUAL INTERCOURSE

There are two profound insights that underlie the slogan "men ought not conceive of women as sexual objects"; both have the generality of scope that justifies the universality with which the feminists apply the slogan; neither can be put as simply as the slogan. The first is that the conception of sexual intercourse that we have in this culture is antithetical to the conception of women as human beings—as persons rather than objects. (Recall that this is congruent with the fact we noted earlier that "man" can be substituted for "humanity," while "woman" cannot.)

Many feminists have attempted to argue just this point. Perhaps the most famous defender of this view is Kate Millett,[4] who unfortunately faces the problem of trying to make a point about our conceptual structure without having adequate tools for analyzing conceptual structures.

The question Millett was dealing with was conceptual—Millett, in effect, asking about the nature of our conception of sexual roles. She tried to answer this question by analyzing novels; I shall attempt to answer this question by analyzing the terms we use to identify coitus, or more technically, in terms that function synonymously with "had sexual intercourse with" in a sentence of the form "A had sexual intercourse with B." The following is a list of some commonly used synonyms (numerous others that are not as widely used have been omitted, for example, "diddled," "laid pipe with"):

     screwed
     laid
     fucked
     had
     did it with (to)
     banged
     balled

humped
slept with
made love to

Now, for a select group of these verbs, names for males are the sub-jects of sentences with active constructions (that is, where the subjects are said to be doing the activity); and names for females require passive con-structions (that is, they are the recipients of the activity—whatever is done is done to them). Thus, we would not say "Jane did it to Dick," although we would say "Dick did it to Jane." Again, Dick bangs Jane, Jane does not bang Dick; Dick humps Jane, Janes does not hump Dick. In contrast, verbs like "did it with" do not require an active role for the male; thus, "Dick did it with Jane, and Jane with Dick.'" Again, Jane may make love to Dick, just as Dick makes love to Jane; and Jane sleeps with Dick as easily as Dick sleeps with Jane. (My students were undecided about "laid." Most thought that it would be unusual indeed for Jane to lay Dick, unless she played the masculine role of seducer-aggressor.)

The sentences thus form the following pairs. (Those nonconjoined sin-gular noun phrases where a female subject requires a passive construction are marked with a cross. An asterisk indicates that the sentence in ques-tion is not a sentence of English if it is taken as synonymous with the italicized sentence heading the column.[5])

Dick had sexual intercourse with Jane
Dick screwed Jane†
Dick laid Jane†
Dick fucked Jane†
Dick had Jane†
Dick did it to Jane†
Dick banged Jane†
Dick humped Jane†
Dick balled Jane(?)
Dick did it with Jane
Dick slept with Jane
Dick made love to Jane

Jane had sexual intercourse with Dick
Jane was banged by Dick
Jane was humped by Dick
*Jane was done by Dick
Jane was screwed by Dick
Jane was laid by Dick

    Jane was fucked by Dick
    Jane was had by Dick
    Jane balled Dick (?)
    Jane did it with Dick
    Jane slept with Dick
    Jane made love to Dick
    *Jane screwed Dick
    *Jane laid Dick
    *Jane fucked Dick
    *Jane had Dick
    *Jane did it to Dick
    *Jane banged Dick
    *Jane humped Dick

These lists make clear that within the standard view of sexual intercourse, males, or at least names for males, seem to play a different role than females, since male subjects play an active role in the language of screwing, fucking, having, doing it, and perhaps, laying, while female subjects play a passive role.

The asymmetrical nature of the relationship indicated by the sentences marked with a cross is confirmed by the fact that the form "—ed with each other" is acceptable for the sentences not marked with a cross, but not for those that require a male subject. Thus:

    Dick and Jane had sexual intercourse with each other
    Dick and Jane made love to each other
    Dick and Jane slept with each other
    Dick and Jane did it with each other
    Dick and Jane balled with each other (*?)
    *Dick and Jane banged with each other
    *Dick and Jane did it to each other
    *Dick and Jane had each other
    *Dick and Jane fucked each other
    *Dick and Jane humped each other
    *(?) Dick and Jane laid each other
    *Dick and Jane screwed each other

It should be clear, therefore, that our language reflects a difference between the male and female sexual roles, and hence that we conceive of the male and female roles in different ways. The question that now arises is, What difference in our conception of the male and female sexual roles requires active constructions for males and passive for females?

One explanation for the use of the active construction for males and the passive construction for females is that this grammatical asymmetry merely reflects the natural physiological asymmetry between men and women: the asymmetry of "to screw" and "to be screwed," "to insert into" and "to be inserted into." That is, it might be argued that the difference between masculine and feminine grammatical roles merely reflects a difference naturally required by the anatomy of males and females. This explanation is inadequate. Anatomical differences do not determine how we are to conceptualize the relation between penis and vagina during intercourse. Thus one can easily imagine a society in which the female normally played the active role during intercourse, where female subjects required active constructions with verbs indicating copulation, and where the standard metaphors were terms like "engulfing"—that is, instead of saying "he screwed her," one would say "she engulfed him." It follows that the use of passive constructions for female subjects of verbs indicating copulation does not reflect differences determined by human anatomy but rather reflects those generated by human customs.

What I am going to argue next is that the passive construction of verbs indicating coitus (that is, indicating the female position) can *also* be used to indicate that a person is being harmed. I am then going to argue that the metaphor involved would only make sense if we conceive of the female role in intercourse as that of a person being harmed (or being taken advantage of).

Passive constructions of "fucked," "screwed," and "had" indicate the female role. They also can be used to indicate being harmed. Thus, in all of the following sentences, Marion plays the female role: "Bobbie fucked Marion"; "Bobbie screwed Marion"; "Bobbie had Marion"; "Marion was fucked"; "Marion was screwed"; and "Marion was had." All of the statements are equivocal. They might literally mean that someone had sexual intercourse with Marion (who played the female role); or they might mean, metaphorically, that Marion was deceived, hurt, or taken advantage of. Thus, we say such things as "I've been screwed" ("fucked," "had," "taken," and so on) when we have been treated unfairly, been sold shoddy merchandise, or conned out of valuables. Throughout this essay I have been arguing that metaphors are applied to things only if what the term *actually* applies to shares one or more properties with what the term *metaphorically* applies to. Thus, the female sexual role must have something in common with being conned or being sold shoddy merchandise. The only common property is that of being harmed, deceived, or taken advantage of. *Hence we conceive of a person who plays the female sexual role as someone who is being harmed* (that is, "screwed," "fucked," and so on).

It might be objected that this is clearly wrong, since the unsignated terms do not indicate someone's being harmed, and hence we do not conceive of having intercourse as being harmed. The point about the unsignated terms, however, is that they can take both females and males as subjects (in active constructions) and thus *do not pick out the female role.* This demonstrates that we conceive of sexual roles in such a way that only females are thought to be taken advantage of in intercourse.

The best part of solving a puzzle is when all the pieces fall into place. If the subjects of the passive construction are being harmed, presumably the subjects of the active constructions are doing harm, and, indeed, we do conceive of these subjects in precisely this way. Suppose one is angry at someone and wishes to express malevolence as forcefully as possible without actually committing an act of physical violence. If one is inclined to be vulgar one can make the sign of the erect male cock by clenching one's fist while raising one's middle finger, or by clenching one's fist and raising one's arm and shouting such things as "screw you," "up yours," or "fuck you." In other words, one of the strongest possible ways of telling someone that you wish to harm him is to tell him to assume the female sexual role relative to you. Again, to say to someone "go fuck yourself" is to order him to harm himself, while to call someone a "mother fucker" is not so much a play on his Oedipal fears as to accuse him of being so low that he would inflict the greatest imaginable harm (fucking) upon that person who is most dear to him (his mother).

Clearly, we conceive of the male sexual role as that of hurting the person in the female role—but lest the reader have any doubts, let me provide two further bits of confirming evidence: one linguistic, one nonlinguistic. One of the English terms for a person who hurts (and takes advantage of) others is the term "prick." This metaphorical identification would not make sense unless the bastard in question (that is, the person outside the bonds of legitimacy) was thought to share some characteristics attributed to things that are literally pricks. As a verb, "prick" literally means "to hurt," as in "I pricked myself with a needle"; but the usage in question is as a noun. As a noun, "prick" is a colloquial term for "penis." Thus, the question before us is what characteristic is shared by a penis and a person who harms others (or, alternatively, by a penis and by being stuck by a needle). Clearly, no physical characteristic is relevant (physical characteristics might underlie the Yiddish metaphorical attribution "schmuck," but one would have to analyze Yiddish usage to determine this); hence the shared characteristic is nonphysical; the only relevant shared nonphysical characteristic is that both a literal prick and a figurative prick are agents that harm people.

Now for the nonlinguistic evidence. Imagine two doors: in front of each door is a line of people; behind each door is a room; in each room is a bed; on each bed is a person. The line in front of one room consists of beautiful women, and on the bed in that room is a man having intercourse with each of these women in turn. One may think any number of things about this scene. One may say that the man is in heaven, or enjoying himself at a bordello; or perhaps one might only wonder at the oddness of it all. One does not think that the man is being hurt or violated or degraded —or at least the possibility does not immediately suggest itself, although one could conceive of situations where this was what was happening (especially, for example, if the man was impotent). Now, consider the other line. Imagine that the figure on the bed is a woman and that the line consists of handsome, smiling men. The woman is having intercourse with each of these men in turn. It immediately strikes one that the woman is being degraded, violated, and so forth—"that poor woman."

When one man fucks many women he is a playboy and gains status; when a woman is fucked by many men she degrades herself and loses stature.

Our conceptual inventory is now complete enough for us to return to the task of analyzing the slogan that men ought not to think of women as sex objects.

I think that it is now plausible to argue that the appeal of the slogan "men ought not to think of women as sex objects," and the thrust of much of the literature produced by contemporary feminists, turns on something much deeper than a rejection of "scoring" (that is, the utilization of sexual "conquests" to gain esteem) and yet is a call neither for homosexuality nor for puritanism.

The slogan is best understood as a call for a new conception of the male and female sexual roles. If the analysis developed above is correct, our present conception of sexuality is such that to be a man is to be a person capable of brutalizing women (witness the slogans "The marines will make a man out of you!" and "The army builds *men*!" which are widely accepted and which simply state that learning how to kill people will make a person more manly). Such a conception of manhood not only bodes ill for a society led by such men, but also is clearly inimical to the best interests of women. It is only natural for women to reject such a sexual role, and it would seem to be the duty of any moral person to support their efforts—to redefine our conceptions not only of fucking, but of the fucker (man) and the fucked (woman).

This brings me to my final point. We are a society preoccupied with sex. As I noted previously, the nature of proper nouns and pronouns in our language makes it difficult to talk about someone without indicating that person's sex. This convention would not be part of the grammar of our language if we did not believe that knowledge of a person's sex was crucial to understanding what is said about that person. Another way of putting this point is that sexual discrimination permeates our conceptual structure. Such discrimination is clearly inimical to any movement toward sexual egalitarianism and virtually defeats its purpose at the outset. (Imagine, for example, that black people were always referred to as "them" and whites as "us" and that proper names for blacks always had an "x" suffix at the end. Clearly any movement for integration as equals would require the removal of these discriminatory indicators. Thus at the height of the melting-pot era, immigrants Americanized their names: "Bellinsky" became "Bell," "Burnstein" became "Burns," and "Lubitch" became "Baker.")

I should therefore like to close this essay by proposing that contemporary feminists should advocate the utilization of neutral proper names and the elimination of gender from our language (as I have done in this essay); and they should vigorously protest any utilization of the third-person pronouns "he" and "she" as examples of sexist discrimination (perhaps "person" would be a good third-person pronoun)—for, as a parent of linguistic analysis once said, "The limits of our language are the limits of our world."

NOTES

1. The underlying techniques used in this essay were all developed (primarily by Austin and Strawson) to deal with the problems of metaphysics and epistemology. All I have done is to attempt to apply them to other areas; I should note, however, that I rely rather heavily on metaphorical identifications, and that first philosophy tends not to require the analysis of such superficial aspects of language. Note also that it is an empirical matter whether or not people do use words in a certain way. In this essay I am just going to assume that the reader uses words more or less as my students do; for I gathered the data on which words we use to identify women, and so on, simply by asking students. If the reader does not use terms as my students do, then what I say may be totally inapplicable to him.

2. It is also interesting to talk about the technical terms that philosophers use. One fairly standard bit of technical terminology is "trouser word." J. L. Austin invented this bit of jargon to indicate which term in a pair of antonyms is important. Austin called the important term a "trouser word" because "it is the use which wears the trousers." Even in the language of philosophy, to be important is to play the male role. Of course, the antifeminism implicit in the language of tech-

nical philosophy is hardly comparable to the male chauvinism embedded in commonplaces of ordinary discourse.

3. Although I thought it inappropriate to dwell on these matters in the text, it is quite clear that *we* do *not* associate many positions with females—as the following story brings out. I related this conundrum both to students in my regular courses and to students I teach in some experimental courses at a nearby community college. Among those students who had not previously heard the story, only native Swedes invariably resolved the problem; less than half of the students from an upper-class background would get it (eventually), while lower-class and black students virtually never figured it out. Radical students, women, even members of women's liberation groups fared no better than anyone else with their same class background. The story goes as follows: A little boy is wheeled into the emergency room of a hospital. The surgeon on emergency call looks at the boy and says, "I'm sorry I cannot operate on this child; he is my son." The surgeon was not the boy's father. In what relation did the surgeon stand to the child? Most students did not give any answer. The most frequent answer given was that the surgeon had fathered the boy illegitimately. (Others suggested that the surgeon had divorced the boy's mother and remarried and hence was not legally the boy's father.) Even though the story was related as a part of a lecture on women's liberation, at best only 20 percent of the written answers gave the correct and obvious answer—the surgeon was the boy's mother.

4. *Sexual Politics* (New York: Doubleday, 1971); but see also *Sisterhood Is Powerful*, ed. Robin Morgan (New York: Vintage Books, 1970).

5. For further analysis of verbs indicating copulation see "A Note on Conjoined Noun Phrases," *Journal of Philosophical Linguistics*, vol. 1, no. 2, Great Expectations, Evanston. Ill. Reprinted with "English Sentences Without Overt Grammatical Subject," in Zwicky, Salus, Binnick, and Vanek, eds., *Studies Out in Left Field: Defamatory Essays Presented to James D. McCawley* (Edmonton: Linguistic Research, Inc., 1971). The puritanism in our society is such that both of these articles are pseudoanonymously published under the name of Quang Phuc Dong; Mr. Dong, however, has a fondness for citing and criticizing the articles and theories of Professor James McCawley, Department of Linguistics, University of Chicago. Professor McCawley himself was kind enough to criticize an earlier draft of this essay. I should also like to thank G. E. M. Anscombe for some suggestions concerning this essay.

Thomas Nagel

Sexual Perversion

There is something to be learned about sex from the fact that we possess a concept of sexual perversion. I wish to examine the concept, defending it against the charge of unintelligibility and trying to say exactly what about human sexuality qualifies it to admit of perversions. But let me make some preliminary comments about the problem before embarking on its solution.

Some people do not believe that the notion of sexual perversion makes sense, and even those who do, disagree over its application. Nevertheless, I think it will be widely conceded that if the concept is viable at all, it must meet certain general conditions. First, if there are any sexual perversions, they will have to be sexual desires or practices that can be plausibly described as in some sense unnatural, though the explanation of this natural/unnatural distinction is, of course, the main problem. Second, certain practices, such as shoe fetishism, bestiality, and sadism will be perversions if anything is; other practices, such as unadorned sexual intercourse, will not be; and about still others there is controversy. Third, if there are perversions, they will be unnatural sexual *inclinations* rather than merely unnatural practices adopted not from inclination but for other reasons. I realize that this is at variance with the view, maintained by some Roman Catholics, that contraception is a sexual perversion. But although contraception may qualify as a deliberate perversion of the sexual and reproductive functions, it cannot be significantly described as a *sexual* perversion. A sexual perversion must reveal itself in conduct that expresses an unnatural *sexual* preference. And although there might be a form of fetishism focused on the employment of contraceptive devices, that is not the usual explanation for their use.

I wish to declare at the outset my belief that the connection between sex and reproduction has no bearing on sexual perversion. The latter is a

This article is reprinted from the *Journal of Philosophy* 66, no. 1 (January 16, 1969), with the permission of the publisher and author.

concept of psychological, not physiological interest, and it is a concept that we do not apply to the lower animals, let alone to plants, all of which have reproductive functions that can go astray in various ways (think, for example, of seedless oranges). Insofar as we are prepared to regard higher animals as perverted, it is because of their psychological, not their anatomical similarity to humans. Furthermore, we do not regard as a perversion every deviation from the reproductive function of sex in humans: sterility, miscarriage, contraception, abortion.

Another matter that I believe has no bearing on the concept of sexual perversion is social disapprobation or custom. Anyone inclined to think that in each society the perversions are those sexual practices of which the community disapproves should consider all of the societies that have frowned upon adultery and fornication. These have not been regarded as unnatural practices, but have been thought objectionable in other ways. What is regarded as unnatural admittedly varies from culture to culture, but the classification is not a pure expression of disapproval or distaste. In fact it is often regarded as a *ground* for disapproval, and that suggests that the classification has an independent content.

I am going to attempt a psychological account of sexual perversion, which will depend on a specific psychological theory of sexual desire and human sexual interactions. To approach this solution I wish first to consider a contrary position, one that provides a basis for skepticism about the existence of any sexual perversions at all, and perhaps about the very significance of the term. The skeptical argument runs as follows:

Sexual desire is simply one of the appetites, like hunger and thirst. As such it may have various objects, some more common than others perhaps, but none in any sense "natural." An appetite is identified as sexual by means of the organs and erogenous zones in which its satisfaction can be to some extent localized, and the special sensory pleasures that form the core of that satisfaction. This enables us to recognize widely divergent goals, activities, and desires as sexual, since it is conceivable in principle that anything should produce sexual pleasure and that a nondeliberate, sexually charged desire for it should arise (as a result of conditioning, if nothing else). We may fail to empathize with some of these desires, and some of them, like sadism, may be objectionable on extraneous grounds, but once we have observed that they meet the criteria for being sexual, there is nothing more to be said on *that* score. Either they are sexual or they are not: sexuality does not admit of imperfection, or perversion, or any other such qualification—it is not that sort of affection.

This is probably the received radical position. It suggests that the cost of defending a psychological account may be to deny that sexual desire is an appetite. But insofar as that line of defense is plausible, it should make us suspicious of the simple picture of appetites on which the skepticism depends. Perhaps the standard appetites, like hunger, cannot be classed as pure appetites in that sense either, at least in their human versions.

Let us approach the matter by asking whether we can imagine anything that would qualify as a gastronomical perversion. Hunger and eating are importantly like sex in that they serve a biological function and also play a significant role in our inner lives. It is noteworthy that there is little temptation to describe as perverted an appetite for substances that are not nourishing. We should probably not consider someone's appetites as perverted if he liked to eat paper, sand, wood, or cotton. Those are merely rather odd and very unhealthy tastes: they lack the psychological complexity that we expect of perversions. (Coprophilia, being already a sexual perversion, may be disregarded.) If, on the other hand, someone liked to eat cookbooks or magazines with pictures of food in them, and preferred these to ordinary food—or if when hungry he sought satisfaction by fondling a napkin or ashtray from his favorite restaurant—then the concept of perversion might seem appropriate (in fact it would be natural to describe this as a case of gastronomical fetishism). It would be natural to describe as gastronomically perverted someone who could eat only by having food forced down his throat through a funnel, or only if the meal were a living animal. What helps in such cases is the peculiarity of the desire itself, rather than the inappropriateness of its object to the biological function that the desire serves. Even an appetite, it would seem, can have perversions if in addition to its biological function it has a significant psychological structure.

In the case of hunger, psychological complexity is provided by the activities that give it expression. Hunger is not merely a disturbing sensation that can be quelled by eating; it is an attitude toward edible portions of the external world, a desire to relate to them in rather special ways. The method of ingestion—chewing, savoring, swallowing, appreciating the texture and smell—is an important component of the relation, as is the passivity and controllability of the food (the only animals we eat live are helpless mollusks). Our relation to food depends also on our size: we do not live upon it or burrow into it like aphids or worms. Some of these features are more central than others, but any adequate phenomenology of eating would have to treat it as a relation to the external world and a way of appropriating bits of that world, with characteristic affection. Displacements or serious restrictions of the desire to eat could then be described as perversions, if they undermined the direct relation between man and food that is the natural expression of hunger. This explains why it is easy to imagine gastronomical fetishism, voyeurism, exhibitionism, or even gastronomical sadism and masochism. Indeed, some of these perversions are fairly common.

If we can imagine perversions of an appetite like hunger, it should be possible to make sense of the concept of sexual perversion. I do not wish to imply that sexual desire is an appetite—only that being an appetite is no bar to admitting of perversions. Like hunger, sexual desire has as its characteristic object a certain relation with something in the external world; only in this case it is usually a person rather than an omelet, and the relation is considerably more complicated. This added complication allows scope for correspondingly complicated perversions.

The fact that sexual desire is a feeling about other persons may tempt us to take a pious view of its psychological content. There are those who believe that sexual desire is properly the expression of some other attitude, like love, and that when it occurs by itself it is incomplete and unhealthy—or at any rate subhuman. (The extreme Platonic version of such a view is that sexual practices are all vain attempts to express something they cannot in principle achieve: this makes them all perversions, in a sense.) I do not believe that any such view is correct. Sexual desire is complicated enough without having to be linked to anything else as a condition for phenomenological analysis. It cannot be denied that sex may serve various functions—economic, social, altruistic—but it also has its own content as a relation between persons, and it is only by analyzing that relation that we can understand the conditions of sexual perversion.

It is very important that the object of sexual attraction is a particular individual, who transcends the properties that make him attractive. When different persons are attracted to a single person for different reasons—eyes, hair, figure, laugh, intelligence—we feel that the object of their desire is nevertheless the same, namely, that person. There is even an inclination to feel that this is so if the lovers have different sexual aims, if they include both men and women, for example. Different specific attractive characteristics seem to provide enabling conditions for the operation of a single basic feeling, and the different aims all provide expressions of it. We approach the sexual attitude toward the person through the features that we find attractive, but these features are not the objects of that attitude.

This is very different from the case of an omelet. Various people may desire it for different reasons, one for its fluffiness, another for its mushrooms, another for its unique combination of aroma and visual aspect; yet we do not enshrine the transcendental omelet as the true common object of their affections. Instead we might say that several desires have accidentally converged on the same object: any omelet with the crucial characteristics would do as well. It is not similarly true that any person with the same flesh distribution and way of smoking can be substituted as object for a particular sexual desire that has been elicited by those characteristics. It may be that they will arouse attraction whenever they recur, but it will be a new sexual attraction with a new particular object, not merely a transfer of the old desire to someone else. (I believe this is true even in cases where the new object is unconsciously identified with a former one.)

The importance of this point will emerge when we see how complex a psychological interchange constitutes the natural development of sexual attraction. This would be incomprehensible if its object were not a particular person, but rather a person of a certain *kind*. Attraction is only the beginning, and fulfillment does not consist merely of behavior and contact expressing this attraction, but involves much more.

The best discussion of these matters that I have seen is in part three of Sartre's *Being and Nothingness*.[1] Since it has influenced my own views, I shall say a few things about it now. Sartre's treatment of sexual desire and of love, hate, sadism, masochism, and further attitudes toward others, depends on a general theory of consciousness and the body that we can neither expound nor assume here. He does not discuss perversion, partly because he regards sexual desire as one form of the perpetual attempt of an embodied consciousness to come to terms with the existence of others, an attempt that is as doomed to fail in this form as it is in any of the others, which include sadism and masochism (if not certain of the more impersonal deviations) as well as several nonsexual attitudes. According to Sartre, all attempts to incorporate the other into my world as another subject, that is, to apprehend him as at once an object for me and a subject for whom I am an object, are unstable and doomed to collapse into one or the other of the two aspects. Either I reduce him entirely to an object, in which case his subjectivity escapes the possession or appropriation I can extend to that object; or I become merely an object for him, in which case I am no longer in a position to appropriate his subjectivity. Moreover, neither of these aspects is stable: each is continually in danger of giving way to the other. This has the consequence that there can be no such thing as a *successful* sexual relation, since the deep aim of sexual desire cannot in principle be accomplished. It seems likely, therefore, that this view will not permit a basic distinction between successful, or complete, and unsuccessful, or incomplete, sex and therefore cannot admit the concept of perversion.

I do not adopt this aspect of the theory, nor many of its metaphysical underpinnings. What interests me is Sartre's picture of the attempt. He says that the type of possession that is the object of sexual desire is carried out by "a double reciprocal incarnation" and that this is accomplished, typically in the form of a caress, in the following way: "I make myseif flesh in order to impel the Other to realize *for-herself* and *for me* her own flesh, and my caresses cause my flesh to be born for me in so far as it is for the Other *flesh causing her to be born as flesh.*" [2] The incarnation in question is described variously as a clogging or troubling of consciousness, which is inundated by the flesh in which it is embodied.

The view I am going to suggest—I hope in less obscure language—is related to Sartre's, but differs in allowing sexuality to achieve its goal on occasion and thus in providing the concept of perversion with a foothold.

Sexual desire involves a kind of perception, but not merely a single perception of its object, for in the paradigm case of mutual desire there is a complex system of superimposed mutual perceptions—not only perceptions of the sexual object, but perceptions of oneself. Moreover, sexual awareness of another involves considerable self-awareness to begin with—more than is involved in ordinary sensory perception. The experience is felt as an assault on oneself by the view (or touch, or whatever) of the sexual object.

Let us consider a case in which the elements can be separated. For clarity we will restrict ourselves initially to the somewhat artificial case of desire at a distance. Suppose a man and a woman, whom we may call Romeo and Juliet, are at opposite ends of a cocktail lounge with many mirrors on its walls, permitting unobserved observation and even mutual unobserved observation. Each of them is sipping a martini and studying other people in the mirrors. At some point Romeo notices Juliet. He is moved, somehow, by the softness of her hair and the diffidence with which she sips her martini, and this arouses him sexually. Let us say that X *senses* Y whenever X regards Y with sexual desire. (Y need not be a person, and X's apprehension of Y can be visual, tactile, olfactory, and so on, or purely imaginary. In the present example we shall concentrate on vision.) So Romeo senses Juliet, rather than merely noticing her. At this stage he is aroused by an unaroused object; so he is more in the sexual grip of his body than she of hers.

Let us suppose, however, that Juliet now senses Romeo in another mirror on the opposite wall, though neither of them yet knows that he is seen by the other (the mirror angles provide three-quarter views). Romeo then begins to notice in Juliet the subtle signs of sexual arousal: heavy-lidded stare, dilating pupils, a faint flush. This of course renders her much more bodily, and he not only notices but senses this as well. His arousal is nevertheless still solitary. But now, cleverly calculating the line of her stare without actually looking her in the eyes, he realizes that it is directed at him through the mirror on the opposite wall. That is, he notices, and moreover senses, Juliet sensing him. This is definitely a new development, for it gives him a sense of embodiment, not only through his own reactions, but also through the eyes and reactions of another. Moreover, it is separable from the initial sensing of Juliet, for sexual arousal might begin with a person's sensing that he is sensed and being assailed by the perception of the other person's desire rather than merely by the perception of the person.

But there is a further step. Let us suppose that Juliet, who is a little slower than Romeo, now senses that he senses her. This puts Romeo in a position to notice, and be aroused by, her arousal at being sensed by him. He senses that she senses that he senses her. This is still another level of arousal, for he becomes conscious of his sexuality through his awareness of its effect on her and of her awareness that this effect is due to him. Once she takes the same step and senses that he senses her sensing him, it becomes difficult to state, let alone imagine, further iterations, though they may be logically distinct. If both are alone, they will presumably turn to look at each other directly, and the proceedings will continue on another plane. Physical contact and intercourse are perfectly natural extensions of this complicated visual exchange, and mutual touch can involve all the complexities of awareness present in the visual case, but with a far greater range of subtlety and acuteness.

Ordinarily, of course, things happen in a less orderly fashion—sometimes in a great rush—but I believe that some version of this overlapping system of distinct sexual perceptions and interactions is the basic framework of any full-fledged sexual relation and that relations involving only part of the complex are significantly incomplete. The account is only schematic, as it must be to achieve generality. Every real sexual act will be psychologically far more specific and detailed, in ways that depend not only on the physical techniques employed and on anatomical details but also on countless features of the participants' conceptions of themselves and of each other, which become embodied in the act. (It is a familiar enough fact, for example, that people often take their social roles and the social roles of their partners to bed with them.)

The general schema is important, however, and the proliferation of levels of mutual awareness it involves is an example of a type of complexity that typifies human interactions. Consider aggression, for example. If I am angry with someone, I want to make him feel it, either to produce self-reproach by getting him to see himself through the eyes of my anger and to dislike what he sees, or to produce reciprocal anger or fear by getting him to perceive my anger as a threat or attack. What I want will depend on the details of my anger, but in either case it will involve a desire that the object of that anger be aroused. This accomplishment constitutes the fulfillment of my emotion through domination of the object's feelings.

Another example of such reflexive mutual recognition is to be found in the phenomenon of meaning, which appears to involve an intention to produce a belief or other effect in another by bringing about his recognition of one's intention to produce that effect. (That result is due to H. P. Grice,[3] whose position I shall not attempt to reproduce in detail.) Sex has a related structure: it involves a desire that one's partner be aroused by the recognition of one's desire that he or she be aroused.

It is not easy to define the basic types of awareness and arousal of which these complexes are composed, and that remains a lacuna in this discussion. I believe that the object of awareness is the same in one's own case as it is in one's sexual awareness of another, although the two awarenesses will not be the same, the difference being as great as that between feeling angry and experiencing the anger of another. All stages of sexual perception are varieties of identification of a person with his body. What is perceived is one's own or another's *subjection* to or *immersion* in his body, a phenomenon that has been recognized with loathing by St. Paul and St. Augustine, both of whom regarded "the law of sin which is in my members" as a grave threat to the dominion of the holy will.[4] In sexual desire and its expression the blending of involuntary response with deliberate control is extremely important. For Augustine, the revolution launched against him by his body is symbolized by erection and the other involuntary physical components of arousal. Sartre too stresses the fact that the penis is not a prehensile organ. But mere involuntariness characterizes other bodily processes as well. In sexual desire the involuntary responses are combined with submission to spontaneous impulses: not only one's pulse and secretions but one's actions are taken over by the body; ideally, deliberate control is needed only to guide the expression of those impulses. This is to some extent also true of an appetite like hunger, but the takeover there is more localized, less pervasive, less extreme. One's whole body does not become saturated with hunger as it can with desire. But the most characteristic feature of a specifically sexual immersion in the body is its ability to fit into the complex of mutual perceptions that we have described. Hunger leads to spontaneous interactions with food; sexual desire leads to spontaneous interactions with other persons, whose bodies are asserting their sovereignty in the same way, producing involuntary reactions and spontaneous impulses in *them*. These reactions are perceived, and the perception of them is perceived, and that perception is in turn perceived; at each step the domination of the person by his body is reinforced, and the sexual partner becomes more possessible by physical contact, penetration, and envelopment.

Desire is therefore not merely the perception of a preexisting embodiment that in turn enhances the original subject's sense of himself. This explains why it is important that the partner be aroused, and not merely aroused, but aroused by the awareness of one's desire. It also explains the sense in which desire has unity and possession as its object: physical possession must eventuate in creation of the sexual object in the image of one's desire, and not merely in the object's recognition of that desire or in his or her own private arousal. (This may reveal a male bias. I shall say something about that later.)

To return, finally, to the topic of perversion: I believe that various familiar deviations constitute truncated or incomplete versions of the complete configuration and may therefore be regarded as perversions of the central impulse.

In particular, narcissistic practices and intercourse with animals, infants, and inanimate objects seem to be stuck at some primitive version of the first stage. If the object is not alive, the experience is reduced entirely to an awareness of one's own sexual embodiment. Small children and animals permit awareness of the embodiment of the other, but present obstacles to reciprocity, to the recognition by the sexual object of the subject's desire as the source of his (the object's) sexual self-awareness.

Sadism concentrates on the evocation of passive self-awareness in others, but the sadist's engagement is itself active and requires a retention of deliberate control that impedes awareness of himself as a bodily subject of passion in the required sense. The victim must recognize him as the source of his own sexual passivity, but only as the active source. De Sade claimed that the object of sexual desire was to evoke involuntary responses from one's partner, especially audible ones. The infliction of pain is no doubt the most efficient way to accomplish this, but it requires a certain abrogation of one's own exposed spontaneity. All this, incidentally, helps to explain why it is tempting to regard as sadistic an excessive preoccupation with sexual technique, which does not permit one to abandon the role of agent at any stage of the sexual act. Ideally one should be able to surmount one's technique at some point.

A masochist on the other hand imposes the same disability on his partner as the sadist imposes on himself. The masochist cannot find a satisfactory embodiment as the object of another's sexual desire but only as the object of his control. He is passive not in relation to his partner's passion but in relation to his nonpassive agency. In addition, the subjection to one's body characteristic of pain and physical restraints is of a very different kind from that of sexual excitement: pain causes people to contract rather than dissolve.

Both of these disorders have to do with the second stage, which involves the awareness of oneself as an object of desire. In straightforward sadism and masochism other attentions are substituted for desire as a source of the object's self-awareness. But it is also possible for nothing of that sort to be substituted, as in the case of a masochist who is satisfied with self-inflicted pain or of a sadist who does not insist on playing a role in the suffering that arouses him. Greater difficulties of classification are presented by three other categories of sexual activity: elaborations of the sexual act, intercourse of more than two persons, and homosexuality.

If we apply our model to the various forms that may be taken by two-party heterosexual intercourse, none of them seem clearly to qualify as perversions. Hardly anyone can be found these days to inveigh against oral-genital contact, and the merits of buggery are urged by such respectable figures as D. H. Lawrence and Norman Mailer. There may be something vaguely sadistic about the latter technique (in Mailer's writings it seems to be a method of introducing an element of rape), but it is not obvious that this has to be so. In general, it would appear that any bodily contact between a man and a woman that gives them sexual pleasure is a possible vehicle for the system of multilevel interpersonal awareness that I have claimed is the basic psychological content of sexual interaction. Thus a liberal platitude about sex is upheld.

About multiple combinations the least that can be said is that they are bound to be complicated. If one considers how difficult it is to carry on two conversations simultaneously, one may appreciate the problems of multiple simultaneous interpersonal perception that can arise in even a small-scale orgy. It may be inevitable that some of the component relations should degenerate into mutual epidermal stimulation by participants otherwise isolated from each other. There may also be a tendency toward voyeurism and exhibitionism, both of which are incomplete relations. The exhibitionist wishes to display his desire without needing to be desired in return; he may even fear the sexual attentions of others. A voyeur, on the other hand, need not require any recognition at all by his object, certainly not a recognition of the voyeur's arousal.

It is not clear whether homosexuality is a perversion if that is measured by the standard of the described configuration, but it seems unlikely. For such a classification would have to depend on the possibility of extracting from the system a distinction between male and female sexuality; and much that has been said so far applies equally to men and women. Moreover, it would have to be maintained that there was a natural tie between the type of sexuality and the sex of the body and that two sexualities of the same type could not interact properly.

Certainly there is much support for an aggressive-passive distinction between male and female sexuality. In our culture the male's arousal tends to initiate the perceptual exchange; he usually makes the sexual approach, largely controls the course of the act, and of course penetrates whereas the woman receives. When two men or two women engage in intercourse they cannot both adhere to these sexual roles. The question is how essential the roles are to an adequate sexual relation. One relevant observation is that a good deal of deviation from these roles occurs in heterosexual intercourse. Women can be sexually aggressive and men passive, and temporary reversals of role are not uncommon in heterosexual exchanges of reasonable length. If such conditions are set aside, it may be urged that there is something irreducibly perverted in attraction to a body anatomically like one's own. But alarming as some people in our culture may find such attraction, it remains psychologically unilluminating to class it as perverted. Certainly if homosexuality is a perversion, it is so in a very different sense from that in which shoe-fetishism is a perversion, for some version of the full range of interpersonal perceptions seems perfectly possible between two persons of the same sex.

In any case, even if the proposed model is correct, it remains implausible to describe as perverted every deviation from it. For example, if the partners in heterosexual intercourse indulge in private heterosexual fantasies, that obscures the recognition of the real partner and so, on the theory, constitutes a defective sexual relation. It is not, however, generally regarded as a perversion. Such examples suggest that a simple dichotomy between perverted and unperverted sex is too crude to organize the phenomena adequately.

I shall close with some remarks about the relation of perversion to good, bad, and morality. The concept of perversion can hardly fail to be evaluative in some sense, for it appears to involve the notion of an ideal or at least adequate sexuality that the perversions in some way fail to achieve. So, if the concept is viable, the judgment that a person or practice or desire is perverted will constitute a sexual evaluation, implying that better sex, or a better specimen of sex, is possible. This in itself is a very weak claim since the evaluation might be in a dimension that is of little interest to us. (Though, if my account is correct, that will not be true.)

Whether it is a moral evaluation, however, is another question entirely, one whose answer would require more understanding of both morality and perversion than can be deployed here. Moral evaluation of acts and of persons is a rather special and very complicated matter and by no means are all of our evaluations of persons and their activities moral evaluations. We make judgments about people's beauty or health or intelligence that are evaluative without being moral. Assessments of their sexuality may be similar in that respect.

Furthermore, moral issues aside, it is not clear that unperverted sex is necessarily *preferable* to the perversions. It may be that sex that receives the highest marks for perfection *as sex* is less enjoyable than certain perversions, and if enjoyment is considered very important, that might outweigh considerations of sexual perfection in determining rational preference.

That raises the question of the relation between the evaluative content of judgments of perversion and the rather common *general* distinction between good and bad sex. The latter distinction is usually confined to sexual acts, and it would seem, within limits, to cut across the other: even someone who believed, for example, that homosexuality was a perversion could admit a distinction between better and worse homosexual sex, and might even allow that good homosexual sex could be better *sex* than not very good unperverted sex. If this is correct, it supports the position—if judgments of perversion are viable at all—that they represent only one aspect of the possible evaluation of sex, even *qua sex*. Moreover it is not the only important aspect: certainly sexual deficiencies that evidently do not constitute perversions can be the object of great concern.

Finally, even if perverted sex is to that extent not so good as it might be, bad sex is generally better than none at all. This should not be controversial: it seems to hold for other important matters, like food, music, literature, and society. In the end, one must choose from among the available alternatives, whether their availability depends on the environment or on one's own constitution. And the alternatives have to be fairly grim before it becomes rational to opt for nothing.

NOTES

1. Trans. Hazel E. Barnes (New York: Philosophical Library, 1956).
2. Ibid., p. 391. Sartre's italics.
3. "Meaning," *Philosophical Review* 66, no. 3 (July 1957): 377-88.
4. See Romans 7:23, and the *Confessions*, Book 8, v.

Sara Ruddick

Better Sex

It might be argued that there is no specifically sexual morality.[1] We have, of course, become accustomed to speaking of sexual morality, but the "morality" of which we speak has a good deal to do with property, the division of labor, and male power, and little to do with our sexual lives. Sexual experiences, like experiences in driving automobiles, render us liable to specific moral situations. As drivers we must guard against infantile desires for revenge and excitement. As lovers we must guard against cruelty and betrayal, for we know sexual experiences provide special opportunities for each. We drive soberly because, before we get into a car, we believe that it is wrong to be careless of life. We resist temptations to adultery because we believe it wrong to betray trust, whether it be a parent, a sexual partner, or a political colleague who is betrayed. As lovers and drivers we act on principles that are particular applications of general moral principles. Moreover, given the superstitions from which sexual experience has suffered, it is wise to free ourselves, as lovers, from any moral concerns, other than those we have as human beings. There is no specifically sexual morality, and none should be invented. Or so it might be argued.

When we examine our moral "intuitions," however, the analogy with driving fails us. Unburdened of *sexual* morality, we do not find it easy to apply general moral principles to our sexual lives. The "morally average" lover can be cruel, violate trust, and neglect social duties with less opprobrium precisely *because* he is a lover. Only political passions and psychological or physical deprivation serve as well as sexual desire to excuse what would otherwise be seriously and clearly immoral acts. (Occasionally, sexual desire is itself conceived of as a deprivation, an involuntary lust. And there is, of course, a tradition that sees sexual morality as a way of controlling those unable to be sexless: "It is better to marry than to burn.") Often, in our sexual lives, we neither flout nor simply apply general moral principles. Rather, the values of sexual experience themselves

280

figure in the construction of moral dilemmas. The conflict between better sex (more complete, natural, and pleasurable sex acts) and, say, social duty is not seen as a conflict between the immoral and compulsive, on one hand, and the morally good, on the other, but as a conflict between alternative moral acts.

Our intuitions vary but at least they suggest we can use "good" sex as a positive weight on some moral balance. What is that weight? Why do we put it there? How do we, in the first place, evaluate sexual experiences? On reflection, should we endorse these evaluations? These are the questions whose answers should constitute a specifically sexual morality.

In answering them, I will first consider three characteristics that have been used to distinguish some sex acts as better than others—greater pleasure, completeness, and naturalness. Other characteristics may be relevant to evaluating sex acts, but these three are central. If they have *moral* significance, then the sex acts characterized by them will be better than others not so characterized.

After considering those characteristics in virtue of which some sex acts are allegedly better than others, I will ask whether the presence of those characteristics renders the acts *morally* superior. I will not consider here the unclear and overused distinction between the moral and the amoral, nor the illegitimate but familiar distinction between the moral and the prudent. I hope it is sufficient to set out dogmatically and schematically the moral notions I will use. I am confident that better sex is morally preferable to other sex, but I am not at all happy with my characterization of its moral significance. Ultimately, sexual morality cannot be considered apart from a "prudential" morality in which it is shown that what is good is good for us and what is good for us makes us good. In such a morality, not only sex, but art, fantasy, love, and a host of other intellectual and emotional enterprises will regain old moral significances and acquire new ones. My remarks here, then, are partial and provisional.

A characteristic renders a sex act morally preferable to one without that characteristic if it gives, increases, or is instrumental in increasing the "benefit" of the act for the person engaging in it. Benefits can be classified as peremptory or optional. Peremptory benefits are experiences, relations, or objects that anyone who is neither irrational nor anhedonic will want so long as he wants anything at all. Optional benefits are experiences, relations, or objects that anyone, neither irrational nor anhedonic, will want so long as he will not thereby lose a peremptory benefit. There is widespread disagreement about which benefits are peremptory. Self-respect, love, and health are common examples of peremptory benefits. Arms, legs, and hands are probably optional benefits. A person still wanting a great deal might give up limbs, just as she would give up life, when mutilation or death is required by self-respect. As adults we are largely responsible for procuring our own benefits and greatly dependent on good fortune for success in doing so. However, the moral significance of benefits is most clearly seen not from the standpoint of the person procuring and enjoying them but from the standpoint of another *caring* person, for example, a lover, parent, or political leader responsible for procuring benefits for specific others. A benefit may then be described as an experience, relation, or object that anyone who properly cares for another is obliged to attempt to secure for him. Criteria for the virtue of care and for benefit are reciprocally determined, the virtue consisting in part in recognizing and attempting to secure benefits for the person cared for, the identification of benefit depending on its recognition by those already seen to be properly caring.

In talking of benefits I shall be looking at our sexual lives from the vantage point of hope, not of fear. The principal interlocutor may be considered to be a child asking what he should rightly and reasonably hope for in living, rather than a potential criminal questioning conventional restraints. The specific question the child may be imagined to ask can now be put: In what way is better sex beneficial or conducive to experiences or relations or objects that are beneficial?

A characteristic renders a sex act morally preferable to one without that characteristic if either the act is thereby more just or the act is thereby likely to make the person engaging in it more just. Justice includes giving others what is due them, taking no more than what is one's own, and giving and taking according to prevailing principles of fairness.

A characteristic renders a sex act morally preferable to one without that characteristic if because of the characteristic the act is more virtuous or more likely to lead to virtue. A virtue is a disposition to attempt, and an ability to succeed in, good acts—acts of justice, acts that express or produce excellence, and acts that yield benefits to oneself or others.

SEXUAL PLEASURE

Sensual experiences give rise to sensations and experiences that are paradigms of what is pleasant. Hedonism, in both its psychological and ethical forms, has blinded us to the nature and to the benefits of sensual pleasure by overextending the word "pleasure" to cover anything enjoyable or even agreeable.[2] The paradigmatic type of pleasure is sensual. Pleasure is a temporally extended, more or less intense quality of particular experiences. Pleasure is enjoyable independent of any function pleasurable activity fulfills. The infant who continues to suck well after he is nourished, expressing evident pleasure in doing so, gives us a demonstration of the nature of pleasure.[3]

As we learn more about pleasant experiences we not only apply but also extend and attenuate the primary notion of "pleasure." But if pleasure is to have any nonsophistical psychological or moral interest, it must retain its connections with those paradigm instances of sensual pleasure that give rise to it. We may, for example, extend the notion of pleasure so that particular episodes in the care of children give great pleasure; but the long-term caring for children, however intrinsically rewarding, is not an experience of pleasure or unpleasure.

Sexual pleasure is a species of sensual pleasure with its own conditions of arousal and satisfaction. Sexual acts vary considerably in pleasure, the limiting case being a sexual act where no one experiences pleasure even though someone may experience affection or "relief of tension" through orgasm. Sexual pleasure can be considered either in a context of deprivation and its relief or in a context of satisfaction. Psychological theories have tended to emphasize the frustrated state of sexual desire and to construe sexual pleasure as a relief from that state. There are, however, alternative accounts of sexual pleasure that correspond more closely with our experience. Sexual pleasure is "a primary distinctively poignant pleasure experience that manifests itself from early infancy on. . . . Once experienced it continues to be savored. . . ."[4] Sexual desire is not experienced as frustration but as part of sexual pleasure. Normally, sexual desire transforms itself gradually into the pleasure that appears, misleadingly, to be an aim extrinsic to it. The natural structure of desire, not an inherent quality of frustration, accounts for the pain of an aroused but unsatisfied desire.

Sexual pleasure, like addictive pleasure generally, does not, except very temporarily, result in satiety. Rather, it increases the demand for more of the same while sharply limiting the possibility of substitutes. The experience of sensual pleasures, and particularly of sexual pleasures, has a pervasive effect on our perceptions of the world. We find bodies inviting, social encounters alluring, and smells, tastes, and sights resonant because our perception of them includes their sexual significance. Merleau-Ponty has written of a patient for whom "perception had lost its erotic structure, both temporally and physically."[5] As the result of a brain injury the patient's capacity for sexual desire and pleasure (though not his capacity for performing sexual acts) was impaired. He no longer sought sexual intercourse of his own accord, was left indifferent by the sights and smells of available bodies, and if in the midst of sexual intercourse his partner turned away, he showed no signs of displeasure. The capacity for sexual pleasure, upon which the erotic structure of perception depends, can be accidentally damaged. The question that this case raises is whether it would be desirable to interfere with this capacity in a more systematic way than we now do. With greater biochemical and psychiatric knowledge we shall presumably be able to manipulate it at will.[6] And if that becomes possible, toward what end should we interfere? I shall return to this question after describing the other two characteristics of better sex—completeness and naturalness.

COMPLETE SEX ACTS

The completeness of a sexual act depends upon the *relation* of the participants to their own and each other's *desire*. A sex act is complete if each partner allows himself to be "taken over" by an active desire, which is desire not merely for the other's body but also for his active desire. Completeness is hard to characterize, though complete sex acts are at least as natural as any others—especially, it seems, among those people who take them casually and for granted. The notion of "completeness" (as I shall call it) has figured under various guises in the work of Sartre, Merleau-Ponty, and more recently Thomas Nagel. "The being which desires is consciousness making itself body."[7] "What we try to possess, then, is not just a body, but a body brought to life by consciousness."[8] "It is important that the partner be aroused, and not merely aroused, but aroused by the awareness of one's desire."[9]

The precondition of complete sex acts is the "embodiment" of the participants. Each participant submits to sexual desires that take over consciousness and direct action. It is sexual desire and not a separable satisfaction of it (for example, orgasm) that is important here. Indeed, Sartre finds pleasure external to the essence of desire, and Nagel gives an example of embodiment in which the partners do not touch each other. Desire is pervasive and "overwhelming," but it does not make its subject its involuntary victim (as it did the Boston Strangler, we are told), nor does it, except at its climax, alter capacities for ordinary perceptions, memories, and inferences. Nagel's embodied partners can presumably get themselves from bar stools to bed while their consciousness is "clogged" with desire. With what, then, is embodiment contrasted?

Philosophers make statements that when intended literally are evidence of pathology: "Human beings are automata"; "I never really see physical objects"; "I can never know what another person is feeling." The clearest statement of disembodiment that I know of is W. T. Stace's claim:

"I become aware of my body in the end chiefly because it insists on accompanying me wherever I go."[10] What "just accompanies me" can also stay away. "When my body leaves me/I'm lonesome for it./ . . . body/goes away I don't know where/and it's lonesome to drift/above the space it/fills when it's here."[11] If "the body is felt more as one object among other objects in the world than as the core of the individual's own being,"[12] then what appears to be bodily can be dissociated from the "real self." Both a generalized separation of "self" from body and particular disembodied experiences have had their advocates. The attempt at disembodiment has also been seen as conceptually confused and psychologically disastrous.

We may often experience ourselves as relatively disembodied, observing or "using" our bodies to fulfill our intentions. On some occasions, however, such as in physical combat, sport, physical suffering, or danger, we "become" our bodies; our consciousness becomes bodily experience of bodily activity.[13] Sexual acts are occasions for such embodiment; they may, however, fail for a variety of reasons, for example, because of pretense or an excessive need for self-control. If someone is embodied by sexual desire, he submits to its direction. Spontaneous impulses of desire become his movements—some involuntary, like gestures of "courting behavior" or physical expressions of intense pleasure, and some deliberate. His consciousness, or "mind," is taken over by desire and the pursuit of its object, in the way that at other times it may be taken over by an intellectual problem or by obsessive fantasies. But unlike the latter takeovers, this one is bodily. A desiring consciousness is flooded with specifically sexual feelings that eroticize all perception and movement. Consciousness "becomes flesh."

Granted the precondition of embodiment, complete sex acts occur when each partner's embodying desire is active and actively responsive to the other's. This second aspect of complete sex constitutes a "reflexive mutual recognition" of desire by desire.[14]

The partner *actively* desires another person's desire. Active desiring includes more than embodiment, which might be achieved in objectless masturbation. It is more, also, than merely being aroused by and then taken over by desire, though it may come about as a result of deliberate arousal. It commits the actively desiring person to her desire and requires her to identify with it—that is, to recognize herself as a sexual agent as well as respondent. (Active desiring is less encouraged in women, and probably more women than men feel threatened by it.)

The other recognizes and responds to the partner's desire. Merely to recognize the desire as desire, not to reduce it to an itch or to depersonalize it as a "demand," may be threatening. Imperviousness to desire is the deepest defense against it. We have learned from research on families whose members tend to become schizophrenic that such imperviousness, the refusal to recognize a feeling for what it is, can force a vulnerable person to deny or to obscure the real nature of his feelings. Imperviousness tends to deprive even a relatively invulnerable person of his efficacy. The demand that our feelings elicit a response appropriate to them is part of a general demand that we be recognized, that our feelings be allowed to make a difference.

There are many ways in which sexual desire may be recognized, countless forms of submission and resistance. In complete sex, desire is recognized by a responding and active desire that commits the other, as it committed the partner. Given responding desire, both people identify themselves as sexually desiring the other. They are neither seducer nor seduced, neither suppliant nor benefactress, neither sadist nor victim, but sexual agents acting sexually out of their recognized desire. Indeed, in complete sex one not only welcomes and recognizes active desire, one desires it. Returned and endorsed desire becomes one of the features of an erotically structured perception. Desiring becomes desirable. (Men are less encouraged to desire the other's active and demanding desire, and such desiring is probably threatening to more men than women.)

In sum, in complete sex two persons embodied by sexual desire actively desire and respond to each other's active desire. Although it is difficult to write of complete sex without suggesting that one of the partners is the initiator, while the other responds, complete sex is reciprocal sex. The partners, whatever the circumstances of their coming together, are equal in activity and responsiveness of desire.

Sexual acts can be partly incomplete. A necrophiliac may be taken over by desire, and a frigid woman may respond to her lover's desire without being embodied by her own. Partners whose sexual activities are accompanied by private fantasies engage in an incomplete sex act. Consciousness is used by desire but remains apart from it, providing it with stimulants and controls. Neither partner responds to the other's desire, though each may appear to. Sartre's "dishonest masturbator," for whom masturbation is the sex act of choice, engages in a paradigmatically incomplete sex act: "He asks only to be slightly distanced from his own body, only for there to be a light coating of otherness over his flesh and over his thoughts. His personae are melting sweets. . . . The masturbator is enchanted at never being able to feel himself sufficiently another, and at producing for himself alone the diabolic appearance of a couple that fades away when one touches it. . . . Masturbation is the derealisation of the world and of the masturbator himself."[15]

Completeness is more difficult to describe than incompleteness, for it turns on precise but subtle ways of responding to a particular person's desire with specific expressions of impulse that are both spontaneous and responsive.

There are many possible sex acts that are pleasurable but not complete. Sartre, Nagel, and Merleau-Ponty each suggest that the desire for the responsive desire of one's partner is the "central impulse" of sexual desire.[16] The desire for a sleeping woman, for example, is possible only "in so far as this sleep appears on the ground of consciousness."[17] This seems much too strong. Some lovers desire that their partners resist, others like them coolly controlled, others prefer them asleep. We would not say that there was anything abnormal or less fully sexual about desire. Whether or not complete sex is preferable to incomplete sex (the question to which I shall turn shortly), incompleteness does not disqualify a sex act from being fully sexual.

SEXUAL PERVERSION

The final characteristic of allegedly better sex acts is that they are "natural" rather than "perverted." The ground for classifying sexual acts as either natural or unnatural is that the former type serve or could serve the evolutionary and biological function of sexuality—namely, reproduction. "Natural" sexual desire has as its "object" living persons of the opposite sex, and in particular their postpubertal genitals. The "aim" of natural sexual desire—that is, the act that "naturally" completes it—is genital intercourse. Perverse sex acts are deviations from the natural object (for example, homosexuality, fetishism) or from the standard aim (for example, voyeurism, sadism). Among the variety of objects and aims of sexual desire, I can see no other ground for selecting some as natural, except that they are of the type that can lead to reproduction.[18]

The connection of sexual desire with reproduction gives us the criterion but not the motive of the classification. The concept of perversion depends on a disjointedness between our experience of sexual desire from infancy on and the function of sexual desire—reproduction. In our collective experience of sexuality, perverse desires are as natural as nonperverse ones. The sexual desire of the polymorphously perverse child has many objects—for example, breasts, anus, mouth, genitals—and many aims—for example, autoerotic or other-directed looking, smelling, touching, hurting. From the social and developmental point of view, natural sex is an achievement, partly biological, partly conventional, consisting in a dominant organization of sexual desires in which perverted aims or objects are subordinate to natural ones. The concept of perversion reflects the vulnerability as much as the evolutionary warrant of this organization.

The connection of sexual desire with reproduction is not sufficient to yield the concept of perversion, but it is surely necessary. Nagel, however, thinks otherwise. There are, he points out, many sexual acts that do not lead to reproduction but that we are not even inclined to call perverse—for example, sexual acts between partners who are sterile. Perversion, according to him, is a psychological concept while reproduction is (only?) a physiological one. (Incidentally, this view of reproduction seems to me the clearest instance of male bias in Nagel's paper.)

Nagel is right about our judgments of particular acts, but he draws the wrong conclusions from those judgments. The perversity of sex acts does not depend upon whether they are intended to achieve reproduction. "Natural" sexual desire is for heterosexual genital activity, not for reproduction. The ground for classifying that desire as natural is that it is so organized that it *could* lead to reproduction in normal physiological circumstances. The reproductive organization of sexual desires gives us a *criterion* of naturalness, but the *virtue* of which it is a criterion is the "naturalness" itself, not reproduction. Our vacillating attitude toward the apparently perverse acts of animals reflects our shifting from criterion to virtue. If, when confronted with a perverse act of animals, we withdraw the label "perverted" from our own similar acts rather than extend it to theirs, we are relinquishing the reproductive criterion of naturalness, while retaining the virtue. Animals cannot be "unnatural." If, on the other hand, we "discover" that animals can be perverts too, we are maintaining our criterion, but giving a somewhat altered sense to the "naturalness" of which it is a criterion.

Nagel's alternative attempt to classify acts as natural or perverted on the basis of their completeness fails. "Perverted" and "complete" are evaluations of an entirely different order. The completeness of a sex act depends upon qualities of the participants' experience and upon qualities of their relation—qualities of which they are the best judge. To say a sex act is perverted is to pass a conventional judgment about characteristics of the act, which could be evident to any observer. As one can pretend to be angry but not to shout, one can pretend to a complete, but not to a natural, sex act (though one may, of course, conceal desires for perverse sex acts or shout in order to mask one's feelings). As Nagel himself sees, judgments about particular sex acts clearly differentiate between perversion and completeness. Unadorned heterosexual intercourse where each partner has private fantasies is clearly "natural" and clearly "incomplete," but there is nothing prima facie incomplete about exclusive oral-genital intercourse or homosexual acts. If many perverse acts are incomplete, as Nagel claims, this is an important fact *about* perversion, but it is not the basis upon which we judge its occurrence.

IS BETTER SEX REALLY BETTER?

Some sex acts are, allegedly, better than others insofar as they are more pleasurable, complete, and natural. What is the moral significance of this evaluation? In answering this question, official sexual morality sometimes appeals to the social consequences of particular types of better sex acts. For example, since dominantly perverse organizations of sexual impulses limit reproduction, the merits of perversion depend upon the need to limit or increase population. Experience of sexual pleasure may be desirable if it promotes relaxation and communication in an acquisitive society, undesirable if it limits the desire to work or, in armies, to kill. The social consequences of complete sex have not received particular attention, because the quality of sexual experience has been of little interest to moralists. It might be found that those who had complete sexual relations were more cooperative, less amenable to political revolt. If so, complete sexual acts would be desirable in just and peaceable societies, undesirable in unjust societies requiring revolution.

The social desirability of types of sexual acts depends on particular social conditions and independent criteria of social desirability. It may be interesting and important to assess particular claims about the social desirability of sex acts, but this is not my concern. What is my concern is the extent to which we will allow our judgments of sexual worth to be influenced by social considerations. But this issue cannot even be raised until we have a better sense of sexual worth.

THE BENEFIT OF SEXUAL PLEASURE

To say that an experience is pleasant is to give a self-evident, terminal reason for seeking it. We can sometimes "see" that an experience is pleasant. When, for example, we observe someone's sensual delight in eating, his behavior can expressively characterize pleasure. We can only question the benefit of such an experience by referring to other goods with which it might conflict. Though sensual pleasures may not be sufficient to warrant giving birth or to deter suicide, so long as we live they are self-evidently benefits to us.

The most eloquent detractors of sexual experience have admitted that it provides sensual pleasures so poignant that once experienced they are repeatedly, almost addictively, sought. Yet, unlike other appetites, such as hunger, sexual desire can be permanently resisted, and resistance has been advocated. How can the prima facie benefits of sexual pleasure appear deceptive?

There are several grounds for complaint. Sexual pleasure is ineradicably mixed, frustration being part of every sexual life. The capacity for sexual pleasure is unevenly distributed, cannot be voluntarily acquired, and diminishes through no fault of its subject. If such a pleasure were an intrinsic benefit, benefit would in this case be independent of moral effort. Then again, sexual pleasures are not serious. Enjoyment of them is one of life's greatest recreations, but none of its business. And finally, sexual desire has the defects of its strengths. Before satisfaction, it is, at the least, distracting; in satisfaction, it "makes one little roome, an everywhere." Like psychosis, sexual desire turns us from "reality"—whether the real be God, social justice, children, or intellectual endeavor. This turning away is more than a social consequence of desire, though it is that. Lovers themselves feel that their sexual desires are separate from their "real" political, domestic, ambitious, social selves.

If the plaintiff is taken to argue that sensual pleasures are not peremptory benefits, he is probably right. We can still want a good deal and forego sexual pleasures. We often forego pleasure just because we want something incompatible with it, for example, a good marriage. We must distinguish between giving up some occasions for sexual pleasure and giving up sexual pleasure itself. When all circumstances of sexual pleasure seem to threaten a peremptory benefit, such as self-respect, then the hope and the possibility of sexual pleasure may be relinquished. Since sexual pleasure is such a great, though optional, benefit, its loss is a sad one.

In emphasizing the unsocial, private nature of sexual experiences, the plaintiff is emphasizing a morally important characteristic of them. But his case against desire, as I have sketched it, is surely overstated. The mixed, partly frustrated character of any desire is not particularly pronounced for sexual desire, which is in fact especially plastic, or adaptable to changes (provided perverse sex acts have not been ruled out). Inhibition, social deprivation, or disease make our sexual lives unpleasant, but that is because they interfere with sexual desire, not because the desire is by its nature frustrating. More than other well-known desires (for example, desire for knowledge, success, or power), sexual desire is simply and completely satisfied upon attaining its object. Partly for this reason, even if we are overtaken by desire during sexual experience, our sexual experiences do not overtake us. Lovers turn away from the world while loving, but return—sometimes all too easily—when loving is done. The moralist rightly perceives sexual pleasure as a recreation, and those who upon realizing its benefits make a business of its pursuit appear ludicrous. The capacity for recreation, however, is surely a benefit that any human being rightly hopes for who hopes for anything. Indeed, in present social and economic conditions we are more likely to lay waste our powers in work than in play. Thus, though priest, revolutionary, and parent are alike in fearing sexual pleasure, this fear should inspire us to psychological and sociological investigation of the fearing rather than to moral doubt about the benefit of sexual pleasure.

THE MORAL SIGNIFICANCE OF PERVERSION

What is the moral significance of the perversity of a sexual act? Next to none, so far as I can see. Though perverted sex may be "unnatural" both from an evolutionary and developmental perspective, there is no connection, inverse or correlative, between what is natural and what is good. Perverted sex is sometimes said to be less pleasurable than natural sex. We have little reason to believe that this claim is true and no clear idea of the kind of evidence on which it would be based. In any case, to condemn perverse acts for lack of pleasure is to recognize the worth of pleasure, not of naturalness.

There are many other claims about the nature and consequences of perversion. Some merely restate "scientific" facts in morally tinged terminology. Perverse acts are, by definition and according to psychiatric theory, "immature" and "abnormal," since natural sex acts are selected by criteria of "normal" sexual function and "normal" and "mature" psychological development. But there is no greater connection of virtue with maturity and normality than there is of virtue with nature. The elimination of a village by an invading army would be no less evil if it were the expression of controlled, normal, natural, and mature aggression.

Nagel claims that many perverted sex acts are incomplete, and in making his point, gives the most specific arguments that I have read for the inferiority of perverted sex. But as he points out, there is no reason to think an act consisting solely of oral-genital intercourse is incomplete; it is doubtful whether homosexual acts and acts of buggery are especially liable to be incomplete; and the incompleteness of sexual intercourse with animals is a relative matter depending upon their limited consciousness. And again, the alleged inferiority is not a consequence of perversion but of incompleteness, which can afflict natural sex as well.

Perverted acts might be thought to be inferior because they cannot result in children. Whatever the benefits and moral significance of the procreation and care of children (and I believe they are extensive and complicated), the virtue of proper care for children neither requires nor follows from biological parenthood. Even if it did, only a sexual life consisting solely of perverse acts rules out conception.

If perverted sex acts did rule out normal sex acts, if one were *either* perverted *or* natural, then certain kinds of sexual relations would be denied some perverts—relations that are benefits to those who enjoy them. It seems that sexual relations with the living and the human would be of greater benefit than those with the dead or with animals. But there is no reason to think that heterosexual relations are of greater benefit than homosexual ones. It might be that children can only be raised by heterosexual couples who perform an abundance of natural sex acts. If so (though it seems unlikely), perverts will be denied the happiness of parenthood. This would be an *indirect* consequence of perverted sex and might yield a moral dilemma: How is one to choose between the benefits of children and the benefits of more pleasurable, more complete sex acts?

Some perversions are immoral on independent grounds. Sadism is the obvious example, though sadism practiced with a consenting masochist is far less evil than other, more familiar forms of aggression. Voyeurism may seem immoral because, since it must be secret to be satisfying, it violates others' rights to privacy.[19] Various kinds of rape can constitute perversion if rape, rather than genital intercourse, is the aim of desire. Rape is seriously immoral, a vivid violation of respect for persons. Sometimes doubly perverse rape is doubly evil (the rape of a child), but in other cases (the rape of a pig) its evil is halved. In any case, though rape is always wrong, it is only perverse when raping becomes the aim and not the means of desire.

Someone can be dissuaded from acting on his perverse desires either from moral qualms or from social fears. Although there may be ample basis for the latter, I can find none for the former except the possible indirect loss of the benefits of child care. I am puzzled about this since reflective people who do not usually attempt to legislate the preferences of others think differently. There is no doubt that beliefs in these matters involve deep emotions that should be respected. But for those who do in fact have perverted desires, the first concern will be to satisfy them, not to divert or to understand them. For sexual pleasure is intrinsically a benefit, and complete sex acts, which depend upon expressing the desires one in fact has, are both beneficial and conducive to virtue. Therefore, barring extrinsic moral or social considerations, perverted sex acts are preferable to natural ones if the latter are less pleasurable or less complete.

THE MORAL SIGNIFICANCE OF COMPLETENESS

Complete sex consists in mutually embodied, mutually active, responsive desire. Embodiment, activity, and mutual responsiveness are instrumentally beneficial because they are conducive to our psychological well-being, which is an intrinsic benefit. The alleged pathological consequences of disembodiment are more specific and better documented than those of perversity.[20] To dissociate oneself from one's actual body, either by creating a delusory body or by rejecting the bodily, is to court a variety of ill effects, ranging from self-disgust to diseases of the will, to faulty mental development, to the destruction of a recognizable "self," and finally to madness. It is difficult to assess psychiatric claims outside their theoretical contexts, but in this case I believe that they are justified. Relative embodiment is a stable, *normal* condition that is not confined to cases of complete embodiment. But psychiatrists tell us that exceptional physical occasions of embodiment seem to be required in order to balance tendencies to reject or to falsify the body. Sexual acts are not the only such occasions, but they do provide an immersion of consciousness in the bodily, which is pleasurable and especially conducive to correcting experiences of shame and disgust that work toward disembodiment.

The mutual responsiveness of complete sex is also instrumentally beneficial. It satisfies a general desire to be recognized as a particular "real" person and to make a difference to other particular "real" people. The satisfaction of this desire in sexual experience is especially rewarding, its thwarting especially cruel. Vulnerability is increased in complete sex by the active desiring of the partners. When betrayal, or for that matter, tenderness or ecstasy, ensues, one cannot dissociate oneself from the desire with which one identified and out of which one acted. The psychic danger is real, as people who attempt to achieve a distance from their desires could tell us. But the cost of distance is as evident as its gains. Passivity in respect to one's own sexual desire not only limits sexual pleasure but, more seriously, limits the extent to which the experience of sexual pleasure can be included as an experience of a coherent person. With passivity comes a kind of irresponsibilty in which one can hide from one's desire, even from one's pleasure, "playing" seducer or victim, tease or savior. Active sexual desiring in complete sex acts affords an especially threatening but also especially happy occasion to relinquish these and similar roles. To the extent that the roles confuse and confound our intimate relations, the benefit from relinquishing them in our sexual acts, or the loss from adhering to them then, is especially poignant.

In addition to being beneficial, complete sex acts are morally superior for three reasons. They tend to resolve tensions fundamental to moral life; they are conducive to emotions that, if they become stable and dominant, are in turn conducive to the virtue of loving; and they involve a preeminently moral virtue—respect for persons.

In one of its aspects, morality is opposed to the private and untamed. Morality is "civilization," social and regulating; desire is "discontent" resisting the regulation. Obligation, rather than benefit, is the notion central to morality so conceived, and the virtues required of a moral person are directed to preserving right relations and social order. Both the insistence on natural sex and the encouragement of complete sex can be looked upon as attempts to make sexual desire more amenable to regulation. But whereas the regulation of perverted desires is extrinsic to them, those of completeness modify the desires themselves. The desiring sensual body that in our social lives we may laugh away or disown becomes our "self" and enters into a social relation. Narcissism and altruism are satisfied in complete sex acts in which one gives what one receives by receiving it. Social and private "selves" are unified in an act in which impersonal, spontaneous impulses govern an action that is responsive to a particular person. For this to be true we must surmount our social "roles" as well as our sexual "techniques," though we incorporate rather than surmount our social selves. We must also surmount regulations imposed in the name of naturalness if our desires are to be spontaneously expressed. Honestly spontaneous first love gives us back our private desiring selves while allowing us to see the desiring self of another. Mutually responding partners confirm each others' desires and declare them good. Such occasions, when we are "moral" without cost, help reconcile us to our moral being and to the usual mutual exclusion between our social and private lives.

The connection between sex and certain emotions—particularly love, jealousy, fear, and anger—is as evident as it is obscure. Complete sex acts seem more likely than incomplete pleasurable ones to lead toward affection and away from fear and anger, since any guilt and shame will be extrinsic to the act and meliorated by it. It is clear that we need not feel for someone any affection beyond that required (if any is) simply to participate with him in a complete sex act. However, it is equally clear that sexual pleasure, especially as experienced in complete sex acts, is conducive to many feelings—gratitude, tenderness, pride, appreciation, dependency, and others. These feelings magnify their object who occasioned them, making him unique among men. When these magnifying feelings become stable and habitual they are conducive to love—not universal love, of course, but love of a particular sexual partner. However, even "selfish" love is a virtue, a disposition to care for someone as her interests and demands would dictate. Neither the best sex nor the best love require each other, but they go together more often than reason would expect—often enough to count the virtue of loving as one of the rewards of the capacity for sexual pleasure exercised in complete sex acts.

It might be argued that the coincidence of sex acts and several valued emotions is a cultural matter. It is notoriously difficult to make judgments about the emotional and, particularly, the sexual lives of others, especially culturally alien others. There is, however, some anthropological evidence that at first glance relativizes the connection between good sex and valued emotion. For example, among the Manus of New Guinea, it seems that relations of affection and love are encouraged primarily among brother and sister, while easy familiarity, joking, and superficial sexual play is expected only between cross-cousins. Sexual intercourse is, however, forbidden between siblings and cross-cousins but required of married men and women, who are as apt to hate as to care for each other and often seem to consider each other strangers. It seems, however, that the Manus do not value or experience complete or even pleasurable sex. Both men and women are described as puritanical, and the sexual life of women seems blatantly unrewarding. Moreover, their emotional life is generally impoverished. This impoverishment, in conjunction with an unappreciated and unrewarding sexual life dissociated from love or affection, would argue for a connection between better sex and valued emotions. If, as Peter Winch suggests, cultures provide their members with particular possibilities of making sense of their lives, and thereby with possibilities of good and evil, the Manus might be said to deny themselves one possibility both of sense and of good—namely the coincidence of good sex and of affection and love. Other cultures, including our own, allow this possibility, whose realization is encouraged in varying degrees by particular groups and members of the culture.[21]

Finally, as Sartre has suggested, complete sex acts preserve a respect for persons. Each person remains conscious and responsible, a "subject" rather than a depersonalized, will-less, or manipulated "object." Each actively desires that the other likewise remain a "subject." Respect for persons is a central virtue when matters of justice and obligation are at issue. Insofar as we can speak of respect for persons in complete sex acts, there are different, often contrary requirements of respect. Respect for persons, typically and in sex acts, requires that *actual present* partners participate, partners whose desires are recognized and endorsed. Respect for persons typically requires taking a distance from both one's own demands and those of others. But in sex acts the demands of desire take over, and equal distance is replaced by mutual responsiveness. Respect typically requires refusing to treat another person merely as a means to fulfilling demands. In sex acts, another person is so clearly a means to satisfaction that she is always on the verge of becoming merely a means ("intercourse counterfeits masturbation"). In complete sex acts, instrumentality vanishes only because it is mutual and mutually desired. Respect requires encouraging, or at least protecting, the autonomy of another. In complete sex, autonomy of will is recruited by desire, and freedom from others is replaced by frank dependence on another person's desire. Again the respect consists in the reciprocity of desiring dependence, which bypasses rather than violates autonomy.

Despite the radical differences between respect for persons in the usual moral contexts and respect for persons in sex acts, it is not, I think, a mere play on words to talk of respect in the latter case. When, in any sort of intercourse, persons are respected, their desires are not only, in fair measure, fulfilled. In addition, their desires are active and determine, in fair measure, the form of intercourse and the manner and condition of desire's satisfaction. These conditions are not only met in sexual intercourse when it is characterized by completeness; they come close to defining completeness.

Sartre is not alone in believing that just because the condition of completeness involves respect for persons, complete sex is impossible. Completeness is surely threatened by pervasive tendencies to fantasy, to possessiveness, and to varieties of a sadomasochistic desire. But a complete sex act, as I see it, does not involve an heroic restraint on our sexual interpulses. Rather, a complete sex act is a normal mode of sexual activity expressing the natural structure and impulses of sexual desire.

While complete sex is morally superior because it involves respect for persons, incomplete sex acts do not necessarily involve immoral disrespect for persons. They may, depending upon the desires and expectations of the partners; but they may involve neither respect nor disrespect. Masturbation, for example, allows only the limited completeness of embodiment and often fails of that. But masturbation only rarely involves disrespect to anyone. Even the respect of the allegedly desirable sleeping woman may not be violated if she is unknowingly involved in a sex act. Disrespect, though likely, may be obviated by her sensibilities and expectations that she has previously expressed and her partner has understood. Sex acts provide one context in which respect for persons can be expressed. That context is important both because our sexual lives are of such importance to us and because they are so liable to injury because of the experience and the fear of the experience of disrespect. But many complete sex acts in which respect is maintained makes other casual and incomplete sex acts unthreatening. In this case a goodly number of swallows can make a summer.

In sum, then, complete sex acts are superior to incomplete ones. First, they are, whatever their effects, better than various kinds of incomplete sex acts because they involve a kind of "respect for persons" in acts that are otherwise prone to violation of respect for, and often to violence to, persons. Second, complete sex acts are good because they are good for us. They are conducive to some fairly clearly defined kinds of psychological well-being that are beneficial. They are conducive to moral well-being because they relieve tensions that arise in our attempts to be moral and because they encourage the development of particular virtues.

To say that complete sex acts are preferable to incomplete ones is not to court a new puritanism. There are many kinds and degrees of incompleteness. Incomplete sex acts may not involve a disrespect for persons. Complete sex acts only *tend* to be good for us, and the realization of these tendencies depends upon individual lives and circumstances of sexual activity. The proper object of sexual desire is sexual pleasure. It would be a foolish ambition indeed to limit one's sexual acts to those in which completeness was likely. Any sexual act that is pleasurable is prima facie good, though the more incomplete it is—the more private, essentially autoerotic, unresponsive, unembodied, passive, or imposed—the more likely it is to be harmful to someone.

ON SEXUAL MORALITY: CONCLUDING REMARKS

There are many questions we have neglected to consider because we have not been sufficiently attentive to the quality of sexual lives. For example, we know little about the ways of achieving better sex. When we must choose between inferior sex and abstinence, how and when will our choice of inferior sex damage our capacity for better sex? Does, for example, the repeated experience of controlled sexual disembodiment ("desire which takes over will take you too far") that we urge (or used to urge) on adolescents damage their capacity for complete sex? The answers to this and similar questions are not obvious, though unfounded opinions are always ready at hand.

Some of the traditional sexual vices might be condemned on the ground that they are inimical to better sex. Obscenity, or repeated public exposure to sexual acts, might impair our capacity for pleasure or for response to desire. Promiscuity might undercut the tendency of complete sex acts to promote emotions that magnify their object. Other of the traditional sexual vices are neither inimical nor conducive to better sex, but are condemned because of conflicting nonsexual benefits and obligations. For example, infidelity qua infidelity neither secures nor prevents better sex. The obligations of fidelity have many sources, one of which may be a past history of shared complete sex acts, a history that included promises of exclusive intimacy. Such past promises are as apt to conflict with as to accord with a current demand for better sex. I have said nothing about how such a conflict would be settled. I hope I have shown that where the possibility of better sex conflicts with obligations and other benefits, we have a *moral dilemma*, not just an occasion for moral self-discipline.

The pursuit of more pleasurable and more complete sex acts is, among many moral activities, distinguished not for its exigencies but for its rewards. Since our sexual lives are so important to us, and since, whatever our history and our hopes, we are sexual beings, this pursuit rightly engages our moral reflection. It should not be relegated to the immoral, nor to the "merely" prudent.

NOTES

1. An earlier version of this paper was published in *Moral Problems*, edited by James Rachels (New York: Harper & Row, 1971). I am grateful to many friends and students for their comments on the earlier version, especially to Bernard Gert, Evelyn Fox Keller, and James Rachels.

2. This may be a consequence of the tepidness of the English "pleasant." It would be better to speak of lust and its satisfaction if our suspicion of pleasure had not been written into that part of our language.

3. The example is from Sigmund Freud, *Three Essays on Sexuality*, standard ed., vol. 7 (London: Hogarth, 1963), p. 182. The concept of pleasure I urge here is narrower but also, I think, more useful than the popular one. It is a concept that, to paraphrase Wittgenstein, we (could) learn when we learn the language. The idea of paradigmatic uses and subsequent more-or-less-divergent, more-or-less-"normal" uses also is derived from Wittgenstein.

4. George Klein, "Freud's Two Theories of Sexuality," in L. Berger, ed., *Clinical-Cognitive Psychology: Models and Integrations* (Englewood Cliffs, N.J.: Prentice-Hall, 1969), pp. 131-81. This essay gives a clear idea of alternative psychological accounts of sexual pleasure.

5. Maurice Merleau-Ponty, *Phenomenology of Perception*, trans. Colin Smith (London: Routledge & Kegan Paul, 1962), p. 156.

6. See Kurt Vonnegut, Jr., "Welcome to the Monkey House," in *Welcome to the Monkey House* (New York: Dell, 1968), which concerns both the manipulation and the benefit of sexual pleasure.

7. Jean-Paul Sartre, *Being and Nothingness*, trans. Hazel E. Barnes (New York: Philosophical Library, 1956), p. 389.

8. Merleau-Ponty, *Phenomenology of Perception*, p. 167.

9. Thomas Nagel, "Sexual Perversion," *The Journal of Philosophy* 66, no. 1

(January 16, 1969): 13; herein, pp. 276. My original discussion of completeness was both greatly indebted to and confused by Nagel's. I have tried here to dispel some of the confusion.

10. W. T. Stace, "Solipsism," from *The Theory of Knowledge and Existence*; reprinted in Tillman, Berofsky, and O'Connor, eds. *Introductory Philosophy* (New York: Harper & Row, 1967), p. 113.

11. Denise Levertov, "Gone Away," in *O Taste and See* (New York: New Directions, 1962), p. 59. Copyright by Denise Levertov Goodman, New Directions Publishing Corporation, New York.

12. R. D. Laing, *The Divided Self* (Baltimore: Pelican Books, 1965), p. 69.

13. We need not become our bodies on such occasions. Pains, muscular feelings, and emotions can be reduced to mere "sensations" that may impinge on "me" but that I attempt to keep at a distance. Laing describes the case of a man who when beaten up felt that any damage to his body could not really hurt *him*. See *The Divided Self*, p. 68.

14. Nagel, "Sexual Perversion," p. 275. .

15. Jean-Paul Sartre, *Saint Genet* (New York: Braziller, 1963), p. 398; cited and translated by R. D. Laing, *Self and Others* (New York: Pantheon, 1969), pp. 39-40.

16. Ibid., p. 13.

17. Sartre, *Being and Nothingness*, p. 386.

18. See, in support of this point, Sigmund Freud, *Introductory Lectures on Psychoanalysis*, standard ed., vol. 26 (London: Hogarth, 1963), chaps. 20, 21.

19. I am indebted to Dr. Leo Goldberger for this example.

20. See, for example, R. D. Laing, *The Divided Self*; D. W. Winnicott, "Transitional Objects and Transitional Phenomena," *International Journal of Psychoanalysis* 34 (1953): 89-97; Paul Federn, *Ego Psychology and the Psychoses* (New York: Basic Books, 1952); Phyllis Greenacre, *Trauma, Growth, and Personality* (New York: International Universities Press, 1969); Paul Schilder, *The Image and Appearance of the Human Body* (New York: International Unversities Press, 1950); Moses Laufer, "Body Image and Masturbation in Adolescence," *The Psychoanalytic Study of the Child* 23 (1968): 114-46. Laing's work is most specific about both the nature and consequences of disembodiment, but the works cited, and others similar to them, give the clinical evidence upon which much of Laing's workd depends.

21. The evidence about the life of the Manus comes from Margaret Mead, *Growing Up in New Guinea* (Harmondsworth, Eng.: Penguin Books, 1942). Peter Winch's discussion can be found in his "Understanding a Primitive Society," *American Philosophical Quarterly* 1 (1964): 307-34.

Bernard H. Baumrin

Sexual Immorality Delineated

Human sexual interaction is essentially manipulative—physically, psychologically, emotionally, and even intellectually. On different occasions of such interaction or anticipated interaction, different weights, emphases, and significance will be given to these factors; so the analysis of their relative force in any given sexual interaction is exceedingly complicated. It will not be my task here to present even a general taxonomy or analysis of these factors (though this is where, in my view, the most fruitful discoveries will be made); rather I shall use this information only in order to delineate the realm of immoral sexual interaction, if there is one.

I start with the thesis that human sexual interaction is essentially manipulative for several reasons. (1) If one were to suppose that the Kantian dictum "never treat anyone as a means only but always as an end"[1] implies that one should never use anyone as a means and that manipulating another for one's own purpose is using another as a means, then every instance of sexual manipulation would be immoral; and that, it seems to me, would perhaps make every human sexual interaction immoral. There seem to me to be several weaknesses in this view, not the least of which is the fact that virtually no one believes the conclusion to be true—that is, that every human sexual interaction involving the manipulation of another for one's own (sexual) ends is immoral. Another perhaps not less important point is that Kant's dictum does not mean that one should never treat anyone in *any* respect as a means, but rather that one should never treat anyone in *every* respect as a means, or not as an end as well as a means. In this form the dictum might be true and useful; otherwise it is piously empty, for it bids us to refrain from the unavoidable.

I dwell on this point only because if there is any sexual immorality, one interpretation of Kant's view seems most straitaway to establish what it is—the manipulation of others for one's own ends. It seems to me that this must be wrong, since sex is manipulation, is using others as means to one's own ends, and I take it as indisputable that nothing that virtually everyone thinks is not immoral is in fact immoral.

(2) A second reason for beginning with the thesis that sex is essentially manipulative is that it eliminates, in gross, any number of quite silly views that espouse the mythology of perfect sexual harmony, of two minds (in the manner of *The Prophet*) conceptually indistinguishable, of two hearts beating as one, of two bodies locked together like bronze equestrian sculptures. It is not that I think these are merely rare occurrences and thus bad bases on which to erect theories and make recommendations; rather I think that they are impossible occurrences and that any theories that rest on or press for them must perforce be mistaken. Thus, I begin (as moralists sometimes do) by admitting the most damaging facts—for they are, in my view, facts—that any theory of sexual immorality must countenance, and then look about to see what is left. For this reason I expand a bit on what I consider the facts to be.

However inherently attractive, desirable, and satisfying to others we think we may be, so much of our thought and action shaped by such thought is concerned with enhancing these characteristics, with making them noticeable or perhaps even remarkable, that it is painfully clear that all of us think of ourselves often enough as awkward, ugly, repulsive, detestable, inept, and laughable to others. The primary point here is that we are frequently taking ourselves in hand, not leaving totally to the chance conjunction of emotional storms the success of our mating instincts. We do not (often) behave as statues sought for their inherent qualities—sexual interaction is a bundle of disparate activities that we try to manage, devoting to it a great deal of energy, foresight, and care. Even when hoping for the perfect spontaneous interaction we at least try to do what will not thwart it. We invite attention and manage what attention we attract. Often we do this ineptly and need to review our errors to understand from them what not to do in the future, and so sacrifice with advancing age and growing wisdom the possibility of the perfect spontaneous interaction. We change the focus of our desire to satisfaction or naturalness or pleasure or some other piece of the ideal sexual interaction that is promulgated in our sexual mythology. But all along from the primping and swaggering teenager to whatever age the reader is, memories of the management of one's encounters charm or horrify. Perhaps no one has ever had a perfectly spontaneous sexual interaction, but everyone has spoken to cajole, shifted eyes to charm, acquiesced to trick, clothed to attract, touched to try to thrill, waited for the moment, played on a known weakness, looked for a sign of one's initial success to move the game along. We use our own emotions sexually to change the emotions of others. We seek to know the inner psyche of our partners to enhance at least for ourselves our interaction with them; we want to know their physical responsiveness, their likes and dislikes, for use now or in the future. Who supposes that our interest in such information is scientific, medical, artistic, or philosophic? Who supposes that our interest in such information is sought by us solely to benefit our partner? Is it not patent that even if we wish to benefit a sexual partner, we seek such knowledge at least also for our own benefit, and possibly only for our own benefit.

There appears to be no plausible theory[2] on the basis of which we could justify the use of someone[3] sexually exclusively as a means. This fact does not merely imply that we should never so treat them; it also implies that to some extent we ought to treat them as non-means—that is, it is a positive duty of every sexual interaction that each person treat every other not merely as a means to the satisfaction of their own desires but as someone to whom one owes this positive duty and who has a right to expect implementation of it. This point may not seem to be altogether clear as stated; so I shall restate it in two other ways. First, if a person X has a particular duty D toward someone else Y, it is always appropriate to infer that Y has a right with respect to X that X fulfill D. X's duties to Y exist only if Y has rights; Y has rights against X only if X has duties to Y. A negative duty of X's toward Y implies that Y has a right to expect X not to do whatever the duty forbids; a positive duty of X's toward Y implies that Y has a right to expect X to do whatever the duty calls for.

But not all apparently negative duties are genuinely negative. While I have a genuinely negative duty not to kill anyone, Y has only a right to expect me to engage in behavior that avoids the likelihood of my killing him. He does not have the right to expect me to do this in any particular way, or even in cognizance of his existence. I may do it quite well by avoiding him. But in sexual interaction my behavior involves interaction with another, and I cannot engage in the action in a purely negative way. I am, as it were, constrained to act with someone, and thus all the rights that that person has and all the duties that I have toward that person coexist during that interaction. All the negative duties may be dischargeable by not infringing the other's rights, but the positive duties cannot be satisfied without some other-directed behavior being done that the other has a right to expect. My duty is only apparently negative since my choosing to interact sexually at all creates rights in the other, just as their choosing to so interact creates rights in me.

The second way of putting the point is this: If I have a duty in a sexual interaction to treat Y as other than a non-means, then the class of such non-means treatment is a class of behaviors permissible to me; Y has a right to expect that at least some of my behavior will come from this class, and the implementation by me of at least one such behavior is a positive duty that I have toward **Y**. My failure to perform or appear to try to perform some behavior in the class may properly be regarded by **Y** as a failure to perform my duty, or a violation of **Y**'s rights.

Let me sum up this point by saying that the voluntary choices by **X** and **Y** to engage in a sexual interaction creates in both X and Y new positive duties and rights, and failure by either to do that which fulfills the former violates the latter and is immoral.

But what exactly is this class of permissible treatment of another, some of which each person has a duty to do and some of which each has a right to expect. The class in question has only the following criteria to delineate it thus far: (1) the persons involved must in some positive respect treat each other as non-means; (2) each person properly expects some such treatment; (3) that expectation is based on the apparently voluntary choice of the other to engage in this kind of activity, that is, sexual interaction.

While these factors delineate the class of permissible sexual treatment, they do not do so with sufficient precision, since they exist as well in other than sexual contexts. They can be found in normal contractual situations, for example, undertaking to have someone repair one's car or ordering a meal from a waiter. Nor would it be sufficient merely *to say* that these are the crucial factors in *sexual* situations, since that would leave "sexual" unspecified and thus fail to tell us anything more about what creates specifically sexual rights and duties. What we need to specify for sexual interactions are just those additional factors that differentiate sexual interactions from other similar interpersonal interactions. Those additional factors are: (4) behavior reasonably apprehendable by one person as being intended by another to form an offer of some form or level of sexual interaction creates in the initiating agent a duty to perform in that form or at that level should the offer be explicitly or implicitly accepted; (5) accordingly, the apparent acceptance of such an offer creates a duty toward the initiating agent to perform at least at the behavioral level or in the behavioral form of the acceptance (not necessarily in the form or at the level of the offer).

Thus the initiating agent creates a right in the other properly to accept the offered performance, if the initiative is accepted without modification.

The accepting party may accept, but only with modification, which therefore might entirely discharge the offering party of any further duty.

There is, however, one further factor that is of central importance. The initiating agent, through his or her behavior, implicitly offers the following proposal (this holds even if there are simultaneous offers): (6) *I wish to use you as an instrument for my sexual purposes and therefore undertake to make myself the instrument of your sexual purposes to the extent that you accept my proposal.* Thus, on this view, the crucial element in creating specifically sexual rights and duties is the desire to use another as a means for a certain kind of end and the willingness to offer oneself to that person as an inducement to form a voluntary arrangement. What one is offering is to make oneself the other's means for the satisfaction of their desires. Otherwise one would in fact not be making an offer at all, or at least not a sexual one, since one would merely be behaving in a peculiar way or forcing one's attentions on the other. In either case, the immorality of one's behavior would be obvious. Consider the following examples: (1) A approaches B and suggests charmingly that due to B's attractive characteristics, A would like to make love to B. In response, B invites A to B's home. On arrival A shakes B's hand and leaves. (2) C approaches B and suggests that due to B's attractive characteristics C would like to make love to B. B says no. C becomes more demonstrative. B attempts to leave. C locks the door and proceeds to shower B with attention, while B spends the evening trying to extricate himself. (3) The particulars are the same as in case 1 except that on arriving at B's home B shakes A's hand and goes inside alone.

I think it is clear that the six factors I have set down are interrelated, and although they provide a clear enough test of sexual immorality of the grosser sorts, it is not altogether clear what their force is on a more intimate level. It is to this subject that I now turn.

If it is immoral to propose to use someone else as a sexual instrument without at the same time being prepared to be used by them as their instrument, then it is also immoral to use someone else as a sexual instrument without permitting oneself to be so used. While the immorality of the unilateral proposal is derived from intending to use someone only as a means, the immorality of the behavior is derived from the actual depersonalization of the other.

To illustrate, let us suppose that A wishes to engage in a specific kind of sexual activity and manipulates B, for example, emotionally and physically, to that end. All along, B anticipates the later occurrence of another kind of sexual activity that B wants, and B's wishes are known all along by A; but A nevertheless avoids doing what B wants. On the view stated above, A's behavior is immoral. It makes no difference that A loves B in some way (otherwise quite satisfactory); if A, knowing what B wishes, nevertheless knowingly fails to do what B wishes and B has done what A wished, then A is immoral. This is so because A has failed to be what he has undertaken to be—namely, an instrument of B's satisfaction.

A would of course not be immoral (that is, would not have violated B's rights) if A had *tried* to do what A reasonably believed B wished; but if A did not try, then A did not discharge the duty owed to B. A has no right to use B without B's having a right to use A; therefore, if A will not let B use A, then to that extent A previously had no right to use B.

Now, one might object that the situations of A and B are not parallel since A manipulated B and A stands ready to be manipulated but is not ready to volunteer. This objection (which arises domestically not infrequently) rests on a confusion: if A knows that B wishes A to do Q and Q is the kind of behavior that must be volunteered by A, then what A must do in order to be B's instrument is Q; for if B is required to manipulate A to engage in the sexual acts included in Q, it is no longer Q that A will do, because part of the definition of Q is that it emanates voluntarily from A. Thus, if A knows that B wishes Q and B knows that A wishes R, then if B engages in R, A is obliged to do Q.

We might speculate that one who never or rarely initiates sexual activity may simply not wish to create duties for himself or rights in others. There might be some psychological explanatory power in such an analysis of the origin of sexual passivity, frigidity, and impotence.

The central point is that if one offers to be used within certain bounds, then if one's offer is accepted, the other person determines what use is to be made of one within those bounds. If one does not intend to be used, one is neither genuinely making nor accepting an offer of sexual interaction, despite the appearances. One might, however, be morally bound anyway to perform as expected because the appearances seemed to create an offer or an acceptance, and might thus put one under a duty to satisfy the good-faith expectations of the other created by one's own behavior. This arises, for example, when one has created the appearances deliberately while knowing more or less how they would be interpreted.

It is, of course, perfectly permissible for one who accepts an offer not to wish to use another. This is not an uncommon occurrence, and I think it springs in part from the frequent failure to realize that rights are created by interpersonal transactions, and not just the ones we have been discussing. Probably part of this unconsciousness of one's rights (as well as of one's duties) comes from the now quite ancient tradition of considering sexual interaction as a romance between feelings, where feelings have been elevated to a sacrosanct position. Thus it appears that many believe that if one's positive feelings change, one is relieved of the burden of responding to overtures based on the now mistaken belief that those positive feelings still exist. Similarly, some believe that if one performs under the influence of a feeling, one's behavior is excusable, as well as explainable. What is especially implausible about views of this sort is that no analysis has as yet been made of feeling that shows it to be of a higher value than any other psychological entity; nor has any analysis been made that shows that behavior caused by feeling has any comparatively privileged position that makes it immune from praise or blame. Of course one might argue that behavior caused by feeling is uncontrollable; but why should that fact, if indeed it is one, make such behavior more valuable than merely rational or calculative or habitual behavior. One can well understand someone's being driven by his feelings to do something he might otherwise not do; but surely there is nothing specially laudable or natural in such action. The intellectual picture of sexuality that we have had for quite some time applauds the natural, the pastoral, the uninhibited, the silent communion of souls; it treats the contrived, the cultured, the controlled, and the merely carnal as contemptible. This legacy of romanticism has endured in our thinking about sex, while all of the intellectual paraphernalia that supported it has long since been swept away by clear thinking and rational criticism.

One might be curious to see what this analysis has to say about the immorality of such sexual interactions as adultery, incest, and rape. Ordinary rape is easily enough dealt with, since its immorality stems from the lack of voluntary participation of one of the parties, thus giving the other no rights and making the rapist's behavior a violation of other rights of the involuntary participant. There are, however, two kinds of rape cases that are more complicated. First, there is the case where the rapist has a good-faith belief that he has received an offer of sexual interaction and views his behavior as the implementation of his acceptance. Such cases depend for their resolution on a careful analysis of the actual behavior of the person raped and what reasonable people would have interpreted it to mean (this problem will be dealt with in more detail later).

Second, there is the possible case of a person who believes that (1) there is a class of persons who can achieve sexual fulfillment only if raped, that (2) he is a person gifted in perceiving who these persons are, and that (3) his activities in this regard are a social duty (I suppose he is also a utilitarian). This case is complicated because number 1 seems true and number 3 is self-supporting; so only number 2 is open to criticism. But if he believes that he is gifted in perceiving those persons who can achieve sexual fulfillment only if raped, then it may be the case that we cannot show him that he is wrong. Thus, if he rapes someone not in the class in question, he is doing both what he believes to be his duty and something immoral. I think there are ways of handling this apparent difficulty, but since it is not especially a problem for my view, I leave it here unresolved.

Adultery, it seems to me, presents no special problems since its immorality, *when* it is immoral qua adultery, springs from the violation by one or more parties of a prior agreement with some other person(s) to preserve some degree of exclusive access. Thus in adultery the very fact of the interaction's existence might be immoral even though no part of the interaction is itself immoral.

There seems to be nothing sexually immoral about incest that is not accounted for by the immorality that springs, on one hand, from adultery and, on the other, from constructive (or statutory) rape. This implies that adult-sibling incest is not immoral and that incest is in general not sexually immoral, even though such interactions might be immoral on other grounds.

When I began to rethink this subject some years ago I approached it from an entirely different direction and uncovered for myself a wealth of complications. In deference to those complications, I have here almost entirely omitted even tangential reference to the domain of directive communication (except in our discussion of rape). However, something needs to be said of it, even if all too schematically. A good deal of the communication of offer, acceptance, counteroffer, scope, seriousness, and detail in sexual transactions occurs by means of customary and special-convention gestures—that is, by behavior whose primary purpose is to transmit information. Gestural communication with or without attendant verbal communication is used in preference to mere verbal communication for a wide variety of purposes and for different sorts of reasons. One of the most interesting is that gestures are by nature ambiguous, both as to what the user intends and the interpreter understands. When used in sexual transactions (as they very often are), they court misunderstanding. Nevertheless, they also preserve the possibility of innovation, of a new agreement, of new levels of behavior. They also permit the avoidance of embarrassments and permit us to overcome our mistakes almost as quickly as we make them. In short, they facilitate the management of our interpersonal relations with less friction, less recrimination, and less pain than if we were relegated to the use only of language stripped of nonverbal behavior.

But it should be remembered as well that gestures and gesturally enriched talk easily lends itself to misperception, and misperception lends itself to disappointment. It is here that we so often fail each other without being immoral; for our duty is to act on what we perceive the other to wish, and the other has only a right to expect us to act on what we perceive and not on what he or she wishes in fact. Our perceptions create the particular character of our duties; thus we may do what we in good faith believe is required of us without doing what is wished. Such sexual failure stems from miscommunication and not immorality.

AN APPENDIX ON UTILITARIANISM AND EGOISM

I think it is obvious that sexually self-interested behavior is not always immoral; so clearly the question is whether it is ever immoral and, if so, when and why. One might begin by seeing whether any clear direction can be given by any standard popular ethical theory. Whatever the merits of utilitarianism are, this is one area where, if there are merits, they are quite obscure. Certainly a sexual interaction might increase the sum total of pleasure or happiness or even good in the world, but certainly not for very many people, and not necessarily for any. And the long-range consequences of the interaction for increasing pleasure, happiness, or good are unprojectible. But even were these difficulties easily set to rest, sexual interaction is not so clearly more beneficial for mankind than is sexual abstinence, unless one were constrained to argue that it has to be engaged in so as to provide future generations who would enjoy a balance of a valued property over a disvalued property. (If it is believed that the future will in fact be worse than the past in regard to the property in question, then the argument would have the opposite thrust—that is, that one should discourage the production of future generations.) Finally, and perhaps most importantly, ought one to engage in sexual interactions (acts of class S) in order to increase the amount of the valued property? Is it in fact a moral duty to do acts of the class S, and if so, ought one do them to increase the amount of the valued property, or just do them simply? This question is of some importance, for it must be asked not only of utilitarians. Suppose that S represents the class of all sexual acts. Then, whether or not one wishes finally to say some S ought not be done, one must ask whether some S ought to be done. That is, are some sexual acts morally obligatory? Utilitarianism, to its credit, does seem to imply that S's that would increase the balance of pleasure over pain (P/p) in the world should be done, and if the opportunity is available, one should do that S that would have this result (in fact one should do that S that *maximizes* this result). But the question remains for utilitarians: Should one do what one does *in order to* increase the balance of P/p? Is increasing P/p the criterion for S's obligatoriness and also the reason why one ought to do S? Would one be immoral for doing S for some other reason? Would sexual immorality for a utilitarian be doing what one ought, but not for the reason one ought, or would it be merely not doing what one ought? The latter answer supposes that the agent not only knows that he ought to do S, but also that he does not think on utilitarian grounds that he ought to do some other act, T. Suppose he believes (on utilitarian grounds) that T will increase the balance of P/p more than S will. Then (on utilitarian grounds) he should do T, unless S will in fact increase the balance more than T. But if he believes T will increase the balance of P/p more than S will he should do T anyway, since he believes (on utilitarian grounds) that S is not as obligatory as T.

Now suppose he believes (on utilitarian grounds) he ought to do S; then it follows that he must believe that S will enhance the balance of P/p more than T. Therefore, if he ought to do S, then he ought to do S *because* it will enhance P/p, and he cannot be said to have a moral duty to do S unless he first determines that S will enhance P/p. If he does S without making this prior determination, he cannot know that doing S is his moral duty; and so he cannot be doing S, if he then does it because it is his moral duty.

It is clear, then, that if utilitarianism is used to support the view that some acts of the class S ought to be done, it is committed to the view that they must be done from the motive to increase the balance of the desired property over its contrary. If this conclusion is correct, then both utilitarianism and Kantianism are pretty much in the same canoe—namely, they share the view that all sexual acts, if they ought to be done, ought to be done from the belief that it is one's duty to do them. And further, any such act not so done might for that very reason be immoral.

I have dwelt on this small point because it seems to me that besides being counterintuitive, it is inconsistent with the view that the manipulative acts I cited at the beginning are not always immoral. This, I think, accounts in part for the fact that neither utilitarians nor Kantians seem to have had much to say about human sexual interaction. They have thought that by sweeping all human activity together they can deal neatly with sex in the same package as lying, assault, and the distribution of bonbons. But this is quite wrong. One does not primp, swagger, wink, cajole, or importune out of duty, nor for the general production in the long or short run of an enhanced balance of P/p; and it is not obviously immoral to do so. It is not obvious that it is immoral to act as we do thoughtlessly, ineptly or irrelevantly; but it is just as obvious that a lightly considered provocative wink whose principal effect is to create pained jealously in another is probably immoral for both utilitarians and Kantians, and either we are much more evil than we think, or these views are just wrong.

Are we then driven at last into the waiting embrace of egoism? Is the final arbitration of sexual morality to be found in a principle that bids us to act only for the enhancement of what we believe to be what we want? Or, put differently, is there nothing sexually immoral save what hinders or thwarts our reaching what we perceive to be what we desire? Versions of an egoistic sexual morality are not difficult to state, but however stated, they seem open to a flaw that militates against their plausibility. That flaw arises from the fact that often (though perhaps not always) sexual gratification, satisfaction, enjoyment, pleasure, and success involves the cooperation (sometimes even the enthusiastic cooperation) of others. Unlike any number of other characteristically moral situations, it is difficult to envision sexual partners as merely passive recipients or victims of our behavior —which we can easily do with, for example, lying, killing, being kind, or being charitable.

In order to have that cooperation that seems desirable (perhaps even necessary), one cannot always do what one desires to do, for fear of alienating the other or of reducing or eliminating the desired cooperation. Whether one then does other than one would dissemblingly (or insincerely) or in a genuine attempt to encourage the desired cooperation, one's behavior is being determined as much by what one perceives the other to wish or desire—or at least not be displeased with—as by what one genuinely desires to do. Thus the egoist (as anyone else similarly situated) is often constrained to behave in accordance with the desires of others in order to try to fulfill his own desires. On his own principles, an immoral act of his would be to do that which he perceives to be counterproductive to fulfilling his goals, and anything offensive to the other might thus be immoral.[4] Thus the only acts that serve self are those that are accepted by the other as serving self as well. The egoist in sex, then, gains little from his or her egoism, for here, as perhaps elsewhere as well, it is not the individual himself who determines what is moral or immoral for him to do, but others who determine it for him. And, of course, they may make that determination on principles quite alien to egoism.

So my criticism of egoism in regard to sexual morality is not that what serves only self is immoral because it is like a kind of theft or deceit, where the services of another are gained by a dissembling larceny; rather, my criticism is that the egoist cannot serve self successfully without serving others successfully. Thus his moral theory does not serve at all as a guide for action, nor even as much of a guide for moral criticism. In short, my view is that whatever the other merits of egoism might be, in sexual matters, it is largely, perhaps entirely, irrelevant.

NOTES

1. "Act so that you treat humanity, whether in your own person or in that of another, always as an end and never as a means only." Kant, *Grundlegung*, IV, p.

429; translated as *Foundations of the Metaphysics of Morals,* L. W. Beck, trans. (Indianapolis, Ind.: Library of Liberal Arts Press), p. 87.

2. The arguments for this conclusion are set out in an appendix to this article, where the two most popular kinds of moral theory, utilitarianism and egoism, are analyzed.

3. I exclude here dead people, animals, and objects of voyeurism, on the theory that we are talking about human sexual interaction and not merely the exercise of one's genitalia or imagination.

4. Cf. Aristotle E.N. IX, 1, 1164a 5-15; IX, 8, 1165b 1-10.

PORNOGRAPHY AND CENSORSHIP

Ann Garry

Pornography and Respect for Women

Pornography, like rape, is a male invention, designed to dehumanize women, to reduce the female to an object of sexual access, not to free sensuality from moralistic or parental inhibition . . . Pornography is the undiluted essence of anti-female propaganda.

Susan Brownmiller, AGAINST OUR WILL: MEN, WOMEN AND RAPE[1]

It is often asserted that a distinguishing characteristic of sexually explicit material is the degrading and demeaning portrayal of the role and status of the human female. It has been argued that erotic materials describe the female as a mere sexual object to be exploited and manipulated sexually .... A recent survey shows that 41 percent of American males and 46 percent of the females believe that "sexual materials lead people to lose respect for women."... Recent experiments suggest that such fears are probably unwarranted.

Presidential Commission on Obscenity and Pornography[2]

The kind of apparent conflict illustrated in these passages is easy to find in one's own thinking as well. For example, I have been inclined to think that pornography is innocuous and to dismiss traditional "moral" arguments for censoring it because many such arguments rest on an assumption I do not share—that sex is an evil to be controlled. At the same time I believe that it is wrong to exploit or degrade human beings, particularly women and others who are especially susceptible. So if pornography degrades human beings, then even if I would oppose its censorship I surely cannot find it morally innocuous.

This article first appeared in *Social Theory and Practice*, 4 (Summer 1978): 395-42. It is reprinted here by permission of the author, with minor revisions, as it appeared in *Philosophy and Women*, edited by Sharon Bishop and Marjorie Weinzweig (Belmont, CA: Wadsworth, 1979).

In an attempt to resolve this apparent conflict I discuss three questions: Does pornography degrade (or exploit or dehumanize) human beings? If so, does it degrade women in ways or to an extent that it does not degrade men? If so, must pornography degrade women, as Brownmiller thinks, or could genuinely innocuous, nonsexist pornography exist? Although much current pornography does degrade women, I will argue that it is possible to have nondegrading, nonsexist pornography. However, this possibility rests on our making certain fundamental changes in our conceptions of sex and sex roles.

I

First, some preliminary remarks: Many people now avoid using 'pornography' as a descriptive term and reserve 'obscenity' for use in legal contexts. Because 'pornography' is thought to be a judgmental word, it is replaced by 'explicit sexual material,' 'sexually oriented materials,' 'erotica,' and so on.[3] I use 'pornography' to label those explicit sexual materials intended to arouse the reader or viewer sexually. I seriously doubt whether there is a clearly defined class of cases that fits my characterization of pornography. This does not bother me, for I am interested here in obvious cases that would be uncontroversially pornographic—the worst, least artistic kind. The pornography I discuss is that which, taken as a whole, lacks "serious literary, artistic, political, or scientific merit."[4] I often use pornographic films as examples because they generate more concern today than do books or magazines.

What interests me is not whether pornography should be censored but whether one can object to it on moral grounds. The only moral ground I consider is whether pornography degrades people; obviously, other possible grounds exist, but I find this one to be the most plausible.[5] Of the many kinds of degradation and exploitation possible in the production of pornography, I focus only on the content of the pornographic work. I exclude from this discussion (i) the ways in which pornographic film makers might exploit people in making a film, distributing it, and charging too much to see it; (ii) the likelihood that actors, actresses, or technicians will be exploited, underpaid, or made to lose self-respect or self-esteem; and (iii) the exploitation and degradation surrounding the prostitution and crime that often accompany urban centers of pornography.[6] I want to determine whether pornography shows (expresses) and commends behavior or attitudes that exploit or degrade people. For example, if a pornographic film conveys that raping a woman is acceptable, then the content is degrading to women and might be called morally objectionable. Morally objectionable content is not peculiar to pornography; it can also be found in nonpornographic books, films, advertisements, and so on. The question is whether morally objectionable content is necessary to pornography.

II

The argument I will consider is that pornography is morally objectionable, whether or not it leads people to show disrespect for women, because pornography itself exemplifies and recommends behavior that violates the moral principle to respect persons. The content of pornography is what one objects to. It treats women as mere sex objects "to be exploited and manipulated" and degrades the role and status of women. In order to evaluate this argument, I will first clarify what it would mean for pornography itself to treat someone as a sex object in a degrading manner. I will then deal with three issues central to the discussion of pornography and respect for women: how "losing respect" for a woman is connected with treating her as a sex object; what is wrong with treating someone as a sex object; and why it is worse to treat women rather than men as sex objects. I will argue that the current content of pornography sometimes violates the moral principle to respect persons. Then, in Part IV of this paper, I will suggest that pornography need not violate this principle if certain fundamental changes were to occur in attitudes about sex.

To many people, including Brownmiller and some other feminists, it appears to be an obvious truth that pornography treats people, especially women, as sex objects in a degrading manner. And if we omit "in a degrading manner," the statement seems hard to dispute: How could pornography *not* treat people as sex objects?

First, is it permissible to say that either the content of pornography or pornography itself degrades people or treats people as sex objects? It is not difficult to find examples of degrading content in which women are treated as sex objects. Some pornographic films convey the message that all women really want to be raped, that their resisting struggle is not to be believed. By portraying women in this manner, the content of the movie degrades women. Degrading women is morally objectionable. While seeing the movie need not cause anyone to imitate the behavior shown, we can call the content degrading to women because of the character of the behavior and attitudes it recommends. The same kind of point can be made about films (or books or TV commericals) with other kinds of degrading, thus morally objectionable, content—for example, racist messages.[7]

The next step in the argument is to infer that, because the content or message of pornography is morally objectionable, we can call pornography itself morally objectionable. Support for this step can be found in an analogy. If a person takes every opportunity to recommend that men rape women, we would think not only that his recommendation is immoral but that he is immoral too. In the case of pornography, the objection to making an inference from recommended behavior to the person who recommends is that we ascribe predicates such as "immoral" differently to people than to films or books. A film vehicle for an objectionable message is still an object independent of its message, its director, its producer, those who act in it, and those who respond to it. Hence one cannot make an unsupported inference from "the content of the film is morally objectionable" to "the film is morally objectionable." Because the central points in this paper do not depend on whether pornography itself (in addition to its content) is morally objectionable, I will not try to support this inference. (The question about the relation of content to the work itself is, of course, extremely interesting; but in part because I cannot decide which side of the argument is more persuasive, I will pass.[8]) Certainly one appropriate way to evaluate pornography is in terms of the moral features of its content. If a pornographic film exemplifies and recommends morally objectionable attitudes or behavior, then its content is morally objectionable.

Let us now turn to the first of our three questions about respect and sex objects: What is the connection between losing respect for a woman and treating her as a sex object? Some people who have lived through the era in which women were taught to worry about men "losing respect" for them if they engaged in sex in inappropriate circumstances find it troublesome (or at least amusing) that feminists—supposedly "liberated" women—are outraged at being treated as sex objects, either by pornography or in any other way. The apparent alignment between feminists and traditionally "proper" women need not surprise us when we look at it more closely.

The "respect" that men have traditionally believed they have for women—hence a respect they can lose—is not a general respect for persons as autonomous beings; nor is it respect that is earned because of one's personal merits or achievements. It is respect that is an outgrowth of the "double standard." Women are to be respected because they are more pure, delicate, and fragile than men, have more refined sensibilities, and so on. Because some women clearly do not have these qualities, thus do not deserve respect, women must be divided into two groups—the good ones on the pedestal and the bad ones who have fallen from it.

One's mother, grandmother, Sunday School teacher, and usually one's wife are "good" women. The appropriate behavior by which to express respect for good women would be, for example, not swearing or telling dirty jokes in front of them, giving them seats on buses, and other "chivalrous" acts. This kind of "respect" for good women is the same sort that adolescent boys in the back seats of cars used to "promise" not to lose. Note that men define, display, and lose this kind of respect. If women lose respect for women, it is not typically a loss of respect for (other) women as a class but a loss of self-respect.

It has now become commonplace to acknowledge that, although a place on the pedestal might have advantages over a place in the "gutter" beneath it, a place on the pedestal is not at all equal to the place occupied by other people (i.e., men). "Respect" for those on the pedestal was not respect for whole, full-fledged people but for a special class of inferior beings.

If a person makes two traditional assumptions—that (at least some) sex is dirty and that women fall into two classes, good and bad—it is easy to see how that person might think that pornography could lead people to lose respect for women or that pornography is itself disrespectful to women.[9] Pornography describes or shows women engaging in activities inappropriate for good women to engage in—or at least inappropriate for them to be seen by strangers engaging in. If one sees these women as symbolic representatives of all women, then all women fall from grace with these women. This fall is possible, I believe, because the traditional "respect" that men have had for women is not genuine, wholehearted respect for full-fledged human beings but half-hearted respect for lesser beings, some of whom they feel the need to glorify and purify.[10] It is easy to fall from a pedestal. Can we imagine 41 percent of men and 46 percent of women answering "yes" to the question, "Do movies showing men engaging in violent acts lead people to lose respect for men?"?

Two interesting asymmetries appear. The first is that losing respect for men as a class (men with power, typically Anglo men) is more difficult than losing respect for women or ethnic minorities as a class. Anglo men whose behavior warrants disrespect are more likely to be seen as exceptional cases than are women or minorities (whose "transgressions" may be far less serious). Think of the following: women are temptresses; Blacks cheat the welfare system; Italians are gangsters; but the men of the Nixon administration are exceptions—Anglo men as a class did not lose respect because of Watergate and related scandals.

The second asymmetry concerns the active and passive roles of the sexes. Men are seen in the active role. If men lose respect for women because of something "evil" done by women (such as appearing in pornography), the fear is that men will then do harm to women—not that women will do harm to men. Whereas if women lose respect for male politicians because of Watergate, the fear is still that male politicians will do harm, not that women will do harm to male politicians. This asymmetry might be a result of one way in which our society thinks of sex as bad—as harm that men do to women (or to the person playing a female role, as in a homosexual rape). Robert Baker calls attention to this point in '"Pricks' and 'Chicks': A Plea for 'Persons'."[11] Our slang words for sexual intercourse—'fuck,' 'screw,' or older words such as 'take' or 'have'—not only can mean harm but have traditionally taken a male subject and a female object. The active male screws (harms) the passive female. A "bad" woman only tempts men to hurt her further.

It is easy to understand why one's proper grandmother would not want men to see pornography or lose respect for women. But feminists reject these "proper" assumptions: good and bad classes of women do not exist; and sex is not dirty (though many people believe it is). Why then are feminists angry at the treatment of women as sex objects, and why are some feminists opposed to pornography?

The answer is that feminists as well as proper grandparents are concerned with respect. However, there are differences. A feminist's distinction between treating a woman as a full-fledged person and treating her as merely a sex object does not correspond to the good-bad woman distinction. In the latter distinction, "good" and "bad" are properties applicable to groups of women. In the feminist view, all women are full-fledged people—some, however, are treated as sex objects and perhaps think of themselves as sex objects. A further difference is that, although "bad" women correspond to those thought to deserve treatment as sex objects, good women have not corresponded to full-fledged people; only men have been full-fledged people. Given the feminist's distinction, she has no difficulty whatever in saying that pornography treats women as sex objects, not as full-fledged people. She can morally object to pornography or anything else that treats women as sex objects.

One might wonder whether any objection to treatment as a sex object implies that the person objecting still believes, deep down, that sex is dirty. I don't think so. Several other possibilities emerge. First, even if I believe intellectually and emotionally that sex is healthy, I might object to being treated *only* as a sex object. In the same spirit, I would object to being treated *only* as a maker of chocolate chip cookies or *only* as a tennis partner, because only one of my talents is being valued. Second, perhaps I feel that sex is healthy, but it is apparent to me that you think sex is dirty; so I don't want you to treat me as a sex object. Third, being treated as any kind of object, not just as a sex object, is unappealing. I would rather be a partner (sexual or otherwise) than an object. Fourth, and more plausible than the first three possibilities, is Robert Baker's view mentioned above. Both (i) our traditional double standard of sexual behavior for men and women and (ii) the linguistic evidence that we connect the concept of sex with the concept of harm point to what is wrong with treating women as sex objects. As I said earlier, 'fuck' and 'screw', in their traditional uses, have taken a male subject, a female object, and have had at least two meanings: harm and have sexual intercourse with. (In addition, a prick is a man who harms people ruthlessly; and a motherfucker is so low that he would do something very harmful to his own dear mother.)[12] Because in our culture we connect sex with harm that men do to women, and because we think of the female role in sex as that of harmed object, we can see that to treat a woman as a sex object is automatically to treat her as less than fully human. To say this does not imply that no healthy sexual relationships exist; nor does it say anything about individual men's conscious intentions to degrade women by desiring them sexually (though no doubt some men have these intentions). It is merely to make a point about the concepts embodied in our language.

Psychoanalytic support for the connection between sex and harm comes from Robert J. Stoller. Stoller thinks that sexual excitement is linked with a wish to harm someone (and with at least a whisper of hostility). The key process of sexual excitement can be seen as dehumanization (fetishization) in fantasy of the desired person. He speculates that this is true in some degree of everyone, both men and women, with "normal" or "perverted" activities and fantasies.[13]

Thinking of sex objects as harmed objects enables us to explain some of the first three reasons why one wouldn't want to be treated as a sex object: (1) I may object to being treated only as a tennis partner, but being a tennis partner is not connected in our culture with being a harmed object; and (2) I may not think that sex is dirty and that I would be a harmed object; I may not know what your view is; but what bothers me is that this is the view embodied in our language and culture.

Awareness of the connection between sex and harm helps explain other interesting points. Women are angry about being treated as sex objects in situations or roles in which they do not intend to be regarded in that manner—for example, while serving on a committee or attending a discussion. It is not merely that a sexual role is inappropriate for the circumstances; it is thought to be a less fully human role than the one in which they intended to function.

Finally, the sex-harm connection makes clear why it is worse to treat women as sex objects than to treat men as sex objects, and why assume the role of "harmed object" in sex; for men have the self-concept of sexual agents, not of passive objects. This is also related to my earlier point concerning the difference in the solidity of respect for men and for women; respect for women is more fragile. Despite exceptions, it is generally harder for people to degrade men, either sexually or non-sexually, than to degrade women. Men and women have grown up with different patterns of self-respect and expectations regarding the extent to which they deserve and will receive respect or degradation. The man who doesn't understand why women do not want to be treated as sex objects (because he'd sure like to be) would not think of himself as being harmed by that treatment; a woman might.[14] Pornography, probably more than any other contemporary institution, succeeds in treating men as sex objects.

Having seen that the connection between sex and harm helps explain both what is wrong with treating someone as a sex object and why it is worse to treat a woman in this way, I want to use the sex-harm connection to try to resolve a dispute about pornography and women. Brownmiller's view, remember, was that pornography is "the undiluted essence of anti-female propaganda" whose purpose is to degrade women.[15] Some people object to Brownmiller's view by saying that, since pornography treats both men and women as sex objects for the purpose of arousing the viewer, it is neither sexist, antifemale, nor designed to degrade women; it just happens that degrading of women arouses some men. How can this dispute be resolved?

Suppose we were to rate the content of all pornography from most morally objectionable to least morally objectionable. Among the most objectionable would be the most degrading—for example, "snuff" films and movies which recommend that men rape women, molest children and puppies, and treat nonmasochists very sadistically.

Next we would find a large amount of material (probably most pornography) not quite so blatantly offensive. With this material it is relevant to use the analysis of sex objects given above. As long as sex is connected with harm done to women, it will be very difficult not to see pornography as degrading to women. We can agree with Brownmiller's opponent that pornography treats men as sex objects, too, but we maintain that this is only pseudoequality: such treatment is still more degrading to women.[16]

In addition, pornography often exemplifies the active/passive, harmer/harmed object roles in a very obvious way. Because pornography today is male-oriented and is supposed to make a profit, the content is designed to appeal to male fantasies. Judging from the content of the most popular legally available pornography, male fantasies still run along the lines of stereotypical sex roles—and, if Stoller is right, include elements of hostility. In much pornography the women's purpose is to cater to male desires, to service the man or men. Her own pleasure is rarely emphasized for its own sake; she is merely allowed a little heavy breathing, perhaps in order to show her dependence on the great male "lover" who produces her pleasure. In addition, women are clearly made into passive objects in still photographs showing only close-ups of their genitals. Even in movies marketed to appeal to heterosexual couples, such as *Behind the Green Door*, the woman is passive and undemanding (and in this case kidnapped and hypnotized as well). Although many kinds of specialty magazines and films are gauged for different sexual tastes, very little contemporary pornography goes against traditional sex roles. There is certainly no significant attempt to replace the harmer/harmed distinction with anything more positive and healthy. In some stag movies, of course, men are treated sadistically by women; but this is an attempt to turn the tables on degradation, not a positive improvement.

What would cases toward the least objectionable end of the spectrum be like? They would be increasingly less degrading and sexist. The genuinely nonobjectionable cases would be nonsexist and nondegrading; but commercial examples do not readily spring to mind.[17] The question is: does or could any pornography have nonsexist, nondegrading content?

IV

I want to start with the easier question: Is it possible for pornography to have nonsexist, morally acceptable content? Then I will consider whether any pornography of this sort currently exists.

Imagine the following situation, which exists only rarely today: Two fairly conventional people who love each other enjoy playing tennis and bridge together, cooking good food together, and having sex together. In all these activities they are free from hang-ups, guilt, and tendencies to dominate or objectify each other. These two people like to watch tennis matches and old romantic movies on TV, like to watch

Julia Child cook, like to read the bridge column in the newspaper, and like to watch pornographic movies. Imagine further that this couple is not at all uncommon in society and that nonsexist pornography is as common as this kind of nonsexist sexual relationship. This situation sounds fine and healthy to me. I see no reason to think that an interest in pornography would disappear in these circumstances.[18] People seem to enjoy watching others experience or do (especially do well) what they enjoy experiencing, doing or wish they could do themselves. We do not morally object to people watching tennis on TV; why would we object to these hypothetical people watching pornography?

Can we go from the situation today to the situation just imagined? In much current pornography, people are treated in morally objectionable ways. In the scene just imagined, however, pornography would be nonsexist, nondegrading, morally acceptable. The key to making the change is to break the connection between sex and harm. If Stoller is right, this task may be impossible without changing the scenarios of our sexual lives—scenarios that we have been writing since early childhood. (Stoller does not indicate whether he thinks it possible for adults to rewrite their scenarios or for social change to bring about the possibility of new scenarios in future generations.) But even if we believe that people can change their sexual scenarios, the sex-harm connection is deeply entrenched and has widespread implications. What is needed is a thorough change in people's deep-seated attitudes and feelings about sex roles in general, as well as about sex and roles in sex (sexual roles). Although I cannot even sketch a general outline of such changes here, changes in pornography should be part of a comprehensive program. Television, children's educational material, and nonpornographic movies and novels may be far better avenues for attempting to change attitudes; but one does not want to take the chance that pornography is working against one.

What can be done about pornography in particular? If one wanted to work within the current institutions, one's attempt to use pornography as a tool for the education of male pornography audiences would have to be fairly subtle at first; nonsexist pornography must become familiar enough to sell and be watched. One should realize too that any positive educational value that nonsexist pornography might have may well be as short-lived as most of the effects of pornography. But given these limitations, what could one do?

Two kinds of films must be considered. First is the short film with no plot or character development, just depicting sexual activity in which nonsexist pornography would treat men and women as equal sex partners.[19] The man would not control the circumstances in which the partners had sex or the choice of positions or acts; the woman's preference would be counted equally. There would be no suggestion of a power play or conquest on the man's part, no suggestion that "she likes it when I hurt her." Sexual intercourse would not be portrayed as primarily for the purpose of male ejaculation—his orgasm is not "the best part" of the movie. In addition, both the man and woman would express their enjoyment; the man need not be cool and detached.

The film with a plot provides even more opportunity for nonsexist education. Today's pornography often portrays the female characters as playthings even when not engaging in sexual activity. Nonsexist pornography could show women and men in roles equally valued by society, and sex equality would amount to more than possession of equally functional genitalia. Characters would customarily treat each other with respect and consideration, with no attempt to treat men or women brutally or thoughtlessly. The local Pussycat Theater showed a film written and directed by a woman (The Passions of Carol), which exhibited a few of the features just mentioned. The main female character in it was the editor of a magazine parody of Viva. The fact that some of the characters treated each other very nicely, warmly, and tenderly did not detract from the pornographic features of the movie. This should not surprise us, for even in traditional male-oriented films, lesbian scenes usually exhibit tenderness and kindness.

Plots for nonsexist films could include women in traditionally male jobs (e.g., long-distance truckdriver) or in positions usually held in respect by pornography audiences. For example, a high-ranking female Army officer, treated with respect by men and women alike, could be shown not only in various sexual encounters with other people but also carrying out her job in a humane manner.[20] Or perhaps the main character could be a female urologist. She could interact with nurses and other medical personnel, diagnose illnesses brilliantly, and treat patients with great sympathy as well as have sex with them. When the Army officer or the urologist engage in sexual activities, they will treat their partners and be treated by them in some of the considerate ways described above.

In the circumstances we imagined at the beginning of Part IV of this paper, our nonsexist films could be appreciated in the proper spirit. Under these conditions the content of our new pornography would clearly be nonsexist and morally acceptable. But would the content of such a film be morally acceptable if shown to a typical pornography audience today? It might seem strange for to change our moral evaluation of the content on the basis of a different audience, but an audience today is likely to see the "respected" urologist and Army officer as playthings or unusual prostitutes—even if our intention in showing the film is to counteract this view. The effect is that, although the content of the film seems morally acceptable and our intention in showing it is morally flawless, women are still degraded.[21] The fact that audience attitude is so important makes one wary of giving whole-hearted approval to any pornography seen today.

The fact that good intentions and content are insufficient does not imply that one's effort toward change would be entirely in vain. Of course, I could not deny that anyone who tries to change an institution from within faces serious difficulties. This is particularly evident when one is trying to change both pornography and a whole set of related attitudes, feelings, and institutions concerning sex and sex roles. But in conjunction with other attempts to change this set of attitudes, it seems preferable to try to change pornography instead of closing one's eyes in the hope that it will go away. For I suspect that pornography is here to stay.[22]

NOTES

1. (New York: Simon and Schuster, 1975), p. 394.

2. *The Report of the Commission on Obscenity and Pornography* (Washington, D.C., 1970), p. 201. Hereinafter, *Report.*

3. *Report,* p. 3, n. 4; and p. 149. Some feminists have proposed reserving the term 'pornography' for morally objectionable sexually explicit material, for example, that which endorses violence, degradation, or conquest of women. For example, in *Take Back the Night,* edited by Laura Lederer (New York: Bantam, 1980) see Gloria Steinem, "Erotica and Pornography: A Clear and Present Difference," p. 23, and Helen Longino, "Pornography, Freedom, and Oppression: A Closer Look," p. 29. I find a morally neutral use of 'pornography' less problematic. See Fred Berger's paper, this volume, pp. 327-351.

5. To degrade someone in this situation is to lower her/his rank or status in humanity. This is morally objectionable because it is incompatible with showing respect for a person. Some of the other moral grounds for objecting to pornography have been considered by the Supreme Court: Pornography invades our privacy and hurts the moral tone of the community. See Paris Adult Theatre Iv. Slaton, 413 U.S. 49 (1973). Even less plausible than the Court's position is to say that pornography is immoral because it depicts sex, depicts an immoral kind of sex, or caters to voyeuristic tendencies. I believe that even if moral objections to pornography exist, one must preclude any simple inference from "pornography is immoral" to "pornography should be censored" because

of other important values and principles such as freedom of expression and self-determination.

6. See Gail Sheehy, *Hustling* (New York: Dell, 1971) for a good discussion of prostitution, crime, and pornography.

7. Two further points need to be mentioned here. Sharon Bishop pointed out to me one reason why we might object to either a racist or rapist mentality in film: it might be difficult for a Black or a woman not to identify with the degraded person. A second point concerns different uses of the phrase 'treats women as sex objects'. A film treats a subject—the meaninglessness of contemporary life, women as sex objects, and so on—and this use of 'treats' is unproblematic. But one should not suppose that this is the same use of 'treats women as sex objects' that is found in the sentence 'David treats women as sex objects'; David is not treating the *subject* of women as sex objects.

8. In order to help one determine which position one feels inclined to take, consider the following statement: It is morally objectionable to write, make, sell, act in, use, and enjoy pornography; in addition, the content of pornography is immoral; however, pornography itself is not morally objectionable. If this statement seems extremely problematic, then one might well be satisfied with the claim that pornography is degrading because its content is.

9. The traditional meaning of "lose respect for women" was evidently the one assumed in the Abelson survey cited by the Presidential Commission. No explanation of its meaning is given in the report of the study. See H. Abelson et al., "National Survey of Public Attitudes Toward and Experience With Erotic Materials," *Tech. Report*, vol. 6, pp. 1-137.

10. Many feminists point this out. One of the most accessible references is Shulamith Firestone, *The Dialectic of Sex: The Case for the Feminist Revolution* (New York: Bantam, 1970), especially pp. 128-32.

11. Richard Wasserstrom, ed., *Today's Moral Problems* (New York: Macmillan, 1975), pp. 152-71; see pp. 167-71. (Herein, pp. 93-106)

12. Baker, in Wasserstrom, *Today's Moral Problems*, pp. 168-169. [Page 264, this volume—eds.]

13. Sexual Excitement," *Archives of General Psychiatry* 33 (1976): 899-909, especially p. 903. The extent to which Stoller sees men and women in different positions with respect to harm and hostility is not clear. He often treats men and women alike, but in *Perversion: The Erotic Form of Hatred* (New York: Pantheon, 1975), pp. 89-91, he calls attention to differences between men and women especially regarding their responses to pornography and lack of understanding by men of women's sexuality. Given that Stoller finds hostility to be an essential element in male-oriented pornography, and given that women have not responded readily to such pornography, one can speculate about the possibilities for women's sexuality: their hostility might follow a different scenario; they might not be as hostile, and so on.

14. Men seem to be developing more sensitivity to being treated as sex objects. Many homosexual men have long understood the problem. As women become more sexually aggressive, some heterosexual men I know are beginning to feel treated as sex objects. A man can feel that he is not being taken seriously if a woman looks lustfully at him while he is holding forth about the French judicial system or the failure of liberal politics. Some of his most important

talents are not being properly valued.

15. Brownmiller, *Against Our Will*, p. 394.

16. I don't agree with Brownmiller that the purpose of pornography is to dehumanize women; rather it is to arouse the audience. The differences between our views can be explained, in part, by the points from which we begin. She is writing about rape; her views about pornography grow out of her views about rape. I begin by thinking of pornography as merely depicted sexual activity, though I am well aware of the male hostility and contempt for women that it often expresses. That pornography degrades women and excites men is an illustration of this contempt.

17. Virginia Wright Wexman uses the film *Group Marriage* (Stephanie Rothman, 1973) as an example of "more enlightened erotica." Wexman also asks the following questions in an attempt to point out sexism in pornographic films: *Does it [the film] portray rape as pleasurable to women? Does it consistently show females nude but present men fully clothed? Does it present women as childlike creatures whose sexual interests must be guided by knowing experienced men? Does it show sexually aggressive women as castrating viragos? Does it pretend that sex is exclusively the prerogative of women under twenty-five? Does it focus on the physical aspects of lovemaking rather than the emotional ones? Does it portray women as purely sexual beings?* ("Sexism of X-rated Films," Chicago Sun-Times, *28 March 1976.)*

18. One might think, as does Stoller, that since pornography today depends on hostility, voyeurism, and sado-masochism *(Perversion,* p. 87) that sexually healthy people would not enjoy it. Two points should be noticed here, however: (1) Stoller need not think that pornography will disappear because hostility is an element of sexual excitement generally; and (2) voyeurism, when it invades no one's privacy, need not be seen as immoral; so, although enjoyment of pornography might not be an expression of sexual health, it need not be immoral either.

19. If it is a lesbian or male homosexual film, no one would play a caricatured male or female role. The reader has probably noticed that I have limited my discussion to heterosexual pornography, but there are many interesting analogies to be drawn with male homosexual pornography. Very little commercial lesbian pornography exists, though lesbian scenes are commonly found in male-oriented pornography.

20. One should note that behavior of this kind is still considered unacceptable by the military. A female officer resigned from the U.S. Navy recently rather than be court-martialed for having sex with several enlisted men whom she met in a class on interpersonal relations.

21. The content may seem morally acceptable only if one disregards such questions as, "Should a doctor have sex with her patients during office hours?" More important is the propriety of evaluating content wholly apart from the attitudes and reactions of the audience; one might not find it strange to say that one film has morally unacceptable content when shown tonight at the Pussycat Theater but acceptable content when shown tomorrow at a feminist conference.

22. Three "final" points must be made:

1. I have not seriously considered censorship as an alternative course of action. Both Brownmiller and Sheehy are not averse to it. But as I suggested in

note 5, other principles seem too valuable to sacrifice when other options are available. In addition, before justifying censorship on moral grounds one would want to compare pornography to other possibly offensive material: advertising using sex and racial stereotypes, violence in TV and films, and so on.

2. If my nonsexist pornography succeeded in having much "educational value," it might no longer be pornography according to my definition. This possibility seems too remote to worry me, however.

3. In discussing the audience for nonsexist pornography, I have focused on the male audience. But there is no reason why pornography could not educate and appeal to women as well.

Fred R. Berger

Pornography, Feminism, and Censorship

It undoubtedly says something about our culture that if one were to mention the name of Richard Lovelace, few people, even in educated circles, will immediately identify the reference and recall the nature of his accomplishments. On the other hand, mention of the name Linda Lovelace will probably produce associations in the minds of the majority, and quite a few will be able to describe her oscular achievements in embarrassing detail. We live in a time when pornography has "come out of the closet" (or dresser drawer). As the topsy-turvy of our time would have it, Ms. Lovelace has become a heroine in circles that would otherwise eschew association with her career.

Symptomatic of the confusion of contemporary political and social thinking, the pornography controversy has faced many of us with a hard dilemma. On the one hand, pornography is sometimes perceived as promoting an ideology that embodies the essence of antifemale sexuality. On the other hand, the ideal of free expression has been so deeply engrained in liberal thinking that the call to suppress communications produces strong visceral reactions. Those of us who are supportive of the central themes in the women's movement have thus faced conflicting pressures on our sympathies.

In an earlier paper, I criticized arguments in favor of censorship of pornography that have been given by what I labeled "conservative" writers.[1] Since that time, some of the most vocal critics of pornography have been radical feminist writers, some of whom favor censorship. I do not believe that their arguments have been fully explored and met by those of us who oppose censorship of pornography. Furthermore, I believe that those arguments have implications for the analysis of freedom of expression that it is important to bring out. Though I continue to oppose censorship, I believe the feminist claims deserve serious attention.

1. THE FEMINIST OBJECTIONS TO PORNOGRAPHY

I shall call the critics to whom I refer "feminists" or "radical feminists," though I do this with reluctance. My hesitation over the label has three sources: (a) I believe that some version of "radical feminism," as a critique of modern society, is true.[2] (b) Many feminists who accept the feminist critique of pornography do not take that critique as sufficient justification for censorship.[3] (c) And, some feminists reject important aspects of the critique of pornography that I shall discuss.[4] The label, then, is misleading if it is taken to suggest that there is a single feminist analysis of pornography and general agreement on the desirability of censorship. Indeed, at certain points in the discussion it is important to bear in mind that some feminists have strong objections to the views I have gathered under the rubric of "radical feminist" arguments for censorship of pornography.

Let us turn to the radical feminist arguments for censorship. These arguments can be understood to have two parts. First, the arguments embody an analysis of the nature and effects of pornography. Second, when fully developed, they provide an analysis of freedom of expression that is designed to justify the suppression of materials that meet the characterization of pornography.

There is considerable agreement among the radical feminist critics on the nature of pornography. A few examples will give the flavor of the essential points of that analysis. In her book, *Against Our Will*, Susan Brownmiller wrote,

> Pornography, like rape, is a male invention, designed to dehumanize women, to reduce the female to an object of sexual access, not to free sensuality from moralistic or parental inhibition. The staple of porn will always be the naked female body, breasts and genitals exposed, because as man devised it, her naked body is the female's "shame," her private parts the private property of man, while his are the ancient, holy, universal, patriarchal instrument of his power, his rule by force over her. Pornography is the undiluted essence of anti-female propaganda.[5]

Andrea Dworkin has expressed her view as follows:

> The pornographers, modern and ancient, visual and literary, vulgar and aristocratic, put forth one consistent proposition: erotic pleasure for men is derived from and predicated on the savage destruction of women . . . The eroticization of murder is the essence of pornography, as it is the essence of life. The torturer may be a policeman tearing the fingernails off

a victim in a prison cell or a so-called normal man engaged in the project of attempting to fuck a woman to death. The fact is that the process of killing—and both rape and battery are steps in that process—is the prime sexual act for men in reality and/or in imagination. Women as a class must remain in bondage, subject to the sexual will of men, because the knowledge of an imperial right to kill, whether exercised to the fullest extent or just partway, is necessary to fuel sexual appetite and behavior. Without women as potential or actual victims, men are, in the current sanitized jargon, "sexually dysfunctional."[6]   *F*

Kathleen Barry has written a book, *Female Sexual Slavery,* that has attracted considerable feminist attention. In a section dealing with pornography, she writes,

> Pornography . . . is the principal medium through which cultural sadism becomes a part of the sexual practices of individuals.
> The most prevalent theme in pornography is one of utter contempt for women. In movie after movie women are raped, ejaculated on, urinated on, anally penetrated, beaten, and, with the advent of snuff films, murdered in an orgy of sexual pleasure. Women are the objects of pornography, men its largest consumers, and sexual degradation its theme.[7]

Finally, the philosopher, Helen Longino, has presented an important and carefully reasoned critique of pornography, which she defines as:

> *verbal or pictorial explicit representations of sexual behavior that,* in the words of the Commission on Obscenity and Pornography, *have as a distinguishing characteristic "the degrading and demeaning portrayal of the role and status of the human female . . . as a mere sexual object to be exploited and manipulated sexually. "*[8]

Later, after elaborating on the characterization, she adds:

> What makes a work a work of pornography, then, is not simply its representation of degrading and abusive sexual encounters, but its implicit, if not explicit, approval and recommendation of sexual behavior that is immoral, i.e., that physically or psychologically violates the personhood of one of the participants. Pornography, then, is verbal or pictorial material which represents or describes sexual behavior that is degrading or abusive to one or more of the participants *in such a way as to endorse the degradation.*[9]

Common to these analyses is the claim that it is essential to pornography that it represent women in a degraded role, serving the pleasure of men as subservient creatures whose *sole* function is to provide sexual gratification for men. As the humiliation of women is the essential source of pornographic pleasure, a central theme of pornography (so the account goes), either explicit or implicit, is the rape of women and infliction of violence on women. Furthermore, an image of female sexuality is promoted that is profoundly false—that of deriving pleasure through being humiliated and degraded (rape is portrayed as unleashing feminine, animal sexual fulfillment). Pornography is thus perceived as degrading women and as promoting a cultural climate that fosters violence against women.

This analysis of pornography, even if accepted completely, does not establish the acceptability of censorship. In addition, there is needed an argument to show that censorship of material—even as characterized—presents no unacceptable violation of the right of free expression. There are three such arguments that can be found in the feminist literature. I shall first list the arguments. I shall then elaborate on them and say what seems to me mistaken in the arguments.[10]

The first argument, which appears to have been made by Brownmiller, holds that the First Amendment was intended to protect political speech and dissent. But, as Brownmiller put it, pornographic materials "have nothing to do with the hallowed right of political dissent."[11] Suppression, then, is not inconsistent with the constitutional right of free expression.

The second and third arguments are sometimes combined, but it is important to keep them separate. One way to illustrate them is through an argument given by Professor Longino. She maintains that the right of free expression is not an "absolute or fundamental right"; it is derived from another right. That further right is illuminated by a distinction between freedom as license and freedom as "independence." The former means doing what one wants. The latter means having "the status of a person as independent and equal rather than as subservient."[12] But, she holds, there is no absolute right to freedom as license. So, in her view, the right of free expression is derivative from the right of "independence." But, pornographic material degrades women, and to the extent that it "supports and reinforces the attitude that women are not fit to participate as equals among equals in the political life of their communities," the fundamental right of independence is undercut.[13] This, and related claims, can be taken to generate different grounds for censorship—the second and third arguments I want to consider.

The second says that pornography degrades women and depicts them in a false light as persons who desire to be dominated and humiliated. It portrays women as appropriate objects of violence by men. In this way women are defamed. Just as libel and slander are not protected expression, so, it is argued, pornography is a form of group defamation that can properly be treated as unprotected.

The third argument takes the analysis one step further. It says that by virtue of the features cited in the second argument, pornography promotes rape and violence against women. Here, the claim is that there is a *causal* connection between the dissemination of pornography and rape and violence. In Professor Longino's version of the argument, it is stressed that since the ultimate right that is at stake is the right to independence or autonomy, and not license—there is no right to do whatever one wants—it is not a violation of anyone's basic rights to interfere with freedom in order to protect women from this sort of harm.

2. RESPONSE TO THE ARGUMENTS

I want to assess these arguments, while elaborating them further. All are, I think, defective as arguments for censorship of pornography. But, a number of points made by the feminist critics deserve careful consideration, and some aspects of their arguments involve important truths or insights.

The first argument—that freedom of expression has as its prime rationale the protection of political speech and dissent—is defective from several points of view. In the first place, it is bad history even of the First Amendment to the United States Constitution; despite Brownmiller's quotation from Chief Justice Burger, the Supreme Court has explicitly rejected the doctrine.[14] Furthermore, the Brownmiller position is inconsistent with that of Professor Longino, who holds that the rationale for freedom of expression is its connection with independence or self-determination. Of course, Longino's claim was not intended as historical, whereas Brownmiller's may have been. Both, however, purport to *justify* certain rather than other modes of expression, and as such, they are not entirely consistent with one another, since not only political speech is useful or requisite for living the life of an autonomous individual.

I should add that I can see no good ground to suppose that there is some *one* justification or rationale for free expression. There are diverse reasons to protect expression, ranging from the need for open discussion of political issues in a democracy, to the likely incapacity of society to determine the truth without open discussion, to the need people have to make and receive unfettered communications in the process of determining for themselves what is true of the world and how they are to live their lives. Moreover, the untrustworthiness of government to wisely wield the censorship power is a strong ground for free expression that is independent of the others, yet compatible with all.[15] If, for example, one studies Supreme Court cases, it is apparent that all of the grounds given above for protecting expression (as well as others) have been drawn on by the Court in its determinations concerning free expression issues.

There is a further point I want to make about the "political speech" doctrine. This view of free expression is sometimes (mistakenly) derived from a conception of free expression championed by Alexander Meikeljohn—a view that has gained considerable support and which has played a role in Supreme Court thinking.[16] Meikeljohn held that citizens, in the capacity of voters, exercise a political office in a democracy. This political function cannot be served properly if citizens do not have access to information and ideas. Freedom of expression, then, is required for citizens to exercise this central political function.

It does not follow, however, nor did Meikeljohn hold, that only political speech and dissent are entitled to protection. The issues that must be dealt with as a voter range over the whole of human life, and the ideas one has of the world and of social life can come in many different forms and from numerous sources. The entire spectrum of human communications—novels, cartoons, poetry, plays, films, and so on—play a role in our acquisition of the special understandings and appreciations of reality that we utilize in the formation of the opinions and attitudes that we bring to our public decision-making. An appreciation of natural resources may be effectively evoked by a film, or through poetic description, and, *via* those means, play a significant role in our understanding of the importance of environmental protection. A play depicting the hopelessness and despair of ghetto life can be more moving and deepen our understanding of the special burdens of many Black Americans than a straightforward, policy-oriented speech. Various fictional accounts of ways of living and behaving that are radically different from our own (presented in diverse media) can enlarge the range of human possibilities open to us and can increase our grasp of the potentialities (both good and bad) of human behavior. They also allow us to try out in imagination ways of being that we cannot (or do not wish to) have first-hand experience of. Such an enlarged vision of possible realities is surely relevant to our decision-making as voters. The political function argument for free expression, properly viewed, justifies the widest possible protection for the widest possible range of modes of expression and of ideas expressed. It must not, therefore, be confused with the doctrine that only political speech is protected. There may be a basis for giving political expression *special* treatment, but there is no ground for regarding other expression as totally outside of the free expression rationale.

Let us turn, then, to the claims that pornography degrades and defames women, and that it promotes rape and violence against women. These should be kept separate, as pornography would be morally objectionable if it degrades women irrespective of further bad consequences, and vice versa. In specific contexts it can be important which objection is at stake.

Both arguments depend on the radical feminist analysis of pornography, which, as we have seen, maintains that it is of the essence of pornography that it degrades women and endorses violence against women. This claim must be examined. Often, it is not made clear what, precisely, is being said about pornography, and it is not an obvious truth that all pornography can be condemned on such grounds.

But, if we are to take it as a meaningful question whether pornography degrades women, then we must eschew attempts to *identify* pornography *by* the sort of characterizing criteria the radical feminists offer. Professor Longino, for example, in her attempt to maintain a clear distinction between "erotica" and "pornography," *defined* pornography by the characteristic: "the degrading and demeaning portrayal of the role and status of the human female."[17]

Longino's definition is paralleled by those of other feminists anxious to distinguish what is objectionable from explicit sexual depictions they regard as acceptable. But, all such definitions suffer serious drawbacks. First, such definitions render the notion of male homosexual pornography incoherent. Second, such definitions make self-contradictory the claim of such other feminist writers as Ann Garry that there *can* be pornography that does not degrade women, which she goes on to describe in its essential features.[18] Third, such definitions of pornography make circular, or logically trivial, the claim that pornography degrades women. It follows from the *meaning* of the term alone that pornography degrades women. That, however, leaves open whether the films shown in adult theaters, or books and magazines sold in adult bookstores, or *Playboy, Penthouse,* and *Hustler* degrade women. Whether they do or not cannot be deduced from the definition of "pornography" alone.

It is one of the merits of Professor Longino's work that she provides an analysis of the ways in which materials can degrade women. That analysis seems to me insightful and I shall draw on it in my subsequent discussion. But, that analysis does not presuppose either the restrictive definition of "pornography" or the claim that pornography degrades women.

Some feminist critics of pornography recognize the limitations of such characterizations of pornography. Professor Rosemarie Tong, for example, does not object to all pornography, only to a variety that she identifies as "thanatic," which she characterizes thus:

> the representation of such degrading behavior is thanatic to the extent that it not only depicts but celebrates (condones) and encourages either the callous frustration of one's own or someone else's preferences as a sexual being or, worse, the intentional violation of one's own or someone else's rights as a sexual being.[19]

It is, of course, part of the feminist attack on pornography to claim that *in fact* it typically *does* degrade and humiliate women. It is not the isolated S-M magazine of an antifemale secret society that is condemned, but wide-ranging, openly available fare that supports a burgeoning industry alleged some years back to have become a four-billion-dollar-a-year business.[20]

The problems of definition are well known in this area, and that fact plays an important role in the arguments against censorship. But, one can come up with definitions that are useful for special purposes. For the present, it is useful to define pornography as visual or written matter that depicts sexual activity or arousal, or the sex organs, in a graphic and explicit way, and in which the predominant themes stressed are of a sexual nature (i.e., are intended, or could be expected, to produce sexual arousal, or, as St. Augustine put it, "genital commotion"[21]). Thus, the display of organs in a medical text would probably not count as pornography, nor would an erotic passage in a long book make the work as a whole pornographic. On the other hand, the definition leaves open the possibility that pornography can have literary or artistic features and, hence, may be true art, as some would claim.[22] It would also include within the genre virtually everything the critics of pornography classify as such. Several "conservative" writers have cited *Fanny Hill* as pornographic, for example, and it meets my definition.[23] (Furthermore, I note that it is not without a measure of literary value.)

The sex in *Fanny Hill* is both explicit and the predominant focus of the work. Some of these writers have rejected Hubert Selby, Jr.'s *Last Exit to Brooklyn* as pornographic,[24] though it contains the most brutal and degrading rape scene I have ever run across in literature. Neither the book as a whole nor that scene is directed at any sexual interest, nor could arousal be reasonably expected as the predominant reaction. (It *was* banned in Britain, however!) The feminist writers I am discussing take *Penthouse* and *Playboy* magazines to be pornographic, and I believe these could be fit in under my definition as borderline examples.

Let us consider the claim, then, that pornography, in its *typical* form, has as a central theme the degradation of women and the endorsement of violence against them. It is noteworthy that many who have studied pornography have found that it typically stresses different themes. For example, several authors who have studied pornography identify as a central theme an image of a societal "pornotopia"—a society in which all social reality is treated as an aspect of the sexual.[25] Susan Sontag, in a searching analysis of *Story of O*, which *could* be taken to express the themes the feminists claim (despite having been written by a woman[26]) takes the central theme of that work to consist in a preoccupation with death.[27] One should be wary, then, of attempts to isolate *the* theme or the predominant message of pornography.

Feminist writers have, however, offered evidence intended to show that the theme of violence against women is regularly endorsed in pornography, and that such materials increasingly feature themes of this sort. One study of "adults only" paperbacks, published between 1968 and 1974, showed that one-fifth of the sex scenes depicted rape, and, typically, that rape is an experience women actually take pleasure in.[28] A study was also done of sexual violence depicted in pictorials and cartoons in *Playboy* and *Penthouse* between 1973 and 1977,[29] from which two feminist writers conclude that it showed the amount of violence in these publications is increasing[30] (although they concede that the total amount is relatively small). These studies, however, do *not* support the charge that violence against women is the predominant theme in pornography. The first, reporting that one-fifth of the sex scenes in adult books involved rape, implies that eighty percent of the scenes did not. Moreover, one must bear in mind that many of the scenes may have been concentrated in books of the sadomasochistic variety. The second study did *not* show a *simple* linear increase in violence in those magazines. (One of the two "raters," in fact, perceived a *decline* of violence in *Playboy* cartoons during the period. Her co-rater, a male who was familiar with the hypothesis that such an increase had taken place, tended to perceive somewhat more violence, though not so much in the cartoons.[31]) More significantly, at the *highest* level of incidence, ten percent of the cartoons and five percent of the pictorials displayed sexual violence. No attempt was made to relate the visuals in the magazines to the articles, editorials, interviews, and so on, that comprise the bulk of the pages, which contain widely mixed messages, but which, I would venture to guess, do *not* endorse violence against women. These studies do *not* show violence and rape to characterize pornography as its dominant theme.

The more plausible claim, then, is that women are typically degraded in pornography in less overt ways. For example, if women are regularly depicted in degrading, second-class roles, or are portrayed as capable of functioning only as sources of sexual pleasure for men, or if the message of a presentation is that it is proper to use and manipulate women as instruments of male enjoyment, then these presentations could be taken to degrade women and to accord them a status that is servile to that of men. There is no doubt in my mind that television commercials regularly defame women in some of these ways; women are depicted as concerned primarily with the whiteness of their wash, the softness of toilet tissue, and whether or not the lines of their panties show when wearing tight slacks. They are rarely depicted as taking significant, serious roles in societal decision-making. The overall image of women, repetitively drawn and reinforced, is that of persons whose roles relate to the home, and whose interests and abilities relate to inconsequential matters.[32] Similarly, there is no doubt in my mind that pornography can sometimes be guilty of portrayals that are degrading in the ways indicated above. To the extent this is true, I believe the feminist critique of pornography is correct. But, I have no reason to believe that pornography is any more to be condemned on these grounds than are other materials. I have not seen any arguments showing that pornography is *typified* by such portrayals. Still, if one admits that pornography sometimes does degrade women, what objections are there to regarding *those* materials as promoting an ideology of violence against women?

To begin with, it is important to stress *how* the degrading messages are conveyed. Unlike the usual sort of expression to which defamation laws apply, pornographic materials usually do not *state* anything degrading about women that is clearly intended as an attempt to convince someone of something. Scenes are portrayed, or pictures flashed, a story proceeds, and so on. The degrading messages consist in those ideas produced *by* the display, or inferred by the reader or viewer, and are not part of the conventional and literal meaning of the language or symbols used. Ideas conveyed in *this* sense, however, are very much a function of context—the surrounding messages, the nature of the audience, the expectations, attitudes, and beliefs of the recipients, and so on. Moreover, the interpretation of the "message" in these cases is always a matter of judgment, and subject to great variation among persons.

The most shocking display of sadomasochistic pictures I have seen was organized by a group of women against pornography. Nancy Friday's books of women's sexual fantasies contain a letter from a woman who had been raped at knifepoint, experienced multiple orgasms during the experience, and who used the experience in later life as the basis of sexual fantasies that she conjures up in order to enjoy intercourse and masturbation more fully.[33] There are several books available to provide information for women directed at increasing sexual pleasure, which contain hand drawings of spread vaginas. In none of these cases were the pictures, reports, or drawings employed to degrade women, nor were degrading messages about women given "endorsement." One can, however, imagine contexts in which the very same items could plausibly be charged with doing so. But, if context is all important, this suggests that there would be insuperable problems of interpretation for any attempt to come up with a workable set of guidelines for defamation laws that would capture the objectionable material, but which would not have a serious "chilling effect" on expression that deals with explicit sex. I am not claiming that there are no objective truths in this area. Indeed, my earlier statement that *some* pornography *does* degrade women was intended as such, and not as a mere expression of subjective feeling or reaction. For purposes of the censorship debate, it is enough that such judgments are difficult, dependent on context, and strongly influenced by subjective reactions, so that agreement is rare and hard to come by.

Furthermore, it is clear that *in fact* there is *considerable* disagreement over the interpretation of particular depictions. One can contrast Susan Sontag's analysis of the *Story of O*, mentioned above, with that of Adrienne Rich,[34] or Angela Carter's analysis of the ideology of de Sade in her book, *The Sadeian Woman and the Ideology of Pornography*,[35] with Andrea Dworkin's analysis in *Pornography: Men Possessing Women*.[36] One feminist writer who went on one of the infamous tours of Times Square led by pornography opponents declared that "it is not promoting the violation and degradation of women, but traditional heterosexual intercourse and gender relations." In her view, there is an important message in pornography for women: that sexuality need not be tied to reproduction or domesticity (or to men, for that matter), and that sexuality is not only for "bad girls."[37] To the extent that women's sexual liberation requires breaking down the good girl/bad girl dichotomy on sexual permissiveness, she regards pornography as not divorced from feminist concerns.

Consider one final example. It is drawn from Beatrice Faust's work entitled *Women, Sex and Pornography*. She notes that in pornographic films there has been a trend to show ejaculation over a woman's face and breasts. She maintains that it is wrong to suppose that this is just an expression of contempt for women. Her explanation is that such scenes serve the need of preserving realism and probably have no greater significance than that:

> One could indicate male orgasm by accelerated thrusts and breathing and then sharp deceleration, but cynics would interpret this as faking. Moreover, the trick is only possible in movies. For most people, male orgasm is identified with ejaculation and, since ejaculating into blank spaces is not much fun, ejaculating over a person who responds with enjoyment sustains a light-hearted mood as well as a degree of realism.
>
> This occurs in both homosexual and heterosexual pornography, so that ejaculation cannot be interpreted as an expression of contempt for women only. Logically, if sex is natural and wholesome and semen is as healthy as sweat, there is no reason to interpret ejaculation as a hostile gesture. Healthy semen is not like feces, which may smell offensive, dirty the sheets, and carry germs. Some women and men enjoy the silky feel of fresh semen, some enjoy the smell and some find it excites the imagination. The ejaculation motif lends itself to elaborate theories, like those surrounding the penis in half penetration, but the simpler explanation is more likely to be the correct one.[38]

I do not mean to endorse Ms. Faust's interpretation; my only point is to show that reasonable people can disagree over what is conveyed by nonliteral expression (and literal expression, too!), and that even supposedly clear examples can generate reasoned disagreement. (Several of the feminist writers I quoted cite the ejaculation phenomenon as evidence of malevolent purpose or effect.) The legal task of ascertaining defamation would present overwhelming courtroom difficulties, and could have disastrous implications for free expression. Both Longino and Tong have outlined versions of the defamation argument, but both require of the defamatory material that it *endorse* the degrading message.[39] Perhaps repetitious occurrence of a type of portrayal has the same effect as an endorsement. (This is precisely what happens in the case, say, of laundry soap commercials.) But is that really a legal concept that can be used to tame the four-billion-dollar-a-year monster industry? If it can, what else would it take with it? Why, for example, limit the defamation to *sexual* themes? Why limit it to defamation against *women*? Surely, defamation of racial or religious groups is objectionable also. But then it is not clear that Shakespeare's *Merchant of Venice,* Wagner's music, and a good bit of feminist writing would not come under attack. (If Andrea Dworkin's characterizations of male sexuality, quoted above, are not defamatory in ways similar to some pornography, then I have not understood what she wrote.) In the course of writing this paper, I discovered that *Huckleberry Finn* had been removed from a school library (ironically, the school was named for Twain) because of its supposed "racist" message. [40]

Perhaps the feminist writers should be reminded that some of the conservative critics I mentioned earlier regard much explicit sexual material as degrading to persons as such; others regard certain *forms* of sexual behavior as degrading, such as homosexual and lesbian sex. When speaking in Texas on the subject of pornography, I was assured by one woman that the problems of the world are due to "all this oral sex!"

It is somewhat distressing that feminist writers who stress the defamation ground for censorship have not sufficiently explored the free expression implications of the "group defamation" concept. [41] The facile assumption cannot be sustained that just because our system can permit prosecutions for individual libel, it follows that there would be no special problem with group libel when applied to pornography. Indeed, there are many who would contend that there is a real danger in the case of defamation of individuals. In fact, the recent history of defamation law reveals it to be in a state of stress, with attempts to circumscribe opportunities for prosecution, e.g., when the defamed person is a public official, a "voluntary limited public figure," or an "involuntary limited public figure." The extent of First Amendment protection may depend on whether one is a "media" defendant, or a "nonmedia" defendant. [42]

Those who believe defamation law *as it stands* poses dangers to free expression are not without basis. A study of fifty-four recent defamation and invasion of privacy cases disclosed an alarming willingness of juries to convict, and, often, to award staggering damages. At trial, media defendants lost four out of five cases, and, when tried before juries, the media lost almost nine out of ten cases. In nine of the cases juries awarded between one million and over forty million dollars. Punitive damage awards for a quarter of a million dollars or more were assessed in seventeen cases, and for over a million dollars in seven cases. Significantly, on appeal, almost three out of four cases were reversed, while almost four out of five damage awards were reduced or rejected.[43]

Let us turn, then, to the "harm" argument—the claim that pornography may be suppressed because it promotes rape and violence against women. It is important to realize that this argument has to maintain two propositions. First, it must hold that the fact that expression is harmful to others constitutes a sufficient ground to suppress it. Second, the advocates of this position must hold that pornography *does* harm women.

The claim that expression may be censored on grounds that it may harm others is not self-evidently true, and has been denied by important theorists of free expression.[44] Consider Professor Longino's account of the rationale of free expression, an account which I believe to be one of the important justificatory bases of free expression. In her view, freedom of expression is not part of a general right of freedom; rather, it is justified by a right of independence (or, as I prefer, autonomy) or status as an equal.[45] This conception of having independent, equal status to others is an important one in the fight for sexual liberation and equality for women. Sexual freedom for women will not be achieved through the notion that "anything goes" in sex, but, rather, through acceptance of women's sexual desires and needs as having equal weight to those of males. It will require a breakdown of the female role as subservient to that of the male. These notions do *not* permit as acceptable all ways of behaving sexually.

The concept of an independent, self-determining person surely implies that one must be free to choose important aspects of one's life—what occupations to pursue, with whom to associate, the sort of lifestyle one wishes to lead, where to live, and so on, irrespective of the wishes of others or the evaluations of others *of* those choices. It is not the *content* of the choice that gives it value from the viewpoint of autonomy, but the fact that it is one's *own* choice.[46] Surely, freedom to read what one wants, and to embrace whatever communications one desires, is crucial to being a self-determining person.

There are, no doubt, limits to the choices that one may exercise in the name of being autonomous. But, it will not suffice to draw those limits by saying that one is not free to have access to communications or to make choices that *can* lead *some* people to do things that harm others. To recognize a right of self-determination entails that we be willing to risk the possibility of harmful consequences from autonomous choices. There is an ironic demonstration of this point available. A journal that has published studies often cited by the radical feminists (indeed, in the *same issue* of an oft-cited study) has also published an article that purports to show that the greater emancipation of women in Western societies has led to great increases in criminal activity *by* women. Such crimes as robbery, larceny, burglary, fraud, and extortion have shown marked increases, as have arson, murder, and aggravated injury.[47] But, freedom of expression would mean little if such facts could be taken as a reason to suppress expression that seeks the further liberation of women from their secondary, dependent status with respect to men.

Still, there *is* a difference between feminist expression urging that the requisites of full personhood be made a reality for women and expression that, at best, plays a role in liberating the sexual psyche, but in some instances degrades women. If, in addition, it can be established that the latter type of expression plays some significant role in promoting rape, we might be somewhat more comfortable suppressing it. What the example above shows, however, is that even *if* we are willing to allow possible harms to others to be a ground for suppression of expression, we need to establish standards for *when* possible harms can play this role. Many free expression theorists would reject the notion entirely, of course; but, even if we beg the question against them, we still require some attention to the issue of criteria.

After considering the sorts of matters stressed by courts when dealing with such matters (e.g., when elaborating the "clear and present danger" test, or when debating government secrecy regulations), I would propose three necessary conditions for determining harms caused by expression, thus warranting censorship. I shall not be concerned with whether there are *further* necessary conditions, or with the conditions sufficient for censorship, since I believe that *none* of the three proposed conditions is met by the case against pornography. The conditions are:

1. There must be strong evidence of a *very* likely and serious harm.

2. The harms must be closely and directly linked with the expression.

3. It must be unlikely that further speech or expression can be used effectively to combat that harm.

The classic case of punishing the false shout of "fire" in a crowded theater illustrates the sort of case that meets the conditions. We should note, of course, that a *true* shout of fire would likely not be punishable, though it could be equally harmful. This shows that the three conditions are not sufficient to justify censorship. In addition, I would stress the importance of the third condition. Free expression theory does not hold that protected expression is never harmful; it insists that in a free society, the proper way to deal with the harmful effects of expression is through further expression. Where that tool is demonstrably not available, the presumption for freedom is undercut.

We need to ask, then, what is the status of research on the alleged harmful effects of pornography, and to what extent are the necessary conditions for justified censorship met. It is well known that the Presidential Commission on Obscenity and Pornography found no significant deleterious effects.[48] More recently, a similar British Committee on Obscenity and Film Censorship (headed by the highly regarded British philosopher Bernard Williams) concluded: "We unhesitatingly reject the suggestion that the available statistical information for England and Wales lends any support at all to the argument that pornography acts as a stimulus to the commission of sexual violence."[49] Furthermore, that report contains a searching critique of allegations that legalization of pornography in Denmark led to an increase in sex crimes. The data, when carefully reviewed, led the Williams committee to conclude: "It is impossible to discern a significant trend in rape which could be linked in any way with the free availability of pornography [in Denmark] since the late nineteen-sixties."[50] On the other hand, the committee noted that there *had* been a marked decline in offences against children, which correlated with the availability of pornography, and which "cannot readily be explained by any other factor."[51]

These reports, however, do not settle the matter. Some of the studies relied on by the American commission have come under attack by feminists and others, and there is more recent research than that reported on by either group that tends to point to certain forms of pornography as promoting harmful attitudes and behavior against women. I want to turn to these recent studies, for I believe that a "harm" case for censorship must rest primarily on this work. Moreover, the results cannot be merely dismissed.

Much of the recent research has been done by groups working with Dr. Neil Malamuth of the University of Manitoba, and by groups working with Dr. Edward Donnerstein of the University of Wisconsin. These studies typically involved the administration of electric shocks by volunteers who had been exposed to various types of pornographic materials, as well as nonpornographic materials, under various conditions. What has most captured public attention has been the fact that some studies showed a greater willingness to administer electric shocks after exposure to pornography depicting certain kinds of rape, viz., where the victim is portrayed as experiencing sexual arousal and enjoyment as an outcome of the rape experience.[52]

What is especially disturbing about this result is that the "message" conveyed is that women enjoy being raped, and that aggressive behavior toward women is a source of sexual pleasure to them. Thus, to the extent that pornographic materials center on such sexual depictions, they may reinforce and foster acceptance of this "rape mythology," and, as the clinical results suggest, they may foster actual aggressive behavior toward women. The concerns that feminists legitimately feel over these results are aggravated further by additional studies designed to gauge the self-reported likelihood that males would commit a rape. After being exposed to a rape sequence of the sort described above, fifty-one percent of the males indicated "2" or above on a 5 point scale, where "1" meant "no chance at all" and "5" meant "highly likely." Such responses tend to be correlated with acceptance of the "rape myth" and with similar attitudes of actual rapists. [53]

What is the significance of these studies for the case of those seeking to censor pornography? To what extent do the studies show that the necessary conditions given above for a "harm" argument to be acceptable are actually met by the case against pornography? The most important point to emphasize is that the recent studies do *not* yield any simple correlation between pornography, aggressive behavior, and rape. Indeed, it is very *unclear* what conclusions are appropriate. For example, one of the studies revealed that the group of men who became more willing to administer the electric shocks after seeing aggressive pornographic films also recommended longer prison sentences for rapists. [54] Could one conclude from this that such materials serve to strengthen the commitment to legal punishment for rape?

As to the degree of aggression perpetrated, I note that Malamuth, writing with one of his collaborators, Seymour Feshbach, states that: "Other investigators have demonstrated that people become similarly aggressive if aroused, for example, by loud noise or vigorous exercise." [55]

Furthermore, the self-reports of males regarding their likelihood to commit a rape must be placed in perspective. The response reported above was predicated on the subjects' being told they would not be caught or punished. When simply asked if they would act as the rapist did, eight-three percent answered "1", i.e., that there was no chance. [56] Furthermore, the level of positive prediction on the hypothesis of not being caught or punished dropped to thirty-five percent in follow-up studies. When these individuals were exposed to a rape portrayal in which significant physical violence was inflicted on the victim, the figure shrank to ten percent, even on the hypothesis of no punishment. [57] I note also that while "3" meant "somewhat likely," "2" was unlabeled;

hence, it is anyone's guess as to what the subjects thought they were agreeing to.[58] Though the results are cautionary (especially if one believes that inhibition caused by social disapproval will be eroded by permitting such portrayals in the media), they hardly demonstrate a strong, likely connection between pornography taken as a whole and the promotion of rape and violence.

Malamuth and Donnerstein, writing jointly in a paper that summarizes the recent research, caution as follows:

> One should not assume that all the research since the Commission's time has shown negative effects on individuals. In fact, the evidence is quite to the contrary. There has been a great deal of research which strongly supports the position that exposure to certain types of pornography can actually reduce aggressive responses. In fact, the reader should keep in mind that pornography has been shown to have many types of effects.[59]

A final point concerning these studies must be made. The researchers, concerned with the effects their studies might have on the male subjects who were exposed to the pornographic materials, undertook "debriefing" sessions designed to dispel the sanctioning of the "rape myth" that might otherwise have been produced by the exposure to the tests. According to Malamuth: "Recent data show that such debriefings are effective in dispelling beliefs in rape myths."[60] While this may raise questions about the strength of beliefs so readily dislodged, it at least shows that there is a noncensorship way of dealing with this sort of effect, viz., *other* expression that calls attention to and refutes the rape myth. Those who oppose censorship must admit the possibility that certain forms of pornography may play a role in the formation of harmful attitude and behavior patterns. But, those who propose censorship must be able to give reasons to think that there are not free expression modes of dealing with those consequences. The research they cite in the case of pornography shows the opposite.

There is one final source of feminist argument I want to discuss. The research I have considered would be somewhat more compelling if it could be shown that there was, in fact, a high correlation between exposure to the particular forms of pornography studied and the commission of acts of rape or other forms of sexual aggression against women. The most significant study of exposure to pornography on the part of sex offenders was done by researchers working with Dr. Michael Goldstein of U.C.L.A., and reported on by the Commission on Obscenity and Pornography. That study concluded that sex offenders in general, and rapists in particular, had had much *less* exposure to pornographic materials of all sorts than the nonrapist, nonsex-offender population used as controls. Moreover, the study revealed that rapists had family backgrounds that were extremely repressive with respect to sex. The study is not without difficulties and it has been subjected to various criticisms.[61] For the most part, these criticisms question the reliability of the results, but they do not show the conclusions to be simply unwarranted. On the other hand, the feminist author Kathleen Barry has mounted an attack on the study designed to undermine the conclusions entirely.[62] If her criticisms are valid, then the only evidence we have that there is *not* a significant pornography-rape link would be undermined. Her most telling points, however, involve serious mistakes.

Barry disputes that the data do show less exposure for sex offenders. She begins with the commission's claim that there had been less exposure to pornography in the adolescent years of sex offenders. She displays a chart showing that in the control group, eight-five percent of the whites had been exposed to pornography as adolescents, seventy-four percent of the Blacks, and fifty-six to sixty-two percent of the sex offenders. (Rapists represented the sixty-two percent figure.) Barry then says that though their figures are lower, the chart shows that the sex offenders had had a high level of exposure to pornography; thus, the commission was wrong to say that the data show that the sex offenders had comparatively little adolescent exposure.[63]

The fact is, however, that the conclusion was not drawn on the basis of the chart. The conclusion was stated by the commission on the following page of the report, on the basis of a *different* chart showing that nearly forty percent of the rapists had never seen photographic depictions of intercourse in adolescence (compared to fifteen percent of the controls), and seventy-six percent of the rapists had seen ten or fewer, whereas well over half the controls had seen eleven or more such depictions. Repetitive exposure of controls versus rapists was on the order of more than 2 to 1.[64]

The Goldstein study, as reported by the Obscenity Commission and in his book, *Pornography and Sexual Deviance,* stated: "It can be seen that across all stimuli and media the rapists reported less exposure to pornography during the past year."[65] Barry displays a chart, based on the commission report, headed "Recent Exposure to Sadomasochistic Movies," in which the rapists are given a seventy-eight percent figure and the controls a seventy-four percent figure. She adds that the study showed both controls and offenders having greater exposure to sadomasochistic movies than to any other form of pornography.[66]

In Goldstein's book there is information on the side of the graph that Barry has left out, and which is also given opposite the percentages in the commission report. It reads: "*never* exposed to stimuli." In other words, the overwhelming majority of controls and sex offenders, including the rapists, had had *no* exposure to sadomasochistic pornography during the prior year. The *only* erotic stimuli the rapists were exposed to less were mouth-genital depictions.[67]

Having set out what I regard as reasonable conditions to impose on an argument for censorship based on the harms caused by expression, I can only conclude that a plausible case has not been made with respect to pornography.

3. CONCLUSIONS

In concluding my discussion, I want to return to points of importance concerning the theory of free expression. That theory is either not taken seriously, or it is not fully understood by some feminist critics of pornography. Neither Rosemarie Tong nor Helen Longino, for example, advocate censorship. Tong concedes that education rather than censorship is probably the best current solution, and, in a concluding section of her original manuscript (not included in the *Take Back the Night* article), Longino concedes that the political climate does not make censorship an approach that is likely to be effective, since it is conservatives who control the judicial system. But, these are not "merely"matters of efficiency, divorced from the freedom of expression principle. The *theory* of free expression commits one to the *principle* that remedies to harms are to be sought through further expression, and the theory of free expression holds that the political climate *always* has the potential for the censorship function to fall into the wrong hands.

Furthermore, there *are* exercises of free expression available that do not involve suppression. Support can be given to writing, publications, and films that are "erotic" and do not degrade or humiliate women.[68] The attempt should be to encourage conceptions of sexuality that are consistent with full and equal status for women.

Those who urge censorship as the solution to perceived harms from pornography should bear in mind that freedom of expression is under a well-financed attack by arch-conservative forces throughout our nation. Freedom of expression may not be indivisible, but violations of it have a way of dragging others along with it. Some of the conservative opponents of pornography regard feminism itself as a great danger to the social well-being of the nation as a whole. They, too, have "evidence" at their disposal—the divorce rate, increases in premarital sex and teen-age pregnancy, increases in abortion, and so on. This is hardly the time to abandon liberal principles without much more compelling evidence of a clear and present danger that can only be dealt with through suppression of expression.

NOTES

1. Fred R. Berger, "Pornography, Sex, and Censorship," *Social Theory and Practice*, 4 (Spring, 1977); 183-209. This paper has been reprinted in several places that may be more accessible: Richard Wasserstrom, ed., *Today's Moral Problems*, 2d ed (New York: Macmillan Publishing Co., Inc., 1979); Alan Soble, ed., *Philosophy of Sex: Contemporary Readings* (Totowa, NJ: Littlefield, Adams & Co., 1980); and David Copp and Susan Wendell, eds., *Pornography and Censorship: Scientific, Philosophical and Legal Studies* (Buffalo, NY: Prometheus Books, 1983).

2. For my version of this critique, see my paper, "The Differences in the Cases For and Against Preferential Treatment Based on Sex and Those Based on Race," in *Proceedings of the Public Policy Conferences on Equality of Opportunity* (Sacramento, 1980), pp. 160-74. (Available through the Philosophy Department, University of California, Davis.)

3. For example, Professor Rosemarie Tong has given an argument that accepts the feminist critique of some pornographic materials, but holds that the legal remedy is probably not the best way at present to deal with the problem. [See, "Feminism, Pornography and Censorship," *Social Theory and Practice*, 8 (Spring, 1982): 1-15.] A strong statement that accepts the critique of pornography, but which rejects censorship, is that of Wendy Kaminer, "Pornography and the First Amendment: Prior Restraints and Private Actions," in *Take Back the Night: Women on Pornography*, ed. Laura Ledered (New York: William Morrow and Company, Inc., 1980), pp. 241-47.

4. See, for example, Ellen Willis, "Feminism, Moralism, and Pornography," in *The Village Voice Anthology (1956-1980)*, ed. Geoffrey Stokes (New York: Quill, 1982), pp. 76-8. Also, Pat Califia, "Feminism and Sadomasochism," *Heresies: A Feminist Publication on Art & Politics*,3 (1981): 30-4; and, in the same issue, Paula Webster, "Pornography and Pleasure," pp. 48-51.

5. Susan Brownmiller, *Against Our Will: Men, Women and Rape* (New York: Macmillan, 1975), p. 201. Also, in *Take Back the Night*, p. 32.

6. Andrea Dworkin, "Pornography and Grief," in *Take Back the Night*, pp. 288-9.

7. Kathleen Barry, *Female Sexual Slavery* (New York: Avon Books, 1979), p. 206.

8. Helen Longino, "Pornography, Oppression, and Freedom: A Closer Look," in *Take Back the Night*, p. 42.

9. Ibid., p. 43.

10. There is an interesting argument presented recently by Professor Frederick Schauer who claims that *some* pornography (which he calls "hard-core") serves

almost exclusively as a masturbatory aid, with no significant communicative content. As such, it is not within the meaning of "speech," and ought not to be considered as constitutionally protected. As he has correctly pointed out to me, this is not an argument for *censorship*, since the materials the argument would permit to be suppressed do not (in his view) constitute expression. The argument is appealing, but it is inconsistent with the feminist objections to hard-core pornography, for those objections maintain that regardless of intention and use, these materials in fact convey ideas and endorse the modes of treatment of women that are depicted. [See Frederick Schauer, *Free Speech: A Philosophical Enquiry* (Cambridge: Cambridge University Press, 1982), pp. 178-88.]

11. Brownmiller, "Let's Put Pornography Back in the Closet," in *Take Back the Night*, p. 254. Brownmiller quotes Chief Justice Warren Burger who stated that protection of "obscene" materials should not be equated with "the free and robust exchange of ideas and political debate."

12. Longino, p. 51. The distinction, and this particular wording, is taken from Ronald Dworkin, *Taking Rights Seriously* (Cambridge: Harvard University Press, 1977), p. 262.

13. Longino, p. 52.

14. Even in cases where "obscenity" has been held suppressible because it is not protected under the First Amendment, the ground has never been that it is not political speech, but that it is "utterly without redeeming social importance," or that suppression is justified in order to protect "the primary requirements of decency," and so on. In *Roth* v. *United States*, 354 U.S. 476 (1957), the Court stated that "all ideas having even the slightest redeeming social importance . . . have the full protection of the [Constitutional] guarantees." In *Paris Adult Theatre I* v. *Station*, 413 U.S. 49, the Court implied that "books, plays, and art," are all encompassed within the protections, so long as they do not "have a tendency to exert a corrupting and debasing impact leading to anti-social behavior."

15. This line of argument is strongly stressed by Schauer. See *Free Speech: A Philosophical Enquiry*, especially, pp. 80-5.

16. Alexander Meiklejohn, *Political Freedom: The Constitutional Power of the People* (New York: Harper & Row, 1948, 1960); and "The First Amendment Is An Absolute," in *The Supreme Court Review 1961*, ed. P. Kurland (Chicago: University of Chicago, 1962), pp. 245-66.

17. Longino, p. 42.

18. Ann Garry, "Pornography and Respect for Women," *Social Theory and Practice*, 4 (Summer, 1978): 395-421; this book, pp. 312-326.

19. Tong, p. 4.

20. See *Take Back the Night*, p. 17.

21. I do not know if the phrase is actually an accurate translation of Augustine's language.

22. See Morse Peckham, *Art and Pornography: An Experiment in Explanation* (New York/London: Basic Books, Inc., 1969). See, also, the interesting and subtle discussion of the matter in *Report of the Committee on Obscenity and Film Censorship*, Cmnd 7772, HMSO (London, 1979), pp. 103-11. (The *Report* is often referred to as the "Williams Report," after its chairman, the philosopher, Bernard Williams.) An important argument for the claim is to be found in,

Susan Sontag, "The Pornographic Imagination," in her book, *Styles of Radical Will* (New York: Farrar, Straus and Giroux, 1969), pp. 35-73.

23. For example, Walter Berns, "Pornography vs. Democracy: The Case for Censorship," *The Public Interest*, 22 (Winter, 1971): 3-24.

24. See Ernest van den Haag, untitled essay in *Censorship: For and Against*, ed. Harold H. Hart (New York: Hart Publishing Co., 1971), pp. 143-63.

25. Stephen Marcus, *The Other Victorians: A Study of Sexuality and Pornography in Mid-Nineteenth Century England* (New York: Basic Books, 1964). Also, David A.J. Richards, *The Moral Criticism of Law* (Encino and Belmont, CA: Dickenson Publishing Company, Inc., 1977), p. 71.

26. An interview with Pauline Reage has been published by the French publisher and writer, Regine Deforges, under the title, *Confessions of O* (New York: The Viking Press, 1975, 1979). In the interview, the author herself stresses as a theme that there is a basic need that is satisfied by humiliation. (See p. 23.)

27. Sontag, especially p. 60.

28. The study is reported on in, Pauline B. Bart and Margaret Jozsa, "Dirty Books, Dirty Films, and Dirty Data," in *Take Back the Night*, pp. 213-14. I have not been able to obtain a copy of the original research.

29. Neil M. Malamuth and Barry Spinner, "A Longitudinal Content Analysis of Sexual Violence in the Best-Selling Erotic Magazines," *The Journal of Sex Research*, 16 (August, 1980); 226-37.

30. Bart and Jozsa, p. 214.

31. Malamuth and Spinner, p. 231.

32. I have given an account that parallels this treatment of pornographic depictions with regard to the mass media in general. See "Racial and Sex-Role Stereotyping in the Media: An Analysis," in *Theories in Practice: The Humanities in Public Life*, ed. Bruce Sievers, forthcoming.

33. Nancy Friday, *My Secret Garden: Women's Sexual Fantasies* (New York: Pocket Books, 1973), pp. 138-40. It is important to emphasize that Ms. Friday, in presenting such fantasies, stressed that "fantasy need have nothing to do with reality, in terms of suppressed wish-fullment," (p. 109). This is ignored by some feminist critics of her work. (See, for example, Diana E.H. Russell, "Pornography and Violence: What Does the New Research Say?" in *Take Back the Night*, p. 231).

34. Adrienne Rich, "Afterword," in *Take Back the Night*, p. 318.

35. Angela Carter, *The Sadeian Woman And the Ideology of Pornography* (New York: Pantheon Books, 1978).

36. Andrea Dworkin, *Pornography: Men Possessing Women* (New York: G.P. Putnam's Sons, 1979, 1980, 1981).

37. Webster, p. 50.

38. Beatrice Faust, *Women, Sex, and Pornography: A Controversial and Unique Study* (New York: Macmillan Publishing Co., Inc., 1980), p. 18.

39. Garry also refers to content that "exemplifies and recommends" attitudes or behaviors. Just when a depiction "endorses" or "recommends" certain conduct, and *what* conduct is endorsed are surely hard questions to answer.

40. Reported in *Contra Costa Independent*, Richmond, California, (April 16, 1982): 7. Apparently, the recommendation of the school's human rights

committee was not acted on.

41. The issue is given some discussion by Rosemarie Tong in the article cited above, and she makes some useful points. This can hardly be regarded as a systematic study of the legal ramifications, especially since the discussion appears to be drawn in large measure from an article written in 1943.

42. An excellent survey of the development and intricacies of defamation law is to be found in, Jerome A. Barron and C. Thomas Dienes, *Handbook of Free Speech and Free Press* (Boston and Toronto: Little, Brown and Company, 1979), Chs. 6 and 7.

43. See "Media Libel Study Charts Rise of Damage Awards," *Publishers Weekly,* 222 (October 8, 1982): 10-14.

44. One of the most compelling arguments for this view is given in, Ronald Dworkin, "Is There a Right to Pornography," *Oxford Journal of Legal Studies,* 1 (Summer, 1981), pp. 177-212. The article is a critique of the "Williams Report" cited above.

45. Longino, pp. 50-3.

46. The argument for this claim is made forcefully in Sharon Bishop, "Self-Determination and Autonomy," in *Today's Moral Problems,* 2d ed., ed. Richard A. Wasserstrom (New York: Macmillan Publishing Co., Inc., 1979), pp. 118-33. See also, Fred R. Berger, *Happiness, Justice, and Freedom: The Moral and Political Philosophy of John Stuart Mill* (Berkeley and Los Angeles: University of California Press, 1983) Ch. V.

47. Freda Adler, "The Interaction Between Women's Emancipation and Female Criminality: A Cross-cultural Perspective," *International Journal of Criminology and Penology,* 5 (1977): 101-12.

48. *The Report of the Commission on Obscenity and Pornography* (New York: Bantam, 1970).

49. *Report of the Committee on Obscenity and Film Censorship,* p. 80.

50. Ibid., p. 83.

51. Ibid., p. 84.

52. The bibliography of this research has become fairly extensive. It is surveyed in a piece jointly authored by Malamuth and Donnerstein, "Pornography: Its Consequences on the Observer," in *Sexual Dynamics of Anti-Social Behavior,* ed. Louis B. Schlesinger (Springfield, IL: Charles C. Thomas), to appear.

53. See, Neil M. Malamuth, "Rape Proclivity Among Males," *Journal of Social Issues,* 37 (1981): 138-157.

54. This result should be contrasted with that of another study in which men and women were subjected to "massive exposure" to what the authors describe as the "least objectionable" type of pornography, that involved neither violence nor rape. Such exposure to the tamer variety produced recommendations of *shorter* prison terms for rapists. [See, Dolf Zillman and Jennings Bryant, "Pornography, Sex Callousness, and the Trivialization of Rape," *Journal of Communication,* 32 (Autumn, 1982): 10-21.] Perhaps a similar study would show a similar result for the class of favored "erotica." Would anyone seriously believe that these varied results would be ground for banning the milder, erotic materials, while permitting the more violent fare because of the stronger punitive attitudes fostered?

55. Seymour Feshbach and Neil M. Malamuth, "Sex and Aggression: Proving the Link," *Psychology Today*, 12 (November, 1978): 112.

56. Neil M. Malamuth, Scott Haber, and Seymour Feshbach, "Testing Hypotheses Regarding Rape: Exposure to Sexual Violence, Sex Differences, and the 'Normality' of Rapists," *Journal of Research in Personality*, 14 (1980): 130.

57. T. Tieger, "Self-reported Likelihood of Raping and the Social Perception of Rape," *Journal of Research in Personality*, 15 (1981): 147-54.

58. Dr. Malamuth kindly provided this information in a letter, in answer to my query.

59. Malamuth and Donnerstein, m.s. p. 4.

60. Malamuth, "Rape Proclivity Among Males," p. 146.

61. The study is reported on in *Report of the Commission on Obscenity and Film Censorship*, Part III, Ch. II; also in *Technical Report of the Commission on Obscenity and Pornography*, Vol. VII (Washington: U.S. Government Printing Office, 1970), pp. 1-90; and in, Michael J. Goldstein and Harold S. Kant, *Pornography and Sexual Deviance* (Berkeley and Los Angeles: University of California Press, 1973). For critical comment, see, Irene Diamond, "Pornography and Repression: A Reconsideration of "Who' and 'What,'" in *Take Back the Night*, pp. 196-7; also, Bart and Jozsa, pp. 211-12; and, H.J. Eysenck and D.K.B. Nias, *Sex, Violence and the Media* (New York: McGraw-Hill, 1978).

62. Barry, pp. 236-41.

63. Ibid, pp. 237-8.

64. *Report of the Commission on Obscenity and Film Censorship*, pp. 279-80.

65. *Technical Report of the Commission on Obscenity and Pornography*, p. 27.

66. Barry, p. 239.

67. Goldstein and Kant, p. 67; *Technical Report of the Commission on Obscenity and Pornography*, p. 29. I note that in the sentence *prior* to the one quoted by Barry, the report refers to the chart as recording "the percentage of 'never' replies." (p. 27)

68. See, for example, *Yellow Silk: Journal of the Erotic Arts*, P. O. Box 6374, Albany, CA, 94706.

HOMOSEXUALITY

Jeremy Bentham

An Essay on "Paederasty"

INTRODUCTION TO BENTHAM'S ESSAY

I have been tormenting myself for years to find, if possible, a sufficient ground for treating them [homosexuals] *with the severity with which they are treated at this time of day by all European nations: but upon the principle of utility I can find none.*

Had these words been penned by a famous social philosopher of the 1980s, they would be noteworthy but not exceptional; written by a social philosopher of the 1880s, they would have been both noteworthy and exceptional; but since the passage was written by a famous English social philosopher of the 1780s, Jeremy Bentham, and since it prefaces what appears to be the first philosophical treatment of homosexuality in the English language, the passage is extraordinary indeed.

Bentham and his fellow utilitarians sought a rational standard against which they could measure the customs and laws of their society. The device they hit upon was the calculus of utility. To employ the calculus one had to conceptualize the social world in terms of acts that were morally neutral in and of themselves, but which acquired value in terms of their consequences. Acts were then held to be moral insofar as their consequences were conducive to human happiness, and immoral insofar as their effects militated against happiness and/or promoted pain, suffering, or any other form of human misery.

The utilitarian project was to measure all customs and laws in terms of the calculus of utility—including, as it turned out, those relating to *"unnatural" sexual acts. Bentham appraised the moral nature of these acts and the laws that criminalize them in three different sets of writings dated c. 1774, c. 1785, and 1814-1816. In each case, when the sexual acts in themselves were regarded as morally neutral and appraised only in terms of their consequences he found that, except in cases of homosexual rape, the most certain consequence of a homosexual act was the pleasure experienced by the participants. There was, therefore, a strong* prima facie *case both against the moral opprobrium with which homosexuality was customarily viewed and against imposing criminal sanctions on homosexual acts. (According to some scholars[1] more than sixty people were hanged for "sodomy" and other homosexual acts in England during the years 1806-1835.) Bentham carefully examined all of the purported negative consequences of homosexual intercourse suggested by his nonutilitarian contemporaries, Blackstone, Montesquieu, and Voltaire—for example, its supposed tendency to corrupt and debilitate practioners, its effects on population, and so on. Weighing these conjectured effects against the historical data supplied by Greek homosexuality, Bentham concluded that since the net consequences of homosexual sex appear not to be harmful, utilitarians must reject the proscription and criminalization of homosexuality.*

Like most of Bentham's writings, his work on homosexuality was not published in his lifetime. The first publication of any of this material occurred in 1931 when C. K. Ogden published some of the 1814-1816 materials as an appendix to his 1931 edition of Bentham's Theory of Legislation. *The essay on "Paederasty" was not published until 1978, when it appeared in the Fall and Summer editions of the* Journal of Homosexuality. *Louis Compton, a professor of English at the University of Nebraska, had rediscovered these materials among Bentham's papers and transcribed the manuscript. Although the style of Bentham's writings reflects the period in which they were written, the thought is remarkably contemporary; the essay is undoubtedly one of the most significant publications in the recent literature on philosophy and sex.—R.B.*

To what class of offences shall we refer these irregularities of the venereal appetite which are styled unnatural? . . . I have been tormenting myself for years to find if possible a sufficient ground for treating them with the severity with which they are treated at this time of day by all European nations: but upon the principle of utility I can find none.

... In settling the nature and tendency of this offence we shall for the most part have settled the nature and tendency of all the other offences that come under this disgusting catalogue.

PAEDERASTY: DOES IT PRODUCE ANY PRIMARY MISCHIEF?

1. As to any primary mischief, it is evident that it produces no pain in anyone. On the contrary it produces pleasure, and that a pleasure which, by their perverted taste, is by this supposition preferred to that pleasure which is in general reputed the greatest. The partners are both willing. If either of them be unwilling, the act is not that which we have here in view: it is an offence totally different in its nature of effects: it is a personal injury; it is a kind of rape.

AS A SECONDARY MISCHIEF WHETHER THEY PRODUCE ANY ALARM IN THE COMMUNITY

2. As to any secondary mischief, it produces not any pain of apprehension. For what is there in it for any body to be afraid of? By the supposition, those only are the objects of it who choose to be so, who find a pleasure, for so it seems they do, in being so.

WHETHER ANY DANGER

3. As to any danger exclusive of pain, the danger, if any, must consist in the tendency of the example. But what is the tendency of this example? To dispose others to engage in the same practises: but this practise for anything that has yet appeared produces not pain of any kind to anyone.

REASONS THAT HAVE COMMONLY BEEN ASSIGNED

Hitherto we have found no reason for punishing it at all: much less for punishing it with the degree of severity with which it has been commonly punished. Let us see what force there is in the reasons that have been commonly assigned for punishing it.

WHETHER AGAINST THE SECURITY OF THE INDIVIDUAL

Sir W. Blackstone [argues that paederasty] is not only an offence against the peace, but it is of that division of offences against the peace which are offences against security. According to the same writer, if a man is guilty of this kind of filthiness, for instance, with a cow, as some men have been known to be, it is an offence / against somebody's security. He does not say whose security, for the law makes no distinction in its ordinances, so neither does this lawyer or any other English lawyer in his comments make any distinction between this kind of filthiness when committed with the consent of the patient and the same kind of filthiness when committed against his consent and by violence. It is just as if a man were to make no distinction between concubinage and rape.

WHETHER IT DEBILITATES—MONTESQUIEU

The reason that Montesquieu gives for reprobating it is the weakness which he seems to suppose it to have a tendency to bring upon those who practice it. (*Esp. des Loix,* L. 12, ch. 6. "11) This, if it be true in fact, is a reason of a very different complexion from any of the preceding and it is on the ground of this reason as being the most plausible one that I have ranked the offence under its present head. As far as it is true in fact, the act ought to be regarded in the first place as coming within the list of offences against one's self, of offences of imprudence: in the next place, as an offence against the state, an offence the tendency of which is to diminish the public force. If however it tends to weaken a man it is not any single act that can in any sensible degree have that effect. It can only be the habit: the act thus will become obnoxious as evidencing the existence, in probability, of the habit. This enervating tendency, be it what it may, if it is to be taken as a ground for treating the / [192] practise in question with a degree of severity which is not bestowed upon the regular way of gratifying the veneral appetite, must be greater in the former case than in the latter. Is it so? If the affirmative can be shown it must be either by arguments *a priori* drawn from considerations of the nature of the human frame or from experience. Are there any such arguments from physiology? I have never heard of any: I can think of none.

WHAT SAYS HISTORY?

What says historical experience? The result of this can be measured only upon a large scale or upon a very general survey. Among the modern nations it is comparatively but rare. In modern Rome it is perhaps not very uncommon; in Paris probably not quite so common; in London still less frequent; in Edinburgh or Amsterdam you scarce hear of it two or three times in a century. In Athens and in antient Rome in the most flourishing periods of the history of those capitals, regular intercourse between the sexes was scarcely much more common. It was upon the same footing throughout Greece; everybody practised it; nobody was ashamed of it. They might be ashamed of what they looked upon as an excess in it, or they might be ashamed of it as a weakness, as a propensity that had a tendency to distract men from more worthy and important occupations, / just as a man with us might be ashamed of excess or weakness in his love for women. In itself one may be sure they were not ashamed of it. . . .

What is remarkable is that there is scarce a striking character in antiquity, not one that in other respects men are in use to cite as virtuous, of whom it does not appear by one circumstance or another, that/he was infected with this inconceivable propensity . . . .

Many moderns, and among others Mr. Voltaire, dispute the fact, but that intelligent philosopher sufficiently intimates the ground of his incredulity—if he does not believe it, it is because he likes not to believe it. What the ancients called love in such a case was what we call Platonic, that is, was not love but friendship. But the Greeks knew the difference between love and friendship as well as we—they had distinct terms to signify them by: it seems reasonable therefore to suppose that when they say love they mean love, and that when they say friendship only they mean friendship only. And with regard to Xenophon and his master, Socrates, and his fellow-scholar Plato, it seems more reasonable to believe them to have been addicted to this taste when they or any of them tell us so in express terms than to trust to the interpretations, however ingenious and however well-intended, of any men who write at this time of day, when they tell us it was no such thing. / Not to insist upon Agesilaus and Xenophon, it appears by one circumstance or another that Themistocles, Aristides, Epaminondus, Alcibiades, Alexander and perhaps the greatest number of the heroes of Greece were infected with this taste. Not that the historians are at the pains of informing us so expressly, for it was not extraordinary enough to make it worth their while, but it comes out collaterally in the course of the transactions they have occasion to relate.

It appears then that this propensity was universally predominant among the ancient Greeks and Romans, among the military as much as any. The ancient Greeks and Romans, however, are commonly reputed as / a much stouter as well as a much braver people than the stoutest and bravest of any of the modern nations of Europe. They appear to have been stouter at least in a very considerable degree than the French in whom this propensity is not very common and still more than the Scotch in whom it is still less common, and this although the climate even of Greece was a great deal warmer and in that respect more enervating than that of modern Scotland.

If then this practise was in those ancient warm countries attended with any enervating effects, they were much more than counteracted by the superiority of [illegible] in the exertions which were then required by the military education over and above those which are now called forth by ordinary labour. But if there be any ground derived from history for attributing to it any such enervating effects it is more than I can find.

WHETHER IT ENERVATES THE PATIENT MORE THAN THE AGENT

Montesquieu however seems to make a distinction—he seems to suppose these enervating effects to be exerted principally upon the person who is the patient in such a business. This distinction does not seem very satisfactory in any point of view. Is there any reason for supposing it to be a fixed one? Between persons of the same age actuated by the same incomprehensible desires would not the parts they took in the business be convertible? Would not the patient / be the agent in his turn? If it were not so, the person on whom he supposes these effects to be the greatest is precisely the person with regard to whom it is most difficult to conceive whence those consequences should result. In the one case there is exhaustion which when carried to excess may be followed by debility: in the other case there is no such thing.

WHAT SAYS HISTORY?

In regard to this point too in particular, what says history? As the two parts that a man may take in this business are so naturally convertible however frequently he may have taken a passive part, it will not ordinarily appear. According to the notions of the ancients, there was something degrading in the passive part which was not in the active. It was ministering to the pleasure, for so we are obliged to call it, of another without participation, it was making one's self the property of another man, it was playing the woman's part: it was therefore unmanly. *(Paedicabo vos et irrumabo, Antoni [sic] pathice et cinaede Furi. [Carm. 16] Catullus. J.B.)* On the other hand, to take the active part was to make use of another for one's pleasure, it was making another man one's property, it was preserving the manly, the commanding character. Accordingly, Solon in his laws prohibits slaves from bearing an active part where the passive is borne by a freeman. In the few instances in which we happen to hear of a person's taking the passive part there is nothing to favour / the above-mentioned hypothesis. The beautiful

Alcibiades, who in his youth, says Cornelius Nepos, after the manner of the Greeks, was beloved by many, was not remarkable either for weakness or for cowardice: at least, [blank] did not find it so. The Clodius whom Cicero scoffs at for his servile obsequiousness to the appetite of Curio was one of the most daring and turbulent spirits in all Rome. Julius Caesar was looked upon as a man of tolerable courage in his day, notwithstanding the complaisance he showed in his youth to the King of Bithynia, Nicomedes. (Aristotle, the inquisitive and observing Aristotle, whose physiological disquisitions are looked upon as some of the best of his works—Aristotle, who if there had been anything in this notion had every opportunity and inducement to notice and confirm it—gives no intimation of any such thing. On the contrary he sits down very soberly to distribute the male half of the species under two classes: one class having a natural propensity, he says, to bear a passive part in such a business, as the other have to take an active part. *(Probl.* Sect. 4 art. 27: The former of these propensities he attributes to a peculiarity of organization, analogous to that of women. The whole passage is abundantly obscure and shows in how imperfect a state of anatomical knowledge was his time. *J.B.)* This observation it must be confessed is not much more satisfactory than that other of the same philosopher when he speaks of two sorts of men—the one born to be masters, the other to be slaves. If however there had appeared any reason for supposing this practise, either with regard to the passive or the active part of it, to have had any remarkable effects in the way of debilitation upon those who were addicted to it, he would have hardly said so much / [194] upon the subject without taking notice of that circumstance.

WHETHER IT HURTS POPULATION?

A notion more obvious, but perhaps not much better founded than the former is that of its being prejudicial to population. Mr. Voltaire appears inclined in one part of his works to give some countenance to this opinion. He speaks of it as a vice which would be destructive to the human race if it were general. "How did it come about that a vice which would destroy mankind if it were general, that an infamous outrage against nature . . .?" *(Questions sur l'Encyclop.* "Amour Socratique." *J.B.)*

A little further on, speaking of Sextus Empiricus who would have us believe that this practise was "recommended" in Persia by the laws, he insists that the effect of such a law would be to annihilate the human race if it were literally observed. "No", says he, "it is not in human nature to make a law that contradicts and outrages nature, a law that would annihilate mankind if it were observed to the letter." This consequence however is far enough from being a necessary one. For a law of the purport he represents to be observed, it is sufficient that this unprolific kind of venery be practised; it is not necessary that it should be practised to the exclusion of that which is prolific. Now that there should ever be wanting such a measure of the regular and ordinary inclination of desire for the proper object / as is necessary for keeping up the numbers of mankind upon their present footing is a notion that stands warranted by nothing that I can find in history. To consider the matter *a priori* [?], if we consult Mr. Hume and Dr. Smith, we shall find that it is not the strength of the inclination of the one sex for the other that is the measure of the numbers of mankind, but the quantity of subsistence which they can find or raise upon a given spot. With regard to the mere object of population, if we consider the time of gestation in the female sex we shall find that much less than a hundredth part of the activity a man is capable of exerting in this way is sufficient to produce all the effect that can be produced by ever so much more. Population therefore cannot suffer till the inclination of the male sex for the female be considerably less than a hundredth part as strong as for their own. Is there the least probability that [this] should ever be the case? I must confess I see not any thing that should lead us to suppose it. Before this can happen the nature of the human composition must receive a total change and that propensity which is commonly regarded as the only one of the two that is natural must have become altogether an unnatural one.

I have already observed that I can find nothing in history to countenance the notion I am examining. On the contrary the country in which the prevalence of this practise / is most conspicuous happens to have been remarkable for its populousness. The bent of popular prejudice has been to exaggerate this populousness: but after all deductions [are] made, still it will appear to have been remarkable. It was such as, notwithstanding the drain of continual wars in a country parcelled out into paltry states as to be all of it frontier, gave occasion to the continued necessity of emigration.

This reason however well grounded soever it were in itself could not with any degree of consistency be urged in a country where celibacy was permitted, much less where it was encouraged. The proposition which (as will be shown more fully by and by) is not at all true with respect to paederasty, I mean that were it to prevail universally it would put an end to the human race, is most evidently and strictly true with regard to celibacy. If then merely out of regard to population it were right that paederasts should be burnt alive monks ought to be roasted alive by a slow fire. If a paederast, according to the monkish canonist Bermondus, destroys the whole human race Bermondus destroyed it I don't know how many thousand times over. The crime of Bermondus is I don't know how many times worse than paederasty. /

WHETHER IT ROBS WOMEN

A more serious imputation for punishing this practise [is] that the effect of it is to produce in the male sex an indifference to the female, and thereby defraud the latter of their rights. This, as far as it holds good in point of fact, is in truth a serious imputation. The interest of the female part of the species claim just as much attention, and not a whit more, on the part of the legislator, as those of the male. A complaint of this sort, it is true, would not come with a very good grace from a modest woman; but should the woman be estopped from making complaint in such a case it is the business of the men to make it for them. This then as far as it holds good in point of fact is in truth a very serious imputation: how far it does it will be proper to enquire.

In all European countries and such others on which we bestow the title of civilized, this propensity, which in the male sex is under a considerable degree of restraint, is under an incomparably greater restraint in the female. While each is alike prohibited from partaking of these enjoyments but on the terms of marriage by the fluctuating and inefficacious influence of religion, the censure of the world denies it [to] the female part of the species under the severest penalties while the male sex is left free. No sooner is a woman known to have infringed this prohibition than either she is secluded from all means of repeating the offence, or upon her escaping from that vigilance she throws herself into that degraded class whom the want of company of their own sex render unhappy, and the abundance of it on the part of the male sex unprolific. This being the case, it appears the contribution which the male part of the species are willing as well as able to bestow is beyond all comparison greater than what the female part are permitted to receive. If a woman has a husband she is permitted to receive it only from her husband; if she has no husband she is not permitted to receive it from any man without being degraded into the class of prostitutes. When she is in that unhappy class she has not indeed less than she would wish, but what is often as bad to her—she has more.

It appears then that if the female sex are losers by the prevalence of this practice it can only be on this supposition—that the force with which it tends to divert men from entering into connection with the other sex is greater than the force with which the censure of the world tends to prevent those connections by its operation on the women. [196]

As long as things are upon that footing there are many cases in which the women can be no sufferers for the want of solicitation on the part of the men. If the institution of the marriage contract be a beneficial one, and if it be expedient that the observance of it should be maintained inviolate, we must in the first place deduct it from the number of the women who would be sufferers by the prevalence of this taste all married women whose husbands were not infected with it. In the next place, upon the supposition that a state of prostitution is not a happier state than a state of virginity, we must deduct all those women who by means of this prevalence would have escaped being debauched. The women who would be sufferers by it *ab initio* are those only who, were it not for the prevalence of it, would have got husbands.

The question then is reduced to this. What are the number of women who by the prevalence of this taste would, it is probable, be prevented from getting husbands? These and these only are they who would be sufferers by it. Upon the following considerations it does not seem likely that the prejudice sustained by the sex in this way could ever rise to any considerable amount. Were the prevalence of this taste to rise to ever so great a heighth the most considerable part of the motives to marriage would remain entire. In the first place, the desire of having children, in the next place the desire of forming alliances between families, thirdly the convenience of having a domestic companion whose company will continue to be agreeable throughout life, fourthly the convenience of gratifying the appetite in question at any time when the want occurs and without the expense and trouble of concealing it or the danger of a discovery.

Were a man's taste even so far corrupted as to make him prefer the embraces of a person of his own sex to those of a female, a connection of that preposterous kind would therefore be far enough from answering to him the purposes of a marriage. A connection with a woman may by accident be followed with disgust, but a connection of the other kind, a man must know, will for certain come in time to be followed by disgust. All the documents we have from the ancients relative to this matter, and we have a great abundance, agree in this, that it is only for a very few years of his life that a male continues an object of desire even to those in whom the infection of this taste is at the strongest. The very name it went by among the Greeks may stand instead of all other proofs, of which the works of Lucian and Martial alone will furnish any abundance that can be required. Among the Greeks it was called *Paederastia*, the love of boys, not *Andrerastia,* the love of men. Among the Romans the act was called Paedicare because the object of it was a boy. There was a particular name for those who had past the short period beyond which no man hoped to be an object of desire to his own sex. They were called *exoleti.* No male therefore who was passed this short period of life could expect to find in this way any reciprocity of affection; he must be as odious to the boy from the beginning as in a short time the boy would be to him. The objects of this kind of sensuality would therefore come only in the place of common prostitutes; they could never even to a person of this depraved taste answer the purposes of a virtuous woman.

What says history?

Upon this footing stands the question when considered *a priori:* the evidence of facts seems to be still more conclusive on the same side. There seems no reason to doubt, as I have already observed but that population went on altogether as fast and that the men were altogether as well inclined to marriage among the Grecians in whom this vitious propensity was most prevalent as in any modern people in whom it is least prevalent. In Rome, indeed, about the time of the extinction of liberty we find great complaints of the decline of population: but the state of it does not appear to have been at all dependent on or at all influenced by the measures that were taken from time to time to restrain the love of boys: it was with the Romans, as with us, what kept a man from marriage was not the preferring boys to women but the preferring the convenience of a transient connection to the expense and hazard of a lasting one.

If it were more frequent than the regular connection in what sense could it be termed unnatural?

The nature of the question admits of great latitude of opinion: for my own part I must confess I cannot bring myself to entertain so high a notion of the alluringness of this preposterous propensity as some men appear to entertain. I cannot suppose it to [be] possible it should ever get to such a heighth as that the interests of the female part of the species should be materially affected by it: or that it could ever happen that were they to contend upon equal ground the eccentric and unnatural propensity should ever get the better of the regular and natural one. Could we for a moment suppose this to be the case, I would wish it to be considered what meaning a man would have to annex to the expression, when he bestows on the propensity under consideration the epithet of unnatural. If contrary to all appearance the case really were that if all men were left perfectly free to choose, as many men would make choice of their own sex as of the opposite one, I see not what reason there would be for applying the word natural to the one rather than to the other. All the difference would be that the one was both natural and necessary whereas the other was natural but not necessary. If the mere circumstance of its not being necessary were sufficient to warrant the terming it unnatural it might as well be said that the taste a man has for music is unnatural.

My wonder is how any man who is at all acquainted with the most amiable part of the species should ever entertain any serious apprehensions of their yielding the ascendent to such unworthy rivals.

Among the ancients—whether it excluded not the regular taste

A circumstance that contributes considerably to the alarms entertained by some people on this score is the common prejudice which supposes that the one propensity is exclusive of the other. This notion is for the most part founded on prejudice as may be seen in the works of a multitude of ancient authors in which we continually see the same person at one time stepping aside in pursuit of this eccentric kind of pleasure but at other times diverting his inclination to the proper object. Horace, in speaking of the means of satisfying the venereal appetite, proposes to himself as a matter of indifference a prostitute of either sex: and the same poet, who forgetting himself now and then says a little here and there about boys, says a great deal everywhere about women. The same observation will hold good with respect to every other personage of antiquity who either by his own account or that of another is represented to us as being infected with this taste. It is so in all the poets who in any of their works have occasion to say anything about themselves. Some few appear to have had no appetite for boys, as is the case for instance with Ovid, who takes express notice of it and gives a reason for it. But it is a never failing rule wherever you see any thing about boys, you see a great deal more about women. Virgil has one Alexis, but he has Galateas [blank] in abundance. Let us be unjust to no man: not even to a paederast. In all antiquity there is not a single instance of an author nor scarce an explicit account of any other man who was addicted exclusively to this taste. Even in modern times the real women-haters are to be found not so much among paederasts, as among monks and catholic priests, such of them, be they more or fewer, who think and act in consistency with their profession.

Reason why it might be expected so to do

I say even in modern times; for there is one circumstance which should make this taste where it does prevail much more likely to be exclusive at present than it was formerly. I mean the severity with which it is now treated by the laws and the contempt and abhorrence with which it is regarded by the generality of the people. If we may so call it, the persecution they meet with from all quarters, whether deservedly or not, has the effect in this instance which persecution has and must have more or less in all instances, the effect of rendering those persons who are the objects of it more attached than they would otherwise be to the practise it proscribes. It renders them the more attached to one another, sympathy of itself having a powerful tendency, independent of all other motives, to attach a man to his own companions in misfortune. This sympathy has at the same time a powerful tendency to beget a proportionable antipathy even towards all such persons as appear to be involuntary, much more to such as appear to be the voluntary, authors of such misfortune. When a man is made to suffer it is enough on all other occasions to beget in him a prejudice against those by whose means or even for whose sake he is made to suffer. When the hand of every man is against a person, his hand, or his heart at least, will naturally be against every man. It would therefore be rather singular if under the present system of manners these outcasts of society should be altogether so well disposed towards women as in ancient times when they were left unmolested.

Whether, if it robbed women, it ought at all events to be punished?

The result of the whole is that there appears not any great reason to conclude that, by the utmost increase of which this vice is susceptible, the female part of the species could be sufferers to any very material amount. If however there was any danger of their being sufferers to any amount at all this would of itself be ample reason for wishing to restrain the practice. It would not however follow absolutely that it were right to make use of punishment for that purpose, much less that it were right to employ any of those very severe punishments which are commonly in use. It will not be right to employ any punishment, 1. if the mischief resulting from the punishment be equal or superior to the mischief of the offense, nor 2. if there be any means of compassing the same end without the expense of punishment. Punishment, says M. Beccaria, is never just so long as any means remain untried by which the end of punishment may be accomplished at a cheaper rate. [200c and 200d are blank]/[201]

Inducements for punishing it not justified on the ground of mischievousness

When the punishment [is] so severe, while the mischief of the offense is so remote and even so problematical, one cannot but suspect that the inducements which govern are not the same with those which are avowed. When the idea of the mischievousness of an offense is the ground of punishing it, those of which the mischief is most immediate and obvious are punished first: afterwards little by little the legislator becomes sensible of the necessity of punishing those of which the mischief is less and less obvious. But in England this offense was punished with death before ever the malicious destruction or fraudulent obtainment or embezzlement of property was punished at all, unless the obligation of making pecuniary amends is to be called a punishment; before even the mutilation of or the perpetual disablement of a man was made punishable otherwise than by simple imprisonment and fine. (It was the custom to punish it with death so early as the reign of Ed. 1st.)

But on the ground of antipathy

In this case, in short, as in so many other cases the disposition to punish seems to have had no other ground than the antipathy with which persons who had punishment at their disposal regarded the offender. The circumstances from which this antipathy may have taken its rise may be worth enquiring to. 1. One is the physical antipathy to the offense. This circumstance indeed, were we to think and act consistently, would of itself be nothing to the purpose. The act is to the highest degree odious and disgusting, that is, not to the man who does it, for he does it only because it gives him pleasure, but to one who thinks [?] of it. Be it so, but what is that to him? He has the same reason for doing it that I have for avoiding it. A man loves carrion—this is very extraordinary—much good may it do him. But what is this to me so long as I can indulge myself with fresh meat? But such reasoning, however just, few persons have calmness to attend to. This propensity is much stronger than it is to be wished it were to confound physical impurity with moral. From a man's possessing a thorough aversion to a practice himself, the transition is but too natural to his wishing to see all others punished who give into it. Any pretense, however slight, which promises to warrant him in giving way to this intolerant propensity is eagerly embraced. Look the world over, we shall find that differences in point of taste and opinion are grounds of animosity as frequent and as violent as any opposition in point of interest. To disagree with our taste [and] to oppose our opinions is to wound our sympathetic feelings and to affront our pride. James the 1st of England, a man [more] remarkable for weakness than for cruelty, conceived a violent antipathy against certain persons who were called Anabaptists on account of their differing from him in regard to certain speculative points of religion. As the circumstances of the times were favorable to [the] gratification of antipathy arising from such causes, he found means to give himself the satisfaction of committing one of them to the flames. The same king happened to have an antipathy to the use of tobacco. But as the circumstances of the times did not afford the same pretenses nor the same facility for burning tobacco-smokers as for burning Anabaptists, he was forced to content himself with writing a flaming book against it. The same king, if he be the author of that first article of the works which bear his name, and which indeed were owned by him, reckons this practice among the few offenses which no Sovereign ever ought to pardon. This must needs seems rather extraordinary to those who have a notion that a pardon in this case is what he himself, had he been a subject, might have stood in need of.

Philosophical pride

This transition from the idea of physical to that of moral antipathy is the more ready when the idea of pleasure, especially of intense pleasure, is connected with that of the act by which the antipathy is excited. Philosophical pride, to say nothing at present of superstition, has hitherto employed itself with effect in setting people a-quarreling with whatever is pleasurable even to themselves, and envy will always be disposing them to quarrel with what appears to be pleasurable to others. In the notions of a certain class of moralists we ought, not for any reason they are disposed to give for it, but merely because we ought, to set ourselves against every thing that recommends itself to us under the form of pleasure. Objects, it is true, the nature of which it is to afford us the highest pleasures we are susceptible of are apt in certain circumstances to occasion us still greater pains. But that is not the grievance: for if it were, the censure which is bestowed on the use of any such object would be proportioned to the probability that could be shewn in each case of its producing such greater pains. But that is not the case: it is not the pain that angers them but the pleasure.

How far the antipathy is a just ground

Meanwhile the antipathy, whatever it may arise from, produces in persons how many soever they be in whom it manifests itself, a particular kind of pain as often as the object by which the antipathy is excited presents itself to their thoughts. This pain, whenever it appears, is unquestionably to be placed to the account of the mischief of the offense, and this is one reason for the punishing of it. More than this—upon the view of any pain which these obnoxious persons are made to suffer, a pleasure results to those by whom the antipathy is entertained, and this pleasure affords an additional reason for the punishing of it. There remain however two reasons against punishing it. The antipathy in question (and the appetite of malevolence that results from it) as far as it is not warranted by the essential mischieviousness of the offense is grounded only in prejudice. It may therefore be assuaged and reduced to such a measure as to be no longer painful only in bringing to view the considerations which shew it to be ill-grounded. The case is that of the accidental existence of an antipathy which [would have] no foundation [if] the principle of utility were to be admitted as a sufficient reason for gratifying it by the punishment of the object; in a word, if the propensity to punish were admitted in this or any case as a sufficient ground for punishing, one should never know where to stop. Upon monarchical principles, the Sovereign would be in the right to punish any man he did not like; upon popular principles, every man, or at least the majority of each community, would be in the right to punish every man upon no better reason.

If it were, so would heresy

If this were admitted we should be forced to admit the propriety of applying punishment, and that to any amount, to any offense for instance which the government should find a pleasure in comprising under the name of heresy. I see not, I must confess, how a Protestant, or any person who should be for looking upon this ground as a sufficient ground for burning paederasts, could with consistency condemn the Spaniards for burning Moors or the Portuguese for burning Jews: for no paederast can be more odious to a person of unpolluted taste than a

Moor is to a Spaniard or a Jew to an orthodox Portuguese.

NOTE

1. Louis Compton, "Gay Genocide," in L. Crewe, *The Gay Academic* (Palm Springs, CA: ETC Publications, 1978).

Michael Ruse

The Morality of Homosexuality

At least half of us have homosexual inclinations at some points in our lives, usually earlier rather than later. Although the figures are not as high, a sizeable group of people in North America have had physical homosexual encounters to the point of orgasm. The number of people who, throughout their lives, are more or less exclusively homosexual in behavior and in inclination is much smaller, but it is, nevertheless, a not insignificant minority. The number of males, as a percentage of the total population, who are totally homosexual all of the time is somewhere between five and ten. The proportion of female homosexuals (lesbians) is quite a bit smaller than males, about one third of the number. That is, around two percent of the female population is exclusively lesbian.[1]

Most people in our society look negatively upon homosexuality. However, a significant minority disagrees, looking upon homosexuality simply as a variant form of sexuality.[2] Hence, as a philosopher, I want to ask: Is homosexuality immoral? Is homosexuality wrong? Is it, in some sense, bad sexuality? I shall concentrate on behavior, and I shall start the discussion by looking at what philosophers of the past have had to say about the morality of homosexual behavior. Then, I shall look at relevant thoughts of contemporary philosophers. Finally, I shall draw some conclusions of my own.

THE MORAL LEGACY OF GREECE AND ISRAEL

If we go back to the roots of our moral thought, then we go back to ancient Greece and to ancient Israel. With regard to homosexuality, you might suspect that we get conflicting messages from these two sources. Supposedly, the Greeks freely indulged in homosexual behavior, and endorsed homosexual liaisons. The Jews, however, set themselves adamantly against any kind of homosexual activity, condemning it as sinful. It would seem reasonable to presume, therefore, that the Greeks found homosexuality to be a morally acceptable form of sexuality, whereas the ancient Israelites had nothing but negative things to say. However, as is so often the case with popular lore, the truth is more complex.

GREECE

It is by no means the case that ancient Greeks openly and freely practiced all kinds of homosexuality, without hesitation or sanction (Dover 1978). The approved form of homosexual conduct was centered on intense emotional relationships, not casual physical activity. Even between homosexual lovers, physical contact was not altogether approved of. It was felt to be something of a giving away before the primitive passions.

Hence, it should come as no surprise to find that when the Greek philosophers wrote about homosexuality, they certainly did not give it an unqualified moral endorsement. Plato provided the fullest philosophical treatment of the moral status of homosexual activity. In one or two famous passages in his dialogues, he acknowledged homosexual inclinations as commonplace (*e.g., Charmides* 155 c-e). Such acknowledgments, however, should not be construed as an endorsement. Although he himself was reputedly exclusively homosexually orientated, Plato was always disapproving of any physical homosexual activity. In the *Republic,* (III, 403), he expressly forbad it between his guardians, as something which involves a triumph of the passions over the reason.[3]

Later, Plato developed the theme that homosexual behavior is always wrong for everyone, basing his case on a thesis which was to have great influence down through the centuries: a thesis which is still definitive for many today. Simply put, Plato condemned homosexual behavior because it is biologically unnatural.

> Our citizens should not be inferior to birds and many other species of animals, which are born in large communities and up to the age of procreation live unmated, pure and unpolluted by marriage, but when they have arrived at that age they pair, male with female and female with male, according to their inclination, and for the rest of their time they live in a pious and law-abiding way, faithfully adhering to the agreements which were the beginning of their love. (Plato, *Laws,* 804 d-e, trans. Dover 1978, pp. 166-7)

For Plato therefore (and, for other philosophers in ancient Greece), homosexual behavior is wrong because it goes against biological nature. Birds and other animals do not behave homosexually. No more should we.

ISRAEL

Turning now to the Judaeo-Christian position on homosexual activity, we find popular opinion to be more accurate. Repeatedly through the Bible, both in the Old and the New Testaments, there are explicit prohibitions against homosexual activity. Thus, in the "Holiness code" of Leviticus, we read:

Leviticus 18:22—Thou shalt not lie with mankind, as with womankind: it is an abomination.

Leviticus 21:3—If a man also lie with mankind, as he lieth with a woman, both of them have committed an abomination: they shall surely be put to death; their blood shall be upon them.

In the New Testament, we find that St. Paul held similar views, and he made it clear that females were not to be excluded from his strictures (Romans 1:26-7; I Corinthians 6:9-10; I Timothy 1:9-10).

In addition to these explicit prohibitions, there are various stories in the Bible that *prima facie* condemn homosexuality. Most famously, there is the story of Sodom and Gomorrah (Genesis 19). The citizens of Sodom supposedly wanted to have homosexual intercourse with two of God's angels. In retribution for these demands, God destroyed the cities and their inhabitants, save only the angels' hosts, Lot and his family. [In fairness, I should say the biblical scholars argue endlessly about the true meaning of the Sodom and Gomorrah story, and there are some who are prepared to argue that it does not really prohibit all homosexual activity. But this does seem to be a minority position. (Bailey 1955; Horner 1978.)]

CHRISTIANITY

The moral legacy of the ancient world, therefore, is that homosexual behavior is wrong. From Greece we learn that it is unnatural, and from Israel we learn that it is a sin against God. Variations on these themes have repeated themselves, again and again, down through the ages, in the writings of Judaeo-Christian philosophers. For instance, St. Augustine, whose philosophical thought was a cross between neo-Platonism and Christianity, set his face firmly against homosexuality.

He saw homosexual acts as a sign of failure to love either God or one's neighbor [Augustine, *Confessions*, III, viii (15)].

Expectedly, the most thorough Christian analysis and condemnation of homosexuality came from the pen of St. Thomas Aquinas (*Summa Theologica,* 2a 2ae, 154, 11-12). For Aquinas, immorality results from the breaking of natural law. This is the law or rule set down by God for us to follow in some way. In Aquinas's opinion, natural law dictates that sexual organs and inclinations are given exclusively for the reproduction of our kind. Only heterosexual intercourse, within marriage, is permitted. All else is against natural law.

Moreover, in Aquinas's opinion certain forms of deviation are doubly wrong, because they are "unnatural" and "vices." There are four kinds of unnatural vice: masturbation, bestiality, homosexuality, and "sex acts where the natural style of intercourse is not observed, as regard the proper organ; or according to other rather beastly and monstrous techniques." Bestiality, in Aquinas's view, was the worst; but homosexuality and masturbation (and the others) were worse vices even than rape.

This conclusion shocks the contemporary sensibility, but Aquinas defended it on the grounds that although rape is a violation against other human beings, it is still a natural form of sexuality. Homosexuality and masturbation, however, are sins against nature; that is to say, they are sins against God Himself. Since sinning against God is worse than man sinning against man (or rather against woman), homosexuality is worse than rape. "The developed plan of living, according to reason, comes from man; the plan of nature comes from God, and therefore a violation of this plan, as by our natural sins, is an affront to God, the ordainer of nature" (*Summa Theologica* 2a 2ae, 154, 12).

In Aquinas's thought, we have a subtle blend of the legacies of Greece and Israel. Homosexuality is unnatural. That is the Greek element. Homosexuality is a sin against God. That is the Jewish element.[4]

MODERN PHILOSOPHERS ON HOMOSEXUALITY

Two great themes have been championed in modern philosophical moral thought. On the one hand, there are those philosophers who feel that the supreme principle of morality must be one which centers on the individual; that is, morality must begin with individual rights and justice. Perhaps, the greatest system of all in this vein was produced by the eighteenth-century German philosopher Immanuel Kant. In contrast, we have the group philosophies. The best known of these is utilitarianism, a system in which principles of morality center on the need to maximize benefits for the entire group. Interestingly, both Kant and one of the founders of utilitarianism, Jeremy Bentham, had things to say about homosexual behavior. More interesting yet, they came to diametrically opposed conclusions.

Kant's ideas on homosexuality are to be found in his *Lectures on Ethics:* actual lectures given by Kant, between 1775 and 1780, and taken down by his students. Throughout these lectures, Kant develops the view that sex is always morally problematic. His reasons for regarding sex in this way become clear if we think of the problem in terms of the second version of his central principle of morality, the "Categorical Imperative": one should treat people as ends in themselves and not as means only (Kant 1959). How can one reconcile sexual activity with treating others as ends in themselves, rather than as means only? Kant's solution to this dilemma was to allow that sex is permissible, if and only if it is part of a love relationship; he held that love is possible only in a monogamous, heterosexual relationship. One enters into an agreement to let another have complete rights over one's own body in return for equal rights over that person's body, because each has given themselves to the other in love (Kant 1963, p. 164).[5]

Why must the mutuality and love that justifies sex necessarily rule out some homosexual equivalent to heterosexual marriage? Because Kant believes that homosexuality is a *crimina carnis*: an abuse of one's sexuality. This abuse comes in two categories. First, there are actions that are contrary to sound reason, *crimina carnis secundum naturam.* These are acts that go against the moral code imposed upon us as humans (e.g., acts such as adultery). Second, there are acts contrary to our animal nature, *crimina carnis contra naturam,* such as masturbation, sex with animals—and homosexuality. *Crimina carnis carna naturam* are the lowest and most disgusting of vices.

> A second *crimen carnis contra naturam* is intercourse between *sexus homogenii,* in which the object of sexual impulse is a human being but there is homogeneity instead of heterogeneity of sex, as when a woman satisfies her desire on a woman, or a man on a man. This practice too is contrary to the ends of humanity; for the end of humanity in respect of sexuality is to preserve the species without debasing the person; but in this instance the species is not being preserved (as it can be a *crimen carnis secundum naturam*), but the person is set aside, the self is degraded below the level of the animals, and humanity is dishonored. (Kant 1963, p. 170)

One cannot be much more adamant in one's condemnation than that.

At virtually the same time as Kant was writing, Jeremy Bentham wrote two essays on homosexuality. For unknown reasons—perhaps prudential—Bentham's writings on the subject were never published (they finally appeared in print in 1978). Curiously, Bentham used virtually the same language as did Kant. He referred to homosexual behavior as an abomination and unnatural, and so forth. However, starting from his utilitarian premises—that the supreme moral maxim is to maximize pleasure and happiness—Bentham drew almost exactly the opposite conclusion from Kant.

Simply put, Bentham argued that if homosexual interactions give you pleasure, then as long as they are not harming others, they are morally acceptable. Indeed, if your tastes point you that way, you should indulge in homosexual activity, because you thereby promote happiness.

> As to any primary mischief, it is evident that [a homosexual interaction] produces no pain in anyone. On the contrary it produces pleasure, and that a pleasure which, by their perverted taste, is by this supposition preferred to that pleasure which is in general reputed the greatest. (Bentham 1978, p. 390)

Beyond this, all that Bentham has to say about homosexuality is simply elaboration and development of his position, and defense against possible objections. For instance, Bentham raises the possibility that perhaps homosexuality as such leads to physical deterioration, and hence is, for that reason, to be avoided. Bentham counters this claim with ease: there are no utilitarian bars to freely chosen homosexual acts.

In short, between Kant and Bentham, we find total opposition Kant thinks the Categorical Imperative has been violated by homosexual activity. Bentham considers free homosexual activity to be endorsed by the utilitarian maxim. Which is right? After we have looked at recent writings, we shall be in a better position to answer this question.

RECENT PHILOSOPHERS ON SEXUAL PERVERSION

Today's moral philosophers, working within the Anglo-Saxon tradition, have had little to say directly about homosexuality.[6] Indirectly, however, they have discussed matters that are pertinent, especially in recent extended and lively analyses of sexual perversion, a label philosophers and lay people often apply to homosexual activity.

The classic paper on the subject is Thomas Nagel's "Sexual Perversion" (1969).[7] In striking contrast to Plato, St. Thomas, Kant, and, indeed the standard literature, Nagel characterizes "perversion" as a psychological state rather than a physiological act. Thus he dismisses the classical view by "declar[ing] at the outset . . . that the connection between sex and reproduction has no bearing on sexual perversion" (p. 248). This declaration made, Nagel describes the psychology of a full, normal, sexual relationship, that focuses on the key element of reciprocity. In such a relationship, a person (let's not prejudge the issue; let's therefore assume that we have a heterosexual relationship) feels an attraction for another person. At the same time, or shortly thereafter, the second person feels a sexual attraction for the first. There is, however, more to full sexuality than this. The two people involved cannot, as it were, simply live in cocoons of their own desires. Each becomes aware of the other's attraction for him (her), and finds this very desire of the other, in itself, stimulating. Thus, in mature sexuality we get a reciprocal shuttling of emotions and desires.

Nagel's analysis of a full sexual encounter provides him with a context in which he develops a definition of perversion. Quite simply, for him, perversions are "truncated or incomplete versions of the complete figuration" (p. 256). In other words, perversion is somehow something less than the full reciprocal type of relationship. Thus, bestiality would be a perversion to Nagel since a human can hardly have the reciprocity required by having sex with a sheep.

What about homosexuality? The conclusion that follows—which, in fact, Nagel himself hints at—is that there is nothing, as such, necessarily perverted about homosexuality (see Nagel 1969, p. 257). One can have a two-way relationship between two people of the same sex, which involves the kind of interaction just described above in heterosexual terms. So, Nagel's model implies the nonperversity of homosexuality.

This being so, questions of morality (deriving from a judgment of perversity) become somewhat moot. But even if Nagel were to judge homosexual activity perverse, he would not thereby at once judge it immoral. Nagel allows that, in some sense, nonperverted sex may well be "better" than perverted sex; but he will not allow that this sense of "better" is to be translated as "morally better." The sense of "better" that Nagel has in mind here is something akin to an aesthetic superiority. The difference between the two kinds of sex—nonperverted and perverted—is probably more akin to the difference between a beautiful and an ugly person, rather than to that between a saint and a sinner. Hence, in Nagel's view, were we to judge homosexual behavior perverse—and I do not think Nagel himself would—we should not then go on to judge it immoral.

Nagel's commentators and critics have agreed that he has caught an important element to sexual relations. They are generally inclined, however, to argue that Nagel describes rather less a notion of perversion and rather more a notion of incompleteness. Sarah Ruddick (1975), for instance, argues that the notion of perversion should be related to the traditional notion of naturalness. In Ruddick's opinion, perverted sex is nonnatural sex. But, what is natural sex? Again, Ruddick opts for a traditional line. The main purpose of sexuality is reproduction. Therefore, in her opinion, only acts that lead to reproduction are natural. All nonnatural acts are perverted. Thus, Ruddick immediately concludes that homosexuality is a perversion (see Ruddick 1975, p. 91).

What then does this say about the question of morality? Like Nagel, perhaps more emphatically, Ruddick goes on to argue that because something is perverted, it does not at all follow that it is necessarily immoral. Indeed, she goes as far as to say that, all other things being equal, "perverted sex acts are preferable to natural ones if the latter are less pleasurable or less complete" (Ibid, p. 96). In other words, although Ruddick would argue that all homosexual behavior is perverted, she does not therefore want to argue that any of this is in any sense immoral.

But, Ruddick does not argue that sex, either heterosexual or homosexual, has no value connotations. Instead, she invokes the notion of incompleteness. On Ruddick's analysis, Nagel's "perversions" are merely "incomplete" sex. Unlike Nagel, she is prepared to argue that this concept does have moral connotations. In particular, Ruddick argues that what she calls "complete sex" acts are morally superior. Why? For three reasons: "They tend to resolve tensions fundamental to moral life; they are conducive to emotions that, if they become stable and dominant, are in turn conducive to the virtue of loving; and they involve a preeminently moral virtue—respect for persons" (Ibid, p. 98). Hence, just as one could have less-than-worthwhile heterosexual activity, so also one could have less-than-worthwhile homosexual activity. But clearly, like Nagel, Ruddick is not arguing that homosexual activity *per se* is morally inferior to heterosexual activity. Ruddick finds nothing inherently immoral in homosexual activity.

Differing more sharply from Nagel is Alan Goldman (1977). He argues that people like Nagel and Ruddick "overintellectualize" the whole sexual scene. He wants to analyse sex simply in terms of physical desires, and of the pleasures that sexual contacts bring. He argues that there is, as such, no morality to be found in sexual relations, either heterosexual or homosexual. The morality is just that which enters into the whole of life. Homosexual rape is morally offensive because it is rape, not because it is homosexual. Rape is morally offensive, not because it is rape, but because someone is being hurt against his (her) will. It is wrong in and of itself, not because it occurs in a sexual context. For Goldman, therefore, homosexuality is not in itself immoral, or moral for that matter.

What about perversion? Like Ruddick, Goldman feels that perversion must be defined in terms of what is natural. But unlike Ruddick, instead of defining naturalness in terms of the purpose of sexuality, whatever that might be, he wants to offer a strictly statistical analysis. "It is a deviation from a norm, but the norm in question is merely statistical" (Ibid, p. 284). A pervert is simply someone who does not have the usual desires. Unfortunately, Goldman does not tell us what precisely constitutes a deviation from the norm. How you decide, presumably, tells you if homosexuality is or is not perverse.

To sum up, there is general agreement that there is nothing immoral *per se* about homosexual activity. Goldman probably sees no value issues at all peculiar to any of today's homosexual activity, although he is rather foggy on the question of perversion. Ruddick would be inclined to label any homosexuality a perversion, but not thereby judge it immoral. Nagel finds value issues peculiar to some sexual activity, but would find homosexuality *per se* neither immoral nor perverted.

IS HOMOSEXUAL BEHAVIOR AGAINST TRUE RELIGION?

Let us turn now to analysis. Since this essay is an exercise in philosophy and not religion, I'll not dwell on Biblical strictures about homosexuality. Let me simply say that, notwithstanding the somewhat intense relationships that are sometimes portrayed in the Bible, for instance that between David and Jonathan, it is hard to conclude that as a Jew or a Christian, one can really view homosexual activity with much favor. Certainly this seems to be the view of many modern churchmen. Pope John Paul II, for instance, has said that while there is no sin in being homosexually oriented, homosexual activity is sinful. (A somewhat dated, but still useful Christian evaluation of homosexual behavior is in Bailey 1955.)

What the Bible says is a problem for believers.[8] Only indirectly, if and when believers force their views on others, is the Bible a problem for the citizens of a secular society. Hence, of significance to us here is simply the fact that Judaism and Christianity certainly give good reasons for the believer to judge homosexual activity to be immoral. Thus, as we move now to more philosophical treatments of homosexuality, we should be sensitive to the fact that believers will probably have religious reasons for drawing negative conclusions. This could lead them to consider their negative philosophical arguments to be more powerful than they really are.

IS HOMOSEXUALITY BAD SEXUALITY BECAUSE IT IS BIOLOGICALLY UNNATURAL?

A key philosophical charge against homosexual activity is that it is "unnatural." "Nature," in this context, is intended to refer to our *biological* nature. Hence, the conclusion is drawn that such activity should be condemned as immoral. This was the cry of Plato, it was echoed by Aquinas and Kant, and it is still with us today. There are a number of points I want to make about this argument.

First, if we mean by "homosexuality is unnatural" that it is never a practice to be found in the animal world—and this is certainly what Plato thought—then the claim is simply false. There is a substantial body of evidence that supports the conclusion that homosexual activity is widespread throughout the animal world. Virtually every animal whose activity has been studied in detail shows some forms of homosexual behavior. Mutual masturbation, anal intercourse, and so forth, are commonplace in the primate world. Similarly, amongst other mammals, we find all sorts of activity that can only truly be spoken of as "homosexual," in some sense. One male will mount another and come to climax. Analogously, females show deep bonds and sexual type behavior towards each other. Sometimes this behavior of animals is manifested just in young animals. In other cases, the homosexual activity is ongoing, if not exclusive (see Weinrich 1982 for details and references).

If homosexual activity is so widespread in the animal world, why has it not been noted before? In fact, it has been noted before; but, with their usual selectivity, people writing on human sexuality have failed to note it or have simply been ignorant about it. Then again, there has been such a fixed notion that homosexuality belongs exclusively to the human world, that people simply have not been able to see animal homosexuality—even when they have been presented with the clearest evidence of it.

A revealing example of this selective vision is given by a recent researcher on mountain sheep. He wrote two books on the subject: one in 1971 and the other a short time later (Geist 1971; 1975). In the first book, there was a great deal of discussion of male dominance and pecking order, with alpha males fighting and subduing beta males. In the second book, the author came right out and said what he had been seeing all along was homosexual activity. The alpha males mount the beta males, having erections and emissions, sometimes involving anal intercourse. Candidly, the author admitted that he simply had not been able to bring himself to think of this as homosexuality. In his own words: "Those magnificent animals, queers?" This case is atypical only in that the researcher was more candid than most. If one's desire is to argue that homosexuality is unnatural, the animal world is certainly not the place to look.

A second pertinent point is that homosexuality might have a biological function in humans. The basic mechanism of the central biological theory of Darwinian evolution is "natural selection"; or "the survival of the fittest." Those organisms more successful at reproducing than others pass on their units of inheritance—their genes—and are thus the organisms most represented in the next and future generations. Given enough time, this process leads to full-blown evolution.

Reproduction is the key to evolutionary success. It is possible, however, to reproduce by proxy. Suppose that, instead of reproducing oneself, one aids close relatives to reproduce more efficiently. Then, in a sense, one is increasing the representation of one's own units of inheritance in the next and future generations, simply because one shares these units of inheritance with close relatives. This vicarious reproduction is known as "kin selection," and it has been very extensively documented in the animal world, particularly in the hymenoptera (ants, bees, and wasps). (For a quick introduction to Darwinism, see Ruse 1982. For more on kin selection, see Wilson 1975 or Dawkins 1976.)

Kin selection in humans provides a possible biological explanation of the homosexual lifestyle, as an alternative reproductive strategy. Recent research has shown that, in nonindustrial societies, male homosexuals frequently fit a pattern one would expect were kin selection operating (Weinrich 1976). These males would probably not be efficient as direct reproducers, because of such factors as debilitating childhood illnesses. They do, however, hold positions in society that can significantly aid close relatives. For example, in many American Indian tribes homosexuals take on the role of the shaman—that is, of a kind of magical figure who has to be consulted by the tribe before great events like battles can take place. The shaman has considerable power and financial influence within the community. He is, thus, in a strong position to aid close relatives (siblings, nephews, nieces, and so on). There is, moreover, evidence that such help actually occurs. It seems plausible to suppose, therefore, that in such cases biology itself has promoted genes for manifesting homosexual inclinations and activity.

If indeed kin selection, or some like process, does operate in a way such as that just suggested, then biology is at least a partial cause of human homosexuality. It would therefore be odd to speak of homosexuality as being "unnatural." If by "natural," you mean that which nature has done, homosexuality would be as natural as heterosexuality. Indeed, forcing homosexuals to live heterosexual lifestyles would be unnatural from a biological point of view, not the converse. (The evidence for the biological foundations of human homosexuality is presented in detail, together with various explanatory models, in Ruse 1981.)

A third point is so obvious that it is usually overlooked. We humans do not live in a world of strict biology. We are cultural creatures, which is why we are so successful as a species. We have speech, customs, religion, literature, art—and even philosophy. To speak of humans as "just animals" is to ignore half the story. Any evaluation of human homosexuality from a natural or unnatural perspective must, therefore, take our culture into account. The fact that we do not always do the things that animals do, does not mean that it is unnatural for us not to do such things. It is simply a reflection of the fact that, by nature, we are not as other animals (Lumsden and Wilson 1981).

Hence, if homosexual activity is part of human culture—and it certainly is in many respects—then to speak of it as "unnatural," judged purely from a physiological perspective, is simply meaningless. It could indeed be true that animals do not practice homosexual activity (although, it so happens that it is not true); it could be true that humans do, in fact, practice homosexual activity (as indeed they do); but, the conclusion would not necessarily be that human homosexuality is unnatural. The conclusion could simply be that such behavior is part of our human nature and not part of animal nature.

Finally, let me point out that even if homosexuality were biologically unnatural, this need not make it immoral. Because we do something which is against our biological nature, it does not follow that the act is wrong. As many philosophers have pointed out, to argue from what *is (i.e.,* biological nature) to what *ought* to be (*i.e.,* the morally desirable) is a fallacy. Whether we do something or not is one thing. Whether it is moral or immoral is quite another. The two are not logically connected.

There are, then, four independent rejoinders to the "unnatural" argument that has dominated both classical and modern discussions of homosexuality: it is false that animals are not homosexual; it is false that homosexuality must be antireproductive and nonbiological; it is false that homosexuality is to be judged without taking note of the cultural nature of humans; and it is false that what is unnatural is necessarily immoral.

THE KANTIAN ANALYSIS

Kant was strongly against homosexuality. Obviously, apart from any religious biases Kant may have had, whatever he himself may have thought, essentially his opposition was based on the homosexuality-as-unnatural thesis. Assuming that the arguments of the last sections are effective, what then of the basic Kantian philosophy? Can one indulge in homosexual activity and yet be true to the Categorical Imperative? Kant himself did not think so. Nevertheless, my own sense of sex in general, and of homosexuality in particular, is that once St. Paul and Plato are put aside, the Categorical Imperative is far less of an impediment to variant sex than its author supposed (see also Baumrin 1975).

The Categorical Imperative demands that people be treated as ends, and not as means only. "Act so that you treat humanity, whether in your own person or in that of another, always as an end and never as a means only" (Kant 1959, p. 47). Nothing in the Imperative itself rules out the possibility of the relationship being a homosexual one, rather than heterosexual. Homosexuals, male or female, fall in love with partners and, under any meaningful sense of the term, treat those partners as ends and not simply as means. Thus, homosexual activity as such is not ruled out by the Categorical Imperative. Indeed, in the right circumstances, a Kantian should rather think that one ought to behave homosexually. (Suppose, for instance, one were faced with a choice of would-be partners, one of the same sex and one of the other sex, and one was oneself drawn homosexually to the same sex partner—and to act otherwise would involve deceit and unkindness.)[9]

THE UTILITARIAN ANALYSIS

Turning to the other great moral theory, let us first distinguish between the two main versions of utilitarianism. There is that associated with the name of Jeremy Bentham (1948), and there is that associated with the name of John Stuart Mill (1910). Bentham argued that the utility against which the consequences of all acts should be judged is any kind of pleasure that one finds desirable. He made no distinction between various pleasures or happinesses. John Stuart Mill, on the other hand, argued strongly that one can grade pleasures and happinesses and that some are much to be preferred to others. In particular, Mill argued that the more intellectual sorts of pleasures are more worthwhile. "Better to be Socrates dissatisfied than a fool satisfied" (Mill 1910, p. 9).

A Benthamite utilitarian appears to endorse homosexual activity just as did Bentham himself. If an individual enjoys homosexual activity, then it is a good thing for that person and she/he should strive to maximize its occurrence. Moreover, assuming that others enjoy it also, he/she should strive to let them enjoy it to the full.

What about Mill? I am not sure that a Millian would be quite as easy about sex as a Benthamite; but with regard to homosexual activity as such, the conclusion seems similar. Certainly, a Mill-type utilitarian would think that activity within a loving relationship, whether heterosexual or homosexual, was a good thing and ought to be promoted. Indeed, as with the Kantian analysis, there will be cases where a Millian (as well as a Benthamite) could urge homosexual activity on someone— not to show affection and not to act homosexually would be wrong.

IS HOMOSEXUALITY PERVERTED?

Is homosexual behavior perverted behavior? With Nagel's critics, I would argue that he described something better called "incomplete" sex than "perverted" sex. But, like Nagel, I doubt that the notion of completeness in itself throws much moral light on sexuality—certainly, it throws no more light than that gained from the traditional moral theories just discussed. If some sex is bad sex, it is not so much because it is incomplete; rather, it is because the sex violates the Categorical Imperative or fails to lead to true happiness.

Does this mean that the notion of sexual "perversion" is an empty one? Not at all. Despite my earlier strictures about the concept of "naturalness" as it occurs in the philosophical literature, I do not want to deny that in some sense the perverted is the nonnatural or the unnatural. But, for reasons given, naturalness cannot be defined in terms of pure biology, as argued by philosophers from Plato to Ruddick. Humans are cultural beings, and what is natural must be understood in terms of culture. Hence, the unnatural—the perverted—is something that goes against cultural norms.

What exactly does this mean? A purely statistical definition, as offered by Goldman, will not do. Being in a minority is not as such nonnatural or perverse. Rather, nonnatural sex is sex that goes against our personal nature as cultural beings. It is something that we simply would not want to do even if we could. Remember the story of Gyges in Plato's *Republic*. He was the fellow who found a ring that enabled him to become invisible. As a result of this, he seized power in the kingdom, killing the king and seducing the queen. We can all understand what Gyges was up to, and even though we may not approve of his actions, we do not find them absurd or weird or nonnatural.

Unnaturalness is something that we simply would not want to do, even if we had gotten Gyges's ring. More particularly, it is something we could not imagine wanting to do. I might not want to murder, even though the ring enables me to do it. I can imagine playing Gyges's role, however. Suppose that, thanks to the ring, I could now spend my days concealed in the corner of a public lavatory, watching and smelling people defecate. I cannot imagine putting the ring to that use. In short, that activity for me, would be unnatural. It would be a "perversion." (Note that not all perversions are necessarily sexual. I am not sure that watching folks defecate would be.)

Thus, I argue that the perverse is the unnatural, where the unnatural is that which goes against what an individual finds culturally comprehensible.[10] The perverse is that which one cannot even conceive of wanting to do, even if one could. Now, this raises a number of questions. First, does the notion of perversion, as defined, have any value connotations? Second, would such value connotations (if they exist) necessarily be moral value connotations? Third, where does this leave the question of homosexual activity? Let me take these questions in turn, briefly.

First, the notion of perversion does have strong value connotations. There is little doubt (except perhaps in minds of academic philosophers), that when we speak of something as "perverted," we mean that it is in some way vile or disgusting. Just above, I gave an example of something I consider a perversion. Would it surprise you to learn that I found it difficult simply to write it down? It shouldn't! It's a perversion! In my opinion, hanging around the lavatories, watching and smelling others defecate, is a thoroughly disgusting thing to do. That is the whole point of my reference to Gyges and his ring. Watching and smelling people defecate is something that I cannot even conceive of wanting to do. I do not want to steal a camera from my colleague's office, but I can certainly conceive of situations where I might do something like this. I do not find the thought of stealing a friend's camera disgusting, although I do find it shameful. Hence, there are strong value connotations involved in the notion of perversion or nonnaturalness.

Second, what of the connection between perversion and morality? Undoubtedly, that which is perverted is often immoral. For instance, strangling a small child and simultaneously raping her is both perverted and grossly immoral. However, this does not mean that the notions of perversion and morality are logically connected. Certainly, that which is immoral is not always perverted. Stealing a colleague's camera would be an immoral act; but it would not be a perverted act.

Are all perverted acts immoral acts? I doubt it. Would my example above be immoral? Perhaps you would think it an invasion of privacy. But what if I waited until the lavatories were empty, and then went in to drink from the urinals? This would be perverted; but, I'm not at all sure that it would be immoral. Of course, the simple fact of the matter is that that which is perverse is often immoral because many things that we cannot even conceive of wanting to do would be immoral things to do. Any connections of this type are contingent rather than logical. Hence, although perversion has with it an element of disgust, which does surely involve values, perversion in itself does not entail a moral repulsion. Therefore, although those who argue that perversion is in some sense bad are right, they are also right when they argue that this badness is not in itself a moral badness. It is more something akin to an aesthetic badness.[11] We are revolted by perversions, but this does not necessarily entail moral condemnation.[12]

Third and finally, what about the connection between homosexuality and perversion? Note that the way in which I have characterized "perversion" makes it a subjective phenomenon, which could vary from person to person within a culture. Some people find certain things revolting, others do not. Expectedly, the same goes for perversions. Thus, for instance, I do not find oral sex a particularly revolting phenomenon. On the other hand, other people find it thoroughly disgusting. For me, therefore, oral sex is not a perversion. For others, oral sex clearly is a perversion.

What does all this mean for homosexuality, especially as it applies to contemporary North America? The answer is relativistic. For some people, homosexuality is indeed a perversion. They find it disgusting and recoil from the very thought of it. Others (not necessarily just homosexuals) do not find homosexual activity a perversion. This is not to say that everybody who finds homosexuality not to be perverted, wants to behave homosexually. But, it is to say that such people could, in some sense, imagine freely doing it—at least, they can put themselves in the place of someone who would want to do it. They are certainly not overwhelmed by a sense of disgust.[13]

Hence, I argue that there is no straightforward answer to the question of whether or not homosexuality is a perversion. Some people regard it as such; others do not. Clearly, we have had something of a change in the last fifty years, with fewer people now thinking homosexual activity perverted. Perhaps, we will continue to see a change. As things stand at the moment, for some people homosexuality is a perversion, and that is all there is to be said on the matter. As a consequence of this, for some people in our society, homosexuality is not the best kind of sex. For them, it is aesthetically inferior sex (more bluntly, it is revolting sex). But this is not to say that those who think this way are therefore justified in inferring that homosexuality is immoral. (Although, I am sure that many do, in fact, conclude this.) For others, homosexuality is not a perversion; it is not in any sense inferior or worse sex

IS HOMOSEXUALITY BAD SEXUALITY?

Let us list the conclusions. First, it is simply bad science to go on arguing that human homosexual activity is biologically unnatural. Even if it were, this would tell us nothing of its moral status.

Second, although religion is *prima facie* hostile to homosexuality (and probably truly hostile), there is nothing in the standard philosophical theories of moral behavior that outrightly condemns homosexual activity. Both Kantians and utilitarians can and should approve of homosexual activity *per se*.

Third, the notion of perversion properly understood does have value connotations; namely, negative values or revulsion and disgust. Undoubtedly, many people in our society do find homosexual activity revolting. For them it is a perversion. However, this is not a universal feeling. There are heterosexuals, as well as homosexuals, who do not look upon such activity as a perversion. For them, homosexuality is perfectly good sexuality.

In response to the title of this essay, therefore, I reply that, in important respects, homosexuality is certainly not bad sexuality. It is perfectly good sexuality. However, many people look upon homosexual activity as a perversion. That is a fact, and no amount of empathetic philosophizing can change this. This is not to say, however, that the possibility of changing people's opinions is not open to us all. As philosophers, caring about human beings, aware of how much hatred today is directed towards homosexuals, we have a special obligation to work toward such change.

NOTES

1. Still standard sources for the statistics on homosexuality are the original Kinsey sex reports, Kinsey *et al* 1948; Kinsey *et al* 1953. The figures given in this paragraph are taken from these reports. They are supported by later studies, for instance Ramsay *et al* 1974; Kenyon 1974.

2. Thanks to Freud and followers, many today look upon homosexuality as less a moral failing and more a sickness. See, for example, Freud 1905; Bieber *et al* 1962. I discuss Freud and the homosexuality-as-sickness thesis in Ruse 1980.

3. In the *Symposium,* Plato has Socrates use homosexual attractions as the first step to contemplation of the Good. But they are only a first step, to be discarded, and they involve no physical activity.

4. In fairness, it must be noted that whatever the theologians may have said, historically the Catholic Church often took a remarkably tolerant attitude toward homosexual activity. See Boswell 1980.

5. I am concerned only with homosexuality in this essay. I explain Kant's position on sex in general because, although he himself certainly thought the Categorical Imperative rules out homosexual activity, I shall argue that Kant's opposition to such activity really comes from other sources. This does not mean that I endorse Kant's general perspective on sex. For an argument spelling out aspects of Kant's thought in a sympathetic manner, see Baumrin 1975.

6. The French existentialists, particularly Sartre (1962) and de Beauvoir (1953) have written on homosexuality. Some of Sartre's important ideas on sexuality have been used by Thomas Nagel, whose work will be discussed. De Beauvoir's views on lesbianism are fascinating, but fall rather more in the realm of the psychological.

7. This has been reprinted in Baker and Elliston (1975), and references are to this reprinting. See pages 268-279 of the present volume.

8. Even if one is a Jew or a Christian, there are time-honored ways of getting around the dictates of the Bible. For instance, one can point out simply that no reasonable person could take all of the dictates of the Bible literally, in this day and age. (Horner 1978 is a sensitive attempt to give a positive Christian account of homosexuality.)

9. In this discussion, I am simply considering basic homosexual activity, essentially between two people who have some feeling for each other. I am not considering possible moral complications, like group sex, since presumably they are not distinctive homosexual matters. However, I must note that male homosexuals are often given to highly promiscuous behavior (Bell and Weinberg, 1978). Were one to think this a moral issue, then as a matter of fact this would be of particular concern in a full analysis of homosexual activity as it typically occurs. See Elliston (1975) for a spirited argument for the value of promiscuity;

although, he does qualify his enthusiasm by allowing the promiscuity as a "limited value in the movement toward a sexual idea," which ideal involves "a full commitment to a single other" (p. 240). I am not sure that much male, promiscuous homosexual activity is properly viewed as moving towards such an ideal. Also, current health threats, such as Acquired Immune Deficiency Syndrome (AIDS), ought to be considered. See Silverstein and White 1977, and *Science 83* (April 1983), for more on these matters.

10. In this essay, I will just deal with perversion at the individual level, where society as a whole is undecided on the subject. This seems to me to be the case for homosexuality in our society today. But, a full analysis of perversion would need reference to when a society as a whole could be said to consider a practice "perverted." This would clearly need discussion of the way most people felt, but would probably also need to refer to other societal beliefs, like religion.

11. A philosophical emotivist could argue that, since ethics is all feelings, morality and perversion collapse together. Since I am not a philosophical emotivist in any usual sense, this is not my worry.

12. If, as Kant argues, one has obligations to oneself, then it might be argued that one ought not degrade oneself by performing that which one finds perverted. But, as will be seen, it does not follow that one must judge others immoral for doing what they do and not find perverted, even though the individual judging does find it to be immoral. Nor, speaking now as an enthusiast for Mill's views on liberty, does it follow that one should at once try to stop that which one would judge perverted. I thus disagree with Devlin's (1965) views about the propriety of legislating on private practices; although, as a matter of fact Devlin himself spoke out against antihomosexual laws.

13. In associating perversion with unnaturalness and disgust, my thinking parallels Slote (1975). However, I see no reason to argue as he does that "the kinds of acts people call unnatural are those that most people have some impulse toward that they cannot or will not admit to having" (p. 263). This may often be true, and perhaps in the case of homosexuality explains the violent emotions engulfing many homophobics. But I deny having even subconscious coprophilic tendencies.

BIBLIOGRAPHY

Aquinas, St. T. (1968). *Summa Theologiae, 43, Temperance* (2a 2ae, 141-54). Trans. T. Gilby, (London: Blackfriars).
Augustine, A. (1909). *Confessions.* Trans. E.B. Pusey, (London: Dent).
Bailey, D. S. (1955). *Homosexuality and the Western Christian Tradition.* (London: Longmans, Green and Co.)
Baker, R., and F. Elliston (eds) (1975). *Philosophy and Sex.* (Buffalo, NY: Prometheus).

Baumrin, B. (1975). "Sexual Immorality Delineated." In R. Baker and F. Elliston (eds) 1975. *Philosophy and Sex*. (Buffalo, NY: Prometheus), 116-128, herein pp. 300-311.

Bell, Alan P. and Martin S. Weinberg (1978). *Homosexualities: A Study of Diversity Among Men and Women*. (New York: Simon and Schuster).

Bentham, J. (1948). *An Introduction to the Principles of Morals and Legislation*. (New York: Hafner).

———, (1978). "Offences Against One's Self: Paederasty," *J. Homosexuality*, 3(4), 383-405; 1(4), 91-107, pp. 385-402.

Bieber, I., H. J. Dain, P. R. Dince, M. G. Drellich, H. G. Grand, R. H. Gundlach, M. W. Kremer, A. H. Rifkin, C. B. Wilbur, and T. B. Bieber (1962). *Homosexuality: A Psychoanalytic Study of Male Homosexuals*. (New York: Basic Books).

Boswell, J. (1980). *Christianity, Social Tolerance, and Homosexuality*. (Chicago: Chicago University Press).

de Beauvoir, S. (1953). *The Second Sex*. (New York: Knopf).

Devlin, P. (1965). *The Enforcement of Morals*. (Oxford: Oxford University Press).

Dover, K. J. (1978). *Greek Homosexuality*. (Cambridge, MA: Harvard University Press).

Elliston, F. (1975). "In Defense of Promiscuity." In R. Baker and F. Elliston (eds) 1975. *Philosophy and Sex*. (Buffalo, NY: Prometheus), 222-243.

Freud, S. (1905). *Three Essays on the Theory of Sexuality*. In J. Strachey (ed) *Collected Works of Freud*, 7. (London: Hogarth, 1953), 125-243.

Geist, V. (1971). *Mountain Sheep: A Study in Behavior and Evolution*. (Chicago: University of Chicago Press).

———, (1975). *Mountain Sheep and Man in the Northern Wilds*. (Ithaca, NY: Cornell University Press).

Goldman, A. H. (1977). "Plain Sex." *Philosophy and Public Affairs*, 6, 267-88.

Horner, T. (1978). *Jonathan Loved David*. (Philadelphia: Westminster).

Kant, I. (1959). *Foundations of the Metaphysics of Morals*. Trans. L. W. Beck. (Indianapolis: Bobbs-Merrill).

———, (1963). *Lectures on Ethics*. Trans. L. Infield. (New York: Harper and Row).

Kenyon, F. (1974). "Female Homosexuality: A Review." In: *Understanding Homosexuality; Its Biological and Psychological Bases*, edited by J. A. Loraine, pp. 83-119. (New York: American Elsevier).

Kinsey, A. C., B. Pomeroy and E. Martin (1948). *Sexual Behavior in the Human Male*. (Philadelphia: W. B. Saunders).

Kinsey, A. C. *et al*. (1953). *Sexual Behavior in the Human Female*. (Philadelphia: W. B. Saunders).

Mill, J. S. (1910). *Utilitarianism, Liberty, and Representative Government*. (London: Dent).

Nagel, T. (1969). "Sexual Perversion." *Journal of Philosophy*, 66, 1-17. Reprinted in R. Baker and E. F. Elliston (eds) 1975. *Philosophy and Sex.* (Buffalo, NY: Prometheus), 247-260, herein pp. 268-279.

Plato (1961). *The Collected Dialogues,* ed. E. Hamilton and H. Cairns. (Princeton, NJ: Princeton University Press).

Ramsay, R. W., P. M. Heringa and I. Boorsma (1974). "A Case Study: Homosexuality in the Netherlands." In J.A. Loraine (ed) *Understanding Homosexuality: Its Biological and Psychological Bases.* (New York: American Elsevier), 121-40.

Ruddick, S. (1975). "Better Sex." In R. Baker and F. Elliston (eds). *Philosophy and Sex.* (Buffalo, NY: Prometheus), 83-104, herein 280-299.

Ruse, Michael (1980). "Are Homosexuals Sick?" In *Current Concepts of Health and Disease,* ed A. Caplan, H. T. Engelhardt Jr., and J. McCartney. (Boston: Addison-Wesley), 693-723.

————. (1981). "Are There Gay Genes? Sociobiology Looks at Homosexuality." *Journal of Homosexuality,* 6(4), 5-34.

Sartre, J-P. (1962). *Saint Genet.* (Paris: Gallimard).

Silverstein, C., and E. White (1977). *The Joy of Gay Sex.* (New York: Simon and Schuster).

Slote, M. (1975). "Inapplicable Concepts and Sexual Perversion." In R. Baker and F. Elliston (eds) 1975. *Philosophy and Sex.* (Buffalo, NY: Prometheus), 261-267.

Weinrich, J. D. (1976). *Human Reproductive Strategy. I. Environmental Predictability and Reproductive Strategy; Effects of Social Class and Race. II. Homosexuality and Non-Reproduction; Some Evolutionary Models.* Unpublished Ph.D. thesis, Harvard University.

————, (1982). "Is Homosexuality Biologically Natural?" In W. Paul, J. D. Weinrich, J. C. Gonsiorek, and M. E. Hotvedt eds. *Homosexuality: Social, Psychological, and Biological Issues.* (Beverly Hills: Sage), 197-208.

Frederick Suppe

Curing Homosexuality

After centuries of acceptance, beginning around 1150 A.D., Christianity began to condemn homosexual behavior as sinful and immoral; such condemnation was well-entrenched by the fourteenth century and continued to be uncontroversial until the nineteenth century[1] when this view came to be challenged on two fronts. First, Karl Heinrich Ulrichs and others argued that homosexual instincts were inborn and thus natural, and advanced the idea that homosexuals were a third or "intersex." Modern incarnations of this innateness hypothesis include theories that homosexuality is genetically caused or that it is due to abnormal hormonal levels during the fetal gestation period. Second, researchers such as Cesar Lambroso and Richard von Kraft-Ebbing began studying sexual deviates and came to the conclusion that homosexual behavior and other sexual perversions were diseases caused by the nervous system, but that hereditary influences predisposed some individuals to the disease. With the rise of psychoanalysis and its expropriation by the medical profession this viewpoint evolved to the modern view that whatever the etiology, abnormal sexual behavior, including homosexuality, was symptomatic of mental illness.[2]

Whether homosexual and other variant sexual behaviors are viewed as immoral (due to inborn deficiencies) or mental disorders, the underlying assumption is that such behaviors are inferior or unacceptable and ought to be suppressed. If possible this ought to be accomplished by producing a cure. Various penances and other disciplines were imposed to cure persons of the sins of homosexuality. Thomas Jefferson was not alone in arguing for castration as a cure for rape, polygamy, sodomy, and bestiality.[3] Later attempts at cure included mesmerism (hypnotism), various forms of psychotherapy, hormonal injections, and more recently aversion or behavioral modification therapy and adaptations of impotence sex therapy. The following underlying themes can be extracted:

(1) Homosexual and other abnormal sexual behavior is intrinsically undesirable and ought to be avoided.
(2) If cures are available then persons who engage in such behavior ought to avail themselves of these remedies.
(3) It is permissible for practitioners to make such cures available.

These typically are construed as moral, not merely prudential, principles.

Until recently, few would seriously disagree with these injunctions. However, due to improved research and understanding of human sexuality and the recent successes of Gay Liberation, they have come under sustained challenge. Work in history, Biblical hermeneutics, and moral theology has challenged the claim that homosexuality *per se* is sinful or immoral.[4] Research has challenged the claim that homosexuality constitutes mental illness with sufficient success that the American Psychiatric Association no longer classifies homosexuality *per se* as a mental illness or disorder.[5] Attempts to demonstrate a genetic, hormonal, or other inborn biological basis for homosexuality have failed to be replicated, have proven methodologically defective, or are untested speculation.[6] Collectively, these developments seriously challenge traditional rationales for construing homosexual behavior as abnormal. When these developments are coupled with recent research on components of sexual identity (see below), which strongly suggest that homosexuality is just a natural variation in human sexuality, we have a *prima facie* case for the denial of claim (1). If homosexual behavior is not intrinsically undesirable and there is no obligation to avoid it, then claim (2) should be rejected as well. Thus, (3) minimally must be restricted to those individuals who desire to have their homosexuality cured.

Still, there *are* ego-dystonic homosexuals who are unhappy with their homosexuality and wish to convert to heterosexuality. The denial of claims (1) and (2) and the restriction of (3) in no way require that such persons refrain from seeking cure or from practitioners providing such cures if available. For doing so would seem to be akin to elective cosmetic surgery—and there appear to be no compelling arguments for the immorality of having a "nose job." Recently, however, several therapists have argued that it is immoral to accept homosexual clients for cure of homosexuality and conversion to heterosexuality even if the person strongly desires such cure and conversion.[7] That is, they are arguing for the denial of (3) and possibly the strong denial of (2):

(4) If cures are available, homosexuals ought not to avail themselves of the cure.

At the heart of their argument is the claim that

> therapists generally regard homosexuality as undesirable if not patho-
> logical. Since therapists are unlikely to work on treatment procedures
> unless they see a problem, it is probable that the very existence of change-
> of-orientation programs strengthens societal prejudices against homosex-
> uality and contributes to the self-hate and embarrassment that are deter-
> minants of the "voluntary" desire by some homosexuals to become
> heterosexual.[8]

That is, change-of-orientation programs for those who seek change are
immoral because

(i) The clients are not really voluntary;
(ii) such programs strengthen societal prejudice and discrimination against
homosexuals.

The first claim surely is overstated. While it is the case that some homosexuals seek cure out of self-hate and embarrassment, and that negative
psychotherapeutic opinions of homosexuality by those who offer such
cure programs may have contributed to such self-hate and embarrassment, these factors are not *always* responsible for persons seeking a
conversion to heterosexuality. Homosexuals can have high self-esteem
and be comfortable with their homosexuality but desire a conversion to
heterosexuality for instrumental reasons such as the desire to sire and
raise children or the belief that discovery of their homosexuality will
effectively preclude a career they strongly desire (e.g., in the military, in
politics, or in any of the various fields where there are legal prohibitions
barring homosexuals).[9] For the latter sorts of clients, the first line of
argument fails to show that offering change-in-orientation therapy is
immoral. Nevertheless, we will see later that there is a point to claim (i).

Thus, if the immorality of cure case is to be made, it will have to be
via the second claim. The following is an expansion and tightening of
key themes in the argument to make the strongest case I can for the
conclusion:

(a) Homosexuality *per se* is intrinsically no more undesirable than heterosexuality.
(b) Insofar as homosexuality *per se* leads to undesirable consequences it is
societal prejudice and discrimination towards homosexuals.
(c) Such prejudices and discriminations are unjust.
(d) It is immoral to cooperate in the furthering of social injustices.
(e) The very existence of programs to cure homosexuality, and the parti-

cipation in such programs, strengthens social prejudices and discrimination toward homosexuals.

Therefore

(f) It is immoral for therapists to attempt to cure homosexuality even if the patient desires it.

Since premise (d) is clearly defensible only as a *prima facie* moral principle, conclusion (f) must be construed as a *prima facie* obligation. The *per se* qualifications in (a) and (b) are crucial since it is possible for homosexuality to be integrated into syndromes or patterns which are undesirable and against which social prejudice and discrimination are just. For example, the Gacey, Atlanta, and other homosexual mass murders combine homosexuality with rape and murder. Such combinations are undesirable and discrimination, prejudice, and sanctions against them are not unjust. But it is the combination, not the homosexuality *per se,* that renders them such.

As is the case with most arguments regarding sexual morality, factual premises carry much of the argumentative burden. Premises (b) and (e) are factual. Premise (a) may or may not be factual; in any case, factual matters will be central to the evaluation of it, and also (c). Thus, before we can evaluate the argument we must turn to a consideration of factual matters—especially since the logic of the argument appears impeccable.

I. SEXUAL ORIENTATION

The condemnation of homosexuality as undesirable has traditionally rested on the assumption that all persons by nature are heterosexual, and hence that deviations from heterosexuality are unnatural, abnormal, or otherwise inferior and undesirable; research on sexual identity has seriously challenged this view. The following components of an individual's psychosexual makeup or *sexual identity* have been adequately identified in the literature: *Biological sex* (the determination whether one is male, female, or hermaphroditic); *gender identity* (one's basic conviction of being male or female); *social sex role* (extent of conformity to physical and psychological characteristics culturally associated with males and females); and *sexual orientation,* which contains the following distinguishable components—*sexual behavior* (patterns of erotic bodily contact with others), *patterns of interpersonal affection* (associations involving varying degrees of trust such as with friends, lovers, and marital partners), *erotic fantasy structure* (sexually arousing patterns of mental images of one or more persons engaged in physical sexual activity or in affectional relationships), and *arousal cue-response patterns* (which sensory cues stimulate or inhibit erotic arousal).[10] These components of sexual identity may or may not be in conformity with each other. E.g., a person may be biologically male but believe himself to be really female, or one's social sex role may be sharply at odds with one's gender. Persons whose behavior and arousal cue-response patterns are exclusively homosexual may have heterosexual fantasies; the analogue occurs for heterosexuals. A person whose fantasy structure and cue-response patterns are overwhelmingly homosexual may engage exclusively in heterosexual behavior. A male who is exclusively homosexual in his behavior, cue-response pattern, and fantasies may confine his affectionate relationships exclusively to females whom he platonically loves, and so on. The terms "homosexual," "heterosexual," and "bisexual" have been applied indiscriminately to all of the various components of sexual identity. It is fairly clear, however, that their application to biological sex confuses homosexuality with hermaphroditism and other gender abnormalities, that their application to gender identity confuses homosexuality with transsexualism, and that their application to social sex role confuses homosexuality with effeminancy in males and tom-boyism in females. Thus, the terms "heterosexuality," "homosexuality," and "bisexuality" are appropriately used only with reference to sexual orientation. While sexual orientation is usually labeled heterosexual, homosexual, or bisexual, in fact these labels can be assigned to the various components of sexual orientation, which may or may not be in accord with each other. Thus, a person can be homosexual in some aspects of his sexual orientation and heterosexual or bisexual in others.[11] Strictly speaking, then, it is illegitimate to classify individuals as heterosexuals, homosexuals, or bisexuals as opposed to, e.g., being homosexual in behavior or heterosexual in fantasy structure or whatever.[12]

Various components of sexual identity became fixed at different times in one's life. Biological sex is determined at or before birth. Gender identity is generally fixed by age three to four. Social sex-role tends to be fixed no later than puberty. Arousal cue-response patterns apparently are not fixed until puberty or adolescence. From birth on (and possibly before), humans are capable of, and frequently experience, erotic arousal and even orgasm.[13] During childhood the stimuli that trigger these responses are highly diffuse and nonspecific, but by adolescence they have become highly directional, specific, and idiosyncratic:

> Young children show an utterly polymorphous sexuality. Before puberty, boys respond with vigorous erections to a great variety of stimulations, often to situations which arouse any kind of intense excitement. Those may include anything from fast rides, getting mad, and seeing fires to reciting before a class or getting home late—in short, any combination of fright, anger, or pain that raises tension and excitement. With the coming of puberty and increased sex drive, this diversity of response quickly narrows down . . . what started as a generalized sexual response to fire engines and to catyclismic events may wind up with its entire investment focused for an instant on the way the light falls onto the dimple on somebody's cheeks.[14]

The normal result of this narrowing process is that the individual develops an idiosyncratic repertoire of highly specific cues that stimulate arousal. These include various physiognomic features, circumstances, modes of dress, personality traits, modes of interpersonal behavior, smells, music, and even more esoteric sources; they almost always include patterns of tactile stimulation. It is one's personal catalogue of what one finds erotic and stimulating. At the same time, one also develops a pattern of aversion responses—cues which tend to inhibit sexual arousal; typically, but not always, these are contraries of what one finds arousing.

Consider the case of Michael, a male homosexual who responds with intense arousal to compact trim buttocks; well-defined pectorals, arms, and shoulders; trim, symmetrical, relatively hairless bodies; "chipmunk mouths"; and just about any trim male wearing nothing other than a leather jacket and motorcycle boots. Contrary cues, such as female subcutaneous fat, fleshy breasts, and splayed hips strongly inhibit his sexual arousal. In Michael's case most of his arousal cues (and the inhibiting ones) are highly *gender correlated* in the sense that *statistically* they are most likely to be characteristics possessed by a particular gender. To the extent that one's arousal cues are same-sex correlated, and one's inhibitory cues are opposite-sex correlated, one's arousal response pattern can be said to be homosexual; and if the statistical correlations are the reverse one can be said to be heterosexual. To the extent that a substantial portion of one's arousal cues are same-gender correlated, a substantial portion are opposite-gender correlated, and there is an absence of contrary gender-correlated inhibitory cues, one's cue-arousal pattern can be said to be *bisexual*. But not all such cues are so gender correlated. It is commonplace for persons to have cues that are inanimate or situational—e.g., low lighting or candlelight, mood music, "baby doll" nighties, lace stockings and garter belts, the feel of rubber or leather, personality traits, talking dirty, slumming, paying, exposure to danger, submission, dominating, among others, as components in one's arousal cue-response repertoire. To the extent that one's arousal cues are not gender correlated one can be said to have an *ambisexual* arousal cue-response pattern.

Apparently, erotic fantasy structures are relatively fixed by adolescence or adulthood if not earlier, although this has not been adequately researched. Homosexual, heterosexual, bisexual, and ambisexual fantasy structures can be distinguished in a manner analogous to that for arousal cue-response patterns.[15] How stable or fixed patterns of affectional preference are, and if fixed by what time, has not been adequately researched. Sexual behavior is more variable,[16] and people are capable of engaging in sexual behavior contrary to their basic arousal cue-response patterns. For example, Weinberg and Williams[17] report that 51 percent of their subjects whose sexual behavior was overwhelmingly homosexual have engaged in heterosexual coitus, and of those 58.5 percent enjoyed it the first time. While male homosexuals generally appear not to have a phobic response to sex with females,[18] in many cases there are just too few arousing cues and too many inhibiting ones for there to be any promise of climactic success; yet with considerable ingenuity, even then coitus can be effected. For example, Michael (whose cue response pattern was described above) once found himself in bed with a voluptuous Rubenesque female. Virtually every obvious physiognomic characteristic she possessed was contrary to his arousal cues, and so were inhibitory in his arousal pattern. In an attempt to counter these, he closed his eyes; but tactile cues informed him of the same features—with the same inhibiting effects. Next they contrived to have him lie on his back, eyes closed; she fellated him to arousal without other bodily contact, and then she mounted him, positioning her body "push-up" style so that there was no contact other than between penis and vagina. While this eliminated the inhibiting cues, there was insufficient positive cue stimulation to keep him aroused—which they finally surmounted by having her further contort her "push-up" posture so as to be able to stimulate him rectally with several fingers without otherwise increasing bodily contact; only then was he able to maintain arousal.

II. CHANGING SEXUAL ORIENTATION

Most therapists claiming to cure homosexuality or convert homosexuals to heterosexuality focus on eliminating homosexual behavior, possibly coupled with initiating heterosexual behavior.[19] Given the fact that people can act contrary to their basic arousal cue-response patterns (see above), the question arises: Does accomplishing this constitute a cure of homosexuality and a conversion to heterosexuality? Suppose Michael really wanted to convert to heterosexuality, and after cure therapy with a willing and contortionist female partner he managed regularly to engage in coital behavior to climax and that, save masturbatory fantasies, he was able to muster sufficient will-power to not engage in sex with any other males. Would he then have become (or "converted to" being) a heterosexual? In his behavior (excluding masturbation), he would be heterosexual. But what if he has to fantasize his partner is a male to effect coitus or resort to masturbation with homosexual fantasies as the major component of his sexual outlet? Is he then a heterosexual? But forget behavior and fantasy: His affectional preferences now may be heterosexual, but his physical preferences and erotic fantasies are not. Moreover, his cue-response pattern is just the same as it was before "conversion"; only now he has learned enough gymnastics with an adept and willing partner to circumvent them—if he masturbates to homosexual fantasies frequently enough. What we want to say here is that he still is a homosexual, one who has learned to fake (bizarrely) heterosexual coitus through mastery of sensory deprivation and gymnastic techniques.

Underlying this assessment is the conviction that in some important sense arousal cue-response patterns and erotic fantasy structures are more fundamental to a person's very sexual being than are sexual behavior or patterns of interpersonal affection; thus one has not cured homosexuality or effected a conversion to heterosexuality unless one has eliminated homosexual cue-response patterns and fantasy structures or replaced them by heterosexual ones. It is precisely because most change therapists concentrate on behavior and make no attempt to assess changes in these other components of sexual orientation that their claims of conversion success are widely viewed with a skeptical eye by sex researchers. Moreover, even the long-term efficacy of such therapies for changing behavior is unclear since follow-up efforts have been few, inadequate, or have involved high levels of noncooperation by former patients.[20]

There is, however, one group of change therapists who have sought to change arousal cue-response patterns and develop tools for assessing success in terms of differential arousal measured in terms of penile engorgement. These are the behavior therapists who typically show erotic slides, supply electroshock in response to homoerotic stimuli, and thereby attempt to inhibit homosexual arousal while stimulating hetero-sexual arousal. The results are equivocal.[21] While they do report con-siderable success in eliminating arousal in response to homoerotic pictures in their sequences, it is unclear whether this amounts to "measuring nothing more than the ability of their patients to become utterly surfeited with sex in the course of a short period of extensive exposure under less than ideal conditions";[22] whether such aversions to particular homoerotic sequences of slides transfer into inhibiting erotic response to persons of the same sex; and whether such methods result in the development of replacement positive responses to heterosexual cues. Further, follow-ups on the long-term effects of such therapy on behavior, fantasy, and cue responses have not been adequate.

In short, then, claims of curing homosexuality, and conversion to heterosexuality, are compromised by conceptual confusion over what cure and conversion consist in; when such confusion is sorted out, as we have tried to do, there is little evidence to suggest that current techniques are capable of altering arousal cue-response patterns or fantasy struc-tures—let alone long-term changes in behavior. Thus, given present therapeutic techniques, it would appear neither that principle (2) obliges homosexuals to seek a cure nor that principle (3) justifies therapists offering such cures. But such conclusions say nothing about the correct-ness of principles (1)-(3) or the contrary claims of (f) and (4).

III. IS HOMOSEXUALITY INTRINSICALLY LESS DESIRABLE THAN HETEROSEXUALITY?

Arguments that homosexuality is less desirable than heterosexuality frequently point out the various negative consequences of homosexual-ity, such as job and housing discrimination, parental and societal disapproval, alienation, supposed difficulties in maintaining homosexual lover relationships, unhappiness, lack of opportunity for having children, loneliness in old age, and others.[23] Such arguments at best establish the *instrumental* superiority or desirability of heterosexuality over homo-sexuality: Our society is such that it tries to make things more pleasant and rewarding for heterosexuals than for homosexuals and other uncon-ventionals. It says nothing about the *intrinsic* values of heterosexuality and homosexuality.

To say that something is intrinsically desirable is to say that *in itself* (as an end and not as a means), it is desirable—independent of its instrumental value as means to other ends. To say that something is intrinsically more desirable is to say that its intrinsic value as an end is superior to that of its comparison. The only arguments I have seen to the effect that homosexuality is intrinsically undesirable (and heterosexuality is intrinsically desirable) are variations on the following three claims:

A. God commands heterosexuality and condemns homosexuality, and it is intrinsically desirable to follow God's commands.

B Homosexuality is intrinsically undesirable, since if everyone were homosexual the human species would die out.

C Part of the essence or nature of a person is to be heterosexual, and it is intrinsically desirable to act in accordance with one's nature or essence.

What God's commands are with respect to heterosexuality and homosexuality is a matter of unresolved theological debate,[24] so much so that (A) provides no convincing grounds for concluding either the intrinsic desirability of heterosexuality or the intrinsic undesirability of homosexuality. Claim (B) obviously embodies a fallacy. If it were correct, so too would be the following: "Being female is intrinsically undesirable, since if everyone were female the human species would die out." Moreover, a homosexual orientation is quite compatible with propagation of the species; we have seen that it is possible for homosexuals to engage in coitus. In ancient Greece, the pattern was for homosexuals to be heterosexually married and raise families: in a totally isolated tribe in eastern Peru, the Amarakaeri, male homosexuality is so dominant that heterosexual intercourse is relegated to the conclusion of long drinking bouts on two or three ceremonial occasions a year—yet the tribe reproduces.[25] As for (C), the very notion of persons having an essence, while once a metaphysical commonplace, today is philosophically suspect.

Even more suspect is the assumption that all persons share exactly the same essence or nature. Rather than pursue this metaphysical claim here, it will suffice to make the following observations: What we know about sexual identity and sexual orientation, the mechanisms whereby they develop, the extent to which one's specific sexual orientation is highly idiosyncratic in arousal cue-response and fantasy patterns, and the extent to which such orientations appear to be fixed are such that, *if* one's sexual orientation is a part of a person's essence or nature, *then* there is great variability and diversity in essences or natures. Assuming that it is intrinsically desirable to act in accordance with one's nature or essence, then it is intrinsically desirable for heterosexuals to act heterosexually and homosexuals to act homosexually. If sexual orientation is not part of a person's essence, then (c) also fails.

Thus, there seem to be no good arguments to the effect that heterosexuality is intrinsically desirable but homosexuality is not, though there may be a case that it is intrinsically desirable that persons act in accordance with their sexual orientations. The notion that intrinsic goods are so comparable that some intrinsic goods are better than others is sufficiently problematical that I see no convincing way of showing that if both heterosexuality and homosexuality are intrinsically desirable the former is more so than the latter—or vice versa. Absent any better arguments for principle (1) I conclude it should be rejected and that premise (a) should be accepted (i.e., that homosexuality *per se* is intrinsically no more undesirable than heterosexuality).

IV. SOCIAL JUSTICE AND SEXUAL ORIENTATION

Premise (c) maintains that social prejudice and discrimination toward homosexuals are unjust. Since this premise implicitly involves prejudice and discrimination and leads to unjust distribution of goods (ranging from jobs, housing, and economic opportunities to such basic necessities as self-esteem and the absence of failure and doubt), the relevant notion of justice is that of distributive as opposed to noncomparative justice.[26] There are competing theories of distributive justice, and this is not the place to attempt developing and defending a comprehensive theory. Nevertheless consideration of two contemporary approaches allows us to assess premise (c). Utilitarian views (whether rule or act) maintain that distributive justice consists in so organizing society that goods are distributed to produce the greatest good or satisfaction for the greatest number. Despite attempts such as Lord Devlin's to argue on utilitarian grounds that it is just for society to discriminate against homosexuals, critical evaluation of these attempts makes it clear that there are no compelling utilitarian grounds supporting such a contention.[27] Coupled with John Stuart Mill's defense of liberty,[28] there are *prima facie* grounds to suppose a utilitarian view ought to condemn prejudice and discrimination as unjust on the grounds of homosexuality *per se*.

The most influential contemporary theory of distributive justice is that of John Rawls. At the heart of his view are two principles of distributive justice:

> First: each person is to have an equal right to the most extensive basic liberty compatible with a similar liberty for others.
>
> Second: social and economic inequalities are to be arranged so that they

are both (a) reasonably expected to be to everyone's advantage, and (b) attached to positions and offices open to all.[29]

So long as basic necessities are supplied to all, these principles do allow differential distribution of surplus goods. Basic necessities include adequate food, clothing, and shelter, as well as such psychological goods as self-esteem; what counts as adequate is culturally relative. With respect to the differential distribution of surplus goods, Rawls's principles require allowing maximal mobility between the classes, on which differential distribution of goods is based, and that the basis for differential distribution must be restricted to differences in individuals for which their possessors can be held responsible—such properties being just grounds for discrimination among persons only if those persons had a fair opportunity to acquire or avoid them. While there are important points of Rawls's theory of distributive justice that are controversial and debatable, most moral and social philosophers would accept the foregoing corollaries to his principles.[30]

Premise (c) addresses itself to both basic necessities and surplus goods. With respect to basic necessities, discrimination on grounds of homosexuality is unjust (as is any discrimination on whatever basis). With respect to discrimination in the distribution of surplus goods, the preponderance of evidence is that persons have no control over their sexual orientations; such orientations are fixed by adulthood and not subject to change or cure. Thus, it follows on Rawls's position that homosexuality or heterosexuality are illegitimate grounds for differential distribution of goods, and a society that discriminates on their basis is unjust.

Other than for basic necessities, this conclusion is restricted to societies such as ours where the therapeutic resources are sufficiently impoverished that sexual orientation cannot readily be manipulated or altered. But suppose we have a society essentially like ours except that there have been therapeutic breakthroughs capable of changing sexual orientations at will—from heterosexual to homosexual, from homosexual to heterosexual, from heterosexual to transvestite, bestialist, or sadomasochist. Suppose further that the society has decided to make fully effective change of sexual orientation therapy available free to all members of society. In such a society it would appear that Rawls's views on justice would allow differential distribution of surplus goods on the basis of sexual orientation (provided, of course, that basic necessities were met and that the inequalities were to everybody's advantage). Rawls's view on when differential distribution of surplus goods is just is a specific version of a more general principle of social justice theory:

> Comparitive [i.e., distributive] justice requires more than that difference in treatment be based on differences in characteristics. The underlying differences between individuals that justify differences in their treatment must be *relevant* differences, and the underlying similarities that justify similar treatment must be *relevant* similarities.[31]

Rawls's theory in effect imposes criteria for determining relevant differences.

Does the free availability of efficacious conversion therapy make sexual orientation a relevant difference that justifies differential distribution of goods on the basis of sexual orientation? Suppose our hypothetical society is one in which reaction to past sexual exploitation of women by men and following certain feminist separatist doctrines has decided on a policy of sexual separatism—in which marriage, sexual activity, and the rearing of children are to be strictly segregated. Only homosexual marriages are sanctioned; heterosexual intercourse is illegal. Procreation is restricted to artificial insemination, where male offspring are raised by the male donor and his lover, and female offspring raised by the mother and her lover. Single parents are discouraged. Finding a totalitarian society repugnant, and aware that total sexual conformity is impossible to "voluntarily" regulate without "big brother" methods that invade privacy illegitimately, a system of sanctions has been imposed that results in a differential distribution of goods that relegates heterosexuals to the lowest socioeconomic categories consistent with Rawlsian justice. Free conversion to homosexuality therapy is provided to enable heterosexuals and other social deviants to escape these sanctions.

Whatever Rawls would say about how just this society is, my intuitions are that it is a fundamentally unjust society, and I suspect that these intuitions would be shared by most readers. If the respective roles of heterosexuals and homosexuals are reversed in our hypothetical society, we obtain a society remarkably close to our own, except that it possesses free efficacious cure therapy. Like our society, the hypothetical one implements heterosexual analogues to (1)-(3). Since we have seen no good reasons to suppose that heterosexuality or homosexuality are intrinsically undesirable or that either is inherently better than the other, it seems that our intuitions should be the same for both societies—they are both unjust since sexual orientation is not a relevant difference justifying differential distribution of surplus goods.

We conclude, then, that regardless of whether the means for cure of homosexuality and conversion to heterosexuality are available, the discriminations addressed by premise (c) are indeed unjust.

The relationships between justice and moral imperatives governing the behavior of individuals within a society are fairly unclear and this is not the place to attempt any systematic treatment of the issues. It does seem to be the case, however, that "the area of justice is a part of morality but not the whole of it."[32] Thus, to act in an unjust manner is to act immorally. Presumably, actively cooperating in the furthering of social injustice does constitute acting in an unjust manner, and so is immoral. Whatever the moral status of nonactive cooperation in the furthering of social injustice (e.g., turning one's back on or refusing to challenge those actively promoting injustice—as in Nazi Germany), in the context of the anticure argument premise (d)—that it is immoral to cooperate in the furthering of social injustice—clearly concerns the active cooperation of the therapist and client, and so we may accept premise (d) as a correct, *prima facie* moral principle. (But see below.)

V. CONSEQUENCES OF HOMOSEXUALITY AND CURE THERAPY

All of the nonfactual premises in the anticure argument have been substantiated; we now turn to the factual premises, (b) and (e). Premise (b) maintains that insofar as homosexuality *per se* leads to undesirable consequences it is due to societal prejudices and discrimination toward homosexuals. If one surveys the homosexuality research literature one will find the following undesirable consequences prominently mentioned:

> inability to enter into lasting relationships
> high numbers of sexual partners
> high incidence of venereal disease
> job discrimination and inability to hold responsible jobs
> housing discrimination
> religious alienation
> exclusion from marriage and raising of family
> loneliness
> liability to arrest, extortion, and blackmail
> mental illness
> depression
> propensity to suicide
> unhappiness
> lack of caring persons in old age

Many of these reflect social stereotypes, and while some have been substantiated by the best available research, many have been repudiated.[33] Male homosexuals do tend to have larger numbers of sexual partners than do heterosexuals, and lesbians tend to have relatively few sexual partners; there is no significant correlation between numbers of partners and emotional stability or maturity, psychological adjustment or happiness. Thus, large numbers of partners is not symptomatic of pathology, although promiscuity often is cited as grounds for discrimination or prejudice against homosexuals. Promiscuity does lead, however, to higher incidences of venereal or sexually transmitted disease, especially high incidences of gonorrhea, hepatitus, and acquired immune deficiency (AID) syndrome are found among male homosexuals. The incidences of venereal disease is quite low among lesbians and relatively monogamous male homosexual couples. Susceptibility to VD is clearly neither a consequence of homosexuality *per se* nor an undesirable consequence due to social prejudice and discrimination. While many homosexuals avoid entangling lover relationships out of fear that such relationships will expose them as homosexuals, and thus make them more liable to societal prejudice and discrimination, many homosexuals who are "out of the closet," to an extent that having a lover will not increase their vulnerability, prefer to engage in promiscuous sexual behavior. Thus, while societal pressure and discrimination may sometimes be a cause of promiscuity, it frequently is not. Other than carrying an increased likelihood of VD, it is unclear that promiscuity is itself undesirable.[34] Many homosexuals combine promiscuous anonymous sex with a stable nonexclusive lover relationship, and many other homosexuals prefer to have nonsexual, close-binding, affectional relationships while confining their sexual activity to anonymous promiscuous sex. While these patterns are alternatives that conflict with the heterosexual monogamous norm, there is no evidence that one pattern is preferable to the other, hence that promiscuous lifestyles are undesirable other than for increased propensity to disease. In any case, these are not consequences of homosexuality *per se,* but of particular homosexual lifestyles that social prejudice and discrimination sometimes do promote.

Job and housing discrimination against homosexuals is frequent and often legally sanctioned. The primary reason it is less extensive than it might be is that most homosexuals are capable of passing as heterosexual whenever they wish, and in job and other circumstances use "passing" as a means of avoiding discrimination. Sometimes this results in the psychological pressures of "living a lie" and can take a serious toll; often it does not. While many homosexuals do engage in stable lover relationships, fear that such relationships may make their homosexuality more visible—and thus invite job and other discrimination—dissuades a number of homosexuals from entering into such relationships. Those who do often try to hide the existence of these associations in ways that ultimately threaten the relationships. Those "out-of-the-closet" gays who openly have stable lover relationships often invite job and housing discrimination as a result. These are clear cases in which societal prejudices and discrimination result in undesirable consequences for homosexuality.

While many sexually active homosexuals enter into heterosexual marriages and raise families, they tend to hide their homosexuality from their families, and if it is discovered the marriage frequently dissolves. The courts have displayed almost uniform reluctance to allow homosexuals to have custody of children—this despite the evidence that homosexuals apparently are as fit to be parents as single parents and that homosexual couples are as fit as heterosexual ones.[35] Occasionally, a homosexual can openly enter into a heterosexual marriage and raise a family, but most heterosexual partners cannot handle this, especially if the person continues to be homosexually active. Other than producing and raising children, homosexual lover relationships can provide the benefits of marriage. Lesbian couples wishing children sometimes resort to artificial insemination (though often it is difficult to obtain medical cooperation),[36] or to anonymous sex with a stranger to produce children to raise. Adoption by homosexual couples usually is impossible without involved subterfuge, so male homosexual couples usually have little opportunity to raise children unless they have custody by a prior marriage (which the courts usually will not consent to if the mother objects); surrogate mothers now offer another legally complicated option. Thus, while an important part of the inability of homosexuals to raise families stems from societal pressure and discrimination (especially as dispensed by the judicial system), much of it is due to the lack of biological means for conveniently providing the children to raise.

It certainly is the the case that theologically questionable moral condemnation of homosexuality (see note 4) has served to legitimize extensive social prejudice and discrimination against homosexuals. Further, many homosexuals are raised in a religious environment that is hostile to and condemnatory of homosexuality. The attendant result is that a person who is coming to grips with his homosexuality often suffers from extreme guilt that may lead to mental health problems, or he may resolve his conflict by joining a gay church (such as the Metropolitan Community Church denomination) and proclaim that "gay is good." Most frequently the result is alienation from religion. Whether alienation from organized religion is undesirable is problematic, but the process by which it occurs for homosexuals frequently is undesirable. This does seem to be a case where religiously sanctioned and encouraged social prejudice, intolerance, and discrimination cause undesirable consequences for homosexuality.

Unhappiness, loneliness, mental illness, depression, and propensity to suicide are popularly exaggerated concomitants of homosexuality. Depending on one's homosexual lifestyle, one may or may not enjoy a higher incidence of these than the heterosexual population. The principle correlates of elevated unhappiness and the other stereotypic symptoms are the lack of acceptance of one's homosexuality, poor integration into the homosexual subculture, and large numbers of sexual problems. While other factors are involved, it appears that societal prejudice and discrimination are the major contributors. The idea that elderly homosexuals are lonelier than elderly heterosexuals or have fewer care resources is a myth.

In many jurisdictions homosexual behavior is felonious, and sometimes homosexuals do get arrested or blackmailed through exploitation of these laws. Homosexual robbery and assault victims often are afraid to report these incidents to the police, especially if they occurred in a homosexual context, for fear of exposure. The illegality of homosexual behavior is sometimes used to justify job and other discriminations—a clear case of the law codifying and legitimizing prevailing social prejudice and discrimination.[37] Available data suggest that while homosexuals are slightly more liable to arrest than heterosexuals, most arrests of homosexuals have little to do with their sexual orientation and that most homosexual men and women have never been arrested, robbed, blackmailed, assaulted, or suffered police extortion on account of their homosexuality. More promiscuous homosexual lifestyles run a significantly higher risk of these consequences. Nevertheless, the threat of such consequences on account of one's homosexuality does add substance to societal prejudices and discrimination in a way that affects the behavior of many homosexuals.

We conclude, then, that while a number of the undesirable consequences of homosexuality are exaggerated, many of them are real and substantial enough to be a cause for serious concern. Some of the risks that obtain accrue to particular homosexual lifestyles rather than to homosexuality *per se*. It is the case that the stereotypical identification of these lifestyles with homosexuality *per se* is often used to justify random discrimination against homosexuals. While some of the potentially undesirable consequences cannot be attributed to societal prejudice and discrimination against homosexuality *per se,* these constitute a major and important cause of undesirable consequences of homosexuality *per se.* Thus, while (b) fails to be defensible, we can accept

> (b') Insofar as homosexuality *per se* leads to undesirable consequences, in large part this is due to societal prejudices and discrimination toward homosexuals.

Premise (b') is strong enough for the remainder of the anticure argument to go through.

We turn now to premise (e), which maintains that the very existence of programs to cure homosexuality and participation in such programs strengthen social prejudice and discrimination toward homosexuals. What evidence is there for this claim? Many homosexuals have perceived the classification of homosexuality as a mental disorder to be one that legitimizes social prejudice and discrimination toward homosexuality; this perception was an important motivation for the successful efforts of gay activists to persuade the American Psychiatric Association to remove homosexuality *per se* from its catalogue of sexual disorders. Despite such declassification, many psychiatrists persist in the belief that homosexuality is a mental disorder; this conviction is especially strong among those therapists who offer and promote cures of homosexuality and conversion to heterosexuality.[38] This suggests there is considerable plausibility to premise (e).

The strongest empirical support for premise (e) comes from labeling or social reaction theory in sociology, which arises out of the social deviance literature and is concerned with the implications of labeling individuals or groups of individuals as deviant.[39] According to the theory, once we impose diagnostic or other negative labels (e.g., "mentally ill" or "homosexual") we accept these labels as the stereotypic reality and thereby treat the persons so diagnosed according to the expectations of the label. Once a person is so labeled, those who relate to the person do so as if the individual possessed the conditions associated with the label, and the person so labeled assumes behaviors congruent with the label. Labeling thus becomes a self-fulfilling prophecy.

> What makes homosexuality "deviant" . . . is not anything about the behavior *per se* but rather the fact that people differentiate, stigmatize, and penalize alleged homosexuals.
>
> Other people's reactions can involve assigning someone a deviant status which often overrides his other statuses. This can influence him to identify and associate with other "deviants" and affect the view he has of himself and the world.[40]

Thus labeling theory implies:

> The labeling of homosexuals as mentally ill causes people to accept these labels as stereotypical reality and to treat persons so diagnosed according to the expectations of those labels.
> In virtue of being labeled mentally ill homosexuals will assume behaviors congruent with the label.

Does the evidence support these implications of labeling theory?

Despite the declassification of homosexuality as a mental disorder in 1973, a substantial proportion of therapists still believe it is a mental disorder. Moreover, a majority of the United States population in 1970 believed that homosexuality is a sickness that can be cured in at least some cases, and that homosexuals should not be allowed to be school teachers, ministers, court judges, physicians, or government officials[41]— all positions one would not want occupied by someone who was crazy. While there may have been some softening of these attitudes since then, such views still appear to be widely held.[42] Collectively, the available evidence tends to support the first implication of labeling theory. The second implication fares less well. Twenty years ago homosexuality was sufficiently invisible that a person discovering homosexual feelings often felt he was the only person like that, and, turning to the available literature,[43] learned that such feelings were rare, abnormal, and indicative of psychopathology. Many apparently accepted such pronouncements, assumed neurotic and other behaviors indicative of mental illness, and sought therapy to cure their homosexuality. However, despite inadequate data, the available evidence suggests that this was a minority phenomenon (although I suspect it was prevalent among those who sought cures), and that the majority of homosexuals did not act in accordance with the predictions of labeling theory.[44] The most important research study applying labeling theory to homosexuality fails to support the second implication, and *inter alia* explains the failure in terms of the ability of most homosexuals to pass at will as heterosexual and the existence of support mechanisms provided by the extensive homosexual subculture.[45] Other recent studies support the same general conclusions. These findings are congruent with the more general evidence on labeling theory, which tends to be confirmatory in institutionalized settings such as hospitals and Alcoholics Anonymous, but equivocal in noninstitutionalized settings.

The evidence on labeling theory thus lends some credence to claim (i) above. A substantial number of Americans accept the labeling of homosexuality as a mental disorder and apply the stereotypic expectations of such labels to homosexuals. Offering and promoting cures for homosexuality for the most part constitutes an act of labeling homosexuality as a mental illness. Thus, labeling theory lends some plausibility to premise (e)'s claim that programs designed to cure homosexuality strengthen social prejudice and discrimination against homosexuals. But we must not exaggerate the strength of such support. Recent studies on homophobia indicate that those who are most homophobic tend to be rural, white persons raised in the Midwest or South; religious, tending toward fundamentalist Protestant; relatively more conservative, less lenient about sex and sexual behavior in general; intolerant of ambiguity; display cognitive rigidity; possess authoritarian personalities; and are opposed to equality of the sexes.[46] The portrait is sufficiently close to what is commonly associated with bigots that there is reason to suspect the labeling of homosexuals as mentally ill frequently serves to legitimize already existing prejudice rather than causing or strengthening it. For these people, if homosexuality were not labeled as a mental illness, other reasons would be found to justify the same prejudice and discrimination toward homosexuals.[47] For such people, one expects that their prejudice toward homosexuality would not diminish one iota if cure programs were eliminated. I doubt very much that the majority of those who are prejudiced against homosexuals, support at least some forms of discrimination (e.g., entrance to certain occupations), and oppose Gay Rights legislation constitute such bigots who are impervious to argument and factual evidence. Rather, I suspect they are persons who grew up with certain prejudices and beliefs (fueled in part by earlier labelings of homosexuality as a mental illness) and if those beliefs are discredited they will modify their beliefs and attitudes. While the existence and promotion of cure therapies probably does not strengthen such prejudices and support discrimination, to the extent that their existence reinforces prior beliefs, alteration in beliefs and attitudes will be retarded; such potential is increased by the prevalent media practice of giving equal time in covering the "controversial topic" of homosexuality to therapists, such as Charles Socarides, who represent the distinct minority of professionals who believe that homosexuality is a curable illness.

The word "strengthens" in premise (e) is ambiguous in that it could mean either *reinforces* or *causes*. The foregoing discussion does indicate that the labeling of homosexuality as a mental illness continues to reinforce prejudice and discrimination toward homosexuality; to the extent that the existence of cure programs and the participation in them perpetuates such labeling, it does reinforce prejudice and discrimination. (This is consistent with there being other practices and forces present in our society that weaken such prejudice and discrimination.) The extent of such reinforcement is unclear, almost certainly is less than it was twenty years ago, and seems to be dependent upon the public visibility of cure programs rather than their very existence. Thus, the following attenuated version of premise (e) seems defensible:

> (e') The existence of well-publicized programs to cure homosexuality and the participation in such programs reinforces existing social prejudices and discrimination toward homosexuals.[48]

So interpreted, our acceptance of premise (d) ("It is immoral to cooperate in the furthering of social injustice") becomes problematic. For while therapist and client are actively participating in the existence of the cure therapy program, the program only serves to reinforce, not cause, prejudice and discrimination—so it is unclear that such participation or the existence of the program constitutes active cooperation in the furthering of social injustice. If it does not, (d) is false and the anticure argument fails to be sound on this interpretation. If it does, then the argument is sound but the force of the argument is weak—the immorality being a mere peccadillo.

If the anticure argument is to have the force its authors intend, we must adopt the causal interpretation of (e), wherein the existence of such programs cause social prejudices and discrimination. A number of meanings of 'cause' have been identified. Sometimes it refers to conditions necessary for an effect to occur. In this sense (e) is false, since it would be possible for there to be prejudice and discrimination against homosexuals even if there were no cure programs. Sometimes 'cause' refers to a sufficient condition. By itself the existence of cure programs is not sufficient to produce prejudice and discrimination. A more sophisticated notion of causality is that C causes E if and only if, under the circumstances E would not have occurred unless C were to occur; i.e., C is among a set of conditions sufficient for E to occur under the circumstances, and E would not have occurred if C were absent.[49] Thus, we might claim that under the present circumstances various factors are sufficient for prejudice and discrimination against homosexuals, and the labeling of homosexuals as mentally ill is one of these; but absent such labeling, such prejudice and discrimination would not occur. Our previous discussion of bigots suggests that this is not the case generally; nevertheless, quite possibly this is the case for a number of individuals.

Thus, to the extent that such labeling causes individuals to become prejudiced and to discriminate, such labeling does cause increased (thus strengthened) prejudice and discrimination. Since the offering of cure programs tends to be part of that labeling process,[50] offering cures would be a part of that cause. What is unclear is whether there are such individuals so influenced by the labeling process, and the extent of their contribution to prejudice and discrimination. We do not possess adequate evidence on this, but it seems quite likely that there were substantial numbers of such persons earlier in this century (before the diagnosis of homosexuality as a mental disorder began to be seriously challenged in the 1960s) and that while today there are fewer such persons, there still are many.

We have found a causal interpretation of (e) on which it quite plausibly is true. A virtue of it is that it is consistent with different etiologies of prejudice and discrimination against homosexuals for different individuals, and thus it is not an excessively strong generalization. Unfortunately, we lack the data to demonstrate that any (and if so how many) individuals evidence this pattern, hence the extent to which (e) so interpreted concerns a significant source of prejudice and discrimination against homosexuals.

It may be that labeling of homosexuals as mentally ill influences people to be prejudiced and to discriminate against homosexuals without meeting the relatively strong contextually necessary conditions of the foregoing analysis. In such cases, we might construe the causal interpretation of (e) as making a statistical claim analogous to "Smoking causes cancer." While there is philosophical disagreement over how to analyze such statistical causality, the basic ideas are that the greater the incidence of C in a population, the greater the probability that E would occur in the population, and that the statistical relationship between E and C is not symmetrical.[51] Thus, the greater the incidence of labeling homosexuality as mentally ill, the greater the level of prejudice and discrimination against homosexuals would be in our population. Ideally, such a statistical causal hypothesis should be tested by a random experimental design or a prospective study. While neither has been done, and there would be difficulties effecting either, the following lends some support to it. Over the last twenty-five years the incidence of labeling of homosexuals as mentally ill by therapists and other experts has been diminishing, and over the same time there appears to be a decline in the incidence of prejudice and discrimination against homosexuals. Furthermore, there is no reason to think that a decline in prejudice and discrimination has caused a decline in labeling. To be sure, such declines in prejudice and discrimination have occurred with the rise and increasing effectiveness of Gay Liberation, and so may be attributed to the effectiveness of that movement rather than to a decline in labeling. However, a key element in Gay Liberation's political activism was to persuade the American Psychiatric Association and other psychological health care professions to declassify homosexuality as a mental disorder as part of an attempt to reduce the stigmatized labeling of homosexuals that was thought to contribute to prejudice and discrimination. This strongly suggests that a reduction in the incidences of labeling of homosexuals as mentally ill was a factor causing a decline in prejudice and discrimination.

Thus, while the evidence is not as strong as one would like, there is reason to think the following version of (e) is defensible on one or the other of the last two views of causality we have considered:

(e") The offering of programs to cure homosexuality typically involves the labeling of homosexuality as a mental disorder or otherwise inferior. Such labeling causes an increase in the incidences of social prejudice and discrimination toward homosexuals.

We provisionally accept this version of (e). Does this weakening of (e) require rethinking premise (d), as was the case for (e')? To the extent that offering cure programs involves labeling of homosexuals, given our prior analysis, such programs do cause prejudice and discrimination and so constitute active cooperation in the futhering of social injustice. Thus, I think we still can accept premise (d). However, the replacement of (e) by (e") requires weakening conclusion (f) to

(f') It is immoral for therapists to attempt to cure homosexuality when such attempts involve the labeling of homosexuality as a mental illness or otherwise inferior.

This applies to most (but not all) therapists currently offering cure therapies.

Conclusion (f') is a *prima facie* principle, and so can conflict with other moral obligations. If a patient presents himself wanting cure of homosexuality and a conversion to heterosexuality, does this produce a conflict of obligations for the therapist? Only if the therapist's cure therapy and actions involve labeling of homosexuality as illness or otherwise inferior. In such cases of conflict, it appears that principle (f') should take precedence simply because there is inadequate evidence to support the contention that existing therapies are efficacious. Rather, the therapist ought to attempt to help the patient to come to terms with his homosexuality and integrate it into a productive lifestyle. Should such efficacious therapies become available, it is less clear how to resolve the clash of obligations. The most reasonable resolution would be to refer the client to a change therapist whose attempts do not involve the labeling of homosexuality as a mental illness or otherwise inferior. Such a referring therapist would thereby honor principle (f') while also providing for the needs of his clients, although he might go out of business in the process if, like many prominent change therapists, his practice is largely concerned with curing homosexuality.

VI. CONCLUSIONS

We have argued for the soundness of a weakened version of the anticure argument, in which premise (b) is replaced by (b'), premise (e) by (e"), and conclusion (f) by (f'). It follows that thesis (3) is acceptable only with serious qualifications that exclude the majority of cure practitioners today. Along the way we argued that thesis (1) should be rejected. It also follows from our discussion that thesis (2) should be rejected—that for homosexuals seeking cure, therapy should be elective rather than obligatory. Claim (4) has not been substantiated. Our acceptance of the anticure argument is, however, tentative since the evidence supporting key factual premises is nowhere as strong as one ideally would desire—despite the fact that what evidence there is more strongly supports these premises than their denials. Better empirical evidence *could* cause us ultimately to reject the anticure argument. This fact, coupled with the extensive recourse to empirical results that we have had to consider in our evaluation of the argument, illustrates that there are important limitations to how far mere philosophical analysis can go in evaluating moral claims. For the defense of moral claims—especially those in sexual morality—typically involves crucial factual claims that cannot be validated philosophically, just as it involves ethical principles that cannot be validated empirically.

The American Psychiatric Association currently classifies a number of other sexual behaviors and orientations, such as bestiality, transvestism, sadomasochism, festishism, among others, as mental disorders. Elsewhere I have argued that there is little empirical evidence supporting their inclusion and that precisely the same criteria used to declassify homosexuality as a mental disorder, if consistently applied, also should result in their declassification.[52] Numerous therapists attempt to cure these "disorders," and it appears that very much the same labeling phenomena occur here as with homosexuality.

Michael Foucault has noted how psychology/medicine in the nineteenth century converted homosexuality from a component in an individual's psychosexual and behavioral repertoire into a species of individual, and thus embarked on a labeling process that *inter alia* codified prejudice and promulgated discrimination against homosexuals.

> The nineteenth-century homosexual becomes a personage, a past, a case-history, and a childhood, in addition to being a type of life, a life form, and a morphology, with an indiscreet anatomy and possibly a mysterious physiology. Nothing that went into his total composition was unaffected by his sexuality . . . It was co-substantial with him, less as a habitual sin than as a singular nature. We must not forget that the psychological, psychiatric, medical category of homosexuality was constituted from the moment it was characterized . . . The sodomite had been a temporary aberration: the homosexual was now a species.[53]

Just as psychiatry and medicine labeled, and thus invented The Homosexual, so too it may have invented The Transvestite, The Pedophiliac, The Sadist, The Masochist, The Voyeur, and so on—all in an orgy of labeling with the effect of causing prejudices and discrimination against such sexual variants. These considerations suggest that, perhaps, analogues to the homosexual anticure argument for other variant sexual behaviors and orientations also are sound. But considerations of these issues would require another investigation.

NOTES

1. John Boswell, *Christianity, Social Tolerance, and Homosexuality* (Chicago: University of Chicago Press, 1980).

2. Vern L. Bullough, *Sexual Variance in Society and History* (Chicago: University of Chicago Press, 1976), chs. 20, 21; John Lauritsen and David Thorstad, *The Early Homosexual Rights Movement (1864-1935)* (New York: Times Change Press, 1974), chs 2 and 3; Michael Foucault, *History of Human Sexuality*, Vol. I (Translated by Robert Hurley; New York: Vintage Books, 1980), pp. 43 *et passim*.

3. Pp. 23-24 in Jonathan Katz (ed.), *Gay American History: Lesbians and Gay Men in the U.S.A.* (New York: Thomas Y. Crowell Co., 1976). See also Bullough, op cit.

4. Boswell, op. cit.; John J. McNeill, *The Church and the Homosexual* (Kansas City: Sheed Andrews and McMeel, 1976); A. Kosnik, et. al, *Human Sexuality: New Directions in American Catholic Thought.* (Ramsey, NJ: Paulist Press, 1977).

5. R. Bayer, *Homosexuality and American Psychiatry: The Politics of Diagnosis* (New York: Basic Books, 1981); F. Suppe, review of Bayer, ibid., *Journal of Medicine and Philosophy* 7(1982):375-381, and "Classifying Sexual Disorders: The Diagnostic and Statistical Manual of the American Psychiatric Association", *Journal of Homosexuality*, forthcoming. Egodystonic homosexuality (roughly homosexuals who are unhappy with their homosexuality and wish to convert to heterosexuality) remains a mental disorder, however.

6. M. Ruse, "Are there Gay Genes? Sociobiology and Homosexuality," pp. 5-34 N. Koertge (ed.) *Nature and Causes of Homosexuality: A Philosophic and Scientific Inquiry* (New York: Haworth Press, 1981); Lynda I. A. Birke, "Is Homosexuality Hormonally Determined?", pp. 35-50 in Koertge, op. cit.; N. K. Gartrell, "Hormones and Homosexuality," pp. 169-172 in W. Paul, et. al (eds.), *Homosexuality: Social, Psychological, and Biological Issues*, (Beverly Hills: Sage Publications, 1982).

7. Gerald C. Davison, "Homosexuality: The Ethical Challenge," *Journal of Consulting and Clinical Psychology* 44(1976):157-162; "Homosexuality and the Ethics of Behavioral Intervention: Paper 1," *Journal of Homosexuality* 2(1977):195-204; and "Politics, Ethics, and Therapy for Homosexuality" (pp. 89-98 in W. Paul, et. al, op. cit). Charles Silverstein, "Homosexuality and the Ethics of Behavior Intervention: Paper 2," *Journal of Homosexuality* 2(1977):205-211.

8. Davison, "Homosexuality: The Ethical Challenge", op. cit., p. 157.

9. In counseling persons at early stages in confronting their homosexuality, I have encountered such reactions. For compelling legal reasons for many such fears, see E. C. Boggan, M. G. Haft, C. Lister, and J. P. Rupp, *The Rights of Gay People: The Basic ACLU Guide to a Gay Person's Rights* (New York: Avon, 1975). Appendix 2 lists 307 occupations where one or more states have licensing requirements such that homosexuals can be excluded on grounds that their sexual orientation is evidence of bad moral character or the illegality of homosexual acts. These range from lawyers (51 states including the District of Columbia), physicians (50), nurses (49), accountants (48), architects (42) to barbers (47), boxer/wrestlers (6), used car dealer (1). Homosexuality is automatic grounds for discharge from the military.

10. M. Shively and J. DeCecco, "Components of Sexual Identity," *Journal of Homosexuality* (1977):41-48; and C. A. Tripp, *The Homosexual Matrix* (New York: McGraw Hill, 1975), ch. 5.

11. Shively and DeCecco, op. cit.

12. Frequently we will use 'homosexual' and 'heterosexual' without qualification. Sometimes this will be for ease of exposition; in other cases it will be because the arguments or claims we are considering are unspecific as to what is meant or otherwise do not distinguish various components of sexual orientation. In both cases we can think of homosexuals as approximating to varying degrees an archetypal homosexual who is exclusively homosexual in all four components of sexual orientation, and heterosexuals as approximating to varying degrees a similarly archetypal heterosexual. 'Heterosexuality' and 'homosexuality' will be used analogously.

13. Orgasm, physiologically, consists of the sudden cessation of vasocongestion and myontonia, which characterize later stages of sexual arousal. It is

distinct from ejaculation and is the same for both men and women, though its subjective experience for men and women may be quite different.

14. Tripp, op. cit., pp. 20-21.

15. Suppe, "Classifying Sexual Disorders," op. cit.

16. A. Kinsey, et. al, *Sexual Behavior in the Human Male* (Philadelphia: Saunders, 1948), ch. 21, esp. pp. 636-659, and *Sexual Behavior in the Human Female* (Philadelphia: Saunders, 1953), Part III.

17. *Male Homosexuals* (New York: Oxford, 1974), p. 213.

18. K. Freund, et. al, "The Phobic Theory of Male Homosexuality." *Archives of General Psychiatry* 31(1974):495-499.

19. This is the case for, e.g., W. H. Masters and V. E. Johnson, *Homosexuality in Perspective* (Boston: Little Brown, 1979); I. Bieber, et. al, *Homosexuality: A Psychoanalytic Study* (New York: Basic Books, 1962); and L. J. Hatterer, *Changing Homosexuality in the Male* (New York: McGraw Hill, 1970).

20. This so far all the works cited in note 19; further it appears that a high proportion of their subjects had bisexual behavior histories and possibly were bisexual in arousal cue-response pattern and fantasy structure.

21. Cf., e.g., N. McConaghy, "Subjective and Penile Plethysmograph Responses following Aversion-relief and Apomorphine Therapy for Homosexual Impulses," *British Journal of Psychiatry* 115(1969): 723-730; "Subjective and Penile Plethysmograph Responses to Aversion Therapy for Homosexuality: A Follow-up Study," *British Journal of Psychiatry* 117(1970):555-560; "Heterosexual Experience, Marital Status, and Orientation of Homosexual Males," *Archives of Sexual Behavior* (1978):575-581. N. McConaghy, D. Proctor, and R. Barr, *"Subjective and Penile Plethysmography Responses to Aversion Therapy for Homosexuality: A Partial Replication," *Archives of Sexual Behavior* 2 (1972):65-78. M. P. Feldman and M. J. MacCulloch, "The Application of Anticipatory Avoidance Learning to the Treatment of Homosexuality: 1. Theory, Technique and Preliminary Results," *Behavioral Research and Therapy* 2(1965):165-183; "Aversion Therapy in Management of 43 Homosexuals," *British Medical Journal* 1(1967):594-597; *Homosexual Behavior: Therapy and Assessment* (Oxford: Pergamon, 1971). John Bancroft, *Review of Feldman and MacCulloch, ibid., *Archives of Sexual Behavior* 3(1974):389-390. S. R. Conrad and John P. Wincze, *"Orgasmic Reconditioning: A Controlled Study of Its Effects upon the Sexual Arousal and Behavior of Adult Male Homosexuals," *Behavior Therapy* 7(1976):155-166. (Works prefaced with an asterisk call into question the efficacy of behavioral modification techniques for changing sexual orientation. See also note 22.)

22. P. 80 of J. Money, "Strategy, Ethics, Behavior Modification, and Homosexuality," *Archives of Sexual Behavior* 2(1972):79-81.

23. While many of these negative consequences are real, their extent frequently is exaggerated. See the discussion in Section V and also C. Silverstein, *Man to Man: Gay Couples in America* (New York: William Morrow and Co., 1981); A. Bell and M. Weinberg, *Homosexualities: A Study in Diversity* (New York: Simon and Schuster, 1978), and R. M. Berger, *Gay and Gray: The Older Homosexual Man* (Urbana: University of Illinois Press, 1982).

24. See the works cited in note 4 above.

25. K. ᴊ. Dover, *Greek Homosexuality* (Cambridge: Harvard University Press, 1978). T. Schneebaum, "Notes on an Isolated Tribe of the Amarakaeri," Department of South American Ethnology, American Museum of Natural History, unpublished, 1958 (as reported by Tripp, op. cit., p. 70).

26. Heɾe I follow J. Rawls, *A Theory of Justice* (Cambridge: Harvard Universit̠y Press, 1971).

27. Seᴇ P. Devlin, *The Enforcement of Morals* (Oxford: Oxford University Press, 1965); and H. L. A. Hart, *Law, Liberty, and Morality* (Stanford: Stanford University Press, 1965). For a comprehensive critical discussion of the issue, see B. Leiser, *Liberty, Justice, and Morals*, second edition (New York: Macmillaɴ, 1979), ch.1. For a utilitarian defense of the morality of homosexuality, sᴇe Ronald Atkinson, *Sexual Morality* (London: Hutchinson, 1965), ch. 6.

28. *On Liberty* (Indianapolis: Bobbs Merrill, 1956).

29. Rawls, op. cit., p. 60.

30. E.g., J. Feinberg, *Social Philosophy* (Englewood Cliffs: Prentice Hall, 1973), ch. 7, esp. p. 108 and W. K. Frankena, "Some Beliefs About Justice", the Lindley Lecture, Department of Philosophy Pamphlet (Lawrence: University of Kansas, 1966) argue the same point.

31. Feinberg, op. cit., pp. 99-100.

32. Frankena, *Ethics*, second edition (Englewood Cliffs: Prentice Hall, 1973), p. 46.

33. See, for example, Bell and Weinberg, op. cit., which is the best empirical study of homosexuality yet mounted, based on the most representative large sample to date For a critical assessment of the study, see F. Sᴜppe, "The Bell and Weinberg Study: Future Priorities for Research on Homosexuality" (pp. 69-97 in Koertge, op. cit.). Factual claims about undesirable consequences below are based on Bell and Weinberg, op. cit., and Berger, op. cit., which constitute important retests of an extensive body of literature summarized in D. Lester, *Unusual Sexual Behavior: The Standard Deviations* (Springfield, Ill.: Charles C. Taylor, 1975).

34. See F. Elliston, "In Defense of Promiscuity." Pp 222-243 in R. Baker and F. Elliston (eds.), *Philosophy and Sex* (Buffalo, NY: Prometheus, 1975).

35. Since child custody generally accrues to mothers, the available data concerns lesbians. See E. Lewin and T. A. Lyons, "Everything in Its Place: The Coexistence of Lesbians and Motherhood" (pp. 249-274 in Paul, et. al, op. cit.) and M. E. Hotvett and J. B. Mandel, "Children of Lesbian Mothers" (pp. 275-286 in Paul, et. al, op. cit.). A few jurisdictions now place gay foster children with gay foster parents.

36. Case Conference Discussion, "Lesbian Couples: Should Help be Extended to AID?," *Journal of Medical Ethics* 4(1978). See also the letters on AID for Lesbians by M. J. G. Thomas and J. M. Cosgrove, *British Medical Journal* 2(1979):495, and by W. McKee, F. E. Hatfield, and D. H. Wilson, ibid 2(1979):669.

37. For an excellent discussion why such laws regulating private, consensual, adult sexual behavior are unjust, see Leiser, op. cit., ch. 1.

38. This is an important theme in Davison's writings cited in note 7. Not all cure therapists share this conviction (e.g., Masters and Johnson, op. cit., do

not), but it appears to be the majority conviction among cure therapists.

39. See, e.g., E. Goffman, *Stigma: Notes on the Management of Spoiled Identity* (Englewood Cliffs: Prentice Hall, 1965); T. Scheff, *Being Mentally Ill: A Sociological Theory* (Chicago: Aldine, 1966) and "The Labeling Theory of Mental Illness," *American Sociological Review* 29(1974):444-452; and Weinberg and Williams, op. cit. For a critical assessment, see W. R. Gove, "Societal Reaction as an Explanation of Mental Illness: An Evaluation," *American Sociological Review* 35(1970):873-884.

40. Weinberg and Williams, op. cit., p. 8.

41. E. E. Levitt and A. D. Klassen, Jr., "Public Attitudes Toward Homosexuality: Part of the 1970 National Survey by the Institute for Sex Research," *Journal of Homosexuality* 1(1974):29-43.

42. E.g., R. Karr, "Homosexual Labeling and the Male Role," *Journal of Social Issues* 34(1973):73-83, found that men who were led to believe a man was homosexual tended to view him far more negatively (e.g., less clean, softer, more womanly, more tense, more yielding, more impulsive, less rugged, more passive, and quieter) than when the same man was assumed to be heterosexual. (Such negative assessments are, of course, standard grounds for "justifying" prejudice and discrimination.) Further, the man who so labeled the other as homosexual was seen more positively for having so labeled the homosexual than when he did not. The study was sufficiently controlled that these differences were due to a difference in attribution, not any change in behavior on the part of the labelee.

43. Often hysteronic works such as E. Bergler's *1000 Homosexuals: Conspiracy of Silence or Curing and Deglamorizing Homosexuals?* (Paterson, NJ: Pagent Books, 1959).

44. I am involved in a long-term research study on the objectivity of behavioral science research using the empirical research literature on homosexuality published in English since 1948 as a case study. When I make claims here and elsewhere such as "the available evidence suggests . . ." I am basing such claims on an examination of a substantial majority of that literature, selected earlier studies, and various historical, biographical, and autobiographical, and other published and unpublished sources. Since the works number several thousand, and the conclusions are based on comparisons and evaluations of such works rather than single specific studies, giving references would be overwhelming, and greatly add to the already excessive number of footnotes in this article.

45. Weinberg and Williams, op. cit.

46. Levitt and Klassen, op. cit., and A. P. MacDonald, Jr., and R. G. Games, "Some Characteristics of Those Who Hold Positive and Negative Attitudes Towards Homosexuals," *Journal of Homosexuality* 1(1974):9-27.

47. W. Paul, "Social Issues and Homosexual Behavior: A Taxonomy of Categories and Themes in Anti-Gay Argument" (pp. 29-54 in Paul, et. al, op. cit.) presents an analysis of reasons used to justify discrimination against homosexuals that tends to support this contention. A good illustration of the attitude is A. Bryant, *The Anita Bryant Story: The Survival of Our Nation's Families and the Threat of Militant Homosexuality* (Old Tappan, NJ: Fleming H. Revell Co., 1977). One suspects that Jerry Falwell also qualifies.

48. "The participation in such programs" includes both therapists and clients. Both are essential to the existence of such programs, and so the phrase is somewhat redundant; for the most part we will ignore it in subsequent discussion.

49. Cf., e.g., S. Gorovitz, "Causal Judgements and Causal Explanations," *Journal of Philosophy* 62(1965):695-711.

50. Therapists who are convinced homosexuality cannot be cured or that homosexuality is not a mental disorder tend to maintain that therapy should help people adjust to their homosexuality. Those who offer cures tend to be most strong in their conviction that homosexuality is a mental disorder.

51. For an elementary treatment of statistical causality, see ch. 9 of R. Giere, *Understanding Scientific Reasoning* (New York: Holt, Rinehardt, and Winston, 1979). Giere's analysis is that statistical causal hypotheses concern the actual population, a hypothetical one X, consisting of the actual population except that everybody has C, and a second hypothetical one K, which is the actual population except that nobody has C. Then C causes E in the actual population if and only if subsequent $\%E^x > \%EK$. The difference between $\%E^x$ and $\%EK$ indicates the strength of the cause C.

52. "Classifying Sexual Disorders: The Diagnostic and Statistical Manual of the American Psychiatric Association", op. cit.; and "The Diagnostic and Statistical Manual of the American Psychiatric Association: Classifying Sexual Disorders," forthcoming E. Shelp (ed.), *Medical Aspects of Human Sexuality* (Dordrecht: D. Reidel).

53. Foucault, op. cit., p. 43.

Joyce Trebilcot

Taking Responsibility
for Sexuality

It is fundamental to feminism that women should take responsibility for ourselves, collectively and individually. In this essay I explore a central aspect of this project: taking responsibility for sexuality. I am particularly concerned here with women taking responsibility for our sexual identities as lesbian or heterosexual.

I write in part out of the struggle within feminism over whether feminism precludes women having affectional-sexual ties with men. As those familiar with feminist theory know, feminists advocate lesbianism on a variety of grounds. Some emphasize, for instance, that because virtually everyone's first erotic relationship is with a woman (mother), lesbianism is "natural" for women, as heterosexuality is for men. Another argument is based on the claim that, in patriarchy, equality in a heterosexual relationship is impossible; even if a man undertakes to renounce male privileges, he cannot do so entirely. A third argument holds that women who are committed to feminism should give *all* their energies to women. I am not concerned here to explore these arguments. Rather, I want to develop the idea of women taking responsibility for our own sexuality, whatever it may be. Feminism requires at least this of us.

Notice first that to take responsibility for a state of affairs is not to claim responsibility for having caused it. So, for example, if I take responsibility for cleaning up the kitchen I am not thereby admitting to any role in creating the mess; the state of the kitchen may be the consequence of actions quite independent of me. Similarly, in taking responsibility for her sexuality, a woman is not thereby claiming responsibility for what her sexuality has been, but only for what it is now and what it will be in the future.

In taking responsibility, a woman chooses to make a commitment about a specific state of affairs. The role of choice here constitutes an important link between the idea of taking responsibility and feminist

421

values, for in feminist value schemes choice often has a central place.[1] Indeed, a feminist theory of responsibility might well involve the thesis that one is not to be held responsible for anything one has not agreed ahead of time to be responsible for.[2]

To take responsibility for one's sexuality, broadly conceived, is to take responsibility for the whole range of erotic/sexual/gender phenomena that are aspects of one's actions, attitudes, thoughts, wishes, style, and so on. In particular, it includes taking responsibility for oneself as lesbian or heterosexual or bisexual, or the celibate version of any of these: celibate lesbian, celibate heterosexual, celibate bisexual. It is to be expected that many women find these male-created labels and perhaps even their feminist redefinitions unsatisfactory.[3] Nevertheless, taking responsibility for one's sexuality does include locating oneself in terms of some such categories—categories that are already available or that one may invent.[4]

A paradigm case of taking responsibility for one's sexuality is coming out as a lesbian.[5] It is characteristic of first coming out, of coming out to oneself, that a woman does not know whether to say that she has *discovered* that she is a lesbian, or that she has *decided* to be a lesbian. The experience is one of acknowledging, of realizing what is already there, and at the same time of creating something new, a new sense of oneself, a new identity. In coming out, one connects up an already-existing reality—one's feelings, one's sensations, one's identification with women—with one's values, i.e., with one's understanding or concept of who one is. This is the sort of process I mean to refer to here when I speak of taking responsibility for sexuality.

The process, then, is one of *discovery/creation*. Notice that there is no simple term for this process in patriarchal language, at least not in English. It might be suggested, for example, that coming out is a matter of interpretation, of interpreting or reinterpreting one's experiences and feelings in a certain way, as evidence of or elements in one's lesbianism. But this way of understanding coming out is incomplete because it captures only part of the process, the discovery part. To discover that one has been a lesbian all along is certainly to interpret past experiences in a new way, as experiences of a closeted lesbian. But coming out involves also deciding to be a lesbian, for now and in the future, which is to say, deciding not to participate in the institution of heterosexuality and to go on loving women. Coming out then is not merely a matter of reinterpreting one's past; it involves taking responsibility for being a lesbian both in the past and in the future.

Another received term that might be thought to apply to coming out is "conversion experience." There is certainly ample patriarchal literature about people undergoing conversions, mostly religious ones. But the idea of conversion doesn't capture coming out either. The patriarchal convert becomes what he was not. The lesbian becomes what she is.

But, it might be suggested, what about the expression "coming out" itself? Doesn't that convey the experience? This expression has been adopted by lesbians from gay male culture and by gay males presumably from the custom of debutantes coming out into society. It emphasizes not the creation of the self, but the presentation of the self to others. It omits, I think, the inwardness of lesbian experience, the fact that coming out is not merely (or at all) a social exercise but a subjective one, a kind of growth.

It is no accident, of course, that there is no term in patriarchy for the experience I am concerned with here, that there is no brief and clear way of accurately referring to it. Taking responsibility for one's own sexuality is not in the interest of patriarchy, which insists, for its own protection, that sexuality is only a given, that we have no role in creating it. The power of men over women in patriarchy, and of some men over others, is maintained in large part through the institution of heterosexuality, which requires not that women take responsibility for our own sexuality but, rather, that women act on rules that are given to us.[6]

Now, before I go on to discuss the meaning of taking responsibility for one's sexuality for heterosexual women, I want to trace briefly how patriarchy insists that sexuality is wholly given, even through changing ways of thinking about sexuality, through changing sexual values.

Consider first the traditional view that establishes heterosexuality as the norm, and lesbianism as a deviation or disease. On this view, one's sexuality is clearly a given only; it is inherited, or acquired in childhood; it is something that happens *to* an individual. This way of thinking about sexuality tends to keep one docile: one is passive, submissive, with respect to it; it is something received entire, not something one contributes to or creates. On this model, the lesbian, who is described as deviant or as suffering some illness or pathology, is supposed to require treatment by an expert: her sexuality, her "deviance," is not something she can take care of herself. On this traditional model, the question of taking responsibility for one's sexuality does not arise for either lesbian or heterosexual. Sexual identity for everyone is something one "gets," something that happens to one; and if it is not okay, then an expert is called in, but the woman herself remains passive.

In some circles this traditional way of conceiving sexuality has been replaced by pluralism. Pluralism rejects the view that only heterosexuality is normal and holds instead, in the spirit of liberalism, that there are alternative "sexual preferences"—lesbianism, bisexuality, heterosexuality—which are all equally acceptable and which can all be equally "healthy." According to pluralism, sexual identity alone does not determine whether one is healthy or ill, normal or deviant. Such determinations are made in terms of how one "adjusts" to one's sexual identity, how well it satisfies one's needs, whatever they may be.

This way of thinking about sexual identity is equivalent to the more traditional view in terms of keeping women docile. Pluralism's message is: "Look, whatever you are, it's okay—don't worry about it. There are differences among us, but we can all live together happily." This message, of course, seeks to drown out the voice of the lesbian who understands lesbianism as part of the struggle against patriarchy. *Her* message is: "Pay attention to what each form of sexuality means for women. They are *not* all the same in terms of equality, in terms of power, in terms of domination." But this thinking is forbidden by an ethic that insists that all the alternatives are equally okay. So laissez-faire pluralism works against women thinking seriously about our sexuality as we must do if we are to take responsibility for it.

A third way of thinking about sexuality is to hold that everyone ought to be pansexual or at least bisexual, and so open to sexual encounters with persons of both sexes. This position is connected with the ideology, if not the practice (which was mainly heterosexual), of the "sexual revolution" of the sixties, and with leftist theories that advocate the release of sexuality from repression. On this view, the theoretical ideal is that everyone should be the same, bisexual. The theory itself tells us what to be. But if we don't have to decide for ourselves, we don't have to compare the different kinds of sexuality and consider reasons for and against them. We are simply to be obedient, to be bisexual, to be open to anything. This position, of course, has special potential for the exploitation of women. And, like the traditional and pluralistic models, it provides no support for individuals' taking responsibility for and defining their own sexuality.

None of these male-created value systems allows room for the idea that one might discover/create one's own sexuality on the basis of one's feelings and one's politics, on the basis of reasons, on the rational-emotional weighing of all one deems relevant. The same is true, of course, of patriarchal science. The scientific study of sexuality seeks to discover causes of lesbianism, and sometimes also of heterosexuality, and there is no space in these causal accounts for women to participate in the creating of our own sexual identities. A feminist theory of sexuality will not be a causal theory in any familiar sense, and will surely include an account of the role a woman herself may play in the development of her sexuality.[7]

It is, I believe, in the interest of all women to take responsibility for our sexuality. "Coming out," as I have suggested, provides a model for this process. But what could it possibly mean to "come out" as a heterosexual? Most heterosexual women accept the identities their conditioning provides for them, and so, it would seem, there is little or nothing for them to discover or create.

But to think in this way is again to fall into the trap of taking sexuality as merely given. Virtually all women can take responsibility for our sexuality. For a heterosexual woman to take responsibility for herself as heterosexual involves acknowledging the experiences and feelings she has that are parts of her heterosexuality, and also making the decision to participate or not in the institution of heterosexuality. Notice that the institution has many facets. It consists not just of sexual activity, but of a myriad of values and practices, including, for example, concepts of love, of couples, of faithfulness; meanings given to various fashions in clothes and personal appearance; ways of behaving with men and with women; and so on. A heterosexual woman taking responsibility decides which of the aspects of the institution she wishes to participate in (if any), and why. She may participate wholly, but if she is responsible, she does so not without thinking, but for reasons that she takes to be good ones.

Some women object to the idea that they should take responsibility for their own sexual identity on the ground that they have no choice, that they are what they are—lesbian, heterosexual—and cannot change. For example, it is not unusual for a feminist to claim that although the weight of *reason*, for her, is on the side of lesbianism, her *feelings* (perhaps as expressed in her fantasies), are irredeemably heterosexual, for she is sexually aroused by men but not by women. If such women sometimes identify as heterosexuals, they may claim that they cannot change the fact that they are sexually attracted to men, which they experience as a given, and so that they cannot take responsibility for their sexuality—that they are caught in a conflict between reason and feeling.

The peculiarity of this position is the assumption that one's feelings must determine one's sexual identity, that is, that one's genital twinges must determine whether one is lesbian, or heterosexual, or both. Granting that some women are sexually aroused only by men, they are not therefore locked into any of the familiar identities or excluded from any. Such women may, in the first place, choose for or against heterosexual *activity*. We know that there are many sexual impulses that ought to be suppressed rather than acted on, and women for whom the weight of reason is on the side of lesbianism have reason not to participate in heterosexual intercourse. It is also true that a woman may choose to make love to or with women, even though she is not sexually aroused. A woman's claim that she is not erotically responsive to women but only to men does not in itself limit her choices as between lesbianism, heterosexuality, or bisexuality, or celibacy of whatever variety. Sexuality is socially constructed; in reconstructing it we need not assume either that erotic feelings should lead to love making or that love making ought to occur only where there are erotic feelings.

Genital *sensations,* then, are not definitive of sexual identity; but clearly genital *activity* has a central role. Although there are, for example, lesbians who regularly engage in sexual intercourse with men (particularly, married lesbians and lesbian prostitutes), lesbian identity in these cases depends on there being special reasons (often economic) for continued heterosexual behavior. In the absence of such special reasons, regular heterosexual activity defeats the claim that one is a lesbian; such a woman would have instead to be identified as heterosexual or bisexual. Similarly, women who believe themselves to be heterosexual or bisexual but regularly engage in sexual activity with women but not with men cannot, in the absence of special circumstances, sustain the claim of heterosexuality.

But what about the heterosexual feminist whose purported reason for engaging in heterosexual activity is just that she takes physical pleasure in it, physical pleasure she can experience in no other way? It would be too great a sacrifice, she says, to give up this pleasure, even for the political and personal benefits she thinks would come from an identification other than heterosexual. In exploring this issue, it often turns out that the physical pleasure is not after all separable from the economic, emotional, social, and other advantages that she gains from heterosexual relationships. For such a woman identification as heterosexual is frequently based not primarily on some genital pleasure, but on a complex understanding of the role of heterosexual activity in her life.

A woman who has such an understanding can correctly be said to be taking responsibility for her own sexuality, even though the inconsistency between her reason (lesbian) and her genital feelings and behavior (heterosexual) remains. For she has come to understand her heterosexual identity not as a fate irrevocably determined by genital sensations, but as a choice she has made on the basis of a variety of factors, a choice pushed upon her, to be sure, by the power of the institution of heterosexuality, but also one that she might not have made and might yet revoke. Indeed, as she comes to understand her sexuality in the process of taking responsibility for it, her sexual identity may itself change, for the process of discovery/creation dialectically transforms preexisting reality.

It seems then that it does make sense to speak of all women—whatever our sexuality is and whatever it may become—as capable of taking responsibility for our sexuality, for discovering/creating our sexuality. I believe that we should take responsibility, for a variety of reasons I can only touch on here. First, if we define our own sexuality, if we are in control, we are more likely to be strong, self-creating, and independent, not merely about sexuality but generally, than if we simply do what is expected of us, that is, conform without question to the norms of heterosexuality. But also, to take responsibility for sexuality requires study and thought about the meanings of the different sexualities, and this consciousness-raising has important political implications. It means that there will be greater understanding among women of how patriarchy operates. It also means that there will be fewer heterosexuals, insofar as serious thought about heterosexuality leads women to withdraw from that institution. It not only contributes to a greater closeness in the women's community but also to a greater solidarity among all women through a lessening of heterosexism, lesbophobia, and lesbian-hating.

Let me focus briefly on this last idea, the connection between taking responsibility and overcoming these forms of lesbian oppression. Heterosexism is the conviction that heterosexuality is superior to other sexual identities; it includes heterosexist solipsism, that is, ignoring the existence of identities other than heterosexual. Heterosexism is commonly manifested in the assumption that everyone is heterosexual, or that lesbians are distant and rare, not one's friends and associates. Taking responsibility for sexual identity raises consciousness about lesbians and so makes women more aware of the presence of lesbians among their families, their friends, and in their workplaces. Heterosexism is expressed also, of course, by overt or subtle denigration of lesbians and lesbian culture. But a woman who takes seriously the project of defining her own sexuality has to consider the possibility that she herself could be a lesbian; having done this, I think, she is less likely to put down lesbians and things lesbian. If she rejects lesbianism, it is a reasoned rejection, not a prejudice (that is, not a judgment made prior to conscientious consideration of the issue). Heterosexism also takes the form of insensitivity, in heterosexual women, to the fact that the special privileges they enjoy as heterosexuals—privileges in jobs, housing, travel, and the like—are not privileges they *deserve* and lesbians do not, but rather, are privileges unfairly awarded to them by the heterosexual/patriarchal system and unfairly denied to their lesbian sisters. Again, women who take seriously their own sexual autonomy are likely to be more aware than others of the injustice of this system of privilege.

Lesbophobia, like heterosexism, may be lessened as one becomes conscious of one's sexual identity as something one has control over. Lesbophobia has a variety of forms. One is simply fear of the unknown: lesbians seem alien and threatening because one does not know what to expect from them. But part of taking responsibility for one's sexuality is finding out about lesbians and lesbianism.

Another form of lesbophobia is fear that I might be or become one too. But a woman who has a sense of responsibility about her sexuality, while she might find the idea of becoming a lesbian scary, knows that if she does identify as lesbian she does so because of her own discovery/decision; she knows that she herself is in control of her sexual identity, and whatever fear she has will be within her control as well.

Finally, lesbophobia may be a fear of being rejected by lesbians, of not being acceptable to them, or to some specific group of them, in terms of their values or standards or styles. This sort of lesbophobia is common among lesbians. But again, for lesbians and nonlesbians, the consciousness of creating one's own values and style mitigates the fear: the question is not after all whether one is acceptable to them, but, perhaps, whether one wants to expand one's own value system so as to include at least parts of theirs, so that one can be part of their group. This is something one can decide for oneself.

Hatred of lesbians, which frequently accompanies both heterosexism and lesbophobia, is, like misogyny, especially sad among women, for it is hatred of oneself, or of parts of oneself. Both lesbian and nonlesbian women can get into hating parts of ourselves and projecting those parts and that hatred onto lesbians. But taking responsibility involves getting in touch with dissonant, unacceptable, threatening, puzzling aspects of ourselves; if we acknowledge those aspects we are less likely both to project them and to hate them. Also, taking responsibility tends to increase self-esteem, and so to squeeze out self-hatred.

There are, then, excellent reasons why women, all women, should take responsibility for our own sexuality. We all *can* do so. For taking responsibility does not require a woman to be in a position to change the material conditions of her life; it requires only that she be able to understand her sexual identity as discovered and created by her in response to the pressures of patriarchy and the promise of the realization of feminism.

NOTES

This paper was originally prepared as a talk for a conference on Women and Mental Health at the University of Oklahoma in the spring of 1982. That version appears in *Women and Mental Health: Conference Proceedings* edited by Elaine Barton, Kristen Watts-Penny, and Barbara Hillyer Davis (Norman, Oklahoma: Women's Studies Program, University of Oklahoma, 1982). The paper was also presented at Union College, Schenectady, New York, in the spring of 1983.

I especially apreciate conversations about the topic of this essay with Sandra Lee Bartky.

1. This is so even though choice is associated with hierarchy and dualism, which most feminist theorists understand to be inconsistent with feminist values.

2. In feminist discourse, the concept of responsibility tends to drop out and is partially replaced by the notion of accountability. Accepting accountability is like taking responsibility in that one chooses what one is accountable for (one is not accountable if one did not make the commitment). Accepting accountability differs from taking responsibility in emphasizing relationships, in emphasizing those to whom one is accountable—one's community, friends, and lover. To urge that women should accept accountability for their sexuality is to urge them to accept membership in a community or to make a commitment to some relationship. In this essay I use the more patriarchal concept of responsibility because my focus is not so much on a woman's relationship to other women as on her giving reasons, perhaps only to herself, for the forms in which she expresses her sexual feelings.

3. For a recent discussion of feminist definitions of lesbianism, see Ann Ferguson, "Patriarchy, Sexual Identity, and the Sexual Revolution," *Signs* 7 (Autumn 1981):158-172.

4. Some rebellious women may resist avowing an identity in these terms on the ground that they do not want to be labeled. But compare rejecting all labels to adopting a deviant's label with respect to their potential for expressing rebelliousness.

5. For accounts of coming out see *The Coming Out Stories* edited by Julia Penelope Stanley and Susan J. Wolfe (Watertown, MA: Persephone Press, 1980).

6. In patriarchy, women may be expected to take some responsibility for aspects of their sexuality, for example, for allowing sexual access only to certain males or for birth control. But the idea that a woman can take responsibility for herself as lesbian or as heterosexual is foreign to patriarchy.

7. Heterosexuality is compulsory (Adrienne Rich, "Compulsory Heterosexuality and Lesbian Existence," *Signs* 5 (Summer 1980):631-660) and chosen

(Marilyn Frye, 'Assignment: NWSA—Bloomington—1980: Speak on "Lesbian Perspectives on Women's Studies," *Sinister Wisdom* 14 (1980):3-7).

Notice too that it may be politically advantageous for gay men to interpret homosexuality as caused, as something they did not choose, in order to protect themselves from being perceived by straight men as breaking the bonds of fraternity.

PEDOPHILIA

Robert Ehman

Adult-Child Sex

While philosophers have recently put into question traditional norms with regard to adultery,[1] promiscuity,[2] sexual perversion,[3] and have maintained that sexual acts are morally neutral,[4] they have not examined adult-child sex. There is no domain of sexuality in which a prohibition is more absolute and more unquestioned; the current categorical moral and legal prohibition against all forms of adult-child sexual contact reminds one in its rigor of previous prohibitions against homosexuality. While perhaps it would be too much to expect that our attitudes on this might become more open, as they have toward homosexuality, we must, nevertheless, not discount the possible effect of rational inquiry. While more difficult here than elsewhere, we must hold fast to Charles S. Peirce's injunction not to block the road to inquiry, and to recall that where there has been the least inquiry, there is probably the most need for it.

In spite of the fact that we tend to condemn all forms of adult-child sex, we more strongly condemn some instances of it than others. If we can take the criminal law as a clue to our attitudes, we tend generally to take a more negative approach toward sexual relations between an adult male and a young girl than toward relations between an adult woman and a young boy, and we are more forgiving of the act the closer the participants are in age.[5] On the other side, I have not found much evidence that we adopt a more negative stance toward homosexual or incestuous sex in this domain than we do toward heterosexual or nonincestuous sex.

The negative attitude toward adult-child sex appears to have begun

431

around the second half of the eighteenth century with a movement to repress the sexual activity of children.[6] In the Middle Ages and in the Renaissance, people regarded the sexual interest and activity of children as a normal state of affairs that did not call for special attention. In the first half of the sixteenth century, young people knew and were allowed to know everything about sex and were sexually active.[7] In the moral and pedogogical literature of the first half of the eighteenth century, there appears no restriction on prepubertal sexual activity. The repressive trend that began in the second half of the eighteenth century eventually led to a vision of the child as asexual and never himself desiring or initiating sexual contact. The move toward this vision of childhood as a time of sexual innocence comes at precisely the same time as the "invention" of childhood as a distinct stage of life in which the child's dress and other modes of conduct were sharply marked off from the adult's. Prior to the eighteenth century, children wore adult clothing, played adult games, attended school with adults, tossed off ribald jokes, and were, of course, a part of the labor force.[8]

The late eighteenth-century vision of the sexual innocence of the child has so deeply imbued our language that we hardly have a term to designate adult-child sex (except this neutral term that I have made my title), one that does not imply that the child is a victim. Hence, sex itself is "abuse," "assault," or "molestation." This bias makes it difficult to put into question the negative moral evaluation of adult-child sex. There is no better example of this than Alan Goldman. For Goldman, sexual acts are morally neutral. However, he finds no other term for adult-child sex than "molestation." He does not mean by the term simply a threatening or violent sexual contact, since he argues that this is the "closest we can come to an act which is wrong because it is sexual." It is wrong because of the "detrimental effects such behavior can have on the future emotional and sexual life of the naive victims"; and there would, obviously, be no need to appeal to the one or the other of these arguments to rule out physical assault or coercion.[9] I suspect that if Goldman had not assumed that adult-child sex is "molestation" of a "naive victim," he would not have been willing to make an *ad hoc* exception to his thesis of the moral neutrality of sexual acts in order to justify a categorical condemnation.

In assessing the prohibition against adult-child sex, I am questioning the cherished vision of the sexual innocence of childhood. Many people want children to be purer than adults, and there is no older and more established symbol of the loss of purity than sexual experience. When these same people envisage adult-child sexual contact, they see the adult as defiling the innocent child. I suspect that it is this, and not the arguments that people commonly advance for the prohibition against adult-child sex, that lies at the root of its acceptance even among those who otherwise eschew sexual puritanism. There is, of course, a remnant of sexual puritanism in this reaction toward adult-child sex, since unless there were something morally problematic and impure about sex, how could it corrupt the child? The attitude toward adult-child sex is the last unquestioned bastion of sexual puritanism.

I shall put to the critical test the two main arguments that people commonly use to justify the claim that adult-child sex makes a victim of a child: the arguments that adult-child sex is harmful to the child and that the child is incapable of valid consent to sex with an adult. The strategy of these arguments is to formulate the issue, not in terms of an unrealistic and problematic ideal of childhood or in terms of sexual puritanism, but in terms of the child's unquestioned right not to be harmed or manipulated in order to satisfy the selfish interests of adults. If the arguments fail, as I shall attempt to show, so also does the strategy; and those who propose to defend current attitudes toward adult-child sex must do so in terms of a model of childhood or of the wrongness of sex apart from marriage or a form of responsible mutual commitment. They must admit to be willing to send a man to prison to preserve a higher incidence of childhood sexual naiveté a bit longer.

HARM

While the contention that adult-child sex harms children is an empirical, and not an *a priori* claim of moral corruption, it is still not easy to evaluate. For although there is a good deal of clinical data on the effects of adult-child sex on the children, there is little in the way of controlled scientific research. There are sound reasons to be suspicious of conclusions based on clinical data alone. The people who come to clinical and legal attention are not necessarily a typical cross section of the relevant population (Koch, 1980). They are apt to be more negatively affected than those who do not come to clinical attention, both because the negative effects bring them to clinical attention in the first place and because there are negative effects from the handling of adult-child sex on the part of parents, medical personnel, law enforcement and school officials, and social workers (Walters 1975; West 1980).

I have been able to find one scientifically rigorous study of the effects of "childhood molestation"; and this will make it possible for us to draw *some* conclusions that have claim to scientific respectability, even though they must, of course, be tentative. Marvis Tsai, Shirley Feldman-Summer, and Margaret Edgar of the University of Washington (1979) made a study of the variables related to the differential impacts on psychosexual functioning in adult women of childhood sexual contacts with adults. The study conducted by Tsai et al., is not only valuable for its own findings, but also for providing an excellent summary and assessment of the available empirical evidence of the effect of adult-child sex on children.

Tsai et al., begin by pointing out what strikes almost anyone who surveys the clinical literature on the subject, viz., that "What little empirical evidence exists regarding the psychological impact of sexual molestation on the child tends to be contradictory (407). One can find what one is looking for: De Francis (1971), Kaufman, Peck, and Tagiuri (1954); Weiss, Rogers, Darwin, and Dutton (1955), all report that molested children experience a negative emotional reaction such as depression, guilt, or loss of self-esteem. Weiss et al., link molestation to phobias and nightmares; Burgess and Holmstrom (1975) find that it leads to unprovoked crying, compulsive bathing, and bedwetting; and Herman and Kirschman (1977), Katan (1973), Peters (1976), Sloan and Karpinski (1942), and Summit and Kryso (1979), all find support for the proposition that childhood sexual experience is a significant determinant of adult psychological disturbances.

On the other side, Yorukoglu and Kemph (1966) studied two cases of incest, one involving a 13½-year-old boy who had sexual relations with his mother since he was 12; the other a 17-year-old girl who had a sexual relationship with her father since she was 12. The study concluded that the children were unaffected by the experience. Bender and Blau (1937) studied sixteen sexually molested children and reported that they were not negatively affected. Fourteen of these children were located for a follow-up study fifteen years later by Bender and Grugett (1958) and only one was "seriously disturbed." Finally, and, I think, most importantly, due to the fact that the data does not arise from a clinical population, Gagnon (1965) and Landis (1956) surveyed college students about childhood sexual experience and found that between 28 and 33 percent of the respondents reported having sexual experience with an adult, but that only 3 to 7 percent reported serious psychological problems arising from the experience. Rascovsky and Rascovsky (1950) go so far as to argue that incestuous experience diminishes a child's chance of psychosis and allows for better adjustment.

Tsai et al., conclude from their examination of the literature that it is "difficult if not impossible to draw any conclusions about the scope and duration of the impact of sexual molestation on the basis of previous research" (408). Moreover, they point out that the "methods employed differ in numerous ways, as to the samples studied, thereby making it virtually impossible to disentangle effects due, for example, to differences among the molested children in terms of age and gender of the child; the relationship between the child and the molester; the acts engaged in; and so forth" (408). They emphasize that the "possible impacts of childhood molestation on adult psychosexual functioning have not been systematically assessed" (408). Their own study is an attempt to provide this assessment.

They select three groups of thirty women each, one a control group without childhood sexual experience, a second group with such experience, but, otherwise, seemingly normal; and a third group seeking therapy for problems associated with their childhood sexual experience. The two main findings are that the women seeking therapy were less well adjusted generally than either of the other groups and, more interestingly, that reports of molestation by the clinical group differed significantly from those of the nonclinical group in such a manner as to suggest a theoretically meaningful explanation of the difference in adjustment. The women in the clinical group were (a) molested at a later age, (b) had stronger negative feelings at the time toward the events, and (c) experienced a higher frequency and longer duration of molestation.

With regard to the differences in age, Tsai et al., suggest that older children are more negatively affected by the act because they feel more responsible for it, are more aware of violating a social norm, and, therefore, are more likely to feel guilt. Because it occurs during the emotional problems of puberty, its impact is thereby increased. The psychosexual problems that arise from the act come about when the negative feelings associated with the childhood sexual experience become attached by stimulus generalization to other sexual and affectionate experiences. The principles of classical conditioning explain why these negative feelings become more strongly attached to other experiences and are more resistent to extinction, the longer the duration and the greater the frequency of the original negative experience. The strong attachment leads to adult psychosexual maladjustment.

The two main causes, according to Tsai et al., of adult psychosexual problems on the part of the sexually molested children are the negative feelings of the children toward their adult partner and their feeling of responsibility for, and guilt from, the violation of a social norm. There is nothing in the study to indicate that there would be a negative impact apart from an aversion to the adult and a violation of a norm. For this reason, the study does not provide the least evidence in favor of a norm prohibiting sexual contact between a child and adult when the child is not averse. On the contrary, the fact that the negative impact of the perceived violation of the norm is a large contributor to the harmful effects of adult-child sex is an argument *against* the norm. There should be nothing surprising in the fact that moral and legal prohibitions impose severe costs on those who violate them and are a factor to be considered in assessing them. The cost of a prohibition always is a *prima facie* consideration against it.[10]

In spite of the cost of the current prohibition and the serious doubt as to whether it protects the child from a substantial risk of harm, one might, nevertheless, defend it to protect against a possible, though undetermined harm, and require, in order to modify it, that we establish more conclusively than we can on the basis of available evidence that adult-child sex is *not* harmful. The argument in this case is precisely analogous to that used by those who maintain that we ought not to allow the use of drugs unless we have established their safety, and ought not to permit pollution unless we have proved that it does not present a health risk.[11]

While there is undoubted benefit in protecting against the possibility of harm, we must be careful, however, not to pay too high a price in foregone benefits ("opportunity costs") or in actual harm. When we restrict a promising drug, not known to be harmful, we may pay a high price for delaying the benefits of use while we test further for possible harm; when we control a pollutant, not known to be harmful, we may pay a high price in more expensive goods, economic stagnation, and unemployment. In both cases, the costs of restrictions are more determinate, although *ex hypothesi* not known to be greater, than the benefits. The situation is precisely the same in adult-child sex. We know the costs of the prohibition; the benefits of it are uncertain. One might argue at this point that we ought to take the most conservative approach toward risk in all of these cases. The "maximum" dictates that we protect against the risk of harm regardless of the opportunity costs. However, we are not in this case dealing merely with lost benefits; we are dealing with genuine risks of harm from the restrictive policies. The most conservative approach does not, therefore, necessarily dictate the restrictions. The "worst case" might be people dying from the delay of the drug, being impoverished and losing their jobs from the pollution control, and being subject to the trauma of guilt and criminal proceedings from the moral and legal prohibition against adult-child sex.[12] When we are more certain of the costs than the benefits of a policy, we have good reason for taking a cautious approach to the policy itself.

While it might be admitted that we cannot justify a prohibition against all acts of adult-child sex, on the ground of the risk of harm from the acts considered in and by themselves apart from the effects of a wider *practice* of acts of that sort, it might, nevertheless, be argued that the relaxation of the prohibition would lead to a wider practice of these acts, which would itself be harmful, not only to the particular children involved in them, but to children generally. The wider practice, presumably, might be harmful either because of a negative cumulative effect, as in the pollution case, or because of reduced protection against abuse, as in the drug case. The harmful polluter does not want everyone to pollute. He would rather have no one permitted to pollute than to have everyone pollute. He finds polluting desirable only so long as others do not engage in it. He benefits from being a "free-rider." There is nothing analogous in adult-child sex. While the wide practice of this would be disadvantageous to those who desire to preserve the model (illusion?) of sexually innocent children, it would not, as in the pollution case, harm those involved in the activity. The participants in adult-child sex have no interest in being free-riders. They would prefer that their acts be widespread rather than prohibited altogether. They would probably prefer a wider practice simply to lessen their sense of being abnormal and to make sexual contacts easier to achieve.

There is, on the other side, a real danger that permitting even harmless adult-child sex might open the door to a more widespread physical and psychological abuse of children. While no one would seriously propose prohibiting all sex in order to protect against adult rape, we do, in fact, take this tact to protect against adult-child sexual assault. Apart from a mere aversion to adult-child sex, there is an important reason for taking this restrictive approach in relation to the child. The child is more easily intimidated by an adult than another adult is, and the child might often find it more difficult to lodge a complaint against abuse or rape. We cannot leave it up to the child to protect himself in this domain as we do the adult. However, there remains the question as to whether this justifies our regarding all adult-child sexual contact as abuse regardless of the facts in the particular case.

The fact that we cannot leave the child responsible for lodging complaints in this domain means that we must investigate all suspected adult-child sex, as we do under current practice. However, while this invasion of privacy is required in order to protect against abuse, the categorical prohibition in its present form is not. The implementation of the categorical prohibition tends, in fact, to be abusive. When society intervenes to impose moral or criminal sanctions against a pleasurable or loving sexual relationship, it runs the risk of producing, by stimulus generalization, damaging negative feelings toward a wide range of sexual and affectionate experiences that can lead to serious psychosexual problems. Moreover, the child, in this case, is bound to regard the intervention, from the perspective of his later life, as unjustified repression, and, for this reason, inconsistent with legitimate paternalism, which demands that a person be able to recognize in retrospect the desirability of the action taken with respect to him.[13]

Instead of considering only whether there has been sex, it would be more consistent with a genuine paternalistic concern for the child to assess the best approach for his own welfare in the situation. There should be several categories. When there is no evidence of physical or psychological harm and the child desires the relationship, the relationship would be permitted, but we would monitor it to detect signs of abuse.[14] Where there is psychological disturbance, but no physical harm or compulsion, the relationship would be enjoined for the welfare of the child. When there is physical harm, and/or compulsion, there would be criminal charges of sexual assault. When an adult makes a child pregnant, we might treat this as a case of physical assault or else simply impose civil liability, depending on what is best for the child. This more flexible approach would enable social agencies to protect children without subjecting them to the trauma of a scandal or criminal proceedings unless this is necessary in the given case. There would be no "statutory rape" in the present sense.

The child is normally under the authority of parents or guardians, not an independent agent, and this raises the question both of the permissibility of sexual relations between the child and his parents or guardians and of the authority of parents or guardians over the sexual conduct of the children under their supervision. The answer to the first turns on whether a sexual relation is compatible with the proper exercise of the parental role. There is, in this case, more than the harm of the particular act involved; there is the general norm of parental behavior. To admit the legitimacy of parent-child sex in any case has implications with respect to the manner in which we conceive of the parental role. While the proper reaction to parent-child incest in a particular case ought to turn on paternalistic considerations of what is most beneficial to the child in that situation, as a general rule we ought to discourage it so far as it negatively affects parental authority and leads to a sexual involvement with the child that interferes with the tasks of parenthood.

The propriety in any case of adult-child sex where the adult has a specific role to play with regard to the development of the child raises questions that do not arise in the case of those who do not have a specified role of this sort, since, in the former, the answers depend on the requirements of the role, not simply on the empirical consequences of the act.

Regarding the right of a parent to exercise authority over the sexual activity of his (or her) children, it is clear that this right ought not to extend to determining the child's sexual partners. The once common authority of the father to arrange and require marriage of his daughter at an early age to a man of his own choosing led to the life-long subjugation of women and was incompatible with the long-term welfare of women as autonomous persons. On the other hand, it is questionable that parents have a right to *forbid* a child's sexual activity unless it is harmful to him. For in the end, it is as intrusive in the sexual life of the child to forbid a sexual relationship as it is to require one. The parent has a duty to protect the child against sexual abuse, but he has no right himself to become abusive in attempting to enforce his own preferences on the child. The use of parental coercion to forbid an otherwise satisfying sexual relationship puts a parent's own fitness into question and counts as a serious form of child abuse in its own right.

CONSENT

The very fact of parental authority over the child presupposes that the child does not yet have the same sort of capacity to make choices as the adult does. He is not yet capable of fully responsible choice, and, for this reason, he is not capable in the full sense of valid consent. The concept of consent in this context is not a mere psychological concept of nonreluctance or desire, but a normative concept prescribing the conditions of rational and responsible choice. To be capable of rational and responsible choice, the person must be free from perceived or actual coercion, must have the relevant concept, and must understand the most important consequences of his act. Apart from these conditions, he cannot in retrospect regard himself as having chosen the act and its consequences and therefore as being liable to answer for it. He cannot regard himself as responsible for an act when someone else coerced him into performing it or when he did not know what he was doing.[15]

The problematic character of the harm argument leads one proponent of a categorical prohibition of adult-child sex to maintain that we ought to justify the prohibition on the ground of the child's incapacity to consent rather than on that of the harmfulness of the act

(Finkelhor 1979). This at once raises the question of why a child's incapacity to consent justifies a prohibition on *sex* when it does not in regard to many other sorts of acts. Finkelhor gives the example of rape, but that is not relevant to the present issue. For insofar as rape requires that the act be *against* a person's consent, it does not apply where a person is not capable of consent. The incapacity of consent is an incapacity to give or to refuse consent. Insofar, on the other hand, as rape requires only that the act be against the *desires* of the person, not all adult-child sex is rape. The very fact that a child is not capable of consent means that we might be permitted on paternalistic grounds to use force to compel him to do things that we could not legitimately compel an adult to do. There is a possible (although, I think, invalid) paternalistic argument to justify the practice of arranging marriages and requiring sex of a child, even though the child does not desire it, on the ground that this is in the child's long-run interest and that the person will in retrospect approve of our act. I suspect that one reason for the arranged *child* marriage is that there is no question of a justification of this sort with regard to an *adult*. The forced sex in this case is not rape in the sense of a violation of the right of the person to choose his own sexual partners, since a person incapable of consent does not have this right. If we are to speak of rape in the context of adult-child sex, it can only mean the use of compulsion to have harmful sex with the child. The prohibition of rape of children is based on harm, not on the right of the child to determine his own sexual life.

The appeal to rape does nothing to answer the question as to why sex requires valid consent. The fact that a child cannot validly consent does, indeed, mean that he does not have a *right* to choose his sex partners as an adult does and that those responsible for him might legitimately forbid sexual conduct that is detrimental to him, in a situation where intervention would not be legitimate in the case of adults. However, the absence of a child's right to decide his own sexual life does not mean that others have a right to forbid a desired, nondetrimental relationship. The child is not without all rights; he has a right not to be harmed, and, in certain cases, a right to protection from harm. The intervention to forbid sex against his will is itself harmful, as is all compulsions, and when the intervention is not justified by benefits, it is itself a violation of his rights and ought to be prohibited. The situation of sex does not appear in principle to be different from other acts. The child has a right to do what he pleases in this as in all other domains unless it is harmful to himself or others.

When a person is not capable of valid consent, we must be more protective of his welfare than when he is capable of it, since the absence of this capability means that he is not able to take responsibility for the harm to which his conduct might give rise. When a child looks back on acts of his own that were detrimental to him, he will rightly blame, not himself, but those responsible for his welfare, for permitting him to harm himself. When an adult acts to harm the child, even without compulsion, he is not only responsible for the harm, but also for violating his duty to protect the child from harm. The child will rightly view this dereliction of duty as itself a further abuse. He will rightly feel betrayed and manipulated without regard for his welfare.[16] There is nothing comparable in the case of an adult who is himself responsible for the consequences of his own acts.

While this means that we are responsible for the harm that arises from our conduct toward those who are incapable of consent in a sense in which we are not responsible for the harm that arises from our conduct toward those who are capable of consent, it does not rule out acts that do not have undue risk of harm. The argument from the incapacity to consent, therefore, brings us back full circle to the harm argument. There is only one ground for ruling out sex for those incapable of valid consent, and that is that the act carries too high a risk of harm. Where it does, of course, we ought to forbid and enjoin it; where it does not, prohibition itself carries an undue risk of harm, and, for that reason, ought not to be invoked.

When we consider whether to have sex with a child in a particular case, we face a more difficult question than the question of social policy with which we have been primarily concerned. For we must recognize the existence of a prohibition that itself can cause serious psychological damage to those who perceive themselves to be in violation of it. The very prospect of psychological damage that puts the norm into question at the same time and for the same reason puts particular acts that violate it into question. While there might still be cases in which we have every reason to believe that the act is harmless, will go unreported, and the child cares nothing for the norm, there is, nevertheless, a danger of miscalculation in this regard, one that makes the act much more risky than it would be in a more enlightened environment. There is a painful paradox when we live under a repressive moral or legal system. The very existence of the repressive norm might make it rational to follow its dictates even when these are otherwise altogether without justification. Even in these situations, however, we are not completely under the subjugation of the norm; we are not merely permitted, but also obligated to attempt to reform it and to free ourselves and society from its yoke. I hope that I have made a beginning toward this end in the domain of my inquiry.

NOTES

1. Richard Wasserstrom, "Is Adultery Immoral?" in *Philosophy and Sex,* eds. R. Baker and F. Elliston (Buffalo, NY: Prometheus Books, 1975), pp. 207-221.

2. Frederick Elliston, "In Defense of Promiscuity," op. cit., pp. 222-240.

3. Sara Ann Ketchum, "The Good, the Bad and the Perverted: Sexual Paradigms Revisited." *Philosophy of Sex* Alan Soble, ed. (Totowa, NJ: Little-field, Adams & Co., 1980), pp. 139-157.

Robert Grey, "Sex and Sexual Perversion," *Journal of Philosophy* 75 (1978):189-199.

Thomas Nagel, "Sexual Perversion," *Journal of Philosophy* 66 (1969).

R. C. Solomon, "Sex and Perversion," *Philosophy and Sex* op. cit., pp. 268-287.

4. Alan Goldman, "Plain Sex," *Philosophy and Public Affairs* 6 (Spring 1977).

5. For comprehensive surveys of current statutory rape laws, see "The Con-stitutionality of Statutory Rape," *Pacific Law Journal* 12:217-233, (January 1981) and Rita Eidson, "Statutory Rape Laws," *U.C.L.A. Law Review.* 27 (February 1980):757-815. While 11 states still have gender discrimination in their statutory rape statutes, 39 states have recently enacted gender neutral sex-offense statutes. 27 states have designated a minimum age for the offender. California's statutory rape law's use of age differentiations to determine the gravity of the offense is typical. For example, in California acts of sodomy or oral copulation on a person under the age of 18 are punishable by a maximum of one year in state prison. If the participants, however willing, include a person over the age of 21, and one who is under age 16, the proscribed act becomes a felony, and the maximum punishment is three years confinement. When the child is under age 14 and the adult is more than ten years older, the punishment for the crime increases to eight years in prison. "The Constitutionality of Statutory Rape," op. cit., p. 231.

The constitutionality of statutory rape laws has been questioned on the ground of sex discrimination in laws that make gender discriminations in the offense (make it illegal to have sex with a girl of certain age but not a boy of that age), and on the ground of the possible violation of procedural right of due process in cases where the "irrefutable presumption of the incapacity of consent" applies to older adolescents. There are also questions with regard to the com-patibility of these laws with the minor's right to privacy, but there is a tendency of the courts to hold that state restriction on the right of minors to have sex is defensible on traditional paternalistic grounds that "young persons frequently make unwise choices with harmful consequences." "Statutory Rape Laws" op. cit., p. 801.

6. Edward Brongersma, "'Indecency' in Moral Offenses Involving Children," *British Journal of Criminology* 20 (January 1980): 22. Brongersma bases his discussion of the history of the sexual practices of children on the thesis of J.M. W. van Ussel. University of Amsterdam 1967. 45. *Vide:* van Ussel. J. M.

W. *Geschiedenis van het seksuele probleem.* Meppel, 1968.

7. Brongersma. op. cit., p. 22; van Ussel 65.

8. Philip Aries, *Centuries of Childhood: A Social History of Family Life* (New York: Knopf, 1962).

9. A. Goldman, op. cit., p. 28.

10. Richard B. Brandt puts this point well in regard to moral prohibitions; it is even more justified in regard to legal prohibitions. "It is clear that there is a *prima facie* case against the moral code prohibiting anything. For what someone wants to do there is (at least normally) some benefit in permitting; he will enjoy doing it, and feel frustrated in being prevented on grounds of conscience. If something is to be prohibited or enjoined, a case must be made out for the long-range benefit of restricting the freedom of individuals, making them feel guilty, and utilizing the teaching resources of the community. Without proof of long-range benefit, any restriction lacks justification." *A Theory of the Good and the Right* (Oxford: Clarendon Press, 1979), p. 293.

11. I am indebted to Professor Elliston for suggesting the example of drug laws to show that we might require a proof of absence of harm to permit an activity, in this case sale and use of a drug.

12. While my concern in this paper is with the harm of the current approach to children, it must be remarked that it seriously harms adults involved sexually with children. They are subject to arrest on a felony charge; and even when the act goes unreported, they live in fear of scandal and prison and might feel guilt. Those who find sexual satisfaction only in children suffer life-long sexual frustration when they *refrain* from the desired act. One might argue that these offenders deserve no sympathy and that it is a mistake of the utilitarian to count the pleasure and pain of offenders and victims on the same scale. However, in this case, there is doubt as to whether the supposed offender is in many cases an offender at all. Summit and Kryso point out that "most pedophiles are gentle creatures. They cherish tenderness and innocence and will back off from fear and resistance in their intended partner," "Sexual Abuse of Children: A Clinical Spectrum," *American Journal of Orthopsychiatry* 48 (April 1978). The offense of the offender in pedophilia is often not only nonviolent, but also, as we have seen, harmless. When we are dealing in this sense with "victimless crimes," it is surely legitimate to consider the suffering of the alleged offender.

13. For an excellent discussion of paternalism as protecting rather than violating the autonomy of the individual, see Gerald Dworkin, "Paternalism," in *Morality and the Law* edited by R. Wasserstrom, (Belmont, CA: Wadsworth Publishing Co., 1971), pp. 107-126. For Dworkin, "we would be most likely to consent to paternalism in those instances in which it preserves and enhances for the individual his ability to rationally consider and carry out his own desires" (125). How either this or "the child's subsequent recognition of the wisdom of the restrictions" (119) could be accomplished by an intervention in a satisfying relationship that paid no heed to the child's own feelings or to the specific situation is hard to see. The present system is not so much paternalistic and puritanical; it is concerned more with upholding a sexual norm than with the well-being of the children.

14. Edmund White provides a paradigm of the sort of relationship that ought to be permissible in his account of an interview with a young man in Boston

with a 12-year-old lover. The relationship began when the child was 9. "I asked him how he'd met his lover." "At the beach. He was there with his mother. He came over to me and started talking. You see, the kids must make all the moves. I wouldn't know how to initiate a friendship with a child. But children do respond to an interest in them . . . . I think they can *feel* the love and fascination. So, he started coming over to my house." "Does his mother know?" I asked. "She knows as much as she wants to. She knows that he was cranky before and had trouble in his schoolwork and that now he's calmer and getting good grades. She *could* know more if she asked her son, but I don't think she wants to know the specifics. She knows we're friends; and what she sees is positive." "Did your friend take the sexual initiative with you?" "Absolutely. I have been into kids since I was twenty-two, and in every case the kids were the aggressors . . . . My current friend wanted to make love right away, 'have some fun', as he said, but I put it off for three weeks." *States of Desire* (New York: E. P. Dutton, 1980), pp. 311-313.

15. There is, of course, considerable latitude for dispute as to the precise conditions of responsible choice. What is to count as a threat? Must there be a threat to intervene to cause harm or simply a threat to withhold a benefit? How adequate must a concept of an action be? In order to consent to a contract or to marriage, how much must the person understand of it? What consequences or far-ranging ones as well? Probable or also improbable ones?

I shall not enter into the issue of the requirements of valid consent and responsible choice, since my purpose is not to decide the requirement of the capacity of valid consent to sex or the proper age of consent, but rather to assess the validity of the categorical prohibition against adult-child sex *prior* to the age of consent.

16. I suspect that this is the fundamental point of the common argument that since children are not the "equal" of adults in an adult-child sexual contact, the adult manipulates the child and takes unfair advantage of him, treating him as a mere means to his own (the adult's) sexual satisfaction without regard for the interests of the child. Those who argue in this manner are correct that the child cannot on his own account adequately protect himself against this sort of abuse as another adult can. However, this does not mean that this manipulation and abuse must occur. The adult might show love and concern for his child partner and, as Summit and Kryso observe in the passage that I have already quoted, back off from anything that they had reason to believe would harm their child partner. The argument that sex with children treats them as mere means to sexual satisfaction assumes both that the sex is harmful and that the pedophile cares nothing for the welfare of his partner; and it, therefore, does not really add anything further to the arguments we have already discussed.

REFERENCES

1. Bender, L., and Blau. "The Reaction of Children in Sexual Relations with Adults." *American Journal of Orthopsychiatry* 7 (1937): 518-600.

2. Bender, L., and A. Grugett. "A Follow-up Report on Children Who Had Atypical Sexual Experiences." *American Journal of Orthopsychiatry* 22(1952): 825-837.

3. Burgess, A, and L. Holmstrom. "Sexual Trauma of Children and Adolescents." *Nursing Clinics of North America* 10 (1975): 551-563.

4. Burgess, A. W., A. N. Groth, and M. P. McCausland. "Child Sex Initiation Rings." *American Journal of Orthopsychiatry* 51 (January 1981).

5. Chaneles, S. "Child Victims of Sexual Offenses." *Federal Probation*, 31 (1967): 52-56.

6. De Francis, V. "Protecting the Child Victim of Sex Crimes Committed by Adults." *Federal Probation* 35 (1971): 15-20.

7. Delora, J., and C. Warren. *Understanding Sexual Interaction.* Boston: Houghton Mifflin, 1977.

8. Feldman-Summers, S.P. Gorden, and J. Meagher. "The Impact of Rape on Sexual Satisfaction." *Journal of Abnormal Psychology,* 88 (1979): 101-105.

9. Finkelhor, David. "What's Wrong with Sex Between Adults and Children?" *American Journal of Orthophychiatry* 49 (October 1979).

10. Finch, S. M. "Adult Seduction of the Child." *Medical Aspects of Human Sexuality.* 7 (1973).

11. Gagnon, J. "Female Child Victims of Sex Offenses." *Social Problems,* 13 (1965): 176-192.

12. Gibbens, T. C. N., and J. Prince. *Child Victims of Sex Offenses.* London: I. S. T. D., 1963.

13. Herman, J., and L. Hirschman. "Father-daughter Incest." *Journal of Women in Culture and Society* 2 (1977): 735-746.

14. Katan, A. "Children Who Were Raped." *Psychoanalytical Study of the Child* 28 (1973): 208-224.

15. Kaufman, I. Peck, and C. Tagiuri. "The Family Constellation and Overt Incestuous Relations Between Father and Daughter." *American Journal of Orthopsychiatry* 24 (1954): 226-279.

16. Koch, Michael. "Sexual Abuse in Children." *Adolescence.* 15 (Fall 1980).

17. Landis, J. "Experiences of 500 Children with Adult Sexual Deviation." *Psychiatric Quarterly Supplement.* 30 (1956): 91-109.

18. Mohr, J. "The Pedophilias: Their Clinical, Social and Legal Implications." *Canadian Psychiatric Association Journal* 7 (1962) 255-260.

19. Mrazek, P. B. "Sexual Abuse of Children." *Journal of Child Psychology and Psychiatry,* (1980): 21-91.

20. Peters, J. "Children Who Are Victims of Sexual Assault and the Psychology of Offenders." *American Journal of Psychotherapy* 30 (1976): 398-432.

21. Rascovsky, M., and A. Rascovsky. "On Consummated Incest." *International Journal of Psychoanalysis* 31 (1950): 42-47.

22. Sloan, P., and E. Karpinski. "Effects of Incest on the Participants." *American Journal of Orthopsychiatry* 12 (1942): 666-673.

23. Robischon, Thomas. "Adult-child Incest: How Harmful Is It?" *Sexology* (April 1980): 26-33.

24. Summit, R. and J. Kryso. "Sexual Abuse of Children: A Clinical Spectrum." *American Journal of Orthopsychiatry* 7 (1978): 417-427.

25. Tindall, R. H. "The Male Adolescent Involved with a Pederast Becomes an Adult." *Journal of Homosexuality.* 4 (1978).

26. Tsai, M., S. Feldman-Summers, and M. Edgar. "Childhood Molestation: Variables related to differential Impacts on Psychosexual Functioning in Adult

Women." *Journal of Abnormal Psychology* 88 (August 1979): 407-417.

27. Walters, David. *The Physical and Sexual Abuse of Children.* Bloomington: Indiana University Press, 1975.

28. West, J. "A Commentary on Brongersma." *British Journal of Criminology* 20 (January 1980): 32-34.

29. Weiss, J., E. Rogers, M. Darwin, and C. Dutton. "A Study of Girl Sex Victims." *Psychiatric Quarterly* 29 (1955): 1-27.

30. Yorukoglu, A., and J. Kemph. "Children Not Severely Damaged by Incest with a Parent." *Journal of Academy of Child Psychiatry,* 5 (1966): 111-124.

Marilyn Frye

Critique

Much of recent liberal moral philosophy about sex and the erotic is a great deal less valuable than it might have been because it originates in a distinctively male or male-identified perspective, serves interests associated with that perspective, and is deceptive on both of these scores. Professor Ehman's essay, "Adult-Child Sex," is a good example of this. It is worthwhile discussing the ways masculine values and perceptions dominate and distort this work, both because this sort of thing makes philosophers get things simply wrong and because such philosophy supports and encourages male dominance. It is also worthwhile to discuss this because in the long-run (though I will not pursue this here) it can shed needed light on many other contaminations of thought, such as those of racism, assumptions of universal able-bodiedness, and the many other structured ignorances that the privileged employ in the practice and maintenance of privilege.

As is common in works of this genre, the primary instrument of obfuscation is abstraction.

At the outset, Ehman invites us to share his assumption that "sex itself" is "morally neutral." Actually, we are not so much invited as required to accept this assumption, on pain of being counted among the "biased" and the "sexual puritans." So warm is the rhetoric of scorn that it seems clear that anyone who will not join in this fundamental assumption will be declared to be "blocking the road" of "rational inquiry." In effect, anyone who denies the assumption does not deserve classification as a philosopher and thus is not qualified for participation in the discourse at hand. This is rather a lot of force for an author to bring to bear in order to achieve agreement on something that supposedly is obvious and easily taken for granted.

447

This force is necessary, I think, not to pry the reader loose from cherished visions of the sexual innocence of childhood (which visions probably prompt disapproval of adult-child sex no more often than they fuel desires for it and for freedom from its prohibition), but to pry the reader's attention and sensibility loose from their moorings in rich experiential knowledge of the many and vivid meanings of sex. What Ehman is after is the detachment of cultural meanings from certain acts that he thinks can be contemplated "in themselves," as a prelude to critical assessment of the values attached to those acts in a particular culture. But what this act of intellectual artifice (a familiar one, to philosophers) accomplishes is detachment from all that informs and quickens moral and political intuition. To embrace such a dogma as "Sex itself is morally neutral" without caveat or qualification is to ignore all one has learned from childhood on about sexuality—sexuality as it is lived in this particular human culture. Whatever acts people engage in as "sex," the parties to them are invariably moving and feeling within a distinctive, complex medium of power, myth, value, and the deliberate manipulation of desire for commercial purposes. To usefully discuss questions about harm and benefit, consent and coercion, as they occur in that context, one has to map out and analyze the currents in this medium. These currents of cultural meaning connect those acts to connotations of dominance and subordination, conquest and degradation, power and powerlessness, violence and victimization, as well as to pleasure or love. In this "semantics" dominance, conquest, power, and violence are "marked" *masculine*. But to earn our stripes as liberals and rational inquirers, we are required to ignore all this.

This separation of moral philosophy from the grounds of moral intuition and political understanding sets the stage for the next move. If "sex itself" is morally neutral, then the only possible justification for any prohibition of any class of sexual acts or behavior must be in terms of the consequences of such acts in those sorts of cases. We must turn to the empirical matter of whether or not some degree of harm is risked by the act or behavior—some harm greater than that presumed to attend the prohibition of anything that is in itself morally neutral. The discussion of the "clinical literature" and the results of "controlled scientific research" that follow is remarkable on several scores.

Here is the vocabulary used to report the findings. *The adjectives:* 'negative', 'better', 'less well', 'psychological', 'psychosexual', 'serious', 'severe', and 'seemingly normal'. *The nouns:* 'effect', 'impact', 'reaction', 'disturbance', 'problem', 'adjustment', 'maladjustment', 'psychosis', 'functioning'. Pseudoscientific psychobabble. The most meaningful terms used are 'guilt', 'self-esteem', 'nightmare', 'compulsive bathing', 'crying', and 'bedwetting'. Surely it is no surprise that the literature soberly seeking correlations between "psychosexual adjustments" or "psychological disturbances" on the one hand and certain events characterized as "sexual experiences" or "sexual contacts" (conceived as themselves bare of moral meaning) on the other, is inconclusive. With vocabulary as empirically void as this, one can show nothing; but one can appear to show whatever one wishes. What does surprise me is that the vacuousness of this literature is claimed by Ehman to justify skepticism in the matter of what harm adult-child sex might do the child, skepticism tilted a bit in favor of "serious doubt" as to whether there is "a substantial risk of harm." Such literature leaves doubt because it is almost totally meaningless, not because it reveals any empirical truth or verifies any empirical hypotheses.

The retreat to this literature leaves us empty-handed, but it also brings in a false posture of empty-handedness assumed in the interest of something like "objectivity." The discipline of "rational inquiry" is presumed to require that we pretend to be ignorant of what we know, as the only way to avoid being helplessly in the sway of prejudice—of traditional, uncriticized, conservative cultural values to which we are attached by training, habit, and emotion.

But we are not ignorant. We all—women, men, girls, and boys— know a good deal about sex and sexuality as they are experienced by persons holding and being held, kissing and being kissed, encountering one's own or another's nudity, fondling and being fondled, fucking and being fucked, when any of these is novel or strange, or when it is familiar; and what it is like to like it or loathe it, to be transported to ecstasy or to despair, to be enlightened or mystified, relieved or frustrated, delighted or stunned, warmed or alienated, excited or bored, feeling powerful or feeling overpowered and frightened, pleased or pained, satisfied or depressed, lying or telling the truth, being lied to or being told the truth, understanding or being bewildered, or any of these things in any combination. In the name of intellectual integrity we are supposed to pretend we know nothing of all this and therefore have nothing upon which to ground reasonable judgments about how it is or would likely be for a child, in this or that sort of situation, to be involved in sexual activity or in a sexual relationship with an adult who holds this or that social position relative to the child; we are required to rest our moral philosophizing instead upon a handful of studies—in fact, in the present case, on just one study. Ehman judges it to be scientifically rigorous, it is apparently the only one his search turned up that even pretends to such merit, and yet we are given no reason to believe that it has been replicated.

We do not, to be sure, know all the same things about all this, and neither conservative nor liberal orthodoxies take much account of what women know. Liberal arguments are generally for extensions of the range of permitted or accepted sex, and they generally take it for granted that sex itself is a good. (This contradicts the first dogma, that sex itself is morally neutral; but that would not defeat the claim that these are both dogmas of a single orthodoxy.) To play the game of liberal moral philosophy, one is expected to assume that in the absence of coercion, force, exploitation, and the contaminations due to superstitious or puritanical prohibitions, sex is to be entered under the "benefits" column in one's utilitarian bookkeeping, as Ehman enters it in his analogies with pharmaceuticals and pollutions. His exposition proceeds as though in cases where sex is "harmless" it can be assumed to be "pleasurable or loving" or "satisfying." There is much evidence, recorded and cited in such sources as the Kinsey and Hite reports, commonplace in woman-only conversation, and revealed by background assumptions in such books as *The Total Woman,* that sex itself is often found by a large number of its participants to be alienating and boring. Many women often find that even where they are not coerced or forced, where they enter the encounter with clear and guiltless erotic desire, sex itself does not bring on orgasm or give satisfaction, not to mention ecstasy or any other of the more pyrotechnic "benefits." In a world in which many people, even if not a majority, find that sex itself is something they would cheerfully do without, and would desire sex only if it is accompanied by other things, like intimacy, personal affection, equality of presence, reciprocity of attention, and so forth, one cannot in good conscience accept as a given and a universal that if only there is no force, coercion or exploitation, sex is something whose prohibition deprives people of a benefit.

The discussion of harm, in Ehman's essay, focusses both on factors that would make a sexual contact a sexual assault and on consequences. If we are convinced that no physical damage is done, that the child is willing and that "science" can be construed as assuring that there is little risk of bad consequences, then there are no further questions; in cases that meet these standards there can be no justification for a general prohibition, social or legal. But I would have more questions: How was it for her? Not: Did this, or is it likely to, result in lifelong psychosexual dysfunction? but: Was it nice? Did she have fun? Was it not soured by ambivalence, confusion, pain, feelings of powerlessness, anxiety about displeasing a partner on whom she is emotionally and materially dependent, fear of pregnancy? And if it is not good, can she, will she, would she dare, make this clear to him? Any woman with reasonably broad sexual experience knows the meanings of these questions. Ehman's discussion of the question of what harm might be done by adult-child sex removes attention and sensibility from the experience itself. An experience can be horrible without precipitating bedwetting or causing "maladjustment." Are we to say it is harmless if it is merely wretched but does not demonstrably cause behavior that parents or clinical psychologists identify as "problematic"?

Ehman would have us philosophize about sex without taking into account either sexual politics or the knowledge of sexual experience that we have first-hand and by way of literature and research. When we take all this into account, *power* and *gender* move into the center of the moral picture. In fact, our attention has been misdirected from the beginning by the use of the phrase "adult-child sex." This gender-washing term diverts our attention from the question of which adults show an interest in sex with which children.

Court records indicate that in the neighborhood of 95 percent or more of adults engaging in sex with children are males, and in the neighborhood of 87 to 90 percent of the children are females. The practice of adult-child sex is gendered. Furthermore, such records indicate that most of the cases involve the child's social or biological father. One survey found that 90 percent of the cases of adult-child sex were father-daughter, stepfather-stepdaughter, or grandfather-granddaughter, and that of the remaining 10 percent, half were father-son.[1] The practice of adult-child sex is "patri-cratic." It has everything to do with gender and the power of the male, the patriarch.

Though some people may indeed object to adult-child sex because they see it as defiling an imagined childhood innocence, many who approach the question from the life experience of a woman in a phallocratic (male-dominated, male-governed, male-protecting) culture are alarmed, not by visions of sullied childhood innocence, but by the enormity of the power-imbalance that obtains in such relationships. As long as the culture is male-dominated, misogynist, and characterized by compulsory heterosexuality for women, most females will have most of their sexual experience in relationships in which, on balance, they have considerably less social, economic, and physical power than their partners and in a context of myth and dogma that would impose male-affirming and female-degrading meanings upon their sexual acts and contacts. That is bad enough, without the addition of the power-imbalance of the adult-child nexus in a culture with little respect for children and the power-imbalance of the father-daughter nexus in a culture in which generally there is much confusion of *father* and *god*. Intellectually and emotionally mature, financially independent adult women have enough trouble knowing their own minds and bodies and defending their pleasure and their integrity in the coercive context of power imbalance that they move in as sexual beings; that a person who is totally dependent materially, in the process of socialization to femininity, and operating with a child's emotional and intellectual resources could do so in the even more coercive context of the father-daughter connection is, in most cases, utterly implausible.[2]

When men explore in imagination (however carefully and with whatever critical sensitivity) the acts and circumstances of sex or sexual relationship between a man and a girl, their situation as men in this society puts them at a double disadvantage for appreciating the dangers for the girl. The experience of men has been almost wholly that of the person in the position of greater power, and it is one of the more dubious privileges of power that it can easily fail to know itself; and then, not knowing one's own power, one also cannot see how the power itself interferes with one's knowing the less powerful other.

As a student's professor, with the power of grades and letters of reference, you ask that student (who is going by the department anyway) to drop something off at the department for you. Though at some level you are of course cognizant of the fact that professors have power with respect to students, you certainly do not feel that you are pressuring this student. After all, you did not threaten to lower the student's grade for refusal to do this small favor, and anyway, you are not that sort and the student ought to know you well enough to know that. But you, unlike, say, the student's roommate, are so positioned, willy-nilly, that if you come to the view that this student is a rather cold or unfriendly person who does not like you much, you could read her/his papers less sympathetically and recommend her/him less warmly, and thus penalize the student for her/his unwillingness to respond to your request with generosity or friendliness. To her/his roommate the student can say, "Drop off your own book; I'm not your servant!" One does not say that to one's professor, whether or not one likes, respects, or feels used by one's professor. That you think you do not allow your feelings about students and theirs about you to affect your grades or recommendations just has no weight in the student's situation; what has weight is the fact that you could—you have that power. Savvy students behave in a generous and friendly way with professors; cruder ones flatter; they are looking after themselves in a coercive situation. Junior professors do the same with department chairpersons. The latter cannot issue a dinner invitation without the former being under some pressure (I do not say irresistible pressure) to accept, and to accept in a manner that indicates an expectation of enjoying the evening. If the chairperson thinks she/he and her/his spouse are witty conversationalists and good cooks, the junior professor is unlikely to challenge this conceit.

If the father thinks he is a sensitive and skillful lover, the daughter he is honoring with his sexual attentions is unlikely to tell him otherwise.

We tend to think of ourselves as good-willed, benevolent, intelligent, and perceptive, and those over whom we have power have every motive to play to our good opinions of ourselves. The structure of power mitigates systematically against their being honest with us about anything that would displease us, and to the extent that one's power takes the form of authority, the structure mitigates even against their being honestly knowledgeable of themselves, since they will not only try to act as we wish but may accept our authority as to what they are and how they feel. The more power one has, the more rigid are these epistemological barriers.

Being in a position of power in a situation not only mitigates against one's having good access to knowledge of the other's wishes and attitudes and the quality of the other's experience, it also tends to make one think precisely that one *does* know what is going on. One's power gives one the feeling of being in control of this situation—that one can make it be what one wants it to be. So if one has good intentions, and means to take care not to harm the other, means to arrange for the other a pleasant, instructive, and satisfying experience, one expects both to be able to do it and to know one has done it. The same power one thinks can be neutralized by one's good will, one expects to use to make the situation and experience a good one.

It is a matter of the structures of power: fathers are in no position to take good care of daughters with whom they are sexually involved, and their daughters are in no position to take care of themselves. There are like problems, even if they are not so heavily over-determined, in any adult-child sexual encounter or relationship.

My own inclinations are anarchistic enough to make me disinclined to argue for criminalization of this or that sort of sexual acts, though in cases of adult-child sex where the adult is totally outside the net of the child's family, the legal prohibition might give the child just the leverage she/he needs to equalize the power in the relationship. But I am inclined to favor social pressure against sexual acts and relationships in any case of marked difference of social and economic power between the parties. (For this principle not to rule out heterosexual relations between adults, perhaps we should have to bring about the feminist revolution. If so, so be it.) The less the difference of age and physical size, the less the difference of power the participants have with others in the surrounding situation, and in the absence of one party's material dependence on the other, the less reason there would be to enjoin children's sexual activity. Perhaps if they experience sexuality between equals in childhood they will have the strength and good sense to refuse anything less in adulthood.

At this point, Ehman would ask, and rightly so, why this should apply to sex and not to all sorts of adult-child activity and interaction. My answer has to do with what sex is *in a culture of the sort we are living in.* Sex, unlike baking cookies, going camping, or playing catch, engages some of our strongest emotions and most desperate needs in an enterprise powerfully associated with dominance and subordination, violence and victimization, a mythology of ladies and whores, queers and Real Men, ideas of "dirt" and "filth," and so on and on; and though it might be otherwise in some other human culture, in this culture, if there is one situation in which people cannot *see* others, are least able to see others' interests as disparate from their own, it is when they are in the sway of erotic desire. There may indeed be other things besides sex that we should discourage adults from doing with children, such as taking them to cockfights; and perhaps fathers should not have control of their children's financial resources, so the whole matter of "buying for" is removed from the politically sticky relationship of the child with its father.

The sexual access of males to females is an absolutely central matter to male supremacy, to masculine identity, and to competition and aggression among men. Men rape "each other's" women in war and in feuds, they prove their masculinity through copulation, they maintain control of women by rape. In a culture such as this, I cannot, myself, shake off my cynicism in the face of any new effort to expand the range of men's sexual access to females. What is gained, and for whom, by putting aside the suspicions rooted in our experience and knowledge of sex and sexual politics, and reasoning airily about "sex itself" between (genderless, positionless) "adults" and "children"? Such philosophy only encourages all of the ignorance that the more powerful have of their power and as a result of their power. What encourages this ignorance also encourages the maintenance of the system that gives it power. Not knowing is the best insurance against the guilty conscience that might make one uncomfortable in one's privileges.

NOTES

1. For references to these studies and others on the incidence of incest and other adult-child sex, see *Conspiracy of Silence: The Trauma of Incest,* by Sandra Butler (Voleano Press, Inc., 330 Ellis Street, San Francisco, California, 94102). If these figures are a fair indication of the general distributions of genders and relations in adult-child sex, it would follow that homosexual males do far less than their proportional share of sex with children, as Bob Baker pointed out to me. Apparently all the cases in which the adult is a woman, plus all the cases in which the adult is a man but not the child's father, account together for only about 5 percent of the cases of adult-child sex. If male homosexuals are about 10 percent of the male population (as some research suggests), then even if male homosexuals were almost all of this 5 percent (and there is no reason to believe they are), then this 10 percent of the male population would be doing less than 5 percent of the adult-child sex. That there is a difference of roughly this magnitude and proportion between homosexual male engagement in adult-child sex and heterosexual male engagement in adult-child sex is quite plausible to me, but runs counter to popular notions of who the "child molesters" are. It might be noted that homosexual males are violating two heavily fraught and heavily sanctioned rules when they have sex with boys, while heterosexual males are violating just one heavily fraught and heavily sanctioned rule when they have sex with girls; if such rules actually have deterrent effect, that might explain the difference in incidence.

2. For narrative of girls and women who have experienced and survived incest, see Butler, op. cit., and also: *Voices In The Night: Women Speaking About Incest,* edited by Toni A. H. McNaron and Yarrow Morgan (Cleis Press, P.O. Box 8281, Minneapolis, Minnesota, 55408), 1981, and *Fight Back! Feminist Resistance To Male Violence,* edited by Frédérique Delacoste and Felice Newman (Cleis Press, 1981). For more general information about child sexual abuse, see *By Sanction of the Victim,* by Patte Wheat (Timely Books, 1978) and *The Best Kept Secret: Sexual Abuse of Children,* by Florence Rush (McGraw- Hill, 1981).

CASE STUDIES

Introduction

The case histories assembled in this section were collected by Dr. Richard Cross of the Rutgers Medical School of the University of Medicine and Dentistry of New Jersey and are used as teaching materials in a Rutgers Medical School course on Human Sexuality. He and his colleagues use these case histories to sensitize students of medicine and the allied health care professions to the issues that they can expect to encounter in the course of their professional duties. The case study entitled "Masturbation," for example, illustrates a situation that can (and, in fact, did) arise in the course of a family practice when a mother brought her worries about her son's excessive masturbating to her family doctor. The case ends when the woman turns to her physician and says "Tell me what I ought to do?" This question sets the issue for health care professionals (and for medical ethicists) quite nicely—what ought the physician do in the circumstances of this particular case?

For philosophers of sex, however, the case is intriguing in a number of different ways. Consider, for example, the woman's dismay at her son's "rythmic noises" and her remark that "he was so engrossed that he never saw me." She does not, it should be noted, conceptualize her reaction in the language of Christian theology. There is no mention of the "sin of Onan," she does not decry her son's act as "unnatural" or as "contrary to Divine Law." On the contrary, she admits that "masturbation is perfectly normal." So the rational elements of her malaise would appear to lie elsewhere. In fact, her sentiments might be rooted in one of the deeper strands of the Western philosophical tradition—the pilot/ship conception of mind and body.

457

At least since the time of Plato, one classical model of the mind-body relationship is that of mind as the pilot/master of the vehicle/servant body. One correlative of this conception is that any inversion of this relationship has been regarded as antihuman, unnatural, and perverse. Thus, to paraphrase St. Augustine, when "lust" leads humans to "lose that dominance to which the body was subject in every part" they become demeaned and bestial. Lust therefore jeopardizes our very humanity. "Engrossing," "rythmic" masturbation, as a paradigm of body dominating mind, is precisely the sort of lust that Augustine—and this mother—condemn as perverse, antihuman, and essentially animalistic.

The concerned mother of the masturbation tale will find support for her reaction not only in the writings of St. Augustine but throughout the Western philosophical tradition. From Aquinas to Kant, from the Romantics to Nagel, philosophers have tended to favor a paradigm of "healthy" sexual intercourse that is other-directed and interactive. Coition is idealized as a physiological analogue of romantic love. Non-interactive, self-engrossed acts (e.g., masturbation) are denigrated, if not as bestial, then at least as incomplete, or lesser, sex.

There is, of course, a different school of philosophical thought that might provide this mother with somewhat less solace. Many contemporary analysts follow the eighteenth-century British philosopher, Jeremy Bentham, in arguing that sexual acts, like all other acts, are morally neutral in and of themselves; consequences alone determine the moral nature of an action. On this view the morality of masturbation depends upon its consequences. Thus, the mother's embarrassment, the boy's enjoyment, and other consequences of the masturbatory act are balanced to determine its propriety.

This simple, altogether typical tale of a mother's dismayed discovery of her son's masturbatory sex life encapsulates a philosophy of sex—and our reactions to this tale enable us to discover our own conceptions of the subject. Dr. Cross's case histories, however, do more than illustrate philosophies of sex; they also provide us with a set of instances against which we can test our nascent philosophical views about such issues as the moral neutrality of sexual acts. For example, in another of his cases, "Bringing Up Children," Dr. Cross presents us with an inversion of "Masturbation"—i.e., with a history of parents who act on the moral neutrality theory and teach their young children to masturbate and to engage in other sexual acts. The reader's reaction to this case history is significant. For if, as Bentham and other philosophers have claimed, the sexual act itself is morally neutral, then consistency requires that the morality of these parental actions should be assessed entirely in terms of the consequences of the act—just as they were assessed in the case of the masturbating boy. Yet, if my own students are a fair sample, many proponents of the moral neutrality theory become somewhat uncertain of their views in this particular case.

The case histories presented here range from matters as mundane as masturbation to the more esoteric subjects of incest, sadomasochism, and zoophylia. They have been selected not only to test the reader's prereflective intuitions about the proper circumstances, locations, and partners for sexual acts, but also as a set of examples that readers can use to reflect on the philosophical theories presented by the other contributors to this volume.

R.B.

Richard Cross, M.D.

Case Studies

MASTURBATION

The thirty-eight-year-old, college-educated wife of a prominent businessman, and a mother of three, comes in to consult you (her doctor) about
her oldest child, a husky boy named Fred.

"I probably shouldn't be bothering you, Doctor, but I am concerned
about Freddy, and I don't know where to go for advice.

"I know masturbation is perfectly normal, but really, he is overdoing
it. Of course, he is no longer a baby, but he is only just fourteen, and
almost every night there are fresh stains on his sheets, and his pajamas
are a mess. I'm ashamed to send his things to the laundry, and I can't
get all the stains out.

"Alex (that's my husband) tried to convince me that I was accusing
him unjustly and that he was just having wet dreams, but I know he's
guilty because last week I caught him in the act. I was sewing in my
bedroom in the late afternoon when I heard rhythmic noises coming
from Freddy's room. I quietly opened the door, and there he was, so
engrossed he never saw me. He had a book in front of him, and the next
day while he was in school I found this hidden in his bottom drawer. It
is disgusting!"

(She hands you a copy of *Fanny Hill*.)

"He's a fine boy, Doctor, and I just want to be sure he's not being
led astray. He's on the football team in junior high, and he goes with a
pretty tough bunch of kids, and I think they must be responsible. Alex
won't do anything; he just says it's normal and not to worry. But I can't
help worrying, Doctor. He's my only boy. Tell me what I ought to do?"

PROMISCUITY AND NYPHOMANIA

A female sophomore from a near-by college is referred to you by Dr.

Blaunitz, Director of Student Health there, because of concern about her promiscuity and nymphomania. She is obviously angry as she comes in and announces:

"The whole problem here is that old Bluenuts is out of Freud country and is forty years out of date. It's okay for a guy to have multiple sex partners, but if a girl does, she must be sick!

"It all started when a guy I've been with got the clap, and I figured I'd better get a check. Dr. Blaunitz asked how many guys I've been with in the last year, and I told him about forty, and he gulped and said that was almost one a week, and I agreed. Then he wanted to know what I thought of them, and I said that if I hadn't liked them, I wouldn't have gone to bed with them, and he asked about love, and I said I didn't much want to fall in love for a while, and he gave me a solemn lecture about how sex was no good unless you were really in love. It never seemed to occur to him that I might know more about my enjoyment of sex than he did.

"Then he demanded that I see a shrink, and when I refused, he threatened to report to the Dean that I was emotionally unstable, and we finally settled on you as an impartial authority.

"So here I am. I like sex. I like variety. I'm not in love, but I've got a lot of good friends. Some day I'll probably fall in love and will limit myself to one guy, but I'm in no hurry, and I figure I might as well enjoy myself. So I have sex 'most every day, sometimes several times a day, with whatever attractive, compatible male may be available, and it suits me and suits them, so why should old Bluenuts interfere?

"Tell him to lay off, will you, Doc?"

ANAL INTERCOURSE

A thirty-three-year-old housewife and mother of three comes to request a rectal examination. Her story is as follows:

"Herb and I have a pretty good sex life, but lately we've gotten bored with the old routine and have been trying out new techniques. I found I liked it when he kissed or fingered my anus, so we decided to try intercourse there. But at first he couldn't get it in, and the harder he tried, the more it hurt. Finally he smeared butter on both of us, draped me over the back of a chair and drove in, but it was no fun for me. Then for a while he stayed quiet, and it began to feel nice and cozy. He hugged me tight and kissed my back and fingered my nipples and vulva. But as soon as he started to pump, it hurt again, and I was mighty glad when he finally finished and pulled out. He said it felt wonderful to him, much tighter than my vagina, but for me it was no fun at all. I lay awake for half an hour, feeling as if I'd been split apart, and I was still sore the next morning.

"A nurse I know pretty well told me I was a fool to let myself be used that way for Herb's pleasure. She said anal intercourse is not only uncomfortable but also messy and unsanitary. She offered to teach me some exercises which would make my vagina plenty tight enough and suggested that if Herb wasn't satisfied with that, there must be something wrong with him.

"Herb says it takes time to get used to this approach, and we should keep trying, but I'm not about to go through that experience again. I wondered if perhaps I had something wrong down there, so I came to see you."

Rectal examination reveals no hemorrhoids, fissures, fistulas or other abnormalities. Sphincter tone is good.

She asks you for advice and suggestions.

DISCREPANCY IN AGES

A middle-aged housewife strides into your office, leans forward and says:

"Doctor, I understand you're Chief of Staff over at the hospital, and I want your help in controlling the chief receptionist over there, a Mrs. Robinson. She has been contributing to the delinquency of a minor, namely my son, Benjamin, and it's got to stop!

"Benjy has only just turned eighteen, and to supplement his allowance, he's been mowing lawns. A month ago he did hers and she invited him in for a Coke and started questioning him about girls and sex. When he naively indicated his ignorance, she offered to answer his questions and then to demonstrate some techniques and before the poor boy knew what was happening, she seduced him.

"Not only that, she has been seeing him two or three times a week ever since. A friend of mine happened to see them together in a motel outside of town and told me. I quizzed my son, and he finally admitted what was going on.

"I try to be broad-minded, Doctor, and I'm sure it's been hard for her to adapt to the widowed state. I don't care how many sex partners she has if they are in her age group, but it's too much when she seduces a boy less than half her age. I guess it's time Benjy learned about sex, but not with someone who's about my age!

"Don't tell me it's none of your business, Doctor, because we are not going to put up with this! Unless you put a stop to it, Mrs. Robinson and you and your hospital are all going to suffer!"

AGE OF CONSENT

The twelve-year-old daughter of a divorced cleaning woman saunters into your office, dressed in the latest style with lipstick and nail polish on, lights a cigarette and says:

"Doctor, I need the Pill, and I hear you'll give it without telling Mom.

"I guess I've been lucky so far. I've had four different guys since I first got the curse a year ago. I've done it most with Ricky, and he always wears a rubber, but that's gonna change.

"You see, he's managed to get me into the Hawks, the best and toughest gang in town. The guys are mostly fifteen and sixteen, and they'll beat the shit out of anyone who lays a hand on one of their gals.

"Getting in is a sort of gang-bang. The new gal takes on all thirteen of the guys, one after the other. Don't look so surprised, Doctor; it ain't that bad. Maria went through it a month ago and says four guys wanted blow jobs, one couldn't get it up no matter what, one came before he got it in, and two more lasted only a few seconds. So there were only five real fucks plus a couple of second helpings. She says all you gotta do is relax and grease yourself up well for the first one, and then each guy leaves you slippery for the next one.

"I was supposed to go this Friday, but I have the rag on and might not be through by then, so they postponed it a week. Ricky says two gals my age got knocked up that way in the last year, and I'd be stupid not to be on the Pill, so here I am. It's not just that one night. I have to be available to any of them whenever they want me, and most of them think it would be a big joke if they knocked you up.

"Don't look at me like that, Doctor. I know this ain't the kind of sex you approve of, but I didn't come here for a lecture. I'm gonna join the Hawks if it kills me! Just give me the Pill so I don't get pregnant."

INCEST

On a Wednesday afternoon in the bar of the Country Club, you are cornered by a middle-aged, local businessman who has obviously had several drinks. He insists on having another with you and drags you off to an isolated table and tells you,

"Doc, I need your help and advice. It's this old college chum of mine. He's got two kids the same age as mine—a boy eighteen and a girl seventeen. They've been bitten by the hippie bug—you know, sloppily dressed, uncouth friends, smoking pot, and always talking about love, as if they'd invented it. My buddy can't do a thing with them, and he's just been sweating it out, hoping they'll outgrow it.

"Well, last night he and his wife went to bed about eleven, and a hour later he came downstairs to get a book, switched on the living room lights, and there were his two kids copulating on the sofa!

"He was so shocked, he could hardly believe his eyes, but the kids took it very casually. They said they'd done it several times before, and so did lots of their friends. They argued that the sex act is the true expression of deep love, that they loved each other, and that it was only natural to express their love this way. My buddy pointed out that incest has been a horrible crime since the dawn of history, but they just accused him of being a hopeless square, tied down by centuries of traditions and inhibitions instead of being free as are the youth of today. They ridiculed his suggestion of going to a psychiatrist.

"He doesn't know what to do. Should he have them arrested for incest? Can he commit them to a mental institution? Should he send the boy away somewhere, even though the girl is probably more to blame? What should he do?"

ZOOPHYLIA

A pert, young housewife enters your office and unabashedly asks:

"What are the dangers, Doctor, of having intercourse with a dog? I guess that's sort of an unusual question, and perhaps I'd better tell you the whole story.

"My husband, Charley, travels a lot, so a couple of months ago, we got a beautiful, big, male police dog. One evening, Charley and I got romantic in the livingroom and made love in front of the fire, while Toby watched with great interest and some excitement. Charley finished before I did and got up to get a towel, saying he'd be right back to clean up and finish me off. But he'd hardly left when I was goosed by a cold nose, and with a loud slurp Toby began the clean-up, and I soon realized that if I relaxed, his tongue would provide the climax I needed. Charley cheered him on and then, not wanting to leave him hung up, rubbed the sheath of his penis till he came too, and we all went to bed well satisfied

"Thereafter, we let Toby watch and clean up whenever we had sex. A week or so later, Charley suggested I let Toby mount me, so we tried it. The first time was not a success. He scratched my back with his fore-paws, and the angle was all wrong. But with a little experimenting, we worked out a very satisfactory technique. We do it in the kitchen so Toby won't drip on the wall-to-wall carpeting. I undress and put on my nylon ski jacket to protect my back. I kneel on a cushion with my knees apart and put my shoulders and head on the floor. Before I'm settled, Toby is on me humping away like mad, and it feels wonderful. He obviously enjoys it too, and Charley gets a kick out of watching us. We do it fairly often when Charley is on the road or just not in the mood. I am usually more interested in sex than Charley is, so it works out fine to have Toby as an added attraction.

"But lately, Doctor, I've begun to wonder if this is normal. Do other women often do this? Are there dangers involved? Can I get any disease from his fluid? Might we get stuck together as dogs do?"

SADOMASOCHISM

The forty-three-year-old principal of an out-of-town high school comes to see you with an infected bite on his penis. He says his wife got overly enthusiastic two nights before. You examine him, prescribe hot soaks and an antibiotic and ask him about a hole neatly punched through his scrotum, needle marks on sides of his penis and welts on his abdomen and buttocks. He laughs them off, saying he and his wife enjoy unusual games. You express concern about his physical and emotional well-being and suggest they see a psychiatrist. He declines but agrees to bring his wife in for a talk.

They come two days later, you repeat your concerns, and she responds:

"Thanks for your interest, Doctor, but I don't think we need that kind of help. Roger and I have a rather unusual lifestyle which admirably meets both our needs but is difficult to explain to the uninvolved. But let us try. Roger, why don't you begin?"

He leans forward in his chair and says, "I guess my basic problem is that I have real difficulty making decisions, particularly when they have impact on other people, and unfortunately my job requires me to do just that. I did fine as a teacher, but as an administrator I'm often in real trouble. I agonize over every decision, analyzing alternatives, fussing over the unknown factors, and worrying that I'll decide wrong and cause all sorts of trouble for innocent people. Memories of past mistakes flood me and fill me with shame and guilt. My insecurity and anxieties may mount to a point where I am unable to decide anything. The papers pile up, the Superintendent blows his top, this increases my anxiety and guilt, and I'm caught in a vicious cycle from which there is no escape, or wasn't till I met Regina, and she showed me a simple way out."

She takes up the story. "I don't know why it works, but there is a way out. If such a person can be *completely* submissive to another human being for a few hours, the cycle is broken. But it does no good to just make promises. He must endure pain and degradation which would normally be totally unacceptable; then his subconscious feels atonement for his mistakes, the guilt and anxiety drain away, and he experiences a feeling of tremendous freedom, peace, and tranquility. He regains his self-confidence, and once again he can function effectively. Of course, the anxieties will again build up, but now he knows how to deal with them. Do you want to add something, Roger?"

"You're doing fine, as always. You see, Doctor, my first wife never understood me. I didn't either, until I met Regina."

She resumes, "There are others who are born to dominate, who enjoy making decisions. Some doubtless end up as captains of industry or army officers or political leaders. But some, by accident of birth or race or sex, are trapped in menial positions and experience tremendous frustration. I, for example, am a practical nurse, carrying out the orders of doctors, ministering to the needs of the sick and the poor in a subservient fashion quite out of keeping with my personality. I've long known that I'd go crazy unless, from time to time, I could utterly dominate another human being. My first husband was much like Roger, and when he died, I knew just what sort of man I needed.

"But let me describe what happened a few nights ago. My good friend, Betty, a widow, came for supper. Roger had been acting uppity, so I made him cook and serve dinner. He did fine till he was serving coffee in the living room and spilled some on her white skirt. I snapped at him that he clearly needed a lesson. He knows this means he has precisely two minutes to remove every stitch of clothes and grovel at my feet. He just made it. I ordered him to apologize to her, and she was quite overwhelmed at all this, since she didn't know of our special relationship, but she recovered enough to remark that she hadn't seen a naked man in three years and even commented on the size and shape of his penis. I ordered him to show her what it was like when erect, and when he was slow to comply, I snapped a clothespin on his nipple, which always brings him to attention. She fondled his phallus and clearly was quite aroused, so I commented on his expert tongue and offered her the use of it. She pulled off her shirt and bra, and he started on her nipples, and soon she wriggled out of the rest of her clothes and spread her legs, and he set to tonguing her with all the little tricks I've taught him. I'd never seen a woman orgasm, but she really had a beaut, and I got turned on and took my clothes off and had him eat me. By the time I came, Betty was horny again and wanted to fuck, so I agreed but ordered Roger not to come. He usually has good self-control, but I guess being in a new woman was too much for him, and he came in her.

"Such disobedience obviously required immediate punishment, so we went down to the basement. Some Masters go in for chains, hoods, gags, etc., but I prefer to make my Slave control himself. I had him hang from a pipe with his eyes closed and told him to sing. That means he can moan or holler when he's hurt. Sometimes I order him to be quiet, and then the slightest gasp means more punishment. Since Betty was the one who might be pregnant, I gave her the whip, but she was not enthusiastic, so I joined in with a length of soft rubber hose, and those were the marks you saw, Doc. They'll be gone in a couple of more days.

"Betty was no good at disciplining, so I figured I'd get rid of her and do the job right. She wanted to be eaten again, so I let Roger down, and he went to work. She loved it, grabbed his tool and began to suck it. Her orgasm was even bigger than the first time. She went into a real spasm and without realizing it, bit his poor pecker half off, which was a hell of a note.

"So that's our story, Doc. I'm a Mistress and Roger's a Slave, and no psychiatrist is going to change that, at least not if I can help it."

Do you agree with her? Would your feelings be different if the sexes were reversed and a sadistic man had made his masochistic wife submit to a friend's desire?

BRINGING UP CHILDREN

A sprightly, determined, gray-haired lady, who has demanded a special appointment, marches into your consultation room and announces:

"Doctor, you have to speak to my daughter. I can't stand to watch her ruin my grandchildren. But let me explain.

"She and her husband have always had liberal ideas about sex, and I have always been careful not to interfere with their lives. I have an old-fashioned belief in things like privacy and modesty, but they and their three children run around naked all summer long and think nothing of barging into the bathroom no matter who is there. I don't approve, but I don't interfere either.

"They discuss sex frankly, which is fine, and in explicit detail, which I question. At least I find it difficult to eat dinner while the techniques of anal intercourse are being described to my seven-year-old grandson. Their bookshelves are full of pornography, which the kids are encouraged to look at. In my day, masturbation was widely practiced, but usually in private and not till adolescence. My daughter and son-in-law have carefully taught their kids to masturbate at about age three and have encouraged them to play erotic games with each other.

"I've learned that they play with their parents too. A favorite parlor game is to unzip Daddy's trousers and rub his penis to watch it get big. Next they play with Mommy's nipples and vulva. Then they watch while Mommy and Daddy have intercourse!

"But that's not all, Doctor. The kids spent last weekend with me. The five-year-old dropped some hints, I asked some questions, and I could hardly believe the picture that unfolded. It seems that my daughter and son-in-law are "swingers," who feel free to swap sex partners with other couples. They give and go to swinging orgies where anything goes, and in public view. And they bring their kids along to watch and share the fun! Imagine these small children wandering among the sweating bodies, passing food and joints (and probably stronger drugs), poking their little hands into various orifices and being fingered in return, watching Mommy bounce on Mr. Jones's lap while Daddy is banging Mrs. Smith! Would you believe that my sweet, nine-year-old grand-daughter is proud of her ability to perform what I believe you doctors call *fellatio ad ejaculationem?* She can only do it on men with small penises, but in another year or two . . . Honestly, Doctor, it makes me feel sick.

"When I confronted her, my daughter frankly admitted that the kids had told the truth. She feels that sex is natural, normal, and healthy and that the more kids know and the earlier they learn it, the better. Teaching masturbation makes much more sense to her than piano lessons (which she hated in her youth). If a child has sound attitudes, watching adults enjoy sex is no more harmful than watching them play tennis. One can really learn about sex only by participating, so why not do so? As to fellatio, she says learning to swallow semen is like learning to eat a raw oyster, and is a much more useful talent in our society. She admits most swingers don't bring their kids to parties, but feels this is hypocritical. Kids should know of and, insofar as possible, participate in everything their parents do. Her kids have learned to be discrete in talking to outsiders; I am to be congratulated in that they obviously regard me as a member of the family.

"I protested that she is depriving them of the mystery, the beauty, the romance of sex, and making them regard it as a purely mechanical act. She responded that she hoped she was eliminating the mystery, since she felt it did more harm than good. She argued that true appreciation of beauty in any field requires knowledge, experience, and technical proficiency. In her eyes, the average American is as well suited to appreciate beauty in sex as she is qualified to be a music critic on the basis of her childhood piano lessons. The kids are still too young for romance, but she can't see why familiarity with sex should interfere with romance when it comes. Their family has repeatedly discussed swinging, and the kids thoroughly appreciate the differences between mechanical sex and sex with love and affection. They understand much better than do most Americans how swinging can enrich the lives and loves of the participants.

"When I suggested that the kids were being exploited, she got mad, insisting that my generation was far more guilty of exploitation than hers. They have never urged or allowed the kids to try anything they didn't want and ask to do. They have frequently discouraged activities they felt the kids were not ready for. Their friends have also been scrupulous in this regard.

"In summary, Doctor, I got nowhere. She was very logical and very wrong. That is surely no way to bring up children!

"I know she respects you and your opinion, Doctor. Please talk to her and try to persuade her to be a little more conventional."

William Vitek

Bibliography

The following bibliography provides the most complete and comprehensive listing of philosophical materials on human sexuality yet available. It is designed to assist teachers and students by offering a compilation of published materials that bear on the issues raised by contributors to this collection. It is also intended to facilitate researchers by identifying useful related materials.

Its entries are divided into three parts. The first contains bibliographies on human sexuality and the social, moral, and metaphysical problems it poses. The second contains anthologies, books, chapters of books, and articles by philosophers, both contemporary and historical. The third and final part lists other pertinent materials from disciplines such as sociology, psychology, political science, history, theology, and women's studies.

PART ONE: LISTING OF BIBLIOGRAPHIES

A Gay Bibliography: Eight Bibliographies on Lesbian and Male Homosexuality. New York: Arno Press, 1975.

Ashbee, Henry Spencer. *Index Liborum Prohibitoru(m).* New York: J. Brussel, 1962.

Astin, Helen S., Allison Perleman, and Anne Fisher. *Sex Roles: A Research Bibliography.* Rockville, Md.: National Institute of Mental Health, 1975.

Banks, J. A., and Olive Banks. "List of Relevant Books and Pamphlets to the Woman Question Published in Britain in the Period 1792-1880." An appendix to *Feminism and Family Planning.* New York: Schocken Books, 1964.

Bullough, Vern L. *An Annotated Bibliography of Homosexuality.* New York: Garland Publishing, 1976.

Bullough, Vern L. et al. *A Bibliography of Prostitution.* New York: Garland Publishing, 1977.

Byerly, Greg. *Pornography, The Conflict Over Sexually Explicit Materials in the United States: An Annotated Bibliography.* New York: Garland Publishing, 1980.

Ch'iu Lyle, Katherine, and Sheldon J. Segal, eds. *International Family-Planning Programs, 1966-1975: A Bibliography*. Tuscaloosa, Alabama: University of Alabama Press, 1977.

Damon, Gene. *The Lesbian in Literature, A Bibliography*. San Francisco: Daughters of Bilitis, 1967.

Dollen, Charles. *Abortion in Context: A Select Bibliography*. Metuchen, N.J.: Scarecrow Press, 1970.

Driver, Edwin D. *World Population Policy: An Annotated Bibliography*. Lexington, Mass.: Lexington Books, 1972.

Equal Rights Amendment Project. *The Equal Rights Amendment: A Bibliographic Amendment*. Westport, Conn.: Greenwood Press, 1976.

Gehr, Marilyn. *Employment Discrimination Against Women, II: A Selected Annotated Bibliography*. Albany, N.Y.: University of the State of New York, State Education Dept., New York State Library, Legislative Research Service, 1975.

Geijerstam, Gunnaraf. *An Annotated Bibliography of Induced Abortion*. Ann Arbor, Mich.: Center for Population Planning, University of Michigan, 1969.

Gittings, B. A. *A Gay Bibliography*. Philadelphia: Task Force on Gay Liberation, American Library Association, 1974.

Goodland, Roger. *A Bibliography of Sex Rites and Customs: An Annotated Record of Books, Articles, and Illustrations in All Languages*. London: G. Routledge & Sons Ltd., 1931.

Hoffman, Frank. *Analytical Survey of Anglo-American Traditional Erotica*. Bowling Green, Ohio: Bowling Green University Popular Press, 1973.

Hughes, Marija Matich. *The Sexual Barrier: Legal, Medical, Economic, and Social Aspects of Sex Discrimination*. Washington, D.C.: Hughes Press, 1977.

Institute for Sex Research. *Sex Research: Bibliographies From The Institute For Sex Research*. Comp. Joan Scherer Brewer and Rod W. Wright. Phoenix, Ariz.: Oryx Press, 1979. Topics include: Sex Behavior, Sex Dysfunctions, Sex Variations, Sexual Response Physiology, Sex and Gender, Sex Counseling, Reproduction and Contraception, Venereal Disease, Marriage, Sex Education, Sex and Society, Legal Aspects of Sex Behavior, and Erotica.

Muldoon, Maureen. *Abortion: An Annotated Indexed Bibliography*. New York: E. Mellen Press, 1980.

Parker, W. *Homosexuality: A Selective Bibliography of Over 3000 Items*. Metuchen, N.J.: Scarecrow Press, 1971.

———. *Homosexuality Bibliography: Supplement 1970-1975*. Metuchen, N.J.: Scarecrow Press, 1977.

Reisner, Robert George. *Show Me the Good Parts: The Reader's Guide to Sex Literature*. New York: Citadel Press, 1964.

Seruya, Flora C., Susan Losher, and Albert Ellis. *Sex and Sex Education: A Bibliography*. New York: R. R. Bowker Co., 1972.

Sharma, Umesh D., and Wilfred C. Rudy. *Homosexuality: A Select Bibliography*. Waterloo, Ontario, Canada: Waterloo Lutheran University, 1970.

Sollito, Sharmon, Robert Veatch, and Nancy K. Taylor. *Hastings Center Bibliography of Society, Ethics and Life Sciences*. New York: Hastings-on-the-Hudson, 1976.

St. Louis Feminist Research Project. *The Rape Bibliography: A Collection of Abstracts*. Ed Netter, editor. St. Louis: The Project, 1976.

Vitek, William. Bibliography of *Philosophy and Sex*. 2nd ed. Edited by Robert

Baker and Frederick Elliston. Buffalo, N.Y.: Prometheus Books, 1984.

Walters, LeRoy. *Bibliography of Bioethics.* Detroit, Mich.: Gale Research Co., 1975.

Warren, Mary Anne. *The Nature of Woman: An Encyclopedia and Guide to the Literature.* Pt. Reyes, Calif.: Edgepress, 1980.

Weinberg, Martin S., and Alan P. Bell. *Homosexuality: An Annotated Bibliography.* New York: Harper & Row, 1972.

PART TWO: PHILOSOPHICAL MATERIALS

A. Anthologies

Arthur, John, ed. *Morality and Moral Controversies.* Englewood Cliffs, N.J.: Prentice-Hall, 1981.

Baker, Robert, and Frederick Elliston, eds. *Philosophy and Sex.* Buffalo, N.Y.: Prometheus Books, 1975. Second Edition, 1984.

Bayles, Michael D., and Kenneth Henley, eds. *Right Conduct: Theories and Applications.* New York: Random House, 1982. Chapters 7 ("Sexual Ethics") and 8 ("Pornography and Censorship").

Beauchamp, Tom L., William T. Blackstone, and Joel Feinberg, eds. *Philosophy and the Human Condition.* Englewood Cliffs, N.J.: Prentice-Hall, 1980.

Bishop, Sharon, and Marjorie Weinzweig, eds. *Philosophy and Women.* Belmont, Calif.: Wadsworth Publishing, 1979.

Bondeson, William B., et al. *Abortion and the Status of the Fetus.* Dordrecht, Holland: D. Reidal Publishing Co., 1983.

Clark, Lorenne M. G., and Lynda Lange, eds. *The Sexism of Social and Political Theory: Women and Reproduction From Plato to Nietzsche.* Toronto: University of Toronto Press, 1979.

Cohen, Marshall, Thomas Nagel, and Thomas Scanlon, eds. *Equality and Preferential Treatment.* Princeton, N.J.: Princeton University Press, 1976.

Cohen, Marshall, Thomas Nagel, and Thomas Scanlon, eds. *The Rights and Wrongs of Abortion.* Princeton, N.J.: Princeton University Press, 1974.

Copp, David, and Susan Wendell, eds. *Pornography and Censorship.* Buffalo, N.Y.: Prometheus Books, 1983.

Eisenstein, Zillah R., ed. *Capitalist Patriarchy and the Case for Socialist Feminism.* New York: 1979.

English, Jane, ed. *Sex Equality.* Englewood Cliffs, N.J.: Prentice-Hall, 1977.

Feinberg, Joel, ed. *The Problem of Abortion.* Belmont, Calif.: Wadsworth Publishing, 1973.

Fitzgerald, Maureen, Connie Guberman, and Margie Wolfe. *Still Ain't Satisfied: Canadian Feminism Today.* Toronto: The Women's Press, 1982.

Gaffney, James, ed. *Essays in Morality and Ethics.* New York: Paulist Press, 1980.

Gould, Carol C., and Marx W. Wartofsky, eds. *Women and Philosophy: Toward a Theory of Liberation.* New York: G. P. Putnam and Sons, 1976.

Grassian, Victor, ed. *Moral Reasoning: Ethical Theory and Some Contemporary Moral Problems.* Englewood Cliffs, N.J.: Prentice-Hall, 1981.

Hall, Robert et al. *Abortion in a Changing World.* New York: Columbia University Press, 1970.

Harding, Sandra, and Merrill P. Hintikka, eds. *Discovering Reality.* Dordrecht, Holland: Reidel Publications, 1982.

Holbrook, David, ed. *The Case Against Pornography.* London: Tom Stacey Ltd., 1972.

Jaggar, Allison M., and Paula Rothenberg Struhl, eds. *Feminist Frameworks: Alternative Theoretical Accounts of the Relations Between Women and Men.* New York: McGraw-Hill, 1978.

Kohl, Marvin, ed. *Infanticide and the Value of Human Life.* Buffalo, N.Y.: Prometheus Books, 1975.

Mahowald, Mary Briody, ed. *Philosophy of Woman: Classical to Current Concepts.* Indianapolis, Ind.: Hackett Publishing Co., 1978.

McConnell-Ginet, Sally, Ruth Barker, and Nelly Furman, eds. *Language in Women's Lives: Literature, Culture and Society.* New York: Praeger, 1980.

Norton, David L., and Mary F. Kille, eds. *Philosophies of Love.* San Francisco: Chandler, 1971.

O'Neill, Onora, and William Ruddick, eds. *Having Children: Philosophical and Legal Reflections on Parenthood.* New York: Oxford University Press, 1979.

Osborne, Martha Lee, ed. *Woman in Western Thought.* New York: Random House, 1979.

Rachels, James, ed. *Moral Problems.* New York: Harper & Row, 1971; 2nd ed., 1975.

Reich, Warren T., ed. *The Encyclopedia of Bioethics.* New York: The Free Press, 1978.

Rorty, Amelie O., ed. *Explaining Emotions.* Los Angeles: University of California Press, 1980.

Rossi, Alice, ed. *Essays on Sex Equality: John Stuart Mill and Harriet Taylor Mill.* Chicago: University of Chicago Press, 1970.

————, ed. *The Feminist Papers: From Adams to Beauvoir.* New York: Bantam Books, 1973.

Roszak, Theodore, and Betty Roszak, eds. *Masculine/Feminine.* New York: Harper & Row, 1969.

Sadler, Richard, ed. *Sexual Morality: Three Views.* London: Arlington Books, 1965.

Sargent, Lydia, ed. *The Unhappy Marriage of Marxism and Feminism.* Boston, Mass.: Pluto, 1981.

————, ed. *Women and Revolutions.* Boston: South End Press, 1981.

Schneir, Miriam, ed. *Feminism: The Essential Historical Writings.* New York: Random House, 1972.

Smith, F. J., and Erlin Eng, eds. *Facets of Eros.* The Hague: Nijhoff, 1972.

Soble, Alan, ed. *The Philosophy of Sex: Contemporary Readings.* Totowa, N.J.: Littlefield Adams and Co., 1980.

Treblicot, Joyce, ed. *Mothering and Feminist Theorizings.* Totowa, N.J.: Littlefield and Adams, forthcoming.

————, ed. *Crying Over Spilt Milk.* Totowa, N.J.: Littlefield Adams, forthcoming

Tanner, Leslie, ed. *Voices of Women's Liberation.* New York: Signet, 1970.

Verene, Donald P., ed. *Sexual Love and Western Morality: A Philosophical Anthology.* New York: Harper & Row, 1972.

Vetterling-Braggin, Mary, ed. *Sexist Language: A Modern Philosophical Analysis.* Totowa, N.J.: Littlefield Adams and Co., 1981.

————, ed. *Femininity, Masculinity, and Androgyny: A Modern Philosophical*

Discussion. Totowa, N.J.: Littlefield Adams, forthcoming.

Vetterling-Braggin, Mary, Frederick Elliston, and Jane English, eds. *Feminism and Philosophy,* Totowa, N.J.: Littlefield Adams and Co., 1977.

Wasserstrom, Richard A., ed. *Today's Moral Problems.* New York: Macmillan, 1979.

B. Philosophical Books and Articles

Abarbanel, Judah. *Philosophy of Love.* Translated by F. Friedeberg-Seely and J. H. Barnes. New York: Gorden Press, 1977.

Abbott, Philip. "Philosophers and the Abortion Question." *Political Theory* 6 (August 1978): 313-335.

Adams, Phyllis. "With an Eye to the Future." In Jaggar and Struhl, pp. 43-44.

Agonito, Rosemary. "The Concept of Inferiority: When Women Are Men." *Journal of Social Philosophy* 8 (January 1977):8-13.

Aldridge, Alfred Owen. "The Meaning of Incest from Hutcheson to Gibbon." *Ethics* 61 (July 1951):309-313.

Alexander, William M. "Philosophers Have Avoided Sex." *Diogenes* 72 (1970): 56-74.

―――― "Sex and Philosophy in Augustine." *Augustine Studies* 5 (1974):197-208.

Alexander, William M., "Grosticism and Hamann's Interpretations of Human Sexuality." Johann George Hamann: *Acta Des Internationalen Hamann-Coccoquims in Lunneberg,* 1976. Edited by Bernhard Gafek. FrankfurtamMain ViHorio Klostermann, 1979., pp. 85-92.

Allen, Christine Gardise. "Sex Identity and Personal Identity (Prolegomena to a Discussion of the Quality of Life)." *Contemporary Issues in Political Philosophy.* Edited by W. Shea and J. King-Farlow. New York: 1976, pp. 93-125.

――――. "Plato on Women." *Feminist Studies* 2 (1975):131-138.

――――. "Nietzsche's Ambivalence About Women." In Clark and Lange, pp. 117-134.

――――. "Women and Persons." In *Mother Was Not a Person.* Edited by M. Anderson. Montreal: Cotent Publishing Limited and Black Rose Books, 1972.

Andreeva, I. S. "Sociophilosophical Problems of Sex and Marriage and the Family." *Soviet Studies in Philosophy* 19 (Fall 1980):44-67.

Annas, George J. "The Supreme Court and Abortion: The Irrelevance of Medical Judgement." *Hastings Center Report* 10 (October 1980):23-24.

Annas, Julia. "Mill and the Subjugation of Women." *Philosophy* 52 (April 1977): 179-194.

Anon, N. "Did Nietzsche Predict the Superwoman as Well as the Superman?" *Current Literature* 43 (1907):633-634.

Anton, John P. "The Secret of Plato's Symposium." *The Southern Journal of Philosophy* 12 (Fall 1974):277-293. Reprinted in *Diotima* 2 (1974):27-47.

Aquinas, Thomas. *On the Truth of the Catholic Faith.* Book 3, Parts 1 and 2. Translated by Vernon J. Bourke. New York: Doubleday, 1956. Reprinted in Verene, pp. 119-133.

Ardley, Gavin. "The Meaning of Plato's Marital Communism." *Philosophical Studies* (Ireland) 18 (1969):36-47.

Aristotle. *De Generatione Animalium.* Books 1-4. Translated by A. L. Peck,

Boston: Harvard University Press, 1943.

———. *Ethica Nicomachea*. Vol. 9, *The Works of Aristotle*. Edited and translated by W. D. Ross. Oxford: Clarendon Press, 1915. Book 8, chaps. 1-4, and Book 9, chap. 8. Reprinted in Verene, pp. 55-65.

———. "Politica." Book 2, chaps. 1-4, in vol. 10. *The Works of Aristotle*. Translated by Benjamin Jowett. Edited by W. D. Ross. Oxford: Clarendon Press, 1921. Partially reprinted in Verene, pp. 48-54.

Atkinson, Gary M. "The Morality of Abortion." *International Philosophical Quarterly* 14 (September 1974): 347-362.

Atkinson, Ronald. *Sexual Morality*. New York: Harcourt, Brace and World, 1965.

Atkinson, Ti Grace. "Radical Feminism and Love." In Jaggar and Struhl, pp. 301-302.

Attig, Thomas. "Why Are You a Man, Teaching this Course on the Philosophy of Feminism?" *Metaphilosophy* 7 (April 1976): 155-166.

Augustine. *City of God*. Translated by P. Levine. Cambridge, Mass.: Harvard University Press, 1966. Book 1, chaps. 16-19; Book 12, chap. 24; Book 14, chaps. 17-28; Book 15, chap. 16; Book 22, chap. 24. Partially reprinted in Verene, pp. 95-118.

———. *Continence*. *Fathers of the Church*. Edited by R. J. Deferrari et al. New York: Fathers of the Church, Inc., 1948-1960; Washington: Catholic University of America Press, 1960-1962, Vol. 14.

———. *The Excellence of Widowhood*. *Fathers of the Church*. Edited by R. J. Deferrari et al. Vol. 14.

———. *The Good of Marriage*. *Fathers of the Church*. Edited by R. J. Deferrari et al. Vol. 15.

———. *Holy Virginity*. *Fathers of the Church*. Edited by R. J. Deferrari et al. Vol. 15.

———. *To Pollentius on Adulterous Marriages*. *Fathers of the Church*. Edited by R. J. Deferrari et al. Vol. 15.

Bacon, John. "Are There Sex Specific Norms?" Unpublished. The Long Island Philosophical Society. Adelphi University: Garden City, Long Island, New York, December 11, 1976.

Baier, Annette. "Good Men's Women: Hume on Chastity and Trust." *Hume Studies* 5 (April 1979): 1-19.

———. "Helping Hume to Complete the Union." *Philosophy and Phenomenological Research*, 41 (1980): 167-186.

Baker, Robert. "'Pricks' and 'Chicks': A Plea For Persons." In Baker and Elliston, pp. 45-64 1st edition and Vetterling-Braggin, pp. 161-182.

Baker, Robert. "'Pricks' and 'Chicks.'" *Philosophy and Sex*, 2nd edition. Edited by Robert Baker and Frederick Elliston. Buffalo, N.Y.: Prometheus Books, 1984, pp. 249-267

Balbus, Isaac D. *Marxism and Domination: A Neo-Hegelian, Feminist, Psychoanalytic Theory of Sexual, Political, and Technological Liberation*. Princeton, N. J.: Princeton University Press, 1983.

Bancroft, John. "Homosexuality and the Medical Profession: A Behaviourist's View." *The Journal of Medical Ethics* 1 (December 1975): 176-180.

Barnhart, Joseph E., and Mary Anne Barnhart. "Marital Faithfulness and Unfaithfulness." *The Journal of Social Philosophy*. 4 (1973): 10-15.

———. "Does the Creator Practice Planned Birth Control?" *Southwest Philosophical Studies*. 5 (April 1980): 90-93.

————. "The Myth of the Complete Person." In Vetterling-Braggin, Elliston and English, pp. 277-290.

Bartky, Sandra Lee. "Toward a Phenomenology of Feminist Consciousness." *Social Theory and Practice* 3 (Fall 1975): 425-439. Reprinted in Bishop and Weinzweig, pp. 252-257; and Vetterling-Braggin, Elliston and English, pp. 22-37.

————. "On Psychological Oppression." In Bishop and Weinzweig, pp. 33-41, and *Philosophy for a New Generation.* Edited by Arthur K. Bierman and Jane A. Gould. New York: Macmillan, 1981.

————. "Narcissism, Femininity and Alienation." *Social Theory and Practice* 8 (Summer 1982).

Baumrin, Bernard H. "Sexual Immorality Delineated." *Philosophy and Sex,* 2nd ed., Edited by Robert Baker and Frederick Elliston. Buffalo, N.Y.: Prometheus Books, 1984, pp. 300-311.

Bayles, Michael D. "Marriage, Love and Procreation." *Philosophy and Sex,* 2nd ed. Edited by Robert Baker and Frederick Elliston. Buffalo, N.Y.: Prometheus Books, 1984, pp. 130-145.

————. "Limits to a Right to Procreate." In *Ethics and Population.* Edited by Michael Bayles. Cambridge, Mass.: Schenkman, 1976, pp. 41-55. Reprinted in O'Neill and Ruddick, pp. 13-24.

————. *Morality and Population Policy.* University, Ala.: University of Alabama Press, 1980.

————. "Genetic Equality and Freedom of Reproduction: A Philosophic Survey." *Journal of Value Inquiry* 11 (1977): 186:-207.

Bayzin, N. "The Androgynous Vision." *Women's Studies* 2 (1974): 185-215.

Beardsley, Elizabeth. "Referential Genderization." *The Philosophical Forum* 5 (1973): 285-293.

————. "Traits and Generalization." In Vetterling-Braggin, Elliston and English, pp. 117-123.

————. "On Curing Conceptual Confusion." In *Femininity, Masculinity and Androgyny.* Edited by Vetterling-Braggin, pp. 249-255.

————. "Degenderization." In Vetterling-Braggin, pp. 155-160.

Beigal, Hugo G. "Sex and Human Beauty." *Journal of Aesthetics and Art Criticism* 12 (September 1953): 83-92.

Beis, Richard H. "Contraception and the Logical Structure of the Thomist Natural Law Theory." *Ethics* 75 (July 1965): 277-284.

Bellicotti, Raymond. "A Philosophical Analysis of Sexual Ethics." *The Journal of Social Philosophy* 10 (September 1979): 8-11.

————. "Women, Sex, and Sports." *The Journal of Philosophy and Sports* 6 (Fall 1979): 67-72.

Benjamin, Jessica. "The Bonds of Love: Rational Violence and Erotic Domination." *Feminist Studies* 6 (Spring 1980): 144-174.

Benn, S. I. "Abortion, Infanticide and Respect For Persons." In Feinberg, pp. 92-104.

Bentham, Jeremy. "Offences Against One's Self: Paederasty." *Journal of Homosexuality* 3 (1978): 383-405 and 4 1978:91-107.

————. An Essay on "Paederasty." *Philosophy and Sex,* 2nd ed. Edited by Robert Baker and Frederick Elliston. Buffalo, N.Y.: Prometheus Books, 1984, pp. 353-369.

Berger, Fred, R. "Pornography, Feminism, and Censorship." *Philosophy and Sex,* 2nd ed. Edited by Robert Baker and Frederick Elliston. Buffalo, N.Y.: Prometheus Books, 1984, pp. 370-390.

————. "Pornography, Sex, and Censorship." *Social Theory and Practice* 4 (Spring 1977): 183-209. Reprinted in Wasserstrom, pp. 337-358; and Soble, pp. 332-347.

————. "Love, Friendship and Utility: On Practical Reason and Reductionism." *Human Nature and Natural Knowledge*. Edited by Nonagen, Perovich, Weidin. Dordrecht, Holland: D. Reidal, 1983.

Berkeley, George. "Letter to Percival, July 29, 1710." In *The Works of George Berkeley*. Vol. 8, pp. 34-35. Edited by A. A. Luce and T. E. Jessop. London: Nelson, 1948.

Bertocci, Peter Anthony. *The Human Venture in Sex, Love, And Marriage*. New York: Association Press, 1949.

————. *Sex, Love, and the Person*. New York: Sheed and Ward, 1967.

————. "The Relation Between Love and Justice: A Survey of Five Possible Positions." *Journal of Value Inquiry* 4 (1970): 191-203.

Bhattacharya, R. D. "Because He is a Man." *Philosophy* 49 (January 1974): 96.

Bishop, Sharon. "Love and Dependency." In Bishop and Weinzweig, pp. 147-153.

Blackstone, William T. "Freedom and Women." *Ethics* 85 (April 1975): 243-248.

Blum, Larry, Marcis Homiak, Judy Housman, and Naomi Scheman. "Altruism and Women's Oppression." *The Philosophical Forum* 5 (1973): 222-247. Reprinted in Bishop and Weinzweig, pp. 200-205, and Gould, *Philosophy and Women*.

————. "Kant's and Hegel's Moral Rationalism: A Feminist Perspective." *Canadian Journal of Philosophy* 12 (June 1982): 2.

Boas, George. "Love" In *Encyclopedia of Philosophy*, Vol. 5. New York: Macmillan Free Press, 1967.

Bolton, Martha Brandt. "Responsible Women and Abortion Decisions." In O'Neill and Ruddick, pp. 39-51.

Bouregeois, Patrick. "Kierkegaard: Ethical Marriage or Aesthetic Pleasure." *Personalist* 57 (1976): 370-375.

Boxill, Bernard R. "Sexual Blindness and Sexual Equality." *Social Theory and Practice* 6 (Fall 1980): 281-298.

————. "The Morality of Abortion." *The Monist* 56 (October 1972): 503-526.

Brink, Andre P. "Literature and Offence." *Philosophical Papers* 5 (May 1976): 53-66.

Brockriede, Wayne. "Arguers as Lovers." *Philosophy and Rhetoric* 5 (Winter 1972): 1-11.

Brody, Baruch A. "Abortion and the Law." *The Journal of Philosophy* 68 (June 17, 1971): 357-368.

————. "Thompson on Abortion." *Philosophy and Public Affairs* 1 (Spring 1972): 335-340.

————. "Abortion and the Sanctity of Human Life." *The American Philosophical Quarterly* 10 (April 1973): 133-140.

————. "Fetal Humanity and the Theory of Essentialism." In Baker and Elliston, pp. 338-354.

————. *Abortion and the Sanctity of Human Life: A Philosophical View*. Cambridge, Mass.: MIT Press, 1975.

Brown, Carol. "Mothers, Fathers and Children: From Private to Public Patriarchy." In Sargent, pp. 239-268.

Brown, Malcom and Jane Coulter. "The Middle Speech of Plato's Phaedo." *Journal of the History of Philosophy* 9 (1971): 405-423.

Burch, Robert W. "The Commandability of Pathological Love." *The Southwestern Journal of Philosophy* 3 (1972): 131-140.

Burns, S. "The Humean Female." *Dialogue* 15 (1976): 415-441. Reprinted in Clark and Lange, pp. 53-59.

———. "The Platonic Woman: Philosophy as a Subversive Activity." Unpublished. Dept. of Philosophy, Dalhousie University.

Cacoullos, Ann R. "The Doctrine of Eros in Plato." *Diotima* 1(1973): 81-99.

Callahan, Daniel. *Abortion: Law, Choice, and Morality.* New York: Macmillan, 1970.

Calvert, Brian. "Plato and the Equality of Women." *Phoenix* 29 (Autumn 1975): 231-243.

Camenisch, Paul F. "Abortion, Analogies and the Emergence of Value." *The Journal of Religious Ethics* 4 (Spring 1976): 131-158.

Caraway, Carol. "Commentary on Rolf Johnson's 'Love, Passion and the Need to Be Loved'." Unpublished. The Society for the Philosophy of Sex and Love. American Philosophical Association, Philadelphia, Pa.: December 28, 1981.

Carrier, L. S. "Abortion and the Right To Life." *Social Theory and Practice* 3 (Fall 1975): 381-401.

Clark, Lorenne M. G. "Reply to Sumner on Abortion." *The Canadian Journal of Philosophy* 4 (Summer 1974): 183-190.

———. "The Rights of Women: The Theory and Practice of the Ideology of Male Supremacy." In *Contemporary Issues in Political Philosophy.* New York: Neal Watson Academic Publications, 1976.

———. "Women and John Locke; or, Who Owns the Apples in the Garden of Eden?" *The Canadian Journal of Philosophy* 7 (December 1977): 699-724. Reprinted in Clark and Lange, pp. 16-40.

———. "Privacy, Property, Freedom, and the Family." *Philosophical Law.* Westport, Conn.: Greenwood Press, 1978.

———. "A Marxist-Feminist Critique of Marx and Engels; or, The Consequences of Seizing the Reins in the Household." Unpublished. Dept. of Philosophy, University of Toronto.

Clark, Lorenne M. G., and Debra J. Lewis. *Rape: The Price of Coercive Sexuality.* Toronto: Canadian Women's Educational Press, 1976.

———. "Liberalism and Pornography." In *Pornography and Censorship: Scientific, Philosophical and Legal Studies.* Edited by D. Copp and S. Mendell. Buffalo, N.Y.: Prometheus Books.

Clark, Lorenne. "The 'Naturalness' of the Family: A Critique." *Laurentian University Review.* 14 (February 1982) 64-78.

Code, Lorraine. "Is Sex of the Knower Epistomologically Significant?" *Metaphilosophy* 12 (July-October 1981): 267-276.

Cohen, Carl. "Sex, Birth Control and Human Life." *Ethics* 79 (July 1969): 251-263.

———. "Sex, Birth Control, and Human Life." *Philosophy and Sex,* 2nd ed. Edited by Robert Baker and Frederick Elliston. Buffalo, N.Y.: Prometheus Books, 1984, pp. 185-199.

Cohen, Howard. *Equal Rights for Children.* Totowa, N.J.: Littlefield Adams and Co., 1980.

———. "Abortion and the Quality of Human Life." In Vetterling-Braggin, Elliston and English, pp. 429-445.

Collins, Margery, and Christine Pierce. "Holes and Slime: Sexism in Sartre's Psychoanalysis." *The Philosophical Forum* 5 (Fall-Winter 1973): 112-127. Reprinted in Osborne, pp. 319-322.

Connell, Richard J. "A Defense of *Humanae Vitae.*" *Laval Theologique et*

Philosophique 26 (February 1970); 57-87.

Cooper, Burton. "Metaphysics, Christology and Sexism: An Essay in Philosophical Theology." *Religious Studies* 16 (June 1980): 179-193.

Copper, W. E. "What is Sexual Equality and Why Do They Want It?" *Ethics* 85 (April 1975): 256-257.

Cordero, Roland A. "The Demise of Morality." *Journal of Value Inquiry* 8 (1974): 187:195.

Cornford, F. M. "The Doctrine of Eros in Plato's *Symposium.*" In *The Unwritten Philosophy and Other Essays,* by F. M. Cornford. Cambridge: Cambridge University Press, 1967, 68-80. Reprinted in *Plato: A Collection of Critical Essays.* Vol. 2. Edited by Gregory Vlastos. Garden City, N.Y.: Anchor Books, 1971, pp. 119-131.

Cosby, Grant. "Abortion: An Unresolved Moral Problem." *Dialogue* (Canada) 17 (1978): 106-121.

Cowburn, John. *Love and the Person: A Philosophical Theory and a Theological Essay.* London: Chapman, 1967.

Cox, Jean W. "The Lawful Expression of Erotic Fantasies: All Our Dreams Come True." *Religious Humanism* 9 (Winter 1975): 17-22.

Crocker, Lawrence. "Meddling With the Sexual Orientation of Children." In O'Neill and Ruddick, pp. 145-154.

Cross, Richard. "Case Studies." *Philosophy and Sex,* 2nd ed. Edited by Robert Baker and Frederick Elliston. Buffalo, N.Y.: Prometheus Books, 1984, pp. pp. 460-469

Costanzo, Joseph F. "Papal Magisterium and *Humanae Vitae.*" *Thought* 44 (September 1969): 377-412.

Cumming, Alan. "Pauline Christianity and Greek Philosophy: A Study of the Status of Women." *The Journal of the History of Ideas* 34 (Fall 1973): 517-528.

Curley, E. M. "Excusing Rape." *Philosophy and Public Affairs* 5 (Summer 1976): 325-360.

Daly, Mary. *Beyond God the Father: Toward a Philosophy of Women's Liberation.* Boston: Beacon Press, 1973.

———. *Gyn/Ecology: The Metaethics of Radical Feminism.* Boston: Beacon Press, 1978.

Dana, Richard H. "Equality in Sexual Behavior." *The Journal of Thought* 15 (Summer 1980): 9-18.

De Beauvoir, Simone. *The Second Sex.* Translated by H. M. Parshley. New York: Knopf, 1952. Partially reprinted in Verene, pp. 318-327.

Dedek, John F. *Contemporary Sexual Morality.* New York: Sheed & Ward, 1971.

De George, Richard T. "Legal Enforcement, Moral Pluralism and Abortion." *Proceedings of the Catholic Philosophical Association* 49 (1975): 171-180.

De Gourmont, Remy. *The Natural Philosophy of Love.* New York: Liveright, 1932.

De Sade, Donatien Alphonse-Francois. *Justine: Philosophy in the Bedroom; Eugenie de Franval and Other Writings* (1791). Translated by R. Seaver and A. Wainhouse. New York: Grove Press, 1965. Partially reprinted in Verene, pp. 295-305.

Dewar, Lindsay. *Marriage Without Morals: A Reply to Mr. Bertrand Russell.* London: Society for Promoting Christian Knowledge, 1931.

Dickason, Anne. "Anatomy and Destiny: The Role of Biology in Plato's View of Women." *The Philosophical Forum* 5 (1973): 45-53.

———. "The Feminine as Universal." In Vetterling-Braggin, Elliston and English, pp. 79-100.

Dillon, Martin C. "Love in *Women in Love:* A Phenomenological Analysis." *Philosophy and Literature* 2 (Fall 1978): 190-208.

———. "Romantic Love, Enduring Love and Authentic Love." Mimeographed, Dept. of Philosophy. State University of New York at Binghamton. 1980.

———. "Sacred Love, Profane Love and Love." Mimeographed, Dept. of Philosophy. State University of New York at Binghamton. 1980.

———. "Toward a Phenomenology of Love and Sexuality: An Inquiry into the Limits of the Human Situation as They Condition Loving." *Soundings* 43 (Winter 1980): 341-360.

———. "Love, Death and Creation." *Research in Phenomenology,* 11 (1981): 190-210.

Dolan, Joseph V. "*Humanae Vitae* and Nature." *Thought* 44 (1969); 358-376.

Drouin, F. M. "Conjugal Love: A Way of Sanctity." *Revue De L'Universite D'Ottawa* 29 (July-September 1959): 153-162.

Dufresne, Nicole (trans.), and Jean Baudrillard. "Forgetting Foucault." *Human Society* 45 (April 1981): 175-193.

Dupre, Louis K. "Natural Law and Contraception." *Proceedings of the Catholic Philosophical Association* 39 (1965): 166-169.

Duran, Jane. "Gender-Neutral Terms." In Vetterling-Braggin, pp. 147-154.

Dyal, Robert A. "Is Pornography Good for You?" *Southwestern Journal of Philosophy* 7 (Fall 1976): 95-118.

Eames, Elizabeth R. "Sexism and Woman as Sex Object." *The Journal of Thought* 11 (April 1976): 140-143.

Edwards, John N. "Incest." *Sex and Society.* Edited by John N. Edwards. New York: Macmillan, 1972, pp. 157-159.

Ehman, Robert. "Adult-Child Sex." In *Philosophy and Sex,* 2nd ed. Edited by Baker and Frederick Elliston. Buffalo, N.Y.: Prometheus Books, 1984, pp. pp. 431-446

———. "Personal Love and Individual Value." *Journal of Value Inquiry* 10 (1976): 91-105.

Elliston, Frederick. "Gay Marriage." In *Philosophy and Sex,* 2nd ed. Edited by Robert Baker and Frederick Elliston. Buffalo, N.Y.: Prometheus Books, 1984, pp. 146-166

———. "In Defense of Promiscuity." In Baker and Elliston, 1st ed. pp. 222-246.

———. "Toward a Phenomenology of Love." Unpublished. Washington, D.C.: American Philosophical Association, December 27, 1978.

———. "Homosexuality and Monogamy." Unpublished. Philosophy Colloquium. State University of New York College at Fredonia, February 25, 1979.

———. "Sex, Marriage and the Law." Conference on Value Inquiry. State University of New York at Geneseo, April 20, 1980.

———. "Philosophy and Sex." Colloquium on Human Sexuality. State University of New York at Albany, April 27, 1982.

Elrod, Eleanor. "Plato's Argument of Equal Opportunity." *The Journal of the West Virginia Philosophical Society* 9 (Spring 1978): 110-127.

Engels, Friedrich. *The Origin of the Family, Private Property and the State.* New York: International Publishers, 1942.

Engler, Barbara. "Sexuality and Knowledge in Sigmund Freud" *Philosophy Today* 13 (1969): 214-224.

English, Jane. "Review Essay: Philosophy." *Signs: Journal of Women in Culture and*

Society 3 (Summer 1978): 823-831.

———. "Sex Equality in Sports." *Philosophy and Public Affairs* 7 (Spring 1978): 269-277.

———. "What Do Grown Children Owe Their Parents?" In O'Neill and Ruddick, pp. 351-356; and Arthur, pp. 147-153.

Epictetus. *The Discourses and Manual.* Book 2, chaps. 18, 22. Translated by P. E. Matheson. Oxford: Clarendon Press, 1916. Reprinted in Verene, pp. 66-74.

Ericsson, Lars O. "Charges Against Prostitution: An Attempt at a Philosophical Assessment." *Ethics* 90 (April 1980): 335-366.

Ezorsky, Gertrude. "It's Mine." *Philosophy and Public Affairs* 3 (Spring 1974): 321-330.

———. "The Fight Over University Women." *New York Review of Books* 16 (May 1974): 32-39.

Evers, Williamson M. "Rawls and Children." *The Journal of Liberal Studies* 2 (Summer 1978): 109-114.

Farley, Margaret A. "Sexual Ethics." In Reich, pp. 1575-1587.

Farrell, Daniel M. "Jealousy." *The Philosophical Review* 89 (1980): 527-559.

Faust, Beatrice. *Women, Sex and Pornography.* New York: Macmillan Publishing Co., 1981.

Feinberg, Joel. *The Idea of the Obscene.* Lawrence, Ks.: University of Kansas Press, 1979.

———. "Pornography and the Criminal Law." *University of Pittsburgh Law Review* 40 (1979): 567-604.

———. "Obscenity, Pornography and the Arts." In *Values and Conflicts.* Edited by Burton M. Leiser. New York: Macmillan, 1981.

———. "Love and Sexuality." In *Philosophy and the Human Condition.* Edited by Tom L. Beauchamp, William T. Blackstone, and Joel Feinberg. Englewood Cliffs, N.J.: Prentice-Hall, 1980, pp. 396-404.

Ferguson, Ann. "Androgyny as an Ideal for Human Development." In Vetterling-Braggin, Elliston and English, pp. 45-69; and Soble, pp. 232-255.

———. "Motherhood and Sexuality: A Feminist-Materialist Perspective." In *Crying Over Spilt Milk.* Edited by Joyce Treblicot. Totowa, N.J.: Littlefield Adams, forthcoming.

———. "Patriarchy, Sexual Identity and the Sexual Revolution." *Signs* 7 (Autumn 1981): 158-172.

———. "On Compulsory Heterosexuality and Lesbian Existence: Defining the Issues." *Journal of Women in Culture and Society* 7 (1981): 158-199.

Fichte, Johann Gottlieb. *The Science of Rights* (1795). First Appendix: "Fundamental Principles of the Rights of the Family." Translated by A. Eger Kreger. Philadelphia: J.B. Lippincott, 1869.

Finnis, John M. "Natural Law and Unnatural Acts." *Heythrop Journal* 11 (1970): 365-387.

———. "The Rights and Wrongs of Abortion: A Reply to Judith Thompson." *Philosophy and Public Affairs* 2 (Winter 1973): 117-145.

Firestone, Shulamith. *The Dialectic of Sex: The Case for Feminist Revolution.* New York: William Morrow, 1970.

———. "Love: A Feminist Critique." In *Philosophy and Sex.* 2nd ed. Edited by Robert Baker and Frederick Elliston. Buffalo, N.Y.: Prometheus Books, 1984, pp. 37-52.

Fisher, Mark. "Reason, Emotion and Love." *Inquiry* 20 (1978): 189-203.

Flanagan, Owen J., Jr. "Virtue, Sex and Gender: Some Philosophical Reflections on the Moral Psychology Debate." *Ethics* 92 (April 1982): 499-512.

Floyd, S. L., and D. Pomerantz. "Is There a Natural Right to Have Children?" In Arthur, pp. 131-138.

Foa, Pamela. "What's Wrong With Rape?" In Vetterling-Braggin, Elliston and English, pp. 347-359; Bishop and Weinzweig, pp. 140-146; and Arthur, pp. 98-108.

Fortenbaugh, W. W. "On Plato's Feminism in *Republic* V." *Apeiron* 9 (November 1975): 1-4.

Fortunata, Jacqueline. "Masturbation and Women's Sexuality." In Soble, pp. 389-408.

———. "Lakoff on Language and Women." In Vetterling-Braggin, pp. 81-92.

Foucault, Michel. *The History of Sexuality. Vol. 1, An Introduction.* Translated by Robert Hurley. New York: Pantheon Books, 1978.

Fourier, Charles. *Harmonian Man: Selected Writings of Charles Fourier.* Edited by Mark Poster. New York: Anchor, 1971.

Fried, Marlene Garber. "In Defense of Preferential Hiring." *The Philosophical Forum* 5 (1973): 309-319.

Frisbe, Sandra. "Women and the Will to Power." *Gnosis* 1 (Spring 1975): 1-10.

Frye, Marilyn. "Critique." In *Philosophy and Sex.* 2nd ed. Edited by Robert Baker and Frederick Elliston. Buffalo, N.Y.: Prometheus Books, 1984, pp. 447-455.

———. *The Politics of Reality: Essays in Feminist Theory.* The Crossing Press, 1983.

———. "To Be and Be Seen: Metaphysical Misogyny." *Sinister Wisdom* 17 (Summer, 1981): 57-70.

———. "Some Remarks on Separatism and Power." In *Sinister Wisdom* 6 (Summer, 1978): 30-39.

———. "Rape and Respect." Coauthored with Carolyn Shafer. In Vetterling-Braggin, Elliston and English, pp. 333-346.

———. "Male Chauvinism: A Conceptual Analysis." In Baker and Elliston, 1st ed. pp. 65-82; and in Vetterling-Braggin, pp. 7-22.

Fuchs, Jo-Ann P. "Female Eroticism in *The Second Sex.*" *Feminist Studies* 6 (Summer 1980): 304-313.

———. "Socialist Feminism: Analysis and Strategy Gleaned from Five Position Papers." Unpublished. Society for Women In Philosophy. February 22, 1975.

Fuller, Margaret. "The Great Lawsuit: Men Versus Men, Women Versus Women.' *Dial* 4 (July 1843): 1-47.

Gardner, R. F. R. "A New Ethical Approach to Abortion and its Implications for the Euthanasia Dispute." *The Journal of Medical Ethics* 1 (September 1975) 127-131.

Garry, Ann. "Pornography and Respect for Women." *Social Theory and Practice* 4 (Spring 1978): 395-421. In Bishop and Weinzweig, pp. 128-139, and Baker and Elliston, 2nd ed., pp. 312-326.

———. "Reflections on 'Women as Sex Objects'." Unpublished. The Society for the Philosophy of Sex and Love. American Philosophical Association, Sacramento Calif., March 25, 1982.

———. "Why are Love and Sex Philosophically Interesting?" *Metaphilosophy* 11 (April 1980): 165-177.

———. "Narcissism and Vanity." *Social Theory and Practice* (Summer 1982):

Garside Allen, Christine. "Plato on Women." *Feminist Studies* 2 (1975): 131-138.

Gastil, Raymond D. "The Moral of the Majority to Restrict Obscenity and Pornography Through Law." *Ethics* 86 (April 1976): 231-240.

Gauthier, David. "The Rationale of Differential Sexual Socialization." Manuscript. Toronto: University of Toronto Press, 1975.

Gellner, E. A. "Ethics and Logic." *Proceedings of the Aristotelean Society* 55 (1955): 157-178.

Gelven, Michael. "Eros and Projection: Plato and Heidegger." *The Southwestern Journal of Philosophy* 4 (Fall 1973): 125-136.

Gendron, Bernard, "Sexual Alienation." *Technology and the Human Condition.* New York: St. Martin's Press, 1977, pp. 114-133. Reprinted in Soble, pp. 281-298.

Gerber, D. "Abortion: The Uptake Argument." *Ethics* 83 (October 1972): 80-83.

Gerber, Rudolf J. "Abortion: Parameters for Decision." *International Philosophical Quarterly* 11 (December 1971): 561-584. Reprinted in *Ethics* 82 (January 1972): 137-154.

Gillespie, Norman C. "Abortion and Human Rights." *Ethics* 87 (April 1977): 237-243.

Godwin, William. *Enquiry Concerning Political Justice and its Influence on Morals and Happiness* (1793). Edited by F. E. L. Priestly. Toronto: University of Toronto Press, 1946, Book 8, chap. 8, pp. 506-513.

Goldman, Alan H. "Abortion and the Right to Life." *The Personalist* 60 (October 1979): 402-406.

―――. *Justice and Reverse Discrimination.* Princeton, N.J.: Princeton University Press, 1979.

―――. "Plain Sex." *Philosophy and Public Affairs* 6 (Spring 1977): 267-287. Reprinted in Soble, pp. 119-138; and Arthur, pp. 85-98.

Gordon, Robert M. "The Abortion Issue." In *The Abdication of Philosophy.* Edited by Robert M. Gordon. La Salle, Ill.: Open Court, 1976.

Gould, Carol C. "The Women Question: The Philosophy of Liberation and the Liberation of Philosophy." *The Philosophical Forum.* 5 (1973): 5-44. Reprinted in Gould and Wartofsky, pp. 5-44.

Govier, Trudy. "Woman's Place." *Philosophy* 49 (July 1974): 303-309.

―――. "Getting Rid of the Big Bad Wolf." *Philosophy* 56 (April 1981): 258-261.

―――. "What Should We Do About Future People?" *American Philosophical Quarterly* 16 (1979): 105-114.

Grad, Mary Lou. "Play as an Ethical Paradigm for Sexual Intercourse." In Gaffney, pp. 162-173.

Gray, Robert. "Sex and Sexual Perversion." *The Journal of Philosophy* 75 (1978): 189-199. Reprinted in Soble, pp. 158-168.

Greene, Andre. "Sexuality and Ideology in Marx and Freud." *Human Context* 6 (1974): 362-384.

Greene, Naomi. "Sartre, Sexuality, and *The Second Sex.*" *Philosophy and Literature* 4 (Fall 1980): 199-211.

Griffin, Susan. "Rape: The All American Crime." *Ramparts* (September 1971): 26-35. Reprinted in Vetterling-Braggin, Elliston and English, pp. 313-332.

Grim, Patrick. "Sexism and Semantics." In Vetterling-Braggin, Elliston and English, pp. 109-116.

―――. "A Note on the Ethics of Theories of Truth." In Vetterling-Braggin, pp. 290-298.

————. "Sexist Speech: Two Basic Questions." In Vetterling-Braggin, pp. 34-52.

————. "Sex and Social Roles: How to Deal with the Data." In Vetterling-Braggin.

————. "Sports and Two Androgynisms." *Journal of the Philosophy of Sport.*

Grisez, Germain Gabriel. "Reflections on the Contraception Controversy." *Proceedings of the Catholic Philosophical Association* 39 (1965): 176-182.

————. *Abortion: the Myths, the Realities, and the Arguments.* New York: Corpus Books, 1970.

Guettel, Charnie. *Marxism and Feminism.* Toronto: The Women's Press, 1974.

Guyon, Rene. *Sex Life and Sex Ethics.* London: John Lane, The Bodley Head, 1933.

————. *Studies in Sexual Ethics.* 2 vols. New York: Knopf, 1948-1950.

————. *The Ethics of Sexual Acts.* New York: Knopf, 1948.

Haack, Susan. "On the Moral Relevance of Sex." *Philosophy* 49 (January 1974): 90-95.

Hall, Diana Long. "Biology, Sex Hormones, and Sexism in the 1920's." *The Philosophical Forum* 5 (1973): 81-96.

————. "Social Implications of the Scientific Studies of Sex." *The Scholar and the Feminist* IV Conference at Barnard College, New York, 1977.

Hamlyn, David. "The Phenomena of Love and Hate." *Philosophy* 53 (1978): 189-203.

Hamrick, William S. "Fascination, Fear and Pornography: A Phenomenologic Typology." *Man and World* 7 (February 1974): 52-66.

Hansen, Linda. "Pain and Joy in Human Relationships: Jean-Paul Sartre and Simone De Beauvoir." *Philosophy Today* 23 (Winter 1979): 338-346.

Harding, Sandra. "Feminism: Reform or Revolution." *The Philosophical Forum* 5 (1973): 271-284.

————. *Thinking about Women: Syllabi for Courses on Philosophical Aspects of Feminism.* University of Delaware, 1975.

Hare, R. M. "Abortion and the Golden Rule." *Philosophy and Public Affairs* 4 (Spring 1975): 201-222. Reprinted in Baker and Elliston, pp. 356-376.

————. "Abortion and the Golden Rule." *Philosophy and Sex,* 2nd. ed. Edited by Robert Baker and Frederick Elliston. Buffalo, N.Y.: Prometheus Books, 1984, pp. 231-248.

Harris, Daniel, "Androgyny." *Women's Studies* 2 (1974): 171-184.

Hatab, Lawrence J. "Nietzsche on Woman." *Southern Journal of Philosophy* 19 (1981): 171-178.

Hegel, G. W. F. *On Christianity: Early Theological Writings.* Trans. T. M. Knox. New York: Harper & Row, 1961, pp. 304-308. Reprinted in Verene, pp. 234-239.

————. *The Phenomenology of Mind* (1807). Trans. J. B. Baillie. London: Allen and Unwin, 1910. Chap. 6, sec. Aa, "The Ethical World."

————. *The Philosophy of Right* (1821). Trans. T. M. Knox. London: Oxford University Press, 1942. Part 3, sec. 1, pp. 105-121.

Hein, Hilde. "A Second Look at *The Second Sex:* The Institutionalization of Otherness." Paper read for Pacific Division of the American Philosophical Society, San Diego, 1976. Worcester, Mass.: Holy Cross College, 1976. Mimeographed.

————. "Obscenity, Politics, and Pornography." *Journal of Aesthetic Education* 5 (October 1971): 77-97.

————. "On Reaction and the Women's Movement." *The Philosophical Forum* 5

(1973): 248-270.

――――. "Women: A Philosophical Analysis." *The Holy Cross Quarterly* 4 (Fall 1977): 4.

――――. "Women: On Liberation From Expectation." *Sounding* (Fall 1974).

――――. "S-M and the Liberal Tradition." In *Against Sadomasochism: A Radical Feminist Analysis.* Edited by Robin Ruth Linden, et al. East Pacific Alto: Frog in the Well Publications, 1982, pp. 83-90.

――――. "Women and Morality: A Women's Place Is in the Wrong." Mimeographed. Worcester, Mass.: Holy Cross College, 1979.

――――. "Libertine, Liberalism, and Liberty." Mimeographed. Worcester, Mass.: Holy Cross College, 1983.

Heise, Helen. "Eyeshadow, Aesthetics and Morality." Society for Women in Philosophy, Los Angeles, 1981.

Held, Virginia. "Marx, Sex, and the Transformation of Society." *The Philosophical Forum* 5 (1973): 168-184. Reprinted in Bishop and Weinzweig, pp. 159-162.

――――. "Reasonable Progress and Self Respect." *The Monist* 57 (January 1973): 12-27.

――――. "Men, Women, and Equal Liberty." In *Promise and Problems of Human Equality.* Edited by Walter Feinberg. Urbana: University of Illinois Press, 1976.

――――. "The Obligations of Mothers and Fathers." In O'Neill and Ruddick, pp. 227-239, and Vetterling-Braggin, pp. 242-258.

Hellegers, Andre E. et al. "Abortion." In Reich, pp. 1-32.

Herbenick, Raymond M. "Remarks on Abortion, Abandonment, and Adoption Opportunities." *Philosophy and Public Affairs* 5 (Fall 1975): 98-104. Reprinted in O'Neill and Ruddick, pp. 52-57.

Higgs, Roger et al. "Lesbian Couples: Should Help Extend to Aid?" *The Journal of Medical Ethics* 4 (June 1978): 91-95.

Hill, John. *"Persona Humana* on Sexual Ethics: An Interpretation." *The Thomist* 41 (October 1977): 540-566.

Hill, Sharon Bishop. "Self Determination and Autonomy." In Bishop and Weinzweig, pp. 68-76.

Hill, Thomas E. "Servility and Self-Respect." *The Monist* 57 (January 1973): 87-104. Reprinted in English, pp. 170-182.

Hoffman, Eric. "Love as a Kind of Friendship." Unpublished. The Society for the Philosophy of Sex and Love. American Philosophical Association, Boston, Mass., December 28, 1980.

Holstrom, Nancy. "Do Women Have a Distinct Nature." *The Philosophical Forum* 14 (Fall 1982): 25-42.

Hughes, John C. "Sexual Harassment." *Social Theory and Practice* 6 (Fall 1980): 249-280.

Hugo, John J. *St. Augustine on Nature, Sex, and Marriage* Chicago: September 1969.

Humber, James M. "The Immorality of Abortion." Eastern Division Meeting of the American Philosophical Association, December 1973.

――――. "Abortion: Fetal Research and the Law." *Social Theory and Practice* 4 (Spring 1977): 127-147.

――――. "Abortion: the Avoidable Moral Dilemma." *The Journal of Value Inquiry* 9 (Winter 1975): 282-302.

――――. "The Case Against Abortion." *The Thomist* 39 (January 1975): 65-84.

――――. "Understanding Sexual Perversion." Unpublished. Southern Society for

Philosophy and Psychology. Louisville, Ky., April 16, 1981.

Hume, David. "Of Polygamy and Divorces." *Essays Moral, Political, and Literary* Vol. 2. Edited by T. H. Green and T. H. Grose. London: Longmans, Green, 1875. 231-239. Reprinted in Verene, pp. 144-153.

———. "Of Chastity and Modesty." In *A Treatise Concerning Human Nature,* Book 3, Part 2. Garden City, N.Y.: Dolphin, 1961.

Hunter, C. K. "The Problem of Fichte's Phenomenology of Love." *Idealism Studies* 6 (1976): 178-190.

Hunter, J. F. M. *Thinking about Sex and Love.* Toronto: Macmillan of Canada, 1980.

———. "On Camp: The Sensibility of Innocent Frivolity." *Journal of the West Virginia Philosophical Society* 9 (1975): 28-30.

"Issues in Reproduction." *Cases in Bioethics from the Hastings Center Report.* Edited by Carol Levine and Robert M. Veatch. Hastings-on-the-Hudson, N.Y.: Hastings Center, 1982.

Jacobson, Paul. "The Return of Alcibiades: An Approach to the Meaning of Human Sexuality Through the Works of Freud and Merleau-Ponty." *Philosophy Today* 22 (Spring 1978): 89-98.

Jaggar, Alison. "Abortion and a Woman's Right to Decide." *The Philosophical Forum* 5 (Fall-Winter 1973): 347-360. Reprinted in Baker and Elliston, 1st ed., pp. 324-337.

———. "Abortion and a Woman's Right to Decide." In *Philosophy and Sex.* 2nd ed. Edited by Robert Baker and Frederick Elliston. Buffalo, N.Y.: Prometheus Books, 1984, pp. 218-230.

———. *Feminist Politics and Human Nature.* Totowa, N.J.: Littlefield Adams, 1983.

———. "Male Instructors, Feminism, and Women's Studies." *Teaching Philosophy* 2 (1977-1978): 247-256.

———. "Political Philosophies of Women's Liberation." In Vetterling-Braggin, Elliston and English, pp. 5-21.

———. "Prostitution." In Soble, pp. 348-368.

———. "On Sexual Equality." *Ethics* 84 (1974): 275-292. Reprinted in English, pp. 93-109; and Bishop and Weinzweig, pp. 77-87.

Jarrett, James L. "On Pornography." *Journal of Aesthetic Education* 4 (July 1970): 61-68.

Johnson, Rolf M. "Love, Passion and the Need to Be Loved." Unpublished. The Society For the Philosophy of Sex and Love. Philadelphia, Pa.: American Philosophical Association, December 28, 1982.

Kaelin, Eugene F. "The Pornographic and the Obscene in Legal and Aesthetic Contexts." *Journal of Aesthetic Education* 4 (July 1970): 69-84.

Kainz, Howard P. Jr. "The Relationship of Dread to Spirit in Man and Woman, According to Kierkegaard." *The Modern Schoolman* 47 (November 1969): 1-13.

Kanoti, George A., and Anthony R. Kosnik. "Homosexuality: Ethical Aspects." In Reich, pp. 671-675.

Kant, Immanuel. "Duties Towards the Body in Respect of Sexual Impulse." In Arthur, pp. 80-84.

———. *Lectures on Ethics: 1775-1780* (1930). Translated by Louis Infield. Indianapolis: Hackett, 1963, pp. 162-171. Reprinted in Verene, pp. 154-164.

———. *Observations on the Feeling of the Sublime and the Beautiful (1763).* Sec. 3, "Of the Distinction Between the Beautiful and the Sublime in the Interrelations of the Two Sexes." Berkeley, Calif.: University of California Press, 1960, pp. 76-96.

———. "The Rights of the Family as a Domestic Society." *The Philosophy of Law (1797)*. Translated by W. Hastie. Edinburgh, 1887. Part 1, Sec. 1.

Kardiner, Abram. *Sex and Morality*. Indianapolis: Bobbs-Merrill, 1954.

Keohane, Nannerl O. "Feminist Scholarship and Human Nature." *Ethics* 93 (October 1982): 102-113.

Ketchum, Sara Ann. "Alienation of Labor and Alienation of Labor: An Analogy." Unpublished. Society for the Philosophical Study of Sex and Love. Eastern Division Meetings of the American Philosophical Association, Boston, Mass., December 1980.

———. "Comment on 'Discrimination and Physical Appearance' by Alan Soble." Unpublished. Western Division Meeting of the American Philosophical Association, Columbus, Ohio, April 1982.

———. "Comments on 'Sex and Sex.'" Unpublished. Oakland, Calif.: American Philosophical Association, Spring 1976.

———. "Female Culture, Woman Culture, and Conceptual Change: Toward a Philosophy of Women's Studies." *Social Theory and Practice* 6 (August 1980): 151-162.

———. "The Good, The Bad, The Perverted." In Soble, pp. 139-157.

———. "Liberalism and Marriage Law." In Vetterling-Braggin, Elliston and English, pp. 247-276.

———. "Moral Redescription and Political Self-Deception." In Vetterling-Braggin, pp. 279-289.

———. "Reply to Peterson." Unpublished. Society For the Philosophy of Sex and Love. Boston, Mass.: American Philosophical Association, December 1980.

Ketchum, Sara Ann, and Christine Pierce. "Separatism and Sexual Relationships." In Bishop and Weinzweig, pp. 163-171.

Kielkopf, Charles F. "On the Structure of Chastity." *Proceedings of the Catholic Philosophical Association* 53 (1979): 164-172.

Kierkegaard, Soren. "The Aesthetic Validity of Marriage." In *Either/Or*. Vol. 2. Translated by Walter Lowrie. New York: Anchor, 1959, pp. 3-157.

———. *"The Diary of a Seducer* (1843). Translated by Fick. Ithaca, New York: The Dragon Press, 1932.

———. *Fear and Trembling*. Translated by Walter Lowrie. New York: Doubleday, 1954, pp. 52-61.

———. *Works of Love (1847)*. Translated by David F. Swenson and Lilian Marvin Swenson. Princeton, N.J.: Princeton University Press, 1946.

King-Farlow, John. "The Sartrean Analysis of Sexuality." *The Journal of Existential Psychiatry* 2 (1962): 290-302.

Kirchner, Landon. "Contemporary Sexuality." *The Journal of the West Virginia Philosophical Society* 8 (Fall 1974): 1-8.

Kleinig, John. "Censorship." *Interchange* (1974): 232-240.

———. "Mill, Children and Rights." *Educational Philosophy and Theory* 8 (1976): 1-15.

Kockelmans, Joseph J. "Merleau-Ponty on Sexuality." *The Journal of Existentialism* 6 (Fall 1965): 9-30.

Korsmeyer, Carolyn W. "Reason and Morals in the Early Feminist Movement: Mary Wollstonecraft." In *Women and Philosophy: Toward a Theory of*

Liberation. Edited by Carol C. Gould and Marx W. Wartofsky. New York: G. P. Putnam and Sons, 1976, pp. 97-111. Reprinted in Osborne, pp. 139-150.

———. "The Hidden Joke: Generic Uses of Masculine Terminology." In Vetterling-Braggin, Elliston and English, pp. 138-153; and Vetterling-Braggin, pp. 116-131.

Kosok, Michael. "The Phenomenology of Fucking." *Telos* 8 (1971): 64-76.

Kraut, Richard. "The Importance of Love in Aristotle's Ethics." *Philosophical Research Archives:* #1060 (1975).

Krell, David Farrell. "Merleau-Ponty on 'Eros' and 'Logos'." *Man and World* 7 (February 1974): 37-51.

Kupfer, Joseph. "Sexual Perversion and the Good." *The Personalist* 59 (January 1978): 70-77.

Kurtz, Paul. "Tolerance Versus Repression." *The Humanist* 32 (1972): 34-35.

Kuykendall, Eleanor. "Feminist Linguistics in Philosophy." In Vetterling-Braggin, 132-146.

Lange, Lynda. "The Function of Equal Education in Plato's *Republic* and *Laws.*" In Clark and Lange, pp. 3-15.

———. "The Politics of Impotence." In *Contemporary Issues in Political Philosophy.* Edited by J. King-Farlow and W. Shea, New York: N. Watson, 1976.

———. "The Politics of Reproduction." Unpublished doctoral dissertation, York University, Toronto, 1976.

———. "Reproduction in Democratic Theory." In *Contemporary Issues in Political Philosophy,* pp. 131-146. Edited by J. King-Farlow and W. Shea. New York: N. Watson, 1976.

———. "Rousseau and Modern Feminism." *Social Theory And Practice* 7 (Fall 1981): 245-278.

———. "Rousseau: Women and the General Will." In Clark and Lange, pp. 41-52.

Langham, Paul. "Between Abortion and Infanticide." *The Southern Journal of Philosophy* 17 (Winter 1979): 465-471.

Larson, Susan. "What Befits a Woman." Unpublished. Barnard College, May 1974.

Lawrence, Barbara. "Four Letter Words 'Can' Hurt You." In Baker and Elliston, 1st ed. pp. 31-33.

Leacock, Eleanor Burke. "Political Ramifications of Engel's Argument on Women's Political Subjugation." In Osborne, pp. 295-297.

Leiser, Burton M. *Liberty, Justice, and Morals: Contemporary Value Conflicts.* New York: Macmillan, 1973.

———. "Homosexuality and the 'Unnaturalness Argument'." In *Social Ethics.* Edited by Thomas Mappes and Jane Zembaty. New York: McGraw-Hill, 1982, pp. 215-227.

LeMoncheck, Linda. "Treating Women as Sex Objects." Unpublished. Occidental College. The Society for the Philosophy of Sex and Love. Sacramento, Calif.: American Philosophical Association, March 25, 1982.

Lenzer, Gertrud. "Gender Ethics." *Hastings Center Report* 10 (February 1980): 18-19.

Lesser, A. H. "Love and Lust." *The Journal of Value Inquiry* 14 (Spring 1980): 51-54.

Leser, Harry. "Plato's Feminism." *Philosophy* 54 (January 1979): 113-117.

Levin, Michael. "Vs. Ms." In English, pp. 216-219; and Vetterling-Braggin, pp. 217-222.

Levine, Carol. "Depo-Provera and Contraceptive Risk: A Case Study of Values in Conflict." *Hastings Center Report* 9 (august 1979): 8-11.

Levy, Donald. "The Definition of Love in Plato's *Symposium.*" *Journal of the History of Ideas* (April 1979): 285-291.

———. "Perversion and the Unnatural as Moral Categories." *Ethics* 90 (January 1980): 191-202. Reprinted in Soble, pp. 169-189.

———. "Response to Hoffman." Unpublished. The Society for the Philosophy of Sex and Love. Boston, Mass.: American Philosophical Association, Decmeber 28, 1980.

———. "Sexual Objectification and the Goals of Sexual Liberation." Unpublished. Convention of the Popular Culture Association and the American Cultural Association, Louisville, Ky., April 1982.

Levy, Steven R. "Abortion and Dissenting Parents: A Dialogue." *Ethics* 90 (Spring 1980): 162-163.

Lingus, Alphonso. F. "Sense and Non-Sense in the Sexed Body." *Cultural Hermeneutics* 4 (December 1977): 345-356.

Linton, David. "Why is Pornography Offensive?" *The Journal of Value Inquiry* 13 (Spring 1979): 57-62.

Lloyd, G. E. R. "Parmenides' Sexual Theories: A Reply to Mer Kember." *The Journal of Hellenistic Studies* 92 (1972): 178-179.

Long, Thomas A. "Obscenity, the Law and Religion." *Iustitta* 2 (Fall-Winter 1974): 5-13.

Lorch, Ingrid. "Sexuality and Intersubjective Knowledge." Unpublished. State University of New York at New Paltz, December 1976.

Louch, A. R. "Sins and Crimes." *Philosophy* 43 (January 1968): 38-50.

Lucas, J. R. "Because You Are a Woman." *Philosophy* 48 (1973): 161-171.

———. "The Lesbian Rule." *Philosophy* 30 (July 1955): 195-213.

———. "Vive La Difference." *Philosophy* 53 (July 1978): 363-373.

Ludwig, Emil. *Of Life and Love.* New York: Philosophical Library, 1945.

Luther, A. R. "Scheler's Interpretation of Being As Loving." *Philosophy* 14 (1970): 217-227.

Luther, Martin. *What Luther Says.* Comp. Ewald M. Plass. S. Louis: Concordia Publishing House, 1959, pp. 132-134, 884-886, 902, 906, 1457-1459. Reprinted in Verene, pp. 134-143.

MacDonald, I. A. "The 'Offence Principle' as a Justification for Censorship." *Philosophical Papers* 5 (May 1976): 67-84.

MacGuigan, Maryellen. "Androgyny and Sexuality: A Comment on Pielke." Unpublished. Mercy College of Detroit.

———. "Is Woman a Question?" *International Philosophical Quarterly* 13 (1973): 485-505.

Macklin, Ruth. "Ethics, Sex Research, and Sex Therapy." *Hastings Center Report* 54 (April-June 1975): 5-7.

———. "Sex Therapy and Sex Research: Ethical Perspectives." In Reich, pp. 1551-1559.

MacMurray, John. *Reason and Emotion* (1935). London: Faber and Faber, 1962. Chaps. 6-7.

Mahowald, Mary B. "Feminism, Socialism and Christianity." *Cross Currents* 25 (Spring 1975): 33-50.

———. "Freedom Versus Happiness, and 'Women's Lib.'" *Journal of Social Philosophy* 6 (1975): 10-13.

Makedon, Alex. "Platonic Education: A Sexual Reinterpretation." Unpublished. 1976.

Marcil-Lacoste, Louise. "The Consistency of Hume's Position Concerning Women." *Dialogue* 15 (1976): 415-441.

———. "Feminisme et Rationalite." *La Rationalite Aujord'hui/Rationalite Today.* Edited by Theodore Gereats. Ottawa: Presses de l'Universite d'Ottawa, 1979. 475-484.

———. "The Grammar of Feminine Sexuality." *The Canadian Journal of Politics and Social Theory* 4 (Spring-Summer 1980): 69-74.

———. "The Historian's Presupposition on Feminism: A Case Study." *The Canadian Journal of Philosophy* 12 (March 1982): 185-200.

———. "Hume's Method in Moral Reasoning." In Clark and Lange, pp. 60-73.

———. "The Trivialization of Equality: The Case of Feminist Writings." In *Discovering Reality.* Edited by Sandra Harding and Merrill P. Hintikka. Reidel Publications, 1982.

———. "Women as Persons." Proceedings of the Catholic Philosophical Association, 53 (1979): 78-87.

Marcuse, Herbert. *Eros and Civilization: A Philosophical Inquiry into Freud.* Boston: Beacon Press, 1955.

———. "Marxism and Feminism." *Women's Studies* 23 (1974): 279-288.

Margolis, Joseph. "Abortion." *Ethics* 84 (October 1973): 51-61.

———. "Homosexuality." In *Justice For All.* Edited by Tom Reagan and Albert Van DeVeer. Totowa, N.J.: Littlefield Adams, 1982, pp. 42-63.

———. "Perversion." In *Negativities: The Limits of Life,* by Joseph Margolis. Columbus, Ohio: Charles Merrill Press, 1975. Chapter 9.

———. "The Question of Homosexuality." In Baker and Elliston, 1st ed., pp. 288-304.

Margolis, Clorinda, and Joseph Margolis. "The Separation of Marriage and Family." In Vetterling-Braggin, Elliston and English, pp. 291-300.

Markovic, Mihailo. "Women's Liberation and Human Emancipation." *The Philosophical Forum* 5 (1973): 242-258.

Markus, R. A. "The Dialectic of Eros in Plato's *Symposium.*" In *Plato: A Collection of Critical Essays.* Vol. 2. Edited by Gregory Vlastos. Garden City, N.Y.: Anchor Books, 1971.

Martin, Michael. "Pedagogical Arguments for Preferential Hiring and Tenuring of Women Teachers in the University." *The Philosophical Forum* 5 (1973): 325-333.

Marx, Karl. *On Education, Women and Children.* Translated by Saul K. Padover. The Karl Marx Library, Vol. 5. New York: McGraw-Hill, 1975.

Mastandrea, Jamie, and Mary K. Duggan. "Language and the Oppression of Women." *Dialogue* 19 (October 1976): 7-14.

Mastiny, Aleta You. "Sexism and Education." *Proceedings of the Far Western Philosophy of Education Society* (1978-79): 137-144.

Mazis, Glen A. "Touch and Vision: Rethinking with Merleau-Ponty and Sartre on the Caress." *Philosophy Today* 23 (Winter 1979): 321-328.

McAdoo, N. A. "The 'Aesthete' and the 'Philistine'." *The British Journal of Aesthetics* 19 (Fall 1979): 331-341.

McConnell-Ginet, Sally. "Linguistics in the Feminist Context." Unpublished. Available from author at Ithaca, New York: Cornell University, Dept. of Linguistics and Women's Studies.

———. "Prototypes, Pronouns, and Persons." In *Boas Sapir and Whorf Revisited.* Edited by M. Mathiot. The Hague: Mouton, 1981.

McCormick, Richard. "Reproductive Technologies: Ethical Issues." In Reich, pp. 1454-1463.

McKissick, Dorothy. "Language, Sex Roles and Women's Self-Concept." Unpublished. Los Angeles: University of California, Dept. of Sociology.

McLaughlin, Eleanor Commo. "Equality of Souls, Inequality of Sexes." In Osborne, pp. 77-86; and *Religion and Sexism*, by Rosemary Radford Ruether. New York: Simon and Schuster, 1974. pp. 59-71.

McLachlan, Hugh V. "Must We Accept Either the Conservative or the Liberal View on Abortion?" *Analysis* 37 (June 1977): 197-204.

McMurtry, John. "Monogamy: A Critique." *The Monist* 56 (October 1972): 587-599. Reprinted in Baker and Elliston, 1st edition pp. 166-177 and Arthur, pp. 120-131.

———. "Monogamy: A Critique." *Philosophy and Sex*, 2nd ed. Edited by by Robert Baker and Frederick Elliston. Buffalo, N.Y.: Prometheus Books, 1984, pp. 107-118.

———. "Sex, Love and Friendship." Paper presented at the American Philosophical Association Meeting. Baltimore, Md.: December 27, 1982.

McNamara, Colleen. "I Just Don't Know if I Can Make It." *Up from Under* 1 (Winter 1971-1972): 34. Reprinted in Jaggar and Struhl, pp. 41-42.

Meager, R. "Obscenity: A New Danger in Literature." *The British Journal of Aesthetics* 5 (January 1965): 57-61.

———. "The Sublime and the Obscene." *The British Journal of Aesthetics* 4 (July 1964): 214-227.

Mechanic, David. "The Supreme Court and Abortion: Sidestepping Social Realities." *Hastings Center Report* 10 (December 1980): 17-19.

Merleau-Ponty, Maurice. "The Body in Its Sexual Being." In *Phenomenology of Perception*. New York: Humanities Press, 1965.

Midgley, Mary. "The Concept of Beastliness: Philosophy, Ethics and Animal Behavior." *Philosophy* 48 (April 1973) 111-135.

Miguens, Manuel. "Christ's 'Members' and Sex." *The Thomist* 39 (January 1975): 24-48.

Milhaven, John Giles. "Christian Evaluations of Sexual Pleasure." In *Selected Papers*. American Society of Christian Ethics, 1976, pp. 63-74.

———. "Conjugal Sexual Love and Contemporary Moral Theology." *Theological Studies* 35 (December 1974): 692-710.

———. "The Grounds of the Opposition to *Humanae Vitae*." *Thought* 44 (September 1969): 343-357.

———. "Thomas Acquinas on Sexual Pleasure." *The Journal of Religious Ethics* 5 (Fall 1977): 157-181.

Mill, Harriet Taylor. *Enfranchisement of Women* (1851). Reprinted in *Essays on Sex Equality*. Edited by Alice S. Rossi. Chicago: University of Chicago Press, 1970.

Mill, John Stuart. *On the Subjection of Women*. London, 1869. Republished by Fawcett Books: New York, 1973. Reprinted in *Essays on Sex Equality*. Edited by Alice S. Rossi. Chicago: University of Chicago Press, 1970.

Mill, John Stuart, and Harriet T. Mill. *Early Essays on Marriage and Divorce* (1832). Reprinted in *Essays on Sex Equality*. Edited by Alice S. Rossi. Chicago: University of Chicago Press, 1970.

Mills, Patricia Jagentowicz. "Hegel and the 'Woman Question': Recognition and Intersubjectivity." In Clark and Lange, pp. 74-98.

Mohr, Richard. "A Non-Liberal Argument For Gay Rights." Unpublished. The Society for the Philosophy of Sex and Love. Philadelphia, Pa.: American Philosophical Association, December 28, 1981.

——. "Gay Rights." *Social Theory and Practice* 8 (Spring 1982): 31-41.

——. "Gay Studies in the Big Ten: A Survivor's Manual." Unpublished, n.d.

——. "Invisible Minorities, Civic Rights, Democracy: Three Arguments for Gay Rights." *Journal of Philosophy* 78 (1981).

Moore, Harold F. "Abortion and the Logic of Moral Justification." *The Journal of Value Inquiry* 9 (Summer 1975): 140-151.

Morawski, Stefan. "Art and Obscenity." *The Journal of Aesthetic Criticism* 26 (Winter 1967): 193-207.

Morgan, Douglas N. *Love: Plato, the Bible and Freud.* Englewood Cliffs, N.J.: Prentice-Hall, 1964.

Morgan, Kathryn. "The Androgynous Classroom." *Philosophy of Education: Proceedings* 36 (1980): 245-255.

——. "Androgyny: A Conceptual Critique." *Social Theory and Practice* 8 (1982): 245-283.

——. "The Moral Politics of Sex-Education." In *Moral Issues.* Edited by Jan Narveson. Oxford: Oxford University Press, forthcoming.

——. "Romantic Love, Altruism, and Self Respect." Manuscript. Toronto: University of Toronto Press, 1982.

——. "Sexuality as a Metaphysical Dimension." In Bishop and Weinzweig, pp. 88-95.

Morreall, John. "Of Marsupials and Men: A Thought Experiment on Abortion." *Dialogos* 16 (April 1981): 7-18.

Moulton, Janice. "Comments on J. Shaffer's 'Sexual Desire'." Unpublished. Psychology Dept., Duke University, November 30, 1977.

——. "The Myth of the Neutral 'Man'." In Vetterling-Braggin, Elliston and English, pp. 124-137; and Vetterling-Braggin, pp. 100-115.

——. "Review Essay: Philosophy." *Signs: Journal of Women in Culture and Society* 2 (Winter 1976): 422-433.

——. "Sex and Reference." In Baker and Elliston, pp. 34-44 and Vetterling-Braggin, pp. 183-193.

——. "Sexual Behavior: Another Position." *The Journal of Philosophy* 73 (1976): 537-546. Reprinted in Soble, pp. 110-118.

Munz, Peter. "The Ethics of Relationship and Solitude." *Humanitao* 11 (1975): 99-113.

Myrna, Frances. "Abortion: A Philosophical Analysis." *Feminist Studies* 1 (Fall 1972): 49-63.

Nagel, Thomas. "Equal Treatment and Compensatory Discrimination." *Philosophy and Public Affairs* 2 (1973): 348-363.

——. "Sexual Perversion." *The Journal of Philosophy* 66 (1969): 5-17. Reprinted in Soble, pp. 76-88; and Baker and Elliston 1st ed. pp. 247-260.

——. "Sexual Perversion" *Philosophy and Sex,* 2nd ed. Edited by Robert Baker and Frederick Elliston. Buffalo, N.Y.: Prometheus Books, 1984, pp. 268-279.

Narveson, Jan. "Semantics, Future Generations, and the Abortion Problem." *Social Theory and Practice* 3 (Fall 1975): 461-485.

——. "Tinkering and Abortion." *Dialogue* (Canada) 17 (1978): 125-128.

The National Commission for the Protection of Human Subjects of Biomedical and Behavioral Research. *Research on the Fetus.* Washington, D.C.: U.S. Dept. of

494   BIBLIOGRAPHY

Health, Education and Welfare, 1975.
Neu, Jerome. "What Is Wrong With Incest?" *Inquiry* 19 (1976): 27-39 Reprinted in Wasserstrom, pp. 300-311.
Newman, Jay. "An Empirical Argument Against Abortion." *New Scholasticism* 51 (Summer 1977): 384-395.
Newman, R. P. "Karl Marx on Women, Marriage and the Family." Unpublished. State University of New York at Fredonia, 1975.
Newton, Lisa H. "Abortion in the Law: An Essay on Absurdity." *Ethics* 87 (April 1977): 244-250.
————. "Humans as Persons: A Reply to Tristram Engelhardt." *Ethics* 85 (1975): 332-336.
————. "The Irrelevance of Religion in the Abortion Debate." *Hastings Center Report* 8 (August 1978): 16-17.
————. "Reverse Discrimination as Unjustified." *Ethics* 83 (July 1973): 308-312.
Newton-Smith, W. "A Conceptual Investigation of Love." *Philosophy and Personal Relations*. Edited by Alan Montefiore. Montreal: McGill, Queen's University Press, 1973, pp. 113-136.
Nicholson, Linda. *Feminism as Political Philosophy*. Unpublished manuscript. Albany: State University of New York, 1982.
————. *Abortion and the Roman Catholic Church*. Knoxville, Tenn.: Religious Ethics Inc., 1978.
Nicholson, Susan T. "The Roman Catholic Doctrine of Therapeutic Abortion." *The Journal of Religious Ethics*. Reprinted in Vetterling-Braggin, Elliston and English, pp. 385-407.
Nickel, James W. "Classification by Race in Compensatory Programs." *Ethics* 84 (January 1974): 146-150.
————. "Discrimination and Morally Relevant Characteristics." *Analysis* 32 (1972): 113-114.
Nietzsche, Friedrich. *Beyond Good and Evil* (1886). Secs. 79, 84, 85, 86, 102, 120, 123, 126, 131, 139, 144, 145, 148, 167, 168, 172, in *The Philosophy of Nietzsche*. Translated by H. Zimmern. New York: Random House, 1954.
————. "Morality as the Enemy of Nature." *The Twilight of the Idols*. Translated by Anthony M. Ludovici. Vol. 16, *The Complete Works of Friedrich Nietzsche*. Edited by Oscar Levy. New York: Russell and Russell, 1964, pp. 26-32. Reprinted in Verene, pp. 186-192.
————. "On Child and Marriage." *Thus Spake Zarathustra* (1885). Part 1, Sec 20; In *The Portable Nietzsche*. Translated by Walter Kaufmann. New York: Viking Press, 1954.
————. "On Little Old and Young Women." *Thus Spake Zarathustra* (1885). Part 1, Sec. 18; in *The Portable Nietzsche*. Translated by Walter Kaufmann. New York: Viking Press, 1954.
Nilsen, Aileen P. "Sexism in English: A Feminist View." In *Female Studies*, Vol. 6. Available from Feminist Press, Old Westbury, New York.
Noble, Mary, and J. K. Mason. "An Almost Absolute Value in History." In *The Problem of Abortion*. Edited by Joel Feinberg. Belmont, Calif: Wadsworth Publishing Co., 1973.
————. "Contraception." In Reich, pp. 204-216.
————. *Contraception: A History of its Treatment by the Catholic Theologians and Canonists*. New York: Mentor Press, 1965.
————. "Incest." *The Journal of Medical Ethics* 4 (June 1978): 64-70.

Nowell-Smith, P. H. "Morality: Religious and Secular." *Rationalist Annual* (1961): 5-22.

Oaklander, L. Nathan. "Sartre on Sex." In Soble, pp. 190-206.

O'Brien, Mary. "Hegel: Man, Physiology and Fate?" Unpublished. Dept. of Sociology, Ontario Institute for Studies in Education, Toronto.

———. "The Politics of Impotence." In *Contemporary Issues in Political Philosophy.* Edited by Shea and King-Farlow. New York: Science History Publications, 1976, 147-162.

———. "Reproducing Marxist Man." In Clark and Lange, pp. 99-116.

O'Connor, Catherine R. *Woman and Cosmos; the Feminine in the Thought of Pierre Teilhard de Chardin.* New York: Prentice-Hall, 1974.

O'Connor, Edward. "Natural Law and Contraception." *The New Scholasticism* 43 (Summer 1969): 432-439.

———. "Abortion, Property Rights, and the Right to Life." *The Personalist* 58 (April 1977): 99-114.

O'Driscoll, Lyla H. "On the Nature and Value of Marriage." In Vetterling-Braggin, Elliston and English, pp. 249-263.

Okin, Susan Moller. "Philosopher Queens and Private Wives: Plato on Woman and the Family." *Philosophy and Public Affairs* 6 (Summer 1977): 345-369.

———. "Rousseau's Natural Women." *Journal of Politics* 41 (1979): 393-416.

———. "Women and the Making of the Sentimental Family." *Philosophy and Public Affairs* 11 (Winter 1981): 65-88.

———. *Women in Western Political Thought.* Princeton, N.J.: Princeton University Press, 1979.

Olah, Suzie. "Impolite Questions of Frederick Engels." *Quest: A Feminist Journal* (March 1970).

Olshewsky, Thomas M. "A Christian Understanding of Divorce." *The Journal of Religious Ethics* 7 (Spring 1979): 118-138.

O'Neil, Charles. "Is Prudence Love?" *The Monist* 58 (1974): 119-159.

O'Neill, Onora. "How Do We Know When Opportunities Are Equal?" *The Philosophical Forum* 5 (1975): 334-346. Reprinted in English, pp. 143-154.

Ortega y Gasset, Jose. *On Love* (1939). Translated by Toby Talbot. New York: Meridian, 1957.

Osborne, Martha Lee. *Genuine Risk: A Dialogue on Woman.* Indianapolis: Hackett Publishing, 1981.

———. "Plato's Unchanging View of Woman: A Denial that Anatomy Spells Destiny." *The Philosophical Forum* 6 (Summer 1975): 447-452.

Ovid. *The Art of Love and Other Poems.* Translated by J. H. Motzley. Cambridge, Mass.: Harvard University Press, 1939. 1:13-17; 2:111-117; 3:123-124, 173-175. Reprinted in Verene, pp. 75-83.

———. *Amores.* Edited by J. Kenney. Oxford: Oxford University Press, 1961.

Palmer, David. "The Consolation of the Wedded." In Baker and Elliston, 1st ed. pp. 178-189.

———. "The Consolation of the Wedded." *Philosophy and Sex,* 2nd ed. Edited by Robert Baker and Frederick Elliston. Buffalo, N.Y.: Prometheus Books, 1984, pp. 119-129.

Parfit, Derek. "Future Generations: Further Problems." *Philosophy and Public Affairs* 11 (Spring 1982): 113-172.

Pateman, Carole. "Women and Consent." *Political Theory.* n.d.

Peterson, Susan Rae. "Against Parenting." In *Mothering and Feminist Theorizings.*

Edited by Joyce Treblicot. Totowa, N.J.: Littlefield Adams, 1982.

———. "Coercion and Rape: The State as a Male Protection Racket." In Vetterling-Braggin, Elliston and English, pp. 360-371.

———. "Feminism, Marxism and Reproduction." Unpublished. The Society for the Philosophy of Sex and Love. Boston, Mass.: American Philosophical Association, December 28, 1980.

———. "The Justification of Sex-Differentiated Norms." Unpublished. The Long Island Philosophical Society. Adelphi University: Garden City, L.I., N.Y., December 11, 1976.

Peterson, Susan Rae, and H. B. Holmes. "Rights Over One's Body: A Woman-Affirming Health Care Policy." *Human Rights Quarterly* 3 (Spring 1981): 71-87.

Pielke, Robert. "Are Androgyny and Sexuality Compatible?" In Vetterling-Braggin, pp. 187-196.

Pierce, Christine. "Equality: *Republic* V." *The Monist* 57 (1973): 1-11.

———. "Natural Law Language and Woman." In English, pp. 130-142; and Gornick, pp. 169-181.

———. "Review Essay: Philosophy." *Signs: Journal of Women in Culture and Society* 1 (Winter 1975): 487-501.

Pierce, Christine, and Margery Collins. "Holes and Slime in Sartre's Psychoanalysis." *The Philosophical Forum* 5 (1973): 112-127.

Plato. "Laws." *The Dialogues of Plato*. 3rd ed. Translated by Benjamen Jowett. New York and London: Oxford University Press, 1892, pp. 739-929.

———. "Phaedrus." *The Dialogues of Plato*. 3rd ed. Translated by Benjamen Jowett. New York and London: Oxford University Press, 1892.

———. "Republic." *The Dialogues of Plato*. 3rd ed. Translated by Benjamen Jowett. New York and London: Oxford University Press, 1892. 3: 144-159. Reprinted in Verene, pp. 29-47.

———. "Symposium." *The Dialogues of Plato*. 3rd ed. Translated by Benjamen Jowett. New York and London: Oxford University Press, 1892. Partially reprinted in Verene, pp. 10-28.

Pluhar, Werner S. "Abortion and Simple Consciousness." *The Journal of Philosophy* 74 (March 1977): 159-172.

Plutarch. *Moralia*. Boston: Harvard University Press, 1965, Vol. 2, Section 219.

Pomeroy, Sarah. "Feminism in Book V of Plato's *Republic.*" *Apeiron* 8 (May 1974): 33-35.

Poole, Howard. "Obscenity and Censorship." *Ethics* 93 (October 1982): 39-44.

Pope Paul VI. *Humanae Vitae*. Washington, D.C.: N.C.W.C., 1983. Reprinted in Baker and Elliston, 1st ed., pp. 131-149.

Pope Paul VI. "Humanae Vitae." *Philosophy and Sex*, 2nd ed. Edited by Robert Baker and Frederick Elliston. Buffalo, N.Y.: Prometheus Books, 1984, pp. 167-184

Poster, Mark. "Foucault's True Discourses." *Human Society* (Spring 1979): 153-166.

Postow, B. C. "Thomas on Sexism." *Ethics* 90 (January 1980): 251-156. In Vetterling-Braggin, pp. 271-278.

Price, Kingsley. "Love Yes, But Maybe Not Sex." *Philosophy of Education: Proceedings* 36 (1980): 317-321.

Proudfoot, Merrill. "How Sex Can Make Us Good." *Philosophy of Education: Proceedings* 36 (1980): 307-316.

Purdy, L. M. "Abortion and the Husband's Rights: A Reply to Wesley Teo." *Ethics*

86 (April 1976): 247-251.
———. "Against 'Vs. Ms.'" In Vetterling-Braggin, pp. 223-228.
———. "Genetic Disease: Can Having Children Be Immoral?" In *Biomedical Ethics*. Edited by Thomas A. Mappes and Jane S. Zembaty. N.Y.: McGraw-Hill, 1980, pp. 468-475.
Purdy, L. M., and Michael Tooley. "Is Abortion Murder?" *Abortion: Pro and Con*. Edited by Robert L. Parkins. Cambridge, Mass.: Schenkman, 1974, pp. 129-149.
Ramsey, Paul. "The Morality of Abortion." In *Moral Problems*. Edited by James Rachels. New York: Harper & Row, 1971; and *Life or Death: Ethics and Options*. Edited by D. H. Labby. Seattle: University of Washington Press, 1980.
Rapaport, Elizabeth, and Paul Sagal. "One Step Forward, Two Steps Backward: Abortion and Ethical Theory." In Vetterling-Braggin, Elliston and English, pp. 408-416.
———. "On the Future of Love: Rousseau and the Radical Feminists. *The Philosophical Forum* 5:1-2 (1973-74): 185-205. Reprinted in Soble, pp. 369-388; Osborne, pp. 122-128; and Gould and Wartofsky, pp. 185-205.
Reagan, Gerald M. "Further Questions About Androgyny." *Philosophy of Education: Proceedings* 36 (1980): 256-259.
Reeves, Robert B. Jr. "Commentary on Rosner's 'Induced Abortion and Jewish Morality.'" *Values Ethics Health Care* 1 (Spring 1976): 225-226.
Reid, Coletta. "Coming Out." In Jaggar and Struhl, pp. 303-309.
Reuther Radford, Rosemary. "Misogynism and Vaginal Feminism." In Osborne, pp. 62-65.
Rettig, Salomon. "A Note on Censorship and the Changing Ethic of Sex." *Ethics* 78 (January 1968): 151-155.
Rhodes, Rosamond. "Reconsidering Infidelity." Unpublished. Hunter College, CUNY (April 1983).
Rice, Lee C. "Homosexuality and the Social Order." In Soble, pp. 256-280.
Richards, Janet Radcliffe. *The Skeptical Feminist: A Philosophical Enquiry*. Boston, Mass.: Routledge and Kegan Paul, 1980.
Richards, R. C. "LeMoncheck on Sex Objectification." Unpublished. California State Polytechnic. The Society for the Philosophy of Sex and Love. Sacramento, Calif.: American Philosophical Association, March 25, 1982.
Ricoeur, Paul. "Wonder, Eroticism and Enigma." *Cross Currents* 14 (1964): 133-141.
Rosen, Deborah. "Toward and Beyond a New Model of Sexuality." Unpublished. University of New Orleans. The Society for the Philosophy of Sex and Love. American Philosophical Association, December 28, 1982.
Rosenthal, Abigail. "Feminism Without Contradictions." *The Monist* 57 (1973): 28-42.
Ross, Stephanie. "How Words Hurt: Attitudes, Metaphor and Oppression." In Vetterling-Braggin, pp. 194-216.
Rossi, Alice S. "Maternalism, Sexuality and the New Feminism." In *Contemporary Sexual Behavior*. Edited by J. Zubin and J. Money. Baltimore: Johns Hopkins University Press, 1972.
———. "Research and Politics on Sexual Gender." Unpublished. Helen Kenyon Lecture. Vassar College, Poughkeepsie, New York, April 24, 1974.
———. "Sex Equality: The Beginnings of Ideology." *The Humanist* 29 (September-October 1969): 3-6.
Rousseau, Jean-Jacques. *Emile: Or on Education* (1762). New York: Basic Books, 1979.

Rowbotham, Sheila. "Imperialism and Sexuality." In Jaggar and Struhl, pp. 314-317.

Roy, Rustum, and Della Roy. "The Autonomy of Sensuality: The 'Final Solution' of Sex Ethics." Unpublished.

————."Is Monogamy Outdated?" *The Humanist* 30 (April-May 1970): 19-26.

Rubenstein, Richard L. *Morality and Eros.* New York: McGraw-Hill, 1970.

Rubin, Gayle. "Talking Sex: A Conversation on Sexuality and Feminism." *Socialist Review* 11 (July-August 1981): 43-62.

————. "The Traffic In Women: Notes Toward A Political Economy of Sex." In *Toward an Anthropology of Women.* Edited by Rayna Reiter. New York: Monthly Review, 1976.

Ruddick, Sara. "Better Sex." In Baker and Elliston 1st ed., pp. 83-104.

————. "Better Sex." *Philosophy and Sex.* 2nd ed. Edited by Robert Baker and Frederick Elliston. Buffalo, N.Y.: Prometheus Books, 1984, pp. 280-299.

————. "On Sexual Morality." In Rachels, 2nd ed., pp. 16-34.

Rudinow, Joel. "On 'The Slippery Slope.'" *Analysis* 34 (1974): 173-176.

Ruse, Michael. "Are Homosexuals Sick?" In *Concepts of Health and Disease.* Edited by Arthur C. Caplan. New York: Reading Adison-Wesley, 1981, pp. 693-724.

————. Are There Any Gay Genes?" *Journal of Homosexuality* 6 (1981): 361-386.

————. "The Morality of Homosexuality." *Philosophy and Sex.* 2nd ed., edited by Robert Baker and Frederick Elliston. Buffalo, N.Y.: Prometheus Books, 1984, pp. 370-390.

————. *Is Science Sexist? and Other Problems in the Biological Sciences.* Hingham, Mass.: D. Reidal Publishing Co., 1981.

Russell, Bertrand. *Anti-Suffragist Anxieties.* London: People's Suffrage Federation, 1910.

————. "Education Without Sex Taboos." *The New Republic* 52 (November 1927): 346-348.

————. "Liberalism and Women's Suffrage." *Contemporary Review* 94 (July 1908): 11-16.

————. *Marriage and Morals* (1928). New York: Liveright Publishers, 1970. Partially Reprinted in Verene, pp. 306-317.

————. "Marriage and the Population Question." *International Journal of Ethics* 26 (1916): 443-461. Reprinted in *Principles of Social Reconstruction.* By Bertrand Russell. London: Allen and Unwin, 1916, pp. 117-136.

————. "My Own View of Marriage." *The Outlook* 148 (March 1928): 376-377.

————. "Ostrich Code of Marriage." *Forum* 80 (July 1928): 7-10.

————. "Our Sexual Ethics." *The American Mercury* 38 (1936): 36-41.

————. "Sex Education." Chapter 12 of *On Education.* London: Allen and Unwin, 1926.

————. "Shall the Home be Abolished?" *Literary Digest* 8 (November 1931): 25-26.

————. "The Status of Women." *The Journal of the Bertrand Russell Archives* (Summer 1974): 3-12.

————. "When Should Marriage be Dissolved?" *The English Review* 12 (August 1912): 133-141.

Russell, John L. "Contraception and the Natural Law." *Heythrop Journal* (April 1969): 121-134.

Ryskamp, John. "The Women's Movement and the Dialectic of Sex: The Failure of Positive Schism." *The Journal of Thought* 10 (January 1975): 46-57.

Sadler, William A. *Existence and Love.* New York: Charles Scribner's Sons, 1969.

Salm, Luke. "Methodological Issues in the Ethics of Human Sexuality." In Gaffney, pp. 148-161.

Sartre, Jean-Paul. "First Attitude Toward Others: Love, Language, Masochism." In *Being and Nothingness.* Translated by Hazel E. Barnes. New York: Philosophical Library, 1956, pp. 478-491. Reprinted in Verene, pp. 254-271.

Saxonhouse, Arlene W. "The Philosopher and the Female in the Political Thought of Plato." *Political Theory* 4 (May 1976): 195-212.

Schedler, George, and Matthew J. Kelly. "Abortion and Tinkering." *Dialogue* (Canada) 17 (1978): 122-125.

Scheler, Max. *The Nature of Sympathy.* New Haven: Yale University Press, 1944.

Schiltzer, Albert L. "Finality of Marriage." *Proceedings of the Catholic Philosophical Association* 23 (1949): 108-117.

Schmickel, Roy. "Determination of Sex by Amniocentesis for the Purpose of Sex Selection." In *Ethics, Humanism and Medicine.* Edited by Marc D. Basson. New York: Liss, 1980, pp. 95-102.

Schopenhauer, Arthur. "Essay on Women." In *Parega and Paralippomena* (1851). Available in translation. Edited by William Durant. *The Works of Schopenhauer.* New York: Simon and Schuster, 1928. Reprinted in *Selected Essays.* Edited by E. B. Bax. London: George Bell, 1900, pp. 338-346.

———. "The Metaphysics of the Love of the Sexes." In *The Philosophy of Schopenhauer.* Edited by Irwin Edman. New York: Modern Library, 1928.

———. "The Metaphysics of Sexual Love." In *The World as Will and Representation.* Vol. 2. New York: Dover Publications, 1958, pp. 533-540. Reprinted in Verene, pp. 174-185.

———. *Studies in Pessimism.* New York: Macmillan Co., 1908, pp. 15, 113.

Schwarz, Daniel. "Four Letter Words: A Symposium." *The Humanist* 29 (September-October 1969): 7-8.

Scruton, Roger. *Sexual Desire.* London: Weidenfeld & Nicholson, forthcoming.

Sennett, Richard. "Destructive Gemeinschaft." *Partisan Review* 43 (1976): 341-361. Reprinted in Soble, pp. 299-321.

Shafer, Carolyn M., and Marilyn Frye. "Rape and Respect." In Vetterling-Braggin, Elliston and English, pp. 333-346.

Shaffer, Jerome A. "Sexual Desire." *The Journal of Philosophy* 75 (April 1978): 175-189.

Shapiro, Ellen. "The Epistemological Significance of Homosexuality in Plato (*Symposium* and *Phaedrus*)." Unpublished, n.d.

Shaw, B. "Sex Discrimination in Education: Theory and Practice." *The Journal of Philosophy of Education* 13 (1979): 33-40.

Sher, George. "Governmental Funding of Elective Abortions." In *Rights and Responsibilities in Modern Medicine.* By Marc D. Baddon. New York: Liss, 1981, pp. 219-228.

———. "Hare, Abortion and the Golden Rule." *Philosophy and Public Affairs* 6 (Winter 1977): 185-190.

———. "Our Preferences Ourselves." *Philosophy and Public Affairs,* 1982.

———. "Subsidized Abortion: Moral Rights and Moral Compromise." *Philosophy and Public Affairs* 10 (Fall 1981): 361-372.

Sherwin, Susan. "The Concept of a Person in the Context of Abortion." *Bioethics Quarterly* (Summer 1981).

———. "Ethical Problems Associated with Human Reproduction Technology." In *Nonmedical Issues and Contraception.* Edited by E. J. Love. The proceedings of a seminar sponsored by the Canadian Committee for Fertility Research (September 11-12, 1979) pp. 149-168.

———. "The Implications of a Sexist Culture on the Doctor-Patient Relationship." *Atlantis* 4 (Spring 1979): 5-12.

———. "Virtues: A Perspective on the Situation of Women." *Atlantis* 3 (Fall 1977): 84-97.

Shute, Sara. "Sexist Language and Sexism." In Vetterling-Braggin, pp. 23-33.

Simon, Robert. "Preferential Hiring: A Reply to Judith Jarvis Thompson." *Philosophy and Public Affairs* 3 (Spring 1974): 312-320.

Singer, Irving. *The Goals of Human Sexuality.* New York: W. W. Norton and Co., 1973.

———. *The Nature of Love: Plato to Luther.* New York: Random House, 1966.

Singer, June. *Androgyny: Toward a New Theory of Sexuality.* New York: Doubleday, 1977.

Singer, Peter. "Ethics and Sociobiology." *Philosophy and Public Affairs* 1 (Winter 1982): 40-64.

Sircello, Guy. "Beauty and Sex." In *Body, Mind and Method.* Edited by D. F. Gustafson. Dordrecht: Reidel, 1979, pp. 225-240.

Slote, Michael A. "Inapplicable Concepts." *Philosophical Studies* 28 (October 1975): 265-271. Reprinted in Baker and Elliston, 1st. ed., pp. 261-267.

Smith, James Leroy. "The Problem of Abortion and Negative and Positive Duty." *The Journal of Medicine and Philosophy* 3 (September 1978): 245-252.

Smith-Rosenberg, Carol. "The New Women and the New History." *Feminist Studies* 3 (Fall 1975): 185-198.

Soble, Alan. "A Marxist Analysis of Women's Alienation and Male Sexuality." Unpublished. Eastern Marxist Scholar's Conference, New York, N.Y., October 17-19, 1982.

———. "An Introduction to the Philosophy of Sex." In Soble, pp. 1-54.

———. "Beyond the Miserable Vision of 'Vs. Ms.'" In Vetterling-Braggin, pp. 229-248.

———. "Comments on Lemoncheck, Sullivan and Richards." Mimeographed. Moorhead, Minn.: Moorhead State University, 1982.

———. "Marxism and Pornography." Mimeographed. Moorhead State University, 1982.

———. "Masturbation." *Pacific Philosophical Quarterly* 61 (July 1980): 233-244.

———. "Physical Attractiveness and Unfair Discrimination." *Applied Philosophy* 1 (April 1982): 36-64.

Solomon, Robert C. "Emotions and Choice." In Rorty, *Explaining Emotions,* pp. 251-281.

———. *Love: Emotion, Myth and Metaphor.* New York: Doubleday and Co., 1981.

———. "Love and Feminism." *Philosophy and Sex,* 2nd ed. Edited by Robert Baker and Frederick Elliston. Buffalo, N.Y.: Prometheus Books, 1984, pp. 53-70.

———. "Sexual Paradigms." *The Journal of Philosophy* 71 (1974): 336-345. Reprinted in Soble, pp. 89-98.

———. "Sexual Perversion." In *Philosophy and Sex.* Edited by Robert Baker and Frederick Elliston. 1st ed., pp. 268-287.

Solomon, Robert C., and Judith Rose Sanders. "Sexual Identity." In Reich, pp. 1589-1596.

Solovyev, Vladimir Sergeyevich. *The Meaning of Love.* Trans. Jane Marshall. London: Geoffrey Bles, 1946. Partially reprinted in Verene, pp. 240-253.

Spender, Dale. *Man-Made Language.* Boston, Mass.: Routledge and Kegan Paul, 1980.

Spurrier, William A. *Natural Law and the Ethics of Love.* Philadelphia: Westminster Press, 1974.

Squadrito, Kathy. "Locke on the Equality of the Sexes." *The Journal of Social Philosophy* 10 (January 1979): 6-11.

Stack, George J. "Sexuality and Bodily Subjectivity." *Dialogos* 15 (April 1980): 139-153.

Stafford, Martin J. "On Distinguishing Between Love and Lust." *The Journal of Value Inquiry* 11 (Winter 1977): 292-303.

Stegeman, Beatrice. "Are Feminist Ideas a Moral Right or a Legal Right?" Unpublished. Collinsville, Ill.: Society for Women in Philosophy, 1975.

————. "But Are There Any Women?" Unpublished. Collinsville, Ill.: Society for Women in Philosophy, 1976.

————. "Contrasting Philosophies of Monasticism in the Modern Ceptic Church." *Bulletin de la Societe D'Archeology Copte,* XX-1969-1970 (1971): 159-165.

————. "The Divorce Dilemma: The New Woman as a Symbol of Contrasting Value Theories in Several Contemporary African Novels." *Critique* XV-3 (Spring 1974): 81-94.

————. "The Preference Problem." Unpublished. Collinsville, Ill.: Society for Women in Philosophy, 1973.

————. "From Theoretical Physics to Practical Politics, Women and Science." Bloomington, Ind.: National Women's Studies Association (Spring 1980).

————. "Several Philosophies on Social Service in the Contemporary Coptic Church." *Bulletin de la Societe D'Archeology Copte,* XXIII-1976-78 (1981): 33-42.

Stenner, A. J. "A Note on the Logical Truth and Non-Sexist Semantics." In Vetterling-Braggin, pp. 289-306.

Sterba, James P. "Abortion, Distant Peoples, and Future Generations." *The Journal of Philosophy* 77 (July 1980): 424-439.

Stern, Bernhard J. "Engels on the Family." In *A Centenary of Marxism.* Edited by Samuel Bernstein. New York: Science and Society, 1948.

Sullivan, John P. "Women as Sex Objects: Some Reflections." Unpublished. University of California at Santa Barbara. The Society for the Philosophy of Sex and Love. Sacramento, Calif.: American Philosophical Association, March 25, 1982.

Sumberg, Theodore A. "Privacy, Freedom, and Obscenity: Stanley vs. Georgia. *The Journal of Critical Analysis* 3 (July 1971): 84-96.

Sumner, L. W. *Abortion and Moral Theory.* Princeton, N.J.: Princeton University Press, 1981.

————. "Toward a Credible View of Abortion." *The Canadian Journal of Philosophy* 4 (September 1974): 163-181.

Suppe, Fred. "Curing Homosexuality." *Philosophy and Sex,* second edition, eds. Robert Baker and Frederick Elliston. Buffalo, N.Y.: Prometheus Books, 1984, pp. 391-420.

Szasz, Thomas S. "The Ethics of Abortion." *The Humanist* 26 (October 1966): 147-148.

————. "Legal and Moral Aspects of Homosexuality." In *Sexual Inversion.* Edited by J. Marmor. New York: Basic Books, 1965, pp. 124-139.

Taylor, Gabrielle. "Love." *Proceedings of the Aristotelian Society.* Supplementary

Volume (1976-77): 147-164. Reprinted in *Philosophy as It Is*. Edited by T. Honderich and M. Burnyeat. New York: Penguin Books, 1979, 161-182.

Taylor, Kriste. "Reference and Truth: The Case of Sexist and Racist Utterances." In Vetterling-Braggin, pp. 307-318.

Taylor, Richard. "The Ethics of Having Love Affairs." *Philosophy and Sex*, 2nd ed. Edited by Robert Baker and Frederick Elliston. Buffalo, N.Y.: Prometheus Books, 1984, pp. 71-92.

———. *Having Love Affairs*. Buffalo, N.Y.: Prometheus Books, 1982.

———. "Love and Friendship." In *Good and Evil: A New Direction*. New York: Macmillan, 1975.

———. "Love and Separation." In *With Heart and Mind*. New York: St. Martins Press, 1973.

Taylor, Roger L. "Sexual Experiences." *Proceedings of the Aristotelian Society* 68 (1968): 87-104. Reprinted in Soble, pp. 59-75.

Teichman, Jenny. "Intention and Sex." In *Intention and Intentionality*. Edited by Jenny Teichman and Cora Diamond. Ithaca, N.Y.: Cornell University Press, 1979, pp. 147-161.

Teo, Wesley, D. H. "Abortion: The Husband's Constitutional Rights." *Ethics* 85 (July 1975): 337-342.

Thalberg, Irving. "Reverse Discrimination and the Future." *The Philosophical Forum* 5 (1973-74): 294-308. Reprinted in English, pp. 161-169.

Thielicke, Helmut. *The Ethics of Sex*. Translated by John Doberstein. New York: Harper & Row, 1964.

Thomas, Laurence. "Sexism and Racism: Some Conceptual Differences." *Ethics* 90 (Spring 1980): 239-250. Reprinted in Vetterling-Braggin, pp. 256-270.

Thompson, Judith Jarvis. "A Defense of Abortion." *Philosophy and Public Affairs* 1 (Fall 1971): 47-66. Reprinted in Arthur, pp. 184-195; and Baker and Elliston 1st ed., pp. 305-323.

———. "A Defense of Abortion." *Philosophy and Sex*, 2nd ed. Edited by Robert Baker and Frederick Elliston. Buffalo, N.Y.: Prometheus Books, 1984, pp. 201-217.

———. "Preferential Hiring." *Philosophy and Public Affairs* 2 (1973): 364-384. Reprinted in Bishop and Weinzweig, pp. 227-236.

———. "Rights and Deaths." *Philosophy and Public Affairs* 2 (1973): 146-159.

Thompson, William. *Appeal of One Half of the Human Race, Women, Against the Pretensions of the Other Half, Men, to Retain Them in Political and Thence in Civil and Domestic Slavery; In Reply to a Paragraph of Mr. (James) Mill's Celebrated "Article on Government."* London, 1825.

Thorne, Barrie. "The Feminist Rethinking of the Family." Unpublished. Conference on Philosophy, Children and the Family. Michigan State University, March 1980.

Timmons, Mark. "Treblicot on Androgynism." *The Journal of Social Philosophy* 10 (May 1979): 1-4.

Tong, Rosemarie. "Feminism, Pornography and Censorship." *Social Theory and Practice* 8 (Spring 1982): 1-18.

———. *Women, Sex and the Law*. Totowa, N.J.: Littlefield Adams, 1983.

Tooley, Michael. "Abortion and Infanticide." *Philosophy and Public Affairs* 2 (Fall 1972): 37-65. Reprinted in Arthur, pp. 214-226.

———. "Infanticide: A Philosophical Perspective." In Reich, pp. 742-750.

Toon, Mark. *The Philosophy of Sex According to St. Thomas Aquinas*. Catholic

University of America Philosophical Studies No. 156. Washington, D.C.: Catholic University of American Press, 1954.

Tormey, Judith. "Exploitation, Oppression and Self-Sacrifice." *The Philosophical Forum* 5 (1973): 206-221, and Gould and Wartofsky, pp. 206-221.

Trebilcot, Joyce. "Taking Responsibility for Sexuality." *Philosophy and Sex.* 2nd. ed. Edited by Robert Baker and Frederick Elliston, Buffalo, N.Y.: Prometheus Books, 1984, pp. 421-430.

———. "Conceiving Women: Notes on the Logic of Feminism." In *Sinister Wisdom* XI (Fall 1979): 43-50.

———. "Sex Roles: The Argument From Nature." *Ethics* 85 (1975): 249-255. Reprinted in English, pp. 121-129.

———. "Two Forms of Androgynism." *The Journal of Social Philosophy* 8 (January 1977): 4-8. Reprinted in Vetterling-Braggin, Elliston and English, pp. 70-100.

Valian, Virginia. "Linguistics and Feminism." In Vetterling-Braggin, Elliston and English, pp. 154-170; and Vetterling-Braggin, pp. 68-80.

Van de Vate, Dwight. *Romantic Love: A Philosophical Inquiry.* University Park, Pa.: Penn State Press, 1981.

Vannoy, Russell. *Sex Without Love: A Philosophical Exploration.* Buffalo, N.Y.: Prometheus Books, 1980.

Veatch, Robert M. *Case Studies in Medical Ethics.* Cambridge,Mass.: Harvard University Press, 1979, chapters 7, 8.

Verene, D. P. "Sexual Love and Moral Experience." In Baker and Elliston, 1st ed. pp. 105-115.

Vetterling-Braggin, Mary. "Some Common Sense Notes on Preferential Hiring." *The Philosophical Forum* 5 (1973-74): 320-324.

Vitek, William. "Bibliography." *Philosophy and Sex,* 2nd ed. Edited by Robert Baker and Frederick Elliston. Buffalo, N.Y.: Prometheus Books, 1984, pp. 471-523.

Vlastos, Gregory. "The Individual as an Object of Love in Plato." *Platonic Studies* 3 (1973): 22-28.

———. *The Encyclical "Humanae Vitae."* Chicago: Franciscan Herald Press, 1969.

———. *Humanae Vitae: A Sign of Contradiction.* Chicago: Franciscan Herald Press, 1969.

Wade, Francis C. "Potentiality in the Abortion Discussion." *The Review of Metaphysics* 29 (December 1975): 239-255.

Warren, Mary Anne. "Do Potential People Have Moral Rights?" *The Canadian Journal of Philosophy* 7 (June 1977): 275-289.

———. "On the Moral and Legal Status of Abortion." *The Monist* 51 (January 1973): 43-61. Reprinted in Bishop and Weinzweig, pp. 216-226.

———. "Secondary Sexism and Quota Hiring." *Philosophy and Public Affairs* 6 (Spring 1977): 240-261. Reprinted in Bishop and Weinzweig, pp. 237-246.

Warren, Mary Ann, Daniel Maguire, and Carol Levine. "Can the Fetus be an Organ Farm?" *Hastings Center Report* 8 (October 1978): 23-25.

Wasserstrom, Richard A. "Is Adultery Immoral?" In Wasserstrom, pp. 288-300. Reprinted in Arthur, pp. 108-120, 1st ed; and Baker and Elliston, 1st ed., pp. 207-221.

———. "Is Adultery Immoral?" *Philosophy and Sex,* 2nd ed. Edited by Robert Baker and Frederick Elliston. Buffalo, N.Y.: Prometheus Books, 1984, pp. 93-106.

————. "Issues of Privacy and Confidentiality in Sex Therapy and Sex Research." In *Ethical Issues in Sex Therapy and Research.* Vol. 2. Edited by Masters, Johnson, Kolodny, and Weems. Boston, Mass.: Little, Brown and Co., 1980, 42-60.

————. "Preferential Treatment." In Bishop and Weinzweig, pp. 247-250.

————. "Racism and Sexism." *University of California Law Review.* Reprinted in Bishop and Weinzweig, pp. 5-20 and (in an expanded version) in *Philosophy and Social Issues: Five Studies.* Notre Dame, Ind.: University of Notre Dame Press, 1980, pp. 11-50.

————. "The University and the Case for Preferential Treatment." *The American Philosophical Quarterly* 13 (1976); 165-170.

Watt, E. D. "Professor Cohen's Encyclical." *Ethics* 80 (1971): 218-221.

Wender, Dorothea, "Olato: Misogynist, Paedophile and Feminist." *Arethusa* 6 (1973):1.

Werner, Richard. "Abortion: The Moral Status of the Unborn." *Social Theory and Practice* 3 (Fall 1974): 201-222.

————. "Hare on Abortion." *Analysis* 36 (June 1976): 177-181.

Wertheimer, Roger. "Errata: A Reply to Abbott's 'Philosophers and the Abortion Question.'" *Political Theory* 6 (August 1978): 337-344.

————. "Philosophy on Humanity." In *Abortion: New Directions For Policy Studies.* Edited by Edward Manier. Notre Dame, Ind.: Notre Dame University Press, pp. 117-158.

————. "Understanding the Abortion Argument." *Philosophy and Public Affairs* 1 (Fall 1971): 67-95.

Westermarck, Edward. *Three Essays on Sex and Marriage.* London: Macmillan and Co., 1934.

Westley, Richard J. "Justifying Infidelity." *Listening* 10 (Winter 1975): 36-44.

————. "Some Reflections on Birth Control." *Listening* 12 (Spring 1977): 43-61.

————. "The Maternal Instinct." *The Philosophical Forum* 6 (Winter-Spring, 1974-75): 265-272.

Whitbeck, Carolyn. "Theories of Sex Differences." *The Philosophical Forum* 5 (1973): 54-80.

White, Stephen W. "Beautiful Losers: An Analysis of Radical Feminist Egalitarianism." *The Journal of Value Inquiry* 111 (Winter 1977): 264-283.

Whitehurst, Robert N. "Open Marriage: Problems and Prospects." Unpublished. n.d.

————. "Sex - In And Out of Marriage." *The Humanist* 30 (January-February 1970): 27-28.

Whiteley, C. H. "Love, Hate and Emotion." *Philosophy* 54 (April 1979): 235.

Wicclair, Mark R. "Is Prostitution Morally Wrong?" *Philosophical Reserach Archives* 7 (1981): 1429.

————. "The Abortion Controversy and the Claim that This Body is Mine." *Social Theory and Practice* 7:3 (Fall 1981): 337-346.

Wikler, Daniel I. "Ought We Try to Save Aborted Fetuses?" *Ethics* 90 (October 1979): 58-65.

Wilder, Hugh T. "The Language of Sex and the Sex Of Language." In Soble, pp. 99-109.

————. "Starter Kit in the Philosophy of love and Sexuality." Hyde Part, N.Y.: Helvetia Press, 1981.

————. "Philosophy of Love and Sexuality: Course Syllabi." Hyde Park, N.Y.: Helvetia Press, 1981.

Wilkes, Kathleen V. "Women in 'Philosophy.'" *Philosophy 54 (April 1979): 236-238.*

Willard, Duane. "Aesthetic Discrimination Against Persons." *Dialogue* (Canada) 16 (1977): 676-692.

Williford, Mariam. "Bentham on the Rights of Women." *The Journal of the History of ideas* 36 (January-March 1975): 167-176.

Williston, Frank A. "A Philosophic Analysis of Pornography." *The Journal of Thought* 7 (April 1972): 95-105.

Wilson, Edward O. *On Human Nature.* Cambridge, Mass.: Harvard University Press, 1978, chapter 6.

Wilson, John. *Logic and Sexual Morality.* Baltimore: Penguin Books, 1965.

———. *Love, Sex and Feminism: A Philosophical Essay.* New York: Praeger, 1980.

Wilson, W. Cody. "Facts Versus Fears: Why Should We Worry About Pornography?" *The Annals of the American Academy of Political and Social Science* 397 (September 1971): 105-117.

Wolff, Robert Paul. "There's Nobody Here But Us Persons." *The Philosophical Forum* 5 (1973): 128-144.

Wolgast, Elizabeth H. *Equality and the Rights of Women.* Ithaca, N.Y.: Cornell University Press, 1982.

Wollstonecraft, Mary. *A Vindication of the Rights of Women* (1792). New York: W. W. Norton, 1967.

The Woman Question: Selections from the Writings of Karl Marx, Friedrich Engels, V. I. Lenin, and Joseph Stalin. New York: International Publishing, 1951.

Women Staff. "Sex in a Capitalist Society." *Women: A Journal of Liberation* 3 Inside Cover. Reprinted in Jaggar and Struhl, pp. 310-313.

"Women's Liberation: Ethical, Social and Political Issues." *The Monist* 57 (January 1973).

Wood, Frederick C. *Sex and the New Morality.* New York: Association Press, 1968.

Wringe, Colin. *Children's Rights: A Philosophic Study.* Boston, Mass.: Routledge and Kegan Paul, 1981.

Young, Iris Marion. "Beyond the Unhappy Marriage: A Critique of the Dual Systems Theory." In Sargent, pp. 43-70.

———. "The End of Marriage." Mimeographed. Rensselaer Polytechnic Institute, Troy, N.Y., 1978.

———. "The Exclusion of Women from Sport: Conceptual and Existential Dimensions." *Philosophy in Context* 9 (Fall 1979): 44-53.

———. "Feminism and Ecology." *Environmental Ethics,* 1983.

———. "Gender Differentiation and Male Domination: An Examination of Chodrow, Harstock and Harding." In *Mothering and Feminist Theorizings.* Edited by Treblicot (forthcoming).

———. "Rights to Intimacy in a Complex Society." *Journal of Social Philosophy,* 1982.

———. "Throwing Like a Girl: A Phenomenology of Feminine Body Component Motility and Spatiality." *Human Studies* 3 (April 1980): 137-156.

———. "Women and Philosophy: New Anthologies." *Teaching Philosophy* 2 (1979): 172-182.

Yudkin, Marcia. "Difference Be Damned." *Philosophy* 55 (July 1980): 392-395.

———. "Transsexualism and Women: A Critical Perspective." *Feminist Studies* 4 (October 1978): 97-106.

Zaitchik, Alan. "Viability and the Morality of Abortion." *Philosophy and Public Affairs* 10 (Winter 1981): 18-26.

Zartesky, Eli. "Capitalism, the Family and Personal Life." In Jaggar and Struhl, pp. 263-270.

Zita, Jacquelyn N. "Glass Closet Liberalism: Liberal Rights and Wrongs (Commentary on Richard Mohr)." Unpublished. The Society for the Philosophy of Sex and Love. Philadelphia, Pa.: American Philosophical Association, December 28, 1981.

PART THREE: OTHER RELEVANT MATERIALS

A. Anthologies

Adams, Elise, and Mary Lou Briscoe, eds. *Up Against the Wall Mother: On Women's Liberation.* Beverly Hills, Calif.: Glencoe Press, 1970.

Aiken, William, and Hugh LaFollette, eds. *Whose Child? Children's Rights, Parental Authority, and State Power.* Totowa, N.J.: Littlefield Adams, 1980.

Ascher, Carol, ed. *Simone De Beauvoir: A Life of Freedom.* Boston: Beacon Press, 1981.

Audre, Lorde, ed. *Uses of the Erotic: The Erotic as Power.* New York: Out and Out Books, 1982.

Baker, Jean, ed. *Psychoanalysis and Women.* Baltimore: Penguin, 1973.

Bardwick, Judith M. et al, eds. *Feminine Personality and Conflict.* Belmont, Calif.: Wadsworth Publishing, 1970.

———. eds. *Readings on the Psychology of Women.* New York: Harper & Row, 1972.

Bazin, Nancy. "The Androgynous Vision." *Women's Studies* 2 (1974): 185-215.

Bell, Robert R., ed. *Studies in Marriage and the Family.* New York: Thomas Y. Crowell Co., 1973.

Bell, Robert R., and Michael Gordon, eds. *The Social Dimension of Human Sexuality.* Boston: Little, Brown and Co., 1972.

Berge, Andre, et al. *Body and Spirit: Essays in Sexuality.* Translated by Donald Atteater, New York: Longmans, 1939.

Bieber, Irving et al. eds. *Homosexuality.* New York: Basic Books, 1962.

Bohanin, Paul, ed. *Divorce and After.* Garden City, N.Y.: Anchor Books, 1970.

Brecher, Edward, and Ruth Brecher, eds. *An Analysis of Human Sexual Response.* London: Panther Books, 1968.

Broderick, C. B., and J. Bernard, eds. *The Individual, Sex and Society.* Baltimore: Johns Hopkins Press, 1969.

Bucher, Glen R., ed. *Straight/White/Male.* Philadelphia: Fortress Press, 1976.

Bunch, Charlotte, ed. *Lesbians and the Women's Movement.* Oakland, Calif.: Diana Press, 1975.

Burg, B. R., *Sodomy and the Perception of Evil: English Sea Rovers in the Seventeenth-Century Caribbean.* N.Y.: New York University Press, 1983.

Buttruff, D., ed. *Women's Language and Style.* Akron, Ohio: University of Akron Press, 1979.

Cott, Nancy F., ed. *The Roots of Bitterness.* New York: E. P. Dutton, 1972.

Curtin, Mary Ellen, ed. *Symposium on Love.* New York: Behavioral Publications, 1973.

Davidson, Kenneth M. et al., eds. *Sex-Based Discrimination.* St. Paul, Minn.: West Publishing Co., 1974.

DeMartino, Manfred, ed. *Human Erotic Practices.* New York: Human Sciences Press, 1979.

Densmore, Dana, ed. *Sex Roles and Female Oppression—A Collection of Articles,* Boston: New England Free Press.

Dubois, B. L., and I. Crouch, eds. *The Sociology of Languages of American Women.* San Antonio, Texas: Trinity University Press, 1967.

Edwards, Lee R., ed. Mary Heath, and Lisa Baskin, eds. *Women: An Issue.* Boston: Little, Brown and Co., 1972.

Edwards, John N. et al. eds. *Sex and Society.* Chicago: Markham Publishing Co., 1972.

Eisenstein, Zillah, ed. *Capitalist Patriarchy and the Case for Socialist Feminism.* New York: Monthly Review Press, 1979.

Ellis, Albert, and Albert Abarbanel, eds. *The Encyclopedia of Sexual Behavior.* London: W. Heinemann Medical Books, 1961.

Farber, Seymour, and Roger H. L. Wilson, eds. *The Potential of Women.* New York: McGraw-Hill, 1963.

Fenstermaker Berk, Sarah, ed. *Women and Household Labor.* Beverly Hills, Calif.: Sage, 1980.

Filsinger, Erik E., and Robert A. Lewis, eds. *Assessing Marriage: New Behavioral Approaches.* Beverly Hills, Calif.: Sage, 1981.

Freeman, Jo, ed. *Women: A Feminist Perspective.* Palo Alto, Calif.: Mayfield Publishing Co., 1975.

Freemantle, Anne, ed. *The Papal Encyclicals.* New York: Mentor, 1956.

Fuller, Arthur B., ed. *Woman in the Nineteenth Century, and Kindred Papers Relating to the Sphere, Condition and Duties of Woman* (1859, Tribune Association). Roberts Brothers, 1874.

Furness, C.F., ed. *The Genteel Female: An Anthology.* New York: Knopf, 1931.

Gager, Nancy, ed. *Women's Rights Almanac.* New York: Harper & Row, 1975.

Gagnon, John H., and William Simons, eds. *Sexual Deviance.* New York: Harper & Row, 1967.

Garskof, Michele, ed. *Roles Women Play.* Belmont, Calif.: Brooks/Cole Publishing Co., 1971.

Gebhard, P. H. et al., eds. *Sex Offenders: An Analysis of Types.* New York: Harper & Row, 1965.

Glazer-Malbin, Nona, and Helen Youngelson Waehrer, eds. *Woman in a Man-Made World.* Chicago: Rand McNally, 1972.

Gordon, Sol, and Roger Libby, eds. *Sexuality Today and Tomorrow: Contemporary Issues in Human Sexuality.* Duxbury Press: North Scituate, Mass., 1976.

Gornick, Vivian, and Barbara K. Moran, eds. *Women in Sexist Society.* New York: Signet, 1972.

Gould, Carol, ed. *Beyond Domination: New Perspectives on Women and Philosophy.* Totowa, N.J.: Littlefield Adams, 1983.

Haire, Norman, ed. *Encyclopedia of Sexual Knowledge.* 2nd ed. London: Encyclopedia Press, 1965.

Hall, Robert., ed. *Abortion in a Changing World.* New York: Columbia University Press, 1970.

Hammer, Signe, ed. *Women, Body and Culture.* New York: Harper & Row, 1975.

Hart, Harold C., ed. *Marriage: For and Against.* New York: Hart Publishing

Co., 1972.
———. ed. *Sexual Latitude: For and Against.* New York: Hart Publishing Co., 1971.
Hartman, Mary, and Lois W. Banner, eds. *Clio's Consciousness Raised: New Perspectives on the History of Women.* New York: Harper & Row, 1974.
Hauser, Philip M. et al., eds. *The Population Dilemma.* Englewood Cliffs, N.J.: Prentice-Hall, 1963.
Heer, David M. et al. *Readings on Population.* Englewood Cliffs, N.J.: Prentice-Hall, 1968.
Heron, Alastair, ed. *Towards a Quaker View of Sex.* London: Friends Home Service Committee, 1964.
Hess, Thomas B., and E. Barker, eds. *Art and Sexual Politics.* New York: Macmillan, 1973.
Huber, J., ed. *Changing Women in a Changing Society.* Chicago: University of Chicago Press, 1973.
Hughes, Douglas, ed. *Perspectives on Pornography.* New York: St. Martin's Press, 1970.
Irani, I.D., and Gerald Meyers, eds. *Emotion.* Haven Press, 1983.
Jerness, Linda, ed. *Feminism and Socialism.* New York: Pathfinder Press, 1972.
Kelly, Alison, ed. *The Missing Half: Girls and Science Education.* Manchester: Manchester University Press, 1981.
Kinsey, Alfred et al., eds. *Sexual Behavior in the Human Female.* New York· Pocket Books, 1965.
Kirkendall, Lester, and R. Whitehurst, eds. *The New Sexual Revolution.* New York: Scribner's, 1971.
Koedt, Anne, Ellen Levine, and Anita Rapone, eds. *Radical Feminism.* Chicago: Quadrangle/New York Times Book Co., 1973.
Kraditor, Aileen, ed. *Up from the Pedestal: Landmark Writings in the American Woman's Struggle for Equality.* Chicago: Quadrangle, 1968.
Kramerae, Cheris, ed. "The Voices and Words of Women and Men." *Women's Studies International Quarterly* 3 New York: Pergamon Press, forthcoming.
Krich, A. M., ed. *The Homosexuals.* New York: Citadel Press, 1954.
———. ed. *The Sexual Revolution.* New York: Dell, 1964.
Lederer, Laura, ed., *Take Back the Night.* New York: Morrow, 1980.
Lerner, Gerda, ed. *The Female Experience: An American Documentary.* Indianapolis: Bobbs-Merrill Co., 1977.
———. *Lesbianism and the Women's Movement.* Oakland, Calif.: Diana Press, 1975.
Libby, Roger W., and Robert N. Whitehurst, eds. *Renovating Marriage.* Danville, Calif.: Consensus Publishers, 1973.
Lifton, Robert Jay, ed. *The Woman in America.* Boston: Beacon Press, 1964.
Livingood, J. M., ed. *National Institute of Mental Health Task Force on Homosexuality: Final Report and Background Papers.* Washington, D.C.: U.S. Government Printing Office, 1972.
Lovenduski, Joni, and Jill Hills, eds. *The Politics of the Second Electorate: Women and Public Participation.* London: Routledge and Kegan Paul, 1981.
Maccoby, Eleanor, and Carol Jacklin, eds. *The Psychology of Sex Differences.* Stanford, Calif.: Stanford University Press, 1974.
MacKinnon, D. M. et al, eds. *God, Sex and War.* Philadelphia: Westminster Press, 1965.
Manier, Edward, et al., eds. *Abortion: New Directions for Policy Studies.* Notre Dame, Ind.: Notre Dame University Press, 1978.

Marcus, Irwin, and John Francis, eds. *Masturbation: From Infancy to Senescence.* New York: International Universities Press, 1975.

Marks, Elaine, and Isabelle de Courtivron, eds. *New French Feminism: An Anthology.* Amherst, Mass.: University of Amherst Press, 1980.

Marmor, Judd, ed. *Homosexual Behavior: A Modern Appraisal.* New York: Basic Books, 1980.

———. ed. *Sexual Inversion: The Multiple Roots of Homosexuality.* New York: Basic Books, 1965.

Masters, William H., Virginia E. Johnson, and Robert C. Kolodny, eds. *Ethical Issues in Sex Therapy and Research.* Boston: Little, Brown and Co., 1977.

McCaffery, Joseph, ed. *The Homosexual Dialectic.* Englewood Cliffs, N.J.: Prentice-Hall, 1972.

McDermott, John F., ed. *The Sex Problem in Modern Society: An Anthology.* New York: Modern Library, 1931.

Morgan, Robin, ed. *Sisterhood is Powerful.* New York: Vintage, 1970.

Morrison, Eleanor S., and Vera Borosage, eds. *Human Sexuality: Contemporary Perspectives.* 2nd ed. Palo Alto, Calif.: Mayfield Publishing Co., 1977.

Mulvihill, Donald J. et al., eds. *Crimes of Violence: A Staff Report to the National Commission on the Causes and Prevention of Violence.* Washington, D.C.: U.S. Government Printing Office, 1969.

Neubeck, Gerhard, ed. *Extra-Marital Relations.* Englewood Cliffs, N.J.: Prentice-Hall, 1969.

Nilsen, Aileen Pace et al, eas. *Sexism and Language.* Urbana, Ill.: National Council of Teachers of English, 1977.

Noonan, John T., ed. *The Morality of Abortion: Legal and Historical Perspectives.* Cambridge, Mass.: Harvard University Press, 1970.

Novak, Michael, ed. *The Experience of Marriage.* New York: Macmillan and Co., 1964.

O'Faolain, Julia, and Laura Martinez, eds. *Not in God's Image: Women in History from the Greeks to the Victorians.* New York: Harper & Row, 1973.

O'Neill, Wiliam L., ed. *The American Sexual Dilemma.* New York: Holt, Rinehart and Winston, Inc., 1972.

Ortner, Sherry B., and Harriet Whitehead, eds. *Sexual Meanings: The Cultural Construction of Gender and Sexuality.* New York: Cambridge University Press, 1980.

Otto, Herbert A., ed. *Love Today: A New Exploration.* New York: Dell, 1972.

Patai, Raphael, ed. *Women in the Modern World.* New York: Free Press, 1967.

Peck, Ellen, and Judith Senderowitz, eds. *Pronatalism: The Myth of Mom and Apple Pie.* New York: Thomas Y. Crowell Co., 1974.

Peck, Joseph, and Jack Sawyer, eds. *Men and Masculinity.* Englewood Cliffs, N.J.: Prentice-Hall, 1974.

Plaskow, Judith, and Joan Arnold Romero, eds. *Women and Religion.* Missoula, Mont.: The Scholar's Press, 1974.

Plummer, K., ed. *The Making of the Modern Homosexual.* London: Hutchinson Publishing Group, 1981.

Reiter, Rayna, ed. *Toward an Anthropology of Women.* New York: Monthly Review, 1976.

Reuther, Rosemary Radford, ed. *Religion and Sexism.* New York: Simon and Schuster, 1974.

Robinson, William J. et al., eds. *Sex Morality: Past, Present, and Future.* New

York: Critic Guide, 1912.

Rosaldo, Michelle Zimbalest, and Louise Lamphere, eds. *Women, Culture and Society*. Stanford, Calif.: Stanford University Press, 1974.

Ross, Susan Deller et al., eds. *Sex Discrimination and the Law: Causes and Remedies*. New York: Little, Brown and Co., 1974.

Rothman, David et al., eds. *Birth Control and Morality in Nineteenth-Century America*. New York: Arno Press, 1972.

Ruitenbeek, Hendrik M., ed. *Sexuality and Identity*. New York: Delta, 1970.

Safilios-Rothschild, Constantine, ed. *Toward a Sociology of Women*. Lexington, Mass.: Xerox College Publishing, 1972.

Sagarin, Edward, and E. J. Donal, eds. *Problems of Sex Behavior*. New York: Crowell, 1968.

Salper, Roberta, ed. *Female Liberation*. New York: Knopf, 1972.

Sargent, Alice, ed. *Beyond Sex Roles*. New York: West Publishing Co., 1977.

Schur, Edwin M., ed. *The Family and the Sexual Revolution*. Bloomington, Ind.: Indiana University Press, 1964.

Schwartz, Gary et al., eds. *Love and Commitment*. Beverly Hills, Calif.: Sage, 1980.

Shepard, Don, ed. *Women in History*. Los Angeles, Calif.: Manland Publishing Co., 1973.

Shores, David L., and Carole P. Hines, eds. *Papers in Language Variation*. Birmingham, Ala.: University of Alabama Press, 1977.

Smith, James R., and Lyn G. Smith, eds. *Beyond Monogamy: Recent Studies of Alternatives in Marriage*. Baltimore: Johns Hopkins Press, 1974.

Stacey, Judith, Susan Bereaud, and Joan Daniels, eds. *And Jill Came Tumbling After: Sexism in American Education*. New York: Dell, 1974.

Stuart, M., and W. Liu, eds. *The Emerging Woman*. Boston: Little, Brown and Co., 1970.

Thorne, Barrie, and Nancy Henley, eds. *Language and Sex: Difference and Dominance*. Rowley, Mass.: Newbury House, 1975.

Welter, Barbara, ed. *The Woman Question in American History*. Hinsdale, Ill.: Dryden Press, 1973.

Wilson, Cassandra, and Noreen Connell, eds. *Rape: The First Sourcebook for Women*. New York: New American Library, 1974.

Wortes, Helen, and Clara Rabinowitz, eds. *The Woman's Movement*. New York: Halsted Press, 1972.

Wynn, John C., ed. *Sexual Ethics and Christian Responsibility: Some Divergent Views*. New York: Association Press, 1970.

Zubin, J., and J. Money, eds. *Contemporary Sexual Behavior: Critical Issues in the 1970's*. Baltimore: Johns Hopkins Press, 1973.

B. Books and Articles

Adams, Milfred. *The Right to Be People*. New York: Lippincott, 1967.

Alcott, William A. *The Young Woman's Guide to Excellence*. Boston: George W Light, 1840.

Alexander, William. *The History of Women from the Earliest Antiquity to the Present Times*. 3rd. ed. London: 1782.

Altman, D. *Homosexual Oppression and Liberation.* London: Allen Lane, 1971.

Archbishop of Canterbury (Fisher). *The Church and Marriage.* London: Church Information Board, 1954.

Astell, Mary. *An Essay in Defense of the Female Sex (*London, 1697). New York: Sourcebook Press, 1970.

———. *Reflections on Marriage (*London, 1706). New York: Sourcebook Press, 1970.

———. *A Serious Proposal to the Ladies, for the Advancement of Their True and Greatest Interest* (London, 1694). New York: Sourcebook Press, 1970.

Atkinson, Grace Ti. *Amazon Odyssey.* New York: Link Books, 1974.

———. *Sexual Relation in Christian Thought.* New York: Harper and Brothers, 1959.

Barker-Benfield, G. J. *The Horrors of the Half-Known Life. Male Attitudes Toward Women and Sexuality in Nineteenth-Century America.* New York: Harper & Row, 1976.

Barnhart, Joseph E., and Mary Anne Barnhart. "St. Paul and Divorce." *Journal of Divorce* 1 (Winter 1977): 141-151.

———. "The Creation of New Desires." In *The New Birth: A Naturalistic View of Religious Conversion.* Macon, Georgia: Mercer University Press, 1981. pp. 121-143.

Baron, Naomi. "A Reanalysis of English Grammatical Gender." *Lingua* 27 (August 1971): 113-140.

Barrett, Michele. *Women's Oppression Today: Problems in Marxist Feminist Analysis.* New York: Schocken Books, 1980.

Barthes, Roland. *A Lover's Discourse.* Translated by Richard Howard. New York: Hill and Wang, 1979.

Bartling, Walter J. "Sexuality, Marriage and Divorce in 1 Corinthians 6: 2-7: 16. A Practical Exercise in Hermeneutics." *Concordia Theological Monthly* 39 (1968).

Beard, Mary. *Woman as Force in History.* New York: Collier Books, 1971.

Bebel, August. *Woman and Socialism* (1885). Translated by Meta L. Stern. New York: Socialist Literature Co., 1910. Translated by H. B. Adams Walther. New York: AMS Press, 1976.

Belok, M. V. "A Forgotten Minority." *The Journal of Thought* 4 (1969): 273-277.

Bem, Sandra, and D. J. Bem. "Training the Woman to Know Her Place." In *Beliefs, Attitudes and Human Affairs.* Edited by D. J. Bem. Belmont, Calif.: Brooks/ Cole, 1970.

Bensen, Donna. *Sexual Harassment: A Hidden Issue.* Project on the Status of Women, Association of American Colleges, 1977.

Betheke Elshtain, Jean. *Public Man, Private Woman: Woman in Social and Political Thought.* Princeton, N.J.: Princeton University Press, 1981.

Beyle, Marie-Henri [Stendhal]. *Love.* Translated by Gilbert and Suzanne Sale. Harmondsworth, England: Penguin Books, 1975.

Blanshard, Paul. "Christianity and Sex." *The Humanist* 34 (1974): 27-33.

Blanshard, Paul, and Edd Doerr. "Is Abortion Murder?" *The Humanist* 32 (1972): 8-9.

Bodine, A. "Androcentrism in Perspective Grammar: Singular 'They', Sex-Indefinite 'He', and 'He or She.'" *Language in Society* 4 (1975): 129-146.

Bosmajian, Haig A. "The Language of Sexism." *ETC.* 29 (September 1972): 305-313.

British Council of Churches. *Sex and Morality* (A Report to the British Council of Churches). Philadelphia, Pa.: Fortress Press, 1966.

Brownmiller, Susan. *Against Our Will: Men, Women and Rape.* New York: Simon and Schuster, 1975.

Buckley, M. J. *Morality and the Homosexual: A Catholic Approach to a Moral Problem.* Westminster, Md.: Newman Press, 1960.

Bullough, Vern L. *The History of Prostitution.* New York: University Books, 1964.

———. *The Subordinate Sex: A History of Attitudes Toward Women.* New York: Penguin, 1974.

Cappellanus, Andreas. *The Art of Courtly Love.* Book 1, chapters 1-4. Translated by John J. Parry. New York: Ungar.

Carballo, Juan Rof. "Eroticism." *Human Context* 2: 320-343.

Catholic Theological Society of America. *Human Sexuality: New Directions in American Catholic Thought.* New York: Paulist Press, 1977.

Catullus, C. Valerius. *Erotica.* Translated by Walter K. Kelly. London: Henry G. Bohn, 1854.

Chasteen, Edgar R. *The Case for Compulsory Birth Control.* Englewood Cliffs, N.J.: Prentice-Hall, 1971.

Chesler, Phyllis. *Women and Madness.* New York: Doubleday, 1972.

Chesser, Eustace. *Is Chastity Outmoded?* London: Heinemann, 1960.

———. *Unmarried Love.* New York: David McKay, 1965.

Chevigny, Bell Gale. *The Woman and the Myth: Margaret Fuller's Life and Writings.* New York: Feminist Press, 1977.

Chodorow, Nancy. *The Reproduction of Mothering.* Berkeley, Calif.: University of California Press, 1978.

Clark, Lorenne. "Rape in Toronto: Psycho-Social Perspectives on the Toronto Offender": In *Sexual Behavior in Canada: Patterns and Problems,* edited by B. Schlesinger. University of Toronto Press, 1977.

———. "Sexual Violence: Group Rape." *Canada: Comparative Contemporary and Historical Perspectives on Violence,* edited by Desmond Ellis et al. McClelland and Stewart, 1982.

Cleugh, James. *The First Masochist: A Biography of Leopold Von Sachermasoch (1836-1895).* London: Anthony Blond, 1967.

Comfort, Alexander. *The Joy of Sex.* New York: Crown Publishers, 1972.

———. "On Advanced Lovemaking." *The Joy of Sex.* New York: Crown Publishers, 1972, pp. 8-15. Reprinted in Jaggar and Struhl, pp. 285-287.

———. *Sex from the Standpoint of Anarchism.* London: Freedom Press, 1948.

Conklin, Nancy F. "Toward a Feminist Analysis of Linguistic Behavior." *University of Michigan Papers in Women's Studies* 1 (February 1974): 51-73.

Connolly, L. W. "Pornography." *Dalhousie Review* 54: 698-709.

Cox, Harvey, "Evangelical Ethics and the Ideal of Chastity." *Christianity and Crisis* 24 (1964): 75-80.

Cox, Jean W. "The Lawful Expression of Erotic Fantasies: All Our Dreams Come True." *Religious Humanism* 9 (Winter 1975): 17-22.

Curran, Charles E. "Homosexuality and Moral Theology: Methodological and Substantive Considerations." *The Thomist* 35 (1971): 447-481.

Dahmer, Helmut. "Sexual Economy Today." *Telos* 36 (Summer 1978): 111-126.

Daly, Mary. *The Church and the Second Sex.* 2nd ed. New York: Harper & Row, 1975.

Davis, Murray S. *Smut: Erotic Reality/Obscene Ideology.* Chicago: University of

Chicago Press, 1983.

DeCrow, Karen. *Sexist Justice.* New York: Random House, 1974.

Decter, Midge. *The New Chastity and Other Arguments Against Women's Liberation.* New York: Coward, McCann and Geoghagan, 1972.

Demant, V. A. *Christian Sex Ethics.* New York: Harper & Row, 1963.

D'Emillio, John. *Sexual Politics, Sexual Communities: The Making of a Homosexual Minority in the United States.* Chicago: University of Chicago Press, 1983.

———. "The Making of an American Homosexual Minority." Paper read at the Conference on Homosexuality. Union College, Schenectady, N.Y. (May 5, 1983).

DeRougemont, Denis. *Love Declared: Essays on the Myth of Love.* New York: Pantheon Books, 1963.

———. *Love in the Western World.* Translated by M. Belgion. New York: Pantheon, 1970.

De Santo, C. "Sex Education Within a Social Context." *The Journal of Moral Education* 3 (October 1973): 345-352.

Detre, Jean. *A Most Extraordinary Pair: Mary Wollstonecraft and William Godwin.* New York: Doubleday, 1975.

Deutsch, Helene. *The Psychology of Woman.* New York: Grune and Stratton, 1944, 1945. Vol. 1, pp. 219-278.

Dinnerstein, Dorothy. *The Mermaid and the Minotaur. Sexual Arrangements and Human Malaise.* New York: Harper & Row, 1976.

Dixon, Marlene. "Why Women's Liberation?" *Ramparts* 7 (December 1969): 57-63.

Doherty, Dennis. *The Sexual Doctrine of Cardinal Cajetan.* Regensburg, Germany: Pustet, 1966.

Donaldson, James. *Woman: Her Position and Influence in Ancient Greece and Rome, and Among the Early Christians.* New York: Longmans, Green, 1907.

Douglas, M. *Purity and Danger.* London: Pelican Books, 1970.

Dubois, B. L. and I. Crouch. "The Question of Tag Questions in Women's Speech: They Really Don't Use More of Them, Do They?" *Language in Society* 4 (1975): 129-146.

Dummet, Michael. "The Documents of the Papal Commission on Birth Control." *New Blackfriars* 50 (February 1969): 241-250.

Dupre, Louis K. *Contraception and Catholics: A New Appraisal.* Baltimore: Helicon Press, 1964.

Durkheim, Emile. *Durkheim: Essays on Morals and Education.* Edited by W. S. F. Pickering. London: Routledge & Kegan Paul, 1979.

Dworkin, Andrea. *Our Blood: Prophecies and Discourses on Sexual Politics.* New York: Harper & Row, 1976.

———. *Pornography: Men's Graphic Description of Whores.* New York: Putnam, 1981.

———. *Pornography: Men Possessing Women.* The Women's Press, 1981.

———. *Woman Hating.* New York: Dutton, 1974.

Edwards, Susan. *Female Sexuality and the Law.* Martin Robertson, 1981.

Ehrenreich, Barbara, and Deidre English. *Complaints and Disorders: The Sexual Politics of Sickness.* Old Westbury, N.Y.: Feminist Press, 1973.

———. *For Her Own Good: 150 Years of the Expert's Advice to Women.* Garden City, N.J.: Doubleday, 1978.

Eller, Vernard. *The Sex Manual for Puritans.* Nashville, Tenn.: Abingdon, 1971.

Ellis, Albert, "Rationality in Sexual Morality." *The Humanist* 29 (September-October 1969): 17-21.

Ellis, Albert, and Albert Abarbanel, eds. "Language and Sex." In *The Encyclopedia of Sexual Behavior.* Vol. 2, pp. 585-598.

——. *The Folklore of Sex.* New York: Charles Boni, 1951.

——. *Sex Without Guilt.* New York: Lyle Stuart, 1958.

Ellis, Albert, and Ralph Brancale. *The Psychology of Sex Offenders.* Springfield, Ill.: Charles C. Thomas, 1956.

Ellis, Havelock. *Little Essays of Love and Virtue.* New York, 1922.

——. *On Life and Sex.* Garden City, N.Y.: Garden City Publishing Co., 1947.

——. *Sex & Marriage: Eros in Contemporary Life* (1952). Westport, Conn.: Greenwood, 1972.

——. *Studies in the Psychology of Sex.* New York: Random House, 1936.

Epstein, Cynthia F. *Woman's Place.* Berkeley, Calif.: University of California Press, 1970.

Erickson, Eric. "Reflections on Womanhood." *Daedalus* (Spring, 1964).

Faderman, Lillian. "Lesbian Images in Turn of the Century American." Paper read at the Conference on Homosexuality (May 6, 1983), Union College, Schenectady, N.Y.

Faust, Jean. "Words That Oppress." In *Women Speaking.* Reprint, KNOW, Inc., P.O. Box 10197, Pittsburgh, Pa. 15232.

Fawcett, Millicent Gattett. *Women's Suffrage.* London: The People's Books, 1912.

Firestone, Shulamith. *The Dialectic of Sex: The Case for Feminist Revolution.* New York: William Morrow, 1970.

Feminist Writers Workshop. *An Intelligent Woman's Guide to Dirty Words: English Words and Phrases Reflecting Sexist Attitudes Toward Women in Patriarchal Society.* Chicago: YWCA, Loop Center, 1973.

Flexner, Eleanor. *Century of Struggle: The Women's Rights Movements in the United States.* Cambridge, Mass.: Belknap Press, 1966.

Foote, Nelson. "Sex as Play." *Social Problems* 1 (1954): 159-163.

Foucault, Michel. *Power/Knowledge: Selected Interviews and Other Writings.* Edited by C. Gordan. New York: Pantheon, 1980.

Francoeur, R., and A. Francoeur. *The Future of Sexual Relations.* Englewood Cliffs, N.J.: Prentice-Hall, 1974.

Frankfort, Ellen. *Vaginal Politics.* New York: Bantam Books, 1973.

Frenkel, F. E. "Sex-Crime and Its Socio-Historical Background." *Journal of the History of Ideas* 25 (July-September 1964): 333-352.

Freud, Sigmund. "'Civilized' Sexual Morality and Modern Nervous Illness." In *The Standard Edition of the Complete Psychological Works of Sigmund Freud.* Vol. 9. London: Hogarth Press, 1959, pp. 187-204. Reprinted in Verene, p. 206-224.

——. *Three Contributions to the Theory of Sex.* New York: Dutton, 1962.

Friedan, Betty. *The Feminine Mystique.* New York: Dell, 1962.

——. *It Changed My Life. Writings on the Women's Movement.* New York: Random House, 1976.

——. *The Second Stage.* New York: Summit Books, 1981.

Fromm, Erich. *The Art of Loving.* New York: Harper & Row, 1956. Partially reprinted in Verene, pp. 272-286.

Gilligan, Carol. *In a Different Voice: Psychological Theory and Women's Development.* Cambridge, Mass.: Harvard University Press, 1982.

Gilman, Charlotte Perkins. *The Man-Made World: Our Androcentric Culture.* New York: Charlton, 1914.

Goldberg, Steven. *The Inevitability of Patriarchy.* New York: William Morrow and Co., 1974.

Goldman, Emma. *Anarchism and Other Essays.* New York: Dover Publications, 1969.

Goldstein, Michael J., and Harold S. Kant. *Pornography and Sexual Deviance.* Berkeley, Calif.: University of California Press, 1973.

Greene, Gerald and Caroline. *S-M: The Last Taboo.* New York: Grove Press, 1974.

Greer, Germaine. *The Female Eunuch.* New York: McGraw-Hill, 1970.

Gribble, Francis. *Rousseau and the Women He Loved.* New York: Scribner's, 1908.

Griffin, Susan. *Rape: The Power of Consciousness.* New York: Harper & Row, 1979.

————. *Pornography and Silence.* New York: Harper & Row, 1981.

Grimke, Sarah M. *Letters on the Equality of the Sexes and the Condition of Woman.* Boston, Mass.: Lenox Hill Pub. and Dist. Co., 1838.

Greenwell, James R. "Abortion and Moral Safety." *Critica* 9 (December 1977): 35-48.

Grummon, Donald L., and Andrew M. Barclay. *Sexuality: A Search for Perspective.* New York: Van Nostrand, 1971.

Guindon, Andre. *The Sexual Language: An Essay in Moral Theology.* Ottawa: University of Ottawa Press, 1976.

Guitton, Jean. *Essay on Human Love.* New York: Philosophical Library, 1951.

Guttmacher, Alan. *Birth Control and Love.* New York: Macmillan, 1969.

Hallet, Judith Pellar. "Ancient Homosexuality: Dover, Boswell and Beyond." Paper read at the Conference on Homosexuality (May 6, 1983), Union College, Schenectady, N.Y.

Hannan, Johann Georg. *Essay of a Sybil on Marriage.* 1775.

————. *Skirts of Fig Leaves.* 1777.

Hardwick, Elizabeth. *Seduction and Betrayal: Women and Literature.* New York: Vintage, 1975.

Hariton, Barbara E. "The Sexual Fantasies of Women." *Psychology Today* (March 1973): 39-44. Reprinted in Jaggar and Struhl, pp. 57-62.

Harris, Daniel. "Androgyny." *Women's Studies* 2 (1974): 171-184.

Hayakawa, S. I. "Semantics and Sexuality." *ETC.* 25 (June 1968): 135-153.

Hayek, Friederich. *John Stuart Mill and Harriet Taylor: Their Friendship and Subsequent Marriage.* Chicago: University of Chicago Press, 1951.

Hecker, Eugene. *A Short History of Women's Rights.* Westport, Conn.: Greenwood Press, 1914.

Hefner, Hugh. "The Playboy Philosophy." *Playboy Magazine* (1962): 65. Chicago: HMH Publishing Co.

Herman, Judith Lewis. *Father-Daughter Incest.* Cambridge, Mass.: Harvard University Press, n.d.

Hiltner, Seward. *Sex Ethics and the Kinsey Report.* New York: Association Press, 1953.

Himes, Norman E. *Medical History of Contraception.* New York: Schocken Books, 1963.

Hite, Shere. *The Hite Report.* New York: Dell, 1977.

Hole, J., and E. Levine. *Rebirth of Feminism.* New York: Times Books, 1971.

Hooker, E. *Final Report of the Task Force on Homosexuality.* Bethesda, Md.:

National Institute of Mental Health, 1969.

Horney, Karen. *Feminine Psychology.* New York: W. W. Norton, 1967.

Hrdy, Sarah. *The Woman that Never Evolved.* Cambridge, Mass.: Harvard University Press, 1981.

Hughes, Douglas A. *Perspective on Pornography.* New York: St. Martin's Press, 1970.

The Humanist. "A New Bill of Sexual Rights and Responsibilities." 36 (January-February 1976): 4-6.

Hunt, Morton M. *The Affair: A Portrait of Extra-Marital Love in Contemporary America.* Cleveland, Ohio: World Publishing Co., 1969.

———. *The Natural History of Love.* New York: Alfred A. Knopf, 1959.

Janeway, Elizabeth. *Man's World, Woman's Place: An Essay in Social Mythology.* New York: Morrow, 1971.

Johnston, Jill. *Lesbian Nation: The Feminist Solution.* New York: Touchstone, 1973.

Jung, C. J. *Aspects of the Feminine.* Translated by R. F. C. Hull. Princeton, N.J.: Princeton University Press, 1982.

Kameny, Franklin E. "The Federal Government vs. the Homosexual." *The Humanist* 29 (May-June 1969): 20-23.

Kanowitz, Leo. *Women and the Law: The Unfinished Revolution.* Albuquerque, N.M.: University of New Mexico Press, 1969.

Katchadourian, Herant A., and Donald T. Lunde. *Fundamentals of Human Sexuality.* New York: Holt, Rinehart and Winston, 1972.

Kempthrone. "Incest and the Body of Christ: A Study of 1 Corinthians VI, 12-20." *New Testament Studies* 14 (1967/68).

Key, Mary Ritchie. *Male/Female Language.* Metuchen, N.J.: Scarecrow Press, 1975.

Kilian, Sabbas J. "The Question of Authority in *Humanae Vitae.*" *Thought* 44 (September 1969): 327-342.

Kinsey, Alfred C. *Sexual Behavior in the Human Female.* Philadelphia: W. B. Saunders Co., 1953.

———. *Sexual Behavior in the Human Male.* Philadelphia: W. B. Saunders Co., 1948.

Kramer, Cheris. "Women's Speech: Separate but Unequal?" *Quarterly Journal of Speech* 60 (February 1974): 14-22.

Lakoff, Robin. *Language and Woman's Place.* New York: Harper & Row, 1975. Reprinted in English, pp. 220-230; and Vetterling-Braggin, pp. 60-67.

Lane, Robert. "Sexual Rights and Responsibilities." *Current* (April 1976): 18-28.

Lasch, Christopher. "The Flight From Feeling: Sociopsychology of Sexual Conflict." *Marxist Perspectives* 1 (1978): 74-95.

Larue, Gerald. *Sex and the Bible.* Buffalo, N.Y.: Prometheus Books, 1983.

Lawrence, D. H. *Pornography and Obscenity.* New York: Alfred A. Knopf, 1928.

———. *Sex, Literature and Censorship.* New York: Viking Books, 1953.

Lazarre, Jane. "Loving Men: Two Aspects." *Feminist Studies* 6 (Spring 1980): 212-217.

Le Chaplain, Andre. *The Art of Courtly Love.* Translated by John Jay Parry. New York: Columbia University Press, 1941.

LeConte, Edward. *Milton and Sex.* New York: Columbia University Press, n.d.

Leighton, Jean. "Prostitution." In *Problems of Sex Behavior.* Edited by Edward Sagarin and Donal E. J. MacNamara. New York: Crowell, 1968.

————. *Simone De Beauvoir on Woman.* Cranbury, N.J.: Associated University Press, 1975.

Lennert, Midge, and Norma Wilson. *A Women's New World Dictionary.* Available from 51% Publications, Box 371, Lomita, Calif. 90717.

Lewis, C. S. *The Allegory of Love.* Oxford, England: Clarendon Press, 1936.

Lewis Herman, Judith. *Father-Daughter Incest.* Cambridge, Mass.: Harvard University Press, 1980.

Licht, Hans. *Sexual Life in Ancient Greece.* New York: Barnes and Noble, 1953.

Lindsey, B. B., and W. Evans. *The Companionate Marriage (1927).* New York: Arno, 1972.

Lingus, Alphonso F. "Khajuraho." *Soundings* 62 (1979): 52-69.

Lopate, Carole. "Women and Pay for Housework." *Liberation Magazine* (June 1974): 8-11. Reprinted in Jaggar and Struhl, pp. 211-216.

Low, Anthony. *Love's Architecture: Devotional Modes in Seventeenth-Century Poetry.* New York: Columbia University Press, n.d.

Luther, Martin. *What Luther Says.* St. Louis, Mo.: Concordia Publishing House, 1959, pp. 132-134, 884-886, 902, 906, 1457-1459.

MacDonald, Robert H. "The Frightful Consequences of Onanism: Notes on the History of a Delusion." *Journal of the History of Ideas* 28 (1967): 423-431.

MacKinnon, Alastair. "God, Humanity, and Sexual Polarity." *Hibbert Journal* 52 (1953): 337-342.

MacKinnon, Catherine. *Sexual Harassment of Working Women.* New Haven, Conn.: Yale University Press, 1979.

MacNamara, Donal E. J., and Edward Sagarin. *Sex, Crime and the Law.* New York: The Free Press, 1977.

Madsen, Axel. *Hearts and Minds: The Common Journey of Simone De Beauvoir and Jean-Paul Sartre.* New York: Morrow, 1977.

Makarius, Laura, and Raoul Makarius. "The Incest Taboo and Food Taboos." *Diogenes* 30 (Summer 1960): 41-61.

Marcus, Stephen. *The Other Victorians: A Study of Sexuality And Pornography in Mid-Nineteenth-Century England.* New York: Basic Books, 1964.

Margolis, Clorinda, and Joseph Margolis. "Alternative Life-Styles and Sexual Tolerance." *The Humanist* 33 (1973) 19-20.

Masters, R. E. L. *Forbidden Sexual Behavior and Morality.* New York: Matrix House, 1966.

Masters, William H., and Virginia E. Johnson. *Homosexuality in Perspective.* Boston: Little, Brown and Co., 1979.

————. *Human Sexual Inadequacy.* Boston: Little, Brown and Co., 1970.

————. *Human Sexual Response.* Boston: Little, Brown and Co., 1966.

————. *The Pleasure Bond.* New York: Bantam, 1976.

Masters, William H., Virginia E. Johnson and Robert C. Kolodony, eds. *Ethical Issues in Sex Therapy and Research.* Boston: Little, Brown and Co., 1979.

————. *Ethical Issues in Sex Therapy and Research.* Vol. 2. Boston: Little, Brown and Co., 1980.

Mathieu, Nicole-Claude. "Notes Toward a Sociological Definition of Sex Categories." *Human Context* 6 (1974): 345-359.

May, Rollo. "Paradoxes of Sex and Love." In *Love and Will.* New York: W. W. Norton, 1969, pp. 37-48. Reprinted in Verene, pp. 328-342.

McCarthy, Sarah J. "Pornography and the Cult of the Macho." *The Humanist* 40 (September-October 1980): 11-20, 56.

McCary, James Leslie. *Human Sexuality; Second Brief Edition.* New York: D. Van Nostrand, 1979.

McConnell-Ginet, Sally. "Our Father Tongue: Essays in Linguistic Politics." *Diacritics* (Winter 1975): 44-50.

———. "Women's Minds and Lives: Making Linguistics Connections." Unpublished. Ithaca, N.Y.: Cornell University Department of Linguistics and Women's Studies, 1979.

McCoy, Charles N. R. *"Humanae Vitae:* Perspectives and Precisions." *New Scholasticism* 44 (Spring 1970): 265-272.

McIntyre, Clara F. "Is Virginia Wolf a Feminist?" *The Personalist* 41 (Spring 1960): 176-184.

McLaren, Angus. "Sex and Socialism: The Opposition of the French Left to Birth control in the Nineteenth Century." *The Journal of the History of Ideas* 37 (July-September 1976): 475-492.

Mead, Margaret. *Male and Female.* New York: William Morrow and Co., 1949.

———. *Sex and Temperament in Three Primitive Societies.* New York: William Morrow and Co., 1935.

Memoirs of Casanova. Translated by Lowell Bair. New York: Ballantine, 1968.

Merchant, Carolyn. *The Death of Nature: A Feminist Reappraisal of the Scientific Revolution.* New York: Harper & Row, 1980.

Millet, Kate. *Flying.* New York: Ballantine, 1975.

———. *The Handbook of Nonsexist Writing.* New York: Lippincott and Crowell, 1980.

———. *The Prostitution Papers: "A Quartet for Female Voices."* New York: Ballantine, 1976.

———. *Sexual Politics.* New York: Avon, 1969.

———. *Words and Women.* Garden City, N.Y.: Anchor Press/Doubleday, 1976.

Mitchell, Juliet. *Psychoanalysis and Feminism.* New York: Pantheon Books, 1974.

———. *Woman's Estate.* New York: Pantheon Books, 1971.

Mohler, James A., S.J. *Dimensions of Love: East and West.* Garden City, N.J.: Doubleday, 1975.

Mohr, J. W., R. E. Turner, and M. B. Jerry. *Paedophilia and Exhibitionism.* Toronto, Canada: University of Toronto Press, 1964.

Monaghan, Patricia. *Women in Myth and Legend.* Junction Books, 1981.

Money, John. *Love and Love Sickness: The Science of Sex, Gender Difference, and Pairbonding.* Baltimore, Md.: Johns Hopkins University Press, 1982.

Money, John, and Anke Ehrhardt. *Man and Woman, Boy and Girl.* Baltimore: Johns Hopkins University Press, 1972.

Montagu, Ashley. *Sex, Man and Society.* New York: G. P. Putnam's Sons, 1969.

Morgan, Elaine. *The Descent of Woman.* New York: Bantam Books, 1972.

Morris, Maxwell H. "The Functions of Sex." *Religious Humanism* 8 (Winter 1974): 31-32.

Moylan, Prudence Ann. "What's in a Word: Women, Language and Taboo." *Listening* 14 (Spring 1979): 92-99.

Nass, Gilbert D., Roger W. Libby and Mary Pat Fisher. *Sexual Choices.* Belmont, Calif.: Wadsworth Publishing Co., 1981.

Nelson, John Charles. *Renaissance Theory of Love.* New York: Columbia University Press, 1958.

Ochs, Carol. *Women and Spirituality.* Totowa, N.J.: Littlefield Adams, 1983.

Ogilvy, James. "Mastery and Sexuality." *Human Studies* 3 (July 1980): 201-220.

O'Neil, Robert P., and M. A. Nonovan. *Sexuality and Moral Responsibility.* Washington, D.C.: Corpus, 1968.

O'Neill, Nena, and George O'Neill. *Open Marriage: A New Life Style for Couples.* New York: M. Evans and Co., 1972.

Ovid. *The Art of Love and Other Poems.* Translated by J. H. Motzley. Cambridge, Mass.: Harvard University Press, 1: 13-17, 2: 111-117, 3: 123-124, 173-175. In Verene, pp. 75-83.

Pappe, H.O. *John Stuart Mill and the Harriet Taylor Myth.* Parkville, Australia: Melbourne University Press, 1960.

Pateman, Carole. "Women and Consent." *Political Theory* 8 (May 1980): 149-168.

Pielke, Robert. "The Rejection of Traditional Theism in Feminist Theology and Science Fiction." *The Intersection.* Edited by Robert Meyers. Westport, Conn.: Greenwood Press.

Pomeroy, Hiram S. *The Ethics of Marriage.* New York: Funk and Wagnalls, 1888.

Pope Paul VI. *Humanae Vitae.* Washington, D.C.: N.C.W.C., 1968. Reprinted in Baker and Elliston, 1st ed., pp. 131-149.

Pope Pius XI. *Casti Connubii.* Encyclical, 1930. Reprinted in Anne Freemantle, ed., *The Papal Encyclicals.* New York: Mentor, 1956.

Pornography: The Longford Report. London: Coronet Books, 1972.

Radzinowicz, Leon. *Sexual Offences.* London: Macmillan, 1957.

Raven, Susan, and Alison Weir. *Women in History.* Weidenfeld, 1981.

Reed, Evelyn. *Problems of Women's Liberation.* New York: Pathfinder Press, 1971

———. *Women's Evolution.* New York: Pathfinder Press, 1975.

Reich, Wilhelm. *The Invasion of Compulsory Sex-Morality.* New York: Farrar, Straus and Giroux. 1971.

———. *The Sexual Revolution: Towards a Self-Governing Character Structure.* New York: Orgone Press, 1945.

———. *The Discovery of the Orgone: The Function of the Orgasm.* New York. Farrar, Straus and Giroux, 1942.

Report of the Commission on Obscenity and Pornography. Washington, D.C., G.P.O., 1970.

Rich, Adrienne. "Compulsory Heterosexuality and Lesbian Existence." *Signs* 5 (1980): 631-660.

Richards, David A. *Sex, Drugs, Death and the Law.* Totowa, N.J.: Rowman and Littlefield, 1982, viz pp. 29-153.

Robinson, Paul. *The Modernization of Sex.* New York: Harper & Row, 1976.

Rogers, Katherine M. *The Troublesome Helpmate: A History of Misogyny in Literature.* Seattle: University of Washington Press, 1966.

Rossi, Alice. "Sex Equality: The Beginnings of Ideology." *The Humanist* 29 (1969): 3-6.

Rowbotham, Sheila. *Woman's Consciousness, Man's World.* London: Penguin Books, 1973.

———. *Women, Resistance, and Revolution: A History of Women and Revolution in the Modern World.* New York: Vintage, 1974.

Roy, Rustum. "Is Monogamy Outdated?" *The Humanist* 30 (1970): 19-26.

Saghir, Marcel, and Eli Robins. *Male and Female Homosexuality.* Baltimore: Williams and Wilkins, 1973.

Salper de Tortella, Roberta. *Female Liberation: History and Current Politics.* New York: Knopf, 1972.

Sanger, William W. *History of Prostitution: Its Extents, Causes, and Effects*

Throughout the World. New York: Harper and Brothers, 1858.

Schulz, Esther. "Education for Human Sexuality." *The Humanist* 28 (May-June 1968): 18-19.

Sears, Hal D. *The Sex Radicals; Free Love in High Victorian America.* Kansas University Press, 1977.

Sheehy, Gail. *Hustling.* New York: Dell Books, 1971.

Sherwin, Robert V. "Laws on Sex Crimes." In *The Encyclopedia of Sexual Behavior,* Vol. 2. New York: Hawthorn Books, 1961, pp. 622-630.

Sherwin, Susan. "When Does a 'Girl' Become a Woman?" In *Nonmedical Issues and Contraception.* Edited by E. J. Love. The proceedings of a seminar sponsored by the Canadian Committee for Fertility Research (September 11-12, 1979) pp. 54-76.

Smith, Kenneth J. "The Last Tango to Nowhere: Sex as Therapy." *Religious Humanism* 8 (Winter 1974): 25-30.

Solanis, Valerie. *Scum Manifesto.* New York: Olympia Press, 1970.

Stanley, Julia P., and Susan W. Robbins. "Goin Through the Changes: The Pronoun 'She' in Middle English." *Papers In Linguistics* 9 (Fall 1977): 3-4.

Stekel, Wilhelm. *Sexual Aberrations.* New York: Liveright, 1930.

Stern, Herold S. "The Concept of Chastity in Biblical Society." *The Journal of Sex Research* 2 (1966): 89-97.

Strachey, Ray. *The Cause: A Short History of the Women's Movement in Great Britain.* London: G. Bell, 1928.

Sunstein, Emily W. *A Different Face: The Life of Mary Wollstonecraft.* Boston: Little, Brown and Co., 1975.

Synan, Edward A. "Four Questions by Adam Burley on the 'Liber Sex Principorum.'" *Medical Studies* 32 (1970): 60-90.

Tapia, Ralph J. "Human Sexuality: The Magisterium and Moral Theologians." *Thought* 54 (December 1979): 405-418.

Taylor, Gordon. *Sex in History.* rev. ed. London: Panther Books, 1965.

Thomas, Keith. "The Double Standard." *The Journal of the History of Ideas* 20 (April 1959): 195-216.

Tiedt, Iris M. "The Possible Biological Origins of Sexual Discrimination." *Impact* 20 (1970): 29-44.

———. "Sexism in Language: An Editor's Plague." *Elementary English* 50 (October 1973): 1073-1074.

Tomlain, Claire. *The Life and Death of Mary Wollstonecraft.* New York: New American Library, 1974.

Tripp, C. A. *The Homosexual Matrix.* New York: New American Library, 1975.

Trotsky, Leon. *Women and the Family.* New York: Pathfinder Press, 1970.

United Nations Study on Traffic in Persons and Prostitution. New York, 1959.

"Vatican Declaration on Sexual Ethics." *Origins: NC Documentary Service* 5 (January 22, 1976): 486-500.

Von Hildebrand, Dietrich. *In Defense of Purity.* Chicago: Franciscan Herald Press, 1978.

———. *Man and Woman.* Chicago: Franciscan Herald Press, 1974.

———. *Celibacy and the Crisis of Faith.* Chicago: Franciscan Herald Press, 1971.

———. *Marriage.* New York: Longmans, 1942.

Weinberg, George. *Society and the Healthy Homosexual.* Garden City, N.Y.: Anchor Books, 1973.

Weinberg, M. S., and C. J. Williams. *Male Homosexuals.* New York: Oxford

University Press, 1974.

Whitely, Charles H., and W. M. Whitely. *Sex and Morals.* New York: Basic Books, 1967.

Wilson, Colin. *Origins of the Sexual Impulse.* London: Panther, 1963.

Wilson, James Q. "Violence, Pornography and Social Science." *Public Interest* 22 (Winter 1971):45-61.

Winick, Charles. "The Desexualized Society." *The Humanist* 29 (November-December 1969): 6-8.

Withey, Lynne. *Dearest Friend: A Life of Abigail Adams.* New York: Free Press, 1981.

"The Wolfenden Report." *Report of the Committee on Homosexual Offences and Prostitution.* Cmd. 247. London: H.M.S.O., 1957. New York: Stein and Day, 1963.

Wollstonecraft, Mary. *Letters Written During a Short Residence in Sweden, Norway and Denmark.* Lincoln: University of Nebraska Press, 1976.

———. *Thoughts on the Education of Daughters.* New York: Garland Publishing, 1974.

———. *A Vindication of the Rights of Woman.* New York: W. W. Norton and Co., 1967.

"Women's Manifesto." *New Left Notes* (July 10, 1967).

Wu, Kuang-Ming. "Neither Male Nor Female." *Religious Humanism* 10 (Autumn 1976): 159-164.

Contributors

ROBERT BAKER	Associate Professor of Philosophy Union College, Schenectady, N.Y.
BERNARD BAUMRIN	Professor of Philosophy City University of New York
MICHAEL BAYLES	Professor of Philosophy University of Florida
FRED BERGER	Professor of Philosophy University of California, Davis
JEREMY BENTHAM	Author, *Introduction to the Principles of Morals and Legislation* (Oxford, 1789)
CARL COHEN	Professor of Philosophy University of Michigan, Ann Arbor
RICHARD CROSS, M.D.	Professor University of Medicine and Dentistry of New Jersey
ROBERT EHMAN	Associate Professor of Philosophy Vanderbilt University
FREDERICK ELLISTON	Senior Research Associate, Ethics Center Illinois Institute of Technology
SHULAMITH FIRESTONE	Author, *The Dialectic of Sex* (New York, 1970)
MARILYN FRYE	Associate Professor of Philosophy Michigan State University
ANN GARRY	Professor of Philosophy California State University, Los Angeles
R. M. HARE	Professor of Moral Philosophy Corpus Christi College, Oxford
ALISON JAGGAR	Professor of Philosophy University of Cincinnati

JOHN MCMURTY — Associate Professor of Philosophy
University of Guelph, Ontario

THOMAS NAGEL — Professor of Philosophy
New York University

DAVID PALMER — Associate Professor of Philosophy
SUNY, College at Fredonia

SARA RUDDICK — Editor, *Working It Out*
(New York, 1981)

MICHAEL RUSE — Professor of Philosophy
University of Guelph, Ontario

ROBERT SOLOMON — Professor of Philosophy
University of Texas, Austin

FREDERICK SUPPE — Professor of Philosophy
University of Maryland, College Park

RICHARD TAYLOR — Professor of Philosophy
University of Rochester
& Union College, New York

JUDITH JARVIS
THOMPSON — Professor of Philosophy
Massachusetts Institute of Technology

JOYCE TREBILCOT — Director
Woman's Studies
Washington University, St. Louis

WILLIAM VITEK — Graduate student in Philosophy
City University of New York

RICHARD WASSERSTROM — Professor of Philosophy
University of California, Santa Cruz